NORTH AMERICAN INDIANS

Chronological chart of Native North American culture areas

Date	MEXICO	SOUTHWEST	SOUTHEAST	NORTHEAST	PRAIRIE-PLAINS	WEST & CALIFORNIA	NORTHWEST COAST	ARCTIC & SUBARCTIC
1900	MEXICO	PUEBLOS APACHE NAVAHO	Removal	IROQUOIS ALGONKIANS	FARMING VILLAGES / U.S. RESERVATIONS	RESERVATIONS / U.S. WARS	FUR TRADE	Home rule (Greenland) / Native Settlement Acts
1700	SPANISH	Coronado	De Soto	European invasion	FUR AND HORSE TRADE	FUR AND SLAVE TRADE		FUR TRADE / Russians
1500	AZTECS	PAQUIMÉ ANASAZI	MISSISSIPPIAN			Spanish contact		European fisheries
1300	TOLTECS		CAHOKIA	Norse	HORSES	HORSES	TRADITIONAL CULTURES	Norse
1100	MAYA	HOHOKAM		Agriculture begins				INUIT
900					PLAINS	TRADITIONAL CULTURES		
700	TEOTIHUACAN		HOPEWELL	MIDDLE WOODLAND	WOODLAND			
500			ADENA					
300					HOPEWELL			
100 A.D. / B.C. 100	OLMEC			EARLY WOODLAND				
300								
500								
700								
900								
1100		Agriculture begins	Poverty point					
1300			Agriculture begins					
1500	Agriculture begins							
8000 PLEISTOCENE								

HOLOCENE

PLEISTOCENE

2nd
edition

NORTH AMERICAN INDIANS
A Comprehensive Account

Alice Beck Kehoe
Marquette University

Prentice Hall
Upper Saddle River, New Jersey 07458

Library of Congress Cataloging-in-Publication Data

Kehoe, Alice Beck, (date)
   North American Indians: a comprehensive account / Alice Beck
Kehoe.—2nd ed.
   Includes bibliographical references and index.
   ISBN 0-13-624362-2
   1. Indians of North America. I.Title
E77.K43 1992
970.004'97—dc20

                                        91-20226
                                            CIP

Production Editor: KERRY REARDON
Acquisitions Editor: NANCY ROBERTS
Copy Editor: KATHRYN BECK
Cover Designer: JOE DI DOMENICO
Prepress Buyer: KELLY BEHR
Manufacturing Buyer: MARY ANN GLORIANDE

 © 1992, 1981 by Prentice-Hall, Inc.
Simon & Schuster / A Viacom Company
Upper Saddle River, New Jersey 07458

Cover photo courtesy of The Heritage Center
of Holy Rosary Mission, Pine Ridge, South Dakota
and Marquette University Archives;
photo by James Strzok, 1977.

Printed in the United States of America

10

ISBN 0-13-624362-2

Prentice-Hall International (UK) Limited, *London*
Prentice-Hall of Australia Pty. Limited, *Sydney*
Prentice-Hall Canada Inc., *Toronto*
Prentice-Hall Hispanoamericana, S.A., *Mexico*
Prentice-Hall of India Private Limited, *New Delhi*
Prentice-Hall of Japan, Inc., *Tokyo*
Simon & Schuster Asia Pte. Ltd., *Singapore*
Editora Prentice-Hall do Brasil, Ltda., *Rio de Janeiro*

CONTENTS

PREFACE

This is a straightforward history of North America. It begins when humans first inhabited the continent, at least fifteen thousand years ago, and it continues, chronologically, region by region, to the present; a most logical and traditional scheme, surely, yet uncommon for accounts of North American Indians. Histories of American Indians usually begin with the European invasions of America. Anthropology texts usually present a series of synopses of the "ethnographic present," the time just before Euro-Americans gained political sovereignty over the Indian society. Popular books use the Indian as a vehicle to carry a more or less mystical world-view or to pander to a thirst for gore. Where, in all of these, are the human beings, the communities, whose ancestries can be traced back to the Paleolithic period, whose sophisticated technologies managed their resources to provide reasonable security, whose astute stratagems should have contained the European advance had it not been coupled with catastrophic epidemics and ecological disturbance? Where are the people who are reasserting their rights and the value of their heritages?

Here you will find the histories of the first nations of North America. Because the continent is so large and diverse, the histories are examined by region, from the rich lands of Mexico, where magnificent cities were built over two thousand years, through eastern and western United States, to the challenges of Canada's forests and Arctic coast. I have weighed the material in published sources against my own experiences as an archaeologist who has excavated in Mexico, the Midwest, and Canada, and as an anthropologist who lived for several years on the Blackfeet Reservation and worked with Cree, Dakota Sioux, Assiniboin, and Ojibwa (and briefly, with Bolivian Aymara) as well. I have benefited greatly from discussions with colleagues, Indian and Euro-American, some anthropologists, and some community workers. Not all the text represents a consensus of scholars or of Indians, but it is my honest effort to build a coherent, factual, unbiased description.

Specialists will take issue with my choices of emphasis or detail in many instances. Sometimes my treatment stems from the sweeping perspective of the book itself: for example, discussing the western Great Lakes peoples in a chapter on the Prairie-Plains highlights the interdigitation of prairie and woodland in central North America and the multiple prehistoric and historic human connections and movements between the two ecological areas. Sometimes, I have made minor adjustments to help the reader, especially in converting radiocarbon "dates" (that is, estimates of elapsed time) into calendar years, primarily through the calibration charts pubished by MASCA (University of Pennsylvania Museum) in its Volume 9, Number 1 Newsletter (later work gives much finer calibrations, but the MASCA correlations are sufficient for a history of this scope). No general study can hope to satisfy specialists, but I do assure readers that there are no hastily tossed-in notions.

My gratitude for help in preparing this book must be extended to hundreds who have befriended me in thirty years of learning about the first nations on this continent. I can single out, initially, Professors Gordon R. Willey and Evon Z. Vogt, whose joint Harvard course clearly demonstrated the necessity of truly continental coverage (including Mexico) and a temporal framework encompassing the human habitation of this continent. Then I must thank my husband, Thomas F. Kehoe, my best colleague and the initiator of most of our joint work. It would have been nice if he had also done the dishes, but then no one's perfect. Among Indian friends who have deeply influenced me, I must thank the late Mae Williamson and Nora Spanish; Earl Old Person; Inez Deiter; Eleanor Brass; Piakwutch; Arthur Brown; Winona Frank; Robert Goodvoice; Joe and Florence Douquette; Max Goodwill; Maxine Smallish; Bea Medicine; JoAllyn Archambault; and Robert K. Thomas (the last three are professional anthropologists). Anthropologists and historians who have directly aided this book through discussion, unpublished papers, or checking sections include: members of the 1977 Wenner-Gren Conference on Early Civilizations of Asia and Mesoamerica, particularly David H. Kelley, James Schoenwetter, Paul Tolstoy, the late Gordon Ekholm, Peter and Jill Leslie Furst, David Harris, the late C. Earle Smith, Jr., and Gordon Whittaker; Juan Alvárez Cuauhtémoc; Paul G. Bahn; Charles Bishop, Arthur Ray, Jr., and their excellent circle; Alan Bryan and Ruth Gruhn; Dena F. Dincauze; Michael Fleet; James P. Gallagher; Susan Gardner; James R. Gibson; Robert S. Gru-

met; June Helm; Jane Holden Kelley; Charles E. Lincoln; Alice Littlefield; Nancy Lurie; Alan Marshall; Carol Irwin Mason; George MacDonald; Linda Manzanilla; David Reed Miller; Jay Miller; John H. Moore; Mary (Chris) Nunley; Wally Olson; James B. Petersen; Bernd Peyer; Harald Prins; Francis Paul Prucha, S.J.; Anthony Ranere; Robin Ridington; G. Micheal Riley; Diane and Jerry Rothenberg; William Simmons; Florence Shipek; Louise Spindler; Michael Stanislawski; Andrea Stone; Norman C. Sullivan; Mark Thiel; Joan B. Townsend; Christy Turner II; Claude Warren; Phil Weigand; David Wilcox; members of the Wisconsin Archaeological Survey, especially James Stoltman; and our Saskatchewan colleagues, particularly George Arthur, Bruce McCorquodale, David Meyer, Grace Morgan, Wayne and Elaine Wright Pendree, and the late John and Jean Hodges. Ellen Kozak clarified legal terms, and more. I thank Leo Johnson, former Milwaukee Public Museum Photography Chief, for his aid in preparing photographs; and the Prentice-Hall staff, especially Stan Wakefield, Anthropology editor, his assistant Audrey Marshall, and Alison D. Gnerre, production editor of the first edition, and Nancy Roberts, Anthropology editor, and Kerry Reardon, production editor, who supervised the second edition with a much-appreciated flexibility. Revision for the second edition was greatly facilitated by Marquette University's star word-processor, Kathy Hawkins, who generously typed the printed text of the first edition into the computer.

Dody H. Giletti deserves thanks for helping me achieve what clarity of thought and expression I can manage; time does not dim her memory. And my parents, Roman and Patty Rosenstock Beck, brought me up in an atmosphere of learning, tolerance, and moral principles that stimulated my intellectual curiosity about my fellow humans and made it easy for me to establish friendships in many communities. This book is part of the fruition of their planting.

Alice B. Kehoe

ACKNOWLEDGMENTS

Grateful acknowledgment is made to the following sources for permission to reprint:

Quotes on pp. 49, 76–77, 80, 81 and 84–85 from *Aztec Thought and Culture* by Miguel León-Portilla, copyright ©1963 by the University of Oklahoma Press.

Quotes on pp. 76–77, and 80 from *Pre-Columbian Literatures of Mexico* by Miguel León-Portilla, copyright ©1969 by the University of Oklahoma Press.

Quote on pp. 106–108 from *Flesh of the Gods: The Ritual Use of Hallucinogens* edited by Peter T. Furst. Copyright ©1972 by Praeger Publisher, Inc. Reprinted by permission of Holt, Rinehart and Winston.

Quote on pp. 113–114 from *A Yaqui Life: The Personal Chronicle of a Yaqui Indian* by Rosalio Moisés, Jane Holden Kelley, and William Curry Holden by permission of University of Nebraska Press. Copyright ©1971 by the University of Nebraska Press.

Quote on pp. 139–142 from *Finding the Center: Narrative Poetry of the Zuni Indians,* translated by Dennis Tedlock, copyright ©1972 by Dennis Tedlock, reprinted by permission of The Dial Press.

Quote on pp 150–151 from *Apache Odyssey: A Journey Between Two Worlds* by Morris E. Opler. Copyright ©1969 by Holt, Rinehart and Winston, Inc. Reprinted by permission of Holt, Rinehart and Winston.

Quote on pp. 185–186 reprinted by permission of the Smithsonian Institution Press from *Smithsonian Institution Bureau of American Ethnology Seventh Annual Report (The Sacred Formulas of the Cherokees),* by James Mooney: "To Take Water for the Ball Play—A 'yunini," p. 396. Washington, D.C.: U.S. Government Printing Office, 1891.

Quote on p. 210 reprinted by permission of the Smithsonian Institution Press from *Smithsonian Institution Bureau of American Ethnology Bulletin 161 (Seminole Music),* by Frances Densmore: "Song for Bringing a Child into the World," p. 172 and "Song for the Dying," p. 174. Washington, D.C.: U.S. Government Printing Office, 1956.

Quote on p. 260–261 reprinted by permission of the Smithsonian Institution Press from *Smithsonian Institution Bureau of American Ethnology Bulletin 30, Part II,* Frederick Webb Hodge, editor, "Tuscarora," J.N.B. Hewitt pp. 843–844. Washington, D.C.: Government Printing Office, 1910.

Quote on p. 290 reprinted by permission from *The Way to Rainy Mountain* by N. Scott Momaday, ©1969 by the University of New Mexico Press. First published in *The Reporter*, January 26, 1967.

Quote on pp. 372–374 reprinted by permission of the Smithsonian Institution Press from *Smithsonian Contributions to Anthropology Number 14 (Anthropology of the Numa: John Wesley Powell's Manuscripts on the Numic Peoples of Western North America, 1868–1880),* edited by Don D. Fowler and Catherine S. Fowler: "Origin of the Pai-Utes," p. 78 and "The Shin-au-av Brothers Discuss Matters of Importance to the People," p. 80. Washington, D.C.: Smithsonian Institution Press, 1971.

Quote on p. 414–415 reprinted by permission of the University of California Press.

Quote on p. 416–418 reprinted by permission from *The Hudson Review,* Vol. III, No. 3 (Autumn, 1950). Copyright ©1950 by the Hudson Review, Inc.

Quotes on pp. 438–439 reprinted from *Kwakiutl Ethnography* by Franz Boas by permission of The University of Chicago Press. Copyright ©1966 by the University of Chicago Press.

Quote on pp. 470–473 by permission of British Columbia Provincial Museum, Victoria, British Columbia.

Quote on pp. 528–529 reprinted from *The People of the Twilight* by Diamond Jenness by permission of The University of Chicago Press. Copyright ©1959 by The University of Chicago Press.

Quote on pp. 528–529 by permission of the Arctic Institute of North America.

Quote on pp. 539–540 from *Naskapi: The Savage Hunters of the Labrador Peninsula* by Frank G. Speck, copyright ©1935, 1963 by the University of Oklahoma Press.

Quote on pp. 569–570 from pp. 12–14, 17–18 by Barre Toelken in *Seeing with a Native Eye* edited by Walter Holden Capps. Copyright ©1976 by Walter Holden Capps. Reprinted by permission of Harper & Row, Publishers, Inc.

Quote on p. 571 from *Fraud, Politics, and the Dispossession of the Indians* by Georgiana Nammack, copyright ©1969 by the University of Oklahoma Press.

Maps on pp. 4, 22, 104, 161, 225, 288, 363, 430, and 481 from Gordon R. Willey, *An Introduction to American Archaeology: North and Middle America,* Vol. 1, ©1966, pp 6, 31, 92–93, 180, 253, 314, 362, 381, and 413. Reprinted by permission of Prentice-Hall, Inc., Englewood Cliffs, N.J.

TO THE READER

North American Indians is a comprehensive history of the humans who colonized North America and developed its nations before this continent became involved in the politics and economics of Europe. It is the history of the descendants of these peoples after this involvement. Because the book is written from the point of view of chronicling the native American nations, there is no sharp break or contrast between "traditional" and "historic" cultures or societies. Claiming such a contrast is racist: it perpetuates the stereotype of "primitive," unchanging tribes bound to an ageless past—the stereotype of the virgin land awaiting in darkness her penetration by European heroes. Rather than "traditions," let us speak of heritages, the languages, knowledge, technology, arts, and values that have been passed on through the generations, not as packages but always dynamic. If you want to anchor an event or person in the text to its time, flip back to the chronology tables at the beginning of each of the principal chapters. You'll see that even for "prehistoric" periods, we can chart change, and the chapters' descriptions of cultural adaptations underline the challenges, and the vitality of Indian nations' responses, from both environments and other nations over dozens of millennia of which the last five centuries are only the best documented.

Many passages slight the complexity of European and Euro-American events and policies affecting American Indians. Selecting the dominant policy or trend, that which, as events turned out, seems to have had the greatest impact, has tended in many instances to reinforce a stereotype of Europeans and their immigrant progeny as ruthless, cruel, glory-seeking money-grubbers. The many, many Europeans and Euro-Americans who were true friends of Indians seem to get soft-pedaled. Some do appear in the text; notice, although they don't shock you; remember, too, those instances of Indians who were looking out for their own interests, befall what may the rest of the nation. Especially notice how often no one directly involved in a situation could have foretold the eventual effects of one decision versus another, how often Indian communities were divided over courses of action, each faction allied with some of the Euro-Americans, each faction sincere, honest, and partly right. If this book leaves you with the impression that Europeans and Euro-Americans spent five centuries perpetuating injustice, so it has seemed from the American Indian point of view, which naturally tends to be less outraged at acts of their own nations that might be excused as reactions to provocation. The European point of view is readily available in hundreds of books. Here, I have tried to present the perspective of anthropologists, historians, and political scientists who study not the dominant powers of today, but the smaller countries and subjugated nations who are increasingly asserting their human rights to life, liberty, and the pursuit of happiness.

There are certain portions of this book that are extremely tedious to read: the lists of languages and named societies in the early historic sections of most of the chapters. These lists are not to be memorized, but please read through once. However small a named nation may be, it and its language are very important indeed to its members. The lengths of the lists also convey the number of independent polities in a region, a feature of the overall political structure—or the significant lack of an overall political structure. Don't forget that America was not unique in being politically fragmented; the number of principalities in Italy or Germany up until this century was similar to the number of "tribes" in a comparable area of America. Language diversity may seem to have been greater in America (and more confusing to read about), but taking into account the very much greater size of America compared to Europe, it

should not be unexpected that linguists recognize six major language stocks (phyla) in America, while Europe has only three (for Europe, Indo-European with many branches, Basque, and Finno-Ugric).

A final note: all dates are given in years according to the modern calendar. This means that most dates for the prehistoric periods have been converted from radiocarbon estimates (often called radiocarbon "dates"). These estimates are never exact, but at best indicate the century in which a site or object was used. If you go on to read archaeological books, you will find that most give radiocarbon "dates"—that is, estimates of age—without converting them to calendar years (which is done by means of published tables) and without rounding them off to the nearest century or half century, as I have done. In my opinion, the nonspecialist reader is given a false impression of historical detail or precision by the usual citations of radiocarbon "dates." The apparent discrepancies between prehistoric dates in this book and in archaeological works is merely the difference between rounded-off estimates converted to calendar years, and the raw radiocarbon estimates.

THE AMERICAS' EARLIEST HUMANS

SECTION 1: PEOPLING THE CONTINENT

The peoples we call the American Indians are the descendants of the original human inhabitants of the American continents. Culturally and physically, they form a set of distinctive groups contrasting with the peoples of the Eurasian, African, and Australian continents. Evidence now available, drawn from the fields of geology, biology, and archaeology, indicates that hunters began moving through the Americas some fourteen thousand years ago, very possibly earlier. Small bands of people continued shifting eastwards and south from the northern continent while earlier settlers increased in population, until by A.D. 1492 there may have been close to fifty million people in North America, from the Inuit (Eskimo) families ranging the Arctic Ocean to the populous nations of Mexico.

There are differing schools of opinion on when the first humans came into the Americas. These schools may be labeled radical, liberal, and conser-

vative, according to their estimates of the validity of alleged evidence for early human occupation. All agree that the earliest Americans came from a northern continent covering what is now Eurasia, the present Bering Strait, and western Alaska.

A radical view is that there have been humans in North America for at least one hundred thousand years, and possibly for one million years. Proponents of this extreme position argue that there were probably more periods during which the sea level was low enough that today's narrow, shallow channel between Asia and Alaska, the Bering Strait, was above water, and there was a single land mass encompassing the present two continents. The principal problem in accepting this radical view is that there is no evidence of human habitation in what is now northeastern Siberia before approximately thirty-three thousand years ago (as evidenced at the Dyuktai site there). It is true that most of northeastern Asia is poorly explored archaeologically, but there have been several well-carried-out Soviet investigations into the prehistory of

CONFLICT OF OPINION ON THE ORIGIN OF NATIVE AMERICAN POPULATIONS

Philosophers point out that there are many "universes of discourse" in which discussants consider certain ideas and facts relevant, others irrelevant. Each universe of discourse includes basic presuppositions that are taken for granted. Arguments between individuals of differing views often arise from disagreement over the acceptability of these fundamental assumptions.

Two often conflicting universes of discourse are science and spirituality. Science is concerned with the testing of information gathered through observation of the phenomena of the natural world. Spirituality is concerned with the search for the ultimate, transcending reality, which includes but need not be limited to the observable natural world. Scientists will not admit as a presupposition that final truths have already been grasped by human minds; in spiritual discourse, it is accepted as an axiom that humans can and perhaps have received the revelation of ultimate truth.

The origin of American Indians is a subject of scientific discourse and also one of personal concern to Americans who are Indians. The latter may bring to their discourse convictions drawn from a feeling—a presupposition—that American Indians are markedly different from all transoceanic peoples. This may seem so obvious to persons who have grown up within Indian societies that it is accepted without question. The implication of this presupposition is that American Indians evolved in North America independently of any connection with humans on other continents. The lack of evidence of protohumans in America is then interpreted to indicate insufficient exploration for such ancient remains.

Scientists do not accept this presupposition of differences, but instead examine the evidence pro and con. The weight of evidence seems to indicate, to scientists, that the remote ancestors of American Indians were part of the human population of what is now eastern Asia and moved into present-day America thousands of years ago. This hypothesis accounts for the many biological similarities between American Indians and other peoples, and for the lesser number of biological differences (chiefly, a narrower range of genetic variations, compared with the total range of genes found among humans in the rest of the world). The hypothesis is compatible with more general hypotheses of biological evolution and population growth and change.

Many American Indians profess to find this hypothesis of an ancient Asian ancestry unacceptable. Their opposition to the scientific conclusions cannot be resolved by arguments from data because they believe that relevant data either have not yet been discovered, or are not recognized by unbelievers. Other data, some say, indicate coincidences, not common origin. The scientists try to restrict their theories to conclusions supported by the data at hand, and believe it is truer to experience to explain similarities by common origin rather than by coincidences.

The basic disagreement lies in the evaluation of the degree of uniqueness represented by American Indian peoples. Scientists do recognize a high degree of uniqueness on the part of American Indians when compared with populations and cultures on other continents, but reject the position that the linguistic, technological, religious, and physical differences are so great that no common ancestry, however remote, can be admitted. The belief of some individuals that myths of the separate origins of American and transoceanic peoples contain final truths revealed to seers in the past rests upon a presupposition outside the scientific universe of discourse.

Spiritual truths exist in a universe overlapping, but not identical with, the scientific universe. Most scientists and lay persons resolve apparent contradictions between these universes by understanding that spiritual discourses refer to a universe greater than the material world, one that our human languages can describe only poorly, and that most of us can at best only glimpse. We separate our scientific explanations of observable data from our deeper convictions of ultimate truth.

This book lies within the anthropologists' universe of discourse. It is a mundane universe without claim to final knowledge of transcendent reality. On the question of the origin of American Indians, as on other issues within the spiritual as well as the scientific universe, the text seeks only to present and interpret the data at hand. Readers looking for explanations derived from myth or revelation must turn to books discoursing on the spiritual universe.

---

eastern Siberia and a great deal of recent work by Japanese archaeologists in their homeland, which was once part of mainland Asia. Soviet, Japanese, Korean, and American archaeologists are now collaborating in conferences and in the field. Both the Soviet and Japanese researchers suggest that Asia north of the temperate latitudes was not colonized by humans until the fully modern physical type *(Homo sapiens sapiens)* had evolved and had developed the complex technology of the Upper Paleolithic period (approximately 35,000 B.C. to 8500 B.C.). The premodern humans *(Homo erectus)* and the protomodern humans *(Homo sapiens neanderthalensis,* or Neanderthal) have not been found beyond southern Siberia and northern China, the edge of the temperate zone.

The radicals base much of their claim for the great antiquity of humans in America upon a site in southern California called Calico Mountain. The site is an alluvial fan (a deposit of soil and gravel washed down from a hillside) in the California desert. On and in this deposit are crudely broken sharp-edged rocks and scattered concentrations of bits of charcoal. Those who believe the site represents human occupation one hundred thousand or

more years ago think the rocks are the stone tools of *Homo erectus* and the charcoal from their hearths. Those who do not accept this claim of great antiquity for Calico Mountain are convinced that some of the rocks were naturally fractured while rolling in the flash floods that contributed gravel to the alluvial fan, and that other rocks were quickly made tools abandoned by Indians hunting in the region in the relatively recent past. The charcoal concentrations are said to be the remains of creosote bushes flamed by lightning. The unprejudiced archaeologist is most disturbed by the unstable nature of the alluvial fan, in which the rocks could have been naturally shifted from their original positions, and by the consequent lack of secure association between the alleged tools (artifacts) and means of dating them, such as charcoal bits or geological layering.

There are a number of other finds of crude stone artifacts that suffer from problems similar to those of the Calico Mountain site. The artifacts lie on or near the surface on fans or hillside terraces that may in themselves have been formed many thousands of years ago, but that on the other hand have been available for camping right up to the present.

MAP 1 Americas' earliest humans

4

Crudity alone does not indicate antiquity for a stone tool, since most people—including you, reader—have at some time picked up a handy stone to break or hammer something, then discarded the stone after use. Only if the artifact lies buried under undisturbed layers of soil, and is closely associated with similarly undisturbed means of dating, can antiquity be accepted.

Archaeologists seeking evidence of early humans in Alaska and in the Yukon in Canada encounter problems similar to those of the Calico Mountain investigators. Logically, the oldest evidence of humans in the Americas should be in Alaska and the Yukon because in the late Pleistocene Ice Age, this northwestern section of present-day America was more than once part of the northern continent including Siberia. During the coldest phases of the Pleistocene, so much water was frozen in the huge glaciers that sea level was lower than today, and the shallow Bering Strait between what we know as Siberia and Alaska was dry land, called Beringia by geologists.

Animals moved east and west over Beringia, and human hunting bands could have followed over the cold plains of tundra, grass and sage, and occasional forest. Mammoths, giant bison, caribou, elk, wild sheep, and horses grazed the Beringian plains. Searching the gravelly outwashes of Yukon rivers, archaeologists have picked up dozens of chunks of mammoth bone that look as if they had been chipped like flint into sharp-edged flakes. Evidence for Beringian humans substituting massive mammoth bone for scarce stone in making artifacts? Or natural breakage of the bone, by trampling mammoths or in raging floods? To test one possibility, archaeologists threw an elephant bone into a cage of elephants to see whether their trampling would break it up into pieces like the Beringian chunks. It didn't, but the single experiment isn't a final answer. We do know that humans butchered mammoths in the Yukon, at Bluefish Cave, but the radiocarbon date for the occupation is 13,500 B.C., well in line with conservative estimates of humans entering America.

Liberal archaeologists assume that the spread of Upper Paleolithic peoples throughout northeastern Asia brought the most far-ranging bands comparatively quickly (within a few thousand years) through Beringia into North America. They might have come even during periods of higher sea level, since the Bering Strait is only 56 miles (90 kilometers) wide. A couple of small islands rising from the middle of the Strait make small boat crossings easier, and in winter, when the shallow Strait freezes, people could walk over on ice. In clear weather, the far mainland can be seen from the coasts.

Forests may have been a more formidable barrier than the Bering Strait. Forests have a low density of game compared to grassy plains, and forests were probably extensive in both Siberia and America from about 60,000 to 23,000 B.C., when increasing cold led to the last major glaciation, about 20,000 to 12,500 B.C. During this last glaciation, mountain valleys and great regions of northern America and Asia were closed off by glaciers, but there were always areas of Beringia open to game and to humans, so no span of time can be ruled out for human migration.

What frustrates liberal archaeologists is that much of that part of Beringia most favorable to human living is now below the sea. Historically, human populations in the Arctic have been most dense along the seacoasts where sea mammals such as seals, sea birds, fish, and shellfish provide food that can be supplemented by land game such as caribou and by river fish. The only remnant of the ancient Beringian coast preserved today and available for archaeological investigation is the Aleutian Islands. Excavated villages in the Aleutians have been dated only back to 7000 B.C.; perhaps earlier settlements were closer to the lower coastline of their time, and have since been flooded by rising sea levels. Underwater archaeology has been attempted off our present coasts, but it seems to work reasonably well only for salvaging historic ships: ancient sites lie under so much mud they can't be found.

HUMAN EVOLUTION

The first mammals appeared some two hundred million years ago. For an extremely long period, mammals lived among and competed for food with dinosaurs, many of which, it is now believed, were warm-blooded like mammals and unlike reptiles. The principal difference between mammals and the later dinosaurs may have been that the female mammals carried their developing young within their body and nourished them with milk after birth, whereas the female dinosaurs laid eggs and fed the hatched young with regurgitated food.

Approximately seventy million years ago, forces within the earth began to break up land masses, causing huge blocks to drift apart. The changes in climate that ensued as the continents slowly moved from one latitude to another, and as the pressures of continental masses drifting against each other forced up mountains, were detrimental to many types of animals, but particularly to the dinosaurs. Most of them became extinct. The mammals, generally smaller than the dinosaurs that perished, were apparently better able to adapt to the changed conditions, in part because they provided better care for their young, perhaps in part because, being smaller, they required less food. Mammals not only survived but, freed from the competition of dinosaurs, invaded many ecological niches (habitats) formerly dominated by the dinosaurs, and increased both in overall numbers and in numbers of species.

Among the little mammals of the period of early continental drift were rodentlike creatures that ran along tree branches catching insects. Their ecological niche, the lower branches of tropical forests, was rich in food, comfortable, and relatively free from competition from other types of animals, since insect-eating birds flew from the higher, more open branches, and true rodents tended to remain on the ground. The tree-dwelling, insect-catching mammals consequently prospered, and mutants able to survive in specialized habitats or more efficient in utilizing the resources of the tropical forests became the founders of new species. Several species of these prosimians (Latin for "before apes") can be recognized among the fossils from tropical regions of sixty million years ago. (Incidentally, many prosimians survive to the present. They include the lemurs you can see at zoos.)

A few million years later, monkeys had evolved. Monkeys differ from prosimians in that they have better-developed vision, more finely coordinated fingers (and toes), and, most important, greater intelligence. These advantages allowed the monkeys to dominate when in competition with prosimians within their habitats. Many prosimians became extinct, while new species of monkeys continued to appear.

During this period, South America drifted wholly apart from other continents (including North America). The primitive monkeys in South America flourished in their tropical forests, but no radically different, new forms of primates (monkeys, apes, and humans) appeared in the relatively stable environment of the South American tropics.Nor did primates evolve in the colder, temperate North American continent.

The Eurasian (Europe and Asia are one continental mass) and African tropics presented quite a different picture. By twenty-eight million years ago, a variety of monkeys were competing with primates having even larger brains, the apes. From then until the present, ape evolution tended to give this stock both greater intelligence and greater body size, which established for the apes a secure place in tropical habitats.

Most of the Eurasian-African apes remained in the forests, but a minority explored the edges of the jungles, attracted to the meat available on the grassy plains. Intelligence was at a premium in this environment, where one competed with lions, leopards, hyenas, and other quick, strong, cunning predators for fleet, sharp-eared game. By two million years ago, natural selection on the tropical grasslands produced from the primates the immediate ancestors of true humans. This type of primate had a larger brain than any other ape or monkey; it stood and ran upright, freeing its hands for carrying things; it was accustomed to making tools to perform tasks better; and it was developing, or perhaps had already developed, well-coordinated social groups whose members regularly helped one another.

Until one half million years ago, humans were restricted to their ancestral tropics. Then, some extraordinarily courageous and inventive individuals discovered how to tame fire. The control of fire enabled humans to live in temperate regions, and much of the world was thereby opened up to immigration. Campfire by campfire, bands of people advanced into northern China, Siberia, and eventually into North America, a continent with no other primates, and South America, where primitive monkeys were the sole representatives of this ancient order of mammals.

Continental drift had separated the Americas from the other continents before the mutations that eventually gave rise to the human species appeared. All American peoples are descended from ancestors ultimately from Eurasia and Africa.

That humans migrated south and southeastward from Beringia into America before or during the last glacial maximum is suggested by a number of finds in Central and South America. It is reasonably certain that people were living at the far tip of South America, Patagonia, by 10,000 B.C. In south-central Chile, Thomas Dillehay excavated butchered mastodon (an extinct elephant adapted to temperate climates) and bits of wooden artifacts and house structures, radiocarbon-dated to 11,000 B.C., in a site called Monte Verde. Possible crude stone tools and charred wood were uncovered in a lower, older stratum at the site. Richard S. MacNeish recovered bones of extinct sloth and horse with crudely chipped stones that might be tools in Pikimachay (Flea Cave) near Ayacucho in the highlands of south-central Peru, where the lowest, oldest occupation layer is dated to 12,000 B.C. Niéde Guidon, an archaeologist experienced in

French Paleolithic sites, exposed a series of occupation layers with stone artifacts in Pedra Furada, a series of massive rock shelters in northeastern Brazil; radiocarbon dates indicate the oldest of layers may be from 30,000 B.C., but whether any artifacts are that old is much debated. Pedra Furada does have simple but clear paintings, in red, of people and animals on its rock walls, and these, some dated to 12,000 years ago, establish human habitation in eastern South America contemporaneous with that in the south (Chile) and throughout North America.

Sites in Mexico and the United States give support, but not absolute proof, for the liberal estimate of the time depth of human residence in the Americas. Hueyatlaco in the Valsequillo region southeast of the Valley of Mexico contained what appear to be butchered bones of horse, of a llamalike American camel, and of mastodon, as

---

RADIOCARBON DATING

The radiocarbon method is the method most commonly used to date American archaeological finds. It is based on the fact that all living organisms take in some radioactive carbon isotopes, which are normally present in the air, and that these isotopes decay at a regular rate. When an animal or plant dies, the amount of radioactive carbon in its tissues is roughly that in the air. During life it is constantly renewed, but when respiration stops it is reduced. After nearly six thousand years, a skeleton or carbonized wood will contain only half the air proportion of radioactive carbon. Physicists can measure the proportion of radioactive carbon remaining in long-dead tissue and calculate from that the number of years since the organism's last respiration. The date so calculated will be approximate, due to variations in the proportion of carbon in the atmosphere over the centuries, and to variations in the concentration of carbon in different organisms (fast-growing organisms such as grasses contain more carbon than slow-growing organisms such as trees). The reliability of a radiocarbon date depends also on the competence of the archaeologist who has excavated the material to be dated: he or she must be skilled in judging whether the material to go to the dating laboratory is truly associated with the occupation layer and artifacts to be dated, or whether it comes from a different layer, perhaps brought down in a rodent's burrow, by erosion, or by digging by later visitors to the site.

---

well as stone artifacts. All of these lay in ancient stream gravels rather than in a stable soil "floor" of a camp, so they have been difficult to date, although a geologist's estimate of 20,000 B.C. for the time the gravels were laid down seems not unreasonable. Tlapacoya in the Valley of Mexico, in modern Mexico City, has what looks like a briefly-used camp, with a couple of small flakes of chipped stone and a possible hearth, radiocarbon-dated to 21,000 B.C. Meadowcroft Rockshelter in western Pennsylvania near Pittsburgh has its lowest human occupation layer dated to 12,500 B.C. Meadowcroft's archaeologist, James Adovasio, was excited by the possibility of older dates, but critics point out that no extinct animal bones, only deer and other modern fauna, occur in the rockshelter layers.

Conservative archaeologists worry that radiocarbon dates have been accepted too readily. Not only do some researchers write as if "10,850 +/- 870 B.C." were a historical date rather than what it really is—the median year in the probable span of years (870 years on each side of the median, that is, the 1,740 years between 11,720 B.C. and 9980 B.C.) within which the assayed plant or animal actually lived— researchers may also be too ready to assume evidence of human occupation was contemporary with the radiocarbon-dated material. Soil movement through freezing and thawing, through water flow, through animal digging (even worm burrowing can move objects), and the simple weight of objects, causing them to gradually sink through soil, can all shift artifacts and bone and wood fragments from separate places of origin into proximity. Conservatives demand the kind of proof that first convinced scientists that humans had arrived in America by the end of the Pleistocene epoch: a distinctively manufactured artifact indisputably contemporary with independently dated material.

That first accepted proof of human antiquity in America was a Folsom spearpoint stuck between the ribs of an extinct species of bison. Discovered near the town of Folsom in northeastern New Mexico in 1926, the find was viewed the next year, 1927, by a blue-ribbon panel of geologists, paleontologists, and archaeologists who agreed that the only reasonable explanation for the stone spearpoint in the bison carcass was that the animal had been killed by a human hunter some ten thousand years ago. The distinctive style of spearpoint, beautifully chipped into a leaf shape, then attached, tongue-in-groove, to a shaft by removing a few long, thin flakes vertically up from the base of the point and inserting the thinned base into a slot in the shaft, is called Folsom after the first find site. Folsom points are frequently discovered with bison remains, suggesting these animals were a favored prey of the hunters. Through radiocarbon dating of charcoal or bone associated with Folsom points (since stone never breathed in carbon isotopes, it can't be radiocarbon-dated in itself), the style is known to have been common around 8500 B.C. For a thousand years preceding (from about 9500 B.C.), a similar style of spearpoint except usually larger and with shorter flakes taken in thinning the base—was in use throughout America. This earlier style is called Clovis, after another New Mexico site, and is more often found associated with mammoth carcasses than with bison. Both Clovis and Folsom styles require extraordinary skill in flintknapping (chipping stone) to achieve the even, rippled surfaces and "fluted"-looking like fluted columns on buildings—thinned bases.

There is no question that by 9500 B.C., humans were in America well south of the grassy plains of Beringia west of the Pleistocene glaciation. Right along the edge of the continent-wide glacier was a narrow tundra inhabited by caribou and musk-ox. The western half of unglaciated North America had park-like alterations of evergreen and oak forests with grasslands grazed by small camels, antelope, and ground sloth. Northeastern North America had subarctic pine forests with moose and giant beaver, while the Southeast had mostly deciduous forests with deer the principal game. The end-Pleistocene hunters of these several great natural zones left campsites testifying to their highly developed technology both in manufacturing stone and bone artifacts and in procuring food and raw materials. East of the Rockies, fluted-base Clovis and then Folsom styles were preferred. West of the Rockies, hunters seem to have preferred hafting their spearpoints by narrowing the base into a stem and then inserting it into a shaft slot, rather than creating a tongue-in-groove fit by "fluting." Fort Rock Cave in eastern Oregon is an example of a site where leaf-shaped stemmed spearpoints, associated with other stone and bone tools and with butchered game bones, occur dated to around 11,000 B.C.

What puzzles archaeologists is that end-Pleistocene sites in Beringia lack fluted-base Clovis or Folsom style artifacts. Fluted-base spearpoints were used in Alaska, but apparently *later* than to the south in the United States. Apparently the "fluted" thinning of spearpoint bases, difficult to achieve, became fashionable in central and eastern America around 9500 B.C.; while west of the Rockies, in Beringia, and in Eurasia, late-Pleistocene hunters preferred less-tricky methods of fitting spearpoints into their shafts. Putting aside the one unusual American technique of thinning spearpoint bases, the technology and economy of American peoples, beginning at least by 9500 B.C. and continuing to the very end of the Pleistocene Ice Age a couple thousand years later, fit into the general pattern of Eurasian Upper Paleolithic cultures. In western Beringia—today, easternmost Siberia—the Ushki site, dated to 12,000 B.C., exemplifies the local variant of Upper Paleolithic hunters, not dissimilar to Paleo-Indian campsites far eastward in America.

Some idea of what life was like for Paleo-Indians can be glimpsed at Debert, a site in central Nova Scotia, Canada. Radiocarbon dates for Debert place its occupation at around 8500 B.C. The excavator found what appear to be the floors of ten tents, arranged in a roughly semicircular camp, each tent with two or more fire hearths and with the door opening south. A scatter of broken fluted points and tools lay on each floor. An eleventh concentration of chips of stone and tools lay just west of the tents, and was probably a lookout where the men of the camp manufactured their weapon points and tools while watching for game. In this area was a hearth in which blocks of chalcedony, a fine-grained silicate stone especially suited to making sharp-edged artifacts, had been heated to render them easier to chip. These blocks of raw material had been carried to the site from an outcrop sixty miles away. From the chalcedony and from other types of stone, the Debert people had made and discarded or lost at the camp 140 whole or fragmentary fluted projectile points, 1,600 scrapers (for cleaning the flesh from hides or for woodworking), and 1,000 small wedges used to split bone, which then could be made into scrapers, knives, or projectile points. Fluted-point makers' campsites similar to Debert have been found from Maine to Colorado, dating to the same period.

At about 8000 B.C., the effects of a drastic change in climate began to be evident throughout the Northern Hemisphere. For reasons still not understood—although various theories have been put forth in explanation—great ice sheets covering thousands of square miles in Canada and the northern United States and in northern Eurasia began to melt more than they accumulated water as ice over the winters. This was not an overnight phenomenon, but one that fluctuated throughout the last Ice Age (Pleistocene epoch) and it was particularly noticeable during the period in which fluted points were made. As the continental glaciers (ice sheets) melted, three effects were felt:

1. The runoff from the melting ice raised the sea level, flooding thousands of miles of coastline even in tropical zones, and in places submerging hundreds of square miles of coastal plain and producing a new coast far inland. The Bering region was thus flooded, and the Bering Strait created. A tremendous number of archaeological sites, the habitats of people who lived near the coasts or hunted on the Bering plain during the late Pleistocene epoch are now lost beneath the ocean.

2. The melting ice gradually freed for human use the northern United States and Canada, where formerly only limited areas, mostly in the West, were habitable. Migrations both northward from the United States, and southeastward from the habitable territories of Ice Age Alaska and Yukon, would be likely. Plants and animals, as well as people, migrated north.

3. The lack of ice sheets in formerly glaciated territories, as well as other factors, caused changes in wind and rainfall patterns throughout North America. These changes, with associated temperature changes, in turn caused changes in the ecology of most regions of North America, not just the north. Forests replaced grasslands, or deserts developed. Animal populations shifted as their habitats did. Some animals became extinct, especially the large grazing animals such as mammoths, horses, American camels, and a very large race of bison, at least in part because the grasslands on which they foraged became much reduced in extent. The ending of the last cold stage of the Pleistocene epoch, about 8000 B.C., was both beneficial, in opening the northern half of the continent for habitation, and detrimental, in contributing to the extinction of many excellent game species.

The warming trend continued, with minor fluctuations, until about 3000 B.C., when winters in North America were in general a little warmer, and overall conditions drier, than at present. The ecological shifts also continued, at a slower pace, after 8000 B.C., with a few mastodon possibly surviving in the Southeast until close to 4000 B.C. (the evidence is debatable), and the High Plains nearly a desert at the climax of the trend to drier and warmer winters. Much of what happened in American prehistory, as throughout the world, can be viewed in an ecological framework as adjustments to changing environmental conditions. Add the need to adjust to increasing populations (which in a sense is another environmental condition for the people in a society), and powerful stimulants to technological and societal developments are visible.

The past ten thousand years (the Holocene, or present, geological era) have seen the human population of North America rise from perhaps a few hundred thousand to many million, and differentiate from a once-universal hunter-gatherer mode of life into hundreds of distinctive life-ways. Most of this population increase and differentiation was the natural growth of reasonably healthy populations in America. There were probably several Holocene migrations across the Bering Strait from Asia into America, the latest perhaps 2000 B.C., but there has been little scholarly interest in determining any but the earlier ones. In addition to migrations of small groups of people in the early and middle Holocene era, there has been definite contact across the Bering Strait throughout the later Holocene era. Since about 4000 B.C., the Bering region has been exploited by sea-mammal hunters and fishermen, historically the Inuit (Eskimos), who live on both sides of the channel and on the larger islands in it, and visit and trade across it. Inuit also traded in the interior of Alaska and southward with the British Columbia Indians. Many ideas and inventions could thus have been traded from Asia to America (or the opposite way) during the Holocene era, but, like the later migrations, diffusion of traded items has received relatively little scholarly attention except when, as in the case of burial mounds, it seems possible to refute any derivation from Asia.

Migration of humans into America is customarily viewed as taking place during two periods. The first was in the late Pleistocene epoch and brought bands of hunters across the Bering region from northeastern Asia into America, then southward and southeastward. This migration is generally assumed to have been largely completed by the time of Clovis, 9500 B.C. American populations then grew by natural internal population increase until A.D.. 1500, when Christopher Columbus sold

Europe the idea of America as a New World of opportunity. The second period of migrations then began. The common assumption of only two so widely separated periods of migration is surely overly simple. But it does emphasize the fact that the development of the native American nations was largely independent of Old World influence; it was the result of the intelligence and abilities of the descendants of the late-Pleistocene and early-Holocene migrants from northeastern Asia.

SECTION 2: CULTURE AREAS

Once humans had migrated throughout the American continent, history was strongly influenced by the climate and resources of each region in which they settled. Many of the differences between the native American nations arose through the development of patterns that more efficiently and fully exploited the resource potentials of the nations' homelands. A knowledge of American geography is therefore a prerequisite to understanding the cultures of American peoples.

The importance of geography to students of American cultures was recognized in the late nineteenth century, in part through the emphasis placed on it by Franz Boas (1858–1942). Boas was born and educated in Germany, where his opportunities for advancement in an academic career were limited by his Jewish origin. He emigrated to the United States, where the remarkable scope of his abilities brought him to a preeminent position in the young discipline of anthropology. We shall meet Boas again in these pages, but at this point we will note only that Boas stimulated many of his colleagues and students to examine the ecology (a term not then used, however) of the various areas in which they recorded American Indian cultures. Chief among Boas's students was Alfred L. Kroeber (1876–1960), who produced in 1931 (and published in 1939) the climax of these researches, *Cultural and Natural Areas of Native North America*.

ANTHROPOGEOGRAPHIE

Germany in the second half of the nineteenth century was a center of progress in both the sciences and philosophy. It was generally assumed that the diversity of phenomena in any field masked underlying regularities, which in turn derived from primordial simple "germs" (in the sense of seeds, which *germ*inate). Many thinkers, scientists and philosophers alike, sought to discover these regularities, or "laws," and primitive forms that developed through time under the influence of these laws. Among the leaders of this quest during Franz Boas's (1858–1942) young manhood were Adolf Bastian (1826–1905) and Friedrich Ratzel (1844–1904). Bastian was a somewhat eccentric world traveler who produced a major ethnography of Asia but is best known for his search for "elementary ideas," from which he assumed all modern cultural phenomena grew. To explain the obvious variety of modern ideas in spite of the hypothesized elementary ideas underlying all human cultures, Bastian invoked the effects of different climatic, ecological, and topographic experiences upon the peoples inhabiting contrasting regions of the world. Ratzel followed up Bastian's direction by producing, in the 1880s, an illustrated encyclopedia of the peoples of the world, arranged according to major geographical regions, so far as these were known at the time. He then condensed this work and developed its theoretical foundation more clearly in a book, *Anthropogeographie,* which brought to fruition the concept, introduced early in the century by the brilliant Alexander von Humboldt, that we cannot understand either history or the cultures of modern peoples without examining the characteristics of the regions they inhabit.

Even before Ratzel's major volumes were published, Boas knew of his work through attending his lectures. Boas was attracted to Ratzel's ideas particularly because Ratzel strove for a thorough grounding in ethnographic fact and because he displayed great caution in speculating on "elementary ideas" or cultural "laws"—qualities that distinguished Boas's work, too.

Discussion of the correlations between environments and cultures in North America had been codified in print by 1896, when Otis T. Mason (1838–1908), an anthropologist with the U.S. National Museum, published a division of the continent into eighteen "environments," the boundaries of which seemed to coincide significantly with cultural differences between peoples. By 1910, Mason had reduced the eighteen regions to twelve, which he now termed "ethnic environments." Clark Wissler (1870–1947), a junior colleague of Boas at the beginning of this century, began on a different tack by grouping aboriginal Indian peoples on the basis of their major food staples. This yielded six areas: Caribou, Bison, Salmon, Wild Seeds, Eastern Maize, and Intensive Agriculture.

Wissler next integrated these with the commonly recognized geographical regions and by 1914 could publish a map of the "Material Cultures of the North American Indians." This map was used in Wissler's 1917 popular survey, *The American Indian,* and through its many editions, this book became the most generally used source of the division of the continent into culture areas.

Kroeber realized that grouping native American societies into culture areas could fulfill two objectives. First, as Mason and especially Wissler had thought, it organized a confusing array of descriptions into packages that the nonprofessional reader could easily grasp. By knowing the geographic location of a tribe, one could predict its major food resources, nomadic or sedentary settlement, political structure, and so forth. Second, Kroeber seized upon the predictive power of the culture areas: by studying the characteristics of culture areas, the anthropologist may better learn what factors of the environment influence human societal development and, having sorted these out, what cultural behavior seems to have purely historical origins. He concluded that the culture area was a "valuable mechanism" in reconstructing the undocumented pasts of the native American peoples.

Acting upon his insight, Kroeber prepared what seemed to him the best possible correlation of cultural differences and geographical boundaries. He found (using Mason's and Wissler's culture areas as a base) that the most meaningful correlations were between vegetation zones and aboriginal cultures. This discovery underscores the importance of food resources in shaping cultures, for vegetation is either directly eaten (as in Wissler's Wild Seeds, Eastern Maize, and Intensive Agriculture areas) or furnishes the food of the animals upon which humans depend (Wissler's Caribou and Bison areas), or the lack of edible vegetation forces reliance upon fish (Wissler's Salmon area, the rocky northern Pacific coast). Vegetation zones themselves reflect climate, topography, altitude, soils, and often human practices such as field clearing and fire drives.

Kroeber felt the culture areas are "geographical units of culture" that correspond "to regional floras and faunas, which are accumulations of species but can also be viewed as summation entities"—in modern words, a total ecology. Culture areas exist because groups of peoples tend to be more like their immediate neighbors than like distant groups, for two reasons: (1) all peoples within a geographical region must adjust their diet, shelter, and other biologically demanded practices to the conditions of that region, and (2) people borrow ideas from and adjust to adjacent social groups. Because climate, topography, and soils, and the vegetation influenced by these, change through time, and because migrations, epidemics, and inventions change human populations, culture areas are inher-

ently unstable. Kroeber reminded his readers of this, and urged that culture areas be considered generalizations. The characteristics of each culture area, he said, are true only for one point in time and, usually, only for the central section of the geographical region. At other periods of time, and in the transition zones between regional ecologies, some, perhaps many, of the characteristics of the culture area will be lacking. (The time at which all the characteristics are found is the cultural climax; the area within which all are found is the culture center.) Culture areas are thus heuristic devices (concepts or techniques useful at the moment) for analyzing the various factors, physical and social, that have influenced the development of a way of life.

Table 1–1 compares Wissler's and Kroeber's culture area divisions to those used in this text, shown in Figure 1–2. The geographical areas underlying the culture areas represent Holocene climate; in the late Pleistocene epoch, the Arctic-Subarctic would have been under ice, its southern margin fringed by tundra, and the Prairie-Plains and Intermontane West a single major geographic zone of grasslands and mountain forests. A good argument could be made for lumping several of the standard Wissler-Kroeber areas to make only three major culture areas for North America: Continental Core, comprising Mexico, the Southwest and America east of the Rockies, north through the St. Lawrence Valley; Pacific Drainage, west of the Rockies from Baja California through British Columbia; and High Latitudes, the subarctic forests and the Arctic. Farming the Mexican domesticates—maize, squashes, and beans—was the basic economy of the Continental Core, cultivation of indigenous plants was the basis of Pacific Drainage economies, and hunting and fishing was the economy of the high latitudes. Though the number and boundaries of culture areas may differ somewhat according to the features that are emphasized, recognition of basic cultural geography must be the backbone of our study of the history of the Indian peoples of North America.

TABLE 1.1   Culture Areas of North America

KEHOE (THIS BOOK)		WISSLER'S FOOD AREAS	OTIS MASON, 1910	KROEBER, 1939
Mexico Southwest	}	Intensive Agriculture	[did not include Mexico] Pueblo	Mexico Southwest
Southeast Northeast	}	Eastern Maize	Gulf Coast Mississippi Valley Atlantic Slope St. Lawrence Lakes	East and North
Prairie-Plains		Bison	Plains	Plains
Intermontane West California	}	Wild Seeds	Interior Basin Columbia-Fraser California-Oregon	Intermediate and Inter- mountain
Northwest Coast		Salmon	North Pacific Coast	Northwest Coast
Arctic and Subarctic		Caribou	Arctic Yukon-Mackenzie	[North sector of East and North]

SECTION 3: THE END OF THE PLEISTOCENE EPOCH AND THE EARLY ARCHAIC PERIOD

It is usually assumed that the Ice Age migrants into North America were highly nomadic hunters who followed herds of mammoth or bison. This assumption contrasts these early migrants with their descendants, who occupied more defined territories and lived off a greater variety of foods, plant as well as animal. The ancestors are called Big-Game Hunters, the descendants Archaic. The assumption and the contrast it asserts exaggerate the difference between the earliest and later American Indians in many areas of the continent.

The hunters who used fluted projectile points to kill mammoth and bison were certainly nomadic. At the Hell Gap site in Wyoming, in a layer dated about 8500 B.C., archaeologists found post molds (soil discolorations from decayed wooden posts) loosely spaced into a circle 6 feet (2 meters) in diameter. This probably was a lightly built hut frame, perhaps covered with skins. It would have been much easier for hunters who had killed a mammoth to move their families and rebuild such a hut or tent near the carcass, than to carry the tons of meat from the kill site to a camp miles away. Moving camp to the vicinity of a generous harvest does not, however, imply that the hunting families were accustomed to travel across hundreds of miles, any more than that the slaughter of a mammoth implies that the families ate nothing but mammoth meat. Towards the end of the Ice Age, a traveler in North America would have found no permanent, year-round towns and no farms, but he or she would have seen that most families stayed within a radius of a hundred or so miles, and, except in a few western grassland regions, did not rely on mammoth or giant bison for their regular food. Evidence for a seasonal round of local movement, rather than wandering, has come from Paleo-Indian sites in Maine, where stones near camp sites were piled to protect, the archaeologists think, caches of meat. Possibly the Paleo-Indian hunters, like historic Inuit in the Arctic, cached meat at the beginning of winter when game animals were fat and freezing temperatures would keep the meat as in a refrigerator over the snowy months. Caches of fine Clovis-fluted spearpoints and blades have also been found in western states, but with carved

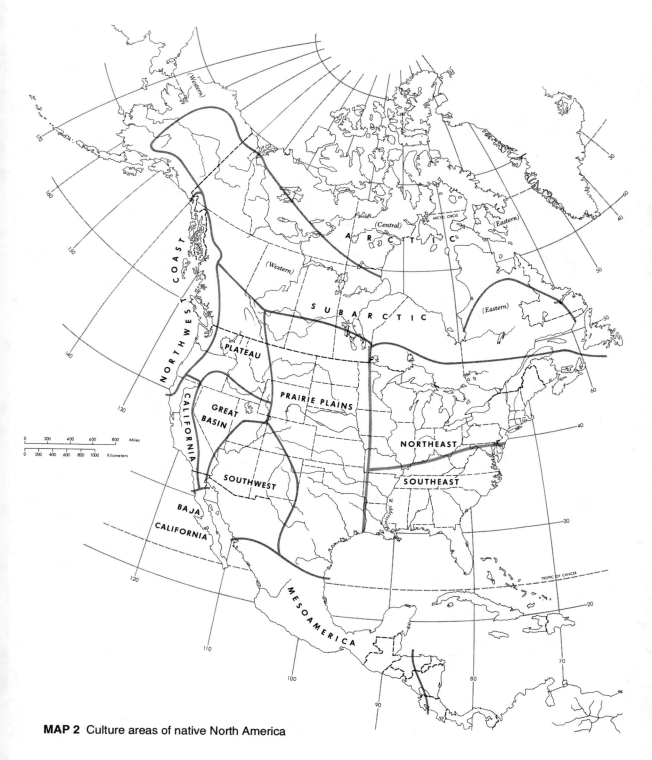

MAP 2 Culture areas of native North America

15

bones, red ocher paint, and in one cache, human bone, suggesting these "caches" were offerings, or sometimes graves, where the community proffered its craftsworkers' art to please a deity. Within the dominant pattern of seasonal rounds were exceptions; adventuresome young people who explored far beyond their people's land and sometimes returned to take colonies to new territories. The continent became populated through a combination of occasional deliberate colonizing ventures and many small shifts along the margins of occupied territories. There is no need to assume that the early migrants were always moving great distances.

The period in North America after the era of the early migrants is customarily labeled *Archaic,* a term that archaeologists have come to apply to mean a way of life in which families shift camp locally from season to season to be near the food resources obtainable at each time of the year. This *pattern* was not really different from the usual life of Paleo-Indians; the difference between Paleo-Indians and Archaic peoples was in the game available, which in the Paleo-Indian era included now-extinct animals larger than any Holocene game in the Americas. Unable to procure a ton or so of meat from a single kill of a mammoth or giant bison, Archaic peoples' economic strategies must have focused on more frequent hunting, more gathering and even cultivation of plants, and development of more methods of storage. As populations increased in nearly every region, political relations had to be created to manage resources effectively.

During the early Holocene period (8000 to 5000 B.C.), three principal culture areas probably existed within the continent: the Western, from the Pacific to the Rockies and including highland Mexico; the Plains, from the eastern edge of the Rockies to the Red River (of the North)—lower Missouri drainage; and the Eastern, from the Midwest to the Atlantic. The far North at this period still contained glacial ice. Many distinctive projectile points and knife blades from the early Holocene era have been collected from eroding gullies and, in the 1930s,

Dust Bowl fields. What is accurately known comes from the lower levels of deep deposits, where it is difficult to uncover large areas of the ancient camps.

Towards the end of the Ice Age, the custom of hafting projectile points tongue-in-groove—the reason why the "fluted" channel or groove was flaked up the Clovis and Folsom blades—went out of favor. Instead, it became customary to merely thin the basal section of the blade before inserting it in what was probably a squared-off, rather than an elongated and rounded, end of the projectile shaft. The earliest of the new fashion in projectile points is called the Agate Basin type, after a site in Wyoming where it was found. Agate Basin blades have been dated between 8500 and 8000 B.C. at the excavations at the Hell Gap site in Wyoming. They are very close in time to the Folsom fluted points. In Saskatchewan, on the Canadian Plains, some Agate Basin-type blades have been discovered that had short Clovis-like channels flaked up from the base, as if the users didn't quite trust the new fashion in hafting. These transitional blades support the inference, derived from details of the flaking technique, that the disappearance of the fluted blade bases in the early Holocene era represents a shift in hafting method but not an end to the technological tradition begun with Clovis.

People interested in ancient America know the early Holocene era for the beautiful stone blades made in this period. These stone blades, some of which were spearpoints, but others of which were knives or, in some instances, apparently nonutilitarian—ceremonial symbols or virtuoso showpieces of the maker's art—are part of the fluted-point technological tradition that earlier produced the Clovis and Folsom projectile points. This Fluted Tradition, as archaeologists refer to it, taught unsurpassed skill in flint knapping. Blades a foot long and less than an inch thick, of translucent glasslike chalcedony, each face (flat side) covered by narrow, shallow, rippling grooves, prove that many Indians of this period mastered a knowledge of the properties of stones and a delicate control that was difficult to achieve. We must realize also that the societies in which these virtuoso flint knappers lived encouraged them to develop their talent, to express artistic urges through stone. After about 5000 B.C., for reasons quite unknown, the appreciation of virtuoso flint knapping declined and few persons bothered to practice the most difficult aspects of the art.

Persistence of the Fluted Tradition technology, in spite of the discarding of the fluting method of hafting, supports the links seen by many archaeologists between the Fluted Tradition, unique to the Americas, and Eurasian flint-knapping technology. Hansjürgen Müller-Beck, a German archaeologist, noticed that not only were the Clovis blades generally similar to Upper Paleolithic stone blades in Eurasia, but that a few of the thousands of Russian "bifaces" (stone artifacts chipped on both faces in finishing, in contrast with long, thin, specialized blades produced by a different technique needing little finishing) had shallow flute channels in the base. Müller-Beck argues that Clovis blades indicate that some of the migrants into North America in the Ice Age carried with them the stone technology developed in western Eurasia by 30,000 B.C.; American archaeologists such as Joe Ben Wheat and Henry Irwin, who excavated the Hell Gap site, claim that this technology persisted in North America until about 5000 B.C. These archaeologists believe that what is important is the basic technology, a set of flint-knapping techniques, not the relatively brief hafting fashion in America that resulted in flute channels on Clovis and Folsom blades.

The early Holocene era saw several types of stone blades within this later Fluted Tradition. All share a lance (or leaf) outline and a thinned, often squared base, as well as the highly skilled flaking technique used to shape and flatten the artifact. The types differ in details of outline, base, and size. Toward the end of the Fluted Tradition, 6000 B.C.-7000 B.C., a popular type was the Scottsbluff (named after finds at the rock landmark in western Nebraska), on which the basal section was nar-

rowed into a stem. An unstemmed variant of Scottsbluff, called Eden, achieves in many examples the ultimate in flint-knapping virtuosity: blades so long, so delicately thin, so exquisitely ripple-flaked it seems unlikely they were put to any practical use.

The early Holocene blades found *in situ* (in the original place of deposition) in an occupation site have been associated with stone scrapers (for scraping hides or planing wood), stone engravers (for incising and cutting bone), stone and bone knives, and occasionally cobblestones that could have been used as hammers or for mashing vegetable foods such as grains, roots, or berries. Evidence for structures in these sites is slight, perhaps the best being the circle of posts mentioned as probably a hut or tent frame from the Agate Basin layer at Hell Gap. Since bone needles and sewing awls are sometimes found in the early Holocene sites, sewn-skin tents could have been prepared as shelters in this period. The 6-foot diameter of the post circle at Hell Gap reminds us that the tents must have been small, because they had to be carried from camp to camp on the backs of the family. Dogs may have been pressed into service to carry small loads on their backs, or the tents may have been fastened to pole frames that the animals dragged, as was done on the Plains before the historic period; no better beasts of burden were available.

In the Eastern and Western culture areas of the early Holocene era, stone blades similar to those on the Plains were made, but in these areas the flaking technique was usually cruder and the projectile points and knives smaller. Archaeologists debate whether to accept the Eastern and Western early Holocene artifacts as variants of the Plains tradition, or to see these three major culture areas as virtually independent. One site in Wisconsin indicates that there was at least contact between people making Scottsbluff and Eden blades and those making the smaller, notched Eastern Archaic projectile points and knives. The site is the funeral pyre of, probably, a youth, and is located on the highest point of a sandy ridge overlooking what is now Lake Michigan. With the body were placed at least a dozen Scottsbluff and Eden blades and one notched Archaic-type point. The cremation seems to date to about 6000 B.C. The artifacts in it, including simple bifacially flaked blades and scrapers as well as the Scottsbluff type and the Archaic point, allow a choice of explanations: the youth's people were among the late practitioners of the Fluted Tradition and had obtained the Archaic point by trade or seizure as a curiosity; or they had learned a newer style of manufacturing and hafting projectile points and blades, whereby they used notches near the base and practiced a combination of the two technologies. The latter interpretation can be supported by the shift, beginning around 6000 B.C., from the American version of the originally Eurasian Upper Paleolithic stone-artifact technological tradition to an American-developed technological tradition that seems indigenous to the Eastern culture area.

The correlation between the climatic changes of the postglacial early Holocene and the technological shift in stoneworking has led some archaeologists, notably Joseph Caldwell (1916–1973), to consider the Holocene developments in North America as progressively more efficient utilizations of postglacial ecological resources. Caldwell believed that later Archaic peoples achieved what he termed "primary forest efficiency," a reasonably comfortable, secure life based on a sophisticated knowledge of the varied resources of the forests of the Midwest and East. He saw this efficiency growing as the peoples experimented with possible food and raw material sources and with tools for harvesting and preparing them. The most intriguing aspect of Caldwell's thesis is his contention that the achievement of primary forest efficiency was so secure and satisfactory that people had little incentive to adopt agriculture in its place. Thus, Caldwell explained the persistence into historic times of the importance of hunting and wild-food gathering in the Eastern Woodlands culture area. Caldwell's thesis is too simplistic—squash

was planted and cultivated in the Eastern Woodlands from 2000 B.C., and after A.D. 900, there was intensive agriculture—but it does draw our attention to the viability of skilled, intelligent hunting and vegetable gathering as a subsistence base for human societies.

Caldwell's area of expertise was the Eastern Woodlands, and he cautiously limited his thesis to that area, but it seems applicable also to the Western culture area. Indeed, a similar concept was proposed by the Utah archaeologist Jesse Jennings in 1956, a year earlier than Caldwell's work was presented in final form. Jennings had excavated Danger Cave, a large rockshelter on the edge of the Great Salt Desert in Utah. Here he found a series of layers beginning at the very start of the Holocene era, 8000 B.C. Excellent preservation of normally perishable wood, fibers, and hides in the dry desert conditions allowed Jennings a remarkably complete picture of the artifacts and diet of the peoples who had camped in Danger Cave. The picture closely resembled the accounts of historic Shoshoni Indians in Utah, and Jennings therefore argued that the basic pattern of human life in the Great Basin of Utah-Nevada-eastern Oregon persisted with no really major changes for ten thousand years, from the formation of modern climatic conditions in the early Holocene era until the Mormon invasion in the last century. Jennings believed that what he called the Desert Culture represents "primary desert efficiency," to borrow Caldwell's terminology. Any other pattern of life would have been more liable to famine.

Subsequent archaeologists and ethnologists have picked holes in portions of Jenning's bold argument, but the notion that some supposedly primitive life-ways are actually quite sophisticated adjustments to their habitats is increasingly favored. In particular, the old assumption that agriculture is always better than hunting and gathering is demonstrably untrue. The lack of intensive maize agriculture in the Western culture area north of the Southwest can be attributed to a shrewd weighing by the native peoples of the labor required by such agriculture against that required by hunting, gathering and cultivation of indigenous plants. Well-designed techniques for exploiting native resources gave as much, and generally more, return per person-hour of labor as maize agriculture would have, and had the further advantage of more reliable harvests, since the native plants, and animals, were better adapted to the local conditions than foreign crops would be. Throughout North America, the early Holocene era gives evidence that techniques and artifacts for efficiently harvesting reliable, abundant local food resources were being developed. The Archaic lifeway of exploiting a variety of local resources was established within a thousand years or so of the melting of glaciers, and persisted in Anglo-America (north of the pre-1846 Mexico-United States border) until the European settlements, although in many areas of the United States it was eventually modified by the introduction of agriculture as an added resource.

RECOMMENDED READING

Fagan, Brian M. 1991 *Ancient North America.* New York: W. W. Norton (distributor for Thames and Hudson). Clear, readable introduction to North American archaeology.

Jennings, Jesse D., ed. 1983 *Ancient North Americans.* San Francisco: W. H. Freeman. Detailed chapters by experts on the prehistory of each culture area of North America, plus a chapter by Stephen Jett on the highly controversial topic of pre-Columbian trans-oceanic contacts with the Americas. There is also a companion volume, *Ancient South Americans*, edited by Jennings.

SOURCES

Adovasio, J. M., J. Donahue, and R. Stuckenrath. 1990 The Meadowcroft Rockshelter Radiocarbon Chronology 1975–1990. *American Antiquity* 55(2):348–354.

Agenbroad, Larry D., Jim I. Mead, and Lisa W. Nelson, eds. 1990 *Megafauna and Man.* Hot Springs, S.D.: The Mammoth Site of Hot Springs, S.D., Scientific Papers, vol. 1.

American Antiquity. "Current Research" (through volume 55).

Arctic Anthropology 1971 Papers from a Symposium on Early Man in North America, New Developments 1960–1970. (2).

Bahn, Paul G. 1991 Dating the First Americans. *New Scientist* 1778: 26–28.

Bryan, Alan Lyle, ed. 1978 *Early Man in America from a Circum-Pacific Perspective.* Edmonton: University of Alberta, Department of Anthropology, Occasional Papers, No. 1.

Caldwell, Joseph R. 1968 *Trend and Tradition in the Prehistory of the Eastern United States.* Springfield, Ill.: American Anthropological Association, Memoir 88.

Clark, Donald W. 1984 Northern Fluted Points: Paleo-Eskimo, Paleo-Arctic, or Paleo-Indian. *Canadian Journal of Anthropology* 4(1):65–81.

Dincauze, Dena F. 1984 An Archaeo-Logical Evaluation of the Case for Pre-Clovis Occupations. New York: Academic Press, *Advances in World Archaeology* 3:275–323.

———1989 Fluted Points in the Eastern Forests. Ms. prepared for symposium organized by O. Soffer for Leningrad, July 1989.

Driver, H. E. 1962 *The Contribution of A. L. Kroeber to Culture Area Theory and Practice.* Bloomington, Ind.: Indiana University Publications in Anthropology and Linguistics 18.

Ericson, Jonathon E., R. E. Taylor, and Rainer Berger, eds. 1982 *Peopling of the New World.* Los Altos, Calif.: Ballena Press (Anthropological Papers, No. 23).

Fladmark, Knut R., Jonathan C. Driver, and Diana Alexander. 1988 The Paleoindian Component at Charlie Lake Cave (HbRf 39), British Columbia. *American Antiquity* 53(2):371–384.

Gramly, Richard Michael. 1988 *The Adkins Site.* Buffalo: Persimmon Press.

Great Basin Foundation, ed. 1985 *Woman, Poet, Scientist: Essays in New World Anthropology Honoring Dr. Emma Louise Davis.* Los Altos Calif.: Ballena Press (Anthropological Papers, No. 29).

Greenberg, Joseph H., Christy G. Turner II, and Stephen L. Zegura. 1986 The Settlement of the Americas: A

Comparison of the Linguistic, Dental, and Genetic Evidence. *Current Anthropology* 27(5):477–497.

Gruhn, Ruth. 1988 Linguistic Evidence in Support of the Coastal Route of Earliest Entry into the New World. *Man* 23:77–100.

Jennings, Jesse D., ed. 1983 *Ancient North Americans.* San Francisco: W. H. Freeman.

Kehoe, Alice B. 1981 Revisionist Anthropology: Aboriginal North America. *Current Anthropology* 22(5):503–517.

Kelly, Robert L. and Lawrence C. Todd. 1988 Coming Into the Country: Early Paleoindian Hunting and Mobility. *American Antiquity* 53(2):231–244.

Kroeber, A. L. 1939 *Cultural and Natural Areas of Native North America.* Berkeley: University of California Press.

Laughlin, William S. and Albert B. Harper, eds. 1979 *The First Americans: Origins, Affinities, and Adaptations.* New York: Gustav Fischer.

Lowie, Robert H. 1937 *The History of Ethnological Theory.* New York: Rinehart & Co.

Lynch, Thomas F. 1990 Glacial-Age Man in South America? A Critical Review. *American Antiquity* 55(1):12–36.

Macneish, Richard S., ed. 1973 *Early Man in America.* San Francisco: W.H. Freeman Co.

Manitoba Archaeological Society. 1982 *Recent Studies in Paleo-Indian Prehistory. Manitoba Archaeological Quarterly* 6(4).

Mithun, Marianne. 1990 Studies of North American Indian Languages. *Annual Review of Anthropology* 19:309–330.

Moratto, Michael J. 1984 *California Archaeology.* Orlando: Academic Press.

Morlan, Richard E. 1980 *Taphonomy and Archaeology in the Upper Pleistocene of the Northern Yukon Territory: A Glimpse of the Peopling of the New World.* Ottawa: National Museum of Man Mercury Series, Archaeological Survey of Canada Paper, No. 94.

Poirier, Frank E. 1977 *Fossil Evidence,* 2nd ed. St. Louis: C.V. Mosby.

Rogers, R. A., L. D. Martin, and T.D. Nicklas. 1990 Geography and Languages. *Journal of Biogeography* 17:117–130.

Rutter, N.W. and C.E. Schweger, eds. 1980 The Ice-Free Corridor and Peopling of the New World. *Canadian Journal of Anthropology* 1(1).

Shutler, Richard, Jr., ed. 1983 *Early Man in the New World.* Beverly Hills: Sage Publications.

Spiess, Arthur E. and Deborah Brush Wilson. 1987 *Michaud, a Paleoindian Site in the New England-Maritimes Region.* Augusta, Me.: Occasional Publications in Maine Archaeology, No. 6, Maine Historic Preservation Commission and Maine Archaeological Society.

Tomenchuk, John and Robson Bonnichsen, eds. 1989 *Abstracts of the First World Summit Conference on the Peopling of the Americas.* Orono: Center for the Study of the First Americans, Institute for Quaternary Studies, University of Maine.

Turner, Christy G., II. 1986 Dentochronological Separation Estimates for Pacific Rim Populations. *Science* 232:1140–1142.

West, Frederick H. 1987 Migrationism and New World Origins. *Quarterly Review of Archaeology* 8(1):11–14.

THE RISE OF THE MEXICAN NATIONS

SECTION 1: THE EARLY HOLOCENE ARCHAIC IN MEXICO

Native American Indian civilizations reached a peak of technological and social complexity and population densities in southernmost North America, what is now Mexico, Guatemala, Belize, El Salvador, and Honduras. This large area is termed by anthropologists *Mesoamerica* (Greek for "Middle America"). The northern sector of Mesoamerica is a desert, but south of a line extending from the Panuco River in the Mexican state of Veracruz, on the Gulf of Mexico to the east, westward through the Mexican states of Hidalgo, Mexico, and Michoacán to Colima on the Pacific, is the "core," or "nuclear," set of regions where the great Mesoamerican nations flourished.

Mesoamerica contains dramatic contrasts in topography and climate. Two rugged mountain chains separate tropical jungle coastal strips from their interior lands. These mountain chains are the Sierra Madre Occidental on the west, a continu- ation of the Rockies, and the Sierra Madre Oriental on the east. These two great north-south chains are loosely joined by an east-west series of volcanoes, still active, if at the moment quiescent, across central Mexico. Habitable areas are the jungly Pacific and Atlantic coastal strips, and plateaus and basins between the mountain ridges in the interior. Because the interior plateaus are high, they enjoy a pleasant temperate climate in spite of being so far south. Many sections of the interior plateaus tend to be semiarid, since moisture blowing in from the coasts is frequently trapped by the escarpments of the Sierras and falls back onto the humid rain forests of the hot coastal plains. A few hours' travel in Mexico can take one from clammy, lush, vine-tangled jungle near the sea, up frighteningly steep, fog-shrouded escarpments, through cold, silent pine forests, then down past snow-capped volcanoes into a broad, flat valley with cactus and mesquite on its edges, but a cottonwood-shaded river meandering through rich farm fields in the middle. This ecological diversity meant that the

Map 3 Mexico

Gulf of Mexico

TEXAS

NORTHWESTERN

SIERRA MADRE OCCIDENTAL

SIERRA MADRE ORIENTAL

NORTHERN FRONTIER

La Quemada

BAJA CALIFORNIA

TROPIC OF CANCER

R. Panuco

R. Soto La Marina

Tamuín

MICHOACAN

HIDALGO

Tula

Valley of Mexico

Teotihuacán, Tenochtitlán

Cholula

MORELOS

PUEBLA

Tehuacán Valley

SIERRA MADRE DEL SUR

Río Balsas

Tajín

VERA CRUZ

La Venta

San Lorenzo

OAXACA

Monte Albán

SIERRA DE OAXACA

TEHUANTEPEC

TABASCO

CHIAPAS

Palenque

SIERRA MADRE

Izapa

Kaminaljuyú

GUATEMALA

Tikal

PETÉN

YUCATÁN

Dzibilchaltún

Chichén Itzá

Uxmal

Río Bec (Becan)

BELIZE

Cuello

R. Belize

R. Ulua

HONDURAS

EL SALVADOR

NICARAGUA

Lake Nicaragua

Nicoya Peninsula

COSTA RICA

PANAMA

20

100

90

10

International Boundaries

Mexican State Boundaries

0   100   200 Miles
0   100   200 Kilometers

MEXICO CHRONOLOGY

Period	Date	WESTERN especially VALLEY OF MEXICO	EASTERN especially MAYA LOWLANDS	PERIPHERAL COASTAL LOWLANDS	OAXACA
PERIOD	1970				
MEXICAN	1940	Indian Affairs under National Indigenist Insitute (INI) First Inter-American Indigenist Congress, Pátzcuaro; indigenismo strengthened Cárdenas' socialist programs' ejido movement REVOLUTION			
	1855	Díaz dictatorship, oppression of Indians Juárez reform			
	1821	MEXICAN INDEPENDENCE			
POST CLASSIC	1700	Indians become peons	last Maya independent ruler conquered		Zapotecs
	1600	Indian population at lowest			Mixtecs
	1521	Cortés and Tlaxcalan allies conquer			
	1400	Aztec empire builds Aztecs		T O T O N A C S	
	1200	"Chichimec" invasions ← T o l t e c s →	(Northern Yucatán Maya continue)		M O N T E A L B Á N
CLASSIC	1000		← M a y a C l a s s i c	T A J Í N	
	800	Teotihuacán burned			
	600	T E O T I H U A C Á N			
	400				
	200				

A.D.
B.C.

200	
400	PRE
600	LATE
800	MIDDLE
1000	EARLY
1500	
2000	ARCHAIC
2500	
3000	
4000	
5000	
7000	PLEISTOCENE

PRECLASSIC

ARCHAIC

PLEISTOCENE

Cuicuilco

Tlatilco

Large varieties of maize developed

Maize appears, Tehuacan Valley

Iztapan

Tlapacoya, Hueyatlaco

Founding of Tikal, Becan, other Maya cities

Cuello a village

OLMEC

San José Mogote

Maize, squashes cultivated

native nations could obtain a great variety of products, generally without excessive transportation costs.

For purposes of cultural analysis, Mesoamerica's nuclear area has three principal geographical divisions: Western Mesoamerica, or Mexico proper, the semiarid highlands west of the Isthmus of Tehuantepec and the southern Gulf of Mexico; Eastern Mesoamerica, or the Maya area, lowland tropical forests east of the Isthmus of Tehuantepec and the Gulf of Mexico's southern shore, an area including the Maya-occupied Yucatán Peninsula; and the Peripheral Coastal Lowlands, a lowland tropical zone extending from the Pacific shores of Chiapas in Mexico, Guatemala, and El Salvador, through the narrow Isthmus of Tehuantepec (a break in the mountains west of Chiapas), and into the broad, flat coastal plain of Veracruz and Tabasco bordering the Gulf of Mexico. The earliest great Mexican nation, the Olmec, lay at the north end of the Isthmus of Tehuantepec, but came to be eclipsed by the Mexican and Mayan nations to the west and east, respectively.

We have seen that some of the earliest evidence for humans in the New World comes from Mexico, though it is poorly dated in the case of Hueyatlaco in the Valsequillo area of the state of Puebla, and poorly represented in the meager remains from the most ancient deposit at Tlapacoya in the state of (Valley of) Mexico. The most arresting artifact of these earliest known humans in Mexico is a sacrum, or rump bone, from a llama (American camel). The bone was carved to look like the head of an animal, perhaps a coyote or peccary (American wild pig). Near the carved bone were some crude flakes of stone and bone. These artifacts came from a low position in a late Pleistocene rock layer, the Becerra, underlying the Valley of Mexico. These finds from Tequixquiac, as the site is named, are accepted as authentically Pleistocene in age, but unfortunately have not been precisely dated.

In the upper portion of the Becerra formation, other sites have been found, dating from near the end of the Pleistocene epoch. At Tepexpán, again in the Valley of Mexico, a human skeleton was found, along with a few crude stone and bone artifacts. At the Valley of Mexico village of Santa Isabel Iztapán is the spectacular find of two imperial mammoths butchered by humans. Artifacts discarded beside the enormous bones of the mammoths include an Agate Basin blade, two smaller Fluted Tradition blades or projectile points (one of the Lerma type common in Mexico and the West, and one described as s "crude Scottsbluff," perhaps better termed an Alberta point or knife), several simple knives of stone, and some scrapers chipped from obsidian, a natural volcanic glass abundant in the Valley of Mexico. The Iztapán mammoths have not been precisely dated either, but both their geological position in the Becerra formation and the artifacts with them suggest a date of about 8000 B.C.

The Mexican interior plateaus' tendency to aridity increased in the Holocene era as the global effects of the continental glaciers decreased. The mammoths were soon victims of, we guess, a debilitating combination of shrinking grasslands and hunters picking off too many young beasts. (There is a high proportion of young animals among the

The Iztapán mammoths and the artifacts with them are displayed as they were originally found, in one of the many exhibit halls of the imposing modern Museo Nacional de Antropología (National Museum of Anthropology) in Chapultepec Park, Mexico City. A day at this magnificent display of the greatness of the Mexican peoples is a must in any visit to Mexico.

mammoth skeletons that have been found in sites, evidencing slaughter by humans.) Early in the Holocene, Mexican hunters were forced to seek smaller game, and probably the collecting of wild vegetable foods became more important as meat became less easily procured.

Two major research projects, one in the Tehuacán Valley of the state of Puebla and one in the Valley of Oaxaca (pronounced Wa-ha-ca) in the state of the same name, have traced the shift from hunting and gathering to agriculture in Mexico. Both projects employed several specialists in the natural sciences, such as botanists, to work with the archaeologists in the field to ensure that significant data would not be overlooked or misinterpreted. The first project, in the Tehuacán Valley, was directed by Richard S. MacNeish, who later discovered the twelve-thousand-year-old evidence of humans in Pikimachay in Peru. The second project, in Oaxaca, was directed by Kent V. Flannery. Both scientists chose their valleys for investigation with great care, looking for ecological conditions fairly typical of much of interior Mexico, yet including dry rockshelters in which plant remains might be well preserved.

Flannery, in what has become a classic paper (Flannery 1968), analyzed the results of both his own and MacNeish's research in terms of how the ancient Mexicans utilized their environmental resources. He was able to determine with considerable certainty what the ancient peoples who camped in the rockshelters had eaten, because for evidence he had not only cut bones showing butchering marks, cut rinds, stalks, pits, and seeds of plants—none of which could have grown inside the dry caves—and chewed quids of tough maguey, but also the actual feces of persons who had relieved themselves thousands of years ago in the corners of the caves. Specialists who closely examined these well-dried feces, called coprolites by polite archaeologists, had indubitable proof of what some campers in the caves had consumed. From the coprolites, other "macrofossils" (remains visible to the naked eye), and the "microfossil"

(needing microscopes to be seen) plant pollens analyzed from the soils of the cave floors, Flannery discovered that in the early Holocene era, from around 8000 B.C.to about 5000 B.C., Mexicans in the interior highland valleys depended upon six principal food resources: maguey (century plant), a cactuslike plant, now grown for its juice which is distilled into tequila, but in ancient times cut for its central pith, which can be roasted and eaten; prickly-pear cactus, whose sweet fruit and young leaves can be eaten; mesquite, a bush bearing edible pods; seed-bearing grasses, including amaranth (pigweed), foxtail millet, and maize (Indian corn); deer; and rabbits. In addition the people collected, when convenient, a variety of less important foods, such as avocados and other fruits, acorns, pine nuts, turtles, birds, rodents, peccary, raccoons, opossums, and skunks.

During the dry winter season, people lived in small groups of one or a few families and concentrated their food-getting efforts on deer hunting. Early winter is the mating season for deer, and the animals are fat, are less wary, and cluster together at this time. If the hunter was unsuccessful, the family ate roasted maguey hearts and kapok (ceiba) roots, not very appetizing but something to avert famine. When summer, the rainy season, arrived, many families gathered at localities where there was an abundance of ripe prickly pears, avocados, mesquite pods, or amaranth seeds. While they harvested these foods, they set traps for small game and probably organized animal drives, all the men, women, and children forming a great circle around a valley floor and then closing in, beating the bushes and yelling, and clubbing and spearing the rabbits and other animals as they ran inside the human net.

Flannery argues that this Archaic exploitation of a variety of seasonally abundant resources is built upon a basic schedule set by the ripening of the preferred plants and the habits of the game. The exact times of ripening varied somewhat from year to year, depending on weather, and any one locality might have a poor harvest some years but better harvests others, so there was a need for flexibility within the basic schedule. Flannery's principal point is that no one food resource was sufficient in amount and in filling nutritional needs, or available for year-round use to support families; therefore, the people had to plan to move on every few weeks to the next resource.

MacNeish and Flannery both emphasize that the peoples of the Mexican Archaic period were intelligent and alert, experimenting and innovating to improve their comfort and security. One focus of innovation was on developing stone choppers, mashers, and grinding mills and mortars to better process vegetable foods, including the various grass seeds that could be ground into flour for porridge and tortilla-type bread. Another focus, and one that would radically change Mexican lifeways, was on modifying the conditions in which their preferred food plants grew.

As early as 7000 B.C., the natives of Oaxaca seem to have been cultivating beans, squash, pumpkins, and a primitive maize. Note that the word is *cultivating*. These Mexicans were most probably clearing patches of ground along the river below their favorite rockshelters, loosening the soil with sticks, putting the seeds of the preferred plants in the soil, moistening the planting spot, and occasionally removing weeds. They would return to the rockshelters to harvest the wild foods seasonally abundant nearby, and incidentally take whatever could be harvested from their little garden patch. What they were *not* doing, what they could not afford to do, was settling down and staking the lives of the families upon good harvests from planted fields. At 7000 B.C., families survived by traveling from one bountiful wild food resource to another. To save some walking from the best campsites, and to be sure of having the time to gather good minor foods such as beans, squash, and maize even when all hands were busy every day harvesting the principal seasonal resource, such as mesquite pods, people planted the "extra" foods conveniently close. They noticed that the beans and squashes and maize from the patches they had

prepared often grew a little larger than what they collected from the wild: not only were the garden patches convenient, but cultivation allowed the plants to achieve their maximum yield, a worthwhile return for the planning and work invested in the patches.

Of all the plants cultivated in the early Holocene era—beans, squash, pumpkins, amaranth, avocado, chili peppers, bottle gourds, foxtail millet, and maize (and possibly prickly pear and maguey, which don't grow from seeds)—maize is the plant that would have most rewarded its cultivators. Curiously, no real wild maize has ever been found. Maize is the cultivated form of a grain, teosinte, that looks much more like a tall grass. About 7000 B.C., someone somewhere in southern Mexico (or possibly northern South America) noticed an odd teosinte stalk with larger, rounder seeds. By planting seeds from this mutant, the discoverer began development of a new species dependent on human cultivation. With properly prepared soil, sufficient moisture and sunlight, and weeding, the seeds are large and numerous and set on long cobs. Recent experiments and observations suggest that many of the varieties of maize are not simply additional mutations, but products of a complex interplay between genetic potential and soil nutrients, moisture, and light. Maize, with no true wild forms, is, in a sense, an artifact, an object manufactured by human skill.

Between 7000 B.C. and 2000 B.C., Mexicans in the highland valleys invested increasingly greater time and effort into producing their food. Around 5000 B.C., the major part of the diet of the people in the Tehuacán valley came from cultivating maize, amaranth and foxtail millet, beans, squashes, avocado, zapote (a fruit), and chili peppers. Bottle gourds grown in the gardens provided containers. Around 2300 B.C., maize with large cobs much like some varieties still grown was being consistently produced in Tehuacán fields. A couple of centuries later, bottle gourds were joined by a second nonfood plant, cotton, cultivated to produce string and cloth. At the time, 2000 B.C., people began giving up spring collecting of wild foods in order to work full-time on their farms. It was a risk, neglecting food now and betting on a sufficient harvest months later, and it meant sweating and grunting in the fields—hard, dull labor, when one could easily be picking sweet, juicy prickly pears or stripping mesquite pods from the low trees. The risk and the sweat could produce more and bigger seeds and fruits than anyone could gather wild, so many a young couple ignored Grandma and Grandpa fidgeting with the gathering baskets, and set out, wooden hoes over their shoulders, for the fields cleared from the thickets by the rivers.

The shift from gathering to cultivating as the subsistence base had been gradual, but radical in its effects. First, it required the development of storage methods and facilities more ambitious than those used to save the gathered wild foods. Remember, the basis of hunting-gathering was seasonal movement. There was little effort to save quantities of food from any one resource because it was difficult to transport and unnecessary when the next season's resource ripened. Cultivators remain near their fields, eliminating the transportation problem. Techniques for drying and safely storing many foods had been known for thousands of years, but with the shift to dependency on cultivated plants there was a new concern with perfecting these techniques and building permanent granaries.

The second effect of the shift to full-time cultivation was a lifting of the necessity for multifamily social groups to break up in the seasons when wild foods were not abundant. Formerly, during the dry winter, men went deer hunting, alone or with a brother, brother-in-law, or friend; wives and children camped, setting traps for rabbits and small game and tending the roasting pits where the tough maguey was slowly cooking, to be ready if nothing better was caught. The deer and the maguey were scattered, and the families had to scatter to find them. Only during the summer and early fall, when grasses, fruits, and nuts were ripe in great numbers, could many families camp together and enjoy gossip, songs, stories, dances, the ministrations of

experienced healers, and the opportunity to attract lovers. Cultivation on a permanent basis changed this. With the fields concentrated, the granaries of the families concentrated, true villages developed and the benefits of social life could be indulged in year-round.

The commitment to agriculture had as its social consequence, then, the fostering of permanent multifamily social groups that were free to create long-term, complex, and cooperative endeavors. Hunting-gathering had constrained each adult couple to become self-sufficient so as to survive the lean winters when food was scanty and scattered. Alliances, even of two families, were temporary, for winter wanderings could end with families dozens of miles apart, choosing to camp for the summer with relatives and friends not seen for several years rather than trek back to those they camped with the previous summer. When, in contrast, the same families worked in adjacent fields and returned each evening to adjacent houses, year in and year out, more efficient societies could be arranged, with people specializing in the production of items for which they had talent and trading these for other necessities that they could not make so well. There was also personnel enough for impressive ritual music and dramatic performances, and these individuals were available evening after evening for rehearsal. Monumental buildings to house properly the performances and the icons carved and painted by gifted artists were feasible, for the workers were always in residence. Trade became more popular as people saw that they could invest in bulky or delicate things that would be both useful and safe in the houses.

To summarize, hunting-gathering had stimulated human experimentation with food-getting techniques and apparatus, but had repressed inventiveness in social arrangements and constructions needing large numbers of persons. Agriculture built upon the earlier experiments and released the constraints of a life organized to fit movement from resource to resource.

By about 2000 B.C. in Mexico, the culmination

THE "AGRICULTURAL REVOLUTION"

We tend to assume that the cultivation of plants and herding of animals is a totally different way of life from the gathering of wild foods and hunting of game. Agriculture is thought to mean mastery of the environment, giving people control over their needs. Following this reasoning, the great British archaeologist V. Gordon Childe (1892-1957) used a Marxist model to claim that cultivation, by changing, as it appeared to him, the mode of production of food, constituted a true revolution. He termed this the Neolithic Revolution, occurring as it did in the Eurasian Neolithic period of the middle Holocene era. Childe theorized that the Neolithic, or Agricultural, Revolution was the first of only three true Marxist revolutions; the other two being the Urban Revolution, when the clustering of thousands of people in permanent communities again, he thought, radically changed the relationship of people to modes of production; and the Industrial Revolution, when mechanical energy was substituted for living energy.

Childe's theory was a brilliant extrapolation of Karl Marx's thinking onto new data coming from twentieth-century archaeological excavations, but it suffered from a lack of first-hand experience of hunting-gathering societies. Largely stimulated by Childe, archaeologists such as Robert Braidwood, working in western Asia, and Richard MacNeish, working in the Americas, have surveyed and excavated what should have been the critical centuries of Neolithic Revolutions in these continents. Each of their major research projects has included zoologists and botanists with anthropological training who have closely observed the modern peasant farmers of the study regions as well as the excavated data. Kent Flannery, a generation younger, directed a similar project. The results of these investigations have demonstrated that (1) there was no short critical period in which people's relationships to the principal modes of production were revolutionized, and (2) there is not so major a difference between traditional hunting-gathering and subsistence agriculture. Many present-day prehistorians therefore feel that Marx's model does not apply to the study of human life before the advent of historic class-structured societies, although Childe did help us appreciate the ultimately drastic effects of full-scale agriculture on human social relations.

---

of increasingly sophisticated food collecting had been achieved. Symbiosis—mutual interdependence—had appeared, humans relying upon a plant, maize, that had been selectively bred to cluster many seeds upon thick, tough stalks (cobs). The plants could be propagated only by the intervention of the humans, who alone could dislodge the seeds from the cobs and plant them sufficiently far apart that the young shoots would not suicidally compete with one another. What had begun in the Old World Paleolithic period and been continued in the American Paleo-Indian period of the late Pleisto-

cene-early Holocene era—selective harvesting of the plants and animals that best repaid human time and effort, given the available technology—had developed through improvements in the technology and increasing nurture of the preferred species until, in Mexico, human social organizations came to be profoundly affected. The selected plants benefited from humans working hard to provide optimum conditions for growth and fruit bearing, and varieties that could not survive in the wild, such as maize—true domesticates—flourished in fertile fields near rivers, lakes, or springs. The people who cultivated the fields received the benefit of yields of nutrients per acre vastly greater than would usually be found in the wild, with the additional, calorie-saving convenience of having the fields close to good dwelling locations. No drastic changes in social organization had yet appeared, but they were budding.

Regional differences became more pronounced in Mexico as the Archaic period gave way to the Preclassic epoch. In the interior highland plateaus, communities around lakes slaughtered quantities of the ducks that winter there, and also went into the hills stalking deer during the winter. In the coastal lowlands, warm climate permitted two or even three crops to be raised each year, and the people concentrated on their fields year-round, gaining protein by fishing, collecting shellfish, and hunting deer in the vicinity. We know the societies in the various regions of Mexico had been in contact at least intermittently over thousands of years, part of the evidence for this being the diffusion of food crops into regions where the wild ancestors of the plants do not occur. For example, beans are native to the Pacific coast, chili peppers to the Gulf coast, and pumpkins and related squashes, as well as maize may have originated on the semiarid slopes of southern Mexico and adjacent Guatemala. By 2000 B.C., all these excellent foods were being grown in many sectors of the "core" of Mesoamerica, whether highland valleys or coastal lowlands. Only human agency could have carried these cultigens (cultivated plants) into so many regions.

During the millennium between 2000 B.C. and 1000 B.C., Mesoamerican societies transformed themselves from simple communities of households engaged in subsistence pursuits to complex organizations tying thousands of persons into the production and exchange of goods and services. This millennium saw the end of the Archaic period and the beginning of the Preclassic period for most of the populations in the core area of Mesoamerica. An Archaic way of life did persist in northern Mexico, but the core sprouted civilization.

SECTION 2: THE PRECLASSIC PERIOD

Many archaeologists term the Preclassic period in Mesoamerica the "Formative period." That term is not chosen here in order to emphasize that Mesoamerican societies—like societies everywhere—have been and are continuously changing, forming, and reforming. Between approximately 1500 B.C. and the time of Christ, Mesoamerica was creating the social structures, the technology, the artistic canons, and the ideologies that became the great civilizations of the Classic period of the first millennium A.D. In the sense that the earlier two millennia were the period of a concentration of critical innovations, the foundation of the Classic civilizations, this Preclassic epoch was indeed a "formative" period par excellence.

V. Gordon Childe recognized ten criteria for distinguishing urban civilizations from simpler societies:

1. settlements of large size and high density
2. territorially based states rather than kinship-dominated societal groups
3. capital wealth, from taxes or tribute
4. monumental public works
5. class-stratified society
6. full-time craft specialists
7. long-distance trade in luxury items
8. representational art, including human portraiture
9. writing
10. true (that is, exact, predictive) science.

Each of these traits appeared in Mesoamerica during the Preclassic period. They seem to have first reached full, sophisticated manifestation in the coastal plains of the north end of the Isthmus of Tehuantepec, in southern Veracruz and adjacent Tabasco, part of the Peripheral Coastal Lowlands division of Mesoamerica.

The distinctive Preclassic archaeological remains from the northern Tehuantepec area are named "Olmec." Historically, part of this region has been the homeland of a relatively small and politically unimportant people called the Olmeca, or in English, Olmecs. Prehistoric discoveries made in the land of the Olmecas were assumed to represent the ancestors of this people, and thus are also referred to as "Olmec." Gradually, during the 1930s, archaeologists began to realize that the Olmec remains had to be at least a thousand years old, and in the 1950s, radiocarbon dates were obtained that demonstrated that the archaeologists' Olmec lived in the first millennium B.C. With so many centuries intervening between the archaeological remains and the historic Olmeca, it is impossible to determine whether the ancient people were the direct ancestors of the historic Olmeca, or what the ancient people called themselves. Some archaeologists think it likely that the ancient Olmecs were the ancestors of the several Indian nations in the northern Tehuantepec region who speak dialects of the Mixe and Zoque languages. There is, at present, no method for unequivocably linking a historic group with a prehistoric one, lacking texts we can read.

"Olmec," then, is the accepted, though probably erroneous, name for the builders of the Preclassic civilization in the northern Tehuantepec lowlands. The Olmec civilization becomes recognizable about 1400 B.C. There are three major centers— San Lorenzo and Tres Zapotes, in southeastern Veracruz, and La Venta, just over the eastern border of Veracruz in Tabasco. San Lorenzo and La Venta have been more fully excavated than Tres Zapotes, and so can be better described.

San Lorenzo

San Lorenzo may have been the leading center of civilization in the earlier portion of the Preclassic period in Mesoamerica. About 1500 B.C., possibly earlier, people living along the Coatzacoalcos River in northern Tehuantepec began to build a platform of sand and clay. One century and millions of basket loads of earth later, the result was an artificial plateau 1.2 kilometers (four fifths

of a mile) long and 50 meters (close to 165 feet) high. On this gigantic platform were constructed nearly two hundred small platforms, usually grouped three around a rectangular courtyard, several somewhat larger mounds, and many clay-lined water-storage reservoirs with long drainage troughs made of basalt, an imported granitic rock. The excavator of San Lorenzo, archaeologist Michael D. Coe, thinks the grouped low mounds were probably bases upon which the houses, perhaps of priests and nobility, were built; the larger mounds may have been bases for temples. If so, the architectural style of San Lorenzo already followed principles that were to dominate Mexican architecture until the Spanish conquest.

If the probable house mounds at San Lorenzo were each the home of a family, then the population living on the artificial platform would have been about one thousand persons (counting father, mother, and an average of three children per family). Coe estimates that about twice this number of individuals may have lived in the vicinity, in hamlets among the maize fields on the natural plain. (Today, the population around the San Lorenzo site is 2,500.) Since the adults in this population had to spend much of their time in farming, homemaking and child care, or craft production, the number of man-hours available for the massive building projects in San Lorenzo seems grossly inadequate for the tasks. Coe suggests that San Lorenzo must have been the capital of a state able to draw men from many miles around to labor on its monuments. While San Lorenzo itself is not particularly large, if it was the acropolis residence of the elite only, and if common people lived in light huts— the climate is warm year-round—among the fields below, then the total settlement, acropolis and associated hamlets, fulfills Childe's criterion of large settlements marking urban civilization. The tremendous manpower requirements for the artificial acropolis and its monuments, plus the uniformity of pottery and other artifacts from this period in a region extending from the Gulf coast to within the adjacent states of Puebla and Morelos, seem to be evidence for a territorially based state. The probability that an elite lived on the acropolis implies a class-stratified society, and since the thousands of laborers working for the state had to be fed, although they may have been paid only a promise of salvation hereafter, it is probable that the state exacted taxes or tribute to support them as well as the elite.

Childe's other criteria of urban civilization are well demonstrated at San Lorenzo. Coe's excavations discovered forty-eight sculptures carved from large boulders, and he estimates there may be hundreds more still buried in the acropolis. "Monumental public works" thus range from the stupendous artificial platform of the acropolis itself, through the public structures on the acropolis (the water-storage reservoirs and the buildings on mounds, which presumably included temples, priests' quarters, and administrative halls), to the monumental structures. These sculptures indicate full-time craft specialists, since many must have been made by highly trained, gifted artists able to devote a lifetime to slowly pecking a 6-foot (2-meter) basalt boulder into a perfectly finished human head. Representational art is amply evidenced by these sculptures, nearly all of which are realistic portraits of men, animals, or anthropomorphic (human-bodied) deities. Long-distance trade in luxury items is indicated by the basalt for the monuments, which can hardly be considered a necessity of daily life, and were quarried 70 kilometers (43.5 miles) away.

Childe's last two criteria, writing and true science, are only weakly represented in the Olmec Preclassic period. Definite writing can be identified only in the late Preclassic period of the Olmec region. Earlier, there are some symbols that resemble hieroglyphs of the Classic writing systems, but these Olmec symbols have neither been deciphered nor observed to be regularly used in message-bearing contexts; they may perhaps be termed protohieroglyphs. Similarly, true science seems to have been in a "proto" stage at the height of Olmec

civilization. Olmec architects were able to lay out their buildings according to a precise orientation, probably by using astronomical alignments but possibly by using magnetism (the Olmecs imported parabolic discs of magnetic iron ore from Oaxaca). A good astronomical calendar may have been developed, but if so, no traces of it have been recognized.

Common people at San Lorenzo lived principally on grain, probably maize, as deduced from the quantities of metates (stone grinding slabs) and manos (stone rollers used to crush the grain on the metates) excavated from the site. Animal protein was obtained from fish and turtles, supplemented by puppy dogs (fat puppies were raised for banquet fare by many Mexican and other Indian peoples) and, rarely, deer. The soil in the region is rich, being renewed frequently by the river's flooding, and the low tropical plain is frost-free, so agriculture regularly yielded a reliable subsistence.

Crafts at San Lorenzo included the laborious working of very hard stones into beads, ornaments, and fine axes as well as into monumental sculptures. Stone carvings must have been performed with stone chisels and abrasion with sand. Metal tools were not known, although iron ores were chipped and then polished like a telescope lens until they became mirrors. Some of these mirrors seem to have been worn as pendants on necklaces, where they would have blindingly reflected light into the eyes of lesser people who approached a lord or high priest standing on a platform wearing the "jewel" on his chest. The parabolic mirrors can also concentrate sunlight at their focal points and thereby ignite tinder, a nice "miracle" for the populace waiting for a sign from the gods. Many of the axes fashioned from the attractive green serpentine were destined for the gods; the archaeologists found them laid as a base for a boulder monument featuring a relief carving of a doglike animal. Another craft in the service of deity as well as humans was pottery. The Olmec potters were masters who made both small, solid-clay human (or anthropomorphic-deity) figurines and larger,

FIGURE 2.1   Olmec stone sculpture, possibly a ruler. Preclassic, c. 800 B.C. (*A. Kehoe*)

hollow, clay ones. They also made pots and dishes, the latter including handsome, dark, open bowls with slightly flaring sides decorated with elegantly executed, strong, simple motifs seen also on the sculptures.

Ideology for the Olmecs focused on concepts symbolized by the serpent and the jaguar. There may have been a myth telling of a woman mated with a jaguar—there are several Olmec sculptures depicting the jaguar covering a lady, though possibly the beast was eating her—and subsequently the birth of a child whose face shows the terrible power of its father. The "were-jaguar," the baby with fanged mouth and angry eyes, is often shown held in the arms or on the lap of a man who may be a priest. Other stone and clay figurines seem to portray the were-jaguar as an adult, sometimes a man with the terrifying fangs and eyes, sometimes an upright jaguar menacing the viewer. Possibly

the jaguar's child was supposed to have been the founder of the Olmec ruling dynasty. As suggested by Peter Furst, who has studied both modern Indian mythologies and the prehistoric art, it is possible that the Olmecs believed, as do many Latin American Indian peoples, that their religious specialists learned to turn themselves into jaguars, to roam the jungle fighting monsters threatening the villagers.

The other major symbol, the serpent, is shown in its natural aspect. In a number of instances, a man sits within the gaping jaws of the serpent, as if within a cave. An echo of this theme may be the carvings of a person seated within a niche, which could be a representation of a cave mouth. It is tempting to interpret these Olmec motifs as the great Mexican artist and prehistorian Miguel Covarrubias did, assuming the jaguar and the serpent had meanings then similar to their meanings in the Spanish-conquest period 2,500 years later, but we can only guess what the jaguar and his child, and the serpent and the man in the cave signified to the Olmecs.

The most impressive pieces of Olmec sculpture are the basalt boulders 6 to 8 feet high carved in the round to represent colossal men's heads. All of each boulder was beautifully finished; the heads were never meant to be placed upon bodies. They seem to be portraits of real men, having a family resemblance but being individually varied. Each wears a hat or wide band, ornamented but reminding us of a football helmet. In spite of the consummate realism of these great portraits, they are as enigmatic as the were-jaguar. Most experts guess the colossal heads are portraits of the succeeding rulers of a dynasty, but this interpretation is only a reasonable supposition, not a surety. An intriguing aspect of the portrait heads is that most were carved not from raw boulders but from stone-block thrones, some with the man-in-a-niche relief. Perhaps after a ruler died, his throne was recarved into his portrait.

San Lorenzo suffered a strange fate in the eleventh century B.C. Dozens of the monumental stone sculptures were hacked and bashed, dragged and set in rows, then buried. Did a messiah arise and preach the destruction of old gods? Was San Lorenzo invaded and its gods destroyed by a foreign enemy? Had the common people been oppressed by their rulers, and did they finally revolt? Whatever the cause, two more generations of people continued to live at San Lorenzo, but no more great sculptures were erected. Then the site was abandoned, with no evidence why.

The demise of San Lorenzo correlates with the rise of another Olmec center, La Venta, situated on a small island in a swamp near the Gulf coast, northeast of San Lorenzo. La Venta was to dominate the northern Tehuantepec from about 1100 B.C. to about 750 B.C. Because San Lorenzo and La Venta are only some 50 miles (80 kilometers) apart, and because late San Lorenzo overlaps in time with early La Venta but was abandoned during the period of La Venta's climax, it seems possible that the Olmec capital moved from San Lorenzo to La Venta about 1000 B.C. The move may have been the result of the lords of La Venta wresting domination from the rulers of San Lorenzo, it may have been a dynastic change occurring when a princess of San Lorenzo, heiress of its domain, became the consort of the heir to La Venta, or it may have been a move prompted by a religious vision calling for the burial of the San Lorenzo gods and the establishment of a "New Jerusalem" at La Venta. The close resemblances in technology, art style, and ideological motifs between San Lorenzo and La Venta indicate that whatever the structure of power, a single national culture continued from the early (Olmec) through middle Preclassic period.

Other Mesoamerican Nations in the Early and Middle Preclassic Period

The Olmec was not the only nation of the Mesoamerican Preclassic period. Closest to the Olmec were the people of the Valley of Oaxaca. In the early Preclassic period, from about 1600 B.C. to about 1300 B.C., there were about twelve communities in the Valley of Oaxaca, all but one hamlet containing five to ten houses and covering 1 to 2 hectares (2 to 5 acres). The exception was the site near the present village of San José Mogote, which covered 3 hectares (7.4 acres) and may have had thirty houses. A typical house of this period in Oaxaca was rectangular, measured 4 by 6 meters (4 by 6.5 yards), was built of small upright posts laced with thin branches, and was then plastered with adobe and finished with a white clay "whitewash." (Construction by adobe on a brushwood-wall foundation is called "wattle [the brushwork] and daub [the adobe].") Eight pits dug west of the houses were used for storage of food and goods, and eventually for trash disposal, each holding about 1.5 cubic meters (2 cubic yards). Food remains in the pits included maize, avocados, deer, rabbits, gophers, and turtles; there were also household appliances such as broken metates and manos, and evidence of dance or ceremonial paraphernalia, including macaw feathers and the shell of a Gulf Coast turtle, historically used for drums. There was no hearth in the house. Instead, portable pottery braziers were used for cooking, a custom still followed in many Mexican Indian households. At the larger village at San José Mogote, an area of 300 square meters (328 square yards) was used for a public building. The small hamlets seemed to have only residences, although one was likely to be raised on a low platform and to contain debris indicating a slightly higher standard of living—more deer bone, bits of imported obsidian, and decorative ocean shells—than the others.

Between about 1300 B.C. and 900 B.C., craft specialization and intercommunity trade is recognizable within the Valley of Oaxaca and in other regions of Mexico. San José Mogote continued to grow, up to perhaps 120 houses covering 20 hectares (49.2 acres), and continued to be the dominant settlement in its section of the Valley of Oaxaca. The villagers raised maize, amaranth, squashes, avocados, and chili peppers; kept dogs and a few turkeys; hunted deer, rabbits, opossums, raccoons, peccaries, turtles, quail, and doves; collected (and perhaps planted) maguey and prickly pear; and on the mountain slopes cut pine for house posts and for cooking charcoal. They quarried chert for stone tools across the river, and they probably traded for salt with a small hamlet at a salt spring an hour's walk away, and for pottery with a hamlet at a good clay source a little further away. Some specialists in San José Mogote obtained magnetite, an iron ore, from localities about 20 miles away and painstakingly polished sections of it into small mirrors. The mirrors, probably worn in necklace pendants, were traded to the Gulf Coast Olmec and also north to other central highland valleys. Fine pottery bowls were another export product of the Valley of Oaxaca. In exchange for the mirrors and bowls, Oaxacans received obsidian, the volcanic glass that made the sharpest cutting implements, from quarries in Puebla, at Teotihuacán in the Valley of

Mexico, and in Michoacán, all to the north, and in rare instances from Guatemala to the southeast. They also received handsome white pottery, turtle shells for drums and conch shells for trumpets, mother-of-pearl mussel shells for ornaments, and shark teeth and stingray spines, probably to arm battle-axes, from the Gulf of Mexico coast of southern Veracruz (the Olmec area), and decorative oyster shells to be made into ornaments, from the Pacific coast.

Oaxaca was thus part of a network of exchange of special products running throughout Mexico. Its own people were self-sufficient and beginning to organize manufactures on an intercommunity exchange, probably through the single large village of San José Mogote with its public building. Compared with the Olmec, however, Oaxacans did not yet feel impelled, or compelled, to labor on stupendous monuments, nor did they provide gifted artists the opportunity to create great sculptures.

A comparable situation was to be found in the Valley of Mexico. Here there was also contact with the Olmecs, so much that local artists were influenced by the Olmec style and motifs in their modeling of the figurines and in pottery, but here again there were no truly monumental works. The population, which has been estimated to total not more than three thousand people, was divided among three villages—Tlatilco, Tlapacoya, and (probably; the site is mostly buried under lava) Cuicuilco—and perhaps half a dozen hamlets. All the sites except two hamlets are situated on the floor of the valley around its lakes; the two exceptions are along the Amecameca Pass through the mountains to the southeast. (The valley-floor sites are now within the urban area of Mexico City. The chain of lakes that occupied much of the valley has been largely drained to allow expansion of the metropolis. Xochimilco, the "floating gardens" south of the city, is a remnant of the ancient lakes.) It is curious that although obsidian was being mined and exported from the rich sources in the Teotihuacán Valley, no evidence has been discovered of settlements in this northeastern arm of the

Valley of Mexico. It may be that an early village was obliterated by the construction of the great city of Teotihuacán centuries later, or it may be that the obsidian was taken by work parties who camped briefly, leaving no remains.

Other valleys in the Mexican highlands seem to have been comparable to the Valley of Mexico in the early Preclassic period. Villages in the Tehuacán Valley had been farming and making pottery for a thousand years, and by the early Preclassic period were turning out technically difficult clay figures showing, as did those from Tlatilco in the Valley of Mexico, knowledge of the Olmec style and motifs. Chalcatzingo, in Morelos, the state bordering the Valley of Mexico on the south, was a village admirably situated near water, good farmland, and a route between the Gulf coastal plain and the Valley of Mexico. West Mexico also was developing farming towns. None of these valleys exhibit evidence of complex civilization at this period.

La Venta

The strange destruction of the monumental sculptures of San Lorenzo about 1050 B.C., and the abandonment of the site at the end of that century marked a widespread series of changes in Mexico. At La Venta, there is what may be an artificial acropolis comparable to and contemporary with the one at San Lorenzo, but the site has not yet been excavated sufficiently to determine this. The principal La Venta site is a quarter of a mile from this earlier center. The main site's most striking feature is a huge artificial mound 32.3 meters (106 feet) high, with a base diameter of 420 feet (128 meters). Presently there is no indication of stairs or ramps giving access up the steep sides to the small flattened area at the top, but twenty-eight centuries of weather beating upon the pyramid have destroyed its ancient surface. It is the oldest known "pyramid," or monumental mound, in North America. Robert F. Heizer, the archaeologist who excavated sections of La Venta and cleared the

pyramid of its jungle overgrowth, speculated that the La Venta Olmec intended to reproduce on their swamp island a volcanic cone such as they had seen in the Tuxtla Mountains 70 kilometers (44 miles) to the west. The Olmec of La Venta as well as those of San Lorenzo obtained the basalt blocks for their colossal heads and the other great sculptures from the Tuxtla Mountains, so the volcanoes, some of which may have been active in the early Preclassic period, may have been considered a sacred place. Perhaps the La Venta people hoped that if they provided such a mountain in their town, the gods would leave the Tuxtla range and reside among the Olmecs. Perhaps they were not naive, but audacious, flaunting their own godlike power in moving mountains.

La Venta was occupied as a ritual center for 400 years, until about 750 B.C. Heizer and his coexcavators found there had been four phases of construction, each initiated by what Heizer calls "massive offerings": rectangular pits ranging in size from 50 by 20 feet (15 by 6 meters), 15 feet (5 meters) deep, to 77 feet (23.5 meters) square, 13 feet (4 meters) deep, lined with basalt blocks or colored clay and filled with imported stone blocks and carefully chosen clays. The most spectacular of these massive offerings was one in which twenty-eight layers of the expensive green serpentine blocks, each roughly the size and shape of an ax head, were capped with a mosaic 15 by 20 feet (4.5 by 6 meters) composed of 485 polished green serpentine blocks laid out to represent a jaguar face wearing a crown. When this mighty "sculpture" of serpentine blocks was completed, it was buried. Above the massive offerings were set two rows of green stone "celts" (ax-head-shaped objects), most of serpentine but some of jade, the rows in the form of a cross. The sacrifice of so much time and energy for the buried offerings suggests that the Olmecs felt that La Venta, otherwise an unimposing locale, was imbued with sacredness. During the Classic and later eras in Mesoamerica, the jaguar was lord of the earth and underworld, and the cross symbolized the four cardinal directions.

These symbols at La Venta, if they had such meanings for the Olmec, may have invoked and acknowledged the presence of the lord of the earth and progenitor of the human race, or at least of its Olmec rulers.

Having paid homage to the jaguar lord of the earth, the La Venta Olmecs would add or enlarge mounds, embankments, and walls, laying out structures with care to preserve the symmetry of the overall plan of platforms matched on each side of the long north-south axis. One feature of the plan was what had been termed a "ceremonial court" outlined with columns of basalt 6 to 11 feet (3 to 4 meters) high. These columns formed naturally in the basalt in the Tuxtla Mountains and were transported to the La Venta swamp. More basalt columns were used for enclosed courts on top of a pair of platforms on the south side of the ceremonial court, and for a tomb with walls and roof. The tomb measured 5 by 2.5 meters (16 by 8 feet). A floor of limestone slabs was covered with a layer of clay muck from the swamp, and in the layer were two sets of human bones coated with red paint. The acid muck had unfortunately nearly destroyed the bones, but it seemed that each set may have been from a child, for what was left appeared too small and light for an adult, and deciduous ("baby") teeth were included in one set. The individuals had not been buried as corpses, but instead the flesh had been stripped or rotted from the skeleton and the bones alone buried as a bundle. Each set of bones had with it a small seated figurine of jade, in one set a male, in the other a female, plus a simpler standing jade figurine of indeterminate sex, jade beads, and jade pendants. Other precious objects were included: with the male figurine, two polished obsidian discs, a mirror of polished iron ore, and a serpentine "celt"; with the female figurine, two jade objects representing hands, another representing a small frog, and a jade imitation of a stingray tail plus real stingray tail spines and one shark tooth. The basalt-columned tomb was worthy of a king, but it seems more likely that the boy and girl (guessing from the sexes of the figurines

with the bones) were sacrifices, not rulers. Within the site there were several other stone constructions, less impressive than this one, that looked like tombs and contained jade and other precious items laid out as if to adorn and accompany a corpse, but in each the acid teased the archaeologist—was the lack of bones due to the effects of the soil, or had there never been a burial in the structure?

A tantalizing glimpse into life at La Venta occurred when the archaeologists uncovered an offering buried within the ceremonial court. Actually, there were dozens of sets of jade and other valuables buried as offerings within the court, but this set, Offering Number 4 in the excavation record, was not just a jumble of prized carvings and beads. For Number 4, a miniature wall of jade columns (four cut from what had been an engraved plaque, plus two more) had been set up. Against this wall leaned a figurine, unusual in having been carved of dark granite. In front of him, four figurines, one of jade and the others of serpentine, march in single file toward a tall, "haughty and commanding" (the excavator says) figurine facing the file. This personage is of a striking bright-green jade with black inclusions. Ten more figurines of serpentine stand about watching the file of four marching along the wall. Dress and posture give no clue to the roles of the four, or of the man leaning against the wall. Were they priests in procession to the high priest or ruler? Captives marching to the conquering lord? Sacrificial victims? Tribute bearers? Youths being initiated to manhood or vocation? The Olmec are expressive, but silent. A curious postscript to the scene is that many years after the construction of the court, someone cut through the floor of the platform above the buried offering as if to check that the sixteen stone men were still performing their ceremony. The La Ventans must have kept very accurate records or plans of their offerings, because the cut is precisely over the scene.

The *floruit* of La Venta marked changes in the Preclassic trade networks. Oaxaca no longer had a market on the Gulf of Mexico for its flat magnetite mirrors; the La Venta Olmecs made their own mirrors, usually of other iron ores, and made them parabolic (concave), which allowed them to be used to ignite tinder and even to throw images, although we don't know whether the Olmecs deliberately used this trick. Obsidian was now preferably traded as finished blades, in the shape of flat prisms with long, very sharp cutting edges. Early Preclassic sources of lower-quality obsidian, which did not permit the manufacture of fine blades, sold less, and two high-quality sources, that in the valley of Teotihuacán and one in Guatemala, sold more to the Olmecs. Trade in shells declined during the middle Preclassic period, conch shells for trumpets being the only species that continued to be demanded by the peoples of the interior highlands.

That there was not a simple diminution of trade, but rather shifts in routes and alliances, is shown by the rise of Chalcatzingo during the middle Preclassic period. Chalcatzingo lies at the foot of a pair of odd, isolated hills that are a landmark along a good route from the Gulf Coast to the Valley of Mexico. Iron ore was traded from Chalcatzingo to the La Venta Olmecs, and, more important, the town is near a source of fine kaolin clay used in the middle Preclassic period as a slip, or wash, on pottery. The popularity of white-slipped bowls throughout Mexico in this period profited Chalcatzingo. The site is interesting not only for the evidence of its economic position, but also because it demonstrates how Olmec ideology and stylistic canons were shared and modified by what seems to have an independent, though allied, polity in the highlands. On the hill slope above their town, the Chalcatzingoans constructed a stone terrace and from it a stone stairway leading to a narrow terrace of the hill, along which are several large boulders carved with intricately interlocked figures. The scenes, or set of figures, are now difficult to view, being on the undersides of the boulders (presumably the boulders rolled over), but men and serpents can be seen, and the motif of the man in the cave. Portable Olmec art—clay

figurines and bowls—has been found at Chalcatzingo, as at other sites in the highlands, but the glories of the coastal-plain Olmec sites, the monumental carvings in the round, are absent. Its beautiful natural setting makes Chalcatzingo an imposing site, but in terms of outlay of labor, it is puny compared with the Olmec artificial acropolis in the coastal swamps.

The Valley of Mexico underwent an increase in population during the La Venta period. There were four large settlements (up to 58 hectares [143 acres]) in the southern portion of the valley, and, more significant, smaller settlements are spaced an hour or two's walk apart around the lake system, suggesting a population sufficiently large to distribute itself fairly regularly over the arable land. Evidence presently available (that is, not destroyed by the urbanization of Mexico City in the center of the valley) indicates that farming was principally carried on along the lower slopes of the edges of the valley, where irrigation ditches were built to channel water to the fields.

Excavations at Tlatilco, well within the present city, have revealed a cemetery containing graves of persons of varying wealth, some interred with only a few simple items of common life, others buried with elegant dishes, ornaments of imported jade and marine shell, and clay figures, a few of Olmec manufacture but most locally made and reflecting the valley artisans' interpretations of Olmec ideology and style. By far the most common figurine-type is a small, solid-clay girl, nude or scantily dressed, frequently wearing necklaces and other ornaments and with hair elaborately arranged. These nubile girls certainly don't look like earth-mother goddesses. The little figures may have been good-luck charms, forerunners of the figures Mexicans today set on the dashboards and hang from rear-view mirrors of their cars. It is unfortunate that what were probably the two largest communities in middle Preclassic period Valley of Mexico, Tlatilco and Cuicuilco, are virtually inaccessible to modern archaeological investigation. Tlatilco has been nearly destroyed by extensive digging for brick clay (which, incidentally, produced the thousands of figures and pots, very few noticed to be associated with other artifacts or structures) and Cuicuilco was buried by the eruption of Xitle volcano. Teotihuacán, the northeastern extension of the Valley of Mexico, exported quantities of obsidian blades, but for the Preclassic period, now shows only evidence of hamlets on the edges of the valley; if there were a big village in the valley center, it lies under the later city of Teotihuacán.

Outside Mexico proper, the probable ancestors of the Maya were farming and evolving more complex societies in both the mountainous highlands of southeastern Mexico and Guatemala and the jungle lowlands of eastern Mesoamerica. The site of Cuello in Belize, in the lowlands, has a series of occupation floors spanning the Preclassic period and continuing into the Classic periods. Bits of charcoal found in trash swept up by the builders of the first definite village at Cuello have been radiocarbon-dated to 3000 B.C., but might be remains of forest fires. On the other hand, they *might* be from cooking hearths, and therefore from a more ancient settlement obliterated when later Cuelloans prepared the foundations of their buildings.

Cuelloans in the first millennium B.C. ground grain, probably maize, on sandstone metates brought from sources of the stone in the Maya Mountains 150 kilometers (93 miles) away. They hunted deer and agouti and also ate snails. A wood-framed building, possibly like modern Maya houses that are plastered and thatch-roofed, was constructed on a low earth platform neatly plastered on the surface. The excavator estimates this early house platform to have been circular and about 3 meters (9 feet) in diameter, again like modern Maya peasants' homes but unlike the impressive buildings of later Classic Maya cities. Pottery technology is sophisticated and well mastered, the shapes of the pottery following fashions found throughout Mexico in this and much of the succeeding millennium—flat, low sided open bowls, bottles, and round, pumpkin-shaped cook-

ing or storage pots. General characteristics of the pottery link it to contemporary sites in Mexico, for example in the Tehuacán Valley; in Central America, for example in Panama; and in northern South America, in Ecuador and Colombia. The very earliest pottery now known in the Americas comes from the northern South American sites and dates to the fourth millennium B.C., two thousand years earlier than ceramics in Mesoamerican sites. This knowledge, and the lack of any crude, experimental early pottery in Mexico, suggests that American pottery making began in northern South America and that the craft was learned by Mesoamericans from contacts to the south. The sharing of inventions, crop plants, and religious concepts such as jaguar and serpent symbols of deity from Mesoamerica through Central America and into South America as far as southern Peru led A.L. Kroeber to call this entire area "Nuclear America."

By the middle Preclassic period, Cuello, like many other Maya-area settlements, had a public building, probably a temple, on a plastered platform. The structure was built of limestone cobbles, the wall finished with plaster. Under the threshold of the door is the dedicatory offering, a sacrifice not of time and energy, as at La Venta, but of a young man, whose corpse was given a plain jar and a string of shell and jade beads to carry into the afterlife. The jade had been mined 400 kilometers (250 miles) away. By the middle Preclassic period, population in the Maya region was increasing, farming was important and water-control systems were being built, and trade or expeditions to remote raw-material sources were a regular part of the proto-Maya economy. Crop plants and pottery styles reflect much wider contacts, but the limited excavations and analyses of the Preclassic period proto-Maya sites have not yet given direct proof of more distant ties.

The ninth century B.C. was the closing era of the middle Preclassic period in Mesoamerica. La Venta was abandoned in the middle of the following century, about 750 B.C.—why, we do not know.

Two innovations in the ninth century B.C. may indirectly be connected with the fall of La Venta and subsequent decline of the Olmec. First, a true planned town was constructed at Monte Negro in Oaxaca, near the present town of Tilantongo. Low platforms were built along regular streets and houses erected on the platforms, usually following the Mesoamerican tradition of a group of four, one on each side of a rectangular patio. Some of the platforms are handsomely faced with cut stone blocks. A system of drainage channels took care of heavy rains and sewage. Pottery found in the mountaintop town included, in addition to very ordinary local wares, some fine ceramics probably obtained from the town of Monte Albán, on the outskirts of the present city of Oaxaca (capital of the state of the same name). Monte Albán was also a mountaintop settlement, but whereas Monte Negro was abandoned at the end of the middle Preclassic period and its remains left undisturbed for the archaeologists, Monte Albán was occupied for many more centuries and rebuilt several times, until its earliest town can no longer be traced. Thus, Monte Negro, not especially important in its own right, is a surviving clue to the emergence of densely occupied, organized towns in the Mesoamerican Preclassic period.

The second notable discovery dating from the ninth century B.C. is a dam at Purrón in the Tehuacán Valley in southern Puebla. The primary purpose of the dam across the valley at this locale seems to have been to control flash floods. A sluice gate allowed management of impounded water. The Purrón dam, 100 meters (328 feet) across, indicates a large-scale community effort to modify the natural environment in favor of human safety and needs. One benefit of the dam was probably irrigation of fruit orchards below it. The Tehuacán Valley is more arid than many other Mexican highland valleys, although there are good springs along its edge (these are now tapped for the bottled mineral waters sold throughout Mexico). Purrón-area occupations dating before the dam have little fruit remains, but once the dam was built, evidence

of fruit eating dramatically increases, implying that the later Preclassic period people took advantage of seepage from the dam's reservoir to nourish orchards. The dam functioned, and was rebuilt when required, until A.D. 800. To the north, in the Valley of Mexico, other farmers of the early first millennium B.C. canalized water flowing down Guadalupe Hill into Lake Texcoco. This canal system controlled flash floods, spreading the water over fields.

The last phase of the middle Preclassic period, beginning about 750 B.C., saw a return of inhabitants to San Lorenzo. It is quite possible that the La Ventans left their great center to rebuild their ancestors' acropolis. The same evidence—defaced and buried monuments—that led us to wonder whether visionaries or enemies were responsible for the end of the original San Lorenzo occupation exists to mark the end of La Venta and leads to the same questions for this site. Strong cultural continuity between late La Venta and the second occupation of San Lorenzo is demonstrated by the presence of the same pottery styles and by the rebuilt structures of the new San Lorenzo, which closely parallel the mounds and platforms of La Venta's latest phase. In spite of the persistence of the Olmec tradition in the late middle Preclassic period, the power that gave the Olmecs preeminence in earlier centuries seems to have declined.

The Oaxacans

Oaxacans were contenders for the leadership that had slipped from Olmec grasp. Oaxaca's capital at Monte Albán had its ceremonial center crowning a very high, steep ridge from which one surveys, as would an eagle, miles of rich farmlands far below. The heart-pounding climb up the ridge leaves the visitor breathless. Then awe is compounded by the stone-faced pyramids, one behind another the length of each side of the ridge, the greatest of them closing the huge plaza at its north and south ends. The construction of this display of the melding of human and natural magnificence seems to have begun by 750 B.C.

Daily life for the common people in the Valley of Oaxaca probably did not change much from the early Preclassic period, when villages like San José Mogote were the sites of the little temples and residences of the chiefs who traded the magnetite mirrors to the Olmecs. What was new was the organization of an increasing population. The shift from societies structured along personal relationships to one defined by territorial and perhaps ethnic (language and customs) criteria must have occurred in Oaxaca about the ninth century B.C. The new concept of nations of thousands dominating homelands may be vividly illustrated in over one hundred bas-reliefs on slabs in Monte Albán. The slabs were carved in the first building period (late middle Preclassic period) of Monte Albán and many were buried by later construction or reused in new buildings, so the original context is lost. Most of the slabs bear a human figure in a grotesque pose. They have been called *danzantes* (Spanish for "dancers"), but dancing they are not. The most tenable interpretation is that each figure is a man captured or killed in battle. Scroll-like lines emerging from the bodies of many *danzantes* may be blood flowing from their wounds. Quite a few figures have accompanying symbols that may be hierogylphs for the town or nation from which the warrior came. One such slab, to be seen at the south end of the plaza, has to the left of the man's head a distinctly Olmec-style head, then below that a jaguar, then what looks like a rope knot. Interpolating from later Mesoamerican hieroglyphic writing, these symbols may have identified the capture (rope knot) of an Olmec "Jaguar-man." (Did the Olmec call themselves the Jaguar People?) Monte Albán was not built as a fortress, but it would have been naturally impregnable, and its founders may have had this in mind when they chose to place their temples and palaces on its top. The siting of Monte Albán cogently illustrates the new society in Oaxaca in the late middle Preclassic period: at the height, priests and rulers commanding armies to slay other nations threatening Oaxaca's superiority; lower, the craftworkers, farmers, and servants who maintained the society; and at the fringes, naked captives from foreign lands.

Mention of the probable hieroglyphs in early Monte Albán carvings brings up the question of the origin of Mesoamerican writing. At the time of the Spanish conquest, there were some eighteen distinct writing systems in Mesoamerica. The systems had varying combinations of realistic pictures, recognizable symbols, and abstract symbols, and varied also in the degree to which they were phonetic. The Spanish attempted cultural genocide by destroying the native Mesoamerican books and persecuting literate nobles and priests clinging to this heritage of knowledge. Now we have only a handful of examples of Mesoamerican books, too little to enable us to learn to read the inscriptions even on all late pre-Columbian Mesoamerican remains. Obviously, it is even more difficult to read inscriptions from earlier centuries, which differ from the late ones as medieval or ancient Greek writing differs from modern English. Archaeologists work to "crack the code" of the Mesoamerican inscriptions in part by trying out readings that could be made if the earlier inscription used the conventions of conquest-period writing, in part by using the methods of cryptographers. From such a combination, we can guess at the meaning of the symbols beside the Monte Albán *danzantes*. It is an exercise in ambivalence, of course—the slab described above could quite possibly represent a priest's soul and the glyphs might read, "He twists his soul [the rope knot] and is transformed into a magical jaguar who visits the deity [the 'Olmec' head]." (The "twisting" of the soul would have been accomplished with the aid of a hallucinogen or sensory-dissociation techniques.) Such an interpretation is as much in line with Mesoamerican thinking as is one of warrior capture.

When writing appeared in Mesoamerica depends in part upon one's definition of writing. Do a few semiabstract symbols constitute writing? Or must one have enough symbols to record complete utterances on any subject? If one agrees on a minimum of only a few glyphs, then Mesoamerican writing is definite by the late middle Preclassic period, probable in the middle Preclassic period (the glyphs on La Venta carvings, none of which have yet been read), and possible in the Tlatilco Preclassic period, when a number of clay and stone cylindrical stamps (usually referred to as seals) were used, probably to print designs on cloth or perhaps on people's skin. Most of the designs are simple geometric or life forms, but some have quite abstract, glyphlike motifs, which are occasionally repeated. The stamps may be exhibiting the beginning, as early as 1500 B.C., of experimentation with symbolic notation.

By early Monte Albán, there is no question that the carved symbols are glyphs, the germs of a writing system. It is no coincidence that attempts at writing appear with the emergence of the state. When everyone knew everyone else, and his or her deeds, in the village, and had little business elsewhere, no one had to read. But when thousands of peasants and traders traveled for days to visit the new towns and their temples, priests and rulers had to devise a constant, silent form of communication to the unceasing throngs. The glyphs served this function, identifying deities and rituals and emblazoning the conquests on which the ruler's claim to power rested.

Another aid to managing the masses was the development of calendars. The historic Mesoamericans strongly believed in astrology. Priests cast horoscopes according to the stars and planets associated with the day on which one was born, and each day was auspicious for some persons in certain undertakings, inauspicious for others. Much of the priests' time was taken up with astronomical observations and calculations. The people followed a 260-day ritual series, or "ritual year," as well as the 365-day solar year, and were particularly observant of the period, every 52 years, when the first day of the ritual year coincided with the first day of the solar year. Glyphs from stelae in early Monte Albán may be interpreted as signifying the 260-day ritual year, which suggests that the organization of the early state was facilitated by the regularization of a calendar of rituals.

The Late Preclassic Period

The late Preclassic period runs from about 500 B.C. to about 100 B.C. Around 300 B.C., the radioactive-carbon content of the atmosphere changed so much that radiocarbon dating, which up to then had given dates of fewer than the true number of years, now begins to give dates older than the true year, making the time span of the period longer than radiocarbon dates for the late Preclassic period had led archaeologists to estimate. This calls into question some of the reconstructions of the prehistory of the era. But the exact number of years an occupation or phase lasted, or the precise year something was built, is not really a vital question in a study of cultural development such as this. The reader brought up in the European cultural tradition, that which dominates American schools, has been taught to remember dates and is apt to feel disturbed upon encountering people who are imprecise about years. Such readers must be patient until we reach the Mesoamerican Classic period, when we return to a better fit between radiocarbon-based time estimates and calendar year spans. About a millennium elapsed between the glory of the Olmec and the power of the great Classic empire of Teotihuacán. This millennium encompasses the late middle and late Preclassic period epochs and the Protoclassic epoch. It is a millennium of the slow decline of the Olmec art style and the subsequent slow rise of the Maya and Teotihuacán styles, a millennium of steady population growth and the founding of many towns, a millennium in which the technological competencies evolved in the preceding centuries continued to be demonstrated, and in which many inventions were made.

Among the significant developments of the late Preclassic period was the improvement of the cal-

FIGURE 2.2 House scene, clay model. Preclassic western Mexico, c. 100 B.C. *(Milwaukee Public Museum)*

endar. As we have noted, astrology was the great preoccupation of Mesoamericans. People were named after the date of their birth, and were given a second name to distinguish them from others born on the same day. (For example, Ce Acatl Topiltzin—Ce Acatl meaning "One Reed," the name of the day of his birth, Topiltzin meaning "Prince"—was the king of the Toltecs, distin-guished by his title from the hundreds of Ce Acatls who were peasants, artisans, or merchants.) Many priests dedicated themselves to the study of astron-omy in order to understand the system they be-lieved to influence fate. A famous king of Texcoco, a nation of the Valley of Mexico allied to the Aztecs, was Netzahualpilli, renowned for his wisdom gained through study of the heavens and discussion with astronomer-priests. (Netzahual-pilli's name, "Fasting Prince," suggests he also shared the ascetic practices of the priest-scholars.) The acme of Mesoamerican astronomical knowledge was reached by the Maya, but the other native nations were able to perform nearly as advanced calculations of eclipses, planetary motions, and stellar cycles. The general structure of the 260-day ritual calendar and the 365-day so-called Vague Year (18 months of 20 days each, totaling 360, plus 5 "unlucky" days, but no leap-year correction) was shared throughout Mesoamerica, each nation varying from the others in details such as day names and name series.

Several buildings in ceremonial centers in Mesoamerica were apparently astronomical observatories with tunnels or slots placed so that the priest sitting within could precisely fix a regular astronomical event—for example, the summer-solstice sun or Venus's rising or setting. The layout of buildings in relation to one another in the ceremonial center also furnished astronomical sight lines to priests standing at certain doorways or corners facing architectural features of adjacent or distant structures. Some of these sight lines no longer "work" because the tilt of the earth's axis has gradually shifted the point at which the star or planet appears or sets; to discover whether the viewpoint had been scientifically positioned, one now needs to consult astronomers' tables giving the degrees of these shifts. Other astronomically oriented constructions are still obvious: at Chalcatzingo, for instance, the rays of the sun setting at summer solstice fall upon the stone terrace and stairway to the carved boulders upon the probably sacred hill.

Late Preclassic Oaxaca built astronomical observatories. Monte Albán exhibits a strongly marked north-south orientation, except for one oddball structure in the middle of the southern section of the plaza. This jarring note, called Building J, is a rectangle with a triangular rear appendage, through which passes a narrow, straight tunnel. The building is oriented with its front stairway toward the northeast and the prowlike rear pointing southwest. Astronomer Anthony F. Aveni has determined that in the late Preclassic period, the rear triangle pointed to the setting positions of five bright stars, and that a person standing on the front stairway would be facing the rising position of another bright star, Capella, when it first appeared before dawn at the season of the passage of the sun through its zenith. Since the movements of the sun and moon through their zeniths on certain days of the 52-year Mesoamerican "century" were thought to signal salvation from threatened world holocaust, Building J may have been a calendar temple, on the stairs of which, as the critical days neared, a learned priest stationed himself to determine from Capella the fatal day itself. On that day, the priest entered a building (P or R—the designation differs on some maps) on the east side of the plaza. Here a narrow vertical slot in the construction provided a sight line to the zenith. We can imagine the hush as the lords and populace of Monte Albán waited for the priest to signal that the sun had stood above his sighting slot and then passed on, the clamor of trumpets of conch and drums of turtle shell announcing that the sun and our world would continue, the hymns of thanksgiving soaring from the throng so close to the sky on that magnificant mountaintop.

A curious twin to Building J at Monte Alban is Building O at a smaller contemporary town, Caballito Blanco, 50 kilometers (31 miles) east of Monte Albán. This building has the same triangle-plus-rectangle form, so unusual in Mesoamerica, as Building J; and like Building J, it is noticeably skewed off the orientation of its fellow structures. However, Building O, while also facing northeast with its prow facing southwest, is not aligned exactly like Building J: the solar phenomenon to be observed from the front stairway of Building O is the summer-solstice sunrise, and the phenomenon on line from the triangle point is the setting of the brightest star, Sirius, that rises before dawn close to the summer solstice. Whether the Oaxacan

FIGURE 2.3 Monte Albán hilltop ceremonial center. Odd-shaped building in foreground (Building J) is an astronomical observatory dating from the Late Preclassic, c. A.D. 200. Behind it and along the sides of the great plaza are platforms on which stood temples and palaces. Not all of the site has been excavated: vegetation covers several of the platforms in the background. For scale, note people on plaza, right background. *(A. Kehoe)*

towns of the late Preclassic period each specialized in one calendar-correlated astronomical sighting, or whether Building O was simply a naive copy of the capital's Building J, accidentally oriented to summer solstice, or, finally, whether the smaller town's priests were ignorant of the Capella sighting marking the crucial day and assumed that summer solstice was what one observed in the northeast—these questions we cannot now answer.

SECTION 3: THE MEXICAN CLASSIC PERIOD

Around two thousand years ago (from the last century B.C. to the first century A.D.), the balance of power and influence in Mesoamerica shifted into a configuration that has characterized Mesoamerica up to the present time: the Valley of Mexico dominates Mesoamerica politically and economically; the other regional centers are constrained by this domination but maintain their own artistic and ideological growth; there are interregna during which defeat of the Valley empire allows leadership by another nation, which is dominated anew by a Valley power. It has been customary to picture Mexico after the Olmecs as being divided into Mexico proper, the Valley-focused western lands, and the Maya realm in eastern Mesoamerica. This is a false division; first, because it does not do justice to the important major western capitals outside the Valley—Oaxaca, Veracruz, Puebla, and the poorly known states along the Pacific—and second, because it does not recognize the periodic extensions of Valley empires into Maya regions. There is, however, a basis for stressing the independence of the Maya in artistic matters. Early in the Classic era, these peoples achieved one of the world's great art styles, expressed in architecture, carvings, and paintings (and very possibly also in literature, which unhappily was nearly totally destroyed by the Spanish). The Mexicans and the Maya may, on this ground, be seen as two parallel civilizations, but it must be understood that the nations were always in contact, a tendency fostered by the major ecological differences between the Mexican highlands and the Maya lowlands. (Again, this is a difference not to be unduly emphasized. There are Mexican lowlands, in Veracruz and along the Pacific, and Maya highlands, in Chiapas and Guatemala. The amount of highlands and lowlands relative to each other differs between West and East Mesoamerica.) The parallel growth of the two civilizations can be traced from the Protoclassic period.

Teotihuacán

Teotihuacán means "place of the gods" in Nahuatl, the language of the Aztecs. A stupendous pyramid, approximately 64 meters (210 feet) high by 210 meters (690 feet) square at the base, hulks over the city. (The exact original measurements are not known because its outer surface was destroyed before the study began.) The city itself spreads over 20 square kilometers (8 square miles), a substantial portion of its valley, which is a northeast extension of the Valley of Mexico. The master plan of the city is based upon an east-west line sighted from the center of the city (where the ancient survey station was established by a cross inside concentric circles, all incised on a stone slab) west to a station (similarly marked) on a hill. The surveyors drew a right angle to this base line and made this north-south perpendicular the axis of the city. The Pyramid of the Sun was constructed just north of the survey station, on the east side of the principal axis. A slightly smaller and more elegant pyramid, the Pyramid of the Moon, was constructed 700 meters (nearly one-half mile) to the north, blocking the north end of the principal axis. Twelve hundred meters (three-quarters of a mile) to the south, the elaborate

Temple of Quetzalcoatl and its broad court are on the east side of the axis, facing the Great Compound, probably the empire's largest market, on the west side. The principal axis has been called, since Aztec times, the Street of the Dead, but it is not really an avenue because between the Great Compound and the Pyramid of the Sun it is broken up into a series of courts. To walk from the Compound to the Pyramid, one must climb up and down the stairs of the platforms running east-west across the axis. These barriers may have been designed to separate the most sacred sector of the city from mundane business, like the series of walls with gates that separated the forbidden City of the divine emperor from the prosaic life of Beijing in China. Beyond the hub formed of the axis from the Great Compound to the Moon Pyramid stretch the hundreds of city blocks, each (varying somewhat in size) an apartment complex housing around twenty families and including interior patios and often small temples. The workshops of the craftsmen seem to have been within the apartment complexes, also. The population of the city at its height, around A.D. 650, is conservatively estimated at 200,000; it may have been thousands more.

Throughout the Preclassic period, the Valley of Teotihuacán was a major exporter of obsidian, which at least from the beginning of the middle Preclassic period, was exported as finished blades. Yet there is no evidence of substantial settlement in this extension of the Valley of Mexico until the late Preclassic period—although it is possible a moderately large village existed during the middle Preclassic period around the springs in the middle of the Valley, its remains lost in the drainage and construction projects of the later city. Existing evidence does demonstrate that in the late Preclassic period, three villages lay on the floor of the valley of Teotihuacán and a number of hamlets were scattered on its edges.

The most important community in the Valley of Mexico area in the late Preclassic era was probably Cuicuilco, a town in the southwestern part of the

FIGURE 2.4 Teotihuacán, view from the top platform of the Pyramid of the Moon at the end of the principal axis. The Pyramid of the Sun occupies the left center (note how its contours repeat the contours of the mountains ringing the valley). In the center distance, left of the principal axis, is the partially-excavated mound of the Temple of Quetzalcóatl and Tlaloc, at the left end of the court thought to be that of the ruler's residence. Across the principal axis or "avenue" (right background) is the Great Compound, probably the city's central market. For scale, note the people in the plaza below the platform in the foreground. *(T. Kehoe)*

Valley of Mexico (just south of the National University on the southern border of Mexico City and beside the freeway [Periférico] leading south). The southern half of the Valley of Mexico had the larger share of the area's population through the Preclassic era, so it is not surprising that the first town with a monumental public work was in this section. The citizens of Cuicuilco built a "pyramid," as it is usually erroneously referred to, about 370 feet (113 meters) in diameter at the base and 60 feet (18 meters) high (its original dimensions can no longer be determined). This construction—in actuality, a mound—consists of three superimposed terraces now above ground. A broad ramp on the mound's west side leads the visitor of today part way up, where the remains of stairs appear and

take one to the top terrace. Excavation has opened an oval room within this terrace. Since the archaeological work was done early in this century, when methods were crude, it is now difficult to unravel the several successive, comparatively crude temples that seem to have been built on the top terrace, or to reconstruct any of them. Just south of the foot of the ramp, the excavators uncovered a circle of boulder slabs set on end, which they believed to be a small shrine. Simple figures were painted in red on the interior side of some of these boulders. About 150 B.C., the volcano Xitle (Nahuatl, for "navel") on the southern rim of the Valley of Mexico erupted and covered much of the southern valley, including Cuicuilco, with many feet of lava. The combination of this lava rock covering the ancient town and the crude excavations of the archae-ologists of many years ago is extremely frustrating today. What little is now to be seen at Cuicuilco cannot be trusted to be more than an approximation of the original finished construction, and practically the entire town is buried under lava rock. Archaeologists have tunneled under the lava here and there, and have examined the openings in it made by commercial excavations for building and road foundations, but the nature and extent of late Preclassic period Cuicuilco is inevitably a topic for argument. The majority of prehistorians guess that it was an important town that may have covered several square kilometers (about one square mile) and that had a population of perhaps ten thousand.

When Xitle's eruption overwhelmed Cuicuilco, the population of the Valley of Mexico had increased to the point that, on the one hand, hamlets were being founded all over the Valley, even in the less hospitable, arid northwestern corner and the high Amecameca Pass, and, on the other hand, thousands of persons lived clustered in towns of around five thousand people covering about 100 hectares (250 acres). Cuicuilco in the southwest and Teotihuacán in the northeast were apparently the largest settlements, each having an estimated ten thousand residents and the latter covering 600 hectares (1,500 acres). Between these major towns were local centers such as Tlapacoya, on what is now the eastern edge of Mexico City, formerly the eastern shore of Lake Texcoco. Towns like Tlapacoya had platform mounds as high as 7 meters (23 feet)—the larger ones were stepped—that were presumably crowned with temples. The smaller towns, as well as Cuicuilco and Teotihuacán, probably had craft specialists and priests to serve the townspeople and peasants in the surrounding hamlets, and were governed by chiefs who made alliances with neighboring towns.

The survivors of the eruption of Xitle were forced to take refuge in the northern half of the Valley of Mexico. They seem to have been attracted to Cuicuilco's old rival, Teotihuacán, which rapidly swelled in population. From this time, in the first century B.C., until the fall of Teotihuacán, about A.D. 800, the city of Teotihuacán was absolutely preeminent in the Valley of Mexico. The city was so attractive that during the first century A.D., many hamlets in the Valley of Teotihuacán and the neighboring Lake Texcoco shore region were abandoned, the people apparently flocking into the metropolis. A fully urban way of life dominated the Valley of Mexico.

The first phase of urban settlement was located in what later became the northwestern sector of the city. This phase, of around ten thousand persons by the end of the first century A.D., had several platform mounds, probably bases for temples and perhaps for palaces and administrative halls also. Homes were tightly clustered, which foreshadowed the apartment blocks that served the city in subsequent centuries. The economy of the early city must have been at least in part based upon the extraction, processing, and export of obsidian blades, but the manufacture of goods such as cloth and pottery for the Valley of Mexico and the performance of rituals by highly trained priests must have also contributed to the city's prosperity, drawing thousands to its markets and shrines. On the outskirts of the city were productive farms benefiting from the rich alluvial soil and numerous springs of the Valley of Teotihuacán. Archaeologist William T. Sanders suggests that the hamlets on the drier slopes of the surrounding hills probably specialized in the cultivation of maguey, rendering the plants' sap into the popular fermented drink pulque and selling jars of the beerlike liquid to the thirsty city workers.

An ancient lava flow underlies the Valley of Teotihuacán. In the lava are many caves, once bubbles in the flow. Southeast of the original city of Teotihuacán, in a locality now called, in Nahuatl, Oztoyahualco ("In a circle of caves"), is a cave composed of a tunnel 103 meters (338 feet) long, meandering from an entrance on the west toward the east, where it ends in four chambers forming a four-petal flower shape. Two more chambers open from the tunnel, one on each side, about one-third of the distance from the entrance. During the period of the first urban development of Teotihuacán, a mound of earth covered with adobe bricks in turn faced with cobblestones—similar to the platform mounds in the center of the city and also to the great mound of Cuicuilco—stood over the chambers at the end of the underground tunnel. At this time, a spring probably ran in the tunnel. Caves in Mesoamerica have often been shrines, associated with the jaguar and/or serpent lord of the underworld (represented by the gaping fanged mouth of these animals), the legendary place whence humankind emerged into life and where the sun, the source of life, travels each night. The Olmec, it will be recalled, pictured a personage (deity? legendary first man? priest? oracle?) seated in a cave or cavelike serpent's mouth. The four-petal flower is a favorite symbol in Mexico, continuing from the early Classic period through the Spanish conquest into the seventeenth century A.D., when native artists still used it as a decorative pattern in churches. The form represents the four quarters of the earth (the four directions) and its center. The four-chambered cave thus may have signified the earth itself—the earth being a womb that always yields water and that once produced humans (a frequent metaphor in conquest-period and historic Mesoamerica)—and also the jaguar lord of the earth, for the markings on the jaguar's pelt are shown as a four-petal rosette throughout Nuclear America.

About A.D. 150, the Teotihuacános began to construct a much more massive mound over the existing mound above the cave. This enlarged mound became the mountainous Pyramid of the Sun, the first of the major structures in the heart of Classic Teotihuacán. The pyramid faces west, and has four superimposed platforms. An early excavator found bodies of children at each of the four corners of each platform, presumably sacrifices dedicating the structure. The finished pyramid had a facing of dressed stone slabs and a temple on the top, neither evidenced now. The tunnel and cave chambers under the pyramid were probably used

for rites during most of the Classic period, since the cave walls were plastered, sectioning walls built and rebuilt, and the chambers modified. At last, about A.D. 550, the entrance to the tunnel was sealed off by the construction of the platform that stands as an annex at the middle of the western front of the pyramid and provides the stairs that bring visitors to the first terrace of the pyramid. Why this platform was built over the entrance to the tunnel, we cannot guess. Exploration in the tunnel and chambers, incidentally, showed the cave complex to be nearly empty, and there was some indication that looters may have entered in the Aztec period, a thousand years after the use of the tunnel.

Prior to the final phase of construction of the Pyramid of the Sun was a period in which the pyramid's truncated top had upon it two temples. During the final phase, there may also have been twin temples on the top of the pyramid. The conquest-era Aztec civilization had two temples side by side (each on its own pyramid platform) in the center of their capital, Tenochtitlán, and this concept of two ruling deities may have been a carry-over from the Teotihuacán civilization. Aztec philosophy and oratory stressed duality, as in the description of the Supreme (translated from Nahuatl):

> And it is told, it is said [the oratorical style was
> to repeat a phrase, using a word with a
> shade of difference in meaning]
> That Quetzalcóatl would invoke...
> She of the starry skirt, he whose radiance en
> velops things;
> Lady of our flesh, Lord of our flesh;
> She who is clothed in black [night], he who is
> clothed in red [day];
> She who endows the earth with solidity, he
> who covers the earth with cotton [clouds]
> And thus it was known, that toward the heav
> ens was his plea directed,
> Toward the place of duality, above the nine
> levels of Heaven.
>
> *(León-Portilla 1963:29)*

A thousand years later, the Aztecs' two principal temples were dedicated to Tlaloc, god of fertility, and to Huitzilopochtli, a warrior god and national patron of the Aztecs. We can be reasonably confident that Huitzilopochtli was not a Teotihuacán deity, since legends invariably associate him closely with the Aztecs. Tlaloc, in contrast, was worshiped throughout Mexico, his name different from nation to nation, but the iconography more consistent. Tlaloc has large, round goggle-eyes reminiscent of a frog and a rectangular open mouth with jaguar fangs. Miguel Covarrubias, the Mexican artist and lifelong student of pre-Columbian Mexican art, argued that Tlaloc evolved, conceptually and iconographically, from the Olmec jaguar symbol. If so, the Teotihuacán "Tlaloc," a thousand years more recent than the Olmec religion, was not only a much more abstract symbol but also a more complex one. The Teotihuacán "Tlalocs" usually are painted in colors associated with rain and storm—blue, green, or black—and carry water pots and lightning, but a few are painted yellow and carry maize plants and cobs and squashes, or are painted red and carry lightning bolts and decorated containers. These Lords of the Storms, or priests representing them, are depicted in processions to a fierce female deity who seems to be the source of all life, both bestowing it and demanding its sacrifice. One of the two temples on top of the Pyramid of the Sun may have been that of the Lord of the Storms.

It is more difficult to guess what deity was enshrined in the other temple on the great pyramid, if indeed there were two. An obvious contender is Quetzalcóatl, "Precious Feather Snake" in Nahuatl, who, like Tlaloc, was worshiped throughout Mexico and may have Olmec roots, in this case in the serpent symbol. The beautiful, rather baroque temple in the Ciudadela compound of Teotihuacán, which is south of the Pyramid of the Sun and opposite the Great Compound market, is decorated with alternating heads of Quetzalcóatls and a scaly, snouted creature (might it be a cayman alligator?) not otherwise seen in the city. The

palace on the west side of the Pyramid of the Moon plaza, the Quetzalpapalotl ("Precious Feather Butterfly") Palace, is entered by stairs flanked by fearsome heads of Quetzalcóatl, represented here as a rattlesnake with a feather design on its back. These instances demonstrate the importance of Quetzalcóatl to the Teotihuacános, who may have believed this deity to fulfill the functions ascribed to him in later times by the Aztecs: patron of human life and the arts of civilization, high priest of all priests.

Another contender for the title of co-deity of Teotihuacán is the goddess who hovers over the Lords of the Storms. Similar in many attributes to the Aztec goddess Xochiquetzal ("Flower Feather" or "Precious Flower" in Nahuatl), she is alternately terrible and beneficent. (Incidentally, the "quetzal" ["feather"] in these deity names refers specifically to the gorgeous and expensive feathers from the tropical quetzal bird. Quetzal feathers adorned royalty and ceremonial objects, and the word "quetzal" came to be synonymous with "precious" [as we say "golden"] and associated with high rank.) In Aztec mythology, Xochiquetzal was once married to Tlaloc and was mother to Quetzalcóatl. She was patroness of fertility, including human procreation, of weaving and painting, and of flowers. A number of murals in Teotihuacán depict a goddess wearing a headdress, sometimes with a green bird—a quetzal?—in the center, sometimes with a four-petal flower. The goddess's hands are extended at her sides, and from her hands flow streams of riches. On other representations, which may be of the same goddess, judging from the repetition of certain iconographic emblems, the figure is, or partly emerges from, a mountain or pyramid with a cave-like interior in which are objects that have been interpreted to be seeds and jade. A mural in the Quetzalpapalotl Palace shows many individuals making offerings to this highly stylized deity. Still other representations include a complex four-part symbol that has been interpreted by the art historian George Kubler to mean the four basic elements of the world: earth, air, fire, and water. (These four basic elements were recognized in Aztec cosmology. This similarity between the Aztec and the classical Eurasian conceptualization of the four elements is curious and unexplained.) If the several varying Teotihuacán icons do represent an earlier version of the Aztec Xochiquetzal, the motifs of the four-petal flower and the four elements fit this goddess, whom the Aztecs believed to be very ancient, the mother of gods, and the female aspect of the Supreme invoked by Quetzalcóatl in the quoted myth.

The rulers of Teotihuacán were probably either believed to be semidivine or were high priests as well as governor. There are several reasons for this supposition: one, the religious aura surrounding the Aztec emperor, and the possibility that Aztec civilization took over the traditions of its predecessors in the Valley of Mexico; two, the importance placed upon the Aztec and other Mexican rulers' performance of rituals of the highest sacredness; three, the preoccupation with religion seen in the Teotihuacán murals and other paintings; and, four, the fact that most monarchs have been titular heads of their state church (the doctrine of separation of church and state being modern). Mexican archaeologist Pedro Armillas and, more recently, René Millon, who directed an intensive survey of the site of Teotihuacán, believe that the compound called the Ciudadela, on the east side of the Street of the Dead and south of the Pyramid of the Sun, was the residence of the rulers and political center of Teotihuacán. This compound has broad platforms north and south of a long, wide central plaza. Palaces were built upon the platforms, and the elaborate temple covered with relief masks of Quetzalcóatl and the scaly creature was placed at the east end, opposite the entrance from the street. (The temple now seen at the site was a relatively early one, and was later covered by a much larger pyramid with a temple.) We do not know whether the temple was dedicated to Quetzalcóatl and/or the scaly creature, or whether these were here subsidiary to the deity of the temple, who may have

been the special patron of the nation of Teotihuacán, and therefore reduced to lesser stature in the mythologies of later Mexican nations. Whoever the deity, the completion of the Early Classic temple was celebrated with the sacrifice of over a hundred people, most of them soldiers ranged around the temple base in a seated position, hands tied behind their backs, but including at least two young women. One group of these eternal guards consisted of six very young men, 18 to 20 years old, six young mature men, and six middle-aged men, all outfitted with weapons and costumes seen in the mural paintings. These men sat against the center of the south wall of the temple; against the center of the north wall was a set of eighteen more persons, seventeen men and one woman. Among the ornaments with the sacrifices were thousands of shell beads carved to look like human teeth, and some real human teeth. Such emphasis on human teeth —a nightmare version of the Tooth Fairy—is unique in Mesoamerican archaeology. The exact center of the temple was marked by the burial of twenty bodies richly ornamented with jade, shell, obsidian, and other precious materials.

The Quetzalcóatl Compound's paired palaces led Millon to wonder whether Teotihuacán had dual rulers, one living in the north palace of the Ciudadela, the other living in the south palace. If this speculation is correct, it would support the inference that the government of Teotihuacán was dominated by religious ideas and personnel, for dual monarchs would strongly reflect the fundamental duality seen in Teotihuacán iconography as well as in conquest-period traditions and cosmology. In practice, too, dual rulers would likely be chiefly occupied in ritual, leaving mundane governance to a single prime minister with clear and undivided jurisdiction.

Millon identifies the Great Compound opposite the Ciudadela as the empire's principal market and the economic center of the nation. The platforms ringing the large plaza of this compound supported buildings that seem to have been different from those in comparable position in the Ciudadela.

Limited excavation in the plaza has given possible evidence of market stalls and food vendors there. The buildings on the platforms may have housed overseers and offices of trade and of tax and tribute collection.

Throughout the 20 square kilometers (8 square miles) of the city of Teotihuacán are the apartment blocks, at least 2,200 of them. Many blocks seem to have been laid out according to a base measuring unit of 57 meters (187 feet), but the city as a whole does not appear to have been rigidly planned, apart from the Street of the Dead's north-south axis and the principal avenue, which runs west from the Great Compound and east from the Ciudadela, though not through them. The apartments within the blocks, and the blocks as wholes, vary in size and finishing: some are lovely series of rooms, the walls tastefully and skillfully painted with scenes from mythology or highly stylized figures, the doors opening into airy patios; others are a multi-plicity of small rooms with niggardly patios—very much tenements. Burials found in the tenements lack expensive goods. Each apartment block, expensive or lowly, was designed as a structural unit with drains running under floors to discharge rain water from the patios. The apartments within the blocks were refinished or modified from time to time, but the underlying drainage system set limits on modifications. The apartment blocks were occupied for generations, and were so basic to the Teotihuacános' notion of a proper residence that small apartment blocks were built in the hamlets on the edges of the valley, though they were surrounded by open land.

Several hundred apartment blocks were workshops as well as residences. Whether these were primarily lineages—caste-like kinship units whose members were ascribed the craft of their fathers (or mothers) by birth, or guilds—tightly organized artisans' unions—or simply areas owned by entrepreneurs employing a number of craftsworkers and furnishing lodging to their families as well as work space, we cannot decide. The greatest number of workshops excavated produced obsidian blades.

Of the over two hundred obsidian workshops, some were clustered just west of the Great Compound, some just east of the Ciudadela, and some just northwest of the Quetzalpapalotl Palace on the west side of the Pyramid of the Moon plaza. These locations on the edges of the sacred center of the city suggest the obsidian workers may have been given a high status, earned by the basis of the wealth and power of the empire in its control of the Mexican equivalent of blade steel. However, other obsidian workshops are scattered in the city, and the ones in the center may merely have produced sacrificial knives, priests' razors, nobles' sharp-edged battle clubs, and the precious, delicate vases and mirrors of polished obsidian used in the temples and palaces. The obsidian used in the Teoti-huacán workshops came not only from the source in the valley itself, but also from mines north of the Valley of Mexico in the state of Hidalgo, where an especially fine volcanic glass of a greenish (rather than the usual black) tint can be obtained.

A second major product of Teotihuacán was pottery. Millon's survey team identified about 150 ceramic workshops. The potters made plain, sturdy cooking pots, storage jars, and serving dishes for common families, and also thin, beautiful vases, cups, incense burners, and cylindrical jars for the elite and the temples. The cylindrical jar, with tripod supports raising it from the ground and a cover with a knob, was usually painted in fresco technique with complex designs or scenes. Quite similar jars were made in China at this period, raising the question of occasional contacts from trans-Pacific voyages. It has been pointed out, also, that the form of the raised cylindrical jar with rounded cover is the form of a granary used for maize storage in many Mexican villages, and this has led some to think that the jars are miniature "granaries" for the jewels of the rich, or for maize kept symbolically in the houses of the gods. But the jars were taken to all the cities of Mexico at the height of the Classic period, A.D. 450 to A.D. 600, and most of them were probably merely a purchase of the wealthy.

Some fifteen identified workshops in Teoti-

FIGURE 2.5 Interior court and rooms, building near the Pyramid of the Moon, Teotihuacán. Carved columns and painted stucco walls are original; the wall seen through the doorway at the top of the steps (rounded stones mortared in cement) is a nonauthentic restoration. *(A. Kehoe)*

huacán manufactured figurines. Most of these were of clay, and took advantage of an innovation, the use of molds to mass-produce items for the market. Many molds were made carefully by talented artists, but the dozens of identical figurines inevitably give a feeling of urban alienation. Small clay effigies to be attached to incense burners and to be used as knobs on pots and jar covers were also mold-produced in these workshops.

Other workshops in the city made metates and manos, other appliances and tools of stone, beads and pendants, and no doubt a variety of long-lost softer products such as cloth, mats, sandals, containers, and hunting and fishing nets. Many artisans must have been employed in the creation of the intricate costumes worn by dignitaries, who are shown in carvings and paintings dazzlingly arrayed in towering feather headdresses and sporting ornaments of jade, gold, and feathers from belt, chest, back, arms, and legs. Out on the west side of the city is a neighborhood that seems to have been an enclave of people from Oaxaca, who lived in Teotihuacán apartment blocks but used Oaxaca-style pottery and buried their dead in the manner of the Oaxaquenos. What they were doing in Teotihuacán is unclear. They do seem to have been making a particular variety of domestic pottery, but do not appear to have been at all wealthy. On the other side of the city, near the road leading south to Puebla, is an area with pottery from Veracruz and the Maya region, possibly the residence and business area of traders from these nations. Evidence of residents from West Mexico seems lacking, and archaeology in West Mexico suggests that this region had its own Classic nation in the lakes district of Jalisco, holding a border against Teotihuacán approximately at the historic Jalisco-Guanajuato border.

How Teotihuacán controlled its foreign trade and how much of its sphere of contact was under its political dominion and how much independently allied, is difficult to assess. Warriors are frequently depicted in Teotihuacán late art, and men outfitted in the style of Teotihuacán warriors are carved on stelae in Monte Albán and in the Maya city of Tikal in Guatemala. At Tikal, the Teotihuacános flank an apparently Mayan ruler almost invisible under his display of emblems of rank. According to the glyphs on the stela, A.D. 445, one of the Teotihuacán warriors is the father of the Maya ruler. Back on home ground, Teotihuacán warriors may be shown wearing realistic headdresses of jaguars or eagles, similar to the costumes of the Aztec nobility's orders of jaguar and eagle knights. This suggests that the power of Teotihuacán may have been carried in the field by armies commanded by an elite corps of aristocratic knights bound to each other by vows in quasireligious orders emulating the eagle, lord of the air, and the jaguar, lord of the earth. During Teotihuacán's last century, about A.D. 700–800, knights occupied at least one luxurious apartment compound and were immortalized there in wall paintings apparently identifying their great generals by name and rank. It is interesting that there are no written (glyph) identifications of individuals in the paintings in the city's central temples and palaces on the "Street of the Dead." This down-playing of personal glory in Teotihuacán's central precinct contrasts with the glorification of Maya kings and conquering rulers elsewhere in Mesoamerica. Creating a state manifestly greater than any of its human leaders may have been the key to Teotihuacán's five-century-long domination of Mesoamerica.

The role of agriculture in Teotihuacán's wealth is overshadowed by the abundant evidence of manufacturing and trade discovered in the archaeological investigations of the city. The little river that flows through the center of the valley was canalized to parallel the east-west avenue, skirting the Great Compound and Ciudadela along their northern walls, and other streams were controlled by similar simple canals. But to what extent these canals were constructed for irrigation, not urban planning, is not yet determined. One problem in reconstructing the ancient agricultural system of the Valley of Teotihuacán is that at least by A.D. 1050, the marshy, spring-fed, fertile land on the southwestern outskirts of the city was being developed into *chinampas,* artificial islands of swamp mud laid on huge log rafts. *Chinampas* stretch for miles around Xochimilco in the southern Valley of Mexico and continue to furnish the bulk of fresh produce to modern Mexico City, as they did to its predecessor, Aztec Tenochtitlán. The "floating gardens" are renewed seasonally by layers of rich mud dredged from the canals around them. In this way the canals are maintained and new topsoil is provided for the fields. With the year-round warmth of Mexico's latitude and the continuous supply of water from the swamps, Xochimilco's *chinampas* yield some of the highest harvest per unit of land to be found anywhere on earth. *Chinampas* on a smaller scale are still farmed in the Valley of Teotihuacán. The problem of determining when *chinampas* were first used in the valley is aggravated by the use today, and for centuries in the recent past, of the land most likely to have been developed the earliest; instead of studying at leisure "fossil" canals, the archaeologists must contend with a system in active operation. Hence, there is certainty only that some *chinampas* were in existence by A.D. 1050. But there is also speculation that this excellent, labor-intensive, high-yield but ecologically nondegrading system was invented earlier, when Teotihuacán was still a living city. If it were not, then the city's hundreds of thousands must have been fed on simple canal-irrigated agriculture

FIGURE 2.6 Youth in traditional-type dugout, removing stalks of previous harvest from chinampa. The field in back of him is a man-made island, the water a canal draining the former swamp. *(T. Kehoe)*

drawing on the valley's numerous springs and small streams, plus, probably, crops grown in the southern Valley of Mexico and transported to the city on rafts plying Lake Texcoco.

Teotihuacán's power came to a violent end about A.D. 800. Fires very likely deliberately set by enemies destroyed the principal temples and palaces in the center of the city. Ordinary people continued to live and work in much of the residential area and farm around the ruins. The city's final century, A.D. 700–800, had been one of a glorification of militarism and war leaders not seen previously in its art. Whether this was in response to increasingly serious threats from would-be-rivals outside the Valley of Mexico, or whether it reflects a new thirst for conquest on the part of ambitious eagle and jaguar knights who fomented overextended campaigns that eventually weakened the empire, we cannot tell. The archaeologist can only note the disappearance of one of the world's major powers in the first millennium A.D. and use the event as the terminus of the Classic period in the Valley of Mexico.

Eastern Mesoamerica: Izapa and Abaj Takalik

The pioneer farmers with well-made pottery who first settled the San Lorenzo site, and who were presumably the ancestors of the Olmecs there, established numerous other villages in the Peripheral Coastal Lowlands and adjacent hills around 2000 B.C. Two such communities, Izapa and Abaj Takalik, are in the piedmont overlooking the Pacific coastal plain on the border between Chiapas (Mexico) and Guatemala. By the time of Christ, Izapa had become a major center enjoying a notable artistic florescence. On the basis of its innovative and powerful bas-reliefs, Izapa is seen as the link between the Olmec tradition and the developing Maya. Abaj Takalik is particularly known for its round boulder sculptures, including a colossal Olmec head, but has a variety of bas-reliefs as well.

Neither Izapa nor Abaj Takalik became a central power, like Teotihuacán, nor did their artistic influence continue once the Maya Classic era emerged. What gives these towns of northern Pacific Guatemala an importance in the late Preclassic period is their raising of stone stelae (slab markers). Izapans carved stelae with dramatic scenes from mythology. Maya Classic culture continued this art form, modifying it to represent real people as well as legends and adding inscriptions marking historical events. Abaj Takalik has stelae carved with calendar dates in the Maya style. Other early stelae with calendar dates have been found north, in Chiapas, and south, in Guatemala, of the Izapa-Abaj Takalik area. These several earliest carved dates all seem to record years in our first century B.C. Raising stelae commemorating historical events is one of the distinguishing features of Classic Maya civilization, although stelae were raised in most other Mesoamerican principalities as well. Stelae are frequently associated with rectangular or drum-shaped stone blocks usually called altars, which more probably are thrones. Both throne and stela are generally placed at the base of a temple pyramid—or to phrase it another way, at the edge of a main plaza in front of a temple pyramid. Stone thrones and stelae were made by the Olmecs as individual pieces; the Izapans took the forms and made them into a pattern, as they took the occasional dramatic portrayals in Olmec carvings and made narrative the focus of their art.

What the relationships of the Izapans were to the Olmecs, their sources for many ideas, and to the Mayas, for whom they in turn were a source, is only sketchily known. Since Izapa's earliest phase features pottery similar to that of the first settlers at San Lorenzo and also to that of villagers along the Pacific coast of Guatemala, to the east, and since Izapa, the Olmec domain, and Pacific Guatemala share a similar humid tropical environment, it is quite possible the Izapans were ethnically related to the Olmecs and to neighboring Guate-

malans. Both the Olmecs and the Izapans probably spoke languages from which descended modern Mixe and Zoque, still used by Indians in the region. The highland Mayans of Guatemala and the relatively lowland Izapans would have found trade mutually desirable, and the Mayans would have been impressed by the large building platforms, the temples, and especially the writhing monsters and heroes melodramatically filling the stelae in the plazas. One stela at the Mayan highland city of Kaminaljuyú (modern Guatemala City) appears to have been sculpted by an Olmec artist. The Mayans were thus drawn into the Mesoamerican Olmec heritage, transmuted through Izapa.

Izapa has also been linked, more controversially, with Peru. The art historian Mino Badner detailed fourteen complex motifs shared by Izapa and the Preclassic period major civilization of Peru, the Chavín. The florescence of Chavín is contemporary with the Olmec, thus antedating Izapa's heyday and suggesting to Badner that Chavín may have been a source of many Izapan motifs. While some of Badner's similarities may be considered too general to be proof of borrowing, others are less likely to be coincidence: the dragon's head from which a useful plant grows (this motif is also incised on Olmec jade celts and is used by the Maya); a man (or spirit-man) wearing an elaborate bird headdress and extended wings, hovering over a scene; a conch trumpeter sounding his instrument over an undulating serpent or dragon; a masked human wrestling a tightly coiled serpent; and a warrior wearing an elaborate plumed headdress and back ornaments (feather bustle?), holding in his left hand his knife and in his right the severed, blood-dripping head of his conquered enemy. Some Izapan motifs are seen in the Moche culture of the north coast of Peru, which was contemporary with Izapa's terminal Preclassic period. Moche, like Izapa, delighted in vivid dramatic scenes, especially of combat. The Izapa warrior is watched by a person sitting in a litter carried by two men and topped with a crouching jaguar; the Moche painted their lords carried in carved litters. Moche and Izapa both show people in boats, animals—especially jaguars—caught in nets, and, most curious, skeletons lecherously erecting the one fleshy organ somehow left to them—the penis. On the Izapan stela, the skeleton's penis (or, according to one writer, umbilical cord), coiled snakelike, is being wrestled with by a human or anthropomorphic deity.

Izapa is not actually on the Pacific coast, not even on a major river, but it is near enough to the Pacific to have been a capital with a dependent ocean port. There was coastwise shipping between northcoast Peru and Ecuador, and between Ecuador and the Pacific coast of Mexico and Guatemala, probably on large, well-designed sailing rafts (the Kon-Tiki type) during the late Classic period, and these sea routes may very well go back many centuries. Both at the very beginning of lowland village settlements, around 2000 B.C., and again in the middle Preclassic period, a few distinctive pottery styles are shared among Veracruz, the Izapa-Guatemala Pacific coast, and Ecuador. The nature and extent, even the very fact, of contacts between southern Mesoamerica and Peru have not yet received enough scholarly attention to be properly understood.

The late Preclassic era in the southern Peripheral Coastal Lowlands was a period of considerable variety. Izapa stands out for its long, smooth history of occupation, flowering in the late-Preclassic period bas-reliefs and stone thrones. To the west in coastal Chiapas was the town of La Perseverancia, apparently larger than Izapa, having great granite-faced earthen platform mounds, but lacking sculpture, as far as is known. The lack of obvious evidence of ritual at La Perseverancia has led to the supposition that it was a trading center or military fortress, but there seems to be little evidence of long-distance trade, nor is there any clear reason why it should have been a military stronghold. It was abandoned at the end of the Preclassic period.

Another large site of the late Preclassic era is Chiapa de Corzo, which contrasts strongly with La Perseverancia in having fine stone platforms, buildings, and sculpture including stelae, one with a date that would be December 7, 36 B.C. in our calendar. Chiapa de Corzo imported expensive ceramic vessels of Maya manufacture, and used them only in its palaces. At the end of the Preclassic period, the stone monuments of Chiapa de Corzo were defaced, mutilated, and buried. Was this a rebellion against Maya overlords in the palaces of the town? Meanwhile, Izapa, which appears to have been more independent of the Maya in the late Preclassic era, continued its long existence, its monuments calmly in their places, and was slowly eclipsed by the Maya centers to the east and later to the north.

The Maya

The small early Preclassic period village at Cuello in Belize, in the southeastern Maya area, grew into a middle Preclassic period community that burned more jungle to make maize fields, constructed a temple on a platform dedicated by the sacrifice of a young man, and possibly began to improve the land for human use by draining swamps. By the late Preclassic period, about 400 B.C., the Cuello Maya became ambitious and razed their old temple, filling in the little plaza with limestone rubble from a source at least 2 kilometers (1.25 miles) away and laying a new temple platform 4 meters (13 feet) high and 80 meters (262.5 feet) long. Cuello may have been stimulated by the power vacuum left by the demise of La Venta, or by the substantial market developed by this period through several previous centuries of expansion of Maya into the Yucatán. Colonization of this broad but initially not especially inviting peninsula had been steady throughout the middle Preclassic period, and contacts among the many seedling towns were a foundation on which profitable trade might be built.

The middle Preclassic pioneers in Yucatán may have emigrated eastward and then northward from the southern Gulf Coast, where they would have been on the border of the Olmec domain, or northward from the mountains of Guatemala. Their late Preclassic descendants were familiar with Guatemala, where fine obsidian from deposits at El Chayal was being worked into blades for export at the town of Kaminaljuyú, in what is today Guatemala City, 35 kilometers (22 miles) away from the source, as early as the middle Preclassic period. Jade from the Motagua Valley in north-central Guatemala, on the edge of the highlands, was also traded north in the middle Preclassic period. Marine shell for beads and pendants would have been a third trade item in demand throughout Yucatán. Salt may have been commercially produced and widely traded, as it was in the Classic period later. The town of Komchen, near Dzibilchaltún and also near salt flats, had a thousand structures covering two square kilometers (0.8 sq. mi.), with six large platforms around a rectangular plaza and a raised roadway 260 meters (286 yards) through the center of the town. The general similarity of pottery styles throughout the Maya lowlands also attests to continuous contracts. In the ideological realm, dedicatory deposits under temples at two sites in Belize demonstrate a sharing of cosmological concepts: at each site there are four small carved jade heads, apparently representing the four cardinal directions, and a pair of flaring jade ear ornaments, and one offering features a mask that seems to signify the duality of life and death. Agriculture would also have been widely shared, and it seems to be have been in the Preclassic period that Maya domesticated turkeys and muscovy ducks.

Archaeological investigation of Maya lowland sites is hampered by the tough jungle cover, and work on early phases tends to be sidetracked by discoveries of magnificent Classic-period temples and carvings. When excavation is directed toward discovering earlier phases, it has frequently been rewarded by unexpected finds as impressive as the pyramid-topped platforms of El Mirador in the Petén near the Mexico-Guatemala border. One El Mirador pyramid structure is 230 feet (70 meters)

high, another 141 feet (43 meters), and a raised road connects the precincts of the structures, with other roads leading out into the countryside. At Cerros in Belize, a contemporary town of 37 hectares (91 acres) was circled by a canal 6 meters (6.5 yards) wide and 1,200 meters (1,320 yards, or .25 mile) long. The Cerros canal linked with drainage canals creating raised fields for agriculture outside the town. Pyramid temples in El Mirador, Cerros, and other Late Preclassic Maya cities and towns were blazoned with huge painted plaster masks of deities flanking the imposing stairways. To claim that certain sites were the major centers of late Preclassic Maya civilization is hazardous: known centers may only be those that had the luck to be excavated. Be that as it may, three towns of the late Preclassic Maya civilization were certainly important centers for the people of their regions and are examples worth describing: Dzibilchaltún, Becan, and Tikal.

Dzibilchaltún, north of the city of Mérida in Yucatán, is in the dry northern plains of the peninsula, where agriculture is not as productive as it is farther south. Maya Dzibilchaltún is one of the largest cities of pre-Columbian Yucatán, but it lacks spectacular ruins, its people having been satisfied, it seems, with simple, chastely adorned buildings on moderate platforms. One unusual feature discovered in Dzibilchaltún is a small building dating from the end of the middle Preclassic period. It is set at the edge of a platform, not on it, is reached by a stair, and has in its floor a channel that leads to a sizable hearth lined with a quantity of potsherds (broken fragments of pottery). The excavator suggests this building may have been a sweathouse (sauna), historically used by Indian religious practitioners as a means of purifying themselves before enacting rituals. Dzibilchaltún was established beside a natural limestone well, or cenote, and water from it could have been led along the channel to the hearth, causing clouds of steam to envelop the priests gathered in the building to cleanse themselves. The city of Dzibilchaltún, like its nearby modern

FIGURE 2.7   Traditional-style Maya house. *(T. Kehoe)*

counterpart, Mérida, seems to have grown into a political and religious hub for the northern sector of Yucatán, primarily because of its central location. It seems to have achieved more or less urban status slightly earlier than Maya cities to the south—in the fourth century B.C. But strangely, it, like Komchen 6 kilometers (3.5 miles) away, failed to maintain itself and was abandoned for several centuries, beginning at the time of Christ. There is no evidence of violent destruction to the city to explain this abandonment.

Becan was a city of central Yucatán. It was founded in the late middle Preclassic period, about 750 B.C., on relatively high ground two-thirds surrounded by marshy depressions. By the final years of the late Preclassic era, about A.D. 250, Becan was a town covering 19 hectares (46 acres), fortified by a ditch 2 kilometers in circumference. The interior side of the ditch was made more formidable by an embankment and perhaps, though it was not discovered in the excavations, a log palisade. The archaeologists calculated that even without a palisade, the embankment would have averaged 11.3

meters (37 feet) in height. With the further protection of the natural marshy depressions, Becan was more heavily fortified than any other Maya lowland city. A hint to the cause of this need for protection may lie in the presence of imported obsidian blades soon after the founding of Becan, which proves long-distance contacts. In contrast, early Dzibilichaltún had few imported materials and probably felt relatively safe in its remoteness from the south.

Within its wall, Becan had over 500 square meters (600 square yards) of plastered pavement; platforms of rubble fill faced with dry-laid limestone blocks and finished with smooth plaster; and buildings that seem to have been open on one long side, with stone base walls up to 1 meter (1 yard) high and the upper wall and roof made of perishable material (poles, mats, or thatch). Some of the platforms and buildings were painted red, and at least one platform was multicolored. The largest platform, 10 meters (33 feet) high and containing 50 square meters (nearly 60 square yards) of surface area on top, was built in four tiers and supported a one-room temple on top. Outside the fortification, smaller platforms are grouped around plazas, no doubt indicating the common Maya residential pattern of houses surrounding patios.

At the end of the Preclassic period, many—but by no means all—lowland Maya cities were importing, or copying, certain fine ceramics for their upper class. Becan, like the greater city Tikal in Guatemala, did not import these elite ceramics, apparently being governed by families content with the best products of their own city's potters. However, the early Classic era, about A.D. 300, saw the introduction of ceramic styles developed outside the Becan region, some in the north of the peninsula and some in the south (the Petén region). The local pottery follows general trends common throughout the Maya lowlands, but in a particular style that appears nowhere except within the fortified area of Becan. This peculiarly extreme localization—together with obsidian imported from the Hidalgo mines of central highland Mexico controlled by Teotihuacán, and with a dedicatory offering of a Teotihuacán cylindrical tripod jar and eleven Teotihuacán figurines placed within what may be a Teotihuacán-style platform (repeating units of sloping wall-cornice-terrace)—implies that Becan's wall may not have withstood the army of Mexico's greatest empire, and that the citadel was now an outpost of Teotihuacán. Several of the figurines in the offering in fact represent Teotihuacán warriors; the other figurines represent the gods who aided them. Since the dedicatory offering was later in the early Classic period, about A.D. 550, than the appearance of the early Classic ceramics, the Teotihuacános may have first merely stimulated more widespread trade among Maya cities but finally invaded as conquerors to control the Maya lowlands better. The period of abandonment at Dzibilchaltún coincides with the early Classic era at Becan; during this period Becan did not import northern Yucatán ceramics, but only styles and vessels from the Petén region to the south. About A.D. 650, Becan seems to have successfully rebelled against the foreign conquer-

ors. Becan's late Classic era was a period of population increase and of intensive agriculture using check dams and terraces, drainage channels in swamps, and *chinampa*-like raised fields (swamp mud dug in draining operations was heaped up as rich topsoil on the fields between canals; the fields were not actually artificial islands, as are true *chinampas*). This late Classic period was the era of the greatest buildings and art in Becan, an era when the local artists, including potters, were encouraged to express their creativity. Becan relaxed her defenses in the late Classic period, dumping trash into the fortification ditch.

In the ninth century, Becan, like most of the lowland Maya cities, experienced what is generally termed a cultural collapse. No more monumental public buildings, whether temples or governmental palaces, were constructed. The cities were not abandoned, for the homes of common people continued to be built. Nor was an upper class lacking, since fine ceramics were imported from the north. Possibly, Becan was conquered by a dynasty from northern Yucatán contemptuous of Becan's past: household garbage was allowed to accumulate in the ceremonial precincts of late Classic Becan. Whatever the cause of the turning away from public art, the ending of the late Classic period reversed the population trend in central Yucatán, as in the south. From that time on, population declined, intensive agricultural practices were gradually abandoned, and the region came to seem backward.

Tikal seems to have been the principal city of the Petén lowlands of southern Yucatán, the region where early-Classic Maya civilization reached its climax. Total population of the kingdom of Tikal, covering 2,500 square kilometers (1000 square miles) at a minimum, was around 400,000 people. The site of the capital, Tikal, was first occupied in the middle Preclassic period, about 800 B.C.; and by 100 B.C. in the late Preclassic period, the city was an important center. In the following early Classic period, Tikal grew to cover 123 square kilometers (nearly 50 square miles), with some 300 large public or elite buildings and thousands of more modest homes. Workshops processed a good-quality flint, abundant in the vicinity, and also imported obsidian. Jade, slate, iron pyrite (for mirrors), granite, and quartzite were other imported stones, and marine shells came in also. Tikal is noteworthy not only for its size and population, which probably reached 50,000 in the capital, but more especially for its exhibition of the Classic Maya art and hieroglyphic writing. Indeed, Tikal has the honor of officially inaugurating the Maya Classic period with its Stela Number 29, carved with the full "Long count" Maya date of 8.12.14.8.15. This is the earliest instance of the recording of a date in the complete calendrical system. The most generally accepted correlation of the Maya calendar with the European, the Goodman-Martínez-Thompson correlation, works out the Tikal Stela 29 date as A.D. 292. (None of the proposed Maya-European calendar correlation formulae gives reasonable Christian dates for all Maya date inscriptions. The various Maya centers may have had slightly divergent calendar reckoning systems, or may occasionally have modified calendars to adjust to accumulated discrepancies with astronomical phenomena.) The numerous fully inscribed hieroglyphic stelae, the quality of the bas-reliefs, and the several impressive temple pyramids, as much as 60 meters (197 feet) high, in the distinctive Maya style of frighteningly steep slopes, attest to Tikal's importance as much as does the size of the city.

At the height of the early Classic period, around A.D. 400, Tikal, as well as Becan and other Maya cities, fell under the domination of Teotihuacán. The earliest known Teotihuacán presence in the Maya lowlands is at a relatively minor town, Altun Ha, near the Caribbean coast in Belize. There, a tomb dating to about A.D. 200 was set inside and near the top of one of the smaller pyramids of the city. Placed above the ceiling of the tomb was an offering of shell ornaments, 85 jadeite and other green stone beads, 22 ceramic vessels, and, most significantly, 13 large knives and 245 chipped effigies of green-tinted obsidian, the obsidian exported from Teotihuacán. Very similar chipped obsidian effigies have been found in smaller offerings in the Quetzalpapalotl Palace and before the Pyramid of the Sun in Teotihuacán, in contexts suggesting the same date as the Altun Ha tomb. Who was the individual in the tomb at Altun Ha? Was he a Teotihuacáno? A nobleman who married a Maya princess of Altun Ha? A conquering general? An adventurer? No stela records the history at this early date.

Two centuries later, Teotihuacános and their exports were common in Maya cities. The most famous example is Kaminaljuyú, in what is now Guatemala City, situated in a highland valley that also contained the major obsidian mines of El Chayal. It may be that Teotihuacán was determined to control all the obsidian in Mesoamerica, and conquered Kaminaljuyú for that purpose. The people of Kaminaljuyú were Maya, but in the late early Classic period they followed Teotihuacán architects' plans, constructing platforms with the typical Teotihuacán profile of a sloping side topped by a vertical cornice on which lies the terrace. It is possible that some of the clay effigies made in Kaminalijuyú were produced from Teotihuacán molds. Both Yucatán and the Pacific lowlands evidence Teotihuacán influence, though nowhere else as overwhelmingly as at Kaminaljuyú.

Why might Teotihuacán be concerned to control the Maya realms? An obsidian monopoly cannot be the whole answer, because the volcanic glass is absent in the lowlands. The empire might have sought to control all stone from which cutting implements and weapons could be manufactured—an arms monopoly, as it were—which would account for the presence of Teotihuacános in many lowland cities, such as Tikal. Another answer, however, may be that Teotihuacán had to control the cacao market if it was to solidly dominate the economics of Mesoamerica.

Cacao (a name we take from Mesoamerican languages, for example *kakaw* in Maya) is a tropical tree bearing edible seeds that can be processed into cocoa and modern chocolate. At the time of the Spanish conquest, cacao beans were the basic Mesoamerican unit of currency. *Chocolatl* (the Nahuatl word for a beverage produced from the beans) was a highly esteemed elite drink. Cacao seeds have considerable caffeine content, and as prepared by Mesoamericans, without milk or sugar, *chocolatl* is a stimulating, definitely adult drink. Jars of the drink were placed in the tombs of Maya nobles, beside the corpse's head. As a unit of currency, cacao beans had the virtues of being durable, portable, rather uniform in size, inherently valuable and in constant demand, regularly produced in limited quantities (limited because the tree will not grow except in certain areas of southern Mesoamerica), and regularly taken out of the market system by consumption. Cacao presumably entered the international Mesoamerican market as a drink, probably in the early Preclassic period. It may be significant that the earliest civilization centered in the Peripheral Coastal Lowlands, where cacao grows. Paul Tolstoy, an archaeologist who has conducted extensive investigations in Preclassic period sites in the Valley of Mexico, speculates that the Olmecs introduced cacao—or rather *chocolatl*—into the Valley of Mexico, and may have based their trade into the interior highlands in part on a demand for this beverage. This cannot be demonstrated because cacao seeds are perishable, so no traces of them have been discovered. The first proof of the importance of cacao in Mesoamerica comes in the early Classic period, when a cacao tree was painted in a mural in Teotihuacán, where it can only have been known as a remote source of the valuable beans. Contemporary Cotzumalhuapa, in the Pacific lowlands of Guatemala (east of Izapa), depicted cacao pods anthropomorphically, as if they were spirits—a not unlikely possibility, considering that the Maya god of trade, Ek Chuah, was also specifically the patron of cacao. Based on this evidence, Lee A. Parsons, who excavated Cotzumalhuapa monuments, postulates that cacao developed as a unit of currency as well as a staple of

international Mesoamerican trade in the early Classic period. He notes that Teotihuacán influence is particularly strong in the Pacific lowlands and in sites such as Kaminaljuyú that controlled major routes for the export of lowland products. Teotihuacán, he suggests, controlled such sources of the cacao export trade from about A.D. 400 until at least A.D. 700. Maya cities in the Yucatán Peninsula, which is outside the prime cacao regions, do not show Teotihuacán dominance to the degree obvious in the cacao lands and export routes.

The Maya middle Classic period (A.D. 400 to A.D. 700), then, was a period in which the first Mesoamerican empire, Teotihuacán, controlled much of the Maya area, either through outright colonies, as at Kaminaljuyú, or through agents in less strategic cities such as Tikal. Teotihuacán symbolized power in its heyday: even outside its direct domination and after its fall, Maya kings had themselves portrayed wearing accoutrements of Teotihuacán military leaders, and sometimes in the blocky style of Teotihuacán art. (Similarly, European kings called themselves "Holy Roman emperors" and modern European leaders have been sculpted in the style of Roman empire art.)

In addition to cacao and Guatemalan obsidian, southern Mesoamerica probably exported copal incense (the one specialty of the Petén district, around Tikal), cotton, sea salt, honey, amber, jade, brilliant bird feathers such as those of the quetzal, jaguar skins, cochineal (a scarlet dye from an insect), rubber, and possibly slaves. The rubber was used for balls for the highly exciting though ceremonial ball games played in one form or another from the late Preclassic period on. The game was basically a kind of basketball played like soccer, the ball to be knocked through a ring high on a court wall, the players usually using knees, hips, and other body parts rather than their hands. The rubber ball being quite hard, players wore heavy belts and other protective devices. The outcome of a game prognosticated future events, and according to carvings, the losing captain could be beheaded. The spread of such detailed, complex, purely arbitrary fashions as this ball game, sculpted and painted so frequently throughout Mesoamerica, prove international contacts as surely as do nonperishable trade objects.

The later part of the middle Classic period, A.D. 534 to A.D. 593 by the Goodman-Martínez-Thompson Christian-calendar correlation formula, is known as "the hiatus" by Maya specialists. No new stelae were erected during these years to mark historic events in the major lowland cities. Parsons suggests the lack of new stelae was the result of Teotihuacán dominance, that power never having gone in for inscribed stelae. Other experts, such as leading Maya archaeologist Gordon R. Willey, are inclined to find the reason for the hiatus in problems within the Maya region. Willey believes Tikal may have ruled the Petén in the early Classic era, been unable to cope with the combination of population pressure and external threats, and lost its power. The hiatus would represent the years in which no one political group was able to seat its leader as a dynastic ruler, and therefore the years in which there was no cause to set up a dynastic-succession marker (which is what many stelae were).

The late Classic period begins about A.D. 600, when stela inscriptions resume in Tikal and other lowland Maya cities. The late Classic Period is the true flowering of Maya civilization. It appears to Willey that whereas Tikal may have ruled the only organized Maya state of the early Classic era (other Maya cities being either independent or Teotihuacán-dominated), in the late Classic era, there were at least six other Maya states besides that of revived Tikal. One of the most brilliant was Palenque, westernmost of the Maya states, located in the foothills overlooking the Gulf coastal plain in northern Chiapas. Palenque was a small, unimportant, but independent town in the early Classic period. Inscriptions in Palenque claim that about A.D. 500, a dynasty was founded that in A.D. 603 gave birth to the great lord Pacal ("Shield"). Pacal ascended the throne while yet a boy, in A.D. 615, following a three-year reign by his mother, the Lady Zac Kuk. One of the most beautiful bas-reliefs in Palenque, beside the grand stairway entrance to Pacal's palace, shows the royal lady bestowing the rulership upon her son. Although—perhaps because—he is shown as physically handicapped by a club foot, Lord Pacal built in his capital a magnificent palace and a pyramid temple, both decorated with an abundance of sensitively molded stucco reliefs bespeaking outstanding artistic genius fostered by an enlightened and ambitious patron. The pyramid temple, known as the Temple of the Inscriptions, reveals Lord Pacal to have favored learning as well as art, for it contains one of the longest of all Maya sculpted hieroglyphic texts. In this text, Pacal's historians and astronomer-astrologers calculated mythic events not only from the beginning of Maya calendrical reckoning (3113 B.C.), but eons back to more than one million years B.C.

Pacal died at the age of eighty in A.D. 683, and was buried in a tomb prepared for him below the base of the pyramid of the Temple of the Inscriptions. Surrounded by painted stucco reliefs depicting the nine Lords of the Night (that is, the underworld), Pacal lies in a sarcophagus covered with a 12-foot (3.5-meter) limestone slab. The lord's proud genealogy is recorded in hieroglyphs around the edge of the slab, and Pacal himself, his twisted foot realistically included, is depicted on the center of the slab, resting in the jaws of the monstrous Underworld but looking upward along the Tree of Life to the Celestial Bird watching him from Heaven.

Pacal was succeeded by his son Chan Balum, who displayed a less aggrandizing, more pious nature, building a set of much smaller, though exquisite, temples east of his father's plaza—the Temple of the Sun and the Temple of the Foliated Cross (tree of life). At this time, Palenque was a city stretching some 7 miles (11 kilometers) along the foothills. It was serviced by stone-lined aqueducts, and its slopes were improved by stone-block faced terraces, some supporting temples and homes, some agricultural plots. The territory governed from this capital included smaller cities in

FIGURE 2.8 Palace of Pacal, Lord of Palenque, A.D. 615–683. *(A. Kehoe)*

FIGURE 2.9 Tomb of Pacal, Lord of Palenque, died A.D. 683. Pacal was buried beneath the pyramid and a temple was built on top. For scale, note people in the plaza and on the steps of the pyramid. *(A. Kehoe)*

the region as well as villages. There is no direct evidence identifying the basis of Palenque's late-Classic wealth, but it could well have been that Pacal seized control of the region's cacao plantations.

Classic Maya hieroglyphs are now beginning to disclose histories. The hieroglyphs combine symbols for whole concepts (ideographs) with symbols for syllables (collectively, these symbols are a *syllabary* rather than an alphabet; in the latter, symbols stand for the breakdown of syllables into their constituent sounds). Translating hieroglyphs is difficult because of uncertainty as to whether a particular glyph is to be read as a sound (syllable) or as an idea (ideograph). Further problems are caused by the existence of several Maya languages,

and no one can be sure what the syllables were a thousand or more years ago in the many different Maya cities, although good guesses can occasionally be made on the basis of linguistic reconstructions. Nevertheless, several scholars agree on the reading of Pacal, Chan Balum, and their dynastic genealogy in Palenque; on the Balam ("Jaguar") dynasty of Yaxchilán, a southern Yucatán city ruled early in the eighth century A.D. by the Lord Shield-Jaguar, who was succeeded in A.D. 752 by the conquering hero Bat-Jaguar, who in turn was related by royal marriage to Lord Bat-Jaguar of the city of Piedras Negras; on the Caan ("Sky") dynasty of Copán, which sent a scion to rule Quirigua; and, at Tikal, the dynasty of Shield Skull, whose son acceded to the throne in A.D. 682. The names

---

MAYA CIVILIZATION

The Maya shared with other Mesoamerican nations traits such as the grouping of buildings around the four sides of a court, the placing of temples on high platforms (truncated pyramids) and other buildings on lower platforms, hieroglyphs, a good calendar combining 260-day ritual "years" with solar years, a cosmology of a layered universe, astrology, iconography using the serpent, the jaguar, a crocodilian dragon, the fanged-mouthed, round-eyed Tlaloc; economically useful plants, and the agricultural triad of maize, beans, and squashes. Agricultural techniques including extensive raised field systems, rituals such as sacrifices and ball games, and technologies of ceramics, weaving, stone dressing and carving, feather ornamentation, and many other crafts were also pan-Mesoamerican, with local variation.

Within these general traditions, the Maya developed a recognizable style of their own and expressed it through variations differentiating the various regions (or, perhaps, kingdoms). Basic to the Maya style was an emphasis on baroque surface ornamentation rather than on severely geometrical architecture; rhythmic line rather than blocking; a dispersed pattern, with ceremonial centers placed without apparent overall plan and then linked by fine roads, rather than a master grid for cities; terrifyingly steep temple pyramids rather than pyramids in the form of massive hulks or elegantly composed blocks; palace or administrative buildings composed of a series of single rooms in line rather than apartments around patios (although some Maya palaces, such as Pacal's at Palenque, were compromises toward the latter form); the corbeled vault roof rather than flat roofs or true arches (three true arches are known from Maya late Classic buildings, but the cumbersome corbeled "arch" was clearly preferred); advanced astronomical-calendrical calculations; the most complete writing system of Classical Mesoamerica, as far as surviving carved-stone evidence indicates; and a religion in which cycles of time were deified, death was a challenge to philosophy and human ambition, and the dragon Itzamná was the principal symbol of godhead.

FIGURE 2.10 Maya nobleman, Classic period, c. A.D. 700. *(Rubbing by G.K. Erskine. Milwaukee Public Museum and Gertrude K. Erskine)*

and titles of the Maya lords are usually accompanied by glyphs that are emblems of the cities they ruled, as well as glyphs meaning "born," "ascended to the throne," and so forth. Rulers who began their reign young are shown on stelae first as richly ornamented youths, then on later stelae as elaborately outfitted warriors standing over crouched captives. These late-Classic carved inscriptions record and glorify the Maya rulers; what they do not record are the philosophy, poetry, or even mundane affairs that we think were written in the folding paper books that were subsequently nearly all burned by the Spanish conquerors. Our knowledge of the Maya from native texts, then, is comparable to what would be known of the Romans if only the Latin inscriptions on triumphal archs and emperors' statues were preserved.

Not quite a century after the fall of Teotihuacán, the dynasties of the cities of the southern Maya lowlands, from Palenque on the west to Tikal and other Petén-district cities on the east, ceased to maintain their greatness. The last stela inscribed with a full "Long Count" date was erected in A.D. 889. The most puzzling aspect of the end of the Maya tradition of monuments is that there was a clear decline in population as well as in artistic production in the ninth century A.D. in the southern lowlands, and a complete collapse in the tenth century, especially in the formerly bustling Petén, which became covered with scrub jungle except for a few poor towns. The decline seems to have begun in the west, including Palenque, and rolled eastward. It did not affect northern Yucatán, which, on the contrary, began a final burst of glory about A.D. 950, postponing its decline until after A.D. 1050.

The cause, or causes, of the Maya "collapse" have been hotly debated. Were the Petén Maya overcome by foreign invaders? There is no evidence of massacres or burning of cities, no replacement of the indigenous people by a new group, except in northern Yucatán, the one region that did *not* experience the tenth-century collapse! Were the Maya elite overthrown by revolts of oppressed peasants? Again, there is no evidence of violence

FIGURE 2.11 Shield-Jaguar, Lord of Yaxchilán, is presented with the symbolic head of a Jaguar Lord of the Underworld by his lady wife on a New Year's Eve, A.D. 720. Classic Maya. *(Rubbing by Gertrude K. Erskine; interpretation by David H. Kelley. Milwaukee Public Museum and Gertrude Erskine)*

in the palaces and grand temples, and there is the loss of almost entire populations within the century. Was there an epidemic? There are no mass cemeteries, no bodies in abandoned houses. Was there a natural catastrophe? No hurricane, flood, or drought would have affected both the Gulf Coast lowlands and the entire southern Yucatán lowlands, earlier in the west and then in the east. Were there severe crop failures? This explanation has some support. The Petén is an indifferent land for intensive agriculture. Even with terracing on slopes and ridged fields in the drained swamps, it must have been difficult for the larger Petén cities such as Tikal, with at least fifty thousand people, to feed their populations from fields of maize, beans, and squashes. One Maya archaeologist,

Dennis E. Puleston, believed families depended upon groves of breadnut trees producing a large, nutritious fruit, plus a variety of other fruits and nuts, and fish from the rivers and swamp canals, to supplement their maize, beans, and squashes. The sophisticated ecosystem reconstructed by Puleston may have been adequate up to a certain population density, but insufficient above that critical level. Analysis of skeletons of common Mayans by physical anthropologist Frank P. Saul demonstrated signs of malnutrition, though not outright starvation, in the last decades of the Late Classic. One possible explanation of this decline in health is that the collapse of the Teotihuacán empire caused a collapse of the economy of the southern Maya lowlands, which may have been too depend-

FIGURE 2.12 Maya Puuc style temple, Chichén Itzá. Late Classic c. A.D. 950. Note the highly stylized deity face motif, repeated twice on each side of the door, on each side of the central head-with-headdress above the door, and again in profile three times on each wall corner; now note that the entire facade of the building is the deity face (upper flanking faces are the eyes, central head the nose, and the door is the mouth). *(A. Kehoe)*

ent on international export. The lords of the Maya states, who had been competing so fiercely to win wars and arrange politically advantageous marriages, may have found themselves bankrupt. The common people would then no longer have had markets for their products. The urban craft-workers would have been especially hard-hit, unable to purchase food and forced to live on the marginal nutrition from kitchen gardens and the few bread-nut trees shading their homes. With too few people able to buy food, the farmers may have reverted to subsistence agriculture, abandoning the drudgery of maintaining the intensively cultivated terraces and raised swamp fields. Thousands of urban families and some farmers would eventually have emigrated, a few to the northern Yucatán cities,

many to previously undeveloped areas such as the eastern coast of the Yucatán Peninsula.

Northern Yucatán in the century beginning about A.D. 950 exhibits a phenomenon as curious as the collapse to the south. The city of Chichén Itzá in the center of northern Yucatán, southeast of Mérida and Dzibilchaltún, seems to have two sectors: one has the baroque lines of the late-Classic Puuc architectural style of northern-Yucatán Maya, the other has the cleaner lines of the "Toltec" style seen also in the Mexican central highlands. It used to be assumed that the Toltecs invaded Chichén Itzá and built their colonial capital next to an existing Puuc Maya city, but recent investigations indicate that the Chichén "Toltecs" and the Maya Puuc were contemporary, and that

Chichén Itzá expressed two complementary concepts through its architecture. The "Maya" sector boasted a plaza with a palace and steep temple pyramid at one end, and among other buildings along the sides, an astronomical observatory (the round structure called the Caracol). The "Toltec" sector also had a plaza, this being ringed by a taller but less steep temple pyramid, a large ball court with its own temples, a magnificent courtyard bordered by columned porticos and a temple pyramid with a columned forecourt, and, on the fourth side, the road to the holy natural well (cenote) into which people were thrown to bring petitions from the populace to the Mayan version of Tlaloc, whom they called Chac. (The "sacrifices" could be children, men, or women. If they could swim well enough to return to the surface and float or tread water for a couple of hours, they would be pulled out and praised for successfully delivering the message.)

What the relationship was between these two contrasting styles in one city, or between Chichén Itzá and the purely Mayan contemporary cities elsewhere in northern Yucatán, is a puzzle. Paintings in "Toltec" Chichén depict armies invading by sea like a hurricane, opposing classic-looking Maya in several battles. It was assumed that once they had overcome that Maya army and executed their king, the invaders may have allowed the conquered people to maintain their own city overlooked by the adjacent new "Toltec" capital. Critics of this interpretation point out that the paintings do not show the gory hand combat seen in murals in Bonampak or Cacaxtla: the Chichén murals may represent a display of military power, a sort of military tattoo. One archaeologist argues that both the murals and the contrasting architectural styles are signs of an unusual dual government developed at Chichén in the late Classic period. In this view, the baroque Puuc-style sector was ruled by a high priest or noncombative governor representing the wisdom and fecundity of the earth, symbolized by Quetzalcóatl (Kukulcan in Maya) the precious-feathered serpent. The more cleanly elegant "Toltec" sector was the domain of Kaku-

pacal, who carries the fiery sun as his round shield. The warrior murals depict, in this argument, Kakupacal's legions facing Kukulcan's peaceful productive peasants, artisans, homemakers, and traders, not to slaughter them but to maintain discipline in their state and defend it. Kukulcan and Kakupacal, plumed-serpent and sun-disk deity, meet in the "Toltec" Castillo pyramid dominating Chichén. The extraordinary contrasting styles in the city were then a unique expression of the profound truth that the power of the state must recognize and respect the power of the masses. The hundreds of columns in the great "Marketplace" colonnaded portico, each column carved as an individual man, are the stone presence of what Europeans call the Third Estate—the people as contrasted with the church and law (First Estate) and the king and his court (Second Estate).

A possibility argued by somewhat more traditional archaeologists is that "Toltec" Chichén was built by a legendary Maya group from southwestern Yucatán and adjacent southern Gulf Coast, a people called the Putun or Chontal (the second name comes from the Nahuatl word for "foreigner," which Maya would be to the Nahuatl-speaking Mexicans). Maya histories recorded by Spanish missionaries centuries later describe the "Itzá" as "foreigners" who invaded Yucatán and built their capital city at the holy well (chichén) of divination in central northern Yucatán—that is, at Chichén Itzá. The Itzá are also supposed to have built the northern Yucatán city of Mayapán about A.D. 1270, and there are similarities between it and Chichén, which was still an active city when Mayapán was constructed. The Itzá are said to have been defeated in Mayapán two centuries later by a rival noble family. Fleeing into the swampy southern Petén (present northern Guatemala), the Itzá built the town of Tayasal (now called Flores) and maintained a tiny kingdom there until 1697, when the Spanish colonial government decided to mop up the last Maya hold-out.

If "Toltec" Chichén Itzá was a "Putun" establishment, it presumably represents ambitious border Maya allied with Mexican groups to the west, all eager to create a new empire in the political vacuum left by the fall of Teotihuacán power. Cacaxtla, in east-central Mexico near Tlaxcala, was at this time a small fortified city on a major route between the Valley of Mexico and Puebla and the east coast. Impressive murals painted on the walls of two buildings in the site show dramatic battles between eagle and jaguar knights and their soldiers. The Teotihuacán symbols that in this period were used by the Maya as emblems of rulers' power mark some of the winning figures, although the art style and general costumes are distinctly Mayan. At Xochicalco in Morelos, southwest of the Valley of Mexico, Maya style influenced the artists who carved a frieze on a principal pyramid, depicting conquering lords over captives from a series of other localities. Maya and Central Mexican peoples were obviously jockeying for dominance, yet freely borrowing ideas and even professional painters. Out of this fluid movement of professional people, no doubt including traders and competing warlords, emerged the Mexican Toltecs.

SECTION 4: THE POSTCLASSIC

Following Aztec histories, the Postclassic period of Mexico includes two empires: first, that of the Toltecs; then, that of the Aztecs. The period ends in 1521, when the Spaniards under Cortés conquered Tenochtitlán, the Aztec capital.

After the burning of Teotihuacán about A.D. 800, no one major power appeared in Mexico for two centuries. The Valley of Mexico had many villages and a few small towns, but no city. Regional states gained a relatively short-lived burst of power, reflected in the final glories of Monte Albán, of Xochicalco in Morelos south of the Valley of Mexico, of Teuchitlán in Jalisco (West Mexico), of Cholula in Puebla to the southeast, of Tajín in central Veracruz, and in the northern Yucatán Maya. There was intensive trade among these regions, indicated by the popularity of fine pottery manufactured in the southern Gulf region and widely used, and by the fashion of decorating palaces and temples with the "Greek key" (stepped-fret) design probably originated by the Tajín somewhat to the north of the fine pottery producers. The capitals of these regional states show little direct evidence of threats from competing nations, but the number of Maya lords depicted in military triumphs during this last century of the Maya Late Classic period suggests that internal glory may have been precariously protected by incessant border skirmishes.

The Toltecs

Toltec Tula lies just north of the Valley of Mexico in the present state of Hidalgo. There was a Teotihuacán outlier called Chingú, with a considerable irrigation system for its fields, only 10 kilometers (6 miles) away. In the Late Classic period, when militarism was so prominent in Teotihuacán, a small plaza with surrounding platforms was constructed at Tula in a style similar to those to the northwest in what is now Guanajato and Querétaro: as Aztec histories stated, "Chichimecs,"—"wild tribes"—from the northern borders of civilization migrated to Tula. By A.D. 1000, Tula had entered its heyday. At its height, the city covered 12 square kilometers (about 5 square miles) and was home to about sixty thousand persons. Situated on a ridge and adjoining lower slopes, it overlooks a junction of two rivers, which probably gave it its initial command over the northern boundary region of the Valley of Mexico.

The city of Tula lacks the overwhelming magnificence of Teotihuacán, or of Chichén Itzá. Tula's ridgetop location precluded laying out a broad master grid plan such as contributed to one's impression of the power of Teotihuacán. The principal structures were, however, oriented 18° east of north, as were so many Mesoamerican centers (and even raised fields in Veracruz; the orientation

FIGURE 2.13 Tajín, Veracruz, principal pyramid. Late Classic c. A.D. 800. The seven stories of the pyramid probably represent layers of heaven, and the niches (square window-like alcoves), one for each day of the ritual calendar, probably held figurines of the deities ruling the days according to the astrological system. *(A. Kehoe)*

probably was to sunrise on spring equinox, when the rainy season begins and crops should be planted). Its dominant pyramid is small compared even with Teotihuacán's Pyramid of the Moon, but it does enjoy the happy preservation of a section of an intricately carved and painted facade, and does have monumental stone figures in warrior dress. Beside the principal temple pyramid, enlarged at least once, are the main ball court, testifying to the importance given to the ceremonial game by the Toltecs, and a palace or hall. The latter contains what is conventionally recognized as the "Toltec" signature (also at Chichén), a many-columned portico and, in the court, a *chacmool*—a stone basin said to be for the hearts of sacrifices, in the shape of a young man on his back, resting on his elbows, his knees drawn up, his head up, and his hands holding the shallow bowl on his abdomen. There are other plazas with public buildings, and thou-

sands of homes, most of them apparently single-story apartment complexes with interior patios, often containing small shrines. The homes were built of stone and adobe, and were sometimes plastered. The residential areas were densely built up, but may not have appeared quite as totally urban as the block upon block of tenements in Teotihuacán's poorer neighborhoods on its flat plain.

The Toltecs are the first historic people of western Mexico, in that books by Aztecs recorded stories of these immediate predecessors. According to the Aztec versions, Tula was founded by Nahuatl-speaking immigrants from the northwest who settled among the long established communities of the central highlands. In the tenth century, not long after Tula was built, the good and wise Ce Acatl Topiltzin Quetzalcóatl ("One Reed [birth date], Our Prince of the Precious-Feathered Ser-

71

pent") came into conflict with a faction of Toltecs who favored continued war and bloody sacrifice of captives to the fierce god Tezcatlipoca. Topiltzin supposedly wished his people to improve their new city, to practice the many crafts and arts and superior agricultural technique he taught them (if this is true, he presumably brought specialists to Tula), and to offer flowers, incense, maize, and butterflies, not humans, to the god he served, Quetzalcóatl, patron of civilization. At first, he was honored—he is shown in a rock carving with the date (in hieroglyphs) A.D. 968—but militarism prevailed and Topiltzin fled with followers to the east, promising to return as the herald of a golden age. (Tragically, the conquistador Cortés landed on the east coast when the calendar cycle had come once again to the year One Reed. The Aztec emperor Motecuhzoma II, well versed in history, believed the strange man who smote down the altars of human sacrifice might be the godly Topiltzin Quetzalcóatl fulfilling the prophecy, and feared to hinder him.) Tezcatlipoca's war-bent worshipers took over Tula and forged an empire that controlled the Valley of Mexico and its borders and sections of eastern Mexico, although the strong state of Cholula (in Puebla) resisted domination. The Toltec empire lasted, according to the Aztec histories, until A.D. 1168, when the emperor Ce Coatl Huemac ("One Snake [birth date] Big Hand") was deposed, fled to a cave in Chapultepec ("Grasshopper Hill"), now in the middle of Mexico City's largest park, and saw his people dispersed.

Maya chronicles pick up the story of Topiltzin. Fleeing to the east, he and his faithful band are said to have arrived in Yucatán in A.D. 987 and to have built the Toltec sector of Chichén Itzá. This may be true, for the dates roughly fit the archaeological evidence, the vision and grandeur of Toltec Chichén fit the leader who may have earlier commissioned public construction in Tula, the Precious-Feathered Serpent is prominent in the temples of Toltec Chichén, and the wonderfully pacific nature of Topiltzin would account for the strange circumstance of a foreign city next door to a Mayan one, neither seeming to wish to obliterate the other. If the Chichén "Toltecs" were in fact "Putun" Maya from the southwest border of Maya lands, this border group may have invaded westward, as seen in the Cacaxtla murals, as well as eastward, and taken over Tula, building a grander central sector in place of the small center constructed a century or so earlier. Postulating the "Putun" Maya as responsible for both Toltec Tula and Toltec Chichén Itzá explains the similarities between so many widely-separated Mexican cities and suggests why the invaders might have allowed the Puuc Maya at Chichén to continue their customs, which would be less alien to western Maya than to Central Mexicans. Prince Ce Acatl Quetzalcóatl may indeed have fought his brother in Mexico over how to dominate the empire they tried to build, Tezcatlipoca retaining Tula while Topiltzin Quetzalcóatl took his army into Yucatán; this aristocratic family would under this view be Putun Maya.

"Toltec" influence can be seen in many Postclassic centers, from chacmools in eastern Yucatán cities to columned halls on the northwestern frontier, at La Quemada in the state of Zacatecas. Sometimes the influence was subtle, as in the modified chacmool on the platform before the Palace of the Governors in Uxmal, a northern Yucatán city. The building itself (it may have been a religious or administrative headquarters, not necessarily a palace) is one of the finest examples of the native Maya Puuc style of the end of the late Classic. Its corbeled niche is one of the masterpieces of architecture. The lack of militarism in Uxmal contrasts strongly with its emphasis in Tula, where warriors are everywhere carved.

One craft introduced in the beginning of the Postclassic had a potential the Toltecs and their Aztec successors failed to fully realize, although in Eurasia the craft had been foremost in weapon development for millennia. This, of course, was metallurgy. Techniques for mining, smelting, and working copper, gold, and silver had been known in Peru for centuries before they were transferred to Mesoamerica about A.D. 850. At that time, metal needles, tweezers, axes, rings and bells and also knowledge of their manufacturing techniques came by sea trade from South America along the Pacific coast to west Mexican ports. The Postclassic Mexicans quickly learned mastery of copper and gold, producing exquisite pieces of great delicacy and the massive embossed discs that inflamed Spanish lust. Little copper or bronze bells shaped like sleigh bells are perhaps the most common Mexican manufacture in metal, and may have been sewn onto dance costumes as their modern counterparts are sewn onto Indian dance outfits. Sophisticated knowledge of alloying copper with tin and arsenic created a variety of bells golden or silver in color and with beautiful sound. Gold was associated with the sun, symbol of life-power, and sheet gold ornamented representations of this symbol. Silver or high-arsenic bronze gave the moon's color, complementing sun-gold creations. The nobility wore brilliant, gold jewelry highlighting the rich greens of jade and turquoise inlays. The few practical tools of metal were small items of bronze—awls, needles, and fishhooks. Iron smelting, which requires a much higher temperature than the smelting of other ores, was never developed.

Aztec histories record the thirteenth and fourteenth centuries A.D. as a period of endemic warfare in the Valley of Mexico. Each section of the valley had its ambitious city-state, some inhabited by descendants of the Tula Toltecs, others by immigrant tribes from the northern frontier of Mesoamerica who were described as wild barbarians, Chichimecs ("Dog clan!"). The legends claim these barbarians arose in seven caves far to the north and wandered as naked savages eating raw meat until by force of arms—notably the bow and arrow, which they introduced into nuclear Mesoamerica—they wrested a place in the civilized lands. One of the first documented Chichimec invasions of the Valley of Mexico occurred in A.D. 1224 and was led by Xolotl Tecuanitzin (Xolotl means "Monster"). Xolotl gained land in the north-central section of the valley and built the capital of Tenayuca, now on the northern edge of Mexico City. The principal pyramid of Tenayuca may still be visited. It exemplifies the persistence of Teotihuacán tradition, passed through the Toltecs, for although the pyramid differs in many details from the ancient ones, it is ringed by the serpent heads of Quetzalcóatl, and on its top it held twin temples, one to the primordial Tlaloc, the other to the fearsome Tezcatlipoca. The latter, whose name meant "Smoking (Obsidian) Mirror," was considered master of the night and of evil and monsters, jaguar lord of the underworld, challenger of warriors, and an omniscient being because all events and the inner thoughts of men and women were revealed to him in his polished black obsidian mirror. It will be recalled that Tezcatlipoca was the god, with his worshipers, opposed by Topiltzin Quetzalcóatl of the Toltecs. That he should be the patron worshiped by the conquering "Monster" is not surprising. What we do not know is whether the basic Mesoamerican religion had diffused to the northern-frontier nomad tribes during the Teotihuacán empire, or whether Xolotl and other Chichimecs adopted civilized religion as well as the other trappings of the civilization they came to rule.

The Aztecs

The Aztecs ("People from Aztlán," a more or less legendary place in the north) were another Chichimec tribe. They arrived in the Valley of Mexico about the same time as Xolotl's group, but were much less successful and had to settle on a marshy little island in the middle of the central lake. The famous legend tells that the tribe was led to this island by its priests, who sought the magic place promised to the people by their patron god, Huitzilopochtli ("Hummingbird on the South [or, Left]"). The priests would know the spot by seeing on it an eagle, perched on a nopal cactus, tearing the heart of its prey (this vision is now emblazoned on the national flag of Mexico as an eagle on a cactus, holding a serpent in its beak). The Aztecs began their capital, Tenochtitlán, upon the uninviting island. Here they found a refuge while they grew in strength, awaiting their destiny promised by Huitzilopochtli. This patron god had himself begun as a ball of feathers taken by a devotee from a temple floor near Tula, and had sprung from the lady's womb fully armed to kill his half-sister and hundreds of brothers who were advancing to murder the mother they falsely believed to have dishonored them by fornicating. This myth strikingly describes the Aztecs: no one noticed their conception, and after their gestation on the reed-encircled island they emerged as the scourge of the many peoples with whom they were culturally half-kin.

During most of the fourteenth century A.D., the Aztecs, who were also known as the Mexica (hence, "Mexico"), were supporters of the city to their west on the shore of the lake. About A.D. 1363, the throne of this city was ascended by Tezozomoc ("Angry Stone Face"), a man of insatiable ambition and arrogance who scrupled at nothing to achieve and maintain his power. In A.D. 1367, Tezozomoc's army, which included his Aztec allies, conquered the city of Culhuacán, on the southwest shore of the lake, the last citadel of the Toltec refugees from the fall of Tula. Shortly afterward, the Aztecs requested of Tezozomoc that he allow them to institute their own king. Very shrewdly, they chose not an Aztec nor a relative of the reigning strong man, Tezozomoc, but a son of the royal lineage of Culhuacán. By this choice they legitimized the claim they would often make—that they, the Aztecs once of far Aztlán, were the true heirs of the Toltec empire.

Tezozomoc died in A.D. 1426, a shivering mummy said to be a hundred years old who still commanded his armies to slaughter all who would oppose his rule. One of his last victims was the king of Texcoco, on the northeast shore of the lake. After Tezozomoc's demise, the son and heir of the king, Netzahualcóyotl ("Fasting Coyote," perhaps a reference to his years of hiding in exile), joined other oppressed Mexicans to war against Tezozo-

moc's heirs. This uprising was successfully concluded in A.D. 1433, when Netzahualcóyotl came again to the throne of his father and sealed the Triple Alliance of Texcoco, the Mexica (Aztecs), and the people of Tacuba, a town near Tezozomoc's capital on the west shore of the lake. The Aztec kingship went in A.D. 1440 to Motecuhzoma I ("Angry Lord"). Motecuhzoma (also spelled Montezuma or Moctezuma) and Netzahualcóyotl, who in effect shared power over the central highlands, were a marked contrast. The Aztec king was set on expanding his domain by war; the Texcocan, who had proved his courage during his exile and the reconquest of his kingdom, preferred to devote himself and his nation's wealth to pacific arts. First and foremost, Netzahualcóyotl was a poet, and his compositions are still admired. He was also, as can be read in his introspective, haunting poems, a philosopher, and he was a man of cultivated taste who designed temples, palaces, and lovely gardens. Practical construction was not neglected by this paragon of a king, who is said to have advised his Aztec colleague in the building of the aqueduct from the clear springs of Chapultepec to the city of Tenochtitlán. Perhaps it was the encouragement of Netzahualcóyotl that stimulated Motecuhzoma I to patronize sculptors and other artists and to have plants of all climates collected and maintained in botanical gardens.

Motecuhzoma I died in A.D. 1468 and Netzahualcóyotl in A.D. 1472. Soon after, the Triple Alliance died from unremitting jealousy and strife between their successors and rivals. Motecuhzoma I was succeeded by his sons, who continued their father's career of conquests, reaching the borders of Mesoamerica. Ahuizotl ("Water Dog"), last of Motecuhzoma I's three royal sons, died during a famine in A.D. 1502, and was succeeded by a nephew, Motecuhzoma II, who could boast a mother descended from the royal Toltec house. (Mexican kings were polygamous, having both many wives, a large number of them princesses of other nations with whom alliances were thereby cemented, and also concubines, commoner girls

FIGURE 2.14 Clay figurine, Remojadas, Veracruz. Classic period. The woman may be represented as deceased, since she holds a bead in her mouth, and jade beads were placed in the mouths of the deceased. *(Milwaukee Public Museum)*

whose beauty or talent delighted the king.) It had been expected that a son of Ahuizotl would become his heir, but this young man was killed in battle, and Motecuhzoma, who had planned to be a priest, took the throne instead. Motecuhzoma II was a superior man to his often cruel father, and emulated his illustrious grandfather and namesake not only in perpetuating wars of conquest, but also in supporting art, learning, and the beautification of Tenochtitlán. His devotion to religious duties was praised. This commitment to his beliefs was his downfall when Quetzalcóatl's prophecy seemed about to be fulfilled with the landing in the east of exotic, bearded white men who would advance upon Tenochtitlán in a fateful year named, as it happened, Ce Acatl—"One Reed"—A.D. 1519.

Controversy will always rage over whether a determined attack by Motecuhzoma's eastern army would have prevented Spain's eventual victory. Probably the Aztecs could not have prevailed, no matter how unyielding, because Cortés was a skilled and shrewd diplomat who, abetted by the bitter, exiled, knowledgeable Aztec woman baptized Doña Marina, maneuvered to enlist on his side the many Indian nations smarting under the Aztec conquests of the past century or resisting constant Aztec threats. What Cortés led, allied with the generals of other Indian nations, was a rebellion. In A.D. 1521, Cortés finally consolidated his victories and formally took over the rule of the Mexican nations subservient to the Aztecs. This date is generally accepted as the end of native Mexican power in Mesoamerica, although Spaniards did not conquer the last Mayan dynasty, the Itzás who had fled Chichén Itzá to found Tayasal deep in the Petén swamps, until A.D. 1697, and did not subjugate the northwestern-frontier nations until the century after that.

IN XOCHITL IN CUICATL

"Flower and song" (*in xóchitl in cuícatl*, in Nahuatl) was a metaphor favored by the Texcocans, the Aztecs, and other Nahuatl-speaking peoples for poetry, the art in which they expressed their most profound thoughts. King Netzahualcóyotl's "flower and song" are epitomized by this example from his compositions:

Is it true that on earth one lives?
Not forever on earth, only a little while.
Though jade it may be, it breaks;
though gold it may be, it is crushed;
though it be quetzal plumes, it shall not last.
Not forever on earth, only a little while.
(Léon-Portilla 1963:72).

Another Texcocan poet, realizing like his king the ephemerality of life, finds solace in friendship and service:

I am come, oh my friends,
with necklaces I entwine you,
with feathers of the macaw I adorn you,
a precious bird, I dress with feathers,
I paint with gold,
I embrace mankind.
With trembling quetzal feathers,
with circlets of song,
I give myself to the community.
I will carry you with me to the palace
where we all,
someday,
all must betake ourselves,
to the region of the dead.
Our life has only been loaned to us!
(Léon-Portilla 1969:80)

To create poetry, "flower and song," was to render the highest service:

> Our priests, I ask of you:
> "From whence come the flowers that enrapture man?
> The songs that intoxicate, the lovely songs?"
> Only from His home do they come, from the innermost part of heaven,
> only from there comes the myriad of flowers....
> Where the nectar of the flowers is found
> the fragrant beauty of the flower is refined....
> They interlace, they interweave;
> among them sings, among them warbles the quetzal bird.
> (*Léon-Portilla 1963:77*)

Princes who had not themselves the gift of "flower and song" called to them poets:

> Thus spoke Ayocuan Cuetzpaltzin [advisor to the lord of Huexotzinco]
> who without doubt knew the Giver of Life....
> Now do I hear the words of the *coyolli* bird
> as he makes answer to the Giver of Life.
> He goes his way singing, offering flowers.
> And his words rain down
> like jade and quetzel plumes.
> Is that what pleases the Giver of Life?
> Is that the only truth on earth?
> (*Léon-Portilla 1963:75*)

The Maya also counseled their people to emulate the lesser creatures:

> You are singing, little dove,
> on the branches of the silk-cotton tree.
> And there also is the cuckoo,
> and many other little birds.
> All are rejoicing,
> the songbirds of our god, our Lord.
> And our goddess
> has her little birds,
> the turtledove, the redbird,
> the black and yellow songbirds, and the hummingbird.
> These are the birds of the beautiful goddess, our Lady.
> If there is such happiness
> among the creatures,
> why do our hearts not also rejoice?
> At daybreak all is jubilant.
> Let only joy, only songs,
> enter our thoughts!
> (*Léon-Portilla 1969:92*)

The Mexico Cortés saw has been described for us by many sixteenth-century Spaniards, among them Bernal Díaz del Castillo, one of Cortés's solders, and Fray Bernardino de Sahagún, a missionary who interviewed elderly Indians later in the century to record their accounts of their people's customs. From the Spanish accounts and the few native books surviving the Spanish zeal to destroy what they saw as the works of the devil, we know that the numerous petty states of Mexico, some under Aztec domination and others independent, were ruled by kings or lords whose claim to their position was based on legitimate descent from the founders of royal lineages. Royalty and nobility spent much effort allying themselves through marriage with other noble houses; occasionally a royal woman was herself the ruler. The upper classes were supported by the profit produced by their estates and, in the case of royalty, by tribute paid by citizens and conquered states as well. Nevertheless, noble ladies were expected to occupy themselves industriously with weaving and embroidering the finest cloths, including those interwoven with brilliant feathers, and with preparing and serving food and *chocolatl* to their aristocratic husbands. Commoners supported themselves through agriculture, mining, manufactures, or portering (goods were transported by boat or human carriers), paying taxes and working a certain number of days per year on estates or national projects. Throughout Mexico, labor needs were met by a flexible system that encouraged men to work on farms when agricultural labor was in highest demand, then at extractive occupations, manufacturing, trade, or war during the dry season.

The common people as well as the nobility were organized into *calpulli*, sometimes termed clans. The exact nature of these residence-based segments of society is not clear, but they were composed of many families each, and most if not all the families in each one were related. The elders and head of each *calpulli* organized the activities of the members, allocated resources to them, enforced local and, in part, national laws, and repre-

sented the members at national councils. Most *calpulli* owned farmland and residential land as a corporation, although some were perhaps more like guilds, their members engaged primarily in a particular craft. Merchants formed special guilds that acted as an arm of the state in trade regulation and in international affairs; the power wielded by merchants, often the sole emissaries of their nation abroad, gave them a high position. Farmers and craftsworkers sold their products themselves in the markets held frequently in the market plaza of each town, where merchants would buy local specialities to sell elsewhere, transporting them by canoe, raft, or human porters, and would merchandise items such as obsidian knives produced outside the district. The markets were very much like those in the regional centers of modern Mexico: sellers of each kind of product grouped together, their wares spread and stacked on the ground or on benches, and food vendors offered snacks or meals. Bartering was possible, but it was also common to buy and sell using fixed units of value, from the small change of cacao beans to the higher values of a finely woven mantle or a goose quill filled with gold dust. Officers of the state supervised the markets, and courts with judges were available to citizens harassed by disputes.

Aztec children all received some formal education. Most went to schools run by their *calpulli*, where the boys were instructed in the martial arts, law and morality, and an occupation. When their country called, the men from each *calpulli* would go to war as a group, led by their own officers. Girls were taught in separate schools, by women, to be mistresses of the housewifely arts. Sons of the nobility and unusually intelligent boys from among the common people attended schools attached to the major temples of the cities. There, they served the priests and were taught to read, write, and calculate, to perform rituals and understand the meanings of religious symbols, and to know the laws, legal procedures, astronomy-astrology, rhetoric, oratory, music, and etiquette. The Aztecs were puritanical and prudish, urging young

FIGURE 2.15 Market at Toluca, central Mexico. Similar markets were held before the Cortés conquest. (*T. Kehoe*)

men to refrain from sexual intercourse until fully able to support a family, and keeping girls strictly chaperoned and segregated in walled schools or in their family homes. Girls and women were so careful to be properly dressed in full blouse and skirt that the oratorical metaphor for "woman" was "skirt and blouse." (Men wore a breechcloth and a cotton cloak knotted over one shoulder.) Laws were observed equally strictly, capital punishment being administered for relatively minor crimes, and even sons and daughters of the royal families are known to have been executed for adultery or other crimes. Perhaps because punishment was so swift and heavy, perhaps because morality was so strongly inculcated in the schools, or perhaps because astrology led people to be rather fatalistic, Aztec citizens were praised by the Spanish visitors as being wonderfully law-abiding.

What disturbed the Spanish most was that the prudent, polite, well-regulated Aztecs, with their rich, busy, honest markets, their respect for the aristocrats, the nobles' cultivated manners and taste, the impressive orators and poets, cities the equal of or superior to any in Europe at the time—

with all these marks of the most refined civilization, the Aztecs worshipped before terrible statues. The Spaniards' passion in overthrowing these statues was not mere intolerance, but heartfelt revulsion at the temples literally reeking of slaughter and decay, at priests whose black robes reminded the Spanish of their own until they saw the long hair intractably matted with human blood. Cortés could not understand how so polished a gentleman as Motecuhzoma could honor the gods in such a brutal manner. The answer has two aspects: First, the Aztecs sincerely believed themselves to have been chosen to maintain the life of the sun, and through it the earth, by rituals of human sacrifice. Second, the very puritanical asceticism that gave such exemplary order to the cities was also expressed in fanatic masochism on the part of the priests, to whom tearing out others' hearts was little beyond their own constant austerity and self-laceration. The man who since youth had spent most of his hours, day and night, on cold stone floors stinking of dried blood, praying unceasingly, slashing his ears, arms, and body and piercing his tongue and penis with maguey thorns to draw the red elixir for the gods—that man would not be disturbed to help lesser men who had enjoyed more of life's pleasures, to make, finally, a greater sacrifice. What is surprising is that the sixteenth-century Spaniards did not more readily compare the Aztec priests to the Catholic masochists, whether saints or flagellants, pursuing their fanatic asceticism in Europe at that very time.

Aztec religion was based on the belief that the earth is subject to cyclical destruction. Four times in the past, the earth and humans on it had been annihilated. The present age would come to its end when a horrendous earthquake engulfed all, and this fifth destruction would be the end of the total cycle, because time and space are related dimensions and there were only five directions (east, north, west, south, and center) for the Aztec. Heroic, cooperative efforts by humans and deities might postpone the holocaust. Any Aztec who shirked his duty as prescribed by the learned priests was betraying his people, his gods, and the world.

Like the Toltecs and probably the Teotihuacános before them, the Aztecs had a strongly dualistic cosmology. Associated with day, light, sky, and the male gender were the sun, Venus as the morning star Quetzalcóatl, Xiuhtecuhtli ("Lord of Fire") and Xiuhcoatl (his "Fire Serpent"), the Aztec patron and war leader Huitzilopochtli, and Cipactli ("Dragon of the East"), counterpart of the Mayan Itzamná. Associated with night, darkness, the earth and underworld, and the female gender were the moon, Venus as the evening star, fertility and vegetation deities such as Tlaloc and Xochiquetzal, and monstrous, toadlike earth herself, Tlaltecuhtli. The four cardinal directions were paired, east and north going with the sun, west and south—and also center, because it is in the earth—with the monster earth. The multitude of deities are reducible to aspects of the two fundamental, opposing, and complementary principles animating the universe.

Ometéotl, the dual principles in their primordial and infinite unity, is the ultimate nature of the universe, and is dynamic. The conflicts and crea-

tions of the deities, as of humans and other earthly creatures, are expressions of this vital dynamism, and nothing more—or less. The Aztecs perceived that the ultimate Giver of Life acts through

the sun, eagle with arrows of fire.
Lord of time, god.
He shines, makes things radiant, casts his rays of light upon them.
His heat is felt, he scorches people, makes them sweat,
he darkens their faces, blackens them, turns them black as smoke.

(Léon-Portilla 1963:51)

The sun, like everything else other than the ultimate self-generating Ometéotl, needs nourishment or it will die. The Aztecs believed that they had been chosen to be the people responsible for keeping the sun alive through feeding him bits of the essence of life contained in beating hearts. With this terrible obligation resting upon them, the Aztec priests became very efficient at swiftly slicing open human chests with razor-sharp knives of the finest obsidian, tearing out the beating heart, and offering it to the sun. Every day as the sun passed through the blue Mexican sky, the priests and the people rejoiced that their efforts had been successful in gaining all humans, all creatures, more life.

It was, of course, glorious to die that the sun and all people might live. Nevertheless, few healthy men or women seemed to volunteer for the honor. The Aztecs therefore instituted formal wars with adjacent nations to capture men for sacrifice. When sufficient captives had been seized by each side, the leaders were supposed to notify their opposite officers and the war should end. A Nahuatl poem describes one of the battles of these flower wars, as they were called:

There is a clamor of bells,
The dust rises as if it were smoke.
The Giver of Life is gratified.

Shield flowers open their blossoms,
the glory spreads,
it becomes linked to earth.
Death is here among the flowers
in the midst of the plain!
Close to the war,
when the war begins,
in the midst of the plain,
the dust rises as if it were smoke,
entangled and twisted round
with flowery strands of death.
Oh Chichimec princes!
Do not fear, my heart!
In the midst of the plain
my heart craves death
by the obsidian edge.

(Léon-Portilla 1969:87-88)

Human sacrifice goes back at least to the Pre-classic era in Mesoamerica, but the Aztecs became obsessed with their mission to preserve the world and sacrificed thousands of persons each year under Motecuhzoma II. Besides the warriors captured in the "flower wars" and in serious wars of conquest, slaves were bought for the purpose. Women and young children were also sacrificed, but they were few compared with the numbers of men. Each deity had his or her preference or appropriate type of sacrifice, and between human sacrifices during festivals, the lesser deities were content with quails and other animals or the priests' own bloodletting. Since all deities were basically aspects of the dual principles, all required nourishment similar to the sun's. But the sun's formal opposite was the earth monster, and she was particularly important to keep fed, because she needed strength each night to gestate the sun in her underworld womb after he fell into her gaping jaws in the west, and to labor and give birth to him each dawn.

The Aztecs did not impose their religion upon conquered nations, but assumed that local variants of the basic Mesoamerican beliefs and purely local deities were no serious threat to the victorious

Huitzilopochtli and the people he led. Not only Huitzilopochtli's success in superseding the principal deities of the Aztecs' predecessors, but Toltec Tezcatlipoca's overthrow of Quetzalcóatl's pre-eminence centuries earlier, fit the Nahuatl cosmology of a dynamic universe. There was no philosophical barrier to accepting both ancient and newly conceived deities, for all were understood, at least by the most educated priests, to be aspects or manifestations of the godhead, Ometéotl. Most Mesoamericans had a very sophisticated realization that religious symbols must be relevant to the traditions and current situation of the ethnic group for whom they are intended, and that it follows that each region would have its own versions of deities. Some icons were universal, or nearly so, in Mesoamerica: serpent, fire, celestial bird, world-supporting tree or tree of life, cave, mountain, jaguar, and maize growing out of the head of a monster. These icons are all present by the end of the Preclassic period, but it is a safe bet that their meanings were not identical in all centuries and all regions. Teotihuacán influence crystallized religious concepts into a widespread, fairly coherent set of deities, including Quetzalcóatl ("Precious-Feathered Serpent"), Tlaloc ("Cave in Which Rain is Kept"), Huehuetotl ("Old Man Fire"), Xiuhcoatl ("Fire Serpent"), and Xipe ("Flayed One"), who puts on a fresh skin symbolizing spring regeneration. The basic stratum (more precisely, strata) of Archaic, Preclassic, Classic, and early Postclassic conceptions and reformulations, adapted by the late Postclassic period to the regional experiences and concerns of dozens of Indian nations, gave Mesoamerica the variety within similarity seen by the Spanish beginning in 1519.

SECTION 5: MEXICAN PEOPLES UNDER SPANISH AND MEXICAN RULE

Cortés left Spain's first foothold in America, the Caribbean islands, to attempt to establish trade between the Spanish in Cuba and the Indian nations of the mainland. Soon after his landing, he realized that the mainland nations were, as far as he saw on the rich east coast, sophisticated states far above bartering for trinkets but promising great wealth. Cortés discovered that many of these states were actively resisting domination by an expanding empire, or had recently been subjugated. A shrewd and disciplined man and a born leader, Cortés wisely determined to ignore his orders from the governor of Cuba and to aim to take over domination of Mexico with the aid of the Aztecs' enemies. He made it clear that he respected the Indians and would treat those who cooperated with him as true allies. Politicking all the way, he marched inland, over a high, less-used route, won a battle against the city of Cholula in Puebla, and entered Tenochtitlán as Motecuhzoma's guest.

Motecuhzoma's conduct has puzzled historians for centuries. It has been common to dismiss him as a weak man totally swayed by barbaric superstition, in spite of the testimony of both Cortés and Bernal Díaz that the emperor was kingly in his bearing, intelligent, and alert. A close reading of the chronicles shows that when he first heard of Cortés's landing and march, Motecuhzoma became very curious to see this exotic marvel from the eastern sea. The emperor encouraged the expendable Cholulans to try to stop the invader, but he was so confident of his own empire's power— and why not?—that the Cholulans' defeat did not disturb him or cause him to mount an Aztec campaign against the strangers. Motecuhzoma, although trained as a priest, had led his armies valorously in battle, and had no doubt that Anáhuac, as the Aztecs called their nation, could prevail when necessary. Therefore, he indulged his desire to see with his own eyes the source of the fascinating stories coming from the east. Motecuhzoma made the fatal mistake of the proud: He underestimated a lesser personage.

Cortés used Motecuhzoma's confidence to chance an incredibly bold move. He and his men told the emperor that they would not permit him to leave the room except as their prisoner. Mote-

cuhzoma acquiesced. Was he frightened for his life? That seems unlikely. Rather, he seems to have played along with Cortés, even going through a ceremony in which he announced to his nobles that he was handing over government to the Spaniard as representative of Charles V, Spain's Hapsburg emperor. Presumably, Motecuhzoma considered this ceremony a farce, since he knew, though Cortés did not, that Aztec emperors were elected by a council of men from the royal family: the reigning king had no power to pass on authority by his own hand. It appears that Motecuhzoma, highly devout and well educated in religious matters, was disturbed by a comet and other unusual omens observed not long before, and was waiting for some sign from Huitzilopochtli as to how best to treat the foreigners who would usurp his office. The sign came in the form of Cortés's impulsive destruction of the god's own shrine in the principal temple, and that of Tlaloc beside it. Motecuhzoma ordered Cortés to leave Tenochtitlán. With his nation undisturbed around him except for this sacrilege, Motecuhzoma was still confident no serious threat was posed by Cortés. Cortés asked for time to ready ships to take his party away from Mexico. The magnanimous emperor granted the wish. The Aztec people, however, were not so forgiving. Plots were discussed to dislodge the interlopers. Motecuhzoma at one point spoke to citizens demanding Cortés's removal, and the angry mob stoned to death the former emperor, who shortly before had been superseded by his brother as a result of the Aztec council's repudiation of his conduct.

The new emperor, Cuitláhuac, pursued the Spaniards out of Tenochtitlán, but was himself killed not long after by a secret weapon the Spaniards unwittingly brought from Europe: smallpox. Introducing the disease to the highly vulnerable American Indians was not deliberate, but it contributed to the Aztecs' downfall. Historians who discuss the event have been engrossed exclusively in military tactics and have neglected to fully consider the possible role of smallpox. Cuitláhuac was succeeded by Cuauhtémoc, who had the unhappy fate of being the last emperor of Anáhuac, the Aztec empire.

In 1520, Cortés had had to march back to the Veracruz coast to fight one of his own countrymen, sent by the governor of Cuba to take him prisoner for disobeying orders. Cortés won and reinforced his troops with the soldiers from Cuba. More important, he enhanced his prestige among the tribute payers to the Aztec and the nations still outside the empire. When he marched back to Tenochtitlán, he enlisted armies from several Indian nations, the largest group being from Anáhuac's eastern neighbor and most formidable foe, Tlaxcala. With about a hundred thousand Indian soldiers, led by their own experienced captains and princes, Cortés advanced on Tenochtitlán, and after a siege of three and one-half months, brought the starving Aztecs to a last-ditch, all-out battle that destroyed much of the beautiful capital city in the lake. Thus, in August 1521, after two years of effort, Cortés became sovereign of Mexico.

For all practical purposes, Cortés was ruler of Mexico until October 1524, when trans-Atlantic letters finally and officially declared the conqueror's subordination to his lawful king's decrees. During the three years of his power, Cortés sought to fulfill the two purposes that had brought him to Mexico and sustained him during his long campaign: the enrichment of the conquerors, and the Christian salvation of the Indians' souls. To fulfill the first goal, Cortés distributed to his fellow Spaniards *encomiendas*, grants of the labor of specified numbers of Indian inhabitants of particular lands. The *encomendero*, or holder of the grant, expected to profit from the work of "his" Indians on farms, at crafts, in mines, in households as servants, or however they might be employed in that district. In return, he was obliged to maintain a church and priest for "his" Indians and to keep arms, as a kind of militia. In theory, the encomienda system was designed—in Europe—primarily to protect commoners from exploitation by feudal lords and to ensure revenues and power to

the Crown. In practice—in America—encomiendas were granted to Spaniards as rewards for service in the conquest. Obviously, most of the soldiers were adventurers, more or less unscrupulous, since no respectable gentleman with a secure position in Spain was likely to go off to fight savages in American jungles. The law distinguished clearly between slaves, who were blacks imported from Africa, and Indians. Indians were not to be uprooted from their homes, were not to be sent to mines or on war expeditions except when levied by the crown's representatives for defense, were not to be made to labor to exhaustion or to the detriment of their own plots of land. The encomendero could require tribute from his grant, but could not expropriate possessions, gold, or women. Legal distinctions somehow became obscure thousands of miles west of Charles's court, and not only legends but a long series of depositions before Charles's officials describe flagrant abuses of Indians by encomenderos.

Cortés himself tried to curb this de facto enslavement of the Mexicans, but even his authority could not prevail. As he was struggling to reconcile his soldiers' expectations of rewards with his sincere respect for his Mexican allies and opponents and his fervent desire to convert all to Christianity, Charles V and his Council of the Indies were reviewing the disastrous effects of encomienda upon the Indians of the Caribbean islands, colonized by Columbus and his party twenty-odd years earlier. Charles's conclusion was that the encomienda system could not be reformed. He therefore ordered Cortés to cease granting encomiendas, and expected that those already given would revert to the Crown upon the death of the grantee. He also appointed a special judge to investigate governance in Mexico, Cortés's authority to be suspended upon this man's arrival. For the next six years, ineffective or, more often, downright unethical officials abetted the ruthless encomenderos exploiting the Indians. When Charles V belatedly learned of the situation in Mexico, through a smuggled letter from the bishop of Mexico, Zumárraga, a fearless Basque, he ordered the incumbent officials suspended while a special commission from Spain rectified the horrors. Then, in 1530, he set up Mexico as a viceroyalty and appointed as viceroy Don Antonio de Mendoza, a member of Spain's most powerful noble family.

Mendoza's arrival in 1535 inaugurated the happiest period of Spanish-Indian relations. Encomiendas were gradually abolished, and authority on the district level was given to a salaried Spanish official, the *corregidor*, who was assisted by a deputy, a constable, and a secretary. Mexico was divided into territorial units—smaller in densely populated regions, larger in the mountains—of a size that could reasonably be supervised by the corregidor and his staff. The corregidor was expected to devote himself primarily to maintenance and adjudication of law and the king's interests, which of course included continuing monetary return but on a long-term basis, not quick and destructive exploitation. The crown ruled indirectly through native Indian *caciques* (local leaders), frequently either the preconquest lord or his heir or another relative. Once the illegal abuses of the encomenderos were curtailed, the life of the common Indian reverted to one much like his life before the coming of the Spaniards. To the majority of Indians, political conditions had even improved: the endemic warfare had been abolished, and human sacrifice ended. The Spaniards in Mexico vividly remembered the glories of the native cities and the pomp and aristocratic manners of the native nobility, and respected those upper-class Indians who adapted themselves graciously to the new order. Many of the Spanish colonists married Indian ladies, including daughters of Motecuhzoma, and some of the sons of these unions boasted more loudly of their native princely blood than of their Spanish fathers. A college was established for highborn native youth and soon produced young scholars fluent in Latin as well as correct Castilian and polished Nahuatl. Native artisans added European techniques to their own and created vigorous, widely praised styles in many media.

Foremost among the champions of native Mexicans in the sixteenth century were the missionary priests brought to convert them and thereby fulfill Cortés' second goal. There had been a debate over whether Indians have souls and are therefore capable of Christian salvation. This debate had been won by the "liberals," who argued pro. The question had really been raised about the Indians of the Caribbean islands discovered by Columbus, Indians in villages, people of scanty clothing and simple-appearing technology. Cortés considered the great complex civilizations of Mexico ample proof that the Indians were fully human and not only capable of reason, but because of it obliged to embrace salvation through Christianity. Charles V agreed and chose, for the most part, "liberals" such as Zumárraga and the newly reformed mendicant orders (the Franciscans, Dominicans, and Augustinians) to bring the Church to Mexico.

The first Spanish missionaries, the famous Twelve, arrived in Mexico in 1524. Later in the century, their fellow Franciscan, Bernardino de Sahagún, published an account in Nahuatl of an open meeting between the Twelve and a group of distinguished Indian *tlamatinime* ("knowledgeable men," or, as glossed by Sahagún, "wise men or philosophers"). The knowledgeable men fearlessly declaimed,

Through an interpreter we reply,
we exhale the breath and the words
of the Lord Who is near, Who is within [omni
    present].
Because of Him we dare to do this.
For this reason we place ourselves in danger....
Allow us then to die,
let us perish now,
since our gods are already dead.

You said
that we know not
the Lord Who is near, Who is within,
to Whom the heavens and the earth belong.

You said
that our gods are not true gods.
New words are these
that you speak;
because of them we are disturbed,
because of them we are troubled.
For our ancestors
before us, who lived upon the earth,
were unaccustomed to speak thus....
In reverence they held,
they honored, our gods.
They taught us
all their rules of worship,
all their ways of honoring the gods....
It was the doctrine of the elders
that there is life because of the gods;
with their sacrifice, they gave us life.
In what manner? When? Where?
When there was still darkness.

It was their doctrine
that they [the gods] provide our subsistence,
all that we eat and drink,
that which maintains life: corn, beans, ama
  ranth, sage.
To them do we pray
for water, for rain
which nourish things on earth....

And in what manner? When? Where were
  the gods invoked?
Were they appealed to; were they accepted
  as such; were they held
in reverence?

For a long time has it been;
it was there at Tula, . . .
it was there at Teotihuacán.

Above the world
they had founded
their kingdom.
They gave the order, the power,
glory, fame.

And now are we
to destroy
the ancient order of life?
Of the Chichimecs,
of the Toltecs...?

We know
on Whom life is dependent;
on Whom the perpetuation of the race de
    pends;
by Whom begetting is determined;
by Whom growth is made possible;
how is it that one must invoke,
how it is that one must pray.

Hear, oh Lords [the Spaniards],
do nothing
to our people
that will bring misfortune upon them,
that will cause them to perish....

We cannot be tranquil,
and yet we certainly do not believe;
we do not accept your teachings as truth,
even though this may offend you.
                           (Léon-Portilla 1963:63–66)

The "doctrine of the elders" had taught that without sacrifices, the world would soon come to an end. In 1524, Aztec tlamatinime accepted that the Spaniards had overthrown Huitzilopochtli, patron god of Anáhuac, but the event did not invalidate their cosmology. Would the Spaniards respect the knowledge of past ages, the knowledge to which even the Spaniards owed their existence?

More months passed. The sun continued to rise in the east each day. Rain came as usual. Crops grew, babies were born. Yet no sacrifices had been offered, other than a few quail, tamales, and drops of blood from the devout, drawn at night in private rooms. Did the ongoing world mean that the doctrine of Teotihuacán and the

Toltecs (the doctrine according to Aztec historians, that is) was wrong?

The Spanish missionaries believed that the Mexicans had renounced their old gods and embraced Christianity wholeheartedly. In fact, the Mexicans had embraced a reinterpretation of their own religion. A few diehards persisted in the preconquest practices, insofar as they could in secret. The majority of the Mexicans of all classes, however, adopted the practices of Christianity as superior means of invoking the gods, to be added to traditional practices that did not openly conflict. Certain elements of sixteenth-century Catholic Christianity were peculiarly compatible with contemporary Nahuatl beliefs. For example, it was easy for a Mexican to accept the doctrine that Jesus' sacrifice upon the cross had redeemed mankind forever, for not only was the notion of human sacrifice to gain salvation basic to Mexico, but the cross itself, representing the five directions of the world (four cardinal points and the center), was a fundamental symbol; the white risen Christ seemed a European version of Quetzalcóatl as the Morning Star; the worship of Jesus' mother seemed to acknowledge the importance of Quetzalcóatl's mother, Omecihuatl ("Lady of Duality"), the primordial female principle; and the Christian Communion echoed Aztec worshipers eating dough representations of their gods.

Charles V's choice of missionaries fostered this confusion. Charles was a champion of the Catholic Counter-Reformation, and upheld the school of thought that urged the preaching of the gospel directly to the people in words ordinary lay people could understand. The Franciscans sent to Mexico gave themselves the task of learning Nahuatl and preaching to the Mexicans in that tongue, as well as establishing colleges where selected upper-class Indian youths could learn Spanish and Latin to assist missionaries in bringing Christianity to the youths' communities. In translating the gospel into terms the Nahuatl speakers could grasp, the missionaries sometimes took preconquest symbols— for example, the cross—and claimed Christian meaning for them. Heretofore rather esoteric Christian symbols might be given a new importance in this New World context. The Sacred Heart was a minor theme in the visions of some medieval European saintly mystics, and in its few depictions it appeared as a stylized European "valentine" heart. In sixteenth-century Mexico, a gory, realistic human heart, shown either alone (as when the Aztec priests had lifted up their sacrifices' hearts), or within Jesus' breast, became a very popular symbol. The heart was often shown radiating flames from its top, a conflation of the Aztec convention of showing blood streaming from the torn-out heart as stylized flamelike scrolls and the Christian mystics' visions of Christ's heart radiating divine grace. So popular did this nonofficial symbol become in Mexico that at the end of the sixteenth century, a Vatican commission explicitly banned its use in churches. (An odd consequence is that shortly after the Vatican investigation's decision, the realistically depicted Sacred Heart began to be used as a symbol by several of the most advanced liberal theologians of France. It is possible, though difficult to prove, that these theologians, who were known to be deeply interested in the Mexican missionary endeavors, saw the Aztec-originated symbol at this time and took it up to convey their own more profoundly spiritual conception of Christ's love.)

The best-known of the Christian-Aztec fusions is the Virgin of Guadalupe. She is said to have appeared first in 1531 to an Indian upon a small hill in the northern sector of the Valley of Mexico, and to have asked that a shrine be erected there for her. By the middle of the sixteenth century, the shrine and a cult celebrating this virgin was well begun. Before the conquest, the Aztecs had a shrine on the same hill for Tonantzin, "Our Lady Mother" (another name for Coatlicue, "Serpent Skirt"), who was identified in some legends as the mother of Huitzilopochtli, the god conceived without intercourse from feathers picked up by the lady in the temple. Associated with fertility, Tonantzin was offered flowers; the Virgin of Guadalupe's miraculous sign was a rose plant flowering upon a dusty hill. Nahuatl-speaking Indians in the Valley of Mexico still address Guadalupe as "Tonantzin." A somewhat less familiar fusion is the Christ of Chalma, who appeared, two years after Guadalupe, in a cave where the Aztec Oztocteotl, "Cave God," had been worshipped. Theologian Juan Alvárez Cuauhtémoc points out that Aztec and other Nahuatl speakers value poetic speech using metaphors extensively, and this facilitates identification of new images with older symbols. Alvárez notes that the Virgin of Guadalupe heralded by bird song and accompanied by flowers manifested *in xóchitl in cuícatl*, "flower and song," for Mexicans the purest worship of the eternal Deity.

The mid-sixteenth century thus became, in retrospect, a golden age in which the citizens of Anáhuac and other domains of central Mexico lived much as they had lived in the previous century—under their native nobility, tilling their fields or practicing their crafts, trading in their markets, and worshiping most of their gods, though with new images and newly composed songs and dances. If their native lords answered to strange rulers, that did not directly affect most of the commoners. The new religious practices brought sincere joy, for families no longer had to dread the seizure of sons or daughters for sacrifice. New crops and livestock broadened the economic base. There was even a small renaissance of Nahuatl literature as Sahagún and others collected accounts from elders of traditional customs and beliefs, second-generation Spanish-Indian nobility wrote histories of their mothers' peoples, and courts turned to native records of genealogies and landholdings to settle disputes.

The snake in the grass at this period was a disease. Motecuhzoma's successor, Cuitláhuac, died in the first smallpox epidemic, 1520. The epidemics of 1545–58 and 1576–81 were more severe, decimating the Indian population of central Mexico. The district of Xochimilco, for example, in the southern sector of the Valley of Mexico, was reduced to 6,000 people in 1563, compared with 30,000 before 1545. Which diseases caused the major epidemics is not known, but smallpox, typhus, and measles appear to have been present. The effects of these diseases would have been exacerbated by secondary illnesses such as pneumonia and by malnutrition resulting when no family member remained well enough to prepare food. The Indians were struck much harder by the epidemics because they had had no previous exposure to the current Eurasian plagues, but Spanish and blacks in Mexico were also affected, although in fewer numbers and not so often fatally.

The outcome of the two major epidemics of the sixteenth century and the continuing high disease rate in Indian communities was a marked loss of population. The low was reached by about 1630, and consequently the government had to cease drafting Indian laborers by community or district for civil work projects. Many areas were virtually emptied of people. Population pressure on farmland eased, and families migrated to abandoned land. The cultivation of *chinampas* decreased, partly because fewer families survived to work them and partly because the availability of land that could be farmed without intensive irrigation or drainage and fertilization made it unnecessary to put so much labor into them. The introduction by the Spanish of ox-drawn plows was another factor inducing farmers to work land extensively rather than intensively, but the plow would have been of much more limited use had there not been so many tenantless fields.

The seventeenth century thus began with a drastic loss of population and the initiation of several long-term trends connected with this loss. These trends continued well into the nineteenth century, and to a greater or lesser degree may still be observed, although they are now reversed. First was the deflation of the Indian social classes—once structured from royalty through nobility and citizens to serfs and slaves—into a single, low class of peasants. The native nobility either merged into the Spanish upper class, primarily through the marriage of women from Indian noble families with Spanish men, or disappeared into a peasantry as a result of losing lands and wealth. The epidemics and other causes of population decline in the sixteenth century affected the native upper classes not only by killing some of the caciques and their wives and heirs, but also by killing the lower class of the Indian community, who upheld the wealth and position of their caciques by their labor and tribute payments. Spanish encomenderos were similarly deprived of labor. In the seventeenth century, a substitute method of exploitation, the *repartimiento*, became popular with the Spanish: Indians were forced to accept cash advances, or goods priced high, against expected harvests, then "sell" the harvested crops at a lower-than-market price to the Spaniards to whom they were involuntarily indebted. If the harvest was poor, the Indians had to buy enough additional cotton, cacao, or whatever to make up the delivered amount demanded. What the Indian paid for the additional produce might be two or three times more than what he received when he delivered his obligated amount.

A second trend was that the Indian communities increasingly were restructured and sometimes relocated. To a certain extent this would have been necessary anyway because of the reduction in population, but it was also a matter of governmental policy to settle the Indians in towns in order to make it convenient to group them into congregations for the church parishes. Clustering the Indians into closely settled towns made it easier for officials to maintain law and order, collect tribute, and force church attendance. By the end of the seventeenth century, the Crown had regularized the layout of Indian towns: each town was allowed by law a square land area of minimum size, separated by a minimum distance from Spanish-owned haciendas, having a one-square-league *ejido*, or common pasture, a suitable amount of land for farms, plus water rights and a woodlot adjacent to the town. The Indian towns were communally held lands allotted to families for their use but not theirs to sell. In principle, this prevented alienation of

land, the base of support, as well as ensuring a stable congregation and an easily administered fiscal unit. In fact, Indians might illegally leave their towns and find homes elsewhere, and not infrequently a whole town might be bought by a Spanish landowner through quasi-legal maneuverings with the duped or conniving Indian cacique, might be expropriated by a neighboring landowner who would eventually claim ownership by right of long use, or might become serfs of the landowner for failure to pay tribute or rents. By the nineteenth century, the old native towns in districts administered by a descendant of the preconquest lords had virtually disappeared; instead, most Indians lived in villages on large haciendas owned by Mexicans of principally Spanish descent. Communal allocation of village lands continued, but the families tended to be in perpetual debt to the *hacendado* (estate owner) and thereby bound to his property. Thus, the severe population decline in the century after the conquest facilitated the reduction of the complex Indian societies of central Mexico to a single class of rural peasants governed by a group of alien extraction and foreign cultural allegiance.

As a gap between the impoverished Indians and the wealthy hacendados widened through the seventeenth and eighteenth centuries, the upper class of Mexico, which identified itself with Spain, felt increasing contempt for the native Indians. No longer would a mestizo (a person of mixed blood) boast of a genealogy including the kings of Texcoco, or even of Motecuhzoma. The greater susceptibility of Indians to diseases was interpreted to indicate physical inferiority, which was also supposedly indicated by short stature (actually a result in part of lack of animal protein in the peasant diet) and dark skin (a consequence of field labor). Mental inferiority was supposedly shown by the Indians' inability to speak Spanish, which the rural people segregated in their Indian towns had no opportunity to use. Any Indian who did pick up Spanish and attempted to work outside his rural collective was labeled *ladino*, "crafty," and was shunned by Spanish and Indian alike.

Indians in Postcolonial Mexico

At the beginning of the nineteenth century, Mexico was divided between Spanish speakers, who alone participated in national politics and the management of interregional and international businesses, and hundreds of separate Indian groups with a considerable degree of internal autonomy, although subject to the economic exploitation of the Spanish-speaking hacendados. Where the haciendas and mines integrated the labor of Indians into the national economy, the upper class's contempt maintained the caste barrier and, by its unwillingness to associate with Indians, permitted by default the continuation of the Indian villages' local self-government. Elsewhere, in the rugged mountains of Oaxaca and the far northwest, and in the formidable jungle of southern Yucatán, Indians existed as tiny republics, seldom visited by representatives of the national government and staunchly claiming they had never been conquered by Spaniards. Not a few were honestly unaware that they were considered to be part of the Mexico that had its capital in Mexico City. Technically, there is some basis for some of the more remote, inaccessible communities, such as the highland Zapotecs and the Yaqui in the northwestern Sierra, to argue that their groups did not sign pacts with Spaniards or Mexicans, and that therefore, never having been under the full jurisdiction of a colonial power, they remain independent. "Rebellions" asserting independence have been a recurrent event in these far northwestern and far southeastern regions of Mexico.

Most famous of these Indian "rebellions" (from the Indian point of view, battles to retain independence) is the War of the Castes in Yucatán. Maya chafed under Spanish domination, and from the beginning of Spanish conquests, Indians fled from Colonial towns and haciendas into the Petén jungles and the highland back-country. Maya remaining in Spanish-ruled areas were from time to time excited by visionaries proclaiming the end of Colonial impositions. Beginning in 1708, for ex-

ample, Maya in the Chiapas mountains reported the appearance of the Virgin Mary promising to aid Indians. In 1712, a Tzeltal Maya girl announced that she had been vouchsafed the news that the Spaniards' God and King had died and the Maya should recognize an Indian Redeemer and an Indian king. Under the new order, Spaniards would serve Indians, and Spanish women be taken as wives by Indian leaders. Sebastián Gómez, a Tzoltil Maya, organized the new kingdom, apparently too much like its hated predecessor, for his fellow Maya soon became dissatisfied with his rule, too, and the Spanish Colonial government was able to reimpose its officers, tripling the number of Spanish priests to maintain closer surveillance over the Chiapas Maya.

In central Yucatán at Cisteil, José Jacinto Uc de los Santos, a Maya claiming the name Canek borne by the last of the royal Itzá, gathered hundreds of his fellows in 1761 to drive out the Spanish. Within a year, his little army was massacred, he and his lieutenants brutally executed, and the village of Cisteil obliterated. Eighty-six years later, in 1847, three leaders of Maya communities in the same central region of Yucatán forged an alliance that nearly ousted the Spanish-Mexican government. Jacinto Pat negotiated with the Mexican government in 1848 and accepted the position of Governor of the Indians of Yucatán; Cecilio Chi broke with his ally, reasserted Maya independence and besieged Mérida, the capital of the province. Observers said Chi probably would have driven the Spanish elite out of Mérida had he maintained the siege, but when the spring rains came, the Maya army dispersed to plant its cornfields. For the rest of the nineteenth century, Maya held most of Yucatán beyond a heavily patrolled zone just east of Mérida. Chan Santa Cruz in the middle of Quintana Roo was the Maya capital and center of the revitalized Maya religion focused on its Talking Cross (*Cruz* in Spanish, hence the independent Maya are known as the Cruzob). This War of the Castes, so called because it was seen as polarizing the two castes, Spanish-speaking Mexicans against Maya,

FIGURE 2.16   Maya rural homestead, Yucatán. (*T. Kehoe*)

is officially said to have continued until a Mexican government offensive in 1901 overcame Chan Santa Cruz. By 1915, Cruzob Maya retook Chan Santa Cruz. The final outcome of the War of the Castes was a retreat of the Cruzobs after a smallpox epidemic decimated them soon after their last victory. Proudly independent, Cruzob descendants still challenge Mexican domination in some Quintana Roo villages. Similarly independent Maya, known as the Lacandón, occupy the eastern Chiapas jungle; they were mostly refugees from Spanish Colonial oppression in Guatemala, and now are resisting takeover of their land by homesteaders, including many Maya, encouraged by the Mexican government to clear the tropical forest for cattle ranches.

The Mexican government did not, and will not, distinguish between Indian communities in the central Mexican valleys, isolated from the national mainstream usually by speaking a native language, by illiteracy, and by poverty, and Indians similarly handicapped who are far from the center. The seventeenth-century creation of an Indian peasantry contrasting with a Spanish-derived upper class was not a result of conquest policies—indeed, it was contrary to the liberal tenets of many sixteenth-century administrators—but the consequence of Indian depopulation, caused primarily by disease, and the attendant contraction of Indian economic and political power. The effect of this degradation of the Indians was the reinforcement of the racist attitude of superiority of eighteenth- and nineteenth-century Mexicans in power.

Mexico won independence from Spain in 1821, taking advantage of the post-Napoleonic breakdown of Spanish authority. The war of independence was a rebellion of Mexican Spaniards and did not really involve the Indians. Even the 1855 accession to power of the Zapotec Indian Benito Juárez did not substantially affect the Indians. Juárez led a reform movement against the conservatives who had ruled Mexico, and established a constitution modeled in part upon that of the United States. But his regime was occupied first with battling the conservatives, then with repelling the French attempt to usurp Mexico through the puppet emperor Maximilian. Defeating Maximilian, Juárez and his party found a resurgence of conservative rebellion, strengthened by Juárez's untimely death in 1872.

Four years later, in 1876, Juárez's successor was overthrown by a revolt led by General Porfirio Díaz, a mestizo from Oaxaca (his mother was a Mixtec Indian) who spurned the humanitarian concerns of the reformers. Díaz ruled as dictator until 1911, leaving the constitution on the books but suppressing any democratic or egalitarian efforts that might interfere with his principal goal, the building of a strong capitalist economy in Mexico. To further this goal, Díaz looked to investments from the United States, itself in the heyday of the "robber barons" of laissez-faire capitalism. Díaz's long dictatorship became a nightmare of oppression for the Indians. Not only were there military campaigns against remote Indian groups—especially the Yaqui of Sonora, who would not acknowledge Mexican sovereignty—but also police support of peonage (enforced labor of debtors) and a good deal of outright slavery, including the shipping of thousands of Yaquis to work, and usually die, on the plantations of Yucatán. Hacendados had for three centuries kept Indian peasants as serfs on the estates by keeping them perpetually in debt to the landowner, but under Díaz, Indians were even dragged from the relative security of their ancestral villages on the haciendas and their services sold to other plantation owners, who could mistreat the unhappy peons, women and boys as well as men, as they pleased.

Díaz was overthrown in 1911, in a revolution that began late the previous year. The following years saw contests between several movements implicated in the revolution. Of principal concern to the Indians were the attempts of Emiliano Zapata, from Morelos, to win agrarian reforms. Zapata's melodramatic career was ended by assassination in 1919, without the accomplishment of his goals, although the new constitution of 1917 did include a provision for restoring ejido lands to the peasants.

Both during Díaz's regime and, more fervently, after the revolution, Mexican intellectuals and political leaders argued over two related themes: whether the Indians were inherently inferior, and whether it was desirable to instill Mexican nationalism in Indians by exterminating the native languages. The idea that Indians were inherently and hopelessly inferior, fit only for peonage, was claimed to be scientific. It was an application of Social Darwinism, the school of thought that believed the contemporary world powers had achieved their positions through natural selection of races with superior genetic endowments for the development of civilization. This "scientific" rationale for the status quo of course appealed to the elite, who preferred such a facile bastardization of Darwin's theory to the bothersome notion that the short and brutalized lives of the lower classes were the result of un-christian exploitation by the capitalists. If the Social Darwinists were correct, it might be that the Indian peasants of Mexico were incapable of education, even of learning to speak Spanish fluently. There was serious advancement of the idea that Indians' mouths were too animal-like to permit them to form Spanish sounds, and that Indian languages, even Nahuatl, could express only crude emotions and kindergarten thoughts. Thus, there developed the curious contention that Indian languages ought to be allowed to flourish, since their speakers could not advance to Spanish, and the linking of this position to conservative, elitist politics, while the argument that Indian languages ought to be exterminated was propounded by liberal, egalitarian "friends of the Indian"!

Prominent in the debates over proper treatment of the Indians in the new constitution of 1917 was the anthropologist Manuel Gamio, who had studied with Franz Boas at Columbia University. Gamio was both an archaeologist, one of the first to use scientific stratigraphic techniques of excavation in America (following a suggestion by Boas), and a Mexican deeply aware of the Indian heritage of his country. He felt that knowledge of the languages and customs of the various Indian groups would be invaluable to the archaeologists attempting to understand and reconstruct the pre-conquest sites, but that he who would benefit from such studies had an obligation to use the principles of anthropology to design and advocate programs aiding the contemporary Indians. Gamio's proposal, expounded in 1916, was to divide the Indians of Mexico into ten districts, and to develop curricula to fit the particular circumstances and needs of each. Because Gamio sought to integrate the Indians as full citizens, he urged that teaching be conducted in Spanish in order to give the Indian students facility in the national tongue. Gamio's innovation, which was reminiscent of the practical curricula used in United States Indian schools, was to forego the customary classics studies of traditional Mexican schools and substitute teaching of hygiene, agricultural methods, consumer protection, and civics. The Valley of Teotihuacán was chosen to be a pilot district for Gamio's plan, and a program following his principles was carried out there, but in 1921 a change in government brought in a new educational policy that decried reinforcement of Indian separateness out of fear that it would promote political separatism.

Although the Obregón regime that took office in 1921 repudiated special programs for Indians, the effect of its politics was little different from what would have resulted from Gamio's proposals. Any village that provided a school building (usually through the donation of materials and labor by cooperating villagers) would be sent a teacher whose salary would be paid by the federal government. The village's *casa del pueblo* (people's house) would be a staging ground where the adults as well as children would learn basic Spanish, arithmetic, and literacy. The adults would be offered instruction in crafts and agriculture, but the children who completed the preprimary program would go on to regular elementary school and eventually to high school. What happened was that Indian villagers were, for the most part, too poor

to manage the expense of keeping a child out of labor and in school in town, where room and board as well as clothes and books required a weekly cash outlay. Therefore, the preprimary schools were the only formal instruction the Indian children received, with rare exceptions, and this continued the separation of the rural Indian peasantry from the Spanish-speaking literate townspeople (who were classed as mestizos or ladinos rather than *indios*, whatever their genetic makeup).

The year 1934 was a landmark for Indian politics in Mexico, as in the United States. Lázaro Cárdenas was Mexico's new president. Himself part Tarascan, Cárdenas was committed to bettering the lot of the working people, Indian and ladino, through Marxist socialism. By 1936 he had inaugurated both a federal Department of Indigenous Affairs and a program to return land to local collectives. The land-reform scheme was applied more in the north, where population density was lower and where the landless people were either militant Indians with a long history of resisting Spanish power, or Spanish-speaking mestizos, many of whom emigrated to the north from central Mexico to obtain land. Though as poor as any others, these northerners were more aware of political rights and more vigorous in demanding them than were (or are) some southern enclaves suspicious of *any* government intervention. The recurring problem with land reform—which had been attempted earlier by Obregón, who repatriated 3 million hectares (approximately 750 million acres) to nearly two thousand pueblos (village communities)—has been that before long, unscrupulous local landowners, caciques, and sharp operators from the cities tend to reestablish large private holdings and de facto peonage. When, near the end of his six-year term, Cárdenas visited the northwestern provinces, he is said to have been told by a delegation of Yaquis who came to his hotel, "Papa Lázaro, do you remember the hospitals, the schools, the lands that you told us about? All that's ended. The hospitals are taverns, the schools are occupied by soldiers, the lands belong to the new rich."

The Department of Indigenous Affairs, unlike the socialist land reforms, outlasted Cárdenas. Its name marked a growing emphasis on problems of poverty rather than on cultural distinctions or race. While everyone realized that the "indigenes" were the *indios*, the euphemism did heighten consciousness that national economic progress depended upon international trade and foreign investments in Mexico, and that, as Porfirio Díaz's dictatorship has exemplified, a focus on the economy vis-à-vis that of other nations, was likely to severely shortchange Mexico's own working class. Thus, the Department of Indigenous Affairs was mandated to concern itself with the betterment and protection of all Mexican natives, whether they were monolingual isolated Indians or ladinos trying to survive as small-town shopkeepers or northern desert farmers. The personnel of the department concentrated upon Indian populations, but in a context of widespread poverty, rather than racial inferiority.

Cárdenas was replaced in 1940 by a more conservative government, but the indigenist movement that had developed strength under his policies continued to grow. The first Inter-American Indigenist Congress met in Pátzcuaro, a Tarascan town of west Mexico, in 1940. Its delegates, who came from most of the Latin American countries, discussed methods and means of improving the economic and political status of the Indian peasantries and, in some nations, tribes. In 1948, Mexico created the semiautonomous National Indigenist Institute (*Instituto Nacional Indigenista*, or INI), with Alfonso Caso, an anthropologist, its director until his death in 1971. The INI replaced the Department of Indigenous Affairs, which had been dissolved in 1946 and its business placed under other government departments, particularly the Department of Education. The significance of the INI has been its relative freedom from direct political interference, which allows it to take an active role in utilizing social scientists, especially anthropologists, to plan, promote, and implement programs that may seem unconventional to bureaucrats or inexpedient to politicians. The INI

works closely with the allied National Institute of Anthropology and History to ground its programs in ongoing studies of the history and traditions of the various Mexican native peoples. Its perspective has moved it from Cárdenas's emphasis on local collectives, which tried to put a new shoe on the same foot that had survived as the minimal unit since the end of the sixteenth century, to an emphasis on districts and regions as the economically viable units of today.

The 1940 Mexican census reported a total population of 19,653,552, of which 5,427,396 were categorized as *indios*. Of these, a total of 2,490,909 spoke an Indian language either exclusively (1,237,018) or bilingually with Spanish (1,253,891). The last two categories, constituting 12.5 percent of all Mexicans, have been considered the prime target of indigenist programs, since they are handicapped economically by their inability to use the national language fluently. As a prerequisite for development programs adapted to regional conditions and problems, Mexico has been divided into eighteen "indigenous zones," which are similar to culture areas (the names preceding "zone" are language groups, the name or names following "of" are states of Mexico):

1. the Yaqui-Mayo zone of Sonora
2. the Mayo zone of Sinaloa
3. the Tarahumara [Rarámuri] zone of Chihuahua
4. the Huichol-Cora-Tepehuan zone of Durango, Jalisco, Nayarit, and Sinaloa
5. the Tarascan zone of Michoacán
6. the Mazahua-Otomí zone of the state of México
7. the Otomí zone of the Valley of Mezquital in the state of Hidalgo
8. the Huastec zone of Hidalgo, Veracruz, and San Luis Potosí
9. the northern Sierra zone of Puebla
10. the Nahua-Tlapaneca zone of Guerrero
11. the Mixtec zone of Oaxaca
12. the Nahua zone of Puebla and Veracruz

13. the Mixe-Chinanteca-Mazateca zone of Oaxaca
14. the Zapotec zone of Oaxaca
15. the Nahua-Popolaca zone of Veracruz [not named in the official list, but of interest are the Totonacs of central Veracruz, who may have been the people of prehistoric Teotihuacán, driven to the east when the great city fell]
16. the Tzeltal-Tzotzil-Tojolobal-Zoque-Maya-Chel zone of Chiapas
17. the Maya zone of Yucatán and Quintana Roo
18. the Chontal zone of Tabasco.

Although these zones are labeled by the indigenous language or languages found in them, geographical and cultural characteristics were also criteria in demarcating them. The zones continue to have validity, even though by 1970 the census counted only 873,545, or 2.1 percent of Mexico's population of 40,183,075, as monolingual speakers of indigenous languages.

The contemporary situation of Mexican Indians was discussed before a special session of the advisory council of the INI in 1971. Gonzalo Aguirre Beltrán, director of the INI, and Alejandro D. Marroquín, chief of the Anthropology Department of the Interamerican Indigenist Institute (an international coordinating agency headquartered in Mexico, formed from the 1940 Pátzcuaro Congress and directed by Manuel Gamio from 1942 until his death in 1960) presented summaries of the tenets and activities of their allied institutes. The crux of their work was the reconciliation of two ostensibly contradictory goals: the popular recognition of the dignity and worth of the indigenous (Indian) cultures, and the integration of members of these cultural groups into the modern national society. Mexico is, and is to be, an ethnically pluralistic nation, but one in which every native-born or naturalized resident should be capable of exercising full citizenship, enjoying a decent standard of health, and having access to economic and social opportunities.

Aguirre Beltrán pointed out that when politi-cians envisioned the development of a national culture, they gave the burden of that development to the Indians. The Indians were expected to learn Spanish and learn about Spanish-derived institutions; no one seriously urged that speakers of Spanish learn Nahuatl or Mayan, or that the nation be organized along the lines of Indian pueblos. The impracticality of Indianizing Mexico rested on two considerations: one, use of a European language and internationally prevalent economic forms was necessary for Mexico to maintain the desired standard of living, and two, with more than fifty extant Indian languages, no single Indian culture could or ought to dominate Mexico. The imposition of the overseas language, religion, and culture had at least ended the fratricidal wars that Cortés had manipulated to pull down the Aztec empire. To prevent a renewal of these clashes, Mexico felt justified expecting the Indians to become bilingual and bicultural, while allowing the Spanish speakers to remain monolingual and conversant only with the national culture.

Marroquín explained that education in the community school was the key plank in the INI programs. After anthropological study of the indigenous language and society by the INI, instruction was to begin in the local language as the medium of attaining basic literacy and learning Spanish. Native people were to be used as teachers and as personnel in the projects that the community wished to initiate. These projects should come from the community, not be ordered by outsiders, and should be carried out by persuasion, not coercion. The school should be the catalyst alerting the community to possibilities and encouraging action. Ideally the schools would be *casas del pueblo* in the centers of the villages. Where rugged topography and poor agricultural resources have resulted in tiny, dispersed hamlets, as in the High Mixteca of Oaxaca and the northwestern Sierra lands of the Rarámuri, Cora, and Huichol, "radio schools" and weekday boarding schools could substitute for more accessible centers.

Complementing the local schools are projects

FIGURE 2.17 Peasant homestead, Morelos, central Mexico. House is built of adobe bricks, with thatch roof. On the left, behind the dead tree, is a round adobe, thatched granary. (*A. Kehoe*)

for raising the health, economy, and arts of the indigenous communities. The INI works with federal Department of Health officials and others to vaccinate communities, maintain medical and dental clinics, educate the people on sanitary measures, and eradicate endemic diseases by a diversity of approaches, including even the provision of clean mills grinding maize into tortilla flour. Roads and bridges and telephone networks have been installed to break down the isolation of many communities. Agricultural projects have used demonstration fields, the provision of improved grain seed, fruit trees, and livestock, and financial credit to help indigenous families better their subsistence and, in many areas, also raise cash crops. Dams and irrigation systems have been built in some needed locations. The INI is also proud of its encouragement of crafts (merchandised and displayed in its museum in downtown Mexico City), its printing of many thousands of primers, texts, and instruction manuals in both Spanish and indigenous languages, and its provision of legal advice to Indians.

Marroquín also discussed the less praiseworthy aspects of the Mexican indigenist movement. The INI, like any institution a generation old, has lost some of the visionary energy of its founders. Bureaucracy has grown to stifle initiative and entangle operations. The INI's lack of top-level governmental power has permitted politicians and functionaries on various levels, national and local, to ignore or subvert INI programs. Money is limited, and too much of it, in Marroquín's opinion, goes to INI salaries rather than to projects. All these complaints could have been prophesied, and are probably inevitable in any national government agency. More fundamental are some other of Marroquín's charges. He did not see that the INI had made any substantial, permanent changes in the relationship of the indigenes to the nation, nor in the situation of the indigenes. They remain impoverished, handicapped in any efforts to gain a fairer share of the national income, and victimized by ladinos. One major obstacle to betterment has been the rapid population increase in the rural regions. The Indian population began to rise in the latter part of the seventeenth century, when the native peoples achieved a degree of immunity to Eurasian diseases. The marked rise in the last few decades has been fueled in part by the very medical and sanitary projects introduced by the INI programs. With improved prenatal and delivery care, baby and child clinics, vaccination, and greater cleanliness, far fewer babies die, and far more grow up to have more babies. (However, contraception is slowly gaining popularity.) The increased populations press heavily upon resources, reducing land per capita to less-than-adequate ratios, diverting development funds into short-term alleviation channels, and driving hundreds of thousands into urban labor markets unable to utilize them. Additional thousands annually seek work in the United States, legally or illegally. Others see the tremendous barriers to achieving their ideals in the national economy and choose to abandon all effort, reverting to a simpler life style in the jungle or mountains. Thus, the INI can count many small victories, many successful local projects, but it has not integrated the Indians into regional socioeconomic systems, it has not created political strength for the indigenes, and it has disappointed hundreds of thousands whose perhaps unrealistic hopes for a more comfortable, not merely less miserable, life have been frustrated.

Another story lies underneath the apparent weakness of government efforts in behalf of Indian communities. Typical of Third World nations, population increase seems to tear at Mexico's construction of a viable economy benefiting all classes. Huge debts to the major industrial powers eat up whatever profits Mexico earns in world trade, and poor citizens desperate for a living work at cut-rate wages. Tourists are appalled at the slums around cities and the stark simplicity of rural villages. Careful examination of census records and descriptions of earlier decades reveals a less discouraging picture. By the 1980s, a substantial number of schoolteachers and local businesspeople have come from poor families, many of them Indian. A study of highland Tarascan communities displaced by the new volcano Parícutin in the late

1940s showed that 40 percent of the villagers' grandchildren were middle-class skilled workers, professionals, or advanced students. Only one community preserves its markedly Tarascan customs and speech, and that one earns most of its income by attracting tourists. Throughout Mexico, traditional Indian villages are home to families with some members living in cities or in the United States. Villagers take modern buses and trucks to utilize city markets, purchasing clothing, radios, and small gas or kerosene stoves. Soccer, bottled beer and soft drinks, comic books and photo novels are as common in the Indian villages as tortillas. Urban relatives drive back to join in picturesque village fiestas and eventually to invest in a comfortable retirement home. Poverty is real, middle-class amenities beyond the means of millions, yet social mobility is also real, and the Indian heritages more and more are seen in celebrations rather than imposed by circumstance.

In 1521, over a hundred complex, class-structured Indian nations, and many smaller independent groups, occupied Mexico. The rebellion against the Aztecs led by Cortés changed the balance of power so that no Indian nation was able to forge another empire. Instead, the Spaniards continued the campaigns the Aztecs and others had been pursuing against the weaker or more remote nations, and over the succeeding three centuries gradually brought all the peoples between the Río Grande del Norte (on the Texas border) and Guatemala under Mexican dominion. The massive mortality from Eurasian diseases inadvertently introduced by the Spanish and their servants robbed the Indians of much of their leadership and talent, and fostered the reduction of the mass of the people to peons. The few surviving nobility either lost their estates or married into the Spanish elite, ceasing to identify themselves as Indian. By the nineteenth century, what the conquistadores had assumed would be a multitude of Indian republics interspersed with Spanish estates had become only thousands of primitive villages, their inhabitants cut off from participation as citizens in Mexican society. The premature reforms of Benito Juárez established goals for humanitarians, but were aborted by the conscienceless acts of the dictator Díaz. The twentieth century has been the era of the unfolding of the revolution, which has made enfranchisement and economic viability of the Indians into principles espoused by every government but so far fully realized by none. A fair summary would be that everything has been dreamed, much has been programmed, something has been accomplished, but little that is revolutionary has been effected. Still, there has been a real amelioration of conditions, a real, if inadequate, opening of educational and economic opportunities, and a spread of genuine concern over the plight of the country's indigenous peoples.

The sincere pride of Mexicans of all classes in their nation's pre-Hispanic heritage, symbolized in the magnificence of the National Museum of Anthropology in Mexico City, has been undermining the caste barriers. Gamio's goal of integration without destruction of the Indian cultures seems possible, though poverty cannot be wiped out overnight.

SUMMARY

When mammoths and other large herd game became extinct in Mexico at the end of the Pleistocene Ice Age, the human inhabitants of this southernmost section of North America scheduled their economies around deer and rabbit hunting, the collection of seasonal harvests of certain wild plants, and the planting of small supplementary crops of squash, maize, and gourds. Gradually, over five thousand years, selective breeding of maize and the addition of new cultigens, including beans, increased the yields and reliability of cultivated plants, until by the second millennium B.C. they had become the staples of the economy, and societies in many areas of Mexico had shifted to sedentary villages beside farm fields in place of seasonal camps.

The Preclassic period, from approximately 1500 B.C. to around A.D. 1, saw the appearance of the first urban communities in Mexico. The Olmecs of the tropical Gulf of Mexico region built several imposing centers of temples and palaces on artificial acropoli, and created the first great art in the form of monumental stone sculptures. Other regions of Mexico participated in the extensive trade of this period. The decline of the Olmec, about 400 B.C., ushered in the Late Preclassic (Protoclassic) period, when two major cultural traditions became clearly evident in Mesoamerica, the Mexican in the western half and the Mayan in the eastern half.

The Classic period covered most of the first millennium A.D. In western Mexico, the city of Teotihuacán in the Valley of Mexico dominated trade, but other nations such as Monte Albán, in Oaxaca, and Tajín, in Veracruz, also built magnificent capitals. In eastern Mexico, not one Maya state seems to have dominated; instead there were several fine cities, each with its own variation of the great Mayan art style. Teotihuacán was destroyed about A.D. 800, and the leading Maya states, in southern Yucatán, seem to have collapsed about a century later, although lesser Maya cities seem to have continued without break.

The Postclassic period lasted from about A.D. 1000 to the Spanish conquests in the sixteenth century. Toltecs built up an empire with a capital just north of the Valley of Mexico, at Tula, and outposts as far as Chichén Itzá in Mayan Yucatán. Toltec power lasted only about two centuries, and was followed in the Valley of Mexico region by battles between contending smaller nations that finally led to the emergence of the Aztecs in A.D. 1440 as the dominant state. In other regions, independent nations pursued their businesses. The most impressive of the states in western Mexico during the second half of the Postclassic period was probably Cholula in Puebla, although by the time Cortés invaded, the Aztec capital of Tenochtitlán was a dazzling city.

Cortés conquered the Aztecs with the aid of armies from Cholula and other Indian nations already engaged in fighting Aztec imperialism. The Spanish incursion might not have changed Mexico so radically had it not brought European diseases that decimated the Mexican population. For three centuries, the Mexican Indian communities, many resettled to be better administered by Spanish colonial officials, labored for an elite that was largely of Spanish descent, although it included some offspring of Indian nobles who had married Spaniards following the Conquest. There was a brief attempt at reform in 1855, when the Zapotec Indian Benito Juárez achieved the presidency, but in 1876 the dictator Porfirio Díaz took over, and although of part Indian heritage, ruthlessly put down efforts by Indians to gain economic or political influence.

During the twentieth century, Mexican governments have more or less promoted a policy of *indigenismo*, studying and to a limited degree encouraging Mexican Indian traditions, but attempting to integrate Indian communities into the national economy and political structure, which is seen to be the only way the growing Indian populations can obtain a better standard of living. Since there are hundreds of distinct native peoples in Mexico, in environments ranging from tropical jungles to high mountain forests, a variety of programs have had to be developed, and progress toward the national goal of economic and educational opportunities open to all has been slow, though the oppression felt by most Indians has been ameliorated. Mexico did not experience in the 1970s the open rebellions by Indians that attracted public attention in the United States and Canada.

RECOMMENDED READING

Wauchope, R., ed. 1964 *Handbook of Middle American Indians*, Austin: University of Texas Press. Standard reference work, although out-of-date in many details and sometimes in perspective.

Archaeology:

Coe, Michael D. *Mexico* (Praeger); *The Maya* (Thames and Hudson). Concise and readable.

Willey, Gordon R. 1966 *An Introduction to American Archaeology*, Vol.1. Englewood Cliffs, N.J.: Prentice-Hall. Best-illustrated general overview of North American including Mesoamerican prehistory. Details out-of-date but no later publication covers so much with such excellent illustrations.

Pre-Columbian Art of Mesoamerica:

Covarrubias, Miguel. 1957 *Indian Art of Mexico and Central America*. New York: Alfred A. Knopf.

Easby, E.K. and J.F. Scott. 1970 *Before Cortés*. New York: Metropolitan Museum of Art.

Modern Mexican Indians:

Case Studies in Cultural Anthropology (series). Fort Worth: Holt, Rinehart and Winston, and Prospect Heights, Ill.: Waveland Press. [Waveland reissues many of the Case Studies series; the Pi-Sunyer and Turner books listed were out-of-print in 1990].

Chiñas, Beverly. *The Isthmus Zapotecs: Women's Roles in Cultural Context*. Prospect Heights, Ill.: Waveland Press.

Kearney, Michael. *The Winds of Ixtepeji*. Prospect Heights, Ill.: Waveland Press. (Zapotec of Oaxaca.)

Lewis, Oscar. *Tepoztlán: Village in Mexico*. Fort Worth: Holt, Rinehart and Winston. (Nahuat near the Valley of Mexico.)

Pi-Sunyer, Oriol. *Zamora: Change and Continuity in a Mexican Town*. Fort Worth: Holt, Rinehart and Winston. (Michoacán.)

Turner, Paul. *The Highland Chontal*. Fort Worth: Holt, Rinehart and Winston. (Chiapas Maya.)

Vogt, Evon. *The Zinacantecos of Mexico*. Fort Worth: Holt, Rinehart and Winston. (Highland Maya in Chiapas.)

Kintz, Ellen R. *Life Under the Tropical Canopy*. Fort Worth: Holt, Rinehart and Winston. (Yucatec Maya.)

Other publishers:

Foster, George M. 1967 *Tzintzuntzan: Mexican Peasants in a Changing World*. Prospect Heights, Ill.: Waveland Press. A shorter companion study is by Cynthia Nelson, *The Waiting Village: Social Change in Rural Mexico* (Boston: Little, Brown, 1964). Both studies deal with Tarascan communities near Lake Pátzcuaro; the Foster study is a classic view now controversial.

Friedlander, Judith. 1976 *Being Indian in Hueyapan: A Study of Forced Identity in Contemporary Mexico*. New York: St. Martin's Press. Particularly valuable in contrasting life in a Nahuat-speaking village in Morelos, where in Friedlander's view the label *indio* denotes an exploited low class, and the romantic version of *indio* is cherished by a group of middle-class mestizo professional people in Mexico City who seek to revive Aztec culture.

Madsen, William 1960 *The Virgin's Children*. New York: Greenwood Press. A classic study of Valley of Mexico Nahuatl-speaking rural Indians.

Wolf, Eric 1959 *Sons of the Shaking Earth*. Chicago: University of Chicago Press. A well-written synthesis of Indian-derived Mexican culture.

Students interested in the political relevance of anthropology should read:

Oscar Lewis's several books, including *Pedro Martínez: A Mexican Peasant and His Family* (New York: Random House, 1964); *Life in a Mexican Village: Tepoztlán Restudied* (Urbana: University of Illinois Press, 1951); and the famous *The Children of Sánchez* (New York: Random House, 1961), about life in the slums of Mexico City. Lewis's pessimistic, Marxist analyses were meant to awaken social consciences to the desperation of Mexico's lowest class. He particularly tried to counter the complacency he felt was engendered by earlier anthropologists' works, especially those of Robert Redfield in *Tepoztlán: A Mexican Village: A Study of Folk Life* (Chicago: University of Chicago Press, 1930), the same village Lewis studied a generation later; *Chan Kom, A Maya Village* (Washington, D.C.: Carnegie Institution of Washington, 1934); and *A Village That Chose Progress: Chan Kom Revisited*. (Chicago: University of Chicago Press, 1955).

Elsie Clews Parsons, ed. *American Indian Life*. Lincoln: University of Nebraska Press, 1967 (1922) Bison Books. Includes three dramatic, imaginative, and ethnographically sound reconstructions of Mexican Indian life (Maya, Aztec, and Northwestern Sierra Tepecano) by pioneer anthropologists. (Tozzer's story of Chichén Itzá rivalries includes the error that Teotihuacán was Toltec, but the story is fun.)

SOURCES FOR THE FIRST EDITION

Symposia:

Adams, Richard E.W., ed. 1977 *The Origins of Maya Civilization*. Albuquerque: University of New Mexico Press.

Aveni, Anthony, ed. 1975 *Archaeoastronomy in Pre-Columbian America*. Austin: University of Texas Press.

Benson, Elizabeth P., ed. 1968 *Dumbarton Oaks Conference on the Olmec*. Washington, D.C.: Dumbarton Oaks Research Library and Collections.

———— 1975. *Death and the Afterlife in Pre-Columbian America*. Washington, D.C.: Dumbarton Oaks Research Library and Collections.

Congrès International Des Americanistes, XLIIe (1976). 1979 *Prehistoric Mesoamerica,* Volume VIII. Paris: Société des Americanistes, Musée de l'Homme.

Culbert, T. Patrick, ed. 1973 *The Classic Maya Collapse*. Albuquerque: University of New Mexico Press.

Edmondson, Munro, ed. 1974 *Sixteenth-Century Mexico: The Works of Sahagún*. Albuquerque: University of New Mexico Press.

Flannery, Kent V. 1976 *The Early Mesoamerican Village*. New York: Academic Press.

Hammond, Norman, ed. 1974 *Mesoamerican Archaeology: New Approaches*. London: Duckworth.

Kehoe, Alice B., organizer. Early Civilizations of Asia and Mesoamerica, unpublished conference, Mexico, June 1977 (sponsored by the Wenner-Gren Foundation and the Ford Foundation). In this chapter I have drawn upon the presentations and discussion of C. Earle Smith, Jr., James Schoenwetter, Paul Tolstoy, Norman Hammond, David Kelley, Gordon Whittaker, Gordon Ekholm, Evelyn Rattray, Merle Greene Robertson, Doris Heyden, Yólotl González Torres, and Peter and Jill Leslie Furst.

Paddock, John, ed. 1970 *Ancient Oaxaca* (2nd ed.). Stanford, Calif.: Stanford University Press.

Wolf, Eric, ed. 1976 *The Valley of Mexico*. Albuquerque: University of New Mexico Press.

Books and Articles not in Symposia:

Badner, Mino 1971 *A Possible Focus of Andean Artistic Influence in Mesoamerica*. Washington, D.C.: Dumbarton Oaks Research Library and Collections (Studies in Pre-Columbian Art and Archeology, No. 9).

Ballesteros-Gaibrois, Manuel and Julia Ulloa Suarez. 1961 *Indigenismo Americano*. Madrid: Ediciones Cultural Hispanica.

Bernal, Ignacio. 1963 *Mexico before Cortez*. Garden City, N.Y.: Doubleday.

———— 1963 *Teotihuacán*. Mexico: Instituto Nacional de Antropología e Historia.

Comas, Juan. 1953 *Ensayos Sobre Indigenismo*. Mexico: Instituto Indigenista Interamericano.

Cheetham, Nicolas. 1974 *New Spain*. London: Victor Gollancz.

Díaz Del Castillo, Bernal. 1800 (London) *The True History of the Conquest of Mexico*. In Harold E. Driver (ed.). *The Americas on the Eve of Discovery*. Englewood Cliffs, N.J.: Prentice-Hall, pp. 112–133.

Dobyns, Henry F. 1966 An Appraisal of Techniques [of Estimating Aboriginal American Population] with a New Hemispheric Estimate. *Current Anthropology* 7:395–416; comments, 425–445.

Drucker, Philip. 1952 *La Venta, Tabasco*. Washington, D.C.: Smithsonian Institution, Bureau of American Ethnology, Bulletin 153.

Drucker, Philip, Robert F. Heizer, and Robert J. Squier. 1959 *Excavations at La Venta, Tabasco, 1955*. Washington, D.C.: Smithsonian Institution, Bureau of American Ethnology, Bulletin 170.

Flannery, Kent V. 1968 Archeological Systems Theory and Early Mesoamerica. In *Anthropological Archaeology in the Americas*. Washington, D.C.: Anthropological Society of Washington.

Gibson, Charles. 1964 *The Aztecs under Spanish Rule*. Stanford, Calif.: Stanford University Press.

Grove, David B. 1976 Chalcatzingo. Paper given at the forty-first annual meeting of the Society for American Archaeology, St. Louis, 1975.

¿Ha Fracasado el Indigenismo? 1971 Mexico: Secretaria de Educación Pública.

Hammond, Norman. 1977 The Earliest Maya. *Scientific American* 236:116–133.

Heath, Shirley Brice. 1972 *Telling Tongues*. New York: Teachers College Press.

Heyden, Doris. 1975 An Interpretation of the Cave Underneath the Pyramid of the Sun in Teotihuacán, Mexico. *American Antiquity* 40:131–147.

Kehoe, Alice B. 1979 The Sacred Heart. *American Ethnologist* 6:763–771.

Kelley, David H. 1962 Glyphic Evidence for a Dynastic Sequence at Quirigua, Guatemala. *American Antiquity* 27:323–335.

———— 1976 *Deciphering the Maya Script*. Austin: University of Texas Press.

Léon-Portilla, Miguel. 1963 *Aztec Thought and Culture*, trans. J.E. Davis. Norman: University of Oklahoma Press.

———— 1969. *Pre-Columbian Literatures of Mexico*,
trans. G. Lobanov and Miguel Léon-Portilla. Norman: University of Oklahoma Press.

MacNeish, Richard S. 1964 The Origins of New World Civilization. *Scientific American* 211:29–37.

Madsen, William. 1967 *Christo-Paganism*. New Orleans: Tulane University, Middle American Research Institute, Publication 19.

Millon, Clara. 1973 Painting, Writing, and Polity in Teotihuacán, Mexico. *American Antiquity* 38:294–314.

Millon, René F. 1955 Trade, Tree Cultivation, and the Development of Private Property in Land. *American Anthropologist* 57:698–712.

———— 1967. Teotihuacán. *Scientific American* 216:38–48.

Modiano, Nancy. 1973 *Indian Education in the Chiapas Highlands*. New York: Holt, Rinehart, and Winston.

Mountjoy, Joseph B. 1969 *On the Origin of West Mexican Metallurgy*. Carbondale: Southern Illinois University, Research Records.

Parsons, Lee A. 1969 *Bilbao, Guatemala*, vol. 2. Milwaukee: Milwaukee Public Museum, Publications in Anthropology 12.

Parsons, Lee A. and Barbara J. Price. 1971 *Mesoamerican Trade and Its Role in the Emergence of Civilization*. Berkeley: University of California Archaeological Research Facility, No. 11.

Pasztory, Esther. 1972 The Gods of Teotihuacán. *Atti del XL Congresso Internazionale degli Americanisti*, Genoa, vol. 1, pp. 147–159.

Pendergast, David M. 1971 Evidence of Early Teotihuacán-Lowland Maya Contact at Altun Ha. *American Antiquity* 36:455–460.

Proskouriakoff, Tatiana. 1960 Historical Implications of a Pattern of Dates at Piedras Negras, Guatemala. *American Antiquity* 25:454–475.

———— 1961. The Lords of the Maya Realm. In John A. Graham (ed.). *Ancient Mesoamerica*. Palo Alto: Peek Publications.

Puleston, Dennis E. 1973 The Manipulation of Environmental Variables by Human Populations and Significant Thresholds. Paper given at the thirty-eighth annual meeting of the Society for American Archaeology, San Francisco, 1973.

Sahagún, Bernardino de. 1951 *Florentine Codex: General History of the Things of New Spain*, trans. Arthur J.O. Anderson and Charles E. Dibble. Albuquerque: School of American Research Monograph 14.

Schoenwetter, James. 1974 Pollen Records of Guila Naquitz Cave. *American Antiquity* 39:292–303.

Stirling, Matthew W. 1943 *Stone Monuments of Southern Mexico*. Washington, D.C.: Smithsonian Institution, Bureau of American Ethnology, Bulletin 138.

Turner, John Kenneth. 1969 (1911) *Barbarous Mexico*. Austin: University of Texas Press.

Voegelin, C.F. and F.M. Voegelin. 1965 Languages of the World: Native America, Fascicle 2. *Anthropological Linguistics 7* (7). Bloomington: Indiana University.

ADDITIONAL SOURCES FOR THE SECOND EDITION

American Antiquity, "Current Research" through vol. 55 no. 4 (October 1990).

Ashmore, Wendy, ed. 1981 *Lowland Maya Settlement Patterns*. Albuquerque: University of New Mexico Press.

Aveni, A. F., E. E. Calnek, and H. Hartung. 1988 Myth, Environment, and the Orientation of the Templo Mayor of Tenochtitlán. *American Antiquity* 53(2):287–309.

Aveni, Anthony, and Horst Hartung. 1986 *Maya City Planning and the Calendar*. Philadelphia: American Philosophical Society.

Benz, Bruce F., and Hugh H. Iltis. 1990 Studies in Archaeological Maize I: The "Wild" Maize from San Marcos Cave Reexamined. *American Antiquity* 55(3):500–511.

Berdan, Frances R. 1982 *The Aztecs of Central Mexico*. New York: Holt, Rinehart and Winston.

Berrin, Kathleen, ed. 1988 *Feathered Serpents and Flowering Trees*. San Francisco: The Fine Arts Museums.

Boone, Elizabeth Hill, ed. 1987 *The Aztec Templo Mayor*. Washington, D.C.: Dumbarton Oaks Research Library and Collections.

Campbell, Lyle, and Marianne Mithun, eds. 1979 *The Languages of Native America*. Austin: University of Texas Press.

Campbell, Lyle, and Terrence Kaufman. 1985 Mayan Linguistics: Where Are We Now? In B. J. Siegel, A. R. Beals, S. A. Tyler (eds.). *Annual Review of Anthropology* 14. Palo Alto: Stanford University Press, pp. 187–198.

Carrasco, David. 1982 *Quetzalcóatl and the Irony of Empire*. Chicago: University of Chicago Press.

Castile, George Pierre, and Gilbert Kushner, eds. 1981 *Persistent Peoples*. Tucson: University of Arizona Press.

Chance, John K. 1989 *Conquest of the Sierra*. Norman: University of Oklahoma Press.

Chase, Arlen F., and Prudence M. Rice, eds. 1985 *The Lowland Maya Postclassic*. Austin: University of Texas Press.

Chase, Diane Z., and Arlen F. Chase. 1982 Yucatec Influence in Terminal Classic Northern Belize. *American Antiquity* 47(3):596–614.

Chippindale, Christopher, Norman Hammond, and Jeremy A. Sabloff, eds. 1988 The Archaeology of Maya Decipherment. *Antiquity* 62 (234): 119–172.

Coe, Michael D. 1987 *The Maya* (4th ed., rev.). London: Thames and Hudson.

Collier, George A., Renato I. Rosaldo, and John D. Wirth, eds. 1982 *The Inca and Aztec States, 1400–1800*. New York: Academic Press.

Conrad, Geoffrey W., and Arthur A. Demarest. 1984 *Religion and Empire: The Dynamics of Aztec and Inca Expansionism*. Cambridge, England: Cambridge University Press.

Crumrine, N. Ross, and Phil C. Weigand, eds. 1987 *Ejidos and Regions of Refuge in Northwestern Mexico*. Tucson: Anthropological Papers of the University of Arizona, no. 46.

Diehl, Richard A., and Janet Catherine Berlo, eds. 1989 *Mesoamerica After the Decline of Teotihuacán A.D. 700–900*. Washington, D.C.: Dumbarton Oaks Research Library and Collections.

Doolittle, William E. 1990 *Canal Irrigation in Prehistoric Mexico*. Austin: University of Texas Press.

Farnsworth, Paul, James E. Brady, Michael J. DeNiro, and Richard S. MacNeish. 1985 A Re-evaluation of the Isotopic and Archaeological Reconstructions of Diet in the Tehuacán Valley. *American Antiquity* 50(1):102–116.

Farriss, Nancy M. 1984 *Maya Society Under Colonial Rule*. Princeton: Princeton University Press.

Folan, William J., ed. 1985 *Contributions to the Archaeology and Ethnohistory of Greater Mesoamerica*. Carbondale: Southern Illinois University Press.

Foster, Michael, and Phil C. Weigand, eds. 1985 *The Archaeology of Western and Northwestern Mesoamerica*. Boulder: Westview Press.

Fox, John W. 1989 On the Rise and Fll of *Tuláns* and

Maya Segmentary States. *American Anthropologist* 91(3):656–681.

Freidel, David A., and Linda Schele. 1988 Kingship in the Late Preclassic Maya Lowlands: The Instruments and Places of Ritual Power. *American Anthropologist* 90(3):547–567.

Grove,David C. 1984 *Chalcatzingo*. London: Thames and Hudson.

Harvey, H. R., and Hanns J. Prem, eds. 1983 *Explorations in Ethnohistory: Indians of Central Mexico in the Sixteenth Century*. Albuquerque: University of New Mexico Press.

Healan, Dan M., ed. 1989 *Tula of the Toltecs*. Iowa City: University of Iowa Press.

Hinton, Thomas B., and Phil C. Weigand, eds. 1981 *Themes of Indigenous Acculturation in Northwest Mexico*. Tucson: Anthropological Papers of the University of Arizona, no. 38.

Hirth, Kenneth G., ed. 1984 *Trade and Exchange in Early Mesoamerica*. Albuquerque: University of New Mexico Press.

Hosler, Dorothy 1988 Ancient West Mexican Metallurgy: South and Central American Origins and West Mexican Transformations. *American Anthropologist* 90(4):832–855.

Lincoln, Charles Edward. 1990 Ethnicity and Social Organization at Chichén Itzá, Yucatán, Mexico. Doctoral dissertation, Department of Anthropology, Harvard University.

McAnany, Patricia A., and Barry L. Isaac, eds. 1989 *Prehistoric Maya Economies of Belize*. Greenwich Conn.: JAI Press, Research in Economic Anthropology, Supplement 4.

McVicker, Donald. 1985 The "Mayanized" Mexicans. *American Antiquity* 50(1):82–101.

Nations, James D., and Ronald B. Nigh 1980 The Evolutionary Potential of Lacandon Maya Sustained-yield Tropical Forest Agriculture. *Journal of Anthropological Research* 36(1):1–30.

O'Connor, Mary I. 1989 *Descendants of Totoliguoqui: Ethnicity and Economics in the Mayo Valley*. Berkeley: University of California Publications in Anthropology, vol. 19.

Papousek, Dick A. 1981 *The Peasant-Potters of Los Pueblos*. Assen (Netherlands): Van Gorcum.

Porter, James B. 1989 Olmec Colossal Heads as Recarved Thrones. *Res* 17/18:22–29.

Riley, Carroll L. 1987 *The Frontier People* (rev. ed.). Albuquerque: University of New Mexico Press.

Sabloff, Jeremy A. 1990 *The New Archaeology and the Ancient Maya*. New York: W. H. Freeman.

Sabloff, Jeremy A., and E. Wyllys Andrews V, eds. 1986 *Late Lowland Maya Civilization*. Albuquerque: University of New Mexico Press.

Sanders, William T., and David Webster. 1988 The Mesoamerican Urban Tradition. *American Anthropologist* 90(3):521–546.

Scarborough, Vernon L. 1983 A Preclassic Maya Water System. *American Antiquity* 48(4):720–744.

Sharer, Robert J., and David C. Grove, eds. 1989 *Regional Perspectives on the Olmec*. Cambridge: Cambridge University Press.

Siemens, Alfred H. 1983 Oriented Raised Fields in Central Veracruz. *American Antiquity* 48(1):85–102.

Stothert, Karen E. 1985 The Preceramic Las Vegas Culture of Coastal Ecuador. *American Antiquity* 50(3):613–627.

Sugiyama, Saburo. 1989 Burials Dedicated to the Old Temple of Quetzalcóatl at Teotihuacán, Mexico. *American Antiquity* 54(1):85–106.

Taube, Karl A. 1989 The Maize Tamale in Classic Maya Diet, Epigraphy, and Art. *American Antiquity* 54(1):31–51.

Wasserstrom, Robert. 1983 *Class and Society in Central Chiapas*. Berkeley: University of California Press.

Weigand, Phil C., and Gretchen Gwynne, eds. 1982 Mining and Mining Techniques in Ancient Mesoamerica. *Anthropology* VI(1–2) (Special Issue).

Wilkinson, Richard G., and Richard J. Norelli. 1981 A Biocultural Analysis of Social Organization at Monte Albán. *American Antiquity* 46(4):743–758.

Willey, Gordon R., and Peter Mathews, eds. 1985 A Consideration of the Early Classic Period in the Maya Lowlands. Albany: Institute for Mesoamerican Studies, SUNY-Albany, Publication No. 10.

3

THE GREATER SOUTHWEST

The Greater Southwest, from southern Colorado and southeastern California south through Arizona and New Mexico into northwestern Mexico, includes four indigenous cultural traditions: the well-known Pueblos; the 'O'odham (Pima and Papago) farmers and their linguistic relatives in northern Mexico; the Yuman peoples of the Colorado River; and the late migrant Navajo and Apache. The three former traditions developed within the Southwest from Archaic bases; the Navajo and Apache seem to have moved into the Southwest only a century or so before the first European explorers there.

Rugged extremes characterize the Southwest as a natural region. Its backbone is the Western Cordillera, the Rocky Mountains passing through the heart of the Southwest and down through Mexico, where the range becomes known as the Sierra Madre Occidental. Along the Sierra Madre, using its sharp ridges and sheer, tortuous canyons as protection against soldiers, live a series of Aztecan-speaking farmers and hunters of whom the 'O'odham are the northern representatives. These latter have adapted to a second type of Southwestern ecology: the desert, comprising low, relatively flat lands crossed by several rivers rising from the mountain snows but, because of high evaporation under the heat developed at these low elevations, supporting only a variety of cactuses and other widely spaced water-retentive plants. The western border of the Southwest is formed by the lower reaches of the Colorado River and its tributaries, particularly the Gila River. The mouth of the Colorado forms a delta at the head of the Gulf of California. Although the whole region is desert, farming is possible in the flood plains of the rivers. One can thus see sharp contrasts between cultivated fields and cottonwood stands following the streams, and tan-colored expanses of bare land dotted with sparse grasses, creosote bushes, mesquite, and cactuses. On the eastern portion of the Southwest, the broad valley of the Río Grande is essentially a similar ribbon oasis in a dry land, but higher elevation provides somewhat denser vegetation on its edges, and tree-covered mountains are visible from much of the valley. The northern sector

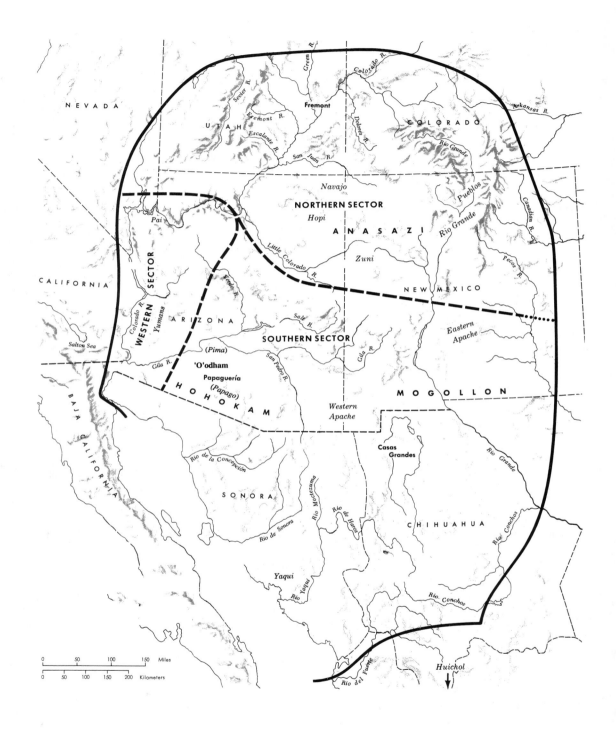

Map 4 The Greater Southwest

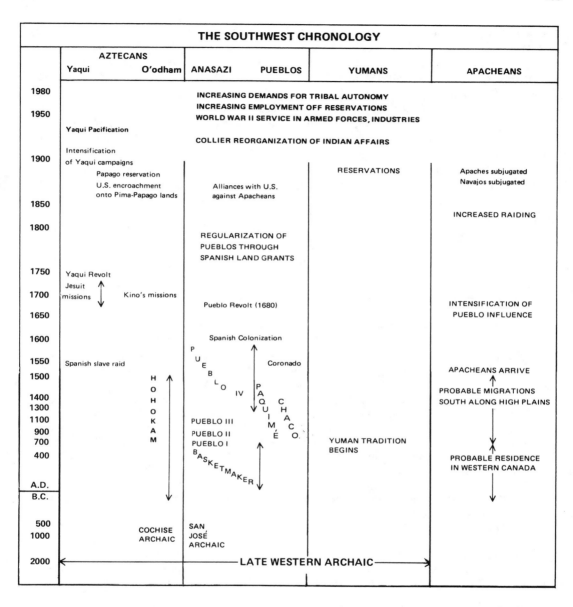

THE SOUTHWEST CHRONOLOGY

	AZTECANS		ANASAZI	PUEBLOS	YUMANS	APACHEANS
	Yaqui	O'odham				

1980 / 1950: INCREASING DEMANDS FOR TRIBAL AUTONOMY / INCREASING EMPLOYMENT OFF RESERVATIONS / WORLD WAR II SERVICE IN ARMED FORCES, INDUSTRIES

Yaqui Pacification

COLLIER REORGANIZATION OF INDIAN AFFAIRS

Intensification

1900 of Yaqui campaigns

RESERVATIONS — Apaches subjugated / Navajos subjugated

Papago reservation
U.S. encroachment — Alliances with U.S. against Apacheans
onto Pima-Papago lands

1850 — INCREASED RAIDING

1800 — REGULARIZATION OF PUEBLOS THROUGH SPANISH LAND GRANTS

1750 Yaqui Revolt

Jesuit
1700 missions — Kino's missions — INTENSIFICATION OF PUEBLO INFLUENCE

Pueblo Revolt (1680)

1650

1600 — Spanish Colonization

1550 Spanish slave raid — Coronado — APACHEANS ARRIVE

1500 — HOHOKAM — PROBABLE MIGRATIONS SOUTH ALONG HIGH PLAINS

1400 / 1300 / 1100 / 900 / 700 / 400 — PUEBLO III / PUEBLO II / PUEBLO I / BASKETMAKER — YUMAN TRADITION BEGINS — PROBABLE RESIDENCE IN WESTERN CANADA

A.D. / B.C.

500 / 1000 COCHISE ARCHAIC — SAN JOSÉ ARCHAIC

2000 ←——— LATE WESTERN ARCHAIC ———→

of the Southwest is a plateau high enough to share with the mountains both savanna meadows and pine forests. The culture area as a whole, then, is unusually diverse ecologically, and in its gamut from desert to forested mountains it is similar to, and indeed an extension of, western Mexico

SECTION 1: THE SOUTHERN SECTOR

The southern sector of the Greater Southwest is the homeland of the Uto-Aztecan-speaking groups of southern Arizona and the adjacent Mexican state of Sonora. Of these, the Arizona 'O'odham

(Papago and Upper Pima, or Pima Alto), and Yaqui are United States citizens, while the Cáhita peoples (Yaqui, Mayo, and Tehueco), the Tepehuan and related Tepecano, the Lower Pima (Pima Bajo), the Rarámuri ("Tarahumara," in the state of Chihuahua), and, south of Sonora, the Cora and Huichol are all citizens of Mexico, residing in four of Mexico's "indigenous zones" (see p. 93). Historically, a group called the Opata spoke a language related to 'O'odham and occupied the mountains between the Tóhono 'O'odham and Lower Pima, but the Opata language ceased to be spoken by the mid-twentieth century, and the Opata are no longer a political entity.

These Uto-Aztecans constitute a block of linguistically and culturally related peoples who dominate northwestern Mexico. A nonrelated group, the Seri, whose language has not been securely linked to any of the major native American language families, lives in the desert of the central Sonoran coast, perhaps pushed into this marginal habitat by the larger population block of Uto-Aztecans. The dominant bloc is, of course, linguistically related to the Nahuatl-speaking Aztec proper, the most powerful nation of Mexico at the time of Spanish contact. At the opposite end of the continuous band of Uto-Aztecan peoples are the Utes of Nevada, whose Great Basin desert environment restricted population concentrations and thereby fragmented their political power. Uto-Aztecan speakers range from some of the most unpretentious peoples of North America to the conquering Aztecs of the contact period's most complex empire. The northwestern Mexico–southern Arizona

THE HUICHOL

The ten thousand Huichol living in remote, roadless mountain valleys in the Sierra Madre of western Mexico have preserved much of the pre-Spanish Aztecan culture. They live in extended-family homesteads (*rancherías*) wherever in the mountains they can cultivate—with the ancient digging stick instead of the plow—their plots of maize, beans, and squashes. The families in each vicinity gather periodically for religious festivals and maintain a building ("temple") for their holy images. Huichol have accepted, from Spanish colonists and missionaries, horses and other livestock, metal tools, coffee, sugar, fruit trees, modified dress styles, and violins, which are in a sense an elaboration on the pre-Spanish musical bow. Their religion superficially resembles folk Catholicism—for example, it includes festivals at Christmas and Easter—but the Christian symbols are a veneer on a persisting northwest Aztecan religion. Franciscan missionaries renewing in 1953, after nearly two centuries' lapse, their efforts in the Huichol community of Guadalupe Ocotán found the people venerating the Virgin of Guadalupe in their church, offering her *muviéri* (ceremonial arrows), votive gourds, and the blood of a sacrificed deer or bull, and lighting within the church a fire representing Tatewarí, Old Grandfather Fire. The Franciscans tried to substitute a new image of Guadalupe, with more orthodox ritual, but in the end had to accept two Guadalupes in the church, the Huichols' (identified by many as Mother of the Eagles), and the Mexican.

"To find our life," as they phrase it, Huichols make a pilgrimage 300 miles through the mountains to the high desert in northwest San Luis Potosí. On this mountain-bordered plateau the Huichol see an ancient and eternal paradise. Peter Furst, an anthropologist who accompanied Huichol on two pilgrimages, records that when his party first arrived, "Ramón [the leader] had taken us by the hand and pointed out everything that made survival and even a reasonably good life possible—edible leaves and seeds and roots, barrel cactus full of thirst-quenching liquids, herbs good for wounds and sickness of all kinds (peyote itself is considered the best medicine of all, effective not only against fatigue but infections and intestinal complaints), and the burrows and lairs of small animals. 'One lives well here,' he said, 'if one has learned well and does not take more than one needs.'"(Furst 1972:170–171).

"Going to find our life"begins in the autumn with the *ranchería* gathered to celebrate the harvest of maize and squash. The spiritual leader, *mara'akáme*, beats a holy drum made of a hollowed oak log covered with a deerskin head and set over burning pitch-pine logs (the heat tunes the drumhead, and the smoke entering and filling the log drum symbolizes the union of male and female). To the beat of the drum, the *mara'akáme* chants the story of the journey to the "Patio of the Grandfathers,"where the peyote cactus grows. Each holy place on the way, each danger spot is enumerated. The children of the *rancheria* listen closely, for their spirits are making the journey as the *mara'akáme* sings: they are hummingbirds, escorted by Elder Brother the Deer. The little flock of children pause by springs (actually in San Luis Potosí) rising from the Rain Mothers, and at last reach their goal, *Miwetuka(me)*, Our Mother, "the one who embraces us,…the one who loves us much." When the children arrive, Our Mother sings, "Now I am content, now I am happy. I will give them life.....Look, my children, I am the one who embraces you. I am the one who gives you your soul." (Furst 1972:150)

Later, during the winter, all the people who wish to make the arduous pilgrimage, in order to gain health, good fortune, peace of mind, or the spiritual experience necessary to become a religious leader, assemble, shed their adult nature by publicly revealing all their sexual experiences, and then as innocent souls are symbolically bound together as knots tied into a cord kept by the *mara'akáme*. After completing in fact the journey earlier flown by the children's spirits, the pilgrims incarnate Tatewarí, Grandfather Fire, by lighting a fire on the edge of the area where they will seek the peyote cactus. They then set off hunting the small, ground-hugging plant that is the physical body of Elder Brother the Deer. The *mara'akáme* first, and then the other men, shoot the first peyote they find with their bows and arrows (some had been playing songs on their bows, to please Deer, as they stalked him). The people sob as the soul of the shot Deer begins to rise to the sky, but the *mara'akáme* presses it back into the cactus, using his hawk-feathered *muviéri* arrow. When Deer's soul has subsided, the *mara'akáme* cuts the cactus out from the ground, taking care to leave the base of the root, which will produce new shoots (hence, Deer never really dies). Next, each pilgrim is given a piece of the cactus to chew, while offerings each has brought are sacrificed by being burnt before the hole in which the cactus grew. The rest of the day is spent in digging peyote until the pilgrims' baskets are full (they will bring the sacramental plant back to their *rancherías* so that those who did not journey may also partake of "our life"). Evening is a joyous celebration of the success of "finding our life,"singing, dancing, and chewing peyote around Tatewarí. Some of the celebrants experience the brilliantly colored visions induced by mescaline, an alkaloid in the cactus. The aim of the pilgrims, and other Huichol who will chew the very bitter cactus at home in festivals, is not to "get high," but to ingest this plant, which demonstrates through the incredibly beautiful "flowers"of the vision that it is indeed the essence of life, both static (plant) and moving (the vision, symbolized by Deer, the largest game animal in the region). The mystic union of the two principal forms of life, born of Mother Earth under Father Sun, makes the innocent pilgrims born again, whether or not they experience a vision.

Leaving the paradise where Elder Brother the Deer browses eternally, the Huichol sing,

We are all the children of,
We are all the sons of,
A brilliantly colored flower,
A flaming flower.
And there is no one,
There is no one,
Who regrets what we are. (Furst 1972:184)

Aztecans are in the middle, physically and politically.

Prehistoric Western Mexico

Western Mexico has been less explored by archaeologists than other regions of the country. The Sierra Madre Occidental is rough terrain, steep slopes and winding, sometimes swampy valleys; the west coast has thick jungles. Traffic normally moved north and south along the coasts from port to port, with river valleys providing routes inland into the Sierra and the Gulf of California giving access to Sonora and the Colorado River system in Arizona. Trade between West Mexico and the Central Highlands connected via the inland corridor linking the Bajío region of Querétaro and Guanajuato, west of Tula and the Valley of Mexico, running northwestward through Zacatecas, Durango, and Chihuahua to New Mexico. This inland corridor was over 2000 km. (1300 miles) long (about as long the total distance between the Valley of Mexico and lower Central America; from Teotihuacán to Kaminaljuyú is about 1700 km., or 1100 miles). When Cortés invaded Central Mexico, the Tarascan kingdom in the West Mexican Highlands opposed the Aztec kingdom and, in turn, Cortés. Western Mexico apparently never was incorporated into Central Mexican empires, and the frontier lay through Jalisco and along the eastern Sierra Occidental foothills.

During the first millennium B.C., Preclassic occupations of western Mexico seem to have centered in the temperate-climate lake basins of eastern Jalisco, around Teuchitlán, and adjacent Michoacán and Guanajuato. Important mineral resources—obsidian, copper ores (including malachite, a blue-green mineral resembling turquoise), gold and silver—can be mined in these highlands, and the lake basins are fertile and easily farmed. Earlier, in the second millennium, villages had constructed building platforms and burial mounds. By the first millennium B.C., towns appeared, with large circular raised plazas around a multilevel circular "pyramid" and broad raised rims on which are built four or eight rectangular, evenly spaced, flat-topped pyramids. (The only comparable circular terraced "pyramid" outside West Mexico is that at Cuicuilco in the Valley of Mexico. Whether there were direct connections between these regions perhaps will never be discovered, since Cuicuilco is buried under Xitle's lava.) Under the West Mexico platforms are chamber tombs entered through shaft tunnels. A wealth of beautiful ceramic vessels and figurines unhappily have attracted commercial art-market looters to the tombs, resulting in these objects scattered to collectors all over the world and knowledge of their original meaning lost.

Continued growth of West Mexican populations in the Classic period of the first millennium A.D. produced denser settlements and larger towns. Teuchitlán on the Santiago River in Jalisco became a ring of towns around Tequila Volcano. Eight to sixteen pyramid platforms are built on the raised rims of the towns' circular plazas, and the towns have ball courts. Probably fifty thousand people lived around the volcano, improving their farms through chinampa-type drained and raised fields along the shallow lake and terraced fields with check dams on the slopes. Trade was extensive, traceable through distinctive, fine-painted ceramics, but no doubt also including the metals, semiprecious stones and obsidians from the region and very likely transshipment of Pacific coastal products. Spondylus oyster shells, in demand for luxury ornaments in Teotihuacán and in Peru, would be one such coastal product. Sea routes incorporated West Mexico with Ecuador and Peru and were the means by which West Mexicans learned metallurgy during the Postclassic era following the fall of Teotihaucán. The Teuchitlán towns (or perhaps we should call them a city encircling the volcanic cone) flourished while Teotihuacán far to the east did, then diminished in the ninth century when Teotihaucán fell. Teuchitlán's culture was distinct from that of Teotihuacán, even though settlements showing strong Teotihuacán influence neighbor the Teuchitlán region; presumably, Teuchitlán traded its products into the Teotihuacán empire through those outposts, and the West Mexican economy reeled when the empire was struck.

Around A.D. 1000, the Teuchitlán region seems to have been invaded by allies of the Toltecs. These invaders may have been the historic Caxcan who held the frontier of Western Mexico against the Spanish for years. Spanish conquistadores described the Caxcans' fortified citadels along the frontier, citadels that were built before Cortés landed. Caxcan towns, with tombs containing a variety of copper implements and ornaments, turquoise, obsidian, and figurines—usually looted before archaeologists could see them—lay below the citadels. Little recognized after the Colonial period, the Caxcan slowly disappeared from history, the last speakers of the language dying at the end of the nineteenth century.

Prehistoric Greater Southwest

North of West Mexico is the huge, arid zone that can be termed, from a United States perspective, the Greater Southwest. This zone runs from Colorado and Utah in the north to Jalisco and Michoacán in the south, and from Baja California in the west through West Texas, Coahuila, and San Luis Potosí in the east, including arid northeasternmost Mexico. Spaniards called this the Gran Chichimeca, the land of the fierce barbarians always threatening the rich civilizations of Central Mexico. The Aztecs had once been Chichimecs, a claim supported by the fact that related Uto-Aztecan languages are spoken from the Aztec domain northwestward through the arid zone. In the Pleistocene epoch, this zone had extensive open grasslands supporting herds of antelope, small camels, deer, ground sloths, and lions and cheetahs. Deer and antelope survived into the Holocene era and their human hunters with them, the humans gradually increasing their reliance on seeds, as evidenced by increases in the numbers of stone seed-grinding metates.

These Archaic people are known as the Cochise. Sites are camps along streams, in the hills at the heads of drainages, and in rockshelters. About twenty-five individuals is the estimated size of Cochise hunting-gathering bands. Dry rockshelter occupations have preserved evidence of the baskets, sandals, and cloth the Cochise wove from wild fibers. Most sites have both chipped- and ground-stone artifacts, including atlatl dart points, knives, scrapers for hides and other instruments for preparing plants such as cactus and yucca, and the stone slab metates with their manos (oval rounded stones held in the hand [mano] to grind corn).

About 1200 B.C., people began planting maize and squash in southern New Mexico. The flour-corn variety they used was bred, perhaps in the Greater Southwest, to grow under arid conditions. No evidence of permanent buildings from this period has been found, although archaeologists now have hundreds of bits of maize kernels and cobs, so it seems the corn was grown to provide a storable grain. This supposition is strengthened by the appearance of storage pits in campsites beginning with this period. Maize, particularly this variety of flour corn, has kernels many times larger, and softer, than the seeds of wild grasses in the arid zone, meaning that the effort of planting and cultivating this maize yielded an abundance of grain and a grain easier to grind than could be obtained from collecting wild seeds.

For the first millennium or so during which Southwesterners planted maize and squash, they continued to shift residence to harvest seasonally abundant wild resources. Archaeologists have looked for their occupations in rockshelters and found packed earth levels indicating fairly regular use of the natural shelters and storage pits, cooking hearths, and, at Cienega Creek in Arizona, a cemetery pit with the remains of at least thirty-six people whose bodies had been cremated and the burned fragments placed in baskets. Because the funeral baskets had been placed into the pit at different times, the cemetery appears to have served a small community for some years.

Shortly after two thousand years ago, that is to say in the Protoclassic period of Mexico, radical changes appeared in the Greater Southwest. By A.D. 300, the zone exhibited a long series of towns from the northern Central Highlands of Mexico, through Querétaro, Guanajuato, Zacatecas, Durango, to Sinaloa and Sonora, Chihuahua, and New Mexico. The craft of pottery was introduced from Mexico, and irrigation agriculture developed. Interestingly, at this time bison hunting was intensified along the northeastern border of the Southwest (New Mexico), perhaps to supply dried meat and hides to the towns.

Along the Sierra eastern foothills in interior Northwestern Mexico (Zacatecas and Durango), villages of rectangular wattle-and-daub, or possibly simply of brush, small houses with low platform mounds appeared in this Protoclassic period. Villagers raised maize, squashes, several kinds of beans, gourds, and cotton in river-valley fields below their homes on adjacent natural terraces or mesa tops. Hunting and wild foods supplemented their crops, and they wove blankets of strips of rabbit skin as well as baskets and cotton cloth. At the same time that settled villages first appear, so

do a few citadel towns along this great trade route. The citadels may have been established to maintain Central Mexico's supplies of turquoise and ornamental Pacific shells, although imports from Central Mexico seem lacking. Although contemporary with each other, the villages are known as Loma San Gabriel culture (and believed to be ancestral to the historic Tepehuan), and the trade-route citadels are termed Chalchihuites culture. More than securing trade was involved in Chalchihuites: at Alta Vista in Zacatecas, the town was not placed for dominating the valley route, but on a low ridge. Its location was chosen to put it right on the Tropic of Cancer, the northernmost point at which the sun at noon seems to reach the zenith of the sky. At the Tropic of Cancer, the sun is at the zenith on only one day, summer solstice. A pair of circles pecked in stone, like those used for surveying at Teotihuacán, on a hill near Alta Vista suggests that Teotihuacán-trained astronomers chose the site and made Alta Vista an observatory. Pillars and walls were constructed to produce dramatic "sun paths"on the equinoxes and solstice. Beautiful, imported painted ceramic vessels at Alta Vista imply ceremonies conducted during these solar events. Under the principal pyramid in the town was a burial crypt with three bodies, older adults, given such precious goods as a conch shell trumpet and a pyrites mirror with painted cloisonné back. To top off the importance of this town, it neighbors a turquoise mine and springs of abundant water—truly a blessed place. Alta Vista and the imposing citadel of La Quemada in western Zacatecas flourished and then were abandoned early in the Postclassic period, between the fall of Teotihuacán and the principal phase of Tula. Halls of columns in La Quemada and neighboring little towns were assumed to link the citadel to the Toltecs, but archaeology shows the popularity of columns in Zacatecas to be earlier than such halls at Tula or Chichén Itzá. The historic Zacatecas Indians were probably the descendants of the population maintaining La Quemada and the great trade route it oversaw.

The valleys of northwestern Mexico were rather densely populated in the early sixteenth century, totaling at least several hundred thousand. Few people lived in the mountains or in the deserts between river valleys. Spanish efforts of conquest began in 1530 with Nuño de Guzmán leading an army that, like Cortés's, included thousands of Indian allies. Guzmán suffered from malaria, and the west coast he invaded harbored hordes of mosquitoes able to serve as vectors for this disease. Typhoid and dysentery also beset Guzmán's army. Eight thousand of his Indian troops died in one epidemic late in 1530. These introduced diseases hit the civilian population as well, and a second hard blow came in 1534 as measles swept in from central Mexico; 130,000 people around Culiacán in Sinaloa were recorded as dying from this one epidemic. Depredations from disease were exacerbated by raids to capture slaves. Irrigation works that for centuries had elaborately channeled water to cultivated fields had to be abandoned for lack of labor to keep them up. Harvests were no longer reliable, and droughts, unseasonable storms, and insect infestations brought widespread hunger, weakening people so that diseases continued to take a heavy toll.

Spanish policy of "reduction" of scattered Indian homesteads into supervised villages reconstituted many Northwestern Indian communities. Families who had fled valley towns to escape slave raiding or because broken irrigation systems turned fields into swamps and bone-dry terraces, were herded into the missions. Life in these missions may not have been radically different from preconquest life for the common people. Much of everyday religion survived through translation into Christian terms, for example the calendar-based cycle of seasonal celebrations of harvests and hunting. Mission villagers had to obey foreign overseers who more or less carried out Spanish policy, where preconquest lords had exercised regional independence; but the work week, half of each given in labor for the overlord in return for paternal provision of subsistence, was much the same. For ordinary men and women, the daily grind and the pleasures of fiestas may not have seemed very changed.

Expulsion of the Jesuits from Mexico in 1767, the outcome of the Spanish monarchy's refusal to agree to Jesuit domination of the mission lands, left the Indian towns free of direct control. The government attempted to restore local autonomy to the Indian towns by chartering them as *comunidades indígenas*, communities holding parcels of land communally. Local non-Indian landowners influenced the allocation of these parcels so that much of the best land remained on private haciendas. Within a few years, as miners and settlers continued migrating into the Northwest from central Mexico, Spaniards and mestizos leased Indian communal lands, especially for winter pasture for cattle, or simply let their herds graze on the Indian land. Because the Indians practised long-fallowing, leaving fields uncultivated for several years to restore fertility, the *comunidades indígenas* appeared to have "extra" land. Letting cattle graze on the fallow fields subverted the restoration of soil fertility in the Indians' marginal agricultural lands. Indians also were pressured to sell their water rights, which often lowered the water table in adjacent sections to below what crops could reach.

The 1910 Mexican Revolution brought reforms that in Northwestern Mexico allowed many Indian *comunidades indígenas* to rebuild their land base as *ejidos*, basically similar to the late-eighteenth-century communal properties. Again, non-Indians with more capital and more political power leased or nibbled at the Indian *ejidos*. Throughout the twentieth century, government and agribusiness enterprises built dams and irrigation systems for commercial crops, even sugarcane, substantially altering large regions. By mid-century, reforms were again demanded. Pedro de Haro, a Huichol, led a campaign against cattle ranchers' inroads that won the Huichol a Presidential Order confirming their titles. Other Northwestern groups, including the Tepecano, Mayo, and Yaqui, mounted similar protests, which by the late 1970s, pitted conservative Indian communities against less-conservative Indians and poor mestizos, all demanding land to live on. Police action against some of the protests killed dozens of people. Politicians were blamed for failing to control, or bring justice to, the squatters; the governor of Sonora was forced to resign. This hardly addressed the problems of limited water, limited arable land, and a population rapidly growing through both natural increase and immigration from elsewhere in Mexico and Central America. Disagreements over whether to maintain subsistence farming or to commercialize *ejidos,* whether to remain separate or integrate more with the mestizos, fight for rights in Mexico or emigrate to the United States, inject bitterness into many Indian communities.

The Yaqui

There are now some four thousand Yaqui Indians living in Arizona, where, in 1964, the United States deeded to them their principal community, Pascua, near Tucson, of 202 acres. Most of the American Yaquis are refugees, or descendants of refugees, who fled north from Sonora during the first third of the twentieth century. Their community is split between their first village on what was the outskirts of Tucson, now swallowed within the city, and New Pascua, the reservation outside the city. The history of the Yaqui can exemplify the history of the Northwestern Mexican Aztecan-speakers.

The Yaqui were one of the Cáhita-speaking (Aztecan) peoples farming along the larger rivers of western Sonora, in northwest Mexico. Their indigenous organizational unit was the *ranchería,* and they generally resembled the 'O'odham in cultural patterns. The Yaquis' first contact with Europeans occurred when they repulsed a Spanish slaving raid in 1533. Their subsequent relationship with Spain and her successor government, Mexico, seems to have been set then, for the Yaqui have been the most fiercely antagonistic of all Mexico's Indian peoples. From 1623 to 1740, the Yaquis accepted Jesuit missionaries and much of their teaching, from Catholicism to agricultural innova-

tions. The *rancherías* were consolidated into eight towns along the Yaqui River, and although many families continued to reside in traditional *ranchería* homesteads, they were officially members of one or another of eight towns. Each town had a set of native "governors,"or officials, who were aided in their duties by men of the Coyote Society, a kind of militia. The Jesuits taught Catholicism in part by means of dramatic enactments of biblical stories and historical legends. Actors in these spectacles formed sodalities with responsibility for carrying out their ceremonies at the appropriate season. Along with "deer dancers,"whose ritual stems from the preconquest period, these sodalities became the framework of the eventually syncretistic Yaqui-Catholic religion that survived the expulsion of the Jesuits in 1767.

Growing dissatisfaction by the Yaquis with the imposition of alien rule through the missions climaxed in 1740 with an armed revolt that drove all the Spanish—missionaries, soldiers, and colonists—out of Yaqui country. The autonomy of the Yaqui towns was confirmed in fact, if not in official policy. Many Yaquis emigrated during the eighteenth century to mines and Spanish haciendas in Sonora to earn income, but emigration for work did not cut off these individuals from continued membership in the tribe. A prickly truce between the Yaqui and the Spanish lasted until Mexican independence in 1821, which established, under the Plan of Iguala, that all Mexicans, regardless of race, were legally Mexican citizens. For the Yaqui, that meant acknowledging Mexican dominion over their eight towns, the payment of government taxes, and conscription into the Mexican army. None of these was acceptable. In 1825, a Yaqui named Banderas led a revolt against Mexico. From that time on, the Yaqui have been in more or less continuous rebellion against Mexico, which has no authority over them, they claim, because the Yaqui nation (the eight towns) never were conquered, nor did it sign any treaties binding the tribe as a whole. (The Mexican government, of course, follows Spanish precedent in considering the Yaqui acquiescence to the establishment of missions to have constituted acceptance of Spanish dominion, and, further, points to several documents drawn up as treaties by the Mexican government at various times and signed by some Yaqui leaders. The Yaquis argue that these leaders were never empowered to sign for the Yaqui nation.) The contest for Yaqui control was intensified by the fact that the Yaqui lands were among the very best farmland in northwest Mexico; Yaqui enjoyment of these lands without even paying taxes was most galling to Mexicans.

The continuing campaign to put down Yaqui power reached a climax in 1903 with the issuance of a new policy to deport Yaqui from Sonora. Over a period of five years, five thousand Yaquis were sold, at sixty pesos each, as slaves to the operators of plantations in Yucatán and Oaxaca. Women as well as men were taken, and there was little concern to keep mothers near their children, much less their husbands. Yaqui families today hear from their grandparents of the terrible hardships suffered by their people under the brutal conditions

YAQUI RELIGION

The Teachings of Don Juan: A Yaqui Way of Knowledge, written by Carlos Casteneda, excited thousands of Americans with its passionate drama of a man glimpsing a strange "other reality" through the tutelage of an American Indian shaman. Anthropologists reading Castaneda's books recognize many concepts and techniques for spiritual revelation common to native religious practitioners, especially in western Mexico—but are Don Juan's teachings really a Yaqui way of knowledge? The question was put to Rosalio Moises, a Yaqui born in 1896 who lived both in the Yaqui River Valley and in Arizona Yaqui settlements, a man thought by many Yaqui to be a sorcerer, and a man deeply concerned with understanding human existence and the lot of his people. Moises "was decisive in his opinion that [Don Juan's] knowledge had been acquired from Mexican sources"(Moises, Kelley, and Holden 1971:xxxiv) and that it was not typically Yaqui. Casteneda himself indirectly confirms this by naming as Don Juan's own principal teacher a supposed Mazatec shaman, Don Genaro: the Mazatec live in Oaxaca, in southwestern Mexico, and culturally and linguistically are unrelated to Yaqui.

Yaqui religion shares with other Aztecans of northwestern Mexico, such as the Huichol, the ancient concept of human life dependent upon Our Elder Brother the Deer, whose spiritual essence browses in a mountain world brilliant with beautiful flowers growing on Our Mother the Earth, under Our Father the Sun. Costumed deer dancers reenact these symbols on the ceremonial ground traditionally called the flower patio. Under Jesuit missionizing, Christian symbols were incorporated into Yaqui religion. The result can be seen in Moises' description of the fiesta held in observance of his aunt's funeral anniversary in 1916:

Over fifty people attended the fiesta. My grandmother Maria had organized the whole thing and she was very happy. Every few minutes she started dancing. She asked permission of the *pascolas* [ritual clowns, similar to Pueblo clowns] to dance as a *pascola*, and they were happy to have her do it; she clowned all night.....[One *pascola*] played all sorts of animals. First he was a raccoon, going up to each of the other *pascolas*, touching and smelling their hands like a raccoon would. The other three *pascolas* buried seeds for the raccoon to dig up and eat. [He] was also a lion, climbing up poles set up outside the ramada. He repainted his face every time he played a new animal.

[There was a] deer [and] *matachines* [originally the Spanish Christians-versus-Moors dance drama, then in Mexico a dance drama of the conversion of Indians to Christianity, but for Yaquis now a men's sodality devoted to the Virgin Our Mother and her promise of cures].....My father's coyote soldiers [the equivalent of the Pueblo Bow Priests' warrior sodality] also danced. *Maestros* [Yaqui priests, who consider themselves the equivalent of non-Indian Catholic priests] recited and sang all night in front of the altar that my grandmother kept in the house. She had about seven *santos* [saint's images] on our house altar.

My grandmother had bought some big firecrackers called *cohetes correos* (running rockets). Two tall poles, one near our ramada and the other about a half mile away, were connected by a cord, to which the *cohetes correos* were attached. When lighted they ran from pole to pole, going as fast as sixty miles per hour. Their final explosion was accompanied by a bang and lots of pretty lights. We set off three of them, which had cost my grandmother at least fifty dollars, about eight o'clock in the evening. Everyone was very happy.....

An abundance of food was available. My grandmother had *atole de panoche* (a sweel gruel), garbanzo stew, flour tortillas, breads, coffee, and chocolate. Barbecue was reserved for the *maestros* and *pascolas*. Nearly every family brought more food.

At daybreak the *pascolas* said a big rainstorm was coming. One rubbed a big drum for the thunder; they flicked their tongues in and out to represent lightning and threw gourds full of water on the crowd. Everyone had to run or get wet.

After the musicians stopped playing about nine o'clock in the morning, they had the deer "play." Three of the *pascolas* acted as deer hunters, using bows and arrows without points. [The *pascola* who played animals] took the part of the hunting dog. [He] made a very good dog, walking on all fours, with a cow's tail attached to his pants.....The deer dancer played the deer.

The crowd stood in two lines outside the ramada, on either side of the three poles stuck in the ground. Children and women ran from line to line and the hunters shot arrows at them, pretending they were deer also. A canteen of homemade wine (*tepache*) had been buried and the "dog" dug it up so the *pascolas* could drink it.

The "deer" hid around the poles for about half an hour; he went through all the motions of a deer hiding in a forest. At one point he surprised one of the hunters and knocked him down. The hunter started to cry, and the other two hunters had to whip him to get him to stop. At the third tree (or pole), the "deer"was caught and the hunters "killed"him. The "dead deer"was then carried to the ramada, where the hunters proceeded to skin, cut up, and weigh the meat. They then started measuring the skin. One *pascola* asked another, "Were you born in a kindergarten?" The other replied, "Yes," beginning to count: "One kilometer, four kilos, fifty miles, thousand, a thousand eight hundred,"and such nonsense. The skin and meat were then sold to the crowd, the money being placed in a little pile. That was the end of the fiesta. All of us who had mourned for my aunt Camilda took off our black bands.

(Moises, Kelley, and Holden 1971:57-59)

on the plantations, and of the tremendous courage of the women who escaped, sought out their children, and walked, barefoot, hungry, ragged, and always threatened with rape and murder, back to the mountains of Sonora, where they could join the furtive camps of the Yaqui guerrillas. The lucky Yaquis ran north into Arizona, where many attempted to aid their people's cause by running supplies to the guerrillas in Mexico. Deportation ended with the overthrow of the Díaz regime in the 1910 Mexican Revolution, but the Yaqui contention for autonomy continued. In 1936, the socialist government of Cárdenas attempted to sound out an end to hostilities, and in 1939, it set up a kind of Yaqui reservation, giving the tribe control of their homeland north of the Yaqui River and a little land south of the river.

The resolution of Yaqui opposition to the government of Mexico came too late to attract all the American Yaqui back to their homeland, although some returned, and many others maintain ties through visits. The American Yaqui settlements had perpetuated the core of Yaqui culture, insofar as that could be divorced from its setting in the beloved and holy Yaqui River valley. In 1906, when thousands of their compatriots were undergoing the Mexican government's "final solution" of genocide for the Yaqui, Arizona Yaqui observed Good Friday and Easter with their Jesuit legacy of reenactment of this most moving story of persecution and ultimate resurrection. The Euro-Americans of Tucson saw the Yaqui celebration as a colorful addition to the entertainment of the town, and encouraged the refugees to repeat this and other rituals. As the Arizona Yaquis had no quarrel with the Arizona Euro-Americans, to whom they were grateful for sanctuary, this encouragement was instrumental in making Yaqui religion the center of Arizona Yaqui life. Town government, Yaqui agricultural techniques, and Yaqui crafts were seen as inappropriate, impossible, or unsatisfactory by most of the Arizona Yaquis, but the consciousness of being a special people was maintained through the revitalization of the historic

sodalities and the performances of their costumed dances. During World War II, a pattern of weekend- or holiday-only participation in the traditional Indian community began to be common, but even long before then, the Yaqui could combine this pattern with wage work and schooling within American society without loss of ancestral history and spiritual heritage. The American Yaqui, separated from their homeland, have not revived Yaqui culture to the degree that their relatives in the Yaqui River Valley have in recent years, but they have demonstrated for several generations now that an Indian tribal identity can be maintained even in the midst of an alien society.

The Hohokam

Among the Protoclassic farming communities extending through northwestern Mexico was one that settled in the flood plain of the Gila River, a tributary of the Colorado River in southern Arizona. There they constructed an irrigation canal 5 kilometers (3 miles) long near the present 'O'odham village of Snaketown, drawing the river waters onto the fertile flood plain.Where only the small camps of the late Cochise Archaic period had existed, a town of permanent square houses was built, its inhabitants working their irrigated fields, manufacturing vessels and human figurines of clay, grinding maize on carefully shaped stone metates, and making ornaments of carved shell from the Gulf of California and of bits of turquoise from mines near Baker, California. Snaketown's irrigation system was maintained, and eventually extended and improved considerably, for some 1,700 years, until A.D. 1450. The people of Snaketown, and of other Arizona sites with similar culture, have been called the Hohokam (from the 'O'odham word meaning "they are used up"). It is generally agreed that the modern 'O'odham (Pima and Papago) are the descendants of the Hohokam.

Hohokam contrast not only with the Cochise of the Archaic period but with later peoples contemporary with early Snaketown: the non-Hohokam lived in small, round houses, in camps or villages smaller than Snaketown, were less dependent on maize and did not irrigate, did not make pottery or clay figurines, did not shape into complete troughs the stone slabs on which they ground seeds and maize; and did not import marine shell and turquoise from the west for use in ornaments.

Strong though the argument is for attributing Hohokam innovations to migrants from Mexico, it has not been easily accepted by many Southwestern archaeologists. It is a peculiarity of the majority of archaeologists who have worked in the U. S. Southwest that they often vehemently reject interpreting Southwestern data in terms of broader contacts and social history. Instead, many explain social change in the Southwest as due to environmental changes. In spite of the inbred prejudice to accept the U. S. Southwest as the northwestern frontier of Mesoamerica, that the Hohokam were, or at least included, emigrants from much farther south in Mexico seems incontrovertible.

Before the massive twentieth-century diversion of its water, the Gila River valley was an attractive green belt through the southwestern desert, profitable for farmers and a good route from the southern Plains to California and the Pacific. Hohokam built on the Gila and its tributaries, along the principal trade route up from the coast in Sonora, and exchanging also with Pueblo villages to the north and east. As the frontier of Mexican civilization, the Hohokam were probably the channel through which Puebloans were initially linked to the technological and religious ideas of the Mexican nations. From the perspective of merchants and generals in the Valley of Mexico, the Hohokam may have been at best a vaguely heard of group who sent precious turquoise down the long, hard route past the great outpost fortresses, such as La Quemada in Zacatecas, to the empire markets. From the perspective of the early Pueblo villages, the Hohokam were sophisticated townspeople who could grow impressive crops, had complex ceremonies on their platform mounds and in their ball courts, and displayed remarkable ornaments, in-

cluding copper bells, shells with chemically etched designs, remarkable mirrors, and headdresses brilliant with the feathers of the macaw, a Mexican bird. Snaketown and other Hohokam towns, with scattered, adobe-covered houses and a relatively low adobe-surfaced platform mound, were remote reflections of the magnificence of Classic Mexican cities, yet they served the Puebloans as models of a cosmopolitan urban style of life.

Hohokam continued to be receptive to Mexican ideas throughout its history in the Southwest. During the Mexican Classic period, cotton was grown in Snaketown's fields and became the basis for a variety of cloths, some of them with lacelike, openwork patterns. Potters decorated their wares with red-painted designs and modeled effigy vessels and censers for burning incense. In the Mexican Postclassic period, copper bells and mirrors made of mosaics of iron pyrites were imported from Mexico, as were rubber balls for the town ball games. People stretched their ear lobes around spool-shaped ear ornaments such as were fashionable in Mexico. Small figurines, some with flat, rectangular bodies on which paint could be mixed, were sculpted in stone. Hohokam artists seemed to reach their finest expression in both ceramics and stone in the early Postclassic. There was a steady population increase, and by the later Postclassic, after about A.D. 900, individual artists' talents seem to have been subordinated to the goal of greater production of goods.

After A.D. 1200, the Hohokam began to decline. A series of long, severe droughts struck the Southwest in the thirteenth and fourteenth centuries, and, in addition to the droughts, a major shift occurred in the climate pattern in the Southwest: winters became longer, and most precipitation fell during the winters (in contrast with the present pattern, which began about 1850, of shorter winters and most precipitation falling during the summers, as rainstorms with quick, erosive runoff). One result of the longer, wetter winters was heavier floods with more deposition of silt along the rivers. This situation may have made maintenance of the Hohokam irrigation systems difficult, or may have caused other problems with the agricultural practices that had been adapted to earlier conditions. Whatever the cause, or combination of causes—and many others have been suggested, including the possibility of raiding Navajos and Apaches stealing crops—by A.D. 1450, Snaketown had been abandoned, and most Hohokam communities had disappeared or were reduced to hamlets.

The 'O'odham

The historic 'O'odham retained many Hohokam traits. 'O'odham are divided into the Akimel 'O'odham, often called River Pima, and Tóhono 'O'odham, Desert Pima or Papago, who live in the region called Papaguería south of the Gila River valley. 'O'odham lived, and many still live, in *rancherías*, communities of family homesteads strung out along streams or irrigation canals or near wells they have dug. The older 'O'odham house was round or oval, with four inner support posts for the roof, a hearth near the door, and walls of woven brush daubed with adobe. This type of house appeared late in the Hohokam period, an oval modifying the rectangular form more common in the earlier Hohokam. Modern 'O'odham houses are again rectangular. Homesteads also contain *ramadas*, open-walled, brush-roofed shelters from the hot desert sun, and other outbuildings.

The several homes in an 'O'odham homestead are usually occupied by an elderly couple and their married sons, who cooperate in maintaining the irrigation system and in farming their maize, beans (particularly the drought-resistant tepary bean) and pumpkins. One older man is recognized as the leader among the related homesteads of a *ranchería*, but there are no traditional formal political offices. Religion focuses on songs celebrating a harmonic world, in which beautiful rain rejuvenates the desert. Costumed masked dancers recreate the desired harmony, which is symbolized also by an abundance of maize, deer, and eagles

(who fly to the clouds where rain abides). Tobacco is ceremonially smoked in cane cigarettes. These elements of spirituality are found in the other Uto-Aztecan-speaking peoples of northwestern Mexico, and, as part of traditional native Mexican religions, were probably present in Hohokam culture too.

'O'odham first had contact with Europeans in 1540 when the Spanish explorer Alvar Núñez Cabeza de Vaca met some in Sonora, near the border between 'O'odham and Yaqui territory. Reading between the lines of history, the ethnohistorian Edward Spicer suggests that at this time there were about thirty thousand 'O'odham, and that although their scattered *rancherías* were found over a north-south span of a thousand miles, their boundaries were areas of conflict with Yaquis, Opatas, and other groups seeking the same sparse resources of arid northwestern Mexico. Some of the southern 'O'odham allied with the invading Spanish against these neighboring disputants, professed interest in Spanish plans to change native life, moved from their *rancherías* into a compact village, and became immediate converts to Christianity at the appearance of the first missionaries in 1591. The Spanish penetration of 'O'odham country was slow, for the silver, gold, and lead mines that drew the Europeans into adjacent territories were few in 'O'odham lands, and the missionary orders were understaffed for the magnitude of the conversion program they undertook. The core of the Spanish program was the "reduction," as they phrased it, of the dispersed Indians into tightly supervised towns. Reduction of the number of Indian settlements was seen as the first and most necessary step in the efficient transformation of the Indians from their native way of life to the European pattern, upon which a Spanish empire could be built. Missionaries often did not approve of the profit-seeking goals of their secular countrymen, but were convinced that only by overseeing the daily activities of the Indians could they eliminate the seduction of non-Christian practices. Thus, whether their aim was to save souls or to open territory to European exploitation, the vanguard of Spanish expansion agreed that a thorough reorganization of Indian societies was desirable. Eventually, even those Indians who had been receptive to European ideas realized their threat, and, in 1740, Lower Pimas (southern 'O'odham), Yaquis, and Mayos rebelled against Spanish domination. This revolt, like the many smaller uprisings before and after it, was put down by Spanish troops using seek-and-destroy tactics. These hostilities intensified the fragmentation of the 'O'odham, some communities becoming increasingly assimilated into the Spanish program, others preserving their independence in mountain refuges.

Northern 'O'odham became the target of Christianization in 1687 with the arrival of the Italian Jesuit missionary Eusebio Kino. Father Kino, like many of his brethren, was sincerely concerned to improve, according to his understanding, the life of the Indians in his charge. He brought in cattle, fruit trees, and wheat, all proving welcome to the 'O'odham. However, his plan of reduction of settlements was hindered by a lack of sufficient priests to staff the new villages he envisioned. Kino's personal popularity among the 'O'odham did not offset the ill effects of Spanish colonization, among them the disruption of 'O'odham territories, introduction of a multitude of diseases, and, regardless of population loss from epidemics, the impressment of many Indians into forced labor in mines and on ranches. The Northern 'O'odham staged a series of surprise raids on Spanish establishments, always disbanding to their *rancherías* after the attacks but usually thereby leading the Spanish troops to massacre whatever 'O'odham they happened to encounter when their reprisal forays failed to find an 'O'odham army.

Spanish efforts to conquer the 'O'odham lessened in the second half of the eighteenth century, but 'O'odham security became increasingly threatened by Apache Indian bands. For most of the nineteenth century, the 'O'odham were the unhappy buffer between Apaches and Spanish towns in northwesternmost Mexico. After the Gadsden Purchase of 1853 put the northern half of 'O'odham

territory under United States control, 'O'odham joined Americans against Apaches. A curious result of this alliance against a mutual enemy was that there seemed to be no need for the United States government to negotiate a treaty with the 'O'odham; they were seen as peaceful and accommodating because they were allies. Small reservations were set aside for Tóhono 'O'odham in 1874 and 1884, but the majority of 'O'odham *rancherías* were outside these reservations and subject to increasing competition from miners (silver and copper mines were opened in Tóhono territory) and ranchers. The scarcity of water in the southern Arizona desert led to numerous conflicts between 'O'odham farmers and Euro-American cattle ranchers. As a result, 'O'odham families often had to forage for wild foods in the desert. While 'O'odham had traditionally harvested cactus fruits and other desert plants in season as important supplements to their crops, and while a few 'O'odham had chosen to be nomadic and rely entirely on wild resources, most 'O'odham were strongly committed to their domestic crops, and losing their traditional water holes or finding their streams depleted by Euro-American dam systems deeply angered them.

A large portion of southern Arizona finally became the official Papago Reservation in 1918. By this time, many Indians, both men and women, were accustomed to working on the railroads, on ranches, and in towns such as Tucson for cash to supplement their own products.

Both Catholic and Presbyterian mission organizations had established agencies and schools for 'O'odham. Tóhono also had their own independent Christian cult elevating San Francisco. The Tóhono chapels to San Francisco featured icons of St. Francis Xavier, but the 'O'odham conception of San Francisco included attributes of St. Francis of Assisi, who was associated with the Franciscan order that took over missionary work in northwestern Mexico after the Jesuits were expelled in 1767. Traditional 'O'odham religion and practices continued, augmented by ideas gathered through exposure to Euro-American culture. An interesting light on evolving 'O'odham society is that the late nineteenth century encroachment of Euro-American ranchers on 'O'odham territory, coupled with a market for 'O'odham baskets among the Colorado River Indians as well as among Euro-Americans, led many 'O'odham to include a desert plant used for basketry among their cultivated crops. Formerly, the people had gathered the wild devil's-claw in the desert; with less open desert, they began to plant devil's-claw seeds in their fields. The importance of maintaining supplies of this fiber can be realized from the estimate of at least 1,400 'O'odham basketweavers today, of which 800 consider this work a full-time occupation.

In 1934, Roosevelt's New Deal reached Indians through the reassessment of the Bureau of Indian Affairs effected by its new commissioner, the anthropologist John Collier. Collier repudiated the earlier policy of denigration of Indian cultures and tried to revive Indian pride by giving reservations greater control over their resources and people. A staunch believer in American democracy, Collier offered each reservation the opportunity to vote for tribal reorganization in the form of an elected council and chief, who would cooperate with the BIA in seeking to improve the economic status of reservation members. The 'O'odham, like nearly all other government-recognized tribes in the United States, accepted Collier's proposal, ethnocentric though it was, and for the first time, 'O'odham *rancherías* were under a formal organization of native leaders—subject, however, to the final decision of the BIA agents.

After World War II, in which 250 'O'odham served in the United States armed forces, a major shift occurred among the 'O'odham. Most young men and women left their reservations at least seasonally to work for wages on Euro-American cotton and cattle ranches and in the cities, not only in Arizona but as far away as Los Angeles. The children of these younger people all attended American schools. The *rancherías* on the reservations were the year-round home of only the middle-aged and elderly, along with some grandchildren whose parents preferred to see them

grow up on their own lands rather than in the low-income neighborhoods of the cities. The off-reservation Indians returned regularly to visit their *rancherías* and participate in native religious and social celebrations, and their income helped support the elders who maintained their traditional pattern of life. Part of the impetus to seek wage work off the reservations is a desire to work in occupations not available on the reservations, but the primary motive is the simple need to find employment at a time when the rapid increase in Indian population has made the reservations too small to provide opportunities for all to obtain even a minimal living. According to 1980 BIA population figures, 14,000 people inhabited the two main 'O'odham Arizona reservations, quadruple the number for which they were established; and this does not include individuals—over 25,000 in 1980— residing off the reservations but continuing to think of them as "home." With so many living in Indian neighborhoods in the cities, 'O'odham are increasingly recognizing their common interests with Indians of other tribes and developing pan-Indian political, religious, and social solidarities. The ancient 'O'odham culture persists, but in a wider universe.

SECTION 2: THE NORTHERN SECTOR

The Colorado Plateau and its southern escarpment in New Mexico and Arizona was sufficiently different in ecology from the southwestern desert to become the border zone of Mexican cultural patterns. The people of this zone gradually acculturated to the Mexican urban model of society, but their habitat rendered this pattern a precarious one.

The Mogollon

Mogollon is the archaeologists' name for the prehistoric cultural pattern practiced in the mountainous region (the Mogollon Rim) of the southern portion of the Arizona-New Mexico state line. Beginning from a Cochise Archaic base, the people of this region began making pottery similar to Hohokam and northwestern Mexican types not long after the Hohokam founded Snaketown. It is therefore surmised that the migration of the Hohokam into southern Arizona excited the interest of their neighbors to the east and led to the adoption of ceramics, increased farming, and more permanent little villages. Further, it is theorized that it may have been through the Mogollon that these traits reached the indigenous peoples on the Colorado Plateau. Efforts to link the Mogollon tradition to specific historic peoples have not been successful; Mogollon peoples entered in the still somewhat puzzling population shifts in the fifteenth-century Southwest, and their descendants may be merged in the historic Pueblos.

What makes the Mogollon worth mentioning in a general survey of North America is their marvelous ceramics. Classic Mimbres potters of the eleventh century A.D. made excellent ware and painted it with great verve and skill in lively black-and-white geometric and animal designs. There were only about twenty villages and perhaps four thousand people in the Mimbres River region in the eleventh century, and none of the villages were architecturally impressive. Their beautiful pottery seems to have been produced mostly for local use, especially to grace interments of the dead. (Often, pots in graves were punched through the bottom so that they couldn't be used any more by living people.) A fisheries specialist studied the depictions of fishes on Mimbres ceramics and concluded that people from this landlocked desert region must have traveled to the Gulf of California, the Sonora coast, about 600 kilometers (400 miles) direct but much farther by foot. Eleven kinds of Gulf fish have been definitely identified from Mimbres paintings, plus there are other depictions not so easily determined. The surprising variety of ocean fishes on Classic Mimbres ceramics indicates Mimbreño travel to Sonora, and suggests the primary purpose of the long treks may have been to import shells for ornaments (thousands of shell ornaments have been found in

Mimbres sites). Mimbreños traded into Chaco Canyon, and the Mimbres culture seems to have disappeared when Chaco disintegrated.

The Anasazi Tradition

The Anasazi (Navajo for "ancient alien ones") were the ancestors of the modern Pueblo Indians. The name applies to the period beginning A.D. 700, but the Anasazi Tradition is seen to go farther back in time. Late Archaic people of the northern sector are known as the San Jose Archaic. Like other groups of the Western Archaic, the San Jose utilized a variety of wild resources obtainable from a series of seasonal camps; like other late Archaic Southwesterners, they planted small amounts of maize and squash. By the first millennium B.C., they seem to have been forming winter villages of perhaps a dozen families in sheltered locations, where they built modest pole-frame huts and cobblestone-filled earth ovens.

The Basketmaker

About 400 A.D.., people of the northern sector began building more substantial dwellings. Archaeologists took note of this shift by calling them Basketmaker instead of Archaic. The term Basketmaker was applied many years ago to the pre-Pueblo sites because several of them were in dry rockshelters in which a variety of basketry remains were preserved but no pottery was found. Basketmaker houses had log foundations around scooped-out floors, walls made of pieces of wood and mud mortar, and roofs probably made of poles and brush. Early Basketmaker houses were round and the floor excavation shallow; later houses tended to be more square, had four interior posts to support the roof, had floors sunk as much as nearly a meter (yard), and sometimes had stone slabs lining the lower walls. It is possible that these changes in house style reflect imitation of the Hohokam. More definite evidence of Hohokam influence, perhaps indirectly through Mogollon practices, is the appearance of pottery in the later Basketmaker period, after A.D. 400. Basketmaker pottery is gray rather than the brown of Hohokam and Mogollon, and several sites seem to show that once the Basketmakers wished to have clay vessels, they experimented with ceramics instead of taking lessons directly from Hohokam or Mogollon potters. Another innovation in the later Basketmaker period was the bow and arrow. Since this weapon first appeared about the same time in the Hohokam towns, it was probably introduced to Southwesterners of both cultural traditions from outside, very likely from the Great Basin or Plains to the north, where arrow points appear somewhat earlier.

The most significant innovation in the Basketmaker period was the use of substantial, carefully constructed storage pits near the houses. Storing food required not only development of techniques for processing and preserving, but different allocations of labor and time—hard work at harvest season, followed by a season that could be filled with activities other than food getting. Bringing food in quantity to a central location allowed more families to live in a community. The storage pits are mute signs of the replacement of nomadic, small-band societies by permanent villages large enough to support more complex religious, political, and economic activities. The changeover was slow, taking centuries, but was encouraged by greater moisture in the later Basketmaker period, which produced both more abundant wild seeds and better crops. Amaranth, chenopods (goosefoot and pigweed), and cactus, as well as maize, were harvested and stored. The changeover during Basketmaker times was not from gathering to farming, but from seasonal camps to permanent villages.

Pueblo Prehistory

The eighth century A.D. saw the inception of the distinctive Pueblo cultural pattern in the northern sector of the Southwest. The climate during this century shifted from longer winters to conditions similar to the present—shorter, milder winters and

heavy summer rainstorms likely to cause erosion. Water rather than frosts threatened farmers' yields: there was not enough water in the soil when crops were germinating in the spring, because of the mild winters and lack of snow, and there was too much water in the storms that hit the dessicated land later in the summer. Anasazi farmers met the challenge of drought and erosion of arable land by constructing check dams and ditch systems across runoff channels, and, where appropriate, terracing fields to conserve both moisture and topsoil. Underlying these efforts was a strong commitment to an urban style of society.

The high, semiarid Colorado Plateau, with its steep-walled canyon streams, is not an environment especially suited to agriculture. Arable land is generally found only on the narrow valley floors or where springs and slope runoff can be channeled at the base of mesas. The most sensible economy for humans in this environment is the gathering of wild plants, supplemented by the hunting of rabbits and deer. Nutritious wild plants native to this environment range from pines producing pinyon nuts and junipers producing berries, in the higher mountain areas, through seed-bearing amaranth and chenopods on lower ridges, to a variety of cactuses in the driest localities. All of these native plants bear even in dry years, since they are the offspring of those that reproduced throughout the droughts of ancient times. Rabbits and deer are also always obtainable, not necessarily in the same locality each year, but within a couple days' journey by foot. The easiest, most secure life for humans in this region is bands of a few families moving from camp to camp following the ripening of the various wild foods. This, of course, was the Archaic pattern.

The longer winters resulting in greater soil moisture of the Basketmaker period were particularly beneficial to seed-bearing grasses, maize and amaranth among them. These seeds, or grains, are the easiest foods to store in quantity in the drier temperate and subtropical climates. Thus, environmental conditions of the Basketmaker period favored the development of permanent villages using stored grains as their diet staple. When the conditions changed in the eighth century, the Anasazi faced a choice: abandon the villages, reverting to light huts and baskets, nomadism, small social groups, and little investment of labor or time in food getting; or stay in the villages, relocating them where the most arable land could be found, paying for solidly built houses, pottery, accumulations of manufactured goods, and bigger communities by spending long days in the fields and workshops. Contrary to the popular notion that humans always choose the easier way, the Anasazi, like so many other peoples, chose the rewards of hard work. They never forgot how to live off wild foods, since these were always collected around their pueblos, and when severe droughts or disastrous floods ruined crops, families survived by leaving the pueblo to range widely for wild products. But the ideal was always to work on the farms, breaking intermittently for rituals and parties.

Anasazi and Hohokam both valued maize, beans, squashes, pottery, cotton clothing, and adobe-plastered houses, but the two traditions contrast in their valuation of personal and family autonomy. The 'O'odham and, to judge from the loose clustering of their houses, the Hohokam, dislike wall-by-wall settlements, where one must always consider the neighbors' demands. The Anasazi and their Pueblo descendants desire contiguous neighbors and are willing to smother the inevitable irritations. Both traditions believe it is crucial that humans live in harmony with kin and nature, but the 'O'odham avoid getting on each other's nerves by staying somewhat apart, and the Pueblos by inhibiting antisocial behavior and even, insofar as they can be controlled, thoughts. If interpersonal conflicts could not be repressed any longer, a pueblo would divide, one faction leaving to found its own village away from its opponents— but, again, a village, not a return to wilderness. For a millennium and a half, Puebloans have been staunch townspeople, come hell or high water.

The broad outlines of Pueblo prehistory are well known. In the first period, from A.D. 700 to 900, some villages were still clusters of Basketmaker-type pit houses (houses with sunken floors), and others were switching to houses and storage huts built at ground level. Both types of villages (and there were villages with a mixture of house types) continued to build special ceremonial structures resembling the early Basketmaker round houses but dug more deeply into the ground. These structures seem to be the forerunners of the historic Pueblo ceremonial chambers called (in Hopi) *kiva*, and are so named by archaeologists. In the next period, A.D. 900 to 1100, many villages built the family residences in a connected row, like today's town houses or "mom and pop" small motels. One or more kivas would be excavated adjacent to the row of homes. There was increasing use of stone slabs, mortared with adobe, either as facing for pole-and-rock-rubble walls or as the walls themselves. Pottery became an outlet for artistic talent, and featured sophisticated designs painted in black on white backgrounds. No doubt, weaving of cotton was also a medium demonstrating high skill, for it had been an Anasazi crop since the late Basketmaker period; but not much fragile cloth has survived in the ruins. (Historically, Pueblo men did the weaving and women the pottery, but whether this was the ancient practice we cannot tell.)

The third Pueblo prehistoric period, A.D. 1100 to 1300, saw the growth of towns, some housing as many as 1,200 persons, as well as villages. Multistory, multifamily apartment houses were built around large, open plazas in which the kivas were sunk. Many towns allowed entrance to the rooms only through holes in the roof, which were reached by ladders extending from story to story. We guess such awkward entrances were meant to safeguard the families from enemy attack, since in some towns the walls of the first apartments had doors that were later blocked. Small villages continued to exist in the countryside, and families from the towns who had to walk some distance to their fields built summer houses outside the pueblo next to the farms. These unprotected habitations suggest

FIGURE 3.1 Hopi man and boy, 1879, dressed in traditional clothing, and armed with a throwing stick and club for rabbit hunting. *(Smithsonian Institution National Archives, Bureau of American Ethnology Collection)*

that warfare may have been carried out only between the major towns, and only during the winter after the crops were harvested. Contention between towns may have been over arable land, which was becoming increasingly scarce due to erosion of valley floors. Some of the most spectacular fortress towns, the "cliff dwellings" built in clefts in sheer rock-canyon walls, are located near what at the time were unusually good farmlands.

The last quarter of the thirteenth century saw a prolonged, severe drought. The climate also shifted back to longer winters. Towns at the highest elevations, particularly the Mesa Verde communities in southern Colorado, were abandoned, probably because the growing season had become too short for reliable harvests. Localities at lower elevations, particularly the Río Grande Valley in New Mexico, were the scene of new settlements, which could take advantage of the increased runoff from snow at drainage-system headwaters. Archaeologists have tried to trace many of these new or expanded settlements of A.D. 1300 to 1500 back to abandoned towns in the northern border areas of the Southwest, but little agreement has been reached. The western pueblos—those of the Hopi, Zuni, and Acoma—have been continuously inhabited since this late prehistoric period, and some of the eastern, or Río Grando, pueblos have also been continuously inhabited, but whether the new towns of the late prehistoric period were resettlements of refugees from the north, or expansions of Río Grande populations, or mixtures of the two sources, is much debated. Some archaeologists have thought the northern Puebloans simply turned to wild-food gathering as nomads, but in view of the several well-documented cases of towns surviving long droughts by hunting and collecting intensively from the permanent pueblo as a base, it is not likely that reversion to an Archaic economy was chosen by many. Precarious as agriculture has always been in the northern Southwest, resettlement as erosion and flood-plain building alters farming potential has been the rule since the Basketmaker period. Even the largest Pueblo towns were comparatively small as populations go, and vulnerable to falling below the sustaining level even in the absence of major catastrophes. Mergings of smaller groups into larger towns have been common for the Anasazi since at least 1100, and the history of most pueblos is complex.

Chaco Canyon and Casas Grandes (Paquimé)

Trade at the northern end of the Greater Southwest was centered consecutively, during the Postclassic period, at Chaco Canyon in New Mexico and then at Paquimé, also known as Casas Grandes, in Chihuahua. Chaco flourished between A.D. 800 and 1175, Paquimé between A.D. 1150 and 1450.

Chaco Canyon is in northwestern New Mexico on a tributary to the San Juan River of the Four Corners (meeting of Utah, Colorado, Arizona, and New Mexico) plateau. Although the region was inhabited by people in seasonal camps during the Archaic period, and these people had been planting a little maize and squash since early in the first millennium B.C., only in the ninth century A.D. did building begin on the wide canyon floor, where rainfall washes flow down from the uplands above the canyon walls. The basic unit of building was a larger front room with two small rooms behind. This unit was repeated, presumably for each nuclear family in the community, and by A.D. 930 the central construction, Pueblo Bonito, was three stories high with 125 rooms. Then, about A.D. 1000, Pueblo Bonito was enlarged and two smaller pueblos built, one a couple of kilometers (a little over 1 mile) away, the other 5 kilometers (3 miles) away. Fifty years later, a third satellite community was started. By 1100, there were seven big pueblos as well as many hamlets within an 8-square-kilometer (3 square mile) section of Chaco Canyon. Four-story Pueblo Bonito had more than five hundred rooms, and the number of rooms in the set of communities totaled over thirteen hundred, with ninety kivas for religious sanctuaries. Some two hundred thousand trees were used in the construction of this complex, and most of the trees had to be brought many kilometers from the mountain forests. (How the logs were transported has not been determined.) The great buildings were attractively finished with ashlar masonry veneer and adobe plaster.

Estimated population at Chaco in the twelfth century is about six thousand people. They farmed hundreds of plots watered either from the canyon wash or from rainfall collected through an elaborate system of dams and canals. Some of the inhabitants processed turquoise in workshops in the pueblos, but manufacturing does not seem to have been a full-time occupation for many. Cemeteries are just outside the pueblos. Elaborate tombs are not to be found, but a few persons at Bonito were buried with riches: turquoise, jet, shell beads, copper bells, shell trumpets, macaws, and handsomely inlaid or painted objects. One man, who died from a violent blow to the head, was given 11,000 turquoise beads and hundreds of turquoise pendants and other pieces, in addition to other expensive objects. Who such a man was, whether clan leader, high priest, or possibly a warlord, we cannot guess, nor do we have any good evidence on how the Chaco complex was governed.

Remarkably straight roads up to 100 kilometers (60 miles) long connect Chaco Canyon to major pueblos elsewhere in the San Juan region. The main roads are 9 meters (9 yards) wide and secondary roads are half as wide. Roads turn sharply when they must turn and when a road comes to a steep rise, ramps, stairs, or toe-holds were cut into the obstacle. All traffic was on foot, so no curves to accommodate vehicles were required. Signal stations on high points made it possible to link communities visually at night by means of flares or bonfires. Some fifty-five hundred villages contemporary with the Chaco pueblos are known within the San Juan region.

It is clear that Chaco Canyon, and particularly Pueblo Bonito, imported quantities of luxury goods. Thousands of ceramic vessels manufactured in pueblos outside the canyon were carried to it. Turquoise mined in New Mexico 175 kilometers (105 miles) to the southeast, and lesser amounts mined in Arizona and Colorado, were gathered at Chaco; so were shells and ornaments manufactured from shells both from the Gulf of California and farther, on the Pacific coast. Two imports definitely came from Mexican markets, copper bells and macaws (living birds as well as their bright feathers). Cotton cloth was probably manufactured, but no evidence remains of this perishable material. Luxury objects found at lesser pueblos in the San Juan region presumably came through Chaco. Chaco was apparently the great entrepôt for the northern end of the Greater Southwest, and an exporter of precious turquoise to Central Mexico.

Pueblo Bonito and its satellites in Chaco Canyon were abandoned by A.D. 1300. Legends in historic Pueblos say refugees from droughts in the north (the San Juan region) came down to the Río Grande and its immediate tributaries in central New Mexico, settling in near the existing pueblos, doing some trading and some militant threatening if objections were raised. That the refugees may have been Chacoans is suggested by the appearance of irrigation construction similar to some at Chaco, and also pottery styles, in the Río Grande region about 1300. Similar movement down from higher elevations into lower, larger river valleys, along with innovations in canal, as contrasted with floodwater-control, irrigation, occurred in the western Pueblo region in Arizona at this time. Florence Hawley Ellis, an archaeologist who worked closely with modern Pueblos for decades, pointed out that immigrants into a pueblo were expected to use the pottery styles of their host community, as a matter of good manners, so if Chacoans did take up residence among foreign pueblos, the Chacoans would very rapidly "disappear" to the archaeologist tracing and identifying social groups by their pottery styles.

The people disappeared from Chaco Canyon, and suddenly Paquimé was the entrepôt for the Greater Southwest. Not that Chacoans ran, not walked, south to Chihuahua—Paquimé and Pueblo Bonito overlap for a century, the one building up while the other declines. We have no clue to the ethnic affiliation of Paquimé, nor of what language its people spoke. Paquimé soon overshadowed Bonito, and every other pueblo in the northern Southwest. Years of archaeological excavation have not yet uncovered half of the ruin. The multistory buildings, constructed of a kind of concrete rather than ordinary adobe, had a variety of room sizes. Outside the structures of rooms were platform mounds and at least three ball courts. One 14-meter-deep (14-yard) well, with a stair and ladder down to the water, was dug at the site, and spring water carried via canal 3.6 kilometers (2.2 miles) from the source to a reservoir in the town, then through small stone-lined ditches to the homes. Complementing the provision of clean water was a sewer system draining waste water.

Paquimé has less turquoise than Chaco Canyon had, perhaps indicating that the precious mineral passed through the entrepôt rather than remaining with its leaders. Shell is another story. One-and-one-half tons shell, or four million shell artifacts, have been recovered by archaeologists, and nearly all this enormous quantity was found in three storerooms. Needless to say, the shell was imported to this valley within the northern desert, probably the transshipment point between the west-east route from the Sonora coast and the north-south route down through Durango and Zacatecas to Central Mexico. Paquimé did more than move goods along. It produced, apparently on the site, copper bells and other ornaments, and copper "ax money," standardized-weight pieces of copper in outline resembling ax heads. Fine polychrome painted ceramics were a Paquimé manufacture, and cotton cloth probably another. Another valuable Paquimé export produced in the town was macaws, raised in at least seventy pens. Turkeys were raised in other pens. Domesticated turkeys, for eating and feathers, were common in prehistoric Mexico and the Greater Southwest, including historic Pueblos, but Paquimé is the farthest north that macaws seem to have been raised.

What happened to Paquimé, or for that matter, Chaco, is not well understood. Chaco's abandonment seems to be correlated with the droughts of the thirteenth century. It is also correlated with the abandonment of Chalchihuites centers in Durango and with Toltec decline; all these may have been affected by the widespread droughts. Paquimé's rise may be associated with its relatively better water supply, so that it competed favorably with towns more dependent on rainfall. Once its leaders had realized the advantage of consolidating their advantage at the crossing of two major continental

routes by themselves producing valuable, easily transported goods, Paquimé would seem to have been set for centuries of prosperity. Yet when observed by a Spanish explorer in 1584, it was already in ruins. Exactly when it was abandoned has not yet been well determined—1450 is an approximation. Warfare was common in the Greater Southwest in the early sixteenth century, but signs of attack have not been recognized at Paquimé. It is possible that epidemics sweeping north after 1530—two generations before the 1584 notice—killed both a large proportion of the townspeople and also the trade for which they lived in the town. Perhaps Paquimé had been abandoned before the Spanish invasion; if so, no reason presents itself.

The Historic Pueblos

Written history begins for the Pueblos in 1540, when Francisco Vásquez de Coronado and his party of several hundred Spanish soldiers and Mexican Indian servants marched into the upper Río Grande Valley, settled for the winter near a native pueblo, and requisitioned supplies and women from their Indian neighbors. Recalcitrance on the part of the Indians, who could not possibly support an army nearly the size of their own community, was met by the execution of two hundred people of the pueblo. This show of force awakened military opposition by the Indians and led to the slaughter of hundreds more from the pueblos and the destruction of villages. Winning battles by the superiority of firearms and cavalry over foot soldiers with bows and hand weapons did not, in the final accounting, win the goals of war for the Spanish. Finding the Pueblo country both hostile and poor, contrary to rumors of cities of gold, Spain explored the northern Southwest but did not seriously attempt colonization until 1598.

At this time, most of the Pueblos lived in villages of a few hundred persons, up to about two thousand at most, along the Río Grande River in New Mexico. They used the river to irrigate fields on the flood plain and supplemented this land with farms along the lower piedmont, where runoff and springs could be controlled to provide moisture. The climate, then and until the middle of the nineteenth century, was in the pattern of longer winters that in the late prehistoric period had made the lower portions of major drainage systems most favorable for agriculture. Those few Pueblos who did not obtain river-valley land occupied oases where check dams and small reservoirs could create similar conditions. The Pueblos (capitalized, Pueblo means peoples of the Anasazi tradition;

without a capital, pueblo means a town community) are usually divided into Eastern and Western branches. The Western Pueblos were, and are, the Hopi in Arizona, who speak a Uto-Aztecan language related to Shoshonean, and the Zuni in western New Mexico, who speak a language that exhibits few similarities to any others but may belong to the Penutian family. The Acoma in south-central New Mexico speak a Keresan language, one of a group of languages unique to the Pueblos. The Eastern Pueblos, on and near the Río Grande in New Mexico, speak either Keresan lan-

Pueblos and Their Languages

DIVISION	PUEBLO ENGLISH NAME	PUEBLO NATIVE NAME	LANGUAGE	LANGUAGE STOCK
Western	Hopi	Hopituh	Hopi	Tanoan*
	Zuni	Áshiwi	Zuni	Penutian?
	Acoma	Akóme	Keres	(undetermined)
	Laguna	Kawaik	Keres	(undetermined)
Eastern	Cochita	Kochiti	Keres	(undetermined)
	Zia	Tseya	Keres	(undetermined)
	Santo Domingo	Kiua	Keres	(undetermined)
	Santa Ana	Tanava	Keres	(undetermined)
	San Felipe	Katishtya	Keres	(undetermined)
	Taos	Teotho	Tiwa	Tanoan*
	Picuris	Picuria	Tiwa	Tanoan
	Sandia	Nafiat	Tiwa	Tanoan
	Isleta	Tuei	Tiwa	Tanoan
	San Juan	Okeh	Tewa	Tanoan
	Santa Clara	Xapogeh	Tewa	Tanoan
	Pojoaque (Pueblo group in mixed village	Pojoageh	Tewa	Tanoan
	San Ildefonso	Poxwogeh	Tewa	Tanoan
	Nambe	Nambe's	Tewa	Tanoan
	Tesuque	Tetsugeh	Tewa	Tanoan
	Jemez	Walatowa	Towa	Tanoan
	Pecos (abandoned 1838)	Péaku	Towa	Tanoan
	Hano (moved to Hopi land after 1680 rebellion)		Tewa	Tanoan

*Tanoan is distantly related to Uto-Aztecan and also to Kiowa (a Plains group).

FIGURE 3.2 San Juan (Tewa) pueblo, 1879. Maize is drying on the roof in the foreground. *(Smithsonian Institution National Anthropological Archives)*

guages or one of the divisions of Tanoan, a stock that separated in ancient times from Uto-Aztecan and is grouped in the Aztec-Tanoan major linguistic family. The Eastern Pueblos bore the brunt of the Spanish invasion. Their total population seems to have been roughly fifty thousand, in about seventy villages. Unlike the Aztecan-speaking peoples of northwestern Mexico, whose population for each major language group was comparable to the Pueblo total, the Pueblos at the time of Spanish invasions were not scattered in *rancherías* but were already in compact, organized villages. The Spaniards therefore did not need to spend much effort in "reducing" the settlements to manageable mission stations, but could immediately institute the second phase of their program, the establishment of missions and military posts. This program began in earnest in 1598, with the arrival of Juan de Oñate and a colony of several hundred soldiers, Spanish settlers, their Mexican Indian servants, and missionaries. Oñate had been given a contract by the Spanish government to found towns, obtain the allegiance of the native Indians to the Spanish crown, promulgate their conversion

to Christianity, and profit by whatever mining and trade he could develop.

For about a generation, Spain's program in New Mexico proceeded slowly but without serious impediments. Many colonists were discouraged by the poverty of the country, which contrasted with the mineral resources of the Aztecan-speaking lands to the south. Missionaries were, as always seemed to be the case in New Spain, too few for the magnitude of the conversion task they faced. The Puebloans gave nominal allegiance to the King of Spain. Individual pueblos suffered sometimes dangerous depletions of their food stores under the demands of colonists and soldiers, and hostility occasionally flared over violence or arbitrary, arrogant orders from Spanish captains or priests; but on the whole, New Mexico seemed to be moving steadily toward fulfillment of Spanish policy. The principal interest of the colonists and their officials in New Mexico was financial reward. Toward this end, they drew upon the aboriginal trade in salt and hides, furthered Pueblo production of cloth, attempted to expand trade in Pueblo farm and pinyon-nut crops, and, since none of these was highly remunerative, added traffic in human beings, sold as slaves. Spanish colonist households and ranches came to rely on the labor of enslaved Indians, mostly captives taken by Apache bands raiding Plains Indian camps and villages. The Apaches traded the captives to Pecos and other easternmost pueblos, where Spaniards could obtain them as slaves. The Spanish market for slaves encouraged the Apaches to escalate the extent of their raids and lured the Comanches into the same business. By the end of the seventeenth century, the short-sighted Spanish slave market had made much of eastern New Mexico and adjacent Sonora untenable: pueblos were abandoned under the constant harassment of the Apaches, and travel along the old route into Mexico could be attempted only by large convoys under heavy armed guard. In addition to entering Pueblo trade, the Spanish officials took tribute from each pueblo. The Puebloans, having apparently agreed to Spanish dominion, had to pay taxes. As in Mexico, the community as a whole was taxed, its *alcalde* (Spanish-appointed native magistrate) being charged with collecting the sum of goods and produce and delivering it to the Crown officers. Pueblos were also required to furnish labor to work the Crown and mission estates. There was always a temptation for colony officials to order more tribute and more labor than was required by the Crown and skim off for their private benefit enough of each to nourish their ambitions for wealth. Only the missionaries were in a position to protest the often exorbitant exactions of the officials, but their concern tended to be linked with complaints that civil demands prevented the Indians from giving sufficient labor to the mission.

Difficult as it was to meet the impositions of church and state, the pueblos were more disturbed by the harsh regime enacted by the missionaries to ensure the practice of Christianity. After compelling the community to build a church large enough to accommodate all residents, plus a residence, storage buildings, and stables for the mission, the priests required every member of the pueblo to attend morning Mass daily. Anyone who did not appear, or who sneaked out during the Mass, was punished. Public flogging was the most common penalty. The Franciscans who ran missions in the seventeenth-century Southwest were adamantly opposed to all native religious practices, unlike many of the first missionaries in Mexico a century earlier, who sought to reinterpret native symbols in Christian terms. The Pueblos' missionaries banned the indigenous dances, the costumes, and symbols, such as the scattering of maize meal and the setting of feather-tufted sticks beside altars. Kivas were raided, their contents of masks and other religious paraphernalia destroyed, and their leaders severely dealt with, even hanged as idolators or witches. Spanish civil officials complained that the missionaries were too rigorous, that they denied the people social entertainments and prevented them from staging secular rituals welcoming the visits of the governor or trading parties. In 1661, the Franciscans tried to totally wipe out the *katcinas*, (masked dancers personifying spirit beings), in spite of the governor of New Mexico's view that many katcina impersonations were harmlessly amusing, and in spite of the church's policy in Mexico of avoiding blanket condemnations of native practices.

The years 1667 to 1672 witnessed severe drought in New Mexico. Pueblo crops failed, and the Apaches, who depended on captured produce and livestock to supplement their hunting and gathering, intensified their raids. Puebloans had also been suffering throughout the century from European diseases. Now they saw evidence on all sides of disharmony in the universe: plants not growing; people sickening; enemies attacking; violent, arrogant aliens making serfs of the most dignified men and women; the cloudless sky hard and burning, season after season. What conclusion could a sensible person reach? Obviously, their religious tradition was correct in teaching that the proper performance of their indigenous ceremonies was necessary to maintain the beneficial harmony of the universe; the ceremonies had not been per-

FIGURE 3.3   Bow Priesthood (hunters) ceremonial dance, Zuni Pueblo. *(Milwaukee Public Museum)*

formed as they should have been, and evil was rampant. Tinder was laid for a conflagration. The spark was the seizure and flogging, in 1675, of forty-seven Pueblo leaders accused of fomenting revival of native religion. One of these men was a Tewa from San Juan, Popé. Hiding from the Spanish in the northern Pueblo of Taos, Popé organized a rebellion. The fruit of his efforts was reaped in 1680 for all the Pueblos, except the southernmost of those on the Río Grande (the Isleta and the Piros, a Tanoan-speaking group). Attacks by Pueblos upon their resident missionaries and other Spaniards, and by an army of men from most of the

Tanoan-speaking groups, plus many Keresans, upon Sante Fe, the capital of New Mexico, drove all the Spaniards south into Mexico at El Paso. The Piros went with the Spanish, and over subsequent generations virtually lost their Pueblo identity. The rebel Pueblos reestablished their native customs, augmenting them with the desirable Spanish introduction of wheat, fruit orchards, and livestock. (In 1980, the Pueblos celebrated the tricentennial of the revolt.)

Independence was enjoyed for twelve years. Then, between 1692 and 1696, Spanish soldiers and colonists returned to New Mexico, fighting pueblos individually. By the end of four years,

Spain had again achieved dominion over the Pueblos. Open armed rebellion had been, in the long run, futile. Pueblo spirit remained strong, but took a new tack: overt submission to Spanish rule, covert continuation of native government and religion. The head priests of the Pueblo kivas and other religious societies constituted a governing council that appointed less important men—usually Bow (war) Society leaders, who traditionally acted as pueblo police—to the Spanish offices of pueblo governor, lieutenant governor, sheriff, and work-project organizer. These public officers were changed yearly, and their decisions could be vetoed by the council of priests and their chief. Thus, the Pueblos maintained their traditional conception of secular power and business as subordinate limbs of the central body of ceremonies through which humans strengthen the equilibrium, or harmony, of the universe. A combination of wary secrecy on the part of the Puebloans and a diminished missionary program during the remainder of Spanish domination allowed the scheme to succeed.

The eighteenth century and the first half of the nineteenth century was a period of Pueblo persistence in the face of steadily declining population and constant threat from nomadic Athabascan (Apache and Navajo) and Shoshonean (Comanche and Ute) raiders. The western pueblos of the Hopi and Zuni had only intermittent contact with Spaniards or Mexicans, who feared to travel through the raiders' haunts, particularly when the precarious subsistence farming and lack of mineral resources in Hopi and Zuni country offered no inducement. Spanish officials did occasionally come to the Hopi to entice them and the several Eastern Pueblo refugee groups settled among the Hopi after 1680 to move to the Río Grande region, where they could be at least superficially managed. Some of the refugees returned, but the Tewa community of Hano would not, and they still live on the Hopis' First Mesa. Franciscan missionaries also came from time to time, stimulated by Jesuit rivalry, but they had more apparent success with Navajos near the Hopi villages than with the Hopi themselves.

Eastern Pueblos needed to be more cunning than the Hopi and Zuni to carry on their traditions, since missionaries and Mexican and Spanish colonists lived adjacent to or even within the Pueblos. In most Pueblo communities, a core remembered the disasters that seemed to result from lapses in rituals preceding 1680. This core conspired to fulfill their ceremonial obligations and enforce secrecy on the villagers; Puebloans who would not support the traditionalist core left, willingly or not, to join Spanish-American communities. The decline in Pueblo populations was thus from two kinds of causes, death from disease and raids, and the siphoning off of individuals who either disagreed with the dominant faction in a community or who were captured and sold as slaves by raiders.

Pueblos fought against Mexican oppression in 1837 and then against United States conquest in 1847, a fight suppressed by the massacre of 150 Taos people. When the United States took over the northernmost Southwest in 1848, it recognized Spanish land grants, including those made to Indian pueblos. Puebloans allied with United States troops against Athabascan and Shoshonean raiders. In 1876, the United States Supreme Court decided that Pueblos occupied the same status as Spanish-Americans in New Mexico, that they held the same kind of land tenure, and that they should therefore not be treated as Indians (in other words, they were not to be considered wards of the government). In spite of this decision, in 1882 a presidential executive order created a reservation for the Hopi, to protect their land base against the inroads of Navajo neighbors. That purpose was ill-served by an agreement to make a large part of the Hopi Reservation a Joint Use Area where both peoples could graze their flocks; within eighty years, population growth in both groups led to each demanding exclusive use of the Joint Use Area, and a long, drawn-out lawsuit. Other pueblos seemed open to take-over by non-Indian business operators: Acoma in 1884 became embroiled between competing trading-post owners wanting to lease the entire pueblo. The Acoma decided to sign with a

German-Jewish immigrant, Solomon Bibo, who had married Juana Valle, granddaughter of a governor of the pueblo. A year later, Bibo was elected governor of Acoma, the only non-Indian to ever hold that post. He quickly brought in a teacher and set up a school in the town, but that aroused opposition among the people concerned to preserve their own culture. The Bibos left (and Mrs. Bibo, in time, became a successful businesswoman in the couple's San Francisco enterprises).

The 1876 Supreme Court decision was reversed in 1913, when the Court found the Pueblos entitled to benefits enjoyed by other Indians, including land wardship. The court cases stemmed from the infiltration of non-Pueblo settlers into Pueblo lands. During Spanish domination, both Spanish and Mexican colonists and enclaves of local mestizos, often the descendants of enslaved Indians, had slowly increased in numbers, competing with Pueblos for arable land. After the United States Civil War, and especially after the nomadic raiders were controlled in the 1880s, Anglo-Americans had come into the Southwest in much greater numbers. These new immigrants wanted farms, ranches, and town sites; many had enough capital to buy large tracts and import substantial herds of livestock or build expensive irrigation systems. With arable land and good range naturally so limited in the Southwest, considerable pressure was applied to old residents, Spanish-American and Puebloan, to sell out. The 1913 decision indicated that the government thought it necessary to step in to preserve the integrity of Pueblo communities; but not until 1924, when the Pueblo Lands Act was passed, did the government have an instrument to recover lands.

Government concern over Pueblo landholdings did not extend to other aspects of Pueblo life. At the same time territory was being returned to pueblos, the Bureau of Indian Affairs continued its longstanding policies of removing Indian children to boarding schools in which all native culture was suppressed and of discouraging native religions. Agents attempted, too, to change Pueblo farming practices to resemble Euro-American models. Some of their innovations were good, but many tended to destroy cooperative work groups and sometimes the fields themselves. The notion that Pueblo farmers were intelligent people whose methods had been proved best for local conditions by generations of experiment was not accepted by the BIA. The overlord had changed, but the Pueblos still needed to fight the imposition of foreign values, still needed to use cunning and secrecy to preserve their cultures.

John Collier's 1934 "New Deal" for Indians was to many Puebloans yet another threat to their culture. Pueblos were ruled by priests because only people who devoted years to learning religious knowledge were thought to have the wisdom to maintain pueblos. The Tewa call these well-trained leaders the Made (or Finished) People. Collier's proposal for democratically elected representative councils and elected chiefs did not recognize the importance Puebloans place upon preparation for leadership and did not account for the centrality of sacred knowledge in guiding decisions affecting the community. Only the pueblo of Santa Clara initially accepted Collier's recommendations; and a half-century later, in spite of the exposure of thousands of Puebloans to the American democratic procedures extolled in schools, towns, and the armed forces, only five more pueblos (Isleta, Laguna, Pojoaque, San Ildefonso, and Zuni) have adopted tribal constitutions and councils on the American model.

A basic component of Collier's program was the promotion of native crafts through the Indian Arts and Crafts Board, which hired persons, usually non-Indian, to organize production of crafts, determine the most marketable types, and develop merchandising outlets. As a rule, these arts-and-crafts specialists tried to encourage each tribe to draw from its own tradition rather than follow individual tastes and ideas gleaned from intertribal gatherings and popular media. Collier saw a revival of native tribal craft traditions as contributing both to the reservation economies and to pride in the native heritage. The Pueblos, having been sedentary for over a thousand years, had nurtured craft skills in a variety of goods, including kiva painting, pottery, weaving, and woodworking. The Spanish had taught Puebloans metalsmithing. A market for Pueblo crafts had already grown among tourists, especially along the Santa Fe Railroad, which used Pueblo artisans' work to advertise the allure of its route west. María and Julian Martínez of San Ildefonso Pueblo had become quite famous for their experiments in reviving lustrous black-on-black pottery. The Arts and Crafts Board thus found the Pueblos fertile for its enterprise. Pottery and silverwork brought in significant income to many Pueblo families. Some artists studied the artifacts unearthed by archaeologists from the ruins of their ancestors' pueblos and reproduced the techniques and styles that they found. The arts-and-crafts movement was important in continuing the viability of ancient material culture, but there was a flip-side to the benefits: craftworkers were discouraged from producing items that did not appeal strongly to Euro-American buyers, and the popularizing of Indian motifs led to the horrendous souvenirs that compete with the real crafts—coarse pots painted with Day-Glo zigzags, machine-woven blankets, and stamped tinny jewelry with fake turquoises. Tourists' visits to pueblos seemed a likely outgrowth of the Arts and Crafts Board and railroad promotions, but the Pueblos were not interested in making money from zoolike displays of their way of life. Not only would the dignity of the people be demeaned by the presence of paying onlookers around the villages, but the effectiveness of the pueblos' religious rituals could be hindered by the interruptions of ignorant aliens.

Euro-Americans at the Pueblo ceremonies had been troublesome for centuries. First, the Spanish missionaries had forbade Pueblo religious practices. Then, in the late nineteenth century and the twentieth century, some overzealous anthropologists had tried to ferret out the secrets to which only initiated men should be privy. Finally, a series of Protestant and Catholic missionaries supported by pre-Collier officials had claimed that Pueblo religion was debauched and must not be perpetuated. A Religious Crimes Code drawn up in the Bureau of Indian Affairs proscribed a long series of these "pagan" practices. In 1924, the All Pueblo Council, a meeting of the Pueblo governors formally organized in 1922, protested the BIA policy of placing Indian children in Christian mission schools and refusing to allow them to receive instruction in their native religion. The policy was subsequently rejected by Collier's administration, but out in the Indian communities, there was often considerable lag in implementing new directives, particularly when agents' personal convictions did not change with the policy reversals.

The problem of handling anthropologists' inquiries and the nuisance of blundering tourists remained and discouraged the opening of most ceremonies to public viewing. To protect the naturalness of customary daily life and the viability of the rituals they believe necessary, the Pueblos have consistently refused to capitalize on their attraction as exotic and colorful non-Westerners within easy driving distance of millions of Euro-Americans. Not all Puebloans adamantly adhere to their centuries-old traditions, however. Probably in prehistoric days, dissidents left pueblos to found new communities that departed in custom, to a degree, as well as in miles, from the old home. Certainly, this fissioning of villages and apostasy of individuals continued through the historic period. World War II seemed to accelerate the rate of departure of dissidents. Large numbers of young Pueblo men and women served in the armed forces or worked in war-production factories or on large, non-Pueblo farms. Some of these young people were not content with the subsistence farming and theocracy of their pueblos. Others may have been willing to return to a traditional life, but found their villages becoming overpopulated.

The postwar years saw a marked increase in the rate of population growth, which rendered the Pueblo lands inadequate to sustain all their younger families. In the 1980s, there were over ten

FIGURE 3.4 Hopi woman in traditional everyday dress making baskets outside her home. *(Smithsonian Institution National Anthropological Archives)*

thousand Hopi, seven thousand Zuni, over four thousand Laguna, three thousand each in Acoma, Isleta, and Santo Domingo, and hundreds in each of the smaller pueblos. Thus, more or less willingly, many Pueblo families have found it necessary to leave the old villages to found new communities or to work in the cities. Those who did not wish to abandon their native religion, and many who intend to retire to their home villages, have softened the cleavage that formerly existed between each pueblo and all outsiders. Intermarriage between pueblos, fostered by young people from many pueblos meeting in high schools and at their jobs, has also been a factor in lessening some of the pueblos' outward uniqueness, although the basic core of beliefs and ethos seems strong.

Pueblo Culture

Many aspects of Pueblo culture—town life, agriculture, and crafts—have already been sketched. The core of organization and beliefs should be delineated more explicitly. Western and Eastern Pueblos contrast in social organization but share many religious practices and concepts. The Western Pueblos, Hopi and Zuni, are organized on the basis of descent from legendary ancestors, each group believed to have moved into the pueblo in ancient times, bringing some sacred knowledge or ability. Their descendants inherit the right and obligation to conduct the ritual or activity contributed by their founders. Husbands traditionally lived in their wives' homes, and if divorced, moved out, back to their mother's or sister's house. Each descent group maintains a kiva, or ceremonial chamber, and owns ritual paraphernalia. The descent group is symbolized by an ear of maize, decorated and placed upon an altar in the chamber. Men of the group, led by one of the oldest, lead prayers and perform rituals together. Persons from other groups may participate, but the responsibility for the success of the ceremony rests

FIGURE 3.5 Hopi men emerging from a kiva in Walpi pueblo, 1900. *(Smithsonian Institution National Archives, Bureau of American Ethnology Collection)*

with the hosts. Integration is achieved in the Western Pueblos by residents having memberships in several organizations that are somewhat overlapping in function and that recruit without reference to descent affiliation. There are, first, the katcina dance associations, headquartered in kivas, whose male members impersonate the katcina spirits in rituals designed to call these ancient beings to the pueblo, bringing rain and prosperity with them. All Hopi children were initiated into the katcina cult when they were six to ten years old; while at Zuni, all boys were initiated. There are the village-function organizations, whose members are charged with performing both the ritual and practical business of war, hunting, policing, and castigating offenders against public morality. Then there are medicine societies, which are joined by individuals who survive certain illnesses and who are then charged with aiding others to recover. There are kin relationships extended to include many persons in and beyond the pueblo; women look out for the young men who are sons of their

brothers and male cousins, and the "aunts" and "nephews" enjoy joking about each others' sexual skill. Finally, there are informal social parties of friends. These various groups create multiple, crosscutting ties between pueblo residents, which counteract the divisiveness that might otherwise result from bonding on the basis of descent groups. That inherent divisiveness surfaces in political controversies, which tend to invoke legendary rights and duties ascribed to opposing leaders seen as representatives of their ancestral groups.

The Eastern Pueblos' social structure is built not on clans, but on the moiety system (dividing the village in two). The Keresans have matrilineal descent groups serving principally to promote extended family cooperation and prevent close inbreeding. Keresan pueblos are organized on the basis of the moieties Squash and Turquoise. In most of the pueblos, individuals residing on the north side of the village belong to one, those on the south side to the other. Each moiety maintains a kiva. The moieties are charged with carrying out

FIGURE 3.6 Hopi men personifying katcinas of the Powamu ("Bean-planting") ritual, Walpi pueblo, 1893. *(Smithsonian Institution National Anthropological Archives)*

major village ceremonies, including the katcina dances, which are associated with the kivas. The business of the village is supervised through the medicine societies, it being required that the chief (often termed *cacique*, a Caribbean-Spanish word) and his assistants be members of these societies. Public morality is guarded by the two "clown" societies, Koshare and Kwirena, whose members dress in outlandish but drably colored costumes and cavort between sets of the sacred dances, mimicking with slapstick humor those who do not conform to the Pueblo ideal of circumspect, self-effacing, polite behavior. Government officials, schoolteachers, missionaries, tourists, anthropologists, and Navajos are favorite targets of the ritual clowns, whose exaggerated gestures and nonsense speeches hold up to ridicule these antagonists of Pueblo tradition. Two major activities outside the village are given to the war and hunt associations. The former are now extinct, but the latter are still active, conducting rituals through which the power of the large hunting animals is passed to human hunters.

Tanoan pueblos operate through the moieties of Summer, which organizes and supervises village activities from spring equinox to autumn equinox, and Winter, from autumn to spring. The Tanoans have the same types of associations as their western neighbors—indeed, in some instances they have modeled a ceremonial organization upon a Keresan one. The principle of duality is pervasive in Tanoan pueblos, which are divided not once, but twice (that is, into quarters), which classify a tremendous number of objects and activities as belonging to one or the other moiety, and which see dual duality (quartering) in the structure of the world as well as of the pueblo. Nevertheless, the Tanoans express the underlying unity of the world and the pueblo by the devices of pairing an official from each moiety on many important occasions, and of considering the priesthoods to be "in the middle": above and linking the moieties. From west to east among the Pueblos, a visitor would pass from communities emphasizing descent groups, through the Keresans with some recognition of such groups, to the Tanoans, among whom both parents' families are equally and in the same way important and in which inheritance is given to both sons and daughters. All the pueblos have medicine, katcina, clown, hunt, and (formerly) war associations; but in the west, the rain-bringing katcinas and rain-calling medicine-society rituals are the most important religious activities, and among the Tanoans, war associations were especially active. These shifts in emphasis no doubt are correlated with the Western Pueblos' greater dependency upon rainfall for agriculture, contrasted with the Tanoans' river-fed fields and the Western

Pueblos' greater isolation and hence protection from enemies. The Tanoans' position along the eastern border of the Southwest, where they were open to attack from Apaches, Plains Indians, and Spaniards was a factor in the continued activity of the war associations.

Throughout the Pueblos, religion pervades social life. Each pueblo is literally the center of its world, a world bounded on the four quarters by holy mountains or hills and containing within it lakes and shrines where contact may be made with spirits. In the pueblo, in its plaza or in a room in the home of its chief, is "earth mother navel," a small, tunnel-like pit said to connect with the spirit world below and to be the point from which the prosperity of the pueblo radiates out. Symbols of the good things of the world, including seeds of all food plants, wild and cultivated, are enshrined within this center of the pueblo's world. The people of the pueblo are divided into classes according to the degree of religious knowledge they have attained. For the Tewa, these classes are (1) the *Seh t'a* ("Dry Hardened People"), the common young people and uninitiated persons, so called because they are like their ancestors who had emerged from the sacred primordial lake and hardened on the dry earth but had not yet attained spiritual advancement; (2) the *Towa é* ("Persons"), the executive officers of the pueblo, who are likened to the six pairs of brothers (a pair for each of the six directions, including zenith and nadir) who assisted the primordial Chiefs, Mountain Lion the Hunt Chief, the Summer Chief, and the Winter Chief; and (3) the *Patowa* ("Made People"), the leaders of the pueblo, who have attained their offices through study and practice of spiritual and ritual knowledge. Invisible to ordinary humans are three classes of beings: (1) the "Dry Food [People] Who Are No Longer" -that is, the souls of commoners; (2) the souls of Towaé; and (3) the souls of Made People, who join the "Dry Food Who Never Did Become," or spirits in the primordial lake who did not emerge at the beginning of human history. These spirits include the katcinas, who are invoked

FIGURE 3.7 Hano (Tewa) pueblo women inside a home, 1895. The woman on the left kneels at bins in which maize is ground. Figurines of katcinas hang on the wall above her. *(Smithsonian Institution National Anthropological Archives)*

to visit the pueblo and are at these times given physical "hardened" form by dancers in costumes embodying attributes of the individual katcinas.

The Made People have the duty to perpetuate the pueblo world as it should be by retreating to the kivas to pray before altars on which symbols of life and goodness (such as maize and tufts of downy feathers that look like rain clouds) are displayed. Many of the prayer retreats conclude with public ritual dances dramatizing to the common people the focus of the leaders' retreats. The orderly, dignified, beautifully dressed, and anonymous dancers singing of the good aspects of life are at these performances contrasted with the ritual clowns, dirty and ugly, whose grotesque, madcap, highly individualistic behavior parades before the public what is undesirable to the pueblo. The proper, selfless prayer retreats of the Made People are believed to preserve the ancient cooperation between humans and Dry Food Who Never Did Become, a harmonious relationship in which plants will happily grow, game animals will come to the hunter, rain clouds will release their water, and beauty will fill the senses. Most of the ceremonies are held during the winter, when the world seems to be running down and the work of the Made People is clearly needed to restore warmth and life. (Anthropologists have pointed out that the holding of more of the ceremonies in winter prevents conflict with the demands of agriculture for time and labor, and that, further, the distributions of food at the feasts that accompany the ceremonies help families with small fields or poor harvests get through the winter without need to beg from more prosperous families.) Pueblo cosmology thus emphasizes the centrality of the human community, its continuing ties to the beings of the Creation, and the obligation of all persons, but especially the learned, to work for the common good;—for if they fail to do so, if people harbor evil thoughts and shirk duties, then they are responsible for bringing disaster upon all.

Pueblo culture is distinctive, complex, and well integrated. Ties to Mexico are clear—maize, macaws kept for their decorative feathers, New Mexico turquoise found used in Valley of Mexico artifacts—but not so easy to evaluate. It seems likely that the Mexican agricultural village, with its pottery and rectangular adobe houses, was in its Hohokam manifestation the model for Mogollon

and then Anasazi development. Some anthropologists are convinced that Pueblo religion, too, should be seen as the reworking of Mexican concepts carried in with macaws, or learned by those who took the turquoise south. Parallels with Mexico are numerous: the six directions; the Earth Mother in whom are caves, some of them leading through tunnel openings (*sipapu*, "earth navel") to the human world; the ancient elderly fire god Huehueteotl; the hunt chief Mountain Lion of the North, paralleling the jaguar as lord of the hunt and earthly power; the eagle as symbol of celestial power; the Hopi god Sotuqnang-u, whose attributes of a horn, when seen masked, and a star-shaped hat, when unmasked, identify him with Quetzalcóatl; the Corn Mother, or goddess of maize; and the rain katcinas, who, like Tlaloc and his tlaloques, or helpers, have a leader and lesser

---

THE ZUNI LEARN TO HONOR MAIZE, THE STAPLE OF THEIR LIFE

This is an episode from the myth "In the Beginning," narrated March 29, 1965, at Zuni by Andrew Peynetsa. It was translated by Dennis Tedlock and Joseph Peynetsa. Note that Tedlock uses capital letters to render loud-voice emphasis, small print for low, dropped voice, and syllables above or below the line to indicate change in pitch, in order to recapture the narrative poem as it was told.

FAR OFF AT ASH WATER [the Milky Way]
at the spring
of the Ritual Clowns
the Clowns had their beginning.
THEY CAME ALONG
until they came to the Middle Place [Zuni].

At that time
we were irresponsible.
It seems that we didn't love
our mothers
all the kinds of corn.
Our elders, our grandfathers, our grandmothers, the people who lived before us
DID NOT LOVE THEM, and so
the Corn Mothers ABANDONED them.
The CORN MOTHERS A ABANDONED THEM
and went toward the coral [dawn].

THERE IN THE CORAL OCEAN
out in the water
a goose
nestled the ears of corn
and NO WAY
to bring them back was known.
THERE WAS NO SEED CORN.
They were living
WITHOUT SEED CORN.
They were full of anxiety.

Even the priests
though they were wise
did not know HOW TO GO ON LIVING.
The CLOWNS were summoned.

When the Clowns were summoned
Nepayatamu [the primordial Clown]
came to the Priest Kiva.

He entered the Priest Kiva:
    "My fathers, my children, how
have you been?" "Happy, our child
sit down," they told him, and he sat down. When he sat down

the Sun Priest questioned him: "NOW, our father, CHILD
we have summoned you HERE.
PER HAPS, AS WE HAVE IN MIND
you might
find our Corn Mothers.

Our Corn Mothers aren't here, they've GONE somewhere
Because we were irresponsible
    we lost the sight of our mothers.
Since
you are an extraordinary person
perhaps
you might find them.
You might bring them back to us."
… … … … … … …
Then Nepayatamu told them:
"THERE WILL BE FASTING.
IF YOU WANT IT
IF YOU ARE WILLING
to go into fasting
then I will look for them."
That's what he told them.
The priests
went to thinking.
They went to thinking.
They talked.

Their House Chief said
   "Well then
this is the way it will be:
WE ARE WILLING, for truly
we were irresponsible and lost our mothers, and so
we will go into fasting, we are WILLING to fast." ...
[Nepayatamu went to the ocean in the east, and a duck ferried him]
until they came to where the goose lay.
"My mother, my CHILD
how have you been passing the days?" Nepayatamu said.
   "Happily, our FATHER.
So you've come," she said. "We've come."
"Indeed
FOR WHAT REASON
have you entered upon our roads?
Perhaps it is because of a WORD of some importance
that you have entered upon our roads, for you would not do this for no reason,"
   that's what
the goose
told Nepayatamu. "YES, in TRUTH
my mother, my CHILD:
there at the Middle Place our fathers, the PRIESTS
have lost the sight
of their MOTHERS
all the kinds of corn.
Because they have ABANDONED us
I am looking for them." "Indeed.
BUT DO THEY REALLY LOVE THEM?" she asked NEPAYATAMU.
"Yes
it must be that they really love them.
WHAT THEN?"
Nepayatamu said.
"I am nestling them.
Right here I'm nestling them
but if you
have set a day for them
THEN ^{THEY}
will certainly have
that day.
Through THEIR FLESH

the women
among our daylight children
will have good flesh.
Their flesh will smell of corn."
Those
were the words of the goose.
"But if THIS is what you want
perhaps you will be very CAREFUL.
YOU ARE IN NEED
so you may GO AHEAD and take them JUST AS THEY ARE

and THAT will be IT.
But IF YOU HAVE DIFFICULTY on the way
then that's the way it will have to be."
Those were the words
she spoke to Nepayatamu.
    "NOW
our father, CHILD
you may hold them in your arms," she told him.
(From Tedlock 1972:288-295)

ones, and play a ball game (thunder is the noise of their kicked wooden ball) associated with the coming of rain and duplicated by human men in a ritual game. Yet neither Pueblo society nor religion offers one-to-one replication of Mexican models. Considering that Tanoan is one branch of the Aztec-Tanoan language stock, it is possible that much of the Pueblos' religion and basic concepts of social organization developed relatively independently from a very old common cultural base from which stemmed also Mexican culture, or at least much of Aztec culture. The most reasonable view is that Pueblo and Mexican similarities indicate both a most ancient shared ancestry and continued contacts by trade and migrations through many subsequent centuries. Pueblo culture can be fully understood only in the context of its position on the northern border of Mexico, but it is not a derivative of Mexico. In meeting the challenge of building sedentary towns in the marginal environment of the northernmost Southwest, the Pueblos forged a pattern that seems to justify their concept of each pueblo existing at the navel of its world.

SECTION 3: THE APACHEANS

When the Spanish entered New Mexico in 1540, the plateau north of the Pueblos was inhabited by small bands of people speaking an Athabascan (Dene) language and raising maize, beans, and squash, but relying on hunting and wild-food gathering to a greater extent than was usual for the Pueblos. These Athabascans came to be called Apaches. They occupied the country abandoned by the Pueblos several generations earlier.

Classification of American Indian languages has revealed the startling fact that Apachean, the language of the communities on the Southwest's northern frontier, is closely related to Indian languages of western Canada. All other Athabascan-stock languages are spoken by peoples in Canada and the Pacific Northwest. The greatest number of shared words and grammatical features can be found between Apachean and Sarsi, the language of a historic bison-hunting people in southern Alberta, Canada. Ancestral Apacheans (including Sarcee) moved from the western Subarctic forests onto the northwesternmost High Plains about two thousand years ago. They used bows and small, sharp, beautifully flaked arrowpoints (known as Avonlea points) to slaughter bison they drove into pounds. The linguistic relationships seem to indicate that several centuries before European contact, a few of these Athabascan hunting bands in what is now the Canadian province of Alberta moved south along the high plains just east of the Rocky Mountains. Families that remained in southern Alberta, allying with the more numerous, Algonkian-speaking Blackfoot, are the historic Sarcee. The Apacheans are those who continued south into Montana and Wyoming and through the western high Plains, where some added agriculture to their economy, using lands deserted by the Pueblos on the Colorado Plateau, and others remained no-madic bison hunters, ranging through western Texas and Oklahoma. The latter were met by Coronado in 1540. By about 1700, the Kiowa-Apache had allied with the Aztec-Tanoan-speaking Kiowa, with whom they gradually shifted into the southern Plains.

The distinction between agricultural and non-agricultural Apacheans correlates with environ-mental differences that became effective as the Apacheans infiltrated the more-or-less unoccupied areas between the Pueblo farmlands. This en-croachment was possible because the Apacheans, moving in groups of a few families and oriented toward wild resources, could live off country that could not support the agricultural towns of the Pueblos. The success of the encroachment was ensured by the readiness of the Apacheans to raid: the Puebloans were put on the defensive guarding their food stores and were prevented from making retaliatory attacks by the difficulty of finding the elusive little Apachean camps in the back country. Not all contact between Apacheans and Puebloans was hostile, however, especially before the nine-teenth century: Apacheans regularly traded meat and hides in Pueblo towns, and often wintered beside the walls of the towns. After the Pueblo Revolt of 1680, the host-guest relationship was reversed for several decades, Pueblo refugees camping with Apacheans to escape Spanish re-tribution. The result of two centuries of extended visits was a rough distinction, which intensified after 1680, between the more strongly Pueblo-in-fluenced Apacheans—the Navajo and the Western Apache, who came to be grouped into White Mountain, Cibecue, San Carlos, and Tonto bands—and the Eastern Apaches, who showed more Plains influence—the Kiowa-Apache, Lipan, Jicarilla, Mescalero, and Chiricahua. The Navajo and Western Apache are farmers and have matrilineal descent groups; the Eastern Apache have traditionally been primarily bison hunters, and emphasize the solidarity of relatives of the same generation rather than the tie to the mother and her lineage.

The Navajo

The Navajo are now the largest single Indian tribe in the United States, approaching two hundred thousand members—twenty times the number of Navajos in the 1860s—and holding 9 million acres of reservation. Governed by a vigorous tribal council drawn from local district "chapters," the Navajo Nation, as it styles itself, has come to be a force to be reckoned with in the Southwest and in government Indian policies.

The earliest trace of the Navajo may be hogan logs determined by the pattern of their tree rings to have been cut in A.D. 1491. Hogans, round houses of forked poles and brush covered with earth, have historically been distinctively Navajo. Even today, a more solidly constructed, log-walled hogan is preferred by many Navajo families, although in the seventeenth century some Navajo built rectangular stone homes (*pueblitos*) resembling small Pueblo houses. Early Navajo sites, as also later ones, ap-pear to have been camps occupied for a few months at a time by about twenty to thirty people, what today is called an "outfit" of cooperating related families. Hunting, gathering, and limited agricul-ture were practiced, and a note in Coronado's expedition record describing a raid by nomads a generation previous (about 1525) suggests raiding was also part of the economy.

The seventeenth and eighteenth centuries were a period of considerable incorporation of Pueblo technology, and some Spanish technology via Pueblos, into Navajo culture. The Navajos may have picked up agriculture in Colorado during their prehistoric trek southward, but in the Southwest they expanded, taking both Pueblo crops and meth-ods and Pueblo agricultural ritual symbols. Span-ish introductions of livestock to the Pueblos were accepted by the Navajos in this period. Navajos learned weaving from the Pueblos, though again with some Spanish influence, and blankets from the wool of their own sheep became a source of income, sold to other Indians and Spanish, as well as household staples. Pottery styles shifted, though never reaching the degree of artistic eminence of some Pueblo craftworkers. Baskets were probably a pre-Southwest Apachean product, but basketry continued in the Southwest under Puebloan influence. Many spiritual ideas and practices were borrowed by Navajos from the Pueblos, of which the most well known are sand paintings, ephemeral designs made by sprinkling colored sands and maize meal on the floor. These are common in Pueblo ceremonial chambers, but among the Navajo they became larger, more complex, and a focus of ritual. Matrilineal descent groups are said to be a form of social organization copied by Navajo from the Pueblos, but a tendency toward emphasizing mother-daughter ties is common among all Athabascans, in Canada as well as in the Southwest. The total picture is, then, one of a broad reworking of Navajo cultural patterns under Pueblo and, sometimes indirectly, Spanish examples, with the Navajo taking a great deal of technology and material traits but consistently molding and reinterpreting them in terms of older Navajo values. This occurred even when refugee Puebloans stayed on in Navajo territory as clans traced to Pueblo ancestors. Particularly expressive of Navajo values have been the Navajo retention of small, scattered camps instead of pueblo towns, and the continuing emphasis in religious rituals on restoring individuals to health and prosperity rather than on community-wide goals.

The nineteenth century was one of escalating raids by the Navajo and other Apache. The Apacheans now owned sufficient horses, originally obtained from Spanish ranches, to mount cavalry attacks that were frighteningly successful against the immobile villages and fields of the Pueblos and Spanish-Americans. Where the earlier, pedestrian Apacheans had stolen crops (the name Navajo is said to mean in Tewa "they take from the fields"), their horse-borne descendants could run down and massacre, as well as pillage, townsmen. Raiding was more profitable than trading, which became much less regular than before. The serious threat posed by the Apacheans stimu-

lated several Pueblo groups to ally with the Spanish, and later with Mexicans and then Anglo-Americans as the Southwest's national affiliation changed. Occasionally, the retaliators managed to surprise Navajo camps and kill defenseless women and children; often Navajo youngsters were captured and sold as slaves to Spanish households. Important as raiding had become to Apachean economy, the Navajos never allowed it to dominate, but consistently kept up their farms and managed their flocks. Their relatively sedentary life, restricted to areas with water for crops and herds, encouraged craftwork, to which in the nineteenth century was added silversmithing learned from the Mexicans.

The United States, coming into the Southwest at the conclusion of the Mexican War, attempted to end Apachean raiding by making treaties with chiefs. Since the Apachean leaders were no more than men whose advice was respectfully listened to, but by no means always followed, the agreement of any "chief" bound only himself, and then for only as long as seemed politic. Unhappily, while United States officers made sincere efforts to negotiate peace, United States soldiers expropriated Navajo pastures to graze Army livestock. Navajos from several bands then organized, in 1860, an attack upon the U.S. Fort Defiance, built deep in Navajo territory near what is now the Arizona-New Mexico border. The attack failed, but because the U.S. troops were soon pulled out, the Navajo thought they had succeeded in defending their land. The truth was, the troops left to join the Civil War battles. Then, in 1863, Union commanders cautioned the government to guard the Southwest so that California would not be cut off. The redoubtable Colonel Kit Carson was sent to Fort Defiance with orders to control the Apacheans, especially the numerous and well-supplied Navajo.

Carson had more serious business than revenge. Instead of fighting Navajo men and stealing children to sell as slaves, Carson marched his troops through the Navajo canyons, methodically destroying fields and herds. Men who resisted were killed, but women, children, and men whose discretion tempered their valor were taken to camps where they were provided with food and promised new homes if they would submit to government regulation. Most of the Navajo—eight thousand out of about ten thousand—were thus forced by the threat of starvation out of their territory and onto the "Long Walk" across New Mexico to Fort Sumner. There they stayed for four years, until 1868, supposedly to learn new farming techniques, the building of adobe houses, Christianity, and literacy. But most Navajos, having little interest in any of these alien ideas, simply collected their rations and mourned the loss of their freedom. Crowded conditions and the poor diet made the people vulnerable to disease, especially to smallpox, which killed over two thousand Navajo in 1865.

With the Civil War over, the need to closely control the Apacheans declined, and the obvious misery of the imprisoned Navajos—Fort Sumner was, in effect, a large concentration camp—led to a relaxation of the government policy. The Navajos were permitted in 1868 to return across New Mexico to their former territory on both sides of the Arizona–New Mexico state line. They could again take up their accustomed farming practices, and they were issued sheep, goats, and a few other livestock.

Navajo population, and the population of Navajo livestock, especially sheep, increased steadily after the return to the homeland (*Dinétah* in Navajo [equivalent to Denedeh in the Northern Dene languages]). The Navajo Reservation was expanded several times (which left the Hopi Reservation in the middle, completely surrounded!). By 1934, administrators in Collier's Bureau of Indian Affairs were convinced that the Navajo had more livestock than even their large reservation could support. John Collier, who passionately believed that American Indians are models of egalitarian communal societies, suspected that the wealthy Navajo owning over a thousand sheep (and using profits to buy trucks and trading posts)

were undermining the moral purity of the society he admired. More pragmatic officials listened to the engineers planning the Hoover Dam on the Colorado River, who claimed that overgrazed Navajo land would turn into a Dust Bowl and silt up the dam's reservoir. This threat was sufficient to instigate a BIA order that nearly half the Navajo flocks be disposed of, by killing if no market could be found. The Navajo resisted the order, claiming that the land was not being overgrazed, that their subsistence economy should not be judged by the same criteria that applied to the profit-seeking Euro-American farms. Government agents, frightened by the specter of a dust bowl in the Southwest like that developing in Oklahoma, insisted on carrying out their orders, even to the slaughtering of thousands of animals with no compensation to the Navajo owners. Deep bitterness ensued, not only between Navajos and Euro-Americans, but also between the minority of Navajos who agreed with the government assessment of the reservation situation and the majority of Navajos who did not.

The cause célèbre of Navajo stock reduction has led most observers to assume that sheep are the most important factor in the Navajo economy and the most valued of Navajo possessions. In fact, farming is the basis of reservation Navajo livelihood, and Navajo settlements are situated where farming is best, the flocks pasturing if they can in the vicinity of the fields. Truly pastoral peoples move with their animals to the best pastures; the Navajo compromise between the interests of the flocks and agriculture, giving somewhat more weight to the latter. Sheep are important as the regular source of protein in the daily diet, for their wool—which, woven into blankets, brings in cash as well as furnishing the hogan—and as a sign of prosperity. Navajo families love to see large herds of sheep around their home because they are proof of the family's industriousness and managerial ability, and guarantees of warmth and dinner—if the crop fails, then one can eat mutton alone. Sheep were the Navajos' gold: demonstration of present prosperity, and security for the future. The stock-

FIGURE 3.8 Navajo homestead, 1925. The log hogan at left is insulated with earth at its base; an anthropologist photographs a young man in front of the open ramada in which his wife is weaving at an upright loom. *(Milwaukee Public Museum)*

reduction program hit the symbol of Navajo reputation and comfort, and was perceived as a campaign to destroy Navajo society, not just sheep. This became particularly apparent beginning in 1937, when permits to keep stock were limited to 350 sheep (or the equivalent in grazing needs) per owner. The first phase of stock reduction had been a sweeping destruction that disproportionately hit poorer families for whom losing ten sheep could mean the difference between maintaining a flock or having none. The second phase of capping the number per owner was meant to dismantle the social hierarchy in the tribe, leveling the few wealthy families to the common status. What the limit of 350 sheep accomplished was the crash of market-oriented stock-raising plus abolition of

family economies based on livestock alone. Three hundred and fifty sheep-equivalent permits meant fewer than 350 sheep, because horses needed for herding and transport took some sheep permits, and no family could supply all its annual needs maintaining a flock never more than 350 head. The net result was general hardship: more crowding on limited arable land and more people seeking wage work—in the middle of the Great Depression of the 1930s.

World War II distracted the Navajo from the conflict over stock reduction. Several thousand young men and women joined the armed forces, where some used their native language to communicate war intelligence, Navajo serving as a ready-made code impenetrable to the enemy. Thousands more Navajo left the reservation to work. The effect of this unprecedented large-scale exposure to Euro-American society was to make off-reservation employment more tolerable and to spur demand for American schooling so that Navajo might obtain better-paying, more prestigious skilled and professional positions. A number of Navajo veterans took advantage of the G.I. Bill to attend college. The potential of using American political and legal strategies to advance Navajo goals was now appreciated, to the point that Navajo sophisticated in these matters from long residence away from the reservation were elected to tribal-council leadership.

The Navajo Nation was among the first to establish innovative schools directed by its members. These schools seek to stimulate Navajo young people to mesh a love for their tradition with the skills needed to exercise power within American society. The Rough Rock Demonstration School for children and the Navajo Community College developed curricula that not only prepares students for advanced skill-training and college programs off the reservation, but includes courses in Navajo language, literature (myths, legends, and traditional and modern poetry), and philosophy. The Navajo pioneered a public-health program that brings together Euro-American medical doctors and Navajo diviners and curers as consultants. This program recognizes that the physically oriented Western medical treatments can be complemented by the spiritually oriented Navajo treatments, that Navajo patients should not be forced to choose between these two components of their illness. The program seems particularly suitable for the Navajo because Navajo religion focuses on rituals designed to restore to health persons who are "out of kilter" with the world (from guilt over violating proper behavior, from fright occasioned by strange incidents, or from too much intimacy with alien ways, as when living in Euro-American towns or schools). Thus, the emotional disturbance felt by a Navajo away from home, a disturbance that can impede recovery from organic illnesses, is directly

handled by Navajo ritual. This kind of disturbance may be greatest for Navajo in hospitals, where the effect of crowds, sterility, and strange furnishings and food is heightened by knowledge that the building contains dead people: the Apacheans have a horror of corpses and the spirits of the dead. (It is said that this horror repelled the Navajo from the Ghost Dance religion so popular with most other tribes of the American West at the turn of the century.)

Other innovations of the Navajo Nation include concerted efforts to extend the jurisdiction of the tribe over its members and territory in both individual and corporate matters, to develop a stronger reservation economy without damaging traditional values (that is, without disparaging elders or bringing in Euro-American interpersonal competitiveness), and to place well-trained and capable Navajo in professional roles on the reservation. Some observers have claimed that these moves to give Navajo the best of two worlds have exacerbated conflicts, creating a high level of anxiety for many people and increasing accusations of witchcraft within the tribe, but there is no way of determining past incidence of conditions that were never freely discussed and that were not subjects of inquiry by pre-Freudian visitors. In any case, the extraordinary population increase of the Navajo in this century precludes any possibility of strict adherence to past centuries' culture patterns—except that most basic of Navajo patterns, the thoughtful incorporation of neighboring peoples' useful traits.

The Apaches

Apaches and Navajos (originally collectively called *Apaches de Navahu* by the Spaniards) began to diverge at the end of the seventeenth century. Navajos were those Apaches who surrounded the Pueblos, and with whom the Pueblo refugees found safety after the 1680 Pueblo Rebellion. The Navajos absorbed much Pueblo culture and came to base their economy on farming and sheepherding, supplemented by wild foods and raiding. The other Apaches, those farther from the Pueblos, had less intensive contact with Puebloans. The Apaches picked up some Pueblo traits, such as the use of wood-and-leather painted and decorated masks in ritual dances, but they retained more of their earlier cultural emphases, including a valuation of mobility. The Apache other than Navajo have not been willing to burden themselves with large flocks of sheep, although they prize horses and cattle; they have lived in quickly constructed thatch huts *(wickiups)* rather than building the more substantial, earth-insulated, log or stone hogans; and they have not taken up the crafts of weaving and silversmithing that require capital investment, although the beautifully made Apache baskets show the artisan talent among the Apache. The divergence became significant to all peoples in the Southwest when, during the eighteenth century, raiding became an integral part of Apache livelihood, not merely supplemental as for the Navajos, who had greater investments in crops and sheep.

The prevalence of Apache raiding prevented Pueblo or Spanish settlement during the eighteenth century and much of the nineteenth century in a good part of southern New Mexico and in the Arizona–New Mexico–Sonora border region. Through this section of mountains, high valleys, and low, arid desert the Apaches galloped, seizing livestock and, to a lesser extent, crops, manufactures, and woman and child captives and then disappearing into the landscape. Hunting livestock had replaced hunting bison. From time to time, Apache bands took in refugees, but these were usually other Apaches or Plains Indians similarly oriented to hunting, not agricultural Pueblos. Most of the Apaches planted a little maize, beans, and squash, but the fields were the responsibility of women, part of their food gathering; men concerned themselves principally with procuring meat. The nineteenth-century Mescalero and Chiricahua usually did not even bother with such limited farming, relying entirely on predation (hunting game and livestock) and the acorns, pinyon (pine) nuts, mesquite beans, and saguaro cactus fruit collected by the women.

The United States' post-Civil War goal of controlling all Indians within the nation's borders encompassed, of course, the Apache. Because these people were not dependent upon fields and flocks of slow-moving sheep, the United States forces could not conquer them by Carson's policy of ravaging farms. Five reservations were marked out for the Western Apache, supposedly land remote from Euro-American settlements and resources, and band by band, Apaches were cajoled into moving onto the reservations. By late 1872, enough had been lured by the promises of peace and rations that a campaign could be mounted under General Crook to secure the remaining Apaches by arms, using Apache scouts from hostile bands to lead soldiers to camps where, as with the Navajo earlier, resisting men were killed and the remainder of the people dragged to the designated reservation. The Eastern Apaches were included in this policy, and were eventually reduced to two reservations in New Mexico, the Jicarilla and the Mescalero, the latter also including the Lipan and some Chiricahua. Before that final settlement, however, the Chiricahua had been taken as prisoners to Florida, held in the Southeast until 1894, removed to Oklahoma at that time, and not permitted to choose their place of habitation until 1913. A few Apache camps were never subjugated, and hunted and raided in the mountains of northern Sonora through about 1930.

Meanwhile, the remoteness of the Western Apache reservations had been breached by the discovery of minerals in the region. Euro-Americans staked mining claims, sometimes scoffing at the reservation status of the land, sometimes bribing BIA agents. The ensuing scandals confirmed in many Apaches a cynical attitude toward American rule. Nevertheless, seeing no real alternative, most Apaches followed government directives to build irrigation systems and expand farming on the reservations. Until the Collier administration, the BIA had rejected cattle ranching for the Apache, but Collier's icono-

FIGURE 3.9 Apache in camp, late 19th century (wickiup in background). *(Smithsonian Institution National Anthropological Archives)*

clastic staff decided ranching was the most sensible utilization of the Apache country. The San Carlos Reservation, in particular, enjoyed a profitable ranching operation. Men who could not be employed on the tribal ranch worked as cowboys outside the reservation, or in mines, on farms, or at other types of wage work. The Mescalero Apaches in New Mexico, taking advantage of the mountains in their territory, have recently developed a new industry: the Inn of the Mountain Gods Resort, a handsome and far-from-inexpensive lodge with facilities for rusticating urbanites. Of some forty thousand Apaches in the 1980s, over half did not live on Apache reservations.

The trend toward sophisticated business management by tribal councils does not mean that Apache, any more than Navajo, are rejecting their traditions. It is true that not every Apache girl is now transformed into a woman by the *Nai'es* ceremony, but many families do continue to spend considerable sums to host this ritual in which a daughter, having experienced her first menstruation, is imbued for four days with the power of Changing Woman, she who never grows old, who through her two sons conceived by the fire of the sun and by water, taught the Apaches their ways. "Molded" by a priest, the girl emerges prepared physically and spiritually for long and prosperous womanhood, and while she focuses Changing Woman's power, other Apaches can stand near her and be blessed. *Nai'es* symbolizes the focal importance of women to Apache life and their power to transmit Apache culture so that it never grows old and feeble. A similar ceremony is held for young Navajo girls, but the Apache version is more public and most clearly illustrates the benefit to the whole community of traditional values of strength, industriousness, and family responsibility. Many Apache realize that their rituals embodying these values are quite compatible with goals of economic improvement and a respected place in American society.

LEARNING TO BE AN APACHE

In-the-Middle, a Mescalero Apache man born about 1885, told his autobiography to anthropologist Morris Opler in the 1930s. Among In-the-Middle's memories:

Old Lady Yube died quite a while back. One day I was at her camp at Rinconada. I used to stay with these people. I was a little boy, but old enough to know things. I was lying in the shade. A cedar waxwing was coming toward me. I was just about to shoot it when she looked up (she was weaving a basket) and said, "Don't shoot!" I put down my arrows.

The bird stayed here and sang. She said, "I hope it means nothing but good." It looked like she was talking to that bird. She said, "Don't say anything against that bird. It's coming to help me, to help me make baskets and to sell my baskets, and to tell me about the herbs and about the bites of animals and how to cure them."

"Can I shoot these birds?"

"No, do not shoot them. Shoot any birds but these."

"All right, as long as you tell me not to, I won't shoot them."

She said to me, "That bird is good in many ways. Good birds like these we should not bother. To shoot birds that we have no use for is no good. They sing around camp. If you are sad and don't feel well, when they sing you feel better." She put her basket away and spoke to me, and I listened. "Life-giver sends us these birds. They tell us many things. They are too small to use. So it's best to leave them alone. It's just like you, now. Suppose that you were small and the bird was large and it came to you and wanted to eat you. How would you like it?"

"Oh, I wouldn't let any bird eat me. I'd kill it."

"No, I'm telling you this for a lesson, to show you that you should leave birds alone."

The only toothache I had was right there. It happened to me right where she spoke to me that time. I couldn't stop crying. She said, "Now watch and that bird will come."

I was wishing and wishing it would come. It didn't come all day. Then it came. It looked at me and was afraid to light. I said, "Bird, I'm sick; I can't hurt you." The bird sat there and sang.

Then the old woman came out. She heard it singing. She talked to it and it sang on the palm of her hand. She spoke to it, and it took something out of its mouth and put it in her hand. She took it and rubbed it all over my jaw where it was sore. It was sticky and felt good. It felt as if the pain was all being pulled out. That night I slept soundly, and the next day the swelling was down. She did this four times, and then my toothache disappeared. I didn't go to the doctor at all. When she did it, she sang songs and the bird sang also.....

Whenever I see this bird I thank him. I say, "Thank you for curing that toothache so many years ago." Ever since then I like to watch the birds all the time.

This little episode illustrates many aspects of being an Apache: the relaxed childhood in which children practice adult skills—for In-the-Middle, hunting—informally, "for fun"; the gentle lesson taught spontaneously at the moment the child is responsive; the lack of distinction between spiritual and practical matters, with the emphasis on living in harmony with all phenomena; the ill consequences of evil desires (the child's toothache following his move to kill needlessly); the crucial importance of animals lending their spirit power to cure illnesses; the greater efficacy of curing at night; the technique of curing by pulling or sucking out evil things that have magically invaded the body; the magic number four; and the power of songs.

(Opler, 1969:55-57)

SECTION 4: THE WESTERN SECTOR: THE YUMANS

In the valley of the lower Colorado River and its tributary the Gila River and on the semiarid plateau of northwestern Arizona above these rivers live a series of small groups of people speaking languages called Yuman, part of the Hokan linguistic stock common in California. The best known Yumans are the Havasupai, who farm the floor of the Grand Canyon. Closely related to them are the Yavapai and the Walapai (*Pai* is their own term for their people), who have been principally hunters on the plateau, where the Havasupai join them for half the year. Along the lower Colorado, from its mouth upstream, were the Cocopa, whose language suggests a relationship with southern-California Hokans, and then the Yuma (also called the Quechan), the Halchidhoma, the Mohave, and, on the Gila, the Maricopa. These "River Yumans" had a material culture that seems like a simplified version of the Hohokam, while the Pai showed a few Puebloan traits.

During the late Archaic period, the inhabitants of this western border of the Southwest combined hunting, as evidenced by chipped stone dart points, with the collecting of seeds, nuts, and other vegetable foods, evidenced by grinding slabs, a few stone mortars and pestles, and relatively large stone implements for cutting and mashing plants.

By about two thousand years ago, more carefully finished stone knives and drills were becoming common. Houses were light structures of poles and brush, and although they were probably built anew in each seasonal camp, it was customary for families to return each year to campsites where resources were unusually abundant.

After the Hohokam settled on the Gila, their downstream neighbors the Yumans (assuming, as seems likely, that the Yumans have occupied their territory since prehistoric times) imitated, in a creative fashion, the immigrants' culture. Maize, beans, and squash were planted, not after constructing irrigation systems, but simply in the receding floodwaters of the lower Gila and Colorado. Brown pottery was made, sometimes by molding vessels inside baskets, an easy technique scorned by highly professional potters. Houses were copied from the Hohokam. Trough metates were pecked out for grinding maize. The prehistoric Yumans seem to have taken items that would make food procurement and preparation easier, or handier, but to have refused, as would their descendants, to compromise their independence by enslaving themselves to care for elaborate material goods.

Coronado's lieutenant Alarcón probably met Yumans in 1540, but the Spanish did not establish any relationship with the Yumans until Father Kino explored the Colorado River in 1698. Kino was not able to follow up the friendly invitations extended to him by the Yumans, and no mission was sent until 1779, when Franciscans attended by a small troop of soldiers began a program cut short by the massacre of all the Spaniards in 1781. The Pai knew of the Spanish and their activities through their friends the Hopi, but, with the Hopi a buffer between them, remained untouched. Not until the 1850s, when Euro-Americans began traveling through Yuman country on the way to gold in California, did Yumans face the threat of conquest. The discovery of gold and lead in Yuman territory, and the attractiveness of Pai land for cattle ranching, brought increasing numbers of intrusions into the region, with escalating competition for water and other resources. By 1880, the several Yuman peoples had been allotted reservations, which they accepted as it became increasingly obvious that capitulation to the Bureau of Indian Affairs was inevitable.

On the reservations, the Yumans farmed, sometimes impeded by government-built irrigation systems that failed in floods, several times invaded by Euro-Americans who usurped farmland if the irrigation system seemed to be working. The Mohave were forced during World War II to accept thousands of relocated Japanese from the West Coast and then, when the Japanese had been released, to allow Hopi and Navajo families to settle on what was considered surplus land on the Mohaves' Colorado River Reservation. While the Mohave had a relatively large reservation, the Yumans and the three Pai groups claimed that their lands had been unlawfully expropriated, and these claims have been upheld by the U.S. Indian Claims Commission, which has granted the tribes monetary compensation. The Havasupai have derived some income from tourists visiting the Grand Canyon. All the Yumans, like other Indians, find wage work off the reservations necessary for at least some of their population. There were, in the 1980s, some seven thousand Yumans.

Yuman culture differs from the cultures of other Southwestern people. The Yumans seem to shy away from complexity, whether in technology, social organization, or ritual—a contrast with the Pueblos. They were said to particularly appreciate sensual pleasures, from love-making to hand-to-hand manly combat. Battles among themselves were frequent, but furtive raiding despised. What few material possessions a person accumulated were burned—along with the house, in many instances—on a funeral pyre. Much credence was given to individual revelation through dreams, although group discussion of dreams explicated them in terms of the accepted mythology, thereby tending to standardize beliefs. All these characteristics of Yuman culture—"loose" sexual behavior, warlike intergroup contacts, the destruction of material goods at funerals, emphasis in religion on songs invoking power during dream journeys to the realm of spirits—were anathema to the missionaries and BIA agents who dealt with the Yumans in the late nineteenth and early twentieth centuries. Add to their "depraved" traits the fact that the few thousand Yumans, unlike the many more Navajo or Pueblos, posed no serious economic problem even when hundreds who had lost game and water rights were reduced to begging at the railroad towns, and the lack of interest in these native Southwesterners may be understood. Nevertheless, Yumans evolved a comfortable adaptation to the limited resources of the western edge of the Southwest, and a "hang-loose" style compatible with the philosophy of many late-twentieth-century Americans.

At the End of the Twentieth Century

Contemporary Southwestern Indians can be described as underdeveloped nations struggling to rebuild their economies and regain some degree of independence. These Indian nations, after conquest by Spain's colonizing empire, have been internal colonies of Mexico and the United States. Economically and politically, America's Indian nations closely resemble Europe's former overseas colonies in Africa and Asia. For generations, European overlords extracted raw materials from their colonies, denying the native peoples not only the right to govern themselves but also the right to independently manage business enterprises. Wages were kept low, if they were paid at all; workers were forbidden to unionize; and profits were kept by the colonial owners and used for purchases and investments in the home country rather than the colony of origin. Banks would not lend money to native workers. Education was limited and segregated, with the schools for native children providing only elementary level instruction or vocational training. Use of the native language was discouraged and the native culture was said to be primitive and immoral. This paragraph describes American Indians as well as African, Asian, and Pacific island colonies. It is, as ethnohistorian Francis Jennings put it, the "cant of conquest."

World War II destruction undermined European nations' control of foreign colonies, and the development of late-twentieth-century industrial, transportation, and communication technology made the earlier pattern of exploitation obsolete. It was cheaper to let foreign colonies govern themselves while international banks and diversified corporations manage the extraction of raw materials. Giving independence to internal colonies is not so easy. Both in Mexico and the United States (and Canada), Indian nations have been expected to be self-supporting at a subsistence level and to provide cheap temporary labor as needed in mines, Euro-American agribusiness, and fighting forest fires. Integrating Indians into the national economy even at this level of a reserve labor pool proved risky to the dominant society. Where the Union of South Africa dealt with its native nations by imposing strict segregation, the United States and Mexico claimed liberal political policies advocating respect for human rights and unrestricted opportunity for social mobility. American Indians could not legally be held in poverty and peonage. World War II drew thousands of Indians into national service, both in the armed forces and in war industries, and there Indians learned their citizenship gave them rights of self-determination.

The second half of the twentieth century marks a major shift in the histories of American Indian nations. First, many Indians who had been in the armed forces or worked in cities during World War II and afterward entered colleges. A large proportion of the first generation to enroll in colleges found themselves ill-prepared by their reservation or Indian boarding schools and without much counseling or support from the colleges. In an era of civil rights reform and demands for equal opportunities for all segments of the American population, Indians succeeded in demanding improvements in their schools and support offices in colleges. The second generation after World War II's young adults has substantially increased its percentage of college graduates. Fueling this increase is the high birth rate on Indian reservations (high birth rates are generally seen in underdeveloped nations, in part the result of limited education and poor medical services). Reservations cannot possibly provide agricultural employment for all the new generations. Even if only a tiny percentage of the rising population of Indians enters professional and managerial fields, that is still enough to build organizations and networks to increase the political and economic power of the Indian nations.

Exactly this has happened. Perhaps the most obvious example is CERT, the Council of Energy Resource Tribes, founded in 1975. Navajo, Jicarilla Apache, Hopi, Acoma, Jemez, Santa Ana, Zia, and Laguna Pueblo were among the founding tribes, joined by Northern Plains and Western tribes. (We refer to the members of CERT as "tribes" because they are legally recognized as such by the United States. A federally-recognized tribe may or may not be the same as an Indian nation. For example, the Hopi are a federally-recognized tribe but they consider themselves to be thirteen independent communities.) CERT coincided with the U.S. Congress passing the 1975 Indian Self-Determination and Educational Assistance Act and, the previous year, the Indian Financing Act, both aimed at stimulating economic development on reservations through giving more autonomy to tribal governments and reservation enterprises. Through contacts pursued by La-Donna Harris, a Comanche married to a (non-Indian) U.S. senator, CERT was able to work directly with the federal Department of Energy, circumventing and challenging Bureau of Indian Affairs policies and operations. As a result, oil, gas, and coal production on Indian reservations has been more effectively monitored, producing larger royalties to the tribes and giving them a voice in regulating these enterprises. In turn, the power gained through more money and influence on energy production translates into more political clout. Indians are still a small percentage of the population of the United States, but they are in a position to exercise disproportionate decision making concerning the exploitation of the United States' energy resources.

At the end of the twentieth century, Indians in the Southwest have by no means reversed the injustices they suffered through four centuries of colonial domination. Water rights are perhaps the most crucial economic issue: throughout the Greater Southwest, agribusiness irrigation and the water demands of modern cities are rapidly depleting a severely limited resource. Water is taken from rivers, turning many into dry depressions most of the year, and even worse, the water table is falling drastically. Indian agriculture, businesses, and villages are small compared with the Euro-American agribusiness corporations and cities. Tóhono 'O'odham totally lost all the arable land on the Gila Bend Reservation when the U.S. Army Corps of Engineers built a downstream dam against the tribe's wishes. This project periodically flooded the reservation, destroying farm fields and leaving weed seeds that quickly turned the land into unmanageable thickets. After years of litigation, the U.S. Congress voted in 1986 to compensate the tribe for its irreparable loss by paying it $30 million to buy a new reservation, relocate homes and community buildings—and buy water rights!

Assertion of rights to cultural resources grows along with demands to right economic injustices. The most famous case in the Southwest has been the return of Blue Lake to Taos Pueblo. It was President Theodore Roosevelt who decreed in 1906 that the lake should be included in the new Taos National Forest (now Carson National Forest, reminding the Navajos of their 1860s trauma). Taos Indians could make their usual pilgrimages to their shrine at the lake, but non-Indians could graze stock, take timber, or enjoy recreational activities around the holy sanctuary. In 1924, after continuing pleas from Taos to restore their holy place, Congress offered money in compensation for the loss of Taos land. The pueblo persisted in begging for their sanctuary. At last, in December 1970, Congress gave in to pressure from a number of national organizations rallying to the pueblo's concern, and Blue Lake, with 48,000 surrounding acres, is now legally protected from desecration. Zuni, Zia, and Cochiti Pueblos have similarly received protection for shrines where they worship. On the other hand, in spite of the 1978 American Indian Religious Freedom Act, the Hopi have not succeeded in preventing commercial development of the San Francisco Peaks, where they believe their katcinas reside.

Hopi katcinas are disturbed by skiers slaloming over their heads while VCRs all over the country play videotape versions of New Age films with Hopi language titles, and the viewers munch chips made from Hopi blue corn. Friends of "the Indian" flock to towns near the pueblos to march in support of Hopi claims, or Navajo claims, to the Joint Use Area, or maybe the supporters don't believe the tribes are disputing (the Hopi are called the Peaceful People) and think they are protesting strip mining coal on holy Black Mesa. Sages retell the "Hopi prophecy" in popular "Indian religion" seminars; this has been promoted by a Hopi named Thomas Banyacaya who was appointed in 1948 by one of the village chiefs to tell the outside world the conservative Hopi would not give up their autonomy nor follow United States customs in negotiating for land and rights. Banyacaya's appointment came during a meeting of traditional chiefs (that is, not Tribal Council members) called by one, Katchongva, who believed that the atomic bombs dropped in 1945 had been the fulfillment of a revelation that a time would come when Hopi religious teachings would save the world. Banyacaya has enjoyed a considerable audience for his Hopi teachings on the need for peace and harmony with natural forces, but the basic demand for Hopi autonomy is seldom heard, much to the chagrin of the Hopi. It's much pleasanter for the American public to listen to sweet "Songs of the Fourth World" than to give up land, and water, and dollars to communities held down as internal colonies for four centuries.

SUMMARY

The Greater Southwest can be divided into four major sections: the Aztecan-speaking peoples of the south, whose prehistoric ancestors were the Hohokam and northwestern Mexican Loma San Gabriel, Chalchihuites, and other regional cultures; the Pueblos of the north, whose ancestors were the Anasazi; the Yuman speakers of the west along the lower Colorado River and its tributaries; and the Apacheans, who invaded from the north late in the prehistoric period. Hunting and gathering, supplemented by a little maize and squash cultivation after about 1000 B.C., was the basic economy of the Southwest until the first millennium A.D.

Hohokam, in southern Arizona, appears to have been the northernmost of a series of Mexican peoples combining agriculture and long-distance trade in the first millennium A.D. Their historic descendants are the 'O'odham (Pima and Papago), who continue to live in small hamlets (*rancherías*) and farm their homeland, although hundreds now are forced to seek employment off their reservations as the growing population exceeds the traditional resources of the reservations. Aztecan-speaking groups occupying northwest Mexico include the

Huichol, Cora, Mayo, Tepehuan, Tepecano, Rarámuri (Tarahumara), and Yaqui, the last with a refugee colony in Tucson, Arizona. Like the 'O'odham , the northwest Mexican groups lived by irrigation agriculture, fishing, and deer hunting. Disease epidemics, beginning with Spanish invasion in 1530, coupled with enslavement and forced labor in mines, severely decimated the population, and twentieth-century agribusiness enterprises imperiled their remaining lands. Contemporary Indians range from those who persevere in subsistence farming, often in mountain country, to those who live in Indian villages but work for wages where they can find employment, and to urban families, some with professional careers, who return to the villages to celebrate fiestas.

Peoples in the northern sector of the Southwest began building more substantial shelters and making pottery about A.D. 400, and about A.D. 700 shifted into a cultural pattern that continued into the historic period as that of the Pueblos: densely populated towns of adobe or stone multifamily dwellings, a dependence on maize agriculture requiring irrigation, and complex ceremonies organized by permanent priesthoods who cooperated in governing the towns. Spanish conquest, beginning in 1598, overlaid a colonial set of officers over the native set, which in many towns were underground, ruling through puppet governors acceptable to the Spanish and, later, United States agents. Severe droughts in the late prehistoric period had caused relocations of many (Anasazi) Pueblo towns, but the cultural traditions persisted and to a considerable degree have continued through today in the Pueblos.

The Yumans, who include the Havasupai on the floor of the Grand Canyon, began about two thousand years ago to cultivate maize, beans, and squash, taking advantage of the annual floods of the Colorado and its tributaries to provide water for the farms bordering the streams. Unlike the Hohokam and the Anasazi (Pueblos), the Yumans did not build towns, but lived in *rancherías*. Lacking towns, they did not attract the attention of Spaniards interested in colonies, and except for a mission lasting only from 1779 to 1781, the Yumans remained autonomous until United States incursions in the 1850s, when Euro-Americans came in seeking gold, lead, or land for cattle ranches. Yumans were forced to accept reservations by 1880, and like other Southwestern Indian groups, have continued to farm these lands while many tribal members who cannot obtain land on these limited reservations are employed away.

Apacheans migrated south from western Canada along the High Plains in the late prehistoric period. In the early sixteenth century, some were nomadic bison hunters and others combined bison hunting with limited agriculture in Colorado. Apacheans raided Pueblos, but also traded peaceably, and after the defeat of the Pueblos in their revolt of 1680 against Spanish rule, many Apachean camps were host to Pueblo refugees. From these several centuries of contact, Apacheans took over numerous Pueblo customs, but never so many as to obscure the independence of the Apacheans, who continued to live in camps or small settlements, rather than in highly organized towns as did the Pueblos. During the eighteenth and early nineteenth centuries, the Apacheans became notorious for their raids on Indian and Spanish settlements. These were finally ended in 1863, when the fields and herds of the Navajo, especially, were destroyed by United States soldiers to prevent the Apacheans from blocking United States access to the Pacific during the Civil War. The Navajo and the groups known as Apache were, one by one, forced onto reservations during the next four decades. Most have developed ranching and sheepraising, but rapidly increasing populations strain the reservations. Mining of coal and uranium offered some economic relief to the Navajo, but most of the people have been distressed by the despoiling of the landscape and the threat to human health of these enterprises, and many reject these industries.

RECOMMENDED READING

Archaeology:

Cordell, Linda S. 1984 *Prehistory of the Southwest.* Orlando: Academic Press. Well-written, especially in thoroughly discussing how archaeologists arrived at their interpretations. (Note that this volume is restricted to the U. S. Southwest.)

Fagan, Brian M. *Ancient North America.* New York: Thames and Hudson (distributed by W.W. Norton).

Aztecans:

Joseph, Alice, Rosamond B. Spicer, and Jane Chesky. 1949 *The Desert People: A Study of the Papago Indians.* Chicago: University of Chicago Press.

Spicer, Edward H. 1961. Yaqui. In E.H. Spicer (ed.). *Perspectives in American Indian Culture Change.* Chicago: University of Chicago Press, pp. 7–93.

Underhill, Ruth M. 1979 *Papago Woman.* New York: Holt, Rinehart and Winston.

Pueblos:

Dozier, Edward P. 1970 *The Pueblo Indians of North America.* Prospect Heights,Ill.: Waveland Press. Dozier, an anthropologist, was a native of Santa Clara Pueblo.

——1961. Rio Grande Pueblos. In E.H. Spicer (ed.).*Perspectives in American Indian Culture Change.* Chicago: University of Chicago Press, pp. 94–186.

——1966. *Hano: A Tewa Indian Community in Arizona.* New York: Holt, Rinehart and Winston. Dozier contrasts the immigrant refugee Río Grande Tewa Hano with the Hopi, their hosts for three hundred years.

Sando, Joe S. 1976 *The Pueblo Indians.* San Francisco: Indian Historian Press. Sando is a native of Jemez Pueblo and writes from a more activist viewpoint than Dozier did.

Apacheans:

Basso, Keith H. 1970 *The Cibecue Apache.* Prospect Heights Ill.: Waveland Press.

Downs, James F. 1972 *The Navajo.* Prospect Heights Ill.: Waveland Press.

Kluckhohn, Clyde, and Dorothea Leighton. 1962 *The Navaho.* Garden City, N.Y.: Doubleday. More depth than Downs's shorter account.

Vogt, Evon Z. 1961 Navaho. In E.H. Spicer (ed.).

Perspectives in American Indian Culture Change. Chicago: University of Chicago Press, pp. 278–336.

See also E.C. Parsons (ed.). *American Indian Life.* (Lincoln: University of Nebraska Press, Bison Books, 1967 [1922]). The section on the Southwest includes excellent accounts of Havasupai and Mohave Yumans as well as dramatic vignettes of Apache, Navajo, and Zuni.

SOURCES FOR THE FIRST EDITION

Bailey, L. R. 1966 *Indian Slave Trade in the Southwest.* Los Angeles: Westernlore Press.

Basso, Keith H,. and Morris E. Opler, eds. 1971 *Apachean Culture History and Ethnology.* Tucson: University of Arizona Press, University of Arizona Anthropological Papers, No. 21.

Ellis, Florence Hawley, and Laurens Hammack. 1968 The Inner Sanctum of Feather Cave: A Mogollon Sun and Earth Shrine Linking Mexico and the Southwest. *American Antiquity* 33 (1):25–44.

Furst, Peter T. 1972 To Find Our Life: Peyote Among the Huichol Indians of Mexico. In P.T. Furst (ed.). *Flesh of the Gods.* New York: Praeger, pp. 136–184.

Haury, Emil W. 1976 *The Hohokam.* Tucson: University of Arizona Press.

Hedrick, Basil C., J. Charles Kelley, and Carroll L. Riley, eds. 1974 *The Mesoamerican Southwest.* Carbondale: Southern Illinois University Press.

Hester, James J. 1962 *Early Navajo Migrations and Acculturation in the Southwest.* Santa Fe: Museum of New Mexico Press, Museum of New Mexico Papers in Anthropology, No. 6.

Hodge, Frederick Webb, ed. 1910 *Handbook of American Indians North of Mexico.* Washington, D.C.: Smithsonian Institution, Bureau of American Ethnology, Bulletin 30.

Irwin-William, Cynthia. 1967 Picosa: the Elementary Southwestern Culture. *American Antiquity* 32 (4):441–457.

———Paleo-Indian and Archaic Cultural Systems in the Southwestern United States. In A. Ortiz (ed.). *Handbook of North American Indians, Southwest,* vol 9. Washington, D.C.: Smithsonian Institution Press, pp. 31–42.

John, Elizabeth A.H. 1975 *Storms Brewed in Other Men's Worlds.* College Station: Texas A&M University Press.

Kroeber, A. L. 1939 *Cultural and Natural Areas of Native North America.* University of California Publications in American Archaeology and Ethnology, vol. 38. Berkeley: University of California Press.

Moises, Rosalio, Jane Holden Kelley, and William Curry Holden. 1971 *A Yaqui Life.* Lincoln: University of Nebraska Press.

Nahmad Sittón, Salomón 1972 *El Peyote y los Huicholes.* Mexico City: Sep/Setentas.

Opler, Morris E. 1969 *Apache Odyssey.* New York: Holt, Rinehart and Winston.

Ortiz, Alfonso. 1969 *The Tewa World.* Chicago: University of Chicago Press.

Ortiz, Alfonso, ed. 1972 *New Perspectives on the Pueblos.* Albuquerque: University of New Mexico Press.

Schoenwetter, James and Alfred E. Dittert, Jr. 1968 An Ecological Interpretation of Anasazi Settlement Patterns. In B.J. Meggers (ed.). *Anthropological Archeology in the Americas.* Washington, D.C.: The Anthropological Society of Washington.

Spicer, Edward H. 1962 *Cycles of Conquest.* Tucson: University of Arizona Press.

Tedlock, Dennis. 1972 *Finding the Center.* New York: Dial Press.

Voegelin, C. F., and F. M. Voegelin. 1965 *Languages of the World: Native America,* Fascicle 2. Bloomington: Indiana University, Anthropological Linguistics 7 (7).

Weaver, Thomas, ed. 1974 *Indians of Arizona.* Tucson: University of Arizona Press.

ADDITIONAL SOURCES
FOR THE SECOND EDITION

Adams, William Y. 1983 Once More to the Fray: Further Reflections on Navajo Kinship. *Journal of Anthropological Research* 39(4): 393–414.

Ambler, Marjane. 1990 *Breaking the Iron Bonds.* Lawrence: University Press of Kansas.

Aveni, Anthony F., Horst Hartung, and J. Charles Kelley. 1982 Alta Vista (Chalchichuites), Astronomical Implications of a Mesoamerican Ceremonial Outpost at the Tropic of Cancer. *American Antiquity* 47 (2): 316–335.

Bailey, Garrick, and Roberta Glenn Bailey. 1986 *A History of the Navajos.* Santa Fe: School of American Research Press.

Baugh, Timothy G., and Frank W. Eddy. 1987 Rethinking Apachean Ceramics: The 1985 Southern Athapaskan Ceramics Conference. *American Antiquity* 52 (4):793–798.

Bee, Robert L. 1981 *Crosscurrents Along the Colorado.* Tucson: University of Arizona Press.

Bronitsky, Gordon. 1990 Solomon Bibo: Jew and Indian at Acoma Pueblo. Albuquerque: *The Link,* Jewish Federation of Greater Albuquerque.

Campbell, Lyle, and Marianne Mithun, eds. 1979 *The Languages of Native America.* Austin: University of Texas Press.

Clemmer, Richard O. 1978 *Continuities of Hopi Culture Change.* Ramona, Calif.: Acoma Books.

Cordell, Linda S. 1984 *Prehistory of the Southwest.* Orlando: Academic Press.

Ellis, Florence Hawley, and Andrea Ellis Dodge. 1989 The Spread of Chaco/Mesa Verde/ McElmo Black-on-White Pottery and the Possible Simultaneous Introduction of Irrigation into the Rio Grande Drainage. *Journal of Anthropological Research* 45(1):47–52.

Feher-Elston, Catherine. 1988 *Children of the Sacred Ground.* Flagstaff, Ariz.: Northland Publishing.

Folan, William J., ed. 1985 *Contributions to the Archaeology and Ethnohistory of Greater Mesoamerica.* Carbondale: Southern Illinois University Press.

Foster, Michael S., and Phil C. Weigand, eds.1985 *The Archaeology of West and Northwest Mesoamerica.* Boulder: Westview Press.

Hickerson, Nancy P.1988 The Linguistic Position of Jumano. *Journal of Anthropological Research* 44(3):311–326.

Iverson, Peter. 1981 *The Navajo Nation.* Albuquerque: University of New Mexico Press.

Jett, Stephen C., and Peter B. Moyle. 1986 The Exotic Origins of Fishes Depicted on Prehistoric Mimbres Pottery from New Mexico. *American Antiquity* 51(4):688–720.

Kintigh, Keith W. 1985 *Settlement, Subsistence, and Society in Late Zuni Prehistory.* Tucson: University of Arizona Press, Anthropological Papers of the University of Arizona, no. 44.

Lamphere, Louise,.ed. 1989 Special Issue on Navajo Ethnology. *Journal of Anthropological Research* 45(4).

Mathien, Frances Joan, and Randall H. McGuire, eds. 1986. *Ripples in the Chichimec Sea.* Carbondale: Southern Illinois University Press.

Nabhan, Gary Paul, and Amadeo Rea. 1987 Plant domestication and Folk-Biological Change: The Upper Piman/Devil's Claw Example. *American Anthropologist* 89(1):57–73.

O'Brien, Sharon. 1989 *American Indian Tribal Governments.* Norman: University of Oklahoma Press.

Ortiz, Alfonso, ed. 1979 *Handbook of North American Indians: Southwest,* vol. 9. Washington, D.C.: Smithsonian Institution.

—1983 *Handbook of North American Indians: Southwest,* vol. 10. Washington D.C.: Smithsonian Institution.

Parker, Linda S. 1989 *Native American Estate.* Honolulu: University of Hawaii Press.

Riley, Carroll L. 1987 *The Frontier People,* rev. ed. Albuquerque: University of New Mexico Press.

Salinas, Martín. 1990 *Indians of the Rio Grande Delta.* Austin: University of Texas Press.

Sando, Joe S. 1982 *Nee Hemish: A History of Jemez Pueblo.* Albuquerque: University of New Mexico Press.

Schrader,. Robert Fay. 1983 *The Indian Arts & Crafts Board.* Albuquerque: University of New Mexico Press.

Simmons, Alan H. 1986 New Evidence for the Early Use of Cultigens in the American Southwest. *American Antiquity* 51(1):73–89.

Snipp, C. Matthew. 1989 *American Indians: The First of This Land.* New York: Russell Sage Foundation.

Speth, John D., and Susan L. Scott. 1985 The Role of Large Mammals in Late Prehistoric Horticultural Adaptations: The View from Southeastern New Mexico. In D. Burley (ed.). *Contributions to Plains Prehistory.* Edmonton: Archaeological Survey of Alberta, Occasional Paper No. 26, pp 233–266.

Trennert, Robert A., Jr. 1988 *The Phoenix Indian School.* Norman: University of Oklahoma Press.

Trombold, Charles D. 1990 A Reconsideration of Chronology for the La Quemada Portion of the Northern Mesoamerican Frontier. *American Antiquity* 55(2):308–324

Upham, Steadman, Kent G. Lightfoot, and Roberta A. Jewett. 1989 *The Sociopolitical Structure of Prehistoric Southwestern Societies.* Boulder: Westview Press.

Upham, Steadman, Richard S. MacNeish, Walton C. Galinat, and Christopher M. Stevenson. 1987 Evidence Concerning the Origin of Maiz de Ocho. *American Anthropologist* 89(2):410–419.

Walker, Willard, and Lydia L. Wyckoff, eds. 1983

Hopis, Tewas, and the American Road. Middletown, Conn.: Wesleyan University.

Weiss, Lawrence David. 1984 *The Development of Capitalism in the Navajo Nation.* Minneapolis: MEP Publications.

White, Richard. 1983 *The Roots of Dependency.* Lincoln: University of Nebraska Press.

Whiteley, Peter M. 1988 *Deliberate Acts.* Tucson: University of Arizona Press.

Whiteley, Peter M. 1985, 1986 Unpacking Hopi "Clans."

Journal of Anthropological Research 41(4):359–374 and 42(1):69–79.

Wilcox, David R. 1988 Avonlea and Southern Athapaskan Migrations. In L.B. Davis (ed.). *Avonlea Yesterday and Today.* Saskatoon: Saskatchewan Archaeological Society, pp. 273–280.

Wills, W. H. 1988 *Early Prehistoric Agriculture.* Santa Fe: School of American Research Press.

——1989 Patterns of Prehistoric Food Production in West-Central New Mexico. *Journal of Anthropological Research* 45(1):139–157.

THE SOUTHEAST

The southeastern United States is not a sharply bounded region. Climate and cultural pattern alike shift by small degrees from the climax of the relatively densely populated, complex societies of the semitropical Gulf coastal belt, northward to the more scattered villages of the colder states. Historically, the vegetation of the Southeast has been dominated by pines, which were maintained by regular firings of the underbrush designed to provide good browse for the prime game, deer. Oak and other deciduous trees, many bearing edible nuts, cover the uplands rising to the great forested domes and ridges of the Appalachian Mountains. Cypress trees flourish in the extensive swamps that, with tidal marshes and lagoons along the coast itself, ring the region on the east and south. Rainfall is ample, feeding the streams that rush down the Appalachians, hurtle over the fall line where the piedmont abuts the wide coastal plain, and then meander with their rich loads of silt toward the sea. Whether they gathered from the wild or raised crops, people found most of the Southeast blessed with resources.

The core of the Southeast runs from the Savannah River in Georgia south to, but not including, the Florida peninsula, and from the Atlantic west to east Texas. Muskogean and other languages of the Macro-Algonkian language phylum were spoken in this core. Bordering the core on the north are three cultural and environmental regions: the continuation of the Atlantic coastal plain, inhabited by more Algonkian speakers; the Appalachians, inhabited by Macro-Siouan speakers; and the inland plateau, with both Algonkians and Siouans, which meets the eastern edge of the Plains where a series of Siouan-phylum languages were spoken. South Florida, ecologically a tropical outlier, was taken over in the nineteenth century by refugee Muskogeans filling a vacuum left a century before by the destruction of peoples whose names, but not languages, have been recorded. Linguistically, the Siouan block of Cherokee, Yuchi, and Catawba in the Appalachians and adjacent piedmont contrast with the Muskogeans of the core, but culturally no strong distinctions can be made. This chapter will therefore treat the Southeast as a whole, rather than dividing it into sectors.

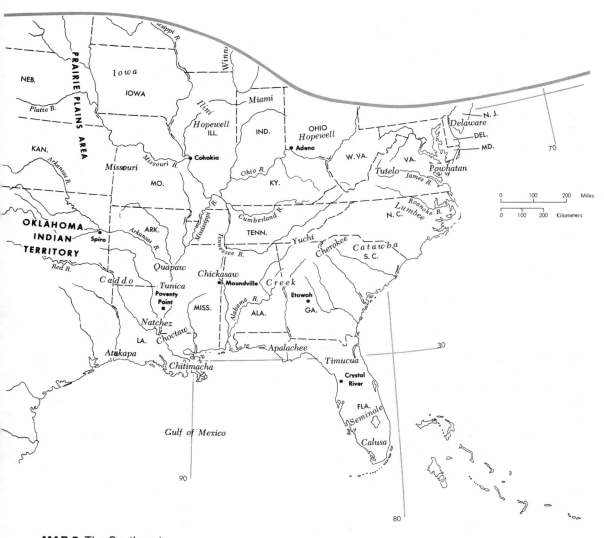

MAP 5 The Southeast

SECTION 1: THE ARCHAIC AND "EARLY WOODLAND" PERIODS IN THE SOUTHEAST

The Southeast would have been a desirable habitat for humans during the late Pleistocene glaciations. Parklands of mixed forests and grassy prairies, more diverse than any Holocene region, harbored a richer variety and greater density of animals than would be found in historic times. Among the game animals were mastodons and ground sloths, as well as deer. Along the Gulf coastal zone, the South American capybara (a very large rodent) and a giant armadillo flourished in tropical warmth.

Finding the remains of the early human occupations in the Southeast has been severely challenging. Most early campsites are presumably either deeply buried under tons of alluvium in the river flood plains or submerged under fathoms of water on the continental shelf, the broad portion of the Ice Age coastal plain drowned when the released waters of the melting glaciers caused rising sea levels. Searching for more accessible early sites, archaeologists have excavated rockshelters and caves and surveyed the natural terraces on the edges of river valleys. Clusters of crudely flaked pebble choppers on some of these terraces suggest to some the presence of "pre-projectile point" Pleistocene foragers who had not yet learned, or invented, tipping weapons with stone points. Crudeness is not in itself diagnostic, so many archaeologists refuse to accept the pebble tools as anything more than choppers that may have been made by travelers and campers of any period, who would have carried with them their carefully made finer tools but left behind the heavy choppers quickly knocked out on local pebbles. Excavations in rockshelters and beside mineral springs have been able to prove human occupation at the final stage of the Pleistocene epoch, when Paleo-Indians made fluted projectile points. Quantities of fluted stone points have also been collected from plowed fields, borrow pits, and other disturbed localities where cultural and dating context has been destroyed. These "orphan" finds, like the fluted points excavated scientifically, probably date from about 10,000 B.C. to 8000 B.C. Earlier occupation in the Southeast, although possible, has not been demonstrated.

Early Archaic begins in the Southeast at the close of the Pleistocene epoch about ten thousand years ago. Triangular dart points fastened to shafts by binding secured around deeply indented ("corner-notched") bases are diagnostic of the Eastern Early Archaic. The significance of the change-over from fluted-base, lance-shaped stone weapon points and knives to the smaller, triangular, notched-base forms is itself inconclusively debated by archaeologists: does the new style represent the invasion of a new ethnic group who

displaced or absorbed the Paleo-Indians, or was it really only a rather trivial technological innovation? About two thousand years later, tangs ("stemmed points") replace notches for hafting points and knives. Such fashion changes help the archaeologist to roughly date "orphan" stone artifacts or the sites on which the artifacts appear.

Surveys of sections of the Southeast reveal dozens, even a hundred or more, identifiable Early Archaic sites in river basins. (Federal and state laws, stimulated by the National Environmental Protection Act of 1966, have since that year mandated surveys and testing to identify archaeological data threatened by construction projects. As a result of this "CRM" [Cultural Resource Management], our knowledge of the prehistory of North America has been markedly expanded.) Along the Savannah River in Georgia, for example, Early Archaic people seem to have wintered on the coastal plain and spent summers in smaller camps on the cooler uplands. They obtained good-quality chert for their stone tools by quarrying outcrops along the Fall Line where the streams drop down to the coastal plain. Some of the best chert was carried from a source 300 kilometers (180 miles) away. A probable winter settlement contained pecked and ground stone adzes, and a whetstone for sharpening one, in addition to the common flaked knives and scrapers. Red ocher in the site, with a stone tablet on which it had been ground into pigment, may have been used in hide tanning, or for painting. Cobblestones had been utilized as manos for grinding on stone slabs, probably in the preparation of plant foods. The adzes suggest woodworking, even the possible building of winter houses with planed log frames.

About 5500 B.C., an apparent increase in human populations in the Southeast had achieved a density at which more stable settlements seem to have developed at least in the western inland-plateau portion of the region. (On the coastal plain, the sea-level rise, which lessened only after 4000 B.C., meant an impoverishment of resources: old forests were destroyed, and the growth of marshes and shellfish beds was hampered by local fluctuations in shoreline.) A site in western Tennessee, beside the Tennessee River, lacks evidence of houses—tents may have been the shelters—but had round graves with corpses in a bent position. Debris indicated hunting of turkeys and most of the larger animals, fishing, nutcracking, and possibly seed grinding in rough stone mortars. Deer were the preferred game, valued for their hides and bones (used for tools) as well as for their meat. Domesticated dogs may have aided hunters; some dogs' owners loved them enough to bury them as if they were human. Beads made from hollow bird bone, from animal canine teeth, and from stone ornamented these ancient Tennesseans, who no doubt also created perishable costumes, wooden tools, containers, carvings, and basketry.

For us today, the most spectacular Southeastern sites from around 5000 B.C. are waterlogged Windover and Little Salt Springs. Little Salt Springs was a village along a mucky slough that was the cemetery for perhaps as many as a thousand corpses. The bodies were laid on branches and wrapped in grass to protect them from the mud. At Windover, close to two hundred corpses lay in the cemetery, and, as at Little Salt Springs, they had been placed on branches and wrapped or dressed, here in cloth. Wooden stakes around the burial gave added protection to the deceased at Windover. Wooden bowls, tools such as digging sticks, stone and shell artifacts, and, at Little Salt Springs, a wooden tablet with a bird carved on it were given to the dead in these cemeteries. One young teenager buried at Windover had a bottle gourd, probably a container, and a bottle gourd was found also at Little Salt Springs. Since bottle gourds historically are cultivated plants, and since they do not seem to have been native to Florida, these gourds may indicate that the early Middle Archaic people of Florida were planting this easily-grown, useful species. The cloth preserved in the airless peat at Windover is especially precious, for this craft seldom is recovered: at Windover, two varieties of twined fabrics have

been identified. Twining is slower to produce than true weaving (in twining, the horizontal weft thread is twisted around each vertical warp thread rather than shuttled in and out as in weaving), but it makes a strong fabric and pretty designs can be worked in. In Peru where the extremely dry coastal desert preserves an abundance of ancient fabrics, twining was earlier than true weaving. Interestingly, the earliest twined fabrics in Peru are, like those at Windover, from around 5000 B.C.

As early as this Middle Archaic period, beginning some eight thousand years ago, the Appalachians cut eastern North America into two great provinces. The interior, western province, from the west flanks of the mountains to the prairies on the farther edge of the Mississippi Valley, seems to have been the more favorable habitat for humans, possibly in part because the network of broad rivers in the Mississippi drainage facilitated trade. The Atlantic slope, eastward from the Appalachians, was not a difficult place to make a living, but it lacks any easy means of north-south communication. This seems to have retarded the development of complex societies, whose specialists would have needed widespread trade to support their activities, whether administrative or artisan. Contacts between human groups east of the Appalachians were frequent, but there is no natural channel system inviting journeys of a thousand miles, as does the Mississippi and its great tributaries.

The Atlantic-slope Middle Archaic period shared, in spite of the absence of communication by navigable north-south rivers, several styles of stone artifacts. Projectile points and knives were given squared or tapering stems instead of the rounded base notches fashionable west of the Appalachians. Atlantic-slope styles occur from eastern Florida to eastern Canada, a continuity that may have been fostered by the attraction of high-quality flaking stones, carried as much as two thousand kilometers (1,200 miles) from their sources. The warming trend climaxing in the "Thermal Maximum" (a period of less harsh

THE SOUTHEAST
CHRONOLOGY

1970	Indian Activism	Eastern remnants win recognition
1964	U.S. Civil Rights Bill	
1954	U.S. Supreme Court ends segregated schools	
1934	Indian Reorganization Act	
1907	Oklahoma statehood Allotment of Five Tribes land	
1887	Dawes Allotment Act; Lumbees recognized ("Croatans")	
	Civil War	
1850		
	Removal	
1830	Removal policy begins Creek War	
1800	Euroamerican invasion of inland Southeast	
1700		
1600	Carolina (deerhide and slave trade begins)	
	De Soto	
1500		
1200	Cahokia	
1000		
500		

LATE WOODLAND

MISSISSIPPIAN

MIDDLE WOODLAND

AD	
BC	Hopewell
500	
	Adena
1000	EARLY WOODLAND
1400	Poverty Point built
2000	Cultivation of grains, squash
3000	Earliest pottery
3500	
5500	MIDDLE ARCHAIC
8000	EARLY ARCHAIC
10,000	PALEO-INDIAN

LATE ARCHAIC

winters) during the late-Middle Archaic period brought mixed oak forests throughout the eastern seaboard, encouraging similar human cultural patterns throughout this eastern province. Movements along the now-drowned coast would have constantly fanned inland as groups went up rivers to falls where fish on spawning runs could be taken. Communication probably took place when families congregated seasonally at these generous fishing stations. Innovations in technology could have passed fairly rapidly from valley to valley as individuals met at the fish runs, at quarries, or while hunting or trapping. Perhaps bands in adjacent valleys staged fairs in the summer when food was abundant and the living easy, to exchange manufactures, feast, gamble, dance, and…ah, avoid inbreeding by widening the pool of eligible mates.

By 3500 B.C., the beginning of the Late Archaic period, sea level was stabilizing. Shellfish beds grew along the coasts; so did middens of discarded shells as humans enjoyed the succulent morsels. People can't live on shellfish alone—imbalance of diet aside, the time required for cracking or steaming is considerable compared to the yield in calories—but communities did settle beside shellfish beds to have one of their several food staples handy. From the beachside settlement, hunters and gatherers went out and fishermen launched their canoes. People ignored the smell of the mounds of opened shells, as people today ignore the smell of oil wells, factories, or manured fields from which they get a living.

The proliferation of shell middens in the Atlantic province during the Late Archaic period raises questions about the derivation of the peoples using the shellfish beds. Were they descendants of the communities of the western province who were already establishing settlements at mussel beds in rivers such as the lower Tennessee during the Middle Archaic period? Were they descendants of Atlantic-slope communities whose earlier camps beside the less extensive shellfish beds of Middle Archaic times have been drowned by the sea? Or might they have included some colonists from northern South America, paddling across the Caribbean?

Startling as the notion of South American immigrants may be, it is suggested by the introduction into the southeastern Atlantic province of conch-shell gouges and "celts" (digging implements?) and, somewhat later, pottery, often associated with ring-shaped villages consisting of clean, open plazas encircled by dwellings and refuse dumps. The purpose of the village layout may have been to ensure good drainage by leveling and ditching. The earliest of these pottery-using Southeastern villages is dated around 3000 B.C., and the cultural pattern persists for a thousand years. Closely similar pottery and ring villages with heavy accumulations of shell refuse occur during the same period in northern South America from Panama through Colombia, where the pottery appears somewhat earlier than in the United States sites. Arguing against the postulation of colonization by large communities from South America is the fact that the Southeastern villages used stone artifacts quite distinct from those in South America, and buried their dead in the small, round graves characteristic of their predecessors, the Middle-Archaic Southeasterners. The most reasonable reconstruction of events is probably that South Americans occasionally migrated to, occasionally traded with, northeastern Florida and Georgia, traveling in large dugouts along the Gulf Stream current, making known to the Southeasterners the virtues of properly drained village foundations and of pottery. At least eight communities rebuilt their villages to contain a central plaza, and many more adopted the new ceramic containers.

The Late Archaic period in the Southeast involved much more than just the appearance of pottery and the occasional ring villages. Population density reached peaks that in some areas were never to be surpassed. Deer continued, as they would until nearly the present century, to be the preferred game. Raccoons, otters, birds, turtles, fish, and shellfish were regular supplementary protein sources, and nuts furnishing vegetable protein and oil were gathered in quantities and stored for winter consumption.

Cultivation of plants became established in the Southeast during the second millennium B.C. It has been suggested, though there is no particular evidence for it, that the ditched enclosures of ring villages may have been built to drain soil for growing crops, as in the raised fields of northeast South America and Central America. The plants that were first cultivated in the Southeast were principally indigenous, except for the Mexican domesticates pumpkins and squashes. Four seed plants were cultivated in the Southeast: sunflowers, chenopods (goosefoot), marshelder (also called sumpweed), and maygrass. Chenopod seeds preserved in Salts Cave, Kentucky, had been popped. Hickory nuts were by far the most popular nuts, although acorns and walnuts were eaten; the hickory nuts, like the sunflower seeds, were valued for the oil that could be pressed from them, and the nuts could be ground into a flour. Blueberries, strawberries, persimmons, and other fruits, probably wild, were enjoyed. Direct evidence of maize dates only from about 500 B.C.

A hint that Late Archaic communities may have been more sedentary than those in earlier times comes from ground-stone artifacts—time-consuming to manufacture and some too heavy to be worth carrying to camps—becoming common in this period. Most attractive were the beautifully polished weights used with *atlatls* (spear throwers), for which carved antler hooks (used to hold the butts of javelin shafts in place) have also been discovered. These weights are popularly called banner stones and bird stones because they were shaped in geometric or bird shapes, the design enhanced by careful selection of elegantly banded rocks for the raw material. Cradling one of these little sculptures in one's hands brings alive the pride its maker must have felt in his skill in supplying the families of his village with good meat, hides, and bone. Late Archaic craftsworkers turned out flat-bottomed bowls from soapstone (steatite) and sandstone, heavy ground-stone axes, and smooth, polished pestles, as well as bone awls and flaked-stone dart points, knives, scrapers, and per-

forators, all similar to earlier Archaic tools. Net sinkers of ground stone found at some sites indicate fishing nets; fragments of other fabrics show that both twined and woven cloth and baskets were made.

Archaeologist James Ford remarked that "the people of eastern North Ameria began to be relieved of the boredom of spare time about" 1400 B.C. (Ford 1966:191). Both agriculture and large, planned towns come into the Southeast at this time. Continuity seen between everyday life in the town and Late Archaic villages indicates a persistence of native populations in the Southeast. Ford believed that Olmec merchants crossed the Gulf of Mexico and went up the Mississippi River to near Vicksburg, where they established a town as headquarters for extensive trading ventures into the Midwest and Southeast. This town is known as Poverty Point—so called, it is said, because the site is, oddly, impoverished in pottery (actually, because the local plantation was satirically named Poverty Point). In other respects, Poverty Point is more impressive: 1,207 meters (39,060 feet) across, it consists of six octagon-shaped, concentric, man-made ridges that comprise 18.6 kilometers (11.5 miles) of embankments. Four "avenues" pass through the embankments. Bayou Macon, an ancient tributary of the Mississippi, is the eastern edge of the town and cuts off what would have been the eastern section of the octagons. Houses, probably light wooden structures in this hot climate, were built on the tops of the embankments. The central plaza was made level by carrying in soil, ending up after several resurfacings with as much as a meter (one yard) of fill over some sections of the original ground. Bird-shaped mounds 23 and 18 meters (75.5 and 59 feet) high, and a conical mound 6 meters (20 feet) high lie within the town. The stupendous quantity of earth moved at Poverty Point is reminiscent of the huge artificial platform built at contemporary San Lorenzo in Mexico.

According to Ford's interpretation—not, however, accepted by many other Southeastern archaeologists—Olmec merchants formed an elite group at Poverty Point. Either they or native leaders founded other towns in the lower Mississippi Valley and nearby tributaries, maintaining trade with Poverty Point and possessing artifacts typical of it. The common people were locals who continued to make and use their traditional Late Archaic atlatl weights, dart points and knives, ground-stone axes, and round stones used in bolas to catch game (stones tied to cords and thrown so that the weights cause the cords to wind around the prey's legs). Ford suggested the ground-stone axes with grooves to secure the handle, the bolas, and the Archaic technique of drilling stone with a tubular, rather than solid, bit were taken from the Southeast to South America at this time. The Olmec merchants brought in, he claimed, the stone-flaking techniques that produced narrow sharp blades, the use of solid drill bits, sandstone saws, pottery, female figurines, and the celt style of ax, including imitation jade celts of a relatively soft, green stone. While stone beads and pendants were long made in the Southeastern Archaic period, Poverty Point beads include some very fine small jasper and other semiprecious stone examples, some shaped as birds or insects; the consummate skill of the artists who produced these creations suggests they may have been employed by wealthy Olmec.

In view of the excellent and abundant ceramics of the Olmec and other Mexican Preclassic peoples, it seems strange that only a few hundred pottery sherds (out of many thousands of artifacts) have been found at Poverty Point. Those few sherds include some thick vessels with plant-fiber tempering (added to the clay to prevent the pot from cracking as it dries), of the same type as the earliest Southeastern pottery in the shell-midden villages; some vessels tempered with ground fired clay, a custom of the Veracruz Preclassic people of Gulf Coast Mexico, but one that persisted for over a thousand years in the lower Mississippi Valley; and some pots tempered with sand. Contrasting with the paucity of pottery, there were eleven times as many soapstone-bowl sherds as potsherds. To add to the anomaly of this elaborate

town that had so little desire for ceramic pots, the most abundant artifact at Poverty Point was a fired clay ball. Numbers of these were heated in fires, then dropped into bowls of water to bring the liquid to cooking temperature, or rolled into pits to be the heating element of earth ovens.

Ford's contention that Poverty Point was planned by Olmecs is strengthened by the orientation of the principal mound—8° west of north, similar to the orientations of Olmec centers. Olmec interest in magnetic stone is echoed at Poverty Point, where the green stone used for apparently ceremonial axes is magnetic, and where hundreds of well-shaped, polished plummets of iron ores, including magnetite, have been recovered. Astronomy was another concern of the Poverty Point architect. At equinox, an observer atop the highest mound and facing across the lower ramp and terrace on its east side sights the sunrise. Two of the "avenues" through the concentric embankments may have been aligned to sunset at the solstices.

It would be expected that Olmec merchants would have brought seed maize to their headquarters town. The selection of prime agricultural land along the river for this and smaller, culturally related towns in the lower Mississippi Valley heightens the expectation. The only evidence adduced for agriculture, however, is a Mexican-style metate and several manos at Poverty Point. Archaic-style mortars and pestles, and simple stone grinding slabs, were also found. Ford and his collaborator, Clarence Webb, excavated before modern archaeological techniques for recovering plant remains had been developed, so knowledge of plant use at Poverty Point has had to await more recent excavations. Maize was grown on circular, raised embankment fields in South Florida early in the first millennium B.C., but evidence for Poverty Point contacts has not been discovered in the Florida sites.

Adena

Ford and Webb hypothesized—contrary to the common assumption of local independent development—that from Poverty Point, traders paddled up the Mississippi, the Ohio, the Missouri, the Arkansas, and many tributary rivers to collect fine flints and other stone, copper, and probably a variety of perishable goods. Suppliers learned of the great mounds dominating the trading capital, perhaps visited it themselves, and were stimulated to organize their own people to glorify their beliefs and leaders with monuments of earth. A few centuries after the founding of Poverty Point, a center of symbolic earthworks and burial mounds developed in the Ohio Valley. Known as Adena, this cultural pattern spans the first millennium B.C. It is marked by conical earth mounds up to 20 meters (66 feet) high covering log buildings with burials on the floor or in a pit, or covering basins in which corpses had been cremated. In this latter respect, the Adena mounds are similar to the conical mound at Poverty Point, which covers a crematory. Many Adena sites also, or instead, have circular earthen embankments about 100 meters (328 feet) in diameter. Unlike the Poverty Point octagonal embankments, these circles do not seem to have had houses; dwellings seem to have been scattered over the landscape in clusters of two to five, rather than congregated into towns. Presumably, the circles enclosed plazas where the population of a district would gather for ceremonies.

Apparent dispersal of Adena homesteads may reflect an economy in which cultivation supplemented hunting, fishing, and the gathering of wild plant foods. No maize has been identified in Adena sites, although there has been a discovery of maize pollen in a Late Archaic village occupation in southern Illinois. Direct information on the diet of people who were probably Adena comes from the analysis of feces preserved in naturally mummified bodies found in Salts Cave, close to Mammoth Cave in Kentucky. Radiocarbon dating puts the bodies in the first millennium B.C. Squash and gourds must have been planted and cultivated; quash was grown in Kentucky and Missouri already in the second millennium B.C. Sunflower

seeds, amaranth, chenopod (goosefoot), and marshelder (sumpweed) in these human feces were probably cultivated grains constituting an important part of the daily diet. Hickory nuts and acorns were another important daily food source, especially in the lean months of winter and early spring when the people relied on their stored supplies. Bits of fish scale and bone, shell, fur, and feathers show that fish, game, shellfish, and birds had been eaten; happily for the archaeologist, the consumers were not always very finicky about thoroughly cleaning their catch. The people realized their need for greens, and in early spring made an herb tea of wild lilies and iris and perhaps also ate the buds; chenopod leaves may have been eaten as greens, too. There was usually plenty of roughage in the diet, but at times people felt they needed a laxative, and for this purpose they scraped a sulfate mineral, mirabilite, from the walls of the cave. Another mineral, gypsum, was also mined from the cave, but its purpose has not been detected.

Adena artifacts include continuations of late-Archaic-style trends in projectile points and other stone tools and in polished atlatl weights. Ungrooved ground-stone axes came in fashion, and a few axes were made of copper. Pottery was made with crushed-stone temper, a characteristic of Woodland ceramics. Many variations of weaving were practiced. Roughly rectangular stones are thought to have been hoes. Bone awls have been found along with small stone blocks deeply carved, usually only on one side, with stylized curvilinear designs, a favorite one showing a raptorial (hunting) bird. These blocks may have been stamps used to print designs, possibly (considering the awls) for tattooing. Stone tube pipes were frequent. One beautiful pipe is an effigy of a man who seems to be singing and dancing. He wears big, spool-shaped earrings and a breechcloth with a snake figured across the front. His hair is carefully arranged, apparently gathered in broad rolls over the top of his head, and his feet are bare, although some of the people in Salts Cave had comfortable woven-fiber sandals. We cannot tell, but his ear spools may be copies of copper ones: Lake Superior copper was imported by the Adena for many ornaments, as were conch shells from the Atlantic.

SECTION 2: MIDDLE WOODLAND

Hopewell

At the end of the first millennium B.C., heretofore unremarkable communities in Illinois began to eclipse the Adena in the Ohio Valley. The rise of this new power, Hopewell, coincided with a warmer phase in climate, which probably encouraged cultivation of maize, although this imported plant did not displace the already-domesticated indigenous seed plants as the basis of the Hopewell diet. Maize found at a few Hopewell sites is a type with small, hard kernels on small cobs, not much of a rival to the sunflowers and chenopods well suited to the temperate climate of most of the Southeast. This maize may have been eaten as sweet corn rather than dried and ground into flour. Hoes made from stone or from the shoulder blades of bison and deer, have been found in, or in fields near, Hopewell sites. Some of the hoes show a peculiar polish, suggesting they had been used to chop holes in prairie sod; sunflowers or maize could have been planted in these holes. Squash and gourds were also grown. Deer, turtles, turkeys, smaller game, and mussels continued to be heavily relied upon; hickory nuts, acorns, walnuts, grapes, berries, and wild plums were gathered. Settlements show both fairly substantial cabins, the earliest such dwellings to appear in Eastern Woodlands archaeology, and also light shelters for outdoor activities and sleeping in summer. Many Hopewell communities were built on river terraces beside flood plains where the indigenous seed grains would flourish. There are river valleys in Ohio that exhibit one Hopewell hamlet after another, neighbors without towns. River terrace villages were advantageous not only for agriculture but also for fishing and for access to the many regions connected by the Midwest's great network of streams.

Above all, Hopewell was the integration of thousands of villages throughout the East into a system in which material goods were moved in the service of political leaders marked by well-defined status symbols. The villages clearly reflect local traditions deriving from the Late Archaic and Early Woodland periods. They remained villages or loosely clustered farmsteads dependent upon hunting and nut gathering as much as upon grain cultivation, instead of consolidating into towns that would be forced to farm intensively to sustain larger populations. The communities of a district nevertheless were subject to leaders who could exact labor to erect impressive geometric embankments, platforms, and conical burial mounds. From the Great Lakes to the Gulf of Mexico, eastern Kansas to upstate New York, these leaders exchanged ideas and exotic ornaments for their tombs.

Hopewell has been explained as the conquest of the Midwest by a warrior tribe from central Illinois, and as the spread of a religious cult of the dead. Neither explanation fully fits what is known about the Middle Woodland period of the Southeast and Midwest. It seems more reasonable to interpret the rise of Hopewell as a shift in the East's center of power and wealth from the initial trading headquarters at Poverty Point, far down the Mississippi, to the central Mississippi and Ohio valleys, which were closer to the sources and the major transportation routes of the most valuable trade materials. Peoples along this northern margin of the Southeast probably were encouraged during Early Woodland times to organize the production and shipment of valued goods, allowing capable men to deal with buyers on behalf of the whole community. In time, such men were able to extend and consolidate their power, legitimizing it by appropriating to themselves symbols such as hawks, bears, stags, and snakes, ostentatiously displayed in rare and expensive materials worked by trained craftsmen. Probably allying the Illinois and Ohio valleys, these chiefs forged trade networks supporting their upper-class positions.

By A.D. 1, southern Ohio was the richest land in America. It featured man-made embankment avenues up to 2.5 miles (4 kilometers) long, circles and other geometric figures 1,000 feet (350 meters) in diameter, and occasionally mounds with huge snake or bird effigies. Conical earth mounds 70 feet (21 meters) high covered cremations or log tombs, some of them obviously of a great man accompanied by sacrificed wives and retainers, with symbols of power cut out of sheet mica from the southern Appalachians, hammered out of Lake Superior copper or silver, and carved on tobacco pipes of fine-grained stone. Handsomely decorated Woodland-type (crushed-stone-tempered) pottery, copper celts, panpipes of reeds covered with copper, copper ear-spools, woven fiber headdresses decorated with thin copper ornaments, fine stone blades, and beads of meteoric iron, copper, Atlantic shell, many stones, and bear—even grizzly-bear—teeth additionally furnished the tombs. Hoards of obsidian from Yellowstone Park in the Rockies prove the great distances commanded by Hopewell trade. Bits of cloth preserved through having been wrapped around copper objects reveal fine weaving, including in one instance a delicate gauze that required hundreds of hours of spinning and weaving to construct. Thread for these fabrics was spun from fibers of indigenous plants such as milkweed and basswood inner bark. We glimpse how Hopewell people looked to each other through figurines carved in stone or modeled in clay: their dress was simple loincloth or skirt, they often wore necklaces and spool-shaped ear-lobe ornaments, and they arranged their hair carefully.

The Hopewell period, from its beginning about 100 B.C., through its flowering around A.D. 1, to its decline by A.D. 500, coincided with Hohokam's establishment in the Southwest. It was also the final Preclassic period and the period of the early Teotihuacán empire in Mexico. No evidence of contact between Hopewell and either of these cen-

ters has been recognized. Hopewell was river-oriented, and does not seem to have pushed beyond the dry Plains and the Rockies into the Southwest. Hopewell pottery does resemble some decorated wares found in Veracruz, Mexico, some centuries earlier, and some on the Pacific coast of Guatemala even earlier. For that matter, similarities can also be seen to pottery from Indochina and the Philippines dating from the first part of the Polynesian migrations, in the second millennium B.C. These widespread occurrences of certain pottery-decoration techniques and designs could be connected, but the gaps between the occurrences, in both time and space, are uncomfortably large. Lower Mississippi Valley occurrences seem to date *after* the development of Illinois Hopewell, and could have been stimulated *by* Illinois. Ear spools are another item whose Olmec and Hopewell examples are very similar, but they have not been found in the intervening time or region, although if they had been made of wood in the lower Mississippi Valley, no traces would remain. Though some occasional contacts between Hopewell and Mexico must have occurred, Hopewell has strong indigenous roots in the Late Archaic of the central Midwest. Stimulated by Poverty Point, nourished by a steadily increasing population that grew indigenous grains as a food staple, Hopewell chiefs built a climax of art, organization, and intellectual concepts still echoing among their descendants today.

Hopewell suffered a decline in its central Midwest heartland around A.D. 350. A cooler phase of climate, which was to persist for about three centuries, set in. Cultivated grain harvests would have been subject to destructive frosts much more often in this cooler period than during the Hopewell climax, and many supplementary foods, such as hickory nuts, would also have become less plentiful. For about two centuries, Hopewell groups fought to maintain their territories and resources, fought inexorable nature, and fought each other. Defensible hilltops in the Ohio Valley became fortified refuges for the villagers who farmed below. Time and again, communities of people may have preserved their lives in these strongholds only to face famine as enemies stole or destroyed their crops. Since Hopewellians had maintained diversified subsistence strategies, loss of cultivated grain supplies probably did not inflict starvation, but it would have forced all the working members of a community to spend more time finding and processing food. Traders and craftsworkers could no longer be supported as full-time specialists; chiefs would receive less tribute and have less to command. Peoples of the central Midwest reverted to more egalitarian, autonomous villages exploiting the wide variety of local foods. One typical central-Illinois settlement cultivated squash and gourds and probably chenopods, gathered nuts and wild seeds, caught deer, turkeys, smaller game, turtles, fish, and mussels—but apparently cultivated no maize. Trade routes linking half the continent collapsed, and richly garnished tomb mounds were no longer built.

South of the original Hopewell climax region, maize could still be grown with security. The societies of the Southeast had been part of the Hopewell network, producing mica, conch shells, and probably perishable goods to exchange for copper and fine-quality flints from the north. The Southerners built towns with both conical burial mounds and truncated (flat-topped) pyramidal mounds (as at Poverty Point), for example, Pinson Mounds in western Tennessee, which features five large platform mounds and at least six conical burial mounds. Pinson Mounds superficially looks like a Mississippian-period town, but, unlike Mississippian sites, at Pinson there is no evidence of buildings on top of the platform mounds, nor of populous settlement around mounds-bordered plazas. Hopewell people seem to have left their hamlets to come to their mounds only for ceremonies. The Southerners employed Hopewell pottery-decorating techniques, and their pottery designs also showed the influence of Hopewell. Other traits distinctive of the Southeast appeared in this period: a beverage drunk during ceremonies, probably the

"black drink" stimulant tea of historic times, and the custom of drying out corpses in a charnel house, then burying the bones tied in a bundle. A variant on this has been discovered at the Fort Center site in central Florida, where, adjacent to a low platform mound that may have held a charnel house, was an artificial pond in which was built a wooden platform outlined with pine posts carved into turkeys and other birds, panthers, dogs, foxes, and bears. Partially dried corpses bent and wrapped in mats were placed on this platform guarded by the carved animals and large birds. When Hopewell declined, the southern towns continued to enjoy a comfortable life, Gulf Coast artists reaching their peak of skill and inspiration just about the time the distinctive Hopewell style disappeared in the North.

Some archaeologists argue that the Gulf Coast climax owed some of its impetus to contacts with the northern Maya across the Gulf of Mexico. A large site in northwest Florida, Crystal River, has two rounded burial mounds and two truncated platform mounds, as well as a plaza, a smaller mound on which were dwellings, and a shell trash heap. Two crude stelae are set upright, one on each side of the burial mound in the center of the town, not adjacent to the mound but far enough away that each seems to have been placed approximately halfway between the two platform mounds. Each is roughly at the point to which the ramp of the platform mound nearest it is oriented. One stela has a simple human figure carved on it, the other appears plain (but may have been defaced). Both stelae have in front of them a deposit of food remains, probably an offering, and the decorated stela has before it a cluster of chert flakes as well. To Ripley Bullen, the archaeologist who excavated Crystal River, the stelae looked like an unlettered attempt to copy the focal area of a Maya city. Charcoal from the food offering was radiocarbon-dated to about A.D. 500, too late to postulate Crystal River as a port of entry through which Mexican ear-spools, for example, might have reached Hopewell. It is possible, however, that this hint of a Floridian's visit to a Maya city indicates contacts across the Gulf that continued into the succeeding Mississippian period.

SECTION 3: THE MISSISSIPPIAN AND PROTO-HISTORIC PERIOD

The colder and wetter phase of climate that probably contributed to the decline of Hopewell in its heartland gave way about 750 A.D. to a less rainy and somewhat warmer phase in the Midwest. Coincident with this return to more favorable growing conditions for maize was the introduction into the region of a new variety of maize, Northern Flint. Northern Flint has two advantages over earlier, Middle Woodland varieties of maize: it has larger cobs with larger kernels (eight rows instead of the ten to twelve rows of earlier, smaller cobs), and it matures more quickly, allowing successful cultivation in shorter growing seasons. In the Eastern Woodlands, as in the contemporary American Southwest, eight-rowed maize seems to have been a critical factor in the development of town-based societies along the regions' northern frontiers.

Mississippian is the name given to the cultural pattern beginning about A.D. 750 in the huge drainage system of the Mississippi River. In the center of this river network at what is now St. Louis, at the confluence of the Missouri and Mississippi a few dozen miles above the Mississippi's junction with the Ohio, is the Mississippian city of Cahokia. Ringing Cahokia were independent societies trading with the city. Cahokia itself seems to have been largely abandoned after about A.D. 1450, but many of the lesser Mississippian-period settlements continued into the protohistoric period of the seventeenth century. Mississippian is the last prehistoric period in the Eastern Woodlands.

Mississippian seems to have crystallized out of the Lower Mississippi Valley and Gulf Coast agricultural societies flourishing throughout the decline of Hopewell. The profitable Eastern types of

Northern Flint and Eight-rowed maize allowed an expansion of agricultural towns northward. These were outposts or colonies, not merely canoes of traders. Where in the Middle Woodland period ritual centers were built amid the villages of local populations, in the Mississippian period distinct new towns appeared on the richest farmland in the major river valleys, while up on the bluffs and along creeks, Late Woodland villages continued local cultural traditions. Stockades around many Mississippian towns suggest these colonies often faced raids from the indigenous peoples.

The immediate source of the early Mississippian cultural pattern cannot be determined, but it probably was in the Lower Mississippi region. One town in this region, the Davis site, on the region's western border in easternmost Texas, can be linked with the founding phases of Cahokia, which began about A.D. 950, and Baytown sites in the state of Mississippi are said to compare closely with Kincaid, a Mississippian town on the lower Ohio River in Illinois. Sometime in the Middle Woodland period—the Davis site was excavated before the discovery of radiocarbon dating, so its occupation span is estimated from a single radiocarbon date on maize cobs in the collection from the excavation—an agricultural town was established on a river terrace in the rolling country where the southeastern pine forests meet the edge of the Plains. Houses in the town were comfortable, round structures 20 to 30 feet (6 to 9 meters) in diameter, their pole walls probably thatched-over. These houses were apparently built by the same construction technique observed to have been used in the early historic period by the Caddo living in the region. The pottery in the town at this time includes some vessels decorated by techniques typical of the later Preclassic period in Mexico. Subsequently, a flat-topped platform mound was built over a portion of the town's residential area, and the house style changed to a square shape. The platform mound was L-shaped, 250 feet (76 meters) long by 150 feet (46 meters) wide, and at least 17.5 feet (5.3 meters) high; very likely, it was originally considerably higher, but historic plowing induced heavy slope wash. Another large, but apparently oval, platform mound and a conical mound now 45 feet (14 meters) in diameter and 21 feet (6.4 meters) high also lie within the town, but they have not been excavated by archaeologists. The abundance of artifacts over the entire river terrace indicates that by about A.D. 700 (very much a guess date), the Davis site was the largest town in eastern Texas. It is not surprising, then, that a few pottery sherds of the Davis-site style occurred at Cahokia, evidence of contact between the well-established southern town and the newer city at the hub of inland America.

Cahokia's urban expansion began about A.D. 950. Within a century, it had attracted thousands of families into the largest city north of Mexico, a city covering nearly 5 square miles (15 square kilometers) with a population estimated at thirty thousand. Substantial but lesser towns were strung out along the banks of the Mississippi, the Missouri, the Illinois, and the Kaskaskia rivers, and they all converged on Cahokia. The city was the seat of power and commerce up to about A.D. 1350, precisely as is St. Louis today, directly across the Mississippi from Cahokia. Interstate Highway 70 and 55 crosses the northern sector of Cahokia. The area, known as the American Bottoms, was important in the Hopewell period, became supreme in the Mississippian, and is important again, an example of the persistent value of rich farmland at the node of a transportation network.

The focus of the city of Cahokia is the greatest of its platform mounds, which is called Monks Mound because a small Trappist monastery was once situated there. Today, Monks Mound is 100 feet (30 meters) high (originally, a conical mound on the top terrace made it even higher), 1,037 feet (316 meters) north-south, and 790 feet (241 meters) east-west, larger than a football field. Its 22 million cubic feet (623,000 cubic meters) of earth make it half the size of Teotihuacán's Pyramid of the Sun, although it is five times larger than the next largest Mississippian mound (at Etowah, Georgia). Monks Mound, like other major mounds north of Mexico, was built entirely of earth (clay, silt, and sand), raised in stages over about two centuries. It headed a large plaza surrounded by smaller (but still impressive) mounds, some conical, some truncated. Subsidiary plazas surrounded by mounds lie off Cahokia's principal plaza and in its satellite towns: over 100 mounds have been counted in Cahokia, and dozens more were destroyed by the building of St. Louis across the river. Wooden structures plastered with adobe stood on at least some of the flat-topped mounds. In some instances they may have served as mausoleums for the royal lineage, in other instances as palaces for the living ruler. These structures of wood lacked the magnificence of the great masonry temples and palaces of the Mexican capitals, but set on their imposing mounds, the Mississippian rulers' domiciles had a monumentality that must have awed all visitors.

Huge wooden posts 30 inches in diameter were erected in plazas and on some platforms at Cahokia. One archaeologist suggests that certain sets of posts were used to observe the equinoxes and solstices. Other posts, one of which has been discovered to have been within a fenced platform, probably served as central symbols in rituals. (The Mandan of North Dakota, whose ancestors participated in the Mississippian network, raised such a post to represent Lone Man who taught the people their most vital ceremonies. The cedar post stood in the plaza in the center of the village, the lodges of the priest and leading families on the north side of the plaza. A fence of cottonwood planks shielded the Lone Man post from the casual business of the village.) Lined up directly south of the southwest corner of Monks Mound, across and south of the principal plaza, a huge post was set up during the city's first phase (circa A.D. 1000). Later, the post was taken out, its pit filled in, and a corpse on a bed of pierced shell discs placed in this key spot. Young men and women were sacrificed to accompany the person in death, bearing with them offerings including a wooden staff covered with

FIGURE 4.1 Cahokia, Monks Mound. Mississippian period, c. A.D. 1100. This entirely manmade earth platform is 100 feet (30 meters) high, 1,037 feet (316 meters) in length. Originally temples and possibly a ruler's residence were built on top. The mound is not restored. *(T. Kehoe)*

sheet copper, quantities of mica, hundreds of arrows in sets imported from the four corners of the Cahokian trade empire, and nineteen beautifully finished chunkey stones (for a game similar to bowling, in which a stone disc is rolled down an alley as players throw sticks to intercept it). The group of bodies was covered with a small earth mound, itself later embedded within a much larger mound.

The burial offerings with the personage in Mound 72, as this is now called, summarize the major trade contacts of the Mississippians. Copper, of course, came from Lake Superior. Mica came from the southern Appalachians. The arrow points encompassed raw materials and styles indicating sources in Wisconsin, Tennessee, and the east Texas–Oklahoma region. Elsewhere in Cahokia, shells of conch and other species indicate exchanges with people on the Atlantic Ocean. Decorative motifs such as the falcon eye, which was used throughout the Southeast in the Mississippi period, are further evidence for extensive communication.

On the fertile river plain beyond the city were hamlets of square wattle-and-daub houses beside fields of maize, beans, and squashes. Mississippi-

ans used versions of raised fields, square or rectangular plots in which the topsoil was heaped into wide, wide-spaced ridges (not individual "hills"), which facilitated drainage and gave a little protection against unseasonable frosts. The "Three Sisters," as the Iroquois call them—maize, beans, and squashes—were for the first time in the Eastern Woodlands raised together in quantity to provide the larger share of daily diet. Agricultural staples were supplemented by deer, turkeys, migratory waterfowl (Cahokia is on the Mississippian Flyway), and fish ranging from sturgeon to catfish, bullheads, suckers, and drum, with many of the latter species so small they must have been caught in nets or traps. Turtles, small game, and shellfish were minor sources of food. It is usually assumed that deer and turkeys must have been obtained on hunting trips into the forests on the uplands, but recognition of probable turkey pens attached to Late Woodland houses in Ohio suggests the Mississippians may very well have kept domesticated turkeys. The high proportion of young-mature— prime eating—deer, one and one-half to three years old, in the trash of some sites of this time makes it likely deer were rounded up and driven into fenced runways where the desired animals could be culled

FIGURE 4.2 Mississippian village archaeological excavation near Cahokia (air view). Rectangular outlines are house foundations; large circles beside the house in the right foreground are probably sweatlodges; smaller circles outside houses are storage pits. For scale, note workers in houses, right foreground. *(J.W. Porter, FAI-270 Project Director, University of Illinois, Urbana. Photo by Jeff Abrams.)*

and the older ones allowed to escape and continue breeding. The general Indian practice of burning off forest to promote deer browse would have facilitated such harvesting methods. Perhaps, too, much of the meat, bones (for tools), and hides required by the Cahokians were traded to them by the Late Woodland villagers who lived out beyond the metropolitan area. Fish and, in season, ducks and geese were available in quantity near the city; it is possible that such fish as catfish were fish-farmed in the sloughs of the American Bottoms.

Mississippian towns and cities similar to, though not as large as, Cahokia occurred from southern Wisconsin (Aztalan site) to eastern Okla-

homa (Spiro) on the west, through Moundville in Alabama on the south, to Macon and Etowah in Georgia on the east. Fringing these stereotypically Mississippian centers were settlements reflecting the persistence of the local cultural traditions. Complicating the picture are regional adaptations of the Mississippian cultural pattern. These adaptations lacked the great mounds and formal plazas of the true Mississippian towns and sometimes, too, their heavy bastioned stockades, but used pottery, hoes, arrowheads, and other artifacts in a general Mississippian style. The underlying trend seems to have been toward increasing reliance upon maize agriculture, so much more profitable with the larger Eight-rowed and Northern Flint varieties. The Mississippians themselves, seizing the best river-bottom farmlands, consolidated into planned, fortified towns—they were, in short, urbanizing. The regional Mississippian-derived societies were frontier people expanding agriculture to the northeast, north, and west; coeval with these frontier societies, the Gulf Coast and lower Mississippi Valley societies and the Late Woodland groups in the invaded territories remained autonomous.

European explorers in the sixteenth and seventeenth centuries met all three types of late-Mississippian-period cultural patterns. Striking links between the true Mississippian and several historic Southeastern societies were provided by explorers' descriptions of the towns with plazas and mounds, and especially the accounts of mortuary customs. The similarity among symbols in the major Mississippian cities of Cahokia, Moundville, Etowah, and Spiro led archaeologists to assume a religious cult had evangelized among Mississippians. Some attributed this supposed cult to Mexicans (Toltecs or Maya); others guessed it was late enough in time to have been a reaction to the disruptions induced by de Soto's expedition. More recent investigations have shown that motifs of the "Southern Cult" were used throughout the five centuries of Mississippian culture, that they differ significantly from any one particular Mexican religious system, and that they long antedate de Soto. Most tellingly, the motifs and their contexts correlate so well with early historic accounts that it seems clear the documents describe customs that have been characteristic of the Mississippian cities from the twelfth century and that had developed from even earlier ideas.

The Southeastern Ceremonial Complex, as the "Cult" was more properly termed, was a set of symbols of rank and power. Imperishable archaeological remains indicate the falcon was the metaphor for conquering power and, by extension, the sweep of virile power through lands and generations. Explorers tell us the king of the Natchez, in the lower Mississippi Valley, was titled the Great

Sun: his symbol was probably the circle or eye without falcon marking, and perhaps the hand with an eye on the palm. Arrows in stylized bows ("bilobed arrows") are frequent motifs. They seem to represent both the weapon and, by the resemblance of the arrow flanked by a pair of rounded bow ends (or possibly it was a javelin lying on an atlatl shaft between the finger-holds) to the male genitals, the virility of the weapon's user. Other favorite symbols are the rattlesnake, the pileated woodpecker, human skulls, and long bones. The symbols are found on sheet copper, engraved shell plaques and bowls, stone tablets and pendants, and fine pottery, and are painted on cloth. They are placed with personages buried in the platform mounds—evidently rulers, other royalty, and perhaps high priests and war leaders (who were often men of the royal family, and thus entitled to mound burial). Copper, shining like the sun, seems to have been royal. From explorers' narratives we learn that sheet copper, embossed or cut into shapes such as imitation hawk feathers, was combined with real hawk feathers and the bright feathers of other birds into resplendent headdresses. Mantles of cloth covered with brilliant feathers also adorned royalty—as in Mexico—but are not preserved archaeologically. High-status men carried ceremonial staffs made of copper and finely polished or skillfully flaked stone. The staffs were shaped like war clubs or tomahawks, but were too fragile to have been wielded in earnest. The kings were furnished in death with bowls made from conch shells, which historically were containers for the "black drink" with which men purged themselves before rituals. While most of the burial mounds seem to have contained kings and nobility, buried alone or with sacrificed retainers, a few burials hint at the sacrifice of impersonators of sacred figures. For example, at Etowah, four men wearing feather and copper headdresses and carrying copper celts were found lying in the square tomb chamber, one along each side.

Another set of symbols probably symbolizes Mississippian cosmology. An equal-armed cross with a circle in the middle, or within a circle, represented the cosmos (the four arms are the cardinal directions) and repeated the sun symbol. Historically, the congruence of fire and sun is shown in ceremonies in which four logs, one brought from each direction, are placed in the form of a cross to feed the newly kindled ritual fire in a town plaza. A carved stone figurine from Cahokia is a woman kneeling within a feline-headed serpent's coil. The tail of the serpent turns into a vine curling up the woman's back; round fruits, perhaps gourds, hang from the vine. On the woman's back is a square bundle with a strap that passes around her shoulders. The woman wears only a skirt, and in her right hand she holds an adzelike implement, apparently a large blade lashed at a right angle to a handle. She seems to be hitting or scraping the serpent's back with this tool. If it is a Mississippian hoe, she may be planting something in the serpent's back. This, and the vines, hint that the woman embodies a cosmological concept like the historic Hidatsa Grandmother-Who-Never-Dies, the life of the earth whose mate is a giant serpent. Grandmother-Who-Never-Dies protects the gentle Corn Maidens in her lodge during the cold winter months, then sends them out to the Hidatsa women's fields in spring for the human women to nurture. What is in the Cahokia figurine's pack is anybody's guess—the pack might be a cradleboard, or it might hold a harvest, or the rodlike carving on its top might be meant for lightning associated with summer rains. Whatever the figurine, and another, simply carved woman found nearby, represent, they show that the Mississippians balanced male symbols with female.

Human sacrifice, kings in feather mantles, elaborate plumed headdresses, rattlesnakes and skulls, cities with platform mounds surrounding plazas—all suggest relationships between the Mexican and Mississippian societies. Analysis, however, demonstrates the long indigenous roots of many superficially Mexican Mississippian traits: towns with mounds and plazas back to Poverty Point, carnivorous-bird symbols back to Adena and Hopewell. Kingship and sacrifice are common developments in relatively dense sedentary societies dependent upon agriculture. Parallel development from a Preclassic base, introduced into the Southeast at Poverty Point, can account for most of the similarities between the Mississippian and Mexican cultural patterns. Nevertheless, contacts did occur. Maya trade across the Caribbean occasionally stopped in Florida. Filed teeth on individuals buried in Cahokia suggest that Mexicans visited the Mississippian capital or that Cahokians traveling in the Mexican empire came home beautified in a fashion rare in the lands beyond the Chichimecs. Ideas and small objects also probably passed from Mexico to the Southeast, and from the American Southwest to the Southeast, or back, via the Chichimecs themselves, the materially impoverished hunting and gathering peoples of arid southern Texas. When the cactus fruits ripened, these peoples held festivals lubricated by fermented cactus juice. Adventurers from all the borders of the arid country participated in these fairs, exchanging stories and trading or gambling for items exotic in their own lands. Chichimecs such as the Jumano in the early historic period carried such objects as bits of French lace or Spanish chain mail across Texas as they hunted and traded. They were always sure of a welcome in the towns of the Caddo in east Texas, the Wichita in Oklahoma, the Pecos Puebloans in New Mexico, and the Mexicans, because in spite of their lack of material goods, they could relate fascinating descriptions of strange peoples and pass on souvenirs. In the prehistoric period, the ancestors of the Jumano and other "wild Chichimecs" must have similarly capitalized on their peregrinations. Thus, Maya traders, Chichimec tale-tellers, and Mexican and Cahokian travelers probably all intermittently reinforced the tendencies to common ideas between Mexico and the Southeast, tendencies fed by an ancient contact base and by parallel demographic trends supported by maize agriculture. No Toltec invasion should be read in the generalized Mexican-Mississippian similarities.

SECTION 4: THE EARLY HISTORIC PERIOD, 1513–1607

The majority of Southeastern peoples spoke languages belonging to the Muskogean language family, including Muskogee proper, spoken by the people called in English the Creeks, living in Georgia and Alabama; Choctaw and closely related Chickasaw in Mississippi; Alabama and Koasati in Alabama; Hitchiti in Georgia; and Apalachee in northwestern Florida. Seminoles, a tribe formed in the historic period, speak Mikasuki, closely related to Hitchiti, or Seminole Creek; formerly, a few spoke Hitchiti. Many Mississippian towns must have used Muskogean languages, but no firm identification for specific sites can be made. Algonkian languages have been thought by some linguists to be very distantly related to Muskogean. Southeastern Algonkian languages include Algonkian proper, spoken by the people of Powhatan's confederacy in Virginia; other peoples, including the Pamlico, along the Atlantic coast from North Carolina northward; and Shawnee in Kentucky.

Other major Southeastern languages include Cherokee, a branch of Iroquoian spoken in the southern Appalachians in the Carolinas, Georgia, and Tennessee; and the closely related Tuscarora, formerly further east in North Carolina. Catawba, bordering the Cherokee in South Carolina; Tutelo in western Virginia; Ofo; and Biloxi in southern Mississippi (the latter said to have come from the Ohio Valley) are Siouan languages. Yuchi, on the Cherokees' southern border in Georgia; Tunica, once on the Yazoo River and then in Louisiana; Chitimacha in southern Louisiana, and to its west, Atakapa are languages apparently unrelated to others. Of these "language isolates," only Yuchi is still spoken (in Oklahoma, where the Yuchi now live). Caddo, a language family, was spoken by the Caddo proper in the Louisiana-Texas-Oklahoma border region, on the western edge of the Southeast.

Many languages spoken in the Southeast became extinct before anyone was interested in re-cording them. Among these are the languages of peninsular Florida: Timucua in the north, Calusa in the southwest, Ais in the east, and several others spoken by smaller societies. Timucua seems related to Warao, spoken by Indians in the Orinoco Delta of Venezuela, whose ancestors may have paddled across the Caribbean to Florida as early as 3000 B.C. The lower Mississippi languages are also extinct, some, like Taensa, never recorded, and others, like Natchez, preserved in small vocabularies barely adequate to hint of the affiliations of the speakers.

The earliest Europeans in the Southeast were Spanish. Florida was probably sighted in 1499, but the first known landing was in 1513, by Juan Ponce de León. Hostile Indians, probably Calusa, met his explorations. This hostility is thought by some historians to indicate prior landings by slavers from Cuba, but it may be no more than the general belligerency noted by early observers throughout the Southeast, endemic warfare responsible for the heavy fortifications of Mississippian towns. Ponce attempted to establish a colony in Florida in 1521, again found the Indians eager to attack, and this time received a fatal arrow wound from them. Two subsequent colonizing ventures by Spaniards in that decade were equally disastrous. Four survivors from the last of these expeditions—Alvar Núñez Cabeza de Vaca, who wrote an account of his extraordinary trek, and three other Spaniards, one of whom was black—lived among the coastal Texas Indians for several years, learning the techniques of the shamans until they were sufficiently skilled to combine these with Christian prayer rituals and earn reputations as powerful healers. Welcome in this capacity in every Indian town, the men worked their way across Texas to the American Southwest and then down to Spanish outposts in northwestern Mexico. Cabeza de Vaca's report stimulated two major explorations north of Mexico, Coronado's through the Southwest beginning in 1540, and that of Hernando de Soto, a conquistador who had fought in Pizarro's conquest of Peru, into the Southeast in 1539.

De Soto was better equipped to seize the Southeast than Pizarro had been in Peru. Six hundred heavily armed soldiers were aided by over one hundred servants, to be supplemented by Indian porters who would be borrowed or seized from native chiefs. Two hundred horses and three hundred pigs accompanied the army. The horses proved crucial in giving the Spaniards the advantage in several battles with Indians; the pigs did not impress the Indians so deeply, but did thrive in the rich forests in spite of their long marches. The substantial party of over one thousand (not counting the pigs) worked its way north to the Savannah River, across the Appalachians, down almost to Mobile Bay, northwest to the Mississippi River, across it and up the Arkansas River to the edge of the Plains (where they were within about 300 miles [about 500 kilometers] of Coronado's party), and then—seeing they had passed from the populous towns into unpromising wild land—back to the Mississippi. De Soto died there, of fever, in 1542. A year later, 311 Spaniards, with 100 Indians they had enslaved, reached Mexico again. The expedition had completely failed in its objective of finding and conquering another Peru. What it had accomplished was a horrifying display of European inhumanity, and very likely the inadvertent destruction of the Mississippian powers.

When de Soto's army reached an Indian town, it demanded bread, bearers, and women. Occasionally, town leaders would offer gifts of these requirements, plus finely dressed white deerskins and fresh-water pearls. The gifts, when freely offered, seem to have signified the town's wish to ally with the Spaniards against another nation. More often, de Soto kidnapped the chief or members of his family who came out to deal with the strangers, forcing the townspeople to succor their leader by supplying the demands of the captors. At times, de Soto didn't bother parlaying with the town, but attacked, seizing the supplies and personnel wanted and destroying houses, fields, and citizens his army couldn't use. These tactics were not new to Southeasterners, who emulated the falcon in dropping swiftly down upon enemies, but the scale of de Soto's demands and reprisals seems to have been unprecedented. The total population of many towns was no greater than de Soto's horde, so to provision that army left the town bereft of food and a substantial proportion of its able-bodied men and women. We have only the archaeological record of what happened after de Soto's army moved on, but we can suppose that the severely weakened town suffered famine, could not plant adequately for the following year's food supply, could not resist depredations by their traditional enemies, and succumbed easily to infectious diseases. This last was probably the most dangerous outcome, for while the Spaniards camped in the town, raping the women, they must have communicated the fevers and agues of which they themselves regularly complained and frequently died (de Soto among them). Some of these diseases were of European origin, to which the Indians had poor immunity. Others may have been endemic in the Southeast. But what killed was not so much the disease as the malnourished victims' lowered ability to maintain general metabolism while combating the infection. De Soto did not consciously devastate the provinces he expected to claim, as Pizarro had Peru, but his heedless brutality made him a juggernaut crushing the towns in his path.

The sixteenth century saw the end of the full Mississippian cultures insofar as large platform mounds were no longer built when European settlements began in the seventeenth century. A prevalent opinion ascribes the fall of the Mississippians to epidemics of European disease introduced by de Soto, but this explanation is too simplistic and denies the considerable persistence of Mississippian cultural patterns even through the eighteenth century (and today, in much modified form). For more than a century after de Soto, there were few attempts to found outposts in the Southeast. The French raided Spanish treasure ships homeward bound up the Gulf Stream off Florida, and the Spanish countered by halfheartedly establishing missions in northeastern Florida and along the Georgia coast, attaching small garrisons to these new towns built beginning in 1565. The missionaries, first Jesuits and Franciscans, then only Franciscans after 1572, followed the policies developed in Mexico and the American Southwest of gathering Indians into a planned community ruled by the church, teaching European agriculture and crafts, and introducing wheat, fruit trees, and livestock. Native Indian rulers were accepted as allied noble lords governing their own fiefs but expected to contribute laborers or soldiers to Spanish enterprises. Since one purpose of the missions was to guard the Spanish sovereignty, and since de Soto and later explorers had found no riches in the interior, the posts were strung along the Atlantic coast where French harassment and a couple of attempts at colonization were concentrated. The interior, where the Mississippian societies lay, was neglected.

Archaeological research has filled in the historical picture. Indian towns along the de Soto route through the Southeast have cemeteries where dozens of people were buried at the same time, sometimes several in one grave, in the years immediately following 1540. It seems likely that these deaths indicate epidemic disease. A few Indian skeletons from 1540 show sword stabs in the bone; most were men, but one skeleton was an elderly woman killed by sword thrusts into her thigh. Twenty years after de Soto, Tristán de Luna returned to Florida, sending some of his men north into Georgia to seek out the rich towns described by De Soto's party. Nothing as impressive as de Soto's Coosa towns, or Etowah, could be discovered, only smaller villages. Luna wondered whether de Soto's men had lied; recent archaeological excavations demonstrate that they had not, but the nation had been severely weakened and impoverished by the ravages of the Spaniards and the diseases they brought with them. Not only were no more large platform mounds built after the sixteenth century, existing large mounds were no longer maintained after about 1630, nor were palisades kept up. Many inland towns, including some

of the Coosa nation occupying western Georgia, were abandoned late in the sixteenth century, the surviving populace either constructing small villages in their homeland or migrating downriver toward the fall-line river towns through which trade was oriented in the seventeenth century. Thus the "mysterious disappearance of the Moundbuilders" is no mystery. The Mississippian kingdoms were decimated by epidemics, most disastrous in the principal towns where de Soto's army had spent the most time, destroyed food stores, and waged battles. The rattlesnake emblem of Coosa was no more flaunted by her troops. The remnant of the nation shifted the capital downstream, with only three villages in the Coosa heartland a century after de Soto, compared to at least eleven in 1540. Historically, the Coosa would become one of the principal Creek confederacy towns.

By the middle seventeenth century, after 150 years of a few much-touted expeditions and a number of minor colonizations along the Atlantic coast, more to prey upon (French and English) or guard (Spanish) the Spanish treasure galleons than to exploit the land itself, Europeans had yet to directly affect most Southeastern Indians. Some people still lived in towns of up to three or four hundred households, or several thousand people; others lived in villages of a few hundred. "Town," among Southeastern Indians, usually refers to not just a semiurban settlement but to its suburban villages as well, the set forming an independent political and economic unit governed through a council. Shelter consisted of square or oval houses of wattle-and-daub, thatch, or cane-mat covering. South Floridians needed only open-walled pavilions, and other people often built small, heavily plastered cabins set in pits for winter use, next to better-ventilated houses for the warmer months. Maize, pumpkins, dried meat, and skins usually were kept in separate storehouses, which, with the summer and winter houses, might form three or four sides of a household courtyard, rather like typical Mexican residences. In the center of the town was a flat, open square, ordinarily reserved

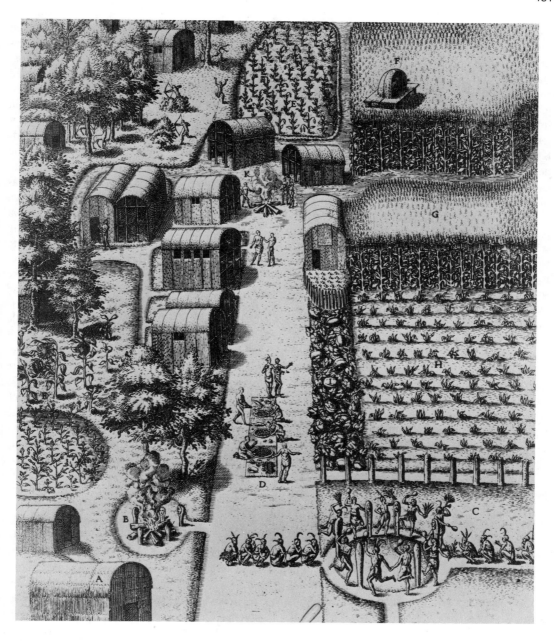

FIGURE 4.3 Town of Secoton (southern Algonkian), on the Pamlico River in North Carolina, about 1585. In upper right, a man sits on a platform to frighten off birds from ripe maize; upper left, men hunt deer; lower, a feast is laid out as a ritual dance is being performed. Note the variety of crops, including sunflowers (left center). *(Smithsonian Institution National Anthropological Archives)*

for the men, surrounded by rectangular, three-wall buildings open to the square. Councils were held in these buildings, the men arranged in them by status. A more substantial building, rounded in shape, might be set off the square and used as a temple, although many rituals were held publicly in the open square. Towns also contained ossuaries, roofed platforms upon which lay chests or mat bundles of the bones of deceased chiefs, gathered neatly after the flesh had rotted or been stripped off (in some areas, itinerant specialists called buzzard men went from town to town to perform this task). A stone, wooden, or wood-and-cloth representation of a protective spirit sat on the platform with the remains of the chiefs, and a priest might sleep beneath it, praying constantly. When enemies overcame a town, they desecrated its ossuary, scattering the bones and looting it of the pearls, copper ornaments, fine mantles, and other furnishings of the departed. (Thus, de Soto unwittingly followed local custom when he ravished the ossuary-temples in his lust for treasure.) Palisades and ditches encircled towns. Beyond these were the fields of maize, squashes, and beans and always a creek or river for washing, drawing water, and fishing. On the edge of town lands were forests where deer and turkeys and, to a lesser extent, smaller mammals, bear, cougars, and bison were hunted and where nuts and medicinal plants were gathered.

Political groups in the Southeast varied from autonomous towns to sets of towns acknowledging by tribute and subordination the greater power of one in the set. It appears that rule of one town over others was generally achieved by the prowess of a chief who extended his domain by alliances and by threats backed by displays of force. For example, in 1607, the Jamestown colonists dealt with Wahunsenacawh, called Powhatan after his home town, who was chief of several Algonkian-speaking towns by hereditary right and who added dozens more by conquest until, it was claimed, over two hundred communities obeyed his commands. As was customary, Powhatan symbolized his paternal position in these towns by taking from most

of them a lady as wife, who lived in her own town and entertained her husband and his retinue (including other wives and concubines) when he visited. Another facet of the same custom led Powhatan to offer one of his daughters, called Pocahontas, to an Englishman at Jamestown in marriage, a sign of relationship between the settlements. (The young woman, Amonute, was of adventuresome spirit, which is what the pet name "Pocahontas" meant. She had been married briefly to one of Powhatan's captains when in 1613 she was captured and held for ransom by the Jamestown colonists. Attracted to John Rolfe, she was pleased at the opportunity to bind the two nations. After bearing her new husband a son, Thomas, she traveled to England, dressed in Elizabethan finery and was presented to Queen Anne as a princess. Unhappily, like most of the American Indians taken to visit European courts in the seventeenth century, "Pocahontas" soon fell ill and died, in 1617, as she, John, and little Thomas prepared to return home.)

Conquerers like Powhatan, with real power over their subjects, were the exception. More typical were chiefs who were selected from among the men of a traditional noble lineage by the town council, which was composed of all the respected older men. These chiefs, like modern constitutional monarchs, represented their polities, led ceremonies and the daily council meeting, and advised, but could not coerce, the citizens. An executive assistant to the chief managed much of the administration of the town and might speak for him. Warfare was led by other men—war chiefs—unless the chief was exceptional, like Powhatan. War chiefs might be members of the chiefly lineage, but in many instances they were simply effective leaders, particularly skilled in oratory as well as being known for their bravery and resoluteness. Along the Gulf, including the Natchez in the lower Mississippi Valley, social stratification distinguished nobility from commoners and attended the chiefs with so many badges of rank that they approached semidivine status: they were carried on litters, the paths before them were swept, fine mats or carved stools were used for their seat, fan- or

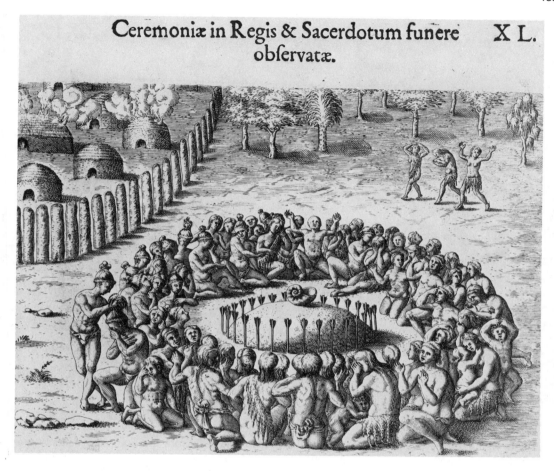

FIGURE 4.4 "Ceremonies at the Death of a Chief or of Priests," drawn at an Algonkian town on the coast of North Carolina. *(Smithsonian Institution National Anthropological Archives)*

parasol-bearers accompanied them, copper head-dresses and necklaces ornamented them, and spouses, servants, and townspeople were sacrificed at their funerals. Ladies of noble lineage did not work like commoner women, and one Florida lord threatened a mission with dire consequences if the convent school persisted in expecting his daughter to perform menial tasks alongside her classmates. Further north, such highly institutionalized stratification did not appear, and the respect shown to a chief was likely to have been earned by his wisdom and devotion to his town.

Most Southeastern peoples emphasized affiliation through the mother's family (matrilineality), and both Muskogeans and Cherokees recognized sets of persons related, or believed to be related in the distant past, through common female ancestors (conventionally, these sets are referred to as "clans"). Matrilineal affiliation meant, incidentally, that children of European fathers and Indian mothers were full members of their mothers' towns, entitled to the same rights and expectations as any other Indian. The Muskogeans and Cherokees shared also the concept of dividing offices

Qua ratione Floridenſes de ſeriis rebus deliberant.   XXIX

FIGURE 4.5 Timucua council, 1562 or 1564–65, presumably to discuss the European visitors (lower left). Women prepare the "black drink" tea served in conch shell cups to the councillors so that they may purify themselves. *(Smithsonian Institution National Anthropological Archives)*

within towns, and the towns of confederations, into White and Red, with White persons and towns to argue for peace, exercise self-restraint, and give sanctuary, and Red to be belligerent and lead wars. In actuality, White and Red were not always easily distinguished, but the concept was a valuable device of checks and balances.

The highlight of the year for most Southeasterners was the New Year celebration, held when the new crop of maize became ripe enough to eat. This Green Corn Ceremony, or Busk (from the Creek [Muskogee] *posketa,* "a fast"), occupied several days. Men thoroughly cleaned the public buildings and central square of the town, renewing the

mound (nowadays a low one) in the square that symbolizes the earth itself, and women cleaned the homes. The people fasted to let all the old year's food pass from them, and might more actively purge themselves with plant infusions. The men drank quantities of a tea high in caffeine, the "black drink" made from the dried and roasted leaves and twigs of a holly. This decoction was enjoyed on all formal occasions, but its stimulant effect caused it to be considered vital in rituals. All fire in the town was extinguished, and then the priest, assisted by younger men, kindled a new fire, the earthly manifestation of the power seen in the sun. Logs of seven species of tree fed the fire, bringing it into conjunction with these other forms of life on earth. Brands from the new fire relit the hearths in the homes. Sweet ears of new maize could now be roasted and enjoyed. The chief exhorted the people to be virtuous and prayed with the priests that they prosper. Dressed in their best, men and women performed dances expressing their joys at the harvest and their hopes for success in all endeavors in the new year. Feuds and grudges were officially forgotten forever, and those exiled because of crimes could rejoin the community. The Busk revitalized the community's sense of commitment, to each other, to their land and the living things upon it, and to the Master of Breath, as the Creeks termed the Almighty.

Games were important events in Southeastern Indian life. Every town had its chunkey yard and its ball-game field. Chunkey could be relatively staid: as the chunkey stone, a carefully shaped and smoothed disc, was rolled along a well-packed alley, players threw poles in its path, winning points when a pole and the chunkey stone came to rest together. Preventing one's opponent's pole from gaining a point figured in the game. Bets were placed on the outcome, which stimulated high excitement as the game progressed. Ball games were always wildly animated. Lacrosse is the modern version of the traditional Southeastern ball game, in which each player used a net-ended stick to whack a baseball-sized ball between a pair of goal posts, set as in football (or as much as a half-mile [nearly a kilometer] apart). Variations of the ball game include football, in which a larger ball was kicked; a game in which the ball was thrown with the hands; one in which the smaller ball was putted along the ground with sticks, a sort of field hockey; and a single-post game in which both sides, using lacrosse sticks or hands, strove to hit the ball above a mark, winning extra points if a player made the image fastened to the top of the pole. Teams had dozens of players, and injuries frequently resulted as sticks were brandished in the melees. Games were regularly held between towns, each team composed of the most athletic young men of the sponsoring town. There were heated preliminary arguments over whether men married into, rather than native to, a town should be allowed to play for that town—as in collegiate and Olympic sports today, the "amateur" status of some competitors was a bit of a fiction, and an athlete's choice of residence could be swayed by the rewards he might expect. Winning teams were entitled to wear special plumes; losing towns felt disgraced and thirsted for their opponents' blood in the following year's contest—intertown ball games were often referred to as "little wars." Less fierce games were played between sets of "clans" within a town, or between men and women, with the women allowed some advantage to offset the greater strength of the other side. Straight gambling games, using marked fruit pits, grains, or cane sections as dice or requiring players to guess where a marked object was hidden (for example, in which of several moccasins), were popular. Powhatan's people frequently played a mentally exacting game in which a set of fifty-one small split reed sections were held by a player, who threw some of the reeds in front of his opponent. The object was to instantly estimate the number of pieces thrown before one, and the Jamestown colonists were amazed at how accurately a player could call out the number even as the reeds were thrown.

A CHEROKEE INCANTATION FOR WINNING THE BALL GAME

Listen! Ha! Now where the white thread has been let down, quickly we are about to examine into (the fate of) the admirers of the ball play.

They [our opponents] are of—such-and-such descent. They are called—so and so. They are shaking the road which shall never be joyful. The miserable Terrapin has come and fastened himself upon them as they go about. They have lost all strength. They have become entirely blue.

But now my admirers of the ball play have their roads lying along in this direction. The Red [color of life] Bat has come and made himself one of them. There in the first heaven are the pleasing stakes. There in the second heaven are the pleasing stakes. The Pewee has come and joined them. The immortal ball stick shall place itself upon the whoop, never to be defeated.

As for the lovers of the ball play on the other side, the common Turtle has come and fastened himself upon them as they go about. Under the earth they have lost all strength.

The pleasing stakes are in the third heaven. The Red Tlaniwa Hawk has come. The pleasing stakes are in the third heaven. The Red Tlaniwa Hawk has come and made himself one of them, that they may never be defeated. The pleasing stakes are in the fourth heaven. The Blue [probably the recorder's error; it should be Red] Fly-catcher has made himself one of them, that they may never be defeated. The pleasing stakes are in the fifth heaven. The Blue [Red] Martin has made himself one of them, that they may never be defeated.

The other lovers of the ball play, the Blue Mole has come and fastened upon them, that they may never be joyous. They have lost all strength.

The pleasing stakes are there in the sixth heaven. The Chimney Swift has made himself one of them, that they may never be defeated. The pleasing stakes are in the seventh heaven. The Blue [Red] Dragon-fly has made himself one of them, that they may never be defeated.

As for the other admirers of the ball play, the Bear has just come and fastened him upon them, that they may never be happy. They have lost all strength. He has let the stakes slip from his grasp and there shall be nothing left for their share.

The examination is ended.

Listen! Now let me know that the twelve [innings] are mine, O White Dragon-fly. Tell me that the share is to be mine—that the stakes are mine. As for the player there on the other side, he has been forced to let go his hold upon the stakes.

Now they are become exultant and happy. Yu!

(Mooney 1891:396)

This incantation was recorded in Cherokee syllabary by A'yu^{n}ini ("Swimmer"), an Eastern Cherokee doctor-conjurer, in his private manuscript book. He sold a copy of the book in 1887 to James Mooney for deposit and preservation in the Bureau of American Ethnology. The incantation is recited by the conjurer as his town's team stands in the river, partaking of its life and power. A red bead is held in the conjurer's right hand and represents his team; a black bead in his left hand represents their opponents. As he chants, the conjurer watches the beads, which begin to move in his hands, the red bead faster, predicting success, the black bead slowly, auguring ill for the opponents. (Should the opposite occur, the conjurer knows formulas to negate the beads' prediction.) The incantation refers to the mythical ball game between the flying creatures and the earthbound ones, which, of course, the flyers won. One by one, the champions of the mythic game join our team; one by one, mythic losers drag down our opponents, and the gambled stakes are ours!

FIGURE 4.6 Cherokee annual ball game (lacrosse), Qualla Reservation, North Carolina, 1900. *(Smithsonian Institution National Anthropological Archives)*

Two impressions stand out as we survey the Southeast at the beginning of the historic period. First, in contrast with the American Southwest, there are no strong differences between groups of Southeasterners. As the topography and climate gradually change from the Gulf Coast-lower Mississippi region northward through the upland plateau to the southern Appalachians, so the degree of social stratification gradually diminishes, but the basic cultural patterns of towns—allied or warring, farming the alluvial flood plains, fishing and hunting, playing chunkey and lacrosse, their deceased chiefs honored in ossuary temples—this pattern holds throughout the Southeast. The diversity of languages suggests great antiquity for the delicate balance of autonomous communities similarly exploiting the environment and constantly in contact, though often in contact through war.

Second, the resemblances between the Southeast and Mexico are tantalizing. The layout of towns, the presence of both platform and conical mounds and central plazas, the frequency of square houses and the tendency toward rectangular household compounds around courtyards, the importance of ball games, feather mantles, the symbols of rank, the New Year ritual with its rekindling of fire and incorporation of direction cosmology, human sacrifice, and, of course, maize, beans, and squashes—all seem generalized Mesoamerican patterns, yet none are identical in detail to any Mexican culture. The relationships across the Gulf of Mexico may never be unraveled.

SECTION 5: EUROPEAN COLONIZATION, 1584–1856

The date 1584 marks the establishment of permanent European settlements in the American Southeast: Spanish soldiers attached to Franciscan missions from St. Augustine in Florida running northeastward through Timucua territory and up the Atlantic coast into Georgia and South Carolina. By 1633, missions were strung along the road westward through Florida into Apalachee country at the western base of the peninsula. These Spanish enterprises were designed to secure the country for the empire and Christianize the Indians. Leaving native governments intact so far as they did not obstruct the Spanish purpose, the Spaniards in Florida, as in Mexico, did not encourage immigration of Spanish farming families. Instead, the Crown preferred entrepreneurs who could exploit the country, for material gain or for converts, with a minimum of Spanish personnel and support. Spanish colonization was moderately successful, by its goals, for more than a century until an expedition of English and Indian soldiers in 1704, operating under the counterclaims of the (European) War of the Spanish Succession, ravaged the Timucua and Apalachee mission settlements. St. Augustine hung on, incorporating Indian refugees into its mestizo population, although the Spanish officially abandoned Florida in 1763 at the conclusion of the (European) Seven Years' War.

Spanish thrusts northward reached Chesapeake Bay, where in 1571, Jesuits attempted a mission but were killed by Indians led by a chief, "Don Luis," abducted ten years earlier by a Spanish exploring expedition. French Huguenots had tried a colony on the coast of South Carolina, a venture to which English assistance was considered in 1563. In 1585, a privately financed but court-approved English colonization effort set a party on Roanoke Island off what is now southernmost Virginia. Two years later, a carefully prepared colony included married couples with children, a few unmarried Englishwomen as well as Englishmen, and two Croatan Indians from the Cape Hatteras area south of Roanoke. The Croatans included Manteo, who had been picked up in a 1584 exploratory voyage and (apparently willingly) brought to England where he had learned the language and familiarity with English customs. Manteo, of the

noble class among the Croatans, was to rule the Roanoke territory as Queen Elizabeth's vassal, protecting the English colonists. He seems to have done so, but the colony struggled rather than thrived, leaving Roanoke Island for a better setting near, or among, Indian towns on the Chesapeake. English sponsors' failure to send reinforcements and new supplies as promised must have heightened the colonists' appreciation of Indian hospitality. Unhappily, the colonists who survived to 1607 apparently were executed by Powhatan just prior to the Jamestown settlement. Whether Powhatan intended to frighten off invaders, or had some other provocation, is not known. One fact must be emphasized here: from the very beginning of English colonization in 1585, Englishmen disappeared into the native Indian communities. In many instances, the Englishman chose the freer life of a man married into an Indian town (where matrilineal affiliation would guarantee his children family status in the town) over obedience to the authoritarian discipline of the colonies; sometimes, Englishmen were captured to be slaves by Indians. The same openness to recruits into the society that allowed Indian refugees to merge with other towns, allowed Europeans to join. Later, this openness allowed colonial traders to establish homes with women of the towns they worked with, and produced a class of Indians whose British fathers had given them enough knowledge of colonists' ways to enable the sons and daughters to serve as interpreters and agents.

Roanoke Colony was a new venture in southern American colonizing. It was to create land for landless English families, and develop the cultivation of subtropical crops such as olives, wine grapes, sugar, and fruits that Britain otherwise had to purchase from Mediterranean nations, chiefly her rival, Spain. Coasting along Chesapeake Bay had shown the English explorers that much of the land there appeared fertile but uncultivated (because the English didn't realize that Indian agriculture used long-fallowing, letting the land rest for years, to restore nutrients to the soil; some land may have been abandoned due to recent hostilities between Algonkian nations along the coast). In 1607, a second colonizing enterprise settled Jamestown on the James River. More military in character than the Roanoke colony, the Jamestown group wanted to trade for corn with the local Indians. Offering copper, prized like gold by the Southeastern peoples, the English were received by Powhatan and granted the food supplies they needed. Later, the British would disparage Indian habits of work and economy, forgetting that Powhatan's Pamunkeys had cultivated, stored up, and could easily spare enough corn to maintain a whole unexpected settlement of strangers.

Uninvited houseguests soon tax the patience of their hosts, and the Jamestown colonists were no exception. If Powhatan was no longer inclined to jeopardize his people's long-term food stocks by continuing sales to the Englishmen, the Englishmen took weapons in hand and forced villages or individual families to part with their supplies. During the winter of 1609–10, Powhatan's soldiers besieged the Jamestown fort, but gave up without overcoming it. Hundreds of new colonists, again mostly armed men, were landed on the James come spring of 1610. Sporadic battles continued until the truce of 1614 cemented with Rolfe's marriage to Pocahontas. Her father died the year after she, and the Pamunkey chief Opechancanough became leader of the Powhatan nation. Carefully dissembling his intentions when confronted by the English invaders, Opechancanough organized his own and neighboring nations' forces and in March of 1622—after colonists murdered a respected Pamunkey priest—launched a broad attack on the colony settlements, killing a quarter of the English. Ten years the war continued, the English following a policy of regularly raiding Indian farms and newly harvested crops, providing themselves with free food and causing great hardship among the Indians. In a 1624 battle, for example, English muskets drove the Pamunkeys away from fields ripe with maize sufficient to feed four thousand people for an entire year. The Anglo-Powhatan War became a war of attrition, supported by the musketeers whose guns kept Indian bowmen out of range of the colonist settlements. Finally, in 1646 Opechancanough was killed in a battle and a peace treaty signed with his successor who agreed to pay annual tribute to the King of England and vacate the lands demanded by the King's colonists.

The English settlement, in 1670 at Charlestown on the coast of South Carolina, began an era in which the Southeast ceased to be seen by Europeans as the remote fringe of their battlegrounds and became a land desirable in itself. The Englishmen were out to earn profit. A century and a half had taught Europeans that the Southeast held no precious minerals, nor any native empires ready-organized for feudal exploitation. Entrepreneurs in the Southeast had to set their sights lower. They gauged the Indian towns could supply two products commanding a good return in Europe's markets: deer hides and human slaves.

Beautifully tanned deer hides had always been valuable exchanged as gifts, fines (five hundred finished skins compensated the family of a murder victim, two pounds' weight compensated a dog's owner for its death), or in trade between Indians. Piles of hides were accumulated in town storehouses, to be used as needed. Plugging into this native exchange was easy, although the enormously increased market eventually affected the Indian economies by pressuring Indian women to spend much more time tanning (and taking less pride in the quality of their craft), and also stimulating a demand for packhorses to carry the hides to market. Twenty years after its founding, Charlestown alone was exporting 54,000 deer hides annually, climaxing at 121,355 hides in 1707. The trade continued to be profitable until about the time of the American Revolution. There was danger of overhunting in many areas, but most of the Southeast is ideal deer habitat, particularly under Indian settlement, when cleared fields were interspersed with forest, creating extensive edge areas. With good meat an inevitable by-product of deer slaughtered for the hide trade, the trade was not inherently disruptive to Southeastern Indian societies, where hunting was the normal and proper occupation for most men.

The slave trade also built upon pre-European practices, but exacerbated these nefarious tendencies to a genocidal degree. De Soto had observed that captives taken in attacks upon enemies were often kept, the children adopted, the women becoming concubines, and the men crippled sufficiently to prevent escape and used as laborers. The English let it become known that they would trade knives, axes, clothing, ornaments, guns and ammunition, and liquor for captives. War could now be profitable. Where formerly the goal was to kill an enemy, supposedly in revenge for enemy killing of a member of one's own group, the goal now should be taking captives as well as satisfying vengeance. Indian slaves were worth only half as much as blacks, because blacks seemed to survive better laboring on plantations, but the ready availability of Indians in contrast with the cost of transporting blacks from Africa kept the demand for Indians constant. Some captive Indians were used in the South, but most were sold into the West Indies, where the late seventeenth-century plantations were more developed than in the South, or into New England where local Indian communities were far decimated. English traders not only bought Indian captives and urged warfare to gain captives, but sometimes personally led parties of warriors against their enemy towns in order to raid for slaves. Year after year, thousands of Indians were thus torn from their homes amid slaughter and destruction.

While the English colonists on the Atlantic seaboard pursued—often all too literally—Indian slaves and deer hides, the Spanish in Florida warily watched the attrition of her claim to America north of Mexico, and the French moving down the Mississippi projected the establishment of their own colonies throughout America. Maneuvering through alliances with the Indian groups, the representatives of England, Spain, and France sought both to augment their mother countries' and their

own wealth and to gain advantages and control that ultimately would benefit their nation in the long-standing rivalry in Europe that was contested between 1701 and 1714 as the War of the Spanish Succession (Queen Anne's War in America). In the Southeast, Creeks decimated the Apalachees around Spanish missions in the Tallahassee region, ostensibly because the Apalachees were demanding too high a price for the horses they customarily sold to the Creeks (Muskogee), who in turn supplied the Carolina English traders with these horses in exchange for guns, clothing, and other goods. Burning the Apalachee mission towns and selling several thousand of the people into slavery, the Creeks abetted the English moves against the waning power of Spain. Skirmishes with the Choctaws and Chickasaws, who were supplied with guns by the French in southern Alabama and Mississippi, made the Creeks instruments for testing French strength in southern America. The only final outcomes of these harassments were the dispersals of Indian peoples from their native, or from refugee, lands.

Canny as the European commanders might be, the Indians were no fools. After a decade of instigations by the rival Europeans, the Creeks, in particular, who occupied the fertile center of the Southeast, began to realize they were often seen as pawns. Ignorant of the niceties of the power struggle triggered by the death of the Hapsburg emperor of Spain, the Creeks came to realize that England, France, and Spain were equally vulnerable and could be played against each other to the benefit of Creek pockets. Between 1712 and 1717, Creek leaders worked out an opportunistic policy of neutrality toward the three European nations ensconced in southeastern America. They first agreed to peace with the French governor, then swore allegiance to Spain, sending several Creeks to Mexico City as sureties of good faith, and finally sealed their relationship with the English by marrying a lady of the chiefly lineage of Coweta, a leading town, to an English colonel's son. (That the groom's mother was Indian and the bride rumored to have an English father did not lessen the symbolic and practical value of the match.)

Meanwhile, other Indian peoples resisted encroachment and exploitation by Europeans by direct challenges. The Yamasee had moved from northern Florida into Carolina, attracted by the English trade. They were aware of the rivalries between the three European colonizing nations, and very much aware of rivalries between the several English colonies of Virginia, North Carolina, and South Carolina, rivalries played out by traders scorning the capacities of any colonies other than their own. By 1715, English creditors of Yamasee were seizing their debtors' wives and children to sell as slaves for payment of the Indians' accounts. The Yamasee rose against the traders and recruited Creeks and Apalachee refugees to join in raids. Creeks invited Cherokees to come in. Knowing the hardscrabble pioneer farms and the poorly supplied Carolina colony towns, the Indians along this frontier had good reason to believe their united effort could drive the invaders out forever. Unity between the formerly warring Indian nations was not easy to achieve. The English persuaded the Cherokee to murder the Creek envoys. Indians discovered that whatever traders had said about each other, with war declared, the governors of the colonies could embargo Indian trade and thus deprive Indians of ammunition, a necessity since firearms' greater range made traditional native weapons ineffective. Within a year, the Yamasee War was over with the English position enhanced.

In the western Southeast, the Natchez attempted repeatedly to rout the French, in 1716, 1722, and 1729–31. Indian neighbors of the Natchez gave refuge to their families uprooted by the battles, but reneged on joining in full-scale war. The Choctaw fought with the French against the Natchez. At the beginning of the eighteenth century, the Natchez numbered about four thousand; within a generation, the tribe was reduced to about three hundred in 1731, as hundreds were killed, hundreds were sent away as slaves, and a few

hundred were scattered among the Chickasaws, the Creeks, and later the Cherokees.

The eighteenth century was a century of guns, promises, and battles fought by Indians on their homelands against armies supplied by European empires. Should the colonists and Indians tire, European conflagrations—the War of the Austrian Succession (1740–48) and the Seven Years' War (1756–63) —renewed enmities. Within Britain, England's campaign to conquer Scotland, culminating in Scotland's final defeat in 1745, pressured thousands of Scottish families to flee to the American colonies, while young English men and women were encouraged to seek their fortunes in America, relieving Britain's employment problems. The century between 1690 and 1790 saw the European population of the Southeast increase from about fifty thousand (mostly on the coast) to one million; and on top of that, black slaves held by the colonists increased from about three thousand to one-half million. As the Europeans flooded in, importing ever-increasing numbers of Africans as slaves, the Indian populations were hit again and again by smallpox and other epidemics.

As the eighteenth century progressed, the expansion of European settlement more than matched slave raids in danger to the Southeastern Indians. Georgia colony was founded, complicating Indian relationships with Carolina English. Tobacco became a profitable export crop in Virginia, after zealous promotion abroad by the investors in the Jamestown colony. Cotton promised to be a second valuable export. Both crops required much hand labor, which encouraged slavery and its reciprocal, a class of gentry on large estates, into which their capital was invested. One effect of the rise of plantations in the eighteenth-century South was the driving of families without capital to the lands at a distance from the seaports, there to compete for river valley farmland with the Indians who had always preferred the forest-rimmed flood plains inland to the swampy coastal plain. This incursion of European families into the interior was the most serious long-term threat, but of more immediate effect was the roving about of unscrupulous traders, amoral adventurers, and other black sheep unwilling to conform to the laws in the colony towns. Many of these men claimed to intend to settle as farmers. But their intemperate language and its escalation to actual theft, rape, and murder was echoed by younger Indian men ambitious to achieve reputations as warriors, consistently undermining the laudable negotiations of colony governors and mature Indian leaders. Demon rum, freely circulating in the frontier taverns and hotly demanded by Indian men from the traders, goaded many an encounter into a fight entailing repercussions among kin and friends on both sides.

 Intrusion of European settlement into prime Indian land, coupled with Indian expectation of European weapons, tools, and clothing obtained in trade for deer hides and slaves, shifted Indian polities from autonomous towns to confederacies attempting to match the colonies in manpower and effective organization. Such a market orientation of the political economy was foreshadowed by the importance of trade, and of its regulation, in the prehistoric Mississippian nations and their predecessors; but in the historic era, the critical advantage of firearms made the arms trade essential as no earlier trade had been. The political underpinning of the armament race was abetted by Europeans, some (particularly Scots who hated the English) allying with the Indians against the English colonists, others unconsciously promoting Indian unity by projecting upon the natives European concepts of nationhood. Thus, in 1730, Sir Alexander Cuming, a Scot loyal to Britain, took it upon himself to seal the Cherokees to English friendship by traveling through the Cherokee country collecting town leaders who would discuss a treaty, conveying seven of these Cherokee to London to ceremoniously make a pact with King George in person, and pushing one leader, Moytoy (a priests' title) of the town of Tellico, to represent all his countrymen as "Emperor of the Cherokees."

Ultimately far more important than Moytoy was Attakullaculla (Leaning Wood), a young Cherokee

in the delegation to England. Attakullaculla was a slightly built man who impressed people with the intelligence animating his face. In addition to his experience in England, he had been a prisoner of the Ottawas in French Canada, where he had come before the governor in Quebec. When his cousin Connecorte became First Man of Chota, one of the mother towns of the Cherokee, Attakullaculla was named his assistant, the second most-respected office in the entire Cherokee hierarchy. During the 1750s, the wisdom and diplomatic skill of Connecorte, called "Old Hop" by the English because he was lame, and Attakullaculla, called the "Little Carpenter" for his mastery of the craft of putting together treaties, brought the Cherokee towns closer to the appearance of a unified state than the towns had ever been. Nevertheless, it was barely a veneer of unification, carpentered by the sagacity of the two men trained in religion. When Connecorte succumbed to old age at the end of the decade, his successor in office failed to exert similar influence. By 1768, the gravity of the constant border skirmishes with English intruders led the Cherokees to recognize Oconastota, Great Warrior (war general) of the confederated Cherokee, as leader above even the First Man. Warriors, traditionally excluded as such from the highest councils, now sat as a body beside the Beloved Men, signifying that the Red Path had to be weighed equally with the White Path of peace. In both structure and overt values, the Cherokees were modifying their ancient system to better meet the overwhelming threat of English invasion.

One incidental consequence was the erosion of the power of the Cherokee women, who had always sat in the councils, observing although not actively participating. Attakullaculla remarked to the English governor in Charleston that it was strange no English women were to be seen in the colony's council chamber. Europeans were on the whole oblivious to the presence of Indian women at official conferences and tended to assume that the roles of the Beloved Women in town rituals and the occasional female town chiefs, not infrequently encountered in the early historic period, were auxiliary or temporary. Women of influence such as Mary Musgrove Bosomworth (Coosaponakeesa) of the chiefly clan of the Creeks of Coweta, a mother town of that people, were uneasily treated as appendages of their husbands by the English: when she was given in marriage to Colonel Musgrove's son (by an Indian mother), she was seen as a token of the alliance of Coweta and Carolina, and when she subsequently became a major landowner, trader, and negotiator on the Creek-Carolina border, she was assumed to be an agent of others rather than legitimately a personage in her own right by birth and experience. In 1749, she asserted herself to be "queen" of the Lower Creeks, probably meaning that she had by then become matriarch of the chiefly lineage of Coweta. But instead of recognizing this office, the Georgia Board council first tried to discredit her by claiming she was a half-breed of poor parentage, then briefly jailed her, and finally tried to ignore her by dealing directly with male headmen. Coosaponakeesa was beyond the comprehension of the English officials (though her English last husband seemed to have no difficulty understanding her status and rights). To the English in the Carolina and Georgia governments, she could not be a leader because she was a woman, could not be a legitimate Indian because her father was said to be European, could not be a merchant and landowner acting independently in business because she was married. That she grew up as a Creek and that in Creek society she was entitled to all the status and powers she exercised could not sway the Englishmen, whose education had taught them that theirs was the only conceivable proper order.

The American Revolution toppled the major Indian peoples in the East. France had been removed from the Southeast a decade earlier, at the conclusion of the Seven Years' War in 1763. At that time, France had ceded southern Alabama to England and Louisiana to Spain, which kept a few missions in the territory until 1773. English colonists interpreted the defeat of France as opening up the West to the Americans. By 1769, the Shawnee in the upper Ohio Valley clearly realized the threat and tried to excite the Cherokees and Creeks to ally with them in a united Indian expulsion of the Europeans. Such an effort had been proposed in 1757 by Yahatastanage, The Mortar, headman of the Creek town of Okchai, who had invited Chickasaws and Catawbas as well as Shawnees and Cherokees to join a campaign against the English. The French and their friends the Choctaws were to support the more eastern Indians. The Mortar's plans disintegrated, in large part because the French were unequal to the task of supplying the guns, ammunition, and household necessities that the Indians would require from them if the English trade were ended. When the Shawnee, inflamed by Iroquois relinquishment to the English of lands that the Shawnee hunted, revived the idea of all-out unified Indian attack, The Mortar set out anew to bring it about. A continuing war with the Choctaws diverted Creeks, however, and English agents persuaded a number of Creek and Cherokee towns to withhold commitment. Indian hesitation played into the intrigues of the colonists: in 1773, over 2 million acres (850,000 hectares) of Creek land was ceded to Georgia to satisfy English traders' demands for payment of Creek debts.

Cherokees had been embroiled in war with England since 1759. Their lands were so devastated by the English army's scorched-earth policy that by 1762 they had to accept further English settlement. When in 1775 the American rebels informed the Indians that a new nation was being forged, most of the Indian nations associated the Americans with the more lawless of the colonists, and refused to fight with the rebels. The Indians were not fond of the British Crown, but the loyalist side seemed most likely to continue supplying the necessities (particularly including ammunition) that Indians had been relying upon for nearly a century. The Revolutionary War battles in which Indians participated were a continuation of the long series of actions by the Southeastern nations in defense of their lands. Within each nation, however, were some who, through hatred of the British or friendship for an American, wished to aid the rebels, or at least hinder the British. These minority factions caused bitter dissension within the Indian nations. In 1779, a Huron Indian from the north, Kessinqua, came through the Southeast urging implementation of the old plans to mount a unified Indian attack on the entire frontier. The wartime cessation of trade proved instrumental in reducing Indian resistance, though not in mollifying the sentiments of the opposing factions, neutralist, pro-British, and, smallest of all, pro-American. The Creeks made a treaty of peace with the Americans in 1783, ceding 800 square miles (20,000 square kilometers). The Cherokees would not accept a treaty until 1794, although a few of the towns had given in to the Americans as early as 1777. Once, Attakulla-culla had worked tirelessly to maintain the fragile restraints he hoped would enable his people to survive, but during the 1780s, Tsiyugunsini (Otter Lifts It, or Dragging Canoe), said to be his son, led implacable warriors who scorned the old Beloved Men pleading for the White Path. The Cherokee war, nearly a generation long, severely impoverished the people materially and also spiritually, for the leadership of the priests—men such as Conne-corte and Attakullaculla—had been displaced, the striving for harmony symbolized by the White Path and created by the counsels of the Beloved Men had been neglected, and eventually even the annual series of celebrations of Cherokee love of the Almighty had been telescoped to the single Green Corn Festival. The Southeastern Indian nations ended the eighteenth century abandoned by the British, treated as defeated enemies by the United States, their leaders debilitated, forlorn in the face of rapidly enlarging incursions into their heartlands.

The year 1794 also marked the first removal of Southeastern Indians west across the Mississippi in order to preserve there an autonomous community free from European intervention. The Bowl, a Cherokee headman, and his men had killed several European colonists traveling down the Tennessee River. Rather than face disciplinary action from the Cherokee leaders negotiating the peace treaty, and unhappy with the prospects for the Cherokee in their homeland, The Bowl and his people first went directly west across the Mississippi, then southwestward in two moves, to the Arkansas River and then to Texas, establishing, in effect, a colony of Cherokee. The action of The Bowl's group coincided with the beginning of sentiment among many of the most liberal and humane Americans that it would be in the best interests of the Indians to consolidate them in a territory far beyond the existing frontier. States' rights, vociferously chanted by the southern border citizens who had the most to gain by ignoring federal policies protecting fertile Indian lands, could become a license for depredation. The numbers of lawless men roaming the frontier threatened the safety of Indian families and might debauch their youth. Legalistic minds were convinced that Indians could not, under the United States Constitution, continue as enclave nations within the United States: if their members did not wish to live simply as citizens of the United States, but would adhere to their native forms of government, they must remove outside of the Union. To the Euro-Americans, all of whom were immigrants or immediate descendants of immigrants, emigration to a new land to preserve liberty and improve family circumstances was an obvious resolution of a difficult situation.

Southeastern Indians had legends of migrations from the west or the north, and during the early historic period there are many records of families, factions, or even towns emigrating to new territory. But in the legends the nations were seeking ideal homelands, and in the historic instances only sections of groups moved, usually relatively short distances. Few Indians at the close of the eighteenth century had any inclination to abandon the lands of their forebears, certainly not for the poorer soils and more extreme climate of the trans-Mississippi West. Most Southeastern Indians wished to incorporate the pleasanter aspects of European colonial culture into their persisting native societies. Livestock, cotton, wheat, fruit orchards, year-round cabins more comfortable in winter, metal tools and kettles became common around Indian households. The adoption of European clothing lent Indians the appearance of respectability rather than savagery before colonists, although the scanty coverings traditional to southern Indians were better suited to the warmer months. The more ambitious Indian farmers purchased black slaves. The value of literacy in English and familiarity with legal and business practices in the states led families to send one or more sons to school, some as far away as missionary colleges in New England. John Ridge, son of the well-to-do Cherokee Kahnungdaclageh (Walks on the Mountaintops), called Major Ridge, and his cousin Gallegina (Buck Watie), known as Elias Boudinot, both married missionaries' daughters they had met while finishing their education in Connecticut. Intensification of missionary efforts, especially by Protestants, persuaded many Indians to profess Christianity during the first decades of the nineteenth century. By the end of the generation following the close of the Revolutionary War, there was every indication that Southeastern Indians were adapting their cultural patterns to fit into a United States of settled farmers and craftsmen: Indians were learning European techniques of spinning, weaving, sewing, blacksmithing, and other trades and reducing their dependence upon hunting and exchanging skins for European manufactures.

Adoption of the appurtenances of Euro-American life was not, however, the solution to the pressures upon the Southeastern Indians. The invention of the cotton gin in 1793 made cotton plantations a profitable investment for persons with capital enough to buy large tracts of land and numbers of slaves. Because cotton rapidly depleted the soil, planters either bought up as much prime land as possible or moved plantations to new land. Both strategies dispossessed less affluent Euro-Americans as well as Indians. The rich de-

manded what was left of the best Indian bottom lands, and the poorer Euro-Americans wanted the smaller acreages that would support family farms, if not plantations. The more Indians shifted to the Euro-American economy, the more they were hated as competitors who denied Euro-Americans the opportunities for which they, or their parents, had emigrated. This competition influenced federal officials to favor removing Indians from the Southeast to open the lands to Euro-American settlement, as did a second factor: the Indians could not be trusted to protect the United States borders. Throughout the eighteenth century, they had played one European power against another, and during the Revolution, the majority had refused to fight with the rebels. If the Indians could be removed beyond the Mississippi, the United States would have a solid bloc of her own citizens massed against the Spanish frontier to the south. Within that block, no dissatisfied Indians would roam, threatening families on their homesteads and peddlers on the roads. Removal of the Indians thus became a strategy of the Secretary of War, pursued openly and also surreptitiously by such means as government "factories," government trading posts where Indians were encouraged to go into debt, eventually to repay by ceding land.

The first three decades of the nineteenth century laid the foundation for the pattern that was to persist throughout the century. The federal government considered itself a government of the Euro-Americans, whose desire to live in security upon their own homesteads must be the ultimate basis of all policies. Philosopher-statesmen such as Thomas Jefferson believed it was the natural inclination and inherent right of all men to own by freehold the means of their family's subsistence; any government that obstructed this basic urge of men was wicked and sooner or later doomed. The catch in the generous respect held by Jefferson and his colleagues toward the common man was, of course, their definition of "man": no women, blacks, Asians, or American Indians need apply, and males from Ireland, Scotland, Germany, and the Latin countries were accepted with reservation. Jefferson said that Indians should be taught the "arts of civilization" (that is, Euro-American culture) and protected from colonists' onslaughts while they were learning, a period that he assumed would be at least a full generation. Jefferson believed, however, that full-blood Indians were probably incapable of fully participating in Euro-American society. His expectation was that children of Indian-European marriages would, with help, overcome the hindrance of a less-than-full share of European "blood" and become assimilated into the United States, while full-blooded Indians would move westward territory by territory before advancing Euro-American settlement and eventually be forced over the Rockies into Spanish California. American policy should therefore be to alleviate humanely the darkness of the heathen as long as his land was not demanded by the increase in Euro-American population, but to inexorably remove all Indians beyond the frontier whenever homesteading land became scarce. The implementation of this policy appeared hypocriti-cal, seeming to encourage Indians in the hope that if they lived like Euro-Americans they would be able to enjoy the security of American citizens, yet over and over again seizing even the handsome brick mansions of wealthy, educated Indian plantation gentry. The key to the policy was the tortured reasoning of Chief Justice John Marshall, who ruled in 1831 (following an 1823 decision holding that the British "discoverers'" title to American lands was superior to that of native Indians) that Indians did not constitute nations able to treat with the United States as powers with natural rights to their lands and people; instead, they were "dependent nations" living in sufferance within the claims of the United States. Indians had no inherent rights. Marshall thus created a strange class of creatures, outside the guardianship of the United States Constitution but not possessing any comparable polity of their own. The bitter irony of the ruling is that it was given in a case brought by the Cherokee nation against the state of Georgia's intrusions upon Cherokee sovereignty defined in the constitution written and ratified by the Cherokee Nation in 1827.

SEQUOYAH

The Cherokee are justifiably proud of their people's literacy in their own language, written in a syllabary of eighty-six letters plus six symbols indicating which Cherokee dialect was intended. (Most letters stand for a consonant-vowel combination, similar to shorthand symbols.) When the Cherokee nation was formally established in 1827 with its constitution and laws, it set up a printing press to publish documents, books, and a newspaper in the Cherokee syllabary, which nearly all adults and older children could read and write with ease. The Cherokee were probably the most fully literate of all nations in 1827.

Cherokee literacy was achieved through the teachings of Sikwayi, or Sogwili (Horse), whose name is usually spelled Sequoyah in English. According to James Mooney, an ethnographer with the Bureau of American Ethnology who obtained information from Sequoyah's second cousin, Sequoyah was born about 1760 and brought up in Tuskegee town, in what is now Tennessee. Sequoyah's mother was a sister of the chief in Echota town, and his father was said to be a Euro-American trader or possibly soldier, whose surname is given as Gist, Guest, or Guess. The father did not remain long with his Cherokee wife, and Sequoyah grew up speaking only Cherokee, among conservative families. In 1809, during a conversation, he was struck with the thought that literacy in their own language would give the Cherokee advantages similar to those enjoyed by the English. By 1821, copying the shapes of some letters from an English speller and inventing other letters, Sequoyah had constructed a complete and efficient writing system for his people. The magnitude of the feat is better grasped when it is realized he had to analyze a complex, inflected language with six dialects and discover its basic phonemic structure a century before scholarly linguists developed the concept of the phoneme. Presenting his perfected syllabary to the leaders of his nation in 1821, he won their approval and immediately began an each-one-teach-one literacy campaign, traveling in 1822 to Arkansas Territory to bring literacy to the Cherokees who had already emigrated west. The next year, he settled among the western emigrants. Although crippled from a hunting accident, he determined in his later years to work with the languages of other Indian peoples and, as he traveled, to seek information on a band of Cherokee believed to have moved beyond United States territory, losing contact with the Nation. Sequoyah's first two journeys, in 1841 and 1842, by oxcart to peoples beyond the frontier, were successful in that his small party of Cherokee were welcomed everywhere, but whether he felt he had progressed toward a grander project, perhaps literacy for all Indians, is not known. The next year, 1843, Sequoyah went into northern Mexico, primarily in search of the "lost" Cherokee. In August he became ill there and died before friends alerted to his condition were able to reach him.

A somewhat different biography is told by one of Sequoyah's descendants, writing under the name of Traveller Bird. This story, passed on from Sequoyah's daughter Gedi, places Sequoyah's birth about 1766. He was the son of Sogwiligigagei (Red Horse), a member of the Anisahoni clan, and grew up, called by the same name as his father, in a Cherokee town on the Sumac River in North Carolina. Thus, according to this modern Cherokee biography, Sequoyah was a full-blooded Cherokee. His father was conservative, a follower of the belligerent Tsiyugunsini (Dragging Canoe). Father and son fought in defense of their homeland and bitterly hated Attakullaculla, whose career of compromises they considered betrayal. Sequoyah's family tradition claims that the Cherokee had a syllabary, called *Gohwelodi* (One Writes), from time immemorial, that Sequoyah's father was a scribe for his town, and that in 1795 the conservative faction decided to make the whole Cherokee Nation literate in *Gohwelodi*, which until then had been the secret knowledge of priestly scribes. The decision was stimulated in part by the fact that so many scribes had been recently killed in battle that Sequoyah was perhaps the last, and in part by the proposal to bring Moravian missionaries to the Cherokee (Mooney gives the date of the Cherokee council meeting with Reverend Steiner as 1800). Disseminating the *Gohwelodi* would ensure its survival, and literacy in their own language would strengthen the Cherokee to resist missionary influence. Two years later, while Sequoyah was engaged in teaching the syllabary, he had a dream whose interpretation by the priest-diviner of his town resulted in his emigration west. By 1799, Sequoyah and several other Cherokee families had settled in Comanche country in east Texas, near the colony led by the Cherokee chief Dustu (Spring Frog). In 1816, Sequoyah and his wife, who were aiding Cherokees in the homeland to emigrate, were captured by the "progressive" followers of Major Ridge. Since only trusted conservative Cherokee had been taught the *Gohwelodi*, the "progressive" faction being considered traitors, The Ridge did not know the syllabary. He and his followers accused Sequoyah and his wife of witchcraft practiced by means of the secret symbols, branded the couple, and cut off Sequoyah's fingers and ears to punish him and mark him a sorcerer. Sequoyah and his wife returned to their Texas settlement. Texas independence forced them and other Cherokee to move into Mexico in 1836. Three years later, Sequoyah and his sons returned to Texas to fight with Cherokee of

The Bowl's colony against Euro-Americans attempting to take over the land. Sequoyah was fatally shot by soldiers in the ensuing battle on the Brazos River in June 1839.

Which biography is more accurate? Mooney was an experienced and gifted ethnographer, deeply sympathetic to Indians, writing less than a half-century after Sequoyah's death. His biography drew on many contemporary papers and the memories of a number of Cherokee, particularly Eastern Cherokee at Qualla. Traveller Bird writes a century later, claiming to draw upon family tradition. A proud Cherokee, still harboring resentment over the faithless and cruel treatment the Cherokees suffered from the United States, Traveller Bird repudiates the supposed Euro-American father of Sequoyah, emphasizes persecution of the conservatives by those who, from the conservative viewpoint, were traitors to their people, and asserts the Cherokee syllabary had been known for many generations before Sequoyah and was presumably prehistoric, "engraved by their forefathers [on] ancient thin gold plates" (Traveller Bird 1971:84). Traveller Bird's Sequoyah is a patriot fighter who again and again sacrificed his comfort, health, loved ones, and at last his life for his people, but he is not the extraordinary genius whose intellectual feat earned him admiration, a medal, and a pension from the United States. Sequoyah's daughter Gedi is quoted by Traveller Bird as saying that the famous portrait of her father is actually a portrait of another Cherokee, Thomas Maw, and that the medal (and pension?) was given to George Gist, who assuredly was not Sequoyah.

The truth probably lies between the two biographies. Mooney's informants had never been close to the Cherokee faction that emigrated to Texas before the removal policies of the American government were implemented. The second cousin of Sequoyah from whom Mooney obtained biographical data was of Euro-American and Natchez as well as Cherokee ancestry, and had been educated as a youth in mission schools. Traveller Bird implies that such a person would not have been trusted by Sequoyah's faction. Sequoyah's descendants are likely to have had information not known to eastern Cherokees even in Mooney's era. On the other hand, it seems improbable that the Cherokee should have from prehistoric times a complete syllabary engraved on thin gold plates, like the Book of Mormon. If they had a writing system, why was it not on deerskin parchment or on paper, both of these in use in Mesoamerica, or on bark sheets, hide, or wood, as used by other Siouan speakers and by Algonkians? More probably, the Cherokee had a set of symbols that were mnemonic aids to the priests: such symbols were basically ideographs, although some might have phonetic value, and were (and are) learned by priests of both the Iroquois and the Algonkians, north of the Cherokee. Sequoyah may well have learned such a set in training for a priestly office in his town, and determined—perhaps through a chance conversation, perhaps through a council of conservatives concerned that esoteric Cherokee knowledge should not die—to convert the ideographic system to one so simple and so flexible that every Cherokee could easily express in it any thought. The secret of the elite would become the common tool of the people, forged by a brilliant mind illiterate in English but aware of the phonemic premise underlying European writing. However Sequoyah came to present his syllabary in 1821, his symbols were then modified by missionaries so that they could be better reproduced by printing presses: the system is Sequoyah's, but the symbols presently used are not identical to his.

Both biographers can at least agree that it is beautifully appropriate that the man who gave his beloved people the literacy through which their traditions have been preserved is commemorated in the sequoias, those tallest evergreens of warm red wood.

In consequence of the arbitrary and superficially paradoxical behavior of the United States and its agents, the Southeastern Indian nations (as they considered themselves by this time) were rent with civil strife. Optimists such as Kahnungdaclageh (Major Ridge), a Cherokee leader, strove to prove to the United States that they must be accepted into citizenship or conceded the powers of a foreign nation. More conservative and, as it turned out, more realistic Indians such as the Creek Osceola fought each incursion of colonists. The "progressives" and the "traditionalists" each had ample evidence to support their belief in the wisdom of their moves, and ample evidence to discredit the opposition's arguments. Neither side was able to fully accept the unhappy truth that military prowess and moral justification were alike ineffective in halting the American juggernaut. The Creeks came to a true civil war in 1813, when the "Red Sticks" followers of Tecumseh fought United States troops at Horseshoe Bend and fled to Florida, still a Spanish domain, when Tecumseh was killed. Refugee Creeks in Florida battled again to retain their autonomy and culture in the Seminole Wars of 1817–18 and 1835–42 (the latter costing $20 million and fifteen hundred American soldiers' lives but leaving some five hundred Seminoles, mostly of Muskogean origin, in Florida). The Cherokee factions assassinated each other (or they would say, executed traitors) for decades. The nineteenth century was a classic picture of frustrated underdogs turning against each other in their despair.

Conflict became crisis at the end of the 1820s. In 1825, Secretary of War Calhoun had recommended to President Monroe that an "Indian Line" be proclaimed along the western borders of Arkansas and Missouri to the headwaters of the Mississippi, with Euro-American settlement prohibited west of the line and Indians encouraged to take claims in this territory beyond the states. (For a full generation, Southeastern Indians unwilling to suffer any more depredations from Euro-American colonists had been emigrating west of this suggested line.) Monroe's successor, Adams, accepted Calhoun's policy but took no action to implement it. At the end of 1828, the state of Georgia forced the federal government to move on the issue by declaring that within six months, all Indians within the state (including the Cherokee Nation with its constitution and government for its treaty-fixed lands) would come under Georgia laws. The conflict between states' rights and federal jurisdiction feared since the creation of the United States had clearly come to a head—and to aggravate the crisis, it became known in 1829 that there was gold in Cherokee land in Georgia.

The entire United States became embroiled in the controversy precipitated by Georgia's decree. Andrew Jackson was elected president on the strength of his belief that the only solution to conflict with Indians was their removal beyond the Indian Line. His party, dominant in the South, used the "Indian question" as a rallying point. The opposition party responded by marshaling sentiment against removal. The result was cleavage of the voting populace, and its representatives, into a Southern bloc championing states' rights, slavery, and Indian removal, and a Northern bloc favoring a stronger federal government, emancipation of slaves, and the Indians' right to their ancestral lands. Deeper than the North-South division was a challenge of the states with more heterogeneous populations to the Puritan-founded New England states. New York Dutch Reformed Church leaders and Southern Baptists agreed on the benefits to Indians of removal, but Boston-based Congregationalist and Presbyterian missionaries (who had been receiving federal funds to "civilize" the Southeastern Indians) announced that true Christianity lay in securing the Indians in their homelands. The 1820s Indian-removal conflict was a rehearsal of the 1850s conflict ostensibly over slavery that culminated in the Civil War. Indian removal was an inflammatory issue betraying unresolved weaknesses in the structure of the United States.

Jackson's party won in a close presidential vote. In May, 1830, President Jackson signed the Removal Act. According to the act, the United States was to mark out districts within its western territory not claimed by existing states, and was empowered to exchange such districts for land held by Indians within the states. Indians were to be reimbursed for improvements they had made on the land they were exchanging, and money was allocated to pay for the costs of this reimbursement, for expenses of travel to the new districts, and for the necessities of the first year of reestablishment in the district. The act did not state that all Indians within the states had to be removed, and Jackson assumed the "mixed-bloods" would choose instead to enroll as individual residents in the states, remaining on their farms. After a removal agreement had been forced upon the Choctaws at Dancing Rabbit Creek in 1830, one-third of the Choctaws attempted to register their intention to stay with the government agent appointed to their tribe; he ignored his directives, refused to perform the lawful requests presented to him, and finally granted 69 stays out of a census population of 19,554. The Creeks in 1825 executed William McIntosh of Coweta for treason against the nation by signing a land cession agreement at Indian Springs. Under an 1832 treaty, their council agreed to cede the nation's lands *provided* the United States would set up reservations and guarantee the preservation of Creek laws on their own territories; their stipulations were disregarded, and when 1,500 Euro-American colonists invaded their lands in Alabama, the United States failed to protect Creek rights. Militia from the state of Georgia attacked Creek refugees from Alabama, and Creeks fought back; that gave the Secretary of War a reason to send federal troops from the Seminole War north in 1836 to destroy Creek camps; and by the end of that year, 14,608 Creeks had been expelled from their homeland, many of the men chained and handcuffed. The Cherokee attempted to fight in the courts to uphold their earlier treaty rights: Supreme Court Chief Justice John Marshall's 1831 landmark decision (*Cherokee Nation vs. Georgia*) proved this course of action futile. Overridingly

concerned with the case's threat of precipitating a destructive confrontation between the powers of the Supreme Court versus those of the President, Marshall ingeniously created a new status for Indian nations, "domestic dependent nations." As such, Indian nations' sovereignty was respected only so far as the United States federal government wished to grant it; the sovereignty of Indian nations as foreign nations was no longer inviolate. At New Echota in December, 1835, The Ridge's faction signed an agreement of removal, which was then approved by the U.S. Senate by one vote in spite of Ross's faction's refusal to be party to the business. The act that on paper made it possible to exchange Southeastern Indian lands for western lands had been interpreted to make it inevitable that the exchanges take place.

Stories of the "Trails of Tears" between the Southeast and Oklahoma have frequently been told. The Choctaws were the first tribe to go. The pattern of their removal was followed by the succeeding tribes. First, the Indians were gathered in camps until everything was ready for their journey. These concentration camps were crowded, hygiene was poor, and food rations tended to be inadequate and of low quality, so the health of the Indians deteriorated. Once it was decided all was ready (a decision allegedly procrastinated in many instances until the local contractors for supplies had raked off all the funds they could possibly hope to get away with), a minimal number of oxcarts were brought for the aged, ill, and children to ride in. Other Indians could ride their own horses, if they had any, or walk, carrying what they could. Indians' livestock were driven alongside the procession of people. Ten miles per day was the best progress that could be hoped for. At night, people slept under wagons or with no shelter, because not enough tents had been provided. Food was bought en route by the army officers in charge of the march. Even the lowest bidders on the supplies, whom the officers were obliged to select, charged exorbitant prices to the captive buyers and often gave spoiled food. Much of the march took place during the winter, resulting in heavy loss of life from pneumonia. Those who journeyed during the summer suffered from heat and insects, impassibly muddy roads, and, to cap it off, a cholera epidemic. Some of the officers in charge were callous, but there are records of compassionate and deeply concerned officers who strove to alleviate suffering, only to be overwhelmed by the initial poor planning, chicanery by unscrupulous contractors, lack of decent roads, and, of course, their era's ignorance of the causes of disease. When the exhausted, sad survivors reached their new territory, the same inadequate planning and problems with supplies continued to plague them. The United States spent over $5 million (1830s dollars!) on Choctaw removal. About two thousand Choctaws managed to evade removal, wandering landless around Mississippi. This extraordinary sum, then, was expended upon only two-thirds, at most, of a population of fewer than twenty thousand people, and was so ineptly or dishonestly spent that even those strong enough to arrive in Oklahoma were woefully impoverished. The results of the Choctaw removal dismayed those who had seen removal as benign, confirmed the remaining Southeastern tribes' determination not to follow, and yet had no effect upon the removal policy. Even the belated realization by some Mississippi shopkeepers that the Choctaws had been better customers than the colonists who replaced them did not ameliorate the inexorable push for removal. The Southeastern tribes were pawns in national politics, game for speculators, victims of a nation whose government was based on precarious compromises influenced by moneyed interests.

The Choctaw removal was followed by the removal of the Creeks, who, after being dislodged from their lands, were hunted and driven into the concentration camps and thence to Oklahoma by 1837 and 1839. The several hundred Creeks who had taken refuge in the Florida swamps were pursued during the Seminole War of 1835–42, which petered out as the majority of the Seminole (a blanket term for people from several Muskogean-speaking groups who had come to Florida at various times in the historic period) were rounded up and forced to Oklahoma. The Cherokee were evicted in 1838 "with unspeakable brutality," according to the usually dispassionate ethnohistorian John Swanton, who also asserted that the "treaty of removal [was] repugnant to nineteen-twentieths of the tribe" (Swanton 1946:80). A few hundred Cherokee who had hidden out in the mountains were finally allowed, in 1842, a reservation in the North Carolina Appalachians. The Chickasaws moved west group by group for ten years, beginning in 1837, avoiding some of the worst experiences of their predecessors by purchasing much of what they needed, including transportation by steamboat to the Arkansas River, out of tribal funds instead of relying upon the United States agents to care for them. (Officers in charge of some parties of other tribes had also chartered steamboats, but the practice was considered unnecessarily expensive.) Within a dozen years of the passage of the Removal Act, the Five Civilized Tribes of the Southeast (so called because so many Creek, Choctaw, Chickasaw, Cherokee, and Seminole utilized Euro-American patterns of farming, household, dress, and local government) were resettled in Oklahoma on the edge of what Americans called the Great American Desert.

Settling in Oklahoma, the Five Civilized Tribes organized as nations. The Cherokees who had come west to the Arkansas Territory before the 1837 Treaty of Removal already had a government with a general council headed by first, second, and third chiefs enacting written laws. Cherokees in their homeland boasted of their national government and constitution, and when they joined their compatriots in Oklahoma, there was tension over which council should rule. But the greater numerical strength of the emigrants carried their principal chief, John Ross, into power. Ross's father was a Scotsman and his mother had only one Cherokee grandparent, but Ross consistently aligned himself with the Cherokees and served as a political leader for the nation from the age of 27, and as principal

FIGURE 4.7   Cherokee family at home, Qualla Reservation, North Carolina, 1888. Woman at right pounds maize in a log mortar; maize grows directly behind the cabin clearing. Lacrosse sticks are laid on the logs of the cabin, to the right of the door. *(Smithsonian Institution National Anthropological Archives)*

chief from age 38 to his death nearly forty years later. His opponents at the merging of the Cherokees in Oklahoma in 1839 were, on the one hand, the chiefs of the western Cherokees, and on the other, the small faction earlier in favor of removal, led by Major Ridge, his brother Oowatie, and their sons John Ridge, Elias Boudinot (Buck Watie), and Stand Watie. Although The Ridge and Oowatie were full-blood Cherokee who had grown up as traditional hunters, and Ross was one-eighth Cherokee and school-educated as a youth, Ross was considered to be the more conservative Cherokee because of his longer opposition to removal. The conflict was ended rather quickly with the assassination of The Ridge, his son, and Boudinot in June, 1839, the murders being justified as the proper penalty for the victims' having signed a removal treaty without bringing it to the full council. The western Cherokees tried to hold out for greater representation, but under negotiations conducted by a United States Army officer, they were pressured into accepting a constitution and government basically the same as those drawn up for the Cherokee Nation in 1827. The structure of the government was modeled upon that of the United States, and the only major divergence from United States law and structure was the reservation of all land to the Cherokee Nation, with improvements upon the land individually owned but forbidden to be conveyed to United States citizens. Dual citizenship was not recognized, although the Cherokee Nation sent representatives to the United States capital. Similar governments were adopted by the Chickasaws and Choctaws, and a less elaborate constitution by the Creeks. Seminoles were finally given a place in Indian Territory in 1856, on land purchased for them by the United States from the Creek Nation. Belatedly, the emigrant Seminoles began to organize on the model of their neighbor Indian nations.

SECTION 6: POSTREMOVAL HISTORY: 1856 TO THE PRESENT

For more than a century, the postremoval affairs of the Five Civilized Tribes and other Southeastern Indians resembled a dreary television series in which tired rewrites of the hackneyed plots are difficult to distinguish from reruns. Indian nations constructed towns, schools, tribal government buildings, farms with substantial homes, yet they were not secure. When the Chickasaws removed, they bought some of the Choctaw land; when the Seminoles removed, they were given land bought from the Creeks; the Cherokees in 1867 took the Delaware and, in 1870, the Shawnee into their land; some Catawba settled in the Choctaw Nation; the Caddo in 1859 fled brutal harassment in Texas by taking up land in Indian Territory. So it went—parcel by parcel the lands of the Indian nations were ceded. Then, in 1854, Kansas and Nebraska were admitted to the Union as states in spite of their lying west of the Indian Line. Jefferson's vision of Euro-American colonists advancing stage by stage to the Rockies was being fulfilled.

The Civil War hastened the inroads upon the Indian nations. Most Indians of Southeastern origin aligned with the South, in part because many held black slaves, in part because Oklahoma Indian Territory was nearly surrounded by southern states and resistance to them would have been suicidal. The consequences of the Civil War were, therefore, a replay of the consequences of the Revolutionary War—seizure of Indian lands and pillaging of their goods, the people rendered destitute whether they chose one side, the other side, or neutrality. New treaties were negotiated in 1866, not only with the Confederate Choctaw and Chickasaw and with the schismatic Cherokee, but with the Creeks, who had sent a large force, although not all of their men, to fight with the Union. The western half of Indian Territory was taken from the Five Tribes to be used to settle other Indians. North-south and east-west strips of land were pulled out for the construction of transcontinental railroads. Freed slaves were to be made citizens of the Indian nations, although the Chickasaws never accepted this provision. The United States also insisted that the nations in Indian Territory meet in intertribal council to allay differ-

ences. Reconstruction in postwar Indian Territory was quite literally that. Battles and raids had destroyed homes, barns, and implements, left fields to weeds, and scattered or killed livestock. It was a second beginning in the territory for the Five Tribes, a recapitulation of what they had undergone after removal. This time it had to be carried out without the assistance of slaves, who were building their own homes and farms as freedmen, and with a reduced Indian population. As they had earlier, the Indians constructed houses and outbuildings, plowed with oxen or horses, kept beef cattle, hogs, chickens, and turkeys, planted maize, cotton, wheat, fruit orchards, and vegetables, generally made their own clothing in Euro-American style, and purchased dishes and metal tools and pots. Children attended schools supported by tribal funds administered by the tribes' United States Government agents. Under a policy initiated in the Grant presidency, these agents were nominated by, or at least acceptable to, Christian missionary churches, each missionary denomination being given one or more tribes in fief, as it were. The Indian nations continued their constitutional governments. There was thus little to outwardly distinguish the Indians in the eastern sector of Indian Territory from Euro-American frontier settlers. They worked hard and lived comfortably, and many, especially the mixed-bloods and black freedmen, engaged in trade or business such as blacksmithing and keeping boardinghouses. (A note on "blood": it is a stereotype that the "full-bloods" are conservative and the descendants of Indian–non-Indian marriages are "progressive" or acculturated. As in the example of The Ridge and John Ross, the stereotype frequently does not hold. What has happened is that conservative individuals are *labeled* full-blood and acculturated individuals mixed-blood, confirming the stereotype in disregard of fact.)

As had happened after the Revolutionary War, the Five Tribes came to live in a manner that would justify their being given full United States citizenship and the rights that that implies. All that marked the Indians were their languages, their religious beliefs—which, for many, were held in addition to Christianity—a few social dances and religious festivals (principally the Green Corn New Year's celebration), and the concept that land belonged to the people in common rather than to individuals. Only this last belief diverged from the attributes of the dozens of other ethnic groups who had been readily integrated into the United States. Common land came to be seen as the chief barrier to, or basic safeguard of—depending on whether one held a Euro-American or Indian point of view—Indian cultural loss. Although Indian national land tenure had been no obstacle to prosperity—in 1846, the Creek Nation in Oklahoma already produced enough corn to export 100,000 bushels to alleviate the famine in Ireland—this fact was ignored in Washington. Missionaries, who now strongly influenced, if not controlled, Indian affairs, preached that Christian virtues flourished on individual family homesteads but somehow were incompatible with commonage (forgetting, apparently, that English commonages had been broken up only at the beginning of the previous century). If the Indians could be made to live on family allotments, the argument ran, they would have taken the last step from savagery to civilization. The United States Government agreed with the missionaries' position because allotting land in homesteads of, say, 160 acres (65 hectares) per family would immediately free a great deal of Indian land for Euro-American colonization and would facilitate further acquisitions as families died out or wished to move. In 1879, a bill was presented to Congress to allot Indian lands in severalty. Such an action was clearly outside the powers of the United States according to nearly all its treaties with Indians, but the Indians had long since learned that Washington usually abrogated treaties unilaterally when voters clamored. In spite of staunch opposition from the Indian nations, and demurrers from the several members of the House Indian Affairs Committee and some other Euro-Americans, in 1887 the act,

sponsored by Senator Dawes of Massachusetts, to allot Indian lands by quarter-section to family heads was passed.

The Dawes Act did not apply to the Five Civilized Tribes, whose lands were held under patented titles. The Five Tribes hosted an intertribal council in 1888 for twenty-two other tribes in an attempt to help the other Indian groups resist allotment, but protest was useless. In 1889, the land in western Indian Territory remaining on reservations after the tribes there had been allotted homesteads was opened to Euro-American ownership as Oklahoma. Many Oklahomans seem to have had difficulty figuring out the boundary between their state and the Five Nations to the east, and illegal colonization was rampant. Dawes headed a commission to investigate the situation, and surely no one could have been uncertain of the recommendations he would make! In 1898, the Curtis Act extended allotment to the Five Civilized Tribes, and for good measure gave the United States jurisdiction over their schools and abolished their constitutional governments. In 1906, an amended law provided that the original practice of holding allotments in trust but granting the allottees citizenship be changed: thenceforth, holders of allotments in trust would not be given full citizenship, while Indians judged to be competent to protect their own interests (the test was whether the man had managed his farm competently, regardless of his ability to deal with English-speaking businessmen) would have their homesteads taken out of trust and be given citizenship. A 1904 petition by the Five Civilized Tribes to admit Indian Territory to the Union as an Indian state to be named Sequoyah was rejected, and in 1907, the new state of Oklahoma was admitted with mixed population. The twentieth century thus brought the dissolution of the century-old formal Indian nations.

Resistance to dissolution was especially strong among the Cherokee. When in 1896 it became clear that the Dawes policy would be extended to the Five Tribes, conservative Cherokees belonging to the Ketoowa Society (Ketoowa was a ceremonial name for the Cherokee) set up a committee led by Redbirth Smith, one of their members. The committee retrieved wampum belts symbolic of the tribe from a former chief's son and carried those to the old traditionalists of the Cherokee, Creek, and Shawnee, asking for instruction in traditional customs and for advice according to the ancient White path. (In this way, the Ketoowa Society followed the Cherokee practice of respecting the counsel of the elderly, peace-inclined Beloved Men, contrasting these with younger, belligerent Red warriors.) The wampum bearers' pilgrimages stimulated conservatives in the other four tribes to create the Four Mothers' Society of conservatives from all Five Civilized Tribes. The Four Mothers pragmatically retained lawyers and sent representatives to Washington to impede, if possible, the threatened allotment. When their efforts failed, thousands of conservatives, prominent among them the Cherokee, chose passive resistance, adamantly refusing to sign up for their allotments, even though their refusal left them destitute and, in 1902, led to Redbird Smith and other leaders being jailed. Passive resistance continued. The Ketoowa Society dropped from the Four Mothers' Society, its members no longer participated in Cherokee tribal politics, and instead they revived ceremonial grounds in local communities. By 1916, the conservatives had reconstructed White towns and the seven clans, two aspects of traditional Cherokee social structure that had not been carried on in Indian Territory. A priest at each ceremonial ground was ritual fire-keeper. All-night series of traditional dances were again held at the town-square grounds. Allotment had the unforeseen effect of recrystallizing tradition for a large segment of the Five Tribes.

The years after 1906 were years of avid, unscrupulous purchasing of Indian allotments by Euro-American speculators and farmers. Indians were further victimized by Euro-Americans administering the funds accruing to minors and to adults considered incompetent to manage their own incomes. These funds included annuities from the United States, rent from leased allotments, sales of land, and, beginning in the 1920s for many Oklahoma Indians, royalties on oil from allotted lands. High-handed dealings with Indians, the acceptance of bribes from speculators and businessmen, and rake-offs on payments enriched scores of Oklahomans who foisted themselves on people helpless in the face of the intricately interlocked wealth and power of the Euro-Americans surrounding them.

Relief from dispossession coincided, unhappily, with the Dust Bowl and the Depression. Beginning in 1934, John Collier's New Deal administration reversed the erosion of Indian land titles as the land itself eroded in the dust storms. The Red Cross had to rescue many Indians from famine during the winters. Most of the Five Civilized Tribes were in the wooded eastern portion of Oklahoma, and so escaped the worst of the Dust Bowl. With the aid of the Collier administration's loans and extension agents, during the last of the 1930s, many families were able to invest in basic machinery, stock, or other necessaries for lifting themselves out of abject poverty. Relative poverty, however, continues to characterize the majority of conservative members of the Five Tribes. Most Indians can obtain better income only by leaving their rural communities for urban employment. In this they parallel the Euro-Americans of eastern Oklahoma, who have been migrating from the region for decades. The Indians have been more reluctant to migrate, whether from a desire to continue living in communities where they speak their native language and share beliefs, or from a hard-headed appraisal of the opportunities for poorly educated, untrained members of racial minorities. Official population figures (rounded off) for the Five Civilized Tribes in Oklahoma in the 1980 census were: Creek, 15,500; Seminole, 5,000; Chickasaw, 6,000; Choctaw, 24,000; Cherokee, 60,000.

Oklahoma today has a great number of persons who claim to be part Indian, generally part Cherokee, but neither know nor participate in Indian life. In 1980, the total population reported as Cherokee was 232,000, far and away the largest tribe in the country, but with a much smaller percentage on reservations than is true for the two next largest tribes, the Navajo and the Sioux. The United States Bureau of Indian Affairs has encouraged "mixed-bloods" to represent Indian tribes and govern tribal councils, on the grounds that familiarity from childhood with Euro-American society renders these individuals more capable of dealing effectively with that society as it impinges upon Indian communities. This encouragement has become notorious in the case of the Cherokee, who have become divided between the conservatives ("full-bloods") subsistence-farming in the hills and the "progressives" in the urban middle class of the state of Oklahoma. In continuation of the withdrawal of the Ketoowa Society from politics, the conservatives feel discouraged from participation in tribal government. The gap between conservatives and the politically powerful "mixed-bloods" seems to be widening as eastern Oklahoma loses its Euro-American small farmers, who mixed socially with their Cherokee neighbors and shared many concerns with them. Texas ranchers have been buying large blocks of former farmland once occupied by these rural Euro-Americans; much other land, including many square miles of flat bottomlands, has been turned into recreational lakes and parks. This "modernization" of eastern Oklahoma has been isolating the conservative Indians and decreasing their opportunities for local or part-time employment. The conservative Indians of the Five Civilized Tribes in Oklahoma have retained (in the case of the Creeks) or revitalized (in the case of the Cherokee) much of their basic cultural pattern. Communities may appear to be dispersed along the hollows in the hills, but they continue to focus on the "town square," or ceremonial ground, and continue to. be religious congregations as well as social and informal governmental units. While an increasing number of Indians openly adhere exclusively to their traditional religions, the majority are also practicing and believing members of Christian churches that

evolved from missionary foundations, such as the Cherokee Baptist Church. Sermons and hymns in these churches are often in the Indian language, and Bibles are available in the native language, although the manner of worship tends to resemble rural Southern Protestant worship behavior. The Green Corn New Year's festival is the principal Indian religious celebration, and is held at the community's square ground. The traditional open cabins for men's groups ring the square, one on each of the four sides laid out according to the cardinal directions. A low mound still lies northeast of the square. A series of the traditional dances precedes the ritual kindling of the new fire, which will burn on the four logs forming the cross of the cosmos. The physical and spiritual cleansing accomplished by purging and by "going to water," a basic Southeastern ritual of immersion in a running stream, remains an important component of the celebration. The traditional ball game and night-long social dancing around fires enliven the festival.

One of the traditional Creek dances, the Stomp Dance, is not only a favorite of young people of the Five Tribes, but has been spreading to Indian young people throughout North America (occasionally to the disapproval of conservative Plains elders, to whom it appears lascivious). A young man leads the Stomp Dance, circling the fire counterclockwise (or, more properly, countersunwise) with a fast, stamping step. Behind him comes a young woman wearing rattles attached to her legs. As the leader dances, he shouts out lines of songs, often humorous, and is answered antiphonally by the rest of the dancers in line behind him. (This leader-response pattern is similar to the West African song style carried by black slaves to the South, but seems to have been indigenous to the Eastern Woodlands Indians. Its popularity may have been reinforced by its similarity to the style enjoyed by the blacks among the Indians and used in a somewhat lesser extent in the rural Southern Protestant churches.). The Stomp Dance is great fun, like a conga line snake-dancing along a street as the stomp leader winds his fellow celebrants into a spiral and out again as they circle, repeating a figure found in Southeastern Indian design for centuries. The last dance, as night turns into dawn, is the Drunken (more properly, Wild) Dance, a final fling for men and women together that would certainly be banned from conservative Plains pow-wows. These social dances are held for pleasure during the summer months at most of the square grounds, as well as during the Green Corn Festival. Indians who have accepted urban employment drive home to their original communities for a weekend of visiting and Stomp Dancing, managing some of the best of both worlds for the price of a few gallons of gas.

Strong as are the values and beliefs of the Five Civilized Tribes in Oklahoma, their formal organizations do reflect twentieth-century adaptations. When John Collier as Commissioner of Indian Affairs in 1934 offered the Indian Reorganization Act, part of Franklin Roosevelt's New Deal, the Creek petitioned the federal government to recognize their own constitution and tribal government. This was granted, and the forty-two towns of the Muscogee Nation (the Oklahoma nation spells "Muskogee" with a "c") elected a Principal Chief and then a council. After the federal government's 1975 Indian Self-Determination and Educational Assistance Act, consolidating a shift in Federal policy toward increased Indian control of Indian affairs, the Muscogee Nation obtained Economic Development Administration and other grants to build housing, a hospital and clinics, tribal archives and education services, and a model farm. In 1984, the Muscogee Nation instituted a new means of creating revenue through bingo halls attracting non-Indians by offering larger prizes than state laws allow (not subject to state jurisdiction, Indian reservations can set their own gambling laws). Through this variety of enterprises, the Muscogee Nation is entered upon what could be seen as its fourth reconstruction since European invasions of its homeland.

The hard-core or lucky Indians who avoided removal from the Southeast founded communities that in several instances were incorporated into reservations; others failed to obtain protection. The remnant Cherokee, now called the Eastern Cherokee, who hid in the Great Smokies from the troops ferreting out Cherokees for removal were assisted by a Euro-American, William Thomas ("Wil-Usdi" in Cherokee) who had been informally adopted, after his father died, by his widowed mother's Cherokee neighbor, Yonaguska. Thomas used the Cherokees' reparations for property damages to purchase land for the Indians—who by law could not own any in North Carolina—and acted as agent for the people. For a century, these Cherokee on the Qualla reservation eked a living out of the high, narrow valleys. A school was not established until 1880, although a few youth apparently received some education prior to that, and even went on to attend Duke University. In 1882, the U.S. Supreme Court ruled, in a question of state jurisdiction, that the Eastern Band of Cherokee, some fourteen hundred people, was a tribe and outside state governance. This ruling was reversed by the Court in 1886, a motion that was countered by the Cherokee, in 1889, organizing as a corporation for legal purposes, although one governed through an elected chief and tribal council. The subsistence farming that had been, and to a lesser degree continues to be, the tribe's mainstay was threatened in the 1920s by the enforcement of stock-fencing rules that prevented the Indians from utilizing steep and forested land for livestock forage; by the enforcement of prohibitions against burning underbrush, which, according to the Cherokee, was necessary to maintain the quality of the forest for hunting and timber; and by the chestnut blight, which destroyed a species that had been important to the Cherokees for nuts, wood, and livestock mast.

Not until after World War II did the Qualla economy strengthen. The development of the Great Smoky Mountains as a national park bounding on the Qualla lands brought hundreds of thousands of tourists. Most of the crush of motels, restaurants, and souvenir shops profiting from the hordes of tourists are owned and operated by Euro-

FIGURE 4.8 Seminole man in a dugout canoe. *(Milwaukee Public Museum)*

Americans, although the tribal council runs a motel and shop. But at least there is seasonal employment close to home for hundreds of Cherokee on the payrolls of these establishments, and an apparently bottomless market for crafts in spite of the competition from imported plastic imitations. The Cherokee attempt to present their story to the tourists through a museum containing a reconstructed traditional village and through the popular outdoor theatrical pageant *Unto These Hills* reenacting the drama of removal. Authentic Cherokee culture is struggling, however, against the readiness of entrepreneurs and the public to stereotype Indians in the Plains image. Cherokee dress in fancy Lakota Sioux "war-bonnet" headdresses and buckskin costumes to be paid for posing for pictures. Tourists overlook Cherokee cabins beside plots of maize, beans, and pumpkins as they strive for a glimpse of tipis and horses. The increasingly common modern houses and the industries invited to the reservation by the tribe to provide year-round employment are of no interest to the average vacationer. The ultimate effect of tourism and industrial employment, and of the schooling that trains young Cherokee for these opportunities, perhaps cannot be foretold, but the persistence of Cherokee tradi-

tion to the present encourages the expectation that it will not be lost. The Cherokee language is still generally used, Cherokee medicine and "conjuring" (the English term the Cherokee use for their native doctors and sorcerers) are seen as efficacious, cooperative labor through the Gadugi organization is valued, and the Cherokee ethos of harmony through indirection, consensus, and, if necessary, withdrawal, is honored. The reservation in North Carolina is now twelfth-largest among United States Indian reservations, with a population of about five thousand.

Seminoles are the most famous of the Indian holdouts in the Southeast. Total population of Seminoles was slightly over ten thousand in 1980, only a portion living on reservations. Around six hundred (in 1980) Muskogees who see themselves as Creek rather than Seminole live without a reservation in northwest Florida; this community has been recognized as Indian by the State of Florida since 1975. Florida now has four Seminole enclaves, one (Hollywood) on the east coast between Miami and Fort Lauderdale and three in the interior of south Florida. The residents of Brighton Reservation, north of Lake Okeechobee, speak Muskogee (Creek), and the three more southern reservations speak Mikasuki (also spelled Micco-sukee), the related Muskogean language similar to Hitchiti. Large portions of the interior reservations are swamps that support a rich wild-animal population but are impossible to utilize for commercial livestock or crops without considerable capital investment in drainage. Venison remains the principal meat of the Seminole, with smaller game, fish, birds, some home-raised maize and garden produce, and purchased corn meal and other foods also utilized. The cash for purchases comes from seasonal agricultural labor on Euro-American agribusinesses and the sale of crafts to tourists. Efforts to improve Seminole economics include an industry invited to the Hollywood reservation, development of commercial-quality pastures on drained land, the replacement of the local scrub cattle with potentially profitable beef varieties, and government jobs ranging from managing the tribal grocery to teacher-aide and Neighborhood Youth Corps projects. Tourism has been increasing in Seminole territory with the completion of modern highways through central Florida. Seminole costume, a colorful adaptation of nineteenth-century Euro-American styles featuring multiple bands of intricately appliqued ribbons, is still worn by many women every day. Many families continue to live in chickees, the open-sided, palmetto-thatched platform shelters, although these are being replaced by concrete-block houses less well adapted to the climate and also by better-adapted, light, wooden houses with a continuous screened window around all four sides. These features interest tourists, even though the chickees are likely to have electricity powering a sewing machine, washing machine, television, radio, and amplified guitar. The basic Muskogean cultural pattern has prevailed until the present, with few adults speaking English, matrilineal clans persisting, and the ethos of indirection and respect for individual autonomy dominant. The Seminole Tribe is incorporated, with the Miccosukee separately organized since 1965, but the Seminole consider each family independent and are generally unwilling to surrender

autonomy to any hierarchical structure. This characteristic is, of course, an exaggeration of the traditional Muskogean ethos, which valued compromise as a means towards achieving a consensus on cooperative action. The Seminole are the descendants of those Muskogeans and other refugees who most doggedly resisted surrendering their independence. Whether the Seminole ethos and canons of interpersonal behavior stressing a quiet tone and the avoidance of confrontation even in conversation (it is good etiquette to look past the person one is speaking to, or on the ground, behavior that causes Euro-Americans to label the Indians "shy"), can survive the onslaught of general schooling in which Euro-American teachers try to "bring out" the "shy" children, and the screaming aggression of radio DJs and television, will soon be seen.

The Choctaws are the second-largest tribe of Indians still in the Southeast, exceeded only by the Cherokee. The two thousand who clung to Mississippi have doubled in number and, like nearly all other Indian populations, have a relatively high birth rate and total increase; the 1980 census reported fifty thousand Choctaw, although it reported fewer than five thousand in Mississippi and Louisiana. Their territory in central Mississippi was officially recognized by the Bureau of Indian Affairs in 1918, after futile efforts in 1903 to remove them to Oklahoma and allot them homesteads under the extension of the Dawes policy. Prior to the belated move of the Bureau to purchase and hold as tribal trust the historic Choctaw land, the Indians had first suffered destitution because they had lost their farms and could not find wage employment in the slaveholding Deep South, and then, after the Civil War, had settled as sharecroppers on Euro-American-owned farms. Establishment of the reservation confirmed the separation of the Choctaws from the Mississippi upper caste of Euro-Americans (who classed the Indians as nonwhites) and from the lower caste of blacks, a status steadfastly rejected by the Indians. Choctaw churches and then Choctaw schools protected the Choctaws' pride, although outside the

SEMINOLE SONGS FOR BIRTH AND DEATH

Omalagi (Let Us All Go), called Susie Tiger in English, was a Seminole woman born at a time when her people feared they would all be removed to Oklahoma. Her family was able to remain in their homeland, and, by 1933, she was living with the Brighton band, using her knowledge of traditional Muskogee medicine to aid the sick and women in childbirth in her village. She sang these doctor's incantations for the pioneer ethnomusicologist Frances Densmore.

Song for Bringing a Child into the World

You day-sun, circling around,
You daylight, circling around,
You night-sun, circling around,
You poor body, circling around,
You wrinkled age, circling around,
You spotted with gray, circling around,
You wrinkled skin, circling around,
Boy [/girl], come!

Song for the Dying

Come back.
Before you get to the [flowering] tree, come back,
Before you get to the peach tree, come back,
Before you come to the line of fence, come back,
Before you come to the bushes, come back,
Before you get to the fork of the road, come back,
Before you get to the yard, come back,
Before you get to the door, come back,
Before you get to the fire, come back,
Before you get to the middle of the ladder, come back.
[Name of patient], come back, come back!
(Densmore 1956:172, 174)

Choctaw communities the Indians were excluded from all white-only areas. The consequences of the rigid caste system of central Mississippi and the Choctaw refusal to share the status of blacks were isolation of the Choctaw socially, reflected in the virtual absence of intermarriage with either of the dominant castes and restricted economic opportunities. The lack of a Choctaw high school until 1964 meant Choctaw young people had no educa-tion beyond the elementary grades, for they could not attend the white high school and would not attend the black one. This limited education in turn prevented Choctaws from obtaining employment other than low-paying agricultural labor, even after racial discrimination in employment lessened. Agricultural employment began a steep decline in central Mississippi (as in eastern Oklahoma) after World War II. Some Choctaws followed their

Euro-American and black neighbors to urban employment, as far as Chicago and Dallas, but most, accustomed to speaking Choctaw, preferred to remain in the Choctaw communities. The passage of the Civil Rights Act in 1964 accelerated two trends that made this preference possible for many. First, racial discrimination in regional industries was no longer defensible, and this, coupled with the availability of high-school training, opened numbers of jobs to Choctaws. Second, the Bureau of Indian Affairs and the Choctaw Tribal Council channeled or created white-collar and paraprofessional jobs for the reservation. The decline in sharecropping, improvement of highways, and increase in jobs in the tribal headquarters have stimulated the growth of the headquarters community into a town, Pearl River, with modern housing as well as schools and services for the Choctaw. From 1973, in response to Choctaw insistence, the BIA agent for the tribe has been a Choctaw, and the agency has coordinated services rather than, as usual on reservations, dictated policy. The tribal Chata Development Company, chartered in 1969, constructed a shopping mall, many homes and other buildings, and an industrial park that gives employment to over a thousand people, in firms ranging from an automobile-parts factory to a greeting-card producer. Clustered around Pearl River, Choctaw families can maintain their language and ethos—especially including wide participation in ball games, American as well as the native stickball—without sacrificing the comforts of an American standard of living.

The fourth officially recognized Indian tribe in the Southeast today is the Alabama-Coushatta (Koasati), Muskogean speakers who drifted west during the eighteenth century and were living in independent Texas during the removal era. In 1854, these people were given a reservation in eastern Texas. During the 1950s, with the federal-government push to terminate responsibility for Indian tribes, the administration of the Alabama-Coushatta reservation was transferred to the state of Texas. Younger people on the reservation no longer speak Alabama or Coushatta, but Texas has exploited the Indian presence in encouraging the development of tourism in the area, which otherwise has only timber as an economic resource. The 1980 census listed a little over one thousand Alabama-Coushatta.

SECTION 7: "OTHER" INDIANS IN THE SOUTHEAST TODAY

The three officially recognized principal tribes of the Southeast—the Cherokee, Choctaw, and the two Seminole tribes (Seminole and Miccosukee)—organized in 1968 as the United Southeastern Tribes of American Indians, Inc. Affiliated, they expected to have greater influence on federal programs and to be able to share techniques for improving their peoples' conditions. More recently, federally recognized tribes allied under the name United South and Eastern Tribes. Louisiana Indians, unrecognized by the Bureau of Indian Affairs as local tribes, also formed a common organization. There are communities in Louisiana who consider themselves to be Biloxi, Tunica, or the related Chitimacha, Coushatta, or Houma (a Muskogean-speaking group), and there are three Choctaw bands. At the beginning of this century, Biloxi and Chitimacha were still spoken by elderly members of these groups, and there was one last Ofo speaker; but English—or in the case of Houma, Acadian French—was already the language generally spoken.

These remnants of displaced peoples, including hundreds of families from the Atlantic Southeast that fled to western Louisiana in the nineteenth century, have been isolated groups. Valuing their own cultures, they often encouraged young couples to remain with the bride's family ("matrilocal residence"), as had been customary, and recognized chiefly lineages when selecting leaders. Herbal and spiritual curing practices and songs have been the components of native tradition persisting most completely, along with material items including basketry and the use of blowguns in hunting. (It is not generally known that Southeastern Indian basketry was a fine art as well as practical, with a wide variety of forms and techniques. The art is continued today, with classes organized for skilled Choctaw, Chitimacha, and Koasati to teach younger Indian women.) The anthropologist Frank G. Speck, with wide experience among Southeastern Indians, remarked in 1938 that he judged the Houma as Indian as most other Indians of the Deep South, at least in physical appearance, but the Bureau of Indian Affairs has been unwilling to recognize them and the other isolated bands as Indian.

Asserting their Indian ancestry (without denying Euro-American intermarriage), the Louisiana Indians, like the Mississippi Choctaw, resisted being classed as blacks although they admitted they were nonwhite. In consequence, they usually had no schools or special facilities, lived marginal existences and were discriminated against in employment, illiterate, unable to obtain legal protection, usually landless, and alleged by the whites to be promiscuous and "degenerate." The Houma, in the Mississippi Gulf Coast region, collected shrimp and trapped muskrat, but as the shrimping industry came to use larger, mechanically equipped boats, the Houma shrimpers became unable to compete with their Euro-American counterparts. Moreover, muskrat trapping became depressed because of the formation of Euro-American trapping companies that leased tracts and because nutria escaped from fur farms and overran the muskrat swamps (there is no market for wild nutria fur). The Houma claim land that is now producing oil, but have been unable to support their claims in court. This lack of a secure land base not only makes Houma life economically precarious, but also undermines the persistence of Houma communities. Kinship, especially as marked by surnames, is the basis of community ties, rather than common land or clustered residence. Without strong formal organization, ethnic religion congre-

gations, or stable, delineated territory, Houma lack a structure that can accommodate "weekend Indians," families working in cities who maintain community membership as Indians by driving home frequently for visits and festivals.

The 1970s rise in political consciousness among urban Indians and the revival of interest in Indian traditions among young Indians both on and off reservations has favored the acceptance of the scattered mixed-blood Indians of Louisiana as legitimately Indian. A Koasati community in Allen Parish obtained federal recognition as an Indian tribe in 1971; this community of three hundred people still uses Koasati as its daily language. Now being incorporated in school programs, the community chooses a chief from a traditional lineage to advise and assist the elected tribal chairman and council, but it supports its culture with enterprises including commercial production of Christmas trees. In 1981, the United States formally recognized the approximately one hundred Tunica-Biloxi (combined from the two ancestral groups) as a tribe, entitled to federal aid. Many more Indians in Louisiana, descendants of the Atlantic-state refugees, are popularly termed "Red Bones," apparently a corruption of the West Indies black expression "Red Ibo" (Ibo is an African nation)—that is, "Indian 'Ibo'"! Compared with the United Southeastern Tribes, the Louisianans have few resources and much greater discouragement.

On the Eastern seaboard, the Catawba retain a small reservation under South Carolina, not federal, jurisdiction. Catawba is no longer spoken, but the craft of pottery has persisted to bring in cash that supplements farming. Most of the Catawba were converted to the Church of Jesus Christ of Latter-day Saints (the Mormon Church), which found some welcome among Southeastern Indians because it gives Indians a much higher status than blacks. Powhatan's Confederacy in Virginia declined rapidly after Opechancanough's defeat in 1645 (Opechancanough had succeeded to leadership when his brother Powhatan died). Nat Turner's slave rebellion in 1831 caused many Virginia Indians who had intermarried with blacks to be dispossessed. A number of persons today can nevertheless trace their descent from the Pamunkey (335 in 1980, plus 320 Powhatan), Chickahominy (850 recognized in the 1980 census), and other Algonkian-speaking groups of the confederacy. Many of these persons are proud of their Indian ancestry, study their heritage, and participate in powwows and similar intertribal events. The Pamunkey and the Mattaponi occupy state-legislated reservations stemming from their Treaty of 1677 with the Colony of Virginia. Other Virginia Indians, when lack of official records made it impossible to document their Indian descent sufficiently to win Federal recognition as Indian tribes, sought state recognition. Six "citizen Indian" groups obtained it, the Rappahannocks, the Chickahominy and Eastern Chickahominy, and the Upper Mattaponis in 1983, the Nansemonds in 1985, and the Monacans (the only group descended from Siouan speakers; the others are all from Algonkian nations) in 1989.

The Eastern Creeks, incorporated in 1971 as the Creek Nation East of the Mississippi, are a core of about six hundred people (86 legally counted as Creek) around the town of Attmore, Alabama. The community centers in tracts of land granted to a Creek named McGhee to reward his work as a guide to Andrew Jackson's forces. The Indians lived on small plots in forested country from which they extracted a little cash through cutting timber and collecting turpentine. Each Indian hamlet had a communal hall serving as church and school supported entirely by parents of the community. In 1947, Calvin W. McGhee instituted a lawsuit against the county school board to demand that the county provide qualified teachers and schools, or busing to the white county high school, for the McGhee and other Creek children. The success of this lawsuit brought in one teacher who mentioned to Mr. McGhee that the federal government had recently created an Indian Claims Commission. McGhee and other Creek leaders then, in 1950, organized as the Perdido (the name of a local stream) Band of Friendly Creek Indians to press,

in conjunction with the officially recognized Oklahoma Creeks, the claims of Eastern Creeks. The eventual judgment in favor of the Creeks brought them not only some money but respect in place of discrimination from the Euro-Americans of their area. Researching the land claims had taught McGhee and other Creeks much that had been forgotten by the Eastern Creeks, and heightened their pride in their heritage. McGhee created and costumed an Indian dance group, became active in pan-Indian activities, recognized an elderly herbalist as an Indian "medicine man," and at his death in 1972 left a vigorous and politically sophisticated Indian band emerging from poverty to relative comfort and strong ties with national Indian interests. The Poarch Creeks in northern Florida followed the Alabama path and received Federal recognition as an Indian tribe in 1984.

The Southern two-caste social system has favored the persistence of many groups of people who cannot document descent from a specific Indian tribe, but who insist they are primarily Indian, or Indian-white, rather than black. Scholars studying these groups suggest they should be termed "tri-racial isolates:" genetic tests indicate heredity from all three races and sufficient inbreeding (encouraged by miscegenation laws) to justify claiming distinctiveness. These genetic tests suggest that the groups cited below are about one-fifth Indian in ancestry, the remainder about equally divided between Euro-American and black. (Note that a greater component of their ancestors may have been culturally Indian than the genetics substantiate, since children with one Indian parent were considered Indian.) The principal tri-racial isolates in the South are the Lumbees of North Carolina, the Haliwa (in *Hali*fax and *War*ren Counties) of North Carolina, the Wesorts or Brandywine of Maryland, the Red Bones of Louisiana and Texas, the Brass Ankles of South Carolina, the Upper Cumberland River Cherokee of Kentucky, the Nanticokes or "Moors" of Delaware, the Guineas of the West Virginia–Ohio area, the Person County Indians of North Carolina, and at least a dozen other sets of families with long local histories of social isolation. There are, in addition, several isolates who resist classification as blacks but from whom genetic studies do not support the claim of Indian ancestry. The most numerous of these are the Melungeons of Alabama, Tennessee, Kentucky, and Virginia and the Cajans (not Louisiana Cajuns) of Alabama. The social isolation of these groups, as well as of the part-Indian isolates, stems in part from their bearing the economic stigmata of poorly educated people eking out subsistence on marginal land, in part from the persistence in some (but by no means all) communities of frontier cultural behavior rather than American middle-class proprieties, and in part from the discrimination suffered by those whose color, hair, or features fit the stereotype of some black ancestry. Breaking out of poverty by migrating to urban employment has been these peoples' avenue of escape from discouraging discrimination fed by the poor schooling they receive in their home localities. Poverty perpetuated by lack of education or training has been the key factor; the frontier cultural behavior can be considered an adaptation to poverty and lack of access to the institutions of the dominant castes. The tenuousness of the alleged racial attributes supposedly marking these isolates becomes clear when researchers discover that surnames and kinship ties, not appearance, are used in the localities to recognize members of the isolates.

The largest of the tri-racial groups claiming to be Indian are the Lumbees centered in Robeson County of North Carolina. A swampy area near the South Carolina border, the county was economically marginal until drainage projects were built in the twentieth century. The Lumbee, named from the Lumbee (sometimes spelled Lumber) River in Robeson County, are descended from frontier farmers found on the land by the first English and Scot homesteaders in the early eighteenth century. The farmers had no deeds to their land and appeared to be of mixed Euro-American and Indian ancestry. They resisted the settlement of the officially encouraged immigrants, but adjusted, like Indians of recognized tribes of that period, by

becoming enclaves practicing subsistence farming, materially similar to the more recent settlers but socially segregated. In 1835, North Carolina consolidated and strengthened the dominance of its Euro-American population by disenfranchising all "persons of color," Indians as well as blacks. Ensuing decades of frustration exploded in 1864 when Confederate home guards executed three Lumbee men for deserting a labor project to which they had been drafted, along with black slaves. Henry Berry Lowry (or Lowrie), a young relative of the executed men, recruited fellow Lumbee for what became a ten-year guerrilla war. Defeat of the Lowry Gang coincided with North Carolina's first real effort to build schools for all its youth. The Lumbees discovered that no provision was made for "persons of color" who were not black. Refusing to become black by sending their children to the only schools open to nonwhites, the Lumbees worked to obtain an Indian school, and through it, status as a third caste. Their county's representative in the state assembly was an amateur historian. Weighing his constituents' claim to be Indian against their lack of documented tribal identity, he suggested that they might be descendents of the colony Walter Raleigh set up on Roanoke Island in 1587. When a supply ship belatedly returned to Roanoke in 1591, no colonists were left, and the only possible clue to their fate was the word CROATOAN carved on a tree. If Raleigh's group had taken refuge with the Indians of Croatan town, a small, independent, Algonkian-speaking band, and eventually intermarried and moved with their hosts inland as the frontier developed, their descendants might have been the mixed-bloods farming in what became Robeson County. Satisfied with this historical possibility, in spite of its lack of documentation, the legislator in 1885 successfully introduced a bill designating his petitioners Croatan Indians and giving them separate schools. Two years later, not just a school but a normal school able to provide secondary education and teacher training was opened for the "Croatans." (This institution grew into a four-year college and then, in 1969, Pembroke State University.) Oddly, the aura of descent from Sir Walter's Lost Colony did little to ameliorate the discrimination and denigration to which the "Croatans" were subjected. In 1911, they petitioned the legislature to be known simply as "the Indians of Robeson County." This was apparently unsatisfactory too, so in 1913 the agreeable legislators "restored" their "ancient" name—Cherokees! With this, the Robeson County Indians requested that the federal Bureau of Indian Affairs take them as the "Siouan Tribes of the Lumber River." The Bureau of Indian Affairs could not discover justification for this claim, and refused. Finally, in 1953, North Carolina allowed the name Lumbee Indians to be recognized for the third caste in Robeson County, accepting the derivation from what is said to be the original Indian form of the name for the Lumber River, and in 1956, the United States recognized them as Indians, *but* not entitled to the federal benefits received by other tribes.

There are now at least thirty thousand Lumbees, one-third of the population of Robeson County. With such a large population, the Lumbees have enough political power to secure basic rights to land and education. Many families have moved to Baltimore for employment, and by occupying apartments in the same few blocks have created a Lumbee colony in that city. Lumbee do not speak any Indian language and have no distinctively Indian customs passed down through the generations in Robeson County, nor do many Lumbee look very obviously Indian. What makes them Indian is their shared sense of descent from people who were in North Carolina when the frontier was first forming, people who were not immigrants in the established colony and certainly were not slaves. This consciousness of descent from the precursors of the dominant castes in the South was recounted in 1940 in an "Indian pageant" developed with the assistance of Ella Deloria, a Lakota Sioux anthropologist (a student of Franz Boas) sent to Robeson County by the federal Farm Security Administration. Beginning in 1976, the Lumbees

have annually staged a drama, "Strike at the Wind," focusing on Henry Berry Lowry. Several Lumbee, including nationally known lawyers and legal scholars, have become active in pan-Indian activism, in addition to continuing to assert their Indian identity vis-à-vis the whites and blacks of Robeson County. The Lumbee-led United Indians of America helped a number of other nonrecognized Southeastern Indian communities achieve state recognition, at least, during the 1980s.

Lumbee success in gaining status as Indians rather than "persons of color" encouraged other North Carolina tri-racial isolates. Some of them had Lumbee teachers in their schools and have maintained intimate contact with Lumbee tactics and leaders. The Waccamaw Sioux, now numbering fifteen hundred members in three communities, obtained Lumbee teachers for their elementary school, built in 1933, and later for their high school. They finally were recognized by the state as an Indian tribe in 1971. In 1965, Indians in Halifax and Warren Counties persuaded the North Carolina legislature to designate them Haliwa Indians (they combined the names of the two counties to obtain a "tribal" name). The Haliwa Indian Club, organized in 1957, acts as a tribal council deciding, among other concerns, who may be classed as Indian in Halifax and Warren Counties. Some North Carolina Indians elsewhere have not yet come up with "tribal" designations, but remain, for example, "Sampson County Indians." By the early 1970s, the various Indian groups, including the Lumbees, had formed the Eastern Seaboard Coalition of Native Americans. With this organization the Lumbees and others are working to gain reservations and economic benefits available under Bureau of Indian Affairs programs. The "tri-racial isolates" are losing their isolation as they affirm their Indian status.

SUMMARY

By 2000 B.C. (the Late Archaic period), Southeastern Indians had developed their basic subsistence economy: deer supplemented by turkeys, other large birds, smaller game, fish, and shellfish for protein, and nuts and grains (maize and/or chenopods and amaranth) for carbohydrates. Houses of poles, wattle, and thatch were grouped in villages, some with central open plazas. About 1400 B.C., a planned town with a large plaza, a conical burial mound, and truncated pyramidal platform mounds was built on the lower Mississippi River, possibly as an Olmec trading outpost. From this period on, the Southeast was tied into a trading network stretching from Texas and Florida to the St. Lawrence River and the Great Lakes. In the first millennium B.C. and until A.D. 350, the Adena along the Ohio and then the Hopewell in Illinois and in Ohio evidenced stratified societies constructing massive earthworks and burying leaders in tombs furnished with skilled artisans' products often made from materials imported from locations a thousand miles away. The northern border of the Southeast experienced a decline between A.D. 350 and A.D. 750, perhaps caused by a climatic phase less suited to cultivated crops. After A.D. 750, the Midwest developed the Mississippian culture pattern, with large towns living on intensive cultivation of Northern Flint, an improved variety of maize for temperate America. Lower Mississippi Valley and Gulf Coast societies had not been affected by whatever had caused the decline in the Midwest, and had continued throughout the first millennium A.D. to grow in population and settlement complexity. These Deep South societies traded with the Mississippian and may have been sources for some of its population and cultural traits.

De Soto, the first European explorer of the Southeast, visited many Mississippian towns in 1540. His chroniclers describe stockaded towns that were independent or subordinate to one among a set of towns and were governed by chiefs who had been given many symbols of elevated rank. The bones of deceased chiefs were kept in town temples, sometimes built on platform mounds, and were attended by priests. These towns with plazas

and platform mounds were late Mississippian. The fully historic period begins in the seventeenth century. There seems to have been a population decline in the latter sixteenth century, perhaps brought about by European diseases inadvertently introduced by de Soto's and other expeditions (whose members record much suffering from disease in their parties; de Soto himself died of a fever in the lower Mississippi Valley). Creations of Mississippian society that were costly in manpower, such as platform mounds, seem to have been abandoned by the seventeenth century. Southeastern Indians then continued to live in autonomous or confederated towns with central public plazas surrounded by men's meeting lodges and a temple. Societies were structured upon matrilineal clans, which were represented in town councils chaired by chiefs. Ritual distinctions between White, or peace maintained by diplomacy and compromise, and Red, or war, articulated relationships between younger and older persons and between towns. The highlight of the year was the Green Corn Festival, celebrating New Year and the beginning of harvest with the kindling of new fires, prayers of thanks to the Almighty, dances, and ball games.

Euro-American colonization began on the relatively underpopulated Atlantic coast, with its extensive swamps. Trade in deer hides and captive Indians to be sold as slaves grew rapidly after it commenced in 1670 between Indians and English colonists in Carolina. English settlement inland invaded the homelands of the principal Indian groups, the Muskogean speakers and the Cherokees. Indians adopted Euro-American material items, especially crops, metal tools, houses, and clothing, and during the eighteenth century were slowly forced to adjust their political practices to better meet the threat of Euro-American conquest. By the early nineteenth century, the Creek and Cherokee nations, as well as the Choctaw and Chickasaw just west of them and the Seminole who had moved into Florida, had a number of leaders living like Euro-American gentry upon plantations, and the bulk of their people possessing most of the appurtenances of their Euro-American neighbors. For this reason, these five Indian groups came to be termed the Five Civilized Tribes. Notwithstanding their demonstrated capability to fit within American society, during the 1830s and 1840s most of the thousands of members of the Five Civilized Tribes were evacuated from their homelands and removed with much suffering to eastern Oklahoma. These removals were designed to free the Southeast for Euro-American settlement and to guard the United States' western border from France, Spain, and western Indians with a buffer of civilized tribes placed before the solid bloc of Euro-Americans east of the Arkansas River.

After removal, the Five Tribes in Oklahoma Territory replayed their earlier history of building prosperous farms and towns under their native governments, only to be manipulated into giving them up, parcel by parcel, under the United States policies of forcing the Indians westward before Euro-American expansion. In 1887, the Dawes Act struck at the heart of Indian societies by allotting tribal land to individual families. Millions of acres of Indian land were declared surplus and no longer reservation, or lost as unscrupulous Euro-American speculators gained title to the homesteads of politically friendless Indians. The Indian Reorganization Act of 1934 halted the loss of most remaining land, but, coming during the Depression and Dust Bowl conditions, could not immediately improve the situation of Oklahoma Indians.

After World War II, eastern Oklahoma experienced an exodus of rural individuals into urban employment. The more conservative Indians, lacking education or training to obtain better jobs, found themselves in economically depressed regions. Indian activism, begun in the 1960s, is ameliorating the poverty of many conservative families and allowing young Indian people to take advantage of economic opportunities without feeling pressured to reject their Indian heritage. One component of that heritage, the Stomp Dance, has become an object of pan-Indian sharing as one of the most popular social dances for young Indian men and women.

In the Southeast, remnants of the Five Civilized Tribes and mixed-blood enclaves of families probably descended in part from coastal Algonkian Indians or other smaller groups persisted on marginal lands. Through the late nineteenth century and early twentieth century, they resisted being lumped with blacks in the Southern two-caste social structure. Discriminated against as "persons of color," barred from white schools and refusing to send their children to black schools, they agitated for separate Indian schools. Usually poorly educated or even illiterate, and with little or no land, the small communities of tribal Indians and the "tri-racial isolates" one by one have been winning recognition as Indians and demanding participation in Bureau of Indian Affairs programs that would benefit them. The most successful of these groups have been the Seminoles, Choctaws, Eastern Creeks and Eastern Cherokees among the tribal remnants, and the Lumbees among the "tri-racial isolates." The success of these groups has called attention to the persistence of substantial Indian populations (160,000 people according to the 1980 census) in the Southeast today in spite of the earlier policies of removal.

RECOMMENDED READING

Blu, Karen I. 1980 *The Lumbee Problem: The Making of an American Indian People.* Cambridge, England: Cambridge University Press.

Fagan, Brian M. 1991 *Ancient North America.* New York: W.W. Norton (distributor for Thames and Hudson).

Gabarino, Merwyn S. 1972 *Big Cypress: A Changing Seminole Community.* Prospect Heights, Ill.: Waveland Press. Vivid personal picture of modern Seminole.

Hudson, Charles M. 1976 *The Southeastern Indians.* Knoxville: University of Tennessee Press. Readable generalized description of culture and history.

Merrell, James E. 1989 *The Indians' New World.* Chapel

Hill: University of North Carolina Press. History sensitive to the viewpoint of the indigenous Indians.

O'Gorman, Edmundo 1961 *The Invention of America.* Bloomington: Indiana University Press. Fascinating discussion of the revolution in European cosmology occurring during the fifteenth and sixteenth centuries, and its importance to America.

Swanton, John R. 1946 *The Indians of the Southeastern United States.* Washington, D.C.: Smithsonian Institution, Bureau of American Ethnology, Bulletin 137. The classic, encyclopedic compendium of information on the subject. Includes hundreds of vivid descriptions directly quoted from early visitors.

Wax, Murray L. 1971 *Indian Americans.* Englewood Cliffs, N.J.: Prentice-Hall, Inc. Includes excellent chapter on Oklahoma Cherokees.

Wright, J. Leitch, Jr. 1981 *The Only Land They Knew.* New York: The Free Press. Well-written history of the Southeast Indians.

SOURCES FOR THE FIRST EDITION

Appleby, Joyce. 1978 The Social Origins of American Revolutionary Ideology. *Journal of American History* 65:935–958.

Baerreis, David A., and Reid A. Bryson. 1965 Climatic Episodes and the Dating of Mississippian Cultures. *The Wisconsin Archeologist* 46:203–220.

Bender, Margaret M., and David A. Baerreis. 1979 Further Light on Carbon Isotopes and Hopewell Agriculture. Paper presented to the 1979 Midwest Archaeological Conference, Milwaukee, Wisconsin.

Berry, Brewton. 1963 *Almost White.* New York: Macmillan.

Bowers, Alfred W. 1950 *Mandan Social and Ceremonial Organization.* Chicago: University of Chicago Press.

Brown, James A. 1973 Spiro Art and Its Mortuary Contexts. In E. Benson (ed.). *Death and the Afterlife in Precolumbian America.* Washington, D.C.: Dumbarton Oaks Research Library and Collections, pp. 1–32.

———— 1977 The Southern Cult Reconsidered. *Mid - Continental Journal of Archaeology* 1:115–135.

Bullen, Ripley P. 1966 Stelae at the Crystal River Site, Florida. *American Antiquity* 31:861–865.

Chomko, Stephen A., and Gary W. Crawford. 1978 Plant Husbandry in Prehistoric Eastern North America: New Evidence for its Development. *American Antiquity* 43: 405–408.

Corkran, David H. 1962 *The Cherokee Frontier.* Norman: University of Oklahoma Press.

———— 1967 *The Creek Frontier.* Norman: University of Oklahoma Press.

Densmore, Frances. 1956 *Seminole Music.* Washington, D.C.: Smithsonian Institution, Bureau of American Ethnology, Bulletin 161.

Dial, Adolph, and David K. Eliades. 1972 The Lumbee Indians and Pembroke State University. In J.Henry (ed.). *The American Indian Reader: Education.* San Francisco: Indian Historian Press, pp. 51–60.

Fairbridge, Rhodes W. 1977 Discussion Paper: Late Quaternary Environments in Northeastern Coastal North America. *Annals, New York Academy of Sciences* 288:90–92.

Fenton, William, and John Gulick, eds. 1961 *Symposium on Cherokee and Iroquois Culture.* Washington, D.C.: Smithsonian Institution, Bureau of American Ethnology, Bulletin 180.

Fischer, Ann. 1968 History and Current Status of the Houma Indians. In S. Levine and N.O. Lurie, (eds.). *The American Indian Today.* Baltimore: Penguin Books, pp. 212–235.

Fogelson, Raymond D. 1977 Cherokee Notions of Power. In R.D. Fogelson and R.N. Adams, (eds.). *The Anthropology of Power.* New York: Academic Press, pp. 185–194.

Ford, James A. 1969 *A Comparison of Formative Cultures in the Americas.* Washington, D.C.: Smithsonian Institution Press.

Fowler, Melvin L. 1969 Middle Mississippian Agricultural Fields. *American Antiquity* 34:365–375.

Fowler, Melvin L., ed. 1969 *Explorations into Cahokia Archaeology.* Springfield: Illinois Archaeological Survey, Bulletin 7.

———— 1975 *Perspectives in Cahokia Archeology.* Springfield: Illinois Archeological Survey, Bulletin 10.

Gearing, Fred. 1962 *Priests and Warriors.* American Anthropological Association, Memoir 93.

Gilbert, William Harlen, Jr. 1943 *The Eastern Cherokees.* Washington, D.C.: Smithsonian Institution, Bureau of American Ethnology, Bulletin 133, Anthropological Paper 23.

Gregory, Hiram F. 1977 Jena Band of Louisiana Choctaw. *American Indian Journal* 3:2–16.

———— 1978 Personal communication, May 23, 1978.

Griessman, B. Eugene, ed. 1972 The American Isolates. *American Anthropologist* 74:693–734, 1276–1306.

Griffin, James B. 1966 Mesoamerica and the Eastern United States in Prehistoric Times. In R. Wauchope, (ed.). *Handbook of Middle American Indians*. Austin: University of Texas Press, pp. 111–131.

Gulick, John. 1960 *Cherokees at the Crossroads*. Chapel Hill: Institute for Research in Social Science, University of North Carolina.

Hall, Robert L. 1973 The Cahokia Presence Outside of the American Bottoms. Paper read at the Central States Anthropological Society annual meeting, St. Louis, 1973.

Hodge, Frederick Webb, ed. 1910 *Handbook of American Indians*. Washington, D.C.: Smithsonian Institution, Bureau of American Ethnology, Bulletin 30.

Illinois Archaeological Survey, ed. 1965 Middle Woodland Sites in Illinois. Illinois Archaeological Survey, Bulletin 5.

Keel, Bennie C. 1976 *Cherokee Archaeology*. Knoxville: University of Tennessee Press.

Kellar, J.H., A.R. Kelley, and E.V. McMichael. 1962 The Mandeville Site in Southwest Georgia. *American Antiquity* 27:336–355.

Kilpatrick, Jack Frederick, ed. 1966 *The Wahnenauhi Manuscript: Historical Sketches of the Cherokees*. Washington, D.C.: Smithsonian Institution, Bureau of American Ethnology, Bulletin 196, Anthropological Paper 77.

Kroeber, Alfred L. 1939 *Cultural and Natural Areas of Native North America*. Berkeley: University of California Press.

Kupferer, Harriet Jane. 1966 *The "Principal People," 1960: A Study of Cultural and Social Groups of the Eastern Cherokee*. Washington, D.C.: Smithsonian Institution, Bureau of American Ethnology, Bulletin 196, Anthropological Paper 78.

Larson, Lewis H., Jr. 1971 *Archaeological Implications of Social Stratification at the Etowah Site, Georgia*. Society for American Archaeology, Memoir 25, pp. 58–67.

Littlefield, Daniel F., Jr. 1977 *Africans and Seminoles*. Westport, Conn.: Greenwood Press.

Mooney, James. 1891 *The Sacred Formulas of the Cherokees*. Washington, D.C.: Smithsonian Institution, Bureau of Ethnology, Seventh Annual Report, pp. 307–397.

———— 1900 *Myths of the Cherokees*. Washington, D.C.: Smithsonian Institution, Bureau of American Ethnology, Nineteenth Annual Report, pp. 3–576.

Munson, Patrick J., Paul W. Parmalee, and Richard A. Yarnell. 1971 Subsistence Ecology of Scovill, a Terminal Middle Woodland Village. *American Antiquity* 36:41–431.

Newell, H. Perry, and Alex D. Krieger. 1949 *The George C. Davis Site*. Society for American Archaeology, Memoir 5.

Ogden, J. Gordon, III. 1977 The Late Quaternary Paleoenvironmental Record of Northeastern North America. *Annals, New York Academy of Sciences* 288:16–34.

Paredes, J. Anthony. 1974 The Emergence of Contemporary Eastern Creek Indian Identity. In T.K. Fitzgerald (ed.). *Social and Cultural Identity*. Southern Anthropological Society, *Proceedings* 8:63–80.

Prucha, F. P. 1969 Andrew Jackson's Indian Policy: A Reassessment. *Journal of American History* 56:527–539.

Prufer, Olaf H. 1965 *The McGraw Site*. Cleveland: Cleveland Museum of Natural History Scientific Publications, n.s. 4(1).

Quinn, David B. 1977 *North America from Earliest Discovery to First Settlements*. New York: Harper and Row.

Reed, Nelson, A., John W. Bennett, and James Warren Porter. 1968 Solid Core Drilling of Monks Mound: Technique and Findings. *American Antiquity* 33:137–148.

Satz, Ronald N. 1975 *American Indian Policy in the Jacksonian Era*. Lincoln: University of Nebraska Press.

Schoenwetter, James. 1974 Pollen Analysis of Human Paleofeces from Upper Salts Cave. In P.J. Watson (ed.). *Archeology of the Mammoth Cave Area*. New York: Academic Press, pp. 49–58.

Sears, William H. 1977 Seaborne Contacts between Early Cultures in Lower Southeastern United States and Middle through South America. In E.P. Benson, (ed.). *The Sea in the Pre-Columbian World*. Washington, D.C.: Dumbarton Oaks Research Library and Collections, pp 1–15.

Stoltman, James B. 1974 *Groton Plantation*. Cambridge, Mass.: Peabody Museum of Archaeology and Ethnology.

Traveller Bird. 1971 *Tell Them They Lie*. Los Angeles: Westernlore Publishers.

Van Every, Dale. 1966 *Disinherited: The Lost Birth-*

right of the American Indian. New York: William & Co.

Vickery, Kent D. 1970 Evidence Supporting the Theory of Climatic Change and the Decline of Hopewell. *Wisconsin Archeologist* 51:57–76.

Voegelin, C. F., and F. M. Voegelin. 1965 *Languages of the World: Native America,* Fascicle #2. Bloomington: Indiana University, Anthropological Linguistics 7(7).

Wahrhaftig, Albert L. 1968 The Tribal Cherokee Population of Eastern Oklahoma. *Current Anthropology* 9:510–518.

Wahrhaftig, Albert L., and Jane Lukens–Wahrhaftig. 1977 The Thrice Powerless: Cherokee Indians in Oklahoma. In R.D. Fogelson and R.N. Adams,(eds.). *The Anthropology of Power.* New York: Academic Press, pp. 225–236.

Wardell, Morris L. 1938 *A Political History of the Cherokee Nation, 1838–1907.* Norman: University of Oklahoma Press.

Watson, Patty Jo, and Richard A. Yarnell. 1966 Archaeological and Paleoethnobotanical Investigations in Salts Cave, Mammoth Cave National Park, Kentucky. *American Antiquity* 31:842–849.

Webb, Clarence H. 1968 The Extent and Content of Poverty Point Culture. *American Antiquity* 33:297–321.

Wilkins, Thurman. 1970 *Cherokee Tragedy.* New York: Macmillan Co.

Wing, Elizabeth S. 1977 Subsistence Systems in the Southeast. *Florida Anthropologist* 30:81–87.

Witthoft, John. 1949 Green Corn Ceremonialism in the Eastern Woodlands. Ann Arbor: Museum of Anthropology, University of Michigan, Occasional Contribution 13.

ADDITIONAL SOURCES FOR THE SECOND EDITION

Anderson, David G., and Glen T. Hanson. 1988 Early Archaic Settlement in the Southeastern United States: A Case Study from the Savannah River Valley. *American Antiquity* 53(2):262–286.

Blanchard, Kendall. 1981 *The Mississippi Choctaws at Play: The Serious Side of Leisure.* Urbana: University of Illinois Press.

Blu, Karen I. 1980 *The Lumbee Problem.* Cambridge: Cambridge University Press.

Brandon, William. 1986 *New Worlds for Old.* Athens: Ohio University Press.

Brasseaux, Carl A., and Michael J. Leblanc. 1982 Franco-Indian Diplomacy in the Mississippi Valley 1754–1763: Prelude to Pontiac's Uprising? *Journal de la Société des Américanistes* 68:59–71.

Brecher, Kenneth, and William G. Haag. 1983 Astronomical Alignments at Poverty Point. *American Antiquity* 48(1):161–163.

Brose, David S., and N'omi Greber, eds. 1979 *Hopewell Archaeology.* Kent, Ohio: Kent State University Press.

Campbell, Lyle, and Marianne Mithun, eds. 1979 *The Languages of Native America.* Austin: University of Texas Press.

Chapman, Jefferson, and Gary D. Crites. 1987 Evidence for Early Maize (*Zea Mays*) from the Icehouse Bottom Site, Tennessee. *American Antiquity* 52(2):352–354.

Claassen, Cheryl. 1986 Shellfishing Seasons in the Prehistoric Southeastern United States. *American Antiquity* 51(1):21–37.

Crites, Gary D. 1987 Human-Plant Mutualism and Niche Expression in the Paleoethnobotanical Record: A Middle Woodland Example. *American Antiquity* 52(4):725–740.

Dincauze, Dena F. 1989 Geoarchaeology in New England: an Early Holocene Heat Spell? *The Review of Archaeology* 10(2):1–4.

Dobyns, Henry F. 1983 *Their Number Become Thinned.* Knoxville: University of Tennessee Press.

Doran, Glen H., David N. Dickel, and Lee A. Newsom. 1990 A 7,290-Year-Old Bottle Gourd from the Windover Site, Florida. *American Antiquity* 55(2):354–360.

Doyon-Bernard, S. J. 1990 From Twining to Triple Cloth: Experimentation and Innovation in Ancient Peruvian Weaving (ca. 5000–400 B.C.). *American Antiquity* 55(1):68–87.

Drechsel, Emanuel J. 1982 Structure and Function in Mobilian Jargon: Indications for the Pre-European Existence of an American Indian Pidgin. Ann Arbor: *Proceedings, Second Annual Symposium on Historical Linguistics and Philology.*

Finger, John R. 1984 *The Eastern Band of Cherokees, 1819–1900.* Knoxville: University of Tennessee Press.

Fitzhugh, William W., ed. 1985 *Cultures in Contact.* Washington, D.C.: Smithsonian Institution Press.

Ford, Richard I., ed. 1985 *Prehistoric Food Production in North America*. Ann Arbor: Museum of Anthropology, University of Michigan, Anthropological Papers, no. 75.

Fritz, Gayle J. 1984 Identification of Cultigen Amaranth and Chenopod from Rockshelter Sites in Northwest Arkansas. *American Antiquity* 49(3):558–572.

Gardner, Paul S. 1987 New Evidence Concerning the Chronology and Paleoethnobotany of Salts Cave, Kentucky. *American Antiquity* 52(2):358–367.

Gradie, Robert. 1984 Colonizing Pigs. In W. Cowan (ed.). *Papers of the Fifteenth Algonquian Conference*. Ottawa: Carleton University, pp. 147–169.

Green, Michael D. 1982 *The Politics of Indian Removal*. Lincoln: University of Nebraska Press.

Griffith, Benjamin W., Jr. 1988 *McIntosh and Weatherford, Creek Indian Leaders*. Tuscaloosa: University of Alabama Press.

Hann, John H. 1988 *Apalachee*. Gainesville: University of Florida Press.

Hantman, Jeffrey L. 1990 Between Powhatan and Quirank: Reconstructing Monacan Culture and History in the Context of Jamestown. *American Anthropologist* 92(3):676–690.

Harn, Alan D. 1986 The Eveland Site: Inroad to Spoon River Mississippian Society. Paper presented at Society for American Archaeology, 51st annual meeting, New Orleans.

Hatch, James W., Joseph W. Michels, Christopher M. Stevenson, Barry E. Scheetz, and Richard A. Geidel. 1990 Hopewell Obsidian Studies: Behavioral Implications of Recent Sourcing and Dating Research. *American Antiquity* 55(3):461–479.

Hickey, Joseph V. and Charles E. Webb. 1985 *The Lyons Serpent: Speculations on the Indian as Geographer*. Emporia, Kan.: Emporia State University, Research Studies XXXIII(4).

Keegan, William F., ed. 1987 *Emergent Horticultural Economies of the Eastern Woodlands*. Carbondale: Southern Illinois University, Center for Archaeological Investigations, Occasional Paper No. 7.

Kersey, Harry A. 1975 *Pelts, Plumes, and Hides*. Gainesville: Florida Atlantic University Press.

———— 1989 *The Florida Seminoles and the New Deal, 1933–1942*. Boca Raton: Florida Atlantic University Press.

King, Duane H., ed. 1979 *The Cherokee Indian Nation: A Troubled History*. Knoxville: University of Tennessee Press.

Kniffen, Fred B., Hiram F. Gregory, and George A. Stokes. 1987 *The Historic Indian Tribes of Louisiana*. Baton Rouge: Louisiana State University Press.

Knight, Vernon James, Jr. 1986 The Institutional Organization of Mississippian Religion. *American Antiquity* 51(4):675–687.

Laub, Richard S., Norton G. Miller, David W. Steadman, eds. 1988 *Late Pleistocene and Early Holocene Paleoecology and Archeology of the Eastern Great Lakes Region*. Buffalo: Buffalo Society of Natural Sciences, *Bulletin*, vol. 33.

Lerch, Patricia B. 1990 Pan-Indianism and Identity among the Waccamaw. Paper read at 89th American Anthropological Association annual meeting, New Orleans.

Lincoln, Charles E. 1985 Cahokia and the American Bottom: Evolutionary Sequence or Social Hierarchy? Seminar paper in possession of author.

Lynott, Mark J., Thomas W. Boutton, James E. Price, and Dwight E. Nelson. 1986 Stable Carbon Isotopic Evidence for Maize Agriculture in Southeast Missouri and Northeast Arkansas. *American Antiquity* 51(1):51–65.

Mainfort, Robert C., Jr. 1988 Middle Woodland Ceremonialism at Pinson Mounds, Tennessee. *American Antiquity* 53(1):158–173.

McLoughlin, William G. 1990 *Champions of the Cherokees: Evan and John B. Jones*. Princeton: Princeton University Press.

Merrell, James H. 1989 *The Indians' New World*. Chapel Hill: University of North Carolina Press.

Milanich, Jerald T., and Charles H. Fairbanks. 1980 *Florida Archaeology*. New York: Academic Press.

Milanich, Jerald T., and Susan Milbrath. 1989 *First Encounters*. Gainesville: University of Florida Press.

Munson, Patrick J., ed. 1984 *Experiments and Observations on Aboriginal Wild Plant Utilization in Eastern North America*. Bloomington: Indiana Historical Society, Prehistory Research Series VI(2).

O'Brien, Michael J. 1987 Sedentism, Population Growth, and Resource Selection in the Woodland Midwest: A Review of Coevolutionary Developments. *Current Anthropology* 28(2):177–197.

O'Brien, Patricia J. 1988 Cahokia: The Political Economy and Economic Capital of the 'Ramey' State. Unpublished paper, presented in part at the 12th International Congress of Anthropological and Ethnological Sciences, Zagreb, Yugoslavia.

O'Brien, Sharon. 1989 *American Indian Tribal Govern-ments*. Norman: University of Oklahoma Press.

O'Donnell, James Howlett, III. 1982 *Southeastern Frontiers: Europeans, Africans, and American Indi-ans, 1513–1840: A Critical Bibliography*. Bloom-ington: Indiana University Press.

Palmer, Stanley H., and Dennis Reinhartz, eds. 1988 *Essays on the History of North American Discovery and Exploration*. College Station: Texas A&M Uni-versity Press.

Paredes, J. Anthony. 1990 Pan-Indianism and the Larger Society. Paper read at 89th American An-thropological Association annual meeting, New Orleans.

Peebles, Christopher S. 1986 Paradise Lost, Strayed, and Stolen: Prehistoric Social Devolution in the Southeast. In M.Richardson and M.C. Webb (eds.). *The Burden of Being Civilized*. Athens, Ga.: Univer-sity of Georgia Press, pp. 24–40.

Perdue, Theda. 1979 *Slavery and the Evolution of Cherokee Society, 1540–1866*. Knoxville: Univer-sity of Tennessee Press.

Perttula, Timothy K., and James E. Bruseth. 1983 Early Caddoan Subsistence Strategies, Sabine River Basin, East Texas. *Plains Anthropologist* 28(99):9–21.

Philips, James L., and James A. Brown, eds. 1983 *Archaic Hunters and Gatherers in the American Midwest*. New York: Academic Press.

Powell, Mary Lucas. 1988 *Status and Health in Prehistory: A Case Study of the Moundville Chief-dom*. Washington, D.C.: Smithsonian Institution Press.

Prentice, Guy. 1986 An Analysis of the Symbolism Expressed by the Birger Figurine. *American Antiq-uity* 51(2):239–266.

Prucha, Francis Paul. 1981 *Indian Policy in the United States*. Lincoln: University of Nebraska Press.

——— 1984 *The Great Father*. Lincoln: University of Nebraska Press.

Purdy, Barbara A. 1988 American Indians After A.D. 1492: A Case Study of Forced Culture Change. *American Anthropologist* 90(3):640–655.

Quinn, David Beers. 1985 *Set Fair for Roanoke*. Chapel Hill: University of North Carolina Press.

Reeves, Carolyn Keller, ed. 1985 *The Choctaw Before Removal*. Jackson: University Press of Mississippi.

Riley, Thomas J., Richard Edging, and Jack Rossen. 1990 Cultigens in Prehistoric Eastern North Amer-ica. *Current Anthropology* 31(5):525–541.

Rountree, Helen C. 1989 *The Powhatan Indians of Virginia*. Norman: University of Oklahoma Press.

——— 1990 "Indian Country" in Ole Virginny. Paper read at 89th American Anthropological Association annual meeting, New Orleans.

Sears, William H. 1982 *Fort Center*. Gainesville: University Presses of Florida.

Sheehan, Bernard W. 1980 *Savagism and Civility*. Cam-bridge: Cambridge University Press.

Smith, Bruce D. 1989 Origins of Agriculture in Eastern North America. *Science* 246:1566–1571.

Smith, Bruce D., and C. Wesley Cowan. 1987 Domes-ticated Chenopodium in Prehistoric Eastern North America: New Accelerator Dates from Eastern Ken-tucky. *American Antiquity* 52(2):355–357.

Smith, Bruce D., ed. 1978 *Mississippian Settlement Patterns*. New York: Academic Press.

——— 1990 *The Mississippian Emergence*. Washing-ton, D.C.: Smithsonian Institution Press.

Smith, Marvin T. 1987 *Archaeology of Aboriginal Culture Change in the Interior Southeast*. Gaines-ville: University of Florida Press.

Snipp, C. Matthew. 1989 *American Indians: The First of This Land*. New York: Russell Sage Foun-dation.

Steponaitis, Vincas P. 1986 Prehistoric Archaeology in the Southeastern United States, 1970–1985. *Annual Review of Anthropology* 15:363–404.

Voss, Jerome A., and John H. Blitz. 1988 Archaeologi-cal Investigations in the Choctaw Homeland. *Ameri-can Antiquity* 53(1):125–145.

Wells, Samuel J., and Roseanna Tubby. 1986 *After Removal: The Choctaw in Mississippi*. Jackson: University Press of Mississippi.

Weslager, C.A. 1983 *The Nanticoke Indians—Past and Present*. Newark: University of Delaware Press.

White, Richard. 1983 *The Roots of Dependency*. Lin-coln: University of Nebraska Press.

Williams, Robert A., Jr. 1990 *The American Indian in Western Legal Thought*. New York: Oxford Univer-sity Press.

Williams, Walter L., ed. 1979 *Southeastern Indians Since the Removal Era*. Athens: University of Geor-gia Press.

Witthoft, John. 1967 Glazed Polish on Flint Tools. *American Antiquity* 32(3):383–388.

Wood, Peter H., Gregory A. Waselkov, and M. Thomas Hatley, eds. 1989 *Powhatan's Mantle*. Lincoln: University of Nebraska Press.

Wright, J. Leitch, Jr. 1981 *The Only Land They Knew*. New York: The Free Press.

Yerkes, Richard W. 1988 The Woodland and Mississippian Traditions in the Prehistory of Midwestern North America. *Journal of World Prehistory* 2(3):307–358.

Young, Mary. 1989 Tribal Reorganization in the Southeast, 1800–1840. Paper delivered at the Newberry Library Conference on Themes in American Indian History II, Chicago, February 17, 1989.

5

THE NORTHEAST

Northeastern North America may be divided into four areas: (1) the Atlantic coastal plain and piedmont, from the Mason-Dixon line (Maryland and Delaware) north to southern Maine; (2) the Maritimes—for our purposes, northern Maine as well as the Canadian Maritimes of New Brunswick, Nova Scotia, Newfoundland, and southeastern Labrador; (3) the St. Lawrence River-lower Great Lakes (Erie, Huron, Ontario), excluding the river's mouth (in the Maritimes); and (4) the Boreal forest and tundra of northeastern Canada. None of these regions is sharply bounded either ecologically or topographically. All, except the tundra on the far north, are dominated by forest cover, although the three more southern regions contain river and coastal meadows, some once maintained by Indian burning. The Appalachians form a massive series of ridges and domes cutting the Atlantic slope from the continental interior, but the Delaware Water Gap, the Mohawk Valley, and the St. Lawrence give comfortable access to the Midwest. The Northeastern Indians were the true "red men," so called because the northern peoples covered exposed portions of their skin with a mixture of bear grease and red-ocher pigment for protection from wind chapping and cold in the winter and mosquitoes and flies in the summer. These were the storybook Indians who skulked through dark forests, canoed blue waters, offered armloads of furs, and gave us the words tomahawk, squaw, papoose, wigwam, squash, powwow, and sachem. The "Last of the Mohicans," Hiawatha, Squanto, and the Iroquois chiefs "straight as a pine tree" lived in the Northeast. Here the stereotypes are the oldest and the most strongly distorted by propaganda. Here the myths to legitimatize English conquests were constructed. The Iroquois carve grotesque, twisted masks for the spirits of their forests; these false faces could represent the Indians themselves as created in nearly five centuries of their enemies' tracts, novels, and history books. Winnowing a valid story from the sheaves of documents on the Northeast is a challenging task.

Inuit (Eskimo)

Norse

Naskapi

Montagnais

L'Anse aux Meadow

Beothuk

Ojibwa

Cree

BOREAL FOREST
(CANADIAN SHIELD)

Nipissing

MARITIMES

Ottawa

Algonkian

Abenaki

Micmac

Malecite
Passamaquoddy
Penobscot

LAURENTIAN LAKES

Huron

Tionontati
Neutral

Mohawk
Oneida
Onondaga
Cayuga

Massachusett

Seneca

Mahican

Wampanoag

Green Bay

Narragansett

Menominee
Winnebago

Erie

Pequot

Susquehannock

Delaware

ATLANTIC SLOPE

MAP 6 The Northeast

225

SECTION 1: THE ARCHAIC, EARLY WOODLAND, AND MIDDLE WOODLAND PERIODS

Human population in the Northeast shows a slow and steady rise from the Paleo-Indian period through the Late Archaic period. Until about 4500 B.C., Northeastern people were primarily hunters, of deer in the southern sectors, caribou in the north, and sea mammals along the northern coast. Most of the evidence of human habitation is no more than scattered finds of one or a few stone projectile points. The rarity of campsites may at least in part reflect preference for living near the coast, where seals and swordfish would have been attractive resources. Unfortunately, this supposition cannot be tested because up to 100 kilometers (about 60 miles) of the former coastal plain has been drowned by the rise in sea level between the end of the Pleistocene epoch and 4500 B.C. Attempts to discover archaeological remains by using divers or dredges on this underwater continental shelf have not been successful. If the guess is correct that humans would have clustered where sea and land resources are equally accessible—near the coast—then the lone projectile points recovered from the Early Archaic period represent hunting trips, probably for deer, elk, and bear, taken by people who used only the most temporary shelter when stopping overnight inland. Their villages will have disappeared. A hint at the life of Middle Archaic people in the Northeast comes from the death of one of their children at the Strait of Belle Isle, where the Quebec and Labrador boundary faces Newfoundland across the sea channel. Here, about 5300 B.C. in radiocarbon years, a young teenager (whether boy or girl could not be determined) was buried face down in a sandy pit. Two fires were lit, one on each side of the body. A walrus tusk was placed in front of the face, three stone knives, a harpoon, and a set of red-ocher and graphite (lead) pebbles, with an antler tine for crushing and mixing them into paint, were put with the body, and a cache of stone and bone projectile

points was laid near the head. A bone pendant and a whistle with three stops hung on a cord around the youth's neck. One of the shovels used to dig the grave pit, a section of caribou antler, was discarded in the pit. Over the torso a slab of rock was laid, then sand was heaped into the grave, then two parallel rows of three slabs of rock set upright were placed over the grave, and finally the whole was buried under a low mound of sand topped with three layers of boulders from a nearby stream. The excavators estimated that it would have taken the adults of the whole hunting band, say fifteen to twenty families, a week to dig the grave pit and then construct the mound. Presumably not everyone who died was given such elaborate and expensive (in terms of labor) burial; why this young person was so honored (or singled out) we cannot know. We are grateful that the grave tells us that as far north as southern Labrador and as early as around 5300 B.C., walruses and caribou were hunted by the same people (confirming our hypothesis that coastal and inland resources were both utilized by the typical band of the period), that efficient toggle harpoons were already invented, that mineral pigments were mixed for paint, that musical whistles were made, and that people invested as much as a week in ceremonies.

The Late Archaic

The Late Archaic period, from about 3000 B.C. to about 700 B.C., was an optimal period in the Northeast. The sea level had stabilized about 4500 B.C., allowing the growth of beds of shellfish. The climatic thermal maximum of the warming trend beginning at the end of the Pleistocene epoch encouraged the spread as far north as southern New England of hickory trees, which provided nuts for human food—both oil and flour, if ground—and mast for deer. Salmon, smelt, shad, herring, and alewives had established annual runs, sturgeon could be speared in the rivers, and cod, bass, swordfish, and other fish could be taken with hooks. The list of faunal remains from an

THE NORTHEAST CHRONOLOGY

1980	Strengthening of Indian communities, demands for recognition as Indian
	American Indian Movement nationalistic activism begins
1960	
	Revival of New England Algonkian nationality
1900	
	Surviving Algonkians in southern New England detribalized
	Eastern Algonkians in Ohio removed west
1800	Handsome Lake's revival
	Iroquois on reservations
	American Revolution
	French America ceded to Britain
1700	
	King Philip's War
	Hudson's Bay Company established
	Huron towns exterminated
	Pequot War
	Champlain allies with Hurons; Dutch colonization, New York; English colonization, New England
1600	
	League of the Iroquois founded
	Cartier on the St. Lawrence
1500	Newfoundland commercial fisheries begin Europe-America fur trade

LATE WOODLAND

1000	Agriculture begins, southern Northeast Norse in Labrador, Newfoundland

A.D.	**MIDDLE WOODLAND**
B.C.	

"EARLY WOODLAND"

700	
1000	**LATE ARCHAIC**
3000	**MIDDLE ARCHAIC**
4500	**EARLY ARCHAIC**
7000	**PALEO-INDIAN**

occupation site on an island in Penobscot Bay, Maine, dated 3000 B.C. demonstrates the richness of resources harvested by Northeastern Late Archaic people: deer, moose, seal, walrus, beaver, mink, sea mink (an extinct species), river otter, fisher, bear; swordfish, cod, sturgeon, sculpin;

mallard, black and old squaw ducks, Canada goose, loon, eagle; and shellfish. Plant remains were not recovered from this site, which would have been too far north for the hickories and sweet acorns that were valuable foods south of Maine.

Relatively dense populations attained by the Late Archaic period, 3000 B.C., maintained cultural traditions that were, in part, adaptations to regional environments but also, in part, stylistic traditions probably marking ethnic heritages. In the Southern sector, the peak in hickory and white oak (which bore "sweet" acorns having relatively little tannic acid) around 2000 B.C. is associated with the northward spread of a southern type of Late Archaic culture pattern, called Lamoka in the interior and Susquehanna on the Atlantic slope. At the Lamoka site, from which the interior pattern is named, in central New York south of the eastern part of Lake Ontario, excavations have revealed a substantial village of about twenty-seven houses, rectangular in shape and measuring around 16 by 12 feet (4.9 by 3.7 meters). Small, round hearth pits and a few large, long rectangular roasting beds full of charred acorns were used by the villagers for food preparation, and pits deep and wide enough for a person to stand in were used for food storage. Situated on a lakeshore, the people hunted deer with atlatl-propelled javelins and with spears, and fished with nets and with hooks. Their manufacture of wooden objects is attested by stone celts, adzes and chisels, and beaver-tooth knives. Lamoka cemeteries show that corpses were interred with a selection of artifacts useful in daily life, although there does not seem to have been any thought of furnishing the deceased with all necessary tools. In southern New England, cremations were common, some of the cremated bone being deposited with red ocher and artifacts, these also usually burned, in burial pits. What look like burial pits without human bone are also known: one in Massachusetts contained a heap of charcoal, a separate deposit of red ocher, several projectile points, two atlatl weights (one broken) and an unfinished weight, and a piece of graphite. It was common to deposit in these pits, whether or not human crema-

tions were included, caches of stone projectile points and knives, many of them well used and some not yet finished. An archaeologist who has studied these burial pits suggests they may have been part of annual life-renewal ceremonies (similar to historic Southeastern Green Corn Festivals) held when the hickory nuts and acorns ripened: new fire may have been kindled, red ocher symbolizing lifeblood and the dawning sun offered, and food and the knives used for it ritually consumed.

The Maritime Archaic, Maine through Newfoundland and southern Labrador, has burial pits resembling those of the southern New England Archaic, but typically more heavily sprinkled with red ocher (therefore, sometimes called the Red Ocher Culture). Both these and sites of the Laurentian Archaic of the St. Lawrence-eastern Great Lakes region ("Laurentian" means "of the [St.] Lawrence") contain ground-stone celts, adzes, and gouges for heavy woodworking, very likely the manufacture of dugout canoes. An innovation in this period among these peoples is the use of slate and copper for elegantly thin, smooth knives, axes, and spearpoints, as well as for pendants and, in the case of copper, beads and bracelets. Half-moon-shaped knives like Inuit ("Eskimo") ulus (blubber knives) are particularly interesting. The development of these broad but thin-bladed, smooth-cutting implements was probably linked to their excellence in slicing large fish and sea mammals, since swordfish and seals were extensively used on the coast, sturgeon and seals quite far up the St. Lawrence estuary, and sturgeon in the interior. "Bayonets" of polished ground slate in Maritime Archaic burial pits have been interpreted as imitation swordfish swords, perhaps for ceremonial purpose. Along the western Great Lakes, the prime source of copper, copper implements dominate and slate is rare, while in the East, where slate deposits occur along the northern Appalachians, the inverse is true. In these two regions, identical forms are found worked in each material, which suggests continued contacts all along the Great Lakes, the St. Lawrence, and the Maritimes. Finds of copper in the eastern province, and Atlantic shell far inland, prove contacts. Even wider extensions of trading and visiting are indicated by the presence in Ontario of artifacts of North Dakota's Knife River flint (a glasslike chalcedony that can be flaked into a very sharp edge) and the presence as far south as Connecticut of artifacts of beautiful Ramah chert from Labrador.

The boreal forest and tundra of the far northeast interior are underlain by glacier-scoured outcrops of bedrock granite called the Canadian Shield. In this region, a relatively impoverished Shield Archaic population adapted to the low game density and the smaller number of species supported by the thin soil of this most recently glaciated region. Caribou must have been the principal game, in contrast with the elk and moose hunted by the Laurentians, and the deer farther south. Fish must have been an important, if less prized, daily food, as it continues to be for the Indians of the region. Edible plants are few and could not have been staples, a marked contrast with the economy of the southern Northeast Archaic peoples. An absence of heavy woodworking tools suggests the birchbark canoe was substituted for the dugout, which would have been cumbersome in the frequent portaging necessary on the Shield. Of all the Late Archaic populations, the Shield Archaic culture persisted most strongly because it adapted well to a relatively harsh environment that allows few alternatives to the humans who live in it. In many respects, the contemporary Cree and other Algonkian-speaking peoples of the Shield forests exhibit a Late Archaic cultural pattern.

The close of the Late Archaic period in the southern Northeast, about 1400 B.C. to 800 B.C., is marked by the use of simple, round bowls cut out of soapstone (steatite). These bowls, as well as pit ovens and small platforms of rocks, were favored means of cooking in this period. Most of the stone bowls have been found in small campsites along streams or in sheltered spots on the coast, which suggests the bowls were carried in canoes and left near the landing places when their owners went on occasional overland hunting trips. All the habitation sites of this period are small, and have no preserved evidence of dwellings, which may have been tents (also carried in the canoes) or light pole and bark wigwams. Deer, turkeys, turtles, and, on the coast and estuaries, oysters and clams were hunted, fish were netted, and nuts gathered and stored in pits for winter use. Concern continued to be shown for the dead through burials of either corpses or cremation remains in pits, some of them quite large, on the tops of hills. Knives and projectile points, "killed" soapstone bowls (a hole punched through the bottom rendered the bowl "dead" to use), pigment and a stone for grinding it, an adze, and a strike-a-light rock for kindling fire were customarily placed with the dead, who were then covered with the ashes and food scrap from a funeral-feast fire and finally liberally sprinkled with powdered red ocher.

The "Early Woodland" Period

Slightly later, but overlapping with the terminal Late Archaic soapstone-bowl use, is the earliest type of pottery in the Northeast, called Vinette. The pottery was built up by paddling into cone-shaped jars. Sometimes the jars were left plain; otherwise their surface was roughened by stamping with a toothed or fabric-wrapped block. Alternately, the pots may have been constructed inside a coarse bag that was impressed on the damp clay surface during the paddling to even the vessel, and then was removed as the vessel dried and shrank. The roughened surface helped prevent the pot from cracking during drying because lines of cleavage were cut short by the alternation of ridges and troughs; the same purpose was served by the practice of adding crushed, heated stone "temper" to the clay if it did not naturally contain grit. The style of dark-brown, surface-roughened, grit-tempered jars persists, with many variations in detail, from its introduction about 1100 B.C. into the early historic period (about A.D. 1700). It appeared throughout the forested Northeast and Midwest, and is therefore called the Woodland ceramic tradition.

The closest similar pottery around 1100 B.C. is, surprisingly, in northwestern Europe. "Woodland"-style pottery is also found at this time in northern Asia, where its antecedents go back to the earliest pottery known in the world, that in northeastern Asia dating to the close of the Pleistocene epoch, 9000 B.C. The Vinette pottery certainly does not resemble the vegetable-fiber-tempered, smooth-surfaced, open bowls that are the early ceramics of the Southeast, nor the fine, smoothed, often painted, ceramics that come into the American Southwest centuries later from Mexico. It would be easiest to attribute the introduction of pottery into the Northeast to migration or trading contacts from the Bering Strait through the boreal forest of Canada to Ontario, but efforts to find Woodland—or any—pottery in the Canadian Northwest have not been successful. Pottery making might have been independently invented in the Northeast, perhaps stimulated by acquaintance with Southeastern ceramics. It is, on the other hand, possible, though far from proved, that pottery making was introduced into the Northeast by boat across the North Atlantic from Scandinavia. Since the Scandinavians at this period, like the Maritime and Laurentian Archaic peoples, caught deep-sea fish and sea mammals, they had seagoing boats (probably dory-sized frames covered with sewn hides caulked with grease, of which Irish curraghs are the modern descendants; that hide-covered curraghs can cross this northern ocean was proven a few years ago in a National Geographic-sponsored test by Tim Severin). Island-hopping from Newfoundland to Greenland to Iceland to the Faroes to Europe, or in the opposite direction, the cod fishermen from one continent may have met their counterparts from the other and exchanged ideas. Pictures pecked in rocks (petroglyphs) showing men in boats, in both Scandinavia and Canada indicate the importance of boats to the peoples on each side of the Atlantic.

Archaeological convention separates the Late Archaic period from the Early Woodland period by the appearance of pottery, but in fact there is strong continuity of cultural traditions to about 700 B.C. An innovation more significant than pottery in the "Early Woodland" period is the manufacture of tubular tobacco pipes, which indicates the use and probable cultivation of tobacco and perhaps new religious ritual. Tobacco is an American plant, and smoking must have come into the Laurentian area from the south. Evidence from the Archaic and Early Woodland periods of plant cultivation other than that presumed for tobacco seems to be lacking in the Northeast, although one archaeologist has noticed that edible wild onions seem to grow on Late Archaic sites in southeastern Ontario, and not generally outside the sites, which leads him to postulate that the Late Archaic people collected onions and either planted them or stored them in pits near their dwellings. The first millennium B.C. seems to have suffered a cooling climatic phase that caused a decline in hickory trees along their northern border in the Northeast. Population seems to have declined along with the important food processed from hickory nuts. While the Midwest was experiencing the Adena and then Hopewell climax of population growth, ceremonial constructions, and trading, the Northeast "Early Woodland" saw a persistence of Late Archaic patterns apparently adapting to a reduced food supply. The Northeast was not isolated from Midwestern developments, since Adena artifacts and mounds resembling Adena and Hopewell mounds occur in western New York and in Ontario along Lakes Huron and Ontario, but nothing in the Northeast seems to have attracted Hopewell trade. No more than an occasional projectile point brought east by an adventurer hints at the Hopewell presence across the Appalachians. Added to the decline in edible nuts and the lack of raw materials that would bring in trade, the Early and Middle Woodlanders in the Northeast faced a decline in swordfish (in the Gulf of Maine) and the replacement of deer by moose (in Maine and adjacent Canada). The cooler water now in the Gulf of Maine was more hospitable to soft-shell clams than to swordfish, which meant a drastic shift in protein availability per hour of human labor. The cooler forests with less mast and browse for deer could support only a much lower density of moose, again meaning many more man-hours of labor (in stalking) per pound of meat obtained. Along the Labrador coast, the first "Eskimo" appear, migrating down from the Arctic coast with their highly specialized culture adapted to the far northern ocean. Only on the Canadian Shield was there little change, other than the introduction of Woodland pottery, from the Late Archaic period through the Middle Woodland period: the Shield Archaic population was already adapted to the resources of a cold forest, and continued to hunt caribou and fish, unaffected by the regression in the deciduous forests and in the Gulf Stream to the south.

The Middle and Late Woodland Periods

The Middle Woodland period in the Northeast, from the last few centuries B.C. through the first millennium A.D., is a period of small nomadic communities living off a broad, diversified range of naturally occurring foodstuffs—meat, fish, fowl, acorns, hickories where persisting, grapes, chenopod (goosefoot) seeds, and shellfish. Houses were rectangular, though with rounded corners, up to 35 by 20 feet (10.7 by 6 meters) in dimension and constructed of poles probably covered with slabs of bark, as was standard in later times. Burials show that the dead were fitted out for the next world with finely carved antler combs; bracelets and necklaces of pendants and beads of stone, copper, and shells (some from southern waters); clothing decorated with sewn-on beads; tobacco pipes; and a variety of useful tools—but usually not pottery or food. The earlier custom of liberally sprinkling red-ocher powder over the corpse continued, although the cremations of the earlier period went out of fashion.

The earliest evidence of domesticated plants in the Northeast dates to about A.D. 1000 and marks the beginning of the Late Woodland period. Maize, beans, squashes, and sunflowers began to be raised in the southern and Laurentian-Lakes sectors of the Northeast, no doubt imported from the adjacent Midwest or possibly the South. Northeastern maize is the large-kerneled (eight rows to the cob) flour corn, raised also in the Ohio Valley Fort Ancient cultural group in this period, but different from the smaller-kerneled Mississippian maize raised around Cahokia. Summers in the Maritimes and, of course, on the Shield were too short to raise dependable crops of any of these plants, but people from these regions did travel south to trade hides and furs, and meat, if close enough to avoid spoilage, for surplus maize. A series of related trends seems to have begun: populations increased; the number of people in a community increased; people became more sedentary, building corn-cribs or man-size storage pits and making larger pottery vessels and houses; competition began for arable land and convenient hunting territories and fishing stations; warfare became endemic, forcing communities to build heavy palisades around defensible sites usually inconveniently far from water (raids rather than sieges were the usual tactic); and endemic warfare led, by A.D. 1300, to terrorist tactics including torture and public feasting on the bodies of enemy warriors. All of these trends are attested by archaeological evidence, particularly in central New York, where the Owasco cultural pattern of the early Late Woodland period is traced into the historic Iroquois tribes.

The advent of agriculture and its apparent reversal of the slow population decline that began in the first millennium B.C., coincide with the termination of burial ceremonies that were so important a part of the social fabric of Northeastern communities from the early Late Archaic period. The Late Woodland dead were respectfully interred, but their graves are simple. Archaeologist William Ritchie suggested that the Owasco shifted their concern from the individual welfare of their members and an annual ritual of affirmation of the social group through community funeral feasts, to emphasis on cooperative farming affirmed through group celebrations of the stages in the agricultural cycle. The importance of the living community was perhaps underscored by the escalating threats to it from enemy raids. The Northeast during Late Woodland times remained largely outside the principal Mississippian trading networks, as it had been on the edge of the Hopewell sphere. In western and northern New York state, where rivers flow through rich agricultural land toward the Great Lakes and Ohio River transportation systems, the Iroquois incorporated Mississippian agriculture. Their farms became the northeastern frontier of agriculture in America, and probably the frontier for Mississippian trade. When Cahokia's power began its apparent decline in the fourteenth century, Upper Ohio groups were eager to take advantage of greater independence in trade, continuing the frontier position of the Iroquois north and east of them. Iroquois, in response, fortified their settlements and maneuvered alliances to assert their competence in managing trade.

One of the most radical shifts in balance of power seen in history is the sudden importance gained by the Northeast when the European trade began at the close of the Late Woodland period. The resulting rapid decline in the Midwest's economic and political power was an exacerbation of the slower shift of the preceding two centuries as Iroquois developed their capacity to dominate the Laurentian-Lakes region. Culminating in the confederation of five nations in the League of the Haudenosaunee—the famous League of the Iroquois—what had been peripheral to American centers of population and power was poised to assert newly forged capability to dominate the Eastern Woodlands. The early sixteenth century was as devastating and revolutionary for the Northeast as it was for Mexico, and, as in Mexico, the repercussions of the events of this century affect us still.

SECTION 2: THE NORTHEAST DURING THE PROTO-HISTORIC LATE WOODLAND PERIOD

By A.D. 1200, the trends marked by the initiation of maize agriculture, trends that can be traced

through the Owasco of central New York, had crystallized into cultural patterns that were described by the first European explorers in the Northeast, three centuries later. The convention of labeling blocks of time in Northeast prehistory "Late Archaic," "Early Woodland," and "Middle Woodland" obscures the contrast between the Northeast and the South and Midwest, where Poverty Point, Adena-Hopewell, and Mississippian societies were climaxes of cultural complexity that are appropriately labeled eras. The Northeast, on the other hand, exhibits strong continuities marked only gently by a flowering during the relatively warm Late Archaic period. Continuities can be discerned among terminal Middle Woodland, Owasco, and the Iroquoian tradition that grows from Owasco, and to a greater degree between Middle Woodland and Late Woodland Algonkians, but the similarities in technology and the genetic continuum cannot hide the great social changes that made life between the St. Lawrence and Delaware Bay very different after A.D. 1300 than it had been only a few generations previously.

The Northeast was inhabited by members of two major language stocks, the Eastern Algonkian and the Iroquoian, a group of languages related to Cherokee and possibly distantly to Siouan. Algonkians occupied the major portion of the Northeast. From north to south, they included the Naskapi hunters on the Labrador tundra and the related "Montagnais" in the forests of Labrador, with the Cree in Quebec to the west forming a set of closely related languages and social groups; the Beothuk of Newfoundland, whose few survivors scattered, ceasing to be an ethnic group, early in the nineteenth century before their language was adequately recorded, and who are therefore not definitely known to be Algonkians; the Micmac (called Souriquois in the seventeenth century; Micmac means "allies") of the Canadian Maritimes; the Maliseet (or Malicite; known as Etchemin before the eighteenth century) and Passamaquoddy just south of the Micmac, in New Brunswick and Maine; the Penobscot and Abenaki (sometimes spelled Wabanaki) of Maine; the speakers of Algonkian dialects in Massachusetts, including Natick, Narragansett, Wampanoag (Pokanoket), and possibly Pennacook in New Hampshire; the Pequot and Mohegan of Connecticut, the Mahican of the upper and the Wappinger of the lower Hudson, the Montauk on Long Island, and the Delaware Lenape, themselves divided into Delaware proper in the South, the Munsee in the north; and the Piscataway (Conoy) and Nanticoke, whose territory bordered that of Powhatan in Virginia. The Shawnee are sometimes included among the Eastern Algonkians, although they were more usually found in the Ohio Valley. The Delaware and their neighbors, the Conoy, the Nanticoke, and the Shawnee all claimed to have migrated eastward to their historic territories. On the basis of linguistic analysis, which demonstrates similarities between Central (Midwest) Algonkian and Eastern Algonkian languages from Connecticut through Powhatan's Confederacy, all these groups from the Pequot through Powhatan might have come into the Atlantic Slope region during the Late Woodland period; if so, whom they displaced is a puzzle. The Atlantic Slope from the Arctic to the Southeast was historically Algonkian-speaking.

One more set of Algonkian speakers occupied the Canadian Shield interior of Quebec and Ontario. The related languages of this group include Algonkian proper (also spelled Algonquin), Ottawa, Ojibwa (often spelled Chippewa in the United States), and the western offshoot of the Ojibwa in Manitoba and Saskatchewan, the Saulteaux (pronounced "Soto"), or Bungi. The entire Canadian Shield has thus been dominated by Algonkian-speakers, which has given rise to speculation that the Shield Archaic people, and possibly even the whole of the Northeast Archaic, were speakers of ancestral Algonkian.

Solidly planted in the beautiful and fertile country of the eastern Great Lakes and upstate New York has been the bloc of Iroquoians, whose languages became separate from the related Cherokee and Tuscarora of the Southeast probably three

thousand years ago. The Iroquoian languages are: the Five Nations group of Seneca and Cayuga, dialects spoken by the westernmost tribes of the original Iroquois League in central New York; Onondaga, the central of the Five Nations; Oneida, the next-to-the-easternmost of the Iroquois League tribes; and Mohawk, the easternmost of the league; then the Huron group, rivals of the League who lived in Southern Ontario, including the Huron (in their own language, Wendat, or Wyandot in the United States) on the lake of their name (which, incidentally, is not an Indian word but was French slang for "ruffian"); and the Tionontati (or Petun, or Tobacco nation), just west of the Huron. Other historic Iroquoian speakers, no longer extant nations, include the Neutral, who refused to take sides in the rivalry between Huron and Iroquois, their neighbors to the north and south, respectively, of Lake Ontario south of the Tionontati; the Erie, south of the lake of that name; and the Susquehannock, on the river (Susquehanna) named after them, who were sometimes included, after 1690, in the "Conestoga". Because the Iroquois and the Cherokee seem to intrude into a huge region otherwise largely Algonkian, early scholars assumed the Iroquoians had migrated eastward from presumed Siouan relatives in the western and upper Mississippi Valley. However, the archaeological demonstration that the Iroquois cultural pattern can be linked trait by trait with the early Late Woodland Owasco in the heart of Iroquois territory, and with similar early Late Woodland societies in southern Ontario, has convinced most contemporary scholars that the historic Iroquois territory was Iroquoian from at least A.D. 1300, and very possibly earlier.

The Iroquois

The Iroquois are the better known of the two major cultural groups in the protohistoric Northeast. This is, in part, because the Puritan colonists of Massachusetts waged genocidal wars in the seventeenth century to conquer Algonkian lands;

in part, because the large and strongly organized Iroquois towns forced alliances with both French and British to a greater degree than did the smaller, less intensively agricultural Algonkian communities; and, finally, in part, because the League of the Iroquois came to be seen as a model of federal political structure when the framers of the new United States were seeking examples of the heretofore unusual (in Europe) form of government. The propaganda published by the Puritans to justify their attempts to take over Algonkian territory, and the proclivity of European intellectual tradition to set up contrasts, have given some the impression that all the Algonkians were nomadic children of nature while the Iroquois were a civilized nation. But careful reading of the historic sources and the archaeological record suggests that in the southern and Laurentian-Lakes sectors of the Northeast—those regions in which maize agriculture was usually reliable as the basis of the food supply—the protohistoric Iroquois and Algonkians were quite similar in economy, community organization, and technology. The real contrast was that forced by ecology between the agricultural peoples and those who lived north of the climatic zone with at least 130 frost-free days annually. With fewer than 130 frost-free days regularly occurring each year, even the varieties of Northern Flint maize carefully selected by the Indians for maturation under borderline ecology could not produce dependable crops. Therefore, peoples north of this zone had to rely on hunting and fishing for subsistence and could not build large, sedentary towns. It happened that at historic contact, all the Iroquois were agricultural and the nonagricultural north was exclusively Algonkian-speaking, but this must not cloud the fact that the Atlantic Slope from southern Maine through the Carolinas was occupied by agricultural Algonkian towns.

From the end of the fourteenth century A.D., most Iroquois nations maintained towns about two acres (one hectare) in extent, heavily fortified with as many as three parallel rows of log palisades

buttressed with thick wickerwork and provided with platform bastions from which archers and stone throwers could defend the town. Towns were usually on hilltops far enough from streams that canoes could not silently glide within shooting distance. Fields of maize, beans, squashes, and sunflowers (raised for the edible seeds) surrounded the town, on the hill slopes as well as the flood plains. These fields were cleared by the slash-and-burn method of killing trees by girdling and then burning off the dried brush and trees, a method that returns valuable nutrients to the soil in the form of ashes. Inside the town were rows of as many as fifty houses, each occupied by several families usually related matrilineally (ideally, sisters and their families). Some towns seem to have emphasized division into clans, presumably matrilineal, to the degree that each clan apparently had its own house, which could be as long as 400 feet (122 meters) by 22 feet (6.7 meters) wide. The longhouses were framed with sapling posts probably bent over at the top and lashed together to form a rounded building, like a quonset hut, that was covered with large slabs of elm bark lashed to the frame. Along the center of the top of the house were openings so that smoke could escape. Below, down the center of the floor, were a row of hearths. This central alley was marked by a row of posts on each side, 7 feet (2 meters) in from each outer wall, partitioning the house into semiprivate rooms for the nuclear families within the clan. Against the walls were constructed wooden benches on which furs were laid for bedding. Each adult woman kept her food supplies and family's clothing and utensils in her family cubicle, and cooked for her family over the hearth in the central alley adjacent to her cubicle. The clan also kept a common store of food, hides, furs, and other necessities to supplement member families' production, if required, and to host visitors. Outside the longhouses, corncribs and smoking racks kept stores to replenish those within the houses. Maize, beans, squashes (including pumpkins), acorns, butternuts, hickory nuts, wild plums and cherries, and probably blueberries (which are seldom identified archaeologically) were dried for year-round use. Deer were the principal game, but beaver, bear, elk, rabbit, woodchuck, and porcupines were caught, as well as the furbearers fox, lynx, wolf, marten, and muskrat, turkeys, Canada geese, passenger pigeons, and grouse among birds, turtles, frogs and toads, and pike, walleye, bullhead, and sturgeon among fish. Tobacco was grown and smoked in stone or clay pipes, which were often carved or molded into animal or human faces. Little simple human faces were also commonly made on pottery, which usually took the form of round vessels with high, decorated rims. The Iroquois fondness for little faces on pots and pipes may indicate that the False Face societies, whose members carve grotesque masks out of living tree trunks to lure the spirits of the forest into houses to cure people, were already popular among the Iroquois at that time. No cemeteries were located close to settlements, and the few that have been discovered, in one case a mile from a town, consisted of burials in small, unfurnished graves. Town sites seem to have been occupied for one to three generations, eventually being rebuilt perhaps 10 miles (16 kilometers) away where soil and wood had been allowed to regenerate through as much as a century.

The preceding generalizations apply especially to central New York Iroquois, and, among them, most particularly to the Onondaga, whose history has been traced back in detail by archaeologists. There are variations on the pattern as close as the Mohawk, whose villages used large storage pits, while the Onondaga preferred above-ground storage. More significant variation occurs among the Ontario Iroquois, who kept their dead in charnel houses until the skeleton could be disarticulated and buried as a bundle with others in a mass grave. A funeral feast for the individuals at their deaths was probably repeated as part of a town-wide or even intertown memorial ceremony when the accumulated dead were finally interred. Historically, this Feast of the Dead became a ritual for cementing alliances as well as affirming the continuity of communities.

The Algonkians

Agricultural Algonkian settlements apparently never reached the size of the larger Iroquois towns. Many were palisaded at the time of historic contact, but archaeological research indicates Algonkian villages were usually open, even when contemporary Late Woodland Iroquois were clustered behind fortifications. The smaller size of Algonkian communities and the number of camps, rather than sedentary villages, in Algonkian territories suggest the Algonkians placed less reliance on maize and more on hunting, fishing, and shellfish gathering than did the Iroquois. This probably reflects the Atlantic Slope's advantage in access to sea mammals (seals and whales), sea sturgeon and swordfish, cod and other deep-sea fish, runs of salmon, shad, herring, and alewives, and oyster and clam beds. In other words, the richness of sea as well as land resources gave the Eastern Algonkians more economic options than the inland Iroquois could command, and less incentive to labor at planting and weeding. Politically, the diversity of options allowed the Algonkians to adopt alternative economic styles that avoided the competition and resulting conflict that led to Iroquois fortifications. The Europeans, who came from several centuries of comparable competition and conflict, rightly judged the Iroquois to be more like themselves than were the Algonkians, but it certainly does not follow that life in the Late Woodland period was better for the Iroquois than for the Algonkians. From the Algonkian point of view, Iroquois had to compensate for their inland location through agriculture and trade.

North of the zone with at least 130 frost-free days, there was a border area in Maine in which maize, beans, and squashes were planted in relatively small garden patches, perhaps with a few

FIGURE 5.1 Ojibwa family making a birchbark canoe in a shade shelter. Bark wigwam home is in the left background (early twentieth century). *(Milwaukee Public Museum).*

local wild-food and medicinal plants. No great effort was expended in daily cultivation, as Iroquois did, since frosts could easily destroy the crop. If they didn't, garden harvest was enjoyed in the fall, but the gardens were not relied upon for year-round staples. North of Maine and the St. Lawrence-Lakes, crops were not even attempted. Agriculture in the Late Woodland period seems definitely to have been limited by ecology, not by choice. Cultural continuities across the ecological boundary of agriculture are evidenced not only by related languages, but by tool styles, canoes, and a preference for wigwams, dome-shaped frames of bent saplings tied together at the apex and covered with sheets of birch bark, slabs of elm or conifer bark, mats, or hides, according to local availability.

The wigwam seems to have been a Middle Woodland house that the Iroquois gradually extended into the longhouse, while among the Algonkians the original form persisted. That the longhouse grew as the matrilineal clan became the basic economic unit among the Iroquois, and that the wigwam persisted among Algonkians, who kept the nuclear family or two-family cooperative the basic unit, reflect increasing differences in sociopolitical structure between Late Woodland Iroquois and Algonkian. In the early historic period, southern New England Algonkian community leaders who sheltered widowed or orphaned persons and hosted visitors extended their wigwams into, as it were, short longhouses. House form and socio-political form were thus tied in the Northeast, and similarities in wigwams between agricultural and nonagricultural Eastern Algonkians are linked with similarities in economy and social structure. In line with this, the most northerly Algonkians tended to have the smallest wigwams (ten feet [three meters] in diameter at the base), or even only a small, conical tent of poles covered with bark or hides, both of which fit the very low population density and marked seasonal dispersal of families.

The coastal northern Algonkians came down to the sea in the summer to hunt seals and whales and collect shellfish. Fall and spring found them camped by stations, such as rapids, where they

---

PENOBSCOT MOOSE HUNTING

In a region where large [moose] bulls are known to range, a camp is made at evening, and everything is kept quiet.....About two o'clock [A.M.], several long, loud, and tremulous calls are given on the moose-call, or "horn"...a sheet of birch bark rolled into the shape of a megaphone....The first long call, lasting sometimes nearly half a minute, is to signal the district.....If a bull is within hearing he will proceed to answer and approach. When an answer is received, a luring call is again given, after which all is kept quiet until a few hours before sunrise. The bull is, during this time, approaching cautiously from a point possibly several miles away. Just before daybreak, about four o'clock, another encouraging call may be given, with the horn held straight out, and then turned down. About daybreak the final trial is made to bring the bull within range. The delay is made purposely until enough light comes to see to aim....In making the last calls, the operator spreads out a little flat space on the dead leaves and holds his call within six or eight inches of it, the mouth pointing downward. More of a squealing tone is incorporated into these calls, representing moose-passion, to hurry the bull's approach. By this time he may be heard trampling down the bushes and thrashing the thickets with his antlers in impassioned rage. The hunters make ready, and a few whispered words of warning precede the last call, which is meant to bring the bull into sight. When his huge form appears in the dim light, he is shot. With shouts the hunters dash to the spot where he stood, and if there is light enough examine the traces of blood....If the blood is dark, the bull has been mortally wounded and may be looked for not far away. If, on the other hand, the color is light, the hunters decide how severe the wound may have been, and whether it is worth while to track the animal.

Let us imagine ourselves under somewhat different circumstances, accompanying the same hunters after moose in a canoe, upon some lake or river. Here the time chosen is also early morning or around dusk. The canoe is paddled noiselessly along near the shore where the game is known to come. At frequent intervals the bow man gives a call with the bark horn pointed up into the woods lining the banks. When he gets an answer he puts an appealing note into the call. Paddling is stopped. So is the bull lured to the bank where he thinks a cow is feeding. Now the operator takes a canoe bailer, or his bark horn, and dips up some water, pouring it out to make a sound like a cow raising her dripping mouth from the stream, or better to imitate her urinating. The bull, seeing the shadowy form of the canoe and hearing the splashing noise, comes out. Now the man paddling in the stern backs the canoe away from the spot and the bow man gets ready to shoot. When the big bull has reached the place he finds that his quarry has retreated from him, and becomes furious. Here while he stands deep in the water the marksman shoots him. Keeping the canoe at a safe distance the hunters 'ait till he succumbs, or paddle ashore to follow him if he takes flight. The Indians, of course, in both cases have to take into consideration the direction of the wind, and many other details which mean much to the success of the hunt.

When still-hunting moose, or other game, the hunter carries a shorter and smaller call, about nine inches long and three wide at the flaring end. Through this he grunts at intervals as he goes through the woods, so as to deceive moose, and formerly caribou, that might be in the neighborhood. The crackling twigs and occasional grunts sound innocently like another moose moving through the woods. This trick is also used at "carries" or portages, in order not to alarm game that may be started up. It also served as a definite call for caribou; a few short grunts being the signal. In the old days when a moose, deer, or caribou was shot with an arrow they say it was not necessary for the shot to be fatal at first because if the arrow penetrated almost anywhere between the ribs the animal would lie down after he had run awhile and roll on the arrow to dislodge it, so driving it in farther until it would result fatally.

(Speck 1940:39-42)

---

could best catch quantities of the seasonally running fish that, after being dried, were winter staples. When ice formed, families moved out by ones and twos onto the interior uplands to hunt deer, elk, moose, bear, and beaver. Berries and edible tubers were gathered and, like meat and fish, dried for use when fresh food was no longer available. Bags of dried food were critical when storms kept families holed up in their wigwams or tents. To transport dried food, bedding and clothing furs, and utensils, and, when caught, fresh carcasses, sleds were pulled in the winter, usually by men, and canoes of birch bark or sometimes moose hide paddled in warm weather. Snowshoes enabled the hunting families to move camp and pursue game in winter. Northern Algonkian life appears simple, but in fact rested upon highly sophisticated technology and knowledge of the environment. Genuises of the order of Henry Ford and the Wright brothers must have invented the variety of traps that in effect let the hunter wait at dozens of animal trails simultaneously, and the weirs and fish traps that brought in basket loads of fish to be assembly-line gutted, filleted, and laid on drying racks by the women. Even the simple conical rolled-bark moose call is part of a fund of animal-behavior data that professional biologists spend years acquiring. It could be argued that the average northern Algonkian adult had a broader range of technical expertise and finesse than the average adult in agricultural communities, Indian or European. This expertise guided the seasonal movements of families and enabled them to garner a comfortable living with less daily labor than is required in Euro-American society today.

The social organization of the northern Algonkians has been the subject of considerable debate. During much of the historic period, it was characteristic of the inland peoples to gather in numbers of up to several hundred at good fishing lakes in summer. In winter, family bands of a man and his grown sons with their wives and children moved into the forest. Each of these patrilocal bands controlled a trapping territory that was inherited patrilineally (from father to son). The furs from the territory were traded at the post of a European fur factor (head trader), often located on the popular fishing lake, and were usually sufficient to provide the families with the guns, ammunition, steel traps, cloth, flour, tea, lard, needles, and other European manufactures they wished to obtain. The question debated has been whether the Indians were patrilineal and patrilocal before the establishment of their symbiotic relationship with the fur companies. One reason to doubt that they were is that the Labrador caribou hunters, especially the Naskapi, who have been less heavily involved in the fur trade than the Cree inland, are not patrilocal and do not stress patrilineality. The most recent opinion is that patrilineality was fostered by the European factors and later the government officials, who, because of their own background, assumed patrilineality was "natural." With power to designate who should trap where, and with whom, first derived from the trader's power to give or withhold credit and supplies, and now fixed in game-management laws, the Euro-American favored patrilineal arrangements among the hunters. The aboriginal situation may instead have favored matrilocality based on a young man going to live and hunt with his bride's family. Parents were concerned to keep their daughters in the family camp until the young couple had amply demonstrated the capability to support themselves and their children and to exercise mature judgment (that is, until they had demonstrated mastery of the expertise needed to live comfortably in the boreal forest or the tundra). By the time parents felt at ease about a couple's ability, they might be aging and becoming dependent upon the son-in-law's hunting. Also, the young man had probably worked out good cooperative hunting practices with his brothers-in-law. The matrilocal arrangement thus tended to persist although it was not obligatory.

Aboriginally, the families who summered at a fishing lake most likely discussed together where each would prefer to winter, and, under the guidance of the experienced elders, came to agreements on territories for the coming season. The next year, territories would be worked out anew, since not all the previous year's families would have returned to the same lake, and in any case, hunters and visitors would have brought word of shifts in animal densities and migration routes. Because of matrilocality in the first years of marriage, men were intimately familiar with at least two territories, the one their parents favored and that frequented by their in-laws. This broadening of a man's expertise helped him assess the potential of areas and make wise choices in selecting where,

and what, to hunt. It probably made him more amenable to accepting the summering group's recommendation on a winter territory, since he was not strongly tied emotionally to one locality. Thus, while the reasons for matrilocality were to allow parents to recruit good husbands for their daughters and good fathers for their grandchildren and to assure themselves they had not erred in these choices—or, if they felt they had, to give them opportunity to train the young men—a valuable result of matrilocality was the extension of hunters' expertise and flexibility, which maximized the opportunities for healthy families in a region where these attributes are vital. Note that matrilocality does not mean matrilineality: the northern Algonkians did not own fixed territories or many material goods, nor did they have political offices, so there was little concern with inheritance. In contrast, the Iroquois, with fixed lands and political offices, were quite concerned with inheritance, which among them was matrilineal, yet they were not strongly matrilocal.

SECTION 3: EUROPEAN CONTACTS WITH THE NORTHEAST

In A.D. 985, Bjarni Herjolfsson, a Norse merchant native to Iceland, followed his father to a new Norse settlement led by Eirik Thorvaldsson (Erik the Red) in Greenland. Bjarni's ship was blown off course in a storm and wandered for some days in a heavy fog. When the weather cleared and Bjarni sighted land, he realized that he must be southwest of Greenland in the vicinity of heretofore unknown country. Beating his way back to Greenland, he reported his discovery to Eirik. This appears to have been the first reasonably uncontroverted European discovery of America.

Claimants to the title of discoverer have been resurrected from hundreds of myths, legends, classical and medieval writings, alleged stone monuments and markers, and supposed pre-Norse artifacts, stone constructions, and even "mooring holes" in seaside rocks. Some of the evidence, such as the stone tower in Newport, Rhode Island, is accepted by all scholars as a seventeenth-century, or even later, Euro-American construction of unusual but not unheard-of- design (the tower was the Rhode Island governor's windmill). Some of the evidence, such as the inscriptions on Mystery Hill, New Hampshire (which tourists may pay admission to view), is subject to the readings of self-trained epigraphers whose enthusiasm seems to outrun their critical faculties. Some of the evidence, such as the Kensington Rune Stone from Minnesota, has been judged an outright hoax or misunderstood innocent fakery. In the case of the Kensington Stone, what had seemed crude errors in the runes are now argued to represent a particular dialect, Bohuslan, of medieval Norse, and to substantiate the claim it was carved by a fourteenth-century Norse expedition to the far western end of the Great Lakes-St. Lawrence route. The weighing of the evidence is unfortunately beclouded by a scholastic "Monroe Doctrine" that induces many American scholars to reject all suggestions of pre-Columbian contacts between America and other continents and to label proponents of possible evidence as crackpots. Imperialist attempts to justify European colonization have denied both American Indians *and* pre-Columbian Europeans any claims to rights by prior discovery. The heat of the arguments over the first European discovery is not from scholarly debate, but from chauvinistic contentions over which Old World nationality may seize the glory of the capture of the virgin land.

Among the resurrected claimants, the earliest would be Neolithic-period fishermen from Scandinavia who did have the boats to island-hop via the Faroes, Iceland, and Greenland to the Labrador-Gulf of St. Lawrence region. That these fishermen did venture out to sea some distance is proved by the bones of cod, an offshore fish, in their settlement debris near the Scandinavian coasts. The waning warm climatic period that had climaxed in the third millennium B.C. would have

made the north Atlantic somewhat more hospitable for voyagers than it became in colder periods later. Evidence for Neolithic transatlantic contact is the apparently abrupt appearance of Woodland pottery, similar to contemporary Scandinavian pottery, in the Northeast around 1000 B.C. and, less striking, the popularity of ground-slate knives on both sides of the north Atlantic during the Late Archaic and contemporary Scandinavian Neolithic. On both sides, the slate knives were probably preferred for slicing sea mammals and cod, which was equally important to the subsistence of the maritime peoples on each side of the northern ocean. Because the peoples on each side seem to have been fairly matched in courage, boats, and a compelling reason to venture on the deep sea, contact could have been initiated from either side. Some petroglyphs (pictures pecked in rock) in eastern Canada are said to resemble petroglyphs in Scandinavia believed to date from its Bronze Age, around 1000 B.C. Symbols with the pictures are said to be short written inscriptions in a heretofore unrecognized Scandinavian alphabet. Since the explanation for the Scandinavian examples is as controversial as that for the American ones, few archaeologists or historians want to spend time seriously considering the possibility of authenticity. No solid proof of contact has been recognized.

The next claims are for the Phoenicians and Libyans (Egyptians), whose seafaring prowess was grudgingly acknowledged by their rivals on the north shore of the Mediterranean, the Greeks and then the Romans. In the first millennium B.C., Phoenicia built a sea trade using a series of colonies around the Mediterranean, the most famous being Carthage in North Africa. Rome's victory in its Punic Wars with Carthage stifled the possible growth of a Phoenician-tradition empire, made the Phoenicians and Carthaginians conquered enemies to be denigrated, and swung the balance of European history to land rather than sea expansion for a millennium, for the Romans were poor sailors, although great road builders. It is quite possible that in the first millennium B.C., eastern Mediterranean or North African ships sailed to Brazil or to the Caribbean and then up along the Gulf Stream, but none of the evidence presently available has convinced the more critical scholars.

After the Roman defeat of Carthage, the next claimants are the Celts of Britain and Brittany. They were regular traders across the Irish Sea and along the western coast of Europe in large hide-covered curraghs (constructed like birch bark canoes but much longer and broader and with a sewn hide, not bark, skin), as well as in wooden vessels. The curraghs, which in canvas-covered versions have survived to this century in impoverished communities in Ireland and Portugal, were highly seaworthy on the Atlantic swells and were easily beached, much safer for ocean sailing and for landing than Columbus's caravels. The most famous Celtic curragh voyage was that of Saint Brendan, an Irish monk whose exploration about A.D. 500 is described in legend and in Latin. The next most famous is the colonizing voyage of a Prince Madoc of Wales in the twelfth century. Petroglyphs said to be inscriptions in Celtic in the ogham alphabet are adduced as proof of Celtic travels in America. Because ogham uses sets of straight lines rather than varied cursive symbols such as form our alphabet, most of the alleged inscriptions are rejected, explained as tally marks, glacial ice scratches, plow scratches, or natural cracks in rock. That many of the claimed ogham, and other supposed ancient, inscriptions are in remote areas of the West—western Oklahoma, Utah—where it is difficult to imagine anybody traveling, reduces credibility. The one likely ogham petroglyph recognized in Newfoundland came probably from an Irish slave of the Norse settlement scratching his name on a rock while he herded sheep. The weight of scholarly opinion is that Brendan did sail the north Atlantic to Iceland, but probably not farther west, and that Madoc is a myth, not even an actual person. One problem with Celtic claims is that until the Viking raids of the eighth and ninth centuries, there seems to have been little reason for Celts to explore westward. Their tiny kingdoms were busy with coastwise trade, and the prominence of the St. Brendan legend itself suggests that a circuit from Ireland to the Azores and Iceland defined the limits of their world.

Norse Contacts with the Northeast

And now Eirik, hot-headed exile from Norway carving out a colony on Greeland's glacier-backed shore. About ten years after Bjarni's landfall, Eirik's son Leif bought Bjarni's ship and attempted to backtrack the merchant's route, hoping to find timber and grazing lands to relieve the limitations faced by his family's Greenland colony. Leif coasted past heavy forest, probably Labrador, and came ashore to winter on meadowland farther south, probably Newfoundland. Several years passed after Leif's return to Greenland before his report attracted colonists. About A.D. 1004, Leif's younger brother Thorvald and a merchant named Thorfinn Karlsefni, who had recently married a widowed lady of the Greenland colony, set out with several ships of men, some women, and cattle to Leif's outpost. According to family histories (sagas), a colony was established, but squabbles over women, too few of whom had come to allow each man a wife, and fear of attack by natives caused the group to return to Greenland after three years. One Norse settlement, radiocarbon-dated to A.D. 1000, has been identified at L'Anse aux Meadows on the northern tip of Newfoundland, on the Strait of Belle Isle. The site consists of several small houses and two larger rectangular ones conforming to Norse building styles, a smithy, and a small number of Norse artifacts—a bronze pin and a spindle weight—that testify to the care with which the Norse ordinarily kept their possessions. L'Anse aux Meadows settlers sailed across the Gulf of St. Lawrence to the Canadian mainland to collect food, evidenced by butternut shells in a house. There are no inscriptions at the site, but a few miles away, lichen-covered lines on a rock have been interpreted as perhaps ogham, the runic alphabet used in first-millenium-A.D. Ireland. Since two Celtic slaves were mentioned to have been included in Karlsefni's expedition, the inscription may have been carved by these men. Unhappily, only one line of the inscription is legible, and it seems to say no more than "land of" or "son of."

It is likely that Greenland Norse continued to cross Davis Strait to Labrador to cut timber, which could not grow in Greenland, throughout the existence of the Greenland colonies—that is, until the cooling climate of the fifteenth century apparently made even southwestern Greenland uninhabitable for domestic livestock, the basis of Greenland Norse economy. It is quite possible that the Norse trapped some furs and bartered for more from Indians and Eskimos during the lumber expeditions: sable, the fur of martens found in Labrador and westward, was particularly valuable in the medieval period and would have added greatly to the Greenlanders' ability to pay for the many manufactures they desired from mainland Scandinavia and Iceland. Valuable ivory, the tusks of walrus, and walrus hides, to be used for the toughest ships' rigging, were also in demand in Europe, so walrus would have been another lure to the Greenlanders to hunt and barter across Davis Strait. The records of the Church diocese that included Iceland and Greenland state that in 1327, the Norse Greenlanders paid 400 walrus-ivory tusks in tithe, a number that would have required the Norse to hunt or trade extensively in northwest Greenland and adjacent Canada, far to the north of their colony settlements. The greatest number of Norse artifacts on the American side occur on Ellesmere Island, closest to Greenland. Here, excavations have recovered bits of Norse woolen cloth, chain-mail armor, iron boat rivets, part of a wooden barrel, and Norse-smelted iron knife blades, all scattered within Thule Eskimo villages. How the Norse looked to the Thule on the west side of Davis Strait is conveyed to us by a little wooden figure, carved in Thule style, of a man in the long woolen hooded coat worn in medieval Europe. A cross decorates the front of the coat.

Did the Norse influence the Indians, or vice versa? The sagas linger on the battles and murders waged by Norse against natives. They imply that the Norse constantly expected trouble and would not trust natives. Karlsefni at least once let natives approach his colony to trade, but forbade his people to give any weapons. In one saga, the natives are satisfied to trade furs for milk from the Norse cows, presumably an unprecedented novelty; in another saga, red cloth as well as milk is exchanged for the furs. The goal of the Norse with Eirik's sons was colonization rather than furs, and the sagas give no indication that any kind of intercourse with the American natives was usual or sought after. Icelandic records other than sagas that mention Greenland or "Markland" (Labrador) are brief, listing tithes or noting a Norse ship coming direct from Markland because it was caught in storms. Perhaps one custom of the Beothuk reflected Norse contact: when European men raided Beothuk camps, as they frequently did in the late eighteenth century, the Beothuk women frantically pulled down their robes, exposing their breasts in the hope (often vain) that the gunmen would spare women. No other Indians seem to have used this gesture so regularly. Now one saga tells that when a large force of natives, who could well have been Beothuk, attacked Karlsefni's colony, the Norse men retreated. Eirik's fierce daughter Freydis ran after her menfolk, calling upon them to fight. Stumbling across the body of one of the slain Norse, and realizing that, pregnant, she could not catch up with her men, Freydis grabbed the dead man's sword, turned to face the pursuing natives, pulled down the upper part of her dress, and slapped the sword against her breasts before brandishing it. The natives stopped short and then retreated. Freydis no doubt intended her dramatic gesture to shame her men into more valiant action, but the natives apparently understood the woman's gesture as a signal that the fight should not be continued. Was the white-skinned woman's gesture repeated in vain generations later by hapless Beothuk women in the slaughter of their people?

European Contacts with the Northeast in the Early Historic Period

The next chapter in European contacts with the American Northeast inaugurates the historic period. In the 1470s, agreement between the king of Denmark and merchants of the Hanseatic League of northern German cities excluded British ships from participating in the Iceland cod fishery, then, as now, a substantial segment of the British economy. To rectify this blow to their income, several shipowners and merchants at the port of Bristol in England sent out ships in 1480 and 1481 to cruise west of Ireland in search of a legendary island, Brasil. The real incentive for these explorations may be guessed from the quantity of salt, suitable for preserving fish, taken along. The 1480 trip was unsuccessful; the outcome of the 1481 trip is unclear. Ten years later, Bristol again sent out ships that might have been searching for, or exploiting, new fishing grounds. Then, when Cabot announced the discovery of Newfoundland in 1497, a correspondent of Columbus mentioned in a letter to him that Cabot's island was the one already discovered by "the men of Bristol."

Cod fishing on the Newfoundland Banks, with the fish processed on the shore of Newfoundland, was rapidly established as a West Atlantic industry by boats from Portugal, England, and France between 1501 and 1512. The fishermen who would make the twenty-day trips out, work feverishly through the short northern summer, and then sail the long distance back were (and are) for the most part independent men who had little influence on, or interest in, their national governments. Indeed, except for some Normans, the French were nearly all Bretons and Basques, fervently separatist, non-Gallic peoples. There is, therefore, very little documentation on the sixteenth-century Newfoundland fishery after the first decade of post-Columbian jockeyings for power in America. It would seem that none of the European rulers realized at this time the potential income from furs that could be gained in America, although the cod fishermen probably exchanged knives for furs and Indians came down to the seashore where the Europeans were working.

During that first decade, the Portuguese Corte Real had seized fifty Indians, perhaps Micmac, from the Canadian Maritimes and sold them for slaves in Lisbon, and a French ship brought seven Indian men, again perhaps Micmac, to France as curiosities (it was intended, and may have been accomplished, to return them home on a subsequent voyage). Three Indian men, hawks, and an eagle were taken to England for display. This pattern of seizing Indians, or their goods, continued throughout the sixteenth century; for example, in 1580 an English ship touched at Maine, noticed an Indian lodge in which 300 moose hides were stored, and helped themselves to this bounty with no consideration of payment. No wonder that three centuries later, Penobscot told of the first sight of Europeans causing an old man to recall, "I could not withhold the tears that rushed upon my brow."

In 1534, Jacques Cartier initiated the formal, royally sponsored French effort to gain more than the duties on salt cod from the New Found Land. In the previous decade in southern Newfoundland, the Portuguese had founded a small colony of fishermen-farmers from the Azores. Those colonists grazed cattle that survived longer than what seems to have been an unsuccessful settlement. Cartier planned to push westward past Newfoundland, hoping to find a sea passage to China but interested also in discovering warmer and more fertile land that eastern Newfoundland offered. In the Gulf of St. Lawrence, he achieved his secondary objective, plus two important introductions: to the Micmac, who pestered Cartier to trade knives and beads for furs, refusing to accept his initial rejection of the pelts they waved at him on sticks from their canoes; and to the Huron Iroquois, who had come down to the ocean to fish for mackerel but traded the few furs they had along as robes and agreed to let Cartier take with him two Huron youths, Domagaya and Taignoaguy, sons of the chief, Donnaconna. The following year, 1535,

Cartier returned with the youths, who now advised him of the route up the St. Lawrence to Donnaconna's town, Stadacona, at the foot of the Rock of Québec. Leaving his ships moored there, he continued by longboat up the St. Lawrence to Stadacona's rival town, Hochelaga, under Mount Royal (Montréal). From the summit of the great hill he saw the St. Lawrence just west of him roar through the Lachine Rapids and realized that there was no route to China that way. (A century later, the Sieur de la Salle named the rapids La Chine—"China"—in ironic note of Cartier's dashed goal.) Retracing his journey, Cartier stopped at Stadacona and decided to winter there. Holed up in the fort his men built, Cartier and his crew eventually fell ill from scurvy. Domagaya saved most of them by urging them to drink a decoction of arborvitae (northern cedar) bark, brought and prepared by Stadacona women, who administered the medicine to their own people when the meat and dried-maize diet of late winter resulted in this Vitamin-C deficiency. Next spring, when the weather permitted, Cartier resumed his voyage home, with Donnaconna and his sons plus seven other Iroquois, all surprised to find themselves hostages on the French vessels. None of the Indians were to see their home again. Donnaconna made the best of his captivity, regaling the King of France with tales of marvels. The Iroquois were revenged when the king and nobles of the court helped finance two expeditions of colonists sailing under Cartier in 1541 and the Sieur de Roberval in 1542. Each group spent a miserable winter near Quebec, collected quartz and iron pyrites thinking they were diamonds and gold, and by autumn was back in France—except for those who had died of scurvy among Roberval's party, which had not made friends of the Indians. No more colonies went out from France to Canada during the sixteenth century.

Cartier's expeditions received the royal limelight, but they contrast sadly with the continuing but unheralded success of the cod fishers and, beginning in 1527, the Basque whalers around Newfoundland. Twenty-odd ships were to be found in St. John's harbor there each summer in the 1540s. British, French, Portuguese—they all found plenty of room on the Newfoundland Banks—and on shore, they packed their holds with dried, salted cod and stowed marten and other furs where they could, and beat back across the North Atlantic before the cold set in. By 1580, four hundred ships, the number now augmented by some Spanish vessels, rendezvoused in Newfoundland. The majority processed cod on shore, but others merely packed catches in brine and spent little time on shore. At the Strait of Belle Isle, the Basque whalers had large fireplaces and warehouses for rendering whale oil—what remained of a carcass would be slid back into the sea—and facilities for processing walrus, a game also pursued by the Bretons. A few of the Basque men and boys might winter over in cabins in the coves. Hostilities between the European powers occasionally stimulated privateers to seize ships and cargoes in Newfoundland, but generally the harbors were reasonably peaceful and disputes between seamen were settled by councils of the captains in port.

The entire sixteenth century was an era of regular but unspectacular trade in the Canadian Maritimes. The Indians, primarily Micmac, brought furs and received for them knives, hatchets, and beads. Neither Indians nor Europeans considered the trade anything more than a supplement to the fish and sea mammals that were for both sides the primary reason to come into the Gulf of St. Lawrence. Nevertheless, the supplement was important. For the European crews, the extra money gained through the furs would be an incentive to sign up for the rough voyage and the relentless, exhausting work of filling the hold before the weather worsened. For the Indians, the metal cutting-implements were tremendous labor-saving devices on two counts, time otherwise spent on manufacturing stone or bone tools (including procuring suitable stone from localized outcrops), and time spent on rechipping or regrinding quickly worn edges, or on substituting a new tool, for the metal tools kept an edge longer and could be more easily resharpened than most native cutting implements. In the short view, Indian technology was nearly as efficient as European: one skilled in its use could cut wood or meat about as fast with a native stone or bone tool as with metal. In the longer view, taking into account the entire manufacturing procedure and the expected longevity of the implement, the metal tool was much cheaper. For this reason, metal knives and hatchets were in constant demand in America. The Micmac and other Algonkians on the mainland shores of the Gulf of St. Lawrence found it profitable to trade not only for their own needs, but to supply interior peoples, especially the Iroquois, with whom they traditionally bartered meat and robes for maize. To protect their middleman profits, the Algonkians apparently attempted to prevent Iroquois from coming into the Gulf. The St. Lawrence became a battleground, and sometime during the latter sixteenth century a no man's land. Stadacona and Hochelaga were abandoned, their people probably finding refuge in Iroquois towns farther west. The historic polarization between the seaboard Algonkians and the inland Iroquois was established.

The Five Nations of the Iroquois

The League of the Five Nations of the Iroquois was established, acording to eighteenth-century sources, in the late sixteenth century. Iroquois tradition tells of constant warfare, between Iroquois towns and between Iroquois and Algonkians. One bereaved by this warfare was a Mohawk man, Hiawatha (Haion'hwa'tha', He Makes Rivers). Crazed by grief for his murdered family, Hiawatha fled into the forests, living like a cannibal monster in the Iroquois myths. One day, Hiawatha met Dekanawida (whose name, appropriately, meant "Two river currents flowing together"). The charismatic goodness of this man, said to have been a Huron miraculously born of a virgin, reawakened in Hiawatha his humanity. Dekanawida confided to Hiawatha plans to free their peoples from the horrors of war by allying all the Iroquois in a grand league, a longhouse over the whole land in which each Iroquois nation would sit as a brother with brothers. The visionary felt himself unequal to the task of forming the league because he suffered a speech impediment. Hiawatha, however, was an imposing man with a fluent tongue. Together, in the time-honored fashion of the wise leader who relies upon his executive assistant to make his speeches (as among the Cherokee and Creek), Dekanawida and Hiawatha might be effective in restoring sanity and peace to their nations. Hiawatha was inspired. Tirelessly, the two men traveled up and down the land, from town to town to town, Hiawatha fervently preaching the alliance outlined by Dekanawida. Most Iroquois were at first hesitant to trust the plan to contain their enemies. Thadodaho (also spelled Atotarho), an Onondaga leader, relentlessly opposed Hiawatha. In a dramatic showdown, Hiawatha's superior spiritual power overcame the evil Thadodaho: it is said Hiawatha combed out of the Onondaga's hair the snakes that had marked him as a fearful sorcerer. Then the five nations—Mohawk, Oneida, Onondaga, Cayuga, and Seneca—came together, fifty great chiefs meeting in a grand council at the principal Onondaga town, in the center of the alliance territory. The five nations were as one family, abolishing blood feud among themselves and replacing it with payment to the injured party from the aggressor's family. The fifty chiefs would meet again at Onondaga's council fire to resolve disputes among themselves and coordinate defense against outsiders. Whenever one of the chiefs died, his brother chiefs would come to his town to convene the Condolence Council, a lengthy and beautiful ritual calling the grief-stricken to look again upon the light, the sky, the sun, to let their friends' pity wipe away their tears, to requicken, to return to the activities of life, and finally, to present to the council their replacement for the deceased, thus perpetuating through the generations the Longhouse of the Five

Nations. The Great Law (Kaianerekowa) of the League, overriding local conflicts, is pictured as a heaven-touching great white pine tree, an eagle in its upper branches searching out events below, its four tap roots anchoring it to east, to north, to west, to south. All peoples may shelter under its wide branches, around the council bench set by its trunk. Weapons should be thrown into the underground stream ("bury the hatchet") that flows away from the Tree, to be carried into oblivion.

Only the Iroquois in central New York, south of Lake Ontario, were members of the League of the Five Nations. The Huron, the Tionontati, the Neutral, the Erie, and the Susquehannock were outside the League, and except for the precariously situated Neutral, were enemies of the Five Nations. The effect of the League was not so much to bring peace as to secure a large tract of fertile land from the attrition of frequent small raids, and in this way to allow more extensive farming that could support relatively large expeditionary forces from the League warring upon more distant towns. With the metaphorical Longhouse of the League thus a bastion, the five allied nations exercised in the seventeenth and eighteenth centuries a power unprecedented in the Northeast. This power challenged the Eastern Algonkians and the Hurons over control of the European trade.

Beginning in 1581, Norman and Breton merchants sent out ships expressly to trade for furs on the St. Lawrence, in addition to the ships going to Newfoundland for cod. For an investment of forty crowns in trade goods, a captain in 1583 brought back four hundred crowns' worth of furs. Such profit spurred competition. By 1588, the King of France's recently discussed plan to found a colony on the St. Lawrence for agriculture, mining, and trade had been scuttled by the clamor of Breton merchants for free trade in a country they insisted was good only for furs. In 1600, an abortive French colony was planted, not at a locality favorable for farming, but at Tadoussac, where the Saguenay River flowing from the northwest interior comes into the head of the Gulf of St. Lawrence. Here

Montagnais and other Algonkians had become accustomed to gather each summer with furs not only from their own trapping, but many more collected from interior tribes (including Hurons) in exchange for European goods. Both the Algonkians and the Europeans at Tadoussac found the trade a windfall, and they celebrated by singing, dancing, and feasting together.

The Seventeenth Century

The first decade of the seventeenth century foreshadowed its whole. In 1606, the Dutch entered the Northeast fur trade, inaugurating the threefold competition that Holland, France, and England would continue for generations. In 1607, an English settlement was attempted at the mouth of the Kennebec in Maine, which established the British interest in colonizing New England. In 1609, Samuel de Champlain left the French colony he had set up the previous year at Quebec to travel to the lake that bears his name and into what is now Vermont, accompanying a war party of Algonkians and Hurons against the Mohawks. Champlain's gun, suddenly barking from what had appeared a close-ranked attack of Indians, killed the three Mohawk leaders. It also entangled the French firmly on the Huron-Algonkian side of the protracted Iroquois wars. By the end of the first decade, in 1611, the fur trade in the Northeast had fully shifted from its desultory beginning as an adjunct to the Newfoundland fishery. The Montagnais and other Algonkians gathered at Tadoussac cannily waited until enough European ships had arrived that the Indians could bargain, playing one European against the other, for higher prices for the furs. Waiting at Tadoussac, the Indians forfeited some of the fishing, hunting, and plant harvesting formerly carried on in summer, relying on traded European foodstuffs such as dried peas to substitute. In 1611, Champlain rendezvoused with Algonkians and Hurons well up the St. Lawrence at Montreal, and, realizing the trading advantages of a location within reach of the

Huron and interior Algonkian territories, planned to eventually build a post there. Its second century found the Northeast fur trade moving deep into the St. Lawrence-Great Lakes inland system as European colonies began to fringe the Atlantic.

European attention began to focus on the Iroquoians in the seventeenth century. The Algonkians on the Canadian Shield north of the Huron—the Algonkian proper, the Nipissing, and the Ottawa, from east to west—were accustomed to visiting Huron towns to trade, often wintering at these towns. Huron men also traveled north to trade at Algonkian camps. Furs, meat, dried fish, and hides, simply tanned or sewn into clothing, some beautifully embroidered with dyed porcupine quills, were the Algonkians' stock to exchange for maize and tobacco grown by the Huron and Tionontati. The extent and importance of the Northern Iroquois (Huron, Tionontati)–Northern Algonkian trade throughout the Late Woodland period is shown by the quantities of Ontario Iroquois pots mixed in campsites with non-Iroquois pottery and other artifacts, well north of the limits of maize agriculture. When in the early seventeenth century the Huron began to procure European implements and beads, adding these to the agricultural products they had formerly offered, the Ottawa and peoples farther west, even the Siouan-speaking Winnebago on Lake Michigan in Wisconsin, looked to the Huron as the principal trading nation of the Northeast.

The Huron received some trade from the south: black squirrel skins, for which they gave cloaks to the Neutral; other warmer-climate skins; gourd containers; and conch shells that originated in the Gulf of Mexico. During the historic period at least, this trade did not include the Five Nations Iroquois. Aboriginal trade in the Northeast seems to have been mainly north-south, following north-south-trending river valleys and crossing climatic zones that fixed the ranges of the animal and plant products forming the bulkier part of the trade goods. Minerals such as catlinite from Minnesota, used for pipes, and North Dakota Knife River "flint" (actually chalcedony) may have zigzagged

along the north-south barter points to reach eastern consumers. The Five Nations had little to offer the Hurons, having no local specialities and less easy access to different regions than did the Hurons. Like the Hurons, the Five Nations could produce quantities of maize sufficient to trade and to supply men out on extended journeys. As long as the Huron held power in southern Ontario, they could shut out the Five Nations from the lucrative middleman role between fur producers and French suppliers. The Five Nations' other possible trading contacts, with the English to the east or the Dutch and Swedes to the southeast, were blocked in part by Algonkian peoples, particularly the Mahican along the Hudson around the Dutch trading point built at Albany in 1614, and in part by the Iroquoian-speaking Susquehannocks aggressively establishing control of European trade in Chesapeake Bay and the lower Delaware River, as well as along the Susquehanna Valley. (Two Virginia English traders had the sense, in the 1620s, to cultivate Susquehannock friendship by paying good prices for beaver pelts carried to them by the Susquehannocks. The traders were assisted by a settler of African origin who had learned to speak Susquehannock. When Maryland Colony authorities intervened in the cosy relationship in 1638, the Susquehannocks transferred their patronage to Swedish traders on the Delaware.) Susquehannock aggression displaced several smaller Algonkian nations, including the Nanticokes and Lenape, from their territories; especially during the Anglo-Powhatan War of the 1620s, these unfortunate Algonkian nations around the Chesapeake were in the pincers of two expanding forces.

The Five Nations Iroquois were not content to labor at manufacturing stone cutting-implements, to make do with fragile ceramic pots, or to ornament themselves with duller-colored, difficult-to-produce bone, shell, or stone beads, when other nations were enjoying metal cutting-implements and kettles and extravagantly bright ornaments cheaply purchased (in terms of hours of Indian labor needed). Iroquois men had little work to do around their towns once the fields were planted in late spring, since women did the routine weeding and cultivating. The peace of the League meant that relatively few men were needed to guard the towns: war parties along the borders of the League lands frightened off foreign invaders. The Five Nations thus had the manpower and the economy to support a large volume of trade during the summer. All they needed was to overcome the peoples who controlled the existing trade—the Hurons, Susquehannocks, and Mahicans. The Hurons managed the routes to the best fur lands (on the Canadian Shield), the Susquehannocks patrolled the southern route to where English, Dutch, and Swedes preferred competitively priced goods, and the Mahicans the route to wampum manufacturing centers along Long Island Sound from New York through Massachusetts, where skilled Algonkians drilled the bead medium and symbol of exchange from quahog shells.

Intensification of French, English, and Dutch fur trading after 1610 intensified Iroquois efforts to gain through it. During the 1630s the Five Nations trapped as much beaver as they could find within their own territories, seriously reducing the population of that animal, and also harassed Hurons, Susquehannocks, and Mahicans. Beginning in 1640, the Five Nations made themselves the scourge of Indians traveling the St. Lawrence, robbing them of furs that could be traded to the Dutch on the Hudson, where the Algonkians had been much weakened by the New England Pequot War of 1637 and by New Netherland's new policy of "ruining and conquering" Indians to secure land for Dutch colonization. The Dutch hoped they could weaken the Hurons and their French allies by attracting the Five Nations Iroquois to Dutch posts and encouraging the League's aggressive pursuit of the principal middleman role. In 1649, the Five Nations accomplished their goal. The previous year, the League had set real armies, rather than many small war parties, upon Huron towns, destroying three of them. The next spring, two more large Huron towns were destroyed by a

League army of a thousand men who, contrary to usual practice, had wintered over on the border rather than journeying home for the season. These intensive campaigns are known as the Beaver Wars. Conventional accounts assume Dutch muskets sold to League members tipped the balance of power in favor of the Five Nations, but the number and effectiveness of the guns available at this time through Dutch suppliers seem inadequate to give Iroquois a real advantage; the radical change in size and deployment of troops probably was the critical factor. (Epidemics of European diseases raged through the Northeast again and again in these years, but both sides in conflicts suffered apparently equally.) In any case, the Huron were broken. With so much of their food stores and fields burned, and with their men unable to go to trade with the interior peoples because of Iroquois threats to themselves en route and to their families at home, the Huron salvaged what they could, set their homes on fire, and scattered to find refuge among their French and Indian allies. The Five Nations now commanded the bulk of the fur trade and could divert it from the St. Lawrence to their friends the Dutch on the Hudson.

By the mid-seventeenth century, the English had become an increasing threat to Indians and European rivals alike. The 1607 settlement in Maine had been decimated by scurvy and the survivors returned to England the next year, carrying furs and sassafras (used as a tonic) to sell. During the summer of 1611, an English ship sailed from Maine to Martha's Vineyard, off Cape Cod's southern shore, stopping several times to seize Indians and quiz them on the resources and farming potential of their homelands. Betting on a surer thing, Bristol capitalists had begun a colony in southern Newfoundland, where they hoped to develop agriculture and exploit fishing until they were strong enough to control the Newfoundland fisheries to English benefit. Effective settlement in New England began in 1620 with the "Pilgrims" at Plymouth in Massachusetts, strongly augmented ten years later by the Puritan colony at Boston on

Massachusetts Bay. Contrasting with French, Dutch, and earlier English colonists, the Massachusetts settlers were determined to settle as families in a new land, not merely work as agents of resource exploiters based in the European ports. The religious fervor that animated them, that had, in their conviction, set them apart by God's grace from their sinning countrymen, persuaded them that perseverance through the trials God would send them would in time gain them God's material blessing as well as eternal salvation. Whereas some of the early French attempts at settlement brought over a strange mix of convicts and young aristocrats, neither class intending to work very hard, the Puritans believed that sweaty physical labor was man's lot. Coupling the determination to build a new and virtuous England at any cost (for the cost would be God's test of their worth) with a greater number of initial colonists (fifteen hundred for Massachusetts Bay) and a much higher proportion of families than had come to other American colonies in the Northeast, the Puritans were a new kind of power in the region. The Puritans claimed that God had prepared New England for them by sending an epidemic to kill off the Indians just before the Plymouth landing. Epidemics do seem to have occurred every few years among Indians in the historic period, and a severe one had raged from 1616 to 1618.

An estimate from carefully analyzed documents puts seventeen thousand European men in eastern Canada in 1580, fifteen thousand of them engaged in the Newfoundland fisheries and two thousand more in whaling. A certain number of this total remained on board the "wet fishing" boats that packed the cod fresh in salt and returned to Europe directly from the offshore banks, but the greater number probably came on shore, and of these, many would have had close contact with Indians, trading and whoring. Throughout the sixteenth century, then, and continuing after it, first hundreds and then thousands of European men yearly left the crowded, dirty streets of that continent and a month or so later were breathing into the faces of Algonkian Indians. Smallpox is generally considered to have been the greatest killer—it took Europeans as well as Indians—but a variety of respiratory diseases nurtured in the closely built, poorly ventilated homes of the European lower classes were transmitted as well to the Northeast Indians, whose practice of shifting settlements had generally prevented endemic diseases cycled through accumulations of garbage and slops. That other pox, syphilis, must also have been transmitted to Indians when the all-male crews were released from the boats. Syphilis probably was endemic in the Caribbean and was introduced to Europe by Columbus's crews, since there was a frightening epidemic of it in Europe in the late 1490s, when it appears to have been more virulent than it is now and was claimed to be a new pox. North of the American tropics, syphilis may have been unknown. If it was carried to eastern Canada by European sailors, it would not only have killed many Indians outright, but would have left some survivors sterile or with reduced fertility. The sixteenth-century Eastern Algonkians were thus likely to be afflicted with the two horrible poxes of contemporary Europe, plus respiratory diseases they had not previously experienced. Cartier's account indicates that in late winter, Indians as well as Europeans were liable to nutritional deficiencies such as scurvy. Even though the Laurentian Iroquois, at least, knew a remedy for scurvy, the unbalanced late-winter diet would have left the Indians with lower resistance to infections. The Indians were surely correct in asserting that since the appearance of Europeans at the beginning of the sixteenth century, native populations had been extensively reduced by disease.

Europeans saw Northeastern Indian farmlands as "unimproved" nature. Instead of totally destroying the natural vegetation of a field, as the European farmer did, and then turning over the soil, the Indian left nut and fruit trees standing, left stumps and rocks, and then broke up the soil, scraping it into ridges or hills separated by relatively wide runoff channels. Maize kernels were individually placed, three or four to a hill, and beans and squashes planted between the maize seedlings. Hand cultivation and planting several different crops together were, to the European, characteristics of gardening but not of full-scale farming. Many centuries earlier, two factors had established the different type of agriculture in Europe: first, the small seeds of European grains (wheat, barley, rye, and oats) were best planted by scattering broadcast over a thoroughly broken soil; second, the plow was the most efficient instrument for preparing fields for the grasslike European grains, and the plow was best used where it could be drawn steadily through long fields. Trees and rocks, nuisances to the plowman because they interrupted his course and damaged his plowshare, could be ignored by the Indian with a hoe. European grains grew too thickly to permit any other crops to be mixed in their fields, but maize grew best when it was more widely spaced, and vine crops such as beans and squashes could flourish in between. The difference between European and Indian agriculture was not a difference between "advanced" and "primitive" technology in the seventeenth century, but a difference between the grasslike European grains and the tall, stout American one. Maize can, of course, be grown with European-derived, plowed-field techniques, but it need not be; European grains cannot be grown as an economic staple by the techniques developed in America for maize. Seventeenth-century Europeans were not, however, sophisticated ecologists when they evaluated Indian agriculture. They saw only that the Indians did not totally clear their fields and used techniques that in Europe were appropriate to small-scale gardening of minor crops, and they concluded that the Indians had not "improved" the land and were not really farmers.

Indian economy was misunderstood by the Europeans in another respect, too. European protein came from livestock penned or herded continuously. Supplemental protein came from dried fish produced by specialists and marketed; for the poor, it came from lentils and similar plants. Indian protein came from deer who grazed unattended in the unfenced parkland around settlements. Supplemental protein came from fish caught and processed by the community as a whole, from game other than deer, and from beans. Deer in the agricultural Northeast were domestic stock in the sense that annual burning over of the parklands by their Indian proprietors maintained the browse that kept the deer population in numbers and density sufficient to be a dependable, reasonably cheap (in hours of labor) resource. Indians did not hunt a wild animal; they harvested an animal population symbiotic with them. The degree of symbiosis was much less than that between the European livestock and farmers, but the principle was similar: humans maintained pasture for the animals they would slaughter. The European colonists did not appreciate this similarity, nor did they accept the basic similarity between Indians congregating at spring and fall fish runs to net, spear, and trap in weirs quantities of food that the fishermen's wives dried, and the European boats congregating in summer at the Newfoundland Banks to catch fish, some of which the crew dried.

The differences between European and Northeastern Indian economies in the seventeenth century were differences in capital outlay and occupational specialization. The intensive labor input that went with European (and with Mexican Indian) occupational specialization produced quantities of foods and goods that maintained dense populations. The Northeastern Indians, having adopted the labor-intensive economy of agriculture only a few centuries earlier, had not yet built up population densities that encouraged occupational specialization. Maize, deer, and fish were the basis of the Indian economy but were harvested directly by every family, with relatively low capital outlay. As practiced in the Northeast, the agricultural economy, with its free-ranging livestock (deer), required more land per person than did the intensified European regime—about one-fourth again as much land. (North of the maize-growing zone, much more land per person was necessary, because the vegetational base of the food chain was much less dense than in the concentrated grain fields and burned-over parklands to the south.) Because Northeastern Indian villages evidenced little capital investment compared with European villages—lightly built houses and storage cribs; no barns, fences, or mills—and because the villages were somewhat farther apart than English villages tended to be, consonant with the Indians' need for more fallow land (they did not have livestock manure to use for fertilizer) and "pasture" for deer, the Europeans did not as a rule recognize the sophisticated adaptation the Indians had made to their homeland. To most Europeans, the Indians in their leather clothing appeared almost as wild as the game in the forests, with as little claim to respect.

The notion that the country had been depopulated for their benefit, and that in any case the Indians were of no account, let the Puritans take up land with little compunction, even when, as frequently happened, the meadows were clearly former Indian cornfields. During the first few years of Massachusetts colonization, there seems to have been no apprehension by the Indians of the real threat posed above them. Squanto (Tisquantum) came by during Plymouth's first planting season and instructed the Englishmen how to raise maize, which they realized was likely to do better in this new land than English grain might. Squanto's advice to fertilize the maize with a fish in every hill may not have been Indian tradition, but perhaps a French technique that Squanto learned either during the couple of years he had lived in Europe after being seized in 1614 and sold as a slave in Spain, or after he had managed to reach Newfoundland and begun working his way down the coast to his home. In spite of his adventures, Squanto was kindly disposed toward the new arrivals from overseas, and apparently did not counsel his sachem (chief) at Mattapoisett to be alarmed. The Plymouth settlers relied heavily on Squanto's knowledge and suggestions and found them good. The pattern set those first few years encouraged the heavy influx of colonists that began in 1630.

The founding of the Massachusetts Bay Colony in 1630 coincided with expansion of Dutch colonization to the south in New Netherland (New York). Both colonies wanted the intervening land and fur trade in Connecticut. Adding to the pressure, dissident English critical of the Bay Colony's authoritarian government were looking for land outside that government's jurisdiction, and that government was determined to enforce its jurisdiction over all New England. As early as 1637, the competition came to a head: the head belonged to a Pequot Indian. Convoluted reasoning in Massachusetts had reached the conclusion that the Pequots, who were themselves asserting dominion over smaller groups such as the Niantic, bore the ultimate responsibility for a couple of murders of Englishmen in previous years. Although neither man had actually been killed by Pequots, the Pequots as the most powerful group in Connecticut should be liable, said the English authorities, for the deeds of all Indians in the region. Extravagant demands for compensation, plus the surrender of the alleged murderers, were made by Massachusetts to the Pequot leaders, who were willing to give substantial amounts of wampum and beaver and otter furs but not the fortune asked, and who could not surrender men belonging to other sachems' groups. To punish the hapless Pequots, Massachusetts sent an armed force to surprise a Pequot town on the Mystic River at a time when most of its men were away. Accompanied by Mohegan and Narragansett Indians, with whom the Pequots had disputed territory, the Englishmen attacked the Pequot town, burned it down, and indiscriminately slaughtered even women and children whom the Narragansett would have saved. Estimates of the number massacred lie between three hundred and seven hundred people, few of them fighting men. A force of Pequot warriors rushing with their principal sachem Sassacus from the main Pequot town five miles away arrived in time only to be shot down by the English guns before their bowmen could come within arrow range. A few more such battles, and the Pequots as a nation were exterminated. The survivors became refugees with the Mohegan under sachem Uncas, formerly a minor leader, or with compassionate Narragansett. The Dutch kept their trading post near Hartford, Connecticut for a few years longer, but it was Massachusetts that opened the rich Connecticut Valley to European settlement.

For a generation, the agricultural Algonkians of New England and New York tried to accommodate the rapidly increasing European inroads on their lands. Puritans seem to have sometimes made up deeds to farms after the Indians had been dispossessed. Both Puritans and Dutch harassed Indian neighbors. Over and over an Indian complained that a European farmer's cattle had trampled his maize. Even when an Indian had copied his neighbor's practice and fenced his field, the fences seemed to break down mysteriously in the night. The local town magistrate would order offending settlers to watch their cattle, but seldom fined them or recompensed the Indian. If an Indian killed the animal that had wasted his family's food supply, townfolk cried for death in retribution. Governors and the Indian sachems prohibited the sale of rum and other liquor to Indians, but traders and settlers flaunted the law and took advantage of Indians who were drunk to get them to sign over land or sell furs for a pittance.

Beginning in 1644, the Puritans took over Indian communities—it is not always very clear how—recording that their sachems submitted themselves and their people to Puritan rule, which meant that the Indians were forced to dress and follow Puritan proprieties and profess Christianity, or else be flogged. According to its charter, Massachusetts Bay Colony was supposed to place the conversion of Indians to Christianity high in its priorities, but the charter directive seems to have been pursued most zealously when the "Praying Indians" needed to be exhibited to the satisfaction of the colony's backers from England, or when they could be used in attacks on other native peoples. There was also a continuing, though not much publicized, seventeenth-century trade in Indian

slaves. The Iroquois nations and, probably to a lesser extent, some of the Algonkians kept slaves, most of them said to be captured through war, since slaves' children were considered free-born citizens. In 1645, one Puritan suggested that they, too, capture Indians in war and sell them, the money to be used to purchase black slaves in place of the less hardy Indians. Southeastern Indians, it will be recalled, were sold in New England as slaves, too. As in the Southeast, no matter how conciliatory the Indians were to the colonists, they could never be safe from land encroachment and personal attack.

By 1671, the Wampanoag sachem Metacomet, whose father had been the massasoit ("great chief") of the area in which Plymouth Colony lay, was finding it increasingly difficult to keep peace with the expanding Puritans. He was compelled to sign a treaty that declared him subject to Plymouth. Metacomet, who was called King Philip by the English, must have been unhappy over the treaty and its implication that he who was leader of a confederacy of a number of Indian towns in southern Massachusetts was less than any man in Plymouth colony (since he had no say in its government). In 1675, a "Praying Indian" who had been sent to instruct Metacomet to read (whether he would or not), but who was rumored to have contented himself with writing Metacomet's will to provide for his own benefit, came to the governor claiming that Metacomet was planning war against the English. Quakers from Rhode Island intervened, talking with Metacomet and reporting war could probably be averted, but Plymouth prepared to fight. Colonists left their homes, retreating to better protection. An Indian said to have been seen stealing from one of the abandoned houses was shot. His people asked the nearby garrison why he had been killed, and overheard a youth in the garrison say, "It was no matter." Enraged, the Indians left and the following day shot their man's murderer. War was on.

King Philip's War was a real war. Both traditional and some "Praying Indian" towns rose against neighboring colonists, while colonist forces, sometimes composed of hired mercenaries as well as real colonists with families, staged surprise attacks upon Indian towns, massacring women and children whose men were in the field. As in the earlier Pequot War, colony competition lay beneath many of the thrusts against the Indians. Metacomet fled to the upper Connecticut River Valley, in the winter of 1675, continuing to fight from there. The governor of New York saw an opportunity to promote the territorial claims of the Duke of York over the entire Northeast by engaging "his" Indians, the Mohawks, to join the war. The Mohawk were delighted to fall upon the Algonkians, who had once blocked them from the fur trade and still disputed it. Metacomet's hope of raising forces in New York and Connecticut was dashed, and he was driven back to the New England coast and killed in August 1676. Many of his people, including his wife (herself a sachem) and children, were sold into slavery in the West Indies. By one recent reckoning, about two thousand Indians were slaughtered in battle, three thousand turned out from their homes and food stores to die, and one thousand sold into slavery from captivity. About two thousand survived as refugees in groups outside New England, and perhaps four thousand remained in New England, many of these in Rhode Island, Martha's Vineyard, and Nantucket Island, where colonists had respected a measure of Indian rights and thereby earned the natives' friendship. King Philip's War was the final phase in the destruction of Eastern Algonkian power under the onslaught of massive European immigration. The Five Nations Iroquois became the dominant Indians in the Northeast, and the fur trade the dominant interaction between Europeans and Indians.

SECTION 4: THE FUR TRADE

From a field of five nations—England, France, Spain, Portugal, and Holland—each hoping in the sixteenth century to achieve domination in the American Northeast, the competitors had narrowed by the late seventeenth century to England and France. Both had realized by this time that extractive industries such as the fur trade and the cod fishery could not be simply combined with the establishment of self-sufficient agricultural colonies. The fur trade and the fishery were international businesses based on intercontinental systems of supply and management; they could not be fully exploited by American-based administrators engaged also in farming or community development. Stimulated by a lucrative European market, especially for beaver, the fur trade emerged as America's prime growth industry in the eyes of English and French capitalists.

The beaver trade was quite complex. The Algonkians had been accustomed to wearing robes made of six to eight beaver skins, well scraped of flesh and gristle inside and then sewn together. During the tanning process, animal marrow and brains had been rubbed into the skins to soften them, and in the year or so a beaver robe would be worn, it would be further softened by the wearer's body secretions and the grease that Indians rubbed on their skin to protect themselves from insects or winter chapping. The well-worn beaver robes that the Indians were about to consider rags were the pelts most desired by the European traders: the *castor gras,* or coat beaver. The robes were taken to France, picked up there by Dutch vessels, brought to northern Russian ports, where by a secret process the fine inner wool was combed out, and then were transported as sacks of beaver wool to Amsterdam. The Russians kept many of the combed-out robes to be made into fur garments, since the long outer fur remained on the skin. Amsterdam sold the beaver wool to felters in France and England who processed it into an exceptionally sturdy felt preferred for hats. The most heavily worn beaver robes could be combed right in France, because the months of rubbing had loosened the wool, and the cost of buying processed wool from Russia via Amsterdam thereby avoided. The French and English managers of the trade wanted the well-greased coat beaver, particularly coats made from beaver caught in the winter, when their wool undercoat was thickest *(castor gras d'hiver)*. Winter beaver skins dried but not worn as robes *(castor sec,* or parchment beaver) were good, but because they incurred the cost of Russian combing, they were bought for less than *castor gras.* Least desired were "summer" beaver, those caught in summer, when they had little wool, and beaver from south of the Canadian Shield ("Illinois" beaver), where the animals grew bigger but did not develop very thick down. As the demand for beaver-felt hats expanded, some French felters shaved the hair from the pelts, ruining them as furs but short-cutting the Dutch-Russian expense. After 1685, the center of beaver-felt hat making shifted from France to England with the immigration of Huguenot craftsmen. A final complication in the market demand for beaver came from the recycling of hats, which, when discarded by aristocrats, were cut down and made into smaller hats for the less fashionable, or stiffened with gum and sold in Spain. When the hats were nearly worn out in Spain or Brazil, they were resold by the Portuguese to Africans.

Back in America, beaver skins were bought from the Indians by weight or bulk. This made it advantageous for the Indians to sell the large southern beaver and the stiff, thick parchment beaver, and meant that they received less for the desirable *castor gras* from northern territories. To encourage them nevertheless to bring in the *gras,* managers instructed the traders to accept only that type of beaver pelt. This backfired early in the eighteenth century, when stockpiles of *castor gras* were so great the felters would not accept any more. That angered the Indians, who had put a year or more into wearing the robes to the proper *gras* condition. Thus, the fur trade was beset by problems of supply and demand so complex that no one could control the market. Requiring heavy outlay of capital in fitting ships and hiring men to journey thousands of miles into interior America, plus warehouses and brokers in Europe, the fur trade was a high-risk business

beyond the capability of small, private entrepreneurs. It was a business for wealthy adventurers.

In 1670, England chartered the Governor and Company of Adventurers of England Trading into Hudson's Bay. Prince Rupert, cousin of the King, a duke, three earls, and lesser-titled but well-to-do men had formed the company after subscribing to trading voyages to Hudson Bay in 1668 and 1669. These voyages had been directed by two Frenchmen raised in Canada, the Sieur des Groseilliers and Pierre Esprit Radisson, who had explored the western Great Lakes and some of the country north of Lake Superior in 1659–60. Groseilliers and Radisson had gone independently, contrary to regulations then in effect in French Canada forbidding traders to go to the Indians' communities to obtain furs. (This was considered a threat to the authorities who supervised, and taxed, the trading at the official collection depots on the St. Lawrence.) Fined upon their return, Groseilliers and Radisson tried to raise backing for a trading venture by ship to the interior through Hudson Bay, first seeking funds in France, which they thought might be more liberal than the Canadian authorities, then in New England, and finally in England. Here the court was much intrigued by the plan to bypass the French and go directly to the source of the prime northern beaver. The success of the first two English voyages, which met the Cree at James Bay, the southernmost section of Hudson Bay, proved the value of the plan, although it was fourteen years before the Hudson's Bay Company earned enough profits over its expenses in constructing ships and facilities to be able to pay dividends.

By the 1680s, the fur trade had three centers. The English at Albany, New York, received the furs collected by the Five Nations Iroquois from Great Lakes peoples. The French on the St. Lawrence relied on the Ottawas, to whom some Hurons had fled, to bring them furs gathered from the Cree, Ojibwa, and other Algonkian speakers, and the Siouan-speaking Assiniboin, all of whom had since the 1640s become accustomed to coming together each summer at the Sault Ste. Marie between Lakes Superior and Huron in order to trade. The English Hudson's Bay Company was trading directly with the Indian producers, mostly Cree, who came down the rivers (northward) to the Bay. The French disputed the English claim to "Rupert's Land," the great watershed of Hudson Bay, and also to the Great Lakes trade brought in by the Iroquois. The Iroquois disputed the Ottawa hegemony. The governor of French Canada, Denonville, was instructed to war upon the Iroquois as well as to secure the northern trade with new posts in the interior and the seizure of English posts. Denonville had little success in the south, merely confirming the Iroquois alliance with the English by such ploys as seizing Iroquois men returning from the hunt and sending them to France as galley slaves. His efforts in the north were better rewarded, several English posts falling into the control of the French. The contests between the French and the English, and the French and the Iroquois, were to continue for nearly a century, until the conclusion of the "French and Indian War" (Seven Years' War) at the Treaty of Paris in 1763 gave Canada to the British.

By the mid-seventeenth century, the Indians of the Northeast were so deeply involved in the fur trade that they were moving into the status of a proletariat. They relied upon European manufactures for their daily needs, in many instances having already lost their own technologies in stone implements, weapons, and pottery. Metal knives, axes, chisels, awls, needles, and kettles, guns, and woolen cloth seemed so cheap compared with the labor needed to make the native analogs that obsolete skills died with the elders. Glass beads and metal ornaments became essential to the self-respect of every Indian. Liquor was eagerly sought after. The set pattern became a canoe journey, often of hundreds of miles, in late spring to a rendezvous—Sault Ste. Marie or Michilimackinac between Lakes Michigan and Huron—or a post where the bundled beaver pelts from a winter's work were exchanged for most of the tools, the ammunition, much of the clothing, and the tea,

tobacco, and flour used by a family during the year. The pelts were exchanged at a standard rate set by the administrators of the trading companies, but the price was augmented by "presents," the value of which were determined by the competition out in the Indian territories. "Presents" were supposedly tokens of friendship and alliance, and refusal to give presents certainly ended friendships and alliances, but the real function of the presents was to allow the traders some flexibility in rates. If liquor was available, a drinking orgy ensued. The Hudson's Bay Company tried to prohibit liquor, but independent, illicit traders undermined the prohibition, using liquor as the inducement for Indians to patronize their posts. When the trade was concluded, the Indians visited the large summer fishing camps, the original attraction of the Sault Ste. Marie, where dancing, courting, gambling, sport contests, public announcement of new leaders chosen to replace deceased ones, and the honoring of valorous deeds could be enjoyed. Gifts of trade goods and furs were lavishly distributed, and feasting indulged in. Waning summer brought consultations on families' preferences for winter hunting territories, and the dispersal of the great conclaves of one or two thousand persons into hunting bands of twenty-five to thirty.

The fur-trade pattern of living, which varied from region to region and decade to decade, retained most of the subsistence skills, some of the technology, and in modified form the social organization of the prehistoric Northeast beyond the agricultural zone. In technology, metal replaced most of the stone, bone, and ceramic artifacts, but not all Indians were persuaded at once to make the change, and for some tasks, bone artifacts are still made today. For example, excavation of an eighteenth-century trading post on the Saskatchewan River in central Canada exposed a quartzite knife and sherds of a native ceramic cooking pot just outside the wall of the post, suggesting someone had prepared a meal with old-style utensils although metal substitutes were available a few steps away. The same excavation produced a hide scraper made by serrating the end of a moose or elk leg bone, an implement identical to ones used in Cree reserves along the Saskatchewan River today—the ancient-type artifact persists because metal substitutes tend to tear a hide.

Changes in social organization came about through the European traders' imposition of their own hierarchical organization upon their Indian customers. Traders found it easier to deal with a single representative of a group of trappers, buying their furs as a lot and leaving it to the Indians to distribute among themselves the goods received in exchange. Traders also assumed they would have greater control over trappers if a leader were made responsible for the activities of a group. To promote this European style of organization, traders selected a man whom they judged to be, or to have the potential to be, a leader from each group of trappers journeying together, and presented to this leader a decorated cloth coat and hat that would mark him as the "captain." The new "captain" was delighted with the extra gifts, but seldom had the power to coerce the men with him to trap more and to patronize "his" trader exclusively, as the trader expected. As more and more trading posts were established in the interior on the Canadian Shield, hunting bands in a locality tended to congregate at the post (which was often conveniently at a summer fishing camp), in contrast with earlier years when the bands sent a few men on a long canoe journey to posts on the seacoast. What became a trading-post community was the coalescence of perhaps five or six hunting bands of twenty-five to thirty persons each. The nuclear bands, or even families within the bands, continued to fan out from the post to set up trap lines and to hunt for meat. Adherence of families to one post, with occasional winter visits as well as the principal summer trading visit, allowed the trader to know and deal with individual families, and thereby shift the trade-imposed leadership from a band captain to male heads of families. This transference of the European model of a patriarchal family to the northern Algonkians encouraged trap-line partner-

ship of fathers and sons and discouraged the traditional matrilocality. The proletarianization of the Indians, as they became the line workers in the fur-trapping industry, thus included shifts toward European patterns of work group and family.

With more time, as well as incentive, to trap once they no longer had to manufacture stone, bone, and ceramic artifacts, Indians produced many more pelts than they had aboriginally, and began to threaten the survival of beaver as a species. Hunting out one locality may promote the proliferation of the animals, since the young in neighboring localities find no competition as they move out from the parental territory, but if intensive trapping depopulates an entire watershed, the few beaver who escape may not find mates, and extinction within a region can ensue. One historian has suggested that epidemics of tularemia and perhaps other diseases may have been carried to America by the rats, dogs, and livestock embarking from European ships, and may have raged through the forests, killing wildlife and humans alike. Since diseases usually spread to the interior by contacts between aboriginal inhabitants, especially the Indian middlemen in the fur trade and their remote suppliers-customers, decades before direct European invasion, no good documentation of such epidemics can be expected. Not only beaver but also moose and caribou seemed to disappear from many regions, no doubt in part because Indians hunted out the region within a couple days' journey from a trading post, but perhaps also as a result of imported disease.

The fur-trade "front" advanced westward throughout the eighteenth and nineteenth centuries, leaving behind lands with almost no beaver and few moose where Indians were forced to subsist on rabbits and fish, rounded out with flour-and-lard bannock biscuit baked from trade provisions, a poor diet that lowered resistance to disease. Social organization deteriorated, too. No longer could ambitious people gain prestige by lavishly distributing gifts at big summer encampments, for with the decline in beaver, no one could amass any

FIGURE 5.2 Midewiwin, Chippewa (Ojibwa), end of the nineteenth century. The Midewiwin ("Midé People") is a ritual society of doctors among the Upper Great Lakes Algonkians. Following several days of spiritual training for the initiates, the Society invites the public to come to its ceremonial lodge for therapy. *(Smithsonian Institution National Anthropological Archives)*

quantities of trade goods. No longer were interband alliances important: the relationship between the family and the local trader, mediated by the community around the post, was the dominant one. Income came from trapping muskrat, marten, and other furs, all more difficult to secure than beaver because, as the Indians described them, beaver seem human in living openly in lodges easily discovered, while the other fur bearers are furtive. Some men supplemented trapping income by hunt-

ing meat for the trading-post operator and his employees. There was almost no other means of earning necessities in the northern forests. From the later seventeenth century in the Maritimes through the nineteenth century in western Canada, Indians found that the heady affluence of first engagement directly with the European traders (following some years of receiving used goods secondhand from Indian middlemen) lasted only a generation or so, and left the sour taste of poverty. The decline of large game and beaver and the substitution of the less bold smaller fur bearers and food game meant many more hours of labor expended to meet the price of a tool, a length of cloth, or an item of store food. In effect, the Indian proletariat offered the fur traders abundant labor and met low wages.

After 1821, the Hudson's Bay Company exercised a true monopoly over Rupert's Land, the interior of Canada granted the company in its charter. The 1763 Treaty of Paris had ceded Canada to Britain, and in 1821 the North West Company, an association of independent traders who had been competing with "the Bay" for decades, merged with the official traders. The Bay's monopoly in Rupert's Land, a country with no other industry but the fur trade, allowed it to insist on conservation procedures that did eventually restore beaver populations and prevent muskrat extinction, but this laudable change was accompanied by greater power over the Indians of Rupert's Land and greater hardship for them until their game densities had appreciably increased.

SECTION 5: IROQUOIS ASCENDANCY AND DEFEAT

The Iroquois in the seventeenth century enjoyed a security denied to the Algonkians of the Northeast. Dutch and then English governors of New York favored channeling the fur trade through the Iroquois to Albany, where it could conveniently be regulated and taxed. To protect the trade, settlement by Europeans was proscribed in Iroquois territory. Algonkians had the land on the seaboard, where Europeans arrived and built ports, while Iroquois land in central New York had much less commercial value. Balancing resources against political power, the Dutch and the succeeding English colonial governments felt little compunction in dispossessing coastal Algonkians, who were only an impediment to colonization and whose principal value lay in what they could bring

sold as slaves or, later, hired at wages less than what European settlers would accept. Iroquois land resources, on the other hand, were too remote from the ports to be desirable for colonization, so the Dutch and British governments allied with the Iroquois by letting them collect the furs beyond their homeland and used them as a barrier to French expansion. Iroquois and Algonkians both suffered from epidemics, but where the Algonkians were harassed into smaller and smaller groups until their impoverished little enclaves were virtually invisible on the Atlantic Slope, the Iroquois, treated with respect as allies, were able to maintain their strength by taking in refugees from other nations (including Hurons and many Algonkians).

The century of on-again, off-again wars between England and France that finally ended in 1763 usually involved joint forces of European soldiers, colonial militia, and Indian men. The Five Nations generally fought with the English, who referred to the Iroquois fortified towns along the colony borders as "castles." Smaller parties of Mahicans and other nations within English territorial claims often joined the English-Iroquois forces. The French enlisted Christian Iroquois settled at Caughnawaga (now spelled Kahnawake) near Montreal and other nations along the St. Lawrence and north of the Great Lakes. The American battles were sometimes stimulated by local grievances or ambitions, sometimes fomented by directives from Europe. None were conclusive, since European negotiations could nullify American gains. Indians were often victims in local uprisings such as Bacon's Rebellion in Virginia in 1675-76, when frontier settlers attacked the Susquehannock town at Accokeek Creek near the head of Chesapeake Bay, and massacred many other Indians in scattered homes. Susquehannock fought back but could not hold their territory won only a generation earlier, and their refugees joined Five Nations towns. This inconclusiveness of inter-European battles and success of colonists' campaigns against coastal nations benefited the Five Nations Iroquois, whose service as the buffer between contesting colonies and additional force in wars, as in King Philip's War, continued to be valued.

War parties of Iroquois also attacked Indians and occasionally colonists to the south and west. According to the historical documents, many war parties were independent adventures unsanctioned by the chiefs. The Iroquois, like most of the Southeastern Indians, classed warriors below the more mature town and league chiefs. Warriors were supposed to be impetuous young men eager to win glory, chafing at the chiefs' preference for discussion and diplomacy rather than fighting. Since the chiefs' power was over internal affairs and could not control men outside the territory of the Five Nations, war parties were beyond the jurisdiction of Iroquois government. The sorties of warriors were thus ostensibly exercises of young men out to gain a name. Armed through the Albany trade, the bold warriors did terrorize broad areas as far away as Virginia to the south, Wisconsin to the west, and Canada to the north. A route south along the edge of the Allegheny Mountains from Five Nations territory to western Virginia and the Ohio country was known as the Warriors' Path. Their chiefs' polite disapproval notwithstanding, the Iroquois independent war parties were an instrument for maintaining Iroquois power, and perhaps official disapproval masked private commendation.

It was in the Iroquois interest to pose a continuous threat to the peoples to the south and west as well as to the north. The French with their Algonkian allies, the Ottawa and Nipissing, and the Christian Iroquois at Caughnawaga (Kahnawake) consistently sought to expand their fur trade at the expense of the English. French exploration of the Mississippi was the foundation for attempts to circumvent the Iroquois-English domination south of the Laurentian-Lakes zone by routing trade from Louisiana along the Mississippi, then north to Lake Superior or over the Wisconsin River–Fox River linkage to Green Bay on Lake Michigan. During the late seventeenth and the eighteenth centuries the French established forts to protect their trade along the Great Lakes–Mississippi passage. They hoped to attract the Ojibwa, Sioux, Miami, Fox, and other nations around the western Great Lakes and in the northern Midwest, and also to draw Cree and Assiniboin to posts nearer their hunting grounds than the English posts on Hudson Bay. French efforts were hampered by the cheaper prices the English could offer at Hudson Bay, where goods were shipped at much less cost than the French suffered for their long canoe transport, and by the Indians' opinion that English goods were of better quality or were better designed for their needs than French goods. (Many European manufacturers produced items specifically modified for the American trade.) Quality gave the Iroquois an advantage, since as middlemen they could not offer prices as low as those given directly by the English at distant Hudson Bay. Teganissorens, an Onondaga leader, used a 1701 treaty between the Five Nations and the English in Albany, New York to draw upon English goods to consolidate Iroquois trading into the Northwest Territory along the Great Lakes. The combination of quality goods and military threat kept the Iroquois potent in the interior fur trade.

Iroquois diplomacy complemented Iroquois armed power. Onondaga sachem Daniel Garacontié led the movement to negotiate using the Confederacy as a united front against European encroachment. At the close of King Philip's War, in New England, and Bacon's Rebellion, in Virginia, in 1677, the term "Covenant Chain" was introduced during negotiations between Mohawk and Maryland Colony. The term was popularized in the 1680s and continued in use for nearly a century, until Britain's victory over France in 1763. Britain wanted to forge a chain of allies along her colony borders by a series of covenants, or treaties, and to this purpose regularly convened meetings of Iroquois leaders and British envoys (at one point including a bright and ambitious Pennsylvania printer named Benjamin Franklin). Iroquois called the agreements "clasped hands." Heavy wampum-bead belts exchanged at the treaty meetings symbolized the clasping of hands at the frontier. One interesting effect of the long series of Covenant Chain meetings came from Indian insistence that Iroquois diplomatic protocol be honored, impressing upon the British the formality of Iroquois law and government. European notions of "rude savages" had to be modified at least for the Iroquois, and when rebel Americans searched for precedent for a federal form of representative democracies, Franklin could describe the League of the Iroquois whose delegates so obviously came from a successful confederation.

The American Revolution posed a dilemma for the Iroquois. From what they could observe, it was a fratricidal war between Englishmen, one that seemed none of their business. The British, however, expected their traditional allies the Five Nations to aid them. Many Iroquois—who were now Six Nations, the Tuscarora refugees from North Carolina having joined as "children" of the league between 1712 and 1715—had little love for the Americans, who had been pushing into the Ohio Valley where the Shawnee and other nations whom the Six Nations claimed to be protecting lived and hunted. In 1774, this country had been the scene of attacks and skirmishes let loose when Euro-American land jobbers massacred Indians in retaliation for the loss of some horses. John Logan, a Cayuga chief's son married to a Shawnee, was bereaved of his family by the massacre and undertook revenge. At the parley concluding the local war, he made the famous oration reported by Thomas Jefferson that asks, "Who is there to mourn for Logan? Not one." Shawnee, Delaware, Wyandot (of Huron descent), and western Iroquois fought with Logan, but the League refused to officially sponsor the war, and mediated a peace with the governor of Virginia. When the Revolution broke out, the Six Nations decided that so long as both British and rebels respected Iroquois sovereignty over the Six Nations homeland and the Ohio-region protectorate, the Iroquois would remain neutral.

THE TUSCARORA SUE FOR PEACE: A PETITION TO THE PROVINCIAL GOVERNMENT OF PENNSYLVANIA, JUNE 8, 1710

Meeting with two commissioners from Pennsylvania, in the presence of five Conestoga chiefs and the head chief of the Shawnee, at Conestoga, Tuscarora ambassadors delivered a petition for peace between their harassed people in North Carolina and the encroaching European colonists. The clauses of the petition were each symbolized in a ceremonial belt of wampum:

"By the first belt, the elder women and the mothers besought the friendship of the Christian people, the Indians and the government of Pennsylvania, so they might fetch wood and water without risk or danger.

"By the second, the children born and those about to be born, implored for room to sport and play without the fear of death or slavery.

"By the third, the young men asked for the privilege to leave their towns without the fear of death or slavery to hunt for meat for their mothers, their children, and the aged ones.

"By the fourth, the old men, the elders of the people, asked for the consummation of a lasting peace, so that the forests (the paths to other tribes) be as safe for them as their palisaded towns.

"By the fifth, the entire tribe asked for a firm peace.

"By the sixth, the chiefs asked for the establishment of a lasting peace with the government, people, and Indians of Pennsylvania, whereby they would be relieved from 'those fearful apprehensions they have these several years felt.'

"By the seventh, the Tuscarora begged for a 'cessation from murdering and taking them,' so that thereafter they would not fear 'a mouse, or anything that ruffles the leaves.'

"By the eighth, the tribe, being strangers to the people and government of Pennsylvania, asked for an official path or means of communication between them."

The Pennsylvania commissioners received the petition with arrogance. On the counsel of the Conestoga chiefs witnessing the meeting, the Tuscarora wampum belts were then sent to the Five Nations Iroquois, who were moved to take the petitioners into their League.

(Hewitt, in Hodge 1910:843-844)

Iroquois conditions for neutrality were soon violated. Rebel troops went into Mohawk country, taking Oswego and arresting Sir John Johnson, whose father Colonel William Johnson had been Superintendent of Indian Affairs for New York, had learned Mohawk and married a Mohawk woman, Molly Brant. Molly's brother Thayendanegea (Joseph Brant) was a staunch advocate of the British, and the incursion of rebels into Mohawk land and the threat to Sir John gave weight to Thayendanegea's arguments against acceptance of the Americans' pleas to avoid the conflict. In 1777, the majority of the Iroquois, acting as independent warriors because an epidemic at Onondaga had killed three League sachems there and no League decision could be made until its council fire was ritually rekindled before the full roster of sachems, agreed to fight with the British. Only some Oneida, with Tuscarora and Stockbridge (refugee Algonkian, mostly Mahican), took up arms on the rebel side. (Much as the Algonkians had suffered from the colonists, they seem to have been able to identify with the rebels' cause against the Crown. Crispus Attucks, the first person killed in the Boston Massacre of rebels, was a Massachusetts Indian on his mother's side, although his father was black. Attucks, like many of the coastal Algonkians of his time, was a sailor by occupation.)

Iroquois action against the American rebels concentrated on laying waste the New York frontier, driving the colonists back toward the seaboard. Iroquois effectiveness spurred Washington to mount a careful campaign against them in 1779, wasting the Indian lands as they had devastated their opponents'. Oneida only were spared, to be destroyed in revenge by Thayendanegea's forces coming down from the St. Lawrence. By early 1780, only two of some thirty Six Nations towns were still habitable. Maize stores had been burned with the houses. What succor the British could give to their allies could barely maintain life. Iroquois men continued their raids of desolation along the frontier from Canada to West Virginia, in spite of the plight of their families in refugee camps around Niagara, until the British surrender in 1783. Then the Iroquois came to negotiate their own peace with the United States, for the British did not include their Indian allies in the Crown's capitulation.

A series of meetings in 1784, 1785, and 1786 between United States representatives and Indians established in United States law the rebel nation's position that Britain's surrender included the surrender of her Indian allies, who forfeited under conquest their lands. The purpose of the post-Revolution treaties was to convey this position to the Indians and grant them reservations within their former (according to the United States) territories. Since Britain had not stipulated in her surrender that she took responsibility for her Indian allies, and since the Indians did not admit that they had been defeated, the Indian delegates to the treaty conferences were shocked at the United States' position. Many would not sign the documents of cession of land. Nevertheless, holding the Indians to be conquered peoples powerless to demand terms to their own liking, the United States held as in force the "agreements" signed by various Indians (some alleged to have been drunk) recognizing United States dominion over all the lands south of the St. Lawrence and the Great Lakes and east of the Mississippi. Within this Northwest Territory, the Shawnee, Delaware, Wyandot, some Ottawa, and Ojibwa (called Chippewa, an alternative spelling of the native name Otchipwa) were given a set of reservations in Ohio. The Six Nations were given reservations in New York. None of the Indian peoples felt the treaties were just, but none judged themselves strong enough to battle the nation that had just ousted Britain, so the treaties stood.

SECTION 6: THE IROQUOIS IN THE NINETEENTH AND TWENTIETH CENTURIES

The few remaining years of the eighteenth century following the Revolutionary War were years of adjustment for the former British allies. Thayendanegea—more often known by his English name of Joseph Brant—headed a settlement of his Mohawk followers, other Iroquois, and even some Delaware on a reserve granted by Britain on the Grand River in Ontario. There he lived like a European aristocrat, with

uniformed black servants attending his table laid with fine china and crystal goblets; that he was a war leader and not a sachem made no difference to New York State officials who in 1797 happily got his signature on a treaty selling eight million acres of Mohawk land in the state. By 1803, relations between New York and Canadian Iroquois were strained to the point that the Six Nations League meeting at Onondaga formally excluded the Canadian émigrés from the League, although the Grand River people continued to consider themselves true Iroquois and set up their own council. The peoples of the former Iroquois protectorate in the Ohio country, led by the Shawnee, confederated and resisted the takeover of their lands until the Battle of Fallen Timbers in 1794 forced a new treaty, this one recognizing Indian rights to their homelands. Negotiations after this battle, not only with the Ohio peoples but also with the New York Iroquois, drew up new reservations but made at least token indemnification to the Indians for their cessions, and promised farm implements, livestock, and instructors in farming and smithing. To defray some of the costs of these aids to "civilization," the United States government invited Christian missionary organizations to cooperate in providing both goods and personnel. Some Indian communities, such as the Seneca led by Cornplanter (Kaiionytwa'ko), whose father was said to be a New York colonist, favored adopting the Euro-American pattern and planned gristmills, sawmills, spinning, and weaving as well as European-style farming. Others, such as Red Jacket (so called from a coat given him by a British officer; his personal name was Otetiani, and he bore the sachem's title Shagoiewatha), also a Seneca, could not be shaken from the conviction that traditional Iroquois ways were best for the Iroquois. Willingness to adopt Euro-American practices, as well as Euro-American occupied land, thus came to divide the Indians affected by the post-Revolution treaties.

The very last years of the eighteenth century were particularly unhappy for the Iroquois. They had to build new settlements on reservations. Most constructed crude log cabins roofed with bark, draftier than the bark-shingled longhouses. The traditional seasonal cycle continued—clearing and planting fields in the spring, hunting and fishing in the summer, harvesting in the fall, and going on long hunts in the winter. War parties no longer went out in summer, however, and their cessation left young men unemployed, restless, uneasy about how they would make names for themselves. Fur trading continued, with Pittsburgh a popular post. The debauchery that for two centuries had accompanied trading worsened: on the one hand, all the men were now in the trading parties, and on the other, in the absence of hostilities and amid the proliferation of traders, families were usually present when the trading goods, including whiskey or rum, were obtained. Orgies of drunkenness came every spring after the furs were sold. Prudent mothers took their children and hid out in the bush for days while men and old women whooped it up in the villages, brawling and wrecking cabins. Frustrated by the ending of the warrior's and middleman trader's roads to glory, many men beat their wives even when they weren't drunk, a shocking departure from the traditional Iroquois man's cool self-control (no doubt cushioned in the traditional longhouse by the constant presence of all the clanswomen and their families). Upset and anxious, people became convinced that witches had to be behind the misery. Suspicions riled the villages. The four principles recognized by the Iroquois to be the foundation of sound life and society were losing force: bodily health and its social equivalent, peace, no longer prevailed within villages; personal strength and civil authority were failing; truth and righteousness were neglected; and the League with its overriding law was broken.

Cornplanter's family was as much disturbed as those who attempted to follow more traditional Iroquois patterns. In May 1799, Cornplanter's village was the scene of days of drunken revelry after the return of men from trading furs at Pittsburgh. One elderly woman died after drinking herself into a stupor alone outside at night. After the whiskey was gone, the community held the Corn Planting Ceremony, and with it a memorial feast for a daughter of Cornplanter who had died late that winter. People talked about the death and felt it might have been engineered by an old woman reputed to be a witch. Fearing further sorcery, Cornplanter's sons openly executed her by stabbing. Then, on June 15, Cornplanter's half-brother, who bore the sachem's title Ganiodayo' (It Is a Very Large Lake, or "Handsome Lake"), came to the point of death. Suffering from a long illness, he fell unconscious. His daughter, with whom he lived, summoned his brother and nephew to attend the dying man. After two hours, Handsome Lake awoke and announced he had been visited by three spirits who warned the people against drinking and witchcraft. On August 7, Handsome Lake, who had remained ill, informed Cornplanter he would go on a second spiritual journey, and lapsed into a longer trance. Handsome Lake's visions during this trance were recounted to form the Gaiwiio', the Good Word (Gospel) or Message of Handsome Lake, the doctrine of what would be called the Longhouse Religion of the Iroquois.

Curiously, western New York from 1790 on was for half a century a hotbed of religious prophets and revivals. The year 1799 witnessed the culmination of several years of mounting religious enthusiasms among the immigrant Euro-American Christians who left poor New England farms and the already well populated Atlantic Slope for the homesteading lands opened up by the defeat of the Iroquois. A Quaker missionary living in Cornplanter's village heard Handsome Lake's account of his spirit's tour of the Above, and told Cornplanter that Christians had had similar visions. While spiritual revelations were certainly not unprecedented among Indians, Handsome Lake's credibility must have been enhanced by the parallel revelations and revivals flourishing among the Iroquois' non-Indian neighbors. It was soon concretely strengthened by a letter from President Jefferson, writing in 1802 after Handsome Lake had visited him in Washington, that he urged the Iroquois to follow the advice and precepts of the prophet.

Handsome Lake's dramatic recitation of the Good Word sent by He-Who-Holds-the-Sky reformed Cornplanter's people. They gave up whiskey: the Pittsburgh traders had to give them sugar-water as the customary lubricant for dealing! They gave up the wild night dances and gambling with cards their men had learned from the Euro-Americans. Men began to take over labor in the fields, as Euro-American men did, freeing the women to work in the houses, which now were usually log or frame cabins sheltering only the nuclear family. Handsome Lake did not advocate abandonment of all Iroquois customs. He did not approve of sending children to school, seeing no need for his people to read or write. (Cornplanter's son Henry had been educated in Philadelphia and since his return had been a source of dissension in the community, championing Euro-American ways.) Handsome Lake continued to believe in witches, as did many Euro-Americans in rural New York, and believed they should be executed. Although farms were worked individually, he urged that produce be shared in the community rather than sold. More important, he reaffirmed Iroquois religious beliefs and the value of the major traditional rituals, the Green Corn Festival, the Harvest Festival or Thanksgiving, the Midwinter New Year's Festival, the Thanks-to-the-Maple when sugar-making time arrived, the Corn Planting Festival, and the Strawberry Festival. Component rituals within the festivals, including the communion feast of the sacrificed white dog, the Great Feather Dance honoring the Sky Holder, and the holy Bowl Game of throwing lots, were to be continued. Handsome Lake did claim that the secret medicine societies, including the False Faces, should be banned, apparently concerned that they inclined toward witchcraft, but the Iroquois would not accept such a proscription.

Most of the Good Word's reforms were already instituted in Cornplanter's community when Handsome Lake went into his first trance. The visions gave the stamp of divine approval to the secular efforts to better the society. Other Iroquois communities were attempting to improve their deteriorated condition, and welcomed Handsome Lake to preach. A beautiful set of wampum belts appeared, the traditional mnemonic symbols of a message, recording the Good Message. Western nations sent delegates to discover the Word and a better life. A Shawnee prophet, Tenskwatawa (Open Door [to revelation]), in 1805 experienced a trance and vision in which the Master of Life spoke, not for the adjustment that Handsome Lake preached, but for the repudiation of all things European. Tenskwatawa and his brother, Tecumseh (One Who Springs [like a panther]) led the trans-Appalachian Indians to war, which was aborted at the Battle of Tippecanoe (Ohio) in 1811. Handsome Lake, a generation older than the Shawnee brothers, staunchly opposed war and kept many Iroquois out of the War of 1812. He preached continuously, dying in 1815 at Onondaga. His Gaiwiio' had been learned verbatim by several of his disciples, and is still memorized by the Longhouse religion preachers. The wampum belts with the Message are reverently kept at Tonawanda, a Seneca reservation where Handsome Lake's grandson lived.

The Iroquois have been unusually successful in maintaining their prereservation cultural pattern. President Jackson's government wanted to include the Iroquois in his scheme of removal beyond the Mississippi, but missionaries to the Iroquois, especially the Quakers, argued against removal and won exemption for them. The missionaries carried their own threat to Iroquois cultural survival, particularly in their conviction, shared by most educated Europeans of the nineteenth century, that individual ownership of land was the necessary base for civilization. Allotment in severalty of the Iroquois reservations was strenuously opposed by most Iroquois women, who realized it would break the power they exercised through their clan-based, cooperative farm-work groups, force them and their children into a dependency upon husbands who would not always be equal to the task of supporting them, and constrict the economic base. The traditional pattern of the Iroquois had distributed subsistence production and household maintenance among all the adult women so that none was excessively burdened and all families adequately provided for. It left the men free to go out in search of additional income. After the move to reservations, this pattern continued—first, in men hunting and trapping furs to trade; then, beginning early in the nineteenth century, in men felling and rafting timber; in the latter part of the century, in railroad work and construction; and, most recently, in skilled factory work and professions. Iroquois men have become famous for their aptitude for high-steel construction work: apparently, a lack of cultural inculcation of a fear of heights plus an encouragement of bravado have allowed the girders of skyscrapers and bridges to replace the warpath in bringing renown and material rewards to young Iroquois men. Except for a colony of Mohawk and other Iroquois high-steel workers and their families in New York City, most of the Iroquois have been able to live on their reservations, commuting to employment in the cities of upstate New York and southern Ontario.

Preservation of Iroquois spiritual beliefs and practices has centered on the Handsome Lake "longhouses" (community halls), where worship of the Good One, He-Who-Holds-the-Sky, in the forms of traditional rituals follows the recitation of the Gaiwiio'. Because the rituals require representatives from the various clans to take ceremonial offices, the Longhouse religion has been instrumental in keeping alive the clan structure and titles, which no longer function to any significant degree economically or politically (the Oneida community in Ontario even reckons band membership patrilineally). Outside the longhouses, there has been strong persistence of native herb doctoring (much of which is at least as effective as

over-the-counter medicines) and "fortune telling" (divination), and presumably witchcraft practices as well as belief. The False Faces still exorcise illness and evil at the Midwinter New Year's Festival and in the spring and fall. As Handsome Lake would have wished, membership in the False Faces is no longer so secret. The False Faces clown as they stir the ashes in the fireplaces in the homes and dance, begging the tobacco and cornmeal mush they should be given, but their incarnation of the dangerous force in the earth opposed to He-Who-Holds-the-Sky is a serious expression of Iroquois cosmogony, and the spiritual power with which the masks are imbued is deeply respected. Christian churches on every reservation discourage the "pagan" practices, but traditional religion has consistently held a substantial number of Iroquois, not infrequently receiving Indians who have become dissatisfied with Christian sects either over spiritual interpretations or because the church has espoused economic or political changes repugnant to the Iroquois member.

On some reservations, political institutions have shown the most divergence from Iroquois tradition; on others, they have been retained as part of the core of being Iroquois. The greatest break came among the Seneca, who in 1848—that year in which democratic republican uprisings shook so much of Europe—followed younger, educated Seneca men in abolishing the sachems and instituting instead a republican Seneca Nation with a written constitution and elected officers. The ostensible reason for the change in government was the malfeasance of the sachems in selling off Seneca land for which they had been offered bribes, but the spirit of the times, the clamor of idealists for the end of inherited privilege, plus a much-discussed new constitution for New York State, must have affected the new Seneca leaders. The most radical element in the Seneca change was the disenfranchisement of women. Where traditionally the matrons of the clan had nominated sachems, kept the power to depose any who failed to perform their duties properly, and could instruct speakers to represent the women's views in League councils, now Seneca women had neither the vote nor representation in government. (Ironically, in the summer of the same year of 1848, Euro-American women meeting in a village called Seneca Falls demanded the United States recognize women's rights.) Not until 1964, the year of the United States Civil Rights bill, was the vote restored to Seneca women.

Iroquois in Canada were officially deprived of their traditional council of sachems by a government act in 1924 requiring an elected tribal government. Like the Pueblos, the Six Nations Iroquois on the Grand River reserve in Ontario let the Euro-Canadian-imposed tribal council, which very few elected, be the community's front in dealing with the government while the sachems' council, with its ancient titles and beautiful ritual, continued to be the de facto internal government. The Grand River community's claim, first made soon after Thayendanegea obtained the land from Canada in 1784, that a majority of league titles were to be found among them, that there were enough persons from each of the six nations to reconstitute the League in Grand River, and therefore that the League council in Ontario was more legitimate than that convened after 1784 in Onondaga, made the continuance of the traditional sachems especially precious to Grand River.

The Oneida have been the only one of the original Five Nations to have been uprooted from the Iroquois homeland. In 1785, they had taken in the Stockbridge and Brotherton (Algonkian) Indian communities, which had coalesced into New England mission villages but subsequently had been driven out by Euro-American settlement expansion. With the Mohawk nearly all resettled in Canada, the Oneida became the eastern border of the Iroquois and bore the brunt of attempts to wrest Indian land for Euro-Americans. In 1820, a Caughnawaga Christian Iroquois named Eleazar Williams who was employed as an Episcopal missionary to the Oneida began to work on schemes to remove the Oneida to Green Bay, Wisconsin and thereby free their land for the speculators of the notorious Ogden Land Company. Williams's services to the Ogden Company were, of course, gratefully rewarded. By 1831, Williams, other missionaries, and government officials had maneuvered the Stockbridge and Brotherton groups to Wisconsin, to land ceded by the Menominee. By 1838, in spite of resistance by the Oneida chiefs, land near Green Bay was obtained from the Menominee and Winnebago for Oneida. By 1846, the Oneida lands in New York had been sold and most of the people removed to Wisconsin. Only the Oneida who had earlier moved to a reserve on the Thames River in Ontario or who had joined the Grand River community remained within ancient Iroquois territory. Williams, incidentally, did not profit as he thought he should from his machinations with Oneida land and missionary salary, and in 1853 tried a new scheme: he passed himself off as the Lost Dauphin of France, Louis XVII, and created a quite remunerative stir.

The Wisconsin Oneida, meanwhile, worked to build a home on a new frontier, and, although they lost most of their land after the 1887 Dawes Act Allotment, they have a small reservation from which some commute to employment in Green Bay and others move to Milwaukee, Chicago, Detroit, and other cities, returning to visit. The Wisconsin Oneida were among the first contemporary reservations to take advantage of independence from state jurisdiction to create high-stakes bingo games, drawing thousands of non-Indians to gamble on the reservation. The Oneida games began in 1976 as a project of two reservation women to raise funds for school programs, a health center, a nursing home, and day care needs. Busloads of bingo players rolled in, attracted by bigger prizes than their local church or American Legion post could legally offer. In 1990, the Oneida Tribe announced that one-half million players at its "First American Games" had brought in $45 million in revenue for 1989. Games are played in a large, gymnasium-style hall with convenient snack bar and cigarettes on sale at a bargain price since no state tax need be paid. ("Well, we Indians

FIGURE 5.3 General Ely S. Parker, 1828–1895. Member of the Tonawanda Seneca Iroquois, Ely Parker was selected by his people to obtain a Euro-American education in order to represent their interests to the United States government. Parker became a civil engineer, during the Civil War served on Grant's headquarters staff, and subsequently was named Commissioner of the Bureau of Indian Affairs by President Grant. Among his own people, Parker was selected to succeed to one of the sachem titles of the Seneca. Parker was the most prominent of a number of Iroquois who struggled throughout the nineteenth and twentieth centuries to maintain the autonomy of their nation. His grandnephew Arthur C. Parker was a leading scholar of Iroquois history and culture in the early twentieth century. *(Smithsonian Institution National Anthropological Archives)*

invented tobacco smoking," an Oneida replied when a visitor remarked that cigarettes are harmful, "but we kept it for religious worship.") Next to the bingo hall is a handsome, 202-room Radisson Inn to accommodate players who want an overnight holiday. Thanks to the lure of gaming, the 2,470-member Oneida Tribe now employs nearly 800 people, reducing reservation unemployment from 1976's 40 percent to 18 percent in 1989 (still four times the rate for non-Indians in the surrounding counties). Bingo enabled the reservation to build the health, school, and community facilities it wanted and to extend its financial base to convenience stores, a commercial printing shop, and the ambitious Oneida Research and Technology Center, designed to be a competitive research and development industrial park.

Mohawks from St. Regis, a reserve on both sides of the New York–Quebec border, have in recent years been leading a resurgence of Iroquois nationalism that has gained international prominence. The movement began in 1968, and was soon identified with AIM, the American Indian Movement. In December of that year, the Mohawks blocked the international bridge at Cornwall to protest attempts by Canada to curtail free movement of Indians over the border, a privilege granted in the Jay Treaty of 1794 between the United States and Canada. The Mohawk action reflected the position that the Jay Treaty clause on freedom of Indian movement was based on the sovereign status of Indian nations, which could not be abrogated by any treaty to which they were not a party. The minor issue was the freedom of the border, which, Canada has ruled, does not hold because it has never passed legislation implementing the intent of the Jay Treaty (the United States implemented the rights of persons in the 1924 Immigration Act, but ruled in a 1937 case involving a St. Regis woman that Indian goods are not exempt from duties). The fundamental issue was the sovereignty of the Mohawk Nation over Akwesasne (Where the Partridge Drums), the Mohawk name for the reserve.

To publicize their position and raise money for the legal expenses of arrested protesters, the Mohawk nationalists began printing a mimeographed newsletter called Akwesasne Notes. A non-Indian, Gerald Gambill, who had been a community-development worker, volunteered to aid the Mohawks in publishing Akwesasne Notes and in expanding their traveling information group, White Roots of Peace (a referral to the traditional

metaphor of the League of the Iroquois as a tree of peace that sends its white roots into all the five nations' lands). Akwesasne Notes rapidly grew into a semimonthly newspaper with a circulation of over one hundred thousand. Its staff moved to an abandoned summer camp in the Adirondack Mountains in New York, claiming the land was rightfully Mohawk. Books, posters, and calendars supporting native sovereignty against colonialist oppression, as well as crafts, were distributed through Akwesasne Notes, and its staff exemplified its adherence to communal principles and rejection of material affluence in its camp village, named Ganienkeh, and the White Roots group. By 1977, the Akwesasne Notes leaders had matured from a local protest conclave to influential counter-culture spokespeople. Gambill, who in 1969 had been adopted into the Bear Clan of the Mohawk with the name Rarihokwats (He Digs Up Information), was rejected from his adopted nation because he advocated, and seemed to practice, a private visionary leadership demanding an asceticism incongruent with actual Indian traditions. (Akwesasne Notes wryly mentioned that he who would abjure toilet paper would claim to be "holier" than other staff members.) The pragmatic orientation of the Ganienkeh group permitted them to accept relocation from the Adirondack camp to a site close to the Canadian border.

The new editor of Akwesasne Notes was most concerned with effective presentation of the political issues of sovereignty and genocide. The December 1977 issue of the Notes gave extensive coverage to the meeting of delegates from the International Indian Treaty Council, founded in 1974, with the United Nations Non-Governmental Organizations in Geneva, Switzerland in September 1977. The report stressed the common grievances of Indians from both North and South America, their insistence on following alternative lifestyles, and the political repression of their leaders. The Notes proudly described a precedent for the 1977 Geneva conference, the attempt of a Cauyga sachem, Deskaheh (Levi General), to interest the League of Nations in Geneva in 1920 and 1923 in the issue of Iroquois sovereignty. Deskaheh had traveled using an Iroquois Nation passport, the only nation in which he would acknowledge citizenship, and the Iroquois, fifty years later, repeated his symbolic gesture. The Akwesasne Mohawk took on the role of a Hiawatha in building a confederation that can renew the power of the Iroquois nations and restore their leadership. One clue to Mohawk leadership in contemporary Iroquois resurgency is the fact that some three thousand people speak Mohawk, while the other Iroquois languages are spoken by only dozens or a few hundred persons. Mohawk constitute one-third of the approximately forty thousand United States Iroquois. There are over ten thousand members of the Six Nations Reserve, the largest Iroquois reserve on the Canadian side, and again the Mohawk dominate as one-third of the total, the remainder fractionated among the other Iroquois national groups plus a couple of Algonkian origin.

After a decade of proliferation of reservation high-stakes bingo, in many instances organized and operated under contract by non-Indian businessmen, opposing forces became apparent. On the one hand, operators proposed adding Las Vegas–type casinos with slot machines, poker, craps, roulette, blackjack, and off-track sports betting. There could be no doubt that non-Indians would flock to spend money in these reservation casinos as they did in the bingo halls; during the first *month* of the Santee Sioux Tribe's casino in Flandreau, South Dakota, nearly one hundred and sixty thousand patrons bet 8.5 million dollars (out of that came the winners' takes and operating costs, then 18 percent of the profits was paid to the Tribe, the non-Indian developer pocketing the rest; but in the second month, the Tribe demanded 60 percent, claiming that was in the contract). On the other hand, an increasing number of Indians feared evil effects from casinos: the possibility that organized crime would move in was very real (in 1990, the FBI charged that a non-Indian supplying slot machines to the New York St. Regis Mohawk reservation

was connected to a New York City crime boss), and many reservation families came to feel that glitzy casinos attracting gamblers are contrary to the moral values they want to instill in their children. The issue came to a head on St. Regis (Akwesasne) in 1989, when both the U.S.-recognized Tribal Council and traditional Mohawk Nation Council requested outside assistance in their efforts to curtail the illegal casinos and commercial bingo halls. New York State police arrested one casino owner, and minutes after they took him away, a group of Mohawk men smashed the slot machines in his hall. Complications ensued when young Mohawk men organized a "Six Nations Warrior Society" calling for expulsion of foreign (that is, New York State) police, insisting the "Warriors" would maintain order within Mohawk territory. Both the Tribal Council and traditional League chiefs condemned the "Warriors" for failing to respect (or even seek) the authority of properly-constituted chiefs. Oren Lyons, an Onondaga chief and also a history instructor in the State University of New York at Buffalo, and Jacob E. Thomas, a Cayuga chief from Six Nations Reserve who teaches in Trent University's Native Studies program, published careful discussions of the situation created by heedless profiteering through gambling and its equally damaging opposition by heedlessly violent young men. The two learned chiefs reminded their people that the term "warrior" comes from English, not the Iroquois languages which have words simply referring to "young men"; Chief Thomas stated that the Great Law of the League had superseded any earlier office of "war chief"; that since Dekanawidah, the only legitimate power lies with the formally recognized Confederacy Chiefs representing their six nations. The 1989 St. Regis battle marked an alignment between culturally conservative and more assimilated Indians united in rejecting violent tactics bloodying the reservations. "Sovereignty" should not mean strong-arm rule by anyone, whether Bureau of Indian Affairs or self-appointed vigilantes with AK-47 rifles.

Iroquois population includes nearly forty thousand counted in the U.S. 1980 census, plus ten thousand on the Six Nations Reserve in Ontario. The Mohawk, with a total of close to eighteen thousand, were the largest Iroquois nation, followed by the Oneida with nine thousand, Seneca with nearly eight thousand, Cayuga with nearly four thousand, and Onondaga with one thousand; there were three thousand Tuscarora. The Wyandot (Huron) counted eleven hundred.

SECTION 7: THE ALGONKIANS IN THE NINETEENTH AND TWENTIETH CENTURIES

Eastern Algonkian groups experienced differing careers, according to whether they were within Iroquois hegemony, in New England, in the Canadian Maritimes, or in the Subarctic. The desirability of a region for European settlement, a factor influenced by climate, resources, and market accessibility, determined the strength of the pressure to dispossess Indians from their homelands. But other factors, such as the labor market, criteria of social class, and what might be termed ethos—value judgments derived from religion, ideology, and historical experience—also acted upon the persistence of Indian peoples, incumbent or removed.

The Delaware, or (in Algonkian) Lenape, comprise the many Algonkian groups living at the beginning of the seventeenth century between the Hudson and Delaware rivers. This position made Albany the convenient major trading station and brought the Delaware into conflict with the Five Nations Iroquois. Southward trading was contended for by the Susquehannock, who pushed the Delaware away from the Chesapeake Bay Virginia trade. By the late seventeenth century, the Iroquois and Delaware had worked out an agreement whereby the two confederacies might be to each other as man and woman, in the Iroquois metaphor: the Iroquois would range widely and fight to dominate far peoples, while the Delaware would maintain their homeland, withdrawing from competition with the Iroquois as long as the latter protected the Delaware lands from intruders. This relationship lasted until 1755, when the Delaware judged the Iroquois to have failed to fulfill their obligation.

Westward removal of the Delaware began in the eighteenth century and accelerated after 1730. In a number of instances, removal seems to have been the reaction of Delaware people who saw their land tainted by the anger and ill feeling developing with European encroachment, and feared the disharmony would cause misfortunes to anyone on the land, however righteous their position. (The Iroquois also practice withdrawal rather than prolonged confrontation, but they do not so readily assume the object of dissension has become imbued with spiritual danger.) In other cases, removal was imposed by the colony, backed by Iroquois allies. One notorious swindle occurred in 1737 when Thomas Penn got Delaware and Minisinks (Munsee) to agree to sell him the amount of land a man can walk into in a day and a half. Penn got trained runners ready and off from earliest dawn to midday the following day, making his Walking Purchase immeasurably larger than the Delawares had expected. By the time of the Seven Years' War, in 1755, most Delaware had retreated over the Appalachians and were in the Ohio Valley. Their fighting men, allied with French and with other Indians, attempted to hold this country against the British, but eventually lost most of it after the Indian extension of the conflict (1763–66) under the Ottawa leader Pontiac was defeated. After the American Revolution, most Delaware moved to Indiana, some to Missouri with Shawnee emigrants, and some to Canada, settling on the Thames River in southern Ontario or with the Six Nations Iroquois, although a few families remained in Pennsylvania farming like colonist neighbors or working as laborers. The nineteenth century opened on Delaware grouped in small independent communities, feeling their backs against the wall. Tenskwatawa the Shawnee Prophet and his brother

Tecumseh the general were eagerly received as they urged a repudiation and repulsion of the Europeans. Tenskwatawa, indeed, was only one in a series of prophets preaching a return to the true native life among the Delaware. Shortly before his vision, Beate, a Munsee woman who had joined and then rejected Moravian mission Christianity, experienced messages from angels foretelling catastrophe if the people did not reform and reinstitute sober worship of Delaware spiritual forces. Prodded by this prophet, the Delaware revived the Green Corn Festival and the Big House harvest ceremony, modifying the rites to emphasize the recitation of visions. Before her, the Delaware had listened to a man named Neolin whose message from the Master of Life inspired Pontiac as a generation later, Tenskwatawa inspired Tecumseh.

Religious faith was powerless against United States expansion, the Delaware losing their Indiana reservation and removing to Missouri during the 1820s, then in the next decade to Kansas, and finally in 1867 to Oklahoma, where land was purchased from the Cherokee in the northeastern section of the state. Other Delaware had gone to Texas and allied with the Comanche, Caddo, and other tribes in that area, ending up with their hosts in Indian Territory in Oklahoma. During the nineteenth century, a number of Delaware men distinguished themselves as guides, scouts, and interpreters on the western frontier; it was said of Black Beaver, a Delaware, that "his services...were invaluable to military and scientific explorers of the plains and the Rocky Mountains." Delaware men also fought on the Union side in the Civil War.

Delaware culture persisted as a distinctive pattern until about 1930 in the main settlement among the Cherokee. After 1924, the Big House ceremony, the principal Delaware ritual, fell into abeyance, revived only during World War II in hopes it would protect the lives of the Delaware young men in that conflict (it did—all returned home). Young people growing up during the 1940s ceased to speak Delaware. The office of chief was discontinued. Because the people in the Delaware communities can trace kinship between all their families, young persons were forced to marry outside; by the early 1950s, only three married couples were both Delaware, and the youngest of these were in their late thirties. The younger Delaware were not, however, losing their Indian identity. Most were adherents of a peyote ritual religion (the Native American Church) established around 1880 by John Wilson, a Caddo-Delaware who had been introduced to the revelatory cactus by Comanche and had been vouchsafed visions of a new belief system syncretizing Peyote, Christ, and the Big House ceremony. Delaware families frequently attended pan-Indian powwows in Oklahoma. The Delaware had become a tribe in the seventeenth century when European colonists working out a political alliance with the Iroquois lumped the Algonkians along the Delaware watershed as a tribe subject to the Iroquois. The Delaware were recognized as a tribe as they were bumped from pillar to post through the nineteenth century. When the United States no longer cared to deal with a Delaware polity, the people who considered themselves Lenape—an ethnic, not a national, designation—became fragmented, losing their imposed political character but not their basic ethnic identification. In the 1980 census, nearly fifty-five hundred people identified themselves as Delaware (of these, 130 are Munsee).

East of the Hudson, the Algonkians who survived King Philip's War in 1676 found themselves increasingly falling into peonage, incurring debts that they were forced to work out by indenturing themselves or their children to Euro-American masters for a stipulated number of years. The threat of indenture was often held over an Indian to induce him to sell his land to settle his debts. In the early eighteenth century, small tracts of land on which Indian communities lived were decreed reservations that could not be alienated from the Indians except by consent of the colony government. To engage this protection, the Indians waived their claim to any additional land in the colony. These last-ditch efforts to preserve a modicum of land under the truncated rule of the group's hereditary sachem counterweighed the dispersal of Indians as slaves or long-term indentured peons on Euro-American farms, where they were classed with the black slaves.

Throughout the eighteenth century and the first part of the nineteenth, a principal occupation of New England Algonkian men was whaling. For the first few decades, "shore whaling" was practiced: the animals were harpooned when they came within sight of lookouts on or close to shore. By the middle of the eighteenth century, whales were too seldom found close inshore to sustain the business, and ships began to regularly hunt as far north as Davis Strait, between Greenland and Labrador. Algonkians formed substantial proportions of the crews of many of these whalers, where they mixed with Portuguese from the Azores and blacks as well as with Euro-Americans (as you can read in Herman Melville's great novel, *Moby Dick*). Indian men enlisted more or less freely on the whalers; many were eager to earn shares in the lucrative catch, others were indentured, working off a debt. Shopkeepers' records show that in the mid-1700s, Nantucket Island Indian whaling crewmen merited credit four times an ordinary colonist's yearly wage. Those who had families left them to plant maize and other crops, in the traditional pattern of the agricultural Northeast in which farming was carried out by sedentary women while their men ranged in pursuit of game or trade. Christian missionary efforts among the Algonkians intensified during the eighteenth century in New England, and, in at least one instance, spurred a complaint of Nantucket Indians, in 1747, to Massachusetts Colony that whaling captains forced them to kill and process whales sighted on the Sabbath, depriving the crewmen of the day that they devoted to studying the Bible.

New England as well as the South recognized two castes, "whites" and "persons of color." Crispus Attucks was one example of the mixing of Indians and blacks that resulted from the common employment of both and their common status. Not only were blacks and Indians together as slaves, or slaves and indentured servants, freed blacks worked with Indians, and they and Portuguese sailors looked for women among their Indian friends' families. In the nineteenth century, the small Algonkian communities on the Atlantic Slope as far north as southern Maine included many persons of mixed racial descent: as in the South, they were "tri-racial isolates," insisting that the Indian component in their ancestry placed them above blacks in the societal hierarchy. Again as in the South, their children often received a limited and poor education because they were not welcomed in white schools and would not attend black schools, although the Indian communities had no funds to maintain adequate teachers. Land base for many communities has been parcels of 50 to 200 acres (20 to 80 hectares) given to them to hold communally by seventeenth or eighteenth century colonial proprietors. Members of these communities kept small farms, fished and gathered shellfish, cut and sold firewood and lumber if the reservation had woods, and peddled crafts—especially wood splint baskets, made by a technique learned from Swedish colonists on the Delaware around 1700, and passed on from Indian to Indian until all groups in the Northeast knew it; and it, more than traditional Indian baskets, became identified as an Indian speciality. Indians worked on Euro-American farms and, on the part of the women, as household help. A significant number of families valued freedom to continue a seasonal round of movement, now usually including seasonal labor, to continue living in wigwams and refuse occasional offers of small parcels of land for Euro-American–style farming. A few communities had developed salable skills, for example, stone-masonry among the Narragansetts of Rhode Island. The remaining Algonkians in the Northeast United States lived quietly in poverty on marginal small tracts, virtually ignored.

Those Indian communities led by missionaries, such as the Stockbridge (who consisted of Mahican, other, smaller Algonkian groups, and a group of Munsee, a Delaware subgroup) received no more consideration than the "pagan" groups. Many Stockbridge men enlisted quickly on the American side in the Revolutionary War, and thirty of them were killed. Hendrick Aupaumat, from the Stockbridge, was promoted to Captain by George Washington, and after the war became a leader of his people, served as United States spokesman at a 1792 treaty meeting with the Old Northwest nations, fought against Tecumseh in General Harrison's army, and, in 1808, secured a letter from President Thomas Jefferson approving Aupaumat's selection of land in Indiana, adjacent to the Miami and Potawatomi, for a new home for the Stockbridge. With the War of 1812 intervening, it was ten years before Stockbridge families moved from their refuge with New York Oneida to the Indiana territory; no sooner had they arrived, than they discovered the Miami and Potawatomi had been pressured to sell out to open the country to Euro-American colonists, and the Stockbridge were expected to move west, too. Christian or "pagan," "civilized" or still living a traditional Indian culture, Indian was Indian in the eyes of President Monroe's government. Captain Aupaumat sent his son Solomon (who would be his successor as chief) to Washington to protest, to no avail. Solomon Aupaumat then traveled to Wisconsin and bought land from the Menominee, leading the Stockbridge settlers there in 1822. Mohegans (whose mid-seventeenth-century sachem Uncas was *not* the "Last of the Mohicans" in spite of novelist James Fenimore Cooper's title) who had become a "praying town" during the 1740s Great Awakening evangelism, had been led by their minister Samson Occom in 1785 to refuge with the New York Oneida. Occom had traveled through England in 1769, strongly impressing listeners there with the force of his preaching. Western New York harbored the Mohegan and their friends in their village called Brothertown for two generations until, like the (Mahican and Munsee) Stockbridge and most of the Oneida themselves,

the "Brotherton Indians" ended up emigrating to eastern Wisconsin. Some Munsee who were living in Canada joined the emigrés. Disputes over the validity of the Menominee and Winnebago land sales to the eastern Indians caused several moves in northeastern Wisconsin, as well as the further emigration of many Stockbridge and Munsee west in 1839, eventually settling in Indian Territory (Oklahoma). Reservations were finally recognized for the Stockbridge-Munsee and the Brothertons in 1856. The 1980 census listed slightly more than fifteen hundred Stockbridge-Munsee (some in Oklahoma) and 173 Brotherton.

Twentieth-century Northeast United States Algonkians are physically varied, their communities usually evidencing their tri-racial heritage. As racial caste barriers have fallen, younger members of these communities have been able to obtain better schooling and skilled or professional employment. The increasing ease of integration has not meant a loss of identity as Indians. Instead, there has been a slowly growing pride in that identity throughout this century. The ethnologists in the Smithsonian's Bureau of American Ethnology worked hard to discover and record what had become of the Algonkians of the Northeast, and in the face of general skepticism were able to demonstrate the continuation of Algonkian communities from the colonization period. Frank G. Speck was indefatigable in countering the myth that all the Indians of the Atlantic seaboard south of Maine had become extinct. His championing of the validity of these communities' claims to being Indian, the respect he showed to the elderly who remembered their languages and rituals, if only in fragments, and his encouragement of reviving the Indian heritages brought him the gratitude of hundreds of Eastern Algonkians. One Virginia Algonkian man employed in New York City during the 1950s organized an Indian dance group there named in honor of Dr. Speck. Besides the leader's family, the group included Long Island Algonkians, Mohawks whose fathers worked on high steel, and one Quechua youth whose parents had emigrated from the Peruvian Andes! Indian dancing, in fact, became a major rallying point for the Algonkian communities. Most had retained a summer festival, the Green Corn gathering stripped of "pagan" ritual. The festival was a big family reunion, with a Sunday service in the community church, track and field games, contests, dancing, and picnicking. Gradually, after World War I, some participants wore costumes copied from books on Indians or purchased from western reservations, and Indian dancing was recognized (much of it learned from Iroquois, Great Lakes, or Oklahoma Indians, but a portion probably persisting locally). In 1926, the Algonkian Council of Indian Tribes was formed in New England. It lasted only a few years, but with the 1934 Indian Reorganization Act some of the Eastern Algonkians, such as the Narragansett, reinstituted a tribal organization. (The Narragansetts, who had officially dissolved their tribe in 1880, created in 1934 the offices of chief, prophet, and medicine man as well as a tribal committee. The Wampanoag, descendants of Metacomet's Pokanoket, organized in 1928 as the Wampanoag nation with similar offices.) The summer festivals became powwows, and tourists flocked to them to watch the peace-pipe rituals and dancing.

One century after the Wampanoags on western Cape Cod and the Narragansetts in Rhode Island were legally dissolved as tribes, both communities filed claims contending that the states of Massachusetts and Rhode Island had erred in proceeding, in 1870 and 1880, respectively, to deal with the tribes without the consent of the United States Congress. The Indians' cases rest on the 1790 Federal Non-Intercourse Act, which restricts jurisdiction to deal with Indian tribes to Congress. Under the Act, states wishing to take over Indian land are required to obtain Congressional approval. The act in 1790 was intended to regularize the expansion of the United States, check unscrupulous purchases likely to excite Indian hostilities, and prevent conflicts between states each claiming to have purchased a particular parcel. Apparently, neither Massachusetts nor Rhode Island realized,

after the Civil War, that the 1790 Act was applicable to their absorption of small tribes wholly within their state boundaries. The climate of opinion in the late nineteenth century was so strongly in favor—among Euro-Americans—of allotting communal Indian land and terminating the "barbarian" status of Indians that the benevolence of tribal dissolution was questioned by no one except the impoverished Indians themselves. Rhode Island clearly considered itself to be carrying out an enlightened and liberal action when it paid the Narragansetts generously for their land, which was too poor for much except sheep raising, and took over responsibility for indigent Indians.

The climate of opinion in the 1970s veered so far as to see detribalization as genocide. The Narragansetts in 1975 and the Wampanoags in 1976 filed suit to regain lands transferred to the states. The Wampanoag case, which received the most publicity, was fought by the town of Mashpee on Cape Cod, whose land had been Wampanoag. The town retained James St. Clair, the lawyer who represented Richard Nixon during the Watergate scandal. St. Clair argued that, in 1870, when the Mashpee Indian district (established in 1637 as a Plantation for the displaced Pokanokets) became the town of Mashpee, the census listed 89 percent of the district residents as "black," and that the Wampanoags had no Indian language, religion, or culture, or any of the powers of sovereign states. Therefore, stated St. Clair, the Wampanoags are not, were not in 1870, and have not consistently since 1676 (the year of the defeat of "King Philip") been a tribe. Not being, or having been in 1870 or 1790, a tribe, according to St. Clair, he concluded that the act of 1790 did not apply to Massachusetts' action, and that the Wampanoag claim should be rejected. On March 24, 1978, the federal judge and jury (on which no Indians sat) accepted St. Clair's argument and dismissed the Wampanoag claim. One month earlier, a White House work group commissioned by President Carter's administration had developed an agreement with the Passamaquoddy and Penobscot nations of Maine to settle their claim for nearly two thirds of the state of Maine, a claim also based on the 1790 Non-Intercourse Act. This settlement would give the two tribes several hundred thousand acres of timberland, several million dollars, and continuation of state aid to the tribes. The crucial difference between the Wampanoag and Maine cases, according to the Massachusetts court, is that Penobscots and Passamaquoddys have never legally ceased to be tribes, while the Wampanoags have not been recognized in that status by the United States. The Wampanoag defeat seems peculiarly poignant in that the Mashpee group refused to join Metacomet in 1675, and that because they had been neutral they were not disturbed in their settlement on Cape Cod until the resort town of Mashpee experienced a boom in the 1970s. The New England court cases were among the more pressing stimulants to formalizing a set of "Procedures for Establishing That an American Indian Group Exists as a Tribe," to be followed under the 1978 Federal Acknowledgment Project within the Bureau of Indian Affairs. Under the Procedures, the petitioning group has the burden, and considerable legal expense, of presenting facts supporting the claim to Indian tribal status. This proof centers on demonstrating continuing existence as a bounded, self-governing community; it does not require the community continue to use an Indian language, religion, or culture as St. Clair demanded in defending the resort town against the Wampanoags. Ironically, the Wampanoags' official Medicine Man, John Peters (Cjigkitoonuppa John Peters Slow Turtle) has been Executive Director of the State of Massachusetts' Commission on Indian Affairs, and a Wampanoag Indian Program using Wampanoag and Narragansett staff is a popular section of Plimoth Plantation, the reconstructed Pilgrim settlement at Plymouth. The 1980 census listed two thousand Narragansett and (in spite of the Mashpee ruling) nearly as many Wampanoag.

The Wabanaki Confederacy—the name Wabanaki means "eastern (daybreak) land people"— was a historic alliance of Abenaki bands, Passamaquoddy, Penobscot, Maliseet, and Micmac, in Maine and the Canadian Maritimes. The confederacy seems to have been an expression of the close linguistic and cultural relationships of these Algonkian groups who realized the importance of submerging petty differences in the face of seventeenth- and eighteenth-century Iroquois military excursions. Wabanaki chiefs, like League of the Iroquois sachems, met in council and symbolized the kinship of their peoples by identifying the peoples, from west to east, as elder to younger brothers, and by ceremonially attending the installation of new chiefs replacing retired or deceased leaders. Formal confederacy ceremonies petered out in the middle of the nineteenth century, although fear and hatred of the Mohawk lasted somewhat longer.

Wabanaki peoples became the object of Jesuit Catholic missionaries in the late seventeenth century. The Jesuits shrewdly challenged the native powwow (Massachusetts Algonkian *pauwau;* a cognate word is found in all the Northeast Algonkian languages), or doctor, the "medicine man" who, as the Algonkian word signifies, "dreams" or has mystical contact with power beyond that known by ordinary persons. The many epidemics allowed the missionary and the powwow to each try his cures. The powwow's remedies from native plants, effective for many precontact ills, were powerless against European diseases, and, seeing this, powwows unfortunately told their patients and the patients' families that the case was hopeless and the victim should be prepared to die. The Jesuit then marched in, announced the case was not yet hopeless, prayed over the victim and had them kiss a crucifix, and reaped the benefit of slow natural recovery strengthened by renewed hope and the taking of nourishment again. Although belief in the native cosmology and herb medicines wavered very little, French Catholicism was grafted on. The missionaries organized late-winter settlements where families gathered after the prime of the furs had passed and the trapping season was winding down. Beginning as permanent villages with a church and school, in the nineteenth century

FIGURE 5.4 Micmac couple beside their bark lodge, New Brunswick, 1870s. *(Smithsonian Institution National Anthropological Archives)*

these settlements became small reservations. In the middle twentieth century, government desires to centralize administration consolidated many of the small communities and brought the residents into the agency towns, where new Euro-American— style housing, schooling, and welfare services could be provided at greater convenience to the bureaucrats.

Hunting and fishing continued to be activities of major economic importance to Wabanaki until late in the nineteenth century, in spite of mission and government efforts to make the people agriculturalists. (Indians planted potatoes, maize, beans, and squashes in gardens, but realized better than the Euro-Americans that farming could never be more than supplementary in the northern climate.) For the Gulf of St. Lawrence people, hunting included seals and porpoises until around 1870. Cash was obtained by the sale of beaver and other furs, and of splint baskets and wooden objects such as bowls and implement handles, which came to be called "Indian wares." In 1889, a woolen mill was built in Old Town, Maine, adjacent to the Penobscot community. It gave employment to Indians who wished it, but there was otherwise little wage employment available. Some men began going as far as Minnesota to work as lumbermen.

The first half of the twentieth century saw a continuation of reliance upon hunting and fishing for subsistence, augmented by sale of crafts to neighboring Euro-Americans who used the items in farm and household work, and increasingly supplemented by skilled or urban employment. Frank Speck mentions a Penobscot man who "has accompanied a Geodetic Survey party to Alaska as woodsman, been 140 feet below water in a caisson building the Bath Bridge, defied the 'bends,' scrambled along four-inch steel girders two hundred feet above the river as a riveter, spent four years with the Canadian forces on the German front, carpenters, and is now awaiting a date to guide sportsmen on the Allagash and St. John rivers" (Speck 1940:310). Since World War II, wage employment far from the reservations has been the major support of the Wabanaki peoples, supplemented principally by government welfare payments to children, the aged, and the disabled. Whole families regularly go to harvest potatoes and blueberries in Maine, and to Boston and other cities in New England and eastern Canada for factory employment. Home usually continues to be the reservation, and children may be left with grandparents there while parents work in the city, in part because the rural or semirural reservation seems more wholesome than urban slums, in part to ensure that the children absorb Indian ways and values. The Indians working on the potato or blueberry harvests are migrant laborers trucked in as crews by middlemen (who may be themselves Indian) and housed in minimal fashion on the farms. Working in Boston or other large cities, the Indians rely on relatives to share apartments, rides to jobs and home to the reservations, and tips on finding employment. Certain bars are known as Indian hangouts and facilitate Indians keeping in touch with one another in spite of often shifting residence. Since the late 1960s, organizations such as the Boston Indian Council and the Friendship Centres in Canadian cities, which began as coalitions of concerned Euro-Americans and Indians but have shifted to stronger Indian leadership, provide meeting halls, recreation, agency referral services, legal aid or referrals, craft, Indian language and powwow-dancing classes, and, not least, identifiable political groups that can work within the urban political structure.

Having retained tribal status and reservations, and with less intermarriage than occurred in southern New England, the Maine and Maritime Algonkians are more obviously Indian than the Cape Cod Wampanoag. Wabanaki material culture is nevertheless very largely Euro-American, even such remnants as bark wigwams for summer or traditional distinctive dress having disappeared almost entirely during the early twentieth century. Native languages persist in the home, and everyone uses English, or English and Canadian French, outside. (Speck noted that in the early twentieth century, some Penobscot women would speak only Penobscot, not because they could not handle English, but because they considered their own people so superior to Euro-Americans that speaking the inferiors' language was beneath their dignity.) Summer festivals persist, but by the middle of the twentieth century, these had generally become church festivals accompanied by Euro-American social dancing and baseball games. Wooden "Indian wares" are made by very few, while tourist souvenirs are increasingly sold; splint baskets remain an important craft bought by the potato farmers. Spurred by the rise of pan-Indian political movements in the late 1960s, Oklahoma-style Indian costumes and dancing are appearing in Northeast Indian powwows, and Algonkians have

FIGURE 5.5 Naskapi family camped at Moose Factory, Ontario, about 1935. *(Smithsonian Institution National Anthropological Archives)*

become active in the National Indian Brotherhood (of Canada) and the American Indian Movement. The strongest persistence of Indian cultural patterns seems to lie in the retention of native values and interpersonal relationships. Respect and tolerance for each individual's autonomy, sharing of resources, love of the beauty of the land, and conviction that spiritual power is pervasive and the basis for fortune and health characterize thousands of Northeast Algonkians today as they did centuries ago. Population figures for the late twentieth century list, in round numbers, one thousand Abenaki in Quebec, one thousand each for Penobscot and Passamaquoddy in Maine, two thousand Maliseet in New Brunswick, and over ten thousand Micmac in four Canadian Maritime provinces.

These social characteristics are prominent among the Naskapi of Labrador, whose edge-of-the-Arctic country did not attract Europeans, and whose dependence on the Barren Ground (tundra) caribou prevented them from trapping sufficient forest-animal furs to engage in more-than-token trading. Consequently, the Naskapi retained a largely aboriginal culture pattern into the twentieth century, and, compared with the Algonkians to the south, still do. The beginning of some "modernization" came when, about 1916, the caribou herds changed their migration paths, leaving many Naskapi stranded without food and forcing them to seek relief from the Hudson's Bay Company stores on the coast. In 1924, a Roman Catholic mission to the Naskapi at the Davis Inlet (Labrador) post was initiated, first part-time and then, since 1952, with a year-round resident missionary. The missionary, working in cooperation with the provincial government, developed a commercial-type fishery for cod and arctic char among the Davis Inlet Naskapi during the summer. This, as well as the increased consumption of Euro-American goods bought with its proceeds, were innovations for the Naskapi, who had virtually neglected marine resources until the fishery was instituted in 1961. The move from tents to houses also came for the Davis Inlet Naskapi in 1967. Traditional Naskapi culture remains strong throughout the winter, when the families leave the coast village to hunt caribou in the interior. Traveling by dog sled—an innovation, along with rifles, early in this century—groups of a few hunters and their wives and children camp in the scattered clumps of trees on the border of the open tundra. The meat of caribou and other animals shot or trapped is shared around the camp, and caribou skins are distributed so that every family has what it needs for clothing, but the pelts of fur bearers are kept by the trappers. Although the missionary persuaded the Davis Inlet Naskapi to give up the songs and dancing thought to enhance hunting power, the people in the camps continue to handle caribou carcasses with great respect, extracting every smidgeon of food and taking extreme care that none is sullied by touching the ground. Such reverence will avoid displeasing the quintessential Caribou, the spirit that can let animals come to the hunter or can hinder them.

The values expressed by the Naskapi wintering in canvas tents on the edge of the tundra so that they can subsist on caribou shared among the families hold also for several thousand Cree in northern Quebec. Here, around James Bay in what had been the Hudson's Bay Company's Rupert's Land, the fur-trading economy continues, with moose hunting and fish the principal food sources and winter fur-trapping bringing income to provide rifles and ammunition, other tools, clothing, tea, tobacco, and flour, outboard motors for canoes, snowmobiles, and gas. With families wintering in post villages where the children attend school and bush planes land regularly to bring in mail and supplies and take out individuals needing medical attention, these Cree, unlike the Naskapi, are thoroughly meshed into the national economy. Quebec's plan for massive hydroelectric development of the James Bay watershed, announced in 1971, threatened to drown large sections of the most valuable moose and beaver lands in the region, and thereby deprive the Cree (and Inuit ["Eskimo"] around the northern portion of the Bay) of their livelihood. Cree and Inuit bands protested, and gained support from conservation and native-rights organizations in southern Canada. The Quebec government tried to placate the native peoples with an offer of $100 million to be paid over ten years. The offer was rejected: it failed to recognize that the people were not asking for compensation for land or potential earnings, but for the land itself and the animals whose spiritual essences joined the spirits of men and women there. Smally Petawabano, young chief of the Mistassini Cree, testified that young men and women who have completed secondary schooling were choosing to return to the traditional life of hunting and trapping rather than taking industrial employment in cities. Motorized transportation, modern rifles, and the security of government assistance have reinforced the ancient way of life in the subarctic.

SUMMARY

Hunting, fishing, and gathering of nuts were the foundation of Indian economies in the Northeast until A.D. 1000. Populations in the Late Archaic were relatively large, but declined thereafter as the climate became too cold for hickory-nut trees, producers of the region's staple carbohydrate food, and also too cold for swordfish, a major coastal resource off northern New England. Agriculture after A.D. 1000 supported increasing populations in New York, the St. Lawrence Valley, and southern New England; north of these areas, hunting and fishing continued to be the resource base.

European contacts with the Northeast are documented beginning A.D. 1000. (Alleged "Iberian," "Celtic," and "Phoenician" antiquities in New England do not generally resemble European antiquities. Most of the New England structures are probably post-A.D. 1630). The Norse expeditions of A.D. 1000 incurred hostilities and did not result in colonies, but desultory trade occurred, and the extent of trade between Norse Greenland and Labrador from the eleventh to the fifteenth centuries may be greater than the lack of documents can indicate. Europeans began to strongly affect Northeastern Indian life at the end of the fifteenth century, when large-scale exploitation of the Newfoundland fisheries rapidly developed. Trading for American furs accompanied the fishing. Later in that century, the League of the Iroquois was established.

Colonization by French in Canada, English in New England, and Dutch in New York proceeded through the seventeenth century. The Pequot and King Philip's Wars dispossessed the New England native peoples, epidemics and harassment reduced native occupancy of the middle Atlantic seaboard, the Iroquois wrecked the Huron nation, and the peoples of the Canadian Maritimes were severely reduced by diseases and the impoverishment that resulted from the fur trade bypassing them. The establishment of the Hudson's Bay Company in 1670 opened the exploitation of the interior of northern North America by Europeans.

The second half of the eighteenth century saw Britain achieve dominance in the Northeast, only to lose the southern sector in the American Revolution. One effect of the Revolution was the reduction of Iroquois power. The demoralized Iroquois communities turned, after 1799, to the "Good Message" taught by the Seneca prophet Handsome Lake, a religion affirming Iroquois values by tailoring practices to the cultural pattern imposed by the postwar situation.

The Removal Act of 1830 led to a second removal for many Northeastern peoples who had sought refuge in the Ohio Valley. The survivors of these nations eventually were settled in Indian Territory in Kansas and Oklahoma. Most of the Iroquois successfully resisted removal, although there is an Oneida colony in Wisconsin, a Seneca-Cayuga reservation in Oklahoma, and several Iroquois communities on the Canadian side of the St.

Lawrence, on the north edge of their historic territory. Public conviction among Euro-Americans in the second half of the nineteenth century that communal property was the mark of barbarians led to the detribalization of the small Indian communities that had survived in New England.

The second half of the twentieth century has seen the revival of Indian nationalism in the Northeast. The hunting peoples north of the St. Lawrence had persisted in the fur trade developed in the eighteenth century, and are now beginning to demand more recognition of their needs by both the fur trade corporations and the government of Canada. Their resistance to being dispossessed by hydroelectric development in the James Bay region has brought them into national politics. New England Indians have been restoring tribal organizations and suing for lands, or compensation for lands, taken from them without action of Congress as required by federal law. Several Iroquois have become leaders in petitioning international organizations to support American Indian nationalism. Micmac have been working to raise the standard of living on their reserves and also have been participating in pan-Indian activities. After five centuries of interaction with European entrepreneurs and colonizers, the Indian peoples of the Northeast have neither disappeared nor been subjugated.

RECOMMENDED READING

Dickason, Olive P. 1992 *Canada's First Nations: A History of Founding Peoples.* Norman: University of Oklahoma Press.

Fagan, Brian M. 1991 *Ancient North America.* New York: W. W. Norton.

McGee, H.F., ed. 1974 *The Native Peoples of Atlantic Canada: A Reader.* Toronto: McClelland and Stewart.

Parsons, Elsie Clews, ed. 1967 [1922] *American Indian Life.* Lincoln: University of Nebraska Press.

Speck, Frank G. 1976[1940] *Penobscot Man.* New York: University of Pennsylvania Press.

Trigger, Bruce G. 1990 *The Huron* (2nd ed.). Fort Worth: Holt, Rinehart and Winston.

Trigger, Bruce G., ed. 1978 *The Northeast,* vol. 15, Handbook of North American Indians. Washington, D.C.: Smithsonian Institution Press.

Tuck, James A. 1984 *Maritime Provinces Prehistory.* Ottawa: National Museums of Canada.

Wallace, Anthony F.C. 1969 *The Death and Rebirth of the Seneca.* New York: Random House.

SOURCES FOR THE FIRST EDITION

Akwesasne Notes, vol. 9, 1977 (4,5); vol. 10, 1978 (1,2). Rooseveltown, N.Y.: The Mohawk Nation.

Americans for Indian Opportunity, Inc. 1973 *Facts About American Indians in Wisconsin.* Racine: Johnson Foundation.

Bailey, Alfred Goldsworthy. 1969 *The Conflict of European and Eastern Algonkian Cultures 1504–1700,* (2nd ed.) Toronto: University of Toronto Press.

Berkhofer, Robert F., Jr. 1963 Protestants, Pagans, and Sequences Among the North American Indians, 1760–1860. *Ethnohistory* 10:201–216.

Bishop, Charles A. 1974 *The Northern Ojibwa and the Fur Trade.* Toronto: Holt, Rinehart and Winston of Canada.

————1977 Aboriginal Cree Social Organization. Paper presented at the Ninth Algonquian Conference,. Worcester, Mass., October 1977.

Boissevain, Ethel. 1956 The Detribalization of the Narragansett Indians. *Ethnohistory* 3:225–245.

————1959 Narragansett Survival. *Ethnohistory* 6:347–362.

————1975 *The Narragansett People.* Phoenix: Indian Tribal Series.

Brasser, T.J.C. 1971 The Coastal Algonkians. In E. B. Leacock and N. O. Lurie, eds. *North American Indians in Historical Perspective.* New York: Random House,. pp. 64–91.

Canadian Association in Support of the Native Peoples. 1973 *Bulletin* 14(1).

Ceci, Lynn. 1975 Fish Fertilizer: A Native North American Practice? *Science* 188:26–30.

Conkling, Robert. 1974 Legitimacy and Conversion in Social Change. *Ethnohistory* 21:1–24.

Cook, Sherburne F. 1973 Interracial Warfare and Population Decline Among the New England Indians. *Ethnohistory* 20:1–24.

Cox, Bruce, ed. 1973 *Cultural Ecology.* Toronto: McClelland and Steward.

Cross, Whitney R. 1950 *The Burned-Over District.* New York: Harper & Row.

Dincauze, Dena. 1976 *The Neville Site.* Cambridge, Mass.: Peabody Museum Monographs, no. 4.

————1978 Personal communication.

Duran, Elizabeth C., and James Duran, Jr. 1973 Indian Rights in the Jay Treaty. *Indian Historian* 6:33–37.

Fenton, William N., ed. 1951 Symposium on Local Diversity in Iroquois Culture.Washington, D.C.: Smithsonian Institution, Bureau of American Ethnology, *Bulletin* 149.

————1953 The Iroquois Eagle Dance. Washington, D.C.: Smithsonian Institution, Bureau of American Ethnology, *Bulletin* 156.

————1965 The Iroquois Confederacy in the Twentieth Century. *Ethnology* 4:251–265.

————1971 The Iroquois in History. In E. B. Leacock and N. O. Lurie, (eds.). *North American Indians in Historical Perspective.* New York: Random House, pp. 129–168.

Fitzhugh, William W., ed. 1975 Symposium on Moorehead and Maritime Archaic Problems in Northeastern North America. *Arctic Anthropology* 12 (2).

Funk, Robert E,. and Bruce E. Rippeteau. 1977 Adaptation, Continuity and Change in Upper Susquehanna Prehistory. Amherst: Man in the Northeast, Inc.

Gadacz, René R. 1975 Montagnais Hunting Dynamics in Historicoecological Perspective. *Anthropologica,* n.s. 17:149–167.

Guillemin, Jeanne. 1975 *Urban Renegades.* New York: Columbia University Press.

Hawk, William. 1977 Blood Quantum and Ethnic Identity Among Coastal Algonkian Remnants. *Proceedings* of the Central States Anthropological Society 3:31–36.

Heidenreich, Conrad. 1971 *Huronia.* Toronto: McClelland and Stewart.

Hendry, Jean. 1964 Iroquois Masks and Maskmaking at Onondaga. Washington, D.C.: Smithsonian Institution, Bureau of American Ethnology, *Bulletin* 191, Anthropological Paper 74.

Henriksen, Georg. 1973 *Hunters in the Barrens.* Toronto: University of Toronto Press.

Hickerson, Harold. 1960 The Feast of the Dead Among the Seventeenth Century Algonkians of the Upper Great Lakes. *American Anthropologist,* n.s. 62:81–107.

Hodge, Frederick Webb, ed. 1910 Handbook of American Indians. Washington, D.C.:Smithsonian Institution, Bureau of American Ethnology *Bulletin* 30.

Hodge, William H. 1975 The Indians of Wisconsin. In *Wisconsin Blue Book*. Madison: State of Wisconsin, pp. 96–102.

Hoople, Joanne, and J.W.E. Newbery. 1974 *And What About Canada's Native Peoples?* Ottawa: Canadian Council for International Co-operation.

Indians, Resort Fight Over Ownership, Milwaukee Journal, Oct. 20, 1977, Sec. 3, p. 18.

Innis, Harold A. 1962[1956] *The Fur Trade in Canada* (rev. ed.). New Haven: Yale University Press.

Jennings, Francis. 1975 *The Invasion of America.* Chapel Hill: University of North Carolina Press.

Kroeber, A.L. 1939 *Cultural and Natural Areas of Native North America.* Berkeley: University of California Press.

Martin, Calvin. 1978 *Keepers of the Game.* Berkeley: University of California Press.

McGhee, Robert, and James Tuck. 1977 Did the Medieval Irish Visit Newfoundland? *Canadian Geographical Journal* 94:66–73.

Michels, Joseph W. 1968 Settlement Pattern and Demography at Sheep Rock Shelter. *Southwestern Journal of Anthropology* 24:66–82.

Miller, Jay. 1974 The Delaware as Women. *American Ethnologist* 1:507–514.

———1975 Kwulakan: The Delaware Side of Their Movement West. *Pennsylvania Archaeologist* 45:45–46.

Morison, Samuel Eliot. 1971 *The European Discovery of America: The Northern Voyages.* New York: Oxford University Press.

Mowat, Farley. 1965 *Westviking.* Boston: Little, Brown.

Newcomb, William W., Jr. 1956 *The Culture and Acculturation of the Delaware Indians.* Ann Arbor: University of Michigan, Museum of Anthropology, Anthropological Paper 10.

Newman, Walter S., and Bert Salwen, eds. 1977 Amerinds and Their Paleoenvironments in Northeastern North America. *Annals,* New York Academy of Sciences 288.

Quinn, David B. 1977 *North America from Earliest Discovery to First Settlements.* New York: Harper & Row.

Ray, Arthur J. 1974 *Indians in the Fur Trade.* Toronto: University of Toronto Press.

Ricciardelli, Alex F. 1963 The Adoption of White Agriculture by the Oneida Indians. *Ethnohistory* 10:309–328.

Rich, E.E. 1967 *The Fur Trade and the Northwest to 1857.* Toronto: McClelland and Stewart.

Ritchie, William A. 1965 *The Archaeology of New York State.* New York: Natural History Press.

Ritchie, William A., and Robert E. Funk. 1973 *Aboriginal Settlement Patterns in the Northeast.* Albany: University of the State of New York.

Rogers, Edward S. 1962 *The Round Lake Ojibwa.* Toronto: Royal Ontario Museum.

Rothenberg, Diane. 1976 Erosion of Power—An Economic Basis for the Selective Conservatism of Seneca Women in the Nineteenth Century. *Western Canadian Journal of Anthropology* 6:106–122.

Salisbury, Richard F. 1976 Transactions or Transactors? In B. Kapferer (ed.). *Transaction and Meaning.* Philadelphia: Institute for the Study of Human Issues.

Sauer, Carl Ortwin. 1971 *Sixteenth Century North America.* Berkeley: University of California Press.

Saum, Lewis O. 1965 *The Fur Trader and the Indian.* Seattle: University of Washington Press.

Segal, Charles M., and David C. Stineback. 1977 *Puritans, Indians, and Manifest Destiny.* New York: G.P. Putnam's Sons.

Severin, Timothy. 1977 The Voyage of "Brendan." *National Geographic* 152:771–797.

Smith, Wallis. 1973 The Fur Trade and the Frontier. *Anthropologica,* n.s. 15:21–35.

Starbuck, Alexander. 1924 *The History of Nantucket.* Boston: C.E. Goodspeed.

Thomas, Peter A. 1976 Contrastive Subsistence Strategies and Land Use as Factors for Understanding Indian-White Relations in New England. *Ethnohistory* 23:10–18.

Tooker, Elisabeth. 1964 An Ethnography of the Huron Indians, 1615–1649. Washington, D.C.: Smithsonian Institution, Bureau of American Ethnology, *Bulletin* 190.

Trelease, Allen W. 1960 *Indian Affairs in Colonial New York: The Seventeenth Century.* Ithaca, N.Y.: Cornell University Press.

Trigger, Bruce G. 1969 *The Huron.* New York: Holt, Rinehart and Winston.

Trudel, Marcel. 1973 *The Beginnings of New France 1524–1663 (trans. Patricia Claxton).* Toronto: McClelland and Stewart.

Tuck, James A. 1971 *Onondaga Iroquois Prehistory.* Syracuse: Syracuse University Press.

———1971 An Archaic Cemetery at Port Au Choix, Newfoundland. *American Antiquity* 36:343–358.

Tuck, James A., and Robert J. McGhee. 1976 An Archaic Indian Burial Mound in Labrador. *Scientific American* 235:122–129.

Voegelin, C.F., and E. M. Voegelin. 1964 *Languages of the World: Native America,* Fascicle One. Anthropological Linguistics 6(6). Bloomington: Indiana University.

————1965 *Languages of the World: Native America,* Fascicle Two. Anthropological Linguistics 7(7). Bloomington: Indiana University.

Wallace, Anthony F.C. 1956 New Religious Beliefs Among the Delaware Indians 1600–1900. *Southwestern Journal of Anthropology* 12:1–21.

Wallis, Wilson D., and Ruth Sawtell Wallis. 1955 *The Micmac Indians of Eastern Canada.* Minneapolis: University of Minnesota Press.

Weslager, C.A. 1972 *The Delaware Indians.* New Brunswick: Rutgers University Press.

ADDITIONAL SOURCES
FOR THE SECOND EDITION

Akwesasne Notes, 1989, 1990 vols. 21(3), 22(1), 22(4). Rooseveltown, N.Y.: Mohawk Nation Council of Chiefs.

American Antiquity, Current Research, reports through vol. 55 no. 4 (October 1990).

Aquila, Richard. 1983 *The Iroquois Restoration.* Detroit: Wayne State University Press.

Axtell, James. 1985 *The Invasion Within.* New York: Oxford University Press.

Baker, Emerson W. 1989 "A Scratch with a Bear's Paw": Anglo-Indian Land Deeds in Early Maine. *Ethnohistory* 36(3):235–256.

Barreiro, Jose, ed. 1987 Special Issue on the Iroquois Great Law of Peace. *Northeast Indian Quarterly* 4(3).

————1990 *The Web* [newsletter, Cornell University American Indian Program], April.

Bishop, Charles A. 1986 Territoriality Among Northeastern Algonquians. *Anthropologica* n.s. 28(1-1):37–63.

Blancke, Shirley, and C. John Peters Slow Turtle. 1990 The Teaching of the Past of the Native Peoples of North America in U.S. Schools. In P. Stone and R. MacKenzie, (eds.). *The Excluded Past.* London: Unwin Hyman, pp. 109–133.

Bourque, Bruce J. 1989 Ethnicity on the Maritime Peninsula, 1600–1759. *Ethnohistory* 36(3):257–284.

Bradley, James W. 1987 *Evolution of the Onondaga Iroquois.* Syracuse: Syracuse University Press.

Brandon, William. 1986 *New Worlds for Old.* Athens: Ohio University Press.

Calloway, Colin G. 1987 *Crown and Calumet.* Norman: University of Oklahoma Press.

Campbell, Lyle, and Marianne Mithun, eds. 1979 *The Languages of Native America.* Austin: University of Texas Press.

Ceci, Lynn 1982 The Value of Wampum Among the New York Iroquois: A Case Study in Artifact Analysis. *Journal of Anthropological Research* 38(1):97–107.

Cowan, William, ed. 1984 *Papers of the Fifteenth Algonquian Conference.* Ottawa: Carleton University.

————1985 *Papers of the Sixteenth Algonquian Conference.* Ottawa: Carleton University.

Cox, Bruce Alden, ed. 1987 *Native People, Native Lands.* Ottawa: Carleton University Press.

Dincauze, Dena F., and Robert J. Hasenstab. 1989 Explaining the Iroquois: Tribalization on a Prehistoric Periphery. In T.C. Champion (ed.). *Centre and Periphery.* London: Unwin Hyman, pp. 67–87.

Dobyns, Henry F. 1983 *Their Number Become Thinned.* Knoxville: University of Tennessee Press.

Dobyns, Henry F., Dean R. Snow, Kim M. Lanphear, and David Henige. 1989 Commentary on Native American Demography. *Ethnohistory* 36(3):285–307.

Dowd, Gregory Evans. 1990 The French King Wakes Up in Detroit: "Pontiac's War" in Rumor and History. *Ethnohistory* 37(3):254–278.

Engelbrecht, William. 1987 Factors Maintaining Low Population Density Among the Prehistoric New York Iroquois. *American Antiquity* 52(1):13–27.

Fenton, William N. 1987 *The False Faces of the Iroquois.* Norman: University of Oklahoma Press.

Fitzhugh, William W., ed. 1985 *Cultures in Contact.* Washington, D.C.: Smithsonian Institution Press.

Fixico, Donald L., ed. 1987 *An Anthology of Western Great Lakes Indian History.* Milwaukee: University of Wisconsin–Milwaukee American Indian Studies.

Ford, Richard I., ed. 1985 *Prehistoric Food Production in North America.* Ann Arbor: Museum of Anthropology, University of Michigan, Anthropological Papers, No. 75.

Foster, Michael K., Jack Campisi, and Marianne Mithun, eds. 1984 *Extending the Rafters*. Albany: State University of New York Press.

Given, Brian J. 1981 The Iroquois Wars and Native Firearms. In M.F. Guédon and D.G. Hatt, (eds.). *Papers from the Sixth Annual Congress, 1979*. Ottawa: National Museums of Canada, National Museum of Man Mercury Series, Canadian Ethnology Service Paper, no. 78, pp. 84–94.

Gonzalez, Ellice B. 1981 *Changing Economic Roles for Micmac Men and Women*. Ottawa: National Museum of Man, Mercury Series, Canadian Ethnology Service Paper, no. 72.

Gramly, Richard Michael 1986 Palaeo-Indian Sites South of Lake Ontario, Western and Central New York State. In R. S. Laub, N.G. Miller, and D.W. Steadman, (eds.). *Late Pleistocene and Early Holocene Paleoecology and Archeology of the Eastern Great Lakes Region*. Buffalo: Buffalo Society of Natural Sciences, vol. 33., pp. 265–280.

Green, L. C., and Olive P. Dickason. 1989 *The Law of Nations and the New World*. Edmonton: University of Alberta Press.

Grinde, Donald A., Jr. 1988 Iroquois Political Theory and the Roots of American Democracy. Unpublished paper prepared for projected volume, *Indians and the U. S. Constitution*.

Grumet, Robert S. 1980 Sunksquaws, Shamans, and Tradeswomen: Middle Atlantic Coastal Algonkian Women During the 17th and 18th Centuries. In M. Etienne and E. Leacock, eds., *Women and Colonization*. New York: Praeger, pp. 43–62.

———1990 National Historic Landmark Theme Study: Historic Contact, Indians and Colonists in Northeastern North America, 1497–1783. Distribution Draft I (ms.). Philadelphia: United States Department of the Interior, National Park Service, Mid-Atlantic Region.

Guralnick, Eleanor, ed. 1982 *Vikings in the West*. Chicago: Archaeological Institute of America, Chicago Society.

Hanna, Margaret, and Brian Kooyman, eds. 1982 *Approaches to Algonquian Archaeology*. Calgary: Archaeology Association of the University of Calgary.

Hauptman, Laurence M. 1981 *The Iroquois and the New Deal*. Syracuse: Syracuse University Press.

———1986 *The Iroquois Struggle for Survival: World War II to Red Power*. Syracuse: Syracuse University Press.

———1988 *Formulating American Indian Policy in New York State, 1970–1986*. Albany: State University of New York Press.

Jackson, L. J. 1986 New Evidence for Early Woodland Seasonal Adaptation from Southern Ontario, Canada. *American Antiquity* 51(2):389–401.

Jennings, Francis 1984 *The Ambiguous Iroquois Empire*. New York: W. W. Norton.

———1988 *Empire of Fortune: Crowns, Colonies, and Tribes in the Seven Years War in America*. New York: W.W. Norton.

Jennings, Francis, and William N. Fenton, eds. 1985 *The History and Culture of Iroquois Diplomacy*. Syracuse: Syracuse University Press.

Johansen, Bruce E., and Elisabeth Tooker 1990 Commentary on the Iroquois and the U. S. Constitution. *Ethnohistory* 37(3):279–297.

Johnston, Basil H. 1989 [1988] *Indian School Days*. Norman: University of Oklahoma Press.

Keegan, William F. 1987 *Emergent Horticultural Economies of the Eastern Woodlands*. Carbondale: Southern Illinois University Center for Archaeological Investigations, Occasional Paper No. 7.

Kelley, David H. 1990 Proto-Tifinagh and Proto-Ogham in the Americas. *The Review of Archaeology* 11(1):1–10.

Landsman, Gail 1985 Ganienkeh: Symbol and Politics in an Indian/White Conflict. *American Anthropologist* 87(4):826–839.

———1988 *Sovereignty and Symbol*. Albuquerque: University of New Mexico Press.

Latta, Martha A. 1987 Iroquoian Stemware. *American Antiquity* 52(4):717–724.

Little, Elizabeth A. 1987 Inland Waterways in the Northeast. *Mid–Continental Journal of Archaeology* 12:55-76.

———1988 Nantucket Whaling in the Early 18th Century. In W. Cowan (ed.). *Papers of the Nineteenth Algonquian Conference*. Ottawa: Carleton University, pp. 111-131.

Little, Elizabeth A., ed. 1990 Southern New England Archaeology and Ethnohistory: The Late Woodland and Contact Periods (papers presented at the 1989 Northeastern Anthropological Association meeting, Montreal). *Bulletin of the Massachusetts Archaeological Society* 51(2): 49-82.

Mason, Ronald J. 1981 *Great Lakes Archaeology*. New York: Academic Press.

May, Elizabeth 1990 Update from Cultural Survival (Canada). *Cultural Survival Quarterly* 14(4):69–70.

McGhee, Robert 1984 Contact Between Native North Americans and the Medieval Norse: A Review of the Evidence. *American Antiquity* 49(1):4–26.

Morrison, Alvin Hamblen 1976 Dawnland Developments: Toward Better Understanding of Wabanaki Participation in the Fur Trade, 1500–1700. Paper presented at 75th annual meeting, American Anthropological Association, Washington D.C.

Morrison, Kenneth M. 1984 *The Embattled Northeast: The Elusive Ideal of Alliance in Abenaki-Euramerican Relations.* Berkeley: University of California Press.

News from Indian Country 1990 vol. 4(15), 4(16), 4(17). Hayward, Wis.: Indian Country Communications.

Nicholas, George P., ed. 1988 *Holocene Human Ecology in Northeastern North America.* New York: Plenum Press.

O'Brien, Sharon. 1989 *American Indian Tribal Governments.* Norman: University of Oklahoma Press.

Oneida Tribe of Indians of Wisconsin. 1990 Fact Sheet. Oneida Wis.: Administrative Offices, Oneida Tribe.

Pastore, Ralph T. 1987 Fishermen, Furriers, and Beothuks: The Economy of Extinction. *Man in the Northeast* 33:47–62.

Petersen, James B., and Nathan D. Hamilton. 1984 Early Woodland Ceramic and Perishable Fiber Industries from the Northeast: A Summary and Interpretation. Pittsburgh: *Annals of Carnegie Museum* 53(14):413–445.

Porter, Frank W., ed. 1986 *Strategies for Survival.* New York: Greenwood Press.

Power, Marjory W., and James B. Petersen. 1984 *Seasons of Prehistory: 4000 Years at the Winooski Site.* Montpelier: Vermont Division for Historic Preservation, Agency of Development and Community Affairs.

Prins, Harald E. L. 1989 Natives and Newcomers, Mount Desert Island in the Age of Exploration. In A. McMullen and D. Kopec, (eds.). *An Island in Time.* Bar Harbor, Me.: The Robert Abbe Museum, Bulletin XII,. pp. 21–36.

Prins, Harald E. L., and Bunny McBride 1989 A Social History of Maine Indian Basketry. In *Maine Basketry: Past to Present.* Waterville: Maine Crafts Association/Colby College Museum of Art, pp. 5–33.

Prucha, Francis Paul. 1981 *Indian Policy in the United States.* Lincoln: University of Nebraska Press.

———1984 *The Great Father.* Lincoln: University of Nebraska Press.

Richter, Daniel K. 1983 War and Culture: The Iroquois Experience. *William and Mary Quarterly* 40:528–559.

Richter, Daniel K., and James H. Merrell, eds. 1987 *Beyond the Covenant Chain: The Iroquois and Their Neighbors in Indian North America, 1600–1800.* Syracuse: Syracuse University Press.

Riley, Thomas J., Richard Edging, and Jack Rossen. 1990 Cultigens in Prehistoric Eastern North America. *Current Anthropology* 31(5):525–541.

Roberts, Arthur 1986 Palaeo–Indian/Archaic Transition on the North Shore of Lake Ontario: The Lithic Evidence. In R.S. Laub, N.G. Miller, and D.W. Steadman (eds.). *Late Pleistocene and Early Holocene Paleoecology and Archeology of the Eastern Great Lakes Region.* Buffalo: Buffalo Society of Natural Sciences, vol. 33, pp. 281–293.

Rowlett, Ralph M. 1982 1,000 Years of New World Archaeology. *American Antiquity* 47(3):652–654.

Salisbury, Neal. 1982 *The Indians of New England: A Critical Bibliography.* Bloomington: Indiana University Press.

———1982 *Manitou and Providence: Indians, Europeans, and the Making of New England, 1500–1643.* New York: Oxford University Press.

Simmons, William S. 1983 Red Yankees: Narragansett Conversion in the Great Awakening. *American Ethnologist* 10(2):253–271.

———1986 *Spirit of the New England Tribes: Indian History and Folklore 1620–1984.* Hanover: University Press of New England.

Simmons, William S., and Cheryl L. Simmons, eds. 1982 *Old Light on Separate Ways: The Narragansett Diary of Joseph Fish, 1765–1776.* Hanover: University Press of New England.

Snipp, C. Matthew. 1989 *American Indians: The First of This Land.* New York: Russell Sage Foundation.

Starna, William A., and Ralph Watkins 1991 Northern Iroquoian Slavery. *Ethnohistory* 38(1):34–57.

Sullivan, Norman C. 1989 On a Darkling Plain: A Study of the Demographic Crisis of the Huron Indians. Doctoral dissertation, Department of Anthropology, University of Toronto.

Tanner, Adrian, ed. 1983 *The Politics of Indianness.* St. Johns: Memorial University of Newfoundland, Institute of Social and Economic Research, Social and Economic Papers, No. 12.

Tooker, Elisabeth 1988 The United States Constitution and the Iroquois League. *Ethnohistory* 35(4):305–336.

Trigger, Bruce G. 1976 *The Children of Aataentsic: A History of the Huron People to 1660.* Montreal: McGill-Queens University Press.

———1985 *Natives and Newcomers: Canada's "Heroic Age" Reconsidered.* Montreal: McGill-Queen's University Press.

Trigger, Bruce G., ed. 1978 *Handbook of North American Indians* vol. 15: *Northeast.* Washington, D.C.: Smithsonian Institution Press.

Upton, L. F. S. 1979 *Micmacs and Colonists.* Vancouver: University of British Columbia Press.

Williams, Robert A., Jr. 1990 *The American Indian in Western Legal Thought.* New York: Oxford University Press.

6

THE PRAIRIE-PLAINS

The Rocky Mountains cast a long shadow, a rain shadow. Air passing over the mountains is cooled and drops its moisture, depriving land east of the range. Sagebrush and grass grow, but there is insufficient water falling to nourish trees except along streams. Conditions are especially arid in the southern Plains, where high temperatures increase evaporation of moisture. To the north, sagebrush declines and grasses predominate into Alberta and Saskatchewan, where long winters retard moisture loss sufficiently for groves of poplars to survive. To the east, similar gradations appear: first, heavier grass cover; then, clusters of trees among the meadows, as the effect of moisture-bearing winds from the Arctic and the Gulf of Mexico is felt. The northern border of the Plains is a poplar (aspen) parkland of groves and meadows, giving way to the pines and spruces of the subarctic boreal forest; the eastern border is the rim of the Mississippi Valley; the southern border is arid Mexico. Swaths of parkland extend across the Mississippi through Illinois, carrying prairie vegetation as far as some tributaries of the Ohio. Grasslands, the ecology of the Prairie-Plains culture area, thus extend from central Canada through Texas, and from Alberta, Montana, Wyoming, and Colorado to Wisconsin, Michigan, Indiana, and Missouri. Their eastern boundary is a fuzzy one, maintained in the Midwest by Indians firing the meadows against encroaching trees, lapping around the wooded thickets that penetrate deep into the Plains along the entrenched rivers.

Bison were the principal inhabitants of the Prairie-Plains grasslands. Sixty million of them are estimated to have lived in the region in the nineteenth century. They provided hunters with lean, flavorful meat, sweet white fat, hides for lodge covers and winter robes, bones for knives, scrapers, and awls, horns for ladles and spoons, wool for weaving, and even tails for fly swatters and ribs for runners of children's sleds. Where cattle now graze, skittish bison were an apparently limitless reservoir of all the necessities of life.

MAP 7 The Prairie-Plains

THE PRAIRIE-PLAINS
CHRONOLOGY

1970	Wounded Knee protest AIM founded
1960	Government policy of relocation into cities
1950	
1945	World War II—Indians into armed services, industries
1940	
1935	Collier Administration, BIA Dust bowl drought, economic depression
1930	
1920	Native American (Peyote) Church incorporated
1910	
1900	
1890	Allotment of Plains reservations under Dawes Act Ghost dance religion begins; Sitting Bull murdered; Wounded Knee Massacre Wovoka's vision
1885	Peyote religion begins with Kiowa, Comanche
1880	Bison herds disappear
1870	Custer's defeat Treaty of Laramie with western tribes Minnesota uprising: Some Santee to Canada; Winnebago disperse
1860	Grass dance popularity begins
1850	Mesquakie return to Iowa Some Kickapoo to Mexico Removal of Midwestern Agriculturists to west of Mississippi after Blackhawk's War
1825	Some Potawatomi move west of Mississippi
1800	Cheyenne nomads on High Plains Some Kickapoo in Texas Ilini confederacy defeated Assiniboin, Cree hunt for fur trade
1775	Dakota use horses
1750	Blackfoot, Gros Ventres, Crow use horses; Kiowa and Shoshoni pushed south Mandan, Hidatsa begin trading horses
1725	Sioux, Cheyenne moving to North Dakota
1700	Pawnee, southern Siouans use horses Wichita and Caddo use horses
1675	Chiwere and Dhegiha Siouan migrations west
1650	Indians begin to use horses
1600	Spanish ranches established
1540	Coronado explores to Wichita towns
1500	Shoshoni enter Wyoming Apacheans in Colorado Farming towns fortified Blackfoot on Northwest Plains
1400	
1300	Farming villages up Missouri to North Dakota
1000	Farming villages in Central Plains
500	Bow and arrow; Apacheans enter Northwest Plains

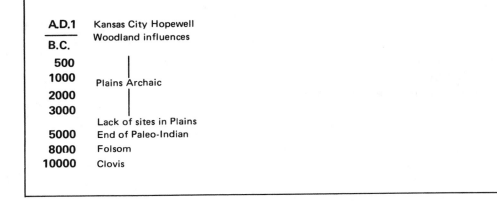

A.D.1	Kansas City Hopewell
B.C.	Woodland influences
500	
1000	Plains Archaic
2000	
3000	
5000	Lack of sites in Plains
	End of Paleo-Indian
8000	Folsom
10000	Clovis

The earth unfolds and the limit of the land recedes. Clusters of trees, and animals grazing far in the distance, cause the vision to reach away and wonder to build upon the mind. The sun follows a longer course in the day, and the sky is immense beyond all comparison. The great billowing clouds that sail upon it are shadows that move upon the grain like water, dividing light…. The sun is at home on the plains. Precisely there does it have the certain character of a god.

…My grandmother…was ten when the Kiowas came together for the last time as a living Sun Dance culture. They could find no buffalo; they had to hang an old hide from the sacred tree. Before the dance could begin, a company of soldiers rode out from Fort Sill under orders to disperse the tribe. Forbidden without cause the essential act of their faith, having seen the wild herds slaughtered and left to rot upon the ground, the Kiowas backed away forever from the medicine tree. That was July 20, 1890, at the great bend of the Washita. My grandmother was there. Without bitterness, and for as long as she lived, she bore a vision of deicide.

Now that I can have her only in memory, I see my grandmother in the several postures that were peculiar to her: standing at the wood stove on a winter morning and turning meat in a great iron skillet; sitting at the south window, bent above her beadwork, and afterwards, when her vision failed, looking down for a long time into the fold of her hands; going out upon a cane, very slowly as she did when the weight of age came upon her; praying. I remember her most often at prayer. She made long, rambling prayers out of suffering and hope, having seen many things….

Once there was a lot of sound in my grandmother's house, a lot of coming and going, feasting and talk…. There were frequent prayer meetings, and great nocturnal feasts. When I was a child I played with my cousins outside, where the lamplight fell upon the ground and the singing of the old people rose up around us and carried away into the darkness. There were a lot of good things to eat, a lot of laughter and surprise. And afterwards, when the quiet returned, I lay down with my grandmother and could hear the frogs away by the river and feel the motion of the air.

(Momaday 1969:7–12)

Climatic changes shifted the boundaries of the Plains north or south, eastward or westward. The bison population shifted with the boundaries, expanding as the grasslands expanded (apparently during the last centuries before European contact), declining into small herds on the better-watered fringes and valleys during the climax of the post-Pleistocene warming trend in the third millennium B.C. Human population correlated with the bison, heavier when and where rich grasslands and parkland supported numerous bison, sparse when and where aridity made grasses and animals fewer. There was no good alternative to bison as the staple food for humans on the Plains: maize requires more water than is naturally available in most of the Plains, there are relatively few wild vegetables or nuts, and, before the modern dams, there were few fishing lakes and streams. No other mammal approached the numbers of the bison, or yielded such a quantity of meat. At least at the time of historic contact, humans and bison were in symbiosis, the humans living off the herds, the herds flourishing on the prairies periodically fired by the humans to encourage the tender grass sought by the bison.

Dependence on bison gives a unity to the native cultural traditions of the Prairie-Plains. Climatic differences and historic situations allow a division of this basically homogeneous broad culture area into three sections: the eastern section, or Prairie, where maize agriculture was practiced in the valleys, with a northern strip from Michigan through Minnesota where wild-rice harvesting substituted for maize; the Northern Plains and bordering parkland, where bison hunting became commercialized into the production of pemmican to supply the Canadian fur trade's need for provisions; and the Southern Plains, where raiding the Southwestern pueblos and ranches became an economic resource.

SECTION 1: THE ARCHAIC AND WOODLAND PERIODS

Late styles of originally Fluted Tradition, lance- or leaf-shaped stone knives and projectile points—the Scottsbluff type—persisted on the Plains somewhat longer than they seem to have in the Eastern Woodlands. A small lanceolate type, the McKean, has even been radiocarbon-dated on the northern Plains to about 1700 B.C. The full-size Plano knives and points of the Scottsbluff type were common up to about 5000 B.C. on the Plains, and possibly until some centuries later in the northwestern extension of the Plains grasslands to the corner of the Yukon territory and northwestern Alberta. The persistence of Fluted Tradition technology on the Plains no doubt reflects the viability of a late-Pleistocene kind of economy based on the nomadic pursuit of herds of large game (here, the bison). Holocene Plains grasslands would not have been as rich as the low-latitude tundra grasslands of the glacial periods of the Pleistocene, as may be inferred from the extinction of the mammoths and the huge species of Pleistocene bison, but still the grasslands under the rain shadow of the Rockies were better pasture than the forests of the East. With the persistence of the game herds for which Fluted Tradition technology had been developed, humans would have had little incentive to adopt radically new tools or weapon fittings such as were being experimented with in the East, where greater ecological changes were occurring.

Climatic change did begin to affect the Plains in the sixth millennium B.C. Atlatl points and knives fastened to shafts and handles by the aid of side or corner notches on the blade's base appear on the Plains about 5500 B.C., and soon come to be more common than the Plano lance heads. The new style may represent influence or possibly migration from the Early Archaic period of the Eastern Woodlands, but it appears on the Intermontane Plateau (the high valleys between the major ranges of the Rockies) in Idaho about the same time it does on the Plains. Sites with the notched knives and points contain mostly butchered bison remains if on the High (western, drier) Plains; if on the peripheral Plains or Plateau, they contain primarily bison plus other game such as elk and, on the

Plateau, mountain sheep. All sites appear to be short-term hunters' camps occupied by people who used a variety of regional resources, including small animals and even shellfish, if available. It is possible that the increasing winter warmth and consequent increasing aridity of the Plains forced the descendants of the Plano spearmen to rely somewhat less on the prime big-game herds and more on lesser prizes. Another hypothesis favored by some archaeologists is that the long decline in prime game, from the extinction of mammoths through the diminution of bison, stimulated the Plano peoples to move northward (where the higher latitude meant a cooler climate and better grass), eventually into the corridorlike northwest extension of the Plains in northern Alberta, where the last vestiges of really big game held out. This hypothesis assumes that as the Plano peoples vacated the main sections of the Plains, Eastern Archaic peoples moved in, bringing their preferred notched atlatl points and knives. The simplest explanation, and quite a plausible one, is that no substantial migrations occurred, but only the spread of innovations in blade and weapon technology, and that the greater variety of food resources found in Plains Archaic sites compared with earlier Plains sites is due chiefly to the excavated Plains Archaic sites having been camps, whereas most of the earlier sites that have been excavated have been kills. So few early sites have been thoroughly studied that perhaps no generalizations ought to be made about them.

As the Holocene warming trend progressed, a lack of human habitation remains on the High Plains becomes evident. Was the region too arid to support people? Did people abandon the region for pleasanter areas with better game resources? Population density at this time in North America could not have been so great that groups were forced to remain in inhospitable deserts because more advantageous localities were securely held by more powerful societies. The absence of sites on the High Plains between about 5000 and 3500 B.C. can also be argued to be an absence of evidence due to

subsequent erosion of the most habitable spots, which of course would have been near water in this arid period. It is therefore uncertain whether the High Plains were truly a deserted desert during the climatic thermal maximum, or whether a limited Plains Archaic occupation continued there as it did on the peripheries of the Plains.

By about 2500 B.C., aridity on the High Plains was lessening and the bison population was recovering from its low. For the next two thousand years, sites are small camps exploiting the local fauna and sometimes using grinding stones, presumably to process amaranth and chenopod seeds, although direct evidence of what was ground has not been observed. Hunters camped at the edge of the Rockies in Wyoming collected pine seeds and several kinds of berries, as well as rose hips, wild onions, and juniper bark and yucca to shred and twist into rope. Similarities in artifacts and settlement patterns among the Plains, the Intermontane Plateau, and the southern portion of the boreal forest north of the Plains suggest all shared an Archaic cultural configuration, and copper artifacts in the drainage of the South Saskatchewan River demonstrate contacts between Northwestern Plains Archaic and Old Copper Late Archaic of the upper Midwest.

The developing Woodland societies in the East began to influence the Prairie-Plains region about 500 B.C., when corner-notched atlatl points and knives somewhat larger than the usual Plains Archaic types came into fashion. Real change began a few centuries later, around A.D. 1, when Hopewell trade and burial customs reached the central Missouri River region, from Kansas City north into central South Dakota. Villages appeared in this region along the river valleys. Oval pole wigwams were the permanent homes, probably supplanted by hide tipis when the community was out on an extended hunt. Bison were the principal source of food, with elk, deer, antelope, bear, beaver, and grouse also taken, along with small creatures, turtles, and occasionally fish. Maize was cultivated around Kansas City, but apparently not farther north in the Dakotas. Adjacent to some of the villages were stone or log tombs covered with earth mounds that held the remains of as many as fifty people. The corpses were partially disarticulated and arranged into a bundle, a practice that would have facilitated the carrying of the community's dead from wherever they may have died, let us say on a hunt, to the village cemetery mounds. Ornaments and utilitarian artifacts were deposited with the dead, but there is no reason to suppose any of the bodies represent sacrifices. In lack of status differentiation within the tombs, and in lack of ostentatious offerings, these Plains Woodland mounds contrast with contemporary Hopewell mounds in the Midwest. Marine shells such as conch, olivella, and dentalium and small copper beads attest that the Plains Woodland peoples were in the Hopewell trade network. The wide distribution of fine chipping stone, such as the glassy brown chalcedony from the Knife River area of central North Dakota, suggests the Missouri and its tributaries carried long-distance trade within the Plains as well. It is possible that some of the olivella shells in South Dakota mounds of this period may have come from the Pacific coast, perhaps over the route that Lewis and Clark took so many centuries later.

A second source of change appeared in the northwestern Plains about A.D. 250: arrow points made on delicate flakes challenged the popularity of the Middle Woodland atlatl points. The arrow points were used to shoot bison at close range as the animals milled in corrals. They represent a different technique of hunting than that associated with atlatls, which were designed to be effective with javelins thrown from a moderate distance when stalking game. Bows and arrows, and the highly efficient impounding method of obtaining bison with which the arrows were associated, became dominant over the Northern Plains during the next few centuries, the Middle Woodland bison hunters adapting their weapon technology and presumably their hunting methods to the new model. Archaeology does not indicate whether any par-

ticular ethnic group introduced the arrow point into the Northern Plains, but its earlier appearance in the northwestern sector hints that it may have been Athabascans (Dené). They may have occupied Alberta and Montana until about A.D. 750, then begun moving south along the western High Plains in the somewhat warmer and moister climatic phase taking effect at this time, and eventually settled in the peripheral Southwest in Colorado, adding limited maize agriculture to their resources. According to this hypothesis, the appearance of the first true arrow points in the northwestern Plains about A.D. 250 marks the first movement of the Apacheans on their southward migration from the Canadian forests to the American Southwest.

SECTION 2: THE LATE PREHISTORIC PERIOD

The slightly warmer and moister climatic phase that drew the early Mississippian peoples northward into Illinois, and that encouraged the Anasazi Pueblos to devote themselves to agriculture, attracted agricultural settlement up the Missouri Valley, too. About A.D. 850, villages of substantial rectangular houses were built in the central Plains as far north as central South Dakota. The homes were framed with wooden posts set along a shallow depression cut into the soil, and were covered with earth. This insulated them well. Hearths near the entranceway, a short corridor higher than the interior floor level, helped air circulate without losing heat within the home, although the houses must have been dark and smoky. Villages were usually constructed on terraces or bluffs above the river flood plain, and the villagers made their fields below, raising maize, beans, squashes, chenopods, amaranth, and domesticated sunflowers. An abundance of bison bone in the village garbage dumps proves that these early Plains agriculturists, like their historic descendants, were committed to extensive hunts and did not rely only on the produce of their fields.

Agriculture, in fact, utilized successful hunts, for the principal agricultural tool was a hoe made from a bison shoulder blade. Harvests were protected by being stored in deep, barrellike pits sunk into house floors. Trade with the Mississippians is shown by shells and an occasional Mississippian pot, but the essential independence of the early Plains agriculturists is indicated by their pottery, an amalgam of Woodland and Mississippian ceramic traits manifested in several regional variants.

Farmer-hunters had expanded up the Missouri River as far as central North Dakota's Knife River, a tributary of the Missouri north of Bismarck, by A.D. 1150. During the droughts of the fourteenth century A.D., villages in south-central South Dakota seem to have been abandoned, but the northern villages and those in the central Plains of Nebraska and Kansas continued. These populations grew steadily, filling stream valleys with hamlets and contributing to the repopulation of the earlier-colonized region. When this section of the arable Missouri flood plain was reoccupied, competition for farmland seems to have developed. After A.D. 1450, villages are larger, with as many as one hundred houses compactly clustered, and most of these permanent towns are fortified with bastioned stockades and ditches. The round style of earth-insulated pole house typical of the central Plains came to replace the rectangular style along the Missouri. Simple small versions of these round houses, with poles laid against stringers lashed to four sturdy posts set around a central hearth, were built as hunting lodges, or hide tipis were used, when the community marched out to procure stores of meat and skins. The uppermost layers of Plains village sites frequently contain European trade items, establishing the late prehistoric communities as the forebears of the historic Hidatsa, Mandan, and Arikara of North Dakota and the Pawnee and Wichita of Nebraska and Kansas.

Not only Missouri Valley populations expanded. That population increased and fully agricultural economies were established in the Upper Midwest-Prairies in the Mississippian Period seem

to be facts. Whether these facts indicate a resurgence of Middle Woodland (Hopewellian) societies that retrenched in the middle of the first millennium A.D., or only straight population growth eventually requiring adoption of agriculture to feed its numbers, or colonial expansion of the Mississippian state, is much debated. A curious regional group is the Effigy Mound culture of the second half of the first millennium across southern Wisconsin and adjacent eastern Iowa. These people built low earth mounds in the shapes of birds, panthers, bears, deer, turtles, lizards, circles and straight lines. Occasionally, an animal shape was carved out of the ground, sort of a mound in reverse. Usually there are groups of these mounds, representing different animals and geometric shapes. Small villages with evidence of hunting, harvesting wild foods, and limited agriculture are near the mounds, but not necessarily next to them. A few mounds had one or a few burials, but many contain nothing. What the mounds symbolized is anybody's guess, and guesses have ranged from "totems" (symbols of the makers' groups, such as might be "Panther Village" or "Hawk Band"), to spirits invoked in ritual, to star maps in which the shapes represent constellations. Why effigy mounds were no longer constructed in the later Mississippian/Late Woodland period, after about the eleventh century, is as much a question as why they were constructed for the several centuries previous.

Mississippians built a palisaded town with flat-topped and conical mounds in south-central Wisconsin, a site designated Aztalan in the nineteenth century by Euro-American settlers who thought it might be the fabled Aztlán, homeland of the Aztecs. Aztalan's occupancy coincides so closely with the heyday and decline of Cahokia that it seems indisputable that the northern town was an outpost communicating by river with the great Mississippian capital. Aggressive defense of this outpost is attested not only by its palisade wall, but also by chopped pieces of human bone in trash: nearly all the human bone is from young men of fighting age. Mississippians may have waged a campaign of terror against uncooperative local groups by threatening to torture and cannibalize enemy captives (as the Iroquois did in historic times). Lesser trade routes linked many smaller towns, including new villages apparently located to produce valued materials such as galena, a mineral mined on the western Illinois-Wisconsin border and traded into central Illinois (while Cahokia, farther south, got its galena mainly from nearer Missouri mines). One of these villages excavated in southwestern Wisconsin showed cultivation not only of corn, squash, sunflowers, and probably chenopods, but also the introduction of a similar seed-grass, maygrass, from Illinois and the first tobacco raised so far north, in Wisconsin. As one goes north into Wisconsin, massive built mounds are replaced by ingenious facing-off of natural promontories and drumlins (glacier-deposited ridges) to make them look like Mississippian platform mounds; just how many of these pseudomounds there were is tricky to determine. At any rate, mounds seem to cease at the northern limit of maize agriculture, central Wisconsin and Minnesota.

Oneota is the term given to the agricultural societies that covered the Upper Midwest beginning in the eleventh century. Oneota may have absorbed Effigy Mound people, or it may be that once Mississippians had colonized the Upper Midwest, indigenous people themselves shifted to a dependence on maize agriculture and participation in regular trading enterprises. A changed culture is evident in human skeletons from this period, who were afflicted with far more dental cavities and bone porosis, a sign of anemia probably due to the effect of a great deal of maize in their diet, which blocked the absorption of iron. Counteracting these unfortunate consequences of maize as dominant in the diet was less incidence of children's growth being affected by occasional lack of food or bouts of illness. In contrast to earlier cultures, Oneota, with its stores of maize, seems to have been consistently able to meet basic food needs year-round. A final interesting observation from Oneota skeletons is that tuberculosis appeared for

the first time at about A.D. 1000, throughout the Upper Midwest. Effigy Mound communities had enjoyed a fairly good (for nonmodern conditions) life expectancy until that time, but when Mississippians and Oneota appeared in Wisconsin, the death rate increased and life expectancy dropped to the point that population maintenance would have been affected. Disappearance of Effigy Mound culture thus may in part have been an effect of higher mortality resulting from a new epidemic, much as occurred seven centuries later with European invasions. The source of the Mississippian tuberculosis epidemic has not been satisfactorily determined, but since tuberculosis was already endemic in Europe, and A.D. 1000 was the time of the Norse efforts to colonize the Gulf of St. Lawrence region, it is possible that the disease was carried by Norse and moved up the St. Lawrence and through the Great Lakes, either in the persons of Norse voyagers or through Indian traders and communities originally infected on the Gulf of St. Lawrence.

Western Oneota were surely ancestral to the historic Siouan-speaking nations of the same region. Excavations of Late Prehistoric fields show that hundreds of acres were cleared and Mississippian-type ridge-and-furrow crop beds constructed. Soil was improved by mixing in ash and charcoal. Maize was planted in little hills on the ridges, with 3,000 planting hills per acre (7,400 per hectare) and a yield of about 23 bushels of corn per acre (57 bushels, or 17 tons of dry shelled corn, per hectare). Important as maize was, Oneota communities carefully continued harvesting, probably through cultivation, temperate-zone seeds and collecting nuts to supplement the nutrients in maize and ensure food in case of maize crop failure. Hunting—of deer, elk, and bison—and fishing further enhanced food supplies and nutritional needs. In the forests north of the Oneota, around the western Great Lakes, are a series of large villages, some palisaded or even fortified with a ditch around the palisade, like Late Prehistoric towns in North Dakota. Because these large, Late Woodland and

Protohistoric villages are beyond the limit for maize and where historic Indians relied on harvesting wild rice, it is assumed—although wild-rice sowing, harvesting, and processing leaves little archaeological trace—the prehistoric communities also relied on this lake-grass grain. Mining Lake Superior copper ensured these northern villages would be in contact with Oneota and, beyond them, other Mississippians needing the metal.

Northern Prairie peoples in western Minnesota fissioned several times, and bands were consequently siphoned off to the west, where they concentrated more fully on bison hunting. The earliest may have been the ancestors of the Blackfoot who may have migrated along the north-westward-trending parkland bordering the Plains, through eastern North Dakota and southern Manitoba to western Saskatchewan. Here, a pretty country of low, rolling hills with aspen groves, streams in broad glacial-outwash valleys, and stretches of sweeping grasslands maintained a relatively high density of game: bison, antelope, elk, and beaver. Here, on both sides of the Alberta-Saskatchewan border, the Blackfoot lived from at least A.D. 1400, camping in bison-hide tipis for a few days or weeks, as the success of the hunt or the attractions of berry bushes, prairie turnips, or sheltered winter-lodge sites dictated. Impounding of bison herds by luring and then stampeding them into corrals provided the depended-upon staple, but other game was stalked or trapped; fish were disdained. All possessions had to be carried on the backs of humans or dogs, or in bundles lashed between two short poles (the travois) tied to a dog's shoulder harness so that the animal could drag the burden. Dogs were carefully bred large and strong for this purpose, but could never approach the capacity of horses for transportation. Thus, the people could own only a few material goods, and their tipis were small, 8 to 10 feet (3 meters) in diameter at the base. Still, the Blackfoot found their life comfortable, and when the fur trade approached their country in the late eighteenth century, they felt little incentive to modify their basic pattern. This contentment

with their Northwestern Plains life indicates to some researchers a much longer habitation in the region, possibly a couple of millennia; archaeology can't flesh out the bare remnants of material culture sufficiently to name either language or ethnic affiliation of Northwestern Plains hunters before about A.D. 1400.

Most of the High Plains at the end of the prehistoric period was probably more hunting territory than settlement areas. The focus of settlement was toward the parklands bordering the Plains on the northeast, the north, and along the foot of the Rockies on the west, plus the deeply entrenched, wooded stream valleys of the Missouri river system where the agricultural villages located. Bison herds themselves sought the parklands and wooded valleys for winter shelter, and it was in this ecology that elk and beaver would be found. The open grasslands, with their strong constant wind, would have been favored in summer, when heat and insects annoy animals and their human predators in the wooded areas. Human utilization of the High Plains would have then, as later, been correlated with bison-herd movements: out into the seas of grass in spring and summer, and back into the aspen groves or willow and cottonwood stream thickets when cold threatened. Wherever they traveled, the people took note of valley rimrocks and similar sharp breaks in the topography where a corral could be hidden below a drop-off or at the head of a coulee. These "kettles," as the Blackfoot called them, were the crucial feature of Plains life, the primary means of harvesting bison.

Along the foot of the Rockies, peoples such as the Kutenai exploited the canyons and passes of mountains as well as the edge of the High Plains. In June they moved into valleys at the base of the Rockies to dig camas root and other edible plants as well as to hunt elk and deer. As the summer wore on, they climbed into the high meadows along the passes where edible plants matured later than at lower altitudes, and where at the end of summer bighorn sheep and elk were migrating. The approach of winter brought the people down, to the intermontane valleys or the river valleys entering the High Plains, where bison, elk, and deer as well as humans could escape the deepest snows.

This pattern of utilizing the high country as well as the bison plains had been developed in the Archaic period by about 5000 B.C., persisted to the mid-nineteenth century in some areas, such as Montana, but was broken in the central High Plains about A.D. 1450 when Shoshoni moved east through the Wyoming mountains to the northwestern Plains. These Shoshoni had been living in the Great Basin of Utah and southernmost Idaho, unacquainted with the resources of the high mountain meadows of the Rockies. They took over the Green River basin of Wyoming and continued to expand, north into Montana and south into Colorado, displacing the indigenous peoples—possibly the Kutenai—and introducing a different exploitative pattern concentrating on bison, antelope, and elk and neglecting the high country.

The southern High Plains during this period experienced the acculturation of the Apacheans to the Southwestern Pueblos. Perhaps the Shoshoni expansion had displaced Apacheans, too. Reestablished in the Southern Plains, the Apacheans took up small-scale farming as an addition to bison hunting. The Southern Plains was also occupied by nomadic hunters who had abandoned agricultural pueblos during the great drought of the fourteenth century, turning to intensive bison exploitation instead. The Kiowa, who are related by language to the Tanoan-speaking pueblos of New Mexico, may represent some of these Puebloans turned to exclusive hunting. Parties of bison hunters on extended trips from the Southwestern pueblos were an additional element in the late-prehistoric Southern Plains. A final element was the nomads of western Texas and adjacent northern Mexico, peoples such as the Jumano, whose material possessions were very few but who enjoyed visiting and trading meat on all sides of the Southern Plains: to the east Texas–Oklahoma Caddo villages, to the Wichita, to Pecos and other pueblos in New Mexico, and to towns in northern Mexico.

SECTION 3: THE ERA OF THE HORSE

Spanish ranches established in New Mexico early in the seventeenth century trained Indians to handle and care for the horses being bred for Mexican markets. These Indians quickly realized the advantages horses could bring the nomadic hunting peoples on the Plains. Indian use of horses in the Southwest may have begun by 1630; by 1659, Apache raids on ranches were capturing as many as 300 horses in one swoop. During the 1680s, Wichita and Caddo in Texas were obtaining horses across the Southern Plains. A decade later, Pawnee and several southern Siouan peoples—Missouri, Oto, Kansa, Ponca—had horses, and the Pawnee sometimes used them to pursue bison. Soon after the commencement of the eighteenth century, the Comanche, an offshoot of the Shoshoni, made horse raiding and trading an important occupation, later in the century bringing the animals each year to a rendezvous in the Black Hills of South Dakota, where a number of peoples met to trade. Comanche also passed horses north to their relatives the Shoshoni, who in turn traded some to peoples on the Intermontane Plateau and eventually down the Columbia River. Eastward, horses reached the Mandan, on the Missouri in central North Dakota, about the time the first French fur traders came to them from the opposite direction, in 1739. Two years later, Mandan were selling horses to traders. Horses became a major object of trade in the Mandan towns, which, because of their permanence, had been markets for the Northern Plains for several centuries. Nomadic peoples of the Northern Plains, the Blackfoot, Gros Ventres, and Crow, may have obtained their first horses from the Mandan; the Blackfoot and allied Gros Ventres were using horses by 1754. Horses of Spanish origin continued to move east, coming into use among the Prairie Dakota (including Yankton and Teton bands) in the 1760s and among the Sauk on the Wisconsin River in the upper Midwest by 1775. Ojibwa migrating onto the northeastern Prairie to hunt bison early in the nineteenth century learned to use horses, as did the Cree who had preceded them.

Obtaining horses required obtaining knowledge of their proper care, knowledge of harnesses, saddles, and other gear, and skill in handling the animals. Thus, the spread of horses throughout the Plains and Prairie attests the widespread peaceful trade and alliances that enabled the diffusion of the imported complex. Other practical techniques, ideas on social organization and rituals, information on political events, and European items, including guns, native manufactures and processed foods, passed along the same networks as did horses. These networks were the mechanism by which the Plains was maintained as a culture area.

Use of the horse opened for Plains nomads the possibility of accumulating wealth. A family with a string of horses could carry poles and cover for a tipi 20 to 40 feet (6 to 12 meters) in diameter, a commodious and pleasant home. They could carry many sacks of dried meat, berries, and prairie-turnip flour, changes of clothing and beautiful costumes for ceremonies and feasts, ritual paraphernalia, and heavy robes for bedding. Elderly persons and toddlers could ride when camps moved. Comfort no longer meant only a full stomach and a fire. A well-furnished tipi of expertly tanned bison hide, insulated from drafts by an attractively painted liner hung from halfway up the tipi, rivaled any earth lodge or wigwam in comfort. Horses became the key to a much higher standard of living on the High Plains, and soon became symbol as well as key.

Historic Plains Indians appeared so dependent upon horses that anthropologist A.L. Kroeber believed the Plains could not have been inhabited before horses were brought into the region. Archaeology demonstrated this notion was untrue, but it is true that population increased dramatically on the Plains after the advent of the horse. The increase was due in part to the attraction Plains nomadism held, once nomadism no longer meant giving up all but a bare minimum of possessions. In part, however, the migrations of several peoples onto the Plains were displacements caused by the invasions of eastern Indians and Euro-American settlers into the Midwest. Villages might not have been directly threatened, but hunting territories surrounding Midwestern villages became overused and disputed, and under this pressure, a number of communities in the Prairie abandoned farms, making bison hunts the basis of year-round life instead of, as formerly, a complement to agriculture. Nomadic life utilizing horses necessitated close attention to grazing requirements, so that the historic Plains Indians selected their camps to provide for herds of horses as well as human needs, and horse pasture could be as vital as hunting territory.

The Crow and Hidatsa

Leaving agriculture to concentrate upon bison hunting was not a new event in the historic Plains. The Blackfoot and the Kiowa had probably done this in the fourteenth century. The Crow (Absaroka or, more phonetically, Apsáalooke) were once bands of the Hidatsa living in villages on the Knife River, north of the Mandan on the Missouri in North Dakota. Their tradition claims that they separated from the other Hidatsa, apparently about A.D. 1700, after a quarrel between leaders. Crow and Hidatsa are dialects of a Missouri Siouan language; differences between the Crow and Hidatsa dialects, and among Hidatsa villages, suggest that, in fact, several bands had been independent for a couple of centuries previously, and that the quarrel was only a particularly memorable episode in which bands asserted autonomy. Nor did the quarrel produce total isolation: individuals and families moved from Hidatsa villages to Crow camps, or vice versa, and whole bands visited one another for protracted periods. Those Hidatsa bands that lived in tipis, devoting themselves to hunting around the headwaters of the Missouri in south-central Montana and adjacent Wyoming, came to be called Crow; the Hidatsa who occupied permanent villages of earth lodges and combined farming with seasonal hunts were the historic Hidatsa of North Dakota. The two principal divisions traded heavily with each other, the Crow bringing horses from Comanche and Shoshoni and the Hidatsa supplying agricultural produce, for the Crow raised only tobacco for religious ceremonies. By the mid-nineteenth century, the Crow controlled the central Montana-Wyoming border region, fine grasslands on the high country east of the Rockies, but with foothill ranges varying the ecological conditions. The 1851 Treaty of Fort Laramie recognized this Crow territory, and, unlike most Indian nations, the Crow were able to negotiate a reservation in south-central Montana and remain in this desirable homeland. It is somewhat ironic that although the Crow have never been removed from their homeland, by the 1980s, one-third of the land within the reservation had been sold to non-Indians and another third is leased to non-Indians. There were seven thousand Crow listed in the 1980 census.

The Blackfoot

Three allied groups, the Kainai ("Bloods"), the Siksika ("Blackfoot"), and the Peigan (Pikuni), form the Blackfoot nation. Occupying the parklands and plains of western Saskatchewan and southern Alberta when first contacted by a European in 1690, the Blackfoot at that time professed no interest in making long journeys to sell furs; or perhaps they were not impressed by the Hudson's Bay Company employee sent to contact them, an adventuresome teenager named Henry Kelsey. During the first half of the eighteenth century, the Blackfoot were engaged in defending their western border against Shoshoni expansion. Allying with the Athabascan-speaking (Dené) Sarsi, the Blackfoot held their border along the front range of the Rockies and gradually pushed the Shoshoni south again, until by late in the century the principal threat came from Crow hunting in central Montana. After 1830, fur and hide trading posts built on the upper Missouri

added contention over access to the posts as well as into the hunting grounds and the distant Indian nations who might accept Indian middlemen traders. Enmity between Blackfoot and Crow, with central Montana the wide boundary between the nations, continued throughout the nineteenth century, but by the 1850s began to be eclipsed by the inroads of Euro-Americans. A first treaty in 1855 exchanged United States gifts and promised annuity payments for Blackfoot forbearance of rapidly increasing traveling, trading, and establishment of missions and government agencies in Montana. A popular pass through the Rockies between the systems of the Missouri River, flowing southeast, and the Columbia River, flowing west to the Pacific, lay in southern Peigan territory. Traffic on this route, and homesteaders' interest in the ranching and wheat potential of the region, pressured the United States agents to make northern Montana a reservation in 1873, then to begin breaking up this Great Northern Reservation (similar to the Great Sioux Reservation in the Dakotas) into very much smaller tribal reservations in 1888. Since no bison had been seen, much less slaughtered, for four or five years by then, the Indians could not resist settling around the agencies handing out food rations. The Southern Peigan took the north-central Montana Blackfeet (U.S. spelling) Reservation; the Bloods, Blackfoot (Siksika bands); and Northern Peigan decided to accept the Dominion of Canada reserves granted them in Canada's 1877 Treaty No. 7. Whichever side of the 49th parallel, these truly High Plains running to the abruptly towering Front Range of the Rockies are good only for range land, and cattle raising has been the principal, though inadequate, economy for the Blackfoot during the past century. In 1980, there were twenty-two thousand Blackfeet counted in the U.S. census.

The Cheyenne, Arapaho, and Gros Ventres

The Cheyenne and the Arapaho are peoples who have historically been often allied. Both, with the

Gros Ventres and Blackfoot, speak Algonkian languages. Cheyenne peregrinations are better documented than those of the other three Plains Algonkian nations. In the seventeenth century and quite possibly in the late prehistoric period, Cheyenne communities were to be found on the prairies of southern Minnesota, where they combined farming with hunting. At the beginning of the eighteenth century, Cheyenne moved west from Minnesota. Endemic warfare between the Cheyennes' Minnesota neighbors, the Dakota Sioux, and Ojibwa (also called Chippewa or Saulteaux), both attempting to secure the rich bison, elk, and beaver resources of the Minnesota prairie, seems to have been the spur to the Cheyennes' move. They set up at least one village on the Sheyenne River in eastern North Dakota, still within the moister prairie with its abundance of game, but far enough from the French trading posts on the Great Lakes to be beyond the territory craved by the Dakota and Ojibwa.

On the Sheyenne, the eighteenth-century Cheyenne lived very much as did the Mandan and Hidatsa on the Missouri River to the west. An excavated Cheyenne village had sixty-two round earth lodges within a semicircular fortification ditch that ended at the bluff edge of the village, above the river. The height of the village gave its defenders a good panorama of the surrounding country. Maize, beans, and squashes were cultivated, probably on the flood plain. Bison bone was abundant in refuse pits, and some horse bones proved that the Cheyenne of the second half of the eighteenth century could ride to the hunt.

This first historic removal of the Cheyenne failed to bring them relief from the attacks of Assiniboin and eventually again of Ojibwa, who had for some years refrained from fighting the Cheyenne in order to trade European goods to them for agricultural produce, but who came to believe that the Cheyenne constituted a threat. Fur-trade posts in the Canadian parklands, north of North Dakota, bypassed the Dakota and Ojibwa. This, combined with severe declines in the game population of the upper Mississippi region, resulting perhaps from a combination of European animal diseases and overhunting stimulated by the fur trade, put the Dakota and Ojibwa in such a precarious position that they could not tolerate the Cheyenne in the desirable Sheyenne River area. By the last decade of the eighteenth century, Cheyenne had abandoned their earth lodges and become wholly nomadic tipi dwellers, transporting their furnishings and stores on horses as they hunted bison. Women continued to prepare and plant fields of maize and beans in river bottom land on the Plains, particularly along the eastern edges of the Black Hills of South Dakota. Combining long summer hunts with returns to the fields when the crops ripened reduced the scale of farming, necessitating trading trips to Arikara villages on the Missouri River near the North Dakota–South Dakota border to obtain maize.

Out on the plains, the Cheyenne met a cognate group, the Sutai, whose language was a dialect of their own but who had earlier adapted to the nomadic bison-hunting life. The Sutai allied with the Cheyenne, taught them the Sun Dance ceremony, let them share in the protective power of the sacred Medicine Hat (bison horns with fur attached, said to have been given to the young man Erect Horns by the Old Lady who is Mistress of both bison and maize). By the mid-nineteenth century, the Sutai were incorporated as a band of the Cheyenne, and hunted in and defended a territory in eastern Colorado and western South Dakota that included access to the Black Hills. This power lasted only a generation: when the bison herds failed, in the 1870s in the Southern and Central Plains and by 1884 in the Northern Plains, Cheyenne had to yield before United States army campaigns against them and accept reservations that split the nation, one sector in 1869 taking a western Oklahoma settlement (with Arapaho) and the other, in 1884, land adjacent to the Crow reservation in southern Montana. In 1980, there were a total of ten thousand Cheyenne.

According to tradition, the Arapaho and the Gros Ventres (who were also called Atsina, a

Blackfoot term, and in their own language 'Aa'ááániinéninah, "White Clay People,") were once a single people. In the late prehistoric period, the Gros Ventres probably occupied south-central Saskatchewan and adjacent northwestern North Dakota, and the Arapaho the country to the southeast, in eastern North Dakota and Minnesota, north of the Cheyenne. The Arapaho farmed as well as hunted bison; the Gros Ventres probably only hunted, for their country bordered the High Plains, where at this northern latitude maize agriculture was generally unsuccessful. Historically, the Gros Ventres tended to ally with the Blackfoot, their neighbors to the west, and the Arapaho with the Cheyenne. The Arapaho shifted southwest with the Cheyenne in the late eighteenth and early nineteenth centuries. The Gros Ventres also moved to the southwest, but a shorter distance: into northeastern Montana as their allies, the Blackfoot, were pushed out of western Saskatchewan by Cree and Assiniboin at the end of the eighteenth century. The association of the Arapaho with the Cheyenne, who several times fought the Blackfoot, tended to separate them from the Gros Ventres, but there are many recorded instances of Gros Ventres and Arapaho camping together, and these encampments sometimes included families or parties of Blackfoot. Extermination of the wild bison herds around 1880 forced all these nations, bereft of their principal subsistence base, to reservations. Some Arapaho had moved with their Southern Cheyenne friends to share a western Oklahoma reservation, other Arapaho took a reservation at Wind River in Wyoming with Eastern Shoshoni. The Gros Ventres in 1887 took an eastern Montana reservation, sharing with Assiniboin (and a legally unrecognized Métis community).

The Mandan and Hidatsa

The Mandan and Hidatsa who occupied the agricultural towns on the Missouri and its tributaries in North Dakota both speak Siouan languages. The Mandan appear to have been the pioneers in settling the trench of the Missouri in the Plains. Their ancestors were probably those who built rectangular earth lodges in southern South Dakota beginning in A.D. 1150. About A.D. 1450, they regrouped in central North Dakota, building fortified towns of round earth lodges. It is likely that at this time they began to make their towns market centers. Dentalium shell from the Pacific coast in Mandan village sites in North Dakota is a clue to the widespread trade in the late prehistoric Plains. Travel may have been on foot, since the rivers of the High Plains are full of sand bars that discouraged the use of canoes, although the Mandan and Hidatsa constructed round, hide-covered coracles (called bull boats) to ford the Missouri and carry supplies on it. Bison-hunting nomads not tied to maize fields had plenty of time and were not likely to be concerned if a trading journey occupied two years or more. The permanency of the Mandan towns along the principal river of the Northern Plains made them a beacon for nomads, and the surpluses of maize and other produce raised by the Mandan attracted those who hunted to the north and west, where agriculture was not feasible. Some might try to raid the Mandan stores—hence the town fortifications—but other nomads realized the long-term advantage of peaceful visiting and carried such light but precious items as the dentalium and olivella shells, obtained at the Rockies from Plateau peoples in contact with Columbia River groups, and exchanged these exotic and perhaps magical ornaments for hospitality and maize. The occurrence along the Knife River and in central North Dakota of brown chalcedony of the highest quality for making flaked-stone tools also attracted nomads to the Mandan neighborhood.

The Hidatsa were very similar to the Mandan. The Hidatsa comprised three groups: the Hidatsa proper, the Awaxawi, and the Awatixa. The Awatixa claim to have lived in agricultural villages at the junction of the Knife and Missouri rivers since time immemorial; archaeology suggests since

FIGURE 6.1 Hidatsa village in winter, 1833. Men in foreground are playing the hoop and pole game, attempting to spear the hoop; earth lodges are in the background. *(Smithsonian Institution National Anthropological Archives)*

about A.D. 1550. The Awaxawi had agricultural villages on the prairie of eastern North Dakota and western Minnesota, presumably north of the Cheyenne and adjacent to the Arapaho, and the Hidatsa proper are said to have been nomadic bison hunters north and west of the Awaxawi in central North Dakota. Some of these Hidatsa took the advice of Mandan who suggested that if they desired maize so much, they should raise sufficient to satisfy their needs; other families preferred to continue to hunt on the High Plains to the west and rely on trade to get some maize. These latter were the nucleus of the Crow. Archaeology on Hidatsa sites shows that the Hidatsa were sedentary communities retaining some of their own distinctive heritage, although they took over many Mandan traits.

The Sioux

The Sioux have been the prototype of Plains Indians, indeed of Indians in general. Historic Sioux eagle-feather headdresses are the symbol of Indianness recognized throughout the world, the Hunkpapa Sioux leader Sitting Bull may be the best known of all Indians, and the two confrontations of United States forces and Sioux at Wounded Knee, in 1890 and 1973, have been major rallying points for public support for Indian grievances. The Sioux have seven principal divisions, each with subdivisions: the four Eastern or Santee Dakota: Mdewakanton, Wahpekute, Sisseton, and Wahpeton; the Middle: Yankton and Yanktonai ("Little Yankton"); and the Western, the Teton, whose dialect uses "l" in place of "d" and thus the name Lakota. In the seventeenth century, the various Sioux bands occupied most of Minnesota, between the Cheyenne to the south and the Ojibwa (Chippewa) in Wisconsin. The Santee in northeastern Minnesota harvested wild rice from the marshy lakes of the region, making the seeds of this grass their principal grain and planting maize only as a supplement to it. They made maple sugar in the early spring, and relied upon deer as much as upon bison. These resources, especially the deer, were equally important to the Ojibwa, and brought the two nations into constant conflict, exacerbated in the eighteenth century by competition for fur bearers and for command of the French trade. The Yankton and Yanktonai lived in the parklands border of the Prairie and made more extensive bison hunts, although they also pursued forest game and, like the Santee, fished and made gardens as supplementary resources. The Teton (Lakota) were Prairie people for whom the bison was the major resource. As the fur trade of the western Great Lakes and Mississippi Valley became established around the beginning of the eighteenth century, the prairie-oriented Lakota Sioux—the Yankton, Yanktonai, and Teton—chose to shift westward into the eastern Dakotas where game resources were greater. Here on the broad zone between the Woodlands and the High Plains, the Yanktonai became middlemen in trade between the Teton Lakota and the Santee closely involved with the French traders. As early as 1707, a Yanktonai record tells that a metal knife was exchanged for a horse in their village. A century later, thousands of Sioux congregated at the Yanktonai town on the James River in northeastern South Dakota, the Lakota giving horses, bison robes and tipi covers, and antelope-skin clothing for Santee walnut-wood bows, smoking pipes of the holy red catlinite stone quarried in southwestern Minnesota, and guns and kettles from European posts. The Yanktonai themselves traded with the Mandan and the Arikara to their west on the Missouri River, securing large ceramic pots from them

and following their styles in dress, village plan, earth-lodge dwellings, and the use of the bullboat (the hide-covered round coracle or, among the historic Yanktonai, rowboat-shaped boat).

Historically, the Lakota were nomads ranging on both sides of the Missouri River in the Dakotas. Their seven subdivisions—Sicangu (Brulé), Oglala, Sihasapa (Blackfoot [not the same as the major Algonkian-speaking tribe of this name]), Minneconjou, Sans Arc, Oohennonpa (Two Kettle), and Hunkpapa—prospered until the Lakota outnumbered the combined Santee and Middle bands. This population and the wealth they built up in horses, which gave them the means to transport possessions and also stores of food, hides, and pemmican to trade, and enabled their men to select and train fine mounts for hunting and battle, resulted in the nineteenth-century Lakota constituting the principal threat to Euro-American domination of the Plains.

Other Siouan-speaking groups inhabited the Prairie in historic times. There were two sets, the Iowa, Missouri, and Oto, who speak dialects of the Chiwere language; and the Omaha, Osage, Ponca, Kansa, and Quapaw, who speak Dhegiha dialects. Winnebago, a language spoken by a nation in southern Wisconsin, is closely related to Chiwere. Tradition recounts that the Chiwere, including the Winnebago, lived in northern Wisconsin, and the Dhegiha in the western Ohio Valley. The Chiwere began migrating south and west, first dividing from the Winnebago, who remained in eastern Wisconsin, then dividing at the junction of the Rock and Mississippi rivers, where the Iowa remained, and finally dividing into Oto and Missouri, the former traveling up the Missouri River to the Nemaha River at the corner where Kansas, Nebraska, and Missouri meet, and the latter journeying down the Missouri into the state of that name. The Dhegiha say they went down the Ohio to its confluence with the Mississippi. There the Quapaw went south, earning their name, which means "downstream," and the others went north as the Omaha, "upstream." After many wanderings, the people dispersed along the Missouri, the Osage band in western Missouri, the Kansa across the Missouri River in the northeastern section of the state that bears their name, the Omaha bypassing the Oto and Iowa, now in western Iowa, to settle above them in northeastern Nebraska and adjacent South Dakota, where the Ponca band separated, moving west along the Niobrara River. Most of these movements apparently took place during the seventeenth century. In this period, the western bands—Ponca, Omaha, Oto, Iowa, and Kansa—learned to make earth lodges and took up other customs of the Arikara and neighboring Plains village nations, while the Osage retained the pole wigwam but covered it with bison hides obtained on twice-yearly hunts to the west. Their congeners farther up the Missouri drainage went out on similar hunts, the Ponca claiming that they were accustomed to reaching the Rockies, and that they built the enigmatic "medicine wheel" of stones in the Bighorn Range of Wyoming.

During the eighteenth century, the Dhegiha nations gained considerable power through their strategic position on the trading frontier: their excursions westward not only could bring in bison, they also were the means of contacting Plains nations beyond regular French and British trading posts. Both middleman trade of European goods from these posts for furs, and raids to capture Indians for sale as slaves to the post agents (who in turn would sell the slaves to the eastern colonies' plantations and even ship them to the Caribbean slave markets) expanded Dhegiha territory. This changed drastically in the nineteenth century after the eastern nations were removed to Indian Territory. Chiwere and Dhegiha, and the Plains Caddoans, were pressured to move out of the farmlands of the lower Missouri and its tributaries—valleys they had focused upon more intensively from the beginning of the Mississippian period, when maize, squash, and sunflower crops became an important part of their subsistence, complemented by deer and bison hunting and harvesting wild foods along the stream valleys.

The middle decades of the nineteenth century were a nightmare of shifts for the Prairie nations. Like the Eastern nations a generation and more earlier, these farmers faced a steady increase in the foreign traders and then settlers invading their lands. Government agents urged them to live like Euro-Americans, but when they took up imported crops, tools, and clothing, they learned the intent was that they give up their communal way of life. Many, like the Easterners before them, decided a move hundreds of miles westward away from the colonists was the best solution, even though it meant sacrificing lands dear to them from their history and valuable as farmland. Thus by midcentury, what is now Kansas was flooded with refugees pioneering its valleys: Chiwere-speaking Iowa, and the more foreign great number of Algonkian speakers—Delawares and Shawnees, Sauk, Kickapoo, Potawatomi, Chippewa, Ojibwa, Ottawa, Miami, Piankashaws, Peorias, Weas, Kaskaskias. All had to live from territory formerly used only by Osage and Kansa. Then the Euro-American colonization front reached Kansas. Land cessions were again demanded by the United States, from native and refugee nations alike. Kansas and Nebraska were opened to colonization in 1854. After the Civil War, the United States custom of providing homesteading land for veterans exacerbated pressure on Kansas Territory, and an army was prepared to defeat recalcitrant Indians as it had defeated Confederates. Adding to Indians' hardship, the tremendous demand for bison so reduced the herds in the Central Plains that they were nearly extinct in that region by the mid-1870s (a decade before their final disappearance in the Northern Plains). Unable to maintain food stores when their strenuous hunting journeys failed, the many nations in Kansas made final moves to reservations in Oklahoma in that decade. The 1980 census showed these populations (some numbers rounded off) for these nations: Chiwere-speaking Iowa, 950, and Oto, 1,500 (the Missouri are no longer a recognized nation); Dhegiha-speaking Osage, 7,000; Kansa (Kaw) 677; Quapaw, 950;

Omaha, 3,100; and Ponca, 2,100—the last three, plus the Winnebago (5,200) with Nebraska reservations; and of the Algonkian-speakers, Delaware, 5,400; Shawnee, 4,500; Sauk and Mesquakie, 3,400; Kickapoo, 2,400; Potawatomi, 9,800; Ottawa, 6,500; Miami, 2,400; and Peoria, 645.

Another Siouan-speaking group is the Assiniboin, or Stoney (their name is an Ojibwa term meaning "those who cook with stones"). The Assiniboin language is related to Dakota, and tradition makes the Assiniboin a branch of the Yankton. In the mid-seventeenth century, the Assiniboin lived north of the Middle Sioux, on the Minnesota border and in adjacent southern Manitoba, a parkland and prairie country, but hunted also to the north into the boreal forest. Already at this time they were allied with the Algonkian-speaking Cree, the westernmost of the subarctic forest Algonkians, living in Ontario and Manitoba. Assiniboin and Cree were among the suppliers of furs to the French trade on the St. Lawrence, via the Algonkian network. When the British intruded into the fur trade with their Hudson's Bay Company in 1670, conflicts between Indian groups developed, fed by rivalry between the agents of the two European nations. The Assiniboin broke off relations with their relatives the Sioux to cement their ties with the Crees. For a century, until France ceded Canada to Britain at the conclusion of the Seven Years' War in 1763, the Assiniboin and Cree together handled a good part of the interior Canadian fur trade, bringing pelts down in canoes to the posts on Hudson's Bay and returning with trade goods, many of which they would exchange with the Blackfoot and other nations for next year's cargo of pelts.

The entrance of Hudson's Bay Company and independent Euro-Canadian traders into the interior after 1763 took this middleman role from the Assiniboin and Cree. Coincidentally, the horse was becoming available on the Northern Plains. A new business developed: supplying pemmican (dried bison meat, pounded with fat and often dried berries) to the interior trading posts and to the brigades

of canoes that linked them to the ports. The Assiniboin began to concentrate on bison hunting on the grasslands of southern Saskatchewan, often joined by Cree families who obtained horses from the Assiniboin. Cree, in turn, maintained closer ties with the trading posts, and were able to provide guns to defend the lands from which the two allies had pushed the Gros Ventres and, to a lesser degree, the Blackfoot, lands that they were attempting to prevent the Sioux from taking. These lands in southern Canada were particularly desirable because the rich grasslands where the bison summered were edged by the parklands where both the bison and the Indians could shelter in winter, and where the Indians could find firewood. The Assiniboin and Cree continued their profitable alliance on the Saskatchewan Plains until the end of bison hunting in the last third of the nineteenth century. When the disappearance of their subsistence staple and the incursions of the railroads and colonization forced them to give up full autonomy, Assiniboin settled on both sides of the 49th parallel, with reserves in Alberta and the Fort Peck (shared with Lakota) and Fort Belknap (shared with Gros Ventres) reservations in northeastern Montana, accepted 1888 and 1887. The 1980 U. S. census identified four thousand Assiniboin within the United States.

The Caddoans

Although the Sioux are the popular stereotype of Plains Indians, the Caddoan speakers of the central Plains have far more right to be considered the original Plains Indians. These three peoples—the Wichita of central Kansas, the Pawnee of central Nebraska, and the Arikara, a Pawnee offshoot on the Missouri in southern South Dakota—may well be the descendants of the farmers who settled the river valleys of the central Plains beginning about A.D. 1150. The people lived in square earth lodges scattered in open villages along terraces and cultivated fields of maize, beans, squashes, and

FIGURE 6.2 Pawnee village of earth lodges, Nebraska, 1871. Bundles of tipi poles are stored over the house entrance, to be used when the family goes off hunting. *(Smithsonian Institution National Anthropological Archives)*

sunflowers on the flood plains, they hunted bison and antelope as well as smaller game, and took fish.

A change occurred about A.D. 1450, possibly due to drought or the colder climate that marked the fifteenth through nineteenth centuries: many villages seem to have been abandoned, and population regrouped into larger, compact, often fortified towns of circular earth lodges in Nebraska, but of round, thatch-covered lodges in Kansas. One of these "Quivira" towns in Kansas, probably a Wichita community, was visited by the Spanish exploring expedition under Coronado in 1541; the Spaniards' Southwestern guides knew the Wichita country from trade between it and the Río Grande pueblos, attested by Puebloan pottery in Kansas

sites. As trade over the Plains developed in the seventeenth century, the Arikara on the Missouri mainstream gained in importance while their more numerous Pawnee relatives, on shorter rivers, exerted less influence. The Arikara also began to recognize common interests with the Mandan upstream, in spite of the different languages. The Pawnee and Wichita, situated on the Spanish frontier, suffered frequent depredations from raiding Apache and Comanche, so much so that in the Southwest, "Pawnee" became, for a time, synonymous with "slave." Slave-raiding was a threat from the east, too, in the eighteenth century, for Quapaw, Osage, and other lower Missouri nations were urged by both British and French traders to capture

FIGURE 6.3 Caddo village, about 1870. Homes are thatched, open kitchen and work sheds (left and unfinished, foreground) have bark roofs. *(Smithsonian Institution National Anthropological Archives)*

their western neighbors for sale to the colonies. By the mid-eighteenth century, conditions had improved, the Pawnee and Wichita acting as middlemen in trade between the Comanches and the French who were located with other Caddoan nations in the lower Mississippi region. The intrusions of the Dhegiha Siouans into the territory on the west side of the Missouri threatened the Wichita and Pawnee in the late eighteenth century, causing the Wichita to move south to the Red River along the present Oklahoma-Texas boundary, and the Pawnee north to the Platte from villages on the Republican River in southern Nebraska. Within a few years, the Pawnee reoccupied some of their former lands and felt secure enough to send out raiding parties of their own into Mexico, as well as to hunt bison out on the Plains. Skidi Pawnee brought European trade goods south into Wichita

towns whose inhabitants raised surpluses of maize, tobacco, and other crops to regularly supply western Plains groups such as the Comanche with quantities of horses to trade. Thus throughout the eighteenth century, lucrative three-way trade flourished, the freely-interchanged elements being European goods, horses (Indian-bred and also stolen), and Indian agricultural products.

The removal policy of the United States toward the Indians of the Southeast ended Pawnee hegemony. Delaware, Shawnee, Sauk, and Mesquakie (Fox) needed land. In 1833, the United States made a treaty with the Pawnee under which they were themselves removed, to the north side of the Platte, although they were to be allowed to hunt south of that river. They settled on the Loup River, territory they had used since the prehistoric era. For the remainder of the century, the Pawnee were pressured by United States Indian agents and missionaries to give up their long bison-hunting treks and concentrate on sedentary farming. For a brief decade immediately after the U.S. Civil War, Pawnee men joined the United States army as Scouts, fighting against the Sioux who for a century had been attempting to dispossess them of the trans-Missouri hunting grounds. In 1874, Nebraska had become so inviting to Euro-American settlers that the United States government pressured the Pawnee to vacate their ancestral home and remove to Indian Territory in Oklahoma. The Wichita suffered similar buffeting and also ended on a reservation in Oklahoma; like the Pawnee, they were severely reduced in numbers by disease and the ill effects of refugee impoverishment. The Arikara were affected less directly by United States intervention in their lives, but were harshly affected by epidemics, especially of smallpox, and they ended a series of moves by joining, in the 1850s, the postepidemic survivors of the Mandan and Hidatsa in a single village, called Like-a-Fishhook, beside Fort Berthold on the Missouri in North Dakota. In 1980, the census listed twenty-five hundred Pawnee, seven hundred Wichita, and fifteen hundred Arikara.

The Numic Peoples

Uto-Aztecan speakers contested the western sector of the High Plains with Apacheans and the westernmost Algonkians, the Blackfoot and Gros Ventres. There seems good archaeological data to support the inference of a migration of speakers of Numic (also called Shoshonean), the "Uto" (from Ute, one of the groups) of Uto-Aztecan. Ancestors of the Numic speakers probably lived in the western Great Basin—that is, in southeastern California and southern Nevada. Around A.D. 1000, Numic speakers apparently began to fan out north and northeast through Nevada and Utah, reaching southern Idaho by A.D. 1250. The reason for this movement is not obvious: there was a spread of a somewhat attenuated Anasazi Puebloan

culture—not necessarily any migration of peoples—into the Fremont area of southern Utah at this time, but it does not appear to have threatened the Numic people somewhat to the west. Whatever the stimulus—and simple population increase may be the explanation for the fanning out in the low-density resource ecology of the Great Basin—the Shoshoni, northeasternmost of the Numic peoples, reached the Front Range of the Rockies in Wyoming about A.D. 1450. They were not a mountain people, but adapted to hunting bison, antelope, and lesser game and collecting pine nuts along the low slopes of hills bordering the sagebrush deserts of the Great Basin. This adaptation they continued while advancing along the western edge of the High Plains, only substituting limber pine nuts for the pinyon they enjoyed in the Basin.

Sometime in the seventeenth century, it is estimated, the Shoshoni in Wyoming broke into two divisions, the Shoshoni in Wyoming and Montana, and the Comanche who moved southward into eastern Colorado. Here, the Comanche competed with the Apache for hunting territory and in raids upon the Spanish and Pueblo settlements in New Mexico. Throughout the eighteenth century, Comanches procured Spanish horses, by fair means and foul, and redistributed the animals in trade to their cousins the Shoshoni and to unrelated peoples such as the Pawnee and Wichita; expanding and protecting their horse trade was a focus of Comanche strategy for one and one-half centuries. In the early eighteenth century, the Spanish refrained from pursuing the Comanche as avidly as their depredations might have warranted, because the Comanche were thought to be a buffer discouraging French advance across the Southern Plains. As the century progressed, French guns coming through the Caddo-speaking towns made the Comanche increasingly dangerous. Belatedly, the Spanish attempted to control the Comanche frontier, but they never succeeded. The Comanche sometimes traded with villages near their own territory, but relied upon raids deep into the Spanish domain to replenish their herds of horses and stores of agricultural produce and European goods. Trading was secondary to raiding for the Comanche, since raiding not only kept them adequately supplied with what they needed from others, but also protected their hunting range by frightening off those others.

The Comanches' power continued well into the nineteenth century as they warred upon Texas during its independence and fought the nations removed from the Midwest into Indian Territory. With the Kiowa and Kiowa-Apache, Cheyenne, Arapaho, and Osage, northern Comanche mounted an unprecedented massive attack in 1854 on the emigrant Indians but were repulsed by a coalition of Sauk, Mesquakie, and Potawatomi out on their regular bison hunt. As United States colonization gradually surrounded them, intruding into territory used not only for hunting but also for pasturing the horses they so profitably traded; and as diseases and the reduction of bison herds weakened them, the Comanche were forced to sign treaties, and, in 1874, they themselves were removed to a reservation in Oklahoma. Nine thousand Comanche were listed in the 1980 census.

The Plains Shoshoni never reached the degree of power wielded by the Comanche. About 1730, mounted Shoshoni in southern Alberta, then the border of their territory, overwhelmed a force of still horseless Blackfoot. But within a few years, the Blackfoot and Gros Ventres had obtained guns from the Cree and Assiniboin and drove the Shoshoni, who lacked the weapon, southwestward again. From the mid-eighteenth century, the Shoshoni hunted along the western edge of the Plains in Montana and Wyoming, but could barely hold this land. Blackfoot and Cheyenne attacked their camps and took captives to sell or keep as concubines; Lewis and Clark's famous guide Sakakawea was such a Shoshoni, sold to the Hidatsa and there taken by a French-Canadian voyageur. Sakakawea, more fortunate than most captives, was left with her own people on Lewis and Clark's return journey. She probably died in

South Dakota in 1812, although some claim she lived with the Wind River band of Shoshoni in Wyoming until death from old age in 1884. Establishment of a fur-trade rendezvous in the Bridger Basin in Wyoming in 1825 became an advantage to the Plains Shoshoni, although Bridger's post was oriented toward the intermontane peoples and independent trappers and caused the Wyoming Shoshoni to have fewer contacts with the Comanche and Crow than with the Utes, the Flathead, and the Bannock Shoshoni of Idaho. The mid-nineteenth-century prosperity of the Wyoming Shoshoni continued through their placement on a reservation on the Wind River, in their habitual territory, in 1863, but ended in the decade of the 1880s, when bison disappeared, the income from furs was reduced to one quarter of what it had been, and farming also failed. There were nearly ten thousand Shoshoni recorded in the 1980 census, the majority of them in the eastern groups.

The Kiowa

Kiowa is related to the Tanoan pueblos of the Río Grande in New Mexico, particularly to Jemez in the north-central part of the state. In the nineteenth century, the Kiowa were nomadic bison hunters in the southwestern Plains, and were allied with the Comanche, whom they joined on raids into Mexico. Surprisingly, a century earlier the Kiowa were in south-central Montana, and both their tradition and that of the Shoshoni who would have been their neighbors there agree that the headwaters of the Missouri in Montana was their aboriginal homeland. From their earliest records in the mid-eighteenth century, too, the Kiowa counted as one of their bands a group of Apache known as the Kiowa-Apache, who retained their own Athabascan language through at least two centuries' residence with the Kiowa.

Since maize farming was impossible in the northwestern Plains, the Kiowa and Kiowa-Apache were wholly nomadic bison hunters. The Kiowa, like the Shoshoni, were friendly with the

Crow in spite of sharing the same general range. Allied with the Crow, the Kiowa felt the hostility of the Blackfoot, traditional enemies of the Crow, and then of the Cheyenne and Arapaho moving west. Cheyenne and Arapaho pressure forced the Kiowa and Kiowa-Apache south along the mountains. At the Black Hills, they were pushed back by the Sioux. On the upper Arkansas, they met the Comanche and managed to work out an alliance after a period of fighting. Eventually, in 1840, they concluded peace with the Cheyenne and Arapaho. These five peoples—Comanche, Kiowa, Kiowa-Apache, Cheyenne, and Arapaho—hoped to preserve the Southern Plains for their use against settlement by Euro-Americans or the Eastern nations removed to the west. But the alliance was, in the long run, futile, and in 1868, the Kiowa and Kiowa-Apache joined the Comanche on an Oklahoma reservation. Nearly seventy-four hundred Kiowa were listed in the 1980 census.

The Sarsi, Plains Cree, and Saulteaux (Bungi)

On the northern border of the Plains in the historic period were three peoples whose dependence upon the bison qualifies them as members of the Plains culture area. The Sarsi (Sarcee) are an Athabascan (Dené) group who hunted along the upper Saskatchewan River in Alberta, just northwest of the Blackfoot. They were allies of the Blackfoot and often joined their bands, but recognized their kinship with the Dené of the forest to the north and with the Apacheans, visiting and occasionally intermarrying with Kiowa-Apache and Apache in the Southwest. The Plains Cree and Plains Ojibwa, the latter commonly known as Saulteaux and, in their own language, Bungi, speak Algonkian languages and, until the nineteenth century, were simply the western bands of the Cree and Ojibwa, the Cree using the forests and parkland of the Canadian Prairie Provinces and the Ojibwa living around Lake Superior and in the forests to the north. As described earlier, the fur trade intensified

the exchange network in the central Canadian forests between the Algonkians north of the maize-growing zone and the Iroquoians (especially the Huron) within the northern boundary of this zone. Through the eighteenth century, the Cree allied with Assiniboin along the western frontier handled a major portion of the European trade, but after British victory in 1763, they lessened their middleman role and turned more to producing pemmican for the trading posts. The nineteenth-century Assiniboin were more fully Plains dwellers; the westernmost Cree remained more in the parkland border, although they rode out on long hunts into the grasslands. The Bungi moved just behind the westernmost Cree, using the parkland and the Manitoba prairie for bison hunts in the nineteenth century. Because the Saulteaux were more skilled trappers than most of the westernmost Cree, the Saulteaux could make a living on the forest edge abandoned by the Cree as being, for their purposes, hunted out. Nevertheless, they too were attracted to the bison herds and allied around 1800 with some Ottawa displaced from their former role in the fur trade, then later with occasional Cree or with French-Canadian voyageurs married into the country, to mount parties to hunt on the prairie. Both the Plains Cree and the Saulteaux adopted the basic Plains culture, from bison-hide tipis to the Sun Dance, but both continue to prefer living within the parkland and retain some knowledge of the resource-exploitation skills, the myths, and the magic of their Woodland forebears. (Both Plains Cree and Saulteaux say that their Woodland relatives practice malevolent as well as beneficial magic, but that they themselves, the Prairie dwellers, renounced malevolent sorcery.) The extinction of the bison herds in the early 1880s forced the Plains Cree and Saulteaux to accept reservation settlement, mostly on small reserves in Saskatchewan, Manitoba, and Alberta, although a relatively large Saulteaux community lives on the Turtle Mountain reservation in northeastern North Dakota (where they are called Chippewa), and there is a Plains Cree band with some Saulteaux ("Chippewa-Cree") on Rocky Boy's Reservation in north-central Montana. Descendants of Cree and Saulteaux women married to French trappers and traders form the ethnic group called Métis in Canada, people who combined bison hunting and pemmican trading with some farming in river valleys of Manitoba and Saskatchewan until the bison herds were exterminated. The Government of Canada was unwilling to treat them as "natives" and give them reserves, or even accept their French-custom form of laying out homesteads, leading to two rebellions of Métis, in 1870 and 1884. Métis have since then struggled against racial prejudice and lack of resources, as disadvantaged on these accounts as Indians but without even the treaty provisions held by Indians. Métis communities can be found on some Indian reserves, for example, Rocky Boy's and Fort Belknap Reservations in Montana.

SECTION 4: PLAINS CULTURE

The preceding section demonstrates the complexity of Prairie-Plains history. A striking uniformity nevertheless marks the entire region, divisible only into Plains village (agricultural) nations and nomads. Subsisting upon bison herds seems to constitute a relatively narrow adaptation, one that was not compatible with many institutions of Eastern peoples. The adoption of the horse loosened the restrictions imposed by this adaptation and promoted a bravura that has impressed everyone from explorers to moviegoers, yet the cultures of Plains peoples remained powerfully shaped by environmental limitations.

Plains Peoples and the Bison

The foundation of Plains culture was the Plains bison, a gregarious herbivore closely related to cattle. For most of the year, bison cows formed a small herd led by a mature cow. Calves born in the spring and yearlings accompanied their mothers,

while the bulls grazed, a few together, apart from the cow herd. Late summer brought the bulls and cows together in the rut, then after some weeks the sexes separated again as winter blew in. This basic pattern was modified by grazing conditions, particularly when, during the Late Prehistoric and historic era, grasslands flourished, in part because of annual extensive firings of the prairie by Indians. The abundance of tender grass in early summer drew many herds together and resulted in uncountable thousands of bison feeding side by side on the open plains. Inevitably, these incredible masses, these herds of herds, broke up into their constituent small cow herds and peripheral bulls in late autumn and browsed their way back to the aspen parklands, river valleys, or deep coulees where the wind-stunted trees broke the forces of blizzards so that snow remained soft enough to paw through to the grass beneath. Indian life from the prairies west of the Mississippi Valley to the Rockies was predicated upon the pattern of bison movement: small bands of a few families wintered in the shelter of the wooded parklands and valleys, joined other bands in summer for large encampments, and broke up into small bands again during the autumn. Tents, clothing, tools, and food were packed on the backs of the people and on large dogs carefully bred for size and strength and trained also to drag travois (pairs of poles with a crossband on which goods are loaded).

Bands of twenty-five to one hundred people were the basic unit of Plains society because this number could manage a bison drive, the most efficient method of securing a livelihood on the Plains. The drive began with the construction of a corral of poles and brush beneath a steep bluff about 70 feet (21 meters) high, or at the end of a ravine. The corral fence did not need to be very strong, as long as the brush woven into it was thick enough that no light penetrated the fence; bison are too stupid to test a wall that looks solid. While most of the men labored to build the corral, the camp's spiritual leaders prayed to the Almighty to grant success to the drive. The Blackfoot kept "buffalo stones," usually fossil ammonites—a spiral shell that somewhat resembles a curled-up sleeping bison—in medicine bundles as tokens of the Almighty's gift to mankind of this game. According to the Blackfoot myth, a woman scrounging in a thicket for food for her family during a time of famine was called to by one of these "buffalo stones." It had taken pity on her people and sang to her the chant that invokes a herd. She carried the little token to the camp, where the elders learned the prayer. Since then, whenever the prayers for a drive were sung, the tokens were taken out of their bags and rubbed with red ocher, symbolizing the life given to us by the Almighty. (Blackfoot families still keep *iniskim*, these buffalo stones, but now they are tokens for general prosperity.) During the ritual, young men scouted for a herd. When they sighted animals, the youths ran back to camp with the information, and the people deployed for the drive; bowmen and people with clubs crouched around the corral, other men and women hid behind little piles of stones or brush on the upland above the corral or along the narrowing valley if it was in a ravine, and one honored young man was sent to call in the herd. At the sight of the bison, the young man sang a magical song that sounds like the bleating of a bison calf. The cows, who of course were the center of the herd, moved toward the singer. He stepped slowly in the direction of the corral, staying downwind of the herd and singing, and gradually increased his speed until the herd was abreast of the hidden gauntlet. Suddenly, the people at the open end of the drive lane leaped up, yelling and waving robes. The bison panicked and stampeded down the lane, past the lines of jumping, shouting people, until the lead cow teetered on the brink of the unseen dropoff. Behind her pushed the herd; she tumbled down, followed by the dozens of other animals, their hoofs hooking frantically but futilely into the fragile lip of the bluff. The herd struggled to its feet in the corral and milled past the armed men who had clambered onto the fence. Soon, dozens of prime animals lay dead, and men and women entered to butcher. The next couple of days were a time of joyous hard work as the camp hacked and stripped and slivered the harvest, snacking on rich organs and sweet, white backfat from the hump. Frequently, more animals were slaughtered than could be processed, since there was no way to allow part of a herd to escape the corral. Thin sheets of lean meat were hung on pole racks to dry into jerky for pemmican, marrow bones were chopped up and boiled until the "bone butter" could be skimmed off, the prized tongues were presented to the ritual leaders whose prayers had brought in the herd, and even the dogs, released from the muzzles put on them during the drive, feasted.

Horses lightened the work of harvesting bison by permitting the rapid surround of a herd, a kind of instant corral obviating the labor of building a fence or the risk of losing a herd if it stampeded too soon or in the wrong direction. Camps that owned a sufficient number of fast, responsive, well-trained mounts kept specially for bison hunting enjoyed freedom from the onerous work of corral building. Hence, every band aspired to accumulate sufficient horses to use the best exclusively for the hunt and others for the chores of moving camp and traveling. Breeding so large a herd of horses would be slow, so people attempted to reach the band's goal by stealing from enemies—Spanish ranchers or other Indian groups. Depleting competitors' herds of horses not only enhanced a band's hunting but might curtail the enemy's use of adjacent territory and impoverish their power to dispute a range. Horses thus became the goad for the endemic warfare of the historic Plains. An ambitious young man could gain prestige, comfort, and the lady of his heart by raiding a camp and driving its horses home. Among the Blackfoot, young women often accompanied their husbands, dashing in beside them to seize horses, fighting off pursuers with them, and sharing both booty and renown. A Piegan Blackfoot woman named Running Eagle led many successful raids herself, and so did a Gros Ventre, Woman Chief, captured as a child and brought up by the Crow.

Competition over hunting ranges and trade and raiding for booty were not results of coveting horses, for both existed before horses were available, to judge by the fortifications around Pueblo and Plains villages prior to the mid-seventeenth century. The displacement of so many Eastern Woodland and Prairie peoples onto the Plains did intensify competition, and the economic importance of horses for packing supplies of meat, dried-prairie-turnip flour or maize, and trading materials,for rapid bison hunting, and for raiding for more horses, did act as a constant stimulus to hostilities. By the beginning of the the nineteenth century, horses had become the instrument and also the symbol of prosperity and power on the Plains. Bison remained the foundation of Plains culture patterns, but horses had become the focus of strategies to achieve the good life. Securing good pasture for horse herds was as necessary as hunting; the Plains nomadic nations were pastoralists, working to maintain their domesticated herds, as much as they were hunters.

The band of a size to operate a bison pound continued to be the basic unit in Plains societies, and, even when wealthy in horses, a camp continued to drive bison into pounds as an alternative to the mounted surround, especially in winter. The camp acknowledged the leadership of a man experienced in hunting and respected for courage and good judgment. The final say in decision making might be that of a matron whose strength of character and wisdom had become the rock upon which the families depended. With men frequently away on raids, trading expeditions, or hunting, women were the mainstay of daily life in camp and the arbiters of all that concerned the family. They needed to be brave, strong, and independent to care for and protect the children. They processed nearly all the raw materials brought into the camp, transforming carcasses into comfortably furnished tipis stocked with handsome clothing and nutritious provisions. Men were generally considered incapable of mastering crafts other than weapon making, and were inept even in slicing meat for

pemmican. The Old Lady, as she was and is titled, who brought up a family in fine tipis, whose skills all admired, whose age proved her to be blessed by the Almighty—hers was and is the quiet but firm voice none will gainsay.

Families in a camp were held together by their willingness to follow its leader. Many of the families were related, but some were attracted by the leader's reputation or by friendship with another family that perhaps was related to the leader or one of his (or her) close companions. Dissatisfaction with a leader or a quarrel between families caused persons to abandon one camp and join another. Frequently, one or a few families in a camp were from a different ethnic group than the majority. Groups normally hostile to each other, such as Blackfoot and Plains Cree, would accommodate a tent of erstwhile enemies who might have been hunting or traveling alone, going to the same trading post or village, or linked by marriage or friendship. In one famous instance, the Plains Cree leader Poundmaker (Pitokanowapiwin) was adopted by the Blackfoot chief Crowfoot (Isapomuxika, "Crow Indian's Big Foot," referring to a raid incident), who saw in the young Cree man a resemblance to Crowfoot's own son recently killed in a raid against Cree. A Plains camp was an open and fluid group accepting individuals with relatively little prejudice against their ethnic origins. Fraternal comradeship and cooperation were stressed, to the extent that the kin terms for "brother" and "sister" were used to address and refer to cousins as well as actual siblings, and were extended to bosom friends and young persons, such as Poundmaker, informally adopted. A camp was like an extended family, and the leader was expected to show a parental concern for everyone in the camp, including the aged, whose needs were provided by the active younger men and women.

Plains Social Structure

Individualism and cooperation were the attributes prized by Plains Indians. Antithetical though these

FIGURE 6.4 Plains Cree family (late nineteenth century). Their horse is pulling a travois on which goods are packed; tipis are in background. *(Milwaukee Public Museum)*

two may appear, in Plains societies cooperation could not be coerced and so became an individual option. But normally it was freely given, because it contributed to the giver's security as much as to others' benefits. Ordinarily, no one compelled another, not even parents their children. However, when the band was moving through territory where hostiles roamed, or was involved in bison hunts, the high value placed on personal autonomy was abrogated in favor of discipline that would protect the group and contribute to the effectiveness of the hunt. At these times, a formal organization of active men policed the camp and had authority to prevent individuals from breaking rank and to humiliate any who tried to do so. These organizations functioned somewhat as men's clubs, often putting up a meeting tipi in the big summer multiband camps, holding feasts, dances, games, and rituals for the protection of members,

and aiding members in times of crisis. Wives frequently participated in the club activities, and might even be required to join with their husbands, but they usually did not use the club's tipi as a place for lounging and visiting. Five groups—the Mandan, Hidatsa, Arapaho, Gros Ventres, and Blackfoot—had a series of these organizations; the first for boys in their early teens, then one for youths entering adulthood, then one or more for adult couples, and finally a club for elderly men retired from hunting and war. An organization dominated by women leaders whose rituals symbolized the coming of bison was part of the set. The Blackfoot called their organizations the All-Comrades' Societies. Although nearly all adults belonged to these organizations, membership came through a group of comrades buying the emblems and rights to the rituals of a group from its members, who then bought into the next higher organization themselves. Poor, ineffectual men who could not get together the horses and goods to purchase a membership could remain throughout their lives in a younger men's organization while their former comrades advanced through the normal career. Plains groups other than these five had clubs whose members were of different ages, and which were usually lifelong associations. The Plains Cree, thinking of themselves as small, independent camps little different from those of their cousins in the forest, had only one "police" society to which all active, respected men belonged, while groups like the Crow, who had lived in larger, sedentary towns, had two or more societies that challenged each other to demonstrate superiority in the hunt, in warfare, in wealth, and in the talents and beauty of their wives. Even when societies were rivals, as among the Crow, they were integrative mechanisms that promoted a sense of fraternal solidarity among members drawn from the many quasi-independent camps of an ethnic group.

The sedentary village nations had a greater number of formal organizations than did the nomads. The towns were structured, like Pueblo towns, on the basis of clans (affiliated lineages supposedly descended from a common ancestor), and lineages were the primary unit of cooperation. Among the Hidatsa, rights to farmland and a residence were inherited through the mother's lineage, while the father and his lineage were obliged to oversee the spiritual training of young people and consider them for priestly office. A similar emphasis on the matrilineage as the unit concerned with an individual's residence and livelihood was found in the other town-dwelling peoples, except for the Chiwere and Dhegiha Sioux, who considered the patrilineage the more fundamental unit. Clans carried out some rituals, but other ceremonies were community-wide and organized on that level. Still other rituals and shows of spiritual power were presented by priest-therapists' societies independent of clan associations. The villages were the theaters for festival cycles expressing through symbols and rituals the history of the people, their relationship to other beings, and their hopes for the blessings of the Almighty. Priests were highly trained, capable of conducting long, complex, beautiful ceremonies, and able also to manifest spiritual power through the sleight-of-hand of master magicians, most impressive persuasion to the pragmatic who might otherwise doubt spiritual reality. The governance of villages and the confederation of allied towns were managed by councils of representatives from the clans, chaired by chiefs from lineages that traditionally produced leaders.

Nomads who had come from sedentary communities, peoples such as the Cheyenne, retained vestiges of their former structures. The Cheyenne recognized themselves as a distinct nation under a supernaturally sanctioned ruling council of forty-four chiefs chosen for ten-year terms from among the older, most respected men. The Council deliberated all matters concerning the Cheyenne people as a whole, and expected that their decisions, reached in discussions to which the public might listen, would be obeyed by all Cheyenne. If the Council concluded that peaceful relations could not be maintained with a foreign power, military societies (popularly called Dog Soldiers) mobilized and waged war. Nomadic nations with no recent history of sedentary origins, such as the Blackfoot and Comanche, lacked formal governing councils, although it was customary for leaders to gather to discuss mutual concerns when several bands camped together in the summer.

The Sun Dance

Throughout the Plains, the Sun Dance was a major ceremonial drawing thousands of persons into summer encampments. If so many were to be fed, the camp had to be held in the season when bison herds began congregating, but before the rut. Village nations were the exception to the universality of the Sun Dance, although they had annual rituals that resembled the Sun Dance in some respects. These nations, with stores of dried maize, beans, squashes, and pemmican, did not need to gear gatherings to bison movements; instead, they spaced their ceremonies over the year. Nomad peoples were constrained to adapt social affairs to ecological cycles: most of the businesses that in towns occurred over the year had to be compressed by the nomads into the few summer weeks when grass was most lush on the open plains. Trading, gambling, visiting friends from other bands, games and sports competitions, and seeking a compatible spouse or comrade were individual incentives to rendezvous at large camps. Leaders were drawn to these camps to adjudicate disputes and discuss policies and strategies for allied bands. Above all, participation in rituals was a magnet. Multiband rendezvous offered the rituals of the sodalities, a range of therapists to help the ill or those suffering misfortune, and the general benefit believed to be derived from the Sun Dance. Great summer rendezvous could be, and very occasionally were, held without Sun Dances, but a Sun Dance could not be held without a large gathering, for the priests who led it and the persons who vowed to take active parts in it were scattered through the bands that normally rendezvoused. The desire of so many to gain spiritual renewal through the potency of the Sun Dance, a ceremony beyond the capability of any one band to mount, made the Sun Dance a major integrating mechanism for Plains societies.

The Sun Dance is usually a four-day ceremony—four being the "magic" or ritually potent number for many American Indians—sponsored by a person impelled to do so as a spiritual sacrifice to the Almighty in acknowledgment of aid at a time of crisis. Ordinarily, a person would invoke help from his or her spirit protector; in a very serious crisis, especially the dangerous illness of a loved one, aid might be sought from the Thunder, voice of the Almighty; in extreme desperation, one would pray directly to the Almighty Power, which is most blindingly manifested in the Sun. If the extreme crisis was satisfactorily passed, the beseecher felt obliged to show gratitude for this bless-

ing by sacrificing effort, wealth, and comfort in sponsoring a Sun Dance. When he or she had amassed enough goods and promises of support from kin and friends to handle the considerable expenses of a multiband ceremony, the vower would notify the band leaders and priests qualified to conduct a Sun Dance. The priests begin preparations many weeks in advance. As the rendezvous draws near, persons who had vowed to make lesser sacrifices to the Almighty if aid appeared during lesser crises, or persons who hoped to gain the favor of the Almighty in their careers or for their families, would mention that they too would participate within the holy lodge. Once most of the bands have arrived at the encampment, preparations for the dance enter their final stage. The head priest and four assistants sit in a special tipi, rehearsing the ritual and making the needed symbolic items. Older people gather leafy boughs to screen the lodge, cut poles for its frame, and select a tree for its center pole. The ceremony begins at dawn when a party goes out to the selected tree, warily encircles it as if scouting out an enemy force, then with a shout rushes to it and chops it down. The trimmed trunk is dragged to the camp and brought in through the morning mist with whoops of victory and the shooting of muskets. Later in the day, when the circular open frame of the holy lodge is up, the community assembles for the raising of the center pole. Dozens of men stand along ropes tied to the pole, the head priest chants prayers, and then suddenly, as the priest's voice climaxes in intensity, the pole seems to leap into the air and then settle into its footing. The audience disperses while assistants complete the holy lodge by leaning the boughs against the stringers of the lodge, constructing a low, circular barrier of leafy brush inside it to separate the dancers from the drums in the middle, and hanging on the center pole items donated by families in the communities as sacrifices to the Almighty. (In the nineteenth century, guns were frequently sacrificed. Today, most families purchase several yards of brightly colored satin to be hung from the rafters of the

FIGURE 6.5   Sun Dance camp, Plains Cree (1975). Over one thousand people attended this ceremony, held over a long weekend. Sun Dance lodge, with hanging prayer banners, is in center. *(T. Kehoe)*

FIGURE 6.6   Frame of sweat lodge. Plains Cree. *(T. Kehoe)*

lodge, waving as prayer-bearing banners.) The top of the center pole is forked, and in the fork is a large bundle of brush representing, or serving as, the nest of the Thunderbird, messenger of the Almighty.

Dancing begins when all is constructed. Those who had vowed to dance would have fasted and abstained from sexual relations. The priests purify themselves in the sweat lodge, a low wigwam over a pit of heated stones on which water is thrown to envelop the people inside in a sauna that cleanses their every pore. Dancers range themselves around the wall of the Sun Dance lodge, behind the low barrier, men on one side, women on the other. Priests, drummers and singers, and devout elders sit in the inner portion of the lodge, where incense from sweetgrass and sage burned before a bison-skull altar symbolizes the Almighty's gift of sustenance to humanity. To the rhythm of the chanted prayers, the dancers stand in place, monotonously rising on the ball of the foot and then coming down as they blow tunelessly on short whistles made of eagle bone. All the while, the dancers fix their eyes on the top of the center pole, where their gaze is led to the infinite sky of the Almighty. (The name Sun Dance comes from the Sioux "Sun-Gazing Dance," which emphasizes the fixed attention of the participants on the ineffable Almighty.) Some vow to dance throughout the ceremony, taking no food and no liquid except for the rain water that the Almighty might briefly bless them with during the ceremony. Others vow to dance for shorter periods. Throughout the days of the ceremony, the camp is decorously quiet, knots of people sitting on the grass surrounding the dance lodge and joining silently in the prayers. If there is gambling or secular singing, it takes place on the fringes of the camp. The ceremony closes with the dancers and priests filing out of the lodge and the spectators entering to circle and touch the holy center pole. When the camp breaks up, the Sun Dance lodge, with the items sacrificed hanging in it, is left untouched for the Almighty to reclaim through natural decay.

The basic form of the Sun Dance was remarkably similar throughout the Plains among the no-

mads, which suggests that it may have been a relatively recent introduction, perhaps in the late eighteenth century. Its popularity must have been due in part to its capacity to include any number of participants, and in part to the wonderful aptness of the lodge as a symbol: transient, open to the sky, walled with leaves, it perfectly expresses the circle of the universe within which humans reside, while the center pole, *axis mundi*, draws our souls toward the Almighty Power that gives us being. Each ethnic group added to the basic form its own symbols, such as the Tai-me figure of the Kiowas signifying the Kiowa people, and features such as noted men and women recounting their moments of glory, or, a spectacle popularized by the Sioux, ambitious young men torturing themselves by attaching thongs passed through their flesh to the center pole or to bison skulls and then pulling against the thong until it tears loose. (The Sioux think this would especially excite the pity of the Almighty, and earn blessing as well as the respect of the human audience. Among other peoples, self-torture was considered self-glorifying and not in the best taste.) The Sun Dance was in a sense a universal religion, emphasizing the individual's relationship to the Almighty and open to participants of any ethnic background, sex, age, or physical and social condition. The particular ritual details practiced in a camp tied the Sun Dance to the heritage and traditions of the people making up a majority of the camp but were not considered the exclusive way to worship the Almighty.

Medicine Bundles

"Medicine bundles" were the focus of most Plains rituals, both among nomads and in towns. They are similar to the collections of sacred symbolic objects kept in the "navel" at the traditional center of a Pueblo town, or to the objects in the sancta of Mexican temples. On the Plains, bundles usually contain preserved skins of small animals and birds or portions of larger ones such as bison horns and eagle feathers, each symbolizing the spirit that took

FIGURE 6.7 Piegan Blackfoot camp, 1833. About four hundred lodges are in this camp. *(Smithsonian Institution National Anthropological Archives, Bureau of American Ethnology Collection)*

the form of that creature to communicate with humans. There may also be seeds and other parts of plants, symbolizing life and the seasons, and usually sage or sweetgrass, the aroma of which is pleasing to all beings. According to legend, strangely shaped stones such as fossils may have been the embodiment of a spirit that revealed a ritual to a people's ancestors. Marine shells or stone arrowheads may represent the danger of dealing with spiritual force, in that such an object may shoot death if unwisely handled. Holy objects are wrapped up, along with rattles to be used to accompany chanted prayers, in layers of hides and cloth. The bundle is ceremoniously opened when supplicants wish to gain spiritual power or blessing in a time of need. Each object is reverently displayed by a priest who has been trained in the ritual, and then the priest and assistants sing prayers invoking the spirit symbolized by the object. The most potent objects are pipes, or, more exactly, pipestems (calumets), many of which are carved from the soft, red stone quarried near the

surface in southwestern Minnesota. (The historic painter-ethnographer of early nineteenth-century Indians, George Catlin, is honored in the name of this stone, catlinite.) Pipes are the medium in which tobacco is transformed into the incense that rises to the Almighty. The strong native tobacco used in ceremonial pipes has a mild consciousness-altering effect, too. So, pipes have been the object par excellence for calling forth contact between sufferer and the power that may help them. As the Thunder, visualized as a tremendous bird whose wings darken the sky and whose eyes flash with shattering brilliance, is the most awesome manifestation of Almighty Power seen by humans, the sacred pipes are the purest symbol of rapprochement to the Above. They tend to be associated with Thunder and, through this association, to signify justice, honor, and the sacredness of all life. Thus, quarrels must be put aside if a holy pipe is brought out, and pipe-bundle keepers were the solemn peace keepers in a camp or town.

Conclusion

Plains cultures were primarily variants of Eastern Woodland patterns, as would be assumed from the origins of many of the historic Plains peoples. From this perspective, the Plains village nations had the most complete traditional patterns, and the nomads a stripped version in which portability determined whether a trait could be retained. Stressing resemblances between Plains and eastern customs fails to illuminate the inventiveness of the Plains people in not only adapting to a relatively restrictive environment of extreme temperatures and limited variety of food resources, but in developing such highly efficient techniques and aids as the bison pound, the tipi, and the round earth lodge, and such social mechanisms as the multicamp sodalities, the Sun Dance, and the medicine bundle, which, carried and opened any place, made spiritual help available wherever a people roamed. The activities at the great summer rendezvous demonstrate that simple as a small band's winter camp might appear, the band was part of a larger and complex society, which, especially for the formerly agricultural nomads, might be termed an "intermittent town." For most of the year among the nomads, the sodalities, the priesthoods, the therapists' association and training programs, the markets, and the governing council lay dormant. When grass and congregating bison permitted, all these were requickened, to function actively for a few summer weeks. The importance of the rendezvous can be glimpsed in the fact that at least some bands designated reliable persons to be calendar keepers and tally each day so that the band would know when to start toward the rendezvous. At least two constructions of small boulders on hilltops, one in the Bighorn Range in Wyoming and one at the end of the Moose Mountain Upland in Saskatchewan, are astronomical alignments from which a calendar keeper could determine the summer solstice. The Bighorn "medicine wheel" is claimed by the Ponca, and the Saskatchewan construction has been shown by archaeological as well as astronomical research to be two thousand years old, thus indicating that great rendezvous on the Plains may go back to the Hopewell era. The concept of "intermittent town" implies that the differences between Plains villagers and nomads was not so major. (Indeed, this is also suggested by the fact that the Plains villagers, like the midwestern communities, decamped en masse twice a year on long hunts.) Further, it underlines the richness of Plains life, a life well supplied with high-protein lean meat— producing the tallest peoples in North America—and good shelter and clothing, and a life with plenty of time for fine craftwork, ritual and poetry, enjoyable visiting and dancing, and production of surplus hides and pemmican for the European markets from which weapons, tools, and ornaments came. The Plains nomads were in no sense foragers, in no way primitive. In conjunction with the thousands of town-dwelling Plains Indians, they were civilized in style, although they had no city walls.

SECTION 5: THE NINETEENTH CENTURY AND POSTBISON PLAINS LIFE

The first half of the nineteenth century saw the simultaneous florescence of the stereotyped bravura style of horse-riding nomads on the Plains, and the invasion of the Euro-American style carried by settled-in trading posts, United States troops, and eastern Indian nations removed to Indian Territory. As population grew in the United States east of the Mississippi, fed during mid-century by boatload after boatload of famine-driven Irish peasants and desperately poor Scandinavians, consciousness rose among leaders in the United States that it must be the "manifest destiny" of this nation to push ever westward, sweeping the "wild" peoples eventually into the Pacific. The self-serving righteousness drawn from the conviction of manifest destiny fueled a series of wars of conquest, exacerbated by the anomaly of "civilized" Indian nations colonizing the eastern Plains. The wars were finally ended by what seemed to both sides an act of God, the extermination of the bison herds that supported the Indian combatants.

The Displacement of the Midwestern Agriculturists

Lost in the shuffle were the Midwestern peoples displaced from the Ohio-Mississippi drainage. At first historic contact in the mid-seventeenth century, Lake Michigan was surrounded by Algonkian-speaking peoples except for the Chiwere-Siouan Winnebago on its central western shore. The Ojibwa (Anishinabe is their own name for themselves) were hunting and fishing along the northern shores of Lakes Huron, Michigan, and Superior, and holding trade rendezvous at the strait between Lakes Superior and Huron, the Sault Ste. Marie—hence the name Saulteaux applied to western Ojibwa. Michigan between Lakes Huron and Michigan was occupied by five principal peoples: the Sauk, the Fox (Mesquakie), the Mascoutens, and the Kickapoo on the east and the Potawatomi on the west. Two more Algonkian groups—the Miami in Indiana and the Illinois in the state of their name—held the "bottom" of Lake Michigan on the map. North of the intervening Winnebago, the Algonkian Menomini occupied northern Wisconsin.

The Menomini, like their Dakota neighbors to the west, harvested wild rice as a staple of their food resources. The other nations were far enough south to raise maize, squashes, and beans to complement the deer and fish they hunted. Predictably, considering their sedentary, agricultural foundation, these nations were more formally organized, with corporate patrilineal clans, than were the Menomini, whose clans had less property to control. Living in an agricultural zone proved in the end the downfall of the Indian nations of Michigan, Indiana, and Illinois. Eastern Indian groups and

then Euro-Americans coveted their land. Only the Menomini have been able to retain their homeland, in northern Wisconsin beyond the prime agricultural zone. Even they were pressured between 1848, when they had ceded the last of their territory to the United States, and 1854 to remove west of the Mississippi into Minnesota, but negotiations by their Chief Oshkosh won them a reservation in a section suited only to lumbering. In 1908, a sawmill was built on the reservation to process timber cut by the tribe on a sustained-yield basis; by the middle of this century, the Menomini community seemed to have a sound financial base, with several million dollars in a tribal treasury and employment in logging and the mill. Allotment under the 1887 Dawes Act had been successfully resisted, in a region where, even by the 1950s, there was little attraction to Euro-American entrepreneurs. The Menomini Tribe was advanced at this time as a prime candidate for the federal government's policy of terminating its treaty status with Indian peoples. Menominis claim that it was represented to them that they would have to agree to termination in order to receive a judgment awarded to them after long litigation over Bureau of Indian Affairs mismanagement of their timber. Termination for the Menomini was passed by Congress in 1954, and took effect in 1961 when the Menomini reservation officially became a county of the State of Wisconsin, with the reservation land, forests, and mill incorporated as assets of Menomini Enterprises, Inc. Control over these assets was vested in two trusts, one of them managed by a bank in Milwaukee, rather than given directly to the Menomini shareholders, many of whom were decreed incompetent toward their own financial affairs without any hearing on the matter. When it became apparent that the sawmill alone could not support all the expenses of running a county, the Enterprise's Board of Directors entered into an agreement with a nationally operating Euro-American businessman to build a resort and vacation homes. "Legend Lake" involved damming streams to create new recreational lakes, construct-

FIGURE 6.8 Che'mon (Mrs. Louise Caldwell), Menomini native doctor, in ceremonial dress, early twentieth century. *(Milwaukee Public Museum)*

ing expensive houses, and installing all the roads and utilities wealthy Euro-Americans would wish. Menomini consternation over such wide-scale destruction of their homeland reached a climax when the people realized that the vacation homes were to be sold, not leased, to outsiders. By 1970, concerned Menomini were joining a newly formed organization to battle the voting trusts and the threatened sale of land. Within two years, the organization had seen its greatest hope to lie in a restoration of the tribe's former status under its treaties, and had persuaded Wisconsin's congressional representatives to introduce a bill to return

the tribe to its pre-1954 status. Such a bill was passed in 1974. The Menominis are once again a federally recognized Indian tribe receiving the benefits due under their treaties. They had resisted nineteenth-century efforts to displace them, only to fall victim to twentieth-century efforts to impose Euro-American enterprise upon them. Two decades of bitter fighting, not only between Menomini and their Euro-American business advisors, but also between Menomini who favored militant tactics and those who found such tactics distasteful, ensued before the Menomini were restored to their traditional status: a community with a scarcity of jobs, isolated within a forest and by the unsavory stereotypes of Indians held by many in the Euro-American towns surrounding them, but at least a community with its homeland secure.

The conclusion of the War of 1812 initiated a series of treaties that nibbled away chunk after chunk of Indian territory west of Lake Huron. A village and its adjacent arable land would be reserved to its occupants, but the hunting and berrying lands between villages, and the fishing streams, were thereby opened to settlement by outsiders. When Black Hawk (Makataimeshekaikiak), a Sauk general who had led battles against the Osage and the Cherokee (which points up the domino effect of Indian removal in the Southeast), returned in 1829 from a regular extended winter hunt to find Euro-American homesteaders not just on the village's farmland but actually living in his house, he organized a stand against further encroachment. Weakened by the failure of many of the villages to unite in his campaign, Black Hawk fought battle after battle, retreating westward until at last, in the summer of 1832, most of his band were killed by United States troops, refugees were halted by the Sioux, and Black Hawk and his aide Nahpope were captured by Winnebago and delivered to their opponent. After a month in prison, Black Hawk was put on tour through United States cities as the Romans had triumphantly led their conquered enemies through their capital. Black Hawk then retired to the Sauk community that had earlier removed to Iowa.

The Mesquakie had also removed to Iowa. For the previous two generations, the Mesquakie, with their allies the Sauk, the Kickapoo and Mascoutens, and the Potawatomi, had been able to use the lands in Illinois and adjacent Indiana and Wisconsin once controlled by the Illinois (Ilini), a confederacy of six groups including the Peoria, Cahokia, and Kaskaskia. In 1769, a Kaskaskia had imprudently killed the Ottawa leader Pontiac, general of an Indian campaign to route the British from Michigan during the last year of the Seven Years' War. Although the murder occurred during drunken revelry at a Cahokia town, the Michigan nations found it grounds to wage unrelenting war upon the Ilini, and succeeded in reducing them to two small villages protected by the French fort at Kaskaskia in southern Illinois. What is now Iowa then became the western edge of the territory of the five nations formerly confined to Michigan, and its prairie-border ecology, not much different from that of southern Michigan, was comfortable for them.

By September 1833, there could be no doubt that Indians were powerless to remain in the agricultural zone around Lake Michigan. Black Hawk's defeat tolled the knell of Indian occupation. A treaty conclave was arranged at Chicago, a new little town. Much of the negotiations at the conclave were conducted by sons of French and British traders who had married Indian women. Although these offspring could not be considered legitimate members of any of the Indian nations around lower Lake Michigan, all of whom reckoned affiliation through the father's line into their basic societal unit, the patrilineal clan, the English-speaking, biologically half-Indian men were most readily accepted by government agents as representatives of the Indians. Since the Chicago treaty included large money payments to traders to quash debts allegedly owed by Indians, the traders' sons had a considerable stake in the outcome of negotiations. The treaty of 1833 decided that all the Indian nations involved would remove west of the Mississippi, receiving lands equivalent to those they had surrendered plus expenses and compensation. On paper, the terms looked decently cognizant of the just claims of the Indians, but in practice they were windfalls for traders and opportunistic Euro-American suppliers. It is not surprising that many Indians remained dissatisfied, and factionalism within Indian communities was heated up by differing attitudes toward the treaty.

The decade after 1833 saw the removal of the agricultural Indians from Michigan, Indiana, Illinois, and Wisconsin. Most of the Potawatomi made one or more moves until they were settled on a reservation in northeastern Kansas. A substantial

FIGURE 6.9 Winnebago and Chippewa (Anishinabe) gambling, 1941, on a northern Wisconsin reservation. A Winnebago man hides a ball under a fur pad "moccasin" while a teammate drums. The Chippewa opponent tries to guess under which "moccasin" the ball lies. Bets are placed on the guesser's success. *(Milwaukee Public Museum)*

segment of Potawatomi instead traveled northeastward and were allowed refuge in southwestern Ontario. A few families eluded government agents and remained in the Midwest, but had to forfeit their arable lands and scrounge a living in forested northern Michigan and Wisconsin; a Catholic group managed to negotiate a supplement to the 1833 treaty permitting them to remain in southwestern Michigan. (In 1901, a descendant of the chief who had obtained the concession announced he was reclaiming another parcel of land reserved to these Pokagon Potawatomis: a strip along the city of Chicago's Lake Michigan waterfront; just a beach in 1833, but now known as Chicago's Gold Coast. Newspapers played up the claim that public

opinion then considered hilarious.) By 1980 there were a total of nearly ten thousand Potawatomi.

The Winnebago removed to Minnesota, which they had been infiltrating for years, but were forced out in 1862 after a Dakota uprising inflamed Euro-American clamor against all Indians. The unfortunate Winnebago were driven to South Dakota, but from there escaped to their linguistic cousins the Omaha in northeastern Nebraska. A community of Winnebago remain with the Omaha, while a number of families managed to stay or return to Minnesota or Wisconsin. The largest segment of Winnebago are now in central Wisconsin, lacking land and climate for farming and therefore, like the Potawatomi presently in the Midwest, hunting, trapping, fishing, harvesting cranberries, and working as laborers. The Wisconsin Winnebago have gravitated toward the resort area of Wisconsin Dells, where supplemental income can be gained by selling baskets and other crafts to tourists and participating in "ceremonials" staged for the vacationers. Development of three bingo halls in the 1980s radically changed the Wisconsin Winnebagos' economy, providing employment and capital for other enterprises. Over five thousand Winnebago were reported by the 1980 census.

The Mesquakie vacated their Iowa home for Kansas, but in 1854 pooled money and delegated a committee to return to Iowa and purchase a block of land. Many Mesquakie then returned to Iowa where they remain in a community near Tama, inviolable because their land is not a government reservation but legally the purchased property of a corporation, the Mesquakie tribal community. The return of the Mesquakie to Iowa was stimulated in part by resentment of United States government elevation of a Sauk politician, Keokuk, to official chieftainship, although Keokuk neither belonged to the clan that possessed the hereditary claim to chieftainship nor enjoyed the confidence of his people. The Sauk had removed from Iowa with their allies the Mesquakie and resided with them for a generation in Kansas, where the Iowa lived adjacent after agreeing, in 1837, to exchange land east of the Missouri River for land west of it. Fourteen Iowa led by the civil chief White Cloud ((Mahaska) and the war leader Neumonya went to England and France in 1843, performing dance exhibitions arranged by the American painter George Catlin, meeting politicians and the King of France, and studying European society. Returning home in 1845, the Iowa had noticed the poverty of the poor in European cities as well as the magnificence of the elite. Their sophisticated knowledge of Europe assisted them in developing, with their Sauk neighbors led by Nesourquoit, a viable farming community life similar to that of many Cherokees: daily clothing and tools were much like those of Euro-American settlers, although a core of tra-

ditional religion, social structure, and values remained strong. In 1867, the Sauk were pressured into ceding their eastern Kansas reservation in exchange for one in Oklahoma Indian Territory. Nesourquoit's Sauk, by now led by Mokohoko, hung on in Kansas along with some of their Iowa neighbors, but most made the final move to Oklahoma. In 1980 there were nearly thirty-five hundred individuals identified as Sauk or Mesquakie (the census doesn't distinguish between the two) and a thousand Iowa, the majority of the three nations in Oklahoma.

The Miami had removed to Kansas early, by 1827, except for one village in the Wabash River homeland that persisted as a corporate group until 1872, when its land was divided into individual family holdings. The immigrant Miami were pushed out of Kansas into Indian Territory and have continued there in Oklahoma. The Miami proper, plus two separately recognized Miami bands, the Wea and the Piankashaw, have perpetuated their confederation with the remnants of the Ilini, now known as the Peoria and including descendants of the Kaskaskia. The 1980 census reported 2,330 Miami and 645 "Peoria." Of all the upper Midwest languages, only Miami and the related Ilini dialects are no longer spoken by anyone.

The Kickapoo

Kickapoo history parallels that of the Cherokee in many respects. The Kickapoo were the southernmost of the upper Midwest Algonkians, first at the western end of Lake Erie and then in Illinois, and in this position were heavily exposed to Euro-American colonists. Their vulnerable position caused the Kickapoo to cede their land in 1819, and, within five years, nearly all were relocated to the Osage River in southwestern Missouri. Here, many of the Kickapoo and about two hundred Potawatomi were members of a community led by Kenekuk. Like the Seneca prophet Handsome Lake (Ganiodayo') and the

Shawnee prophet Tenskwatawa, brother of the war leader Tecumseh, Kenekuk had been a deeply disturbed and frustrated man until he experienced a revelation of an acceptable way of life for the harried Indians. Kenekuk's occasional attendance at frontier Methodist church and camp services gave him a valuable perspective on his native beliefs. He urged his people to abjure liquor, form monogamous marriages exclusively, and give up clan corporate economics in favor of Euro-American-style family farms. To weaken the power of the clan lineages, he urged that clan medicine bundles be neglected, but he taught that other Kickapoo rituals should be maintained. Thus, he worked out a pattern in which the material culture and social organization of the Kickapoo and their Potawatomi friends were sufficiently similar to Euro-American patterns to appear compatible with United States expectations, but the core of language, religion, and community identity was Kickapoo, protected from missionary and government-agent attacks by the visible veneer of similarity to colonists' norms. That Kenekuk's vision was as viable as Handsome Lake's is attested by its survival into the present on the Kickapoo reservation in Kansas, where they moved in 1833. At that time, some dissatisfied Kickapoo went to Texas, although most of the Kickapoo, who had apparently absorbed the Mascouten by the time of their first removal, seemed willing to take up the prairie land in Kansas.

In 1837, several hundred Kickapoo left Kansas to hunt in Texas. Although the earliest migrants into Texas seem not to have been recorded, Kickapoo had been serving the Spanish crown as early as 1775, protecting a portion of Texas from southern Plains raiders and receiving a land grant in recompense. Thus, the factions that left the Kansas reservation in the 1830s were choosing a Plains border alternative living arrangement already at least two generations old among the Kickapoo. In 1839, an independent Texas decided the Kickapoo might be more dangerous than reliable, and exiled its Kickapoo community, which went on to Indian Territory in Oklahoma. Some of these Kickapoo, in concert with a group of Seminole, journeyed to Mexico in 1850 to ask to renew the kind of relationship their fathers had held with Spain. Mexico granted land on its northern frontier in Coahuila, in exchange for resistance to Apache and Comanche raids. Most of the Kickapoo and the Seminole and Potawatomi with them were induced to return to the United States in 1859, but enough Kickapoo for one small village, plus several dozen black slaves of the Seminole who would not go back into slavery, stayed on in Coahuila, the blacks in a settlement a few miles from that of the Indians. About two hundred Kickapoo from Oklahoma joined the Coahuila village in 1862, wishing to avoid the United States Civil War and also angry because a railroad was to be allowed through their reservation. Ten years later, an illegal United States cavalry raid upon the Kickapoo community in Mexico shot many men and dragged women and children captive all the way back to imprisonment in Oklahoma, eventually to be put on a reservation there. Survivors in Coahuila have persevered, in a village of Woodland wigwams incongruously set in the northern Mexican desert. This Mexican Kickapoo community maintained ties to relatives in Oklahoma, crossing the border at Eagle Pass, Texas, on visits. After World War II, increased opportunities for agricultural laborers in the region brought Kickapoo to Eagle Pass seeking jobs, and shopping. By the 1970s, some families kept cheaply constructed shelters in the town, remaining long enough to obtain food stamps to stretch their meager incomes. Townspeople objected to the "shacks" and arranged for land to be purchased for the Indians outside Eagle Pass. Legally, this 1986 reservation is for "the Texas Band of the Oklahoma Kickapoo Tribe," and its members are considered to be under Oklahoma Kickapoo jurisdiction; practically, the Texas residents continue to go back and forth to the Mexican Kickapoo settlement, using the Texas reservation as a base to obtain employment and medical and shopping opportunities not available to them in Mexico. United States Kickapoo listed in the 1980 census totaled nearly twenty-four hundred.

Kickapoo, Sauk, Mesquakie, Potawatomi, Miami, and Ilini—the first four with reservations in both Kansas and Oklahoma, the last two in Oklahoma—plus Delaware, Ottawa, and Shawnee on Oklahoma reservations, and, of course, the Five Civilized Tribes, totaled many thousands of Eastern Indians dumped into the eastern Plains after 1830. The needs of these many families for land and game reverberated upon the struggles of the Prairie peoples who had shifted a century earlier to the same lands. Add to these the need to feed the increasing number of trading posts, military forts, wagon trains, and homesteads of Euro-American settlers, and clearly the resources of what is, after all, a semiarid country were being seriously strained. Epidemics of smallpox, cholera, and other diseases decimated Indian communities and robbed them of countless capable adults, yet the total number of Indians was still large for a region subject to drought. Finally, after the completion of the transcontinental railroad in 1869 made bulk shipments out of the Plains profitable, the wholesale slaughter of bison for boxcar loads of hide contributed to the intolerable strain.

The 1870s became a decade of wars to end all wars on the Plains. In 1876, Sioux and Cheyenne annihilated the unfortunate troops led by the glory-seeking George Custer; most other battles threw well-supplied United States forces against Indians burdened with the provisioning and protection of their families. President Grant had declared his policy on Indian affairs a "peace policy": the army would force peace upon the Indians. Back in the metropolitan East, the policy sounded, and indeed was meant to be, humane. In operation, it was often carte blanche for the military to harass and sometimes massacre Indians away from their allotted agencies, where agents and their missionary colleagues exhorted the people to give up their holy symbols and rituals, break up long-standing polygamous marriages, and work long, backbreaking hours on farms plagued by lack of rain and by grasshoppers. Beginning about 1880, the bison herds were no more seen. This disappearance of the foundation of Plains life was the final blow to peoples who had suffered every other misfortune imaginable in their lives. Armed resistance had to collapse, yet cessation of hostilities could bring no respite, for the subsistence agriculture taught by government agents was an eastern ideal quite unsuited to the Plains, and the only alternative was bare survival on meager, often wormy, imported government handouts of flour, lard, salt pork, and a few beef.

The incredible disappearance of the bison and the rapid subjugation of so many proud and courageous nations seemed a message from the Almighty. Christians interpreted the message to be vindication of their efforts to force Indians to accept Christianity and the Euro-American cultural pattern. Indians felt they must have transgressed moral imperatives, and searched their souls to discover how they might rectify their situation to regain a decent life. A Dakota woman, Wananikwe, who claimed to have narrowly escaped from an attack by Custer on her camp in 1876, shortly before the general's own final battle, began soon after her adventure to preach a new religion, the Dream Dance. She had ascended to heaven, she said, where the Almighty gave her a consecrated Drum, larger than any drums usually used. Power was in that Drum, and all who came in peace with an offering of tobacco could find through that power ease of mind and relief from tribulations. Enmity among Indians had destroyed them. Friendship through the peace of the Drum could save them. Wananikwe went to her people's traditional enemies, the Chippewa. She was welcomed and converted many to her beliefs, demonstrating the validity of her revelation. The Dream Dance, a ritual held sometimes weekly around a large beautifully decorated drum in an arbor, home, or hall, spread rapidly to all the peoples of the upper Midwest and their relatives in Kansas. The Almighty has not yet fulfilled an early promise to Wananikwe to paralyze all nonbelievers (Indian and non-Indian) by a tap on the great Drum Above, but the Dream Dance has proved to be a consolation and hope to thousands of Indian people, who find its gatherings their inspiration to live morally within a spiritual as well as physical community.

The Ghost Dance

Wananikwe spoke to people who had not been wholly dependent upon bison. Those who had, the historic Plains groups, were not yet convinced of the totality of bison extermination when Wananikwe evangelized around 1880. The young Dakota woman's message was ignored by the bison hunters. Then the unthinkable happened: the bison were no longer on the face of the earth. Anthropologist Clark Wissler reported that "the Indians were closely confined, supported by rations and urged to become agriculturists. In many cases these unfortunate people set doggedly at their difficult task, presenting one of the most pathetic spectacles of modern times. With this new life their social ideals and machinery were decidedly out of joint. According to the testimony of one who came to manhood during this period, many young men were so overwhelmed by the vacuity of the new life that they took to suicide or other less direct ways of throwing their lives away" (Wissler 1916:869). A new prophet now spoke, a Paiute man from a high sagebrush valley in Nevada. This man, Wovoka, called Jack Wilson by the rancher who employed him, brought a new hope to the desperate thousands throughout the Plains.

Wovoka was a native of Mason Valley on the Walker River Reservation in Nevada. The Northern Paiute of Walker River traditionally lived by fishing, supplemented by gathering grass seed, berries, and pinyon (pine) nuts and by hunting deer, antelope, and rabbits. About 1850, the Walker River Paiute obtained sufficient horses to mount raids upon the mining camps and ranches beginning to be established in their territory. In 1860, a cavalry post was built to protect the pony express

route running north of Walker Lake, and a reservation was set up for the Paiute who congregated at that lake for fishing. The Paiute were promised government aid in developing agriculture on their reservation, and were eager to do so, but the aid was years in coming and barely adequate when it did appear. Meanwhile, the Paiute were encouraged to obtain employment as seasonal labor on the Euro-American farms and ranches blossoming in the valleys. Many did so, proved excellent workers, and were befriended by some of their employers, who tried to teach them English, Christianity, and Euro-American housing and clothing preferences.

Epidemics struck the Walker River Paiute in 1868 and 1869. At this time Wodziwob, also called Fish Lake Joe, a leader of a more southern Paiute band, was on the Walker River Reservation, probably to fish. He experienced a revelation that a train would come from the east bringing on it the recently deceased parents of reservation people. During the autumn gatherings accompanying the pinyon (pine) nut harvest of 1869, Wodziwob preached that the Paiute should bathe and paint themselves with white, black, and red paint daily and should dance the traditional Round Dance in anticipation of the train. (The transcontinental railroad had just been completed.) A simple ceremony performed throughout northwestern North America, the Round Dance, or Prophet Dance, symbolically repeated the sun's journey—that is to say, the annual cycle of Power Above that seasonally invigorates life on earth. During the dance, individuals who had experienced visions—sometimes within the dance itself—admonished the people to avoid immorality and selfishness, which would be displeasing to the Almighty. Circling like the life-giving sun, and resolved to conduct themselves in a manner that would attract spiritual power to their food quests, the people in a Round Dance felt they were reinforcing their prospects of prosperity. Wodziwob coupled this ceremony with his prophecy of negation of the effects of the epidemic.

Far from restoring the game depleted by destruction of much of its habitat by Euro-American

FIGURE 6.10 Wovoka (Jack Wilson), the Paiute prophet, in 1891, three years after his vision. Wovoka here is in his mid-thirties. *(Smithsonian Institution National Anthropological Archives)*

farms, Wodziwob's Round Dances seemed to have the opposite effect. A drought in 1871 left the people bereft of even their grass seed and pinyon nuts. Nor had the railroad carried back their departed relatives. The Walker Lake people ceased to expect a magical return of prosperity and channeled their energies into reservation farming, with government tools and seed at last available. Wodziwob himself reported he had revisited the land of the dead, seen only shadows instead of the happy people he had seen earlier, and realized he had been misled when an owl was the only creature that acknowledged him from the shadows. Wodziwob's prophecy had been carried to other sections of Nevada, to Oregon, and to California, where it inspired fervent Round Dancing among the persecuted Indians there. In California, the ceremony became the basis for revived native beliefs that remain viable today.

Wovoka was a boy of about ten during the excitement over Wodziwob's prophecy. Wovoka's father was a shaman whose vision experiences enabled him to be a leader of his band. The youth Wovoka had been aided by a rancher named Wilson, who had the young Paiute join his own family for Bible study and prayer. Wovoka worked regularly for Wilson and thus came to be known as Jack Wilson. Wilson's ranch was north of the

FIGURE 6.11 Wovoka, the Paiute prophet in later life. *(Milwaukee Public Museum)*

Walker River Reservation, and Wovoka lived on the ranch, but not cut off from his people: he had married, and resided in a small tule-reed wickiup (a round, thatched hut) in a camp with other Paiute families. The Paiute wore Euro-American clothing, and Wovoka hunted with a gun, but in all other respects they lived in a traditional native manner, the seasonal ranch work being an alternative to some earlier gathering expeditions but allowing enough of the older pursuits to keep the families' diets traditional. In spite of the rancher's endeavors to make Jack a Christian, Wovoka followed his father's beliefs and practices and even as a young man was said to know how to control the weather, as his father had been able to do.

About 1888, Wovoka began leading Round Dances. In the winter of 1889, he fell ill with a high fever. Apparently, he was still ill when a total eclipse of the sun occurred over Mason Valley. Wovoka feared that the sun had died. He himself was lifted into the Above. God, he said, showed him the Paiutes from the past, young, happy, hunting, gathering, and enjoying games. Then God instructed him to go back to earth to tell the people to cease war and quarreling, to work rather than steal, to love one another and accommodate to the Euro-Americans. If the people obeyed God's commands, they would eventually be reunited with their loved ones in the happy world above. God gave Wovoka the Round Dance as the means for relaying the message to the people, and gave him also power over the weather and power for curing.

Wovoka's dramatic vision during the eclipse excited the Paiute. There was nothing novel in Wovoka's practices, though his message stressing peace and accommodation to Euro-American patterns and his Christian-like promise of reunion with the dead in heaven differed from the former prophets' emphases. The young man's fervency, coupled with his tall, strong appearance, reputation for good character, and shamanistic techniques, brought him an immediate following. Songs were composed conveying allusions to his vision. The Paiute danced frequently.

Word of the Paiute prophet spread rapidly through the Plains in 1889. Deprived of bison and with little other game to hunt, their attempts at crops frustrated by drought and grasshopper plagues during the 1880s, the Indians on the reservations had plenty of time to discuss the news of supernatural revelation. The prophecy and the renewed Round Dancing to what were now known as Ghost Dance songs were quickly taken up by all Paiute and by nations with whom they were in contact: the Utes, the Shoshoni, the southern- and central-California peoples (Mission Indians and those living along the Pit River), and the Walapai and Cohonino to the southwest. A Shoshoni delegation to learn firsthand from Wovoka, now being called a messiah, brought along an Arapaho who was impressed by the prophet and proselytized the new religion among his people. From the Arapaho, the news came to the other Plains nations. Many were skeptical. Some reservations sent delegates to confirm or expose, as the case might be, the alleged prophet. The delegates traveled by train, participated in Walker Lake Ghost Dancing, observed and spoke with Wovoka, and were converted. From their enthusiastic reports, the Cheyenne, Gros Ventres, Arikara, Mandan, Hidatsa, Assiniboin, and Teton Sioux took up the ceremony. An intertribal delegation from Oklahoma brought the dance to the Caddo, Pawnee, Wichita, Oto, Comanche, and Kiowa. Other Plains nations were not drawn to the Ghost Dance. Some, of course, had only recently been proselytized by the Dream Dance revealed to Wananikwe and were still engrossed in her prophecy, which was similar to Wovoka's in its emphasis upon peace.

THE ORIGIN OF THE GHOST DANCE

This gospel was related in 1961 by the leader of a Dakota congregation of the Ghost Dance religion. It is the sacred gospel taught to this community about 1900 and recited ever since at the prayer meetings of the congregation. It is, strictly speaking, the origin of Wilson's disciple's Ghost Dance religion. It is recited with reverence, only to those mature enough to ponder its meaning and understand its power to transform despair into joy. Please read it with reverence.

Around 1890, there was a man by the name of Kicking Bear, who had a brother-in-law named Short Bull, with whom he was closely associated. Kicking Bear lost a daughter; she died, he roamed the plains, downhearted, unable to forget his loss. One night he saw a dream vision, stating that "all he worried about is known by Him Who gives power. There is a place where the dead souls gather." This he believed because it seemed to be *wakan* [spiritual, wonderful].

He started off to find a spot where he could discover this, traveling through Montana to Nevada until he faced a mountain of rock. Halfway up was a house occupied by a shaman. Kicking Bear and Short Bull were welcomed by the occupant, all shaking hands. The occupant told them the purpose of their visit, saying, "You are looking for the soul of your deceased daughter; you firmly believe there is a place where souls gather. You are right."

This man was named Jack Wilson. He told them he could help them to see the deceased child among the souls. "You have to go further west, and there you will meet a bunch of people, a tribe, who have the power that they can enable you to see your child, a spirit in spirit-land. This group of people are overseers above the spirits, through the supervision of the Almighty Power. This tribe is the Thunderbirds, the mediators of the Almighty Power."

Jack Wilson had built a sweat lodge and placed in it sage. He laid Kicking Bear on the sage, covered him with a buffalo robe, and fanned him with an eagle fan. This put Kicking Bear into a trance, when he was able to go and see what Jack Wilson had promised him.

When, as he was in a trance, Kicking Bear approached the spirits' camp, he was walking on land. The camp was so big he couldn't see across it. He saw all his deceased relatives, father and mother, and among them his daughter. As far as he could see, the dwellings on both sides of him, left and right, had food (that is, meat) but none offered him food to eat. The dishes were wooden bowls like my great-grandfather's feast bowl, no metal. He was satisfied, seeing his daughter and the tribe of spirits, and was about to return, when they said to him, "You've come this far, you might as well see the Creator, the Power that guides all things." He was taken to see a Being, a Person Who was very magnificent. This person gave him a pipe and sweetgrass, and told him to stand upright and offer the pipe and grass to Him. He would then hear and answer them. The Creator thus confirmed the ancient way of praying to Him and emphasized it was to be continued.

Another instruction Kicking Bear got was, "You thought your child had died and gone forever, but that's not the case. She has joined another tribe. When you rejoin your own tribe on earth, tell the people, 'You are never happy when a person dies. You cut off your braids, and are downhearted. That's not pleasing to the One Who gave them life.' When you get back to earth, take a ball of earth, dampen it, put it into the fire, and take it out. You will see it has turned perfectly red. Powder it and mark your face with it, as a token of happiness pleasing to the Power." He told him, "When one of the earthly beings—the humans—passes away, leave them where they pass away, so their bones turn into dust. You make a scaffold and lay them up there; this is not right. The birds can eat them. The body comes from the earth, and there is where it should return. You should bury in the earth."

Now as he was descending, it seemed to him that he was very near the sun. As he was coming down, he sang a song:

I've come on high.
The Father enabled me to beat that height.

There was nothing holding him as he was coming down, but he was floating slowly down like the eagle feather on the pipe he had been given. He had been told that when he returned to his people, they should dance to that song, with an eagle feather tied to their hair. That's where wearing eagle feathers on their head began.

When he awakened from this sleep, he was in the same place where he had started, with all these instructions and visions clearly remembered. When he awakened, he told his companions what he had seen. He had left out some things, which Jack Wilson put in, straightening out his dream for him. Apparently Jack Wilson had seen where he traveled.

Before this, when a family lost a member, some men would shove a sharpened stick through their flesh and leave it there, some women would cut themselves to show they were in mourning, for a year. Since Kicking Bear told of his dream, this kind of self-cruelty was done away with. Since then, they turned it into a kind of religious dance: on the seventh day, they gathered on a high hill and sang songs pertaining to what Kicking Bear had seen. Men and women joined in happiness, wearing the eagle feathers and the paint Kicking Bear had prepared.

Crossing the Rockies, Wovoka's story became inflated. He was said by some to be Christ. He was said to foresee an apocalypse in which the world would be restored to a pre-European Eden, well stocked with bison. He was said to claim shirts could be imbued with the power to stop bullets. Back home in Mason Valley, Nevada, Wovoka emphatically denied such teachings, but out on the Plains, rumors could not be scotched. The Lakota, bitter over losing the Black Hills, which had been reserved to them but were taken when gold was discovered in them, were especially prone to wondering whether Wovoka's power might be used in battle. Government agents, uneasy because they knew the Lakota had been unjustly deprived of land both beautiful and full of game, imagined that the "messiah" incited Indians to rebel. During the autumn of 1890, agents for the Sioux ordered these people to cease their Ghost Dancing. Naturally, most were unwilling to do so, although many were willing to discuss the matter with the agents and reach a reasonable compromise. Sitting Bull (Tatanka Iyotanke), the Hunkpapa chief and a noted spiritual leader, suggested that he and government agents should visit Nevada together and determine the truth of the new religion. This intelligent idea was ignored, and Sitting Bull declared that he could not in good conscience forbid a ceremony that seemed to have its basis in revelations from the Almighty.

As winter approached, the Lakota grew nervous. Their rations had been drastically reduced in 1890, for the fourth year in a row, and they were hungry. A new and totally inexperienced agent, appointed in reward for political favors in Washington, called for government troops. The soldiers frightened hundreds of families on the Rosebud and Pine Ridge reservations in South Dakota to flee in panic into the Badlands nearby. The local Indian agents were asked to make lists of dissident leaders and forward these to the military for arrest. Sitting Bull was foremost on his agent's list. A first suggestion was to invite his friend William F. "Buffalo Bill" Cody to talk with him and defuse the situation, but the Standing Rock Reservation agent, whose jurisdiction included Sitting Bull's home, preferred to handle the matter himself. At daybreak on December 15, 1890, Indian police reinforced by government troops surrounded Sitting Bull's cabin and ordered him to accompany them to prison. As the leader waited at his door for his horse to be saddled, one of the angry villagers fired a gun. Two policemen flanking the chief immediately discharged their pistols into Sitting Bull. It does seem to be true that Sitting Bull had declared he was ready to fight to the death against the invidious United States, but his murder was a shockingly hasty action unjustified by the circumstances of the unrest around his home.

With Sitting Bull dead, other Lakota realized that the combination of bitter winter weather and several thousand well-armed troops made discretion the better part of valor. The camps in the Badlands broke up. Big Foot (Sitanka) was supposed to be hostile to government policy, but he, famous for his skill in diplomacy, agreed to travel to the Pine Ridge Agency to assist a meeting of Lakota leaders in resolving the economic and political crisis. His entire village rode with their ill and aged chief. Because the Pine Ridge agency grounds were already filled with envoys and their supporters, Big Foot's band was told to camp at the Catholic mission at Wounded Knee Creek. On the morning of December 29, 1890, Big Foot's men were gathered between their tipis, pitched in the valley bottom near the creek, and an array of troops with rifles and four machine guns. The men surrendered guns upon the order of the troop commander. Soldiers then searched the tipis and discovered forty more guns. While the search was being conducted, the Indians were talking, in Lakota, about resisting; most of the men wore the "ghost shirts" supposedly impregnated with invulnerability through the Ghost Dance ceremonies. Guessing that the young men were concealing guns under their blankets, the soldiers began frisking them. A deaf young man struggled with soldiers trying to take his gun, and it discharged into the air. At once, the arrayed troops fired into the camp. The soldiers in front and the Indian men closed in desperate hand-to-hand combat, which caused the death of sixty soldiers, while above their heads the machine guns lobbed dozens of heavy shells per minute into the tipis. Over two hundred Indians, including Big Foot lying in bed, were slaughtered. Particularly horrifying was the soldiers' pursuit of fleeing women and children through the snow. Mothers and babies were shot again and again and left to dye the cold white field with their red blood. The tragedy was perpetrated by new recruits from the East, whose heads had been filled with Wild West tales and slogans.

Popular accounts have it that the Ghost Dance died at Wounded Knee. To the contrary, the true Ghost Dance, the pacific doctrine preached by Wovoka, was untouched by the cruelty inflicted upon Big Foot's band. Disciples continued to take the train to Nevada, to hear again the prophet's words, join him and his people in their dance of renewal, and bring back blessed eagle feathers (symbolic of Wovoka's visit to the Above) and cans of a red ocher dug by the Paiute near their holy mountain, Mount Grant. By diluting this with local red ocher, all participants in a Plains Ghost Dance could be painted with the blessings of Wovoka's Power. Wovoka continued to advise visitors, manipulate the weather, and restore the ill to health until his death in 1932. Many followers wrote to him from their scattered reservations, in Saskatchewan as well as in the United States, and he mailed eagle feathers and holy paint to them. He traveled to San Francisco and to Oklahoma, a deeply respected shaman and spiritual guide. An earthquake in Nevada three months after his death was attributed to the rocking of the universe caused by his soul completing its final entry into heaven.

The year 1890 was revolutionary on the Plains. The last wild bison had been hunted less than a decade before. The most recalcitrant Lakota had been forced onto reservations. For a decade, Indian children had been attending schools, some at Carlisle in Pennsylvania, others closer to home at Chilocco in Oklahoma, near the Kansas border, and at Haskell in Kansas. At these boarding schools, youth from the many Indian nations were mixed, compelled to speak English, and urged to abandon their parents' ways. The Pax Americana allowed adults to travel freely and safely. Most Indians were finding themselves pushed onto individual family allotments under the recently passed Dawes Act. Concomitantly, Euro-American farmers were leasing these allotments, giving the Indian owners income without toil. Health was generally poor, affected by unsanitary conditions in the cabins that government agents advocated in place of the tipis that formerly had been regularly moved to clean grass, by pollution in the streams, by poor nutrition and even hunger much of the year, and by the rise in tuberculosis and other long-lasting diseases, including malaria and venereal diseases. A half-century or more of shifts from one settlement or territory to another, usually under pressure from the United States or hostile Indians, of raids and, increasingly, genocidal contests between desperate nations, of epidemics, of harassment by agents and missionaries determined to destroy every vestige of native culture—all had left the Indian peoples decimated, frustrated remnants of communities.

Into this nadir came the message of the strong, confident, yet gentle man from Nevada. He affirmed the value of the threatened native cultures, he held out hope that good and the ancient life would be experienced again, that parents and children would be reunited in defiance of the multitude of deaths suffered. The Paiute, less buffeted than most of the nations on the Plains, heard Wovoka's message and understood he was urging accommodation to the foreign hegemony. The Plains nations paid less attention to the doctrine of accommodation and grasped at the hope of a return to the proper life of past days. Hence, in 1890 and for a few years more, thousands who accepted the Ghost Dance danced fervently in prayer. Dancers regularly fell into trances, often induced by dance leaders through hypnotic concentration upon eagle feathers (to waft the dancer's soul to the Above), saw the happiness in heaven, and prophesied upon regaining consciousness. Their visions frequently instructed them to revive one or another neglected traditional institution. Through the sanction of Ghost Dance trances, the beleaguered native cultures were strengthened. This effect of the Ghost Dance, plus the abandonment of farms while people gathered to await with prayer what on the Plains was often believed to be imminent apocalypse, angered the government agents charged with "civilizing" the Indians. Ghost Dancing was banned, and leaders jailed. The result of opposition was the movement of the religion underground, meetings secretly arranged for locations away from the ken of agents. Therapeutic rituals were usually also held "underground," and medicine-bundle openings as well. The Sun Dance was generally in abeyance, because it required the tall center pole which was difficult to erect without calling attention to the gathering around it. The 1890 Ghost Dance was thus the context in which native beliefs and many practices, even

quasi-ceremonial but exciting games symbolizing the opposition of spiritual forces, survived the severe disruptions of the early reservation period.

Everyone eventually realized that Wovoka was not, as Plains people had hoped, a magic messiah. Many listened anew to his message and found what he really preached to be a comforting inspiration to live, as one present-day believer put it, a "clean, honest life." Congregations continued to gather to sing the beautiful Ghost Dance prayers, exhort one another to respect the teachings of their tradition, cooperate, and enjoy celebratory meals together. When the last of the original converts to the Ghost Dance died, in the early 1960s, the religion seemed gone, but revival of militant pride in Plains beliefs during the 1970s requickened interest in the Ghost Dance religion, as it had revived its predecessors eighty years ago.

Peyotism and the Grass Dance

Other belief systems and ceremonies spread on Plains reservations, too. The two most important were peyotism and the Grass Dance. The former is a religion; the latter was secular although it resembled religious ceremonials in form and usually opened with prayer. Peyotism is a set of sectarian variations on a ritual apparently developed about 1885 by Kiowa and Comanche on their Oklahoma reservation. The ritual takes place in a tipi, in the center of which is a fire and a low mound altar of earth, commonly in the shape of a half-moon or crescent moon. On the altar is a "grandfather" peyote, a large specimen of a little cactus that grows only in northernmost Mexico along the Río Grande. The cactus has mild hallucinogenic properties, producing vividly colored visions if taken in sufficient quantity. Having an unpleasant taste, peyote is not enjoyed, and many, perhaps most, participants in a ritual take only a small amount as a communion sacrament and do not achieve visions. Peyote is not addictive, and therefore not a narcotic. Peyote rituals are led by four ceremonial officers, or chiefs, who initiate the singing of prayers, ritual smoking of tobacco, the sharing of water at midnight and a sunrise meal of meat, maize, and fruit. (Modern ceremonial meals may consist of canned beef, Crackerjacks popcorn, and canned peaches.) The ritual is nightlong, and the following morning is a time for "after-church" visiting on the grass outside the tipi and an ordinary "feed," or secular meal.

Where the Ghost Dance around 1890 was group-oriented, peyotism, like the twentieth-century Ghost Dance religion, is oriented to the individual, offering personal experience of revelation (visions) through the sacrament, peyote, said to be given by God to Indians for this purpose. "The white man has the Bible, the Indian has peyote," one is told by peyotists. Most peyote sects consciously incorporate Christian elements and see themselves as syncretizing the best of the traditional Indian and Christian religions by acknowledging the truth of Christianity but holding it to be couched in culture-specific terms drawn from European experiences. Peyotism expresses the same faith in a Supreme Being and recognition of Christ's message of loving forgiveness, using symbols familiar to the Plains Indian experience and imparting a deeper spirituality in its small, fire-lit nocturnal congregations pulsed by drum and rattle beats. A peyote church was legally incorporated in 1914 in Oklahoma, and in 1918 nationally as the Native American Church. The church has a very loose structure, the primary purpose of legal incorporation being to secure recognition of the right of its members to the free exercise of their religion, including the taking of peyote as a sacrament, a right that was frequently abrogated, as recently as 1990 in a case upheld 6–3 by the Supreme Court, by zealous Euro-American officers of the law who assumed the mild hallucinogen was "dope" and its rituals "orgies." Peyote meetings are now held in Indian communities from the Midwest through the West. Peyotists frequently also practice their traditional ethnic ceremonies. Individuals who hereto-

fore had lapsed into alcohol abuse or immoral behavior have found the strong interpersonal support proffered at peyote meetings literally lifesaving. Peyotism is certainly not an Alcoholics or Wife Beaters Anonymous, but the solemn yet dramatic night meetings, the eye-to-eye contact between priests and congregation in the circle within the tipi, the belief that peyote cures as well as prophesies, draw many groping for salvation to these meetings and hold them to a more constructive life course.

Readers will recall from Chapter 3 the importance of peyote to the Huichol and other Aztecan peoples of the Sierra Madre Occidental in Northwest Mexico. Peyote rituals in Mexico go back at least to the Classic period. Mexican rituals have only the most general similarities to the standard ritual underlying the variations of the sects within the Native American Church. That ritual may be derived from southeastern Plains towns (Chiwere and Dhegiha Siouans, Pawnee, and Wichita) that in the nineteenth century developed a secret society possibly originating in a hunting-success ceremony among the Wichita. This type of ritual was also known on the Oklahoma reservations of the Apache, Comanche, Delaware, and Tonkawa. The Tonkawa, a people of the barren desert of northeastern Mexico and southern Texas, are said to have been especially fond of the ritual, and so are possibly the ultimate source from which the Wichita borrowed. The ritual's form was much like that of the post-1885 peyote ritual in the United States, but it used the mescal "bean," the seed and pod of a laurel-like shrub that grows in Tonkawa territory. Mescal "beans" contain potent chemicals that induce a blinding red vision and also vomiting. The red, the color of blood, apparently represented success in hunting and war, and the vomiting was thought to purge the celebrants of all evil matter. During the 1890s, the safer and milder peyote, with its possibility of producing beautiful colored visions, apparently was substituted for the violently uncomfortable mescal, and with the addition of interpretation syncretizing Christianity with common Plains spiritual concepts, peyote became the basis of a religion having general appeal.

The Grass Dance was the immediate ancestor of the modern powwow. The Dhegiha Siouans had sodalities for men with records of valor in war. These men were entitled to wear headdresses made of deer-tail hair stiffly erect, like a helmet crest, and also fanlike feather bustles, called crow belts, over the breechcloth in back. Since the deer-hair "roach" and the crow belt were the prerogatives of proven warriors, a certain aura of taboo surrounded them. The Pawnee had a festival every spring when Thunder was first heard again. In this festival, priests and therapists displayed their spiritual powers through illusionist, shamanistic techniques, dressing in costumes indicating their animal-spirit colleagues and performing such feats as seeming to rip up a victim as a bear would and then bringing the person back to life, or plunging the hand unscathed into a boiling kettle and retrieving a portion of meat. The Oglala Lakota had similar shamanistic performances. Terms for the boiling-kettle trick in the languages of the Dhegiha, Dakota, and Pawnee suggest a single origin and the diffusion of the trick with its name from whoever was the originator to the other nations. The shamans' trick and the ceremonial display of warriors' honors became associated, presumably because success in battle was assumed to indicate spiritual power supporting the warrior. About 1860, the Lakota said, Lakota learned from the Omaha a dance for warriors and the making of deer-hair roaches and crow belts, the regalia of the dancers. Before setting out for war, Lakota in this new version of the soldiers' sodality would perform the dance and also confirm their spiritual power by the boiling-kettle demonstration of imperviousness to harm. (The performers, of course, knew it was a trick, probably aided by rubbing a plant preparation on the hand and arm. The purpose of the demonstration was to convince the literal-minded laypeople of the reality of the intangible power felt by the initiates.) The Lakota added new songs to the dance. In the 1890s, frustrating idleness on the Plains reservations encouraged more frequent meetings for social as well as religious purposes. What Clark Wissler termed the "unnatural proximity" of the various nations in Oklahoma made diffusion of innovations rapid and likely. The Lakotas' "Omaha Dance," known also as the Grass Dance, became very popular among young men throughout the Plains. Its songs, mostly Lakota, were exciting and appealing, its dance, reminiscent of the pawing of an enraged bison bull, vigorous. Its association with warriors gave it a cachet of virility.

In the early reservation period, the Grass Dance retained the formal organization of the soldiers' sodalities and treated the roaches and crow belts somewhat as medicine bundles, restricting the number that could be made and treating them with the respect due to symbols of power. Generosity, a necessary attribute for any leader, was manifest by gifts given to spectators at Grass Dances and by organized efforts by some Grass Dance sodalities to attend to the needy in the community. Thus, a young man on a reservation, made restless by the prohibition of war and the paucity of hunting, could channel his energies into perfecting the showy dancing, participating in the preparations for hosting, and joining displays of generosity in the Grass Dance. The prestige so achieved was pale compared with that of his father in the days of independence, but it was reasonably satisfying.

Because the Grass Dance was avowedly secular, it could be attacked by agents and missionaries only on the grounds that it wasted time and siphoned money into community feasts rather than household savings. If a Grass Dance was held with festivities on the Fourth of July—or July 1, Dominion Day, in Canada—the authorities could hardly object. Grass Dances, popularly known to tourists as "the war dance," were also performed when Indians were paid to put on "ceremonials" at resorts that capitalized on the romantic attraction of "real Indians" nearby, resorts that implied in their advertising that Indians adjacent meant a setting of untouched primeval beauty. Under these

FIGURE 6.12 Plains Cree boy dancing the Grass Dance in a powwow. *(T. Kehoe)*

circumstances, heirloom crow belts were kept wrapped up or sold to museums, and young men vied with one another for ever more gaudy costuming ideas. Oddly, as the feather bustle became a sunburst of brightly dyed turkey feathers around a glinting mirror, as a second feather sunburst was added to be worn on the upper back, and as plumes were added to the roach, the dancer came more and more to resemble the gorgeously plumed noblemen depicted in paintings and sculpture of late prehistoric Mexico. Since the crow belt probably was a version of the Mexican belt ornamentation, preserved in Caddoan culture from late prehistoric contacts and executed in dull-toned feathers for want of parrots and quetzals, the modern brilliance of a male dancer is, in a sense, more authentic than 1890s crow belts.

Along with the secularization of the Grass Dance and the development of spectacular cos-

tumes went the innovation of dance contests, with prizes given to the men who most perfectly executed the Grass Dance according to agreed-upon rules, such as stopping instantly when the drum stopped and having not even the tiniest down fluff become detached from the costume when dancing. The Grass Dance is now often called the War Dance even by Indians in Oklahoma. At Northern Plains powwows, it has become the "men's traditional dance," the focus of contests with first prizes running to hundreds of dollars. Exhibition troupes of Indian dancers do the Grass Dance at world's fairs and tourist festivals in the major cities of Europe as well as North America. (One Dakota champion dancer was inspired to make up a new costume with a turn-of-the-century-style crow belt of brown eagle feathers replicating a Thunderbird's tail, when he saw such a crow belt in the Musée de l'Homme in Paris while touring.) Euro-American Boy Scouts imitate the Grass Dance steps and costume when they "Indian dance," and a few young Euro-American men have become so proficient that they have successfully competed in powwow contests.

In reaction to the semiprofessionalization of the Grass Dance, for which a suitable costume may cost five hundred dollars or more, and in which niceties of posture are as formalized as in ballet, an alternative men's dance, the Gourd Dance, gained popularity among the Plains Indians during the 1970s. The Gourd Dance was an organization of Southern Plains and Prairie warriors in the nineteenth century. The Kiowa and Comanche continued to perform this dance, among others, on their Oklahoma reservation. In 1969, a Ponca American Legion post decided to make the Gourd Dance, which some of the Poncas had learned from Kiowa, Comanche, Cheyenne, or Arapaho friends, their post's special presentation. The performance was well received, and other Indian groups in Oklahoma and Kansas, and then elsewhere in the Plains, took it up. The Gourd Dance uses only a blanket, sash, and bandolier as costume over ordinary street clothes and has an easier, less vigorous step than the Grass Dance. Its songs are considered excellent, too. Thus, older men, less athletic men, and men who can't or won't spend hundreds of dollars on a costume are enthusiastically adopting the Gourd Dance. The spread of the Gourd Dance from powwow to powwow in the 1970s illustrates the vitality of Plains Indian culture today.

The Twentieth Century

The first decade of the twentieth century was a period of routinization of the reservation. The Ghost Dance became a religion for guiding one's life, as Wovoka intended, rather than the magical act for restoring Eden that some of the most unhappy Plains groups had briefly made it. Peyotism spread as an alternative to ethnic traditional religion and Ghost Dance alike, a syncretism with Christianity that affirmed the

validity of Indian experience as no Euro-American Christian churches would. The stick game, or hand game, played by opposing teams for stakes to the tune of lively songs, had been revived under sanction from a Ghost Dance vision and was both a recreation and a declaration of determination to remain Indian. Families were pushed into cabins on their allotments, but paradoxically were encouraged to lease their allotments (agents were pressured by Euro-Americans in the vicinity to make these lands available), which gave the Indians leisure to gather frequently. The Sun Dance was seldom held, and brutally terminated when it was attempted, but private therapeutic rituals could not be regulated, and continued along with traditional secular social dances, some learned from neighboring nations. Government agents recognized whom they would as chiefs, but those nations who had had hereditary chiefly lineages remembered who was entitled to the role. Children were taken from their parents and kept in boarding schools, often for years without a visit home so that they would grow up "civilized," but usually hurried home to the reservation as soon as they were permitted and "returned to the blanket," no longer very fluent in their own language (or in English, either) but sure that they did not want the menial jobs available to them away.

World War I drew into service many young Indian men eager to fight gloriously as their grandfathers had. Ceremonies to bless the soldiers with spiritual protection were revived, and when the war ended, some Sun Dances were held in thanksgiving, a purpose that agents found difficult to damn although they still discouraged the form. The 1920s were a period of relative prosperity for many reservations, crops and cattle thriving in what all but the elderly felt to be their real home. Unhappily, the terrible droughts and consequent dust storms of the early 1930s on the Plains coincided with the international Depression, and hit Plains Indians hard. Plows had wrecked Indian farms as native farming with hoes never did. Crops and cattle failed, and no jobs were to be had in towns. Indian youths were taken into the Civilian Conservation Corps, and some men and women were given Works Project Administration employment, but the physical discouragement of living in the Dust Bowl in the Dirty Thirties, as many on the Plains termed the decade, disheartened people almost as much as the poverty did.

Plains reservations followed most other Indian communities in acceding to the reforms, meant to be democratic and humanitarian, of John Collier in the new Roosevelt administration. Tribal councils and chairmen were elected and discussions begun on ways to improve farming and bring in jobs for the reservations. World War II answered this need, young men again volunteering eagerly for service, and women and men unsuited for the armed forces taking off-reservation employment on farms and in industry, many of them in large cities such as Chicago, Denver, Los Angeles, and Seattle. The termination of wartime employment brought some of the migrants back to the reservations, but many continued to work in the cities, driving hundreds of miles "home" to attend powwows and other celebrations on weekends. Some of these city dwellers left their children to grow up with grandparents on the reservation rather than in the poorer neighborhoods of cities where many Indians were forced to live, through discrimination if not through low income. The Eisenhower administration's policy of relocating Indians to centers of employment, particularly the larger cities, encouraged many young adults on the reservations to try to find jobs outside, but poor education, and again discrimination, doomed most to such unsatisfactory work and living conditions that they returned within a year.

The second half of the twentieth century has seen radical shifts in Plains Indian experiences and expectations. High birth rates and a reduction in mortality, although not nearly to as low a rate as is typical for Euro-Americans, have almost doubled Indian population and have caused especially severe strains on today's young adults, who cannot

possibly all be accommodated with jobs on the reservations. The result has become twofold: stronger pressure to prepare Indian young people for urban employment or for managerial positions on and near reservations, and the rise of younger persons to leadership from which they can work to develop local sovereignty and create new jobs. The consolidated-school movement put these young people, and now their own youngsters, on yellow buses to day schools, many of which integrated them with Euro-American town and rural children. Whether the schools were integrated or not, their curriculum was standard, and was designed to lead to higher education instead of to the peasant skills that the traditional Indian boarding school taught. There has been much decrying of the "irrelevance" of the standard Euro-American curriculum to the daily life of reservation Indians (a problem recognized by the Collier administration in the Bureau of Indian Affairs, which printed several series of appealing primers with facing texts in, for example, Lakota and English, the stories and illustrations portraying Indian children reasonably realistically). Nevertheless, more Indian youth were now encouraged to aspire to the professions, and after many found universities hopelessly bewildering and cold, a number of colleges hired Indians who had managed to complete programs, employing them to counsel Indian students, and opened Indian Studies institutes or programs offering courses on topics of personal or practical interest to Indian students, such as traditional religions, Indian languages, and legal relationships between Indians and government. Sophisticated graduates, a number of whom are also veterans of the armed forces, are asserting the rights and privileges of their nations under the treaties and as citizens of the United States. In Canada, the emphasis is on treaty rights and the principle of confederation, even stronger in Canada than for Indians in the United States, invoked by Canadian Indian organizations to support sovereignty of Indian nations on a par with the sovereignty of provinces.

FROM AN ETHNOGRAPHER'S NOTEBOOKS

1972: Earl Old Person is chairman of the Blackfeet Tribal Council and former executive secretary of the National Congress of American Indians. His reservation, in Montana, is that of the South Peigan division of the Blackfoot. Mr. Old Person, one of the leaders who emerged in the 1960s, is chatting with old friends in his Tribal Council office. He mentions that the previous autumn, he represented American Indians at the gala anniversary celebrated by Iran. The Shah of Iran spent an hour discussing economic programs for grasslands with him, he said. Then he remarked, speaking of the Peigan, "There is a very strong feeling about the land and its use. There is a feeling that capable Indian people should be given first chance at using land, rather than the highest bidder. Many Indians can't bid as high for leases as whites, so they lose out." The conversation turned to recent events on the reservation. "The Medicine Lodge [Sun Dance] is a great sacrifice. Young people put it on this year. They came to the council asking for money to put it on. This takes the meaning out of it. This boy came, saying he had dreams he should put it on. A few years ago, a[nother] group had asked the council for money for a Medicine Lodge. If the sponsor gets someone else to pay for it, the sponsor devoting to it only his time, then the meaning is lost. People participated in the ceremony who had not the right qualifications for the role. People made their bone whistles instead of having them given to them and they giving gifts to the givers."

Jim (not his real name), a South Peigan in his late fifties, is talking in his home: "People are saying this [heavy] rain is due to the Medicine Lodge not being run right. The Medicine Lodge people had been collecting money for their camp all over, Choteau, Cut Bank.... Then the merchants wouldn't contribute to our North American Indian Days powwow, saying they'd already given.

Jim and his wife own a painted tipi, a spiritually powerful symbol of a vision. The tipi originally belonged to her father. Jim described how the old man had become ill with cancer, and had decided, "You folks, just go ahead and take this tipi.' The cover was old, so he bought canvas and spread it out, and made a little smudge [of sweetgrass incense] and prayed for long life and happiness." Jim copied the painted animals on cardboard, part by part, taking the copies to the old man, who could hardly see, until finally the copies met with his approval. Jim's first tries were "too natural," according to the old man. Then Jim drew the animals on the canvas. He made the triangles representing mountains along the bottom with a cardboard, stretching a rope to get a straight line, and used a tin can bottom for the circles representing fallen stars. "It took two days to paint the whole thing. All the while, the old man and old lady sat by, smoking. The deer on the tipi were seen in a vision by the old man, seeking a vision high on a mountain by Cougar Lake. 'You do a lot of hunting. That black deer, he owns everything, all the game. You can kill my young ones. Here is my Old Lady,' said the deer, appearing as a man." Later, Jim's father-in-law had gone up again "and saw the man and the woman too. The woman said to him that though he hadn't seen her in the first vision, she had been sitting back of her man. This would have been back in the 1890s, real old. The old man had slept high on the mountain, where the trees are little, on a ridge just big enough to sleep on. He went up with leaves of sage in his moccasins, a pipe, matches and sweetgrass for a smudge, plus a blanket or two to wear." Insikim ("buffalo stones," which bring prosperity) go with the tipi, but Jim and his wife can't find them anymore.

Later, Jim remarked that their home, a ramshackle place without plumbing, was supposed to be bulldozed, and they were to be given a new government-built house in town, but they opposed this. He and other Blackfoot feel that if one has raised a family of children successfully in a house, it is a place of good luck, and places of good luck should not be destroyed.

Mary (a pseudonym) owns a Thunder Pipe. It had belonged to her mother. The bundle hangs on the wall of the main room of Mary's small house, high enough so it will not be disturbed. Mary remembers her mother had kept"about a hundred tin cups" tied and hung up with the bundle, to serve people who came to its ceremony. That was before paper cups were available. We are invited to the opening of Mary's Pipe bundle. Nearly thirty persons are present, not counting us and Mary and her husband. The sponsor of the ceremony is a man whose brother has just had open-heart surgery. One man who will dance with the holy Pipe has lung cancer. A young Crow man, attending with his parents and sister, is just out of the hospital after a serious illness. A woman here fears for her husband who is a fire-fighter. Mary has consented to go through the bundle-opening ceremony so that these people may be helped by the Almighty through the Pipe.

1975: Joe Douquette, a Plains Cree elder, is talking in the sunny yard of his home: "We don't worship the sun, the moon, the stars, we respect these things. The sun, the moon, the stars, the trees, the lake, the water, these things we don't play with. They were put on earth for us to respect, to show us what is beautiful. The tree [center pole] in the Sun Dance is not worshiped, it is there to lead the people to look up, to look up to God, not down to the ground. The sun always follows the same road, never changes. The seasons change, the months, but the sun never changes his direction, his road. This is the direction they go in the dances. The white people dance any way, but the Indians respect their dances, they always go in the same direction [as the sun]."

1973: Robert (not his real name), a Santee Dakota man in his fifties, is talking in our camp at the end of Standing Buffalo Reserve in Saskatchewan, one of several given by the Canadian government to bands of Sioux refugees from the 1862 Minnesota uprising: "'Medicine bags' usually went from father to son, or grandson or brother's son. 'Born to be a medicine man' means a child will be 'groomed,' then for four or five years go through regular sweat-lodge baths, fasting, and so on. To be a medicine man one must work one's way up through the grades. The organization is tightly controlled; just anyone cannot decide to be a medicine man. One who gains power only for himself is not as popular as one who gains power for the tribal benefit. ('Grooming' is old people sitting around smoking the pipe and talking, always positively, of good things—very seldom on negative topics. Young people would sit and listen and thus get indoctrinated. My father would come at noon and sit with the family—ten children—and talk thus, almost always on positive, good things.)
    "Chieftainship is hereditary [among the Dakota], to the chief's son, of if there is no son, to son-in-law or nephew. This keeps politics separate from religion. A chief's child learns [public] speaking and such, which a commoner child does not learn. The Election Act has made chiefs elective, but Alec Buffalo's great-great-grandfather was a chief who signed the treaty in Minnesota, Alec's forefathers for five generations, since 1851, have been chiefs, now Alec is the present Standing Buffalo Reserve chief. Standing Buffalo was Alec's grandfather."

Gloria (a pseudonym), a Plains Cree aged about forty, was brought up in a boarding school and later employed by the Indian Affairs Branch. We are in her office. "Next summer I hope to be working out of the Fort Qu'Appelle office. I asked for a transfer because I want to get back to the spiritualism of the reserves. City life is incompatible with the spiritualism of Indians—the Indian is close to nature.

"My girlfriend and I attended a Sun Dance. We wanted to be initiated [participate within the Lodge], so we fasted all day. We were prayed over by the old-man leader. He spoke Cree so fast I could catch only a few words although I speak Cree. The spirits were supposed to be talking through him. My friend and I were urged to join the other women in praying at the end of the day. I was surprised at how the women wept with emotion. (I asked; they say emotion was why they wept.)

"My husband was brought up 'white man' off the reserve. He was very aggressive, a powerful man; he had greatness [an office in a national Indian organization], but the last couple of years he has lost power. Now he is unemployed; we live on my earnings. Nothing he tries seems to succeed. Something is affecting him adversely from the spirits. Some time ago, he was given a bear claw and visited a medicine man, who prayed over him and the bear claw, then told him that if things don't improve he should return to him. Things haven't improved, but he hasn't returned. I hope living on a reserve will bring him to Indian spiritualism.

"Someday I hope to have a vision and be granted wisdom. I know a young man who was advised by a medicine man to fast for four days out in the wilderness to get a vision. I don't know whether that young man did, but I know many still do but don't talk about it. But I'd be too afraid to try it, out alone at night in the wilderness.

"There is a rebirth of spiritualism among Indians—not that it ever really did die, although some thought so. But morals—drugs, divorces—are at a low point among Indians, as among others."

Three days later, we are at the File Hills Powwow on Starblanket Reserve, a Plains Cree reserve near Standing Buffalo in the Fort Qu'Appelle Agency district. This is a typical Northern Plains powwow, on a reserve headed by a vigorous and able young man, Noel Starblanket, who will before long be elected president of the National Indian Brotherhood of Canada. What catches our eye? The Royal Canadian Mounted Police constable in scarlet dress uniform dutifully paying a dollar admission as a non-Indian, then presenting a trophy to the winner of one of the men's dance competitions? The capable, confident officers of the Federation of Saskatchewan Indians opening the powwow? The beaming young couple, married yesterday, with their bridal party, all in their wedding formals, in procession around the arena to an honoring song sung by one of the"drums"? John Goodwill from Standing Buffalo, in his handsome beaded buckskin suit and eagle-feather bonnet, acting as M.C. and interjecting some Sioux whoops into this Cree-sponsored event? What really caught our eye was the clown, a large man in a shapeless woman's dress, long fake braids hanging from a round pink skullcap, false nose with blue false ears attached, face painted red with broad silver and blue mouth, a sign flapping over his buttocks. In one hand he carries an eagle-feather ceremonial fan, in the other a short horse-tail whip. He dances slowly, peering at the audience. He is a ritual clown, a strange creature who will gently whip laggard dancers so they do not forget that in the dance they show respect to the Almighty that enables us to live.

FIGURE 6.13 Ceremonial clown in Plains Cree powwow. *(T. Kehoe)*

Plains reservations have contributed a substantial proportion of the Indians in the larger cities. (Plains reservations include, of course, those of the former Eastern and Midwestern peoples removed in the nineteenth century to Kansas and Oklahoma.) The proximity of the different peoples in and near Oklahoma, their mixing in the boarding schools, their friendships during wartime and subsequent relocations facilitated interethnic marriages producing homes in which English was usually spoken and neither parent's native tradition was strongly maintained. Even when both parents are from the same ethnic group, the older Indian attitude that middle-aged and elderly adults are the ones properly concerned with spiritual and historical knowledge, while younger people are too busy with growing families and obtaining a livelihood,

has left youngsters in the city, seeing their grandparents on the reservation only on visits, untutored in their tradition.

During the later 1960s, the flowering of the "counter-culture" of younger Americans rejecting military involvement, money grubbing, impersonalization, pollution, and similar perceived consequences of "the Establishment way" promoted a supposed American Indian ethic as one alternative. The Indian was held to be satisfied with subsistence rather than determined to accumulate goods, communal, respecting individuals, a conservationist—a mythic figure embodying all the traits opposite to those decried in powerful Euro-Americans. Like those in the counter-culture, the Indian was an underdog. Young urban Indians were attracted to this positive image of their background. They were also attracted to the excitement and heady camaraderie of militant protest actions.

In 1968, a core group of angry Chippewa in Minneapolis, which is unusual among larger cities in that most of its Indian residents are concentrated in an Indian ghetto neighborhood, organized to force city, state, and federal governments to improve services to this Indian neighborhood and cease discriminatory practices or benign neglect. Their goals and tactics coalesced with those of Indian protests elsewhere, such as those of the Akwesasne Mohawk, and the national American Indian Movement was formed in 1968, meeting in Minneapolis. As the movement grew, it forged its variant of the counter-culture image of the Indian, heavily colored by the Lakota stereotype first popularized in the collaboration of Buffalo Bill Cody and Sitting Bull. This is not entirely inappropriate, since the Lakota are the largest group of Plains Indians and one of the largest Indian groups in North America, second only to Navajo in the United States. Nevertheless, the image of what it means to be Indian carried by many AIM members and sympathizers could be a source of conflict when the AIM attempted to organize on non-Lakota reservations. (Two young AIM men had poor success on the Blackfeet Reservation in 1972. They wore their hair in two braids, Blackfoot woman's style. Real men, among the Blackfoot, wear three braids.) A generalized, simplified image readily assimilated by newcomers promotes unity in AIM but disturbs proud members of non-Lakota groups who see the stereotype threatening to negate their own ethnic heritages.

AIM capitalized upon Plains history by joining a major confrontation between Oglala and the United States government at Wounded Knee. The site of the 1890 massacre had become a hamlet containing the Catholic mission near which Big Foot's band had temporarily camped, Episcopal and Church of God missions, and a large "trading post" that sold groceries to local Indians and souvenirs to tourists led to the crossroads by signs on major highways advertising "Mass Burial Grave."

Although the "trading post" was on the Pine Ridge Reservation, it was owned and operated by Euro-Americans, as were the missions. Late in 1972, AIM had been asked by Pine Ridge Oglala disputing the policies of recently elected Tribal Chairman Richard Wilson to help them protest what they believed to be collusion between Wilson and non-Indian businessmen who would profit from contracts for government-financed housing on the reservation. The housing designed for Pine Ridge and the adjacent Rosebud reservations, both Lakota, had been a sore point for several years; government codes required that the homes be built in clusters on sewer and water lines, but the Lakota wanted homes scattered in open hamlets, each house just within hailing distance of its neighbors, as had become traditional on the reservation. AIM had been on Pine Ridge earlier in 1972 to force action against two young Euro-American men who had roughed up and humiliated a middle-aged Oglala man, Raymond Yellow Thunder. Yellow Thunder died as a result of the beating, but the only charge filed had been manslaughter, the murderers' excuse that all had been drinking. Incidents similar to the 1972 murder had occurred previously, and many Oglala wanted a harsher prosecution of the murderers to lessen the likelihood of recurrences. AIM had also, in November 1972, staged a much-publicized trashing of the Bureau of Indian Affairs headquarters in Washington, D.C., at the conclusion of a prolonged march called the Trail of Broken Treaties. Tribal Chairman Wilson was unwilling to tolerate local challenges to his administration or to allow AIM to protest on his domain. AIM alleges that his stiff opposition to their faction was fed by Euro-Americans who claimed AIM to be a "Communist-front" organization. Wilson called in armed FBI investigators and U.S. Marshals to protect his office in the village of Pine Ridge. Dissident Lakota and their AIM visitors then decided to stage a symbolic stand at Wounded Knee.

The 1973 Wounded Knee confrontation lasted from late February to mid-May. For seventy-one days, Russell Means, an Oglala who was a national leader in AIM, and AIM organizers from other Indian nations orchestrated a highly visible drama pitting roughly two hundred and fifty Indians— about the number massacred in 1890—against a besieging ring of United States forces. Supporters from other Indian groups such as Akwesasne and other Iroquois, and from non-Indian civil-rights organizations, including blacks as disparate as Angela Davis and Ralph Abernathy, came to Wounded Knee to demonstrate their espousal of the AIM position, while many who could not travel to South Dakota, including about two thousand North Carolina Lumbee, paraded elsewhere to indicate support. The approximately fifty AIM members who had come to Wounded Knee thought of themselves as a warriors' society patterned on the nineteenth-century sodalities, comrades defending their women, children, and elderly at the request of three Oglala matrons. (The three Pine Ridge women who had sought AIM's aid in ousting Wilson in fact continued to play leading roles at Wounded Knee. Many other women were active defenders of the besieged community, although the military experience of a number of the men in Vietnam made them the obvious choice to plan and execute tactics during the siege.) Attempting to conform to the earlier sodalities, the Lakota and AIM allies invoked spiritual power through Leonard Crow Dog, a spiritual leader from Rosebud Reservation. At one point during the siege, Crow Dog led a Ghost Dance ritual. The final demands of the Wounded Knee protestors were twentieth-century. They insisted that the government should honor the 1868 treaty the Lakota had made, the treaty that made all of western South Dakota a Sioux reservation. Their position on the intent of the treaty was that the Lakota should be governed by their several band leaders—the "traditional chiefs," in their words—and that Richard Wilson and the Tribal Council elected under the 1934 Indian Reorganization Act could not function as a legitimate Lakota government.

The siege was finally lifted and the protestors dispersed with promises to discuss their demands, although the government representatives negotiating with spokespeople from Wounded Knee consistently reminded the Indians that Washington did not and would not recognize the "Independent Oglala Nation" they had declared, that Washington would not hold provisions of the 1868 treaty sacrosanct if they had been overridden by later actions and statutes, and that only Congress in session had the power to change statutes such as the Indian Reorganization Act. In plain words, Richard Wilson remained the man Washington recognized at Pine Ridge. Little was accomplished for the Oglala who opposed Wilson. Much was accomplished, on a broad canvas, for AIM. National television, both regular and radical newspapers and magazines, and the international news services had featured the Indians' protest for over two months. Coming only a little more than a year after Dee Brown's catchily titled *Bury My Heart at Wounded Knee* had been on the bestseller lists, the AIM "media event" reawakened popular sympathy for the plight of the Indian. Street-smart urban Indians had assaulted the echelons of power and hacked out a base from which the disaffected could contend with all who had seemed to deny them status and a living decent by American standards, whether these oppressors were reservation cliques, the Bureau of Indian Affairs, or city agencies.

Out of the limelight, Plains Indian communities have been aggressively attempting to climb out of the low place they occupy in the statistics of life expectancy, housing, education, and employment. Many reservations seek out light industry, from pencils to mobile homes to electronics assembly, although the isolation of most reservations has made it difficult for them to industrialize. Tribes are demanding better royalties and more control over the exploitation of oil, soft coal, and other minerals under reservations. Here, the problem is often to upset long-standing agreements between corporations and a few "mixed-blood" families fluent in business dealings, so that the majority of the people can derive more benefit from the tribal income. Encouraged by President Nixon's 1970 speech to Congress stating, "Indians can become independent of Federal control without being cut off from Federal concern and Federal support," twenty-six Northern Plains tribes formed the Native American Natural Resources Development Federation. Within a year, the organization was succeeded by CERT—Council of Energy Resource Tribes—and encompassed Southwestern and Northwestern tribes in addition to the Plains and Great Basin reservations with oil or coal. Water rights, both in terms of hydroelectric energy and for irrigation, uranium mining, and the polluting effects of power plants, especially the coal-fired one built on Navajo land to supply distant Southwestern cities, were considered part of the CERT agenda. CERT's intent was to examine critically the leases through which non-Indian corporations took energy from the reservations, turning these contracts around from the ridiculously low royalties and lack of local control permitted by the Bureau of Indian Affairs. Indian control, reasonable recompense, and proper financial accounting should be initiated. Ultimately, CERT tribes hoped not only to guard their lands and mineral resources from damaging exploitation but to gain income to broaden reservation economies.

Cattle ranching and modern wheat farming have been developed on most reservations, but although these are the agricultural endeavors best suited to the Plains, neither can support large numbers of persons on limited land. The huge Army Corps of Engineers projects from the 1930s to the 1960s to control and change the Missouri River Basin was supposed to bring irrigation and electrification to many Indian reservations from Montana and Wyoming through the Dakotas. Very little of the expected agricultural benefits materialized; very much of the Dakota reservations' best river bottomlands, with their rich soil, timber, water, and pleasant homesites, disappeared under the big reservoirs apparently aimed primarily at providing recreation to a general public able to

afford power boats and water-skis. Ecologists have been seriously recommending restocking Plains reservations with bison, better suited to the range. The Crows have developed a large herd on their Montana reservation. Mixed bison-beef cattle breeds promise easier handling than bison, which cannot be really domesticated, and lean, flavorful, marketable meat. Making life on the reservation viable for the many who prefer to remain close to their kin, their language, and special customs rather than conform to Euro-American urban patterns is a challenge accepted by leaders throughout the Plains.

Against the discouragement of poverty and powerlessness, one modern institution, the pow-wow, has become a center around which Indians of every age and political leaning can gather. Pow-wows are really a phenomenon of the second half of the twentieth century. The general form and content go back to nineteenth-century summer encampments and early twentieth-century Fourth-of-July or annual-fair celebrations. Since the 1950s, these have been linked into circuits, each reservation scheduling its powwow at the same weekend each summer, if possible, so that people can plan to attend one after another in succession, from June into early September. The host reservation prepares a large campground, sets up a canvas "big top" or arena with bleachers, arranges for basic "rations" of meat, bread, and perhaps fruit or canned goods to be distributed free to Indian families, and leases space to soft-drink entrepreneurs and amusement-ride proprietors. A thousand or more people usually camp for several days at a powwow. Non-Indian spectators are admitted for a fee to the bleachers, although a few Euro-American families or young people who are friends of the host group often camp with the crowd. Formal events, beginning in the afternoon and lasting until midnight or later in the arena, consist of Indian social dancing, alternating with contests for men's and women's "traditional" and "fancy" dancing, and giveaways to honor individuals in the community recently deceased or to be noted for prestigious

FIGURE 6.14 Honoring procession for recently deceased young man (his photo is being carried), Blackfoot powwow. *(T. Kehoe)*

accomplishments, and to demonstrate the host group's appreciation of visitors from other reservations. Honoring giveaways begin with the honored person's family parading around the arena as an honoring song is sung, and then standing in a receiving line along one side of the arena while the master of ceremonies calls out from the announcer's booth the names of persons who should come up to take gifts from the pile brought in. Gifts are often blankets and sheets, dollar and five-dollar bills, and sometimes shirts. Very special friends are given hand-sewn quilts. Visitors from other reservations may expect buckskin-fringed or beaded jackets or vests or other examples of the host group's crafts. The giveaway is considered to be the purest of all Indian activities, uniquely Indian in its use of generosity to enhance the reputation of the honored person, a cogent contrast to the Euro-American custom of giving gifts *to* the person. Families' giveaways are financed by the pooled resources of the family, and many amount to several thousand dollars. Gifts to visitors from other reservations are usually donated by members of the host group. The money for prizes, preparing the camp, buying the rations, paying the M.C. and the "drums" (groups of singers, about six or eight around a large bass drum) who provide the music for the dances and honoring songs, is taken from

FIGURE 6.15 Giveaway during Plains Cree powwow. The young man with the bullhorn (right center) calls out names of people to whom the family of the honored person wishes to give gifts. *(T. Kehoe)*

tribal funds or the proceeds from leases and spectators' fees. This cash is administered by a hardworking committee in which, as the M.C. usually reiterates, "no one makes any money."

The purpose of a powwow is fun in the Indian manner: visiting friends and making new acquaintances, enjoying a stick game (also called hand game), and dancing and listening to this year's hit parade of songs in the Plains Indian musical style, presented by a series of "drums" who have been practicing together all year, composing some songs and picking up others as they travel the circuit. The powwows seem to be the answer to the dilemma of being Indian but speaking English and going to Euro-American schools or employment. At the powwow, one is immersed in a crowd of Indians, hears the drumbeats and the distinctive Plains singing, sees the brilliant Grass Dance costumes, and eats chunks of beef and frybread. For three days, one feels totally Indian through and

through. Then, with social identity reinforced in a most pleasurable way, one can go back to the other world relaxed and secure, remembering that there is more than clocks and shoving and TV. And for many, there will be visits to the reservation other weekends, for a Sun Dance or Pipe-bundle opening or shaman's therapy. Plains culture lives.

SUMMARY

The Prairie-Plains is the broad central region of North America, from the northern Mississippi Valley-western Great Lakes to the Rockies, in which open grasslands predominate. Herds of bison formed the principal resource for humans in the region until 1885, and native societies in the region adapted to the bison-based economic and social-structure pattern characteristic of the Plains since the late Pleistocene epoch.

FIGURE 6.16 Stick game, Blackfoot powwow. Team on the right is passing a small marked piece between their hands while some drum and sing (this team drums with sticks on the board before them). Opposing team must guess which hand of which person has the marked piece. Decorated upright rods in the ground beside the board, right center, are tallies on gambling. *(T. Kehoe)*

Before European entrance, there were two types of Plains-Prairie cultures. One, on the Midwestern prairies and, after A.D.1150, along the Missouri Valley as far as central North Dakota, combined maize, squash, beans, and sunflower cultivation with bison hunting. This was a basic northern Midwestern pattern differing from Eastern Woodland cultures of the Ohio Valley and Northeast only in that a greater percentage of bison was available compared to deer; the domination of deer as a meat source shifts to a domination of bison as one moves west toward the grasslands. The pattern characterized the Late Woodland/Mississippian period, from about A.D. 800 to European incursions; the Middle Woodland period of the preceding thousand years was similar but raised little maize, cultivating instead the indigenous temperate-zone grains. On the northern border of maize agriculture

in the Midwest, near the present Canadian-U.S. boundary, wild rice substituted for maize. Historically, the town-dwelling societies of the Prairie and Plains river valleys spent spring-planting and late summer-harvest seasons in their villages of sod-covered houses, then trekked out of their river-valley communities to live in tipis, hunting bison on the open grasslands. The Mandan, Hidatsa, Arikara, Pawnee, and Wichita are the best known of these peoples.

The other pattern was one of year-round nomadic life in tipis, west and north of the sector in which maize cultivation is profitable. The principal means of procuring the staple, bison, was to lead a herd into a corral hidden under a bluff or in a ravine, where the animals could be slaughtered and the meat prepared and dried for storage. The Blackfoot, Gros Ventres, Crow, Kiowa, Shoshoni, and probably Apacheans lived by this pattern before European contact. Trade was conducted between groups at summer rendezvous and at the villages.

After A.D. 1600, Indians began to take horses from Spanish ranches in New Mexico. Horses made possible the accumulation of more goods, from large tipis, food stores, and dress clothes to pemmican and hides to trade. In the eighteenth century, the use of horses became common throughout the Plains, and a lucrative market developed to supply horses to English and French colonies in the Southeast, and, in the nineteenth century, to traders and emigrants in the West. At the same time, Eastern nations were being displaced from their homelands and were resettling on the prairie. Some prairie nations, such as the Cheyenne and Sioux, gave up their agricultural villages in order to become full-time bison hunters farther west. On the High Plains, westward-moving prairie groups met eastward-expanding Numic speakers—Shoshoni and Comanche.

The nineteenth century was one of great population loss, from heavy warfare and from epidemics. Southeastern and then Midwestern Indian nations removed after 1830 to the frontier took hunting and horse-pasture lands needed by the indigenous nations and those who had moved onto the Plains a generation or two previously. By mid-century, immigration by Euro-American colonists and traders and the establishment of a number of military posts put even greater pressure on the limited resources of the Plains. After 1868, the transcontinental railroad made bulk transport economical, encouraging the slaughtering of bison for the hides alone. Droughts of the 1870s were the final problem, causing the failure of crops planted by many Indian nations and weakening the few remaining bison herds. After 1885, no more wild bison herds could be found. The economy of the Indian nations of the Plains was totally shattered, and all who had previously resisted relocation were forced to move to reservations, where they tried to survive on government rations that were often inadequate. Under these drastically changed conditions, and with agents and missionaries avidly forbidding the practice of native religions, new religions appeared in the 1890s. The foremost of these were the Ghost Dance, taught by the Nevada Paiute Wovoka (Jack Wilson), and rituals using peyote as a sacrament. Both the Ghost Dance and peyote religions taught accommodation to Euro-American patterns while affirming the value and validity of the Indian experience and Indian beliefs.

Indians on the Plains—where many Eastern nations also have reservations—were just beginning to enjoy at least the prospect of minimal prosperity when the combination of the Depression and the Dust Bowl hit in the early 1930s. Government relief measures prepared some Plains Indians for employment off the economically inadequate reservations, and World War II drew greater numbers away, into the armed services and into defense industries in cities. The trend toward off-reservation employment continued after the war, fed by a high rate of population increase among Indians. Indians from Plains reservations have been leaders in national Indian organizations, and the historic nomads' culture has become the stereotype for all Indians.

RECOMMENDED READING

Deloria, Ella Cara. 1988 *Waterlily.* Deloria was a Lakota who worked with Franz Boas at Columbia University but decided to return to South Dakota to work directly for her own people. Considered too novelistic and never published until after Deloria's death, the book oriented around the heroine Waterlily is a vivid account of early nineteenth-century Lakota life.

DeMallie, Raymond J., ed. 1984 *The Sixth Grandfather: Black Elk's Teachings Given to John G. Neihardt.* Lincoln: University of Nebraska Press. The text of *Black Elk Speaks,* treasured by thousands as an "Indian Bible," is here given as Nick Black Elk actually dictated it, as well as in the literary version prepared by writer Neihardt, and a fascinating life of Black

Elk—Oglala holy man, European traveler, and Catholic catechist—is added.

Grobsmith, Eleanor. 1981 *Lakota of the Rosebud: A Contemporary Ethnography*. Oglala Lakota life on the reservation, 1970s.

Jones, David E. 1972 *Sanapia, Comanche Medicine Woman*. Prospect Heights, Ill.: Waveland Press.

Kehoe, Alice Beck. 1989 *The Ghost Dance: Ethnohistory and Revitalization*. New York: Holt, Rinehart and Winston. Covers the Ghost Dance and both the Wounded Knee events, the 1890 massacre and the 1973 siege. The second part of the book contrasts several social-science interpretations of the historical data.

Marriott, Alice. 1952 *Greener Fields*. Garden City, N.Y.: Doubleday. A vivid first-person account of an ethnologist among the Kiowas in the 1930s. (1945, *The Ten Grandmothers,* Norman: University of Oklahoma Press; a Kiowa woman's life, is also excellent.)

McFee, Malcolm. 1972 *Modern Blackfeet*. Prospect Heights, Ill.: Waveland Press.

Momaday, N. Scott. 1969 *The Way to Rainy Mountain*. Albuquerque: University of New Mexico Press.

Mooney, James. 1973 [1896] *The Ghost-Dance Religion and Wounded Knee*. New York: Dover Publications. Mooney interviewed Wovoka in his wickiup and the Wounded Knee massacre observers, and then compared the 1890 prophet and events with other prophets, Indian and non-Indian. A classic, and exciting.

Parsons, Elsie Clews, ed. 1967 [1922] *American Indian Life*. Lincoln: University of Nebraska Press.

Ritzenthaler, Robert E., and Pat Ritzenthaler.1991 [1983] *The Woodland Indians of the Western Great Lakes*. Prospect Heights, Ill.: Waveland Press.

Wax, Murray L., Rosalie Wax, and Robert V. Dumont, Jr. 1991 (reissue) *Formal Education in an American Indian Community*. Prospect Heights, Ill.: Waveland Press. A landmark study of a Lakota school, emphasizing the dominant influence of the peer group.

Wedel, Waldo R. 1961 *Prehistoric Man on the Great Plains*. Norman: University of Oklahoma Press. Somewhat dated but the fullest introduction to Plains archaeology.

Wilson, Gilbert L. 1981[1927] *Waheenee*. The life of Maxidiwiac, "Buffalo Bird Woman," a Hidatsa born in the mid-nineteenth century, was written by anthropologist Wilson to describe the customs and experiences of Hidatsa in the early reservation period.

Maxidiwiac was the mother of Goodbird, whose life "as told to" Wilson was also published *(Goodbird the Indian* by Edward Goodbird, 1985[1914], Minnesota Historical Society Press). Both biographies are wonderfully illustrated in *The Way to Independence,* by Carolyn Gilman and Mary Jane Schneider (Minnesota Historical Society, 1987), with hundreds of photographs and drawings showing the neglected period when people like Maxidiwiac and her brother Wolf Chief created a way of life still Indian though no longer focused on bison; Wolf Chief operated a local general store.

SOURCES FOR THE FIRST EDITION

Akwesasne Notes. 1974 *Voices from Wounded Knee*. Rooseveltown, N.Y.: The Mohawk Nation.

Albers, Patricia C. 1978 Pluralism in the Native Plains: 1670–1870. Manuscript, forthcoming: The Santee (Eastern Dakota). In R. DeMallie (ed.).*Handbook of North American Indians.* Washington, D.C.: Smithsonian Institution Press.

Baird, W. David. 1972 *The Osage People*. Phoenix: Indian Tribal Series.

Bataille, Gretchen M., David M. Gradwhol, and Charles L.P. Silet, eds. 1978 *The Worlds Between Two Rivers*. Ames: Iowa State University Press.

Bowers, Alfred W. 1965 *Hidatsa Social and Ceremonial Organization*. Washington, D.C.: Smithsonian Institution, Bureau of American Ethnology, Bulletin 194.

Bruner, Edward M. 1961 Mandan. In E. H. Spicer (ed.). *Perspectives in American Indian Culture Change.* Chicago: University of Chicago Press, pp. 187–277.

Butler, B. Robert. 1978 *A Guide to Understanding Idaho Archaeology: The Upper Snake and Salmon River Country*. Pocatello: Idaho Museum of Natural History.

Cash, Joseph H. 1976 *The Potawatomi People (Citizen Band)*. Phoenix: Indian Tribal Series.

Cash, Joseph H., and Gerald W. Wolff. 1975 *The Ponca People*. Phoenix: Indian Tribal Series.

Clifton, James A. 1977 *The Prairie People*. Lawrence: Regents Press of Kansas.

Collins, Michael B. 1971 A Review of Llano Estacado Archaeology and Ethnohistory. *Plains Anthropologist* 16:85–104.

Corrigan, Samuel W. 1970 The Plains Indian Powwow:

Cultural Integration in Manitoba and Saskatchewan. *Anthropologica* 12:253–277.

Dempsey, Hugh A. 1972 *Crowfoot.* Edmonton: Hurtig Publishers.

Denig, Edwin Thompson. 1953 *Of the Crow Nation.* Washington, D.C.: Smithsonian Institution, Bureau of American Ethnology, Bulletin 151, Anthropological Paper 33.

Edmunds, R. David. 1976 *The Otoe-Missouria People.* Phoenix: Indian Tribal Series.

Ewers, John C. 1955 *The Horse in Blackfoot Indian Culture.* Washington, D.C.: Smithsonian Institution, Bureau of American Ethnology, Bulletin 159.

———— 1958 *The Blackfeet.* Norman: University of Oklahoma Press.

Flannery, Regina. 1953 *The Gros Ventres of Montana.* Washington, D.C.: Catholic University of America Press.

Fletcher, Alice C., and Francis La Flesche. 1972 [1911] *The Omaha Tribe.* Lincoln: University of Nebraska Press.

Frideres, James S. 1974 *Canada's Indians.* Scarborough, Ont.: Prentice-Hall of Canada.

Gearing, Frederick O. 1970 *The Face of the Fox.* Chicago: Aldine Publishing.

Grinnell, George Bird. 1972 [1923] *The Cheyenne Indians.* Lincoln: University of Nebraska Press.

Hickerson, Harold. 1962 *The Southwestern Chippewa.* Menasha, Wis.: American Anthropological Association, Memoir 92.

Hilger, M. Inez. 1952 *Arapaho Child Life and Its Cultural Background.* Washington, D.C.: Smithsonian Institution, Bureau of American Ethnology, Bulletin 148.

Hittman, Michael. 1973 The 1870 Ghost Dance at the Walker River Reservation: A Reconstruction. *Ethnohistory* 20:247–278.

Hlady, Walter M., ed. 1970 *Ten Thousand Years.* Altona: Manitoba Archaeological Society.

Hodge, Frederick Webb. 1910 *Handbook of American Indians.* Washington, D.C.: Smithsonian Institution, Bureau of American Ethnology, Bulletin 30.

Hodge, William H. 1973 Ethnicity as a Factor in Modern American Indian Migration: A Winnebago Case Study with References to Other Indian Situations. Paper given at the Ninth International Congress of Anthropological and Ethnological Sciences, Chicago, 1973.

Howard, James H. 1956 An Oto-Omaha Peyote Ritual. *Southwestern Journal of Anthropology* 12:432–436.

———— 1957 The Mescal Bean Cult of the Central and Southern Plains: An Ancestor of the Peyote Cult? *American Anthropologist* 59:75–87.

———— 1961 The Identity and Demography of the Plains-Ojibwa. *Plains Anthropologist* 6:171–178.

———— 1965 *The Ponca Tribe.* Washington, D.C.: Smithsonian Institution, Bureau of American Ethnology, Bulletin 195.

———— 1974 The Culture and Acculturation of the Canadian Dakota. Ms., Ottawa: Canadian Ethnology Service. (Published 1984 as *The Canadian Sioux,* University of Nebraska Press, Lincoln.)

———— 1976 The Plains Gourd Dance as a Revitalization Movement. *American Ethnologist* 3:243–259.

———— 1976 Yanktonai Ethnohistory and the John K. Bear Winter Count. *Plains Anthropologist,* Memoir 11.

Hundley, Norris, Jr., ed. 1974 *The American Indian.* Santa Barbara: American Bibliographical Center, Clio Press.

Jablow, Joseph. 1951 *The Cheyenne in Plains Indian Trade Relations 1795–1840.* New York: J.J. Augustin, Monographs of the American Ethnological Society, 19.

Johnson, Elden, ed. 1974 *Aspects of Upper Great Lakes Anthropology.* St. Paul: Minnesota Historical Society.

Kaye, Barry, and D.W. Moodie. 1978 The Psoralea Food Resource of the Northern Plains. *Plains Anthropologist* 23:329–336.

Kehoe, Alice B. 1964 The Ghost Dance Religion in Saskatchewan: A Functional Analysis. Ph.D. dissertation, Harvard University.

———— 1970 The Function of Ceremonial Sexual Intercourse Among the Northern Plains Indians. *Plains Anthropologist* 15:99–103.

———— 1976 Old Woman Had Great Power. *Western Canadian Journal of Anthropology* 6:68–76.

Kehoe, Thomas F. 1973 *The Gull Lake Site.* Milwaukee: Milwaukee Public Museum.

Kemnitzer, Luis S. 1976 Structure, Content, and Cultural Meaning of Yuwipi: A Modern Lakota Healing Ritual. *American Ethnologist* 3:261–280.

Kenner, Charles L. 1969 *A History of New Mexico-Plains Indian Relations.* Norman: University of Oklahoma Press.

La Barre, Weston. 1938 *The Peyote Cult.* New Haven: Yale University Press.

Lehmer, Donald J. 1966 *The Fire Heart Creek Site.* Lincoln, Neb.: Smithsonian Institution, River Basin Surveys.

Lesser, Alexander. 1978 [1933] *The Pawnee Ghost Dance Hand Game*. Madison: University of Wisconsin Press.

Lowie, Robert H. 1916 Plains Indian Age-Societies: Historical and Comparative Summary. New York: American Museum of Natural History, Anthropological Papers 11, Pt. 13.

———— 1917 Notes on the Social Organization and Customs of the Mandan, Hidatsa, and Crow Indians. New York: American Museum of Natural History, Anthropological Papers, 21, Pt. 1.

Madsen, David B., and Michael S. Berry. 1975 A Reassessment of Northeastern Great Basin Prehistory. *American Antiquity* 40:391–405.

Maestas, John R. 1976 *Contemporary Native American Address*. Provo: Brigham Young University.

Mallory, Oscar L. 1979 One Man's Bread—Another Man's Weeds. *Saskatchewan Archaeology Newsletter* 54(1):15–21.

Mayhall, Mildred P. 1962 *The Kiowas*. Norman: University of Oklahoma Press.

Meyer, Roy W. 1967 *History of the Santee Sioux*. Lincoln: University of Nebraska Press.

———— 1977 *The Village Indians of the Upper Missouri*. Lincoln: University of Nebraska Press.

Miner, H. Craig. 1976 *The Corporation and the Indian*. Columbia: University of Missouri Press.

Momaday, N. Scott. 1969 *The Way to Rainy Mountain*. Albuquerque: University of New Mexico Press.

Neuman, Robert W. 1975 *The Sonota Complex and Associated Sites on the Northern Great Plains*. Lincoln: Nebraska State Historical Society.

Nurge, Ethel, ed. 1970 *The Modern Sioux*. Lincoln: University of Nebraska Press.

Ray, Arthur J. 1974 *Indians in the Fur Trade*. Toronto: University of Toronto Press.

Reeves, Brian. 1973 The Concept of an Altithermal Cultural Hiatus in Northern Plains Prehistory. *American Anthropologist* 75:1221–1253.

Reid, Kenneth C. 1977 Psoralea Esculenta as a Prairie Resource: An Ethnographic Appraisal. *Plains Anthropologist* 22:321–327.

Ridington, Robin. 1978 *Swan People: A Study of the Dunne-za Prophet Dance*. Ottawa: National Museums of Canada, National Museum of Man Mercury Series, Canadian Ethnology Service, Paper 38.

Ritzenthaler, Robert E., and Frederick A. Peterson. 1956. *The Mexican Kickapoo Indians*. Milwaukee. Milwaukee Public Musuem.

Schlesier, Karl H. 1974 Action Anthropology and the Southern Cheyenne. *Current Anthropology* 15:277–299.

Schusky, Ernest L. 1975 *The Forgotten Sioux*. Chicago: Nelson-Hall.

Secoy, Frank Raymond. 1953 *Changing Military Patterns on the Great Plains*. New York: J. J. Augustin, Monographs of the American Ethnological Society, 21.

Shames, Deborah, ed. 1972 *Freedom with Reservation*. Madison: National Committee to Save the Menominee People and Forests.

Sharrock, Susan R. 1974 Crees, Cree-Assiniboines, and Assiniboines: Interethnic Social Organization on the Far Northern Plains. *Ethnohistory* 21:95–122.

Shimkin, D.B. 1942 Dynamics of Recent Wind River Shoshone History. *American Anthropologist* 44:461–463.

Slotkin, J.S. 1957 *The Menomini Powwow*. Milwaukee: Milwaukee Public Museum.

Stewart, Omer C. 1972 [1961] The Native American Church and the Law. In D.E. Walker, Jr. (ed.). *The Emergent Native Americans*. Boston: Little, Brown, pp. 382–397.

Syms, E. Leigh. 1977 Cultural Ecology and Ecological Dynamics of the Ceramic Period in Southwestern Manitoba. *Plains Anthropologist,* Memoir 12.

Taylor, John F. 1977 Sociocultural Effects of Epidemics on the Northern Plains: 1734–1850. *Western Canadian Journal of Anthropology* 7:55–80.

Tyson, Carl N. 1976 *The Pawnee People*. Phoenix: Indian Tribal Series.

Unrau, William E. 1971 *The Kansa Indians*. Norman: University of Oklahoma Press.

———— 1976 Removal, Death, and Legal Reincarnation of the Kaw People. *The Indian Historian* 9:2–9.

Voegelin, C.F., and F.M. Voegelin. 1964 Languages of the World: Native America, Fascicle 1. Bloomington: Indiana University, *Anthropological Linguistics* 6.

Weist, Katherine M. 1973 Giving Away: The Ceremonial Distribution of Goods Among the Northern Cheyenne of Southeastern Montana. *Plains Anthropologist* 18:97–103.

Weltfish, Gene. 1965 *The Lost Universe*. New York: Basic Books.

Wendland, Wayne M. 1978 Holocene Man in North America: The Ecological Setting and Climatic Background. *Plains Anthropologist* 23:273–287.

White, Robert A. 1974 Value Themes of the Native American Tribalistic Movement among the Dakota Sioux. *Current Anthropology* 15:284–303.

Wissler, Clark. 1914 The Influence of the Horse in the Development of Plains Culture. *American Anthropologist* 16:1–25.

——— 1916 General Discussion of Shamanistic and Dancing Societies. New York: American Museum of Natural History, Anthropological Papers, 11, Pt. 12.

——— 1941 *North American Indians of the Plains.* New York: American Museum of Natural History.

Wood, W. Raymond. 1965 The Redbird Focus and the Problem of Ponca Prehistory. *Plains Anthropologist,* Memoir 2.

——— 1967 *An Interpretation of Mandan Culture History.* Washington, D.C.: Smithsonian Institution, Bureau of American Ethnology, Bulletin 198.

——— 1971 *Biesterfeldt: A Post-Contact Coalescent Site on the Northeastern Plains.* Washington, D.C.: Smithsonian Institution Press, Smithsonian Contributions to Anthropology, no. 15.

——— 1974 Northern Plains Village Cultures: Internal Stability and External Relationships. *Journal of Anthropological Research* 30:1–16.

Wood, W. Raymond, ed. 1977 Trends in Middle Missouri Prehistory. Plains Anthropologist, Memoir 13.

Wright, Gary A. 1978 The Shoshonean Migration Problem. *Plains Anthropologist* 23:113–137.

NOTE:

Much of this chapter draws on my own research in the Northwestern Plains, from 1956 to the present. My husband, Thomas F. Kehoe, has been my collaborator in many of these research projects, both archaeological and ethnographic.

ADDITIONAL SOURCES FOR THE SECOND EDITION

Albers, Patricia, and Beatrice Medicine, eds. 1983 *The Hidden Half.* Washington, D.C.: University Press of America.

Ambler, Marjane. 1990 *Breaking the Iron Bonds.* Lawrence: University Press of Kansas.

Anderson, Duane C. 1987 Toward a Processual Understanding of the Initial Variant of the Middle Missouri Tradition: The Case of the Mill Creek Culture of Iowa. *American Antiquity* 52(3):522–537.

Anderson, Gary Clayton. 1984 *Kinsmen of Another Kind.* Lincoln: University of Nebraska Press.

——— 1986 *Little Crow.* St. Paul: Minnesota Historical Society Press.

Baugh, Timothy G., ed. 1986 Current Trends in Southern Plains Archaeology. *Plains Anthropologist,* Memoir 21, 31(114), Pt. 2.

Benn, David W. 1989 Hawks, Serpents, and Bird-Men: Emergence of the Oneota Mode of Production. *Plains Anthropologist* 34(125):233–260.

Bieder, Robert E. 1986 *Science Encounters the Indian, 1820–1880.* Norman: University of Oklahoma Press.

Blaine, Martha Royce. 1980 *The Pawnees: A Critical Bibliography. Bloomington: Indiana University Press.*

Boyd, Susan H. 1978 This Indian Is Not an Indian: Labelling Play in Powwowdom. In M.A. Salter (ed.). *Play: Anthropological Perspectives.* West Point, N.Y.: Leisure Press.

Bozell, John R. 1988 Changes in the Role of the Dog in Proto-Historic Pawnee Culture. *Plains Anthropologist* 33(119):95–111.

Brasser, Ted J. 1982 The Tipi as an Element in the Emergence of Historic Plains Indian Nomadism. *Plains Anthropologist* 27(98):309–321.

Burley, David, ed. 1985 *Contributions to Plains Prehistory.* Edmonton: Archaeological Survey of Alberta, Occasional Paper No. 26.

Cadwalader, Sandra L., and Vine Deloria, Jr. 1984 *The Aggressions of Civilization.* Philadelphia: Temple University Press.

Campbell, Gregory R., ed. 1989 Plains Indian Historical Demography and Health. *Plains Anthropologist* Memoir 23, 34(124), Pt. 2.

Campbell, Lyle, and Marianne Mithun, eds. 1979 *The Languages of Native America.* Austin: University of Texas Press.

Carlson, Leonard A. 1981 *Indians, Bureaucrats, and Land.* Westport, Conn.: Greenwood Press.

Clifton, James A. 1987 Wisconsin Death March: Explaining the Extremes in Old Northwest Indian Removal. *Transactions of the Wisconsin Academy of Sciences, Arts and Letters* 75:1–39.

——— 1984 *The Pokagons, 1683–1983.* Lanham, Md.: University Press of America.

Clifton, James A., ed. 1989 *Being and Becoming Indian.* Chicago: Dorsey Press.

——— 1990 *The Invented Indian.* New Brunswick: Transaction Publishers.

Davis, Leslie B., ed. 1988 *Avonlea Yesterday and*

Today: Archaeology and Prehistory. Saskatoon: Saskatchewan Archaeological Society.

Davis, Michael G. 1988 The Cultural Preadaptation Hypothesis: A Test Case on the Southern Plains. Doctoral dissertation, Department of Anthropology, University of Oklahoma.

DeMallie, Raymond J., and Douglas R. Parks, eds. 1987 *Sioux Indian Religion.* Norman: University of Oklahoma Press.

Denny, J. Peter. 1991 The Algonquian Migration from the Columbia Plateau to the Midwest, circa 1600 B.C.: Correlating Linguistics and Archaeology. Paper presented at the 22nd Algonquian Conference. Ottawa: Carleton University Press.

Dewing, Rolland 1985 *Wounded Knee.* New York: Irvington Publishers.

Dippie, Brian W. 1982 The *Vanishing American: White Attitudes and U.S. Indian Policy.* Middletown, Conn.: Wesleyan University Press.

Doherty, Robert. 1990 *Disputed Waters: Native Americans and the Great Lakes Fishery.* Lexington: University Press of Kentucky.

Edmunds, R. David 1983 *The Shawnee Prophet.* Lincoln: University of Nebraska Press.

Elias, Peter Douglas. 1988 *The Dakota of the Canadian Northwest: Lessons for Survival.* Winnipeg: University of Manitoba Press.

Epp, Henry T., and Ian Dyck, eds. 1983 *Tracking Ancient Hunters: Prehistoric Archaeology in Saskatchewan.* Regina: Saskatchewan Archaeological Society.

Farr, William E. 1984 *The Reservation Blackfeet, 1882–1945.* Seattle: University of Washington Press.

Feest, Christian F., ed. 1987 *Indians and Europe.* Aachen: Edition Herodot, Rader Verlag.

Finney, Fred A., and James B. Stoltman. 1986 The Fred Edwards Site: A Case of Stirling Phase Culture Contact in Southwest Wisconsin. Paper presented at Society for American Archaeology 51st annual meeting, New Orleans.

Fixico, Donald L., ed. 1987 *An Anthology of Western Great Lakes Indian History.* Milwaukee: University of Wisconsin–Milwaukee American Indian Studies.

Fleckner, John A. 1984 *Native American Archives.* Chicago: Society of American Archivists.

Ford, Richard I., ed. 1985 *Prehistoric Food Production in North America.* Ann Arbor: Museum of Anthropology, University of Michigan, Anthropological Papers, No. 75.

Fowler, Loretta. 1982 *Arapahoe Politics, 1851–1978.* Lincoln: Univeristy of Nebraska Press.

——— 1987 *Shared Symbols, Contested Meanings: Gros Ventre Culture and History, 1778–1984.* Ithaca: Cornell University Press.

Frey, Rodney 1987 *The World of the Crow Indians.* Norman: University of Oklahoma Press.

Gallagher, James P. 1990 Prehistoric Field Systems in the Upper Midwest. In W. Woods (ed.). *Late Prehistoric Agriculture: Observations from the Midwest.* Springfield: Studies in Illinois Archaeology, No. 7, Illinois Preservation Agency.

Gallagher, James P., and Constance M. Arzigian. 1991 A New Perspective on Late Prehistoric Agricultural Intensification in the Upper Mississippi River Valley. In W. Green (ed.). *Native American Agriculture: The Origins, Development and Significance of Prehistoric Farming.* Iowa City: Office of the State Archaeologist of Iowa, Report No. 19.

Galloway, Patricia, ed. 1989 *The Southeastern Ceremonial Complex: Artifacts and Analysis.* Lincoln: University of Nebraska Press.

Gibbon, Guy. 1990 Tribalization and Its Causes in Central Minnesota. Unpublished manuscript.

Gibbon, Guy, ed. 1990 *The Woodland Tradition in the Western Great Lakes.* Minneapolis: University of Minnesota, Publications in Anthropology, No. 4.

Gilman, Carolyn, and Mary Jane Schneider. 1987 *The Way to Independence.* St. Paul: Minnesota Historical Society.

Grange, Roger T., Jr. 1989 The Functions of European Artifacts in Pawnee Culture: Evidence from the Pike-Pawnee Village, Nebraska. Paper presented at the First Joint Archaeological Congress, Baltimore, Md.

Green, William 1987 A Prehistoric Frontier in the Prairie Peninsula: Late Woodland Upland Settlement and Subsistence Patterns. Paper presented at 52nd annual meeting, Society for American Archaeologists, Toronto.

——— 1990 Patterns and Processes of Early Mississippian Inter-societal Contacts within the Cahokia Interaction Network. Paper presented at 52nd annual meeting, Society for American Archaeologists, Las Vegas.

Green, William, James B. Stoltman, and Alice B. Kehoe, eds. 1986 *Introduction to Wisconsin Archaeology.* Special issue (vol. 67[3–4]) of the *Wisconsin Archeologist.* Milwaukee: Wisconsin Archeological Society.

Greiser, Sally Thompson. 1985 Predictive Models of Hunter-Gatherer Subsistence and Settlement Strategies on the Central High Plains. *Plains Anthropologist,* Memoir 20, 30(110), Pt 2.

Grobsmith, Elizabeth S. 1989 The Impact of Litigation on the Religious Revitalization of Native American Inmates in the Nebraska Department of Corrections. *Plains Anthropologist* 34(124):135–147.

Hanna, Margaret, and Brian Kooyman, eds. 1982 *Approaches to Algonquian Archaeology.* Calgary: Archaeology Association of the University of Calgary.

Hanson, Jeffrey R. 1986 Adjustment and Adaptation on the Northern Plains: The Case of Equestrianism among the Hidatsa. *Plains Anthropologist* 31(112):93–107.

Herring, Joseph B. 1990 *The Enduring Indians of Kansas.* Lawrence: University Press of Kansas.

Hittman, Michael. 1990 *Wovoka and the Ghost Dance: A Source Book.* Carson City, Nev.: The Grace Dangberg Foundation.

Howard, James H. 1981 *Shawnee!* Athens: Ohio University Press.

Hoxie, Frederick E. 1984 *A Final Promise: The Campaign to Assimilate the Indians, 1880–1920.* Lincoln: University of Nebraska Press.

Iverson, Peter, ed. 1985 *The Plains Indians of the Twentieth Century.* Norman: University of Oklahoma Press.

Johnson, Alfred E. 1984 Temporal Relationships of Late (Plains) Woodland Components in Eastern Kansas. *Plains Anthropologist* 29(106):277–288.

——— 1987 Late Woodland Adaptive Patterns in Eastern Kansas. *Plains Anthropologist* 32(118):390–402.

Johnson, Elden. 1991 Cambria and Cahokia's Northwestern Periphery. In J.B. Stoltman (ed.). *New Perspectives on Cahokia.* Madison: Prehistory Press.

Jorgensen, Joseph G., ed. 1984 Native Americans and Energy Development II. Boston: Anthropology Resource Center.

Keyser, James D. 1986 The Evidence for McKean Complex Plant Utilization. *Plains Anthropologist* 31(113):225–235. With "Comment on McKean Plant Utilization" by Thomas W. Haberman, *ibid.* pp. 237–240.

Lawson, Michael L. 1982 *Dammed Indians.* Norman: University of Oklahoma Press.

Lees, William B. 1985 Dakota Acculturation During the Early Reservation Period: Evidence from the Deerfly Site (39*LM*39), South Dakota. *Plains Anthropologist* 30(108):103–121.

Lopach, James J., Margery Hunter Brown, and Richmond L. Clow. 1990 *Tribal Government Today: Politics on Montana Indian Reservations.* Boulder: Westview Press.

Mason, Ronald J. 1981 *Great Lakes Archaeology.* New York: Academic Press.

McCollough, Martha. 1990 Horse Trading Between the Southern Plains and the Eastern United States During the Eighteenth and Nineteenth Centuries. Paper presented to the Plains Anthropological Society annual meeting, Oklahoma City.

Medicine, Bea. 1982 Native American Resistance to Integration: Contemporary Confrontations and Religious Revitalization. *Plains Anthropologist* 26(94):277–286.

Meyer, David. 1985 *The Red Earth Crees, 1860–1960.* Ottawa: National Museums of Canada, National Museum of Man Mercury Series, Canadian Ethnology Service, Paper No. 100.

Michlovic, Michael G. 1983 The Red River Valley in the Prehistory of the Northern Plains. *Plains Anthropologist* 28(99):23–31.

Miller, J. R. 1990 Owen Glendower, Hotspur, and Canadian Indian Policy. *Ethnohistory* 37(4):386–415.

Milner, Clyde A., II. 1982 *With Good Intentions: Quaker Work Among the Pawnees, Otos, and Omahas in the 1870s.* Lincoln: University of Nebraska Press.

Moore, John H. 1987 *The Cheyenne Nation.* Lincoln: University of Nebraska Press.

——— 1988 The Dialectics of Cheyenne Kinship: Variability and Change. *Ethnology* 27(3):253–269.

——— 1989 The Myth of the Lazy Indian: Native American Contributions to the U. S. Economy. *Nature, Society and Thought* 2(2):195–215. See also (1987) "The Cheyenne Indians Within the American System of Hired Labor," *Soviet Ethnography* 5:111–118.

Moses, L. G. and Raymond Wilson, eds. 1985 *Indian Lives.* Albuquerque: University of New Mexico Press.

Nock, David A. 1988 *A Victorian Missionary and Canadian Indian Policy.* Waterloo: Wilfrid Laurier University Press.

O'Brien, Sharon. 1989 *American Indian Tribal Governments.* Norman: University of Oklahoma Press.

Paredes, J. Anthony, ed. 1980 *Anishinabe: 6 Studies of*

Modern Chippewa. Tallahassee: University Presses of Florida

Peroff, Nicholas C. 1982 *Menominee DRUMS.* Norman: University of Oklahoma Press.

Perttula, Timothy K., and James E. Bruseth. 1983 Early Caddoan Subsistence Strategies, Sabine River Basin, East Texas. *Plains Anthropologist* 28(99):9–21.

Perttula, Timothy K. and Paul McGuff. 1985 Woodland and Caddoan Settlement in the McGee Creek Drainage, Southeast Oklahoma. *Plains Anthropologist* 30(109):219–235.

Peterson, Jacqueline, and Jennifer S. H. Brown. 1985 *The New Peoples: Being and Becoming Métis in North America.* Lincoln: University of Nebraska Press.

Pettipas, Leo, ed. 1983 *Introducing Manitoba Prehistory: Papers in Manitoba Archaeology.* Winnipeg: Manitoba Department of Cultural Affairs and Historical Resources, Popular Series No. 4.

Prucha, Francis Paul. 1984 *The Great Father.* Lincoln: University of Nebraska Press.

Rodell, Roland L. 1991 The Diamond Bluff Site Complex and Cahokia Influence in the Red Wing Locality. In J.B. Stoltman (ed.). *New Perspectives on Cahokia.* Madison, Wis: Prehistory Press.

Ross, Thomas E. and Tyrel G. Moore, eds. 1987 *A Cultural Geography of North American Indians.* Boulder: Westview Press.

Samek, Hana. 1987 *The Blackfoot Confederacy, 1880–1920.* Albuquerque: University of New Mexico Press.

Schneider, Mary Jane. 1983 The Production of Indian-Use and Souvenir Beadwork by Contemporary Indian Women. *Plains Anthropologist* 28(101): 235–245.

——— 1984 An Investigation into the Origin of Arikara, Hidatsa, and Mandan Twilled Basketry. *Plains Anthropologist* 29(106):265–276.

——— 1986 *North Dakota Indians.* Dubuque: Kendall/Hunt.

Schusky, Ernest L., ed. 1980 *Political Organization of Native North America.* Washington, D.C.: University Press of America.

Shimkin, Demitri B. 1986 Eastern Shoshone. In W.L. D'Azevedo, ed. *Handbook of North American Indians,* vol. 11 *Great Basin.* Washington, D.C.: Smithsonian Institution Press, pp. 308–335.

Smith, Craig S. 1988 Seeds, Weeds, and Prehistoric Hunters and Gatherers: The Plant Macrofossil Evidence from Southwest Wyoming. *Plains Anthropologist* 33(120):141–158.

Smith, Donald B. 1987 *Sacred Feathers.* Lincoln: University of Nebraska Press.

Snipp, C. Matthew. 1989 *American Indians: The First of This Land.* New York: Russell Sage Foundation.

Spector, Janet, and Elden Johnson, eds. 1985 *Archaeology, Ecology and Ethnohistory of the Prairie-Forest Border Zone of Minnesota and Manitoba.* Lincoln: J & L Reprint Company.

Spielmann, Katherine A. 1983 Late Prehistoric Exchange between the Southwest and Southern Plains. *Plains Anthropologist* 28(102):257–272.

Sullivan, Norman C. 1990 The Biological Consequences of the Mississippian Expansion into the Western Great Lakes Region: a Study of Prehistoric Culture Contact. In S.M. Nelson and A.B. Kehoe, eds. *Powers of Observation: Alternative Views in Archeology.* Washington, D.C.: Archeological Papers of the American Anthropological Association, No. 2.

Tanner, Helen Hornbeck, ed. 1987 *Atlas of Great Lakes Indian History.* Norman: University of Oklahoma Press.

Tarasoff, Koozma J. 1980 *Persistent Ceremonialism: The Plains Cree and Saulteaux.* Ottawa: National Museums of Canada, National Museum of Man Mercury Series, Canadian Ethnology Service, Paper No. 69.

Thistle, Paul C. 1986 *Indian-European Trade Relations in the Lower Saskatchewan River Region to 1840.* Winnipeg: University of Manitoba Press.

Thornton, Russell. 1987 *American Indian Holocaust and Survival.* Norman: University of Oklahoma Press.

Trigger, Bruce G., ed. 1978 *Handbook of North American Indians,* vol. 15, *Northeast.* Washington, D.C.: Smithsonian Institution Press.

Unrau, William E. 1979 *The Emigrant Indians of Kansas: A Critical Bibliography.* Bloomington: Indiana University Press.

Unrau, Wlliam E. and H. Craig Miner. 1985 *Tribal Dispossession and the Ottawa Indian University Fraud.* Norman: Oklahoma University Press.

Vennum, Thomas, Jr. 1982 *The Ojibwa Dance Drum: Its History and Construction.* Washington, D.C.: Smithsonian Institution Press.

——— 1988 *Wild Rice and the Ojibway People.* St. Paul: Minnesota Historical Society.

White, Richard. 1983 *The Roots of Dependency.* Lincoln: University of Nebraska Press.

Wiegers, Robert P. 1988 A Proposal for Indian Slave Trading in the Mississippi Valley and Its Impact on the Osage. *Plains Anthropologist* 33(120):187–202.

Wilson, Terry P. 1985 *The Underground Reservation: Osage Oil.* Lincoln: University of Nebraska Press.

Wood, W. Raymond, and Margot Liberty, eds. 1980 *Anthropology on the Great Plains.* Lincoln: University of Nebraska Press.

7

THE INTERMONTANE WEST
AND CALIFORNIA

Tremendous forces deep within the earth well upward within the mid-Atlantic and mid-Pacific, slowly but inexorably pushing the crust of the earth away. Far from the sources of pressure, the force from the east and the force from the west meet, buckling the land. East and west, the strain shows in sharp escarpments rising to the snowy peaks of the Front Range of the Rockies and the Sierra Nevada. Between these ranges are innumerable mountain ridges running roughly north-south in parallel to the great mountain walls. Along the United States border with Canada in British Columbia and eastern Washington, the headwaters of the Columbia River lie in a broad, high valley. To the south, in eastern Washington and Oregon and adjacent Idaho, are lava plains dotted with volcanic peaks and craters. South of these, which, with the Columbia-headwaters trough forms the Columbia Plateau, are many thousands of square miles of flat valleys separated by eroded older mountain ridges, a landscape the geographers call the basin-and-range region. Most of Nevada and Utah is basin-and-range country.

The western slopes of the Sierra and the Rockies, obstructing the moisture-laden winds from the Pacific, carry dense forests of firs and other evergreens. Cut off from this moisture, the intermontane plateau and basin are sagebrush deserts, relieved by marshes where streams from the slopes lose velocity in the flat valleys and flow slowly into catchment lakes, and by pines on the lower slopes and firs on the upper slopes of the ranges. Parklike grassy meadows occur throughout the Intermontane West, although their total area is much less than that of sagebrush desert.

California constitutes a geographic province in itself. California the geographic region is somewhat smaller than California the state, since it comprises only the portion west of the crest of the Sierras. This portion includes a long north-south trough in central California, between the Sierra and the Coast ranges that make the central California shore ruggedly picturesque. Northern California's topography is mountainous, the Klamath range bridging the Coast ranges and the Sierra with sharp

THE INTERMONTANE WEST AND CALIFORNIA CHRONOLOGY

	GREAT BASIN	PLATEAU	CALIFORNIA
1975			Alcatraz occupation
1950	Ute land claim settled	National Indian brotherhood develops in British Columbia	Termination partially revoked / Termination of BIA responsibility / War industries
1925			"Okie" immigration
1900	Ute lands allotted / Paiutes to reservations	U.S. reservations allotted	Reservations individually allotted
1875	Wodziwob (1870)	"Bannock War" British Columbia reserves / Shoshoni to reservations / Smohalla's religion	Ghost dance, religious revivals
1850	Paiutes dispossessed / U.S. treaty with Utes	Euramerican colonization / U.S. treaties	Euramerican Gold Rush, settlement
1825		Euramerican missions (1834) / Fur trade established (1820)	Mexico secularizes missions
1800	Spanish explore Basin	Lewis & Clark (1805)	Russian contacts / Spanish missions
1750		Shoshoni obtain horses	
1700	Ute obtain horses		
1650	Spanish settle on southern border		
1550			First Spanish contact
1500			

FREMONT

Numic Expansion

Salmon processing increases
Shoshoni enter

Climate improves

Drier warmer maximum

Lower eastern Basin uninhabited?

Woodworking developed
Plateau culture pattern developing

Historic culture patterns established

California culture pattern developing

Fish netted

WESTERN ARCHAIC

A.D.
B.C.

1400
1300
1200
1100
1000
900
800
700
600
500
400
300
100
500
1000
2000
3000
4000
5000
6000
7000
8000

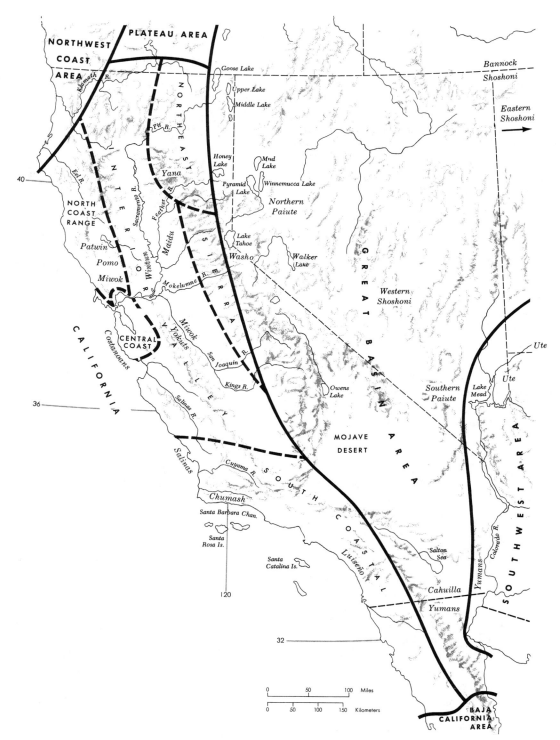

MAP 8 The Intermontane West and California

steep spines walling narrow valleys with dense rain forest. Quite the opposite is seen in southern California, where desert grasses cover rolling hills and estuary marshes mediate between sea and land. Chaparral covers hills in the southern half of California, but groves of oaks frequently occur where streams, springs, and sheltered lees provide sufficient water.

This chapter discusses three geographic provinces, the Plateau, the Great Basin of Nevada and Utah, and California. The east and west boundaries are sharp but broken by good passes. To the north, the Plateau narrows into slimmer, more heavily forested intermontane valleys in British Columbia. In California, the country north of the Klamath Mountains, in the state of Oregon, looks to the Northwest coast and will be discussed in the next chapter. South, the Basin grades into the Southwest's Colorado Plateau and western deserts, into which southern California also opens. All three of the geographic provinces treated in this chapter share a dominant semiarid climate enriched by the denser vegetation on the abundance of mountain slopes. Culturally, the vegetation and climate the regions shared facilitated communication and the diffusion of cultural patterns, making the Intermontane West with California one basic culture area that includes a number of subareas.

SECTION 1: THE WESTERN ARCHAIC CULTURAL PATTERN AND ITS PERSISTENCE

The West at the beginning of the Holocene era, about 8000 B.C., was a uniformly more inviting land than it has become. Blue water glinted, mile after mile, where now stretch hot sands and alkaline flats. Conifers covered lower slopes now dotted with sagebrush and juniper. As one archaeologist who has worked in the desert basins wistfully noted, the greater number of perennial streams in the early Holocene era meant there was then water and shade in basins that today give no

relief to people working in the scorching sun. In this early period, humans hunted big and moderate-sized game and waterfowl, fished, and gathered vegetables and nuts. These resources were relatively abundant in and around the many valley lakes. People camped in valley meadows and groves or in rockshelters overlooking the lake shore. There was travel between valleys, but no need to trek distances to hunt or collect food.

The trend to warmer, drier winters that climaxed after 3000 B.C. destroyed this Eden. While there had earlier been fluctuations in the levels of lakes, now many of the lakes totally disappeared. California and the western Great Basin, with streams fed by Sierra snows, kept their populations, which were more confined to the major stream valleys but were able to continue their comfortable lake-shore and flood-plain harvesting, supplemented by hunting on the lower slopes. On the Plateau, which is far enough north that cooler temperatures retard evaporation, more time and labor probably had to be expended in getting a living, to judge from the increase in small animals taken, the probable introduction of net fishing, and the manos and metates and mortars and pestles that appear in greater numbers in sites. (Net fishing may indicate a decrease in big game fish that could be speared, a decrease that forced people to spend hours weaving and repairing nets to pull in small fish that once may have been ignored. Grinding stones, whether the flat slab or trough metate or the bowl-shaped mortars, indicate a need to collect and process grass seeds—wild grains—and nuts. Considerable work is involved in gathering and grinding wild seeds, so life at these sites was less easy than it probably was before 4000 B.C.) In the eastern Great Basin, much of the lower elevations seems to have been virtually abandoned, people moving to the uplands and the ranges where mountain sheep become a prime food resource.

The climate ameliorated and cultural patterns shifted about 1500 B.C. Mountain sheep became the most important game throughout the Plateau, supplemented by bison, elk, and deer. Apparently, meat was sufficiently abundant that seed collecting declined. Large areas of the eastern Great Basin seem to have remained uninhabited for another thousand or even two thousand years. People returned to the drier northwestern Great Basin (the Oregon-Idaho-Nevada border area), resuming occupation in creekside and lakeside rockshelters. In one such shelter in a narrow creek valley, remains of a round pole-and-thatch wickiup much like that in which the ethnographer Mooney interviewed the Paiute prophet Wovoka in 1892 suggest that the overhang was a winter dwelling site. Human feces preserved in the dry rockshelter proved that the inhabitants ate antelope and smaller mammals (mostly rabbits and marmots), crayfish and shellfish, wild onion, sego-lily bulbs, cherries, rose hips, prickly-pear cactus pads (eaten baked), seeds of sedge, sunflower, and goosefoot (chenopod), and termites and ants. A few bison and deer were secured. Hunting was performed with atlatls that projected darts, at least for the larger game. Small animals were probably trapped by snares. Baskets, well preserved in the dry shelter, were used in quantity, and woven bags and mats, but there was no pottery. Twisted plant fiber, especially sagebrush bark, was woven into sandals. Leather manufactures were not found in this site, although stone tools suggested hide-working. Seeds, including cherry seeds, were cracked or ground on stone metates with manos, and these plus various other foods and implements were stored in grass-lined pits dug into the floor of the shelter. Similar inventories come from other rockshelters in the western Great Basin and, later, in Utah.

California at this time, roughly 2000 B.C., became more strongly differentiated from the Great Basin to the east. Contacts across the Sierra were fairly frequent, attested by Pacific Coast olivella and abalone shells in sites east of the mountains, but marine foods and acorn oaks made California richer than the valleys watered from the eastern slopes. As techniques for exploitation of these resources improved, and as population grew, California became a distinct culture area. An Archaic

cultural pattern persisted in the Basin from the early Holocene era, about 7000 B.C., to late in the nineteenth century A.D., although with major fluctuations in areas occupied. The Plateau shared in the persistence of Western Archaic traits, with a shift to emphasize mountain-sheep hunting, at least until the thirteenth century A.D. and, by some criteria, into the nineteenth century. Such persistence demonstrates how early the Indians of the arid West developed effective resource-harvesting techniques. Because the exceptional dryness of many rockshelters used by these peoples preserves normally perishable woven products, we can see that the basketry arts for which Great Basin women are historically noted had been invented early in the Archaic period, perhaps earlier yet in the Paleo-Indian period.

SECTION 2: THE GREAT BASIN

The Indians of the great American desert have been said to typify the simplest of human societies. They were to be found in small bands of only a few families, they were nearly naked, they lived in roofless windbreaks, they ate grasshoppers and wild-grass seeds, and they wove baskets but did not make pottery. Nineteenth-century Euro-Americans sweltering in woolen clothing and eating hardtack and salt pork imported from the East, watched these people living off the arid land, relaxing in the shade of their airy homes, and judged them to be inferior to the noble horsemen battling on the Plains. This attitude was only partially modified by early-twentieth-century anthropologists. In the 1930s, Julian Steward visited many of the Great Basin Indian communities to interview their elderly members on the prereservation cultural pattern. Steward hypothesized that the poor resources of the desert would have severely limited the human inhabitants' capacity for elaboration of social institutions. He assumed that where resources appear to be few and widely scattered, people would be forced to spend nearly all their time gathering food and thus have little time available for either manufactures or social performances. Furthermore, the low density of food resources would result in a low density of humans, too few in any locality to need or to maintain complex social institutions. Interviewing Indians who had been born in the second half of the nineteenth century, when Euro-American immigration displaced their families from their ancestral territories, Steward believed he had confirmed his hypothesis. His classic monograph, *Basin-Plateau Aboriginal Sociopolitical Groups,* published in 1938, cogently set forth the limiting and dispersing effect of the arid environment upon its human inhabitants. Relying upon Steward's study, the Utah archaeologist Jesse Jennings interpreted his discoveries in the deep midden of Danger Cave, bordering Great Salt Lake, as exemplifying the "Desert Culture" described by Steward. Jennings saw very little cultural change during the millennia Danger Cave had been intermittently occupied, and concluded that the exigencies of living in the desert had early molded a human adaptation that was the only viable response to the desert until Mormon colonization.

Perhaps because it would be rather boring to excavate site after site that only replicated Danger Cave, younger archaeologists in the 1960s were critical of Jenning's "Desert Culture" and, by implication, of Steward's pictures of the aborigines of the Great Basin. Emma Lou Davis was one of the first to modify the classic interpretation. Working directly with Paiute living at Mono Lake on the western edge of the Basin in California, Davis drew up a detailed map of the localities utilized by these Paiute for subsistence, surveyed the localities for signs of habitation, and finally excavated sites she had found. Her reconstruction of aboriginal Paiute life does not contradict Steward's, but it changes the emphasis from restriction to successful exploitation through intelligent planning. Partly through Davis's work, other archaeologists analyzed their data as tests of Jenning's model of

the "Desert Culture," and concluded that Steward had led Jennings to overlook a critical fact: Danger Cave is adjacent to a lake. All the early Western Archaic sites, and many of the later ones, are really not desert camps but lake-shore or stream-plain settlements. True, each habitat is separated from others by desert, but the desert was not the habitat. Why had Steward not realized this? Because his informants had been displaced from their parents' homes by Euro-American colonization. Mormon and subsequent Euro-American settlement had not altered the ancient pattern of human utilization of the relatively narrow watered habitats of the Great Basin, but had merely replaced the earlier users with the immigrants. Steward's displaced informants were atypical of aborigines of the Great Basin.

At the time of historic contact, in 1776 (marking the exploration by the Spanish missionary Escalante), the Great Basin was the territory of speakers of the Numic languages, the "Uto-" of Uto-Aztecan. These include, from the west, Mono, spoken by the Mono Lake Paiute; Northern Paiute (also called Paviotso) and related dialects, Snake in eastern Oregon, and Bannock Shoshoni in southern Idaho; Shoshoni throughout the heart of the Basin, including the dialects Gosiute, Panamint, and the eventual western-Plains Wind River (Wyoming) Shoshoni and the Comanche; and Southern Paiute with related dialects, Ute, Chemehuevi on the Colorado River, and Kawaiisu in the Mohave Desert of southernmost California. Various lines of evidence suggest that the Numa—a general term for all these peoples—were originally in southeastern California and adjacent southern Nevada along the eastern valleys of the Sierra. About A.D. 1000 they began to expand north and east—why is not known—covering the Great Basin, reaching to the southern Plateau by A.D. 1300, and breaking across the Rockies into Wyoming about 1450. If this reconstruction of Numa history is correct, who occupied the Basin before Numa expansion? The only non-Numic group historically in the Basin is the Washo, whose language is an isolate within the Hokan phylum (the majority of Hokan languages are in and west of the Sierra, in California). Washo folklore implies a very long residence in their territory around Lake Tahoe, in the eastern Sierra on the border of the Basin. Their material culture has been typical of the Basin adaptation, no more and no less similar to that of prehistoric sites in the western Basin than was that of the historic Numa. The rather plain brown pottery found in the uppermost layers of many Basin and southern Plateau sites is generally thought to be Numic, and to mark the expansion of Numa peoples. Potteryless Hokan could therefore be the predecessor of the Numa in the western Basin, where the abundance of basketry mirrors the importance of basketry to the historic Washo. Such a simple interpretation is complicated by the fact that basketry was important and abundant among the Numa, too, not to mention the ethnically unidentified prehistoric Fremont, and by the possibility that pottery diffused as a technological innovation across ethnic lines, independent of population movements. The only safe conclusion is that we do not know what peoples lived in the Great Basin before the late prehistoric era.

The Fremont

Utah between around A.D. 500 and 1450 was occupied by a series of agricultural groups known as the Fremont. These are subdivided into regional variants, but share the cultivation of maize, beans, and squash, the construction of comparatively more substantial houses and storage chambers than would be found in the Western Archaic, the manufacture of gray pottery, and the depiction of ritual and war parties in rock pictographs. Early Fremont seems to coincide with a climatic phase of somewhat increased moisture that brought the expansion of grasslands in many localities in the Basin. This climate allowed both the cultivation of a small-cobbed maize similar to that grown in New Mexico during the previous two millennia, and great use of wild seeds, including chenopod, amaranth, and pickleweed. Then, coincident with

Pueblo I on the Colorado Plateau to the south, Fremont began raising its own variety of a large-cob, good-flour maize, Fremont Dent. With this profitable cultigen, maize became increasingly eaten, yet never to the exclusion of wild seeds. Instead, both the quantity and kinds of wild-grass seeds collected and consumed rose along with the consumption of Fremont Dent. In northern Utah, bison and waterfowl were protein sources for Fremont populations, while to the south, antelope and rabbits were predominant meats. Some Fremont sites are small villages usually of round pole-and-brush houses built over shallow excavated floors, accompanied by adobe or stone above-ground granaries or stone-lined storage pits. Other Fremont sites are camps in rockshelters or open tipi sites; these probably represent the forays of hunting parties out from the villages.

Hints of the social side of Fremont life come from clay figurines, most of them representing the head and upper torso of women bedecked in bead necklaces, some wearing short fiber skirts such as early historic Basin women did; and from pecked or painted rock drawings depicting costumed characters who may be spirits, or persons enacting them in ritual, and men with large, decorated shields, presumably off to war. From one perspective, Fremont looks like a northern extension of the Southwest, a persistence of the immediately pre-Pueblo Basketmaker cultural pattern beyond the urbanizing Anasazi Pueblo. From the opposite direction, Fremont looks like an intrusion of a High Plains bison-hunting people through the Wyoming Rockies into Utah, where they came into contact with local Archaic peoples desultorily cultivating a low-yield maize. About the time of this contact (roughly, A.D. 900), the Archaic cultivators succeeded in breeding a stable, high-yield dent maize, or perhaps obtained from the Southwest a dent that was modified into Fremont Dent in Utah.

Archaeological data seems to support both theories of the origin of Fremont, as Puebloid or as Northeastern, depending on which traits, or which region—from Nevada, through Utah, into southern Idaho—one emphasizes. We can at least state that

Fremont is a Great Basin development influenced by the Pueblo Southwest. It is possible that the northeastern variants of Fremont might represent southward-migrating Apacheans, moving in from the Plains and picking up agricultural, pottery, and basketry techniques from the Anasazi-influenced (or related?) southern Basin Fremont. Southern regional variants of Fremont might have included northern outliers of Anasazi nations (that is, ancestral Pueblos) and very possibly also ancestors of the Utes and Paiutes, whose early nineteenth-century cultural pattern was quite similar to that of Fremont. The disappearance of the Fremont cultural pattern about A.D. 1450 is usually attributed to invasion and competition from the Numa peoples, although the result of several centuries of drier climate causing flash-flood arroyo cutting in formerly arable canyon floors may have contributed to the demise.

The Cultural Pattern of the Great Basin Peoples

Great Basin peoples were dispersed in small family groups around lakes, along streams, and beside springs. The usual camp was of one to a few couples, their youngsters and adolescents, and widowed or elderly parents or aunts. It was not uncommon for two sisters to jointly marry one husband. If sisters did not share a household, it was necessary that there be included a grandmother, or a nearly grown girl, for there had to be a woman to baby-sit while the other woman worked to gather food. The baby-sitter occupied herself with weaving baskets and mats, processing food, and other useful stationary tasks as she watched and attended to the little ones, while her co-wife, daughter, or cousin moved about steadily beating seeds into carrying baskets, cutting tule or cattail reeds, digging up edible roots, or picking berries—gathering whatever food resource was ripe. Men were farther away from camp, driving fish into weirs where they could be speared or netted, shooting ducks from blinds, setting snares

or pulling from their burrows various rodents, or stalking or ambushing mountain sheep or deer if in the vicinity of the slopes harboring these game animals. In late spring, groups of women dug up camas (a marshy meadow lily bulb) or wappato ("Indian potato," a tuber), drying and pounding quantities to store as meal. The Indians knew that breaking up the soil by digging the bulbs and tubers improved the next year's harvest, as they knew that by breaking off the old stems of the leafy plant called Indian spinach, they caused many tender edible leaves to grow the following year. Entire families worked together during the autumn harvest of pinyon nuts, bending the branches of the bushy pines down, beating off the cones full of soft nuts, then leaving the older women to clean and roast the nuts and finally grind them into a compact, storable flour as the younger people continued collecting more and more nuts. Each family group carried as many basket loads of processed nuts and seeds and dried meat as it could manage, caching additional quantities in grass-lined pits covered with brush and stones. Nondomesticated foods were supplemented by maize, beans, and squashes cultivated in fields watered by springs, streams, or washes where water running down could be saved through check dams. People also sowed native seed grasses in suitable fields burned off and lightly hoed to provide optimum growth for the indigenous grains.

Great Basin families were loosely grouped into bands named after their principal local food resource. These named bands merely reflected the tendency to remain in the territory of one's childhood, where most of one's relatives were to be found. Young men, in particular, often traveled long distances visiting other bands, perhaps deciding to remain with a family whose daughter was attracted to the new youth. Whole families might change band affiliation after quarreling with neighbors, suspecting sorcery, or striking up a new friendship when relatively large numbers of people came together at localities where the pine nuts or another resource were especially abundant. Essen-

FIGURE 7.1 Southern Paiute family in camp, early 1870s. The woman is grinding seeds on a stone metate with a stone mano. *(Smithsonian Institution Office of Anthropology, Bureau of American Ethnology Collection)*

tially, the band consisted of the inhabitants of a territory who shared its resources—hence the naming of the band after its principal local food—and was not a political body. When people moved into a new locality, they were expected to ask its residents for permission to share the resources. Leadership in a band was usually hereditary but ostensibly the exercise of spiritual power by a gifted person in order to aid his or her fellows. Traditionally, persons dreamed they were blessed by a spirit to exercise a specific power. The

dreamer was obliged to learn the pragmatic aspects of this power, or suffer illness and misfortune. One man might have the power to capture rabbits. A "rabbit boss" or "captain," he would send messages around a territory announcing that he found it propitious to drive rabbits in such-and-such a valley in late summer or autumn, when the animals were fat. All the families in the territory would gather at the rabbit boss's camp at the valley. Most families had wide-mesh nets. The nets were strung out in a great circle around the valley, and then the

FIGURE 7.2 Southern Paiute playing their version of the gambling game generally known as the hand game; Paiute call this "Kill the Bone." Early 1870s. *(Smithsonian Institution National Anthropological Archives)*

rabbits were driven into them by the horde of men armed with sticks and clubs. Those rabbits not killed when first sighted were slaughtered in the nets. An "antelope boss," blessed with power to take antelope, organized an antelope drive that worked much like the rabbit drive, except that the game was often driven into a corral. On the uplands, mountain sheep were taken by organized parties of hunters with dogs, the men spaced along a drive lane behind boulders or in blinds so that the sheep could be stampeded into a narrow pass or cirque. Whenever a drive was held, there was a festival atmosphere, not only because quantities of fresh meat plus extra to dry for weeks ahead would be available, but also because there would be enough people for exciting gambling games, singing, dancing, gossiping, and courtship. These festive times were precious, for once a drive had been held in a valley, it would be hunted out and some years would have to pass before another could be staged there. Thus, only a few drives, at most, could be held in one year, and those would be at widely separated locales. Band leaders had responsibility for negotiating sharing of resource harvests, intergroup trading, and resolution of conflicts, and were expected to make speeches, even within their own camps, exhorting everyone to live by the highest moral principles.

The human population of the Basin was dispersed in small groups matching the oases and the zones of resources along the ranges. They traveled seasonally to a series of ecological niches because, with rare exceptions, no one camp had a sufficient quantity of food within walking distance to sustain even one family for more than a few days or weeks. Furthermore, the people had to be sophisticated naturalists and dieticians to maintain even the relatively low-density population they had achieved. Plains Indian techniques of game impounding and berry and bulb or root collecting were practiced, but added to these were California-area techniques of nut processing and fishing and Basin specialties of grass-seed and insect collecting. Both the small wild-grass and cattail seeds and the insects (grasshoppers, crickets, certain caterpillars, and fly larvae) that were locally very abundant in season were roasted with coals and then ground, like pine nuts, into a dehydrated "flour" that was compact to store and transport and highly nutritious. Similarly sophisticated was the Basin development of weaving to produce light, strong containers to carry the foods and babies the long distance from camp to camp, and the making of blankets out of rabbit fur. This all-purpose, warm covering, the only warm clothing used, was as light and transportable as the woven containers and had the further virtue of utilizing the most abundant animal skin available.

Two border areas of the Great Basin amplified the harvests of wild foods. The Southern Paiute of southern Utah and Nevada farmed maize, beans, squash, and sunflowers in small fields in valley bottoms adjacent to streams or springs. The natural moisture of these sites was augmented by brief irrigation ditches. Land suitable for farming was limited; most families obtained some, but supplemented crops with the more reliable and abundant grass seeds. Standard native American agriculture was thus known and practiced to the extent permitted by the arid environment, and was regularly augmented by the gathering of wild seeds. In Owens Valley in southeastern California, Northern Paiute practiced a somewhat different technique to increase

plant food resources. Owens River and its tributaries were fed by snows in the high Sierra bounding the valley to the west. The resident Paiute constructed miles of irrigation canals to extend the available ground water to the wild foods in the valley. None of the "American trinity" of maize, beans, and squashes was planted; only indigenous roots, bulbs, and grains benefited from the irrigation. Irrigation from perennial streams or from springs onto flood plains was the basic technique of the lower Colorado Yuman-speaking peoples on the western periphery of the Southwest. The Northern Paiute may have adapted the technique from Yumans to the south, either on the Colorado or in southern California. Why the Paiute in Owens Valley did not plant maize in their valley-bottom fields is not known. Their neglect of maize suggested to some observers that they picked up the idea of irrigation from Euro-American immigrants in the middle of the nineteenth century, or possibly a generation or two earlier through contact with Indians subjugated on the plantations of the Spanish missionaries on the western side of the mountains. However, archaeological investigation has shown that from the earliest discovered evidence of human habitation, 4000 B.C., to about A.D. 650, Owens Valley people established their principal settlements near the river, in the zone where, historically, edible root plants were irrigated. There seems no way to discover whether these early villages irrigated roots, but neither is there any way to disprove irrigation. In these earlier periods, Owens Valley people also occupied temporary camps in the desert scrub of the valley, where grass seeds would be harvested, and upland camps, where hunting would have been most profitable. After A.D. 650, pine nuts seem to have become much more important than they had been previously, and riverside occupation was reduced. Then, after A.D. 1300, riverside settlement increased while hunting stations in the desert scrub and in the uplands became more rare. Again, these settlement data do not bear directly upon irrigation, but they do allow the probability of it, especially after A.D. 1300.

FIGURE 7.3 Southern Paiute women harvesting seeds, early 1870s. *(Smithsonian Institution National Anthropological Archives)*

NUMIC TALES FROM THE SOUTHERN BASIN

I.

Once upon a time the Shin-au-av [Wolf] brothers met to consult about the destiny of the Numas. At this meeting the younger said, "Brother, how shall these people obtain their food? Let us devise some good plan for them. I was thinking about it all night but could not see what would be best, and when the dawn came into the sky I went to a mountain and sat on its summit and thought a long time and now I can tell you a good plan by which they can live; listen to your younger brother. Look at these pine trees: their nuts are sweet; and there is the fruit of the Yucca, very rich, and there is the apple of the cactus full of juice. On the plain you see the sunflower bearing many seeds; they will be good for the nation. Let them have all these things for their food and when they have gathered a store they shall put them in the ground, or hide them in the rocks. And when they return they shall find abundance and having taken of them as they may need shall go on. And yet when they return a second time there shall still be plenty, and though they return many times as long as they live the store shall never fail, and thus they will be supplied with abundance of food without toil." "Not so," said the elder brother, "for then will the people, idle and worthless and having no labor to perform, engage in quarrels, and fighting will ensue and they will destroy each other, and the people will be lost to the earth. They must work for all they receive." Then the younger brother answered not but went away sorrowing.

The next day he met the elder brother and accosted him thus: "Brother, your words were wise; let the Ute people work for their food. But how shall they be furnished with honeydew [a sweet secretion]? I have thought all night about this, and when the dawn came into the sky I sat on the summit of the mountain and did think, and now I will tell you how to give them honey-dew. Let it fall like a great snow upon the rocks and the women shall go early in the morning and gather all they may desire and they shall be glad." "No," replied the elder brother. "It will not be good, my little brother, for them to have much and find it without toil, for they will deem it of no more value than dung and what we give them for their pleasure will only be wasted. In the night it shall fall in small drops on the reeds which they shall gather and eat, and then will it taste very sweet, and having but little they will prize it the more." And the younger brother went away sorrowing but returned the next day and said, "My brother your words are wise; let the women gather the honey-dew with much toil by beating the reeds with flails. Brother, when a man or a woman, or a boy, or a girl, or a little one dies, where shall they go? I have thought all night about this and when the dawn came I sat on the top of the mountain and did think. Let me tell you what to do: when a man dies, send him back when the morning returns again, and then will all his friends rejoice." "Not so," said the elder, "the dead shall return no more." The little brother answered him not, but bending his head in sorrow went away.

One day the younger Shin-au-av was walking in the forest and saw his brother's son at play, and taking an arrow from his quiver slew the boy and when he returned did not mention what he had done. The father supposed that his boy was lost and wandered around in the woods for many days and at last found the dead child, and mourned his loss for a long time.

One day the younger Shin-au-av said to the elder, "You made the law that the dead should never return: now you know how it is yourself; I am glad that you were the first to suffer." Then the elder knew that the younger had killed his child and he was very angry and sought to destroy him, and as his wrath increased the earth rocked, subterranean groanings were heard, darkness came on, fierce storms raged, lightning flashed, thunder reverberated through the heavens, and the younger brother fled in great terror to his father Tov-wots [Rabbit] for protection.

[This stormy upheaval is said to have produced the Kaibab Plateau and the Cave Lakes near Kanab, Utah.]

II.

Si-chom-pa Ka-gon [Old Woman of the Sea] came out of the sea with a sack filled with something and securely tied. Then she went to the home of the Shin-au-av brothers carrying her burthen with her, which was very heavy, and bent her nearly to the ground. When she found the brothers she delivered to them the sack and told them to carry it to the middle of the world and open it, and enjoined upon them that they should not look into it until their arrival at the designated point, and there they would meet Tov-wots, who would tell them what to do with it. Then the old woman went back to the sea disappearing in the waters.

Shin-au-av Pavíts [the Elder] gave the sack to Shin-au-av Skaits [the Younger] and told him to do as Si-chom-pa Ka-gon had directed, and especially enjoined upon him that he must not open the sack lest some calamity should befall him. He found it very heavy and with great difficulty he carried it along by short stages and as he proceeded, his curiosity to know what it contained became greater and greater. "Maybe," said he, "it is sand; maybe it is dung! who knows but what the old woman is playing a trick!" Many times he tried to feel the outside of the sack to discover what it contained. At one time he thought it was full of snakes; at another, full of lizards. "So," said he, "it is full of fishes." At last his curiosity overcame him and he untied the sack, when out sprang hosts of people who passed out on the plain shouting and running toward the mountain. Shin-au-av Skaits overcome with fright, threw himself down on the sand. Then Tov-wots suddenly appeared and grasping the neck of the sack tied it up, being very angry with Shin-au-av Skaits. "Why," said he, "have you done this? I wanted these people to live in that good land to the east and here, foolish boy, you have let them out in a desert."

(Collected and translated by John Wesley Powell in 1871 from Southern Paiute.)

(Fowler and Fowler 1971:78, 80–81)

Whatever the antiquity of Owens Valley irrigation of indigenous root foods, this irrigation plus the relative abundance of grass seeds and pine nuts in this Basin-margin habitat allowed permanent villages in the valley, each village considering itself the manager of a surrounding territory that gave it resources from the river, the flood plain, the desert scrub, the pinyon groves, and the Sierra uplands, where deer and mountain sheep browsed. These Northern Paiute differed from other Numa in having larger, year-round communities and in traveling much less, since most resources could be obtained within 20 miles (30 kilometers) of the sedentary village. In these respects the Owens Valley Paiute were more Californian than Basin. The fundamental question of whether the Owens Valley Northern Paiute ought to be said to be agricultural does not really rest on the possible origins of their irrigation, but should be considered in the context of other Basin food-amplifying practices. Several other Numa peoples regularly burned over grasslands and broadcast chenopod seeds on this fertilized ground where competing plants had been checked. Thus, it is clear that the Numas' profound knowledge of the plants of their habitats either led directly to their modifications of the environments of preferred plants—as long as the time and labor of such modifications did not jeopardize the harvesting of other resources—or led them to take and adapt cultivation techniques from the farmers to the south. Full-scale agriculture could not develop in the prehistoric Basin because climatic conditions did not permit reliable subsistence agriculture: irrigable land was very limited, frosts were a hazard in many areas, and investing much time in coaxing maize up, and thereby neglecting other resources, was a gamble that might pay off only in famine. Euro-Americans could live exclusively by farming in the Basin only because they brought livestock and plants better adapted than maize to drier, cooler conditions, and could supplement their produce with imported food and goods. Indian peoples of the Basin adopted cultivation techniques, for both indigenous plants and domesticates brought in from other regions, that reliably and economically augmented the total harvests. The sum of Basin subsistence practices was variety: a variety of foods and a variety of techniques of gathering and processing them. The Numa were not agricultural, but carried utilizing natural resources to an art bespeaking skills and ingenuity fully comparable to those of any sedentary farming nation.

The Utes

The Utes composed about a dozen territorial bands in the early nineteenth century, covering most of the present state of Utah (named after them) and the Colorado Plateau, from the mountains south of Great Salt Lake eastward to the Front Range of the Rockies. Establishment of reservations in 1861, 1863, and 1868 reduced the Utes to what the Mormon colonists considered wasteland: in southern Colorado, the Muache and Capote have the Southern Ute Reservation and the Weeminuche the adjacent Ute Mountain Reservation; in northeastern Utah, the combined Uintah-Ouray Reservation is home to the Taviwach (Uncompahgre), Parusanuch, Yampa, Uintah, Pahvant, Timpanogots, Sanpits, and Moanunts.

The first Numa to be affected by European invasion were the Utes. On the northern border of the Southwest, they had been accustomed to trading with Anasazi pueblos. Spanish settlement in the Río Grande Valley in the seventeenth century brought Utes to these new sources of trade. The potential usefulness of horses was quickly realized by the Utes, who, with the Apache, their neighbors to the east, were the first Indians to make pack and riding horses integral to their cultural pattern. Horses enabled the Utes to travel out of the mountains and onto the plains to hunt bison and to carry the fruits of the hunt back to their mountain-valley homes. To hunt the bison herds more effectively, and to protect themselves against the Plains peoples who resisted Ute incursions, the Utes kept together in bands under recognized leaders. Utes did not, however, become Plains dwellers. After a bison hunt, they retreated to their traditional Basin-border lands, holding antelope and rabbit drives and gathering seeds and roots. Limited grazing in their homeland prevented them from accumulating large herds of horses such as the Comanche bred

on the Plains after A.D. 1700. Instead of maintaining their required number of horses by breeding, the Utes traded to the Spanish for horses, usually giving a captive or one of their own children. In the latter case, the child was not a slave but a foster child who was to be trained as a shepherd or cowboy in exchange for his labor, and who could return to his Ute relatives. This practice continued well into the nineteenth century. The treaty-period chief Ouray, born about 1820, spent his youth as a shepherd with a Hispanic family. During the eighteenth century, Utes added to their stock by raiding Plains camps and occasionally Spanish settlements. Ute women as well as men took part in the raids, which were seen as primarily sources of needed items rather than as arenas for martial exploits.

The United States made a treaty with Utes at the close of the war with Mexico, in 1849. The following decade brought pressure on the Ute hunting domain from Plains peoples, many of whom, of course, had themselves been removed from their ancestral homes. Supplied with more horses and more guns, these Indian Territory residents harassed Utes attempting to hunt bison. Restricted to the Colorado Plateau and border areas, the Utes could not obtain enough game to support their populations and had to raid for subsistence. The next decade, the 1860s, severely increased pressures on the Utes. They were to have a large portion of western Colorado as their reservation, but discovery of gold near Denver brought in Euro-American miners and a clamor to confine Indians to narrow sections of less desirable country. The Utes were shunted about, and the lands they had negotiated to retain whittled away again and again: in 1864, 1868, 1873, 1878, 1882, 1888, and finally in 1897 and 1899, Ute households were allotted homesteads in severalty and more than half the reservation acreage was opened to Euro-American ownership.

Under Chief Buckskin Charlie, who had succeeded Ouray as principal leader of the Utes in 1880, Utes made sincere efforts to adapt to Euro-

American patterns, attempting farming and schooling for the children. Euro-Americans had bought the better parcels of Ute land, however, and what remained in Ute hands gave poor returns. Many Ute, those who had most eagerly taken up farming among them, realized the emptiness of agents' promises of a good life through agriculture, and moved away from the agency to live as before in wickiups and to gather wild foods. Though they managed to survive, with the help of rations issued by the agency in return for labor from the men of the families, these Utes were much impoverished compared with their parents, since the "wild" portion of the reservation had meager resources and the valleys where once the Utes hunted and gathered were settled by Euro-Americans. The only employment available to them was occasional seasonal work on the Euro-American farms. Although the 1895 agreement to sell Ute lands "in excess" of the allotments to families had stipulated that the proceeds from the sale should be invested in, among other enterprises, sheep, it was thirty years before an agent implemented the agreement by purchasing sheep and organizing marketing of wool. Malnourishment made the people vulnerable to tuberculosis and other fatal diseases.

Real improvement in Ute living conditions began only after 1950, when the United States Court of Claims judged that the Utes had indeed been defrauded of much of their decreed territory and were entitled to millions of dollars in compensation. The tribe (organized as such under the 1934 Indian Reorganization Act) decided to distribute a portion of the compensation to each family, to be used to improve its home or meet similar needs, and to invest a substantial amount in projects for general betterment, from bringing in electricity, telephone service, water for homes and for irrigation, and vocational and professional training for tribal members, to developing livestock and timber enterprises, tourism, and Ute-owned, Ute-managed local businesses. A generation after the court judgment, these plans are still being slowly realized; some depend upon legal decisions on water

rights contended between the tribe and Euro-American neighbors. Meanwhile, older patterns of leasing grazing, oil, and gas rights persist. Also persisting are nineteenth-century traditional and early-reservation beliefs and patterns of social interaction. The Utes' principal religious and social ceremony, the late-spring Bear Dance, is regularly held on the three Ute reservations. In addition, the old social dances, in which women may use a "lame" foot-dragging step supposed to represent women dragging quantities of loot from a raid, and in which they bring in men whom they wish to partner, are widely participated in. About 1890, the Utes adopted the Plains Sun Dance from the Shoshoni as a means of restoring spiritual power and health. In 1870, the Utes had taken the first Paiute Ghost Dance, preached by Wodziwob, in hopes of revivifying their threatened culture. Twenty years under United States domination proved the futility of that hope, but did not destroy Ute convictions of the truth of their spiritual knowledge. The Sun Dance was established as an occasion for all Ute to congregate in prayer, listen to sermons from their wisest leaders and priests, obtain relief from malaise through the remedies and shamanistic techniques of their own doctors, and, if strongly motivated, dance to receive visions and increased power. Unlike many Plains Sun Dancers, Utes who had pledged to sacrifice in worship by dancing moved back and forth between the perimeter of the holy lodge and the center pole, rather than dancing in place. By the third day of this more vigorous movement, dancers could expect to be exhausted to the point of becoming open to visions. The Numa peoples who took the Sun Dance in the reservation period thus adapted it to their own forms of religious worship, and their active dancing plus the expectation that some participants would fall and be granted visions was similar to the form that went out to the Plains at this time as the 1890 Ghost Dance. Utes who turned to the Sun Dance ameliorated their reservation misery not through miracles, but through the belief that the concentration of spiritually gifted Indians would have some efficacy against the diseases so sorely afflicting the malnourished, ill-housed people. Tuberculosis was thought to be the worst of these. Sun Dances did not cure the diseases—in the late 1920s, one quarter of the Ute population suffered from tuberculosis and/or the eye disease trachoma—but they were thought to have held them somewhat in check, and Sun Dances continue to uplift Ute hearts. In 1980, the U.S. Census listed nearly six thousand Utes.

The Paiutes

Paiutes and Utes are closely related, with some bands (for example, the Antarianunts and the Kaiparowits) as easily considered Ute as Paiute. Ethnohistorians name about sixteen bands (including the Chemehuevi) in Arizona and southern Nevada and Utah as Southern Paiute, while most of Oregon and Nevada, plus northeastern California and southwestern Idaho, was Northern Paiute country. One historian put twenty-one names on a map as representing that number of Northern Paiute bands, but the Paiute themselves recognize primarily residential groupings in geographic regions rather than political entities. Beginning in the 1840s, the Oregon Trail and the California Trail were used by thousands of emigrating Euro-Americans, their cattle and horses, dislocating the Northern Paiute and eventually, after colonization of the interior valleys and mining claims from 1859, forcing the Northern Paiutes to Pyramid Lake and Walker River Reservations in western Nevada or to small Indian Colonies elsewhere in that state, Oregon, or California. Southern Paiute were pushed onto reservations during the 1870s. Kaibab and Shivsits Reservations, one on each side of the Utah-Arizona border, and Chemehuevi Reservation, on the California side of the lower Colorado River, remain; several Southern Paiute reservations were terminated by the U.S. government in 1954, although there was some restoration in 1980, and small Indian Colonies also remain.

Paiute history is not dissimilar to Ute history. Euro-American impingement began with wagon trains traveling across the Basin to Oregon and California in the 1850s. Horses and cattle on the wagon trains consumed grasses and shoots the Paiute would have harvested, and disrupted game habitats. Emigrants were trigger-happy, shooting Indians they thought might attack, or taking revenge for fights and pilfering by wantonly murdering whatever Indians they found. During the 1860s, most of the Paiutes were persuaded or pressured to move to reservations. Mormons began proselytizing Indians, and initiating a program, which continues today, of taking Indian children into Mormon homes to cut them off from their parental culture. Mormons and other Euro-Americans also proliferated in the lands around water sources, cutting off all Indians from these prime resource areas. They chopped down pinyon pines for fuel and fence posts. Livestock from their settlements grazed widely, destroying many of the native seed-bearing grasses; former grasslands became sagebrush desert. Pigs often went feral, rooting up the Indian marsh and lake-shore resources and depredating the nests of waterfowl. Wild game could not compete against the livestock and were severely reduced in numbers. If the Indians took some ripening grain from a field, or butchered a steer from the range, a hue and cry was raised to jail the thieves. The subsequent history of the Southern Paiute closely parallels that of their neighbors the Ute, from the terrible health conditions following the continuing attrition of their lands well into the twentieth century, to the eventual favorable settlement in 1970 of land claims against the United States. A complication is that some of the southernmost Paiute, the San Juan Paiute, were not recognized as an Indian nation; and the majority of the southern Paiute, in 1865, were said to have signed a treaty that in fact was not agreed to by any reasonable number of Southern Paiutes and, furthermore, was never ratified by the United States Congress. In 1954, that Congress—which had for nearly a century attempted to maneuver the Southern Paiutes without meeting its own legal criteria for doing so—decreed termination to the Southern Paiutes' Indian status. After reinstatement in 1980, the census of that year claimed only 110 Southern Paiute (out of a grand total of over nine thousand "Paiute," most of these not designated to any particular Paiute group). It was a decade later, in 1990, that the San Juan Southern Paiute were officially recognized as an Indian tribe.

Northern Paiute history is more checkered. There was an attempt to herd Paiute onto a reservation on the Malheur River in eastern Oregon. The peoples at Pyramid and Walker Lakes in Nevada resisted, determined to keep at least the core of their territories and with it the lakes' unique fish runs. Some of the more northern groups moved to the Malheur, which had been selected principally because it was remote from the Nevada regions being overrun by Euro-American mining speculators. In 1878, many, but by no means all, northern Paiute joined angry Bannock Shoshoni (actually a Northern Paiute band living among Shoshoni) in abandoning reservations where they were starving (bison were gone, and government aid amounted to 2 1/2 cents per person per day). Strong military force broke up this last desperate plea for Indian rights, the final blow being the massacre of all the women and children in a Bannock camp of twenty households at Clark's Ford, Idaho. Further retaliation against the Paiute included removing them, plus many families who had not been part of the hostilities, to the reservation of their traditional enemies, the Yakima, in eastern Washington. Among these displaced families was that of Winnemucca, leader of the Pyramid Lake band, who with his father Truckee had been steadfast for peace; even the murder of one of Truckee's sons while the youth and his father were fishing had not provoked this family to condemn the invaders. The continuing injustices finally impelled Winnemucca and his daughter, Sarah Winnemucca Hopkins, to travel east to beg the government to relocate their people. Mrs. Hopkins carried on the

protest in lectures in eastern cities and in a book, *Life Among the Piutes, Their Wrongs and Claims*, which she published in 1883 (it is again available, reissued in paperback by Chalfant Press of Bishop, California). The Paiutes were officially granted permission to leave the Yakima for the Malheur, but were frustrated by agents in the field who would not cooperate. Eventually, Malheur's status as a reservation was rescinded and both its Paiutes and the families who had left the Yakima one by one were neglected by government.

After about 1880, the majority of Paiutes lived on Euro-American farms and ranches as laborers, or in shanty towns on the edges of Euro-American communities. Men worked in haying and harvesting or sheepshearing, women as domestics in Euro-American homes and hotels. Like Jack Wilson (Wovoka), the Northern Paiute 1890 Ghost Dance prophet, most Paiute used their wages for clothing, guns and ammunition for hunting, and some food, but continued to reside in the thatched or tule-mat wickiups and to gather native foods where colonization had not yet destroyed their habitats. Children were left with the grandparents while their parents worked—basically the same pattern as the traditional one, in which older women in camp freed the younger mothers to work at gathering. Wages for Indians were very low, sometimes scandalously so (one brewery paid Indian workers by allowing them to tap as much beer as they could drink at the end of the working day), and most families scavenged in garbage cans in the towns to supplement what they could buy and gather. Disease, of course, took a severe toll. A study made in the late 1930s reported that garbage cans were still a regular source of food, that trachoma affected most families and tuberculosis and venereal diseases many, that infant mortality was high and girls tempted into prostitution, but that, believe it or not, "in comparison with the period from 1880 to 1910, conditions are improved" (Whiting 1950:25).

As among the Utes, old beliefs and practices have persisted in spite of their relative powerlessness against the miseries of the reservation period.

Wodziwob's 1870 prophecies and those of Jack Wilson twenty years later were taken by most Paiute as new revelations in the continuing series normal in Paiute life, rather than as new religions. Peyotism appeared, as among the Utes, but without converting a majority of the people. Unlike the Utes and Shoshoni, the Paiutes did not turn to the Plains Sun Dance. Instead, they relied on private treatments by their own doctors' shamanistic methods. Spiritual power obtained in dreams was the foundation of leadership—Winnemucca and several other late-nineteenth-century chiefs came forward to lead because they had power to ward off bullets, they believed—and was to be used to benefit the community. A formal congregation as in the Sun Dance was not felt to be required. Thus, the Paiute have been materially impoverished, but their cultural pattern has been modified less than those of the many Indian groups who accepted new, if still Indian, religions in the reservation period. There were nearly ten thousand Paiute counted in the 1980 census, the majority of them Northern Paiute.

The Shoshoni

Shoshoni (also spelled Shoshone) formed the northeastern vanguard of Numa expansion. Some pushed onto the Plains, where they became the Eastern Shoshoni. They were located on the Wind River Reservation in Wyoming after the treaty of 1868. Others crossed the mountains during the nineteenth century to hunt bison on the Plains, but spent most of the year west of the Rockies. Western Shoshoni occupy most of Nevada, with the southwesternmost band, the Panamint, just over the California border. Shoshoni thus overlapped, or interdigitated with, their linguistic relatives the Northern Paiute. The least well-known Shoshoni, because the least encountered by Euro-Americans, were the Sheepeaters, who hunted mountain sheep in the mountains of Idaho, wintering on the Lemhi River or in smaller valleys in Idaho and adjacent Montana. In southeastern Idaho were the Bannock

(from their own word Pana'ti), whose language is a Northern Paiute dialect, and who therefore are misnamed Shoshoni. Salmon runs up the Snake and Salmon rivers in Idaho were exploited by all these Shoshoni and by the Northern Paiute having access to these streams in southeastern Oregon and Idaho. Camas, the bulb of a plant related to the hyacinth, was abundant in better-watered prairies of the southern Plateau and was an important resource for the Shoshoni. Salmon and camas supported larger communities among the Shoshoni than could generally be maintained farther south in the Basin.

Horses, reaching the Shoshoni at the beginning of the eighteenth century, reinforced band organization among the Shoshoni on the Plains and those in western Montana and eastern Idaho whose territories had sufficient grass to feed horses. (Over most of the Basin, horses would have competed with people for the grasses, of which humans gathered the seeds. Therefore, Western Shoshoni and Paiutes ate any horses they obtained.) Horse herds limited the Eastern and Northern Shoshoni, like so many other early historic Indian nations, to camps offering good horse pasture, and competition for these localities necessitated stronger organization among families sharing the guarding of herds now vital to their economy. Many Shoshoni of the eighteenth century covered a thousand miles yearly between the camas grounds of central Idaho and the bison plains east of the Rockies. Bison were also hunted on the Snake River plain and other intermontane extensions of High Plains ecology. In at least one instance, an impoundment beneath a rimrock was used, similar to bison drives on the High Plains (and to corraling antelope and bighorn sheep in the Basin). Bison, however, were not as numerous west of the Rockies as they were east of them. The Eastern Shoshoni came to resemble Plains Indians in wearing buckskin shirts and leggings or dresses rather than merely breechcloths or aprons such as seemed sufficient to the Basin Numa, in living in hide tipis rather than thatch or mat wickiups, and in attaching prestige to exploits in war and horse raiding.

FIGURE 7.4 Washakie's camp in the Wind River mountains of Wyoming, 1870. *(Smithsonian Institution National Anthropological Archives)*

Euro-American fur trappers in western Wyoming and Montana and in Idaho were the first aliens to compete with Shoshoni in their historic homeland, beginning in the 1820s. Wagon trains of emigrants during the 1850s affected the Shoshoni less than they did the Paiute, since the majority of the Shoshoni were hunting away from the valley routes of the trains during the summer, when most emigrants came through. Nevertheless, Euro-Americans' thefts and sometimes senseless destruction of Indian food caches were a nuisance, although not as serious as these acts were to the Paiute in the more sere regions of the Basin. Mormons tried settling on the Lemhi River in 1855; permanent Euro-American colonization began in 1860, and was soon augmented by gold prospectors in Idaho. Negotiations between the government and Shoshoni culminated in the placing of over a thousand Shoshoni and Bannock on a reservation at Fort Hall in central southern Idaho in 1869. A smaller reservation was occupied at Fort Lemhi from 1875 to 1907. The so-called Bannock

War of 1878, in which unhappy Bannock and other Northern Paiute were shown the power of the United States government, was followed by the Sheepeater War of 1879, hounding a few families of Shoshonis from the mountains to Fort Hall Reservation. The Indian side of the Sheepeater War consisted of fifty-one persons, only fifteen of them men able to wield arms, and a total of eight guns, two of them antique muzzleloaders. The last Northern Shoshoni to move to Fort Hall were a village at Smith's Ferry on the Payette River, where Indians employed in a sawmill had by the 1870s settled in wooden houses, plowed fields and planted fruit orchards, and kept pigs and chickens. "Civilized" though they had become, they were no more acceptable to their Euro-American neighbors who coveted the Indian farms than the acculturated Cherokees had been to their Georgia neighbors. At the end of the century, this Indian community was driven from its home and onto Fort Hall.

Early reservation arrangements at both Fort Hall and the Western Shoshoni and Northern Paiute reservation straddling the Idaho-Nevada border around Owyhee were excruciatingly slow to be implemented. Agents did not receive the rations they had requested, and had to encourage the Indians to leave the reservations to gather and hunt where they could. With Euro-American farms and towns in so many of the more habitable areas, Indians were banned from localities they had formerly relied upon. One factor triggering the Bannock Wars was a treaty infringement by Euro-Americans who disregarded the allocation of the Idaho location called Camas Prairie to the Indians, and permitted their hogs to root up the precious bulbs of this resource area. Idaho Euro-Americans were also pressuring the government to reduce the size of the reservations in order to open the reserved land for sale to non-Indians. After 1900, Fort Hall Reservation was allotted to its residents under the Dawes Act and "surplus" land sold until only one quarter of the original reservation remained. Much of the Indians' better land became the town and environs of Pocatello, ironically named after a Shoshoni leader. At this time, 1901, the Sun Dance was taken up by the Fort Hall people, who learned it from the Wind River Shoshoni in Wyoming, who in turn had been taught by a Comanche a century earlier and had then been influenced toward a more elaborate form when the Arapaho were placed on that reservation with them. The Idaho Shoshoni had accepted and had never forgotten the 1870 Ghost Dance religion of Wodziwob, and this faith was strengthened among them by the new revelations of Jack Wilson in 1889. But by 1900, the threat that allotment into severalty posed to their community had spurred them to receive a religious form that more clearly emphasized the importance of the community as a congregation and a supportive group for the distressed.

The Shoshoni variant of the Sun Dance was approximately the same as that of the Ute, with the sacrificing dancers going back and forth to the center pole instead of moving in place at their positions around the rim of the lodge. The Shoshoni and the three Ute divisions (Southern,

Northern, and Ute Mountain, the latter the conservative Weeminuche band) visit one another's Sun Dances, fortifying their consciousness of common bonds among the Numa peoples. Fort Hall Shoshoni deviate from the general eastern Numa Sun Dance in recognizing the leadership of women as well as men as Sun Dance chiefs and shamans, a circumstance that encourages women to dance within the holy lodge at Fort Hall; on the other reservations, women's active participation within the lodge has been discouraged, although this attitude is lessening. Peyotism was introduced to the Fort Hall people in 1915 by an Oglala Lakota missionary, Sam Lone Bear, and under his tutelage became established as a form of worship and means to relief from malaise attractive to those who prefer small gatherings and meditative communion. These religious innovations and the persistence of older forms, including the round dances and prayers at sunrise, cushion the impact of poverty upon the Idaho Shoshoni but cannot relieve it.

Fort Hall has better agricultural and grazing lands than reservations farther south in the Basin, but most of the profit from these advantages are gleaned by Euro-Americans leasing Indian allotments. Although Pocatello is close enough to Fort Hall to make employment in its industries and services convenient, Fort Hall people find most of their employment in the seasonal needs of potato farmers and ranchers—that is to say, in the least desirable intermittent jobs. As late as 1950, 4 percent of Fort Hall residents were living year-round in tents. Ten years later, at the beginning of the 1960s, 82 percent of Fort Hall housing was below the minimum standards of rural Idaho Euro-Americans. Half the employable adults on the reservation were unemployed in 1966, and the other half included a large percentage in temporary or part-time jobs. At that time, the median number of years of school completed by adult Shoshoni was nine, some improvement since 1950, when 56 percent of Fort Hall adults were classed as illiterate, but not sufficient schooling to give people a fair chance in the labor market. Thus handicapped, urban relocation has not been a solution for Fort Hall Shoshoni, and very few have attempted it. Not numerous enough to carry political clout, the Shoshoni of the twentieth century have lived in a desert made by Euro-American usurpation of their resources. Shoshoni population approximately equals that of the Paiute, with a total of nearly ten thousand.

SECTION 3: THE PLATEAU

Historically, the Plateau contrasts markedly with the Great Basin in the importance of salmon to Plateau economies and the absence of this fish in the Basin. The contrast is not absolute, not only because the northernmost Basin groups (the Northern Paiute and the Shoshoni) had access to salmon runs in southeastern Oregon and Idaho, but also because the Paiute of the western Basin depended in part on harvesting runs of lake fish in the closed-drainage basins of Pyramid, Walker, and other southern intermontane systems. Nevertheless, crucial differences between the salmon runs, usually abundant but over the long range sporadic, in the Plateau and the less generous, more localized closed-drainage-system fish runs farther south, clearly affected the cultural patterns of the Plateau and Basin. Populations on the Plateau are largest down-river, and decrease as one moves up-river on the main streams and into their tributaries. The decrease correlates with the decrease, going up-river, in overall number of salmon, in number of species of salmon (five in the lower Fraser, for example, but only two in the upper reaches of this river), and in nutrition as the fish exhaust themselves swimming upriver to spawn.

Prehistoric Cultural Patterns

An economy based on relatively intensive production of salmon and "roots" (actually mostly bulbs and tubers) in contrast to the earlier, apparently more generalized, Western Archaic cultural pattern, seems to have appeared only after the climatic temperature maximum of the fourth and third millennia B.C. By the early second millennium, or roughly 1700 B.C., human communities that had abandoned the lowest, most arid sections of the southern Plateau were moving down from their upland refuges, and forest-adapted people were probably migrating south in British Columbia onto the Columbia Plateau. A set of tools for working wood—hard, polished-stone adzes, stone mauls, wedges of antler for splitting logs, and beaver- and marmot-incisor knives—had become common on the Plateau by 500 B.C., and imply that dugout canoes and well-constructed winter houses were in general use throughout the culture area. Direct evidence of the houses, which were built with posts rising from a floor dug about one meter (one yard) below the ground surface, has been excavated in numerous archaeological sites. Conical roofs of poles laid on rafters resting on the posts were probably covered with earth. People as well as light and ventilation entered through a smoke hole at the top of the mound-like conical roof. One example of such a house from early in this period measured 9 meters (nearly 30 feet) in diameter, and another at the same site was even larger, an elongated oval with three stone-lined fire hearths. The size of these houses and the presence of more than one fire hearth suggest they were occupied by extended families. Some sites have only one house, fairly large; others have one or a few large houses and several small ones, the latter possibly not family residences but houses in which menstruating women could keep separate so the peak of womanly power would not negate the health and hunting luck of men (historically, a practice in the Plateau), or sweat lodges where members of the community could purify themselves. The well-insulated, if dark, winter pit houses are situated in sheltered, wooded valleys beside clear tributary streams. Much less archaeological evidence survives for the temporary, mat-covered,

A-frame houses used in summer by historic Plateau peoples. These portable homes would be erected on camas prairies or beside fishing stations on the rivers. It is likely that these sites were heavily utilized after roughly 1700 B.C., because salmon bones become increasingly common from this time on in refuse middens, and because mortars with basketry hoppers, historically used on the Plateau for processing camas bulbs and edible tubers and roots, as well as earth ovens such as were historically used for baking these foods, are found to date from this period. Net sinkers seem to date as early as about 5000 B.C. on the Plateau, and continue in use, attesting to seining as well as spearing and dip netting as techniques used in fishing. Plateau-type fishing has been found to occur in this period as far east as the edge of the Front Range of the Rockies in Waterton Lakes and Glacier National Parks, on the border of central Montana and Alberta. In the first millennium A.D., population in the Plateau was probably as high as could feasibly be maintained, and armed competition for resources may have developed, judging from the violent deaths evidenced in some groups of skeletons from this period.

About A.D. 1300, salmon fishing appears to have been intensified, and a number of relatively minor innovations in the cultural repertoire indicate increased contacts to the south and down-river from the Plateau. These innovations include pottery, dice and counters for gambling games, clay figurines, turquoise, and apparently traded maize, all probably from the south and perhaps carried by the Numa expansion; and Pacific coast shells (abalone, dentalium, olivella, clam, and scallop) and whalebone clubs traded up from the lower Columbia and Fraser rivers. Importation of Pacific shells up-river dates back to 6000 B.C. on the Plateau, but the amount and variety of shells increased in the late prehistoric period. The increase at this time in trade goods and dependence on salmon suggests a shift on the Plateau from a focus on subsistence to commercialization: salmon fishing being a highly efficient mode of garnering subsistence, in terms of time input, people could produce local specialities for trade and travel to commercial centers without jeopardizing family welfare. In contrast, the hunting of mountain sheep, elk, deer, bison, and antelope, which had been more important before this late period, was relatively time-inefficient until horses made possible instant surrounds of herds and the ready transport of quantities of goods. (The rivers of the Plateau are mostly poor for navigation, with many rapids that require portaging.) Population pressure, from both native increase through the centuries plus Numa expansion into the southern Plateau, may have contributed to this increased concern with efficiency in subsistence pursuits, concentration on the most productive resources, and interest in trade.

Horses became available to the southern Plateau through the Shoshoni, early in the eighteenth century, but did not come into use in the northern and western Plateau until the nineteenth century, and in some areas not until the beginning of Euro-American settlement. Those groups who began to use horses before Euro-American domination advanced into the Plateau shifted their cultural patterns much as did the easternmost Numa peoples and the Plains villages that turned nomad. Trips were made over the mountains in summer to hunt bison herds on the Plains or on their grassland extensions into Idaho. The dark pit house was abandoned and hide tipis substituted; sometimes the complete change was not carried out and mat-covered lodges were used year-round, these being as portable as tipis. Many persons clothed themselves in Plains-style shirts and leggings or buckskin dresses instead of the Plateau costume of only a robe for men and a long tunic of mountain-sheep skin or goatskin for women. For protection, groups hunting on the Plains kept together under leaders. Home on the Plateau, most groups selected an intelligent, respected man to be village chief. His responsibilities included organizing moves to the fishing stations and root-digging grounds, advising hunters, and mediating disputes. Several nations, such as the Okanagon on the British Columbia-

Washington border, also designated woman chiefs, who cooperated with and advised their male counterparts. These women did not deal with women alone, but were (and are) deeply respected by all for their sagacity. In spite of having villages organized under managers, the Plateau nations did not confine their members to particular communities, but allowed individuals or families to change affiliation as desired. Certain favorable sites were used year after year for winter villages, although the families using them might differ from one year to another. Organized villages, chiefs, and flexibility of affiliation probably were characteristic of the Plateau before horses became available, and seem to have been present before Euro-American settlement in those regions where the horse was not taken up. These characteristics fit well when the southern- and eastern-Plateau groups became part of the historic bison-hunting, horse-raiding West.

Historically, the Plateau was divided linguistically between two language stocks, Sahaptin on the south and Salish on the north. The ecological and cultural division of the Plateau into a northern, or Canadian, component and a southern, or United States, component does not coincide with the linguistic division, which lies almost two hundred miles (three hundred kilometers) south of the ecological-cultural transition at approximately the international border. Sahaptin is generally considered to be a stock of the Penutian phylum, which includes many languages along the Pacific coast from British Columbia into Mexico. The Sahaptin languages, all within the Plateau, include Nez Perce (a French name today pronounced "Nez Purse," not according to the French mode), and three dialect groups of Sahaptin proper: Yakima, Kititas, Upper Cowlitz, Upper Nisqually, and Klikitat in one; Wanapam, Walla Walla, Wawyukma, and Palouse in the second; and Umatilla, Wyam, John Day, Celilo, Tygh, and Tenino, all along the middle Columbia River, in the third (today grouped as the "Warm Springs"). Molalla and Klamath-Modoc are Penutian-language isolates of the the western Plateau, and Cayuse an

isolate without apparent relations. Observers have noted that the Nez Perce and Sahaptin speakers were frequently bilingual, not only within Plateau Penutian but with Salish, Shoshoni, or Crow as well, reflecting the importance of trade to the historic Plateau. The other major stock on the Plateau, Salish, probably includes the language isolate, Kutenai, spoken by a people at the border point of Montana, Idaho, and British Columbia in the Rockies. Interior Salish languages are: Lillooet, Shuswap, and Thompson in British Columbia; closely related dialects Okanagan, Sanpoil, Colville, and Lake (Senijextee) on the British Columbia–Washington border; in Idaho, the Coeur d'Alene (pronounced "Cur-da-leen"); in Montana and Washington, Flathead, Pend d'Oreille ("Ponduray"), Kalispel, and Spokan; and in Washington on the middle Columbia, Wenatchi. Precisely on the border of the Plateau at the Dalles, the up-river end of the long series of rapids and twisting channels cut by the Columbia River through the Cascades Range before it flows to the coast, were the villages of the Wishram and Wasco, speaking Chinook, a language of the Penutian phylum distinct from Sahaptin. Basically, the Wishram and Wasco belonged to the Plateau culture area, but because they specialized in large-scale production of dried salmon for sale and also hosted trading fairs attended by thousands of persons, their economy was quite different from that of the more typical Plateau peoples far up-river. The prominence of the Wishrams' market town led to the development of a pidgin language, Chinook Jargon, based on Chinook but with Nootka (a Wakashan language spoken on Vancouver Island), French, and English borrowings; a lingua franca understood from California to Alaska along the coast and far into the interior.

In 1805, when Lewis and Clark recorded the first descriptions by Euro-Americans of the Plateau and its peoples, use of horses had modified the cultural patterns of much of the southern Plateau they transversed. The basic adaptation persisted, however, with winter survival in the small villages

FIGURE 7.5 Nez Perce hunting camp, 1871. The woman is preparing pemmican from dried meat. *(Smithsonian Institution National Anthropological Archives)*

in the sheltered valleys dependent upon stores of two principal foods, salmon and "roots" (including the bulbs of the camas). Both types of food were processed into flour, the salmon by being filleted, dried on racks, and then pounded fine, the roots and bulbs by being baked in earth ovens and then pounded. The compacted dried foods were then packed into baskets lined with salmon skin, if for dried salmon, and the baskets placed in small storage houses or in stone- or bark-lined cache pits convenient to the winter settlements. Cakes of dried berries and pounded parched sunflower seeds were also stored. These basic foods would be sup-

plemented by game and fowl hunted on the Plateau or dried bison meat. The adaptation was a continuation of the Western Archaic pattern of exploitation of a variety of wild resources with concentration upon a few of the most abundant, storable foods, although by the late prehistoric period, after A.D. 1300, concentration upon salmon and "roots" had become more pronounced, and hunting concomitantly less so.

The Plateau adaptation was fundamentally similar to that of the Basin Numa, but contrasted in principal resources (salmon, and "roots" more important than seeds) and in the greater population density these permitted. The beliefs of the Plateau people were also similar to those of the Numa, attributing success in any aspect of life to the support of a spirit enhancing an individual's all too limited human power. A round dance during which individuals might go into a trance and see visions when the song of his or her spirit power was performed was customarily held in the winter villages. Spirit power was apprehended through natural phenomena and creatures, so the songs celebrated attributes of the natural world. At the round dances, spiritual leaders would preach moral behavior to the assembly; these sermons might incorporate revelations gained through visions. As was common on the Plains and in the Woodland, Plateau children were sent out to spend a few days alone, fasting and praying, to render them pitiable to a spirit who would appear and promise aid when needed. When the child returned, a shaman in the community would help the child interpret his or her experience and suggest how keeping a symbol of the spirit, avoiding objects or behavior offensive to or intimately connected with the spirit, and remembering the spirit's song would enable the child to benefit from the promise of power throughout life. As among other nations throughout America, individuals trained to diagnose illness or misfortune and treat it with herbs and the incantation of spiritual power were relied upon for medical and psychological therapy; often termed "shamans" in the literature, they are better seen as doctors practicing non-Western medical traditions.

Fur Traders, Missionaries, and Soldiers Invade the Plateau

Fur traders entered the Plateau in 1811, the Hudson's Bay Company from Alberta and United States traders from Montana and Wyoming. Initially, they were welcomed. Plateau peoples were accustomed to trade, and the novelty of the strangers' posts, with flags and ceremonies, brought the curious from hundred of miles away. Among the traders' parties were Iroquois,

twenty-four of whom settled permanently among the Flathead in 1820. The reorganization of the Hudson's Bay Company after it merged with the independent North West Company in 1821 included a directive to educate representative Indian youths in Christianity and British schooling. To that end, two boys, sons of leaders of the Spokan and the Kutenai, were taken in 1825 to the school established at the Red River colony in Manitoba. In 1830, sons of leaders of the Cayuse, Nez Perce, and again Spokan and Kutenai, five in all, joined the first two youths at the Red River school. One of the first youths, named Spokan Garry after a Hudson's Bay Company official, became a well-known leader among the Spokan, advantaged by his fluency in English and familiarity with Euro-American customs. He lived until 1892, but even when he first returned from school for a vacation among his people, in 1829, Spokan Garry was listened to attentively as he described his experiences and retailed what he had learned of Christianity. Stimulated in part by Spokan Garry's accounts of the power of the Canadians, supposedly linked to knowledge to be read from the Bible, four Nez Perce men journeyed in 1831 to St. Louis to learn at first hand of Christian power and to invite missionaries to come teach the Nez Perce the knowledge that had made Christians both rich and relatively immune to disease. Epidemics of smallpox, measles, whooping cough, and other European scourges had at this point severely afflicted the Plateau peoples and led them to wish for Euro-American healers, whom they assumed would appear as spiritual leaders, to deal with the new foreign illnesses. The Indians' apparent native desire for what the Christians supposed to be salvation excited a great deal of sentiment in the United States, and beginning in 1834, both Protestant and Catholic missionaries answered the call. In spite of the deaths of the two older Nez Perce travelers in St. Louis, and of one of the two younger men on the steamboat returning up the Missouri to the West, the Nez Perce and other Plateau peoples were receptive to the missionaries.

Even before the actual arrival of missionaries, many had incorporated Spokan Garry's knowledge and what they had observed at the Hudson's Bay Company posts into a new religion retaining the indigenous round-dance form and its openness to revelations received in trance or visions, but adding an observance of the Sabbath every seventh day, flagpoles, leadership by the "chiefs" (the secular managers of the band) rather than by the doctors, and songs celebrating God the Creator rather than a variety of natural forces and spirits. The missionaries attempted to build on this pseudo-Christian religion that used crosses as talismans but lacked Christ. They encouraged the village leaders to instruct their followers in the new teachings, recognizing certain men as head chiefs, others as subchiefs, and additional men as policemen. They tried to "civilize" their hosts by introducing monogamy even when this would mean the breakup of longstanding happy marriages of sisters to one husband, by establishing farms, sawmills, and Euro-American-style frame houses, and by drawing up codes of laws specifying hanging or flogging for malefactors, punishments quite alien to peoples who tried to settle injurious acts by payment of damages. The missionaries also tried, with much more rapid success, to civilize the country by touting its delights to friends in the United States, urging them to make up parties of immigrants. Most of the first waves of Euro-Americans passed through the Plateau to colonize the Willamette Valley of western Oregon or to settle in California, but gradually the narrower but lovely valleys of the Plateau were chosen by farmers and ranchers who noticed the fine large horse herds maintained, and sold to them, by the Indians in this country. Delaware trappers who had married Sahaptin women and hunted with their in-laws warned them of the serious threat Euro-American settlement posed to Indians.

Steadily increasing pressure by Euro-American colonists led to government-sponsored treaty negotiations in 1855 with the Plateau peoples and their Plains neighbors and enemies, the Blackfoot.

Peace with the Blackfoot would ease Plateau hunters' forays onto the Plains for bison, and must have been a carrot leading many of the Flathead, Nez Perce, and Coeur d'Alene to the treaty. Treaty or no, Euro-American incursions into the richest Indian lands continued. In 1858, a well-armed troop of five companies of United States soldiers marched north in eastern Washington for no very clear reason, and were about to pass through a prime camas prairie, when repulsed by men from Yakima, Spokan, Palouse, and Coeur d'Alene bands. The peace treaty formally ending this "war" declared most of the Indians' territory open for Euro-American settlement. Two years later, in 1860, prospectors for gold (including many Chinese) overran the Plateau, precipitating damaging erosion by destroying the plant cover along stream banks and ruining the fishing, so vital to the Indians, in many of the smaller streams. Through the 1860s and 1870s, the native people were pressured and cajoled onto reservations, which were redrawn after Indian occupancy in order to reduce the boundaries. One band of Nez Perce (in their own language, Nimipu) in the Wallowa Valley in northeasternmost Oregon was understandably reluctant to abandon their beautiful little refuge where their noted horse herds flourished and they had small farms. The government had granted them a section of the Wallowa in 1873; two years later, it bent to demands from Euro-American immigrants and revoked the grant. After two more years of futile pleas from the band's leader, Hinmaton-yalatkit (Thunder Coming Up From the Water Over the Land), known as Chief Joseph from the name given to his father by a missionary, the band was literally driven from its homeland by a military escort intending to ensure its removal to the reservation decreed for the Nez Perce. Minor skirmishes ensued, touched off by a young man revenging the murder of his father by a settler. Hinmaton-yalatkit determined to march his people into Canada, hoping to obtain safety there, as had Sitting Bull and his Lakota after their defeat of Custer the year before. Throughout the summer the band traveled

FIGURE 7.6 Hinmaton-yalatkit, "Chief Joseph" (1832–1904), in 1877. *(Smithsonian Institution National Anthropological Archives)*

a tortuous route through the mountains, evading the armies sent against them, until in October they were surrounded by troops and had no choice but surrender, 1,000 miles (1,600 kilometers) from Wallowa and only 50 miles (80 kilometers) from the international border they sought. (Over a hundred of the Nez Perce, led by another chief, White Bird, did manage to gain Canada and assistance from Sitting Bull and his refugee band there.) Hinmaton-yalatkit and his proud Nez Perce were then sent into exile in Indian Territory, Oklahoma, and were not allowed to return to the Plateau until 1884, and then not to the Nez Perce Reservation of their Nimipu congeners but to the Colville in northeastern Washington, still far from their beloved Wallowa Valley. Considered to be still prisoners of war and forced to share a foreign locality with the resentful native Nespelem and Sanpoil, Hinmaton-yalatkit's Nez Perce refused to accept farmstead allotments or the houses built on them, insisting they were waiting to be allowed to return to the valley they had never agreed to give up. Hinmaton-yalatkit died in 1904 in the tipi he had always lived in, still in exile. Every one of his nine children had died long before him, all but one during the years the family was held in Indian Territory or on the slow return north.

The Yakima

History for the other Plateau peoples in the United States also fell into the familiar pattern. Kamaiakan, recognized at the 1855 treaty negotiations as head chief of the Yakima, had begun to raise cattle as early as 1836, and subsequently developed a farm. The year before the treaty, the Yakima were reported to be growing potatoes, peas, pumpkins, melons, and some maize, intelligently concentrating upon potatoes as the most profitable crop for their country. The horses they and adjacent Plateau peoples bred had been famous for decades. Nevertheless, Kamaiakan and his fellow Yakima were to be deprived of the lands they had selected and invested labor in, and these choice acreages sold for a pittance to Euro-Americans. Kamaiakan himself resisted, captaining several of the fights between 1855 and the major battle of 1858 that has been termed the Yakima War. Twenty-four leading men involved in the war were executed after their surrender; Kamaiakan, wounded in the last battle, escaped into British Columbia and lived impoverished in exile thereafter. He and his people are recorded to have lost eight hundred horses, nearly all their winter stores, and their winter village with all their possessions in it as a result of the final battle in September, 1858. The Yakimas removed to the reservation assigned to them soon

came under the power of a missionary who built up the economic assets of the agency—cattle herds, a sawmill, apple orchards, and good horses—but would not share them with Yakimas who did not accept his dictates. "If I fail to give moral character to an Indian I can give him nothing that does him permanent good. If I can succeed in giving him moral character, then he no longer needs the gifts of government," said the Reverend Wilbur in justifying his policy of distributing treaty-stipulated benefits only to Indians who cut their hair and worked as he decreed (Relander et al. 1955:31). Reverend Wilbur was succeeded in 1882 by a person who was less inclined to flog men and women for infractions of the mission's rules, but who was even more dangerous to the Yakima. He sold off the agency cattle and urged that the reservation be allotted in severalty with the "excess" land, which would be most of the Yakima grant, made available to Euro-American homesteading. This agent, as might be expected, failed to protect Yakima fishing rights at the salmon-netting stations, rights guaranteed them in their treaty and necessary for their sustenance. The Yakimas were forced to share their reservation with destitute Northern Paiute, whom they pitied but distrusted, after the Bannock War, and with a Salish-speaking band, the Sinkiuse, led by Chief Moses (Sispilth Kalch [Seven Shirts]). Although a new agent in 1890 reported he found the Yakima unanimously against allotment of their land in severalty, surveyors were sent out in 1892 to divide the reservation into 80-acre (32-hectare) allotments, one per person, plus a few for Yakima settled outside the reservation boundary. The "excess" land was sold. Under the Dawes Act, an Indian would not ordinarily be allowed to alienate his or her land until twenty-five years had passed, but among the Yakima, as among many other groups, agents sympathetic to Euro-American demands for land obeyed the letter rather than the spirit of the law, declaring a large number of Indians competent to hold fee title to their allotments. Buyers quickly appeared. Those Indians who staunchly refused to sell were persuaded in many instances to lease their allotments, deriving a small annual income in place of the opportunity to develop their own land. As early as 1911, only 2 percent of all the land allotted to Yakima was actually in Yakima hands: the rest was leased out. It was particularly notorious of the Plateau reservations that their irrigable land was soon out of Indian control, and dry scrub left to the reservation residents. At the end of the stipulated twenty-five years, in 1917, the Yakima went to court to protect their remaining land from dissolution, arguing that the Dawes Act did not require but only permitted the granting of fee patent to allotment owners, and that the agents' readiness to declare an owner competent to deal with Euro-American buyers had been so excessive as to violate the intent of the act. The court found for the Yakima.

Yakima access to the major salmon-fishing site at Celilo Falls on the Columbia River, no longer in Yakima territory but with fishing rights retained in the 1855 treaty, had to be fought for in the courts in 1886, in 1905, in 1916, and in 1936. The battle was finally lost in the 1920s with the construction at The Dalles of a dam and reservoir that drowned the ancient and profitable fishing stations. Monetary compensation to the Yakima for loss of the stations has been a poor substitute for the challenge and promise of poising on a pole platform above the foaming falls, swinging the dip net to meet a leaping fish weighing 30 to 50 or more pounds (14 to more than 20 kilograms), swiftly clubbing the frantic, shining creature, and swinging the net again, losing hardly a moment. In the 1920s, salmon no longer appeared in the Yakima River, its water level too lowered by irrigation project drainage. Thus, a half-century after Plains Indians lost the bison herds, the Yakima lost their equivalent basic staple, the huge schools of salmon. In the 1940s, the Yakima Tribal Council instituted logging of the reservation's pine forests, a program requiring considerable capital outlay to construct logging roads. During the nineteenth century, and doubtless for centuries earlier, the Yakima and

other Plateau peoples had fired much of the land in the autumn to maintain grassy parklands of pine, which were easy to move through, supported wild animals and, in the nineteenth century, useful domestic animals as well, and were unlikely to fuel disastrous fires since deadwood did not accumulate. Twentieth-century forestry experts forbade the traditional firings, which resulted in the loss of grazing opportunities and the growth of a tangled, dangerous forest in which good timber was being overwhelmed by straggly firs. Sustained-yield cutting is now partially compensating for the deterioration caused by shortsighted "scientific" practices, as well as bringing income to the tribe. Other tribal enterprises now include irrigation projects that enable Indian farmers to develop orchards, which have been highly profitable to Euro-Americans in the region, and crops such as alfalfa that supplement grazing for cattle. The tribe operates Yakima Executive Aircraft which rents helicopters, air ambulances, and private planes, and trains pilots for these. Wage labor in Euro-Americans' apple and hop harvests remains, however, a significant source of income, along with leasing to non-Indians. Many families still dig roots and bulbs in the spring and gather berries in the summer, drying them by the traditional processes and sometimes exchanging or selling sacks of these foods to families who have abandoned the old practices of—but not a taste for—native cuisine.

A significant action taken by the elected Yakima Tribal Council in 1979 expressed that love of the homeland that inspires so many nations. The Yakima formally adopted a resolution refusing any access, by land, water, or air, of nuclear fuels, wastes, or products onto Yakima territory. Since the Hanford Nuclear installation is only 13 miles (21 kilometers) from the Yakima Reservation and the tribe legally retains the right to hunt, fish, and gather foods on the ceded land of the Hanford reserve, this resolution is no empty gesture. In 1982, Yakima leader Russell Jim succeeded in obtaining from Congress an extension to Indian tribes of states' right to participate in decisions on disposal of nuclear wastes. Both the Council of Energy Resource Tribes (CERT) and the National Congress of American Indians then organized workshops and programs to assist tribes throughout the country to exercise this right intelligently.

The history and present circumstances of the other Plateau peoples in the Unites States parallel those of the Yakima, with variations such as the small size of the Kutenai and Kalispel communities and the location of the Spokan close to the city taking their name, facilitating their employment there and perhaps their unusually high rate of secondary-school completion, enforced by a 1945 Tribal Council decree of police apprehension of and severe penalties for truancy. Other Plateau reservations also tend to have higher proportions of high-school and college graduates than is general for American Indians. This may be linked with the practice of the nineteenth-century Protestant missionaries in the Plateau of actively favoring those Indians who obeyed dictates insisting on church and school attendance, and jailing and dispossessing those who were adamant in their loyalty to native beliefs. Many families who would not send their children to the missionaries' schools never came onto a reservation, knowing that only by suffering the bitter poverty of squatters upon their preempted lands could they continue to live by the tenets of their own faith.

Smohalla

Hinmaton-yalatkit (Chief Joseph) was an example of a person to whom the integrity of their beliefs is worth more than any promise of wealth. The spiritual leader for Hinmaton-yalatkit and thousands of other Plateau Indians in the second half of the nineteenth century was Smohalla, chief of the small band of Wanapam at Priest Rapids on the Columbia River in eastern Washington, adjacent to the Yakima. Smohalla ("Preacher") had been born about 1820. An ambitious man, lacking the tall, imposing figure of Hinmaton-yalatkit and many other leaders, but a

gifted orator, Smohalla at the time of the 1855 treaty was respected for his conduct on the battlefield, his management of his village, and his doctoring abilities. About 1860, not long after the end of the Yakima War, Smohalla challenged the powerful leader of the neighboring Sinkiuse, Chief Moses. Moses believed Smohalla was working sorcery against him, and according to later stories, met him in open fight, severely wounding him. Smohalla, supposedly left for dead, is said to have dragged himself to a canoe and floated down the Columbia until he was rescued and nursed back to health by a Euro-American settler. Rather than return to the scene of his defeat, Smohalla then embarked on a journey to the south, ending in Mexico. Having seen the peoples of the Pacific Coast, he turned north through Arizona and Utah. Whether he did journey that far, he had opportunities to observe foreign religious practices both from Catholic priests proselytizing from a mission established in Yakima territory in 1847, and from a visit by the Mormon leader Brigham Young ten years later to the Lemhi country. At any rate, back with the Wanapam, he claimed he had died, journeyed to heaven, and had been given a message by the Almighty to teach his people.

In stark contrast with Wovoka's message, or that of Handsome Lake, Smohalla preached no accommodation to the invading Euro-Americans. Any farming was evil, for it violated the parental earth. (Digging camas and tubers was acceptable, for the shallow disturbance of the digging stick was, he said, as the sweet pressure of an infant's fingers upon its mother's breast as it suckles.) Indians should remain in their ancestral villages and live by "root" digging, fishing, and hunting. They should celebrate the first fruits and first salmon in season with rituals of communal prayers and dances. Details of Smohalla's rituals, such as ringing bells and priests' wearing surplicelike garments, were borrowed from the Catholic missions, but the form and content of the rituals were basically Smohalla's reworking of Sahaptin traditions. His "church" at his own village at Priest Rapids

FIGURE 7.7 Smohalla (white tunic, center front) and his Sokulk congregation in their Longhouse church. *(Smithsonian Institution National Anthropological Archives, Bureau of American Ethnology Collection)*

was the smokehouse where hundreds of salmon fillets hung over the worshipers. Smohalla, and some of his followers, occasionally fell into trances and upon awakening preached new revelations. To better remember, Smohalla kept a notebook in which he wrote with symbols apparently of his own devising—unless Sahaptin shamans had a traditional mnemonic symbol system (hieroglyphs). Unfortunately, this question has not been pursued by ethnographers. With his well-thought-out and eloquently delivered theology, Smohalla in the 1870s, and to the end of his life in 1895, was the principal force opposing the Euro-American troika of government, missions, and Euro-American colonists. Sahaptins who would not knuckle under to the expropriation of their lands and rights found inspiration and hope, not of immediate relief but of eventual joy, in Smohalla's doctrine. Different as its counsel was, it did resemble Wovoka's and Handsome Lake's creeds in stressing the intrinsic value of a highly moral life.

The reservation period in the Plateau thus sorted the traditionalists from the "progressives," as agents and missionaries termed them, pushing the traditionalists into pockets off the reservations or in more remote sections of them, and clustering the "progressives" near the bounty of the agent and his missionary collaborator. This division persists to a degree today, as does more-or-less traditional Sahaptin religion in modified Dreamer (named after Smohalla's trances) or "Longhouse" rituals. Ideological differences crystallize into factions everywhere—not only among Indians!—and this tendency can be seen among the Salish-speaking groups, but in the case of the United States Plateau Salish, the throwing together by executive order, not by treaty negotiations, of ten nations on one reservation, Colville in northeastern Washington, has confused issues with dialect and community divisions antedating the reservation. (The Colville residents include the Colville proper, Lake, Methow, Sanpoil, Nespelem, and Okanagon, and some Pend d'Oreille, Spokan, Kalispel, and Coeur d'Alene. The remainder of the last four groups live on the Coeur d'Alene Reservation in Idaho, or the Spokan or Kalispel Reservations in eastern Washington.)

Further confusion arises from intermarriage among the nations; for example, the marriages of Spokan Garry's descendants with Coeur d'Alene and Kalispel, his great-grandson Ignace Garry and great-great-grandson Joseph Garry acting as spokesmen for all three nations. Joseph Garry, in fact, after army service during World War II and raising cattle on an inherited allotment on the Coeur d'Alene Reservation, became increasingly active on behalf of all the Northwest Indian nations and in the 1950s served several terms as president of the National Congress of American Indians. Deep though his interests were for his own three neighboring nations, much of his advocacy was futile in the face of the 1950s Congressional policy of terminating federal responsibility for American Indians. The Kalispel in 1963 won a land claims case against the government, only to be told that their $3 million award from the judgment was contingent upon termination. Protesting, they first wrested a "grant" (from their own money) for basic housing to replace the shed-like hovels in which many of their impoverished families lived. It wasn't until 1980, and more court suits, that the Kalispel, with other tribes, gained the interest on their money that the federal government had kept.

The 1980 U.S. census listed these populations for the Plateau nations: Bannock, 490; Cayuse, 157; Coeur d'Alene, 684; Colville (Reservation), 5,456; Flathead, 4,948; Fort Hall Shoshoni, 450; Kalispel, 181; Kutenai, 386; "Northwest Tribes" (Wenatchi, Kalapuya, the coastal Tillamook, others), 276; Spokane, 1,753; Walla Walla, 262; Warm Springs Reservation, 1,336; and Yakima, 6,506.

Plateau Nations in Canada

On the British Columbia side of the Plateau, initial contacts with fur traders in 1811 and regular contact after that shifted the economy toward greater production of furs and dried salmon to trade. Horses were introduced in southern British Columbia late in the eighteenth century, and the Hudson's Bay Company explorers, like their contemporaries Lewis and Clark, could purchase horses on the west side of the Rockies. But the narrower valleys north of the international border did not permit the raising of herds comparable to the large ones of the Nez Perce, Yakima, and other Sahaptin peoples, while the more difficult passes through the Canadian Rockies discouraged annual bison hunting on the plains, as the broader, lower passes facilitated in Montana and Wyoming. This difference in topography similarly discouraged wagon trains of colonists in British Columbia: emigrants came by sea to Vancouver rather than overland, sparing the inland nations depredations and diseases. In any case, colonization of British Columbia was slower than in the adjacent United States because the province was within the domain of the Hudson's Bay Company until 1858, when it became a Crown colony (although the first governor was formerly the Company's chief factor). Under nineteenth-century British imperialism, it was possible for an official to assume, as this first governor did, that *all* lands under the British flag belong in principle to the Crown, and that private persons or corporations enjoy ownership of land by sufferance of the Crown. Such a view granted native Indians rights to parcels of land they had developed with buildings or cultivation, but no ownership of "wild" lands. They might hunt or gather on these wild Crown lands, yet had no more claim to them than any other subject of the Crown. Following this assumption of Crown land being equivalent to undeveloped land, in 1876 a joint commission of the province and the Dominion of Canada began allocating tracts of land to Indian communities as reserves. These tracts were primarily the villages, in valleys close to streams. Indians were assured that they could continue to hunt, gather, fish, and graze their horses and cattle on the unallocated, undeveloped land around the reserves. After 1909, the province declared it would no longer allocate reserves, although it would consider adjusting the boundaries of tracts; in fact, it both reclaimed some reserve acreages and transferred other sections to Indian bands. As happened in the United States at this time, the land taken from reserves often seemed the most desirable, and came under Euro-Canadian ownership. At this time, too, Indians began to realize the impact of what had seemed a minor adjective in the 1876 policy: they retained the right to hunt, and so on, on undeveloped Crown land, but, undeveloped Crown land was becoming less and less of the province. Euro-Canadian homesteaders had bought substantial segments of British Columbia, thereby severely curtailing Indian hunting and gathering territory and preempting Indian livestock from much of the best grazing land. Protest after protest was filed by Indians and by Euro-Canadian friends moved by Indian grievances, but to little avail; the Indians west of the Rockies had not negotiated treaties and courts viewed their titles to land as clouded.

Paternalistic administration of Indian reserves was reinforced by denial to Indians of the right to vote until 1960, and by the consequences of this denial on economic development. Indians could not enter into financial enterprises without explicit approval from their agency superintendents, since the Indians did not have the status of adult citizens but were held to be wards. In other words, they were legally minors: they could not be bound by contracts, and were treated as incompetent to manage financial affairs. Again and again, agents obstructed experienced Indian farmers' decisions on planting, cattle management, or the purchase of implements, sometimes through agents' unfamiliarity with conditions in the West, sometimes, it seems, to undermine Indians' leadership. Only by giving up Indian status (becoming enfranchised) could an Indian handle his or her financial affairs according to his or her own judgment. Giving up Indian status usually meant giving up one's right to a residence and welfare benefits or land on one's reserve and left the Indian without economic resources. Without collateral, he or she could not buy a home, farm, machinery, tools, or a business by the usual method of obtaining capital through mortgage loans. Therefore, few Indians sought the dubious privilege of voting. On their small and for the most part isolated reserves, a few farmed, but most lived by a combination of fishing, hunting, gathering, gardening, perhaps logging or Christmas-tree cutting, and, regularly, the migration of whole families each summer into the state of Washington to pick berries, apples, and hops. The migration was deplored by the agents, who thought that the families would have been better employed farming on their own reserves, but the low return from subsistence farming (and the extraordinary difficulty faced by Indians who attempted to farm on a larger scale, handicapped by their noncitizen status) made the cash from migratory labor a reasonable choice for a reserve family. The fun of summering away from home in company with hundreds of Indians from a variety of Plateau groups added to the attraction of the Washington employment. A small proportion of Indians, notably in the Okanagan Valley, did manage to develop reserve agriculture or, more profitable, cattle raising, but most let land remain in its aboriginal state or leased it to Euro-Canadians.

The tremendous rise in band populations, particularly in the second half of this century, has forced many Indians to migrate to cities to seek not only employment but also simply a place to live. Education levels among Canadian Indians have been rising, especially beginning in the 1960s, but lag behind those of the Euro-Canadian population and therefore disadvantage the Indian in the job market. Discrimination is lessening—not so long ago, British Columbia Plateau Indians generally were segregated at the sides or in the balcony of movie theaters, like blacks in the Jim Crow American South—but many employers have a legitimate hesitation in hiring Indians because they have seen Indian employees quit in order to join friends and relatives in migratory-labor harvests or to fish. The jobs quit were, of course, low-pay, low-prestige, and uninteresting, and the cash from the harvest camps or the value of hundreds of pounds of salmon canned for the winter made the steady job less desirable than it might have appeared to the Euro-Canadian unaware of the alternatives. As long as one retains Indian status, one can usually manage a minimal income from assorted treaty benefits and the sharing of resources on the reserve, a standard of living impoverished by any economic measure but not much worse than struggling in the city at the low end of pay scales. The minimal security in Indian status contributed to a high rate of legal illegitimacy in Indian births because until 1985, an Indian woman who married a man without Indian status (he might be Indian by descent but enfranchised or from a family or band overlooked when the government registered Indians) lost her own Indian status and could not give Indian status to her children. (Status-Indian men could marry non-Indian women without losing either their own or their children's status, and their wives became members of the husbands' bands.) Rather than lose the bottom-line security of Indian status, many Indian women lived in common-law marriages. A challenge to the law by Jeannette Lavell, an Ojibwa unwilling to give up her Indian status or her marriage, angry because the rule discriminated against Indian women, was opposed by organized status-Indian women because they feared an influx of new claimants to the already too meager resources of reserves. The law was amended to allow women enrolled in bands to retain Indian status and give it to their children (but not grandchildren) regardless of their spouses' status, while opponents to the ruling were mollified by a provision that Indian status would not entail band membership unless the band approved it: a new category was created, in Canada, of Indians without specific band membership. The new category can include children of interband marriages, allowing them to receive federal benefits without obliging one or the other parent's band to enroll the children.

Injustices and severe economic problems stimulated Plateau nations, primarily Shuswap and Chilcotin, to form the British Columbia Interior Confederacy in 1945 (when the Dominion government proposed major revision of the Indian Act), and the North American Indian Brotherhood. Under the leadership of Andrew Paull, the latter organization split from the Native Brotherhood of British Columbia, which concentrated upon the coastal communities. From the model of these Indian brotherhoods developed, in 1968, the National Indian Brotherhood which through the 1970s was the officially recognized representative of status Indians in Canada. Following agitation by the N.I.B. to include Indians in the creation of Canada's Constitution, meetings began in 1979 to work out both proper representation of Indian rights in the new Constitution and proper election of representatives of Canada's Indians. By 1981, this second concern was fulfilled by the organization of the Assembly of First Nations of Canada, composed of the 573 official Band Chiefs (or their delegates). The Assembly of First Nations superseded the National Indian Brotherhood; it is seen as structurally equivalent to the provinces in sending its leaders to the national First Ministers' Conferences. At the same time, Indians can be elected to provincial legislatures, and in 1990, a Cree member of the Manitoba Legislature, Elijah Harper, played a crucial role in the rejection of the Prime Minister's Meech Lake Accord on amendments designed to win Québec's ratification of the Constitution.

British Columbia differs from Canada's other western provinces in that it had established provincial control over its lands when it came into Union in 1871. Therefore, federal and provincial governments had to cooperate in setting up Indian reserves, resulting in slow and patchy decisions. In 1874, bands along the Fraser in the southern portion of the province petitioned the government to recognize that the provincial standard of 20 acres per family of five was one-eighth the federal standard. The communities would accept half the federal standard, 80 acres per family, so long as these could be protected. "Some of our best men have been deprived of the land they have broken and cultivated with long and hard labour, a white man enclosing it in his claim, and no compensation given. Some of our enterprising men have lost a part of their cattle, because white men had taken the place where those cattle were grazing and no other place left but the thickly timbered land, where they die fast," the petition stated (quoted in Knight 1978:259). The Indian farmers had bought all their livestock, seeds, and farm machinery with their own earnings. If anyone doubts the veracity of the petitioners' description of their ability to capably farm, two years after the fruitless petition, farmers from the Indian bands won prizes for their wheat and barley in the United States Centennial Exhibition in Philadelphia.

British Columbia Indians are conscious of having been deprived of their ancestral lands and resources without even the whitewash of conventional treaties. They see themselves burdened under a package of poor schooling (teachers with low expectations of Indian pupils, curricula not adjusted to the difficulties of rural children who may not speak English in the home), lack of marketable skills, lack of employment experience, lack of capital or opportunities to borrow capital, substandard houses and nutrition inducing levels of respiratory and skin diseases and infant mortality far above the national averages, and boredom and frustration among the unemployed—half of the adult population—erupting in alcoholism, violence, and suicides—all of these producing an Indian mortality rate much higher, and a life expectancy much lower, than the national rates. These ills are common to most Canadian Indians, but in British Columbia a history of relative affluence in the nineteenth century exacerbates Indian resentment. Combating the package of ills is the increasing pace of demands for more parental input into schools; realistic but sensitive programs for vocational training; programs for giving youth constructive projects and pride in themselves and

their heritage, which, it is hoped, will carry them through discouraging experiences in school and work; and more cooperation between police officers and bands to reduce accidents and the relatively high rate of arrests, which often put Indians into jail for public drunkenness while even more inebriated Euro-Canadians are sheltered in bars or assisted home. Bands are calling in leases and insisting that their members be given the means to farm, ranch, or log on their reserves, or employed in construction. Power, logging, and irrigation projects by outside entrepreneurs that would alter reserve resources are in several cases being resisted, sometimes in coalition with Euro-Canadian environmental-protection organizations. The details of Indian history in the Canadian section of the Plateau have been quite different from those in the southern section, but the results of poverty and finally a resurgence of determination by Indian peoples to assert their rights to self-rule, resources, and opportunities have been parallel in both parts of the Plateau.

The Wishram and Wasco

A border far older than that between the United States and Canada is marked by the Dalles, or Long Narrows, of the Columbia River cutting from the Plateau through the Cascade Mountains to enter the Pacific coastal region. Whereas the Fraser River draining the northern Plateau travels for many miles deep within a spectacularly steep, narrow-bottomed canyon before it dramatically roars out from rock gates into the broad green delta near Vancouver, the Columbia's route through the southern Plateau lies in a broader trench. The trench and the land above are arid, in the rain shadow of the Cascades, but the gentler topography made the Columbia a highway for canoes, foot travelers, and, historically, horses. Few traveled the difficult and dangerous canyon of the Fraser, while thousands went up or down the Columbia each year. Catering to this traffic were the Wishram who had established a series of villages on the north bank of the Columbia at the Dalles, the principal one being at Spedis (also called Spearfish), Washington. The Wishram speak a dialect of Chinook, a Penutian language, and the importance of their locality as a meeting place for travelers and traders gave rise to the lingua franca Chinook Jargon. The Wishram and their neighbors, the Wasco on the south bank of the Columbia, who spoke a related dialect, and Salish and Sahaptin speakers up-river, netted and dried quantities of salmon sufficient to provision thousands of visitors. Plateau Indians came down-river during the summer, after gathering and drying camas and roots in the spring; they fished for salmon on the Columbia as well as traded. Groups west of the Cascades did not move up-river as families to trade, but were represented by chiefs and other wealthy persons leading trading parties. During the summer, three thousand people at Spedis would be gambling, racing, eating, and bargaining—enjoying a great and noisy months-long fair. Slaves, most of them children, were a principal commodity in demand west of the Cascades. Bison robes, Indian-grown tobacco (cultivated in portions of the Plateau as well as on the Plains), and, in the nineteenth century, horses were Plateau products, augmented by some from the Plains, desired by the coastal peoples. A specialty of the host villages at the Dalles, pounded dried salmon, was also bought by parties from the coast, where salmon was dried but the process of preparing the sweet pounded-salmon meal was not known. In return for these interior products, the coast parties traded their canoes, marine shells and shell beads, and fish oil and some fish from their regions. Dried elk and deer meat, bows, and wokas lily seeds were products traded by the peoples of the Willamette Valley, Oregon, and northern California. Craft specialties such as baskets or the handsome parfleches (rawhide cases) and fiber bags manufactured by the Nez Perce were always good sellers at the Dalles markets. By the end of the eighteenth century, European beads, ornaments, and blankets obtained from trading

posts farther north or from ships along the coast were being traded through the Dalles. Furs also moved through this Indian market. European traders were immediately seen as rivals by the Wishram and Wasco, and were not welcome. The invasion of the Northwest by European traders severely undermined the Dalles market, drawing Indians with furs and provisions for sale to the posts offering guns and other imported items not available, or very expensive, at the Dalles. The Wishram could continue to host the gambling and racing through which large quantities of goods changed hands, and of course they could continue to sell food to the gamblers at what some considered steep prices, but the preeminence of the Dalles as the market for the northwestern quarter of North America was lost as more and more European traders established posts during the first half of the nineteenth century.

Missionaries settled at the Dalles in 1838, and introduced European farming. The area was by then depopulated, for during the second half of the eighteenth century, raids of mounted Paiutes and Shoshoni had slowly driven Sahaptins north and west. They in turn dislodged some Salish formerly closer to the Dalles—the Sinkiuse and Wenatchi—and forced them up-river. By about 1800, much of the territory south of the Columbia in eastern Oregon was a sparsely inhabited borderland. Then, in 1830, four successive years of malaria epidemics decimated the Columbia nations from the Cascades west. These peoples exploited a root growing abundantly in swamps, drying and selling quantities in addition to storing much of it as their own staple carbohydrate. Mosquitoes in the swamps apparently picked up malaria from a European trading-post employee or seaman, and epidemics rose each summer of the four years. Europeans at Fort Vancouver (in Oregon Territory) and other posts were afflicted, but most survived, nursed by friends who kept them warm and fed. The Indians were unfamiliar with the disease and insisted, sometimes against the advice of traders at the posts, on the standard native therapy of sweat baths followed by plunges into the cold river. The traders report that this was frequently a fatal shock. Those Indians who avoided or survived the common treatment were liable to die from lack of food and water if all in the village were seriously ill. The survivors of the population alive in 1838 could no longer consider themselves rivals to the Europeans.

Emigrants invaded the Dalles area beginning in 1842, the majority en route to the Willamette Valley to the southwest. Additional missionaries arrived, and introduced the denominational factionalism that bewildered Indians attempting to understand Christianity. The Wishram and Wasco signed the 1855 treaty without protest, and avoided entanglement in the Yakima War that followed. In 1858, the Wasco removed south to the Warm Springs Reservation in central Oregon, and the Wishram north to the Yakima Reservation in Washington. Both reservations were shared with Sahaptins, Warm Springs with Tenino, Tygh, and John Day bands, and Yakima with the Yakima, Palouse, Klikitat, and other groups. After the Bannock War, some Northern Paiutes were settled on the Warm Springs Reservation, but their former enemies the Wasco and Sahaptins excluded the Paiutes from full participation in reservation affairs. On their reservations, the Wasco and Wishram continued their traditional subsistence pursuits of fishing, tuber and bulb digging, and some hunting, and added farming and livestock raising, the latter proving more reliable for human consumption because of damages to crops from insects and rodents. In order to fish for salmon, both Wishram and Wasco returned to the Columbia for the major spawning runs, and some families remained permanently at the old village, Spedis. The village no longer rang with the clamor of the market fair. Euro-Americans had taken trading out of Wishram hands.

With their principal economic activity so diminished, class distinctions among Wascos and among Wishram on the reservations diminished. Noble families, those from which leaders had traditionally come, continued to seek spouses for their young people from other noble families, Chinook or Sahaptin, but more marriages occurred between nobility and members of families that were merely respectable. The United States Emancipation Proclamation and the subsequent Constitutional amendment outlawing slavery affected the Wasco and Wishram by freeing their slaves, most of them Indians from the Pit River region of northern California. Some of these slaves returned to Pit River; others remained on their former owners' reservations as low-class persons. Leadership on the reservations became somewhat confused, in part because each reservation was settled by several groups, each with its own leaders, in part because agents and missionaries appointed chiefs without regard to their family origin, thereby lessening the importance of the noble or "chiefly" families in providing leadership. Agents and missionaries also attempted to stamp out shamanistic curing and divining, and in doing so lessened the overt leadership of the native doctors, although not necessarily their power to influence people.

On the Warm Springs Reservation, the Wasco have been the group most often controlling reservation politics; the Sahaptins are considered more conservative in maintaining Indian ways, and the Wascos better educated and closer to Euro-American patterns, and therefore better able to handle organization, business, and external relationships in what is basically an agency under the Bureau of Indian Affairs. Conversely, Indian religious ceremonies are most often led by Sahaptins, with both Wasco and Sahaptins participating. These ceremonies are classified by some as Longhouse religion, because of their performance in structures resembling traditional large winter houses that would have been home to several families. (There is no connection to the Iroquois Handsome Lake's "Longhouse" religion.) Components of the Longhouse religion come from Plateau winter round dances, from Smohalla's religion, from the Feather-religion variant of Plateau doctrines introduced through revelations in 1904 to a Klikitat, Jake Hunt, and from the Shaker religion revealed

FIGURE 7.8 Umatilla camp, about 1900. The women are drying eels. A wagon is parked to the left of the double tipi. (*Smithsonian Institution National Anthropological Archives, Bureau of American Ethnology Collection*)

to John Slocum (Squsachtun), a Coast Salish from southern Puget Sound who believed himself to have died and gone to heaven in 1881 but to have been sent back to earth to instruct his people and their neighbors in an Indian version of Christianity. Some of the appeal of Slocum's religion lay in his followers' traditional doctoring (including the spirit-filled trembling giving the Shakers their name) that was said to be God's gift, requiring no payment as native doctors had formerly expected. In recent years, missions of fundamentalist Christian churches have been gaining some converts among the Chinooks, as on many reservations. Economically, the Wishram on the Yakima Reservation followed the dominant Yakima in the various occupations open in the area. The Warm Springs Wasco have continued cattle ranching, but since the Warm Springs Reservation Tribal Council invested its settlement for land sacrificed for the Dalles dam in timber sales and a mill, and an

elaborate resort, Kah-Nee-Ta, tapping the reservation's hot springs, the reservation has become a showplace for Indian economic development. A century of co-residence on well-defined reservations with other Plateau peoples has gradually led the Wishram and Wasco to identify themselves primarily as "Yakima" or "Warm Springs" Indians rather than strongly and solely Wishram or Wasco.

SECTION 4: CALIFORNIA

The hunting-gathering Western Archaic societies of the early Holocene era in California developed into regionally differentiated cultural patterns by 3000 B.C. The most distinctive was that of the south-central coast around Santa Barbara and the Channel Islands. A site on Catalina Island exemplifies the adaptation to marine resources. The site is a midden, or refuse heap, of discarded shells and other garbage 200 by 400 feet (60 by 120 meters) across and 2 to 4 feet deep (60 to 120 centimeters), spread over a hilltop on the island's rugged coast. The lower, earlier portion of the midden was mostly abalone shell. As the inhabitants pried the hundreds and hundreds of abalone off the rocks below, the species apparently failed to maintain its population, and the people gradually consumed fewer of the large shellfish and more and more of the smaller mussels. Mixed in with the abalone and mussel shells were bones of fish, including sea bass and sheepshead, and sea mammals. Some of the sea mammals were female seals and their pups, which may have been clubbed as they lay on the rocks. More common were bones of dolphins, porpoises, and whales. The whales may have been stranded, but the dolphins and porpoises were surely pursued in the open water from boats, and it is possible the whales were also actively hunted and killed, as later in the region, with poisoned projectiles. To get to Catalina Island, the inhabitants of the site must have had boats; the numbers of dolphins and porpoises they ate proves that they had fast, highly maneuverable boats, probably canoes, and were skilled and fearless in sea hunting. Whether the people lived year-round on Catalina, or came over only in the summer, could not be determined. Part of the midden covered a slight round depression 20 feet (6 meters) in diameter that might have been a wickiup similar to historic California Indian houses of the region. Among the artifacts lost or discarded in the midden were pitted stones probably used to tenderize abalone by pounding; beads of olivella shell and abalone pendants; beads and crude carvings of steatite (soapstone), which can be mined on Catalina; a cobblestone that had had a rope stuck around it with tar, used perhaps as a net sinker or anchor; several pebbles coated with tar and probably rolled around in a basket to coat the interior and make it waterproof (a historic California Indian technique); and several quartz crystals and polished stone cylinders, the latter termed charm stones, which continued into the historic period in California and which, in the historical period, at least, were amulets.

Sites basically similar to the Catalina midden occur along the California coast from about 3000 B.C. on. Around San Francisco Bay there were hundreds of shell middens, some many feet deep. The interior valleys of California have few shell middens—and these are shallow heaps of mussel shells—but a greater number and variety of mortars and pestles than are found on the coast, which reflects the greater importance of nuts (ground into flour in the mortars) where sea mammals could not be obtained. Interior sites contain bones of freshwater fish which were speared or caught with lines, in contrast with the coast, where nets were used in addition to spears, hooks, and gorges. Deer and elk were, as would be expected, more common in interior sites than on the coast, although deer were part of the diet of the sea-mammal hunters as well as of the shellfish gatherers and fishermen on the sections of the northern and southern coast where sea mammals are few. Population appears to have been increasing in all regions and to have reached a relatively high density in such resource-rich areas as San Francisco Bay after about 2000 B.C. Post-Pleistocene sea-level rise had stabilized by then, although continuing, gradual silting-up of estuaries and bays created mudflats where once there had been rocky shores, and shellfish species shifted as the habitats changed. The richness of life in this period is glimpsed in the abundance of charm stones and ornaments, including mica pendants, prism-shaped splinters of obsidian, bone hairpins that may have been tufted with feathers, beads of birdbone, antler, and shells, and even mortars decorated with shell beads stuck on with tar. Thin bone awls in many sites suggest the innovation of coiled basketry, which in the historic period was a fine art. The fact that most graves contained few ornaments while a minority of graves contained quantities implies status ranking within the communities, and the presence of objects made of raw materials from sources many kilometers distant implies trade to have been significant even in the

Archaic period. In the San Joaquin River delta, low mounds of clay-earth were constructed as cemeteries for several hundred people, presumably the families of a village.

By about A.D. 300, California's regions had set cultural patterns that would persist with little change to the nineteenth century. Population appears to have been fairly stable. The surprisingly high number of skeletons with spearpoints in or fatally close to bone that have been discovered in Middle Period (2000 B.C. to A.D. 300) graves in interior central California is not matched in the Late Period, indicating that combat may have become less frequent (although the introduction of the bow and arrow in the first millennium A.D. may have only changed the mode, and not the frequency, of war; friends of the slain may have extracted arrows from the bodies before burial, whereas in the Middle Period it was customary to leave the weapon tip in the unfortunate's body.) Interpretations of Late Period archaeological sites rely heavily on applying descriptions of historic nations to what are probably their ancestors' occupations. The continuity of basic Archaic patterns in most of California, enriched but not really changed by the perfection of food-procurement and -processing techniques, the development of basketry, and innovations in weaponry, has impressed all students of California prehistory. That the continuity includes persistence of some ideology is suggested by the thousands of years in which quartz crystals and charm stones were prized by Californians. (Some charm stones are obviously phallic, but many bear no discernible resemblance to natural objects or tools.) It will be best to go on to describe the regional culture patterns of California and the historic nations, noting that these culture patterns appear to have been stable for fifteen hundred years or more.

Cultural Patterns of the California Peoples

Stability and similarity of material culture over the California culture area contrasts with a complicated linguistic distribution. Penutian and Hokan are the best-represented language phyla, with Athabascan, Macro-Algonkian ("Ritwan," the term for Yurok and Wiyot as one distant branch of Algonkian) and Uto-Aztecan also in the area. Penutian includes the isolate Klamath-Modoc in northern California in the border linking this area, the Northwest Coast, and the Plateau, plus several language families: Yokuts, in the Central Valley, including the Kings and San Joaquin Rivers and the foothills of the Coast ranges to the west; Maidu, in the Central Valley north of the Yokuts along the Sacramento River and in the Sierra foothills to the east; Miwok, with one language in Marin County north of San Francisco Bay and a second in the Central Valley just east of the Yokuts and into the Sierra foothills to the east, where the closely related Nisenan lived; and Wintun, with Wintun proper between the Coast ranges and the Sacramento River to Mt. Shasta, and Patwin just north of San Francisco Bay. Hokan includes the isolates Washo, on the California-Nevada border at Lake Tahoe (culturally a border Basin area), Yana, in the northeastern Sacramento Valley to Mt. Shasta, and Karok, on the Klamath River in northwest California, plus these language families: Pomo, along the Russian River to its mouth on the coast north of the San Francisco region; Yuki and its sister language Wappo, both spoken north of San Francisco Bay, mostly northeast of the Miwok; Shasta, including Shasta proper, spoken along the Klamath River and the Scott and Shasta rivers in northernmost California, plus Achumawi and Atsugewi, both spoken in northeastern California along the Pit River (hence these two nations are the "Pit Rivers"); Chumash and Salinan, on the south coast and islands around Santa Barbara; and Yuman, of which Diegueño (spoken by the Ipai, Tipai, and Kumeyaay) in southernmost California and related languages extend into Baja California, and of which River Yuman on the Colorado River, spoken by the Mohave, Quechan, Cocopa, and Maricopa, extends into the Southwest culture area. Athabascan languages in California are clustered in the northwest section and include Hupa,

Tolowa, Kato and Wailaki, and Mattole. The two language isolates Yurok, adjacent to the Athabascan groups, on the lower Klamath River, and Wiyot, also in northwestern California around Blue Lake, are collectively called Ritwan and related to the otherwise distant Algonkian phylum. Uto-Aztecan covers much of southern and eastern California, including under the "Uto" branch many of the "Mission" peoples such as the Gabrielino (Kumivit in their own language), Luiseño, and Fernandeño (Pasekwarum), the Serrano (Takhtam), the Cupeño, the Cahuilla at Palm Springs, and the Tubatulabal on the Kern River in the Sierra, with the Kawaiisu to the south between the San Joaquin Valley and the Mojave Desert. The central coast south of San Francisco and the adjacent Santa Clara Valley across the Coast Range were occupied by the Costanoans, once speaking a language closely related to Miwok, now effectively extinct as a nation.

A.L. Kroeber surveyed the peoples, cultural patterns, and languages of California and discerned a rough fit. He recognized three major culture areas in the state. Northwestern California is a land of rugged topography and heavy forests, with a rocky coast and no coastal plain. Its native inhabitants were principally Athabascan and Ritwan (Macro-Algonkian) speakers. Central California encompassed the Central Valley, its Sierra foothills, the Coast ranges and valleys, and the central coast, including San Francisco Bay with its rich shore flats. This central culture area was predominantly Penutian but was bordered by Hokans. Southern California's more rounded mountains and many tidal marshes and lagoons, its semiaridity, and the relative ease of passage between it and the Great Basin made it ecologically suited to, and accessible to, Numic speakers. The postulated homeland of Shoshoneans on the southeastern slopes of the Sierra Nevada in southeastern California may have been a section of Numic territory occupied long before the early-second-millennium–A.D. north and east movement of Numans. California border areas are the northeast, inhabited

by the Penutian Klamath and Modoc, whose culture was oriented toward that of the Plateau, and the lower Colorado River and Baja California border, inhabited by Yumans who are best understood as members of the western subarea of the Southwest. A distinctive California subarea lay along the Channel Islands coast and was formed by the Hokan Chumash, who took advantage of their good harbors and abundance of sea mammals to make sea hunting and fishing an important sector of their economy, along with acorns and grass seeds.

The ecologically distinctive central California area was also an economically specialized region, in which nut flour was the staple food, amply supplemented by deer and small game, birds, fish, ground seeds, and fruit. This economic pattern was essentially an Archaic pattern, and the central California peoples may have more closely approximated the Eastern Late Archaic way of life than any other historic Americans have. Like the Late Archaic peoples in the Eastern Woodlands, the Californians reached a relatively high and comparatively sedentary population in permanent villages, although camps were set up on hunting and gathering trips. Californian nut processing involved more labor than had been necessary in the Eastern Archaic regions because the most common California nuts were the acorn and buckeye, both of which contain poisonous acid that must be leached out in a tedious series of soakings, drainings, and dryings. The final result is a highly nutritious flour usually eaten as a cooked mush, which was sometimes flavored by the addition of ingredients such as protein-rich roasted ground grasshoppers, or baked as an unleavened bread.

None of the American cultigens were raised in California except tobacco. Maize agriculture was practiced only on the southeastern border along the lower Colorado by the Yuman speakers, in the Imperial Valley, and along the Laguna, San Bernardino, and San Jacinto ranges (east of Los Angeles). Why this was so has intrigued many anthropologists. The climate of California is not particularly favorable to maize, because there is little rainfall in summer, but since the nearest agriculturists, those on the Colorado, practiced irrigation, and since irrigation was carried out even for wild plants by the Owens Valley Paiute, the rainfall pattern would not have precluded maize in the river valleys of central California. Some of the southern Californians—for example, the Diegueno (Kumeyaay)—transplanted wild roots to locations where they would grow better, and planted fields of favorite herbs, greens, grasses, and prickly pear cactus. In southern and central California, Indians burned off valley and foothill districts to thin out thicket and to sow, scattering broadcast, grasses from which they would later gather the seed; to promote the growth of clover, which they ate in spring as salad; and to promote browse for the deer they hunted. Like the Eastern Woodland nations, the Californians maintained a symbiotic relationship with deer, providing the animals with good forage through burnings and then harvesting the animals in these seminatural parks, hunting them individually or through drives. Techniques to modify the natural environment so as to increase human food resources were thus utilized.

Trade contacts with Southwestern agriculturalists can be demonstrated (by Hohokam pottery sherds in California sites) for southern California at least by A.D. 600, and they continued into the historic period. Major trade routes connected the Southwest with San Francisco Bay. These routes, which brought Southwestern cotton blankets and turquoise and a little pottery into California, must have brought also some knowledge of Southwestern crops and of the fact that they were planted and cultivated. There is no evidence, however, that any Californians north of the Los Angeles valley's rim experimented with maize agriculture as a food base, although tobacco was grown from seed and cultivated for use in rituals and for its psychotropic effect. Apparently the abundance of acorns, other nuts, grass seed, and a species of sage producing seeds called chia provided their cultivators with so generous and reliable a food base that there was no

incentive to invest time and labor in maize. Certainly the cost of maize in time and effort (including irrigation construction in many areas) would have been greater than the cost of collecting and processing acorns. Leaching and grinding acorns and buckeyes was tedious, but maize must be shelled, soaked in an alkali solution, and ground, too, if it is to be a year-round staple. Another factor in the economics of acorns versus maize would have been the allocation of acorn preparation to women in the village, which would have left men free to hunt and fish for animal protein and hides. While the distant Eastern Woodland peoples made farming a woman's task, the agricultural peoples nearest California, in Mexico and the Southwest, considered it primarily man's work, so some Californians may have seen farming as a conflict with hunting and fishing. Whatever the reasons for Californians' disinterest in maize agriculture, its absence in this relatively densely populated region forces us to realize that conventional farming is one of several strategies to obtain an abundant, storable carbohydrate staple, and not necessarily a superior strategy or the prerequisite to stable communities.

Central California, from the Coast ranges through the Central Valley to the Sierra foothills, supported the densest population (among the densest in all of North America) and the most typical societies in the California cultural pattern. Among these most typical societies were the Pomo north of San Francisco and the Patwin in the lower Sacramento Valley, northeast of San Francisco. The Pomo were Hokan speakers, the Patwin Penutian. Both had access to a permanently flowing river that could be fished, to grassy valley bottoms, and to hills with oaks. The Pomo included groups on the Pacific coast as well. Of the two peoples, the Patwin enjoyed one important resource not available to the Pomo: annual runs of king salmon up the Sacramento River. Patwin population was accordingly somewhat higher than that of the Pomo. Pomo, on the other hand, had access to the ocean-shore clams from which clamshell disc beads, the standard unit of money in most of Cali-

FIGURE 7.9 Wintun home ("ranchería"), northern California, about 1882. *(Smithsonian Institution National Anthropological Archives)*

fornia, were manufactured. Coast Pomo and their neighbors just to the south, the Coast Miwok on the northern rim of San Francisco Bay, minted the money. A description of the Patwin can be a model for the California cultural pattern, but the model must include reference to peoples such as the Coast Pomo, who differed in many details from the Patwin but were linked to them in the large networks tying the many local societies.

Patwin lived either on knolls near the Sacramento River or beside springs in the hills. Several hundred people formed a village, in which they resided in substantial houses built by digging out a round or oval depression 2 or 3 feet (almost 1 meter) deep, banking the excavated earth as a parapet around the house pit, setting up several forked posts and rafters, and finally covering the frame with earth. Each locality—either a single

village or a cluster of hamlets with a principal larger settlement—had in the main village a dance house constructed like the dwellings but larger. The main village was the home of the society's chief, and had a clear area adjacent to his house, more or less in the center of the community, for open-air dances and festivities. The Patwin constructed wickiups of thatch or of slabs of bark over round or conical pole frames when camping away from their village for gathering or hunting, and within the village as retreats for menstruating women, whose presence was thought to endanger males. (The earth-covered semisubterranean house was characteristic of the Central Valley, while hill peoples such as the Pomo generally built only wickiups. Northwestern Californians used planks to build rectangular houses of the type characteristic of the Northwest Coast culture area.) Each

Patwin village, or village-with-hamlets cluster, was a political entity managed by a chief. Chiefs were chosen from noble families, usually the son or younger brother of the deceased chief, but when no competent son or brother was available from the ruling family, a capable daughter might be chosen. The chief was responsible for organizing community businesses and for overseeing the gathering of food, trading, and the presentation of dances and rituals. Surpluses of food and trade goods were stored at the chief's house, where he could use them to entertain visitors as well as aid the needy. No very stringent accounting was kept of chiefs' personal property versus communal stores, so the chief appeared to be, and acted as, the wealthiest person in the community. The chief was assisted by a messenger and a council of elders. Because managing the affairs of the community was considered a full-time job, the chief did not hunt, fish, or gather, as other men did, but relied on the communal contributions stored at his house for his family's needs as well as for his public duties.

A close associate of the chief was the village doctor, who had inherited from his father or grandfather a deerskin bag of charms, herbs, and headdress and rattle, and had been trained for years by the elder man. The doctor diagnosed and cured most diseases by a combination of herbs and magical songs, of which he had learned hundreds. Stubborn illnesses he finally attempted to cure by dressing up as a ghost or spirit and frightening the patient, and then demonstrating to the sufferer that the apparition had been destroyed. The doctor treated broken bones by setting them with splints and binding them. Doctors usually supported their families from their fees rather than by direct food-getting. Chief and doctor were thus full-time specialists, both from leading families and both trained from childhood for their profession if they showed aptitude. Chiefs, as managers, sometimes arranged for their village doctor to demonstrate his power at another community, and received the fee for the performance, paying the doctor from it but keeping a share. Chiefs' power was enhanced by

people's fear that should someone anger the chief or another member of a noble family, the chief would influence his friend the doctor to do less than his best in curing the object of anger when he or she fell ill. Some families had knowledge of poisons, and a chief might ask a person with this knowledge to poison an enemy. This was a difficult as well as serious task, since a mixture of many poisons was thought to be required and took much time to gather and prepare, with the poisoner at risk himself in the final stages if he was not extremely careful to wash thoroughly. Poison was thus not administered lightly, but the threat of poison, abetted by an unwillingness of the doctor to cure, made community members hesitant to criticize or disobey a chief. An incompetent chief could be deposed, and if reluctant to give up power, the threat of poison could be raised against the chief by the opposing faction.

Communities recognized several classes of people: the chief and his noble lineage, who married into chiefly lineages in other communities; specialists, who earned much of their income through their profession or craft; common people, who hunted, fished, gathered, and made undistinguished ordinary implements; "slaves," young war captives, who often escaped or were allowed to return to their homes after serving for a few years; "no-account" persons without family ties, beggars or drifters; and transvestites, of whom there might be two or three in a village, living alone and performing women's tasks or married to a man. (Transvestites were similarly routinely accepted among Plains societies, where the French termed them *berdache*. Plains transvestites claimed they were called to live as the opposite sex in a vision, and some were consequently believed to have more spiritual power than conventional ordinary men. Central California transvestites were thought to be born hermaphrodites—that is, persons who are physically both male and female.) Specialists usually were members of families that prepared certain of their children to carry on the occupation for which the family was noted. In addition to practical training in the craft or profession, the young person was taught lore of the spirit associated with the specialty, and eventually the talisman of the spirit was passed from teacher to son or daughter. Doctors were thus one kind of specialist, whose training and paraphernalia paralleled those of such other specialists as bow makers, chiefs' assistants, highly successful hunters, or, among the Pomo, clamshell-money makers. It was possible, though not very usual, for an unrelated person to apprentice to a specialist, paying him or her fees for instruction. The cost of instruction tended to limit it to members of chiefly lineages or other specialist families, thereby maintaining the class structure of the community. Traders were specialists or chiefs, again from well-to-do families who could help their kinsman with capital and credit. Popular trade items were obsidian, magnesite beads, skins and feathers of woodpeckers and yellowhammers, bows, nets, bearskins, which were used for bedding and as a sign of prestige, and the medium of exchange, clamshell-disc beads. The Patwin counted the beads, but other groups considered this mean and figured the worth of a string of beads by its length, indicating by not closely examining each bead that they trusted the trading partner and were well enough off not to worry over pennies, as it were. Trading was properly done at the chief's residence, another custom tending to maintain class distinctions, although ordinary people might trade between themselves at festivals.

The preeminent craft of Californians was, and is, basketry. Pomo, Patwin, and other central Californians made coiled baskets so fine that they could hold water without tarring, although everyday containers would not be of such quality. Fine baskets, for use in ceremonies and as gifts, are often decorated with delicate, colorful feathers. The most talented basketmakers were (and are) true artists, whose talent creates objects to be enjoyed for their beauty. Basketry techniques were used for a variety of products other than baskets, too. Mats, especially of tule reed, were made for beds and carpets, and bundles of tule were sewn together to make

canoe-shaped boats up to 20 feet (6 meters) long. Blankets were woven of strips of jackrabbit skin, as in the Great Basin, or of goose feathers tied into strips and then treated as warps woven together by threads. Feather cloaks were once made, but the art disappeared in California, as it did in Mexico, when brightly colored European cloth became available. Leather, except for white deer hides, did not interest the Californians, and comparatively little use was made of hides (as in the western Great Basin). Men seldom wore any clothing, and women only short skirts.

The Patwin and other Californians had a strong sense of territory. Each village thought of itself as the people who lived in and used a particular district. Villages were year-round homes, although excursions would be made in the fall to the district's oak groves to collect acorns. There was enough abundance and diversity of food resources in each district that even should the salmon run or acorn harvest be scant one year, other fish such as sturgeon, other nuts and seeds, and deer (which were beaten into nets as well as stalked) would compensate. The Patwin, living on the lower reaches of a major river, were particularly rich in food, and could scorn less-well-situated peoples such as the Maidu who would collect, parch, and grind grasshoppers.

Patwin religious ceremonies featured men with face blackened, decked in elaborate feather headdresses and, in the case of one type, long feather cloaks. These men danced impersonations of spirits. The entire performance was directed by a specialist and attended by the village chief, who urged his people to be generous in paying the dancers for their efforts. Singers and a hollowed-log foot drum set in the floor of the dance house accompanied the dances. The lay public was supposed to think the dancers were really spirits visiting the village to bring health and blessings. Most youths and some young women were initiated into the secrets of the performance. First, they were dramatically seized and shot with a little flint-tipped arrow, and then they were carried into the dance house and made to lie there recovering from their wound, which was said (to the public) to be serious but in fact was slight or even sham. The fright of the initiates and the following enforced stillness in the dance house impressed the young people, who learned that the actual dancers were their older relatives but who learned also that the real spirits did come, invisible, to the village and lent some of their power to the leaders in the ritual. As in most instances of sha-manistic sleight-of-hand and dramatic ritual per-formances, the initiated use startling, uncanny tricks to make the ignorant believe in spiritual power that the instructed persons understand to be intangible but nonetheless true. Some of the young initiates, perhaps urged by a relative among the leaders, would pay fees to learn more of the tech-niques and esoteric knowledge of their elders, and eventually inherit the costume and role of their instructors. Becoming a religious adept was thus a procedure essentially the same as becoming a craft or hunt specialist, or a chief or doctor. All trained by assisting masters, usually older relatives, and, except for the chief, paid fees for instruction and tools of the trade. Men of the chiefly lineage who were suitable to be chosen chief trained as assis-tants to the chiefs, but did not pay fees.

The performances by spirit impersonators have been termed by Kroeber the Kuksu cult, after the name of one of the principal spirits. The organiza-tion of the ritual, the concept of impersonating spirits who journey from their home to the village and back again after the performance, and the belief that the visit of the spirits blesses the com-munity all resemble the katcina dance societies of the Pueblos. Kuksu rituals are found principally in the lower Sacramento Valley east of San Fran-cisco, a long distance from the Southwest but at the end of a trade route from the Pueblo region. As some katcinas are translations of Mexican deities, who are interpreted in the context of Pueblo socie-ties, the Kuksu rituals ("cult" seems too strong a term) may represent the farthest northern extension in the West of Mexican religious ideas, much obscured by passage through the Pueblos and the translation again into Patwin and neighboring con-texts. The Patwin also had a ritual of visits from other, northern spirits—the Kuksu and his fellows, significantly, are said to come from the south—who cause their impersonators, always fully adult men and women, to go insane on the fourth and final day of the ceremony. The costumed dancers rush outside wildly and throw themselves into the swamp, where their friends rescue them and bring them back to the dance house to be cured and revitalized by the director of the ritual. The dan-gerous behavior of the maddened northern spirits' impersonators resembles the rituals of the North-west Coast and contrasts with the benevolent, com-munity-oriented Kuksu and other southern spirits.

Visits from the spirits were important occa-sions, to which neighboring communities might be invited as guests. Following the religious ceremo-nies, people of the village, and guests if present, would enjoy relaxing social dances. Social dances just for the village could be put on whenever recreation was desired. A different type of dance was done by women led by two men. The women held on to a long rope of swan feathers, swaying with it. The rope was thought to be impregnated with spiritual power, so the women held it gingerly but benefited from their cautious contact with it. Special dances were given to mark a girl's debut as a young woman at the end of her first menstrual period, which she had passed in seclusion, attended by older women who spoke to her of the impor-tance of responsible, moral conduct now that she could become a wife and mother. A final type of "dance" consisted of the gambling games played to sets of songs. These could be enjoyed at festi-vals, along with social dances, and of course were especially popular when people from other villages had come, bringing their special products to add interest to the games' pot.

Each Californian community had its own vari-ations and emphases in ceremonies. Northern Pomo, for example, interpret the northern spirits of the Patwin as ghosts, and every few years a com-munity would hold a religious school for its boys or girls, bringing all the boys, or all the girls, around the age of puberty in the upper-class families into the dance house, where they would remain still while the ghost impersonators lectured them on history, morals, and spiritual knowledge. Students' ears and nose septums were pierced at this time so that they could wear ornaments. After four days, the privileged young people emerged, marked by their new jewelry as ready to continue education in a specialty. Commoner boys and girls excluded from the school were marked by their lack of earrings and nose ornaments as unlikely to achieve mastery of any craft or office, and were relegated to the humdrum chores of getting subsistence and making only utilitarian objects.

Southern Californians had neither the katcinalike spirit impersonators nor the dangerous northern ghosts. Their relationship to their immediate ancestors was expressed in annual mourning ceremonies, and their relationship with spirits in taking a psychedelic drug during a ritual. The mourning ceremony ideally was given each autumn, with guests invited from two or three neighboring communities, but most villages might give it only every other year. The ceremony began with rituals commemorating the community's dead and with weeping and crying out to loved ones by those who had been bereaved since the last ceremony. Families from one of the neighboring villages then ritually cleansed the bereaved and presented them with handsome baskets containing new clothing to replace the rags they had been wearing in sign of their sorrow. Long-standing alliances between families in the adjacent communities were the basis for the cleansing and gifts, one family regularly performing the services for its partner and the partner family reciprocating. Visitors to the ceremony donated money (shell beads) to the hosts, who in turn gave the guests food, fine baskets, ornaments, and other desirable goods. Much of the money received was used to pay the singers, dancers, and doctors who put on displays of their shamanistic power. Gifts were also made to the dead, by burning them on pyres. After the

mourning proper had been concluded, the hundreds of people gathered enjoyed feasting, gambling, trading, and social dancing. The mourning ceremony consolidated both the members of the community, who contributed food and wealth to relieve their bereaved kin's sorrow, and the several communities of an area who regularly exchanged host and guest roles.

Spiritual growth was sought by southern Californians in a winter ritual in which those who wanted knowledge and spiritual power fasted from meat for weeks and then took datura, a plant commonly known as jimson weed—*toloache* is its Mexican name. Unlike peyote, jimson-weed root is poisonous if the dosage is not carefully measured or if the plant is too mature. In the toloache ritual, the seekers were supervised by experienced older men who could also help the visionary interpret what he had seen under the influence of the drug. Upper-class adolescents were expected to participate in the datura ritual to gain spiritual understanding and power to become responsible adults. For the initiates, priests would make sand paintings on the ground, using the pictured symbols of the cosmos to teach the youths spiritual doctrines. Sand paintings were similarly used to teach girls in the ceremony marking their first menstruation when they became women.

Many California peoples held ceremonies on the solstices and had codified observations of the lunar months, stars, and sun's movements into calendars, which they corrected at the solstices. Religious dances were also held to impress upon people the power of natural forces seen in condors, eagles, and grizzly bears, or to protect people from rattlesnakes. Whatever the validity of the rattlesnake doctor's claim that his power invoked in a dance would prevent participants from being bitten, the reminder that caution was needed to avoid the fatal creatures when out hunting or gathering must have done some good. (If someone was bitten, he or she was rushed to the rattlesnake doctor, who sucked out the poison.) The beauty of flowers was celebrated by many communities in the spring, the people decking themselves in crowns of blossoms and dancing with bouquets. Flower festivals expressed the joy of Californians in the goodness of life in a land abundant in resources and mild in climate. There was some competition for territory, attested since at least 2000 B.C. by occasional burials of speared victims, but people attempted to keep population in check by normal frequent nursing, by abortion, and at times infanticide. Each community, of a few hundred to perhaps a thousand persons, was deeply attached to its ancestral district and followed a cultural pattern that had been established for over three thousand years. Then came the Europeans, and destruction. From an estimated three hundred and fifty thousand late in the eighteenth century A.D., native Californians were cut down to twenty-five thousand by 1900, dispossessed, denigrated, and despondent.

The Mission Experience

European contact with California began in 1539, when Spanish exploration of the Pacific coast of Mexico carried Francisco Ulloa around the peninsula of Baja California. United States California was reached by the next expedition, under the Portuguese captain Juan Rodríguez Cabrillo, sailing for Spain. Cabrillo died while wintering on San Miguel Island, one of the Channel Islands off Santa Barbara, and his expedition was resumed by his pilot, Bartolemé Ferrelo, who coasted the entire state and reached the central section of the Oregon shoreline before returning to Mexico. Satisfied with the outline of geography brought back by Ferrelo, Spain neglected California for more than a century, even though the English privateer Francis Drake had spent five weeks in 1579 repairing his ship in an anchorage just north of San Francisco and had included in the account of the circumnavigation a description of the fruitful land and admirable people of what he named Albion. Nor did Britain evince any intent of following up Drake's linking of the Miwok country with his own. Neither this

contact, then, nor that of the Spanish explorer Sebastian Vizcaino, who sailed up to Cape Mendocino and named Monterey Bay in 1602, spurred Spain to reach so far beyond the territory it was consolidating in Mexico.

The international situation changed after the conclusion of the Seven Years' War in 1763. Britain was pushing the fur trade west, now that France had been eliminated from Canada, and Russia was slowly moving south from its fur posts in the Aleutian Islands and Alaska. To secure the borders of her American empire, Spain decided in 1769 to found an outpost in Alta California. The governor of Baja California, Gaspar de Portolá, and a Franciscan missionary, Junípero Serra, marched to San Diego and there established a joint military-mission fort. Serra's Franciscans would be guarded and supported by soldiers, and in return would develop a settlement that could victual the soldiers. Farm labor would be performed by local Indians converted to Christianity and "civilized" through regimentation as serfs of the mission. A series of similar mission forts were built by Spain along the southern and central California coast, most in the late eighteenth century but as late as 1823. They followed the policy of the Northwest Mexican missions, "reducing" the native settlements by resettling converts in new, planned communities around the mission buildings. The California missions included dormitories for unmarried converts and clusters of married couples' homes, as well as quarters for the Spanish soldiers.

Franciscan missionaries in California sincerely desired to save the souls of the natives of this farthest northwest province of New Spain. They were also to help preserve Spain's control by cooperating with the garrisons, and they hoped to teach the native Californians to live as European peasants. These several goals did not always fit without strain. If baptizing dying Indians saved souls, it did not maintain mission labor forces or lead to an Indian peasantry; teaching Indians to live as peasants was a less efficient way to support a garrison than merely conscripting them into the mission. The importance of economic development of the mission forced the friars sometimes to turn away possible converts within the mission, while another year the friars might take an escort of soldiers out to Indian villages to bring in "neophyte" labor.

For the Indians, the missions were a disastrous intrusion. At first, missions offered novelty and food during droughts and could draw recruits. Very soon, Indians realized that acceptance of mission hospitality had to be paid for by loss of personal autonomy. Bells tolling in the morning assembled the Indians for allocation of the day's work, which included heavy, tedious, dirty tasks of building in stone and adobe such as native Californians had never done. The unrelenting march of jobs, briefly broken by Sunday respites, contrasted cruelly with the native pattern of intensive food procurement for a few hours or days, alternated with leisure, preparations for ceremonies, and celebrations. And, much of the native pattern of food procurement was pleasant or challenging, rather than dull and sweaty as at the mission. Family life was subordinated to the mission regime, with food doled out from communal kitchens rather than being the responsibility of the families. European ideas of bodily modesty were of course inculcated, and strenuous efforts made to prevent youths and girls from experimenting with sex. Native class distinctions were largely ignored by the friars. Once the Indians realized the price they would pay for tasting novelty, few freely entered the mission.

The Spanish would not abandon their program because it did not agree with the Indians. Indians became serfs, legally bound to the mission. Converts who deserted a mission were often hunted down and dragged back in iron chains to be flogged in punishment. Recalcitrants within the mission, and those who forgetfully broke rules, were also flogged. A high disease rate was bemoaned but accepted. Crowding young people in the damp, unheated, unventilated dormitories, and the communal kitchens were prime avenues for the spread of contagious diseases introduced by the Europeans. Venereal diseases were additional scourges, the result of the Spanish soldiers taking Indian women, sometimes with the woman's compliance, more often by threat. Because of the high disease rate, the population of "neophytes" did not reproduce itself, but had to be augmented continuously with new villagers. Easing the strain on mission food production through excursions of mission Indians to their former communities to join in acorn and similar harvests facilitated the propagation of introduced diseases in the native villages. Decimated villages then considered surrendering to the mission, fearing (or experiencing) hardship because too few able-bodied adults survived. Thus, the missions' policy was to invite Indians to come of their own will, but in practice the need of the missions for labor led to armed intimidation of potential workers, and epidemics and the debilitation from venereal diseases disrupted native economies and eventually brought additional Indians into the missions as refugees. The destruction of native communities was accelerated in the nineteenth century as private ranches developed by Spanish-Mexican colonists around the missions and garrisons recruited labor from the already reduced Indian population.

Russian movement toward New Spain was primarily an extension of sea-otter hunting from the North Pacific southward, although hope of supplying Alaskan posts with food from California was a secondary impetus. In 1806, Russians sailed to San Francisco to purchase supplies. In 1812, a colony was set up on the Russian River north of the San Francisco region. This foggy location never produced enough crops to provision northern colonies, but, as a base for sea-otter hunting, it functioned until 1841, when the animals had been so heavily slaughtered that hunting them was no longer profitable. Pursuit of the otters was a speciality of Aleuts and Siberian Russians. Numbers of these men were stationed at Fort Ross, the Russian California post. Many took wives from the Pomo of the neighborhood, some eventually bringing their Pomo wives and children back to Russia, others leaving the women and children with the Pomo. One result of the close relationship between the Russians and the Pomo was the retention of some Russian words among the California Pomo. Another result of the establishment of Fort Ross was severe competition between the foreign hunters and the California Indians, from the Pomo to the Channel Islands Chumash and other groups, who also hunted sea otter. Unlike Canadian Indians who became suppliers to European markets, trading through posts where employees did very little trapping themselves, the California Indians were not encouraged to supply the Russian trade. Fort Ross thus destroyed the Indians' resource without providing any compensatory business. Other marine resources were not as avidly pursued, but were disturbed by the Russian boats in the narrow offshore zone frequented by the sea mammals. The Russian intrusion, added to Spanish seizure of the California coast by way of San Francisco Bay, knocked out the native peoples who had developed sea-mammal hunting into the basis of a relatively complex society with a dense population. The Coast Miwok who had impressed Drake, the Chumash, the Costanoans, the Salinans, and the Esselen neighboring them were the major groups affected. Farther south, such peoples as the Gabrielino, Luiseño, and Fernandeño were so completely dominated by the Spanish mission-garrison colonies that their very names were replaced by mission names.

The Dispossession of the Californians

Mexican independence secularized the missions in 1834. Indians in the missions were now technically free, but many were coerced by the lay colonists to become peons on the ranches. Secularization really opened up interior California to invasion. Under Spain, the mission-garrison posts were confined to the coastal region by their duty to defend New Spain's northwestern border. Without that imperial duty, private entrepreneurs looked to the sunny Central Valley behind the Coast ranges.

Here, ranching was more profitable, and the larger Indian population, still living cleanly in its ancestral pattern, might furnish labor. Incursions into the interior during the 1820s had met strong resistance from Indians led by such able generals as the Miwok chief Estanislao. The peoples on the eastern side of the Coast ranges and in the Central Valley were also becoming horsemen, raiding both horses and cattle from the ranches and missions. During the Mexican period, from 1834 to 1848, these peoples were fighting the first real threat to their communities. Increased contacts brought open battles where shrewd guerrilla tactics and swift cavalry charges could give the Indians a fair chance of victory, but unhappily, they also brought epidemics and destruction of resources. The epidemics included malaria as well as smallpox and cholera. Resources were destroyed by the scorched-earth strategies used by the colonists against the Indians, and by grazing cattle. A secondary effect of the epidemics was failure to lay in stores adequate to provide sufficient food over the winter, since epidemics were particularly bad in late summer. Through these several causes, many of the interior villages in California were made increasingly vulnerable to dispossession.

United States takeover of California at the conclusion, in 1848, of the war with Mexico coincided with discovery of gold at a colony at present-day Sacramento developed by a Swiss immigrant, Sutter. Euro-American settlers who had been slowly but steadily coming over the Sierra or down from the Oregon Trail suddenly became a flood. This onslaught was especially disastrous to the Indians because the gold seekers did not remain in the valleys, as ranchers had, but swarmed over the hills, where Indians had been accustomed to finding refuge from foreigners. Many of the miners were vicious men contemptuous of anything but money, booze, and sex. Many thought it good sport to gun down Indians on a Sunday afternoon. Others went with their guns to rape Indian women, beating the men who tried to protect them. Round Valley settlers systematically shot the valley's Yuki people, several dozen at a time week after week, between 1856 and 1860. With farmers in the valleys draining the productive marshes and putting cattle on the grasslands, hogs eating the acorns in the foothills, and miners in the hills sluicing mud into the streams, Indians' once diverse and abundant resources were rapidly destroyed. Hungry and homeless, often suffering from syphilis, the California Indians of the 1850s and 1860s became pariahs in their own homelands, the men accepting petty wages for hard laborers' jobs, the women degraded into prostitution, the children beggars. Destruction of Californians' resources was not as dramatic as the extinction of the Plains Indians' bison herds, but it was similarly rapid and devastating.

The United States government had initiated measures to regulate the affairs of Indians in California when that territory came under United States jurisdiction, but it accomplished little against the rabid determination of many immigrants to exterminate independent Indians as so many "varmints" inherently detrimental to the invading cultural system. The Spanish-Mexican system of subjugating Indian communities into laboring for nothing more than cheap food and clothing continued under United States rule, most colonists relying on this nearly free labor. Johann Sutter, for example, sent out a hundred Indians and, interestingly, fifty Hawaiian natives in 1848 to work his mine claim. An immigrant who was briefly employed by Sutter left to develop his own mines, and by paying Indians goods equal in weight to the gold they panned out, profited to the tune of a half-million dollars—1848 dollars! (Compare this to the price of Indian slaves at that time: $50 for a young child, up to $200 for a strong young man or attractive girl.) California's first legislature, convened even before the territory became a state, passed in 1850 an "Act for the Government and Protection of Indians" that provided for the punishment of Indians not only "for any unlawful offense against a white person" but also "for loitering and strolling about, frequenting places where liquor was sold, begging, or leading an immoral and profligate life.... In no case

shall a white man be convicted of any offense upon the testimony of an Indian, or Indians. And in all cases it shall be discretionary with the Court or jury after hearing the complaint of the Indian." Slavery was regulated by requiring that the person who took and wished to keep an Indian minor, euphemistically called an "apprentice," should go with the child's parents or friends before a justice of the peace to establish that "no compulsion was used." In view of the disregard of the testimony of Indians, this requirement would seem to offer poor protection to Indians. Adult Indians had been forbidden to leave their employers since United States takeover of California in 1846; under the 1850 Act, Indians arrested for "vagrancy" were to be forced into employment, and Indians in jail could be bailed out by white men seeking laborers. In each case, the Indian had no choice and was to be paid only in food and necessary clothing. Ironically, California was entering the Union as a "free state" forbidding slavery: there would be no black slaves, no; why should there be when it was cheaper to "indenture" local Indians?

The 1850 Act ordered sheriffs to designate as Indian land, parcels that the Indians occupied and "needed." Confirmation of Indian occupancy rights would follow determination of the principles of transferring land held under Mexican laws to United States jurisdiction. Commissioners from the United States government traveled about California in 1851, meeting with large numbers of Indians and agreeing with them on treaties setting aside sections of land for reservations. In some instances, the Indians removed immediately to these new reservations. The treaties failed to be ratified in Congress when submitted in 1852, because of strong opposition from the California delegation. Representing the views of most of their voting constituents, who, by the law of California, were exclusively "white male citizens," the congressmen from California decried the granting of good valley land and possible mineral rights to Indians and claimed that the amount of land taken out of the public domain for Indian use was extravagant. The concern of the commissioners to allocate to the Indian groups strips running from the valleys into the hills, to ensure sufficient diversity of resources to permit adequate sustenance, directly conflicted with the interests of the Euro-American colonists, and since the Indians had no lobby, much less vote, in Congress, the interests of the colonists won. Eventually, 115 reservations or rancherías (small villages) were marked out for Indians in California.

None of the reservations finally designated were large, and most contain only enough land for residences; none are big enough for community economic development. Consequently, the majority of California Indians have never lived on reservations, first because of the long delay in granting reservations, and then because no attempt was made to provide reservation land for all California Indians, most of whom were technically squatting on Euro-American holdings or renting laborers' quarters. When the 1887 Dawes Allotment Act was passed, a number of California Indians ingeniously filed for homestead allotments on public lands, usually their traditional homelands. A very few Indians obtained comfortable grants, notably the Cahuilla at Palm Springs, some of whom have prospered, though only by fighting city zoning rules adversely affecting their parcels, since their desert oasis became a fashionable location for the homes of millionaires. Most California Indians were permanently dispossessed, and a proportion, particularly in the south in the former mission area, are often assumed by their non-Indian neighbors to be Mexican-American. Several communities of these Indian nations have been petitioning the federal government for official recognition as Indian bands, with entitlement to federal programs for Indians.

Where reservations were granted, in the 1860s and as late as 1929, the usual course of heavy-handed indoctrination of American Protestant culture was followed. President Grant's policy of delegating Indian agencies to church missionary organizations brought several to California reser-

vations. Indian parents at first were eager to have schools made available to their children, but were soon disillusioned by the prejudice shown against their youngsters and their heritage. At Round Valley Reservation in north-central California, occupied by Pomo, Wailaki, Achumawi, Yuki, and others, an agent's insistence on keeping children in a boarding school led to the older boys and girls burning their dormitories—with the tacit approval of their parents, it was said. The young arsonists were severely flogged. In this case, the Indians were befriended by a Methodist minister, who helped them present grievances to an investigation. The minister noted that the agency superintendent was present to hear all complaints, and had virtually unlimited power, through his control over reservation economy and activities and through his recommendations on Indians who wanted to establish themselves off the reservation, to harass any who dared to speak against him. A few years later, in 1919, fourteen rancherías, advised by a Catholic priest at Ukiah, organized as the Society of Northern California Indians, hoping to obtain legal and economic counsel to improve their lot. Southern Californian Indians with similar goals organized the Mission Indian Federation in 1918. Concerns and grievances voiced at the Federation's meetings led to the arrest of fifty-seven members on the charge of conspiracy against the government. This blatant mishandling of well-justified agitation was rectified by the intervention of Euro-Americans in the area in 1922, but the underlying problems were not resolved.

Long before the twentieth-century shift of public attitudes toward Indians brought hope of improvement through political processes, California Indians had sought relief through spiritual aid. The Ghost Dance visions of the Paiute Wodziwob, who prophesied the return of the dead on a train in 1869 when the transcontinental railroad was completed through Nevada, were proselytized in northern California in 1871 by a Pyramid Lake Paiute, Weneyuga (Frank Spencer). A Modoc leader, Doctor George, converted others of his people after hearing Weneyuga, and from the Modoc the doctrine spread south to the Shasta and also to the Tolowa and to other northwestern California Northwest Coast border groups, the Yurok and the Karok. Another Paiute proselytizer, Biritcid, brought the word to the Achumawi, and they in turn told the Yana. As the doctrine spread south to the peoples in north-central California, it revitalized traditional beliefs and rituals, as happened twenty years later when Wovoka's Ghost Dance spread to the Pawnee and other Plains peoples. Norelputus, whose father was Yana and mother Wintun, interpreted what he learned of the Paiute beliefs to demand that earth lodges, the traditional central-Californian dwelling, be constructed for the returning dead (who might march, rather than come by train). Many communities built earth lodges and danced, costumed in paint and feathers as in traditional ceremonies, excitedly awaiting their many friends and relatives who had died in the difficult twenty years of the American inva-

sion. The Ghost Dance movement lasted only a year, lapsing as the dead failed to come. But the religious revival it stimulated continued. Persons who had dreamed of rituals or spiritual messages spoke up, urging their communities to perform new versions of remembered ceremonies. Kuksu spirits reappeared, usually only two, and a new dance, called Bole or Maru, was developed principally for women participants, who wore dresses patterned after Euro-American dresses of the period and held bandannas in their hands. Thus, old and modern were joined in celebration of traditional beliefs adapted to postcolonization conditions. During the ceremonies, the spiritual leaders whose dreams had revealed the manner of adaptation exhorted their communities to abstain from drinking, quarrels, and similar threats to the survival of peoples already pushed into poverty and frequently degraded. Indians who resisted debauchery were told they could look forward to a heaven filled with flowers, where all was peace and plenty.

SONGS OF LATE-NINETEENTH-CENTURY WINTU SPIRITUAL LEADERS

Song by Jim Thomas:
  Above I have heard is where they will go,
  The ghosts of the people rhythmically swaying,
  Above I have heard is where they will go,
  Rhythmically waving dandelion puffs,
  The ghosts of the people rhythmically swaying.

Song by Harry Marsh:
  Above we shall go,
  Along the Milky Way we shall go.
  Above we shall go,
  Along the flower path we shall go.

Song by unknown Wintu poet:
  Above where the minnow maiden sleeps at rest
  The flowers droop,
  The flowers rise again.
  Above where the minnow maiden sleeps at rest
  The flowers droop,
  The flowers rise again.

Song by Sadie Marsh:
>   Down west, down west,
>   Is where we ghosts dance.
>   Down west, down west,
>   Is where weeping ghosts dance,
>   Is where we ghosts dance.

(Du Bois 1939:57)

The Ghost Dance prophecy of a return of the dead did not come true literally, but its theme did bring about a return of faith in old concepts and values and a determination to keep these alive in spite of the deaths of most of those who knew the esoteric details of Kuksu and his fellow spirits. Shamanistic healing was also reinforced. Many of the trained Indian doctors opposed the innovations, but the sucking doctors, a less prestigious class of healers who lacked the inherited medicine bundles of the more formally trained doctors and who cured by claiming to suck disease out of patients with the aid of spirit healers, were encouraged. The Pomo and the Patwin, who seem to have had some of the most elaborate ceremonies before invasion, after 1873 maintained Bole/Maru dances as expressions of religious belief, from time to time adding symbols or ritual acts, some a syncretism of Christian ideas with the native concepts, as one or another leader dreamed it proper. When Wovoka's Ghost Dance religion was talked about, twenty years after Wodziwob's, California Indians rejected it: they had been disappointed once before in Paiute prophecies, and now they had their own religions, deeply rooted in their traditions but adjusted so as to be carried by laboring people who worked long hours as farm hands and domestics, who had little opportunity to apprentice themselves to priests or doctors. The world of the California Indians had been destroyed, but the structure of their universe persisted and formed the core of a new world.

The Ghost Dance religion did not spread to southern California. Indians of western-southern California had been released from the missions without adequate provision for land on which to build communities. Their own villages long since broken up, they dispersed to work as peons on Mexican estates or were allowed to farm small individual plots of former mission land. Anglo-American invasion further fragmented the remnants of southern California Indian communities, affecting those to the east, on the border of the Southwest, as well as those earlier overcome by Spanish colonization. Those who considered themselves descendants of the Indians of western-southern California came to be lumped as Mission Indians. They had been molded by two or three generations of serf status on the Spanish missions, a period in which the most vigorous efforts had been made to stamp out Indian beliefs and practices. There was no appeal for these people in the Ghost Dance: should their parents come back, the mission serfs? No one remembered rituals that had been impossible to carry out for a half-century or more; there was no strong core upon which the Ghost Dance could revive.

From the 1870s to 1950, California Indians were caught in the lowest stratum of society. Their sensible habit of going without clothes had been seized upon by the Victorian colonists (stifled in woolen dress that had originated in cold northern Europe) as a mark of brutishness, and was used to justify brutal treatment of these unfortunates impeding American "get-rich-quick" plans. The little rancherías set aside by a few kindly colonists or bought by citizens' groups were refuges for the Indians in a district. One near a former Maidu village was called, in Maidu, Mixed Village because it contained families from a number of destroyed communities. In these mixed villages, those Indian nations who, like the dominant Euro-American society, had affiliation through the father tended to persist as nations as their surviving men married women from other attenuated nations (sometimes more than one wife), while nations that traditionally affiliated through the mother, such as the Yuki, had their children perceived as belonging to the fathers' nations in mixed marriages. Euro-Americans segregated Indians—their slaves in California—as blacks were segregated in the South, excluding them from businesses, services, and municipal institutions or forcing them to use separate sections of buildings such as movie theaters and to wait in stores until all non-Indian customers had been attended to. Indian children generally attended public schools, since there were too few of them to set up segregated schools except on the few reservations, but teachers tended to

assume the Indian students would do poorly and discouraged them, and Euro-American children were expected to avoid friendships with their Indian neighbors. Seasonal agricultural labor, with a little regular domestic work for women, was usually the only employment made available to Indians, and they were paid the lowest wages. Some Indian women married Mexican-American Californian men or Polynesian ("Kanaka") sailors, or conceived children by Chinese men imported as coolies but forbidden to bring their wives to America. However, Indians tended to join their Euro-American oppressors in prejudice against the other ethnic groups, particularly blacks. Thus after the 1870s, California Indians were more or less stabilized in small reconstituted communities, many were committed to the faith of their grandparents as adapted through Bole/Maru and similar revivals, and most were shut out from participation in Euro-American life except as unskilled laborers.

The Pit Rivers [Achumawi] (except the younger ones who have gone to the Government School at Fort Bidwell) don't ever seem to get a very clear conception of what you mean by the term God. This is true even of those who speak American fluently, like Wild Bill. He said to me: "What is this thing that the white people call God? They are always talking about it. It's goddam this and goddam that, and in the name of the god, and the god made the world. Who is that god, Doc? They say that Coyote is the Indian God, but if I say to them that God is Coyote, they get mad at me. Why?"

"Listen, Bill, tell me…. Do the Indians think, really think that Coyote made the world? I mean, do they really think so? Do you really think so?"

"Why of course I do…. Why not?… Anyway…that's what the old people always said…only they don't all tell the same story. Here is one way I heard it: it seems like there was nothing everywhere but a kind of fog. Fog and water mixed, they say, no land anywhere, and this here Silver Fox…."

"You mean Coyote?"

"No, no, I mean Silver Fox. Coyote comes later. You'll see, but right now, somewhere in the fog, they say, Silver Fox was wandering and feeling lonely. *Tsikuellaaduwi maandza tsikualaasa.* He was feeling lonely, the Silver Fox. I wish I would meet someone, he said to himself, the Silver Fox did. He was walking along in the fog. He met Coyote. 'I thought I was going to meet someone,' he said. The Coyote looked at him, but he didn't say anything. 'Where are you traveling?' says Fox. 'But where are YOU traveling? Why do you travel like that?' 'Because I am worried.' 'I also am wandering,' said the Coyote, 'I also am worrying and traveling.' 'I thought I would meet someone, I thought I would meet someone. Let's you and I travel together. It's better for two people to be traveling together, that's what they always say….'"

"Wait a minute, Bill…. Who said that?"

"The Fox said that. I don't know who he meant when he said: that's what they always say. It's funny, isn't it? How could he talk about other people since there had never been anybody before? I don't know…. I wonder about that sometimes, myself. I have asked some of the old people and they say: That's what I have been wondering myself, but that's the way we have always heard it told. And then you hear the Paiutes tell it different! And our own people down the river, they also tell it a little bit different from us. Doc, maybe the whole thing just never happened…. And maybe it did happen but everybody tells it different. People often do that, you know…."

"Well, go on with the story. You said that Fox had met Coyote…."

"Oh, yah…. Well, this Coyote he says: 'What are we going to do now?' 'What do you think?' says Fox. 'I don't know,' says Coyote. 'Well then,' says Fox, 'I'll tell you: LET'S MAKE THE WORLD.' 'And how are we going to do that?' 'WE WILL SING,' says the Fox.

"So, there they were singing up there in the sky. They were singing and stomping and dancing around each other in a circle. Then the Fox he thought in his mind: CLUMP OF SOD, come!! That's the way he made it come: *by thinking*. Pretty soon he had it in his hands. And he was singing, all the while he had it in his hands. They were both singing and stomping. All of a sudden the Fox threw that clump of sod, that *tsapettia* [little island in a marsh], he threw it down into the clouds. 'Don't look down!' he said to the Coyote. 'Keep on singing! Shut your eyes, and keep them shut until I tell you.' So they kept on singing and stomping around each other in a circle for quite a while. Then the Fox said to the Coyote: 'Now, look down there. What do you see?' 'I see something…I see something…but I don't know what it is.' 'All right. Shut your eyes again!' Now they started singing and stomping again, and the Fox thought and wished: Stretch! Stretch! 'Now look down again. What do you see?' 'Oh! it's getting bigger!' 'Shut your eyes again and don't look down!' And they went on singing and stomping up there in the sky. 'Now look down again!' 'Oooh! Now it's big enough!' said the Coyote.

"That's the way they made the world, Doc. Then they both jumped down on it and they stretched it some more. Then they made mountains and valleys; they made trees and rocks and everything. It took them a long time to do all that!"

"Didn't they make people, too?"

"No. Not people. Not Indians. The Indians came much later after the world was spoiled by a crazy woman, Loon. But that's a long story…. I'll tell you some day."

"All right, Bill, but tell me just one thing now: there was a world now; then there were a lot of animals living on it, but there were no people then…."

"Whad'you mean there were no people? Ain't animals people?"

"Yes, they are...but..."

"They are not Indians, but they are people, they are alive... Whad'you mean animal?"

"Well...how do you say 'animal' in Pit River [Achumawi]?"

"...I dunno...."

"But suppose you wanted to say it?"

"Well...I guess I would say something like *tee-qaade-wade toolol aakaadzi* (world-over, all living)...I guess that means animals, Doc."

"I don't see how, Bill. That means people, also. People are living, aren't they?"

"Sure they are! that's what I am telling you. Everything is living, even the rocks, even that bench you are sitting on. *Somebody made that bench for a purpose,* didn't he? Well then *it's alive,* isn't it? Everything is alive. That's what we Indians believe. White people think everything is dead...."

"Listen, Bill. How do you say 'people'?"

"I don't know...just *is*, I guess."

"I thought that meant 'Indian'."

"Say...Ain't we *people?*!"

"So are the whites!"

"Like hell they are!! We call them *inillaaduwi*, 'tramps,' nothing but tramps. They don't believe anything is alive. They are dead themselves. I don't call that 'people.'...."

(De Angulo 1973 [1950]:76-81)

During this period the United States Bureau of Indian Affairs claimed difficulty in managing its responsibilities in California. The small, scattered rancherías were too dissimilar from most Indian reservations to fit into policies and practices developed for the majority of federally administered Indian land. Strongly paternalistic, the Bureau operated through agents who ran agencies like Victorian fathers dominating families, keeping strict control over Indian "wards." Even on the more common large reservations, those Indian families who remained in hamlets at a distance from the agency enjoyed more freedom than those near the agency; the California rancherías were so scattered that most agents found it impossible to supervise their "wards" as they were accustomed to elsewhere, and concluded the California Indian jurisdictions were unmanageable. The federal government wanted the state of California to take over responsibility for Indians within the state.

California Peoples in the Twentieth Century

In the twentieth century, California became conscious of its colonists' unsavory handling of its native Indians, but did not see assumption of federal obligations as the solution to Indians' plight. In 1927, the state legislature moved to have the state attorney general initiate a land-claim suit on behalf of California Indians against the United States. This was permitted by Congress the next year. The case dragged through the court until California (not its Indians) accepted a settlement in 1944. A per-capita payment of $150 decreed in 1950 was the final outcome of the generation-long case for California Indians. A second land claim was filed in 1947 before the newly created Indian Claims Commission, this time by attorneys hired by the plaintiffs, not by the state attorneys. The second claim was settled in 1964 for a total of a little over $29 million, representing compensation of 47¢ per acre of unjustly seized Indian land. The Indians themselves voted to accept this settlement, though opinion was far from unanimous in favor of acceptance.

While the state of California was prosecuting its Indians' first major land claim, Indians throughout the state were becoming more aware of the dimensions of their grievances. Southern California Indians, longer exposed to colonization and better integrated into the local economy, had included many politically active persons since the beginning of the century. Now, in the 1930s, the political consciousness of central-California Indians was raised by contacts between them and "Okie" migrants flocking in from the Dust Bowl of Oklahoma. Many of these migrants were themselves at least part Indian. Others were sensitive to the class structure in which they and native Indians shared the lowest status, and believed the Indians should join them in maneuvers to improve the lot of agricultural laborers. Indians saw Asiatic immi-

grants and their children force the Euro-Americans to share some of the state's wealth and political power. Chinese and Japanese were not very useful role models because they grew up in large, complex, class-structured, basically capitalist industrializing nations and were accustomed to the nature and demands of such societies, unlike California Indians, who could not easily notice all the implicit principles and expectations of the alien society from which they were largely segregated. Filipinos, however, came from a less-developed nation and tended to be friendlier toward the Indians with whom they worked as agricultural laborers. Filipino men sometimes married Indian women, although their wives' families often showed prejudice against them. Like most "Okies" and like the better integrated southern-California Indians, Filipinos were determined to at least earn a decent wage and obtain security for their families. The Depression years thus brought the California Indians into contact with people who were equally poor but who expected to improve their lot by combining political strategies with hard work. They were in many instances willing to have Indians join them in their protests (it was, of course, wise to have the Indians as part of any strike that might be planned, instead of being available to employers as scab labor).

Possibilities for economic and social improvements increased dramatically for California Indians during World War II. Young men could enlist in the armed forces, where they were more likely to encounter Euro-Americans who thought Indians a welcome novelty than men who were strongly prejudiced against them. Women and middle-aged men found well-paying employment in industries. Both in the armed forces and industry, Indians were strongly reminded what rights should be theirs as American citizens, citizenship having been granted to Indians in 1924. The conclusion of the war left a comparatively large number of California Indians with employment skills and work records sufficient to make it difficult for employers to reject them. Racial discrimination did not end, but it had to be muted, since the stereotypes it rested upon could often be refuted, and there was more real opportunity for assertive Indians. Federal government policy toward Indians in the 1950s noted the economic gains made by many individual Indians in the previous decade and concluded that improvement for all Indians could be hastened by termination of the wardship status thought to be enjoined to reservations and treaty grants. Part of the impetus toward termination of federal guardianship of Indians was, unquestionably, the desire of many Euro-American land developers and corporations to gain access to timber, grazing, resort areas, and minerals that they could lease but not own as long as Indian reservations were intact. Other supporters of termination came from states with few Indians who begrudged their tax monies spent through the federal government on Indians; the same concern led states with proportionately large Indian populations to oppose termination of federal responsibility. Some proponents of termination were naive "friends of the Indian" who knew of the evils perpetuated through the federal structure and thought freeing Indians of that structure would, as with a magic wand, free them of the appurtenances of poverty. Both direct termination of federal responsibility and slower progress through relocation of Indians off reservations into cities dominated policy toward Indians in the 1950s.

California Indians were hard hit by these policies. Termination was included in a bill passed by Congress in 1954. The state of California was loath to take over welfare services to the grossly neglected Indian communities, but federal jurisdiction over forty-four California rancherías was unilaterally terminated in 1958, and federal services and programs to all other California Indians were withdrawn. The outcry against these acts was raised by Indians and the state of California alike. After ten years of pressure, in 1968 the Bureau of Indian Affairs extended many programs to California Indians again, but the coverage is not as extensive as it was before 1958. A cynical observer would note that the reluctance of the state of California to bear the costs of providing services to its Indian citizens, few of whom pay much in taxes since few have large incomes or property, was probably more influential in restoring federal programs to Indians than was any concern that there had been an abridgement of the rights owed to the Indians through the 1851–52 treaties, which, though never ratified, were acknowledged through the claims settlements to have justified Indian expectations of recompense from the United States.

Relocation strongly altered California Indian life. Indians from other areas had begun coming to California with other Dust Bowl refugees during the 1930s; more came during the 1940s to work in war industries. Relocation plans selected Los Angeles and San Francisco as two cities in which employment opportunities and vocational-training availability should attract Indians. The number of Indians in California doubled between 1950 and 1960, due principally to in-migration, and has continued to increase from this source. Before the relocation program, Los Angeles' recognized Indian population was mostly Cherokee, Creek, Choctaw, and Seminole from Oklahoma, with fewer than one hundred in a survey of three thousand Indians claiming descent from a native California group (though many native Indians were missed by the survey). After relocation in 1952, Navajo and Sioux were the largest Indian groups in Los Angeles, with other Southwest and other Plains peoples next in population size and comparable to the numbers of former Southeastern peoples who had come from Oklahoma. As is generally true for Indians in large cities (not, however, in Minneapolis–St. Paul), no real Indian ghetto developed in the two California cities. A number of bars are seen as catering to Indians and have become informal meeting centers for them. There are also formal Indian centers, some run as outreach social-services centers, some through churches or the YWCA, some as social clubs organized by Indians. Several fundamentalist churches have predominantly Indian congregations. These include transplanted Indian Southern Baptists from Oklahoma, where the Cherokees in particular took over the independent local church as a community center, and Pentecostal and other gospel churches, which have been proselytizing very actively among Indians both on reservations and in cities. The majority of migrant Indians in the California cities return to their home reservations fairly often, many remaining on the reservations after experiencing unhappy employment encounters or yearning for the clear air of their people's home. The cities do maintain, nevertheless, a lively Indian population that enjoys powwows, picnics, visiting, and worship together. For the California Indians whose ancestors held the state, the heavy influx of Southwestern and Plains Indians has swamped the native heritage in the cities, substituting Oklahoma and Gallup style powwows for California dances and songs—even for the Bole/Maru, which were first popular because of their beauty as well as their spiritual content. Only in rural areas can the survivors of California peoples be reminded of their true heritage.

The thousands of Indians from other states living in California cities have stimulated a series of political organizations and movements representative of pan-Indian, and in some cases even Indian-Chicano, concerns. These are for the most part distinct from California Indian organizations such as the Ad Hoc Committee on Indian Education, formed in 1967 to improve education for Indians in the state. The pan-Indian organizations range from the American Indian Historical Society, begun in 1964 by Rupert Costo, tribal chairman of the Cahuilla Reservation, and his wife to encourage and publish, in *The Indian Historian,* research in history reflecting Indian points of view, to militantly activist groups. One year after the American Indian Movement became a national organization, in 1968, its members participated in an Indian occupation of then-deserted Alcatraz Island in San Francisco Bay, an action designed to draw public attention to the land needs of Indians and the apparent availability of unused Federal lands. There was discussion of converting the abandoned facilities on the island into a university specializing in Indian studies and sensitive to the problems of Indian students. A college was founded, but at a more practical site in Davis, California. This institution is known as DQ University, the initials those of Deganawidah, whose vision led to the Iroquois Confederacy, and Quetzalcoatl, the Precious Serpent of the Mexican nations and lord of the arts of peace and civilization. In 1978, nine years after the Alcatraz occupation, AIM began its Longest Walk in California, a march of Indians and sympathizers across the continent to a demonstration in Washington, D.C., protesting bills recently proposed to Congress that would curtail or revoke treaty rights of Indians. AIM activities in California were based on the cosmopolitan Indian population in the major cities. The state today has two Indian populations, the migrant-dominated heterogeneous residents of the cities, and the native California Indians who look to the rancherías and reservations of the state for the preservation of their traditions. These have been reviving their languages, teaching them to their children in schools, and building cultural centers functioning as both museums and community activity grounds where young people practicing dances and crafts guided by the elderly absorb also their outlook on their world. Kashia Pomo, the section of the Pomo nation around Fort Ross on the Russian River, organized in the 1970s an agricultural training project, Ya-Ka-Ama (Kashaya Pomo for "our land"), tapping U.S. Department of Labor funds to develop agricultural practices compatible with Pomo values.

Population figures for native California Indians are difficult to obtain because so many of their rancherías and small reservations were officially terminated in the 1950s. Some have been restored to Indian status, but with those petitioning for federal reinstatement plus those earlier unrecognized, there must be thousands of California Indians not listed on official rolls. According to the 1980 federal census, the state had 227,757 Indians, of which over fifty thousand were Cherokee (most immigrant from Oklahoma)!; Cahuilla, Chumash, Diegueño, Gabrielino, Hupa, Karok, Luiseño, Maidu, Miwok, Mono, Pit River (Achumawi), Washo, Wintu, and Yokuts all had between one and two thousand members each, while the Pomo and Yurok had three thousand, (unspecified) "Mission Indians" twenty-five hundred, Costanoans and Wailaki five hundred each, the Shasta, Salinans, Cupeno, and Wiyot three hundred, and fewer for the Serrano, Mattole, Wappo and related Yuki, and Cahto (Athabascan speakers, just north of the Pomo, similar to, and neighboring, the Wailaki). This chapter has not discussed the peoples of northern California whose residence is within the state's boundary but whose cultural pattern is closer to that of the Northwest Coast. These peoples will be described in the next chapter.

SUMMARY

The peoples west of the Rockies developed a Western Archaic cultural pattern early in the Holocene, and maintained it to, or in better-watered regions through, the climax of the Holocene era warming trend around 3000 B.C. This cultural pattern utilized "roots" (most actually bulbs or tubers), seeds, and nuts as the storable diet staple, and supplemented these foods with game. Detailed and extensive knowledge of the growth of plants and the habits of game was the basis of the economy, which scheduled harvesting of a series of food resources as each reached its prime for human use. Technology focused on basketry, including a variety of specialized seed-collecting beaters, trays, and containers, sandals, and, as an extension of basketry technique, the weaving of strips of rabbit fur into blankets. Domed-shaped huts of poles and brush were built. After around 2000 B.C., regional specialization became more pronounced. On the California coast, the hunting of sea mammals, fishing, and shellfish collecting were established as major features of the economy.

Throughout California, acorns processed to leach out the poisonous acid were the carbohydrate staple. In the Great Basin, pine nuts replaced acorns as the staple, and were supplemented by fishing and mountain-sheep hunting. Contemporary with the Pueblos to the south, but mostly disappearing about A.D. 1450, limited maize agriculture was practiced by the Fremont peoples of southeastern Utah. The Plateau nations depend upon salmon, and have techniques for drying the fish and pounding them into a sweet, nutritious meal. Trade was important to the Plateau and California nations, and shell beads manufactured on the Pacific Coast served as money inland as well as near their origin.

European invasions came relatively late to the West. California began to be colonized in 1769, by Catholic missions built to convert Indians and also to support military garrisons with the labor of converted Indians. The Plateau became involved in the British fur trade early in the nineteenth century. The middle third of the nineteenth century brought missionaries to the Southern Plateau, and then (in part through the missionaries' appeals for settlers from the East) an influx of Euro-American colonists that reached flood proportions when gold was discovered in California, in the Basin and along the Columbia. The Utes had been raiding for horses and selling slaves to the Spanish Southwest from the seventeenth century. With Euro-American colonization backed by United States armed forces in California, the Great Basin, and the southern Plateau after 1848, the Indians were dispossessed from their land and resources and, particularly in California, wantonly murdered. Survivors could no longer obtain a living except by working at the lowest wages for colonists, and by scavenging. Reservations were established in the 1860s and 1870s, but these were not as large as most reservations on the Plains. In California, little effort was made to collect all Indians onto reservations, which resulted in many remnant villages with no land or only a few acres. Everywhere in the West, economic hardship and European diseases weakened and decimated Indian communities from the 1830s on (earlier in southern California).

Those nations who occupied United States reservations lost much of their reserved land at the beginning of this century as the result of the application of the Dawes Allotment Act. British Columbia Plateau groups had only small reserves from the beginning of Canadian rule in their region. Irrigable land was particularly likely to be lost by Indians. Economic development of western reservations and reserves has therefore been severely handicapped. Some of the Basin and California groups have obtained monies from settlement of land claims against the United States, but these funds have had to be used to obtain such basic modern necessities as electricity and roads to reservations, and in general have been unable to improve economies except with such limited enterprises as tribally operated motels or sustained-yield timber harvesting. Beginning in the 1950s, California's major cities received thousands of employment-seeking Indians from the Southwest and Plains reservations. Support for activist protests by AIM in 1969 and later, and for urban Indian clubs and powwows, came largely from these urban migrants. Native western Indians have tended to be more rural and more localized in their concerns.

RECOMMENDED READING

Downs, James E. 1966 *The Two Worlds of the Washo.* New York: Holt, Rinehart and Winston. One of the Case Studies in Cultural Anthropology series, this concise volume focuses on the Washo accommodation to Euro-American society while maintaining a core of Washo tradition.

Fagan, Brian. 1991 *Ancient North America.* New York: W.W. Norton.

Kroeber, Theodora. 1961 *Ishi in Two Worlds.* Berkeley: University of California Press. A sensitively told story of the last Yahi Indian, who hid for years in the wilderness of Mt. Shasta after his people had been massacred, and was finally befriended by Professor Kroeber. Made into a TV movie in 1978.

Miller, Jay, ed. 1990 *Mourning Dove.* Lincoln: University of Nebraska Press. The autobiography of the Okanagon woman, Hum-ishu-ma (Christal Quintasket Galler), who wrote *Cogewea.*

Mourning Dove (Hum-ishu-ma) (Christal Quintasket Galler). 1981[1927] *Cogewea.* Lincoln: University of Nebraska Press. Romantic novel of a half-Okanogon young woman struggling to create a satisfying life in early twentieth-century Montana without denying her Indian heritage. The published novel suffers from an overzealous editor's rewriting in fancy flowery phrases but Mourning Dove's mission of bringing alive the Indians and "half-breeds" of her time is grippingly accomplished.

Wheat, Margaret M. 1967 *Survival Arts of the Primitive Paiutes.* Reno: University of Nevada Press. A wealth of photographs and a lively text recording the skills and experiences of an elderly Paiute woman.

SOURCES FOR THE FIRST EDITION

Adovasio, J.M., R. Andrews, and R. Carlisle. 1977 *Perishable Industries from Dirty Shame Rockshelter.* Pocatello: Idaho State University Museum of Natural History, Tebiwa Miscellaneous Papers, No. 7.

Aginsky, Burt W., and Ethel G. Aginsky. 1967 *Deep Valley.* New York: Stein and Day.

Aikens, C. Melvin. 1966 *Fremont-Promontory-Plains Relationships in Northern Utah.* Salt Lake City: University of Utah, Anthropological Papers, No. 82.

——— 1967 Plains Relationships of the Fremont Culture: A Hypothesis. *American Antiquity* 32:198–209.

Aikens, C. Melvin, David L. Cole, and Robert Stuckenrath. 1977 *Excavations of Dirty Shame Rockshelter, Southeastern Oregon.* Pocatello: Idaho State University Museum of Natural History, Tebiwa Miscellaneous Papers, No. 4.

Azbill, Henry. 1971 Bahapki. *The Indian Historian* 4:57.

Bannon, John Francis, ed. 1964 *Bolton and the Spanish Borderlands.* Norman: University of Oklahoma Press.

Baumhoff, Martin A. 1963 Ecological Determinants of

Aboriginal California Populations. *University of California Publications in American Archaeology and Ethnology* 49:155–236.

Bean, Lowel John, and Thomas C. Blackburn, eds. 1976 *Native Californians: A Theoretical Retrospective.* Ramona, Calif.: Ballena Press.

Bean, Lowell John, and Thomas F. King, eds. 1974 *?Antap: California Indian Political and Economic Organization.* Ramona, Calif.: Ballena Press

Bettinger, Robert L. 1977 Aboriginal Human Ecology in Owens Valley: Prehistoric Change in the Great Basin. *American Antiquity* 42:3–127.

Browman, David L., and David A. Munsell. 1969 Columbia Plateau Prehistory: Cultural Development and Impinging Influences. *American Antiquity* 34:249–264.

Butler, B. Robert. 1959 Lower Columbia Valley Archaeology: A Survey and Appraisal of Some Major Archaeological Resources. *Tebiwa* 2:6–24.

——— 1978 *A Guide to Understanding Idaho Archaeology* (3rd ed.). Pocatello: Idaho Museum of Natural History.

Chartkoff, Joseph L., and Kerry K. Chartkoff. 1975 Late Period Settlement of the Middle Klamath River of Northwest California. *American Antiquity* 40:172–179.

Cook, Sherburne F. 1976 *The Conflict Between the California Indian and White Civilization.* Berkeley: University of California Press.

——— 1976 *The Population of the California Indians 1769–1970.* Berkeley: University of California Press.

Cressman, L.S. 1977 *Prehistory of the Far West.* Salt Lake City: University of Utah Press.

Davis, Emma Lou. 1963 The Desert Culture of the Western Great Basin: A Lifeway of Seasonal Transhumance. *American Antiquity* 29:202–212.

Davis, James T. 1963 Trade Routes and Economic Exchange Among the Indians of California. In R.F. Heizer (ed.). *Aboriginal California.* Berkeley: University of California Archaeological Research Facility.

D'Azevedo, Warren L., ed. 1963 *The Washo Indians of California and Nevada.* Salt Lake City: University of Utah, Anthropological Papers, No. 67.

De Angulo, Jaime. 1973 [1950] *Indians in Overalls.* San Francisco: Turtle Island Foundation.

Delaney, Robert W. 1974 *The Southern Ute People.* Phoenix: Indian Tribal Series.

Downs, James F. 1971 California. In E.B. Leacock and N.O. Lurie (eds.). *North American Indians in Historical Perspective.* New York: Random House, pp. 289–316.

Du Bois, Cora. 1939 *The 1870 Ghost Dance.* Berkeley: University of California, Anthropological Records 3:1–152.

Ellison, William H. 1974 [1913] *The Federal Indian Policy in California, 1846–1860.* San Francisco: R. and E. Research Associates.

Euler, Robert C. 1972 *The Paiute People.* Phoenix: Indian Tribal Series.

Fahey, John. 1974 *The Flathead Indians.* Norman: University of Oklahoma Press.

Fields, D.B., and W.T. Stanbury. 1970 *The Economic Impact of the Public Sector Upon the Indians of British Columbia.* Vancouver: University of British Columbia Press.

Forber, Jack D. 1969 *Native Americans of California and Nevada.* Healdsburg, Calif.: Naturegraph.

Fowler, Don D. 1972 *Great Basin Cultural Ecology.* Reno and Las Vegas: Desert Research Institute Publications in the Social Sciences, No. 8.

Fowler, Don D., and Catherine S. Fowler. 1971 *Anthropology of the Numa: John Wesley Powell's Manuscripts on the Numic Peoples of Western North America, 1868–1880.* Washington, D.C.: Smithsonian Institution Press, Smithsonian Contributions to Anthropology, No. 14.

French, David. 1961 Wasco-Wishram. In E.H. Spicer (ed.). *Perspectives in American Indian Culture Change.* Chicago: University of Chicago Press, pp. 337–430.

Gil Munilla, Octavio. 1963 *Participación de España en la Génesis Histórica de los Estados Unidos.* Madrid: Publicaciones Españolas.

Gunn, Joel. 1975 An Envirotechnological System for Hogup Cave. *American Antiquity* 40:3–21.

Hall, H.J. 1977 *A Paleoscatological Study of Diet and Disease at Dirty Shame Rockshelter, Southeast Oregon.* Pocatello: Idaho State University Museum of Natural History, Tebiwa Miscellaneous Papers, No. 8.

Harnar, Nellie Shaw. 1974 *Indians of Coo-yu-ee Pah (Pyramid Lake).* Sparks, Nev.: Dave's Printing.

Hattori, Eugene Mitsuru. 1975 *Northern Paiutes on the Comstock.* Carson City: Nevada State Museum Occasional Papers, No. 2.

Hawthorn, H.B., C.S. Belshaw, and S.M. Jamieson.

1958 *The Indians of British Columbia.* Toronto: University of Toronto Press.

Heizer, Robert F. 1947 *Francis Drake and the California Indians, 1579.* Berkeley: University of California Press.

———— 1953 *Aboriginal Fish Poisons.* Washington, D.C.: Smithsonian Institution, Bureau of American Ethnology, Bulletin 151, Anthropological Paper No. 38.

———— 1974 *The Destruction of California Indians.* Santa Barbara: Peregrine Smith.

Heizer, Robert F., and William C. Massey. 1953 *Aboriginal Navigation off the Coasts of Upper and Baja California.* Washington, D.C.: Smithsonian Institution, Bureau of American Ethnology, Bulletin 151, Anthropological Paper No. 39.

Heizer, Robert F., and M.A. Whipple. 1971 *The California Indians.* Berkeley: University of California Press.

Hester, Thomas Roy. 1973 *Chronological Ordering of Great Basin Prehistory.* Berkeley: Contributions of the University of California Archaeological Research Facility, No. 17.

Hodge, Frederick Webb. 1910 *Handbook of American Indians.* Washington, D.C.: Smithsonian Institution, Bureau of American Ethnology, Bulletin 30.

Irwin, Henry T. 1975 The Far West. In S. Gorenstein (ed.). *North America.* New York: St. Martin's Press, pp. 133–164.

Jennings, Jesse D. 1973 The Short Useful Life of a Simple Hypothesis. *Tebiwa* 16:1–9.

Jones, J.A. 1955 *The Sun Dance of the Northern Ute.* Washington, D.C.: Smithsonian Institution, Bureau of American Ethnology, Bulletin 151, Anthropological Paper No. 47.

Jorgensen, Joseph G. 1972 *The Sun Dance Religion.* Chicago: University of Chicago Press.

Josephy, Alvin M., Jr. 1965 *The Nez Perce Indians and the Opening of the Northwest.* New Haven: Yale University Press.

Kelly, Isabel T. 1932 Ethnography of the Surprise Valley Paiute. *University of California Publications in American Archaeology and Ethnology* 31:67–210.

Knack, Martha C. 1978 Beyond a Differential: An Inquiry into Southern Paiute Indian Experience with Public Schools. *Anthropology and Education Quarterly* 9:216–234.

Kroeber, A.L. 1925 *Handbook of the Indians of California.* Washington, D.C.: Smithsonian Institution, Bureau of American Ethnology, Bulletin 78.

———— 1932 The Patwin and Their Neighbors. *University of California Publications in Archaeology and Ethnology* 29:253–423.

———— 1939 *Cultural and Natural Areas of Native North America.* Berkeley: University of California Press.

Kroeber, A.L., ed. 1923 *Phoebe Apperson Hearst Memorial Volume.* Berkeley: University of California Publications in American Archaeology and Ethnology 20.

Lahren, S.L., Jr., and John L. Schultz. 1973 New Light on Old Issues: Plateau Political Factionalism. *Northwest Anthropological Research Notes* 7:156–184.

Laviolette, Forrest E. 1973 *The Struggle for Survival.* Toronto: University of Toronto Press.

Liljeblad, Sven. 1972 *The Idaho Indians in Transition, 1805–1960.* Pocatello: Idaho State University Museum.

Loeb, E.M. 1932 The Western Kuksu Cult. *University of California Publications in American Archaeology and Ethnology* 33:1–137.

Madsen, David B. 1975 Dating Paiute-Shoshoni Expansion in the Great Basin. *American Antiquity* 40:82–86.

———— 1978 Recent Data Bearing on the Question of a Hiatus in the Eastern Great Basin. *American Antiquity* 43:508–509.

Madsen, David B., and Michael S. Berry. 1975 A Reassessment of Northeastern Great Basin Prehistory. *American Antiquity* 40:391–405.

Meighan, Clement W. 1959 California Cultures and the Concept of an Archaic Stage. *American Antiquity* 24:289–305.

———— 1959 The Little Harbor Site, Catalina Island: An Example of Ecological Interpretation in Archaeology. *American Antiquity* 24:383–405.

Mooney, James. 1973 [1896] The Ghost-Dance Religion and Wounded Knee. New York: Dover Publications.

Opler, Marvin K. 1971 The Ute and Paiute Indians of the Great Basin Southern Rim. In E.B. Leacock and N.O. Lurie (eds.). *North American Indians in Historical Perspective.* New York: Random House, pp. 257–288.

Palmer, Gary B. 1975 Cultural Ecology in the Canadian Plateau: Pre-Contact to the Early Contact Period in the Territory of the Southern Shuswap Indians of British Columbia. *Northwest Anthropological Research Notes* 9:199–245.

Philips, Susan U. 1974 Warm Springs "Indian Time": How the Regulation of Participation Affects the Progression of Events. In R. Baumand and J. Sherzer (eds.). *Explorations in the Ethnography of Speaking.* London: Cambridge University Press, pp. 92–109.

Ranere, Anthony J. 1970 Prehistoric Environments and Cultural Continuity in the Western Great Basin. *Tebiwa* 13:52–72.

Ray, Verne F. 1932 *The Sanpoil and Nespelem.* University of Washington Publications in Anthropology 5.

———— 1939 *Cultural Relations in the Plateau of Northwestern North America.* Los Angeles: Publications of the Frederick Webb Hodge Anniversary Publication Fund 3.

Relander, Click, ed. 1955 *The Yakimas.* Yakima, Wash.: Republic Press.

Ruby, Robert H., and John A. Brown. 1970 *The Spokane Indians.* Norman: University of Oklahoma Press.

Sanger, David. 1967 Prehistory of the Pacific Northwest Plateau as Seen from the Interior of British Columbia. *American Antiquity* 32:186–197.

Shimkin, D. B. 1953 *The Wind River Shoshone Sun Dance.* Washington, D.C.: Smithsonian Institution, Bureau of American Ethnology, Bulletin 151, Anthropological Paper No. 41.

Shipek, Florence Connolly. 1977 A Strategy for Change: The Luiseno of Southern California. Doctoral dissertation, University of Hawaii.

Sorkin, Alan L. 1971 *American Indians and Federal Aid.* Washington, D.C.: Brookings Institution.

Spier, Leslie, ed. 1938 *The Sinkaietk or Southern Okanagon of Washington.* Menasha, Wis.: George Banta, General Series in Anthropology No. 6.

Spier, Leslie, and Edward Sapir. 1930 Wishram Ethnography. *University of Washington Publications in Anthropology* 3:151–300.

Stanbury, W.T. 1975 *Success and Failure: Indians in Urban Society.* Vancouver: University of British Columbia Press.

Steward, Julian H. 1938 *Basin-Plateau Aboriginal Sociopolitical Groups.* Washington, D.C.: Smithsonian Institution, Bureau of American Ethnology, Bulletin 120.

Stryd, Arnoud H., and Rachel A. Smith, eds. 1971 *Aboriginal Man and Environments on the Plateau of Northwest America.* Calgary: University of Calgary Archaeological Association.

Swanson, Earl H., Jr. 1966 Cultural Relations Between Two Plains. *Archaeology in Montana* 7:1–2.

Taylor, Theodore W. 1972 *The States and Their Indian Citizens.* Washington, D.C.: United States Department of the Interior, Bureau of Indian Affairs.

Voegelin, C.F., and F.M. Voegelin. 1964 *Languages of the World: Native America,* Fascicle 1. Bloomington: Indiana University, Anthropological Linguistics 6.

Walker, Deward E., Jr. 1968 *Conflict and Schism in Nez Perce Acculturation.* Pullman: Washington State University Press.

———— 1970 [1965] Some Limitations of the Renascence Concept in Acculturation: The Nez Perce Case. In S. Levine and N.O. Lurie (eds.). *The American Indian Today.* Baltimore: Penguin Books, pp. 236–256.

———— 1973 *American Indians of Idaho.* Moscow: University of Idaho.

Walker, Deward E., Jr., ed. 1972 *The Emergent Native Americans.* Boston: Little, Brown.

Warren, Claude N. 1967 The San Dieguito Complex: A Review and Hypothesis. *American Antiquity* 32:168–185.

———— 1968 *The View from Wenas: A Study in Plateau Prehistory.* Pocatello: Occasional Papers of the Idaho State University Museum, No. 24.

Whiting, Beatrice Blyth. 1950 *Paiute Sorcery.* New York: Viking Fund Publications in Anthropology, No. 15.

Wilke, Philip J., Robert Bettinger, Thomas F. King, and James F. O'Connell. 1972 Harvest Selection and Domestication in Seed Plants. *Antiquity* 46:203–209.

Winter, Joseph C. 1976 The Processes of Farming Diffusion in the Southwest and Great Basin. *American Antiquity* 41:421–429.

Winter, Joseph C., and Henry C. Wylie. 1974 Paleoecology and Diet at Clydes Cavern. *American Antiquity* 39:303–315.

Wright, Gary A., and Susanne J. Miller. 1976 Prehistoric Hunting of New World Wild Sheep: Implications for the Study of Sheep Domestication. In C. Cleland (ed.). *Cultural Change and Continuity.* New York: Academic Press, pp. 293–312.

ADDITIONAL SOURCES FOR THE SECOND EDITION

Aikens, C. Melvin. 1986 *Archaeology of Oregon* (2nd ed.). Portland: U.S. Department of the Interior, Bureau of Land Management.

Ambler, Marjane. 1990 *Breaking the Iron Bonds*. Lawrence: University Press of Kansas.

American Antiquity. "Current Research" through vol. 55(2) (April 1990).

Ames, Kenneth M., and Alan G. Marshall. 1980 Villages, Demography and Subsistence Intensification on the Southern Columbia Plateau. *North American Archaeologist* 2(1):25–52.

Beckham, Stephen Dow, Kathryn Anne Toepel, and Rick Minor. 1984 *Native American Religious Practices and Uses in Western Oregon*. Eugene: University of Oregon Anthropological Papers, No. 31.

Boyd, Robert T., and Yvonne P. Hajda. 1987 Seasonal Population Movement Along the Lower Columbia River: The Social and Ecological Context. *American Ethnologist* 14(2):309–326.

Bunte, Pamela A., and Robert J. Franklin. 1987 *From the Sands to the Mountain*. Lincoln: University of Nebraska Press.

Butler, B. Robert. 1981 When Did the Shoshoni Begin to Occupy Southern Idaho? Pocatello: Occasional Papers of the Idaho Museum of Natural History, No. 32.

Campbell, Lyle, and Marianne Mithun, eds. 1979 *The Languages of Native America*. Austin: University of Texas Press.

Chartkoff, Joseph L. 1988 Exchange and Social Organization in Archaic Cultures of Coastal Southern California. Paper presented at the annual meeting, Central States Anthropological Society, St. Louis, Mo.

Corless, Hank. 1990 *The Weiser Indians*. Salt Lake City: University of Utah Press.

Cox, Bruce Alden, ed. 1987 *Native People, Native Lands*. Ottawa: Carleton University Press.

D'Azevedo, Warren L., ed. 1986 *Handbook of North American Indians*, vol. 11, *Great Basin*. Washington, D.C.: Smithsonian Institution Press.

Fahey, John. 1986 *The Kalispel Indians*. Norman: University of Oklahoma Press.

Feest, Christian F., ed. 1987 *Indians and Europe*. Aachen: Edition Herodot, Rader Verlag.

Garner, Van H. 1982 *The Broken Ring*. Tucson: Westernlore Press.

Gay, E. Jane. 1981 *With the Nez Perces*. Lincoln: University of Nebraska Press.

Getty, Ian A.L., and Antoine S. Lussier, eds. 1983 *As Long As the Sun Shines and Water Flows*. Vancouver: University of British Columbia Press.

Gibson, James R. 1985 *Farming the Frontier*. Seattle: University of Washington Press.

Gidley, M. 1981 *Kopet, A Documentary Narrative of Chief Joseph's Last Years*. Chicago: Contemporary Books.

Glassow, Michael A., and Larry R. Wilcoxon. 1988 Coastal Adaptations Near Point Conception, California, with Particular Regard to Shellfish Exploitation. *American Antiquity* 53(1):36–51.

Goss, James A. 1990 Mother, Mountain, and Bear: Persistent Symbols in North America. Paper presented at the annual meeting, American Anthropological Association, New Orleans, La.

Harten, Lucille B., Claude N. Warren, and Donald R. Tuohy, eds. 1980 *Anthropological Papers in Honor of Earl H. Swanson, Jr.* Pocatello: Special Publication of The Idaho Museum of Natural History.

Heizer, Robert F., ed. 1978 *Handbook of North American Indians*, vol. 8, *California*. Washington, D.C.: Smithsonian Institution Press.

Hittman, Michael. 1990 *Wovoka and the Ghost Dance: A Source Book*. Carson City, Nev.: The Grace Dangberg Foundation.

Jorgensen, Joseph G., ed. 1984 *Native Americans and Energy Development II*. Boston: Anthropology Resource Center.

Knack, Martha C. 1989 Contemporary Southern Paiute Women and the Measurement of Women's Economic and Political Status. *Ethnology* 28(3):233–248.

——— 1990 Philene T. Hall, Bureau of Indian Affairs Field Matron. *Prologue: Quarterly of the United States National Archives* 22(2):150–167.

Knack, Martha C., and Omer C. Stewart. 1984 *As Long as the River Shall Run*. Berkeley: University of California Press.

Knight, Rolf. 1978 *Indians At Work*. Vancouver: New Star Books.

Long, J. Anthony, and Menno Boldt. 1988 *Governments in Conflict?* Toronto: University of Toronto Press.

Madsen, David B. 1983 *Black Rock Cave Revisited*. Salt Lake City: U.S. Department of the Interior, Bureau of Land Management, Utah, Cultural Resource Series, No. 14.

Marshall, Alan G. 1985 "Prairie Chickens Dancing . . . :" Ecology's Myth. In L.W. Attebery (ed.). *Idaho Folklife: Homesteads to Headstones*. Salt Lake City: University of Utah Press, pp. 101–107.

Meighan, Clement W. 1987 Reexamination of the Early Central California Culture. *American Antiquity* 52(1):28–36.

Moore, Robert E. 1985 Early Prophets and Shakers of the Columbia Plateau in Current Reservation Memory. Paper presented at the American Society for Ethnohistory annual meeting, Chicago.

Moratto, Michael J. 1984 *California Archaeology.* Orlando: Academic Press.

O'Brien, Sharon. 1989 *American Indian Tribal Governments.* Norman: University of Oklahoma Press.

Prucha, Francis Paul. 1984 *The Great Father.* Lincoln: University of Nebraska Press.

Rawls, James J. 1984 *Indians of California: The Changing Image.* Norman: University of Oklahoma Press.

Ross, Thomas E., and Tyrel G. Moore, eds. 1987 *A Cultural Geography of North American Indians.* Boulder: Westview Press.

Shipek, Florence Connolly. 1988 *Pushed Into the Rocks.* Lincoln: University of Nebraska Press.

Snipp, C. Matthew. 1989 *American Indians: The First of This Land.* New York: Russell Sage Foundation.

Stoffle, Richard W., David B. Halmo, and Michael J. Evans. 1990 *Native American Cultural Resource Studies at Yucca Mountain, Nevada.* Ann Arbor: Institute for Social Research, University of Michigan.

Thornton, Russell. 1986 History, Structure, and Survival: A Comparison of the Yuki (Ukomno'm) and Tolowa (Hush) Indians of Northern California. *Ethnology* 25(2):119–130.

Tooker, Elisabeth, ed. 1983 *The Development of Political Organization in Native North America.* Washington, D.C.: American Ethnological Society.

Van Winkle, Barrik. 1985 "Indian Ethnohistory" in the Great Basin. Paper presented at the annual meeting, American Society for Ethnohistory, Chicago.

Voget, Fred W. 1984 *The Shoshoni-Crow Sun Dance.* Norman: University of Oklahoma Press.

Walker, Phillip L., and Jon M. Erlandson. 1986 Dental Evidence for Prehistoric Dietary Change on the Northern Channel Islands, California. *American Antiquity* 51(2):375–383.

White, Robert H. 1990 *Tribal Assets.* New York: Henry Holt.

Whitley, David S. 1990 Etiology and Ideology in the Great Basin. Paper presented at the Great Basin Anthropological Conference, Reno, Nv.

Wright, Gary A. 1984 *People of the High Country.* New York: Peter Lang.

Zucker, Jeff, Kay Hummel, and Bob Høgfos. 1983 *Oregon Indians.* Portland: Western Imprints, the Press of the Oregon Historical Society.

THE NORTHWEST COAST

Sharp ridges bristling with firs shoulder into the pounding sea. Rain laps the twisting rivers drowned at their mouths. Footholds for human habitation are narrow shingles backed by dark-green forests. The Northwest Coast of America is a country of blues and greens and dark grey-browns, imposingly beautiful, rich to those who know its resources. It is a maritime region, its densest populations clinging to its shores. Its world is the North Pacific Ocean, looking to Asia, not to the south.

Peoples of the Northwest boast one of the great art styles of the world, expressed in carvings whose power transcends symbols to speak to every viewer of the potent might of the living spirit. Disciplined exuberance is the heart of Northwest Coast art and ceremony, challenge and conquest, and it is also central to a certain chivalry that respects what it seeks to overpower. In totem poles and potlatches, the Northwest Coast societies paralleled the monuments and court displays of Europe, and similarly reflected stratified social classes nurturing talented specialists on the surpluses produced by organized workers. To many Europeans, the Northwest Coast appeared an anomaly, a far corner of the world where one expected simple savages but met rude civilizations. Freed from that European perspective, we can see the Northwest Coast to be situated near the center of its hemisphere, drawing to it ideas and technologies from Asia and America and reworking them under its own clearly articulated values.

The Northwest Coast is conventionally divided into three subareas, Northern, Central, and Southern. The Northern area runs along the Pacific coast from southeastern Alaska through northern British Columbia and the Queen Charlotte Islands. It is inhabited by the Na-Dene (Macro-Athabascan)-speaking Tlingit of southeastern Alaska, the isolate-language Haida of the Queen Charlottes and adjacent mainland, and the Penutian-speaking Tsimshian of northern British Columbia, including the Nass and Skeena Rivers. The Central area includes the central British Columbia coast, most

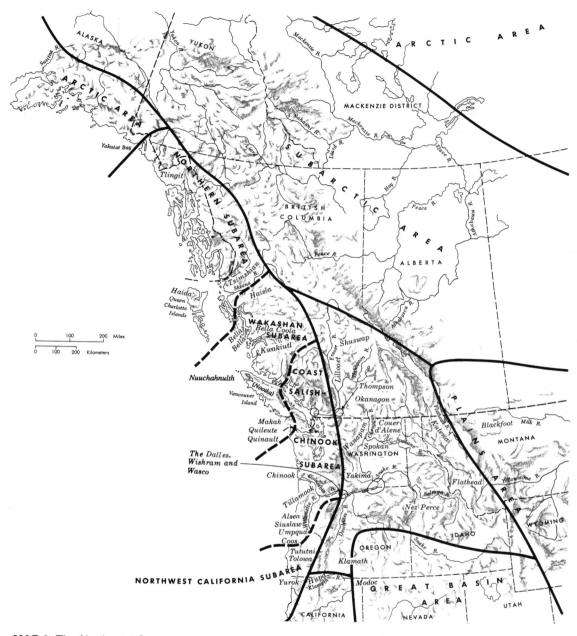

MAP 9 The Northwest Coast

of Vancouver Island and Cape Flattery, the northwestern tip of Washington. The peoples of the
Central area speak languages of two linguistic
families, Wakashan and Salish. From north to

south in the Central area, these peoples are the
Kwakiutl (Kwakwaka'wakw) of the coast and ad-
jacent northern Vancouver Island; the Haisla and
Kitamat and the Bella Bella, speakers of Heiltsuk,

THE NORTHWEST COAST
CHRONOLOGY

1975   Revival of carving, increase in potlatching, spirit dances
       Population increase, increased economic integration into urban U.S./Canada

1950   Repeal of Potlatch Law
       Economic Depression
       Founding of Native Brotherhoods

1900   Allotment of much Indian land
       Potlatch Law
       Reserves set up

1850   Euramerican settlement
       Devastating epidemics
       Hudson's Bay Company establishes permanent posts

1800   Spanish, British, Russian, United States ships explore and trade
       Bering reaches Alaska

1700

1600

1500

1000

500
       "Classical" Northwest Coast culture pattern well established

A.D.

B.C.

       Development of carvers' art, woodworking

500

1000   Increase in trade, including Coast-Plateau contacts

2000

3000   Stabilization of sea level; Northwest Coast settlement pattern established

4000

5000

6000

7000

8000   Early occupations of Northwest Coast utilizing fish and wood resources

10,000

and the Nuxalk (Bella Coola), all on the mainland coast of British Columbia; the Nuu-chah-nulth-aht (Nootka) and related Nitinat on western Vancouver Island, and the Makah on the tip of Washington. All speak Wakashan languages except the Nuxalk, whose language is a Salishan one. The Southern area is inhabited by speakers of Coast Salish languages, from Comox, Pentlatch, and Sliammon (Seshelt or Sishiatl) through Squamish, Halkomelem and Nooksack in southwestern mainland British Columbia; then, around the Straits of Juan de Fuca on the United States–Canadian border, the Lummi, Saanich, Songhees, Clallam, and smaller groups; around southern Puget Sound, the Snoqualmi, Nisqually, Skagit, Snohomish, Puyallup, and other small groups, the principal language being Lushootseed; in western Washington, the Salish Quinault, Chehalis, and Cowlitz, and the Quileute and now-extinct Chemakum, which belong to a separate language family, Chimakuan; and, continuing south, the Salish-speaking Twana (Skokomish and related groups) and the Tillamook and Siletz, in Oregon. The Tillamook and Siletz fit culturally into a lower Columbia River subarea south of the more usually recognized southern Northwest Coast; the Chehalis may be included here as well, and a series of speakers of Penutian-phylum languages, the Lower Chinook, Alsea, Yaquina (not Yakima!), Siuslaw, and Coos, plus the Athabascan-language Umpqua and Tututni. The Penutian Kalapuya of the interior Willamette Valley of Oregon are peripheral to the lower Columbia subarea. The last and southernmost subarea of Northwest Coast culture is in northwestern California, and includes the Yurok and Wiyot, whose languages are grouped as "Ritwan," and are isolates in the Macro-Algonkian phylum; the Karok, who speak a Hokan-phylum isolate; and the Hupa and Tolowa, whose languages are Athabascan. Although the Klamath River is the center of the northwestern California subarea just described, the people known as the Klamath and the related Modoc live on the upper portion of the river and thereby on the border of the Plateau. Their language is a Penutian isolate.

Topographically, the Northwest Coast is dominated by mountains, the Coast Range in British Columbia and the Cascades in the states of Washington and Oregon. These mountains cut off the maritime peoples of the coast from inland hunters and fishermen, except where passes funneled movement through the ranges. The easiest and most popular pass was the valley of the Columbia River, discussed in the section on the Plateau in the previous chapter. The Fraser River, which disgorges in southwestern British Columbia, offered a pass at the head of its broad and lovely delta, but the pass itself was through a formidable canyon; the Fraser's upper valley is deep and narrow, less inviting for travel than the Columbia. North of the Fraser delta, passes climb through mountains and by their difficulty make trade with the interior expensive. Thus, the peoples of the Northwest Coast were oriented to the sea and the coves where villages were situated. Abundance of food in the sea—fish, shellfish, and sea mammals—contrasted with the low density of game in the heavily forested mountains and interior, further influenced the Northwest Coast peoples to view the country behind their villages as a hinterland suited only to the adventurous or exiled. Along the coast, the dissected, rocky terrain tended to isolate communities, resulting in a great number of autonomous societies sharing a cultural pattern and technologies but unaccustomed to recognizing ties.

SECTION 1: PREHISTORY

Investigation of the prehistory of the Northwest Coast is made difficult in many sections of this area by changes in sea level during the early Holocene period as well as in the preceding Pleistocene epoch. The first evidence of humans in the culture area dates to the beginning of the Holocene era, around 8000 B.C. In British Columbia, these earliest people appear to have migrated from the north, although whether along the Pacific coast or down from the Yukon-interior Alaska region cannot yet be determined. Sites on islands indicate the early inhabitants were accustomed to using boats, but they were not exclusively maritime, for they hunted land game as well as fish and sea mammals. In the United States section of the coast, the early inhabitants were Western Archaic, similar to inland peoples except in their greater exploitation of fish, as seen in sites on the lower Columbia and the coast.

Archaeological research has encountered great difficulty investigating some districts of the northern British Columbia coast, such as the homeland of the Tsimshian, where sites earlier than 3000 B.C. may be drowned or hidden by the rain forest. The southern British Columbia coast, which until 3000 B.C. enjoyed a lower sea level and therefore more habitable land, was occupied by hunters of land mammals, sea mammals, and fish. These hunters apparently lived in small settlements. Beginning about 3000 B.C., settlements were built in the formerly wild districts, and many have been more or less continuously occupied through today. The hunting of land mammals, including caribou, which later became extinct along the coast, was important in the third millennium B.C., since the slow stabilization of the sea level had not yet fully established the great annual spawning runs of salmon and eulachon. Land hunting no doubt aided in the maintenance of contacts between the coast and the interior; archaeologists have noticed that in this period, chipped-stone artifacts were often manufactured inland from stone quarried in the river valleys, and carried downstream to be used on the coast, where local stone was ignored or poorly utilized. Once the sea level stabilized after 3000 B.C., permanent winter villages that relied on stores of dried salmon but were close to shellfish beds developed along the coast.

About 1500 B.C. in the United States section of the coast, pit houses similar to those on the Plateau were built and a cultural pattern foreshadowing the historic Northwest Coast can be glimpsed. One pit house of this period in western Washington had on its floor 125 polished stone beads, of chert, jasper, and serpentine, demonstrating the owner's ability to collect beautiful stone from several distant sources and subsidize its laborious manufacture into ornaments. Perhaps it reflects the person's participation in a widespread trade network. What kind of houses were built in the northern sector of the Northwest Coast cannot be told from the poor evidence in excavated sites, but the rarity of adzes and woodworking wedges makes it unlikely that the historic plank houses were constructed; pit houses may have been used in the north, too.

The first millennium B.C. displays the flowering of the distinctive Northwest Coast pattern. Some of the many prehistoric intertidal fish weirs along the coast, designed to trap fish as the tide goes out, have been radiocarbon dated to the first millennium B.C. Along the Oregon coast, sites with offshore bird and halibut bones indicate use of boats on the ocean, in addition to taking land and shore resources including quantities of clams. The Fraser Delta region, around Vancouver, seems to have been a center of development. Carving in stone and probably wood (the latter not preserved there) includes both plain bowls and elaborate ones representing humans or animals holding the container. Small adzes of nephrite, a variety of jade, and ornaments prove the artisans' skill in handling difficult materials. Bark shredders continue in use from the preceding period, suggesting weaving— very likely of the bark rain cloaks so common historically. The existence of heavy woodworking tools by the early first millennium A.D. implies the splitting of the tall cedars, firs, and redwoods into planks and their fashioning into the large canoes and houses typical of known later cultures. The economic basis in this period was definitely that of the historic Northwest Coast: taking salmon, halibut, eulachon, herring, and other fish with nets, lines, spears, traps, and weirs, hunting sea mammals, mountain sheep and goat, deer, and bear, and collecting shellfish and berries and roots. Marine resources, which here would include salmon beginning their runs, dominated. Population was already so high that serious competition for resources involved warfare, attested by a number of burials of young men killed by heavy blows to the upper body, probably by warclubs, and finds of such clubs, trophy heads, and slat armor of the type made popular in Shang Dynasty China in the second millennium B.C. and thence spread along the North Pacific Rim.

After about A.D. 500, the richness of the historic Northwest Coast culture is evident. A variety of specialized, efficient tools facilitated exploitation of the natural resources and production of houses, canoes, boxes of steam-bent cedar, baskets, and ornaments. Many of the tools themselves were so lovingly made, so polished, that they were clearly a joy to own. Obsidian, jade, and copper were used, as were amber beads and pendants, dentalium and many other shells, and whalebone. Clubs of whalebone and stone probably were used in warfare, which may have been an alternative to trade in obtaining the rare or distant materials sought. Defensive forts (sites on top of narrow steep ridges, easily defended) seem to date after about A.D. 1000, suggesting wars became more frequent in the late prehistoric period. Differences from region to region and strong continuities within regions lead to the postulation that the historic peoples of the Northwest Coast were for the most part resident in their eighteenth-century territories for at least the previous two thousand years. Similarities between regions and between the coast and the Plateau seem more likely to be due to trade than to migration on any scale larger than occasional individual adventurers or families fleeing landslides or attacks.

SECTION 2: THE DISTINCTIVE NORTHWEST COAST CULTURAL PATTERN

In spite of the difficulties of archaeological investigations along coasts and in areas where level land suitable for houses is so limited that prehistoric middens are capped by presently occupied homes, the outlines of culture histories on the Northwest Coast have been mapped sufficiently to show that historic Northwest Coast cultural patterns have been well developed since the stabilization of the sea level about 3000 B.C., and that many distinctive traits go back to the first millennium B.C. The greater number of Wakashan- and Salishan-speaking nations, their central position along the coast, and the apparently longer prehistoric sequences in their area (continuous through the Holocene era), in contrast with the lack of human-occupation evidence in the Northern sector before 3000 B.C.—all suggest that the Northwest Coast cultural pattern and many distinctive traits were forged by the ancestors of the Wakashan and Salish communities. From this perspective, the cultures of the Northern sector were developed by nations whose Northwest Coast style of life was in part an environmentally influenced adaptation to coast resources, and in part a borrowing of ideas present farther south in British Columbia. Southern-sector peoples were similarly molded in part by working out techniques successful in harvesting coast resources, and in part by borrowing. (Contrasting environmental adaptations with borrowing of ideas is, of course, a gross oversimplification of the complex interplay between the inventiveness of local people and the many ways in which they can be stimulated by knowledge of neighboring peoples' behavior.) Of the Central-sector peoples, the Kwakiutl have been most thoroughly studied, beginning with the collaboration between Franz Boas and George Hunt, a half-Scotch, half-Tlingit lifetime resident of the Kwakiutl village at the Fort Rupert trading post. This collaboration continued from 1893 to Hunt's death in 1933, and resulted in unparalleled volumes of detail on the southern division of the Kwakiutl. (Boas also trained two Tsimshian men, Henry Tate and William Beynon, who left valuable ethnographies of their nation.) A description of the Southern Kwakiutl can serve as an example of a Northwest Coast people and a base from which comparisons can be presented.

The first English description of a Kwakiutl community was that of Yaculta in 1792. Twelve houses of large split-log planks set in frames of heavy posts constituted the settlement. Each of the rectangular houses sheltered several families, and the total village population was about 350. Nearly ninety log-dugout canoes were drawn up on the beach in front of the houses or in use on the water. The canoes and several of the house fronts were painted with figures. Men and women liberally perforated the rims of their ears, and sometimes their nose septum, to wear numerous ornaments of copper and shell. The men dressed their long black hair with red ocher mixed into grease, and some added the white down of eagles to their hair and painted their faces with red ocher "sprinkled over with black Glimmer that helped not a little to heighten their ferocious appearance" (Gunther 1972:97, quoting Menzies). Women wore skirts, sarongs, or tunics of either deerskin or a coarse cloth woven from mountain-goat or dog wool or from shredded cedar bark. Most men didn't bother with clothing in warm weather, except perhaps a basketry hat with a brim that cut the glare from the water when out fishing or traveling. Chiefs often wore cloaks of sea-otter fur around their shoulders, and in the frequent rainy weather, people protected themselves with conical, tightly woven basketry hats and cloaks or ponchos of woven cedar bark. Fishnets were drying on the beach at Yaculta. Men carried powerful bows backed with strips of sinew; the arrows were often pointed with tips of mussel shell. Spears, slings, clubs, and fishhooks were other implements noticed in the village. A chief invited the European visitors into his house, which they saw had screened-off sleeping alcoves for the several families residing in it. To entertain the visitors, the villagers sang, beating time with anything handy. Some distance from the village, at the border of the forest and a grassy field, the Europeans came upon the community's burial ground. The remains of the deceased were placed in boxes or bundled in mats and then laid to rest in small above-ground, plank houselike shelters. The Kwakiutl were obviously very familiar with trade, both with Indians and with European ships. Regular trading routes went up inlets or followed streams and lakes across Vancouver Island—canoes were portaged where

necessary—as well as extending along the coast. Sea-otter skins were offered to the Europeans in exchange for sheets of copper or a heavy blue cloth, or for muskets, powder, and shot. Iron was not desired; the Kwakiutl said they had all they needed, and were accustomed to making their own knives (one source of iron was said to be Japanese vessels blown across the Pacific and wrecked on American shores). The Kwakiutl impressed the Europeans as shrewd businesspeople.

Kwakiutl society was organized on the basis of houses, each of which was led by a chief who claimed descent from a mythical or quasi-historical personage. Genealogies and events in the histories of the houses were recounted as in the sagas of the Norse. Chiefly lineages generally owned a large residential house for their client families, and the rights to use or display particular designs, songs, ceremonies, and prized heirlooms, such as embossed copper sheets. They also owned local resources, and trespassers upon a lineage's fishing station, berry ground, or mountain-goat-hunting territory could expect to be killed without warning. Chiefs somewhat resembled feudal barons in medieval Europe or Japan, differing perhaps mainly in that the Northwest Coast had no free cities counterbalancing the landed barons, and so far as we can tell, more limited domains than the most powerful in feudal Europe or Asia.

Senior men represented the lineages in village councils and at feasts, and they and the older matrons planned and organized the group's economic activities so that each of the lineage's resources was efficiently harvested and stored. Through such management, each lineage house was usually comfortably supplied with quantities of dried salmon, halibut, cod, and herring, dried herring spawn, berries and pressed dried-berry cakes, seal meat and blubber, eulachon fish oil, skins of fish and sea and land mammals, furs, woven woolen and bark blankets and clothing, a variety of efficient, specialized implements, and all the wooden boxes and baskets needed to contain the stores. Within the house was a section and cooking hearth for each couple and their children plus an area for common stores and slaves' sleeping space. Additional goods could be kept in sheds along the beach below the house. During the summer, houses were often dispersed to the lineage's several resource stations, or several villages congregated at particularly rich stations. In the winter, village houses again sheltered families returned to enjoy elaborate ceremonial performances, their daily needs easily met in the stores amassed in the preceding months.

Kwakiutl, like other Northwest Coast peoples, were highly conscious of social standing. Chiefs were members of an aristocracy that carefully planned marriages to guard against dilution of noble blood and to ally great families of a region. Chiefs employed public speakers to make announcements: it would demean a high-ranking person to speak to commoners. Ordinary persons, as well as aristocrats, usually married outside of their own village and hoped to enhance each offspring's status by choosing a spouse from a thoroughly respectable, well-off family. As many as a fifth or possibly a quarter of the population may have been slaves, most of them said to be war captives; the child of a free man who took a slave woman would be free, while slaves' children were slaves. Slaves and bastards suffered, for they would debase any family they married into. A properly arranged marriage with a high-ranking member of a non-Kwakiutl group was quite desirable, however. Although there was a tendency for men to remain in their natal houses and bring their wives to live there with them, it was common for a woman who expected to inherit a title of rank to stay after marriage, her husband moving in and exercising the man's privileges of that rank in the name of their sons until the boys were adults. Noble women as well as men hosted potlatches. Whether for a son or a daughter, parents sought to arrange marriages and recommend residence choices so that each of their children had the maximum opportunity to do well. Thus, one or more children of a couple might live always in the couple's lineage house, while other children would move to other relatives' or spouses' villages.

As in California, the power of the chiefs was supported by their association with highly trained doctors who were believed to have the capability to send disease into enemies as well as to remove disease from those they pity. One who wished to be a doctor fasted, appearing to be ill, and then disappeared into the forest in back of the village. Experienced doctors went out, found the novice, brought him or her to a graveyard to learn to overcome fear of ghosts, and instructed the person in the secrets of discovering disease (including the use of paid "spies" to report on what the doctor could not personally discover) and techniques of curing, both spiritual and physical (medicinal plants, massage, bringing down a fever by applying cool moss, and so forth). The novice was also supposed to sleep out by the graveyard or another isolated spot to receive dream promises of help from spirit beings. Doctors would not ask for payment, but expected to be rewarded with gifts. Degrees of skill in managing diseases were recognized, as was the possibility that someone not a doctor might have caused an illness by using techniques of sorcery.

Public recognition of social status was obtained at feasts given to announce changes of status. These feasts are called, in English, potlatches (from a Chinook Jargon word, possibly originally Nuu-chah-nulth), and an upper-class person would be the center of a series of them: feasts for announcing the bestowal of an adult name upon a teenager; marriage feasts, when titles were part of marriage gifts; feasts to enhance the social rank of the lineage the person led; and funeral feasts. Upper-class men strove to raise, or at least maintain, the prestige of their titles by distributing costly gifts to other leading families, quantities of everyday items to commoners, and more food than the assemblage could possibly consume (guests took home what they could not eat at the feast). In order to put on an impressive potlatch, everyone in a lineage house worked to provide goods or money and food. The chief usually added to the pooled resources by calling in debts owned to him and perhaps—especially if the official host for the pot-

FIGURE 8.1 Kwakiutl potlatch, late nineteenth century. Guests for a marriage gifts ceremony have disembarked from their canoes (prows in background) as men of the host village (in circle to left of guests) sing a welcome. Gift boxes are piled in the foreground. (*Milwaukee Public Museum*)

latch was a young man—by borrowing from other lineage leaders. During the potlatch, upper-class guests extolled the generosity and ability of the host in formal speeches, and both host-lineage elders and guests orated upon the virtues of their lineage forebears and admonished the young to emulate these illustrious individuals. Dramatic dances of elaborately costumed impersonators of spirit beings enlivened the potlatches, and clowns entertained the audience between acts. While the purpose of potlatches was to pass on titles of rank and their associated privileges—including power of control over specific resources—to designated heirs in upper-class families, they functioned also to distribute surpluses and special local products to other villages, to maintain or inaugurate alliances for political and economic benefit, and to reinforce the cohesion of house groups, who could see rewards for their cooperation.

Summer to the Kwakiutl was a secular season for obtaining the necessities of life. By mid-November, enough stores should have been laid by to last the winter, and the sacred season could officially begin. No one (except slaves) was to work in winter, other than doing daily chores such as cooking. Instead, villages were the scenes of series of potlatches and ceremonial performances. Legendary spirits were believed to hover about the villages through the winter and kidnap people, who then had to be rescued by their friends and freed of the maddening power of the spirit. During the summer, the spirits were away in foreign countries and it was safe for villagers to scatter to the various sources of food. To emphasize the contrast between the secular summer and the sacred winter, people had two names, one for each season.

Winter ceremonials were impressive performances. Most striking were the costumes, which were topped by magnificent carved and painted wooden masks. For one, bearskins might be sewn so that the dancer really appeared to be a bear with a head transformed into a beautiful, stylized, yet terrible spirit-bear's face. For another, eagle feathers might be sewn so closely on a suit that the dancer truly seemed a great bird with an overarching beak. The dancers performed inside the large plank houses, beside a fire and in front of a curtain. Special effects were created with strings invisible in the semidarkness around the dancers, or through trap doors in the plank floor, arrangements hidden behind the curtain, or assistants planted around the house. The masks themselves were often double, hinged so that they clacked, moved, and might open to reveal a transformed face in the inside mask. Dancers practiced sleight-of-hand: one would dramatically stab another, and blood would appear to spurt from the victim, but in actuality it came from a bladder filled with animal blood hidden in the costume. Audiences knew that the performances were ingeniously staged and that the spirits were impersonated, but as in European-tradition theatrical performances, the skills of the actors were employed to communicate profound truths through art.

AN HEIRLOOM COPPER IS CEREMONIOUSLY PURCHASED AT THE FORT RUPERT KWAKIUTL VILLAGE, WINTER, 1894-95

(The chief Owaxalagilis has invited six houses to witness the wealth that proves him a great leader. He will buy the heirloom copper sheet Maxtsolem ("The One of Whom All Are Ashamed"—that is, the one that makes all others seem inferior). To begin the purchase of this renowned heirloom, young men of Owaxalagilis's house have piled 1,200 blankets between two great carved posts at which stands Chief Maxua, who hosts the feast.)

Then Owaxalagilis arose and spoke. He said, "Yes, Chief, your speech was good. You have no pity. Have you finished now asking for more, if I am willing to give your chief 400 blankets more? Answer me now!"... Owaxalagilis sent two young men. They brought the blankets and put them down. Again Maxua took the blankets and spoke:

"Ya, tribes! Do you see now our way of buying? The Kwakiutl, my tribe, are strong when they buy coppers. They are not like you. You always bring the canoes and the button-[decorated] blankets right away. Now there are 1,600 blankets in this pile that I carry here." He turned to the Kwakiutl and said: "That is what I say, Chiefs of the Kwakiutl, to those who do not know how to buy coppers. Now I begin again." He counted the blankets and went on in the same way as before: As soon as ten pairs of blankets were counted, they said aloud, "ten pairs," and the counters said aloud how many tens of blankets had been counted. When he had counted all, Maxua spoke: "Wa, wa! Now I say to you chiefs, of all the tribes it is really enough! I have pity upon my chief. That is what I say, chiefs."

Then Owaxalagilis arose and spoke: "Wa, wa! I say it is enough, Mamaleleqala. Now you have seen my name. This is my name; this is the weight of my name. This mountain of blankets rises through our heaven. My name is the name of the Kwakiutl, and you can not do as we do, tribes. When you do it, you finish just as soon as you reach the 1,000 blankets. Now, look out! later on I shall ask you to buy from me. Tribes! I do not look ahead to the time when you will buy from me. My chiefs! that is what I say, Otsestalis; that is what I say, Wakidis; that is what I say, Maxualagilis; that is what I say, Maxuayalisame. That is what I say for all of you from whom coppers may be bought, by the chiefs of these our rivals, the Mamaleleqala, Wa, wa!"

Then Walas Nemogwis [owner of the copper Maxtsolem] arose and spoke: "Yes, Chief, your speech is true, your word is true. Who is like you, Kwakiutl, who buy coppers and who give away blankets. Long life to all of you, chiefs of the Kwakiutl. I can not attain to your high name, great tribes." Then he turned to his tribe and said: 'That is what I said, chiefs of the Mamaleleqala, that we may beat these Kwakiutl. They are like a large mountain with a steep precipice. Now arise, Yaqalenlis, and speak, Chief! Let me see you that I may look up to you, Chief! Now call your name, Tsonoqoa, you, Chief, who knows how to buy that great copper. You can not be equaled by anybody. You great mountain from which wealth is rolling down, wa, wa! That is what I say, my tribe!"

Then Yaqalenlis arose and uttered the cry of the Tsonoqoa: "Hoo, hoo, hoo, hoo!" and he acted as though he was lifting the heavy weight of the copper from the ground. "You all know, Kwakiutl, who I am. My name is Yaqalenlis. The name began at the time when our world was made. I am a descendant of the chiefs about whom we hear in the earliest legends. The Hoxhoq came down to Xoxopa, and took off his bird mask and became a man. Then he took the name Yaqalenlis. That was my ancestor, the first of the Qoexsotenox. He married Laqoagilayuqoa, the daughter of Walas Nemogwis, the first chief of the great clan Wewamasqem of the Mamaleleqala. That is the reason why I speak. I know how to buy great coppers. I bought this copper Maxtsolem for 4,000 blankets. What is it, Chief? What is it, Owaxalagilis? Come!, did you not give any thought to my copper here? You always say that you are rich, Chief. Now give more, that it may be as great as I am. Give only ten times 100 blankets more, Chief Owaxalagilis. It will not be much, give 1000 more for my sake, wa, wa. This is what I say, Hawasalal; that is what I say, Hexuayus; that is what I say, Wawilapalaso; that is what I say for all of you, chiefs of the Mamaleleqala, Wa, wa!"

(Boas 1966:89-90)

Owaxalagilis accepted the challenge, his young men bringing more piles of blankets. After many more speeches of boasting and challenging, the greatness of Owaxalagilis of the Kwakiutl was established: he had been able to give Walas Nemogwis of the Mamaleleqala a total of 4,200 blankets for the copper Maxtsolem.

SECTION 3: VARIATIONS ON THE BASIC NORTHWEST COAST PATTERN

In many respects, there was a single basic cultural pattern along the entire Pacific coast of North America, from Baja California to Alaska. This pattern included reliance upon fish and sea mammals, which were supplemented by shellfish, deer and other land game, birds, berries, roots, tubers, and bulbs, and seeds; autonomous villages organized on the basis of multifamily houses, recognizing an upper class, commoners, and slaves, managed by a chief assisted by aides and a doctor who could bewitch enemies; and interest in the accumulation of wealth, which could be counted in standard units of value such as shell beads or fur robes (later, blankets). Throughout this long region, men usually were no clothing and women wore skirts or aprons, but both were accustomed to using basketry hats. Maize agriculture was unsuited to this region of frequent fogs, but throughout, people practiced techniques that improved the yields of indigenous plants, cultivating and sometimes transplanting or seeding; camas, for example, was regularly reseeded in burned-over fields. Tobacco was planted, proving that people of the region had been acquainted with foreign agriculture. Population densities were high.

The Pacific Coast is conventionally split into two culture areas on the basis of presence or absence of large conifers (firs and cedars) from which planks can be split. The Northwest Coast thus begins in northern California and uses plank houses and large canoes, dugout or plank; the rest of California as a culture area is the southern portion of the Pacific Coast, and lacks trees that can provide long planks for big houses or canoes. Roughly coinciding with this division is one based on presence or absence of groves of acorn oaks, with California relying on the acorns and the Northwest Coast lacking them. Conifers and oaks overlap in northern California, giving peoples such as the Yurok and Hupa characteristics of both culture areas.

The peoples of northern California have seemed to resemble Northwest Coast peoples more closely than they resemble other Californians. This may be in part because the northernmost Californians built plank houses, and in part because they were outside Spanish-missionary territory and thereby preserved their autonomy and cultural pattern more fully into the modern era than did peoples farther south. Close reading of the early explorers suggests that interest in wealth, class-stratified societies, and similar characteristics of the Northwest Coast did extend through southern California before the mission-garrisons destroyed so much native power. Conversely, some of the flamboyant rivalry recorded between Northwest Coast chiefs seems to be an intensification of an earlier pattern under the stress of the late-nineteenth-century combination of population decline through disease plus disruptions caused by Euro-American-government impositions and entrance into the Euro-American economy.

One curious after-effect of nineteenth-century racism is a prevalent view that the Northwest Coast nations were "primitive hunter-gatherers." Because men did not farm and often went without clothing except for a rain cape, European visitors categorized them as savages. The huge wooden houses with their magnificent carvings, the sleek fast boats and variety of sophisticated fishing and marine hunting equipment, the obvious formal social ranking, the capacity to sell tons of food to colonists, even the fact that these nations did their own metalsmithing—none of these evidences of social complexity and technological mastery seemed to count as the United States and Britain drove to complete their "manifest destiny." When in the twentieth century anthropologists compared societies from different parts of the world, they tended to assume the simplistic notion that Western-style monocrop (one variety of plant per field) agriculture is the only kind of food production. Alternative methods of food production such as Eastern Woodlands multicrop ridged fields and range maintenance for livestock were tagged as "horticulture" (gardening). In regions such as the Great Basin and Northwest Coast where climatic and topographic conditions are radically different from those of Western Europe and eastern America, and food production consequently must be quite different from European practices, native nations were said to be "foragers," a term really referring to soldiers scrounging a countryside for fodder for their horses. Economies were said to be "hunter-gatherer," implying an entirely wild food base. Even after the dispossession of Indians was followed by the reversion of productive fields and pastures to forest, colonists often failed to realize that the unfamiliar practices of the Indians had been means of food production. This blindness to the value of alternative cultural patterns is not yet entirely shaken even within anthropology, with textbooks still describing the Northwest Coast nations as "hunter-gatherers in a rich environment" and calling them "anomalies" in that they had social ranking "without food production." A more realistic understanding comes from recognizing that, as the organizers of the breakthrough 1988 joint American-Soviet exhibit put it, the North Pacific Rim is the "crossroads of continents" where the great trade routes of America and Asia meet. Forming the eastern arm of the North Pacific culture area, the Northwest Coast of America harbored populations quite comparable to any in medieval Europe.

The Northwestern California Peoples

The California peoples along the Klamath River, the Trinity, and the Pacific coast in the northwestern corner of the state include Macro-Algonkian-speaking Yurok and Wiyot, the Athabascan Hupa and Tolowa, and the Hokan Karok. A northern affiliation, perhaps origin, for the Yurok and Wiyot and for the Athabascan speakers is suggested not only by many distantly related languages of these two major stocks north of California, but by such details as the use for money of beads of dentalium shell, from waters off Vancouver Island, rather than clamshell, as in the south. Ethnographers who studied the northwestern California peoples were struck by the importance they placed on the accumulation of wealth, especially heirlooms and rare objects. In contrast with the many North American societies that valued the distribution of goods, disparaging their accumulation, northwestern Californians considered it prudent to retain goods. Young people were exhorted to work constantly, to save, to shun the careless pursuit of pleasure, to fix their ambitions high and bend every effort toward achieving the goal of accumulated wealth. These strictures were aimed particularly at the young people from an upper-class family, which would train its children in formal etiquette with great concern, and might forbid them to play with commoner children. Sexual liaisons were said to be dangerous, distracting people from profitable work and risking entanglements with low-class ne'er-do-wells. A.L. Kroeber remarked that there seemed to be tension in Yurok settlements, everyone busy, worrying, critical of others; a strong contrast, in his experience, with the Mohave at the opposite end of California, who seemed relaxed and ready to enjoy whatever might be offered, once necessary chores were gotten over with.

In the historic period, at least, Yurok and the neighboring peoples were much involved with litigation, demanding indemnities for slander as well as for damage to property, trespassing, and physi-cal injury or murder. One reason to retain wealth was to be able to pay off claimants, and the person of influence was the rich person who could lend money and goods to poorer persons liable for damages. People unable to pay their debts could become slaves, working for the debt-holder or sold by that person to another. The rich enjoyed outfitting performers in dances with valuable headdresses and rare albino-deerskin banners, thereby making the whole community feel indebted to the sponsor. Priests who led thanksgiving ceremonies for harvests of salmon, eels, and acorns were respected too, as were doctors (most of them women). Successful doctors earned wealth in reward for their cures, and so were respected on two counts. Parallels between northwestern-California native values and customs and American capitalist values have often been remarked upon; this may have facilitated movement of modern members of these California Indian nations into the more respected middle-class occupations, where a number are now found. On the other hand, it may only be that the isolation of the deep, narrow northwestern California valleys, poor in commercial resources other than fish and timber, protected these peoples from most of the degradation imposed upon other California native nations. One historian points out that another factor has been the presence of several influential Euro-American settlers championing, rather than seeking to exterminate, Indian rights; these friends included early county sheriffs married to Indian women. Relatively light Euro-American settlement in the region meant that these sympathetic colonists met less opposition than likely in more desired regions of the state.

The Hoopa (that is, Hupa) Reservation, encompassing much of traditional Hupa territory, was established by Congress in 1864. Contrary to the usual sad history, the reservation was not whittled away and is now the largest Indian reservation in California. Hupa population in the 1980 census was nearly two thousand and the tribe's timber resources brought income both directly from sales and through providing wage employment. Along

FIGURE 8.2 Karok man using a dip net to fish for salmon from a platform, Klamath River, California, 1890s. *(Smithsonian Institution National Anthropological Archives)*

with neighboring Yurok (three thousand in the 1980 census), Karok (two thousand), and to a lesser degree the Wiyot (only 243 in 1980), the Hupa have been rebuilding their culture, teaching their language, and reinstituting community religious celebrations. Rituals for curing illnesses had persisted and a public dance commonly held with these rituals had been enjoyed on secular occasions (including a much-recounted episode during World War II when a Yurok soldier at the front taught the Brush Dance step to his non-Indian comrades asking for a "war dance"). Beginning about 1970 as the generation that had last participated in them began to die off, the major "world renewal" festivals were reintroduced, appropriate once more as streams earlier ravaged by Gold Rush mining regained their fish populations and conservation measures brought back elk and deer. The arts of basketry and woodworking attract appren-

tices as the finest creations of contemporary practitioners find display space in museums. Among younger Indians, some have revived traditional customs of daily life such as separation of menstruating women from men, not only to prevent female power from negating that of males, but also to give the women time to focus upon spiritual enrichment as their foremothers did. A very public result of the revival of Yurok, Hupa and Karok spirituality has been a series of challenges to non-Indian incursions onto the riverside and high-country holy places. Judicial injunctions are sought against logging and logging roads that would destroy or pollute these places of spiritual retreat for generations of Indians. Protection for these retreats should be guaranteed by the 1978 Senate Joint Resolution on American Indian Freedom of Religion "including...access to sites." Unfavorable court responses have narrowly construed "access" to mean nonob-

FIGURE 8.3 Karok performing the White Deerskin Dance, 1890s.
(Smithsonian Institution National Anthropological Archives)

struction of access, while Indian petitions have explained the importance of entire routes of prayerful pilgrimage, not merely the mountain lake or river rapids at the end.

The Klamath and the Modoc

At the head of the Klamath River, in northeastern California and adjacent Oregon, lived the Klamath and closely related Modoc, whose languages are Penutian. Much argument has arisen among anthropologists over whether the Klamath and Modoc belong to the Californian, Plateau, or Northwest Coast culture area. The simple truth is, of course, that culture-area boundaries are gentle, not sharp, and that peoples in zones of ecological transition exhibit traits of both—or in this case, all three—of the culture areas they border. The Klamath and Modoc centered in marshes and meadows where they collected camas roots, epos ("wild potato"), and wokas (a pond lily with abundant seeds). Fish, including salmon at the end

of their spawning runs, were the protein staple, and were supplemented by deer and other game from the hills and lava plains and by birds, including waterfowl. The round earth-lodge built over a pit was the winter dwelling; mat houses or wickiups were used in summer camps near resource harvests. In material culture, the Klamath and Modoc thus resembled the Plateau pattern. However, there was more overt emphasis on the acquisition of wealth and its linking with leadership and upper-class status than seems to have been typical on the Plateau. During the nineteenth century, at least, the Pit River (Achumawi) people were frequently captured in raids by the Klamath or Modoc, who kept some to work as slaves for the households of leaders and sold others at the Dalles. Although it is stated that the slaves were not abused, and that after they were freed in 1869, many remained with their former masters' communities, it nevertheless seems to have been the custom for women slaves to have been treated as concubines and consigned to poorer mat lodges adjacent to their masters' warmer earth lodges, and for children of slaves to have been denigrated by those whose mothers were ladies of good local families. Oratory has been esteemed by the Klamath and Modoc, who have tended to follow men who have combined oratorical talent, intelligence, and wealth; women, especially doctors, who had these qualities were invited to participate in councils but—again, at least in the nineteenth century—apparently were not designated "Captains." As in California and the Northwest Coast, leaders and doctors together exercised power, the one through his capability in managing mundane businesses, the other through his or her spiritual power. A list of social and ideological traits thus shows many similarities between the Klamath and Modoc and the people of the coast and interior California. Placing them in this chapter rather than the preceding one is arbitrary.

The more recent history of the Klamath and Modoc is depressingly familiar. A treaty was proclaimed in 1869, following two decades of encroachment of Euro-American immigrants upon the upper Klamath district. For the convenience of the Bureau of Indian Affairs, and to free as much land as possible for Euro-American colonization, the Klamath led by Leleks and Chiloquin, the Modoc led by Schonchin, and some Paiute who lived to the east were placed together on a single reservation, the Klamath Reservation, in Oregon at the northern end of Upper Klamath Lake. Many younger Modoc, in particular, resented the capitulation of their older leaders to United States domination and refused to remain on the reservation. Under Keintpoos (or Kintpuash, "Having the Water Bath"), called Captain Jack by the Euro-Americans, these independent Modocs remained in traditional Modoc territory, at one point collecting rents from Euro-American ranchers using their land. These Modoc were not to be allowed to stay, and by 1873 open battle was being waged against them. Keintpoos and fifty men retreated with their families to the rugged lava beds south of Tule Lake below the Oregon-California border. There was

some sympathy for these Modocs even among Euro-American settlers in the region until the "rebels" coldly murdered a peace commission that insisted on meeting with them in spite of the Modocs' firm refusal to surrender. Military defeat of the Modocs inexorably followed, by June. Keintpoos and three others were hanged, two more leaders were sentenced to life imprisonment at Alcatraz, and 155 remaining Modoc prisoners of war (more than one third of them children) were chained in cattle cars and shipped to Indian Territory, where they were settled on a reservation in eastern Oklahoma. Both the exiled Modoc (some of whom returned to Oregon after 1909, when exile was formally revoked) and the residents of the Klamath Reservation had their lands allotted under the Dawes Act, lost large sections of them, and by the mid-twentieth century were living principally from per capita payments for remaining tribal territory leased for timber exploitation. In 1954, the Klamath Reservation was declared by Congress suitable for termination from federal wardship. By 1956, the Oklahoma Modoc were also terminated as a federally administered tribe. Ten years later, more than half the enrolled Klamath and Modoc resided off the former reservation. A revival of interest in Indian heritage is evident among the Klamath and Modoc, as among so many Indian nations today, and since 1967 the Oklahoma Modoc re-formed a tribal government for their small community and joined the Inter-Tribal Council of the also-terminated Peoria and Ottawa plus other neighbors, the Quapaw, Miami, Eastern Shawnee, and Seneca-Cayuga. The 1980 census counted a little over two thousand Klamath, a majority in their southern Oregon reservation area, and nearly eight hundred Modoc.

The Oregon Coast Cultural Pattern

Along the Oregon coast, the Salish-speaking Tillamook were typical of the peoples who had adapted to this region of rugged shores. Heavy surf discouraged use of the ocean; travel as well as fishing tended to avoid the open Pacific and move instead along the bays and streams. Land was for the most part covered with dense stands of Douglas fir, cedar, pines, spruce, and occasional oaks, maples, and cottonwoods, or, in wet bottomlands, willow. Bracken ferns cover the forest floor beneath the dark conifers. To provide browse for elk and deer, the Indians regularly burned off sections of the otherwise inhospitable forests. Tidal flats were focuses of settlement, for clams, mussels, and other shellfish could be constantly harvested from them, and sometimes whales were beached there, providing a mammoth feast and a marvelous store of oil-rich blubber. Villages of rectangular houses—made of cedar planks lashed between post frames set in excavations a meter or so (about 2 to 5 feet) below ground surface, the roof of sloping planks—and thatched or mat-covered storehouses were built where streams brought fresh water to the coves near shellfish beds. The basic diet was the Northwest Coast pattern of dried salmon, taken during their runs, as the primary staple. Other fish, elk, and deer provided important additional protein; sea mammals were less important. A variety of berries, "roots," crabapples, acorns where available, and other plant foods were also eaten. Trade was frequent but not the basis for great differentiation of wealth or power along the Oregon coast, where topography isolated the small villages from the major avenue of commerce, the Columbia River. Hence, although communities recognized the usual distinctions between upper class, commoners, the poor, and slaves, means and occasions for displaying the distinctions were muted compared with the opportunities enjoyed by the ambitious on the lower Columbia or farther north.

Oregon Coast Indians and their neighbors just over the Cascades in the rich Willamette Valley were forced to deal with substantial numbers of Euro-American colonists beginning in the 1840s. In 1847, Oregon land was to be awarded to Euro-Americans who had fought Cayuse in north-central Oregon after Cayuse had killed a missionary family they believed responsible for a disastrous measles epidemic. That the land belonged to many other Indian nations was ignored. Three years later, Congress passed the 1850 Donation Land Act opening western Oregon to immigrant homesteading; the year *after,* commissioners were instructed to make treaties with the Indian nations. Nineteen treaties were written in 1851, only to be rejected (as happened in California) by Congress. More treaties were written up in 1853 and 1855, some with the same nations that had signed earlier. Congress refused to approve most of these, too. Nonetheless, an aftermath of the 1855 treaties with Plateau nations was the forced removal of hundreds of Plateau Indian people (Shasta, Takelma, Molalla, Kalapuya, Upper Umpqua) to Grande Ronde and Siletz reservations on the central Oregon coast, where already the native Yaquina, Siletz, Alsea, and Siuslaw were joined by their northern neighbors the Tillamook and southern neighbors the Lower Umpqua, Coos, and Tututni. This wholesale warehousing of disparate nations would have been bad enough if the warehouse was legal, but the reservations were mixed in the unratified treaties, leaving all the Indian nations involved without even the minimal protection laws on the books might provide. After unilateral reduction of land in 1875 and then the allotment of the reservations following the 1887 Dawes Act, with sale of "surplus" land, by 1910 three-quarters of the two reservations were lost to Indians, with hundreds of families quietly gone back to their original homes, although now generally as squatters. In the twentieth century, land claims brought by these nations exposed a lawyers' nightmare of documents without legal standing. The final blow was the 1954 Congressional termination of Federal Indian status for all western Oregon Indians. The affected nations organized to fight this unsought decree, and in 1977 the Confederated Tribes of the Siletz Reservation regained Indian status. With the Grande Ronde reservation nations, the total number of these Confederated nations in 1980 was about three thousand.

The Chinook

The Chinook, a series of small nations along the lower Columbia River, dominated the Oregon-Washington coast. Their Penutian language reveals their affinity to the nations along the Columbia and the southern Plateau. Having secured the district in which traffic on the Columbia and along the coast, north and south, converged, the Chinook saw their language become the basis for the lingua franca of the Northwest Coast, Chinook Jargon: Nootka (Nuu-chah-nulth), French, and English terms were added to a simplified Chinook to form a relatively easily learned pidgin. Dentalium shell imported from the Washington–British Columbia border region was the medium of exchange, augmented during the nineteenth century by beaver skins, a medium introduced by the European and Euro-American traders. The Chinook themselves produced, with the aid of household slaves, quantities of dried salmon in various forms—whole, filleted, or pounded into "flour"—dried sturgeon and other river and bay fish, dried seal and sea-lion meat, blubber, oil, dried berries, and wooden canoes. Sea-otters furs were another traded product from Chinook territory, one that was accumulated and displayed as they wore them as cloaks, by Chinook leaders, as well as collected for the market. In return for their own products, the Chinook bought dried wapato and camas and elk and deer meat and skins from the upriver peoples, and dried shellfish and other meat from the peoples of the coastal bays. The baskets and bags in which these products were packed ought perhaps also to be reckoned in the commerce; women wove the variety of such containers while the men hunted or fished. Early explorers such as Lewis and Clark, in 1805, found the Chinook could immediately supply quantities of whatever was asked for—whether several hundred furs, slaves, dried salmon, or bags of other dried foods—and seemed to delight in driving a bargain, although after hours of haggling they might in the end accept a price no

greater than the one initially offered. Chinook women were eager and busy traders, an occupation frequently pursued by women all along the Northwest Coast, especially with foreigners who came to their own ports.

To produce the bulk of their commerce, the Chinook used seine nets. Line fishing, spearing, dip netting, and herring raking brought in additional fish, harpoons secured sea mammals, and spears and bows impaled land game. Like many other Northwest Coast nations, the Chinook themselves did not, it appears, actively hunt whales, but every beached whale was enthusiastically used, its distribution planned and ordered by the village leader. Men performed most of the tasks of procurement and preparation of food, including much of the cooking, while women busied themselves collecting the materials for, and weaving, baskets, bags, and mats, but division of labor was not hard and fast. The drudgery of firewood collecting, shellfish gathering, and other dirty or tiresome tasks was assigned to slaves, who numbered from one to a dozen per household, but free Chinook worked alongside their slaves if not occupied with tasks requiring greater skill. Euro-American colonists in the Willamette Valley in the mid-nineteenth century bought slaves from the Chinook to work their farms.

Chinook winter villages consisted of plank houses with plank gable roofs. As elsewhere along the Oregon-Washington coast, the houses were built in excavated rectangular pits as much as 4 feet (over 1 meter) deep, and thus were half sunk in insulating earth. Around the permanent villages were palisade fortifications. With the approach of summer, Chinook dismantled their houses, stored some of the planks, and took others to serve as the frames of the lighter, shed-roofed houses or the mat-covered houses preferred for warm weather. Each village was politically autonomous, though linked to others by alliances often symbolized by intervillage marriages arranged for the leaders. Typically for the Northwest Coast and California, class stratification was important to the Chinook.

Upper-class persons became village leaders, war leaders, doctors, and chief traders. They owned more slaves than commoners could afford to buy and used them to maintain their household's greater wealth. Freeborn persons were marked by a high, sloping forehead flattened in babyhood by a pad tied down across the cradle, slaves supposedly were marked by their ordinary round heads. But because many slaves were captured as older children from other nations that flattened the forehead, the distinction could apply only to birth status, not necessarily to adult lot. Slaves could be abused or killed by their masters—in one case, a mother had two women slaves killed and buried with her dead child, in hopes the slaves would assist the little one's spirit—but usually they suffered only the hard work and ignominy of their status. They were denigrated by being called only by the name of their original people: a Kalapuya captive, for example, was called Kalapuya instead of a proper personal name.

Class mobility was possible, especially if the commoner (or even slave) had talent for amassing wealth. One legendary route to power and high status was skill in gambling. An unlucky person might become a slave if he had nothing left to wager but himself, and lost that, too, in a game. The person blessed with audacity and sharp mind and eye might play tirelessly, one opponent after another, until even village leaders had to acknowledge his challenge. Then, in true fairy-tale fashion, the ambitious man could make ostentatious presents to an upper-class family until they accepted his request for the hand of their daughter. Children of such a marriage were upper class, but if an upper-class person married one of the lower class who had not distinguished himself or herself, their children would be lower-class. Upper-class families discouraged their children from mixing with commoners, even in play.

Ordinarily, leadership in a village was a formal role passed on from a man to his nephew or son. A leader's daughter or widow could become chief if seen as more capable than available upper-class men. Man or woman, the leader was assisted by other upper-class persons, including one talented in oratory to speak at banquets. These feasts were sometimes called potlatches in Chinook Jargon, but they seem to have been somewhat less ritualized than the British Columbia nations' potlatches, and the intense rivalry between leaders in the display of wealth, recorded by Boas in the late nineteenth century there, was not noted among the Chinook (who did not survive that long as a nation). Chinook feasts were held outdoors in warm weather, and friendly or rival villages were invited to spend several days with the host community, eating, singing and dancing, and leaving with gifts. A pair of feuding villages might attempt to settle their contention during a feast, but if they were unsuccessful, the feast would be followed by a formal battle between men in canoes shooting arrows at each other until one or two on one side were killed. The fighters wore armor of double thicknesses of elk hide made into tunics, or of narrow slats of wood tied together to form flexible corselets. They also wore elkhide helmets or thick basketry hats. These open battles were quite different from stealthy raids upon enemy nations, in which the raiders hoped to breach the fortifications, fire the village, massacre the men, and capture women and children for slaves.

Friendly ties between villages could be maintained during winters, when individuals, rather than whole communities, might be invited to attend a feast in a neighboring settlement. The winter feasts were usually held to aid a doctor in curing someone ill or depressed. Doctors went through years of apprenticeship training climaxed by a public exhibition of the neophyte's spiritual power. This power was evidenced through the apprentice's ability to wound and then miraculously cure himself or herself (presumably this was done with hidden bladders of blood and sleight-of-hand) or walk unscathed over hot coals (possibly achieved through a combination of a plant-juice skin salve and psyching oneself up until the body's natural morphinelike, pain-blocking chemicals are produced). A sufferer attended by a doctor would lie where he or she could clearly see each guest come into the house and hear him or her singing a song of a helping spirit. One of the songs, it would be hoped, would excite the patient's memory of having met a similar spirit when out as a youth seeking such spirit protectors. Then the patient and the guest who sang this song, assisted by the doctor who was familiar with several spirits, could sing to invoke the aid of the sufferer's protector. Some winter feasts would be enlivened by a battle between doctors, one accused of malicious sorcery and the other destroying the evil one's power by feats of superior magic. In one memorable case, a woman doctor whose power was symbolized by a bow and arrow unerringly shot her arrow at her rival's magical knife wherever it was hidden. Blindfolded or lying on the floor, she never missed. The sorcerer's knife lost its power, it was believed, and he was never again able to magically wound people.

After generations of dominating trade from the hub around the mouth of the Columbia, Chinook power declined when the Hudson's Bay Company absorbed its rivals and then in 1824 built its principal regional post at Fort Vancouver commanding both the Columbia traffic and the mouth of the Willamette Valley. Faced with this heavily capitalized competition and attacked by epidemics, the Chinook were reduced to living around Euro-American settlements or moved onto the new reservations after the 1851 treaties that they, like the other Indians, believed to be valid. In 1899, they—the Chinook proper and the closely related Clatsop, Cathlamet, and Wahkiakum—instituted a claim against the United States for uncompensated takeover of their former lands. The action gained them a judgment, rendered in 1912, of $20,000. Again bringing suit, in 1951, for what was blatantly too little for 762,000 acres (308,377 hectares), in 1971 the United States awarded them $75,000, deducting the 1912 settlement from that less than princely sum! Combined legally as The Chinook Nation, the four groups filed in 1979 for federal recognition

as an Indian tribe in order to gain access to benefits normally accruing to United States Indians. The 1980 census counted fourteen hundred persons identified as Chinook.

Puget Sound and Washington Coast

North of the Columbia, native nations can be grouped into those who live along the sheltered waters of Puget Sound and those who face the open ocean on Washington's west coast. Puget Sound peoples had regular contact with Plateau peoples across the Cascades to the east, buying elk and deer meat and hides with dentalium-shell money. Usually, they hosted summer visits of the Klikitat and other easterners, but occasionally they traveled over the mountain passes to hunt or trade. The Snoqualmie living east of Seattle near the mountains hunted along the divide more than did their western neighbors; they even pursued game in the winter by using snowshoes. Peoples on the western coast—the Chehalis, the Quinault and closely related Queets, the Quilete and their relatives the Hoh, and the Makah (a Nootkan offshoot) at the northwestern tip of Washington—were oriented more toward the north and Vancouver Island. Both regions, Puget Sound and the western coast, felt the influence of the British Columbia section of the Northwest Coast, through trade, raiding, and visiting at feasts.

Among the Washington peoples, the more typical Northwest Coast cultural pattern is approached. Although the Chinook lived in large houses in which it was considered desirable to shelter four families, their houses, and those along the Oregon coast, resembled Plateau houses in being sunk partially underground. Chinook also built sweat lodges in each village; these were less common in Washington settlements. Washington houses were seldom in excavations, but on ground level. Some families laid planks on edge horizontally between posts for the walls of their homes, while others set planks vertically in wall trenches. The gable roof was usual in the southern portion of the state, but sloping shed roofs appeared in the north, as in British Columbia. Again as usual in the north, many houses were sixty feet or more in length and thirty-five or forty feet wide (eighteen by twelve meters). Four to six families plus their slaves were said to be the average composition of a house. Two tiers of shelves ran around the walls, the upper for storage and the lower serving as sleeping benches. Hearths usually were set in a row down the middle of a house, one for each family. Loose boards in the middle of the roof could be set at an angle to allow smoke to escape, but might have to be closed in rainstorms, which would make the house dark and smoky but incidentally help preserve all the dried food on the upper racks. Villages were often palisaded, although one Snohomish town near Everett, Washington was reported unfortified because all its inhabitants were commoners who would flee to the forest rather than fight invaders. Most villages built one especially large house, up to 300 feet (92 meters) long, in which to hold potlatches. The village leader and his or her dependents might live in the potlatch house, or it might be reserved for the feasts. Potlatch houses were constructed close to the river or sound so that guests could paddle close, singing and beating time on their gunwales to set the festive mood.

Puget Sound Salish were organized into nations composed of several villages whose chiefs answered to a head chief in a central town. The Snoqualmie's nineteenth-century head chief, Putkadum (Pat Kamin), ruled four districts from the Sound to Snoqualmie Pass through the Cascades. He regularly traveled through the districts, inspecting them and conferring with his subchiefs, aristocrats who were usually related to him by descent or marriage. In this way, the chief ensured labor power, including his own slaves, food, and goods, would be distributed where needed. Each of the districts commanded a strategic fort to control traffic through the domain. Putkadum kept a corps of young men trained and armed for war with him, headquartered at the largest community containing sixteen longhouses, or about six hundred people.

At another Snoqualmie town, a longhouse was used as a crafts center where highly skilled specialists instructed apprentices in the manufacturing technology. Slave labor permitted specialists, both men and women, to work at their crafts without the burden of daily chores. In 1848, Chief Putkadum convened a major regional meeting to discuss strategy for dealing with the new power in their midst, the United States: eight thousand people are said to have attended, two thousand of them capable of prosecuting war. The final outcome of the conference was a decision by Putkadum to sign the 1855 treaty. Incursions by Euro-American colonists gradually displaced the Snoqualmie, turning them into a laboring class in their former territory, but they retained their political organization, and Putkadum's descendant Jerry Kamin was Chief until he died in 1956. Alternative adjustments to United States colonization can be seen in the history of the Duwamish, a Coast Salish nation enjoying the site of what is now the city of Seattle, named after their treaty-period chief Sealth. Although Sealth did not fight the takeover of his land, and his people worked for wages in the new settlement or raised potatoes to sell to the settlers, the Duwamish were removed to other nations' reservations. Many families came back to live on the outskirts of the city of Seattle, where their descendants remain. The Duwamish attempted to gain entitlement to Indian fishing rights but in 1974 were denied on the grounds that they are not a federally recognized tribe; so much for Chief Seattle's goodwill!

Yet another history is that of the Clallam, some of whom, led by their chief James Balch, in 1875 chipped in to purchase land for a settlement near their traditional homeland on the Strait of Juan de Fuca. Jamestown, named after the chief, was a model community, first in the district to build a church although few Clallam were Christian, and soon after a school. Until 1910, the community prospered by continuing its accustomed fishing and plant harvesting; then the state insisted Indians should not be exempt from fishing regulations. Two young men from the community bought com-

FIGURE 8.4 Swinomish (Coast Salish) hauling up a fish trap containing over four tons of salmon, 1938. *(Smithsonian institution National Anthropological Archives)*

mercial fishing boats and began to fish for the market, soon expanding into the selling of the locality's famous Dungeness crabs. By 1918 one of these entrepreneurs had installed a telephone for his business and bought an automobile. After World War II the younger Jamestown Clallam sought employment outside the community, but by 1981, in conjunction with two other Clallam communities and Skokomish Twana, they gained federal recognition and the fishing rights the Duwamish had unsuccessfully sought. Other Puget Sound Salish communities have since the 1970s constructed aquaculture operations such as fish hatcheries and salmon-raising pens. Because so many Puget Sound Salish nations lack federal recognition as Indians, population figures are estimates: in the 1980s, the number of Southern Puget Sound Salish was about eighteen thousand, and another sixteen thousand Coast Salish probably in the northern Puget Sound and adjacent British Columbia area.

Potlatches and Spirit Protectors

Tradition claimed that potlatches were not really ancient among Washington peoples, but were introduced about A.D. 1800. The first Quinault potlatch is said to have excited so much interest that the potlatch house could not accommodate all the visitors. So many of them climbed on the roof to watch through the smoke vents that the roof collapsed, fortunately without killing any of the celebrants. It may be that what was introduced was the highly ritualized British Columbia form of potlatch feast, which perhaps replaced somewhat less formal feasts of local tradition. As elsewhere in the Northwest Coast, it was customary to give potlatch feasts when a young person was introduced into adult society by being given a proper, inherited adult name to replace the child's "nickname"; when a person died, and often a year or more later, when the deceased would be memorialized, and the remains taken from the canoe or wooden box on posts in which they had rested, and interred; and when a village gave thanksgiving for the first salmon of the annual run, or for similar successful hunts. Each potlatch was supervised by the village leader or another wealthy, upper-class person, who gloried in impressing guests from other communities with the abundance of good food, the skill and beauty of dancing, and the generous gifts the host village under his or her direction could present. Sports and gambling games enlivened the hours between speeches and feasting. Leaders and groups of visitors boasted of their prowess in war, hunting, and trading, but rivalry was not the focus of the potlatches, as it seemed to be among the Kwakiutl when Boas observed them at the end of the nineteenth century.

West-coast nations shared with the British Columbia nations several secret societies that gave public performances of dance dramas and magic during the consecrated winter season. Rumor claimed that the members of the societies were cannibals, but the rumor was probably circulated to heighten the drama of the performances, in which, among other feats, the leaders appeared to kill and then revive novices. Puget Sound nations resembled the Plateau more than their salt-water neighbors in holding spirit-protector song performances rather than the highly organized society presentations. For the Puget Sound peoples, the winter brought home the many spirits that otherwise usually traveled around the world. Spirits that had appeared to a youth when he or she went out alone seeking a protector prompted the adult, when the spirit was home in winter, to join with friends, each in turn singing and dancing the song of each person's protector. Wealthy persons would thank their friends by giving gifts after the occasion, commoners would merely reciprocate by attending their friends' gatherings. Some persons' protectors were known as "wealth spirits," and urged their human friends, "You had better throw our money now. I would like to see the people enjoy themselves and to hear all the shamans [doctors] sing

their songs. So you invite so-and-so and such-and-such tribes so I can hear them sing" (Olson 1936:124). Persons with these wealth spirits of course were likely to become famous for the grandeur of their potlatches. Other persons might have a gambling spirit and become rich through gambling skill and good luck, or a warrior spirit urging them to go to battle, or a hunting or fishing spirit, or one that gave talent in basketry to women or talent in the pursuit of food to men. Doctors had more spirits than ordinary people. Their spirits included some who stayed home all year and some who would return when called. Many doctors were aided by spirits who knew the road to the land of the dead and could guide their friend, in a trance, along this road to recapture the souls of dying patients. Doctors with such power over death were never expected to be village leaders—an executive position—but concentrated instead upon gaining and maintaining spiritual knowledge, and advised the secular leaders. These chiefs were likely to have such spirit protectors as Mountain Goat, who surveys the land from the highest elevations and nimbly bounds away from danger.

Northwest Coast Crafts

Washington peoples were familiar with several crafts best developed in British Columbia. The west-coast peoples knew the heavy equipment—canoes and harpoons—designed to kill whales, and many communities had a chief who prepared this equipment, carried out the protective rituals, and recruited crews for whaling. Only the Makah, as an offshoot of the Nuu-chah-nulth, made whaling a regular pursuit, although Quinault also, but less often, hunted whales. The Quinault and the peoples of Puget Sound and Juan de Fuca Strait (northwest Washington) wove blankets on an upright loom, using mountain-goat hair (sometimes bought from eastern neighbors), or the hair of a special breed of woolly dog kept in pens and sheared twice a year, or a yarn made by pounding duck down, mixing it with the fibers of fireweed, and rolling the mixture into thread. Blankets of rabbit-skin strips were also made, as on the Plateau. The Washington peoples had wedges, mauls, and other equipment for felling and splitting large trees and for making dugout canoes (these were often very long and featured handsome painted bows and stern pieces), but their carving was not as finely finished as that in British Columbia. The principal support posts of Washington houses were often carved as simple giant figures rather than as the series of highly stylized creatures on British Columbia "totem" poles. Although on the whole, Washington peoples impressed nineteenth-century Euro-American visitors as "provincial cousins" of the British Columbia Northwest Coast and openly admired the high development of skills among the groups farther north, it was acknowledged that the Coast Salish peoples were not uninventive. For example, only in this region were huge nets stretched on 100-foot (30-meter) high poles to trap whole flocks of migrating ducks—"fishing" in the air, one observer put it (but recall that the Nevada Paiute also trapped ducks in aerial nets).

Ozette, a large Makah village on the northwest tip of Washington state, has provided a remarkable picture of Protohistoric (c. A.D. 1700) Makah life. A mudslide buried several houses in the center of the village strung along the coastal terrace. Continuously wet, the mud preserved everything in the houses. Cooperation between the host Makah and archaeologists revealed the wealth of Ozette before European visits, and enabled the Makah to construct a fascinating museum. A similar project was conducted at the Hoko River mouth, on the coast south of Ozette. Ozette houses had cedar-plank drains feeding into a system of planks and whale bones acting as storm sewers for the village. Inside the buried houses, most wooden objects were decorated with carving and paint. A bowl, no doubt meant for feasts, is carved as a man lying on his back, his belly open as the bowl itself. The little man's realistic face is topped by a glued-on braid of actual human hair. Baskets exhibit a variety of

complex weaves and hold sets of gear for whaling, fishing, weaving, or woodworking. Similarities to historic artifacts permitted the archaeologists and their Makah collaborators to identify such objects as a basketry hood designed to protect a baby's face. No masks were found, suggesting the community may have stored its masks with other spiritually powerful items in particular houses, none affected by the fatal mudslide.

One important difference between the Washington and British Columbia nations is that the latter were not affected by epidemics and colonization so early and so heavily. Consequently, the more northern nations retained their homelands and autonomy when, in the later nineteenth century, the northwestern United States nations had been both decimated and driven into marginal settlements. The few reasonably good descriptions we have of Southern Coast Salish before the 1830 epidemics and following colonization picture populous nations in substantial villages more comparable to the northern nations than is usually realized. In the 1980s, there were two thousand Quinault (including Hoh and Quileute), 425 enrolled Chehalis, and fifteen hundred members of the nonrecognized Cowlitz Indian Nation.

The Coast Salish

Descriptions of Puget Sound Salish apply also, with variation in detail, to the Coast Salish along the Gulf of Georgia between Vancouver Island and the British Columbia mainland, including the lower Fraser River. Over a dozen sets of villages have been recognized and given "tribal" names, such as Sanetch, Cowichan, Nanaimo, or Halkomelem: some refer to dialect distinctions, some to the locality where the villages of a set cluster. From north to south, the Central Coast Salish are the Squamish; the Halkomelem languages speakers, including such local nations as the Nanaimo, the Cowichan, the Musqueam, and the Chilliwack; the Nooksack; the Northern Straits

FIGURE 8.5 Makah gathered at their fishery at the entrance of the Straits of Juan de Fuca, about 1900. *(Smithsonian Institution National Anthropological Archives, Bureau of American Ethnology Collection)*

nations comprising the Saanich, Sooke, Songhees, Semiahmoo, Lummi, and Samish; and the Clallam.

Each community wintered in a permanent settlement whose large plank houses were constructed in one or a few rows convenient to its river or inlet, and each dispersed for about half the year, two or three families camping together in mat lodges near fishing stations, deer- or elk-hunting grounds, or spots for gathering wapato ("Indian potato"), camas, or berries. The Clallam kept watch for whales in their section of the Juan de Fuca Straits and sent out several canoes with harpooners to pursue the animals when sighted. During the summer, the gulf and the rivers were constantly busy with canoes crossing to these various resource-exploitation localities or returning with caches of dried foods to store in the winter

village. Later, in the autumn, canoes full of people dressed in their finest clothing would travel to friendly villages to attend potlatch feasts celebrating a marriage, commemorating dead, or presenting a young person as scion of an upper-class family. Winter was the consecrated season, and in southern British Columbia, the rituals changed as one went from south to north: Southerners held gatherings featuring the singing of individuals' spirit-protector songs, as among the Puget Sound Salish, and only one masked-dance drama; Northerners were more similar to their Wakashan-speaking neighbors in holding several different masked dances.

Historically, at least, the British Columbia Coast Salish distinguished between a grand potlatch, in which other villages were guests and gifts were distributed formally in proportion to the rank of the guests, and less-grand feasts, which might be given more spontaneously, might not have outsiders but only the host's fellow villagers as guests, and in which everyone had an equal chance at gifts placed in the middle of the floor to be "scrambled" for, or distributed in about the same amount to everyone. Puget Sound Salish also had "scrambles," which sometimes became a tussle in which the desired items were wrecked and the winners bought the missing parts from competitors and pieced the objects together. Upper-class families frequently gave "scrambles" and gift distributions in their own villages to erase any reflection upon their proud name from a mistake or embarrassing incident of one of their members, even a child. Commoners could not afford to do so, perhaps could not afford even to host a small feast and gift distribution upon a marriage, and that reinforced their lower status. Ambitious and capable persons could try to rise in status by taking advantage of occasions to be publicly generous, though leading families were slow to recognize and include nouveaux riche in their potlatches.

Contemporary Central Coast Salish are known for their popular heavy sweaters of sheep wool spun by their own process, invented about 1920, using a converted sewing machine. Called Cowichan or Siwash sweaters and sold through Hudson's Bay Company department stores and specialty shops, the handsome hand-knitted sweaters bring designs derived from basketry into a profitable modern medium. (Siwash is the Anglicized version of Chinook Jargon *sawash* meaning "Indian.")

The Nuu-chah-nulth-aht (Nootka)

The Wakashan-speaking peoples of the central British Columbia Northwest Coast—the Kwakiutl, Heiltsuk including Haisla, Kitamat, and Bella Bella, and Nuu-chah-nulth-aht—and the Salish-speaking Nuxalk (Bella Coola) share a cultural pattern described in Section 2 of this chapter. The principal variation from that pattern

is shown by the Nuu-chah-nulth (the Nuu-chah-nulth-aht, Nitinat, and Makah—the suffix "aht" means "people of"), who held the west coast of Vancouver Island and the northwestern tip of Washington across the strait. Vancouver Island Nuu-chah-nulth-aht saw their highly indented coast as two lands, "outside" and "inside." They wintered "inside" at the heads of inlets and moved down to the "outside" open coast for summer fishing and whaling.

Nuu-chah-nulth-aht were famous for their superb seagoing cedar canoes, their pursuit of whales, and their production of dentalium shells, the money unit of the Northwest Coast. Nuu-chah-nulth not only used a variety of canoes for their diverse economic endeavors, they also gave canoes as potlatch gifts and traded them all along the coast. Not only did the Nuu-chah-nulth-aht carve the great canoes from cedar logs, they skillfully split the huge logs to make the long planks wanted for houses, and traded the planks to nations lacking the most imposing cedars. Dentalium shellfish ordinarily live rather deep offshore, but there were a few localities in Nuu-chah-nulth territory where the beds could be reached by an implement consisting of a broomlike bundle of cedar splints fastened to a pole handle elongated by lashing to it a series of extension poles. A narrow weighted board around the top of the broom slid down the bundle and compressed the splints when the implement was pulled up through the water. If the operator had hit a dentalium bed, several of the animals would be caught between the splints and could be pulled out and dropped into a container, where their flesh would be boiled out. The shells would then be dried and lightly polished with sand. Snaring dentalium in this manner was tedious and slow, which ensured that this unit of currency would not lose its value. The combination of production of the best canoes and production of the currency unit gave the Nuu-chah-nulth a power in the regional trade that was reflected in the incorporation of Nuu-chah-nulth words into the Chinook-based lingua franca Chinook Jargon.

The Nuu-chah-nulth third specialty, whaling, was important economically and impressive proof of daring and spiritual and physical strength. Commanders of whaling boats were invariably chiefs from high-ranking families. From elder men in the lineage they had inherited the privilege of learning the rituals and techniques for whaling. Being wealthy, they could have the very large, very finely balanced and sleek whaling canoes built for them, and could commission the gear required for the enterprise. They could recruit crews from their relatives and other men of the village, the crews confident that their families would be provided for while they were out and indemnified in case they failed to return from the dangerous chase. When a whaler planned to go out, he notified his crews to prepare themselves spiritually by abstaining from profane indulgences and practically by getting together and checking over the gear, bailing buckets, and food and water and polishing the hulls of the canoes so they would slip noiselessly through the sea. Once out and a quarry sighted, the canoes would maneuver to a position from which the harpooner could thrust his heavy weapon into the whale, in back of its flipper. The wounded whale would jump and dive, the harpoon line singing as it flew out from the canoe; harpooner and paddlers had to crouch lest the line sweep them out. The steersman for the canoe was the man on whom the most depended: he usually gave the harpooner the signal for the thrust, and it was his skill in holding the canoe advantageously for the hit and afterward in the churning sea that would mean success. A first hit was usually followed by one from the harpooner in a second canoe. The prey would leap, race, and sound for hours, often a couple of days, before it became exhausted enough for the harpooners to kill it with lances. Then the whale's mouth had to be tied shut by a man piercing its jaws and passing a rope through, so that its body would not fill with water and sink. More ropes were secured around the animal to tow it to shore, perhaps now far out of sight if the dying creature had headed out into the open ocean. With many more hours of exhaustive paddling, perhaps aided by men who had come out upon being told of the hit by a messenger rushing back to the village in a small, fast canoe, the whalers would beach their prize. The Nuu-chah-nulth-aht claimed that whaling was developed by two communities who, unlike all the others, lacked salmon streams in their territory. The practice was learned by other Nuu-chah-nulth, but since even the most highly regarded whalers lost more whales than they ever brought in, whaling was the most glorious pursuit but not the basis of the economy.

Nuu-chah-nulth-aht also hunted seals, sea lions, porpoises, and sea otter. Sea-otter fur was always a prestige item, reserved for chiefs' cloaks and, during the nineteenth century, the most valuable fur in the international trade with Russians, British, and United States ships. Nuu-chah-nulth products were important not only for the coastal trade—Indian, and eventually European also—but for trade overland to the Nimkish, a Kwakiutl group on northeastern Vancouver Island who exported quantities of eulachon fish oil stored in "bottles" of kelp (seaweed) floats. Nuu-chah-nulth-aht used whale oil and shark oil from their own hunts to make their dried staples and lean fishes palatable to their taste, but eulachon oil was considered the best, the equivalent of butter to Euro-Americans.

The Northern Northwest Coast Peoples

The Northern Northwest Coast is inhabited by the Athabascan-speaking Tlingit, the Haida, and the Penutian-speaking Tsimshian. These nations have been judged to have produced many of the very finest examples of the great art style of the Northwest Coast. The stout wooden posts supporting the frames of their plank houses and those upon which the coffins of their deceased rested were carved and painted forerunners of the later-nineteenth-century freestanding "totem poles." Their robes of twined and woven mountain-goat hair, called Chilkat "blankets" after one of the Tlingit groups, rank with the

FIGURE 8.6 Haida Skidegate village, early 1880s. *(Smithsonian Institution National Anthropological Archives)*

masterpieces of the weaver's art. Their carved masks have the power to impress even the casual museumgoer. Little Tlingit girls played with dolls whose heads were carved from white marble imported for them from interior Alaska. At first contact with Europeans in the late eighteenth century, these nations had iron knives as well as copper ornaments, and worked both metals. Some copper was imported from interior Alaska native mines; how much iron was salvaged from Asian or Spanish vessels shipwrecked on the American coast, how much traded along the North Pacific rim, has not been determined. Basketry was also an art, again judged to be most skillfully demonstrated by the Tlingit.

In social structure, the Northern nations contrasted with those to the south in recognizing affiliation and inheritance primarily through the mother. Each house was seen as the property of a

matrilineage, and was managed by a man of the lineage referred to as the "house master." A woman usually moved into her husband's house upon marriage, but the upper-class boy was usually sent to live with his mother's brother in her lineage house in order to be schooled by him in the duties and privileges he would inherit as a leading member of the lineage. The Tlingit and Haida organized their lineages into two sets: the Ravens and the Wolves for the Tlingit and the Ravens and Eagles for the Haida. The Tsimshian had four principal divisions, but grouped them two and two when marrying into or joining in ceremonies with the neighboring nations. Each moiety ritually aided the other in carrying out funerals and investitures of officials, and of course considered itself to be the in-laws of the other, since all members of one assumed themselves to be related by descent and could properly marry only persons from the opposite moiety. The formality of lineages among the Northern groups allowed a distinction between housemasters, who were selected by the lineage members from suitable men of their house, and individuals who were wealthy but did not have this official role.

Doctors, men or women, formed a third type of notable person. Many doctors became quite wealthy from the gifts given by the grateful families of their patients, but because the doctors had to maintain their spiritual healing power by frequent fasts and retreats, they could not be as active in leading mundane affairs as the housemasters and ordinary rich people. Tlingit doctors were obliged to let their hair grow, uncut and uncombed, to shelter their spirit helpers, giving doctors a wild and terrifying appearance. (When missionaries and Indian agents forced the Tlingit to conform to Euro-American hair styles, they destroyed the power of these doctors, though one Tlingit doctor was said to have lived to an advanced age unshorn, rendering barbers' scissors useless by his power). As elsewhere, the Northern peoples had upper, commoner, and slave classes. Some of the slaves were bought from traders who imported them from as far south as Washington state.

Trade with the interior of southern Alaska and the Yukon, inhabited by Yupik and Inuit (Eskimo) and Athabascan hunting-fishing groups, was an important and regular activity of the Northern Northwest Coast villages. Native copper, worked into small versions of the embossed and painted shieldlike heirlooms that were made of European sheet copper as soon as it became available, was one traded resource valued on the coast. Furs and moose hides, sometimes sewn into tunics or, later, coats, were also desired, and were sold by the interior peoples for seal hides and oil. Balls of spruce gum were a popular interior product sold to the coast as chewing gum. Walrus-ivory ornaments were desired by the Yupik to the northwest. The Northern Coast participated in the coastal trade as well, voyaging as far as southern Vancouver Island to get dentalium-shell money, abalone-shell ornaments, flicker feathers to decorate headdresses, and slaves. Trade was always carried out with ceremony and was expected to be accompanied by feasting and opportunities for gambling; it was not unusual for whole families to go on trading voyages and stay for months with distant relatives in host villages. Through these visits, cultural preferences and innovations were widely spread and gave the entire long Northwest Coast its distinctive style as well as economic patterns profiting from the marine and riverine resources available to skilled and knowledgeable residents.

SECTION 4: THE HISTORIC NORTHWEST COAST

The Northwest Coast contrasts with every other section of the Americas in its accessibility from Eurasia, specifically eastern Asia and the islands of the Pacific. This accessibility is from two directions: eastward across the Pacific on the Japan Current, which rises near Taiwan, flows past Japan and on past the Hawaiian islands, and swings northward along the American Pacific coast; and north, east, and then southeast along the northern rim of the Pacific with its chains of islands. It was not rare for Asian fishing vessels to be wrecked upon the American coast, and there were trading chains around the Pacific rim that over a few years could pass Asian objects from group to group to Alaska. Neither route was ever regularly exploited by the historic empires of Asia, but each allowed technology and design styles of Asian fishing communities to reach the Northwest Coast. Thus, familiarity with iron, wooden-slat armor, certain hat styles, tattooing, and highly formalized decorative art, including many of its standardized elements (such as ovoids at body joints), are shared by many peoples around the North Pacific. Other, more generalized cultural traits such as masked-dance dramas and the "feast of merit," which combined a memorial to a deceased leader or titleholder, the investiture of his successor, and claim to rank validated by display of wealth, are common all along the Pacific from Melanesia at one end to America at the other, particularly in the "tribal" communities that are ethnically distinct from the ruling peoples of the historic empires. A few traits, such as the ritual of a spiritually powerful person (a shaman in Asia) climbing up a pole into the Above World, symbolized by the Thunderbird, are found in Siberia and the Northwest Coast, possibly diffused through the Inuit, possibly by Siberians employed by the Russian-American Company beginning in the latter eighteenth century. The first historic contacts between Northwest Coast nations and Europeans, unlike first contacts in other sections of America, were therefore not the inauguration of regular contacts between Eurasia and America, but only of documented visits by representatives of European ruling powers.

The Advent of the Europeans

The Russian expedition of 1741 under Vitus Bering was the first to record reaching the Northwest Coast, in Tlingit territory. Russians soon established profitable sea-otter-fur hunting from bases on the Aleutian Islands, where the native Aleuts were forced to pursue the animals for the benefit of their conquerors, but extension of the Russian hegemony was hindered by the fierce resistance of, first, the Chugach Yupik of southern Alaska and then the Tlingit. Extermination of the sea otters from, successively, the Kamchatka Peninsula of Asia, the Kurile Islands, and the islands and peninsula off southwestern Alaska determined the Russians' resolve to build forts in harbors in southeastern Alaska despite Tlingit hostility. Consolidation of formerly independent Russian fur companies into the Russian-American Company, with government support, in 1799 enabled a garrison to be established at what is now Sitka. During the next half-century the Russian-American Company continued its relentless exploitation of sea otters, whose large, very dense pelts were highly valued in China.

Enslaved Aleuts were the principal hunters, and were supplemented by Siberians, Nuu-chah-nulth-aht, and a few Russians. Independent of this officially recognized Russian enterprise, Siberian Chukchi and Bering Strait Inuit traded Russian products out of Siberian posts, into Alaska and British Columbia. Native traders sold indigenous manufactures such as whale fat and fine parkas in addition to the European goods.

The Russian forts in Alaska were provisioned by ships from Siberia and from California, the latter bringing what could be spared from the Russian colony north of San Francisco, Fort Ross, plus foodstuffs bought in San Francisco. There were efforts to develop food-producing colonies in Hawaii, but these were not significant for the Russian Alaskan posts. Shipped thousands of miles, food was of course extremely expensive and often rotting when it reached its destinations in Alaska and the Aleutians. This gave the Tlingit opportunity to profit by supplying Sitka and other posts with provisions. Although in 1802 the Tlingits had destroyed New Archangel, the Russian post at Sitka, after the post was reestablished in 1804 an uneasy dependency of Russians upon Tlingit slowly developed. Tlingits had always camped at Sitka for the herring and salmon runs in spring and summer, and some came to live more permanently adjacent to the Russian fort. A number of Tlingit women married Russian men assigned to the post: sometimes the wife and children accompanied the husband when he returned to Russia, sometimes the family was abandoned, and often the husband remained in the Alaskan settlement and his children formed a class of Creoles employed by the Company. Since the Tlingit reckon descent through matrilineages, the Creoles had rights in Tlingit communities as well as claims upon the Russian government—one factor lessening Tlingit hostility to the invaders. The other factor was the market for Tlingit produce. About 1820, Tlingits had learned from the Russians to grow potatoes, a crop that could supplement the indigenous roots and tubers the Tlingits had already been cultivating in their native habitats. By 1847, New Archangel purchased from Tlingit suppliers not only 40,374 pounds (nearly 20,000 kilograms) of "mutton" (presumably mountain-sheep or mountain-goat meat) and 43,299 pounds (closer to 20,000 kilograms) of halibut, but also 37,200 pounds (17,000 kilograms, approximately) of potatoes. Two years before, less meat had been sold but New Archangel had bought from the Tlingits 246,450 pounds (over 110,000 kilograms) of potatoes. In 1849, the Company had purchased 1,360 logs each 21 feet (7 meters) long from the Tlingits during the course of a year. Tlingits also sold handicrafts and a variety of seasonal foods in lesser quantities than the three principal staples. The Russian market for Tlingit produce continued until Russia pulled out of America in 1867. Note that the standard anthropological descriptions of the Tlingit call them "hunter-gatherers" or even "foragers," a dramatic example of the blinding power of racist ideology.

Russian incursions into Alaska stimulated Spain to send expeditions far into what they claimed was their *Alta California.* Pérez Hernandez was the first of the Spanish explorers. In 1774, he reached the Haida in the Queen Charlotte Islands, and was welcomed by large canoes (many of them as long as the Spanish ships) containing upper-class men in sea-otter cloaks and decorated fine basketry hats accompanied by dancers who ritually communicated peaceful intentions by scattering eagle down upon the water. Britain soon decided that Francis Drake's California stopover of 1579 justified a claim to the North Pacific American coast, and sent James Cook around the world to approach America through the Pacific. Sailing from Hawaii, Cook made a landfall at Cape Flattery, the northwestern tip of Washington, in 1778. Cook continued northward into Nootka Sound, and met welcoming canoes with masked dancers performing upon planks laid across the boats, the paddlers singing and beating time upon the gunwales as they did when ceremoniously approaching the host of a potlatch. Nootka Sound

became the center of contention between Spain and Britain, each dispatching explorers to chart and claim the harbors where sea-otter and fur-seal pelts might be obtained by hunting or trade. The controversy was settled in Britain's favor in 1792, seven years after a Captain Hanna had inaugurated the lucrative trade between the Northwest Coast and China's port of Canton.

United States ships from New England had begun to compete with Britain and Russia in the commerce based on the high prices paid for sea-otter fur in China. Russia was handicapped in that her only entry to China was via inland towns on the Siberian border, which necessitated overland conveyance of the pelts from Siberian ports. The English-speaking traders could unload directly from their ships into the Chinese market, and load directly for the voyage home with Chinese tea, porcelains, and silks. The United States captains worked out a triangular route on which they picked up rum and molasses in the Caribbean on their way around South America to the Northwest Coast, sold these and New England manufactures for sea-otter and fur-seal hides, then struck across the Pacific for Canton, where they obtained the Chinese goods in demand in New England. United States ships were among the best designed of the period, fast and seaworthy. Russian ships were for the most part slow and liable to founder. Russia had an advantage, however, in controlling the highly skilled Aleut hunters. Between 1803 and 1813, United States and Russian traders collaborated, the former with ships and the latter with hunters, dividing between the captains of the two nations the sea-otter furs procured by the hapless Aleuts. Direct pursuit of sea otters was supplemented by trading for the furs with the Northwest Coast natives.

Britain responded by developing an overland route through Canada to the Pacific, reached by Mackenzie in 1793. Officially through the Hudson's Bay Company and unofficially also by the Bay's rival, the North West Company (the rivals merged in 1821), the British established a set of trading posts. These posts attracted Indian settlement, a number of winter villages relocating for the convenience and protection from raids afforded by the foreigners' establishments. Some of the settlements, such as Fort Rupert, in which four former Kwakiutl communities were consolidated, became larger than villages had customarily been in the past. The traders' gardens, cultivated under a policy initiated in 1821 to economize by making posts self-sufficient in food rather than dependent on imported or purchased supplies, may have popularized the cultivation of potatoes and other new crops by the Indians.

British extension of the fur trade overland was paralleled in Oregon by United States traders led by John Jacob Astor, who gave his name to the post he founded in 1811. The American Fur Company focused on the great Columbia River traffic along which Lewis and Clark had been guided, rather than on sea-mammal pelts. Thus, although some sea otter could be obtained off the Oregon and Washington coasts before overhunting nearly exterminated them, beaver were more important in the Oregon trade. The coastal peoples were relatively ignored, except as they traded through the traditional Indian middlemen on the Columbia. A contrast developed in the early nineteenth century between the Oregon-Washington section of the Northwest Coast, little affected by European or Euro-American commerce, and the section north of Juan de Fuca Strait, drawn into a vigorous international trade. The contrast collapsed in the mid-nineteenth century when both sections were invaded by Euro-American colonists.

European diseases, especially smallpox, wreaked their usual devastation on Indians when contacts became common between trading ships and Indians, beginning in the 1780s. The "triangular trade" must have been an especially effective agent of disease communication, with crews going ashore and mingling with crowds on the dirty waterfronts of Caribbean, South American, and Chinese ports before they met Northwest Coast Indians. European diseases also moved down the Columbia River in the early nineteenth century after crossing over the Rockies from the Plains. The terrible smallpox epidemic of the 1830s seems to have been carried to the Pacific peoples by both sea and land. As a result of the toll taken by smallpox, measles, influenza, and other epidemics, hundreds of Northwest Coast villages and their cultivated lands were abandoned during the course of the nineteenth century. Population was further reduced by venereal diseases and then by tuberculosis becoming prevalent late in the nineteenth century as nutrition worsened through increasing use of purchased processed food and as the healthful practice of shifting residence to camps for much of the year was replaced by year-round dwelling in poorly ventilated houses.

At the end of the nineteenth century, most Northwest Coast peoples had only one-tenth of the population they were estimated by reliable observers to have had at the beginning of the century. Severe reductions in population and the consequent merging of formerly independent villages drastically confused the ordering of Northwest Coast societies. Not only did many persons of rank die suddenly without passing on knowledge of ritual or designating heirs, survivors found themselves the single scions of families possessing dozens of titles. The number of recognized titles came to be out of proportion to the number of persons in the community: at Fort Rupert, for example, four formerly autonomous Southern Kwakiutl communities had to work out the relative ranks of the four sets of titles and privileges brought to the trading-post settlement, and exacerbating that problem was the fact that the 658 titles dispersed among approximately eight thousand Kwakiutl in 1835 had come to be distributed among only slightly over one thousand individuals, many of them children, by the beginning of the twentieth century. The fierce rivalry recorded by Boas late in the nineteenth century at Fort Rupert potlatches seems to have been fomented by the disruptions stemming from rapid population decline and realignments, caused primarily by epidemics, though influenced also by economic shifts introduced by the fur trade and later by commercial fishing.

Colonization of the Northwest Coast

Euro-American colonization began on the Northwest Coast during the 1840s. Western Oregon, promoted in the eastern United States as ideal homesteading territory, was the terminus of the Oregon Trail. Dispute over the United States boundary with British Canada focused propaganda and agitation on land to the north that without international imperialist conflict might not have attracted much notice. Establishment of the present border in 1846 promised stability and was followed by the founding of Euro-American colonies in both Washington and British Columbia. Decimation of Indian populations by the epidemics, including malaria, of the previous decade had left some desirable habitable land unoccupied, but Indian communities soon realized the threat posed by the incoming strangers, and many of the Coast Salish, led by the Nisqually chief Leschi and several others, joined in the Yakima War of 1855. Defeat resulted in the hanging of Leschi and the unequivocal acknowledgment of United States rule south of the forty-ninth parallel: treaties made in 1854 and 1855 marked out a number of small reservations for the western Washington nations, others made in 1853 set reservations for the nations of western Oregon and adjacent Washington, and intervening land was "American." North of the border, the Hudson's Bay Company, which had been expanding its system of posts through the 1830s, undertook to manage a crown colony on southern Vancouver Island, around the town of Victoria, in 1849. Through the 1850s, the governor of the colony, Sir James Douglas, developed a policy of compensating Indians for parcels of "improved" land—land actively and continuously utilized—and surveying communities to be held as reserves for bands, but assuming that all "wild" land belonged to the Crown even if Indians claimed it for hunting, plant harvesting, or fishing stations. Implicit in Douglas's policy was the concept that all Canada was owned by the Crown, which could convey title but did not recognize any prior title. By 1866, when the two colonies of Vancouver Island and mainland British Columbia were merged, most of the Indian communities in the coastal section of the province had been allotted reserves, usually the immediate locality of their winter villages. Discovery of gold along the Fraser in 1858 had brought an influx of claimants for the country, which rendered critical the question of Indian land rights and lent the reserves the aura of refuges in spite of the injustice of abrogating Indian title to large territories traditionally theirs. Another smallpox epidemic, touched off by a contagious miner in Victoria in 1862, weakened Indian opposition to the realization of Douglas's policy.

Colonization was not the unmitigated disaster for Northwest Coast Indians that it was for so many other American Indians. A demand for fish, potatoes, and lumber was created in the central sector of the coast similar to that filled by the Tlingits and Haida for the Russians in the northern sector. During the mid-nineteenth century there was, in addition, a market for shark (dogfish) oil and sealskins produced by the Nuu-chah-nulth, and Nuu-chah-nulth seal hunters were frequently employed directly on ships in the fur trade. Provisions supplied for the towns and ships, wage employment, and, especially in Victoria, prostitution (some aristocratic Indian women "rented out" their slave women), brought cash income to Indians just when the near extinction of the sea otter was severely reducing the earlier source of the cash they needed to purchase knives and other desired European goods. Manufacture of tourist curios, particularly wooden masks, became another means of entering commerce, and the Haida developed an art of carving in argillite, a local stone, for this market.

Taking an active and substantial part in the commercial activities of the growing towns, the Northwest Coast Indians of the later nineteenth century enjoyed a fairly steady flow of cash to top off their subsistence pursuits, which continued to be based on salmon and other fish. Harvesting of indigenous plants and land hunting was somewhat curtailed by Euro-American settlement, but flour and other introduced foods could be purchased in place of the native equivalents. Potato farming was so profitable through most of the nineteenth century that Haida attempting to sell potatoes to Fort Simpson in 1841 were killed by local Tsimshian guarding their monopoly there. Chief Legex (also spelled Legaik) married one of his daughters to an officer of the post and established his principal village beside it in 1832. Legex fought to control the Skeena River from its mouth to its head, and the major trading route trails along and intersecting it. (Northwest Coast streams and coast are so rocky that goods were often more economically backpacked along the maintained trails, many with rope-and-plank suspension bridges, rather than transported by boats.) Legex and his soldiers not only controlled access to the Hudson's Bay Company post but insisted the Bay men pay to use his canoes for all traffic on the Skeena. It wasn't until 1892 that the Bay could override the Tsimshian baron and put its steamboat on the river. By that time, another Port Simpson Tsimshian had been skippering his own schooner on regular coastal runs to Victoria for over a decade.

Cash was channeled into gift distribution at potlatches and the payment of craftsmen to prepare dance paraphernalia and the carved poles memorializing the heritage of the potlatch giver. Particularly in the northern sector, remote from the center of colonization in Puget Sound, the Fraser delta, and southern Vancouver Island, there was a florescence of art reflecting the increase in wealth perceived by the Tlingit, Tsimshian, and Haida. Villages and cemeteries sprouted groves of towering poles chronicling the legendary glories of each lineage through series of figures recalling mythical and historic events. (These carved poles are popularly called totem poles, but the figures do not represent totems—symbols of clans—so much as

they do characters in history and legends. The closest European analogy is to heraldic crests and shield devices.) Spurred by the many deaths needing to be memorialized and the problems of maintaining social order in the face of rapid population decline through epidemics and debilitating diseases, the titled people converted their money into blankets and other goods that could be piled up to testify to the worth of the lineage. In the central as well as in the northern sector, each potlatch seemed to reach a new height of expenditure.

The extravagances of the potlatches in communities in which the homes were very sparsely furnished, compared with the Victorian style in contemporary Euro-American homes, and in which wardrobes and other personal possessions were limited, excited the censure of most of the missionaries who had come to "civilize" the Northwest Coast Indians. Lavish public feasts and gift distributions contrasted so markedly with contemporary Euro-American valuation of exclusive private banquets and private display of wealth that the Indian mode was seen as the core of their supposedly Godforsaken heathenism and the prime target for those who would save the natives. The idea that traditional feasts embodied nearly all the worst aspects of Indian life and beliefs was reinforced by the prominence in the central and northern sectors of the cannibal spirit in ritual dramas performed in conjunction with the winter feasts. Supposedly, this spirit implanted in worthy young men a fierce animal power that initially caused the protégé to rage wildly about the village, stripping off his clothes, gobbling food raw, and attacking people as if to eat them alive. Older members of the cannibal spirit secret ritual society attempted to protect villagers from the apparently maddened initiate, and after several days' wrestling with the young man, appeared to have tamed his power so that he would be able to call upon it as he joined other leaders of the community in their endeavors, confining it within normal social behavior. Missionaries did not understand that the cannibal spirit performance is an allegory of human development,

FIGURE 8.7 Tlingit chief's house and totem poles, Cape Fox village, Alaska, 1899. *(Smithsonian Institution National Anthropological Archives)*

an unforgettable enactment of the importance of bringing physical power under the dominion of the social group. The skillfully staged performance in which the novice appeared to actually tear at the flesh of confederates planted in the audience persuaded the missionaries that the Northwest Coast Indians really were cannibals, and needed to be rescued from this most horrendous sin. By 1884, the missionaries had induced the Canadian Parliament to amend the 1880 Indian Act to include a statute making it a misdemeanor, punishable by imprisonment from two to six months, to give or assist in a potlatch or a Tamanawas (Chinook Jargon for "spirit") dance—that is, the winter cere-

monials. This Potlatch Law remained on the books until 1951, although efforts to enforce it died down during its last fifteen years.

Potlatches themselves did not die down, as expected: instead, they were either flaunted and fought in the courts on technicalities of the law, or held more or less surreptitiously. A hiatus in the giving of potlatches during the Depression was the result not of obedience to the law but of inability to raise the large sums of cash necessary to hold respectable potlatches. The 1880s, one full generation after initial Euro-American settlement, saw the establishment of a pattern of Indian life economically but not socially integrated into the

Euro-American pattern. Commercial salmon fishing was industrialized by the building of canneries to process the catch for world markets; Indian women were employed in the canneries as they had traditionally been employed to fillet and dry salmon for their own households' use. Hundreds of Indian men fished from cannery-owned boats for the owners, though it became increasingly common, by the turn of the century, for Indians to own their boat and sell to the canneries. A number of Indian women fished with their men on the boats. Men were employed in lumbering and boat building, and to a lesser degree in mining and transportation (longshoremen, wagon teamsters, steamer and schooner crewmen) as well as in fishing. Entire families from both sides of the border harvested hops in Washington, prizing the games and singing that filled the camps after the day's work. Indian men hunted seals offshore from boats carried out on schooners; dozens of the most adventurous signed on for two-year voyages that took them hunting across the Pacific, wintering over in Japan (where, the young men boasted, Japanese girls much admired them).

Home on the reserves, potatoes for people and oats and hay for horses and cattle were raised. By the 1880s, the large multifamily lineage houses were kept only for feasts; residence was in smaller frame homes similar to those of Euro-Americans. Catholic and Protestant schools were being opened for Indian children, and a majority of Indians were nominally members of the local mission church. Government wardship was enforced as stringently as the budgets and manpower of the agencies allowed, with the agents and missionaries stepping in to manage both business and disputes in a usurpation of the duties of the traditional lineage leaders. In some mission-dominated northern villages, aristocratic men who were unlikely to inherit traditional high office managed to become leaders by taking advantage of government and mission needs for interpreters and assistants, manipulating these roles and entrepreneurial opportunities to achieve recognition as leaders. One missionary, William

Duncan from the Church of England, tried to fulfill the church's goal of creating little English villages by setting up a new community for his Tsimshian converts, a carefully planned mission utopia with a sawmill, cannery, weaving factory, and store, making the congregation appear a model of the Protestant work ethic. Duncan, who was not an ordained minister, was censured by his bishop over his modifications of church ritual to make it more compatible with Tsimshian experience. He then contended with the bishop over whether the church, through the government's recognition of it, or the Indian congregation of Metlakatla had title to two acres of land on which the bishop attempted to build a mission competing with Duncan. In 1886, Duncan and his congregation moved north just across the Canadian-Alaskan border to establish an independent community under United States jurisdiction. In spite of the strong disapproval Duncan met from his own church superiors, his radical revision of Indian life was widely acclaimed as a model for all missionaries and their charges. This model of an economically and socially independent Indian community firmly led by a Euro-American agent was upheld by the government and Euro-Americans until the 1950s. The real pattern of migrant harvesting of berries and then hops in the summer, conflicts between agents and Indians over autonomy, and persistence of potlatches and native religious ceremonies insofar as finances permitted was seen as a deviation from the ideal.

Political Organization among the Northwest Coast Peoples

Northwest Coast Indians contrast with those of other culture areas in that they retained their key economic resource. To the present, they have relied upon salmon and other fish, taken at many of the traditional fishing stations or from their own boats, as the bottom line in their livelihood. When the market has been profitable, they have fished more and earned cash; when, during the

Depression, market prices were low, they retrenched and fished for subsistence. Northwest Coast Indians were thus never reduced to the wrenching despair of those Eastern peoples who were totally dispossessed, or of the Plains peoples whose bison disappeared. From the strength of a basically sound economy, the Northwest Coast Indians could assert their rights to autonomy more cogently and consistently than could most other American Indians.

In the United States section, the whittling down of reservations by allotment under the 1887 Dawes Act was resisted. A 1926 court case filed by the Duwamish and other Puget Sound Indian groups against the United States argued that the 1854 treaties should not be recognized because Governor Stevens negotiated them exclusively in Chinook Jargon, refusing to allow them to be translated from English into the several Indian languages, and that no one could correctly understand the treaties from the distorted interpretations phrased in the limited lingua franca of trade. The 1934 rejection of the claim by the court refused this position, but it illustrates the sophistication of Indian arguments as early as 1926. In Canada, following a decision in 1911 not to hear any more Indian land claims, a royal commission examined all British Columbia reserves from 1913 to 1916 and "adjusted" their boundaries by removing land worth, at that time, $1,522,704 and adding land worth only $444,838. The commission failed to resolve a controversy over whether unused Indian land remained Indian or automatically reverted to the province. It recommended that the government alter its policies to promote enfranchisement for Indians. The first issue, which rested upon the fundamental question of Crown versus Indian title to British Columbia, and the second, which, like the Dawes Act, seemed to be designed to break down Indian nations, spurred many of the native residents of British Columbia to organize, in 1915, the Allied Tribes of British Columbia to battle for their rights. The Allied Tribes had little obvious success: they would not accept local court juris-

dictions and tried to take their cases directly to the British Privy Council, which refused to hear cases except upon appeal from a Canadian court. Over the long run, the Allied Tribes may be said to have achieved, through the organization's intransigence on accepting local jurisdiction, an important statement on the autonomy of British Columbia Indians.

A clearly effective organization of Northwest Coast Indians, the Alaska Native Brotherhood, was founded in 1912 by Tlingit and one Tsimshian from a half-dozen villages who met at Sitka, site of a Presbyterian mission school. All of the delegates—twelve men and one woman— had some formal education and spoke English. (The woman delegate reflects Tlingit acknowledgment of women's abilities. As in other Northwest Coast nations, Tlingit women were active and shrewd traders. Captain Vancouver reported that aristocratic older women were the helmsmen in Tlingit war canoes.) In forming the Brotherhood, the Indians were assisted by Presbyterian missionaries to follow standard Euro-American voluntary-association structure and procedure. Their immediate model was probably the Arctic Brotherhood, a political organization of Klondike settlers who had just won the right to be governed through an Alaskan Territorial Legislature, rather than from Washington. The Alaskan Native Sisterhood was formed in 1923 as a parallel affiliated organization to enable women to work toward those goals they shared with the Brotherhood. The two organizations, operating in tandem, soon became a focus of community life in most of the Tlingit villages. Although the founders included commoner as well as upper-class men, in the villages the local chapters were usually led by upper-class titled men, a system that preserved the aboriginal pattern of clan-based community organization. Each village had a large hall built for Brotherhood/Sisterhood meetings, though available for other community gatherings and, frequently, for basketball games. Local meetings were often run in Tlingit, in contrast with the central conventions held in English, and etiquette and ceremonies from the potlatch were introduced on occasions such as memorials to deceased members or as maneuvers to smooth over disputes or slights.

A leader of the chapter at Wrangell was Charlie Jones, who held the prestigious title Wicekc ("Chief Shakes"), had no formal education, and was responsible for the maintenance of much traditional behavior. The Wicekc nevertheless was instrumental in establishing the Wrangell chapter and then, about 1920, in bringing into the central organization a young Tlingit man, William L. Paul, Sr., who had spent most of his youth attending the Carlisle Indian School in Pennsylvania and then studying law. Paul spent the rest of his life using his legal training and knowledge of United States political structure to lead the Alaska Native Brotherhood. One of the first tests of Paul's capabilities was his defense of the Wicekc, who had gone to vote in the 1922 Alaska primary elections. The Wicekc had voted in previous primary and territorial elections, but this time the poll overseers challenged the right of an Indian to vote as a citizen. Both the Wicekc and Paul's mother, then Mrs. Tamaree, who had come to assist the elderly man with her fluency in English, were arrested. Paul could have argued the case on the basis of the fundamental claim that since the United States had never made treaties with Alaskan Indians, the Indians of the territory were not wards of the government but citizens like other residents of the territory when it was purchased from Russia. However, the cases against Mr. Jones and Mrs. Tamaree were defended on the basis of the Wicekc's prior consistent exercise of citizen's duties, from paying taxes—even though Indians were exempt—and buying war bonds, to voting. The defendants' acquittal thus seemed to leave citizenship for Indians dependent upon exercise of citizens' rights and privileges rather than innate, but it did strengthen the Indians' pride and determination in pursuing their rights and alert non-Indian Alaskans to the potential political clout of Indian voters. Five Tlingit Brotherhood presidents were elected to the Alaska Legislature.

The Alaska Native Brotherhood, representing Haida and some Tsimshian as well as the Tlingit, fought successfully not only for political rights for Indians but also for the right of Indian children to attend public schools, for native land claims, and for an end to discrimination against Indians in theaters, restaurants, and stores and in the purchase of liquor. During the early 1940s, the brotherhood expanded to develop a trade union, the Alaska Marine Workers' Union, that would negotiate with canneries on behalf of fishermen and cannery workers. This union was by no means the first in its area, but with Paul's leadership it became the strongest and a member of the national American Federation of Labor. Within a few years it joined a rival union, which also had some, though not all, Indian leaders, and affiliated with the Congress of Industrial Organizations, ending its Brotherhood association. The Alaska Native Brotherhood has exemplified for over a half-century the power of American Indians to adapt successfully to modern economic and political conditions when their aboriginal economic base has not been destroyed and they have been allowed the basic political rights of citizens. By the 1960s, the Brotherhood and Sisterhood were urging more open celebration of Indian national cultures. This, including impressive potlatches, became easier not only because of the 1946 enactment of the Alaska Anti-discrimination Act, lobbied through the legislature by Paul and the Brotherhood, but more because the 1971 Alaska Native Claims Settlement Act permitted the Tlingit and Haida to form the Sealaska Regional Corporation. Ten years after the Act, Sealaska was on *Fortune* magazine's list of 1,000 top United States corporations. Though its profitability fluctuates with salmon and timber prices, Sealaska continues the Tlingits' and Haidas' tradition of exceptional economic strength.

British Columbia has also had a native brotherhood, organized in 1931 by Tsimshian on the model of the Alaska Brotherhood. It was somewhat the successor to the 1913 Allied Tribes of British Columbia that fought in the courts against the

1912–1916 commission "adjusting" reserve acreages and boundaries. A 1927 amendment of Canada's Indian Act made the solicitation of funds for pursuing land claims a legal offense, clearly jeopardizing the Allied Tribes' work. The British Columbia Native Brotherhood soon included Bella Bella and Nuxalk (Bella Coola), but not until 1942 did it persuade the Kwakiutl, who had their own group, the Pacific Coast Native Fishermen's Association, to join. Prior to this, the Kwakiutl union had been parallel to the Native Brotherhood, which, after intervening in a fishermen's strike on the Skeena River a couple years after the Brotherhood's founding, had functioned as a trade union for Tsimshian fishermen. The 1942 merger came after an attempt was made by the government to collect income taxes from Indian fishermen. The Indians believed this was unfair for two reasons: first, because Canada had never paid them for more than a minuscule portion of the vast lands taken from them for Euro-Canadian settlement, and second, because Indians who lived on crops and livestock raised on Indian reserves were not taxed—therefore, Indians who fished in "Indian waters" should not be taxed. After the merger, the Native Brotherhood became the principal negotiating agent between Indian fishermen and cannery workers and the canneries, sometimes attracting Euro-Canadian and Japanese workers as associate members for this reason, although most non-Indian "marine workers" would join a rival British Columbia union. The Brotherhood has, in addition, pursued other goals similar to those of its Alaskan counterpart. In education, it pushed for better schools, though not necessarily entrance into public schools; it waged strong campaigns for more and better medical facilities (fishing and lumbering are hazardous occupations); and it continued the policy of the Allied Tribes in pressing for land and compensation without admitting Canadian jurisdiction over Indians. Officers of the Brotherhood spoke in Ottawa in 1950, critiquing proposed revisions of the Indian Act and emphasizing their nations' considerable integration into the provincial economy. Two of the speakers were from the northern half of the province—a Kwakiutl and a Haida—where the Brotherhood was strongest, but the third, Andrew Paull, was a Squamish from a Coast Salish group in the southern portion of the province, where the Brotherhood never became firmly established, in spite of Mr. Paull's admirable organizing fervor and ability (he developed the Canada-wide North American Indian Brotherhood). Another officer, Frank Calder, a member of the Nishga division of the Tsimshian, ran for and won a seat in the provincial legislature at this time, the first Indian to be elected to that body.

The Postwar Renascence

The post–World War II phenomenon of rapidly increasing Indian populations has occurred on the Northwest Coast as well as elsewhere, and has brought its characteristic array of problems as well as successes. The small reserves cannot possibly support many agriculturalists, and in Washington and southern British Columbia, they have in many cases become bedroom suburbs for members who commute daily to jobs in cities. Discrimination against Indians in employment has hindered many Northwest Coast individuals, but the relatively good schooling available to Indians in this region, where the pride and economic strength of the upper-class families impressed missionaries and teachers to encourage their children to professional ambitions, allowed a significant number to obtain reasonably prestigious positions, though often at the cost of migrating to major cities elsewhere in Canada or the United States. Commercial fishing has continued to be the principal business of the majority of Indians on the reserves, and can absorb numbers of young people provided the competition from well-capitalized foreign fishing fleets can be met. During the past century, most of the owners of fishing boats from Northwest Coast communities have been upper-class men with claims to traditional leadership titles. Their families trained them for management and supported their purchase and maintenance of equipment, including boats; in exchange, these captains employed clan brothers on their crews. In recent years, commercial fishing vessels have been mechanized and enlarged to such a degree that they are prohibitively expensive for private individuals. Indian captains are seeking to compete by insisting on exclusive rights to traditional fishing stations or grounds, a strategy that has excited angry confrontations with non-Indian commercial fishermen. Both groups agree on petitions to their national governments to restrict access of foreign vessels to North American waters.

Although a number of upper-class Northwest Coast men own fishing boats that have enabled them to compete as equals with Euro-American commercial fishermen, if not against subsidized foreign fleets, and although the proportion of educated professionals among Northwest Coast Indians may be somewhat higher than among Indians of other regions, still it is true that the greatest segment of the Northwest Coast Indian population is employed in the lowest-ranking jobs: crewing on boats, fishing or clam-digging with only hand equipment, logging, unskilled labor, and for women, seasonal cannery work. Migrant harvesting of hops and fruits continues to draw thousands. To cope with their low and erratic incomes, people rely on kin and neighbors, as they did when traditional lineages pooled members' production in the great plank houses. Upper-class families in particular plan to distribute surpluses to others on their reserves, and to visitors: some families cultivate sufficient potatoes or other garden crops to be sure to have a substantial amount available to distribute to every household in the village, or catch a boatload of fish just for distribution, or even purchase a truckload of food for distribution. Women may bake twenty pies at once in order to distribute them. More informally, a skilled fisherman or clam digger may fill his or her small boat, take what the family needs that day, and leave the remainder in the boat on the beach, calling out for people to help

themselves. This concern for distribution marks the upper class and perpetuates the traditional class distinctions, for although anyone who wishes to be considered an Indian is obliged to share when requested or when need is obvious, only the upper-class individuals usually plan for substantial village-wide distributions. The native social structure has thus persisted in large part, with upper-class families continuing to take leadership, to host potlatches ("naming feasts" and "memorial feasts") to announce the investiture of heirs with titles, and even to promote marriages between young people whom the parents deem suitable.

The nadir of Northwest Coast Indian life may have been the 1930s, when the world-wide Depression combined with stern repression of tradition by agents and missionaries to almost bankrupt village life. Recovery slowly gained momentum through the late 1940s and the 1950s as incomes again permitted potlatches, the Potlatch Law itself was repealed, and Euro-Americans realized, from the admiring comments of leading European modern artists and collectors, that the Northwest Coast Indians had produced one of the world's great art styles. The developing tourism industry incorporated Indian carvings into hallmarks of the region, and local Sports Days were promoted into events at which Euro-Americans could be entertained by Indian dances and "war canoe" races. The dances were social dances or invented performances, not true ceremonials, in most instances, and the "war canoes" were Indian-built modifications of Euro-American racing sculls rather than the much heavier dugouts actually used for war raids more than a century ago, but the events brought some income into the Indian communities and were fun for the racers and the many Indians who took advantage of the gatherings to enjoy the old gambling games with their lively songs. Along with the summer shows, winter ceremonials gained greater participation. Traditional religions never died out on the Northwest Coast, although some rituals were forced underground by missionary and agent censure, and others had to be curtailed or modified.

FIGURE 8.8 Nuuchahnulth man in dance costume including "Chilkat blanket" robe, mid-1920s. (*Smithsonian Institution National Anthropological Archives*)

Doctors were the most severely affected, since their uncut hair marked them.

Among the Coast Salish, a new form of Christianity replaced traditional doctoring for many individuals. This was called the Shaker Church—no connection to the Christian Shakers of the eastern United States—founded in 1881 by Squsachtun (John Slocum), a Squaxin from southern Puget Sound. Squsachtun had been a dissolute man, had apparently fallen and seemed to die, then had miraculously revived and begun preaching a Christianity that he said had been revealed directly to him by an angel at the gate of heaven. Squsachtun's rejection of the Bible, which he claimed was supplanted for Indians by his revelation, and other

"heresies" led to confrontations with the resident missionary and his brother, who was the agent for the reservations of the district. Squaschtun and several of his converts were imprisoned in chains for several weeks when they refused to recant. Their overt persecution ended when they consulted a sympathetic attorney who advised them that since they held land under the Dawes Act and voted and paid taxes, they were entitled to all rights of citizens, including freedom of religion. The Shaker Church spread through the first decade of the twentieth century until it was found in Salish communities from Vancouver Island to California, an Indian accommodation of Christianity and, most important, a successor to traditional doctoring in that services included the invocation of the Spirit, manifested through the trembling ("shaking") of believers, to heal the sick and troubled. In Salish villages, the Shaker and conventional Christian churches did not preclude numbers of people participating also in winter Spirit Dances, the old ceremony in which a novice sought to identify the song of a protecting spirit. Obtaining a spirit protector continued to be an important source of strength and ability, and came to indicate also a young person's Indian identity. Some parents dragged a youth or a girl whose behavior worried them into the Winter Dance, hoping that the wayward one would be helped to a better life, and Salish testify that in many cases the parents' goal was fulfilled. In the Wakashan-speaking and northern sectors of the Northwest Coast, which are more isolated than the Salish from Euro-American towns, the traditional elaborate ritual dramas have persisted in essence, though cut down from months-long performances to weekends. Observers carp that sometimes the novice youths seized by the cannibal spirit dance perfunctorily, but it may well be that some of their forefathers did, too. What matters is that although the perform-ances have been adjusted to allow participants and guests to hold their weekday jobs, the dramas and accompanying feasts continue to bind communities, to express native concepts, and to bring to their Indian heritage the hundreds who must spend much of their time following Euro-American patterns in order to make a living.

Seeming to recognize economic achievement among Indians, in 1969 the government of Canada proposed abolishing the Indian Act and the special status of Indians. The outcry against what was perceived by nearly all Indians across the country as its latest and basest perfidy surprised the government. British Columbia Indians organized a Union of British Columbia Indian Chiefs, formally representing most of the bands in the province and determined to advance land claims. A year previous, the British Columbia Association of Non-Status Indians was organized to work on behalf of Indians without federal recognition. Regional organizations of Indian bands are a third political structure, responding to more local needs and issues. Ironically, the 1969 government initiative to remove Indian status galvanized Indians to vociferously reaffirm their resolution to retain that status.

A COAST SALISH BOY BECOMES A DOCTOR

When I was only 3 years old [about 1865], my mother, who was herself a medicine-woman, made me bathe in the river and scrub my limbs with spruce-boughs before breakfast, even through there was ice on the water, and one morning after I had scrubbed myself—I was still only 3—she clothed me with her blessing or power, what we call in our language *swiám'*. Every living creature, you know, possess its special strength or power, something invisible to normal eyes that dwells inside it, and yet can issue from it, giving it power to do the things it wishes to do. Well, that morning she clothed me with her power; she passed her hands over my body, from head to feet, draping her strength over me to shield and fortify me for the trials that she projected for me later. Thereafter she would never allow me to creep into her bed on cold dark mornings, or to receive food from anyone who might be ceremonially unclean. Every night I slept alone in my own little bed, and every morning I bathed and scrubbed myself with spruce-boughs that I might be pure and without taint in both mind and body. By day I played with the other children, and I helped my kinsmen at home and in our hunting camps. My uncles (for my father died soon afterwards) taught me to handle a fishnet, to trap small animals, and sometimes to fire off their guns; yet always I felt that I was different from other children, though in what way I could not understand.

Thus I grew to the age of about 8. Then at intervals throughout one winter my mother called in three of her oldest and best-informed relatives to teach me the ancient history of our people, and the commandments which He Who Dwells Above had imposed upon us when He established us upon this earth. I still bathed night and morning, winter and summer, but so also did other boys of my own age, and many of the men.

Two more years passed uneventfully by, and I reached the age of 10. Then one morning my mother roused me from my bed and said: "Pierre, it is time now that you trained to become a medicine-man. Go back into the woods, but be careful that no one sees you. Whenever you come to a pool, bathe and rub yourself with spruce-boughs, then walk on again. Stay out as long as you can. Remember that He Who Dwells Above has given you power. Pray to Him as you walk along; ask His help; plead with Him to strengthen you for the trials you must now undergo. Don't be afraid, or imagine that you will die. Be of strong mind."

I dressed and stole away into the woods. No one except my mother knew where I had gone, or that I was training to be a medicine-man. I was hungry and cold, for there was snow on the ground and she had sent me away without breakfast, but I remembered what she had told me, and I prayed to Him Who Dwells Above for strength. Twice when I came to pools of water I bathed, rubbed my shivering limbs with spruce-boughs, and hurried on again. But by noon I could bear the cold and the solitude no longer. My mind became weak, my feet turned uncontrollably homeward, and I ran as fast as I could to the house.

It was afternoon when I entered, but my mother paid no attention to me; neither then nor at supper-time did she offer me any food. I crept into my bed, worn out with fatigue and hunger, and fell sound asleep. At daybreak she woke me again and said: "Pierre, you must go back into the woods. Go farther than you went yesterday, and don't come back so early. You are hungry; drink all the water you wish, but don't nibble anything, not even a blade of grass. And remember to keep praying to Him Who Dwells Above."

I cried bitterly and thought that she was terribly cruel to me, but it was of no use; I had to go. I don't remember how far I walked that day or how many times I bathed, but it was late afternoon when I reached home. Although I was famishing, my mother gave me very little to eat and immediately sent me to lie down.....

In the morning she examined me to see that I was warmly clad, gave me some matches but no blankets, and sent me out to continue my fast. I do not remember how many days and nights I stayed away on that occasion, only that before darkness descended I would kindle a fire and gather branches for a bed; but when I did return home, weak and exhausted, my mother fed me very sparingly and sent me out again as soon as I seemed able to endure another trial. So I continued all through the winter. Each time I went out my sufferings seemed a little less, until after the first hour of walking I felt light and vigorous, and was conscious of neither hunger nor thirst.

Spring came, and my mother said to me: "Stop fasting now, Pierre. The sweet briars are budding, and the berries will soon be ripening. They would tempt you to eat, and you would be unable to resist the temptation. Bathe in the woods as often as you wish and scrub yourself with fir-boughs, but do not try to fast."

So from spring to autumn I fished and hunted and played with other boys of our village. But when winter came again I resumed my fasting; I roamed the woods, bathed in its icy pools, rubbed myself with the boughs of the evergreen trees, ate nothing, but drank water copiously and gave it up again. After each bath I prayed to Him Who Dwells Above, and I danced until I fell to the ground exhausted, then at night I slept on beds of branches or in the hollow of some tree. Gradually my skin became hard like the bark of the trees, with which I scrubbed it. No cold could penetrate it; the rain and the snow that fell on me seemed warm....

Four winters I endured this penance. Then at last my mind and body became really clean. My eyes were opened, and I beheld the whole universe.

I had been dancing, and had fallen to the ground exhausted. As I lay there, sleeping, I heard a medicine-man singing far, far away, and my mind traveled toward the voice. Evil medicine-men seemed to swarm around me, but always there was someone behind me who whispered, "Pay no attention to them, for they are evil." And I prayed constantly to Him Who Dwells Above, asking for power to heal the sick, not to cause sickness as did these evil ones.

I reached the place where the medicine-man was singing, a house unlike any that I had ever seen before. He who was behind me whispered: "Go inside. This is he for whom you are seeking, the true medicine-man for whom you have undergone penance all these years."

I entered. The medicine-man was kneeling on the floor, and beside him was his water, in some mystic vessel that was neither a dish nor a basket. He turned and looked at me. "Poor boy," he said. "So you have come at last. Kneel down beside me."

I knelt beside him. In front of us appeared every sickness that afflicts mankind, concentrated in a single human being. "Wash your hands and wrists in this water." I washed them. He grasped them in his own and massaged them, giving them power. "Now lay your hands on that sickness and remove it."

I laid my hands to the patient and cupped his sickness out with them. He rose to his feet, cured. "That is how you shall remove every sickness. You shall chant the song that you have heard me sing and cup out the sickness with your hands. Now go."

My mind reunited to my body and I awoke, but now in my hands and wrists I felt power. I rose up and danced until I fell exhausted again and my mind left me once more. Now I travelled to a huge tree—the father of all trees, invisible to mortal eyes; and always behind me moved the same being as before, though I could not see him. As I stood before the mighty trunk, he said: "Listen. The tree will speak to you."

For a long time I stood there waiting. Finally the tree spoke: "O poor boy. No living soul has ever seen me before. Here I stand, watching all the trees and all the people throughout this world, and no one knows me. One power, and one only, I shall grant you. When you are treating the sick, you shall see over the whole world; when the mind of your patient is lost, you shall see and recapture it."

...My mind returned to my body; I awoke and bathed again in the pool at my side. After my bath I drank copiously of its water.....Then I prayed to Him Who Dwells Above, and I danced till I fell to the ground and lost consciousness. My mind travelled forth again over a beautiful prairie until something tripped me, something hard like stone, and a voice said to me: "Poor soul, go no farther. This is the leader of all things that are upon this earth. You are the first who has come here."

The being who had tripped me stood up and chanted a song. "Take this stone that I use for a pillow," he said. "Hold it in your two hands and kneel down. For a long time I have been watching you, watching your struggles."

As I knelt down, holding the rock in my hands—it was different from all other rocks—the being mounted the back of my head and rubbed my jaw. "You shall heal the sick. Place your lips to the rock and suck it. Suck it once only, but suck it hard." I laid my lips to it and sucked. It became soft like flesh, and something—it was blood—issued from it and entered my mouth. "Don't eject it on the ground, but swallow some of it and rub the rest on your hands." He came down from the back of my head and took the rock from me. "That is how you shall heal the sick. That is how you shall suck away their illnesses. Now go."

I awoke and found myself lying on the ground. Now I had power—power in my hands and wrists to draw out sickness, power in my mouth to swallow it, and power to see all over the world and to recover minds that had strayed from their bodily homes. I was a medicine-man: I could heal the sick, I could banish their diseases, even as my mother had foretold me. But not always. Whenever He Who Dwells Above had decided to take away someone's soul, I could do nothing. This also my mother had foretold me.

I rose from the ground and returned home. My years of fasting were ended.

I think my mother knew what had happened, for she asked no questions, nor did she urge me to stay in the woods again. So I remained at home, and, as soon as I recovered my strength, joined my uncles in the fishing and hunting.

(Jenness 1955:65–68)

Persistence and even revival of traditional ritual dramas and memorial feasts have fostered an exciting revival of arts on the Northwest Coast. Seamen and then tourists had been buying carvings throughout the nineteenth century, and Northwest Coast ceremonial paraphernalia had been increasingly exhibited as art, rather than exotic specimens, in European and American museums since the 1920s. Ironically, foreign appreciation of this great art tradition grew during the years between the World Wars when local enforcement of the government law against potlatches prevented open use of its glories in its homeland. Revival began in the 1950s. Anthropologists of the University of British Columbia's Museum of Man commissioned replications of memorial posts from Mungo Martin (Naqapenkim), a high-ranking Kwakiutl who had learned to carve from his stepfather. Chief Martin taught his art to younger Kwakiutl who aided him in his work, which was carried on in public in a shed in Victoria's Thunderbird Park. The university museum also commissioned work from Bill Reid, whose mother was Haida and the daughter of Charles Gladstone, a noted carver. Reid was brought up as a Euro-Canadian and entered a career as a radio broadcaster, but studied jewelry making. As a young man he began to visit his mother's village and study the works of his grandfather and of his grandfather's uncle and great-uncle, Charles and Albert Edenshaw, great Haida carvers of the nineteenth century. The Edenshaws and Gladstone had worked in silver as well as carving slate. Reid used his goldsmithing craft to develop jewelry in the Haida style of his forebears, as well as joining Douglas Cranmer, a Kwakiutl, in carrying on the wood-carving art after Chief Martin's death in 1962. A gifted non-Indian artist, Bill Holm, collaborated with Reid and others in promoting appreciation of the living tradition of this magnificent art style. Holm has emphasized that the visual arts of the Northwest Coast were, for the most part, intended to be seen in motion in the dance dramas, and that the powerful flow of line in the carvings embodies the dancers' flow of movement; indeed, Holm says, the carver's actions are themselves a kind of ritualized movement akin to dance.

The most ambitious revival is that of the Gitksan, a Tsimshian group on the Skeena River at Hazelton, B.C. In the early 1950s, both Indian and non-Indian residents of the town fostered a revival of interest in the native arts in an attempt to improve the lot of the Indians, who were economically depressed and discriminated against. Heirloom objects were borrowed from the lineage leaders, money was raised, and in 1958 a museum, the Skeena Treasure House, was constructed. Crafts were produced and sold at this museum. Tourist interest and purchases of crafts amply confirmed the community's conviction that production and display of authentic native art could contribute significantly to the economy of the small town. The mayor obtained government grants to supplement what the museum and town could raise, and in 1970 a large park, called 'Ksan, was opened with not only a larger museum but replications of traditional Tsimshian houses and a school and workshop for carvers. Exhibitions of 'Ksan-trained artists' work tour art museums, demonstrating the creative power of the traditional style. 'Ksan stages dramatic performances, and its members give potlatches in its

feast house. Under the impetus of 'Ksan, the young Tsimshian have been interviewing and tape-recording the elderly in order to re-create the Gitksan tradition and understand it so thoroughly that they can use it as their people did in the past to express deeply felt beliefs and prayers. 'Ksan has become breathtaking proof that a renascence has come to the Northwest Coast Indian peoples.

SUMMARY

The Northwest Coast culture area conventionally includes the peoples of Oregon, Washington, British Columbia, and Southeast Alaska who have been dependent primarily upon salmon, marine fish, and sea mammals for subsistence, and who utilize the cedars and firs of the coastal rain forest for houses, canoes, and crafts. These peoples speak a variety of languages belonging to the Na-Dene, Wakashan, Salishan, and Penutian stocks, and the isolate Haida.

Early Holocene inhabitants of the Northwest Coast were less dependent on marine resources than were later people, probably because postglacial fluctuations in sea level did not allow the growth of extensive shellfish beds or the establishment of regular large-scale fish spawning runs. Once the sea level stabilized, around 3000 B.C., the basic Northwest Coast pattern of large, permanent winter villages in protected coves near shellfish beds, and summer camps at fishing stations and localities where berries or edible tubers and bulbs could be harvested, appeared and persisted to the mid-nineteenth century A.D.

Historic contacts with the Northwest Coast began in the mid-eighteenth century, although there were probably earlier contacts with nonliterate marine-oriented nations to the west along the Aleutians and northeasternmost Asia. Russian, Spanish, and English explorers documented the huge, handsomely decorated plank houses, the class stratification, the abundance of food stores, and the sophistication in dealing with strangers and traders characteristic of the Northwest Coast. During the first half of the nineteenth century, Russian and United States ships hunted, and to a lesser extent traded for, sea-otter pelts from the Northwest Coast to sell in China, and the Hudson's Bay Company established a series of trading posts offering imported goods and foods year-round. The northernmost peoples profited from supplying dried meat and potatoes to the Russian garrisons in Southeast Alaska. Euro-American settlement in southern British Columbia and in Washington and Oregon after 1846 opened new markets for native-produced foods, and in the second half of the nineteenth century, the Northwest Coast native nations became commercial salmon fishermen and loggers. Income from these enterprises allowed upper-class Northwest Coast families to retain their traditional leadership and ceremonies, but epidemic diseases decimated the populations and missionary antagonism to native rituals caused much friction.

Missionary and government prohibition and the economic Depression of the 1930s curtailed the great potlatch feasts, but they have been resumed since the economic situation ameliorated after World War II and legal prohibition was repealed. There has also been a revival of the carvers' art and increasing participation in the winter ceremonies, the means by which young people are recruited into the spiritual domain of their ancestral community. Population increase and a serious threat to local commercial fishing from well-capitalized foreign fleets have led many Northwest Coast Indians to seek employment in cities, turning many of the small reserves in southern British Columbia and Puget Sound into bedroom suburbs. Traditional sharing of resources and distribution of foods to the village by upper-class leaders continue even in these communities. Administration of band enterprises, schools, and social-welfare programs employ band members in the villages, strengthening the communities. Overall, the British Columbian and Alaskan Northwest Coast Indian nations, occupying rugged land of little value to Euro-Canadian colonists and highly skilled in surplus production of fish and timber, suffered less radical disruption of their indigenous life patterns than most Indian nations to the south.

RECOMMENDED READING

Codere, Helen. 1961 Kwakiutl. In E.H. Spicer (ed.). *Perspectives in American Indian Culture Change.* Chicago: University of Chicago Press, p. 431–516. A well-balanced, well written history.

Collins, June McCormick. 1974 *Valley of the Spirits.* Seattle: University of Washington Press. Fascinating section on Coast Salish beliefs as well as history and customs; now in paperback.

Fagan, Brian. 1991 *Ancient North America.* New York: W. W. Norton.

Gunther, Erna 1972. *Indian Life on the Northwest Coast of North America.* Chicago: University of Chicago Press. A detailed compendium of descriptions and illustrations of early contacts.

Holm, Bill. 1965 *Northwest Coast Indian Art.* Seattle: University of Washington Press. Holm does not write of "primitive" art: he is an experienced artist who masterfully analyzes a powerful art style that happens to be non-Western.

McIlwraith, T.F. 1948 *The Bella Coola Indians.* Toronto: University of Toronto Press. In two large volumes, McIlwraith records the life of the Bella Coola in the early 1920s, and particularly the winter ceremonials in which he participated. His sensitivity, respect, and enthusiasm give the volumes life.

Stewart, Hilary. 1977 *Indian Fishing.* Seattle: University of Washington Press. Extraordinary details, in line drawings and text, on every aspect of the impressive subsistence technology of the Northwest Coast Indians.

Suttles, Wayne, ed. 1990 *Handbook of North American Indians*, vol. 7, *Northwest Coast.* Washington, D.C.: Smithsonian Institution Press.

SOURCES FOR THE FIRST EDITION

Ackerman, Robert E. 1974 Post Pleistocene Cultural Adaptations on the Northern Northwest Coast. In S. Raymond and P. Schlederman (eds.). *International Conference on the Prehistory and Paleoecology of*

Western North American Arctic and Subarctic. Calgary: University of Calgary Archaeological Association, p. 1–20.

American Friends Service Committee. 1970 *Uncommon Controversy.* Seattle: University of Washington Press.

Barnard, Noel, ed. 1972 *Early Chinese Art and Its Possible Influence in the Pacific Basin.* New York: Intercultural Arts Press.

Barnett, Homer G. 1955 *The Coast Salish of British Columbia.* Eugene: University of Oregon Press.

Birket-Smith, Kaj. 1967, 1971 Studies in Circumpacific Culture Relations. *Kongelige Danske Videnskabernes Selskab Historisk-filosofiske Meddelelser* 42(3), 45(2).

Blackman, Margaret B., ed. 1977 Continuity and Change in Northwest Coast Ceremonialism. *Arctic Anthropology* 14(1).

Boas, Franz. 1966 *Kwakiutl Ethnography.* Chicago: University of Chicago Press.

Borden, Charles E. 1951 Facts and Problems of Northwest Coast Prehistory. *Anthropology in British Columbia* 2:35–52.

———1954 Some Aspects of Prehistoric Coastal-Interior Relations in the Pacific Northwest. *Anthropology in British Columbia* 4:26–32.

———1975 *Origins and Development of Early Northwest Coast Culture to About 3000 B.C.* Ottawa: National Museum of Man Mercury Series, Archaeological Survey of Canada, Paper No. 45.

Bushnell, John H. 1968 From American Indian to Indian American: The Changing Identity of the Hupa. *American Anthropologist* 70:1108–1116.

DeLaguna, Frederica. 1960 *The Story of a Tlingit Community.* Washington, D.C.: Smithsonian Institution, Bureau of American Ethnology, Bulletin 172.

———1963 Mungo Martin 1879–1962. *American Anthropologist* 65:894–896.

———1972 *Under Mount Saint Elias: The History and Culture of the Yakutat Tlingit.* Washington, D.C.: Smithsonian Contributions to Anthropology, 7.

Dewhirst, John. 1976 Coast Salish Summer Festivals: Rituals for Upgrading Social Identity. *Anthropologica* 18:231–273.

Donald, Leland, and Donald H. Mitchell. 1975 Some Correlates of Local Group Rank Among the Southern Kwakiutl. *Ethnology* 14:325–346.

Drucker, Philip. 1951 *The Northern and Central Nootkan Tribes.* Washington, D.C.: Smithsonian Institution, Bureau of American Ethnology, Bulletin 144.

———1958 *The Native Brotherhoods: Modern Intertribal Organizations on the Northwest Coast.* Washington, D.C.: Smithsonian Institution, Bureau of American Ethnology, Bulletin 168.

Drucker, Philip, and Robert F. Heizer. 1967 To Make My Name Good. Berkeley: University of California Press.

Duff, Wilson. 1962 The Upper Stalo Indians. *Anthropology in British Columbia,* Memoir 1.

———1963 Gitksan Totem-poles, 1952. *Anthropology in British Columbia* 3:21–30.

———1957 Prehistoric Stone Sculpture of the Fraser River and Gulf of Georgia. *Anthropology in British Columbia* 5:15–151.

———1975 *Images Stone B.C.* Saanichton, B.C.: Hancock House.

Faulk, Odie B. 1976 *The Modoc People.* Phoenix: Indian Tribal Series.

Fladmark, Knut R. 1976 *A Paleoecological Model for Northwest Coast Prehistory.* Ottawa: National Museum of Man Mercury Series, Archaeological Survey of Canada, Paper No. 43.

Garfield, Viola E. 1938 Tsimshian Clan and Society. *University of Washington Publications in Anthropology* 7:167–340.

Gibson, James R. 1976 *Imperial Russia in Frontier America.* New York: Oxford University Press.

———1978 Old Russia in the New World: Adversaries and Adversities in Russian America. In J.R. Gibson (ed.). *European Settlement and Development in North America.* Toronto: University of Toronto Press, pp. 46–65.

———1979 Personal communication, May 16, 1979.

Goldman, Irving. 1975 *The Mouth of Heaven.* New York: John Wiley.

Gunther, Erna. 1966 *Art in the Life of the Northwest Coast Indians.* Portland: Portland Art Museum.

Haeberlin, Hermann, and Erna Gunther. 1930 The Indians of Puget Sound. *University of Washington Publications in Anthropology* 4:1–84.

Hawthorn, H. B., C.S. Belshaw, and S.M. Jamieson. 1968 *The Indians of British Columbia.* Toronto: University of Toronto Press.

Heizer, Robert F., ed. 1978 *Handbook of North American Indians,* vol. 8. *California.* Washington, D.C.: Smithsonian Institution Press.

Hodge, Frederick Webb. 1910 *Handbook of American Indians.* Washington, D.C.: Smithsonian Institution, Bureau of American Ethnology, Bulletin 30.

Holm, Bill. 1972 *Crooked Beak of Heaven*. Seattle: University of Washington Press.

Holm, Bill, and William Reid. 1975 *Form and Freedom*. Houston: Rice University Institute for the Arts.

Jenness, Diamond. 1955 The Faith of a Coast Salish Indian. *Anthropology in British Columbia*, Memoir 3.

Kroeber, A.L. 1938 *Cultural and Natural Areas of Native North America*. Berkeley: University of California Press.

LaViolette, Forrest E. 1973 *The Struggle for Survival*. Toronto: University of Toronto Press.

Lewis, Claudia 1970. *Indian Families of the Northwest Coast*. Chicago: University of Chicago Press.

MacDonald, George F., ed. 1973 *Archaeological Survey of Canada Annual Review 1972*. Ottawa: National Museum of Man Mercury Series, Archaeological Survey of Canada, Paper No. 10.

———1977 *Archaeological Survey of Canada Annual Review 1975 and 1976*. Ottawa: National Museum of Man Mercury Series, Archaeological Survey of Canada, Paper No. 66.

MacDonald, George F., Charles E. Borden, Donald H. Mitchell, and William J. Folan. 1969 Current Archaeological Research on the Northwest Coast. *Northwest Anthropological Research Notes* 3:193–263.

Mooney, James. 1973 [1896] *The Ghost-Dance Religion and Wounded Knee*. New York: Dover Publications.

Mooney, Kathleen. 1976 Social Distance and Exchange: The Coast Salish Case. Ethnology 15:323–346.

———1976 Urban and Reserve Coast Salish Employment: A Test of Two Approaches to the Indian's Niche in North America. *Journal of Anthropological Research* 32:390–410.

———1978 The Effects of Rank and Wealth on Exchange Among the Coast Salish. *Ethnology* 17:391–406.

Nash, Philleo. 1966 [1937] The Place of Religious Revivalism in the Formation of the Intercultural Community on Klamath Reservation. In F. Eggan (ed.). *Social Anthropology of North American Tribes*. Chicago: University of Chicago Press, pp. 377–441.

National Museum of Man 1972 *'Ksan: Breath of Our Grandfathers*. Ottawa: National Museums of Canada.

Newton, Norman. 1973 *Fire in the Raven's Nest*. Toronto: New Press.

Oberg, Kalervo. 1973 *The Social Economy of the Tlingit Indians*. Seattle: University of Washington Press.

Olson, Ronald L. 1936 The Quinault Indians. *University of Washington Publications in Anthropology* 6:1–190.

Piddocke, Stuart. 1965 The Potlatch System of the Southern Kwakiutl: A New Perspective. *Southwestern Journal of Anthropology* 21:244–264.

Powell, Jay, and Vickie Jensen. 1976 *Quileute*. Seattle: University of Washington Press.

Ray, Verne F. 1938 Lower Chinook Ethnographic Notes. *University of Washington Publications in Anthropology* 7:29–165.

———1963 *Primitive Pragmatists: The Modoc Indians of Northern California*. Seattle: University of Washington Press.

Rohner, Ronald P., and Evelyn C. 1970 *The Kwakiutl Indians of British Columbia*. New York: Holt, Rinehart and Winston.

Ruby, Robert H., and John A. Brown. 1976 *Myron Eells and the Puget Sound Indians*. Seattle: Superior Publishing.

Sauter, John, and Bruce Johnson. 1974 *Tillamook Indians of the Oregon Coast*. Portland: Binfords & Mort.

Snyder, Sally. 1975 Quest for the Sacred in Northern Puget Sound: An Interpretation of Potlatch. *Ethnology* 14:149–161.

Smith, Harlan Ingersoll. 1907 *Archaeology of the Gulf of Georgia and Puget Sound*. Leiden: E.J. Brill.

Smyly, John, and Carolyn Smyly. 1973 *The Totem Poles of Skedans*. Seattle: University of Washington Press.

Spier, Leslie. 1930 Klamath Ethnography. *University of California Publications in American Archaeology and Ethnology* 30:1–338.

Spradley, James P. 1969 *Guests Never Leave Hungry: The Autobiography of James Sewid, a Kwakiutl Indian*. New Haven: Yale University Press.

Sprague, Roderick, ed. 1975 Current Research: Northwest. *American Antiquity* 40:477–479.

Stern, Theodore. 1965 *The Klamath Tribe*. Seattle: University of Washington Press.

Sutherland, Patricia D. 1977 Migration, Diffusion, and Local Development in Northern Northwest Coast Prehistory. Paper presented at the 1977 Calgary Conference on Diffusion and Migration.

Suttles, Wayne. 1951 The Early Diffusion of the Potato among the Coast Salish. *Southwestern Journal of Anthropology* 7:272–288.

———1958 Private Knowledge, Morality, and Social Classes among the Coast Salish. *American Anthropologist* 60:497–507.

———1960 Affinal Ties, Subsistence, and Prestige among Coast Salish. *American Anthropologist* 62:296–305.

———1968 Coping with Abundance: Subsistence on the Northwest Coast. In R.B. Lee and I. DeVore (eds.). *Man the Hunter.* Chicago: Aldine Publishing, pp. 56–68.

Swanton, John R. 1970 *Social Conditions, Beliefs, and Linguistic Relationship of the Tlingit Indians.* New York: Johnson Reprint

Vancouver Art Gallery. 1974 *Bill Reid: A Retrospective Exhibition.* Vancouver: Vancouver Art Gallery.

Voegelin, C.F., and F. M. Voegelin. 1964 *Languages of the World: Native America,* Fascicle 1. Bloomington: Indiana University, Anthropological Linguistics 6.

Waterman, T. T. 1920 The Whaling Equipment of the Makah Indians. *University of Washington Publications in Anthropology* 1:1–67.

———1973 *Notes on the Ethnology of the Indians of Puget Sound.* New York: Museum of the American Indian, Indian Notes and Monographs Miscellaneous Series, no. 69.

ADDITIONAL SOURCES FOR THE SECOND EDITION

Adams, John W. 1981 Recent Ethnology of the Northwest Coast. *Annual Review of Anthropology* 10:361–392.

Ambler, Marjane. 1990 *Breaking the Iron Bonds.* Lawrence: University Press of Kansas.

American Antiquity. "Current Research" through vol. 55(2) (April 1990).

Arima, Eugene Y. 1988 Notes on Nootkan Sea Mammal Hunting. *Arctic Anthropology* 25(1):16–27.

Barbeau, Marius, and William Beynon. 1987 *Tsimshian Narratives 2.* George F. MacDonald and John J. Cove (eds.). Ottawa: Canadian Museum of Civilization Mercury Series Directorate Paper No. 3.

Beckham, Stephen Dow, Kathryn Anne Toepel, and Rick Minor. 1984 *Native American Religious Practices and Uses in Western Oregon.* Eugene: University of Oregon Anthropological Papers, No. 31.

Blackman, Margaret B. 1982 *During My Time: Florence Edenshaw Davidson, A Haida Woman.* Seattle: University of Washington Press.

Boelscher, Marianne. 1989 *The Curtain Within: Haida Social and Mythical Discourse.* Vancouver: University of British Columbia Press.

Buckley, Thomas. 1982 Menstruation and the Power of Yurok Women: Methods in Cultural Reconstruction. *American Ethnologist* 9(1):47–60.

———1988 World Renewal. *Parabola* 13(2):82–91.

———1989 Suffering in the Cultural Construction of Others: Robert Spott and A. L. Kroeber. *California Indian Quarterly* 13(4):437–445.

Campbell, Lyle, and Marianne Mithun, eds. 1979 *The Languages of Native America.* Austin: University of Texas Press.

Carlson, Roy L., ed. 1982 *Indian Art Traditions of the Northwest Coast.* Burnaby: Archaeology Press, Simon Fraser University.

Cole, Douglas. 1985 *Captured Heritage.* Seattle: University of Washington Press.

Feest, Christian F., ed. 1987 *Indians and Europe.* Aachen: Edition Herodot, Rader Verlag.

Fitzhugh, William W., and Aron Crowell (eds.) 1988 *Crossroads of Continents.* Washington, D.C.: Smithsonian Institution Press.

Folan, William J. 1984 On the Diet of Early Northwest Coast Peoples. *Current Anthropology* 25(1):123–124.

Holm, Bill. 1983 *The Box of Daylight.* Seattle: University of Washington Press.

Huelsbeck, David R. 1988 Whaling in the Precontact Economy of the Central Northwest Coast. *Arctic Anthropology* 25(1):1–15.

Isaac, Barry L., ed. 1988 *Prehistoric Economies of the Pacific Northwest Coast.* Greenwich: JAI Press, Research in Economic Anthropology, Supplement 3.

Jopling, Carol F. 1989 *The Coppers of the Northwest Coast Indians: Their Origin, Development, and Possible Antecedents.* Philadelphia: American Philosophical Society, Transaction vol. 79, pt. 1.

Jorgensen, Joseph G., ed. 1984 *Native Americans and Energy Development II.* Boston: Anthropology Resource Center.

Kan, Sergei. 1986 The 19th-century Tlingit Potlatch: A New Perspective. *American Ethnologist* 13(2):191–212.

———1989 *Symbolic Immortality.* Washington, D.C.: Smithsonian Institution Press.

Kan, Sergei, and John W. Adams (eds.). 1987 Two Symposia on Northern North America, *Arctic Anthropology* 24(1).

Kenyon, Susan M. 1980 *The Kyuquot Way: A Study of a West Coast (Nootkan) Community.* Ottawa: National Museums of Canada, National Museum of

Man Mercury Series, Canadian Ethnology Service, Paper No. 61.

Knight, Rolf. 1978 *Indians At Work*. Vancouver: New Star Books.

Lazenby, Richard A., and Peter McCormack. 1985 Salmon and Malnutrition on the Northwest Coast. *Current Anthropology* 26(3):379–384.

Lévi–Strauss, Claude. 1982 *The Way of the Masks* (Trans. S. Modelski). Seattle: University of Washington Press.

Miller, Jay, and Carol M. Eastman. 1984 *The Tsimshian and Their Neighbors of the North Pacific Coast*. Seattle: University of Washington Press.

Mitchell, Donald. 1984 Predatory Warfare, Social Status, and the North Pacific Slave Trade *Ethnology* 23(1):39–48.

Moss, Madonna L., Jon M. Erlandson, and Robert Stuckenrath. 1989 The Antiquity of Tlingit Settlement on Admiralty Island, Southeast Alaska. *American Antiquity* 54(3):534–543.

O'Brien, Sharon. 1989 *American Indian Tribal Governments*. Norman: University of Oklahoma Press.

Prucha, Francis Paul. 1984 *The Great Father*. Lincoln: University of Nebraska Press.

Ruby, Robert H., and John A. Brown. 1986 *A Guide to the Indian Tribes of the Pacific Northwest*. Norman: University of Oklahoma Press.

Seguin, Margaret. 1985 *Interpretive Contexts for Traditional and Current Tsimshian Feasts*. Ottawa: National Museums of Canada, National Museum of Man Mercury Series, Canadian Ethnology Service, No. 98.

Seguin, Margaret, ed. 1984 *The Tsimshian: Images of the Past: Views for the Present*. Vancouver: University of British Columbia Press.

Snipp, C. Matthew. 1989 *American Indians: The First of This Land*. New York: Russell Sage Foundation.

Stearns, Mary Lee. 1981 *Haida Culture in Custody*. Seattle: University of Washington Press.

Suttles, Wayne, ed. 1990 *Handbook of North American Indians*, vol. 7, *Northwest Coast*. Washington, D.C.: Smithsonian Institution Press.

Tollefson, Kenneth D. 1984 Tlingit Acculturation: An Institutional Perspective. *Ethnology* 23(3):229–247.

———1987 The Snoqualmie: A Puget Sound Chiefdom. *Ethnology* 26(2):121–136.

———1989 Political Organization of the Duwamish. *Ethnology* 28(2):135–149.

Tooker, Elisabeth, ed. 1983 *The Development of Political Organization in Native North America*. Washington, D.C.: American Ethnological Society.

Zucker, Jeff, Kay Hummel, and Bob Høgfos. 1983 *Oregon Indians*. Portland: Western Imprints, the Press of the Oregon Historical Society.

THE ARCTIC AND SUBARCTIC

"The Arctic" conjures a picture of bleak, endless ice and snow. In reality, although for some eight months of the year most of the Arctic is snow-covered and long expanses of its seas frozen, winds here expose black rock ridges, there pile up drifts or pack ice into towering fantastic shapes, rendering the landscape varied if chilling. This landscape comes alive in the brief summer under a never-setting sun. Tundra becomes a carpet of mosses and small flowers, blue water gleams in winding stream channels and wide marshes. The Arctic is not an easy land to move about in, but like the High Plains it offers the beauty of great spaces, of light, and of the sculptures of wind, rock, and frost.

The broad area generally included in "the Arctic"—most of Alaska, northern Canada, and Greenland—is not all tundra. Central Alaska is the terminus of the western North American mountain chain, and its Brooks Range raises jagged snowy peaks to form the southern boundary of the North Alaskan tundra coastal plain. A large portion of Alaska and Canada is covered by the coniferous forests of the taiga. Greenland is covered by a tremendous glacier except along its southern coasts. Human ecology in the Arctic adapts to several environments—the seacoast, the tundra, river deltas, taiga forests, and mountain passes.

Overall, there has been one broad division of the human inhabitants. Those who live along the coast are the Inuit, commonly called Eskimo; those who live entirely inland, in the forest, are considered Indian. The division follows both linguistic and ecological boundaries, with the Inuit and the distantly related Aleuts speaking Eskimo-Aleut languages and relying upon sea animals for subsistence, and the Indians speaking Athabascan or Algonkian languages and relying upon forest game and fresh-water fish. It has been traditional to sharply distinguish the Inuit from the Indians, but the common problems of these high-latitude hunters are reason to treat them as variants of a general adaptation to a land of dangerous cold where the capture of other animals is the only mode of human survival.

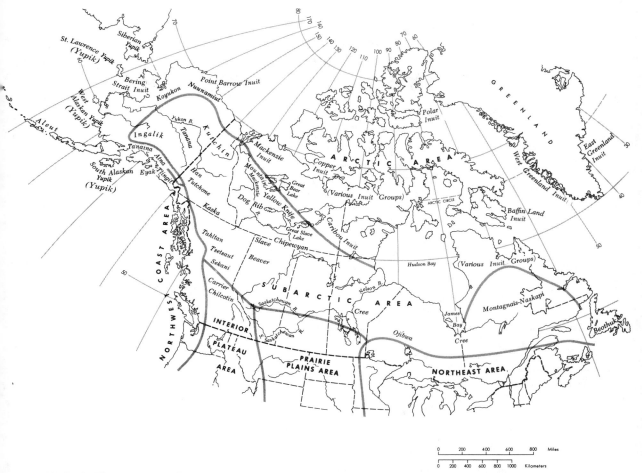

MAP 10 The Arctic and Subarctic

Divisions within the Eskimo-Aleut speakers are, from west to east, the Western and the Eastern Aleuts, occupying the chain of active volcanic islands in the Pacific between Alaska and Kamchatka in Asia; the several dialect groups of Western Eskimoan, termed Yupik, which comprise three distinct dialects or languages in easternmost Siberia, General Central Yupik (including local dialects in Hooper Bay and Nunivak Island) in southwestern Alaska, Central Alaskan Yupik in the interior, and Pacific Yupik with two dialects, Koniag and Chugach, south of the Alaska Peninsula; and the Eastern Eskimoans, or Inupiaq, whose language is spoken with surprisingly small dialect

differentiation from central western Alaska (Norton Sound) through northern Alaska, across northernmost Canada, to and in Greenland. The West Greenlandic dialect of Inupiaq is now the official language of Kalaallit Nunaat, formerly known by its Danish name Greenland; Danish writers frequently call the official language "Greenlandic." In eastern Canada, the language of the Inuit is usually called Inuktitut, although professional linguists use Inupiaq for Canadian as well as Alaskan dialects. Eskimo-Aleut may be distantly related to Chukchi, the language of the principal modern inhabitants of the Chukchi Peninsula of northeasternmost Siberia, closest to America, although

THE ARCTIC AND SUBARCTIC
CHRONOLOGY

1980 Home Rule for Greenland (1979)
Nishnawbe-Aski Declaration (1977)
James Bay Final Agreement
Dene Declaration (1975)
Alaska Native Claims Settlement Act

1970 Organization of Alaskan and Canadian native groups to press claims, foster community development

1960 Shift from bush camps to villages with schools
Greenland becomes Danish county

1950 Defense installations employ Inuit and Indians

1940 World War II invasion of Aleutians (1942)
Tuberculosis reaches epidemic rate
Economic Depression

1930

1920 Shift to greater integration into market economy

1900 Alaska-Yukon Gold Rush (1898)
Protestant missionary impact in Alaska

1870 Canada takes over Rupert's Land from Hudson's Bay Co.
End of Russian jurisdiction (1867)

1850 United States whalers, Hudson's Bay Co. in Yukon, Alaska
Severe decline of large game and beaver in eastern Subarctic

1800 Russian-American Co. fur trade established in Aleutians

1750 Bering expedition discovers Aleutians, Alaska, stimulates Russian conquest of Aleuts
Greenland colonized by Denmark

1700 Hudson's Bay Company intensifies eastern Subarctic fur trade

1650 Fur trade to Siberian Chukchi draws Alaskan Inuit into Russian trade

1600
1500 Newfoundland cod fishery begins fur trade with Montagnais

1400
1300
1200

1000 Norse contacts with Labrador, settlements in southern Greenland
Emergence and spread eastward of Thule Inuit
Dispersion of Athabascans from east-central Alaska

500

AD
BC Ipiutak town with Siberian contacts, western Alaska; possibly Athabascan occupation in upper Mackenzie

500
1000 Dorset cultural tradition begins, eastern Arctic
Norton cultural tradition begins, coastal western Alaska
Arctic Small Tool Tradition retreats from extreme north, colonizes Canadian tundra

2000 Arctic Small Tool Tradition spreads from Alaska to Greenland

4000 Northern Archaic spreads northwest into central Alaska
Stabilization of sea level, retreat of glacier from central Canada; Shield Archaic appears

6000
8000 Paleo-Indians in eastern Canada, Siberian-type hunter-fishermen in Alaska, Aleutians

the proximity of the nations and their centuries-long trade may account for some similarities in languages. Eskimo-Aleut is not apparently related to any American Indian language to the south.

Athabascan speakers occupy the interior of northwestern North America. Eyak in southernmost central Alaska was an independent language distantly related to Athabascan. Roughly from west to east, Northern Athabascan includes: Ingalik, Holikachuk, Kolchan, and Tanaina in central western Alaska; Ahtna, Tanacross and Tanana (not to be confused with the Tanaina), Koyukon, Han, and Tutchone of interior Alaska, east of the preceding; Kutchin (Loucheux) in the northern sector of the Alaska-Yukon boundary region; Tahltan, Tagish, and Kaska of the British Columbia-Yukon boundary region; Chilcotin, Babine, Carrier of interior British Columbia; Sekani in the mountains just north of the preceding two, and the related Beaver in the lower land of northern Alberta to the east; Dogrib, Hare, and Bearlake (Satudene) around Great Bear Lake in the northern sector of the Mackenzie interior; Slavey and Chipewyan (including groups often distinguished as the Yellowknives) around Great Slave Lake in the southern Mackenzie region and in northwestern Saskatchewan; and Sarsi, historically a Plains border people allied with the Blackfoot.

In their own languages, Athabascan speakers refer to themselves by variants of the word Dene or (phonetically) Dinneh or Dené zu, "people" in the sense of "our people." Most of the "tribal" names above are localities, for example the Tanana are Dene on the Tanan River. In some cases, the people prefer a name more common in local use: Ingalik are the Deg Hit'an, since "Ingalik" is merely Yupik for "Indian"; Tanana and Kutchin (Loucheux) use Dineh su (Gwich'in is a more phonetic spelling of Kutchin); Carrier use Dakelne ("Indians"), while Carrier on the Bulkey River are referred to by their neighbor Gitksan Tsimshian as Hagwilget; Beaver are Dunne-za; Dogrib use Done, their pronunciation of Dene; Hare use Ká-sho-gotine, "willow people" in their own lan-

guage; Bearlake use Sahtú-gotine (Satudene); Slavey are Dené Thá; and Chipewyan use Dene. "Koyukon" is an amalgamation of Koyukuk and Yukon Rivers, to cover the Dene in the basins of these watercourses. In the country, there are dozens of local or "band" names. The contemporary political term Dene Nation to cover the great expanse of contiguous Northern Athabascan language groups is closer to the real situation than any anthropologists' or governmental condensation of local terms into a short list of "tribes" or "bands."

On the great shield of eastern Canada, so heavily scoured by Pleistocene glaciers, are the northern Algonkians: the Cree of the forests of Saskatchewan, Manitoba, Ontario, and Quebec, and the related Montagnais and Naskapi (Innu) of Labrador; and the northern Ojibwa (Anishnabai or Anishsinabe) of Manitoba and Ontario, an extension of the Ojibwa whose homeland appears to have been the northern shore of Lake Superior. Like the Dene to the west, the Northern Algonkians live under many locality names.

The three language families of northernmost North America thus broadly coincide with three geographical zones: the Inuit in the true Arctic of icebound coasts; the Athabascans in the western taiga, or boreal forest, which was relatively less affected by continental glaciation and is drained by several major rivers; and the Algonkians in the severely glaciated eastern forest, where drainage has had minimum time to develop and is consequently poor, with a multitude of lakes and short, rapid streams. Neat as this threefold division of language families and geography is, the real division is twofold, between the Inuit, who are coast dwellers exploiting sea mammals, and the Indians—Athabascan and Algonkian—who live within the forests on fish and land game.

SECTION 1: PREHISTORY

The probability that the majority of American Indians are descendants of late Pleistocene and early Holocene migrants from the Beringia region of the Pleistocene Northern Continent has enticed a number of archaeologists to search for evidence of these migrants in northwestern America. Because a portion of Alaska was never glaciated (the center of late Pleistocene American glaciation was far to the east, in Quebec), chances that early occupation sites have been undisturbed seem good. However, the forest cover over so much of Alaska and the sheer size of the territory to be searched reduce the likelihood of finding sites. Only one locality, Bluefish Caves in the northern Yukon, has yielded artifacts from the Pleistocene epoch. At the beginning of the Holocene era, about 8000 B.C., Alaska was inhabited by hunter-fishermen whose stone-tool technology was essentially the same as that of contemporary eastern-Siberian hunter-fishermen. Sites of these peoples appear to be small, temporary camps. On the Aleutian Islands, on the other hand, remains of oval houses 5 to 6 meters (16 to 20 feet) long have been found clustered in a village overlooking the beach. The floors of the houses were cut into the earth to form a shallow pit, and a dome of whalebone and driftwood covered with sod was built over this. Inside the houses were carved-stone bowls and lamps, the latter presumably burning oil rendered from seal blubber. One house was presided over by a carved-stone face similar to the images of deity in historic Aleut homes. The village site has been radiocarbon-dated to 6500 B.C., but its excavators believe such well-established villages may go back to the last retreat of the glaciers in the region, some two thousand years earlier.

The contrast between the relatively large early Aleutian Island villages, with their broad range of tools and furnishings, and the small-camp sites in interior Alaska suggest that the late-Pleistocene inhabitants of Beringia specialized in harvesting the resources of the North Pacific and had little interest in tundra or forest game. Most of the sites of these late-Pleistocene peoples would have been destroyed as the postglacial rise in sea level crept over the ancient seacoasts; the Aleutian village on

a high bluff is an exception. The Aleutian village subsisted principally on whales and the large Steller's sea lion, with seal, sea otter, migratory waterfowl, and fish as supplementary foods. Other communities in other districts along the long North Pacific coast, once unbroken from Siberia into Alaska, may have preferred other sea mammals, perhaps locally more abundant. The basic adaptation was maritime, and included the use of boats.

These North Pacific maritime hunters of the early Holocene era were basically late Northern Continent Upper Paleolithic peoples, sharing the technology and dwelling form common in what is now Siberia. Other early Holocene humans in Alaska and northwestern Canada seem to be related to interior North American Fluted Tradition and Archaic peoples. A number of fluted projectile points or blades have been found in Alaska and the Yukon, but seldom in deep, well-stratified, and carefully excavated sites that would permit reasonably secure dating. Instead, the blades have usually lain on or near the surface on ridges or knolls where the slowness of soil formation under Arctic weather conditions has left very little earth matrix. An exception is a cave in northeastern British Columbia with a fluted knife blade in a lower stratum dated to 8000 B.C. Whether some fluted blades are earlier in Alaska than in temperate regions of North America, or instead all represent northward migrations of temperate-latitude American hunters as the Holocene warming trend caused Plains grasslands and parkland borders to shift northward, cannot be determined. Possibly, some Alaska fluted blades come from early migrants moving south, and others from northward movements several millennia later.

A technological tradition of manufacturing tools with tiny stone blades appears in early Holocene Alaska and seems to continue until perhaps the first millennium B.C. in some regions, sometimes associated with Archaic-style blades or projectile points and sometimes without such different artifacts. There seems to be a northern Archaic cultural pattern contemporaneous with the Archaic farther south in America. This northern pattern used notched-base, relatively heavy projectile points and comparatively heavy, crudely flaked knives, choppers and scrapers, but we cannot distinguish between local technological development in adaptation to environmental resources of the interior, spread of technology under the stimulus of ecological shifts associated with the warming trend, or actual migrations.

As the Holocene climatic trend reached its climax in the third millennium B.C., the sea level stabilized, making possible more intensive human exploitation of coastal resources, and large areas of what is now interior forest were grasslands favorable to bison grazing. (In fact, the forest has in this century invaded much former grassland in Canada's Northwest Territories, grassland that was maintained for bison by Indians firing the districts regularly. Modern efforts to stamp out prairie and forest fires have allowed the browse-poor forests to colonize the grasslands, starving out the bison and robbing the Indians of the best game they formerly hunted.) After about 4500 B.C., regional traditions came to be established in the various areas: sea-mammal hunting continued along the coasts, salmon fishing became a resource base along rivers, musk ox and caribou received attention on the tundra and northern-forest border, and bison were hunted in the southeastern portion of the interior northwest. Freeing Hudson Bay from its glacial cover, gradually completed in this millennium, slowly opened central-northern Canada for habitation.

Around 2000 B.C., a distinctive set of artifacts termed the Arctic Small Tool Tradition was developed, possibly on the tundra of northeastern Siberia, and rapidly spread eastward along the Alaskan and Canadian tundra into Greenland. The bearers of these distinctive tools and weapons may well have been ancestral to the Inuit. Caribou and musk oxen were favored game for them, and they also took seal and walrus, polar bear, birds, and, where available, salmon and trout. At first, their houses in Alaska were 4 meters (13 feet) square, built in

an excavation as much as 1/2 meter (1 1/2 feet) deep, and probably covered with sod. Like later Inuit houses, but unlike the early Aleutian houses entered through the roof, the Arctic Small Tool Tradition houses had a sloping passageway entering the structure at its floor. This sloping shaft provided ventilation while conserving the house's heat under the roof and above the passage mouth. The houses were heated, and food cooked, by fires rather than oil lamps (fuel was driftwood or fatty animal bone), which contrasts with later Inuit practice and suggests that sea mammals, from which oil is extracted, were not as available to the Arctic Small Tool Tradition as to later Inuit. In eastern Canada and Greenland, dwellings seem to have been tents, perhaps of a double thickness of caribou or musk-ox hide in the winter, secured on the ground by stones. Like historic Sami (Lapp) tent homes in northernmost Scandinavia, the eastern Arctic Small Tool Tradition dwellings had a central strip that included a hearth, where food was prepared, and flanking sleeping-sitting sections covered with hides. Archaeologist Moreau Maxwell notes that fuel must have been scarce so far north, and without Inuit oil lamps, the long months of winter darkness must have been bleak for these pioneer northerners. Taking advantage of the climatic thermal maximum, the eastern Arctic Small Tool Tradition peoples spread as far north as to within 700 kilometers (434 miles) of the North Pole.

The slowly cooling climate following the thermal maximum included a few centuries of sharper cold beginning in 1600 B.C. During these centuries the Arctic Small Tool Tradition peoples in the extreme north retreated southward, and others of the same tradition moved westward into the central Canadian Barren Grounds (tundra), and into the Brooks Range of northern Alaska. These movements probably reflect shifts in the ranges of the caribou herds. After the end of the colder period, about 1150 B.C., many sites in the eastern Arctic show a brief hiatus of occupation, although some, in eastern Canada, exhibit continuity into the succeeding cultural phase, which is termed Dorset.

Dorset people occupied the tundra and coasts of the eastern half of northernmost North America for nearly two millennia, about 500 B.C. to A.D. 1100. The Dorset cultural pattern was basically Inuit, with seal and other sea mammals important not only for meat and hides (the hides were used for covering boat frames as well as for tents and clothing), but also for the rendered oil burned in stone lamps for heat and cooking. Dorset people carved bone, ivory, and wood into implements and into masks and small figurines, showing us that they dressed in parka outfits like the historic Inuit. Like the historic Inuit of central Canada, Dorset people built domed shelters of snow blocks ("igloos"—though Inuit *iglu* simply means "house") in regions where driftwood or whalebone was scarce and sod poor. The snow-block house follows the form of conventional Inuit winter homes but can be built quickly anywhere during the winter. This convenience permitted hunters to range farther from their winter villages than they might had they been forced to bring hide tents with them or to return to sleep in the villages. Dorset people differed from the historic Inuit in that they do not seem to have used dogs to pull sleds, although they did have sleds that they apparently pulled themselves; they used harpoons and javelins but not bow and arrow (in spite of the apparent use of this weapon by the preceding Arctic Small Tool Tradition); and their seal hunting technology was not—as might be guessed—as finely specialized as that of their successors. Dorset represents the middle stage in the human colonization of the central and eastern Arctic coast and tundra, initiated by the Arctic Small Tool Tradition and culminating in the Thule Inuit that followed Dorset.

To the west, sea-mammal hunting, including whales and porpoises as well as seals, sea lions, and sea otters, continued to be a focus of human activity on the Aleutians and the coasts of southern and western Alaska. About 3000 B.C., it became increasingly common to manufacture knives and projectile points from slate, sawing and grinding rather than chipping the stone. Archaeologists have debated for decades whether the switch from flaked-stone artifacts to ground slate in northern maritime cultures around both the Pacific and the Atlantic during this time period indicates the diffusion of a new technology or its independent discovery in the widely separated areas. The coincidence of its first appearance more or less within a millennium, and the obvious attraction of this new technology more efficient in slicing fish and sea-mammal flesh, would suggest that an initial development in one maritime region was followed by spread of the knowledge of the technology and then local development of regional styles and variants. If this interpretation is correct, it implies a series of contacts between peoples across the entire Arctic in the third millennium B.C. This is not difficult to believe, considering the unquestioned movement of the Arctic Small Tool Tradition across the American Arctic, the later comparable movement of the Thule Inuit, and the historic trading networks.

While the Aleutian Islanders appear to have maintained a stable cultural adaptation to their unusually rich habitat, Alaskan mainland peoples were working to improve their techniques for exploiting regional resources, visible in sites of the first millennium B.C. In the south and west, salmon were speared in weirs or from scaffolds as they moved up river mouths, providing in dried form a storable staple that supplemented sea-mammal meat and ocean fish such as cod and halibut. Caribou were less numerous but worth the effort of hunting for their skins, preferable for winter clothing. Houses and some stone artifacts continued the types of the western Arctic Small Tool Tradition. One site contained, in addition to dwellings, a large building 12 by 8 meters (40 by 26 feet) that was probably used as a community hall and a workshop for the men of the village. An innovation, in addition to slate working, was pottery: flat-bottomed rounded or nearly straight-sided pots finished by being paddled with a grooved beater. The pottery was not very strong, the paste liberally tempered with fibers that burned out in firing, leaving the wall of the vessel riddled with air spaces. It is assumed that knowledge of pottery came across the North Pacific from Siberia, but it seems odd that it took eight thousand years for this knowledge to pass from the north-temperate latitude of the Asian Pacific coast to western Alaska, and that when it did arrive it had become more crude than the early Holocene pottery of northeastern Asia. If the Alaskans of this period carved for decoration or to produce religious images, they must have done so in perishable material that has not survived. They did inaugurate the custom of wearing highly polished plugs of stone or bone, called labrets, in holes pierced for the purpose in their lower lip or cheeks, a custom that continued among the historic Inuit and on the Northwest Coast. Continuities between the first-millennium B.C. cultures, termed Norton Tradition (after finds around Norton Sound), and later coastal western Alaska cultures including historic Inupiat suggest Norton may be ancestral to Inupiat.

At Bering Strait, seals, walruses, and whales were the dominant subsistence choices of the people. Concentration upon these animals stimulated a great deal of technological invention, perfecting the marvelously light, maneuverable kayak and the more substantial umiak boats, toggling harpoons that exacerbate wounds while attaching the prey to the hunter by a rope, the efficient broad ulu knife with its handle above rather than tangential to the blade, and many other artifacts and techniques. The success of this inventive cultural tradition, fed by the abundance of sea mammals in the North Pacific, is attested to by the large villages appearing by the early first millennium A.D. At one, Ipiutak on Point Hope, Alaska, several hundred substantial houses were arranged in long rows. A wealth of sophisticated carvings in walrus and whale ivory and in caribou antler was found in the site, frequently in graves. Not only local animals but also fantastic or highly stylized creatures were depicted, odd forms, and purely ornamental chains. The dynamic, curvilinear style and the placement of animals in compositions strongly suggest the Ipiutak people were in contact with

Siberians familiar with the great art of nomadic, pastoral Scythians of Central Asia, whose conquests in the first millennium B.C. stretched from China to eastern Europe. This is rendered more probable by the fact that sites of the Bering Strait cultural pattern of the period around the time of Christ are more common on the Siberian than on the American side of the strait. Proof of at least indirect contact with major powers of Asia came in the discovery of a fragment of smelted iron at Ipiutak.

By A.D. 1000, Bering Strait residents, who by now were surely Inupiat, had achieved a highly sophisticated adaptation to the Arctic seacoast. Crews of men in large umiaks pursued whales swimming in narrow channels during their spring and fall migrations; in winter, seals were speared at their breathing holes in the coastal ice; in summer, fish were trapped and caribou could be hunted. Houses were efficiently engineered, the down-sloping entrance tunnel ending lower than the floor to prevent drafts of cold air, the bedding laid upon raised platforms closer to the warmed air caught under the domed roof. Sleds for transporting catches or household goods were sturdier and better designed, although there is no evidence that dogs were yet harnessed to them. Heating-cooking lamps could be made of baked clay as well as of stone, and pottery tempered with stone grit rather than fiber was common, though still coarse and tending to crumble. Caribou-skin clothing consisting of parka, trousers, boots, and mittens must have been sewn for millennia, since Upper Paleolithic Siberian figurines wear such outfits, but in the first millennium A.D., Inupiat women were keeping their bone and ivory sewing needles and awls in beautifully polished and decorated cylindrical bone containers. The finish and ornaments of harpoon heads, bone knives, and other implements show deep appreciation of fine craftsmanship.

Thule is the name applied to this climax phase of late-prehistoric Inuit. (The Greeks called the northernmost land Thule; Greek "Thule," however, was northwestern Europe.) For reasons that are not entirely clear, but probably are related to a somewhat warmer climate at the close of the first millennium A.D., Thule Inuit culture spread very rapidly, south to southwestern Alaska and north and east along the Arctic coast all the way to and around Greenland. Its path was largely that of the Arctic Small Tool Tradition three millennia earlier. One hypothesis is that the warmer climate melted and broke up the sea ice more completely in late spring, causing a later autumn coalescence of ice and resulting in fewer narrow channels hemming in the whales during migration. According to this hypothesis, the Inuit adapted their whaling techniques to the pursuit of the animals in the open sea, using floats to buoy the dead prey and several umiaks to tow it to the village shore. (Aleutian Islanders, less dependent upon whales, paddled home and prayed that the kills be beached by the waves, rather than suffering the arduous labor of towing the whales.) Freed thus from having to live close to the localities where wind and current developed narrow channels, the Thule Inuit moved out from their ancestral districts and followed the whales to the animals' summer feeding grounds in the Arctic Ocean. The use of natural traps to corner whales was not abandoned, but it was no longer the prime technique. The hypothesis that changes in ice formation with concomitant changes in sea-mammal migrations led the Alaskan Thule eastward along the Arctic Coast seems to sensibly explain Thule migration as far east as Amundsen Gulf in the central Northwest Territories. It doesn't explain why they would have persevered eastward across the hazardous jagged ice pack that faced them all year in Amundsen Gulf. Archaeologist Robert McGhee suggests they crossed, or detoured hundreds of kilometers around, this formidable obstacle in order to reach sources of iron in the eastern Arctic: meteoritic iron in Cape York in northwestern Greenland, and iron traded by Greenlandic Norse colonists.

When Thule met other Inuit in Alaska south of the Bering Strait, or the eastern Canadian and Greenland Dorset, Thule technology apparently manifested its superiority and was quickly adopted by the contacted peoples. This technology included regular use of metal blades: like the Northwest Coast nations, Thule Inuit hammered both iron and copper to fit their needs, although as in the Northwest Coast, they do not seem to have smelted iron from rock ore. The relatively small amount of metal they wanted for cutting blades was apparently obtained from combinations of Asian or Norse trade and American copper and meteoritic iron deposits in both the western and eastern Arctic. Thule hunting techniques included trips several days long by dogsled, in contrast to the Dorset restriction to day treks from the family shelter and limitation on load to what a man could pull on a sled; dog teams gave Thule speed, range, and increased capacity for hauling meat home. The archaeological record shows the replacement of Dorset by Thule during the twelfth century A.D., but very little evidence of genocide, such as massacres or destroyed houses. So it seems likely that the Thule migrants' culture, even their western Alaskan language, was accepted by the natives of the lands into which Thule people moved, and that modern Inuit are descended from mixed groups of Thule and natives who, after all, were, like Thule, the inheritors of an Arctic Small Tool Tradition base. At the time of modern European contact, by Britain in the late sixteenth century and Russia in the eighteenth, Thule Inuit formed a continuous band from northwestern Alaska to southeastern Labrador and onto Greenland.

Contrasting with the Inuit, whose history is one of adaptation to the Arctic seacoast and adjacent tundra, are the Indians of the boreal forest and forest-tundra border. In eastern Canada, their history began with the Shield Archaic about 5000 B.C. and continued with what are probably ancestral Algonkians, until by A.D. 1500 the several northern Algonkian peoples formed a continuous bloc from the Labrador tundra to Manitoba. This history has been described in Chapter 5, since from at least the Late Woodland period the Subarctic Algonkians have been linked by trade with the Canadian Maritimes and St. Lawrence–Great Lakes regions. The

Athabascans (Dene) of the western Subarctic, the other ethnic bloc of the Subarctic, probably entered Alaska from Siberia in the early Holocene era. Presumably these ancestral Athabascans occupied some of the camps that yielded artifacts similar to contemporary eastern Siberian assemblages. Considerable use of tiny stone flakes—"microblades"—set along a groove in a bone, antler, or wood handle to form a cutting edge, characterizes the early Holocene era of northwestern America. People with this Northwest Microblade Tradition slowly spread eastward through the western Subarctic, reaching southern Yukon by 4000 B.C. and the Mackenzie Basin by 2500 B.C. Northwest Microblade techniques and implements are recognizably different from the Arctic Small Tool Tradition spreading through the High Arctic in the late third millennium B.C., although Arctic Small Tool might have developed from the same terminal Pleistocene technology from which Northwest Microblade is derived. Around 2000 B.C., the Arctic Small Tool and Northwest Microblade Traditions show a distribution that matches historic Inuit, for Arctic Small Tool, and Dene, for Northwest Microblade, although the distributions may reflect contrasting ecological zone adaptations rather than, or as much as, ethnic differences; archaeology cannot determine whether ancestral Inuit and Dene should be premised.

During the climatic thermal maximum, about 4500 B.C. to about 2500 B.C., a Northern Archaic cultural pattern with artifacts similar to those of interior temperate America spread as far north as north-central Alaska (to the Brooks Range and the Kobuk River, which empties into the ocean just north of Bering Strait). Northern Plains Archaic also spread north in this period, as far as Great Slave Lake's northeastern end, in the southern Northwest Territories. The latter probably were hunting bison, the former caribou. The return of a colder climate brought Arctic Small Tool Tradition, probably Inuit, into these northern borders in Alaska as tundra encroached upon forest, and even down to Great Slave Lake, where artifacts from the period of about 1400 B.C. to 800 B.C. are best classified as variants of Arctic Small Tool types. Non-Inuit, and therefore probably Indian, artifact styles reappear at Great Slave Lake in small numbers about 800 B.C., and by 200 B.C. dominate archaeological assemblages in the region. A major volcanic explosion in the Southwest Yukon at A.D. 750 may have dispersed the Dene in that region, some ending up on the Pacific coast but most remaining within the western boreal forest. The Apacheans would have left the eastern resettlement of Athabascans, perhaps from Alberta, a few centuries later. Athabascan prehistory is really not well documented until its final millennium, a situation in part due to all apparent Athabascan sites being small and often no more than a handful of stone artifacts and chipping debris at a riverside camp or a ridge-top lookout, and in part due to a readiness general among Athabascans to take over useful foreign tools and ideas. As more archaeology is carried out in the huge expanse of Subarctic forests, regional diversity is increasingly recognized, yet the usually poor preservation of any but stone artifacts until the late prehistoric period precludes tying early occupations to historic groups.

The prehistoric record for the Inupiat (Alaskan Inupiaq speakers) and Inuit, the several Yupik groups, and the Aleuts is much fuller than for the Subarctic Indians because the coastal populations have been considerably denser than those in the forests; or perhaps more accurate, because the populations of sea mammals available on the North Pacific coasts and in the Arctic Ocean have been considerably denser than the populations of caribou, moose, and lesser game in the continental interiors. Coastal sites are usually larger and richer in artifacts than interior sites, and on the Arctic coast have the additional advantage of permafrost, which keeps all the debris and other remains of human occupations in cold storage, preserving normally perishable items such as clothing and other hide products. (The ancient garbage from sites in the permafrost still smells like garbage!) Coastal peoples built relatively substantial houses, the ruins of which are not difficult to locate, while the interior Indians used hide-covered pole-frame houses, tents, and lean-tos which leave little or no trace. The preponderance of studies on the coastal Inuit and their ancestors or predecessors creates the impression that the forest Indians have been a minor, literally backwoods feature of the northernmost lands of America. It must be emphasized that although the sea-oriented cultural pattern of the Inuit and their linguistic relatives on the North Pacific coasts supported far larger populations than the tundra or forests, the interior Indians nevertheless colonized and maintained for seven thousand or more years populations throughout the Subarctic interior, a vast area even more challenging to human survival than the Arctic coasts.

SECTION 2: THE ALEUTS

Archaeological remains indicate a probable colonization of at least the eastern Aleutian Islands from the end of the Pleistocene epoch, and a demonstrable continuity of occupation on the larger eastern islands closer to the Alaskan mainland from at least about 2500 B.C. That these eastern islanders were actually Aleuts, direct ancestors of the historic inhabitants and speakers of the Aleut language, cannot be proven by archaeological evidence but seems likely. As population increased in the eastern islands, colonies moved westward, until by 750 B.C. there were human settlements throughout the Aleutian chain. It seems likely that an early Holocene population, represented by a single excavated site on an eastern island, may have been non-Aleut, and that this population was both pushed westward along the island chain and gradually absorbed by the Aleuts.

The Aleut Cultural Pattern

The rich resources of the island coasts and Aleut expertise in utilizing them allowed a population estimated at sixteen thousand persons at the time of European contact in the mid-eighteenth century. Primary to the resources enjoyed by the Aleuts are the abundant tiny plants and animals living in the North Pacific. Fish, birds, and sea mammals feed upon these, either directly or indirectly as carnivores. The rocky islands and islets of the Aleutians and the Alaska Peninsula serve as breeding grounds for sea lions, seals, walruses, and birds. Whales breed farther south, but migrate annually to the North Pacific and Arctic for summer grazing. Since the Japanese Current keeps the Alaska Peninsula and the Aleutians relatively warm, although it causes storms and fog, several varieties of edible shellfish live on the shores and can be harvested even in winter, because no pack ice forms. Those Aleuts who live on the end of the Alaska Peninsula can also hunt caribou and brown bear, but there is no large land game in the islands themselves. Kelp and berries were the principal plant foods available to the Aleuts.

Whales were the most favored food and raw-material resource of the Aleuts. The animals were pursued by crews of men in baidaras, an umiak-type boat with a whalebone frame covered with sea-lion skins. Up to forty men could ride in a baidara, captained by an experienced leader, but usually about ten men made up a crew. Alternately, groups would go out in two-cockpit baidarkas, the smaller kayak with a hide apron stretched across the top to keep water out. In these baidarkas, the forward man was the harpooner and the stern man paddled. When a whale was sighted, a paddle was raised to signal the other baidarkas to close in for a kill. Harpooners were members of families in which esoteric knowledge of whaling was taught to promising boys; the basic secret seems to have been the use of poison from the aconite plant, which was said to cause whales to die three days after being harpooned. Ordinary people did not know of this poison, and believed that the harpooners had great spiritual power enabling them to dig up corpses of deceased successful whalers and prepare a magic potion from human fat to smear

CANOES of OONALASHKA.

FIGURE 9.1 Aleuts in baidarkas, with weapons and (upper craft) float lashed to deck; 1788. *(Smithsonian Institution National Anthropological Archives)*

on harpoon points. Once a whale was successfully struck, the crews usually paddled home and waited while their whaler prayed intently for it to be washed on shore. This occurred in perhaps half the kills. The community closest to a beached whale would rush to it and cut out the harpoon point, note the owner's private mark upon it, and notify the owner of the find. Then the village near the kill and the harpooner's village, if these were not the same, would each take shares of the animal, discarding only the flesh near the wound, where traces of poison might occur.

Steller's sea lion was the second preferred resource. These animals could be speared or clubbed in their rookeries and carried to villages in the boats. Seals and porpoises were other common game, the former speared like sea lions, the latter harpooned from baidarkas. A challenging prey was the sea otter, a large otter with exceptionally fine fur and good meat; Aleut hunters recognized this animal's exceptionally human-like behavior and dressed carefully in handsome ornamented clothes to attract it. Sea otters were chased from baidarkas, either one-man or two-man types, and harpooned with lines attached to the weapon foreshaft so that the otter would not be lost and could be pulled into, or towed by, the boat. Sometimes men crept up on otters on the rocks during storms, relying on the noise of the elements to mask their approach. Pursuing the swift and intelligent sea otter required exceptional skill in handling the baidarka and the harpoon, plus the endurance to search for hours on the water. Aleut boys were carefully trained from early childhood to sit without discomfort with legs stiffly extended, to stretch the arms to obtain maximum leverage in throwing harpoons, and to develop upper-body strength to manage boats in heavy waves and to handle the heavy spears while sitting flat in the baidarka. No European or inland Siberian ever mastered this combination of skills and strengths sufficiently to become reliable sea-otter hunters, in spite of the wealth to be gained from this fur.

Other important food and material sources for the Aleuts were the sea urchin (the favorite food of the sea otter), an animal related to the starfish; birds, which were netted or killed with darts; fish, especially cod, halibut, and sculpin, taken with hooks on lines from boats; shellfish; giant kelp; sarana lily bulbs, wild parsnip, anemone and lupine roots, greens, and berries such as cranberries, gathered by women. Fish, bulbs, and berries were dried during the summer and autumn to be stored for winter use, when storms frequently make it dangerous to attempt to hunt on the sea or even gather shellfish on the beach. Stored supplies usually ran out just about when migrating birds returned in the spring. These birds were thus a critical resource, although a lesser source of meat than sea mammals when measured in terms of yearlong intake.

Not only hides but also the skin of intestines, bladders, and whale tongues were used for clothing, as was fish skin. The damp weather of the Aleutians required waterproof garments as well as warm ones, so parkas of bird skins with the feathers out, or of gut, were made particularly for men to wear while hunting from boats. Sealskin or sea-otter-skin garments were commonly worn by women, who had less need to be concerned with getting drenched. Unlike the Inuit, Aleuts styled their long coats with stand-up collars but no hoods. The warmest, softest, and lightest coats, and the most expensive, were sewn from strips of ground-squirrel fur, often a double layer. Both men and

women wore hide trousers and boots with their ankle-length garments, although many Aleut customarily walked barefoot, even in winter (this was urged upon children, who were consistently encouraged to develop disregard for cold and pain.) Several styles of visor hat carved from wood were used primarily to shield the eyes of men paddling on the sea, with the rank of the wearer signaled by the size and design of his hat.

Coats, caps, and other clothing were often elegantly ornamented with dyed tufts of feathers or hair sewn into the seams and delicate geometric designs worked in appliqué strips along garment borders. Gutskin made gleaming coats that from a little distance resemble tastefully decorated pale silk. Basketry is another art of the Aleut, using a dune grass and twining technique to create flexible or semirigid containers of a great variety of sizes and shapes. As with garments, Aleut women worked colored elements into their baskets for embellishment. Mats, used for seating, as room dividers, and even to line storage shelves, were also woven from dune grass and might include beaver wool in the twining to produce what an early Russian visitor exclaimed was like a velvet carpet. Aleut basketry was, and is, an art that in the hands of some virtuosi became truly precious: museums display examples with more than fifty strands stitched per inch. A contemporary Aleut weaver said that it takes her about a week and a half of steady work to make a little basket "the size of a soup can."

The Aleut house was fairly large, about 6 meters (20 feet) in diameter and oval or a rounded-corner rectangle in shape. The floor was excavated into the ground, and the frame of driftwood timbers or whalebone was roofed with sod. Entrance was through the roof, down a notched log ladder. Around the perimeter of the house interior was a shallow trough in which bedding was placed for sitting and sleeping. Pole frames hung with mats divided these family spaces from the common center of the house, where food was prepared for cooking and then cooked if the weather did not permit use of the outside hearth. Storage shelves ringed the house above the sleeping troughs. European visitors complained of the smell of food waste in the houses, but this didn't bother the Aleuts, who liked fish and meat slightly decayed. Perhaps these foods were easier to digest with the fibers broken down by this process, for the lack of wood forced people to cook over whale-oil lamps or little fires of moss or bone soaked in whale oil, and the limited heat seldom produced thoroughly cooked meat. Seal oil was used generously to flavor and help the food go down; it was said that Aleuts, like Inuit, felt they were starving if they were out of seal oil.

Aleut society was similar to other North Pacific societies in having three classes: the rich, who owned slaves, baidaras, and valuable ornaments such as amber and dentalium shells (the last obtained from the Nuu-chah-nulth producers); ordinary persons, for whom the rich were patrons but who were free to leave one patron for another; and slaves. Slaves were either war captives or orphans lacking kinsmen to protect them, and could be traded for other objects of wealth or use, could be made to labor in household chores, hunting (in two-man baidarkas, the paddler was often a slave, the harpooner his master), backpacking goods for trade, and other onerous tasks, and could be killed at the whim of master or mistress. If slaves married each other, their children were slaves; if in an exceptional case a slave married a free Aleut, the children were free but despised. Rich persons almost always came from well-to-do families, although most wealth was acquired by the individual himself or herself through raiding foreign villages, trading, and using the production of less affluent kinsmen and slaves, of which wealthy households might have three or four. There was great stress among Aleuts on harmony and cooperation between free Aleut, which constrained the well-to-do to share food and materials with other families in the village of about one hundred people. At the same time, the importance of organizers and leaders was recognized, and capable, well-trained individuals from wealthy families were allowed to take the role of village chief. Elders advised the chief, but there was good scope for true leadership by the chief. Whalers were wealthy, but doctors apparently often not, perhaps because Aleuts had less need of their services than did Inuit and Indians, who have had more infant mortality and a shorter life expectancy than the Aleuts with their rich maritime resources.

Aleut households generally contained relatives of the principal couple as well as their children and slaves. Polygamy was permissible, a man was allowed as many wives as he could support (six was the greatest number recorded), and couples sometimes took in a second husband, who worked as an assistant to the first husband. Showing respect toward free persons was emphasized: one who was struck felt fatally insulted and might commit suicide if he was unable to avenge himself. This last ethic occasioned many murders of Russians, who treated the Aleuts working for them as roughly as the Aleuts treated slaves.

The Russian Occupation

European contact with the Aleuts began in 1741 with the voyage of Bering, under Russian sponsorship. Bering himself died of scurvy on an Aleutian island, but survivors of his expedition, including the excellent naturalist Steller, brought back information on the islands and their potential richness in furs. In 1745, a large party of Russian and Kamchadal (Siberian) hunters wintered on a western Aleutian island. Hardly had they landed before they murdered Aleut. Whole villages were cruelly massacred, and some hunters even put poison in stored pounded-root flour so that natives returning to the settlement would be exterminated. Only young women were spared, to be forced into concubinage with the Russians. The massacres were so completely unprovoked and senseless that charges were brought against the hunters in a Russian court and they were punished, but this action had little effect in deterring other Russians from depredations against the Aleuts. Many of the

Russian and Siberian hunters who came to the Aleutians in the employ of merchants and, later, the Russian-American Company were serfs who had little hope of pleasant lives themselves and much experience of brutality.

From 1745 to 1799, the Aleutians were the focus of independently capitalized ventures to extend the Russian fur trade, which had been advancing through Siberia for over a century, to America and its valuable sea-otter skins. The ventures were for the most part profitable, but were beset with poor planning, rivalries between merchants, unwieldy ships that easily foundered, and the challenge of the sea otter itself, probably the most difficult of all fine fur bearers to kill. Neither the Russians nor the Siberians they employed or enslaved had the skill to slaughter enough otters to make a profit from the long and expensive (in ships, provisions, and gear) hunting voyages. Some sea-otter furs were available by trade from the Aleuts, but these animals were among the lesser prey of the natives, and the Aleut were getting most of what they wanted—amber and other ornamental stones, dentalium, and iron hammered into thick-bladed knives—by trading with Pacific Inuit, who in turn traded both with Indians to the south and with Chukchi across the Bering Strait.

Beginning in 1761, Russians imposed tribute in furs upon Aleut villages. It can surely be assumed that the Aleut leaders who agreed to the tribute after receiving gifts of iron kettles, cloth, needles, clothing, and flour had no idea they were now taxpayers to the Czarina of Russia. It was their understanding that in return for the gifts they would allow a few baidarka hunters to live in their villages and would get some sea-otter furs ready to trade the next year. Unfortunately, unlike many Northwest Coast Indians, the Aleuts considered it unseemly to haggle in trade, and relied on middlemen to work out exchanges satisfactory to both parties. Russians had no knowledge of such customs and were pleased with the apparent ease with which trade was effected. They soon became disillusioned with the productivity of these agreements,

and concluded that the only way to exploit the tempting riches of Aleutian fur was to take over the Aleut communities. The people were either forced to relocate to a Russian-established settlement or to accept the transformation of their villages into Russian establishments. All able-bodied men were made to hunt for the Russians, frequently in a new variant of the baidarka, a three-man type with harpooner in front, paddler in rear, and Russian supervisor in the middle. Families of the hunters were hostages for the men's productivity, although a man out for a month or more had no guarantee that he would not return to find that his wife had been abused or his children enslaved. In Russian eyes, the Aleuts were serfs.

When the Russian-American Company was chartered in 1799 by the Crown to regularize the North Pacific fur trade and preserve Russia's claim to America, the serfdom of the Aleuts was set. Their population had been decimated by a half-century of massacres, introduced diseases aggravated by malnutrition when men conscripted for sea-otter hunting could not bring in seasonal foods for their families, and reduced opportunity for conception due to the long absences of the conscripted men. By 1825, fewer than fifteen hundred Aleuts could be counted. On most islands, where several villages had once existed there was only one; and, in many cases, this village was home not only to the remnant local people but also to Aleuts relocated from another island or from the peninsula villages. Groups of Russian and Siberian employees of the company were quartered in the villages to carry out the company's business. With almost no direct supervision from company officers, the men usually treated "their" Aleuts harshly, taking women (in some instances, to establish true marriages and real homes, which would produce the class of Creoles who would be an important component of subsequent Russian-American posts) and working the men to exhaustion. Allowed little or no time to hunt for food, the Aleut men were unable to provision their families adequately, and became dependent upon food purchased on credit from the company stores. Under the Russians, there was little scope for individual acquisition of wealth or display of leadership, the Russians appointing one man chief for each village and expecting him to merely see to it that Russian orders were carried out. Aleut raids upon foreign villages were, of course, forbidden, but there was hardly peace: Aleut rebellion simmered, breaking out in vain fights for freedom or murders of Russians in reprisal for insults.

As an arm of the state, the Russian-American Company sought to bring the Aleuts into conformity with Russian culture insofar as seemed practicable. Material culture, which was adapted to the island conditions, was little tampered with, but societal behavior was affected. Polygamy was frowned upon, and the Aleuts were urged to break up their multifamily households and build smaller homes to be occupied only by one nuclear family. Economic cooperation was not forbidden, but each man had more responsibility for his family than was enjoined under native patterns. Religious and social festivals were banned as pagan.

Missionaries of the Russian Orthodox Church came out to convert the natives to that faith, their task facilitated by a three-year exemption from tribute granted to church members. Ivan Veniaminov, a priest who was the foremost missionary in the Aleutians in the early nineteenth century and was later to be named metropolitan of Moscow, gained the enthusiasm of many Aleuts for his sympathy. He created and taught an Aleut alphabet, preached in Aleut as well as Russian, and, in 1825, founded a school at Iliaka to teach Russian and trade skills to Creole and selected native youths. Veniaminov endeavored to end the inhumane treatment of Aleuts. The Company's second charter, in 1821, stipulated that no more than half the men of a community could be taken away to hunt for the Company, and that the communities should be administered jointly by their chief and the Company officer. With no policing of these directives, and with Veniaminov and his clergy limited in power, there was far less amelioration of Aleut life than might have been hoped, but at least Russian spokesmen for the Aleuts had appeared. No doubt this is one reason the Aleut remained staunch adherents of their Russian Orthodox chapels even after their country was sold to the United States.

The United States Occupation

The 1867 sale of Alaska and the Aleutians—Russian America—to the United States was in part stimulated by the decline in sea otters, which led to the increasing dissatisfaction of Russia with its remote, difficult-to-manage, and, at best, marginally profitable North Pacific colony. Aleuts continued to the end of the nineteenth century to hunt and sell what sea otters they could find, but the United States saw more potential in the fur seal, which had abundant rookeries in the Pribilof Islands, where the Russians had already moved Aleut hunters and their families. In 1870, a San Francisco–based company was franchised to work these rookeries; in 1911, the United States government took over direct control of the Pribilofs and the company town there.

Under the United States, Aleuts were no longer serfs, but they came under stronger pressure to abandon native customs and move into the Euro-American pattern. The Methodist Women's Home Mission Society opened schools, beginning in 1886, and an orphanage. These Methodist missions were actively supported by the United States government through contracts. They pushed the Aleuts to work for wages rather than subsistence, give up their traditional well-insulated sod homes for drafty frame houses expensive to heat, change from the bird-skin and gut coats suited to the damp climate to clammy cloth garments, eat store-bought foods, speak English in place of Aleut or Russian, and of course worship as Methodists. Only the last attempt failed: their Russian Orthodox churches became for the Aleuts a symbol of Aleut tradition (Veniaminov had given them a translation of the Bible into Aleut and services in their language) and kept their congregations. Religious schools teaching in both Aleut and Russian were so clearly sustaining native heritage that the United States authorities closed them in 1912—not until 1973 was Aleut language instruction resumed in island schools.

Development of fur-seal harvesting in the Pribilofs partially compensated for the disappearance of sea otters by the end of the nineteenth century, although to work in the harvest most Aleut men had to absent themselves from home during the months when traditionally they would have been laying in winter food stores. Another compensation was the rise in commercial cod and salmon fishing in the eastern Aleutians. Canneries were built, employing Aleut women and buying fish from Aleut men who had dories. There was an influx of Scandinavian fishermen, a number of whom married Aleuts and settled in the villages near canneries. These men often assisted Aleut in-laws in learning skills necessary for successful commercial fishing, as opposed to subsistence fishing in the traditional Aleut manner. Cod fishing gradually declined in economic value through the first half of the twentieth century, and ceased on a commercial scale in the 1950s, when king crab became profitable. Unfortunately for Aleuts, the crab processors have operated with large, Seattle-based boats, squeezing the self-employed Aleuts out of the economy. Herring fishing was remunerative around 1930, but did not continue to be so.

The 1920s were a decade of intensification of American pressure upon Aleuts. Schools became general, staffed with Euro-American teachers who ridiculed Aleut customs and urged children to plan to move to the mainland. Many Aleut villages obtained substantial cash income by establishing colonies of Arctic foxes on nearby uninhabited islands and harvesting the pelts. Commercial fishing was feasible even without heavy investment in large, motorized boats, the Pribilof fur-seal harvest offered employment, whaling ships hired Aleuts, and in some localities sheep ranches were set up, run by Euro-Americans but hiring Aleuts. Stores in the villages were stocked with food, clothing, rifles, and other goods imported from United States cities. Aleut communities persisted, using Aleut in the homes, sharing slaughtered sea lions and the fish caught in village weirs and seines, maintaining Russian-style steam baths, and enjoying occasional village-wide drinking bouts, a festivity that replaced aboriginal social dances when the Russians simultaneously introduced liquor and banned native festivals.

The Depression affected Aleuts, many of whom, after all, were engaged in the production of luxury furs. John Collier's Indian New Deal reached the Aleutians, and several villages incorporated under the 1936 Alaska version of the 1934 Indian Reorganization Act. They elected councils, contrary to the traditional government of a chief advised by elders. Controversy over this change, seen by many Aleut as an outsiders' effort to destroy Aleut communities by opposing literate younger persons to the older community leaders, can still be observed. Formation of an Aleut regional council, the Aleut League, in 1967 shifted the focus of some issues as the League joined the Alaska Federation of Natives.

The greatest upheaval was World War II, when the Japanese invaded the western Aleutians and were repulsed from their path of conquest by heavy fighting. Rapid establishment of large military bases in the Aleutians spurred an incursion of Euro-American businesses catering to servicemen. In 1942, Aleuts were evacuated from settlements west of Unimak Island (as one cynic notes, the demarcation line spared all the Euro-American–owned salmon canneries, none of them west of Unimak). The evacuees were allowed to take only two suitcases of possessions and were held until 1944 or 1945 in camps in southeastern Alaska, far from their homeland and compatriots. One community, for example, was housed in an abandoned cannery for three years. Poor living conditions in the camps affected health and there was a rise in cases of, and deaths from, tuberculosis. Returning at long last to their villages, the Aleuts discovered their homes had been looted, community facilities destroyed, and land retained by the military, the Coast Guard, and other governmental agencies.

Eastern Aleut communities that had not been evacuated retained their societal structure and economic base, both of which were broken in the western, relocated communities. One study comparing an eastern and a western Aleut village in the 1950s found that the eastern village was based upon a local cannery that bought fish from the Aleut men, many of whom owned their own boats, and employed the fishermen's wives in the processing of their husbands' catches. Both men and women worked very hard, the women being forced to rely upon teen-age girls to manage their homes during the busiest season. Even so, both men and women, and teen-age girls too, expressed reasonable satisfaction with their lives, knowing that they were respected for the responsibility they showed and for their skills and ability to make and act upon intelligent decisions. There seemed to be little alcoholism, although most adults indulged in the social drinking celebrations that during the Russian period became "traditional" Aleut. The prices paid by the cannery for fish were considered low, but because the cannery relied upon the Aleuts for both fish and labor, and had no alternative sources readily available for either, the Aleuts felt they had bargaining power enough to protect themselves.

In contrast, the village that had been evacuated for three years appeared squalid and despairing. Euro-American entrepreneurs eager to cash in on the military buildup cajoled and manipulated the Aleuts of the village to incorporate as a first-class city in late 1941 and to elect a city council of Euro-Americans. After the war, these outsiders continued to exert power over the Aleuts, managing the resources of the locality so as to enhance Euro-American interests and excluding Aleuts from all jobs except for a few of the lowest-paying ones. Instead of training Aleut workers for skilled work and management, the businesses imported non-Aleut from the mainland, ignoring the high turnover rate among these workers. The local Aleut thus had little chance for employment, what they could get was poorly paid, tedious, and denigrated, and their poverty and high unemployment made them despised by Euro-Americans who kept power in the village. The schoolteacher who told children that they should plan to emigrate from the community of "dirty, drunken" natives was supported by those in power, and the teacher who befriended Aleuts and tried to help them organize a food cooperative was dismissed. Protests from the Aleut community finally began to be heard during the 1970s, after the Alaska Native Claims Settlement Act of 1971 brought together native people throughout Alaska to become a political force. The state granted funds for a new high-school building, an alcohol-rehabilitation program was instituted, money was secured for a small boat harbor, aid was obtained to improve homes and social services so that welfare agencies' practice of removing children to non-Aleut foster homes could be curtailed, and land expropriated from the village reverted to its domain. The basic economic and political-power problems of the Aleut villagers were not yet solved, but the nadir seemed to have been passed.

ANCSA, the Alaska Native Claims Settlement Act, radically altered the relationship between the federal government, the state, and the native nations. The Alaska Statehood Act in 1958 granted the new state nearly one-third of "public" land within its boundaries without prior establishment of native nations' territories. Like the Aleuts, most of the Alaskan native nations had never signed treaties and remained on their historic lands, living largely by fishing and hunting. The necessity of formally distinguishing native territories from State of Alaska public land stimulated the 1966 institution of the Alaska Federation of Natives to represent the interests of these nations. Pressured by United States officials and private businesses to clear title to land wanted for oil production development, the Federation agreed after lengthy negotiations to relinquish its members' claims to land in return for establishment of thirteen Regional

Corporations—twelve actual Regions and the thirteenth to enable people of native descent living outside Alaska to obtain benefits—and about two hundred village corporations. Each corporation (except, of course, the Thirteenth Regional one) holds title to land and capital and issues shares to its members. Each was to function like a business and endeavor to produce profits. In expectation of their success, the corporations were required to begin paying taxes in 1991 after a twenty-year adjustment period. In 1980, the Aleut Corporation with fourteen villages had 3,249 shareholders.

SECTION 3: THE INUIT

The Inuit are the largest ethnic group of northernmost America. Popularly known as Eskimo (a corruption of an Algonkian term for Inuit neighbors), Inuit recognize themselves as divided into many small bands or communities, yet sharing related languages and a cultural pattern they consider superior to that of their Indian acquaintances. There is a simple ecological division that correlates with cultural differences between Inuit: most Inuit live along Arctic coasts where the sea freezes during the winter into pack ice, preventing the use of boats but allowing hunting of seals at their breathing holes in the ice. These Inuit speak Inupiaq languages and used the late-prehistoric Thule technological base. (In Alaska, the northern people are usually termed Iñupiaq, Iñupiat, or Inupiat—three spellings of their dialect variation of Canadian "Inuit.") The other division lives along the Pacific coasts where solid pack ice does not form, where hunting of sea mammals from boats is possible most of the year. These are the Yupik groups. This twofold division grossly oversimplifies the variations in Inuit living patterns, but emphasizes the effect of one of the greatest challenges to survival faced by any human society, the blocking of ready access to food sources by the extraordinarily severe winters of the high Arctic.

The Yupik

The Yupik resemble, in general respects, their distant relatives the Aleuts. On the southern mainland, forests come down to the shore and provide timber for wooden-plank houses, small dugout canoes, frames for skin-covered boats, stakes for summer tents and for stretching hides, carved masks, and many other items, a number of them resembling styles of the Northwest Coast Indians adjacent to the southeast. The forests are dense, difficult to penetrate, and poor for hunting, so it is not surprising that excavations into late prehistoric through historic Chugach sites (on Prince William Sound) revealed only a few caribou and mountain-goat bones, in contrast with a preponderance of bones from sea otters, seals, porpoises, sea lions, and whales, many bird bones (loon, cormorant, albatross, coot, eider duck, and eagle), and fish bones (cod and dogfish; few salmon bones were recovered, presumably because the salmon were processed at the fishing station). Of the land animals, marmots were the most common, followed by bears, beaver, land otter, porcupines, mink, and fox. Mussels, cockles, clams, and probably sea urchins were consumed in quantities, a critical resource in spring when winter stores of dried salmon were gone and migratory birds not yet arrived. A nineteenth-century Yupik settlement farther west and north, on the Kuskokwim River in southwestern mainland Alaska, had five family homes and a community hall. The homes were rectangular, with wooden posts and log side walls, but typical of the basic Inuit house in being built in shallow pits and covered with sod, here laid on ceiling of birch bark. Entrance was through a log-lined tunnel opening into an entry room at the house doorway. The community was nestled between a ridge and the river, and it kept the ridge cleared of tree growth in order to prevent surprise attacks. The men of this inland Yupik community traveled up-river in the autumn to hunt caribou, moose, and bear, constructing umiaks of poles from the forest and the skins of their recent slaughter to carry themselves, their meat and additional hides, and the kayaks in which they paddled up, back to the village. Salmon, whitefish, pike, and cod were major foods, taken with nets or in fish traps. Both fish and meat were dried, and a kind of pemmican was prepared of dried meat or fish, berries, and animal oil. Greens such as young fireweed, wild rhubarb, and mushrooms were favored plant foods in addition to berries. Squirrels, hares, mink, marten, land otters, beaver, muskrat, and lynx were trapped, the squirrel skins preferred for women's parkas and other furs traded to the Russian post up-river and, later, its United States successor.

Analysis of the Kuskokwim River settlement showed that technologically and socially it was definitely a basic Yupik pattern, modified to take advantage of forest resources rather than the coastal resources (especially sea mammal) locally unavailable. Houses were lit by stone or pottery animal-oil lamps, although they also contained central fireplaces burning wood. The abundance of wood made it easy for the men of the community to cleanse themselves daily by building a good fire in the community house and then creating a sauna atmosphere with the hot coals and water for steam. Men used the community house as workshop and sleeping quarters, the women and children sleeping in the family homes and the women bringing dinner to their husbands in the community house. In front of the community house stood a pole with a figure carved on top to represent the spirit-animal with whom the leader of the community was associated. Festivals and ceremonies were held in the community house, especially during the winter, when dried food stores relieved people of the need to procure food for a while. The season began with a Halloween-type event, held about the same time as Halloween: two men costumed in amusing wooden masks and ragged clothing would beg from house to house, receiving food from the housewives and feasting on the take with the other men of the village in their community house. Later in the season, there were ceremonies for the dead

and potlatches in which men in masks depicting animals, people, or spirits sang and danced a composition particular to that creature, accompanied on each side by a woman dancing with finger masks. Each village was allied with at least one other through formal partnerships between individuals from the villages, and the communities reciprocated as hosts and guests at each other's festivals. Gambling took the form of the hand game (two teams facing each other, one guessing which hand held the marked piece, the men from the team holding the piece singing in hopes of confusing the guessers). Another entertainment was storytelling by women and girls using a carved bladelike wooden implement, the story-knife, to draw illustrations in dirt or snow; referents such as "man," "woman," "sleeping" were indicated by simple conventional signs that may have made it easy for historic Inupiat to learn syllabic writing. (Inuit across the Arctic, like the Cherokee, learned reading and writing remarkably quickly once a modern system was introduced for their language, and there is a very high rate of adult literacy in Inuktitut.) In 1980, the four ANCSA corporations that are predominantly Yupik (Bristol Bay, Calista, Chugach, and Koniag) had nearly twenty-four thousand members.

The Bering Sea Yuit and Inupiat

Bering Sea Inupiat live in northwestern Alaska, the region in which the historic Arctic Inuit cultural pattern and Inupiaq language are believed to have developed. In many respects they resembled the Yupik. Their homes were rectangular, with floors sunken and tunnels sloping down to below-floor level to provide a cold trap before the low room doorway. Walls were of logs, supplemented with whale or walrus bone if wood was scarce, and the exterior of the house was covered with sod. Central fireplaces, burning driftwood or oil-soaked bones, were present, but seal-oil stone or pottery lamps were standard as well. Around the inside perimeter of the house were plank benches covered with hide

FIGURE 9.2 Inupiat by an upturned umiak, 1895. *(Smithsonian Institution National Anthropological Archives)*

bedding. Dried fish and meat, berries, and extra hides were stored on high wooden racks near the house, in underground cache pits, or in annexes to the house. A sealskin sewn as a bottle held seal oil and was kept handy just outside the house door. Each village had one or, if large, two community halls built like houses but ample enough to hold all the villagers for dances. On ordinary days, the men of the village worked, ate, and slept in the community hall. The business of the men was hunting large game, that of women, processing kills, sewing, and caring for children. Children trapped and shot small game and birds, carried water to the house and slop buckets out to be emptied into the ocean or, in winter, onto sea ice, and ran errands. Both men and women cooperated in fishing, and women frequently took part in the caribou hunts.

Whaling is the focus of Bering Sea communities. Families who camp at a distance from the village to hunt caribou or fish are sure to return for the whaling season in spring. Only a few men—the rich men—owned umiaks and whaling harpoons. These men were (and are) the captains, and their crews are composed of male relatives, including in-laws, and perhaps an unrelated man known to be a good hunter. Crew camp out on the edge of the sea ice, watching constantly for whales migrating along open channels. When one is sighted, the crew rapidly launches its boat and pursues the animal. Kills are towed to the ice edge as close to the village as possible, and are butchered quickly by the successful crew, another crew that came to help dispatch the whale, and all the women, youngsters, and elderly men flocking happily out of the houses. In the autumn, whaling captains give feasts to the community to pray for a good season when the whales return. After the spring season, the captains host thanksgiving feasts where whale meat is distributed to each village member, prepared food is served, and games and dancing take place. The climax of these festivities is the skin toss: a couple dozen merrymakers grasp a large walrus skin fastened to a whalebone frame and toss high from it the captain or his wife, who throw gifts to the crowd as they "dance" far above everyone's head.

Umiak owners—that is to say, whaling captains—are usually the leaders of extended families. Most have inherited the expensive gear, but have been chosen as heir from among the several men in the kindred of suitable age. Thus, the captain has demonstrated leadership capacity and good judgment suited to his position, and has been trained for his task. Prior to this century, the captain learned a complex set of rituals and ritual precautions supposed to be necessary for success in whaling, but after observing the success of Euro-American whalers who failed to follow these rituals, many Inupiat decided simple prayers were sufficient.

After the migrating whales passed by, the Inupiat of the Bering Sea region hunted seals and walrus. Summer brought caribou down from the mountains, and parties of Inupiat traveled by boat to places along the coast or up rivers where the herds were likely to be encountered, and then brought carcasses back to the village in the boats. Boatloads of people also went out to cliffs to gather bird eggs from these rookeries. Families fished, and women and children gathered greens, edible roots, and berries as they ripened. Until this century, there was a great summer trading fair near Kotzebue, up Kotzebue Sound in northwestern Alaska. Inland residents came down the rivers to the Sound to exchange land-game furs, jade, dried fish, and other products for the indispensable seal and whale oils, sea-mammal hides, ivory, and bits of metal and precious blue-glass beads brought from Siberia, directly by Siberian Yuit (Bering Sea Inupiaq dialect variation of "Inuit") or indirectly through Alaskan Inupiat who had crossed Bering Strait.

Although trade with Siberian Yuit was common, and trade occurred also, if less frequently, with the non-Yuit Chukchi of Siberia, the Strait traffic was not always peaceful. Siberians raided Alaskan villages, and vice versa, seizing goods, women, and children to be sold as slaves. Alaska Inupiat raided each other, too, from at least the middle of the first millennium A.D. Prepared for battle, an Inupiat or Yupik man wore wooden- or bone-slat armor covered by a thick rawhide parka, and a wide shielding hat. He would be armed with spear, dagger of iron or ivory, and the sophisticated, powerful sinew-laminated bow used also for hunting. Russian observers of the eighteenth century thought villages were fortified, but they may have assumed that the mound-like, sod-covered winter houses were embankments. Raids in summer would have found many families vulnerable in hide tents, which were much pleasanter living quarters, when weather permitted, than the dark, damp, smoky (but warm) semisubterranean permanent homes.

As summer waned, Bering Sea Yuit and Inupiat worked to lay in a supply of dried fish, and many hunted caribou as well. Autumn was the season to prepare equipment for the stresses of winter, and this included the very important task of sewing warm, watertight clothing. Inupiat women not only were expert tailors, they worked with skins ranging from whale intestine, fish skin, and soft, scraped caribou to bird and squirrel pelts, sealskins, and sea-otter and wolverine furs. Not content with merely serviceable garments, the women appliquéd contrasting bands, decorative furs, and, in the historic period, colored yarn to make their family's appearance handsome and distinctive.

When the sea ice had formed, well-outfitted men went out on it to look for seals' breathing holes. The animals were formerly speared as they poked up their noses for air; now they are shot. Retrieving the dead seal from the sea has always been a challenge. Sometimes it can be hooked before it slips under the ice, but more often it was a struggle to secure it while chopping around its breathing hole until an opening large enough to pull the carcass through was achieved. Seals were also caught in nets set under the ice. After rifles came into general use, many hunters preferred to shoot seals and attempt to retrieve them from small boats hauled on sleds to the edge of an open lead in the ice. However retrieved, the seal would be pulled back to the village on a sled drawn, since the Protohistoric period (the seventeenth century), by dog teams. The idea of harnessing dogs to sleds may have been stimulated by knowledge that Siberians harnessed reindeer, or even knowledge that north-temperate Asian peoples harnessed horses and cattle. Whatever its origin, the use of dog teams became indispensable to most Inupiat and Inuit, in spite of the difficulty of managing teams and the effort needed to obtain fish and meat to feed the dogs. Partly because he hunted for four or more dogs in addition to his family, an Inuit man customarily went out looking for seals every winter day except in the worst blizzards. Youths were taught to endure the cold and the dim light, to remain trigger-alert through countless hours of silent watching for game on the treacherous ice, and to laugh aloud at misfortune; he who seemed bored, careless, or disheartened was mercilessly teased. Adventure appeared in the form of polar bears. This was the one beast that is a real danger to an Inuit hunter, even one with a modern rifle. The man who speared or, in this century, shot a polar bear was admired, and neighbors would gather in his iglu to eat bear meat, help his wife scrape the large, heavy hide, and hear an account of the perilous chase.

Northwestern Inupiat kindreds emphasized patrilineal bonds. A young bridegroom lived and worked with his wife's father for a year but then usually returned with his wife to his own family group. Children were given names traditional to their father's family, under the belief that perpetuation of the name perpetuated also the personality of the former, recently deceased bearer of the name. Elders of the patrilineages were responsible for the training and correct behavior of the mem-

bers of the group, and met together to act as governing council of the village. In most Bering Sea communities, this council was formally organized within the community hall (or, in a large village, one of the community halls). Several men of the village thus had interlocking leadership roles: as rich men owning vital hunting equipment and stores of food, as whaling captains, and as members representing their kindreds on the council. The marked class structure of Pacific peoples to the south seems not to have developed in northwestern Alaska, however. Some persons and families were said to be "better" than others, but overt badges of rank were lacking. Nor were slaves regularly held. Women seized in raids might be kept as concubines and prostituted, in the historic period, to seamen, but slaves as regular sources of labor and prestige were not part of the social system. On the other hand, formal, lifelong trading partnerships with individuals in adjacent districts were an integral component of the social universe.

Religious beliefs of the Inupiat were based on the postulation of a multitude of spiritual forces in the universe. These included the souls of humans and other animals, various seldom-visible dwarfs and monstrous beings, and powerful agents that could be angered by human negligence or evil and visit disaster upon a miscreant's community. To live harmoniously and successfully, an Inupiat formerly regulated behavior by many rituals and proscriptions. If someone became ill or suffered accident or ill luck in hunting, people in the village examined their past conduct to determine whether a slip or contravention of propriety might have unleashed evil. Frequently, the village gathered to witness a doctor invoke his or her familiar spirits or send his or her soul out to discover the source of misfortune. Confession and repentance would set the world to rights once more. Doctors of the Inupiat, like those to the south, underwent long apprenticeships to practicing doctors to learn both the symptoms and physical treatments of illness, and the theories and therapies of spiritual malaise. Mastery of sleight of hand, dramatic drumming on

FIGURE 9.3 Yuit (or possibly Chukchi) in summer camp on the Siberian side of Bering Strait, 1899. Sealskin floats hang from ridgepoles of the hide tent, furs and fur clothing from the lines at the left. *(Smithsonian Institution National Anthropological Archives)*

a single-faced tambourine, and singing impressed and entertained onlookers at curing sessions, but the proof of a doctor's power was in the patient's recovery. Poor outcomes humiliated and cast doubt upon a doctor, and some felt driven to suicide by such exposure of their apparent inadequacy. In accordance with their relatively egalitarian social structure, the Bering Sea Inupiat had no offices of priesthood, nor were doctors usually exempt from ordinary pursuits, although a few very successful ones might be called upon so frequently that they became, in effect, full-time professionals living on fees given as gifts. Most adult Inupiat learned, from a parent or other relative, magical songs to aid them in hunting and other businesses of life. Modern

Inupiat have suggested that these songs, no longer generally used, must have been truly efficacious, considering how their forefathers managed with only homemade harpoons, spears, and bows to bag whales, walruses, polar bears, and other great creatures secured today only by bombs and high-powered rifles. Whatever the truth in this supposition, certainly the songs were critical in providing the hunter with the psychological confidence to persevere against frightening odds.

In a sense, historic contacts with the Bering Sea Yuit began in the mid-seventeenth century when Russians established a trading outpost on the Anadyr River in northeastern Siberia. Expansion of Russian trade was forestalled for decades by the truculence of the Chukchi, but there were sufficient meetings for information on the "Great Land" and its inhabitants beyond the Chukchi domain. Russian trade goods also filtered through the Chukchi to Alaska. Direct contact came in the mid eighteenth century with the exploring voyages of Vitus Bering and others in the employ of Russia, and then, in the later eighteenth century, the arrival of English ships as well. The most important event for the Yuit of this period was the establishment of an annual trading fair in 1789 on the Anyui, a Kolyma River tributary in Siberia some 800 miles (1,300 kilometers) west of Bering Strait. During the first week of March, Russian merchants who had traveled from western Siberia met, at the Anyui fair, Chukchi families who had spent months coming on reindeer-drawn sleds from their peninsula. The Chukchis' most valuable commodity was fur, especially American Arctic-fox and marten skins; American bearskins, walrus-hide thongs, and walrus tusks were also in demand. These items the Chukchi could obtain by trade with American Yuit who had crossed Bering Strait, by traveling across the Strait themselves to trade, or by raiding across the Strait. In return for furs and walrus products, the Chukchi obtained iron kettles, knives, hatchets, needles, scissors, beads, and, increasingly popular, tobacco and smoking pipes. (Yuit learned to smoke tobacco from Siberians, who had learned from Russians, who had learned from western Europeans, who had learned from southeastern American Indians.) Chukchi found their middleman role profitable, but occasionally an American Yuit showed up at the Anyui fair.

Russians were aware of the American source of many of the finest furs sold at the Anyui, but made only limited efforts to tap the source directly. A post was established in 1818 at the mouth of the Nushagak River on Bristol Bay, in southwestern Alaska. The manager of the post was a Creole (Russian father, native mother), Fedor Kolmakov. In 1832 and 1833, posts were built on the Kuskokwim, the next major river north of the Nushagak, and at Saint Michael on Norton Sound. None of these reached the path of trade across Bering Strait;

instead, they drew mostly the Yupik of southwestern Alaska. It may be that the employment of Creoles as explorers and managers in this period tended to focus upon the southwest, where people spoke languages of the same stock as that of the managers' mothers, and discouraged penetration of the north, where Inupiaq was spoken instead. Limited as were the Russian-American Company's foundations on the Bering Sea, the presence of the company proved beneficial in 1838, the year a terrible smallpox epidemic spread north from the Tlingit country. The company sent medical workers to vaccinate as many natives as could be reached, and although in the Aleutians and southern Alaska one-third to one-half of the population perished in the epidemic, vaccinations seemed to halt the disease in Norton Sound, and it did not affect northwestern Alaska.

Until 1848, Yuit and Inupiat contact with aliens was with Russians or Russian-influenced or -supplied Creoles and Chukchi. In the first half of the nineteenth century, some Yuit became primarily traders, traveling far into the Alaskan interior to obtain furs from Indians, and to remote coastal and river Inupiat settlements. Inupiat, and Indians, also traveled on their own accord to the Russian-American Company posts and to the increasingly busy native trading fairs in Alaska, exchanging their families' surpluses of furs, hides, and other products for imported goods and products of other Alaskan regions. After 1848, Inupiat of northern Alaska and the Bering Sea were in contact also with United States whalers, and with Hudson's Bay Company men out of Fort Yukon, which had been built in 1847. Crews of the whaling ships were eager to trade for Inupiat furs, ivories, and women, and sometimes took on an Inupiat crewman; thus, a native of Kauwerak, a village at the mouth of the Kuzitrin River of Seward Peninsula, had been to Hawaii and San Francisco by 1865. Trading ships were well stocked with rum, and it was at this time that Inupiat learned to enjoy liquor.

Russia's sale of Alaska to the United States in 1867 included sale of the assets of the Russian-

American Company to a United States firm that took the name of the Alaska Commercial Company. Guns and European clothing began to come into use among Inupiat in this decade. The United States had little interest in Alaskan natives at the time of purchase, and the government touched them only through the annual cruise of a federal revenue cutter attempting to prevent the sales of firearms and liquor to native persons. Discovery of gold in the Yukon at Klondike in 1897, and then at Nome in Alaska in 1898, brought the famous rush of Euro-Americans. This influx of foreigners fervent to get rich quick was the first major rapid disruption of Inupiat life, but slower alterations had been insinuated a decade or more earlier.

Commercial whaling through the second half of the nineteenth century steadily reduced the population of whales migrating through Bering Strait and into the Arctic Ocean. As whales became scarcer, the commercial whalers turned to walruses to recoup their investments, slaughtering thousands of the animals for their oil and ivory tusks. Walruses do not seem to have been decimated to the point where the subsistence needs of the Inupiat were seriously threatened, but that point was in sight.

Christian mission schools had also been instituted. In the 1870s, the Alaska Commercial Company maintained two schools in the Pribilof Islands and one at Unalaska under the terms of the company's lease to harvest fur seals. More significant were three schools, the only others in Alaska, operated by the Presbyterian Board of Home Missions, at Wrangell (first run by an educated Tsimshian man), Sitka, and Haines. After the Organic Act of 1884 provided local civil government for Alaska, a Presbyterian missionary, Sheldon Jackson, was appointed in 1885 to be in charge of education in the territory. Jackson was a vigorous man convinced that the native peoples of Alaska were savages desperately in need of salvation. He contracted with mission boards to give them federal monies to operate mission schools, and required that all "government" teachers be affiliated Christians practicing Protestant tenets. His inspec-

tion trips of the "government schools" consisted of interviews on board his ship with the teachers. Episcopalian, Moravian, and even Swedish schools were encouraged, being Protestant, but a Russian Orthodox school stemming from the Russian missionary work in the mid-nineteenth century was considered by Jackson to be detrimental to his educational plans. In line with his Protestant principles, Jackson schemed to "civilize the savages" by giving them "regular" work in place of hunting. He claimed that the commercial slaughter of whales and walruses had so depleted the populations of these animals that the Inupiat were starving, and in their weakened condition dying of diseases, too. Other observers, even teachers in Jackson's schools, disputed both the extent of reduction of walruses and the alleged reduction in Inupiat health and population; the nadir of loss from initial exposure to foreign diseases seems to have passed by the 1890s. Nevertheless, Jackson was not to be checked. With funds raised by public appeal, he purchased 16 reindeer from reluctant Siberian Chukchi and got the government revenue cutter to transport them to Amaknak and Unalaska islands. The next year, Jackson bought 171 reindeer and with them set up the Teller Reindeer Station near Port Clarence, close to Bering Strait. Four Chukchi herders were employed to teach Inupiat apprentices the reindeer business, but neither teachers nor students worked as well in this novel "school" as the superintendent for education had envisioned. In 1894, a Norwegian manager and six Sami (Lapp) families plus a single man took over the Teller Station. The same year, an older Inupiat man who worked at the Station was lent 100 reindeer, plus given the 15 deer he and his brothers were due in payment for their work, to be the nucleus of an Inupiat herd. Three years later, nearly all the deer in the Inupiat herd were "borrowed" back to be driven to feed whalers and miners reputedly starving in the far north. In fact, there was no distress in either group; the action only impoverished Antisarlook, the hard-working and benevolent Inupiat herdsman. The original ostensible purpose of the reindeer project, to provide the Inupiat with a better economic base, was lost sight of as Jackson, later in the decade, extolled the potential of reindeer herds as a business venture for Euro-Americans. What the Inupiat gained at this time from the Teller Station was an introduction to skis and a fad for Sami-style boots and hats.

The first two decades of the twentieth century did see a growth in Inupiat cooperative reindeer herds, with animals kept at nine stations. The government now supported the dissemination of reindeer herding, and in 1916 sponsored a festival at which Inupiat could demonstrate their skills with the deer. Herding never appealed to most Inupiat; the necessity of traveling constantly as nomads with the animals conflicted with the Bering Sea Yuit pattern of frequently returning to village homes. Young men employed by the community as herdsmen could not resist coming home often, and failed to adequately protect their animals. The herdsmen did not realize that the deer would overgraze the slow-growing lichen that is their principal food, and districts near the stations soon became useless for reindeer. As the Inupiat reindeer business seemed to fail, by Euro-American standards of business success, Euro-American entrepreneurs muscled in, using greater capital resources and contacts with markets. Inupiat could not compete, and their herds became supplementary subsistence resources.

The Indian New Deal of Collier's administration investigated the situation in the late 1930s and obtained an appropriation to buy up non-Inupiat reindeer and abattoirs, reserving all Alaskan domestic reindeer for native ownership. Roundup and purchasing of reindeer were completed in 1940. Before Inupiat cooperatives could be built into viable businesses, World War II intervened. Military bases in Alaska imported meat rather than develop local sources, and the only strong market for reindeer products in the 1940s was a demand for parkas, especially ones sewn of fawn skins. An Inupiat women's organization in Nome tanned skins and tailored parkas for this market, but the

wartime and postwar defense installations created so many other wage opportunities—which were more exciting, comfortable, and well paid than ceaselessly guarding a herd of reindeer—that reindeer have become a minor resource for Inupiat.

Indigenous products brought cash to Inupiat, subject to fashions around the world. Whale baleen was sold in the late nineteenth century when it was used for corset stays; walrus-tusk ivory was a valuable commodity in that same period; in the 1920s, trapping Arctic foxes for fur kept many Inupiat supplied with rifles, ammunition, traps, clothing, and imported food to supplement what they hunted and gathered. World War II was the agent of greatest change, its impact underscored by the previous years of economic depression after the demand for luxury furs fell. The war brought thousands of Euro-Americans to bases close to Inupiat villages, displaying for young Inupiat the material goods, recreations, and expectations of their Euro-American contemporaries. Hundreds of Inupiat moved to bases or industrial centers to fill the need for labor, or served in the armed forces. The cessation of overt hostilities did not lessen the demand for Inupiat labor because the Arctic was seen as the first line of defense against possible Soviet aggression, and radar and other military installations constructed in the late 1940s and 1950s employed many Inupiat at high wages. Inupiat were fortunate that the construction season coincided with the lull in hunting during the summer. Men could continue to take caribou in autumn, seals from the ice in winter, whales and walruses in spring, and then obtain wage work for the months when women's plant gathering and fishing were dominant and there was little need for male contributions to the traditional subsistence pursuits. Once the Arctic defense system had been completed, there was much less demand for Inupiat labor, and families felt impoverished. However, most men could still feed their families through hunting, and the good hunter continues to be admired and respected.

Traditional Inuit had adequate food, though early spring was often a time of tightened belts.

The food was obtained through the hard work of tough, skilled men and women. Men's work in particular—hunting—was exhausting and dangerous, and carried a high death rate (Inupiat sometimes had to abandon newborn females in order to keep the ratio of hunters to dependents one that would allow for loss of young hunters). Women knew how to hunt, but could not neglect their essential and time-consuming tasks of food processing and sewing warm garments. Families lived in well-engineered, warm, but smoky houses that tended to induce eye problems and respiratory troubles. The twentieth-century shift from traditional Inupiat patterns brought easier and safer work for men, some leisure for women, an end to the pressure to keep population delicately adjusted to local resources, more comfortable though drafty houses, sweetened soft foods, and commercial entertainment. Inupiat were once happy in their traditional life, but their descendants would feel cheated if today they had no more than the traditional pattern. Therefore, the fact that many Inupiat can subsist by traditional hunting, fishing, and gathering does not lessen their need for cash income. Even the family willing to make hunting its primary activity needs cash for rifles, ammunition, modern traps and nets, a snowmobile, and gas. The increased efficiency, ease, and safety of using rifles and snowmobiles rather than aboriginal weapons and dog sleds are so apparent that even those who would reduce the dependence on cash income would want access to these powerful tools. (That snowmobiles don't eat a couple pounds of meat or fish every day, working or not, means that the cost of gas versus dog teams isn't so high when figured in terms of human labor to provide the energy requirement for the snowmobile versus that for the seven or more dogs of a team. And snowmobiles, unlike hungry, tied-up dogs, won't bite babies toddling past.)

A basic problem today is that a large number of Inupiat cannot find enough employment near their homes to pay the very high costs of Euro-American-style living in Alaska. Houses are small, crowded, and without good sanitary provisions; diets are too high in carbohydrates and low in vitamins; and respiratory diseases and dental caries are prevalent. A return to aboriginal eating habits, with their great variety of plants and full use of animal parts, would alleviate diabetes and caries and probably improve health in general, but could not raise the population's health to modern standards unless housing—very expensive to build and to heat in Alaska—were improved. Hence the concern to develop sources of income in the North.

World War II and the postwar military construction boom had made Inupiat aware that fluency in English was a key factor in obtaining better-paying, skilled employment. Earlier, parents had taken their children out to hunting and fishing camps to get their real education for life; formal schooling they could pick up when families happened to be in the village. Now, parents moved from the smaller villages into those with full school programs. An increasing number of teenagers were willing to fly out to the Bureau of Indian Affairs high schools (and some of its institutes in Kansas and Oklahoma) in spite of the regimentation of these boarding schools and the loneliness of living in a world so different from the tundra. With formal education, a generation developed in the 1960s that could negotiate with the United States. One Inupiat leader, Charles Edwardsen, Jr., from Point Barrow, recalls that his moment of truth came when, at the age of sixteen, he read Bancroft's *History of Alaska* in the high school library. That nineteenth-century historian, writing in the heyday of imperialism, wondered why the United States had paid Russia, and not the native peoples of Alaska, for the territory. A century later, the question could become the basis for protest.

Organized attempts to improve Inupiat living conditions effectively began in the 1960s, as construction waned in Alaska. Senator Bartlett of Alaska had formed a committee to investigate and recommend measures to upgrade native housing, and in 1965, hearings before this committee, who visited Inupiat villages, sparked local leadership.

A conference arranged by Bartlett brought these leaders together, stimulating ideas of forming a bloc to work on general problems. In 1966, the state director of the federal Office of Economic Opportunity programs set up an Operation Grassroots to elicit native projects. A series of regional organizations were formed about this time: the Arctic Slope Native Association (consisting of the Inupiat on the land between the Arctic Ocean and the Brooks Range), the Northwest Native Association (northwestern-Alaska Inupiat), the Cook Inlet Native Association, the Chugach Native Association, the Bristol Bay Native Association, the Kodiak Native Association, the Bering Straits Native Association, the Kuskokwim Valley Native Association, and the Tanana Chiefs Organization. Late in 1966, these groups affiliated as the Alaska Federation of Natives. Some of the associations had already begun pressing claims for land, arguing that the United States (or Russia, earlier) had never made treaties with Alaskan peoples to establish United States sovereignty, nor had it ever purchased sections of land, as had been done when states were formed in the eighteenth and nineteenth centuries.

Allied with the land claims were protests against restriction of hunting for subsistence. In 1961, a Barrow Inupiat was threatened with arrest for shooting ducks out of season. Every hunter in Barrow showed up with an illegal duck, forcing the officers to drop the charge against the first man, since it seemed unwise to arrest every man in Barrow. The Inupiat argued that because they were not party to international agreements on migratory-game conservation, they were not bound to such regulations. Less legalistically, they argued that these regulations were meant to curb large-scale commercial operations and should not apply to local subsistence hunting. This argument was acceded to, both for birds and, in 1979, for bowhead whales (although what appear to be reasonable quotas were set for each Inupiat whaling village). Impetus toward a rapid settlement of the Alaska natives' land claims came with the 1968 discovery of a large oil reserve in northern Alaska and the decision by a consortium of oil companies to develop the deposit and market the oil through a pipeline to Valdez, on Prince William Sound in southern Alaska. When the claims were filed in 1966, the United States Secretary of the Interior ruled that no land transactions could be legally completed as long as the claims were in litigation. Eager to begin development of their project, the oil consortium worked with the Alaska Federation of Natives to secure the settlement reached in 1971. Superficially, the settlement appears favorable to native interests: aboriginal rights were recognized, and in return for their surrender, the federal government was to preserve for native communities a total of 44 million acres (nearly 18 million hectares), approximately one-tenth of the state's acreage, plus $962 million. Titles and monies, however, were dependent upon the claimants establishing 225 village corporations to manage the economies of local-district native people, and also 12 regional corporations blanketing the state. Village corporations own surface rights to an area proportionate to village population; the regional corporations own subsurface rights and can derive income also from timber, as well as from investments and businesses. Since not all regions are equally endowed with resources, a formula was included providing that only a portion of a region's income would be held by it; a larger share would be divided among all twelve regions.

The most significant clause in the Settlement Act is the one requiring the regional corporations to be profit-making enterprises. Another noteworthy clause is the twenty-year expiration of the restriction of shares in the corporations to individuals of at least one-quarter native ancestry. From 1991, any person or corporation may freely buy into the corporations. Beginning the same year, the corporations' holdings are taxable. Because the corporations have needed to spend substantial sums on consultants and surveyors merely to select the lands they wish to choose, they incur expenditures before they can control their shares of the settlement monies. NANA Regional Corporation, comprising the Kotzebue area, did well by providing food services to the trans-Alaska pipeline employees, in addition to buying shares in enterprises ranging from United Bank Alaska to electric utilities. Bristol Bay Native Corporation bought a seafood-processing company that has been profitable. The other corporations have had less success in what, upon analysis, can be seen to be an unprecedented task: quickly turning more or less frozen assets—some literally frozen, some immobilized in red tape—into dividend-paying businesses that provide maximum employment to thousands of persons living in small villages scattered hundreds of miles apart and thousands of miles from major urban centers and ports. The task is so prodigious that most observers fear that the Alaska Native Claims Settlement Act will prove to be another Dawes Act, with shares in the corporation being sold to nonnatives in order to meet taxes and debts. Twenty years is a very short time to work out not merely a viable meld of Euro-American capital manipulations and Inupiat-Indian long-term cooperative management of community subsistence needs, but a *profit-sharing* meld. Thus, while on its face the Alaska Native Claims Settlement Act appears benevolent, it has in fact taken nine-tenths of Alaska from the descendants of those who owned it two centuries ago, it has forced every one of those descendants to accept a foreign economic form, and it has threatened these people with the loss of the one-tenth of their patrimony remaining to them if they do not within twenty years invent means of achieving that old utopian ideal, the capitalist business that makes money as it first and foremost serves the best interests, present and future, of the whole community. The three ANCSA corporations that are predominantly Inupiat (Arctic Slope, Bering Straits, and NANA) had fifteen thousand members in 1980.

All Alaskan native peoples have been included in the village-and-regional-corporations scheme, yet even among northern Inupiat there have been considerable differences in economic and societal patterns. One Inupiat leader has noted that the whaling villages such as Point Barrow can easily understand the concept of shareholders receiving dividends from a managed capital resource because this, in effect, was the structure of the whaling-based economy. A variation on this would be the cooperation of members of a northern Alaskan community in hunting the beluga (white whale), which is smaller than the bowhead. Parties of men in kayaks herded schools of beluga into shallow bays where the animals could not maneuver well and were easy targets for harpoons. The catch was, of course, divided into shares—"dividends"—but because each able-bodied man in the community participated directly in the slaughter, there was less of a model for the concept of a few specially trained managers operating a business with little direction from stockholders. This difference would be even more obvious among caribou hunters.

Caribou hunting was an activity engaged in by most Inupiat, particularly in the autumn when hides needed to be obtained for winter clothing. Some Inupiat families preferred to depend primarily upon caribou, supplemented by fish, rather than upon sea mammals. In Northern Alaska, these families were referred to as the Nunamiut, and distinguished from the Tareumiut, or coastal dwellers. (These terms are descriptive, not political. Each term includes several regional groups.) Nunamiut spent most of the year inland on the tundra or in forested valleys. Loosely organized bands drove caribou herds into corrals or killed them at natural traps such as river fords and mountain passes along their migration routes. When rifles became available, at the close of the nineteenth century, the easier method of surrounding a herd and shooting from within rifle range became common. More caribou were taken than needed by the hunters' families in order to have a surplus for trade. Nunamiut felt they required seal or whale oil for lamp fuel as well as for the sauce in which they dipped meat. They also wanted walrus hides for umiak covers and walrus-hide rope. To obtain these necessities, they loaded their umiaks with

FIGURE 9.4   Caribou Inupiat traveling in early October, 1947. *(Smithsonian Institution National Anthropological Archives)*

bales of caribou hides and bundles of caribou sinew for sewing thread, and every summer went to convenient rendezvous at river mouths to meet Tareumiut unloading, from their umiaks, sealskin bags of oil. These summer rendezvous were regular institutions, attended by around five hundred people (Inupiat communities generally averaged about one hundred people, fewer if inland). Men and women set up formal trading partnerships, planning to meet the needs of the partner and giving him or her preference in trading, although they could exchange with additional individuals if they had sufficient goods. Partnerships between men were usually serious, lifelong relationships involving obligations of each partner to host the other if he came to visit; the bond was so close that the two men considered themselves co-husbands to each other's wives. Partners also were competitive in wishing to appear prestigious, and might egg each other on by composing and publicly singing mocking songs, much to the amusement of the assembled community. Women usually had more easygoing partnerships. Although the exchange of basic necessities was the raison d'être of the trading rendezvous, other useful items, such as walrus ivory and mountain-sheep horn for implements, and luxury goods were important in the trade. Both Tareumiut and Nunamiut could obtain the others' basic commodities, the coastal dwellers coming inland to hunt caribou and the inland bands going down to the coast to hunt seal, but by specializing, each could obtain much greater quantities and give its sector a more secure as well as abundant supply. Emphasizing this, the coastal people had rather elaborate rituals, led by the whaling captains for success in whaling; the Nunamiut had parallel rituals led by hunt captains for success in caribou drives. Complementary though the Tareumiut and Nunamiut were, the latter were considered poorer, for they were forced to live most of the year in tents as they followed the caribou herds. Coastal villages had well-built community halls for their ceremonies and potlatch feasts in which they hosted allied communities, but the Nunamiut only erected large tents. In the mid-twentieth century, the employment opportunities at coastal stations and the increasing emphasis on schooling brought the majority of Nunamiut to settle in coastal towns, leaving principally a small conservative Nunamiut band at Anaktuvak Pass in the Brooks Range.

The Central Inuit

Canadian Inuit inhabit some of the harshest regions of the Arctic. Their populations have been smaller than those of Alaska, and they traditionally combined sea-mammal hunting and caribou hunting as seasonal activities rather than specialized pursuits supporting an economic pattern of annual trading. It was they who, lacking driftwood logs or whalebone, invented the snow-block house to substitute for the sod-covered framed iglu. Using the snow-block iglu, which could be constructed anywhere, even on the sea ice, once winter set in, the Central (that is, Canadian) Inuit were more mobile than the Alaskan coastal communities or those on the Atlantic. They tended to dichotomize the year: in winter, people clustered into small villages of snow houses and the men spent every day, unless there was a blizzard, waiting at breathing holes to spear seals, and then sharing the prey in the community; in summer, the village separated into families traveling inland on the tundra to get caribou. It was considered bad luck to engage in "summer" activities, such as processing caribou hide and sewing it into garments, when camped on the winter ice. The dichotomy was modified by people gathering, particularly in the fall, at spots suitable for fish weirs to take quantities of Arctic char, a salmonlike fish, coming down the rivers. The fish were dried and cached to provide food for sled dogs as well as humans. Musk oxen, easy to kill because they stand rather than flee, but never populous except in a few regions, were another resource for many Canadian Inuit in the past. Some Inuit remained year-round on the Barren Ground west

of Hudson Bay, becoming known as the Caribou Inuit from their heavy dependence upon this animal. The Caribou Inuit are said to have been impoverished in material goods compared with other Inuit, no doubt in part because they had to be more nomadic and because they were more likely to suffer famine since they had no other major food source if the caribou herds unexpectedly changed their migration routes, stranding the Inuit at their former hunting stations. Other Central Inuit, on the islands and peninsula of the Arctic Ocean, could sometimes take whales, as attested by whale-bone frames in the ruins of late-prehistoric, Thule-period houses. Ancient villages of twenty or more such houses where no historic settlements occur indicate a higher population in at least some central Arctic regions before historic records begin. Deduction of population figures from archaeological surveys is complicated in northern Labrador by a shift in the early historic period there, the eighteenth century, from villages of four or five nuclear-family houses widely scattered on the outer coasts to settlements of single large rectangular houses in bays with easier access to the interior with its caribou herds. Thirty-odd people lived in one of these large houses, thus the equivalent of the earlier villages; whether the change was in response to greater need for defense, to imitation of European houses, to population increase and consequent politico-economic adjustments—perhaps all of these factors together—cannot be determined. What the eighteenth-century documents tell us is that in that century, several Inuit men became independent traders, brokering the exchange of Inuit products for European manufactures. Tuglavina of Nain, for example, operated a two-masted sailing sloop supplying communities along the southern half of the Labrador coast; he was also widely acknowledged as a powerful *angákok*, the Inuit spiritual practitioner who was both seer and healer.

Archaeological mapping of Inuit villages, hunting locations (often marked by rows of "inuksuk" stone piles, man-size drive lane markers meant to fool caribou into seeing more than the actual number of hunters), and landmark cairns, plus interviews with contemporary Inuit show that families were highly mobile from Thule through present times. People not only could recognize hundreds of landmarks over a home territory of about two thousand square miles (five thousand square kilometers), they could draw accurate, detailed maps of coastlines and interior regions and recite long series of locality names representing travel routes. Children were encouraged to learn these series of names and see how fast they could say them, like tongue-twisters. Add to the locality names the names of all the species, plant and animal, land and sea, and special terms for varieties, weather situations, implement parts, and so on, and the average nineteenth-century Inuit surely knew as many technical terms as any modern engineer. This knowledge was readily admitted by the Scots and Euro-American whaling-ship captains who partnered Inuit hunters from the 1820s to the 1920s, many of them wintering over with Inuit hosts beginning in the 1850s. When in the Arctic, the captains, as well as seamen, usually took an Inuit wife who knew she was a co-wife with a Scots or United States lady, not a circumstance to bother a woman who very likely also shared an Inuit husband with a co-wife. The arrangement really was a regular Inuit practice of two couples from separate communities establishing a long-term partnership sharing food and equipment as well as spouses, and perhaps fostering each others' children to broaden their education; the only difference was the absence of the Scots or United States wife from her Inuit co-husband's embrace. The Inuit children of the partnerships recalled that the ships' captains gave their Inuit parents the respect due them as co-masters of a technically difficult, dangerous, and financially profitable enterprise. Tagak Curley, a president of Inuit Tapirisat of Canada, is the grandnephew of the spiritually powerful whaling boss Angutimmarik, called "Scotch Tom" because he partnered one of the best-known Scottish ship captains.

Decline in population was in part the result of epidemics of European diseases, including a disastrous measles epidemic in 1900 and severe losses from the 1918 influenza pandemic, and in lesser part an adjustment to the declining whale population and a consequence of Inuit clustering near harbors where whaling ships put in and trading posts were established. This clustering, the increased intervillage visiting, and the contacts with Euro-American ships' crews all facilitated the spread of diseases. In spite of the mortality from epidemics, the Inuit of the nineteenth and early twentieth centuries did not feel threatened by outside invasion; rather, most of them welcomed the convenience of the slowly increasing number of regular ship ports of call and trading posts. Once modern rifles were developed, in the late nineteenth century, the longer range accuracy of these guns and the abundance of good steel knives and other tools from trading posts, including strong steel traps, so facilitated hunting that the Inuit felt they were enjoying a golden age. Where their parents had pulled sleds along with their three or four dogs, these Inuit used rifles and commercial nets to collect food to keep enough dogs to make a full team, and their children remembered how they talked about the luxury of putting the little ones and the elderly on top of the sleds as the able adults walked beside the teams.

LAKE EVER-FROZEN

It was a picturesque sight, this train of people and dogs staggering over hill and lake under burdens almost equal in size and weight to themselves. The men carried the tents and weapons, the women the sleeping gear, spare clothing, and cooking utensils, and the little children their own bedding and whatever else their strength permitted. With the packs lying horizontally across their backs they resembled from a distance dark crosses that crept over the snow, now strung out in irregular formation, now filing one behind another in single line, now clustering together with little movement as the train halted to rest. The dogs trailed behind the women and children, their packs, shaped like saddle-bags, beating against their ribs or grooving continuous furrows in the snow.....Slowly we filed across Lake Ever-Frozen and deposited our loads on the shore of a deep inlet at its northern end. In a broad pool created by a stream that foamed down the hill-side a red-throated loon gaily dived and rose to the surface again. Ikpuck seized his fish-trident and raced over the ice to spear it; but just as he reached the margin of the pool the ice gave way, and plunged him in water to his waist. The loon flew up, and the mortified hunter returned to the bank to change his clothing.....

Our jiggling in this corner of Lake Ever-Frozen was very productive for a week, and the new camp with its lines of drying fish among the dogs and tents soon became a replica of the one we had just abandoned. To stand on the ice hour after hour and mechanically vibrate a long line in the clear water below was a pleasantly monotonous occupation when the air was mild, and the sunlight sparkled in the crystalline snow. Even when fogs rolled down on us, and only the dark water-holes at our feet relieved the whiteness all around, there was a comfortable peace in the atmosphere and in the mellowed voices that penetrated from somewhere unseen. The life was in fact too tranquil, too monotonous, for The Runner and his wife. They craved more activity, and spoke of hunting for caribou to the northward.

(Jenness 1959 [1928]:132-134)

The Central Inuit were effectively colonized only in the twentieth century. Canada extended its agents of control onto its Arctic domain only in 1903, sending the North West Mounted Police to set up posts and patrols. The Hudson's Bay Company founded its Arctic posts in the same period. By the 1920s, rifles had largely replaced native weapons, lessening the dependence of hunters upon cooperative strategies. Nuclear-family independence was further nurtured by the development of fox trapping and the selling of the pelts for ammunition and commercial traps, an orientation toward a cash economy in place of the traditional emphasis on kindreds sharing meat. Anglican and Catholic missionaries moved into the central Arctic in the 1930s, and like their predecessors working a generation or two earlier in Alaska, were quite successful in replacing native rituals with Christianity. The death of many Inuit native doctors in epidemics or from tuberculosis, the discrediting of others when they failed to cure sufferers

from the introduced diseases, the skepticism fomented by Euro-Americans flaunting Inuit ritual restrictions, the confidence in rifles' power contrasted with the former need for magical songs to aid the shorter range of traditional weapons—all readied most Inuit to accept the new religion brought by the well-supplied outsiders. Many missionaries had medical training that enabled them to replace the Inuit native doctors in their curing roles as well as in their spiritual leadership.

The 1940s were a decade of severe poverty for most of the Central Inuit, the fur trade hit first by the Depression and then by war, and military activities concentrated more to the west. The Royal Canadian Mounted Police constables and the missionaries helped somewhat with relief supplies. Postwar defense installations, especially the Distant Early Warning (DEW Line) radar system, brought a boom across Arctic Canada. Inuit men were hired for construction and maintenance, both on the military projects and on buildings such as stores and recreation halls responding to the influx of Euro-Canadians. The new international importance of the Arctic awakened government concern for the Inuit. Schools were built, and in the 1960s the Department of Northern Affairs actively encouraged the formation of Inuit community cooperatives to improve the local economic base. Cooperatives organized fish, meat, and hide marketing, house construction in the growing villages, consumer buying, and the development of an art industry, first at Cape Dorset and soon in many villages. Inuit carvings of animals and persons in steatite (soapstone), a soft stone fairly common in the Canadian Arctic, quickly become popular among art collectors in American cities. The Hudson's Bay Company at first was the middleman between the carver and the art retailer, but when the Bay claimed it was glutted with figurines, the government took over marketing through cooperatives, adding print-making in village co-op facilities to the home production of carvings. Inuit had been selling carvings, especially in ivory, to sailors and tourists for over a century, but the organized marketing in southern cities greatly expanded the production in the northern communities.

Northern Affairs staff felt that cooperatives were sufficiently similar to traditional Inuit economic patterns to be well suited to Inuit villages, a means of giving the people self-determination instead of dependency upon government programs and the Hudson's Bay Company prices. (Independent traders and even Révillon Frères had been forced to close Arctic posts during the Depression; only the Bay survived.) In the 1960s, Canadian Inuit co-ops were much less ambitious than the Alaska Native Claims Settlement creations, but still were structured by the Euro-Canadian agents in conformity with industrial-society patterns, and thus were alien to the villagers. Cooperatives certainly improved the material life of many members, were and are an avenue of recruitment for Inuit leaders, and have been more amenable to modification to fit Inuit customs than another economic institution might be; but because they are cash-based, they have not been as easily integrated into communities as the government planners had hoped. Traditional Inuit cooperation is based on long-term personal relationships, including kinship but incorporating individual and family partnerships into other communities. Traditional Inuit cooperating groups have not been governed by shareholders' votes but by respect relationships, younger persons quietly observing and gradually practicing the skills by which success is obtained and respect earned.

With continuing pressure from the Canadian government to industrialize the Arctic, during the 1970s some efforts were made to train Inuit rather than import Euro-Canadians. Gulf Oil Canada, for example, approached the Inuit village of Coppermine, on Coronation Gulf, with an offer to employ the men of the community as a group in oil-exploration work in the Mackenzie Delta. Village leaders were shown the site and nature of the work, and after their recommendation, half the men of the village were flown by Gulf to the sites. Men worked two weeks straight, then were flown back to Coppermine for one week off. This pattern was essentially the same as that followed by men trapping, and so was not disrupting to family life, and the week at home allowed the men to hunt meat for family provisions. Although most of the men performed unskilled labor (a few held skilled jobs), decent wages and treatment in the Gulf camp and time enough to hunt for subsistence produced general satisfaction in Coppermine with the Gulf employment. With the cash from their wages, the men purchased supplemental food such as flour and lard for bannock, the biscuit baked by Inuit and Indians throughout the North; canned fruit, tea, candy, soft drinks, and liquor; clothing; children's toys, radios, and stereos; and capital goods: snowmobiles, outboard motors, boats, rifles, ammunition, and tents. The wages strengthened the subsistence hunting and fishing by enabling the men to go farther, with their snowmobiles or motorized boats, than their fathers could have if they were to return to a sedentary village. Of course, the cost of gas in turn forced most men to work for cash in addition to hunting and fishing. Wages for the Coppermine men supported kindreds (extended families, including adopted people and in-laws), directly through gifts by the men to relatives, especially the elderly, and indirectly through the underpinning of hunting, the proceeds of which were shared among kin. In other Inuit communities, kindreds have continued to be economically important because relatively large boats are required to go to the remote areas where fur seals and walruses can be hunted in numbers, and to transport the hides and meat back to the villages. As in the traditional pattern of whaling, kindred leaders (usually a married couple) pool family resources to obtain the needed boat and equipment, and rely on relatives for the core of their crew (generally male) and processing team (mostly women). Thus, it appears that dependence upon a cash economy is not incompatible with perseverance of Inuit traditional subsistence and societal patterns.

How far the North can be industrialized without doing violence to Inuit life is a prime question, hotly debated. There are, first, the ecological parameters. Tundra is fragile and its flora slow-growing. Land damaged by heavy construction, as for oil rigs and pipelines, can remain visibly scarred for a generation at least. Scarred land cannot be used by game and frightens caribou into new migration routes that may not be able to support as many animals. Industrial processes are apt to poison land and water. One major example was the rendering of lichen, and so the caribou whose chief food is lichen and the Inuit whose chief food is caribou, radioactive from nuclear-testing fallout in the early 1950s. Another example is mercury poisoning from the waste of mines and pulp mills, ingested by fish that in turn are ingested by Inuit and Indian fishermen and their families and dogs. In 1975, Northern Ontario Cree contacted Japanese experts on mercury poisoning (which is also known as Minamata disease after its Japanese occurrence) to help them pressure the Ontario departments of health and natural resources to end

industrial discharge of mercury into northern waters and to give medical aid to the people whom the Japanese scientists diagnosed as exhibiting symptoms of mercury poisoning.

Aside from the environmental issues, industrialization in the North confronts the question of local sovereignty and citizens' rights versus national interests. This question came to public attention in the Mackenzie region, where oil pipelines have been resisted by Indian bands, and especially in the James Bay region of northern Québec, where the Québec government planned a massive hydroelectric project for the 1970s. The James Bay project would have flooded a large area that the government characterized as empty land, but that is hunting and fishing territory for Cree. In 1972, the Indians of Québec Association, founded in 1965, obtained a court injunction against the James Bay Project. Negotiations between the federal and provincial governments, Hydro-Québec, and the James Bay Development Corporation, on the one side, and the Grand Council of the Crees and the Northern Québec Inuit Association, on the other, resulted in 1975 in a settlement whereby Indian rights and claims to 410,000 square miles (1 million square kilometers) of northern Québec were ceded in exchange for 13,300 square kilometers (5320 square miles) of reserve lands, hunting rights over 135,000 square kilometers (54,000 square miles) of land, and a payment of $225 million, to be given over twenty years. The Northern Québec Inuit are peripheral to the James Bay Project but entered the negotiations to protect that periphery of their hunting territories. In 1984, the Inuvialuit Inuit of the Mackenzie delta region agreed to accept title in fee-simple absolute to 90,650 square kilometers (36,260 square miles) of their traditional territory, plus mineral rights to fifteen percent of the territory and $152 million in compensation to be paid over fifteen years. This Inuvialuit Claim settlement represents an important innovation in Canadian policy because it recognizes, through the fee-simple absolute title, the power of the Inuvialuit Land Administration to negotiate use of the territory's resources, independent of the usual process vesting power in the government Department of Indian Affairs and Northern Development.

The outcome of the James Bay Settlement was crystallization of native opposition to any extinguishing of remaining aboriginal title to land. James Arvaluk, president in 1975 of Inuit Tapirisat ("Eskimo Brotherhood") of Canada, publicly expressed his disappointment in the terms of the settlement and stated, "The James Bay Agreement will not be considered a precedent. And Inuit have made it clear...that their land is not for sale" (letter of November 12, 1975 to *Toronto Globe and Mail*). Three Hudson Bay Inuit communities went further and formally withdrew from the Northern Québec Inuit Association. These communities organized as Inuit Tungavingat Nunami and pressed for further, or at least separate, negotiations, insisting that the future needs of their people required more land than the settlement allowed them. Some insist that no extinguishing of native territorial rights can be contemplated. Canadian Inuit have increasingly resisted the government assumption that industrial development of the Arctic is inevitable. Village corporations formed under the James Bay Agreement, somewhat similar to those in Alaska, are entrusted with management of local resources and the provision of local services, at least in principle able to encourage subsistence hunting and fishing and adjust governmental benefits to the Inuit mode of life. Many communities are in fact reviving a more traditional life, not only building local museums and seeing that school instruction is in Inupiaq, but encouraging the use of dog sleds to reduce dependence on wage employment to buy gas for snowmobiles, traditional clothing instead of expensive factory-made outfits, and appreciation of native foods in place of imported junk snacks.

Like the Alaskan Inuit and Indians, the Canadian Inuit did not sign treaties with Britain or another European or Euro-American power. Their claims to sovereignty are difficult to refute. Many Northern Québec Inuit uneasily support Québec separatism in the hope that should that province become independent of English Canada, its northern extension (delegated to it in 1912) would revert to the Northwest Territories, under which united Inuit demands for sovereignty north of the fifty-fifth parallel could better be pushed. The predominantly Inuit northern section of the Northwest Territories would be called Nunavut; in a 1982 election, Inuit voters overwhelmingly favored the establishment of semiautonomous Nunavut, although the Western Canadian Inuit were less enthusiastic than those in the central and eastern regions. The Inuit don't expect to be recognized as a totally independent nation—the land is vast, the population less than thirty thousand Inuit—but autonomy in local affairs and majority power in regional policy decisions seem reasonable goals. If this self-determination is realized, the Inuit would regulate industrial development in the Arctic, curtailing projects that in their opinion threaten their subsistence base and exacting fees from those exploitations that are permitted. Importation of non-Inuit labor would be discouraged, a step that would not only give employment to local people but would also reduce the stress upon Inuit communities posed by numbers of foreign men without families. Inuit would control education in their land, preserving their language with its syllabic script borrowed from the Cree, a script in which in many regions all adult Inuit are literate. Schooling would be adjusted so that families could train their children to live off the land, yet fluency in English and opportunities for formal higher education would be offered, too. Not perhaps the best of both worlds, but their own world improved by some modern buffers against the harsh climate is the goal of many Inuit. Total Canadian Inuit population in 1980 had passed twenty-three thousand, and the rate of population growth, now protected by government intervention against famine and treatable accidents and disease, will demand ingenious solutions to employment needs.

The Inuit of Greeland

Greenland's Inuit have had a longer history of European contact and a more paternalistic recent colonial government than those on the American mainland. Their present status gives them more autonomy than other Inuit. These are contrasts in degree, however, not in kind. Greenland and Labrador, across Davis Strait, form a region now artificially divided by national boundaries. Since the first human settlements of Arctic Small Tool Tradition people about 2000 B.C., through the Dorset cultural phase from 500 B.C. to A.D. 1100, and continuing through the succeeding Thule late-prehistoric phase, this region has been one in which seals have been of primary importance, supplemented by fish, birds, walrus, caribou and/or musk oxen, and, in the historic period, whales. Settlements were on the coasts, in Greenland because the interior is covered by a massive continental glacier, in northeastern Canada because the scrub forests and tundra on the Canadian Shield, heavily scoured by the Pleistocene glacier, supported little game compared with the shore.

Eirik the Red's Norse colony in southwest Greenland, beginning in A.D. 982, coincided with the termination of Dorset Inuit and its replacement by Thule, which seems to represent a relatively rapid migration across Arctic Canada from Thule's apparent origin in northwestern Alaska. The relationship between the resident Dorset and the subsequent Thule Inuit, especially during the thirteenth century A.D., when the shift in cultural inventories is marked, is not clear, but there is sufficient continuity in some Dorset artifact types to suggest the Dorset were either absorbed into Thule populations or acculturated to the newer Thule pattern. Thule people had opportunity for regular contacts with Norse, in Greenland and, less frequently, in Labrador. Since the Norse lived principally from sheep raising, although hunting, fishing, and trapping for furs were also important, Norse and Inuit were not in serious conflict, and

trade was mutually beneficial: The Inuit wanted iron, and the Norse wanted furs and hides to add to their own products when the trading ships from Norway arrived. In the fifteenth century, the climate became colder and the Norse settlements in Greenland gradually disappeared, possibly by some Norse joining Inuit communities. Inuit in Labrador began moving south, as far as Hamilton Inlet, supplanting Indians who had utilized the coast less intensively.

During the seventeenth century, the Inuit became aggressive raiders into the Canadian Maritimes, attracted by the European goods brought by traders and fishing fleets. Iron tools and weapons became common for Inuit, who frequently coldhammered spikes and nails into Inuit artifact patterns rather than taking finished European knives or weapon points. In the eighteenth century, direct trading with Europeans replaced raiding. English, French, and Dutch ships came for whale baleen and oil and for furs, stimulating Inuit to concentrate upon whaling for the first time in the Atlantic region. During this century, the Inuit of Labrador clustered in larger, communal houses to command enough men to make up whaling crews, in contrast with Dorset and earlier Thule settlements of fewer and smaller houses. (Maritime Archaic people in Labrador between 4000 and 1500 B.C. did occupy "longhouses," rows of small rectangular rooms outlined by low stone walls. These may have been connected windbreaks with tents set up inside each "room," although it is quite possible they were roofed rooms. Presumably the Maritime Archaic "longhouses" symbolized as well as housed communities.)

The eighteenth century saw hostilities between Indians and Inuit renewed as the French armed Montagnais to harass Inuit who traded with English ships. A treaty of peace between the two native peoples was negotiated in 1765, at the conclusion of the Seven Years War, but Inuit did not prosper thereafter. Whaling declined in Davis Strait, and with it trading relationships favorable to the Inuit. European diseases took an increasing toll of the native peoples as permanent trading posts and mission stations brought in resident Europeans and induced the Inuit to remain longer in villages, where unsanitary conditions could build up, and to eat less nutritious purchased food. True colonization of the eastern Inuit came with the establishment of missions, in Greenland in 1721 and in northern Labrador beginning in 1752. Denmark asserted its claim to Greenland through the missions, to which were delegated formal education as well as proselytizing in Greenland, and from 1774 through government control of trading. By operating trading stations, the Danish government recovered some of its expenses in administering its colony and sought to protect the Inuit from harmful products such as alcohol, from excessive dependence upon imported goods, and from price gouging.

The first century of Danish control lay upon the Inuit of the former Norse settlement area in southwest Greenland. In 1818, exploration in Northwest Greenland encountered the Polar or Thule Inuit, who at the beginning of the twentieth century were to assist Peary and Henson in traveling to the North Pole, and who from 1910 until the 1930s were the clients of the trader Knud Rasmussen, whose expeditions across the Arctic in the 1920s illuminated a great deal of Inuit life. (Peary hired men as dogsled drivers and hunters, paying them with rifles and ammunition. He also needed boats, and in hiring umiaks he found that men only rowed them when whaling, women otherwise forming the rowing crews. Peary paid his umiak crews with steel sewing needles.) On the east coast, the Angmagssalik were unknown to the rest of the world until 1884. Danish policy for all three areas followed the plan of limited education and trading with encouragement for continuing subsistence hunting. Early in the twentieth century, warming of the Gulf Stream drove seals northward, stimulating the Danish administrators to promote cod fishing off southwest Greenland. Commercial production of cod became a principal livelihood for Inuit in this region by the 1920s, a radical change from hunting particularly because instead of sharing each carcass within the community, the cod

fisherman worked alone or with a partner and sold the catch for money to buy food for his family.

Greenland's position formally changed in 1953, when it became a Danish county rather than a colony in name, and was given two seats in the Danish Parliament. Internal affairs were then to be guided by an elected national council and thirteen local municipal councils. These bodies were only advisory to the Danish central government, and this limitation highlights the frustration of many Greenlanders who believed that incorporation of Greenland into the Danish national structure really lessened autonomy. For example, although Greenland is officially bilingual (its largest newspaper is the *Atuagagdliutit/Grønlandsposten),* there was increased pressure toward fluency in Danish in order to influence Danish politics and economic decisions. Incorporation also threatened to impose Danish judicial judgments upon Greenlanders, who had enjoyed greater leniency in criminal-case judgments because of their traditional handling of social deviation and violence, stressing rehabilitation rather than punishment. Rejection of the older colony status ended, too, the government monopoly of trading, and exposed Greenlanders to cutthroat competitive international markets. Reaction to the new status built through the 1960s and erupted in the 1970s with the formation of two factions, an older group favoring the political equality of Greenlanders with other Danes, and a younger, "radical" group urging truer autonomy, with home rule through the national council and independence from the European Common Market. Control of Greenland's mineral and oil resources was a critical issue. The Home Rule Act passed in late 1978 gave Greenlanders "fundamental rights" to their natural resources, but as several astute critics noted, failed to legally define what was intended. Implementation of the Home Rule Act beginning in 1979 reserved all final authority to the Danish Parliament and specifically kept financial policy, foreign relations and defense under direct Danish control, immediately raising the major issue of subjection to European

Economic Community rules, to which the majority of Greenlanders were opposed. Home Rule for Greenland has been a model for Canadian Inuit and Indians, a basis for the proposed Nunavut and Denedeh provinces; the limitations and issues spotlighted by the Home Rule Act, as well as its positive characteristics, are valuable for guiding efforts to obtain Inuit and Dene autonomy.

A considerable proportion of Greenlanders continues to live principally by subsistence hunting and fishing, with seals the major prey. Denmark tried to develop commercial cod fishing, but as there do not seem to be sufficiently large banks of these fish off Greenland to support an industry, shrimp fishing was promoted as well. Domestic reindeer and sheep have been introduced, but can utilize only limited sections of the country; sheep, in addition, require expensive winter fodder. Fox trapping has been profitable, but is subject to fashion fluctuations. During the 1950s, the large United States air base in Thule employed some of the Polar Inuit (whose village was moved to protect the people from direct exploitation by military personnel and to keep them nearer hunting grounds), but this opportunity declined as jet planes became standard and an Arctic refueling base obsolete. It seems apparent that an independent Greenland cannot support its growing population at a reasonable standard of health and comfort unless it can control some commodities of importance in the international economy. Even the Inuit who are subsistence hunters demand multiroom wooden houses instead of the traditional damp and dark one-room sod iglus, and need rifles, ammunition, steel implements, snowmobiles (except in certain regions of treacherous terrain, where dog-drawn sleds are still used), and motorized boats. They must have modern medical assistance and, with the lessened mortality it brings, schools for the population outgrowing subsistence resources. Like mainland American Inuit and northern Indians, the Greenlanders believe they should control mineral resources within their traditional territories, and that they can supervise limited de-

velopment of these resources that will not destroy the hunting environment but will return royalties sufficient to cover the cash needs of modern subsistence hunters. Thus, in spite of Denmark's less openly exploitative colonization of Greenland, Greenlanders find themselves in the same position as mainland Inuit, and share in their goals. A major difference is that the population of Kalaallit Nunaat (Greenland) passed fifty thousand by 1980, and nearly all these people are Inuit—a strong political majority under Home Rule.

SECTION 4: THE DENE

Dene (pronounced "Din-neh") is the Athabascan word for their own people. When a proposed natural-gas pipeline through the Mackenzie Valley of the Northwest Territories threatened destruction of Athabascan hunting in the region, the native bands organized as the Dene Nation to protest. Strictly speaking, the Dene Nation refers to the Canadian Athabascans (also spelled Athapaskan), but the Dene themselves recognize the affinity of Athabascan speakers on both sides of the foreign-imposed political boundary dividing Canada from Alaska. Dene is the rightful term for these peoples from central and southern Alaska east to the western border of Hudson Bay. Any division of the Dene is arbitrary, for their languages grade into one another through intermediate dialects in several regions, and they did not have rigid territorial or political states.

The greatest number of named groups are in the mountains of interior Alaska and British Columbia: the Upper Koyukuk River people, the Kutchin (also known by the French name Loucheux), Han, Upper Tanana (also called Nabesna), Tutchone, Tagish, Kaska, Tahltan, Tsetsaut (merged in the late nineteenth century with Tlingit, Gitskan, and other neighbors), Mountain, Sekani, Carrier and Babine, and the Chilcotin, the last living on the edge of the Plateau. Living along the Yukon and Kuskokwim Rivers flowing west through Alaska

FIGURE 9.5 Yukon Indians drying fish (late nineteenth century). *(Milwaukee Public Museum)*

are the Ingalik, Holikachuk, Kolchan, Koyukon, and the Tanana and Tanacross. On Cook Inlet and the Susitna River in southern Alaska are the Tanaina (different from the Tanana farther north in the interior). The Ahtna occupy the Copper River basin, east of the Tanaina in southern Alaska.

The second largest bloc of Dene are in the Arctic Drainage Lowlands of the Canadian Yukon and Northwest Territories: the Hare, Bear Lake, Dogrib, Slavey, Chipewyan (not to be confused with the Algonkian "Chippewa," who are properly named Ojibwa) and the allied Yellowknife, the Beaver, and, on the Plains border in Alberta, the Sarsi. Archaeological evidence suggests that the homeland of the Dene was in east-central Alaska, probably including the Koyukuk River basin with its anciently valuable obsidian deposit at Batza

Tena. Continuities in artifact types and settlement patterns also suggest that some Dene had crossed into the Arctic Lowlands as far as Great Slave and Bear Lakes late in the first millennim B.C. These easternmost Dene may have been ancestral to the Chipewyan and Yellowknife.

One historically very small group speaking a Na-Dene language distinct from the Athabascan branch was the Eyak, on the lower Copper River to Prince William Sound in southern Alaska. The Eyak cultural pattern most resembles that of the Tlingit, their neighbors to the east, so this remnant group is best considered a border Northwest Coast people. In the nineteenth century, the Eyak numbered between one and two hundred people living principally by salmon fishing, overshadowed by the Tlingit, to whose customs their own were similar. After an epidemic in the early 1890s, the Eyak abandoned some settlements and clustered in the town of Cordova, where in the 1930s only nineteen individuals could claim to be solely of Eyak descent.

The Dene Cultural Pattern

Dene seem primarily to have been adapted to the flat, forested, mountain-ringed valleys of the northern Cordillera. Historic occupation of the central Canadian Barren Grounds tundra and adjacent northern forest border may be an extension of Dene pushed north by Cree consolidation of their western border during the fur trade era. Caribou have been the foundation of Dene life. Moose, mountain sheep, bison (for southeastern Dene), and bear were other large prey, and fishing supplemented game. Basing their resource needs upon caribou, the Dene, like the Nunamiut Inuit, seek the open lands, the upland valleys, the ridges, and the tundra where the caribou graze. Caribou move in herds of thousands north from wooded regions in the spring to calve on the tundra, wander over the tundra during the summer, congregate on the tundra in autumn for the rut, then migrate south into woods for shelter during the winter. Herds usually, but not invariably, follow the same routes each year, so an efficient hunting strategy is to wait for the herd at the river crossings or mountain passes on the route, slaughtering the animals from canoes as they swim or from ambush as they crowd through a pass. Early autumn, when the caribou are beginning to drift toward the rutting gatherings, is the most valuable period to hunt them, for at this time they are fat; the first growth of their winter coat makes their fur soft and thick; and the fly larvae that infest the animals in spring and summer have hatched, allowing the skin to recover from the holes caused by the insects. In many regions, topography necessitated the construction of corrals, or of long wooden fences set with snares, and the cooperation of several families to drive caribou into the corral or fence where men waited to spear them or shoot

them with arrows. Corrals were especially useful in early winter, when people were preparing for the hardest months ahead. Men noted for their ability to organize successful hunts settled for the winter in localities suitable for caribou drives, and ten to fifty other families might gradually join them in these "meat camps."

The low game density of the Subarctic was compensated for by reliance upon traps and snares, which in effect cloned hunters in untiring wait all along game trails. Men set snares and deadfalls for large game—bears, moose, caribou, and mountain sheep—whose trails could be miles from camps, while women and children set snares for hares, gophers, and birds around camp. Small parties of men, often brothers-in-law, would go out, perhaps for several days, checking the snares and stalking any game whose tracks they noticed. Suggestions on possibly profitable hunting localities were obtained by magical means, such as roasting an animal scapula (shoulder blade) over a fire and observing the direction in which a crack opened, as well as from experience and information eagerly sought from travelers. Fish were clubbed or speared in shallows, trapped, or netted, nets being set under ice in winter when communities settled in beside good fishing lakes. Favorable fishing spots also attracted a dozen or more families in summer to well-known "fish camps." The number of persons at these camps usually was not as great as the number in the early winter caribou-driving meat camps. Vegetable foods include berries, fern roots, lily bulbs, mushrooms, wild onions and wild rhubarb, rose hips, and a turniplike root found in mountain meadows. Unlike Inuit, the Dene did not value as food young willow leaves in spring. Birch sap tapped from the trees in spring was a sweet treat, and people liked to chew spruce gum. Fish were filleted and meat cut into thin strips to dry for storage in caches.

Subarctic winters are extremely cold, but because the Dene, along with the caribou, took to the woods at this season, winds were not as dangerous as they have been for the Inuit on the coasts. Dene shelters therefore have been lighter than the solid Inuit and Aleut winter houses. Among the eastern Dene, tipis of poles covered with moose or caribou hides and banked with snow were common, while in Alaska, log-frame houses covered with moose hides or sheets of bark and moss were often built. Another type of house was a double lean-to of poles covered with bark, spruce boughs, or moss and banked with snow. Two families would occupy such a dwelling, one on each side of a central fire. A single family out trapping or a small group of men might build a single lean-to, relying on a good fire at the entrance to warm the structure. Spruce boughs covered with hides were the usual furniture in Dene aboriginal dwellings, although in Alaska some groups constructed sleeping benches along the walls of the log-frame houses. Dene clothing also differed from that of the Inuit. Coats of caribou hide with separate hoods were sewn rather than parkas, and moccasins rather than boots were worn. The footwear reflected the importance of snowshoes for the Dene, who wear them with moccasins. Indeed, it has been claimed that only the use of snowshoes enabled the Dene to survive in the Arctic Drainage Lowlands. With snowshoes to manage the soft snow of the interior forests, the Dene could pursue game and could travel to better hunting or fishing camps in the winter. Especially in the western areas, aboriginal canoes were made of moose hides over wooden frames; in the eastern lowlands they were made of birch or spruce bark sewn with spruce root and caulked with chewed spruce gum "soldered" on the seams with glowing brands (an early ethnographer observed that wise travelers renewed the gum caulking every evening when they camped on a journey). Toboggans were used to transport loads in winter, and until the late nineteenth century they were pulled by men and women. Not until rifles and commercial fishnets made larger-scale hunting and fishing feasible was it possible to kill and process enough meat and, especially, fish to feed dog teams as well as the human population, nor was there really a need for dog teams before trapping for furs (rather than

meat) became the major winter activity, forcing men to cover longer circuits and travel more rapidly than they had before fur trading came in.

Social units among the Dene were relatively flexible, as befitted people whose food supply was subject not only to population cycles that regularly brought lean years, but also to occasional shifts in game migration routes or favored habitats that would strand the human inhabitants of the former prime territories. The basic unit was the married couple, or man and wives if a hunter could support more than one woman and her children. A young man usually went to live with the family of the young woman the couple's parents had selected; with the Dene, as with the Inuit, a young person's marital preference was taken into consideration, but he or she was expected to obey the judgment of parents in selecting a spouse. The young man hunted with his father-in-law and brothers-in-law, gaining the advantage of their knowledge and training in addition to that provided by his own father and uncles. The young wife had the assistance of her mother in caring for her husband's and babies' needs. When the young family seemed ready for full responsibilities, they were free to move out and set up an independent household, camping with whatever leader they respected. Frequently, brothers-in-law who worked well together, or sisters or sisters-in-law or cousins who liked to cooperate, camped together. Elderly parents kept their dwelling near that of a married child—or children, in the many instances in which adult brothers or sisters formed joint camps— and were provided with meat and other necessities. Moving from one camping group to another was facilitated by recognition of kin ties; nearly all individuals within a region could figure out some blood or in-law relationship to almost any other person he or she might meet. People also had acknowledged partners in neighboring bands, and would rely on them for trade, hunting partnerships, and hospitality. Dene see their social organization as based primarily on the task to be performed by a group, rather than constituted into permanent units, so stability or boundaries are less valued than flexibility.

FIGURE 9.6 Ingalik Dene man ready to fish through ice. *(Smithsonian Institution National Anthropological Archives)*

The western Dene—the Koyukon, Tanana, and Ingalik—have been somewhat more formally organized than the eastern Dene. These western peoples enjoy annual salmon runs that supported slightly higher populations, although not as dense as the Northwest Coast populations to the south. The Tanaina on the Copper River had, in addition to salmon, sea mammals. Reminiscent of the north-

ern Northwest Coast Na-Dene (Tlingit) in social organization as well as in dependence upon salmon, the western Dene had loose matrilineal affiliation; clan is perhaps too strong a term, since the matrilineally affiliated persons did not share corporate ownership of houses or resources, nor did they institute official heads. Individuals in a band knew themselves to be, most commonly, either Crow (or Raven) or Wolf, according to their mother's affiliation. If a Crow, one should marry a Wolf, and of course vice versa. Members of the one division helped those of the other at life crises, from sending a midwife to attend a birth to preparing a corpse for burial. In many areas, there is said to have been a third division, which became reduced in numbers and joined one or the other of the two principal divisions. Affiliation was useful when a Dene traveled, for a Crow was supposed to be able to count on a Crow in any strange community to act as kinsman, and a Wolf to count on a Wolf.

Warfare seems to have been endemic between Dene and their neighbors, especially Inuit, in the historic period (the eighteenth and nineteenth centuries), and probably earlier, to judge from the use of armor by some of the western Dene. Stories about war describe dawn raids upon foreign camps, the enemy clubbing to death the sleeping residents. Revenge, for the death of a kinsman or the kidnapping of a wife, is alleged to have been the motive for raids, but in some cases, defense of territory or the aggressive expansion of a boundary seem likely. Stealing women may have been not uncommon, because when a family had several girls the parents felt constrained to "throw away" a new baby girl who was one too many for the hunters to provide for. Sons were always cared for because they could begin hunting at fourteen or fifteen, supporting rather than burdening the family's critical meat supply. As a result of the imbalance of young men and women caused by occasional female infanticide, an imbalance exacerbated by the custom of good hunters taking two wives, some young men could find no eligible woman to marry and looked to the women of a foreign band. One folk tale tells of a woman so beautiful and so capable in the housewifely arts that she was repeatedly captured and then recaptured, until finally she was called "Woman Who is Stolen Back and Forth." Another tale has such a woman develop sore feet from constantly being forced to travel from one captor to another. Thus, kidnapping for

wives probably did occur and did occasion vengeance raids. Captured women were not always passive: some tales describe how they plotted to lead their husbands to murder their captors. One heroine was so enraged by her captors killing her baby that she escaped, returned to her own people, and she herself organized and led a war party for revenge.

Western Dene resembled their Pacific Yupik and Tlingit neighbors in giving potlatch feasts, ostensibly as memorials to deceased relatives but at the same time as means to impress guests with the host's talents in accumulating goods and generosity in giving. Feasts included performances by masked dancers. Like the "messenger feasts" of the Yupik and Inuit, the western Dene potlatches were formal affairs beginning with ritualized invitations to allied villages. Eastern Dene feasts have been less elaborate, usually involving only the residents of one community and emphasizing thanksgiving and prayer for food abundance rather than gift giving. Eastern Dene feasts traditionally featured drumming (with the single-headed tambourine-type drum, hand-held) and singing, and then group social dancing following the dinner.

The Dene world is full of spirits. Many appear to persons, especially to children who seek them in the forest, and become their helpers. Others may be malicious, dangerous, or the helpers of enemies. Bush Men, ragged and unkempt, are said to lurk around camps and steal children and women. In the past, there was a real threat from raiders, but the Bush Man represents the more generalized threat felt to emanate from the forest, a locus of powers best managed by a caring and cooperating social group. Tales of Bush Men thus serve to teach children, and remind adults, of the value of the community and the possibly fatal result of too much individual independence.

Yet where population densities were kept low by the low food-resource density, the Dene also had to teach children to be self-sufficient and to make and act upon their own judgment. This was done by involving older children in household and hunting activities, giving them latitude to try things

KUTCHIN WINTER LODGES

FIGURE 9.7 Kutchin Dene winter camp, 1848. Man bringing firewood, left, is on snowshoes; a pair of snowshoes stands at right edge of lodge in foreground. Sleds are at left and right centers. *(Smithsonian Institution National Anthropological Archives)*

on their own, and traditionally also by sending children out on ever longer quests for a spirit helper. As the child (boy or girl) wandered alone in the forest, keenly alert for signs of his or her helper, the child became an expert on ecology and animal behavior and confident of his or her understanding of the natural world. When a spirit did speak to a child, dissociated from normal human life by being entirely alone and without food for several days, confidence was bolstered by the assurance of aid from a power greater than that of humans. Children returning from the quest for a helper were seen as wild; they needed to be carefully nursed back to social participation. They were not to recount their experiences, but to reflect on them privately. The quest vision would be reinforced by dreams of the animal who had promised to be one's helper. Some persons had especially

strong rapport with their helper, or gained more than one helper, and were enabled to become particularly successful in hunting and other businesses of life. Some could foretell the future through knowledge brought them by their helper when drumming and singing the helper's song, or when dreaming. Some knew of root medicines pointed out to them in dreams by the helper, gathered the medicines, leaving a pinch of tobacco as thanks on the spot, and administered them to the sick. These doctors usually combined a seance of drumming, singing, and magical extraction of illness with administration of the root, powdered or made into tea. Evil persons could blow power toward one of whom they were jealous or wished to control, causing the victim to fall ill and perhaps die unless a more potent doctor could be called in to nullify the evil power. Spiritually powerful persons formerly tried to bewitch their band's enemies, which at times led to feuds.

Chipewyans say of the spiritually powerful, "They know something a little," emphasizing that what makes them so adept are the morsels of knowledge that come to them in dreams from their helpers. In practice, older doctors noticed young persons who seemed likely to "know something a little" and questioned them, helping them interpret dreams and encouraging them to try to cure. Every normal adult would have a spirit helper and expect that dreams might furnish clues to successful behavior. Those who excelled in an activity were assumed to "know something a little" more than ordinary individuals, and would be allowed to organize activities, such as caribou drives, raids, or trading parties, that required coordination of several individuals. These leaders would make decisions on when and where a camp would move. If the leader's decisions proved ill advised, or if he or she developed an authoritative manner, people ceased to follow his or her directions and changed to a wiser, more polite leader. Exceptions would be leaders who appeared capable of bewitching those who displeased them. People would hope that a more powerful "knower" would battle the feared one, and tales of the awesome conflicts between decent and evil leaders testify to the degree to which Dene canons of interpersonal respect could be warped by ambition or bitterness. On the whole, however, the ethic of noninterference with another's behavior—and its complement, of consideration for others' welfare—was and remains strong in Dene communities. Coupled with this is a value on silence, which contrasts strongly with Euro-American expectations that good fellowship be expressed by words. Silence may be crucial for the hunter approaching his prey, but among the Dene its value was extended. Not only were children taught to be quiet in camps in the bush, but they also learned that those who might "know something a little" could lose some of that knowledge if interrupted when reflecting upon the meaning of a dream. Dene (and also the subarctic Algonkians)

therefore feel that only foolish or malicious people chatter. A group of Dene can be comfortably sociable even when no one says anything, and may be deeply disturbed by Euro-American customs of "polite conversation." These differences in etiquette have given Dene a reputation for being taciturn and unfriendly, and Euro-Americans among the Dene a reputation for intending evil.

The Fur-Trade Period

European contact began for Dene in 1714, when a Chipewyan woman captured by Crees escaped to the Hudson's Bay Company's York Fort. Stimulated by her mention of her people's western neighbors (the Yellowknives) using knives made from copper deposits, the governor of the Company in 1715 sent out an expedition to contact the "Northern Indians," and, in 1717, established Fort Churchill on the southwest shore of Hudson Bay to trade with these peoples. Chipewyans brought furs and musk-ox robes to Churchill, acting as middlemen in trade with Dene farther west as well as bringing in their own catches. From 1769 to 1772, Samuel Hearne, guided by the Chipewyan leader Matonabbee, explored the eastern Dene country for the Hudson's Bay Company. Soon after, in 1778, a post was set up on Lake Athabasca by the independent trader Peter Pond, and from the late 1780s until merger of the North West Company with the Bay in 1821, the rival companies built series of posts in Dene territories. In the same period, the Russian-American Company opened direct trade with western Dene by constructing a post in 1793 at Kenai on Cook Inlet, in Tanaina territory.

For most of the nineteenth century, European trade with Dene was limited in quantity and effect. Chipewyans dominated the eastern Dene trade until the Hudson's Bay Company moved into the Yukon in 1847, and the Tlingit blockaded the hinterland of northern British Columbia and adjacent Alaska until the 1870s, carrying goods to interior Dene trading partners and taking out products ranging from furs to spruce gum for chewing. Tlingit-Dene trade dated from the prehistoric period, but European goods intensified it. Both western and eastern Dene continued throughout the nineteenth century to make subsistence hunting, primarily of caribou, their chief concern, with furs for trading secondary. The Chipewyans even relied more on selling dried caribou meat to provision trading posts than on furs to obtain the iron knives, files, ice chisels (to chop holes for setting fishnets in winter), and kettles they considered necessary. Bows and arrows and spears continued to be hunting weapons, since muskets had less accuracy, though somewhat longer range, and tended to jam in winter.

It was the introduction of rapid-fire repeating rifles late in the nineteenth century that revolutionized Dene life. Rifles imparted greater efficiency in caribou hunting. Instead of laboring to construct corrals and fences and then organizing numbers of people to drive caribou within range of arrows and spears, Dene with rifles could suddenly open fire from a distance upon a herd of caribou and kill a dozen or more before the animals scattered. This allowed more time for nonsubsistence trapping for furs. In this period, also, commercial fishnets became available at the trading posts. Buying ready-made, durable nets with furs replaced spending days making a net. The greater slaughter of caribou made possible by rifles and especially the hauls of fish from the larger number of nets set gave a surplus of food that could support more dogs than had formerly been feasible. Each man could now cover a longer trap line, traveling more rapidly with a dog team drawing his sled. Women could move camp more easily by using their own teams of dogs for sleds. Dene continued to provide their own subsistence needs from hunting, but through the first half of the twentieth century, most men worked during the winter as trappers, supplying luxury furs to the international market. Rifles, ammunition, steel traps, cloth garments, tobacco, tea, sugar, flour and lard for bannock, and yeast and raisins for home brew (it was illegal to sell alcoholic beverages to Indians) became necessities, as iron implements had a century earlier.

Missionaries entered: Anglicans and Roman Catholic Oblate fathers in northern Canada beginning in the 1850s, and Roman Catholics and several Protestant denominations in Alaska after the 1867 purchase ended Russian Orthodox hegemony. As the rifle increased the distance between Dene and the animals they hunted, the feeling of a reciprocal relationship between humans and other creatures diminished, although it did not disappear, and Dene were receptive to Christianity. Leaders who had been respected as "knowing something a little" offered their services to missionaries and became catechists knowing another something a little, while continuing their leadership with their kindreds. People congregated at the Christmas and Easter seasons at the trading posts to exchange furs for supplies and to feast, with the trader and the missionary chipping in to make the New Year's Day celebration the highlight of the social year.

The fur-trade period for the Dene should be seen as several phases, a first one in which Dene on the western and eastern borders of the Northwest were middlemen but the subsistence-hunting economy was little changed, and a second one during the last third of the nineteenth century when a real shift in economic orientation occurred. The first phase began early in the eighteenth century for the Chipewyan, and early in the nineteenth century for the Tanaina, Tanana, and western and northern Kutchin. These peoples used muskets in warfare to guard their positions as middlemen, barring the interior Dene from coming down-river to the trading posts. Some Alaskan Dene on the uppermost reaches of the major rivers did not see a European or Euro-American until around 1900. The second phase of the fur-trade period coincided with initial colonization of Dene territory—that is, with settlements of Euro-Americans—but it was the complex of rifles, dog teams, trap lines, and months spent producing for the market, rather than colonization in a direct sense, that most strongly affected the Dene in this period. One effect of the commitment to trapping for furs to finance purchases was to reduce the basic task group to trapline partners, often a married couple. Women's fishing became a more major component of the subsistence pattern as men were out tending traplines (some women had their own traplines, but generally did not go alone as far and long from camp as men might). Early in the twentieth century, a mercantile economy was estab-

lished in the northern forests in which, the monopoly of the Hudson's Bay Company having ended and the Company itself shifted into merchandising, competing cash-paying fur buyers ended the partnership relations that a century earlier had been essentially a variation on the traditional task-focused and respect-structured relations between Dene.

"MODERN LIFE," 1958

The work-day at the Radar Base began at 7:30 A.M. The Indians at the village allowed themselves about an hour to make the 5-mile canoe trip from the village to the mouth of the river plus the 1-mile walk from the beach to the operations center.....Occasionally, a truck met them at the canoe landing to shuttle the workers to the site....

One group of three Indians, in the charge of a white truck driver, regularly spent the mornings collecting trash and garbage from the mess-hall and other sites and hauling it to the dump. Other crews moved food supplies from the main warehouse to the mess-hall storerooms, unloaded cargo from the incoming planes, or were assigned to special projects such as constructing crude platforms from saplings for carrying an above-the-ground pipe line.....

At 10 o'clock everyone took a 15-minute coffee-break, then returned to their jobs until lunch time. Indians brought their own lunches and ate them in their respective headquarters shacks. On exceptionally cold days those working for Bell went instead to a small, dark furnace room. All whites ate in the mess-hall.

About 1 o'clock the men returned to work. The afternoon was sometimes split by a coffee-break but, unlike the morning break, this was not a regular feature of the work day. About 5:20 P.M. a truck picked up the various crews and brought them to the headquarters areas. The men collected their gear and began the trip home.....

Women, children and old or unemployed men from the village made daily expeditions to the vast Radar Base dump that stretched several hundred yards along the river about 1.5 miles from the major building installations. Some came daily; some, combining visits to the dump with attending their fish-nets, two or three times a week; others intermittently, according to need. At almost any hour from morning to late afternoon, a dozen or so adults and children could be seen at the dump sitting and talking in small groups or casually picking their way through the debris. Some stayed only long enough to load their canoes with discarded packing crates, plywood sheets, damaged steel cots, mattresses, chairs, or whatever else might prove useful, sometimes making two or even three trips the same day. Others came early and spent the day around a fire or, in bad weather, in a temporary shelter hastily constructed from whatever happened to be at hand.

The arrival of a trash or garbage truck brought most people running, each one eager to beat the others to the choicest salvage. Out of deference to the Indians, the mess-hall personnel tried to keep garbage separate from the usable left-overs, and the men on the trucks carefully set the cans down rather than dump them over the side. The women, with sleeves rolled up, plunged their arms into the cans and began filling their boxes with food. After a few minutes, the cans were dumped and returned to the truck, leaving the Indians to pick through the remainder. About 4:30 or 5:00 P.M. those still at the dump loaded belongings and booty into their canoes and returned to the village.....

On Saturday nights...the village took on an unmistakable air of excitement. This was the night for home-brew drinking (illegal) and dancing (forbidden by the missionaries) in private. White men came over from the Base either singly or in small groups to rendezvous with girls from the village. Groups of young Indian men and women, high with excitement or alcohol, occasionally drunk, promenaded boisterously through the village until the early hours of the morning.

Sunday mornings, too, when all people of the village come together dressed in their best clothes for Mass, had its own special kind of excitement. The Base doctor came to the village and held a clinic in the mission after the morning religious ceremonies. A dozen or so other men from the Radar Base came as visitors, some to the mission to attend Mass (although the priest said Mass and heard confessions at the Base on Sunday afternoon), others to buy things at the Hudson's Bay Company store (closed to Indians on Sundays), or, most often, as "tourists."

About half the visitors from the Base remained in the vicinity of the mission and played softball, soccer, or pitched horseshoes with Indian boys and young men, frequently pausing to tease the group of giggling girls who watched and responded in kind. Others, carrying cameras and their pockets stuffed with food or hi-flasks, toured the village taking pictures, generally ending up in more or less secret meetings with girls or unmarried women. In good weather, groups of men from the Base stopped off at the village to pick up an Indian guide for fishing trips.....

The man who works at the Base cannot trap nor, except for sporadic and short-lived forays up-river or along the coast, can he hunt. He has to buy his food from the Company store, supplementing it with whatever fish his women-folk can take from the river. The women may also bring in an occasional rabbit from snares set nearby and, in season, the man can get some ducks and geese at little cost to his job. By and large, however, moose and caribou meat, along with other country food, has been displaced by Spam, canned meatballs, and a variety of canned and packaged foods.....Although the Indians learned, perforce, to build their meals around the tin can, few of them have yet learned to like it. Indeed, the most frequently cited cause of discontent with working at the Base was the aversion to canned food coupled with the lack of fresh meat.....Families who had been on the trap-lines were making a special effort to bring back fresh caribou or moose for sale in the village.....

The dump provided the family with supplementary food, fuel, raw materials for the construction and maintenance of houses and furnishings, and finished articles for a variety of uses.....Indians generally agreed that "we live better" as a result of the establishment of the Radar Base. "People dress better" and "nobody starves to death" were almost universal assessments.....Young men...explained, "it is easier to hunt in the [Hudson's Bay Company] store with my wallet than to hunt in the bush with my gun." Older men appeared reluctant to express a preference for wage-labour. Typically, they said, "it doesn't matter to me." ...Real income seems to have been less important in the decision to forego trapping than more general considerations of economic security.....The wage-earner...had the added security of knowing that a good or a bad year no longer meant the difference between eating well and going hungry.

(Liebow and Trudeau 1962: 195–204)

Rifles and commercial fishnets were the obvious key factors in the new economy, but an underlying major factor in the economic shift must have been depopulation from disease. In 1781, Chipewyans as well as Crees suffered heavily in a smallpox epidemic. Possibly as an aftereffect of the losses of hunters in the epidemic, Dene seen by Alexander Mackenzie on the upper portion of the river named after him looked sickly, whereas those farther down, farther from the epidemic that had come from the southeast, appeared healthy and handsome. Eastern Dene died in considerable numbers during the 1820s from contagious disease, not further identified by the traders who recorded the devastation. Smallpox took a great toll in 1838 and 1839 among all Dene. Whooping cough took many children in the 1840s and 1850s, and other diseases destroyed families in these decades. Scarlet fever was virulent and fatal to many between 1862 and 1865. Diphtheria struck in the early 1880s. Scarlet fever returned around 1897. The influenza pandemic of 1918 reached the Dene, and a second influenza epidemic seems to have been even more severe in 1928. Tuberculosis may be said to have become epidemic among Dene, as among Inuit, during the 1930s. After each of these epidemics, the disruption of subsistence pursuits during the period of illness tended to leave a shortage of dried meat and fish, which caused starvation by late winter. Crisis was aggravated by the sudden deaths of hunters and leaders who "knew something a little." The survivors were forced to seek out other survivors with whom they could form new hunting groups under untested leaders. Thus, the toll of disease was greatly augmented by famine following the actual epidemic and by poor nutrition for months, which in turn made the survivors susceptible to further afflictions and less efficient in hunting and fishing. It has been estimated that the Kutchin, for example, were reduced by five-sixths, from about fifty-four hundred in the eighteenth century to about nine hundred in the 1860s. (By the early 1970s, the Kutchin population had recovered to about twenty-five hundred.)

Added to the disease losses were the losses from intensified raiding and warfare in the first phase of the fur-trade period. The horrendous figures that resulted suggest that the Dene may have been driven into the market economy because it became difficult to operate caribou pounds with shrunken bands, difficult to clothe everyone adequately when so many women seamstresses died, difficult to find time to make fishnets when so few adults remained to hunt and fish. In the context of minimal populations, the efficiency of the repeating rifle and commercial fishnets, which had to be purchased with furs, may have seemed the only means of survival.

The Colonization of the Dene Lands

Colonization first came to the western Dene in the 1860s and 1870s with gold strikes in northern British Columbia and then in Alaska. "The" Gold Rush began in 1898: that year, the Klondike deposits drew forty thousand prospectors through Chilkoot Pass alone. Tent cities erupted at Dawson and other localities on the upper Yukon, ephemeral cities but complete with saloons, brothels, and gambling halls. Dene eager for cash or novelty flocked to these towns, men selling fish and meat or working as laborers on the steamboats, at the river docks, and in towns, women working as laundresses if they accompanied their husbands. The majority of Dene men made excursions for wage labor on the pattern of hunting and trapping, leaving wives and children home in camp. As the gold fever waned, the tent cities emptied and opportunities for Dene men to work as laborers declined. The first decade of the twentieth century was therefore a short boom period for the interior Dene around the upper Yukon, a period in which the Kutchin gave memorable potlatches.

More gradual and ultimately more significant colonization came through incursions more modest than the gold rush. After the United States purchased Alaska, an ambitious plan to link America and Europe through a telegraph line across

Alaska and Russia was launched. With the telegraph line went a series of small stations to maintain it, the stations manned by skilled Euro-Americans imported for tours of duty from the south. This pattern expanded as weather stations and radio stations were constructed. Missions broadened their work by opening schools, particularly in the early twentieth century. For the first decades, not many Dene children attended schools, and of those who did, not many completed more than a primary education. But the presence of missions proselytizing through church and through school and employing a few men at each station had to be accommodated by the Dene of the locality. The missionaries frequently were actively supported by the trader, whose power over purchasing credit could make life easier for those who cooperated with the mission and frustrating for those who opposed it. Even when trader and missionary disliked each other, they affected the local Dene community by pressuring residents to align with one faction or the other. Trading posts increased in number in the early twentieth century; some former whaling ships converted to trading schooners after the end of the baleen market in 1907, independent traders and a few missions set up after the Hudson's Bay Company monopoly was broken at the beginning of the century, and the large firm of Révillon Frères entered competition with the Bay during the 1920s. By establishing a relatively large number of fixed nuclei of trading post and mission, usually at fishing stations, colonists drew the Dene to shorten their earlier pattern of a long annual circuit of fishing, hunting, and wintering camps. After the 1870s, families planned on meeting at the village several times a year to stock up on trading goods and attend religious festivals. Eventually, intensification of trapping relatively close to the post villages, exacerbated in the twentieth century by an influx of non-Indian commercial trappers, so depleted furbearers in the favored regions that in the 1930s and particularly in the 1940s, federal and provincial governments began restricting trapping, issuing licenses to individuals for designated trapline territories and setting quotas. These measures were the final stage in shifting Dene (and Algonkian speakers in the eastern forests) from task-group to nuclear family structure.

Almost unheralded, homesteaders looking for farm and ranch land invaded those northern valleys sheltered from the more extreme Arctic cold. Some settled in northern British Columbia after the earlier gold strikes; some cleared claims in the Peace River basin of northern Alberta, beginning in the 1890s; some came into the Tanana and, in the 1930s, Matanuska valleys of Alaska. The Peace River colonists destroyed most of the bison herds that formed the subsistence base of the Beaver Indians, forcing these bands to hunt instead the smaller populations of moose and woodland caribou in the region. While fur prices held through the 1920s, the intrusions of settlers were not so disturbing, but when the Depression pulled down demand in the 1930s, competition for what market remained coming from better-capitalized Euro-American trappers, and dispersion of game from some of the best lands of the Northwest, increased the hardships felt by Dene.

The Micro-Urbanization of the North

Construction of the Alaska, or Alcan, Highway during World War II marked the initiation of the "micro-urbanization" period of the North. Highway camps employed Dene laborers, some of whom were trained to operate heavy equipment. Once the road was open, trading posts with limited arrays of goods were transformed into southern-style general stores. By the 1970s, many of these stores had developed into small department stores with supermarket sections and catalog desks where customers could order from the major mail-order merchandisers serving millions of southern rural and suburban families. A few large mines with smelters were erected, such as Flin Flon, which processes copper and zinc in northern Manitoba, and Uranium City on Lake

Athabasca. Although the policies of these mines have been to recruit young Euro-Canadian men at high wages for relatively brief terms of employment, some Dene men have been engaged, and the mine towns bring in others as laborers. Oil- and gas-exploration work has also employed some Dene in spite of the preference for imported labor.

The real impact on Dene life during the second half of the twentieth century has been that of the government, United States or Canadian. Soon after World War II, British Columbia and then the federal administration of the Northwest and the provincial governments of the central provinces imposed the requirement of registration of trap lines. The purpose of the new laws was said to be conservation, although the postwar fall in fur prices probably would have been an effective conservation agent in itself. While trapline registration was supposed to merely recognize, in most areas, the status quo, it intruded foreign regulation into economic pursuits that had operated through community agreements. Regulation tended to openly pit one man or family against another, even when, as in many regions of the Subarctic, a bloc of trap lines was registered to a native band. Supervision of trap lines brought government officers into more frequent interaction with Dene, and as a result, conflicts between Dene practices, developed through generations of experience in a region, and regulations derived from theory or experiences in the south were bound to arise.

Augmenting the shift from task group to nuclear family structure was the emphasis, beginning in the 1950s and accelerating in the 1960s, on formal education for Dene in both Alaska and Canada. Pulled from their seasonally nomadic life in bush camps into permanent homes, their villages now centered on the government school. During the previous half-century, many Dene had built log cabins at the trading posts or mission stations, but it had been customary for families to go out on the trap lines in winter, go to fish camps in summer, and sometimes still make up meat camps in early winter. The United States had made some serious

efforts to school Alaskan Dene children by shipping youngsters from the age of five up to residential schools in Alaskan cities or farther south, efforts that saw annual roundups of weeping children torn from agonized parents and herded onto planes. The Canadian government had relied upon missions, which, with more limited funds, had concentrated upon saving orphans rather than uprooting all children. The postwar military importance of the North and the prospect of industrial development brought new government policies of integrating northern residents as fully as possible into national life, either to provide a proletariat for envisioned commercial growth, or for what seemed humanitarian reasons.

United States experience had shown that young people who had spent most of their childhood warehoused in school dormitories were unable to carry on their parents' activities, yet were usually insufficiently educated to win satisfactory employment in cities where racial discrimination and the shyness inculcated by segregation in Indian schools much reduced opportunities even for the few young people who persevered to a high school diploma. There began in the 1950s, then, the construction of schools in Indian and Inuit communities so that families need not be broken up in order to give their children the formal education that is considered the right of every young United States and Canadian citizen. By around 1970, most Dene, like most northern Algonkian and Inuit, lived year-round in wooden-frame houses constructed under government subsidy close to a school. Mothers and elderly persons remained in the villages with the children while the active men went out, often in parties of two, for a week or two at a stretch to tend the trap line or to hunt. In the summer, the family might pile into a boat—a manufactured canoe or dory with an outboard motor—to go to a fish camp, but the increasing use of snowmobiles in place of dog teams meant it was no longer necessary to stockpile dried fish to feed dogs, so the produce of the lake or river upon which the village is situated might be sufficient for a family. Children were growing up lacking experience in the bush, playing spy-versus-spy in imitation of the weekly movie instead of tending snares around a camp. Teenagers pored over clothes in catalogs while their older brothers and sisters played pool and relaxed with a beer in the bar. The presence of Euro-Americans and of members of other native ethnic groups, some of them nurses, store personnel, and other skilled workers, engendered the tenseness that comes from lack of understanding of other cultures' modes of politeness and behavioral cues. Thus the "micro-urban village" replaced the Dene camp as the locus of Dene life.

The Resurgence of the Dene

While government policies directed the Dene into sedentary clusters cut off from intimacy with the natural world, Dene population was rising. The tuberculosis epidemic of the 1930s had at that time been met by transporting hundreds of Indians and Inuit each year to southern hospitals for protracted stays. Chemotherapy developed in the 1950s curbed tuberculosis with minimal disruption of the patient's life. Nurses stationed in the villages radioed requests for air transportation of the ill and injured to hospitals and saved many lives, and vaccinations prevented many more from becoming sick. Respiratory-disease rates and death rates are still much higher in northern native populations than among Euro-Americans, but birth rates are high, too, and the survival rate of infants is many times the rate in past generations. One result of the recovery of the Dene population from its nadir in the late nineteenth century is that hunting camps can again be sustained. This increased manpower for hunting may be one factor stimulating many Dene at the end of the 1970s to return to a greater emphasis on subsistence hunting.

Treaties had been signed in 1899 with the Chipewyan, Yellowknives, and Dogrib and in 1921 with Beaver, Slavey, Mountain, Hare, Bear Lake, and Dogrib. According to the words of the treaties, they ceded Indian "rights, titles, and privi-

leges" to the Northwest Territories to the Dominion of Canada. Recent research has established that many of the illiterate government-identified "chiefs" who made an X on the treaty papers had not been fully informed on the import of the treaty by the Métis interpreters, who perhaps did not understand the treaty provisions themselves. In some instances there is reason to believe that the signatures of recalcitrant local leaders were forged on the papers. Until the 1950s, there was little concern in the Northwest with the treaties. Then, the passage of the revised Indian Act by the government of Canada in 1951 affirmed the Indians' inclusion in federal programs of welfare and assistance, from family allowances and old-age pensions giving small regular cash incomes to parents and the elderly, to education. Indian parents were distressed by the failure of schools to give their children the level of competence in Euro-American skills achieved by most of the Euro-Canadians in the North, but the Indian ethic of noninterference in another's activities kept parents quiet. Alaska Dene had experiences similar to those of their Canadian cousins, although they never signed treaties.

In 1962, Dene from interior Alaska organized at Tanana, led by a young Tanana man, Alfred Ketzler. With some financial aid and advice from the Association of American Indian Affairs, a "friends of the Indian" group based in New York, and the Alaska Native Rights Association, representatives from twenty-four communities discussed their mutual problems. One stimulus to the meeting was the new State of Alaska's imminent selection of 103 million acres (41,682,000 hectares) under the Statehood Act, and the fear that some of the acreage would be land used by the Dene. A second stimulus was conflict between subsistence-hunting needs and the international, federal, and state game laws. The Inupiat men at Barrow had the year before, 1961, staged a successful and well-publicized showdown over their need to hunt eider ducks out of season (out of season according to federal regulations, that is). The Tanana and allied Dene expected that they would need to similarly insist on exemption of subsistence hunting from recreational-hunting regulations and international conservation agreements. At the meeting, several Dene leaders pointed out the difficulties in obtaining financing for homes or commercial ventures encountered by most Indians, who because aboriginal title had never been legally established in Alaska had no ownership of land to build on or use as collateral. To be able to call upon the organizational and land-claim experience of the Tlingit, and ally with them should the Indians of Alaska press claims jointly, the Dene meeting at Tanana voted to affiliate with the Alaska Native Brotherhood, which had been working in southern Alaska since 1912. A voice for the Dene and the Inupiat, who were also organizing at this time, appeared a few months later as a newspaper, the *Tundra Times*, published by Howard Rock, an Inupiat, assisted initially by a Euro-American professional journalist, Tom Snapp.

The formation of the Alaska Federation of Natives, legally established in 1967 after the major meeting of regional representatives in 1966, included Dene as well as Inupiat and Aleut. The Tanana Chiefs Conferences were seen as a model for the federation. In 1971, Alaska Dene won their share in the Alaska Native Claims Settlement Act. Most of the Alaska Dene are members of Doyon, Ltd., the regional corporation mandated by the act that covers a large section of interior Alaska; other Dene are in the Cook Inlet Region, Inc. (principally Tanaina) and Ahtna, Inc. In 1980, the census reported slightly over ten thousand Alaskan Athabascans. *Newsweek* magazine noted in 1978 that Doyon Ltd. is the largest private landowner in the United States. Befitting that status, it invested as a partner in United Bank of Alaska. Many of its shareholders hoped that this and other investments, and leases let for mineral and oil exploration, would bring sufficient income to pay dividends enabling Dene to buy supplies needed for subsistence hunting without being forced to participate in world fur markets or industrial labor.

Alaskan Dene land claims were one stimulus to Canadian Dene examination of their status. The more immediate stimulus was a proposal to build a pipeline through the Mackenzie Valley to deliver natural gas to southern markets. Like the Alaskan pipeline, the Mackenzie Valley pipe would go through fragile ecosystems and disrupt caribou migrations. In 1970, the treaty Indians (members of bands whose leaders had signed the 1899 or 1921 treaties, making the band members legally Indians) organized the Indian Brotherhood of the Northwest Territories in order to formulate and press Dene claims to their lands. By 1973, several of the Dene elected chiefs were in a position to apply to the Supreme Court of the Northwest Territories for a halt to industrial development on 450,000 square miles (1.1 million square kilometers) of the territories. Technically, they filed a caveat, or formal declaration of prior interest in the land, which would prevent any transfers of the land until the declared prior interest had been settled. Justice William Morrow held hearings on the case in a number of communities along the Mackenzie, a procedure unprecedented in its concern that the interests of the people rather than the convenience of the court should be served. The testimonies he heard convinced Justice Morrow that the purported cession of land in the treaties had in many localities been obtained by misrepresentation, outright fraud, or insufficient explanation of the meaning of the English phrases. Justice Morrow then found for the plaintiffs. The government ("Crown") appealed Justice Morrow's decision, it was reversed on a technicality, but that reversal was appealed to the Supreme Court of Canada by the Dene Chiefs. Meanwhile, in 1975, a meeting of representatives from Dene communities, nonstatus (not included in the treaties although socially recognized as Indian) and Métis (of mixed European and Indian descent) as well as treaty Indians, issued the Dene Declaration, a statement of rights focusing on "the right to self-determination as a distinct people and the recognition of the Dene Nation." A year later, 1976, a meeting restricted to the elected chiefs of the twenty-five Dene communities of the territories and the officers of the Indian Brotherhood drew up an agreement on the principles under which the Dene would negotiate with the government of Canada to revise the treaties. This agreement was publicly announced later in 1976 at a general meeting of Dene, although it had been rejected by the Métis who had organized in 1973 as the Métis and Non-Status Native Association [of the Northwest Territories]: the Agreement stressed the importance of international recognition of the Dene as a once-sovereign nation (or people), which the numerically smaller group of Métis feared might deny their rights to cultural patterns differing from those of the dominant Dene.

The Dene Declaration and the agreement drafted by the Indian Brotherhood of the Northwest Territories had received considerable backing from Euro-Canadian organizations and the public, in part because such groups as the Canadian Labour Congress (labor unions) and the New Democratic Party (one of Canada's three major national political parties) recognize that the Mackenzie Valley Pipeline was to be financed largely by foreign capital for foreign economic interests, but in large part because of the Berger Inquiry. Justice Thomas Berger of the British Columbia Supreme Court had represented the Nishga, a Tsimshian-speaking group on the Nass River in northern British Columbia, in their 1969 claim to land. The Nishga had been arguing for their land since 1869, but a century later were at last able to get a court hearing through the efforts of their tribal-council president, Frank Calder, who had become prominent as the first Indian elected to the British Columbia Legislature. After lower-court decisions against them, the Nishga engaged Mr. Berger to argue for them before the Supreme Court of Canada. That court also ruled against the Nishga, on a technicality, but its deliberations revealed a split between the justices on the basic question of aboriginal title. Realizing that the Nishga had good legal arguments for their claim, the governments of Canada and British Columbia began negotiating

for a settlement, which the Nishga insist must not extinguish their title to their land. Having learned much about native views of issues of land rights and use, Mr. Berger agreed to head an inquiry into the Mackenzie Pipeline proposal in 1975. He traveled to each Dene and Inuit community on the Mackenzie and garnered impressive piles of frank and thoughtful appraisals. News media gave ample publicity to the warm, humble judge and the weather-beaten men and women who spoke before him in the small community rooms of the picturesque northern villages. The findings of the Berger Inquiry supported the Dene Chiefs' caveat and position that the pipeline threatened unjustifiable harm to thousands of Mackenzie residents. Construction of the pipeline was therefore delayed, and with wide public approbation the Dene and the Council of Yukon Indians, who had been quietly negotiating land claims for the territory west of the Mackenzie, pushed for establishment of aboriginal title and a consequent recognition of their right to self-determination. The possibility of a federal relationship with the national government like that of the existing provinces of Canada, with territorial affairs administered by Dene and economic power built upon compensation for past Euro-Canadian use of Dene land, is the crux of Dene planning.

Until the promised land, or time, is reached, the Dene continue their orientation toward subsistence hunting, particularly of caribou, supplemented by fish. Trapping is the most common cash-earning occupation of men, along with seasonal wage labor where available. Snowmobiles and increasing use of small chartered planes allow men to extend their hunting and trapping territories far enough to obtain game and furs in spite of the congregation of many families around the village schools. Community involvement in the schools is being encouraged and curricula are being adapted so that they focus more on enhancing students' (adults as well as children) capability to deal with local situations rather than on training for urban life. Paradoxically, many young people are striving to gain sophistication in working with high-level Euro-Canadians while their friends seriously discuss jettisoning Western technology to be able to live truly independently as hunters. A few Dene argue that what is needed is more industrial development, but with adoption of Indian rather than Western work patterns: cooperating "gangs" of workers instead of individuals more or less competing with one another, more flexible work periods allowing men to hunt or feast reasonably often without jeopardizing jobs, and less hierarchical structuring of responsibility. (Similar proposals have been advanced by Western reformers hoping to make European and Euro-American industries more humane.) The Dene realize that although their land is still a colony, it has not been integrated into the Euro-Canadian nation to an irreversible degree. The Dene, like the Inuit, see a real chance of preserving their traditional way of life—indeed, of seeing it blossom as it could not in earlier centuries when infant mortality was high, famines might occur late in winter, and enemy raids were threatening. Total Dene population in Canada in 1980 was approximately twenty-five thousand; this is an estimate which must be rough because the government census excludes from the "Indian" count all non-status Indians, of which there are many in the North because treaty-making there has been late and incomplete.

SECTION 5: THE NORTHERN ALGONKIANS

Chapter 5 introduced the northern Algonkians from the perspectives of the prehistoric Shield Archaic and the historic fur trade. This chapter complements that introduction by describing the northern Algonkians from the perspective of Subarctic cultural patterns and history. Subarctic Algonkians, like the Dene of the western Subarctic, speak a series of dialects and languages grading into one another without clear-cut boundaries. The eastern set comprises Montagnais-Naskapi and Cree, and a second set,

originally west of the first, consists of Ojibwa, Saulteaux, Algonkin proper, and Ottawa. The speakers of the last two, Algonkin and Ottawa, lived directly north of the Iroquois nations in the transition zone between the St. Lawrence Valley and the Subarctic, and collectively were objects of the seventeenth- and eighteenth-century power struggles among the League of the Iroquois (the Five Nations), non-League Iroquois, France, Britain, and the United States. The outcome of the struggles for these two peoples was to reduce the Algonkins to small villages in southern Quebec and adjacent eastern Ontario, and the Ottawa (Odawa) to settlements scattered from Lake Huron and southern Michigan to Kansas and Oklahoma. Their cultural patterns and histories fit into the Northeast culture area. The Ojibwa and their historic offshoot, the Saulteaux, lived west of the Iroquois homelands and consequently were peripheral to the most intense of the fur-trade struggles. They began to expand northward during the eighteenth century in order to trade with the Hudson's Bay Company posts, although French posts established within their Great Lakes territories were more convenient. When the Hudson's Bay Company secured a monopoly on the fur trade, first by Britain's defeat of France in the 1756-63 war and then by merging with the North West Company in 1821, the hundreds of Ojibwa who had over several generations found it profitable to hunt and trap furs in the central Canadian boreal forest began a century of hardship, forced to suffer the Bay's straitened policies of economy because their ancestral homeland around the Sault Ste. Marie, Lake Huron, and eastern Lake Superior was now occupied by stronger groups. Thus, in the nineteenth century, there came to be a population of Northern Ojibwa adapted to Subarctic conditions.

The Cree and Montagnais-Naskapi

The Cree, Montagnais, and Naskapi (Innu) represent the aboriginal inhabitants of the eastern

Subarctic. Their ancestors may have developed, and certainly were included in the late prehistoric pattern of, the Shield Archaic. Algonkian roots could go back seven thousand years to the early postglacial Shield Archaic period. During the Middle Woodland period—the later first millennium B.C. and the first millennium A.D.—pottery was added to the technology of the eastern-boreal-forest inhabitants, presumably spreading from its point of origin or introduction in the Northeast—a point of controversy but possibly the St. Lawrence region. More or less continuous occupations of sites historically attributed to Algonkian speakers date back to the tenth century A.D. In this Late Woodland period, which lasts to historic contacts in the sixteenth and seventeenth centuries, artifacts made of stone and bone show considerable continuity not only from earlier Middle Woodland, but from the Shield Archaic technology, while pottery attests to the trade between northern Algonkians, who offered furs, meat, and birch-bark canoes, and the Iroquoians of the St. Lawrence Valley and eastern Great Lakes, who reciprocated with maize and fishnets. Foreign pottery styles in Algonkian sites demonstrate further trade between probable ancestral Cree and ancestral Ojibwa and Assiniboin.

Cree, Montagnais, and Naskapi are conventional designations for populations of small Algonkian-speaking hunting bands who have never had overarching political structures other than the twentieth-century imposition of Euro-Canadian dominion and the recent native protest groups reacting to it. The Montagnais are the Indians of the forest north of the Gulf of St. Lawrence to the James Bay watershed. Thus, they are principally inhabitants of the province of Québec. Naskapi occupy the Labrador Peninsula, east and north of the Montagnais, the timber edge and tundra. Cree live west of the Montagnais, south and west of James Bay, in Québec and Ontario. As boreal-forest peoples, the Cree and Montagnais hunt moose—and to a lesser degree caribou, bear, and

hares—and trap beaver and other fur bearers. Naskapi are hunters of caribou, the most numerous game on the tundra and timber line. Naskapi and Montagnais dialects are close, and differentiation of the two groups is based on their principal game—moose versus caribou—and, at least in the twentieth century, on the more conservative, traditional hunting life of the Naskapi versus the greater integration into the Canadian economy of the Montagnais. The term *naskapi* signifies a wild and impoverished person, one who is beyond the bounds of civilization, and was applied by Montagnais to those who rejected what Montagnais considered the more proper life; the Naskapis' own term for themselves, Innu, signifies "human beings." Cree are differentiated from Montagnais-Naskapi more by their region, the James Bay and southern Hudson Bay drainages, than by cultural distinctions.

Cree and Montagnais aboriginal dwellings were conical or round wigwams covered with caribou or moose hides or a layer of moss over which birch bark was laid. Innu, living for the most part beyond birch woods, used the caribou-skin tipi. All these northern Algonkians depended on snowshoes to move about in winter, hauling carcasses, tipis, food stores, and other goods on toboggans. During the summer, travel was by birch-bark canoes. The basic social unit was the hunting group, of which the core was the partnership of two or more men, frequently brothers or brothers-in-law. The hunting group supported wives, children, elderly parents and widowed relatives, and younger unmarried brothers. Most groups acknowledged as leader the most successful hunter, who by his success in obtaining game demonstrated wisdom and spiritual power. It was the business of men to shoot and trap larger game and work with the women in fishing, as well as to carve implements of wood and bone as needed. Women fished and snared hares and other smaller game and birds in the vicinity of the camp, to which child care normally confined most women. Parties of women went out gathering berries and the few edible plants of the region, and some women, particularly widows who no longer had small children, hunted game as men did. In crafts, women handled soft materials, processing hides, making birch-bark containers, sewing tipi covers, garments, and robes, and embroidering, originally with porcupine quills and moose hair and later with beads and silk.

Camp was moved several times a year: in the summer, several hunting groups congregated where large numbers of fish could be secured in weirs or traps, or, later, in commercial nets; in September, the fish camps broke up as each hunting group set out to a locality it preferred for hunting migrating waterfowl and moose and bear. If a good kill was made, the whole group moved to the kill site rather than transporting quantities of meat to camp. Fish were regularly taken, though considered a dull staple, inferior to moose. Summer catches were dried, some kept whole for dog food and some cooked over low heat and broken up into powder for better storage as human food. Moose and caribou were cut into thin strips, some of which were dried or smoked for preservation and the rest boiled. Marrow was enjoyed, and fat was rendered and stored, to be mixed with dried meat or fish powder and berries. Grouse and ptarmigan, as well as ducks and geese, were taken, and hares were valued as fresh meat in winter, when large game was difficult to find. Sturgeon were speared, especially when they traveled to spawn. Montagnais and Innu usually moved to the Labrador coast or the Gulf of St. Lawrence coast in summer to hunt seals and fish for saltwater species such as cod. The Innu returned to the tundra or tundra border in the autumn, until this century cooperating to drive caribou into corrals or snare fences. Rifles made this method of hunting unnecessary.

A literally close relationship between humans and their prey existed, late in the nineteenth century, before rifles allowed hunters to shoot from a distance. Sinew-backed (laminated) bows were used until rifles replaced them. They were powerful, but of lesser range than the gun. Therefore, to secure game the human had to bring himself fairly close to the animal, by stalking, driving, or snaring. To achieve this proximity, the hunter needed detailed knowledge of animal behavior patterns and alertness to every clue and cue; having achieved this proximity at the kill, the hunter was very much aware of the prey's emotions. Cree, Montagnais, and Innu understand that humans are but one among many species on earth, and postulate that hunting success depends upon a prey's willingness to support the life of the hunter and his dependents. Such willingness comes through a carefully cultivated rapport between the human and spirits who may appear in animal guise. Young Cree sought relationships with spirits by going out alone to fast for days in the forest, hoping in this state of purity away from the ordinary businesses of camp, a spirit would approach and promise aid in life. Montagnais and Innu were less likely to go out on a vision quest, but expected to be approached by spirits through dreams. Whether a spirit appeared during a solitary vigil or a dream, the recipient consulted an older person—a parent or, more often, a respected native doctor—for clarification of the vision and advice on how to maintain the good will of the spirit helper. No one casually discussed his or her visions, for to do so would destroy the precious rapport between spirit and partner. Often, the spirit desired that a certain design be embroidered or painted upon its human friend's clothing or on a possession such as a leather shot pouch or a bone skinning knife. To carry out the spirit's wish, the human partner might need the help of a spouse, since men ordinarily did not learn to sew well, nor women to carve well, but the spouse would not be told the details of the vision. Spirit helpers informed people, usually through dreams but also through divination techniques such as interpreting cracks in animal shoulder blades held over fires, where game would be found. The spirit helper was considered to be often instrumental in inducing an animal to give itself to the hunter. Hunters and their dependents had also to treat the carcasses and bones of game respectfully and use them thoroughly, or the spirit of the species would

Some men and women dreamt of powerful spirits, or dreamt more frequently of spirits. These persons realized they were called to be doctors. Apprenticeship to a practicing doctor eventually brought the novice familiarity with a variety of medicinal plants and skill in sleight of hand and ventriloquism. Aided by his or her spirit helpers, the adept became a seer able to foretell the future, find lost objects, and report on distant persons. He or she cured sufferers by removing disease by blowing upon or sucking the ill part, and by administering herb concoctions. Wounds and broken bones were treated with poultices and set. Seers usually could persuade their spirit helpers to fly to harm someone believed to be evil, or an enemy. One observer pointed out that through this power the seer acted as attorney for injured persons: One who was cheated or was the victim of malicious machinations visited a seer and informally mentioned his grievance. The seer suggested the plaintiff return in a week or so if the situation was not rectified. At the second visit, the seer summoned his spirit helpers, told them of the injustice, and asked them to effect punishment upon the wrongdoer. It was alleged that the wrongdoer would then sicken, perhaps die, or become the victim of other

THE HOLY OCCUPATION

To the Montagnais-Naskapi—hunters on the barest subsistence level—the animals of the forest, the tundra, and the waters of the interior and the coast, exist in a specific relation. They have become the objects of engrossing magico-religious activity, for to them hunting is a holy occupation. The animals (*awa'cats*) pursue an existence corresponding to that of man as regards emotions and purposes in life. The difference between man and animals, they believe, lies chiefly in outward form..... When addressing animals in a spiritual way in his songs, or using the drum, the conjuror uses the expression *ni·tcimi'·tc ^{c}tc ni·tcatce'^{c}tce'^{c}k,* which means, freely, "you and I wear the same covering and have the same mind and spiritual strength." This statement was explained as meaning not that men had fur, not that animals wore garments, but that their equality was spiritual and embraced or eclipsed the physical.....

The killing of animals, then, entails much responsibility in the spiritual sense..... Requirements of conduct toward animals exist, however, which have to be known and carried out by the hunter. His success depends upon this knowledge, and, they argue, since no one can know everything and act to perfection, the subject of magico-religious science becomes, even from the native point of view, an inexhaustible one.....

The changing conditions of the time force them to eat pork and beef. They realize, however, the impurity of these viands, and attribute their bodily ills, even the decline of their race, to the eating of domestic animals..... The distinction between eating the flesh of the native herbivorous game animals and domestic beasts is of fundamental significance. Native game is to them *notcimi·'umi·tca'm*, "forest food," tantamount in meaning to "pure food."

The holiness of hunting and the holy character of the animals that are hunted has been alluded to. We note a most important and logical belief, at least from the angle of native thought: that the food of the native game animal, the caribou, moose, bear, and beaver, being vegetal substance, and the vegetable kingdom being the original source of medicine agency, the virtues of plant pharmacy are conveyed from the original growths to man through this diet. No wonder, then, the proper food of the tribe being either directly wild fruits or indirectly vegetable through the diet of game animals, that with their food in whatever form consumed, the Montagnais-Naskapi are "taking-medicine." Thus, the native game diet is prophylactic to mankind.....

The material from the northern interior bands can best be surveyed from the transcriptions of the informants themselves:

> To you will be related a story; the caribou-man story. Once an old man and his son were very expert in hunting. And it happened that the son dreamed that he cohabited with caribou. It seemed that he killed a great many caribou. Once, then, it happened that during the winter he said to his father. "I will depart. And I will kill caribou enough for the whole winter. So do not wait for me as respects anything. I will come back. For, indeed, I am going to go with the caribou." Then he sang: "The caribou walked along well like me. Then I walked as he was walking. Then I took his path. And then I walked like the caribou, my trail looking like a caribou trail where I saw my tracks. And so indeed I will take care of the caribou. I indeed will divide the caribou. I will give them to the people. I will know how many to give the people. It will be known to me." [So he sang, and continued:] "He who obeys the requirements is given caribou, and he who disobeys is not given caribou. If he wastes much caribou he cannot be given them, because he wastes too much of his food—the good things. And now, as much as I have spoken, you will know forever how it is. For so now it is as I have said. I, indeed, am Caribou Man *(Ati'k^{c}wape'o)*. So I am called."

(Speck 1977 [1935]:72-73, 78-79, 81)

---

misfortune, unless the wrongdoer was an especially powerful spiritualist, in which case battle might be engaged between the two seers' spirits, the weaker seer to die. In these cases the public served as jury, hearing the evidence from both sides as people talked about grievances, discussing the circumstances and characters of plaintiff and defendant, and rendering judgment. One guilty of wrongdoing might very well sicken with despair, knowing that the victim had enlisted spirits to wreak vengeance and that society concurred. There was usually public knowledge of the seer's action, because the plaintiff's second, formal visit for aid would be attended by the people in the hunting group. The seer would have a small tent or a booth erected, and would be securely bound in a hide or cloth wound with stout cords, and then placed inside the booth. Viewers would see the booth shake violently as spirits came to the seer, talking with their ally in odd voices and weird

languages. At last, the seer would emerge from the booth, miraculously free of the bonds, like Houdini, exhausted but able to report on the probable outcome of the client's case.

The "shaking tent" or "conjuror's booth," as Europeans termed it, was resorted to in the cooler months of the year, when people lived in smaller camps. At the summer fish camps, leaders of the several hunting groups gathered in council to discuss matters of common concern. Among these might be crimes such as murder or unjustified theft. (Someone in dire need was welcome to take what was required for survival from another's cache, but was expected to tell the owner as soon as possible and to repay.) In the historic period, at least, cases have been reported in which the council decided the criminal deserved death, and at once ordered young men of the camp to take the person out and execute him. Whether executions, rather than outcasting, were carried out before European models hunting group. The seer would have a small tent or a booth erected, and would be securely bound in a hide or cloth wound with stout cords, and then placed inside the booth. Viewers would see the booth shake violently as spirits came to the seer, talking with their ally in odd voices and weird languages. At last, the seer would emerge from the booth, miraculously free of the bonds, like Houdini, exhausted but able to report on the probable outcome of the client's case.

The "shaking tent" or "conjuror's booth," as Europeans termed it, was resorted to in the cooler months of the year, when people lived in smaller camps. At the summer fish camps, leaders of the several hunting groups gathered in council to discuss matters of common concern. Among these might be crimes such as murder or unjustified theft. (Someone in dire need was welcome to take what was required for survival from another's cache, but was expected to tell the owner as soon as possible and to repay.) In the historic period, at least, cases have been reported in which the council decided the criminal deserved death, and at once ordered young men of the camp to take the person out and execute him. Whether executions, rather than outcasting, were carried out before European models of justice were imposed upon the northern Algonkians cannot now be determined. Summer fish camp councils more often discussed how best to locate their component hunting groups over the winter and other strategies for general benefit and defense.

Cree near Hudson Bay and Innu in Labrador historically fought neighboring Inuit, and both were occasionally involved in Iroquois onslaughts and French-British hostilities in the seventeenth and eighteenth centuries. Maneuvering over access to European trade led to some of the Inuit conflicts, so it is probable that warfare was at least intensified, if not actually introduced, by European invasion. The tactic of war was raids, and success was thought to depend upon the cooperation of spirit helpers, although body armor of hide over wood or tough hide alone was worn as a practical measure.

Captives were only infrequently taken, since the low density of food resources in the boreal forest on the Shield precluded large human communities or permanent settlements where wealth could be accumulated and displayed through the labor of slaves. Social classes were similarly undeveloped. Leadership was achieved by prowess in organizing successful hunts. The tendency to assume that spiritual power was likely to be passed from parent to child gave offspring of leaders an initial advantage in achieving their parent's role (pragmatically, growing up in a leader's family facilitated close observation of the role model). Some seers wielded considerable influence over the people of a region, but these were usually men or women who had earned respect for success in secular skills as well.

Correlated with the small social units among the northern Algonkians—about twenty in a hunting group, three or four hunting groups to a "band"—went a lack of elaborate ceremonials. Social beginnings and other important happenings were marked by feasts for the residents of a camp. Feasts were appropriate when a youth made his first kill, when a bear was killed, when the community celebrated the season's first trout, moose, beaver, or other important food, and, in present times, for births, sometimes birthdays, marriages, housewarmings in new governmental housing, openings of community halls, and powwows. At a feast, all the residents of the camp or settlement assembled at the host's home or tent, where clean tablecloths had been spread on the floor. Elders took the places of honor at the rear of the tent or room, other men were around the tablecloth, women closer to the door or behind the men, and children against the walls. The host and male relatives cooked the meat, his wife and women relatives the sweet dishes. Tobacco or cigarettes were passed and the adults smoked. (Tobacco has always been obtained through trade, and its use in the boreal forest may have begun in the Protohistoric period.) To open the feast itself, the host cut small portions of the meat being served and placed them in the fire as an offering—or perhaps we should say thanksgiving—to the spirits whose help made the feast possible. Then the food was passed, first to the men, then to the women, and through them to the children. Everyone ate slowly and quietly in deference to the solemnity of thanksgiving; elders might use the occasion to discourse upon correct behavior and values. Among some groups, it was considered necessary for all the food served to be consumed before anyone could leave the tent, which meant that at times guests might feel constrained to gorge until they felt ill. Perhaps more common, and certainly now, guests wrapped in clean cloth whatever food they couldn't comfortably eat and took it home. After eating, men took turns drumming and singing quietly, each to his own song pleasing to his spirit helper. As he concentrated on the beat of the drum and the hum of the tensed line by which it was suspended from a tent pole, a man hoped to hear a message from his spirit helper foretelling hunting success. Feasts were happy events, but religious in tone: a celebration of blessings rather than an occasion for relaxation.

Early ethnographers remarked with surprise that the Cree and Montagnais-Naskapi did not seem to have any gambling games. There were games of chance and games of skill, but no one seemed to bet on the outcomes. One popular amusement, in which scores were counted, was cup-and-pin, which involved attempting to spear carved conical caribou or moose hoof bones with a long bone pin. Another game, enjoyed by Montagnais-Naskapi, was similar in procedure to some forms of divination: a stick was placed in the nose of a muskrat skull and the skull tossed up as a player asked a silly question, such as "Who is good-looking?" The person in the ring to whom the stick pointed when the skull had fallen was the answer to the question, and the next to throw up the skull with a query. Questions could get sticky, such as "Who is sleeping with So-and-so's wife?" but were supposed to be taken in good fun. By the end of the nineteenth century, checkers, played with homemade pieces and board, and European card games were popular among the northern Algonkian adults. Children continued to play traditional games on the theme of hunting, setting up (or having their fathers set up) crudely carved miniature caribou or hares or moose and trying to spear them with darts or hit them with pebbles propelled by the release of a bent thin tapered stick. Little girls were given dolls to dress and toy implements to play with in miniature wigwams, but could join their brothers in more active games in camp.

Traditional cultural patterns were first altered for the Montagnais at the very beginning of the sixteenth century, when British, French, and Portuguese cod-fishing boats put in to the American shore to process the fish they had taken on the Newfoundland Banks. Presumably the Norse had contacted some Montagnais-Naskapi from the eleventh century, but Norse contacts left no recognizable traces in Indian societies. The cod fishers, in contrast, traded iron implements and beads for pelts, and very soon attracted many hundreds of Indians to the north shore of the Gulf of St. Lawrence every summer. Drinking with the native visitors, sleeping with young women who became tipsy or curious for adventure, the Europeans passed on diseases that began to wreak havoc not only along the coast, but far inland as people returned to aboriginal trading rendezvous at lake or rapids fish camps. Partly because European metal implements were cheaper than manufacturing stone implements, and partly, it may be, because skilled craftworkers died suddenly from the new diseases, the imported implements replaced many of the traditional stone and bone implements in northeastern America during the sixteenth and seventeenth centuries. Demand for the imports stimulated more trapping of fur bearers than had probably been done aboriginally, and engendered conflicts between peoples close to the European ports and travelers coming through their territory to trade. The peoples near the ports tried to act as middlemen, skimming a profit by collecting furs inland and selling to the Europeans, while the inland groups tried to circumvent the middlemen. Depopulation from epidemics added to the upsets in traditional relationships among native peoples. These conditions reached a climax in the eastern boreal forests in the mid-seventeenth century, when French Jesuit missionaries battled Indian seers for leadership and French and British competition for furs brought not only European traders and posts but also St. Lawrence Indian trappers and traders into the interior. By the early eighteenth century, much of the southern boreal forest was trapped out and moose were few (epidemics of diseases brought by the domestic animals and rats on the ships of the Europeans may have contributed to the rapid decline of game). The competitive trade shifted westward, leaving the Montagnais-Naskapi dependent on imported implements and desiring cloth garments and glass beads—spirit helpers were thought to be more apt to aid attractively ornamented persons—but with depleted resources.

The Cree occupied the lands south and west of James Bay and south of Hudson Bay that were the prime territory of the second major phase of the fur trade, which began with the incorporation of the Hudson's Bay Company in 1670. Cree developed a symbiosis with traders, both those of the Bay and their competitors, not only bringing in furs but serving as guides and huntsmen provisioning the posts and canoe brigades transporting goods. As the frontier of trade moved westward, Cree remained associated with it. By 1689, decades of skirmishes with the Chipewyans of the Barren Grounds west of Hudson Bay began, the westernmost Cree attempting to prevent the Dene from trading directly with the Bay's post at Churchill. One early historian claimed that several thousand Chipewyan and other Dene men had been killed in battles with the Cree by the middle of the eighteenth century, but these numbers may be exaggerated. Cree did succeed in holding their advantage with the European traders, and drove Dene north and west into the resource-poor transitional forest border, consolidating former Dene territory around the upper Nelson River (which flows into Hudson

Bay from the west) and Lake Athabasca (on the border of Saskatchewan, Alberta, and the Northwest Territories) into a Cree domain. Cree went farther during the early nineteenth century, to the Rockies and onto the northwestern Plains of Alberta and Saskatchewan, where, allied with the Siouan-speaking Assiniboin, some adopted Plains bison-hunting cultural patterns and forced the Blackfoot and Gros Ventres southwestward. By the late nineteenth century, the period of the treaties, the Cree were the dominant Indian ethnic group in central Canada, and were recognized as having two divisions, the Plains Cree and the Maskegon ("Swamp [dwellers]"), called in English the Swampy or Woods Cree. (Forest Cree in their ancestral habitat, are in their own language termed the Muskeko, or "muskeg" [swamp] people, Anglicized as Maskegon.) Each division was economically integrated into the late eighteenth- and nineteenth-century fur trade, the Woods Cree as trappers and post hunters, the Plains Cree as producers of pemmican, the mixture of dried bison meat, berries and fat that sustained the canoe brigades transporting trading goods in and furs out of Rupert's Land, the great domain of central Canada.

One result of the generations-long integration of Cree and Euro-Canadian traders was the formation of the Métis, "Mixed" people, at first the offspring of European men (frequently French-Canadian brigade employees) and their Cree "country wives," then increasingly the children of marriages within the Métis communities themselves. Métis spoke both French and Cree and eventually evolved a creole language from the two. A second formation, the "Northern Métis," developed in eastern Dene country later in the nineteenth and early twentieth centuries as traders married Chipewyan women and their children grew up speaking English and Chipewyan. Métis have had neither the federal protection mandated by treaties nor the political and economic advantages of Euro-Canadian colonists, so that even as they began organizing late in the twentieth century to press claims for land occupied by their forebears, their struggle looked far more difficult, in legal terms, than most Indian claims: neither "aboriginal title" (recognized by treaties) nor official grants or purchases can be documented for Métis occupations. Métis farms followed a French pattern of narrow strips running from the local river up through meadows and arable plots to woodlots on valley slopes. When the new Dominion of Canada began surveying its western regions in 1869, it ignored this pattern and imposed the British survey system of mile-square grids subdivided into square sections. Such a system destroyed the Métis subsistence base dependent upon a variety of local resources available to each family, and when the new government refused to modify its land title system, the Métis in the Red River area of southern Manitoba rebelled, led by the schoolteacher Louis Riel. They lost, and many moved west into Saskatchewan and Alberta. Government surveys followed, and in 1885 the Saskatchewan Métis rebelled, calling Riel from exile to lead them again, with Gabriel Dumont organizing the military aspects of their strategy. Again a well-equipped professional army put down the rebellion, hanging Riel and several other leaders. The Canadian government then set up a Halfbreed Commission to hear Métis land claims, empowering it to issue "scrip" certifying the Métis holder to 240 acres of land but without provision for ensuring the set of resources the Métis family needed. The Commission was dissolved in 1899, leaving many Métis without scrip and more without title to land, scrip or no. Others with scrip-based farms lost them to Euro-Canadian colonists claiming or buying the acreage. In 1938, the Province of Alberta took notice of the plight of its Métis, poorer than anybody in a province hard hit by the Depression plus Dust Bowl drought, and passed the Métis Betterment Act allowing creation of Métis Settlement Associations to homestead Métis Colonies in the province. Of course, by 1940 only marginal land was available for homesteading, and the few Colonies established rapidly outgrew their subsistence potential—a classic case of too little, too late.

Other provinces with Métis populations did not provide even as much as Alberta. The federal government of Canada ceased listing Métis as a census category in 1940, so it is impossible to obtain any official population figures for Métis; one half-million in 1980 is a conservative estimate, one million a generous estimate.

Contemporary Subarctic Cree have found more in common with the Inuit neighboring them to the north. The James Bay Agreement identified these common interests in protecting subsistence hunting and its land base. One major result has been the precedent-setting Income Security Programme begun in 1976 under the Agreement. Those adults who spend more time in "the bush" in subsistence activities (which may include trapping for cash) than in wage employment are entitled to up to $2,400 per year in the equivalent of 1976 dollars (that is, the amount is indexed to inflation). Thus families are insured should disastrously low prices for furs or game depletion threaten their ability to maintain even the very modest existence they have chosen to follow (you might see the Programme as a version of unemployment compensation or minimum wage; it isn't welfare because the recipients must be working "in the bush"). Income Security gives the Cree and Inuit families the means to plan wisely over the long term. It gives their communities security from which to resist exploitation from industrial development aimed, as the James Bay Hydroelectric project was, to benefit southern cities. Continuation of the Indian way of life becomes clearly viable. A population estimate for Woods Cree in 1980 would be at least twenty thousand; a more exact figure is difficult because census figures are based on band memberships, excluding non-status Indians who are especially numerous in the North where treaties date only from the twentieth century and missed many families in the bush.

The Northern Ojibwa (Anishnabai)

As Cree involvement with the fur trade expanded westward, Ojibwa began moving north from their homeland on the north shores of Lakes Superior and Huron around Sault Ste. Marie. From about the 1620s to around 1680, the fish-rich rapids in the narrow channel linking the two Great Lakes was the site of summer fish camps that became trading fairs attended by over a thousand people. Bands at these camps allied themselves through exchanges of gifts and participation in ceremonies such as the Feast of the Dead, a ritual of reinterring the bones of village members who had died during the previous two or three years. Following the deposition of the remains of the deceased in the community grave, guests from other villages or bands were treated to a feast and distribution of gifts. The potlatchlike Feast of the Dead may have originally been a Huron custom, taken up during the seventeenth century by peoples west of the Hurons drawn into the fur trade coming through Huron country. When the Hudson's Bay Company established posts supplied directly by ships from England, the lesser cost of good-quality items from the Bay shifted Indian trade north from the French interior posts and the Sault fair, where the higher manpower costs of canoe transportation made the imported items more expensive. After 1670, Cree traded directly with the Bay, destroying Ojibwa profits as middlemen to the St. Lawrence–eastern Great Lakes French traders. Some Ojibwa went west around Lake Superior to settle less-exploited trapping regions; others went north, attracted both by the furs and by the possibility of trading with the Bay themselves. By 1716, over a thousand Indians congregated at the Bay's York Factory, on Hudson Bay in what is now northeastern Manitoba, to exchange their furs for English goods. Most of these Indians were Cree, some were Assiniboin, and a few were probably Ojibwa. A generation later, in the 1740s, Ojibwa were common in the northern Ontario posts. Cree expansion westward had left fewer Cree in their homeland, which was now depleted of both fur bearers and moose in the formerly rich districts, but the depopulation of the region north of Lake Superior seems to have been due not so much to Cree movements as to constant

warfare between the Cree and Assiniboin and the Dakota striving for their share in the fur trade. Much of the conflict was deliberately instigated by French or British, some officers offering bounties for scalps of their European enemies. Ojibwa were caught up in the hostilities but also had opportunities to infiltrate what had become almost a no man's land.

Ojibwa came to occupy most of the southern half of western Ontario, west to the shore of Lake Winnipeg, by the 1770s. Particularly near their border running along the upper reaches of the rivers draining into Hudson Bay, the northern Ojibwa tended to intermarry and hunt with Cree, producing bands speaking a dialect derived from the two cognate Algonkian languages, Cree and Ojibwa. All of the boreal-forest Ojibwa, not only those on the ethnic border, became similar to the Cree in basic cultural pattern, modifying social and technological features of their ancestral habitat in the northern temperate hardwood forest. Most noteworthy was the dissolution of ancestral corporate villages with patrilineal clans and hereditary leadership. Far from maize agriculture and even, in most sectors, wild rice, the northern Ojibwa ceased to live in permanent communities of over one hundred people and lived instead in hunting groups of twenty or thirty, loosely allied with neighboring groups whom they would meet at the trading posts or in fish camps during the summer. Warfare had become a minor activity for the northern Ojibwa by the end of the eighteenth century, and they had long lost any middleman role in trade, so intercommunity alliances turned into informal networks of kin ties. The Feast of the Dead had disappeared by the nineteenth century along with trading fairs. Instead, the major group ceremony became the Midewiwin, the organization of doctors who annually initiated novices by ritually "killing" and reviving them in the special Midé lodge. The more northern Ojibwa could maintain only an attenuated Midewiwin, with two degrees of membership rather than four and a concomitantly less elaborate ritual. Although the basic social unit was much smaller and even summer gatherings relatively small among the northern Ojibwa, compared with their ancestors and cousins still in the Great Lakes region, the population of northern Ojibwa were dispersed rather than few in total number. The 1780–82 smallpox epidemic decimated the Ojibwa, as other peoples, but from that date the northern Ojibwa population seems to have steadily increased.

Until the merger of the North West Company with the Hudson's Bay Company in 1821, the northern Ojibwa were getting a good exchange for their furs. After the merger, brought about in part by declining profits from the fur trade, the Bay used its monopoly position to enforce unprecedented economies, including a virtual end to the "gifts" through which traders gave Indians better value for their furs in spite of the head office's standardized prices. The Ojibwa were, among other native peoples, the unhappy victims of the economy move. Most unfortunately, not only were beaver and other fur bearers fewer in number after well over a century of intensified trapping, but moose and caribou were much fewer. In many sectors, no large game was normally seen. Whether this decline in meat game was due in part to epidemics of European diseases among the animals, or only to overhunting by a greater number of human predators drawn to the boreal forest by the fur trade, cannot be determined. Whatever the causes, the effect was that for the rest of the nineteenth century, the northern Ojibwa and the adjacent boreal-forest Cree lived principally on fish and hares, the dull famine relief of happier times. The most significant effect of the fish and hare economy was poorer nutrition, since these creatures are lower than moose, caribou, and beaver in fat and in certain necessary trace minerals and vitamins. Poorer nutrition made the Indians more susceptible to infections and less able to recover quickly from wounds or accidents. It became more difficult, too, to keep warm when moose and especially caribou hides could no longer be obtained in needed quantities. Cree and Ojibwa had been accustomed to

wearing caribou-skin tunics with separate sleeves that could be detached in summer, caribou parkas or moose-hide coats with separate hoods, and beaver mittens. In addition, men wore caribou leggings and breechcloths and women, calf-high moccasins of caribou or moose reaching to tunics longer than those of the men. Without their accustomed game, the people had to substitute shirts and coats of rabbit skin cut into strips, twisted as into thread, and woven into a fur fabric. (Whole rabbit skins are thin, and too flimsy for boreal-forest winter clothing. Weaving twisted strips makes a thicker fabric providing better insulation.) Imported cloth and ready-made cloth garments were another substitute, but expensive to purchase. In the nineteenth century, the northern Ojibwa and Cree worked harder and more constantly than their parents had in the more affluent era, but their food and clothing were poorer and their health lower. There are indications in the traders' records that crises of leadership and perhaps faith occurred, since spiritual blessings were believed to be manifest by success in hunting large game. It must have seemed that spirit helpers had deserted the people and that the spirit leaders of the game species were severely displeased; much soul-searching must have gone on to discover how people had offended. There seems to have been an increase in fears and accusations of witchcraft during the nineteenth century, sorcery practices by evil or jealous individuals appearing to be a reasonable explanation of the otherwise inexplicable disappearance of game and rise in ill health.

The Euro-American Presence Intensifies

After Rupert's Land, the domain of the Hudson's Bay Company, became part of the nation of Canada in 1869, government and missionary intrusions stepped up in the boreal forests. The first treaties were signed in 1871 and 1875 in the southern portions of this region. In 1899, 1905, and 1906, treaties were signed with the Indians of much of the rest of the eastern Subarctic, although some

FIGURE 9.8 Woods Cree family in summer camp. Grandmother, in tent, is making birchbark baskets; grandfather is splitting and shaving wood to make frames and handles for his wife's baskets. *(D. Kehoe)*

did not sign until 1929 or 1930. Missionaries, principally Anglican but also some Roman Catholic, began to have an impact in the last quarter of the nineteenth century, although scattered missionaries had been working in earlier decades of that century. It was through the efforts of one of the earlier men, James Evans, stationed at Norway House at the north end of Lake Winnipeg in central Manitoba, that Cree syllabic writing was promulgated. Evans is usually credited with inventing the Cree syllabic-notation system in 1840, but Cree assert that his role was to codify and diffuse a notation system already developed by the Cree. Evans had devised a phonetic alphabet

for Ojibwa in 1837, then tried a syllabary borrowing Cherokee syllabic symbols (without their Cherokee sounds), and by 1843 had worked out the syllabic notations that Cree still use. Midé doctors used mnemonic symbols on birchbark scrolls during their rituals, so the Ojibwa were accustomed to the idea of notation systems. There was little overt opposition to missionaries, and many Indians were easily persuaded to join the church brought to their settlement, but the term "convert" may not be really applicable to many enrolled in the churches. Church attendance and Christmas–New Year and Easter feasts could be added to native forms of worship, and the ethics of

Christianity were not dissimilar to those of Indians, except in the Christian proscription of polygamy. In the twentieth century, it had become common for traditional drumming to be practiced in bush camps, and churchgoing in the trading-post settlement.

Conditions improved in the early twentieth century. Moose and caribou reappeared, relieving people of the monotonous diet of tediously snared hares and netted fish. Fur prices rose, although with fluctuations. Extension of the railways made it possible to bring supplies in to many posts by motor launch, or even tugboats pushing barges, along rivers and lakes from railheads. Bulk supplies thereby came within purchasing range of the Indians in many posts, and they began to use flour, lard, oatmeal, tea, and sugar daily. Canvas tents and canoes, the former lighter to pack and pleasanter than hide tent covers, the latter less fragile than birch-bark canoes, replaced traditional shelters and boats. Cloth became standard for all clothing except winter parkas, mittens, and moccasins. Families built log cabins at the trading posts, using these homes at the Christmas–New Year, Easter, and summer gatherings but continuing to live in tents or wigwams in the bush most of the year. Trapping remained the principal source of cash and, with the hunting of large game, the occupation of most men. Women reverted to the ancient pattern of child care, processing meat and hides, sewing, and snaring hares and setting fishnets near the camp. Frequently, all the adults in a settlement were literate in Cree syllabics (easily transferred to Ojibwa) and so could write to hospitalized loved ones as well as read mission publications. Native doctors administered herbs and made up potions for strength or winning one's beloved—the Cree have become famous for knowing love potions—but their practice as seers was much lessened. One competitor came to be the radio, which, like the seers of old, brought in disembodied voices from a great distance, voices that often could answer queries on the whereabouts and conditions of friends and relatives. One observer noted that the first radio in a Cree settlement elicited interest but not surprise, just as two generations later, a Plains Cree man remarked that it was no great feat for American astronauts to walk on the moon, for the Sun Dance maker and doctor who had ministered on his reserve had often sent his spirit to the moon, and had long ago discovered that it is gray and ashy.

Adverse factors appeared, too, in the twentieth century. Flu epidemics in 1908 and 1918 took a great toll, especially among older people. Then tuberculosis reached epidemic proportions, and during the 1930s and 1940s many persons spent a year or more in southern Canadian sanatoria before resuming normal life, if they recovered. The decline in the fur market during the Depression affected Indians' purchasing power. Prospectors, miners, and Euro-Canadian trappers entered the forests, interfering with native hunting and trapping. It was primarily because of these intrusions that many bands signed treaties with the government, expecting that the treaty would protect their territories. Many, though not all, bands received surveyed reserves including 1 square mile (2.5 square kilometers) per family of five as the basic unit of allocation. These reserves could not encompass all the hunting and trapping lands of a band, particularly because animal populations either fluctuate—hares have a seven-to-ten-year cycle of abundance and depletion—or move. Since the 1821 merger of the fur companies, there has been pressure on Indian trappers to work defined territories in order that the local trading post supervisor could keep track of beaver and other fur bearers and prescribe conservation measures. Post managers recommended that trap lines pass from father to son, which was not alien to the Ojibwa but was to the Cree, who had never made much of descent and inheritance. Government agents gradually replaced trading-post managers as the seat of power in northern Indian communities during the mid-twentieth century, and registration and licensing of trap lines became mandatory in the late 1940s. Some trappers pool or exchange pelts to adjust actual catch to imposed quotas, but the cooperation fundamental to traditional ethics is stifled.

FIGURE 9.9 Cree grandmother baking bannock, in a summer camp. One round loaf, already baked, is by her knee, another is baking in the frypan on the coals (behind the knee of the boy standing at left). *(T. Kehoe)*

The Struggle to Regain Sovereignty

The 1950s brought the major changes in eastern Subarctic life. There was an influx of Euro-Canadians resulting from a combination of stimuli: the resumption of capitalist economic expansion after the hiatus of the Depression and the world war, the construction of radar-based defense installations, and the 1951 revision of the Indian Act, which extended social-welfare policies to the North. Provision of schools at what had been no more than trading posts attracted families to live most of the year in villages, while in at least some districts those who were not attracted were coerced by officials refusing to pay family allowances, old-age pensions, or welfare to families who kept children out of school by remaining in bush camps. Concentration of people in villages forced the hunters and trappers to go farther from home than they had when home was a camp moved to the territory to be exploited. Distance stimulated these men to invest in outboard motors for canoes and, beginning in the mid-1960s, snowmobiles. It was more difficult to keep sled dog teams in villages than in bush camps. In the villages, each family had to stake an area for its dogs and keep them tied up there. When the dogs were not working—that is, when they were in the village—they were fed a minimal diet; hunger and chafing at being tied made the animals restless and vicious, a danger to children. Increased need for cash and a reluctance to leave families in order to spend perhaps two weeks in the forest with only a man partner led many men to prefer wage labor or commercial fishing near the village to subsistence hunting. The government encouraged the development of commercial lake fisheries in the eastern Subarctic, in part because these might absorb some of the younger men who could not be accommodated when trap lines were allocated, and in part because the wild fur market never recovered its early-twentieth-century high. Frozen fish fillets merchandised through supermarket chains seem a surer bet for regular income than furs. Plants for processing and freezing the catch of the commercial fisheries were constructed near some villages. People employed in these plants cleaned fishing hauls as their ancestors had from time immemorial, but now they were enclosed in buildings full of the noise of clanking conveyor belts instead of out on beaches under the summer sun, listening to friends' chatter and children's squeals.

FROM AN ANTHROPOLOGIST'S NOTEBOOK

A Cree Family Camp in the 1970s (Note: Names and identifying details have been changed in these excerpts.) The John family is camped this summer on a small point on Emily Lake. The camp is convenient for Bill to get jobs guiding the businessmen, doctors, and dentists who come to Fisherman's Lodge at the far end of the lake. Mrs. John can more easily sell the birch-bark baskets she makes for tourists if Bill can bring them in and take orders from the lodge guests. It's a pleasant camp, in birch and pine, with a little strip of beach and a couple of pretty rocky islets in the blue water off the point. The gill net is set near the closer islet; early every morning, elderly Mr. John paddles out in his canoe to bring in fish. The family kids about how early the old man goes out; he says he likes the misty-dawn quiet when all the younger people are asleep. That reminds us of the elderly couple telling us they would winter in the small community of Rocky Point instead of the village of Loon Rapids, where their children would be living so that the youngsters could go to school. Old Mr. and Mrs. John say Loon Rapids is too noisy; sometimes they can't sleep because people are partying. Rocky Point is quiet.

There are three canvas wall tents, three fire hearths: one for each mature woman. Elderly Mrs. John cooks for her husband and her two grown but unmarried sons, Bill and the youngest, Robert. In the second tent are her married son, Andrew, his wife, and their youngsters. Andrew's wife cooks for her family at the big fire with the drying racks above it, though Grandma often makes an extra bannock for her grandchildren as a snack. The third, smaller tent is occupied by the Johns' unmarried adult daughter. She keeps a small fire in front of her tent and cooks her own meals. Like many younger Cree women, she is shy with strangers, especially Euro-Canadian men, and remains in her tent whenever my husband is in the camp. Although each woman has her own cooking fire, she takes her and her dependents' share of food from whatever is brought into camp, Mr. John's daily morning fish, the moose Andrew shoots, eggs and bacon and bread and beer Bill buys at the lodge from his pay for guiding and the sales of his mother's baskets to the men who will take them as souvenirs to their wives in Winnipeg or Minneapolis.

August 12: Mr. John is sawing scrap lumber. He shows us the saw he had modified, making a ripsaw edge on one blade edge and a regular saw edge on the other. He doesn't think to mention it, but we notice that the crooked knife he uses so constantly is homemade from a file, with part of the file face intact. We remember how common it is to find prehistoric tools in central Canada that similarly have two different functional edges. Mr. John's present task is to prepare the boards for a grave fence in the Loon Rapids cemetery. The British fur traders and missionaries introduced, more than a century ago, the British custom of that period of constructing a small picket fence around a grave. Mr. John's carpentering skill brings him requests to prepare these fences. He has enough scrap boards, salvaged from the lodge and other Euro-Canadian construction waste, but he'll need nails. His youngest son will catch the daily taxi on the gravel road, opened only last year, that goes past the lodge and on to town, thirty-odd miles (fifty kilometers) away. The town has a mine, an RCMP regional headquarters, a hotel, a small Hudson's Bay Company department store, a competing Provincial Co-op store, and an Indian-Métis Friendship Centre providing rooms, recreation, a meeting hall, and assistance to people in from the villages to shop or look for work. The youngest John son will buy nails, Rit brand dye for his mother to color the spruce root fiber she uses to sew and decorate the baskets she sells, and a twelve-pack of beer, which is much cheaper in town than at the lodge. He might buy a new pair of rubbers for his father to wear over his moccasins—all the older Cree and many younger people protect their moccasins by wearing low-cut over-the-shoe rubbers over them.

August 14: Bill comes back from a day guiding fisherman, and mentions that he saw the RCMP constable at the lodge and asked him whether he had seen his younger brother. Bill is worried. He knows how quickly Indian men are picked up for drunkenness in town, and he's afraid his brother may be in jail. But just as Bill finishes speaking, the young man rather sheepishly comes into camp. He has the nails and Rit dye, but no beer. No one mentions it.

August 15: Bill was hungry late in the morning, so he took one of the whitefish caught this morning, slit and cleaned it on the grass on the edge of the beach, and hung the fillet over a stick propped at a slant over his mother's fire. There are fish fillets hanging on the rack over Andrew's wife's fire, but they are being smoked, and Bill prefers fresh fish to smoked. A couple of bannock are laid on the rack, protected from insects by the smoke, and anyone who wants can break off a piece. This morning, Andrew's younger daughter breakfasted from a single-serving package of Kellogg's Special K, though the older people ate boiled potatoes, bacon, and fish. Andrew was telling us he's shot four moose so far this summer. The last was a cow. Her hide is stretched on a frame leaning against a tree on the edge of camp, for the women to scrape whenever they feel up to such hard work. They cooked every edible part, the head had to cook overnight but was tender and tasty when ready. Long, slender lower leg bones of the moose are next to Mr. John's bed—quilts on a plywood sheet over three logs—near the opening of his tent. He'll whittle these into tobacco pipes to sell at the lodge as souvenirs. The children are, as usual, playing very quietly. (We noticed we are speaking more quietly, too.) The boys are at the water, maneuvering toy boats made of sardine cans nailed to small blocks of wood. Their little sister is watching. She is encouraged to sit with her grandmother or her older sister, who helps the elderly lady with her baskets, but the young girl is lively and restive. The boys' games appeal to her but she is not given boys' toys.

August 16: A man comes up in a canoe with a motor. He had seen a canoe with his son and another teen-age boy tip over near Loon Rapids. The boys have been missing since then; the father is inquiring at every camp, hoping to find them alive. The man won't stay to visit, as people usually do. (Drownings are a common cause of death in the Subarctic.)

The initial effects of aggregation of hunting groups into sedentary villages were often stressful among the Algonkians of the eastern Subarctic, as among the Dene in the west. Children were no longer accustomed to living in the forest and became vociferous. They were constantly with their young companions rather than quietly carrying out tasks in a family camp. Parents found young people would no longer accept parental choice of a spouse, as was traditional among both Algonkians and Dene, but insisting on courting to marry their own, sometimes immature, choices. Youths with some fluency in English were in many localities given better employment than older, respected persons. Alcohol became readily available and drunkenness more frequent, resulting in an upsurge of physical assaults and injuries, and in deaths by exposure. Fatal fires became more common as many families heated wooden-frame or tent-and-board homes with homemade, jerry-built stoves. In communities with rival missionaries, or with conflicts involving RCMP constable, store manager, or missionary, the native people were caught in the tension and sometimes pressured into factions. Québec Indians were made to choose between rival French-language and English schools. The presence of a nursing station or small hospital, and radio communication that would bring in a plane to airlift ill or injured to medical facilities, had the desirable effect of saving victims of accidents and infections and vaccinating children, but an insidious detriment to health was the availability in the village store of refined flour, macaroni, sugar, and sugar-rich packaged baked goods, candies, and soft drinks. Dental caries increased dramatically—even teenagers lost decayed teeth—and many women became obese and developed diabetes.

The greatest threat came from the proliferation of projects for exploiting raw resources in the North for the benefit of temperate-latitude consumers, not only in southern Canada and the United States but also in Europe. The tempo of exploration for these projects increased in the 1970s, after a decade of government construction of all-weather roads into the North. Often, these roads were contrary to the wishes of the northern communities, who found the road construction too destructive to hunting and fishing grounds. The communities asked in vain that instead, "winter roads" be annually opened so that tractor-drawn trains could haul freight economically over the snow. They also asked for help to purchase a bush plane with which they could, without a need to earn a profit, transport trappers and commercial fishermen to distant sites, take out furs and fish, and handle emergencies. International corporations proposed massive timber cutting, pulp and paper processing, mining, and oil and gas extraction; the federal and provincial governments proposed hydroelectric generating systems. The projects were conceived and planned in cities far from the North, by business executives, bureaucrats, and engineers who relied on technical-feasibility reports. Native peoples in the affected areas were not consulted, often not even notified. If pressed, a planner might proceed on the assumption that such economic development automatically creates jobs, but in fact the projects were planned to be highly automated, and the few jobs they might create in the North would be filled by imported Euro-Canadians. The only jobs likely to be available to native people would be of the lowest level, and workers would be expected to give up hunting and fishing except for occasional weekend amusement; any who wanted to work part-time and hunt for subsistence in between need not apply. As an indication of how much good the projects were likely to do the northern economy, it can be noted that most planned to bring in trailer housing for crews because even mines were, as a rule, not expected to be worked sufficiently long to justify construction of permanent houses for employees.

When it was realized, in spite of the lack of publicity and the inadequate translation into native languages of legal agreement, that hundreds of thousands of square miles of hunting and fishing lands would be torn up, clear-cut of trees, and flooded or dried up by dams, that pollution controls were usually low in priority, and that the destruction would remain decades after the resource had been ripped out, the native peoples began to protest. In 1965, the Indians of Québec Association was formed, primarily to protect native interests against national and international exploiters. The IQA participated in negotiating the agreement, signed in 1975, that lifted the injunction brought in 1972 to halt the notorious James Bay Hydroelectric Project. The Cree and Inuit negotiators believed they had obtained the best terms they could against the powerful battery of federal and provincial government and utility corporation lawyers, but a substantial number of Indians and Inuit considered the key to the agreement, the final extinguishing of aboriginal title to lands in return for reserves and money, unacceptable. After the terms of the final agreement were announced in November 1975, the Indians of Québec Association publicly pointed out that the Indians in the agreement were the Grand Council of the Crees (the James Bay Cree), not the IQA, and that the IQA was not a party to the agreement. In common with the national Inuit Tapirisat and the Native Council of Canada, founded in 1970 to represent non-status Indians and Métis, the IQA considered aboriginal rights to anciently occupied lands to be inalienable. This position was maintained also by the Grand Council Treaty Number Nine, an association of the chiefs of the bands signatory to Treaty Number Nine, 1905–1906, the Cree and the Ojibwa of the Hudson Bay drainage of Ontario.

Basically, the majority of spokespeople for Canadian Indians insist that continuation of opportunity for subsistence hunting and fishing be the paramount concern of northern peoples. Projects may be allowed if they do not destroy traditional subsistence resources; if it appears unavoidable that a project will be destructive, or if the financiers claim that sufficient controls would make the project too costly to compete in outside markets, then the project should be abandoned. It is desirable that a project employ, and if necessary, train, local natives, but such jobs are seen as probably temporary and no substitute for subsistence hunting. The

Indian groups say they are willing to share their resources, but they will not sell. They recognize that the North is seen as a colony supplying industrial regions, and they oppose this southern perspective; their view is that the North is their homeland, and is not to be denuded. As the Dene did in 1975, in 1977 the Ojibway-Cree Nation of Treaty Number Nine (Grand Council Treaty Number Nine) issued a statement of rights. In this document, the Declaration of Nishnawbe-Aski, "The People and the Land," the Ojibwa and the Cree listed as their "inalienable rights...

1. the right to self-government.
2. the right to receive compensation for our exploited natural resources.
3. the right to receive compensation for the destruction and abrogation of our hunting and fishing rights.
4. the right to re-negotiate our treaty.
5. the right to negotiate with the elected governments of your society through appropriate levels of representation.
6. the right to approach the judicial, governmental and business institutions of your society in our quest for self-determination and local control.
7. the right of our elected chiefs to deal with your society's elected cabinets on an equal basis.
8. the right to approach other world nations to further the aims of the Cree and Ojibway nations of Treaty #9.
9. the right to use every necessary alternative to further the cause of our people.
10. the right to use all that the creator has given us to help all of mankind.

Recognizing that economic power brings political power, the Grand Council Treaty Number Nine supported its 1977 declaration by establishing the Oski-Pimachi-O-Win (New Life) Corporation, encompassing the Cree and the Ojibwa of that treaty region in a structure aimed at developing a wholesaling and distribution system to improve services and reduce prices at community cooperatives, and a construction branch to improve community housing and possibly to compete with outside firms for large construction projects, as well as coordinating trapping and commercial fishing. Smaller, regional corporations such as the Kuyhana and Windigo had already, by 1977, organized Cree and Ojibwa communities to explore mining development under local control and to open and maintain winter roads. The Treaty Number Nine chiefs, and their fellow Algonkian leaders, hope that with such locally initiated and developed ventures, plus protected hunting, trapping, and fishing, their communities will be able to maintain traditional values while making available desired Euro-Canadian goods and services, from rifles, tools, snowmobiles, bush planes, clothing, and food, to medical aid, business and legal expertise, and schools. They are participating in revisions of curricula to include Algonkian languages and history and instruction in traditional bush skills as well as Western academic subjects. Their goal is to halt the despoliation of their lands so that their children, properly trained in locally supervised schools, can obtain from part-time employment and shares in community enterprises the cash they need for a decent standard of living as they perpetuate their heritage of living off the land in cooperative groups. This is the wisdom gained through decades of frustration and disappointment under policies imposed by strangers.

SUMMARY

The earliest peoples in North America most probably moved south onto the continent during the late Pleistocene epoch, when the present Bering Strait region was all land, part of the Pleistocene Northern Continent. By the close of the Pleistocene epoch, 8000 B.C., there were caribou hunters in the Canadian Maritimes and hunter-fishermen, similar in cultural pattern to contemporary Siberians, in Alaska and the Aleutian Islands. The central Canadian Subarctic remained under glacial ice for several thousand more years. Warming temperatures brought Northern Archaic hunters into western Canada and Alaska around 4000 B.C. Then, by 2500 B.C., an increasingly colder climate can be correlated with the spread of an Arctic-adapted hunting cultural pattern, the Arctic Small Tool Tradition. The peoples of this tradition reached entirely across the American Arctic to Greenland, then in central Canada colonized the tundra west of Hudson Bay. By 1000 B.C., the distinctive Dorset cultural tradition had developed in eastern Arctic Canada. Toward the end of the first millennium B.C., the large coastal town of Ipiutak in northwestern Alaska was skillfully exploiting rich sea-mammal and fish resources and trading into Siberia. At this time, the Athabascans may have been colonizing western Canadian forests. Toward the end of the first millennium A.D., Athabascan Indians were dispersed through the Alaskan and western Canadian boreal forests, and the Thule Inuit, direct ancestors of historic Inuit, migrated eastward from their homeland in northern Alaska, reaching Greenland about the same time as Norse colonists. The eastern Subarctic Algonkian cultural pattern is also evidenced clearly at this time in archaeological sites, showing continuity with the Shield Archaic of the eastern boreal forest, dating back to 5000 B.C., and also contacts, probably through trade, with Late Woodland peoples in the St. Lawrence and Great Lakes regions. Trade with Europeans (Norse) may have occasionally occurred since the eleventh century, but is historically documented only from the beginning of the sixteenth century, when the Newfoundland cod fishery brought Western Europeans each summer to the Canadian Maritimes. In the seventeenth century, the establishment of the Hudson's Bay Company trading posts intensified exploitation of beaver and other fur bearers in the eastern Subarctic, embroiled the Indians in British-French rivalries and hostilities, engaged Cree as middlemen in the trade, and drew some Ojibwa north into the boreal forest of Ontario.

In the Bering Sea region, expansion of the Russian fur trade into eastern Siberia increased Chukchi trade and raids upon the Inuit. During the eighteenth century, Russian ships explored the Aleutians and Alaska, Russian traders massacred many Aleuts and forced survivors to hunt sea otters for them, and, finally, the organization of the Russian-American Company under royal patronage made the Aleutians and Alaska the object of Russian colonization.

Hunting pressure and probably also animal epidemics had sharply reduced game in the boreal forests by 1820. In particular, the Cree and the Ojibwa in central Canada were forced to subsist on fish and hares and to accept whatever prices for fur the monopolistic Hudson's Bay Company would offer. Inuit had been driven from southern Labrador by French fishery posts. Moravian missions in Labrador and Greenland were colonizing both Inuit and Innu. United States whaling ships and new western posts of the Hudson's Bay Company competed with Russia for the trade of Alaskan and western Canadian Inuit and Athabascans. The United States officially took over Alaska as a colony in 1867, and soon after, Canada took over the Subarctic forests and tundra that had been the Hudson's Bay Company domain. It was not until the end of the century that Euro-Americans immigrated in numbers into Alaska and the Yukon. It was at this time, too, that the repeating rifle revolutionized hunting in the Arctic and Subarctic, making cooperative drives obsolete and stimulating fur trapping to pay for ammunition and for commercial nets with which to catch enough fish to support dog teams as well as humans, the dogs being used to facilitate tending traplines.

During the twentieth century, both Inuit and Indians in the Subarctic became more integrated into the international economy. Cloth garments replaced most native clothing, imported flour, tea, and sugar came to be regularly consumed, and families gradually came to live in wooden houses instead of aboriginal sod houses or bark- or skin-covered wigwams or tents. During the 1950s, the strategic importance of the North in Soviet–United States conflict brought intensified colonization to the Inuit and Indians. Greenland became politically a Danish county. Canada built schools and, along with the United States Bureau of Indian Affairs, for the first time made real efforts to impose formal school upon native children. The necessity of keeping children in schools forced both Inuit and Indian families to live permanently in villages rather than for most of the year in camps near subsistence resources. Wage labor for men was encouraged and subsistence hunting discouraged, in spite of the gradual reappearance of prime game—moose and caribou—in the boreal forests over the century.

The 1970s were a decade of resurgence of the native peoples. The Alaska Native Claims Settlement Act, spurred by the pressure of international economic interests to open construction of oil and gas pipelines to southern industrial centers, recognized Inuit and Indian claims to Alaska but organized the claimants into corporations patterned on Western capitalist businesses. The James Bay Final Agreement with Cree and Inuit in Québec was a more traditional claims settlement. Both settlements aroused the opposition of many native leaders by ignoring native concepts of the inalienability of land and of the rights of occupancy (usufruct). As a response to the settlements, the Dene and the Cree-Ojibway (of the Treaty Number Nine district) issued formal declarations of native demands for sovereignty. The Inuit also raised demands for local sovereignty. To reinforce these demands, these peoples are working to develop greater economic power over a base of continuing subsistence hunting. Greenland's internal autonomy under the 1979 implementation of the Home Rule Act became a model for native power.

RECOMMENDED READING

Balikci, Asen. 1970 *The Netsilik Eskimo*. Prospect Heights, Ill.: Waveland Press. Interesting presentation of Central Inuit; especially valuable if Balikci's films of the Netsilik (Education Development Center, Inc., Cambridge, Massachusetts, and National Film Board of Canada) can be viewed.

Bishop, Charles A. 1974 *The Northern Ojibwa and the Fur Trade*. Toronto: Holt, Rinehart and Winston of Canada. Focusing on one trading-post community, the study is enlivened with many frank and candid quotations from the traders' daily journals.

Brody, Hugh. 1981 *Maps and Dreams*. New York: Pantheon. Lively personal account of the conflict between interior British Columbia Athabascans and oil pipeline development.

Chance, Norman A. 1990 *The Iñupiat and Arctic Alaska: An Ethnography of Development*. Fort Worth: Holt Rinehart and Winston. Written for college student readers, focuses on situations of contemporary North Alaska Inuit.

Dickason, Olive P. 1992 *Canada's First Nations: A History of Founding Peoples*. Norman: University of Oklahoma Press.

Fagan, Brian M. 1991 *Ancient North America*. New York: Thames and Hudson (distributed by W.W. Norton).

Jenness, Diamond. 1959 [1928] *The People of the Twilight*. Chicago: University of Chicago Press. Vivid personal account of Central Inuit life before modern disruptions.

Jones, Dorothy M. 1976 *Aleuts in Transition*. Seattle: University of Washington Press. Comparison of two communities, showing the impact of Euro-American policies.

Laughlin, William S. 1980 *Aleuts: Survivors of the Bering Land Bridge*. New York: Holt Rinehart and Winston. Integrates archaeological, biological and ethnographic research for the college student reader.

Maxwell, Moreau S. 1985 *Prehistory of the Eastern Arctic*. Orlando: Academic Press. Detailed, but written with frequent personal observations that put a human dimension into the archaeology.

Nelson, Richard K. 1983 *Make Prayers to the Raven*. Chicago: University of Chicago Press. Sensitive description of interior Alaska Athabascan life, bringing out the Koyukons' ecological knowledge and practices.

Ridington, Robin. 1988 *Trail to Heaven*. Iowa City: University of Iowa Press. Account of the anthropologist's experience of contemporary Beaver (Dunneza) life.

Speck, Frank G. 1977 [1935] *Naskapi*. Norman: University of Oklahoma Press. Sensitive description of the religious base of Naskapi life.

VanStone, James W. 1962 *Point Hope, An Eskimo Village in Transition*. Seattle: University of Washington Press. Among VanStone's many excellent studies of Inuit and Dene, this one captures well the experiences of Northern Alaskan Inuit in recent years.

Willis, Jane. 1973 *Geniesh, An Indian Girlhood*. Toronto: New Press. The young author's poignant depiction of the conflicts forced upon a gifted Cree.

SOURCES FOR THE FIRST EDITION

Ackerman, Robert E. 1975 *The Kenaitze People*. Phoenix: Indian Tribal Series.

———1976 *The Eskimo People of Savoonga*. Phoenix: Indian Tribal Series.

Anderson, Douglas D. 1968 A Stone Age Campsite at the Gateway to America. *Scientific American* 218:24–33.

Aigner, Jean S., ed. 1976 Symposium on Aleutian Archaeology. *Arctic Anthropology* 13(2).

Akwesasne Notes 10 (4):20–21; 11(2):23–24.

Arctic Anthropology 12(1). (Entire issue.)

Balikci, Asen. 1968 The Netsilik Eskimos: Adaptive Processes. In R.B. Lee and I. DeVore (eds.). *Man the Hunter*. Chicago: Aldine Publishing, pp. 78–82.

Basso, Ellen B. 1978 The Enemy of Every Tribe: "Bushman" Images in Northern Athapaskan Narratives. *American Ethnologist* 5:690–709.

Berg, Gosta. 1973 *Circumpolar Problems*. Oxford: Pergamon Press.

Berreman, Gerald D. 1955 Inquiry into Community Integration in an Aleutian Village. *American Anthropologist* 57:49–59.

———1964 Aleut Reference Group Alienation, Mobility, and Acculturation. *American Anthropologist* 66:231–250.

Birket-Smith, Kaj. 1930 *Contributions to Chipewyan Ethnology*. Copenhagen: Gyldendalske Boghandel.

Birket-Smith, Kaj, and Frederica de Laguna. 1938 *The Eyak Indians of the Copper River Delta, Alaska*. Copenhagen: Levin & Munksgaard.

Bishop, Charles A. 1976 The Emergence of the Northern Ojibwa: Social and Economic Consequences. *American Ethnologist* 3:39–54.

———1977 Aboriginal Cree Social Organization.

Paper presented at the Ninth Algonquian Conference, Worcester, Mass., 1977.

———1978 Cultural and Biological Adaptations to Deprivation: The Northern Ojibwa Case. In C.D. Laughlin, Jr. and I. A. Brady (eds.). *Extinction and Survival in Human Populations*. New York: Columbia University Press, pp. 208–230.

Bishop, Charles A., and M. Estellie Smith. 1975 Early Historic Populations in Northwestern Ontario: Archaeological and Ethnohistorical Interpretations. *American Antiquity* 40:54–63.

Boas, Franz. 1964 [1888] *The Central Eskimo*. Lincoln: University of Nebraska Press.

Brody, Hugh. 1975 *The People's Land*. Harmondsworth: Penguin Books.

Bryan, Alan L. 1969 Late Prehistoric Cree Expansion into North Central Alberta. *Western Canadian Journal of Anthropology* 1:32–39.

Buckley, Helen, J.E.M. Kew, and John B. Hawley. 1963 *The Indians and Metis of Northern Saskatchewan*. Saskatoon: Centre for Community Studies.

Burch, Ernest S., Jr. 1975 *Eskimo Kinsmen*. St. Paul: West Publishing.

———1978 Caribou Eskimo Origins: An Old Problem Reconsidered. *Arctic Anthropology* 15:1–35.

Campbell, John M., ed. 1962 *Prehistoric Cultural Relations Between the Arctic and Temperate Zones of North America*. Montreal: Arctic Institute of North America, Technical Paper No. 11.

Canadian Association in Support of the Native Peoples 1974–1978 *Bulletin* 15 (2,3); 16 (1,3,4); 7(1,3); 18 (1,2,4).

Christian, Jane, and Peter M. Gardner. 1977 *The Individual in Northern Dene Thought and Communication: A Study in Sharing and Diversity*. Ottawa: National Museums of Canada, National Museum of Man Mercury Series, Canadian Ethnology Service, Paper No. 35.

Clark, A. McFadyen. 1974 *The Athapaskans: Strangers of the North*. Ottawa: National Museum of Man.

———1974 Koyukuk River Culture. Ottawa: National Museums of Canada, National Museum of Man Mercury Series, Canadian Ethnology Service, Paper No. 18.

———1975 (ed.) *Proceedings: Northern Athapaskan Conference, 1971*. Ottawa: National Museums of Canada, National Museum of Man Mercury Series, Canadian Ethnology Service, Paper No. 27.

Clark, Donald W. 1979 *Ocean Bay: An Early North Pacific Maritime Culture*. Ottawa: National Museums of Canada, National Museum of Man Mercury Series, Archaeological Survey of Canada Paper No. 86.

Cox, Bruce, ed. 1973 *Cultural Ecology: Readings on the Canadian Indians and Eskimos*. Toronto: McClelland and Stewart.

Damas, David. 1969 Environment, History, and Central Eskimo Society. In D. Damas (ed.). *Contributions to Anthropology: Ecological Essays*. Ottawa: National Museums of Canada Bulletin 230, pp. 40–64.

DeLaguna, Frederica. 1956 *Chugach Prehistory*. Seattle: University of Washington Press.

Dene of the N.W.T., n.d. *The Dene: Land and Unity for the Native People of the Mackenzie Valley*. Yellowknife: Dene of the N.W.T.

Dumond, D.E. 1965 On Eskaleutian Linguistics, Archaeology, and Prehistory. *American Anthropologist* 67:1231–1257.

———1969 Toward a Prehistory of the Na-Dene, with a General Comment on Population Movements among Nomadic Hunters. *American Anthropologist* 71:857–863.

———1977 *The Eskimos and Aleuts*. London: Thames and Hudson.

Dunning, Robert W. 1959 *Social and Economic Change Among the Northern Ojibwa*. Toronto: University of Toronto Press.

Feit, Harvey A. 1969 *Mistassini Hunters of the Boreal Forest*. M.A. thesis, McGill University.

Fox, Richard G. 1979 Telling Government to Fool People Somewhere Else. *Reviews in Anthropology* 6:153–163.

Fried, Jacob, ed. 1964 Contact Situations and Their Consequences in Arctic and Subarctic North America. *Arctic Anthropology* 2(2).

Gadacz, René R. 1975 Montagnais Hunting Dynamics in Historico-ecological Perspective. *Anthropologica*, n.s. 17:149–167.

Gallagher, H.G. 1974 *Etok, A Story of Eskimo Power*. New York: G.P. Putnam's Sons.

Gessain, Robert, and Joëlle Robert-Lamblin, eds. 1978 Ecologie, Demographie et Acculturation en Milieu Arctique. Paris: *Actes du XLIIe Congrès International des Américanistes*, vol. 5, pp. 9–107.

Gillespie, Beryl C. 1975 An Ethnohistory of the Yellowknives: A Northern Athapaskan Tribe. In D.B. Carlisle (ed.). *Contributions to Canadian Ethnology, 1975*. Ottawa: National Museums of Canada, National Museum of Man Mercury Series, Canadian Ethnology Service, Paper No. 31, pp. 191–245.

Graburn, Nelson H. H. 1969 *Eskimos Without Igloos*. Boston: Little, Brown.

Graburn, Nelson H. H., and B. Stephen Strong. 1973 *Circumpolar Peoples: An Anthropological Perspective*. Pacific Palisades, Calif.: Goodyear Publishing.

Gubser, Nicholas J. 1965 *The Nunamiut Eskimos, Hunters of Caribou*. New Haven: Yale University Press.

Guédon, Marie-Francoise. 1974 *People of Tetlin, Why Are You Singing?* Ottawa: National Museums of Canada, National Museum of Man Ethnology Division, Mercury Series, Paper No. 9.

Hall, Edwin S., Jr. 1971 Kangiguksuk: A Cultural Reconstruction of a Sixteenth Century Eskimo Site in Northern Alaska. *Arctic Anthropology* 8:1–101.

Harper, Francis. 1964 Caribou Eskimos of the Upper Kazan River, Keewatin. Lawrence: University of Kansas.

Heizer, Robert F. 1943 Aconite Poison Whaling in Asia and America: An Aleutian Transfer to the New World. Washington, D.C.: Smithsonian Institution, Bureau of American Ethnology, *Bulletin* 133, Anthropological Paper No. 24.

Helm, June. 1961 *The Lynx Point People: The Dynamics of a Northern Athapaskan Band*. Ottawa: National Museum of Canada, Bulletin No. 176.

———1976 The Indians of the Subarctic: A Critical Bibliography. Bloomington: Indiana University Press.

Helm, June, and Nancy Oestreich Lurie. 1966 *The Dogrib Hand Game*. Ottawa: National Museum of Canada, Bulletin No. 205.

Henriksen, Georg. 1973 *Hunters in the Barrens: The Naskapi on the Edge of the White Man's World*. St. John's: Memorial University of Newfoundland.

Hippler, Arthur E. 1969 *Barrow and Kotzebue: An Exploratory Comparison of Acculturation and Education in Two Large Northwestern Alaska Villages*. Minneapolis: University of Minnesota.

Hodge, Frederick Webb, ed. 1910 *Handbook of American Indians*. Washington, D.C.: Smithsonian Institution, Bureau of American Ethnology, Bulletin 30.

Honigmann, John J. 1946 *Ethnography and Acculturation of the Fort Nelson Slave*. New Haven: Yale University Press.

———1947 Witch-Fear in Post-Contact Kaska Society. *American Anthropologist* 49:222–243.

———1949 *Culture and Ethos of Kaska Society*. New Haven: Yale University Press.

———1962 Social Networks in Great Whale River. Ottawa: National Museum of Canada, Bulletin No. 178.

Honigmann, John J., ed. 1963 Community Organization and Pattern Change Among North Canadian and Alaskan Indians and Eskimos. *Anthropologica*, n.s. 5 (1).

———1971 The Contemporary Cultural Situation of the Northern Forest Indians of North America and the Eskimo of North America and Greenland. Stuttgart-München: *Verhandlungen des XXXVIII Internationalen Amerikanistenkongresses*, vol. 3.

Honigmann, John J., and Irma Honigmann. 1965 *Eskimo Townsmen*. Ottawa: University of Ottawa.

Hosley, Edward. 1978 The Aboriginal Social Organization of the Pacific Drainage Dene: The Matrilineal Basis. Paper presented at the American Anthropological Association annual meeting, Los Angeles, 1978.

Hughes, Charles Campbell. 1960 *An Eskimo Village in the Modern World*. Ithaca: Cornell University Press.

———1965 Under Four Flags: Recent Culture Change Among the Eskimo. *Current Anthropology* 6:3–69.

Jochelson, Waldemar. 1966 [1933] *History, Ethnology and Anthropology of the Aleut*. Oosterhout N.B., The Netherlands: Anthropological Publications.

Jordan, Richard H., ed. 1978 Symposium on Central Labrador Archaeology. *Arctic Anthropology* 15 (2).

King, A. Richard. 1967 *The School at Mopass*. New York: Holt, Rinehart and Winston.

Krech, Shepard, III. 1978 On the Aboriginal Population of the Kutchin. *Arctic Anthropology* 15:89–104.

———1978 Disease, Starvation, and Northern Athapaskan Social Organization. *American Ethnologist* 5:710–732.

Kupfer, George, and Charles W. Hobart. 1978 Impact of Oil Exploration Work on an Inuit Community. *Arctic Anthropology* 15:58–67.

Lantis, Margaret. 1952 Eskimo Herdsmen. In E.H. Spicer (ed.). *Human Problems in Technological Change*. New York: John Wiley, pp. 127–148.

Laughlin, William S. 1968 Hunting: An Integrating Biobehavior System and Its Evolutionary Importance. In R.B. Lee and I. DeVore (eds.). *Man the Hunter*. Chicago: Aldine Publishing, pp. 304–320.

———1975 Aleuts: Ecosystem, Holocene History, and Siberian Origin. *Science* 189:507–515.

Liebow, Elliot, and John Trudeau. 1962 A Preliminary Study of Acculturation Among the Cree Indians of Winisk, Ontario. *Arctic* 15:190–204.

Lips, Julius E. 1947 Naskapi Law. *Transactions of the American Philosophical Society* 37:379–492.

Malaurie, Jean, ed. 1973 *Le Peuple Esquimau Aujourd'hui et Demain* (The Eskimo People Today and Tomorrow). Paris and The Hague: Mouton.

———1978 Développement Économique de l'Arctique: Avenir des Sociétés Esquimaudes et Indiennes. Paris: *Actes du XLIIe Congrès International des Américanistes*, vol. 5., pp. 109–310.

Mason, J. Alden. 1946 *Notes on the Indians of the Great Slave Lake Area*. New Haven: Yale University Press.

McCartney, Allen P., and William B. Workman, eds. 1974 Festschrift Issue in Honor of Chester S. Chard. *Arctic Anthropology* 11.

McGhee, Robert. 1974 *Beluga Hunters*. St. John's: Memorial University of Newfoundland.

McKennan, Robert A. 1959 *The Upper Tanana Indians*. New Haven: Yale University Press.

———1965 *The Chandalar Kutchin*. Arctic Institute of North America, Technical Paper 17.

Milwaukee Journal, Sept. 1, 1977; Oct. 23, 1977; April 10, 1979.

National Association of Friendship Centres. *The Native Perspective* 1(2); 2(1, 10).

Nelson, Richard K. 1969 *Hunters of the Northern Ice*. Chicago: University of Chicago Press.

———1973 *Hunters of the Northern Forest*. Chicago: University of Chicago Press.

Newsweek, Profits in the Tundra. August 21, 1978:62–65.

Noble, William C. 1971 Archaeological Surveys and Sequences in Central District Mackenzie, N.W.T. *Arctic Anthropology* 8:102–135.

Osgood, Cornelius. 1958 *Ingalik Social Culture*. New Haven: Yale University Press.

———1959 *Ingalik Mental Culture*. New Haven: Yale University Press.

———1971 *The Han Indians*. New Haven: Yale University Press.

Oswalt, Wendell H. 1963 *Mission of Change in Alaska*. San Marino, Calif.: Huntington Library.

Oswalt, Wendell H., and James W. Van Stone. 1967 *The Ethnoarcheology of Crow Village, Alaska*. Washington, D.C.: Smithsonian Institution, Bureau of American Ethnology, Bulletin 199.

Oxendale, Joan. 1969 Reflections of the Structure of Cree in the Spoken English of the Bilingual Crees. *Western Canadian Journal of Anthropology* 1:65–71.

Parker, Seymour. 1964 Ethnic Identity and Acculturation in Two Eskimo Villages. *American Anthropologist* 66:325–340.

Poppe, Robert. 1970 Where Will All the Natives Go? *Western Canadian Journal of Anthropology* 2:164–175.

Price, John A. 1979a *Indians of Canada: Cultural Dynamics*. Scarborough, Ont.: Prentice-Hall of Canada.

———1979b New Books on Indian-White Relationships in Canada. *Reviews in Anthropology* 6:141–151.

Ray, Dorothy Jean. 1975 *The Eskimos of Bering Strait, 1650–1898*. Seattle: University of Washington Press.

Raymond, Scott, and Peter Schledermann, eds. 1974 *International Conference on the Prehistory and Paleoecology of Western North American Arctic and Subarctic*. Calgary: University of Calgary Archaeological Association.

Richardson, Boyce. 1976 *Strangers Devour the Land*. New York: Alfred A. Knopf.

Riches, David. 1974 The Netsilik Eskimo: A Special Case of Selective Female Infanticide. *Ethnology* 13:351–361.

Ridington, William Robbins, Jr. (Robin). 1968 The Environmental Context of Beaver Indian Behavior. Doctoral thesis, Harvard University.

———1978 *Swan People: A Study of the Dunne-za Prophet Dance*. Ottawa: National Museums of Canada, National Museum of Man Mercury Series, Canadian Ethnology Service, Paper, No. 38.

——— n.d. Hunting and Gathering World View in Relation to Adaptive Strategy. Manuscript.

Rogers, Edward S. 1962 *The Round Lake Ojibwa*. Toronto: Royal Ontario Museum.

———1963 *The Hunting Group-Hunting Territory Complex Among the Mistassini Indians*. Ottawa: National Museum of Canada, Bulletin No. 195.

———1967 The Material Culture of the Mistassini. Ottawa: National Museum of Canada, Bulletin No. 218.

Rogers, Edward S., and Mary B. Black. 1976 Subsistence Strategy in the Fish and Hare Period, Northern Ontario: The Weagamow Ojibwa, 1880–1920. *Journal of Anthropological Research* 32:1–43.

Ross, W. Gillies. 1977 Whaling and the Decline of Native Populations. *Arctic Anthropology* 14:1–8.

Savishinsky, Joel S. 1974 *The Trail of the Hare*. New York: Gordon and Beach Science Publishers.

Savishinsky, Joel S., and Susan B. Frimmer. 1973 *The Middle Ground: Social Change in an Arctic Community, 1967–1971*. Ottawa: National Museums of Canada, National Museum of Man Mercury Series, Ethnology Division, Paper 7.

Senungetuk, Joseph E. 1971 *Give or Take a Century*. San Francisco: Indian Historian Press.

Sharp, Henry S. 1975 Introducing the Sororate to a Northern Saskatchewan Chipewyan Village. *Ethnology* 14:71–82.

————1977a The Chipewyan Hunting Unit. *American Ethnologist* 4:377–393.

————1977b The Caribou-Eater Chipewyan: Bilaterality, Strategies of Caribou Hunting, and the Fur Trade. *Arctic Anthropology* 14:35–40.

Sharrock, Floyd W., and Susan R. Sharrock. 1974 *History of the Cree Indian Territorial Expansion from the Hudson Bay Area to the Interior Saskatchewan and Missouri Plains*. New York: Garland Publishing.

Skinner, Alanson. 1911 *Notes on the Eastern Cree and Northern Saulteaux*. New York: American Museum of Natural History, Anthropological Papers, vol. 9, pt. 1.

Slobodin, Richard. 1962 *Band Organization of the Peel River Kutchin*. Ottawa: National Museum of Canada, Bulletin No. 179.

Smallboy, Robert. 1969 Decision to Leave Hobbema (trans. Eugene Steinhauer). *Western Canadian Journal of Anthropology* 1:112–118.

Smith, David Merrill. 1973 *InKonze: Magico-Religious Beliefs of Contact-Traditional Chipewyan Trading at Fort Resolution, NWT, Canada*. Ottawa: National Museums of Canada, National Museum of Man Mercury Series, Ethnology Division, Paper No. 6.

Smith, J.G.E. 1970 The Chipewyan Hunting Group in a Village Context. *Western Canadian Journal of Anthropology* 2:60–77.

————1975 Preliminary Notes on the Rocky Cree of Reindeer Lake (1). In D.B. Carlisle (ed.).*Contributions to Canadian Ethnology, 1975*. Ottawa: National Museums of Canada, National Museum of Man Mercury Series, Canadian Ethnology Service, Paper No. 31, pp. 171–189.

————1978 Economic Uncertainty in an "Original Affluent Society": Caribou and Caribou Eater Chipewyan Adaptive Strategies. *Arctic Anthropology* 15:68–88.

Spencer, Robert F. 1959 *The North Alaskan Eskimo*. Washington, D.C.: Smithsonian Institution, Bureau of American Ethnology, Bulletin 171.

Tanner, Adrian. 1975 The Hidden Feast. In W. Cowan (ed.). *Papers of the Sixth Algonquian Conference*. Ottawa: National Museums of Canada, National Museum of Man Mercury Series, Canadian Ethnology Service, Paper No. 23, pp. 291–313.

Taylor, William E., Jr. and Robert McGhee. 1979 *Archaeological Material from Creswell Bay, N.W.T., Canada*. Ottawa: National Museums of Canada, National Museum of Man Mercury Series, Archaeological Survey of Canada, Paper No. 85.

Townsend, Joan B. 1973 Ethnoarchaeology in Nineteenth Century Southern and Western Alaska: An Interpretive Model. *Ethnohistory* 20:393–412.

————1978 Human Chattels in Southern Alaska. Paper presented at American Anthropological Association Annual Meeting. Los Angeles, 1978.

Trudel, François. 1978 The Inuit of Southern Labrador and the Development of French Sedentary Fisheries (1700–1760). In R.J. Preston (ed.). *Papers from the Fourth Annual Congress, 1977*, Canadian Ethnology Society. Ottawa: National Museums of Canada, National Museum of Man Mercury Series, Canadian Ethnology Service, Paper No. 40, pp. 99–121.

Turner, David H. and Paul Wertman. 1977 *Shamattawa: The Structure of Social Relations in a Northern Algonkian Band*. Ottawa: National Museums of Canada, National Museum of Man Mercury Series, Canadian Ethnology Service, Paper No. 36.

Vallee, Frank G. 1967 *Povungnetuk and Its Cooperative: A Case Study in Community Change*. Ottawa: Northern Co-ordination and Research Centre, Department of Indian Affairs and Northern Development.

VanStone, James W. 1967 *Eskimos of the Nushagak River*. Seattle: University of Washington Press.

————1974 *Athapaskan Adaptations*. Chicago: Aldine Publishing Co.

Voegelin, C. F. and F. M. Voegelin. 1964 *Languages of the World: Native America*, Fascicle One. Anthropological Linguistics 6(6). Bloomington: Indiana University.

Welsh, Ann. 1970 Community Pattern and Settlement Pattern in the Development of Old Crow Village, Yukon Territory. *Western Canadian Journal of Anthropology* 2:17–30.

Wilkinson, Paul F. 1972 Oomingmak: A Model for Man-Animal Relationships in Prehistory. *Current Anthropology* 13:23–44.

Wilmeth, Roscoe. 1978 *Anahim Lake Archaeology and the Early Historic Chilcotin Indians*. Ottawa: National Museums of Canada, National Museum of Man Mercury Series, Archaeological Survey of Canada, Paper No. 82.

Wilson, Ian R. 1978 *Archaeological Investigations at*

the Atigun Site, Central Brooks Range, Alaska. Ottawa: National Museums of Canada, National Museum of Man Mercury Series, Archaeological Survey of Canada, Paper No. 78.

Winterhalder, Bruce P. 1978 [1977] *Foraging Strategy Adaptations of the Boreal Forest Cree*. Ann Arbor, Mich.: University Microfilms.

Wright, J.V. 1972 *Ontario Prehistory*. Ottawa: National Museums of Canada, National Museum of Man, Archaeological Survey of Canada.

Young, T. Kue. 1979 Changing Patterns of Health and Sickness Among the Cree-Ojibwa of Northwestern Ontario. *Medical Anthropology* 3:191–223.

ADDITIONAL SOURCES FOR THE SECOND EDITION

Ambler, Marjane. 1990 *Breaking the Iron Bonds*. Lawrence: University Press of Kansas.

American Antiquity. "Current Research" through vol. 55(2) (April 1990).

Berger, Thomas R. 1985 *Village Journey*. New York: Hill and Wang.

Bielawski, E. 1988 Paleoeskimo Variability: The Early Arctic Small-Tool Tradition in the Central Canadian Arctic. *American Antiquity* 53(1):52–74.

Blackman, Margaret B. 1989 *Sadie Brower Neakok, An Iñupiaq Woman*. Seattle: University of Washington Press.

Boeri, David. 1982 *People of the Ice Whale*. New York: E.P. Dutton.

Brasser, Ted J. 1976 *"Bo'jou, Neejee!"* Ottawa: National Museum of Man.

Braund, Stephen R. 1988 *The Skin Boats of Saint Lawrence Island, Alaska*. Seattle: University of Washington Press.

Brøsted, Jens, Jens Dahl, Andrew Gray, Hans Christian Gulløv, Georg Henriksen, Jørgen Brøchner Jørgensen, Inge Kleivan. 1985 *Native Power*. Bergen: Universitetforlaget AS.

Brown, Emily Ivanoff (Ticasuk). 1981 *The Roots of Ticasuk: An Eskimo Woman's Family Story*. Anchorage: Alaska Northwest Publishing.

Brumbach, Hetty Jo. 1985 The Recent Fur Trade in Northwestern Saskatchewan. *Historical Archaeology* 19(2):19–39.

Brumbach, Hetty Jo, and Robert Jarvenpa. 1990 Archeologist-Ethnographer-Informant Relations: The Dynamics of Ethnoarcheology in the Field. In S.M. Nelson and A.B. Kehoe (eds.). *Powers of Observation: Alternative Views in Archeology*. Washington, D.C.: American Anthropological Association, Archeological Papers, no. 2. pp. 39–46.

Burley, David, and David Meyer, eds. 1982 *Nipawin Reservoir Heritage Study*: vol. 3, *Regional Overview and Research Considerations*. Saskatoon: Saskatchewan Research Council.

Campbell, Lyle, and Marianne Mithun, eds. 1979 *The Languages of Native America*. Austin: University of Texas Press.

Chang, Claudia. 1988 Nauyalik Fish Camp: An Ethnoarchaeological Study in Activity-Area Formation. *American Antiquity* 53(1):145–157.

Condon, Richard G. 1987 *Inuit Youth*. New Brunswick, N.J.: Rutgers University Press.

Conference on Hunting and Gathering Societies. 1990 Precirculated Papers, Sixth International Conference on Hunting and Gathering Societies. Fairbanks: Department of Anthropology, University of Alaska.

Conway, Thor, and Julie Conway. 1990 *Spirits on Stone*. San Luis Obispo: Heritage Discoveries.

Cox, Bruce Alden, ed. 1987 *Native People, Native Lands*. Ottawa: Carleton University Press.

Damas, David. 1988 The Contact-Traditional Horizon of the Central Arctic: Reassessment of a Concept and Reexamination of an Era. *Arctic Anthropology* 25(2):101–138.

Damas, David, ed. 1984 *Handbook of North American Indians*, vol 5: *Arctic*. Washington, D.C.: Smithsonian Institution Press.

Dumond, Don E. 1987 A Reexamination of Eskimo-Aleut Prehistory. *American Anthropologist* 89(1):32–56.

Dyck, Noel, ed. 1985 *Indigenous Peoples and the Nation-State*. St. John's: Memorial University of Newfoundland.

Eber, Dorothy Harley. 1989 *When the Whalers Were Up North*. Boston: David R. Godine.

Feest, Christian F., ed. 1987 *Indians and Europe*. Aachen: Edition Herodot, Rader Verlag.

Feit, Harvey A. 1980 Negotiating Recognition of Aboriginal Rights: History, Strategies and Reactions to the James Bay and Northern Québec Agreement. *Canadian Journal of Anthropology* 1(2):159–172.

———1986 Anthropologists and the State: The Relationship Between Social Policy Advocacy and Academic Practice in the History of the Algonquian

Hunting Territory Debate, 1910–50. Paper presented at American Anthropological Association annual meeting, Philadelphia, December 3-7.

Fitzhugh, William W., and Aron Crowell. 1988 *Crossroads of Continents*. Washington, D.C.: Smithsonian Institution Press.

Fitzhugh, William W., and Susan A. Kaplan. 1982 *Inua*. Washington, D.C.: Smithsonian Institution Press.

Fitzhugh, William W., ed. 1985 *Cultures in Contact*. Washington, D.C.: Smithsonian Institution Press.

Fleckner, John A. 1984 *Native American Archives*. Chicago: Society of American Archivists.

Freeman, Milton M. R., ed. 1976 *Inuit Land Use and Occupancy Project*, vol. 2, *Supporting Studies*. Ottawa: Ministry of Indian and Northern Affairs.

Gagnon, Jo Ann. 1982 *Le Régime de Chasse, de Pêche et de Trappage et les Conventions du Québec Nordique*. Québec: Université Laval, Centre d'Études Nordiques.

Hanna, Margaret G., and Brian Kooyman, eds. 1982 *Approaches to Algonquian Archaeology*. Calgary: Archaeology Association of the University of Calgary.

Hara, Hiroko Sue. 1980 *The Hare Indians and Their World*. Ottawa: National Museums of Canada, National Museum of Man Mercury Series, Canadian Ethnology Service, Paper No. 63.

Helm, June, ed. 1981 *Handbook of North American Indians*, vol 6: *Subarctic*. Washington, D.C.: Smithsonian Institution Press.

Ives, John W. 1990 *A Theory of Northern Athapaskan Prehistory*. Boulder: Westview Press.

Jarvenpa, Robert. 1980 *The Trappers of Patuanak: Toward a Spatial Ecology of Modern Hunters*. Ottawa: National Museums of Canada, National Museum of Man Mercury Series, Canadian Ethnology Service, Paper No. 67.

——— 1982 Intergroup Behavior and Imagery: The Case of Chipewyan and Cree. Ethnology 21(4): 283–299.

Jones, Dorothy Knee. 1980 *A Century of Servitude*. Washington, D.C.: University Press of America.

Jorgensen, Joseph G. 1990 *Oil Age Eskimos*. Berkeley: University of California Press.

Kaplan, Susan A., and Kristin J. Barsness. 1986 *Raven's Journey*. Philadelphia: University Museum, University of Pennsylvania.

Klausner, Samuel Z., and Edward F. Foulks. 1982 *Eskimo Capitalists*. Totowa, N.J.: Allanheld, Osmun.

Krech, Shepard, III, ed. 1984 *The Subarctic Fur Trade:*

Native Social and Economic Adaptations. Vancouver: University of British Columbia Press.

Laughlin, William S., J. B. Jørgensen, and B. Frøhlich. 1979 Aleuts and Eskimos: Survivors of the Bering Land Bridge Coast. In W.S. Laughlin and A.B. Harper (eds.). The First Americans: Origins, Affinities and Adaptations. New York: Gustav Fischer, pp. 91–104.

Lithman, Yngve Georg. 1984 *The Community Apart*. Winnipeg: University of Manitoba Press.

Lytwyn, Victor P. 1986 *The Fur Trade of the Little North*. Winnipeg: Rupert's Land Research Centre, University of Winnipeg.

Maxwell, Moreau S. 1985 *Prehistory of the Eastern Arctic*. Orlando: Academic Press.

McCartney, Allen P., ed. 1982, 1983, 1985, 1987, 1988 *Arctic Anthropology* vols. 19(2), 20(2), 22(2), 24(2), 25(1).

McCormack, Patricia A. 1979 Chipewyans Turn Cree: Governmental and Structural Factors in Ethnic Processes. Unpublished paper presented November 2, 1979.

——— 1987 Fort Chipewyan and the Great Depression. *Canadian Issues/Thèmes Canadiens* 8:69–92.

McGhee, Robert. 1984 The Timing of the Thule Migration. *Polarforschung* 54(1):1–7.

McGhee, Robert, and Magnús Einarsson. 1983 Greenlandic Eskimos and Norse: A Parallel Tradition from Greenland and Iceland? *Folk* 25:51–61.

McGrath, Robin. 1984 *Canadian Inuit Literature: The Development of a Tradition*. Ottawa: National Museums of Canada, National Museum of Man Mercury Series, Canadian Ethnology Service, Paper No. 94.

Miller, J. R. 1990 Owen Glendower, Hotspur, and Canadian Indian Policy. *Ethnohistory* 37(4):386–415.

Morantz, Toby. 1983 *An Ethnohistoric Study of Eastern James Bay Cree Social Organization, 1700–1850*. Ottawa: National Museums of Canada, National Museum of Man Mercury Series, Canadian Ethnology Service, Paper No. 88.

Morrison, Kenneth M. 1990 Baptism and Alliance: The Symbolic Mediations of Religious Syncretism. *Ethnohistory* 37(4):416–437.

Moyles, R. G. 1979 *British Law and Arctic Men*. Saskatoon: Western Producer Prairie Books.

Nichols, John D. 1982 James Evans and the Cree Syllabary. Paper presented at American Anthropological Association annual meeting,1982.

Oswalt, Wendell H. 1990 *Bashful No Longer: An Alas-*

kan Eskimo Ethnohistory, 1778–1988. Norman: University of Oklahoma Press.

Perry, Richard J. 1989 Matrilineal Descent in a Hunting Context: The Athapaskan Case. Ethnology 28(1):33–51.

Peterson, Jacqueline, and Jennifer S. H. Brown, eds. 1985 The New Peoples: Being and Becoming Métis in North America. Lincoln: University of Nebraska Press.

Peterson, Nicolas, and Marcia Langton, eds. 1983 Aborigines, Land and Land Rights. Canberra: Australian Institute of Aboriginal Studies.

Ponting, J. Rick, and Roger Gibbins. 1980 Out of Irrelevance: A Socio-political Introduction to Indian Affairs in Canada. Toronto: Butterworth.

Prucha, Francis Paul. 1984 The Great Father. Lincoln: University of Nebraska Press.

Ray, Arthur J., and Arthur Roberts. 1985 Approaches to the Ethnohistory of the Subarctic: A Review of the Handbook of North American Indians: Subarctic. Ethnohistory 32(3): 270-280.

Ray, Dorothy Jean. 1981 Aleut and Eskimo Art. Seattle: University of Washington Press.

———1983 Ethnohistory in the Arctic: The Bering Strait Eskimo. Kingston: Limestone Press.

Riches, David. 1982 Northern Nomadic Hunter-Gatherers: A Humanistic Approach. New York: Academic Press.

Ridington, Robin. 1990 Little Bit Know Something. Iowa City: University of Iowa Press.

Ross, Thomas E., and Tyrel G. Moore, eds. 1987 A Cultural Geography of North American Indians. Boulder: Westview Press.

Rushforth, Scott. 1984 Bear Lake Athapaskan Kinship and Task Group Formation. Ottawa: National Museums of Canada, National Museum of Man Mercury Series, Canadian Ethnology Service, Paper No. 96.

Schusky, Ernest L., ed. 1980 Political Organization of Native North America. Washington, D.C.: University Press of America.

Scollon, Ronald, and Suzanne B. K. Scollon. 1979 Linguistic Convergence: An Ethnography of Speaking at Fort Chipewyan, Alberta. New York: Academic Press.

———1981 Narrative, Literacy and Face in Interethnic Communication. Norwood, N.J.: Ablex.

Sheehan, Glenn W. 1985 Whaling as an Organizing Focus in Northwestern Alaskan Eskimo Societies. In T. Douglas Price and James A. Brown (eds.). Prehistoric Hunter-Gatherers. Orlando: Academic Press, pp. 123–154.

Shkilnyk, Anastasia M. 1985 A Poison Stronger Than Love. New Haven: Yale University Press.

Smith, David M. 1982 Moose-Deer Island House People: A History of the Native People of Fort Resolution. Ottawa: National Museums of Canada, National Museum of Man Mercury Series, Canadian Ethnology Service, Paper No. 81.

Smith, Donald B. 1987 Aboriginal Rights a Century Ago. The Beaver 67(1):4–15.

———1988 The Life of George Copway or Kah-ge

Smith, James G. E. 1987 The Western Woods Cree: Anthropological Myth and Historical Reality. American Ethnologist 14(3):434–448.

Steegmann, A. Theodore, Jr., ed. 1983 Boreal Forest Adaptations. New York: Plenum Press.

Tanner, Adrian, ed. 1983 The Politics of Indianness. St. John's: Memorial University of Newfoundland.

The Phoenix. 1989 Teme-Augama Anishnabai Fact Sheet. Toronto: Canadian Alliance in Solidarity with Native Peoples.

Thistle, Paul C. 1986 Indian-European Trade Relations in the Lower Saskatchewan River Region to 1840. Winnipeg: University of Manitoba Press.

Tooker, Elisabeth, ed. 1983 The Development of Political Organization in Native North America. Washington, D.C.: American Ethnological Society.

Turner, Christy G., II. 1981 Russian Influence on Aleut Ecology, Culture, and Physical Anthropology. National Geographic Society Research Reports 13:623–633.

Wadden, Marie. 1988 What Do the Innu Want? Peace and Security 3(3):4–5.

Wenzel, George W. 1981 Clyde Inuit Adaptation and Ecology: The Organization of Subsistence. Ottawa: National Museums of Canada, National Museum of Man Mercury Series, Canadian Ethnology Service, Paper No. 77.

Yerbury, J. C. 1986 The Subarctic Indians and the Fur Trade, 1680–1860. Vancouver: University of British Columbia Press.

10

FIRST NATIONS OF NORTH AMERICA ENTER THE TWENTY-FIRST CENTURY

If I knew for a certainty that a man was coming to my house with a conscious design of doing me good, I should run for my life.

Henry David Thoreau, Walden

North America, like the other continents, has had a long history of human population expansion and adaptation to a variety of regional ecologies. Wide networks of trade have been channels of communication for technological, intellectual, and social innovations. The drive to control resources more securely led to wars, countered by alliances. The great maneuvered for power while ordinary men and women looked for the small satisfactions of full bellies, dry beds, companionable friends, and supportive families. Self-evident as it should be that the humans inhabiting North America should have lives and histories similar in nature and sweep to those of humans elsewhere, circumstances of European history created a mythical America that is only now being seriously challenged.

That mythical America was called a virgin land yearning for the embrace of her European lover. The muddled metaphor noted the virgin's red children, children who were said to need a father's guiding hand. Some recent historians have argued that America was in fact so depopulated by recent epidemics when European colonists arrived to settle that the land did look virgin. Though epidemics of introduced diseases did pass from Indian to Indian inland from the coasts in advance of most of the Europeans, the thesis cannot hold for Mexico and can be shown to be incorrect for nearly all of America. Populations in some localities were much reduced before European settlements were initiated in numbers, but few districts could have been honestly perceived as unpopulated. Records of dealings, friendly or hostile, with the native inhabitants amply attest to the prior human occupation of America, and the many treatises on the virgin's red children confirm the invaders' recognition that they had predecessors.

LEGISLATIVE AND JUDICIAL LANDMARKS CHRONOLOGY

1990 Native American Grave Protection and Repatriation Act (Public Law 101-601), United States, requires museums and federal agencies to return human remains, funerary and sacred objects and objects of cultural patrimony to tribes that can show they had belonged to the tribe and had been removed without the tribe's consent. Trafficking in human remains is prohibited.

1990 Elijah Harper, Cree member of the Manitoba Legislature, prevents ratification of Canadian federal-provincial Accord that fails to give Indian nations full standing.

1983 Voight Decision in Lac Courte Oreilles Band of Chippewa Indians v. Wisconsin, United States; Chippewa retain rights to subsistence activities in territories ceded by treaties stipulating these rights.

1982 Canada's Constitution Act sets up Part II, sections 25, 35, and 37 "Rights of the Aboriginal Peoples of Canada," separate from Part I Charter of Rights and Freedoms.

1980 Baker Lake et al. v. Minister of Indian Affairs and Northern Development, Canada; the Supreme Court recognized Inuit "aboriginal rights" to hunt and fish (recognized in 1964 in Skiyea v. The Queen) but denied that their "aboriginal rights" include proprietary title to mineral resources.

1978 American Indian Freedom of Religion Act (P.L. 95-341), United States, stated "American Indian, Eskimo, Aleut, and Native Hawaiian . . . inherent right" to the free exercise of their traditional religions. That this law can be very narrowly interpreted appeared in the 1990 Supreme Court decision upholding the State of Oregon's prohibition against the ingestion of peyote even by members of the Native American Church (Employment Division, Department of Human Resources of Oregon, et. al. v. Smith et. al.), and the 1988 ruling in Lyng, Secretary of Agriculture, et. al. v. Northwest Indian Cemetery Protection Assn., et. al. that the U.S. Forest Service could cut a logging road through a mountain area held sacred and used for religious worship by the Karok, Tolowa, and Yurok tribes of northern California.

1978 Indian Child Welfare Act, United States, protecting Indian tribes' interest in retaining custody of their children.

1978 Oliphant v. Suquamish Indian Tribe, United States; tribes do not have jurisdiction over non-Indians residing on Indian reservations.

1978 Santa Clara Pueblo v. Martinez, United States; Supreme Court ruled that the United States could not enforce its law contrary to tribal government rulings (in this case, the 1968 Indian Civil Rights Act was held not to infringe upon the pueblo's right to limit membership to children of Santa Clara men; Santa Clara women such as Julia Martinez, who married a Navajo, could not enroll their children).

1975 Indian Self-Determination and Education Assistance Act, United States; establishing policy to permit greater governmental and administrative powers to Indian tribes.

1973 Calder et al. v. Attorney-General of British Columbia; Canada recognizes limited aboriginal title, permitting land claims to be negotiated.

1973 Menominee Restoration Act (P.L. 93-197), United States; repealed the 1954 act terminating the tribal status of the Menominee. In effect, this nullified the 1953 federal policy promoting termination of Indian status.

1971 Alaska Native Claims Settlement Act, United States.

1970 Blue Lake restored to Taos Pueblo by Congressional action, United States, after it was expropriated in 1906 for a national forest.

1967 Canada's Supreme Court rules in The Queen v. Drybones that the Bill of Rights applies to status Indians. (Joseph Drybones was a Dogrib protesting the prohibition against selling liquor to Indians.)

1966 National Historic Preservation Act (16 USC 470 et seq.), United States, requires all federal agencies to identify all sites, buildings, etc., under their jurisdictions that have yielded or may yield "information important in prehistory or history." This greatly stimulates archaeological and historical investigations and public knowledge of the value of the country's cultural heritage. The 1979 Archaeological Resources Protection Act (P.L. 96-95) required permits for archaeological work and contained provision for consent of affected Indian tribes if the work impinged on their lands or heritage.

1960 Canada grants citizenship to Indians. (In 1885, a Conservative government passed an Electoral Franchise Bill granting eastern Canadian Indian men the same right to hold office and vote in federal elections as other men: they had only to meet the qualification of an annual income of $300 or more. This franchise for Indians was revoked in 1898 by a Liberal government. The franchise was never extended to Prairie or other western Indians; when the 1885 bill was passed, many Plains Cree and Ojibwa were fighting against Canada in the second Riel Rebellion.)

1959 Williams v. Lee, United States; the Supreme Court ruled that a tribal court has jurisdiction over a contract entered into by a non-Indian with reservation Indians.

1953 House Concurrent Resolution no. 108, United States, states its policy "to end [Indians'] status as wards of the United States;" Public Law 280, United States, gave five states (California, Oregon, Minnesota, Wisconsin, Nebraska) civil and criminal jurisdiction over most Indian lands within their borders.

1951 Revised Indian Act, Canada, repeals prohibition against potlatches.

1946 United States Indian Claims Commission Act; deadline for filing cases was 1951, cases heard until 1974.

1934 Wheeler-Howard (Indian Reorganization) Act, United States, permitted tribes to organize and write constitutions for self-government, and directed the government to consolidate and conserve Indian lands, and encouraged education and economic plans for Indians; the Johnson-O'Malley Act authorized contracts with states to administer educational, medical, and welfare programs on Indian reservations. In 1974, the Johnson-O'Malley Act was amended to encourage Indian direction of such programs.

1924 United States Indians given citizenship, although right to vote denied by several states; Utah the last to enfranchise Indians, in 1960, in state elections.

1908 Winters v. United States (207 U.S. 564), United States; established that irrigation water rights accrued to Indian reservations.

1906 United States Antiquities Act (16 USC 432) establishes national jurisdiction over antiquities.

1903 Lone Wolf v. Hitchcock, United States; the Supreme Court ruled that Lone Wolf, a Kiowa, could not obstruct the implementation of allotment on Kiowa land, regardless of Kiowa consent: the case established Congress' power to unilaterally break treaties. The Court declared the Indians to be "an ignorant and dependent race" that must be governed by the "Christian people" of the United States.

1902 Cherokee Nation v. Hitchcock, United States; the Supreme Court held the United States has the power to overrule Cherokee laws.

1896 Talton v. Mayes, United States, ruled that Indian courts were not bound by United States Constitution provisions.

1889 St. Catherine's Milling and Lumber Co. v. The Queen; Canadian court held that the crown had proprietary estate in Indian land even before treaties, the Indians having only usufructuary rights. (The case was actually over whether the province of Ontario or the Dominion of Canada, via Indian treaties, had rights to the resources of colonized land within the province; the question was who—Indians or Ontario—first held rights to the land.)

1887 Dawes Allotment Act, United States, authorizes the break-up of Indian reservations into individual allotments usually of 160 acres, and the sale of "surplus" lands remaining after enrolled tribal members had received allotments (no provision for later generations); the 1898 Curtis Act gave it power and extended it to the Five Civilized Tribes (Cherokee, Creek, Choctaw, Chickasaw, Seminole) in Indian Territory, soon to be the state of Oklahoma. In 1914, the governments of these five nations were abolished, and they were put under an agency superintendent. The Curtis Act was written by Congressman Charles Curtis, who was part Kansa and Kaw and who became Vice President of the United States in 1928.

1886 United States v. Kagama, United States, narrowly established federal jurisdiction over a Hupa murderer; the Hupa had not signed a treaty with the United States as the Brule Lakota had (the Hupa had been taken over as part of California with the Treaty of Guadalupe Hidalgo, signed with Mexico).

1883 Ex parte Crow Dog, United States, established tribal court jurisdiction over tribal members. (Crow Dog, a Brule Lakota, had murdered Chief Spotted Tail.)

1882 United States v. McBratney, United States, allowed state jurisdiction over crimes committed by non-Indians against non-Indians, although on Indian land.

1876 Canadian Indian Act; amendment in 1884 prohibited potlatches; another in 1885 required Indians to obtain passes from their agent if they wished to leave their reservations (this was impractical to enforce and used principally to restrict "rebels" attempting protests and pan-Indian organizing); and in 1895 Plains giveaways were prohibited.

1832 Worcester v. Georgia, United States; Chief Justice John Marshall ruled that the states do not have jurisdiction over Indian nations within their borders; that the United States comprises three jurisdictional entities, the federal, the states, and Indian tribes. Worcester v. Georgia is one of the most cited cases in United States law because of its impact on questions of states' rights.

1831 Cherokee Nation v. Georgia, United States; Chief Justice John Marshall ruled that the Indians form "domestic dependent nations" over which the United States is guardian, as over wards.

1830 Indian Removal Act, United States, affecting all Indian nations east of the Mississippi.

1823 Johnson v. M'Intosh, United States; Chief Justice John Marshall recognized Indian title, and that the United States, like its predecessor Britain in the 1763 Royal Proclamation, holds the fee in tribal lands.

1797 Jay Treaty gave Indians along the United States-Canada border the right to freely cross.

1790 Trade and Intercourse Act, United States, establishing federal jurisdiction over Indian title and commerce with Indians.

1763 Royal Proclamation (Britain) reserving to the Crown the right to extinguish Indian title. This Proclamation continues to have force, albeit much debated, in Canadian law.

Standard English-language histories and anthropological surveys of the native nations of North America tell more of the European myth than of the American reality. The landing of Columbus is seen as the breaking of a golden bowl of timeless primitiveness. Depending on the historian, the primitives were either said to be relentlessly eradicated until only a tiny broken remnant huddles on reservations, or fought quite literally like the devil until they saw the light and gave themselves up to European missionizing. American history is isolated from European history and from its own past. School textbooks intend to mass-produce American citizens proud of their country and loyal to its institutions; they define the legitimacy of that nation and its institutions, they do not dispute it.

The European settlement of America was a conquest driven by expanding European populations. Recovery had been rapid in Europe after the toll of the Black Death in the mid-fourteenth century. Peasants moved into sparsely settled regions of eastern and northern Europe, seeking land not only for grain for human consumption, but additional land to support the draft and meat animals basic to the European cultural pattern (in contrast with the eastern Asian, Mexican, and Peruvian patterns, in which little meat was consumed and less land needed per capita). Those who could not get land came to towns and ports looking for wage work. This influx of cheap labor sustained the growth of international trade and industrialism, correlated in an economy that always needed new or growing markets. The impact of Columbus's explorations came through Western Europe's recognition that vast potential markets had been discovered, markets in the broadest sense of exchanges of products, both raw materials and finished goods. The Spanish, French, and early British colonies in America were designed to tap American sources of precious metals, furs, dried tobacco, and other high-value, low-bulk materials that could bring profits even after being shipped to Europe. Then, in the seventeenth century, wealthy landowners found that the decline of feudal political structures and rise in central governments meant the end of private troops and their opportunities for riches from war booty. Aristocrats had to plan to obtain their income from their own land through legal levies such as rents. Landholding was tightened up and common lands "enclosed"— that is, allotted and fenced. Peasants who had managed by combining day labor with the keeping of a cow and pig on the village common were forced off, and it was feared they would become a danger to established society, begging and thieving. It was then, in the seventeenth century, that America came to be seen as an outlet for the surplus European population.

In the next three centuries, millions of peasants and urban workers emigrated, keeping the labor supply in Europe low enough to enable those remaining to gradually improve their wages and security. The traditional pattern of relatively high meat consumption could be perpetuated in spite of its wastefulness in terms of efficiently satisfying human needs. In America, the emigrants instituted the cultural patterns developed in Europe: plough agriculture for broadcast grains, stock raising, roads for animal-drawn vehicles, and as soon as a district had sufficient European inhabitants, a money-based market economy. Entrepeneurs recruiting emigrants described America as a new land. Emigration would relieve Europe of landless, surplus laborers and at the same time support industrialization by developing new sources of raw materials and new markets. Hence, European governments, and particularly Britain, which as an island was especially conscious of its limited land base and need for colonization, promoted emigration. If it were advertised that America was already well populated, many potential migrants might be discouraged, but if America was pictured as wilderness needing only an ax to be made habitable, wilderness in which natives of human form were really more beast than human, with no claim to land, then there would seem to be no bar to colonization. It was thus politically astute in Europe to negate the presence in America of native disputants to European hegemony.

Primed to see beastlike savages, emigrants readily interpreted the Indian farms and deer parks as natural landscapes, the lack of vehicle roads as sign of wilderness, the absence of stone buildings north of Mexico as absence of civilization. The myth of the virgin America with no more than red children was projected by Europe to encourage and justify the conquest of the continent for European gain. It persisted through the nineteenth century as eastern North America reached population densities comparable to Europe's and in turn promoted emigration to the western regions of the continent where raw materials and new markets for the eastern American economy could be developed. As the frontier of Euro-American colonization moved westward, so moved the projection of the savage with no more claim to the land than any other beast, the savage in a wilderness that awaited the steel ax.

Dominant images might falsify the presence, claims, and character of the native American Indian, yet the home governments were forced to deal with real Indian men and women. In developing policies, officials had to attempt to satisfy both citizens with economic interests in the colonies—merchants, industrialists, land speculators, emigrants—and those who were concerned with broader implications. These were indirectly influenced by economic interest through theories and philosophies stimulated by shifts and trends in the economic sphere. Through the three centuries of conquest, Western European philosophers developed the concept of natural law, a concept that sanctioned conflict and even genocide by citing competition and killing among animals, although it must be mentioned that the concept of natural law also had a benign influence in asserting an inherent goodness in human beings that was conducive toward recognition of individual rights to "life, liberty, and the pursuit of happiness," if dictatorships could be prevented.

In the nineteenth century, the culmination of imperialism was supported by so-called Social Darwinism, a distortion of the theory of evolution that invoked natural law to support not only the propriety of the stronger killing or enslaving the weaker, but also the promulgation of a hierarchy of peoples purportedly representing progress from simple, primitive types to advanced, conquering nations. A mishmash of Greek myth and selected observations of non-Western peoples and European peasants was organized into a scheme of rankings accepted a priori by officials, missionaries, and even many anthropologists. Truly a Procrustean bed, the evolutionary scheme was made to fit by ignoring or misinterpreting—often without conscious intent—many features of non-Western societies. American Indian societies were labeled primitive because they did not have plough agriculture or smelt iron, and because they were *labeled* primitive, their religions, societal institutions, technology and so on, were described as primitive.

SEEING WITH A NATIVE EYE

My adopted Navajo father…an eighty- or ninety-year-old man in the 1950s…had seen almost nothing of what you and I experience as the "modern, advanced world."…I showed him a two-page spread of the Empire State Building which appeared in *Life* that year. His question was, immediately, "How many sheep will it hold?" I had to admit that I didn't know, and that even if I did know, I couldn't count that high in Navajo; and I tried to show him how big a sheep might look if you held it up against one of those windows, but he was interested neither in my excuses nor in my intent to explain the size of the building. When I told him what it was for, he was shocked. The whole concept of so many people filed together in one big drawer—of course he would not have used those terms—was shocking to him. He felt that people who live so close together cannot live a very rich life, so he expected that whites would be found to be spiritually impoverished and personally very upset by living so close together....

About six months later, when I was at the trading post [I] found a magazine with a picture of the latest jet bomber on it. I brought that to him to explain better what those things were that flew over all the time. He asked the same question in spite of the fact there were lots of little men standing around the plane and he could see very well how big it was. Again he said, "How many sheep will it carry?" I started to shrug him off as if he were simply plaguing me, when it became clear to me that what he was really asking was, "What is it good for in terms of something that I know to be valid and viable in the world?" (That, of course, is not his wording either.) ... When I told him what the jet bomber was for, he became so outraged that he refused ever to go to town, and he died without ever having done so as far as I know. He said that he had heard many terrible things about the whites, but the idea of someone killing that many people by dropping the bomb and remaining so far out of reach that he was not in danger was just too much!

The only other thing that approached such outrage, by the way, was when I explained to him about the toilet facilities in white houses, and I mentioned indoor toilet functions. He could hardly believe that one. "They do that right in the house, right inside where everyone lives?" "No, no, you don't understand. There is a separate room for it." That was even worse—that there could be a special place for such things. A world so neatly categorized and put in boxes really bothered him, and he steadfastly refused to go visit it.....

When we from one culture start looking at the patterns of another culture, we will often see what our culture has trained us to see. If we look at a Navajo rug, for example, we are inclined to say the Navajos use many straight lines in their rugs. And yet if we talk to Navajos about weaving, the _gesture_ we often see is a four-way back-and-forth movement; and they talk about the interaction within the pattern—a reciprocation. Most often the Navajo rug reciprocates its pattern from side to side and from end to end, creating mirror images. My adopted sister, who is a very fine weaver, always talks about this kind of balance.....And she uses circular hand gestures to illustrate. While we are trained to see the straight lines, and to think of the rug in terms of geometric patterns, she makes the geometrical necessities of weaving—up one, over one—fit a kind of circular logic about how nature works and about how man interacts with nature.

(Barre Toelken in Capps 1976:12-14, 17-18)

Europeans and Euro-Americans saw two courses open for dealing with the "primitives." One option was to more or less ignore the primitives and "let nature take its course" in rendering them extinct before the expansion of the more advanced societies. The myth of the "vanishing Indian" was projected to justify this option: supposedly the primitives were bound to die out as their refuges were invaded by a more advanced race, just as the modern species of horse replaced little Eohippus. There was nothing much anyone could do about the situation, said these Social Darwinists, except perhaps reserve little corners of America for the dying race's final accommodation.

Alternately, conquerors might try to raise the primitives to a higher level by teaching them the "arts of civilization"—that is to say, the Western European cultural pattern that was labeled advanced. Raising the primitives was espoused by missionaries who saw it as their Christian duty of loving their neighbors, and by many government officials who felt a moral imperative to aid those persons who fell within their jurisdiction. Government officials tended to be politicians and thereby to be swayed by the wishes of the more powerful of their voting constituents, so government policies have been plagued by vacillation and inconsistency. The force of circumstances upon policies is well expressed in a letter of Sir William Johnson, agent of the British government in dealing with the Indians in eighteenth-century New York, husband of a Mohawk woman and accepted by the Iroquois as a brother-in-law:

I have laid it down as an invariable rule, from wh [sic] I never did, nor ever shall deviate, that wherever a Title is set up by any Tribe of Indians of little consequence or importance to his Majestys interest, & who may be considered as long domesticated, that such Claim unless apparently clear, had better remain unsupported than the Several old Titles of his Majestys Subjects should thereby become disturbed: —and on the contrary, Wherever I found a Just complaint made by a People either by themselves or Connections capable of resenting & who I knew would resent a neglect, I judged it my Duty to support the same, altho it should disturb ye property of any Man whatsoever.

(quoted in Nammack 1969:77)

The essential tension in European and Euro-American traffic with American Indians was, as Johnson indicates, between abstract Justice and the perceived necessity of politically rewarding compromise.

Where political motivations did not induce conflict, Europeans' belief that Western European cultural traditions were overwhelmingly superior and should be adopted by non-Western peoples was sure to prejudice relations with American Indians.

The United States Indian Peace Commission, established by Congress in 1867 to formulate and carry out policy to obtain a final peace (i.e., United States victory and complete subjugation of Indians on its frontier), spoke often of the importance of educating Indians in Christian practice. In 1871, the Riggs missionary family among the Dakota attempted to fulfill this vision by sending bright Indian youth to Beloit College in Wisconsin. These youth were to receive the same academic training as the Euro-American students at the college, and like many of them, go out as ministers and missionaries after graduation. One of the first of the youths was Ohiyesa, called Charles Alexander Eastman in English, a Santee Dakota who completed his education at Dartmouth and then Boston University School of Medicine, earning an M.D. in 1890. Eastman was best in his class at Beloit in mathematics, and eventually published ten books, numerous articles, and was a popular lecturer. Other students sent by the Riggs did well at Beloit. Nevertheless, the Beloit "experiment" in educating Indians was cut out in 1884. Why? because the college had not fulfilled the Commissioner of Indian Affairs' demand for "that thorough industrial training of the pupils contemplated by the law and sanctioned by the Secretary [of the Interior]"…"If you must neglect [something], it should be his literary studies and not his manual labor exercises" (quoted in Rogel 1990:28). Indians might be raised, but they must not be raised too high; what was considered the model of a successful school for Indians, Captain Pratt's institution at Carlisle, Pennsylvania, concentrated on skills that would suit the students for employment as farm or domestic laborers and gave them, at best, an eighth-grade academic level.

The twentieth-century premise of cultural relativism—that the various cultural patterns in the world are alternative modes of adaptation to the problems of survival and reproduction, and that in most respects they are of reasonably equal value in meeting these problems—was not a concept available to thinkers in the three preceding centuries.

FIGURE 10.1 Indian children in a church-run school. (St. Francis Mission, Rosebud Reservation, South Dakota.)

FIGURE 10.1A Boys and their instructor (right background) in the school's carpentry shop, 1919.

FIGURE 10.1B Girls performing domestic duties. The original photo is captioned, "Sioux girls, always industrious at the mission."

Cultural relativism is a revolutionary restructuring of Euro-American views toward what have been competing populations. Perhaps the appearance of cultural relativism is a sign that Euro-Americans felt confident of final conquest of these native nations: rendered helpless to affect Euro-American political and economic events, they can be looked upon benignly and a tiny measure of freedom bestowed.

The Meriam Report of 1928, investigating and criticizing the Bureau of Indian Affairs of the United States, and the subsequent Indian Reorganization Act in 1934 marked the turning point in Euro-American attitudes toward American Indians. The United States shift in policy influenced Canadian policy, although not radically, and coincided with the development of *indigenismo* in Mexico. No doubt the disillusionment and disruption of policies and public attitudes brought on by the world-wide Depression permitted more scope to reformers in the 1930s than they would have gained in a period of capitalist prosperity. It is critical to note, however, that both the Indian Reorganization Act and *indigenismo* were revisions in Euro-American national structures aimed toward economic development of Indian communities within the Euro-American mode. Neither the United States nor Mexico abandoned its longstanding position that the Indian was subordinate within the Euro-American nation and needed regulation by a federal bureaucracy. This position, based on the theory that the Indian had been handicapped by pre-Columbian isolation from the mainstream of Eurasian history, had been founded during the administration of President Jefferson at the end of the eighteenth century. It stemmed from the premise that North America was naturally bountiful in resources for human needs—a favorite line of the propagandists for emigration to America—and that as a result, the American Indian was unaccustomed to work or struggle. Faced with the competition of Europeans trained for hard work, Indians would be exterminated unless the government intervened by placing them beyond the scene

of European settlement—first in the Old Northwest (the present upper Midwest), then in Indian Territory in Oklahoma, and finally on reservations—and there training their children in the activities of working-class Euro-Americans. With this directed schooling, younger Indians would be able to compete with Euro-American laborers and eventually would no longer need bureaucratic supervision. Preserving native cultural patterns was seen as dereliction from the moral obligation to raise the primitive to the salvation afforded by the advanced civilization, according to not only Christian missionaries but also liberals who professed far more concern with the material conditions of life than with souls.

During the challenges to orthodoxy given in the twentieth century, secular liberals rose in influence and Christian missionaries declined. Both Collier in the United States and Cárdenas in Mexico promoted economic reforms for Indian communities, reforms that could include communal enterprises but that should bring the standard and mode of living closer to the national—that is, Euro-American—norms. Collier believed that by structuring Indian communities to conform to the United States democratic model, he allowed Indian self-determination. Apparently he could not realize that the imposition of a European-derived structure and European-derived goals negated his laudable aim. Cárdenas permitted greater latitude to Indian communities, yet did not posit real autonomy as a goal, only what seemed a just share in national benefits. In Canada, frontier conditions in the northern sectors of the country and official sponsorship of church involvement in Indian programs prolonged nineteenth-century attitudes and policies.

The 1960s brought the radical shift in American Indian affairs. Independence movements in Africa and Asia, including the long war in Vietnam first against the French colonial status and then against United States efforts to maintain de facto colonial power, heightened the consciousness of colonization in America. This consciousness was focused by the violent protests staged by several United

States black communities, particularly the Watts ghetto in Los Angeles, in the mid 1960s. Desegregation efforts, slowly building since the 1954 landmark court decision on the unconstitutionality of "separate but equal" public facilities, and civil-rights demands supported by 1964 Congressional affirmation in the Civil Rights Act met frustration through blacks' lack of economic as well as political power. Analyzing these frustrations, Black Power leaders discovered insights in the writings and speeches of Frantz Fanon, a Caribbean black who had been educated in France as a psychiatrist and then devoted himself to the cause of Algerian independence. Fanon, drawing upon Marxist formulations, described the impoverished masses of the European colonies as alienated both physically and psychologically from the decision makers in their societies. Workers and their families were treated as objects in the production process rather than as human beings, and their needs were ignored in favor of increasing the profits of capitalist entrepreneurs. The parallels between conditions described by Fanon and those felt by American blacks in ghettos persuaded these United States leaders that their people suffered from the same type of exploitation as natives in foreign colonies.

The concept of internal colonies was being articulated in this same decade by a Mexican sociologist, Pablo González Casanova. González Casanova demonstrated that although gross national product, income, and other standard indices seemed to show that Mexico was improving its economy, what in fact had been happening for several decades was a widening of the differences between the upper classes, including skilled urban workers, and the lower classes. Construction of new schools and hospitals failed to keep up with population increase, and new industries were based more on technology than on labor, so although some Mexicans from the lower classes obtained education and higher social position, there was a raw growth in the number of the poor. Like Fanon, González Casanova found elements of Marx's classic analyses applicable to the situation in Mexico, and emphasized that exploitation of the lower classes through national policies geared to attracting investment by foreign and elite cosmopolitan Mexican capitalists rendered the Mexican poor, in effect, a colony of the international investors.

In the 1960s, United States Indian leaders refrained from involvement in black protest and civil-rights movements, but were aware of the rhetoric sustaining them. The concept of internal colonies was particularly attractive because it fit well with the traditional Anglo-American political stance of treating American Indian groups as once-sovereign, though defeated, nations. These American Indian communities could claim the same right to self-determination that propelled Algerians and Vietnamese. The recognition that American Indian cultures not only were of intrinsic value, as cultural relativists had been asserting for decades, but should be the base of political autonomy was revolutionary. John Collier tried to preserve aspects of Indian cultural patterns, but it never occurred to him that Indian communities might be freed from the domination of the United States. In an ideological climate still overshadowed by the Social Darwinism that upheld imperialism, Collier—once a crusading urban social worker—sounded only a new variant in the Jeffersonian policy that Indians must be paternalistically guided toward adopting the basic Euro-American cultural pattern. In contrast, the radical position articulated by many Indian leaders in both the United States and Canada in the 1970s, repudiated any necessity of falling into the dominant nations' patterns. Like former colonies in Africa and Asia, American Indians had their own cultural traditions, and should be able to follow them.

Minority protest movements built upon anti-imperialist ideology occurred on all continents during the 1960s and led to the conceptualization of the "Fourth World" of internal colonies, from Australian Aborigines, Scandinavian Sami (Lapps), and American Indians to Bretons in France and Scots in Britain. Under this framework, representatives of several North American Indian nations, as they termed themselves, spoke before the Non-Governmental Organizations of the United Nations in Geneva in 1977, arguing that the United Nations Decolonization Committee should investigate the status of the native American nations under the existing national governments of the Americas. Solidarity with other nonsovereign native nations has also been demonstrated by the attendance of South American Indians and Sami at North American meetings such as the International Indian Treaty Conferences and the 1982 World Assembly of First Nations. Europeans who have become aroused over the poverty and persecutions of colonized peoples have formed organizations, such as the Denmark-based International Working Group for Indigenous Affairs, to raise money and pressure on behalf of these peoples, and to serve as some of the communication links between American Indians and other Fourth World nations. American Indians' refusal to ally with American blacks is founded upon the premise that the rights of American blacks are based upon the rights granted to citizens of the United States, whereas the rights of American Indians are fundamentally those of citizens of Indian nations, over whom the United States should have no sovereignty.

Ironically, while world opinion was responding to colonies' battles for independence, during the 1950s the Republican Eisenhower administration attempted to fulfill the Jeffersonian policy toward American Indians by terminating a century and a half of paternal protectionism. Directed toward individual Indians, the 1952 Voluntary Relocation Program was designed to move Indians off reservations and into cities as private citizens; directed at the tribes, House Concurrent Resolution 108 enabled the United States to end unilaterally the special status of Indian tribal reservations, and Public Law 280 gave states, rather than the federal government, jurisdiction over Indian reservations. Both bills passed Congress in 1953, and it was under them that the Klamath, the Menominee, and several other tribal reservations lost their treaty

rights and privileges. Discussion on these bills and the relocation program was couched in terms of benevolence and claims that Indians would be freed of wardship and placed so as to enjoy the full benefits of citizenship and participation in United States society. In line with Euro-American tradition, few questioned whether the Indians wanted to live as Euro-Americans in the midst of Euro-American cities. Nor did many discussants acknowledge the racial discrimination that has been a serious obstacle to even the minority of Indian persons who managed, in spite of difficulties fostered by Bureau of Indian Affairs practices, to obtain competitive competence in a trade or profession. Relocation was not a new idea: the "outing system" of the BIA boarding schools such as Carlisle placed Indian students with Euro-American families during holidays and vacations—instead of returning them to their families—in order to wean them from a preference for the reservation to one for Euro-American cities or towns. The 1928 Meriam Report had recommended urban relocation to facilitate assimilation, although the unemployment crisis in the cities during the Depression had hindered development of a relocation program. What the Eisenhower administration did was pick up this half-century-old idea and link it with an avowed policy of complete assimilation.

The Trudeau administration in Canada tried the same tactics a decade later, culminating in its 1969 White Paper on Indians. In both countries, urban relocation failed for at least one-third of the Indians in the programs (in Canada, a policy of encouragement was promulgated in place of a formal program). A large number of Indians were insufficiently trained to obtain permanent jobs in cities, lacking even basic fluency in English although resident for six or more years in BIA schools; others found urban living conditions unpleasant and detrimental to their children. Reservations may have rural slums, but at least the air is cleaner than in urban slums. In both countries, the backlash of anger over such blatant disregard of treaty promises consolidated Indian oppostion to government.

As the twentieth century began its last quarter, North American Indians saw themselves at the end of the road to assimilation into the dominant Euro-American cultural pattern. They had discovered, in thousands and thousands of instances, that racial discrimination blocked assimilation. Ideologies popular among intellectuals throughout the world promoted cultural relativism. These factors, one negative and one positive, made it respectable to assert one's Indian heritage and seek to work out a way of life that deviated from the dominant society's basic pattern. Politics now swung away from Jeffersonian policy. In the early 1970s, Presidents Nixon and Ford signed statements and bills recognizing the propriety of Indian self-determination without a penalty of withdrawal of governmental support. All three North American nations—Mexico, United States, and Canada—channeled some federal funds to Indian organizations whose platforms included planks on self-determination. The most lavish outpouring of monies came from Canada, which feared AIM intrusion after the debacle of the 1969 White Paper advocating termination of Indian status. Strengthening Canadian Indian organizations seemed a method of defusing resentment and building resistance to United States Indian interference. The National Indian Brotherhood became the officially recognized lobby for Indian interests on the federal level, and provincial Indian organizations such as the Federation of Saskatchewan Indians were built up to become the liaison between the federal government and its Indian wards. The policy was successful in that AIM did not become transnational, and Canadian Indians continued to attempt to work with rather than against the government, albeit to achieve goals of autonomy that the government would not wish to promote. Mexican Indians have been less vocal and less well organized than their Anglo-American neighbors, in part because the policy of *indigenismo* promises assimilation without total loss of Indian heritage, and in part because illiteracy and poverty are even more oppressive among Mexican than among Anglo-American Indians. As

González Casanova pointed out, methods of formal education reinforce authoritarian conservatism in poor communities, and ignorance and lack of control over political structures result in apparent apathy toward constitutional rights.

Among Anglo-American Indians, veterans of the two World Wars, the Korean War, and the Vietnam War spearheaded effective protests: their period of true assimilation in the armed forces, where there has been little discrimination against Indians in this century, taught them their rights and how to demand them. Mexico has used military service as one means of educating Indian youth, but without the crisis situation of wars, prejudice can be carried over from civilian life into the military and impede integration programs. Thus, with a great deal of public affirmation of the value and persistence of Mexico's Indian heritage, and with Indian problems seen as matters of social class rather than ethnic affiliation, Mexico's Indians have not demanded sovereignty to the degree that Indians in the United States and Canada have.

Conditions of Indians in all three nations make them among the most impoverished of all peoples. State-supported medical intervention has reduced death rates while birth rates remain high, producing rapid population growth since the 1940s and straining all measures to alleviate poverty. One very unfortunate development was a sharp rise in sterilizations, especially of Indian women, in an attempt to curb the birth rate. It has appeared easier, to government-financed medical personnel, to sterilize poorly educated women rather than providing them with contraceptive devices and an understanding of their use. Indian leaders have charged that their federal governments have been pursuing a covert policy of genocide through these sterilizations. Whether or not there is any truth to the claims, the frequency with which Indian women have been coerced into sterilization by hints that the welfare payments which support their children will depend upon their cooperation in this matter, or are sterilized without their informed consent, is another example of the cruelty of paternalism. The paradox of paternalism is that although per-capita expenditures for Indians by the United States government are higher than for any other racial category, and although some twenty thousand federal employees work in agencies set up to serve the half-million Indians on reservations, with approximately $5,000 per family allocated in assistance around 1970, the average income per Indian family at that time was only $3,000–$2,000 *less* than the amount allocated! A 1987 Arizona newspaper investigation quoted BIA officials' estimate that 90 percent of the funds allocated for Indians are used to support the agency bureaucracy, in which Indian individuals have constituted less than one-sixth the staff, and only ten cents of every dollar gets to its Indian targets.

Approximately half of all United States Indians, and more than half of all Canadian Indians, had incomes officially below the poverty level in the 1980 census. (In 1970, it was nearly three-quarters of United States Indians. Note that official designation of "poverty level" may change, instantly shifting families above or below it.) About one-third of all United States and Canadian Indians counted in the labor force are unemployed, and of the remainder, half are considered underemployed; there are also substantial numbers of reservation Indians who don't get counted in these statistics because they never signed up for job searches or training programs. The slippery nature of such statistics can be seen in the difference between 1970 and 1980 on the Montana Blackfeet Reservation: in 1970, 41 percent of adult tribal members were counted "in the labor force," and 27.5 percent of these were unemployed; ten years later, 72 percent were in the labor force and unemployment rose proportionately to 37 percent! In 1970, three-quarters of United States Indians and 87 percent of Canadian Indians lived in housing officially designated substandard, usually one- or two-room cabins, shacks, or cheap frame houses that are each inhabited by about a dozen people, lack plumbing, and are heated by dangerous wood-burning stoves or space heaters. Concerted efforts to improve Indian housing during the 1970s, fueled by funds channeled to reservations to weaken the attraction of AIM and other rebels, resulted in a high number of new houses but failed to change the statistic that Indian housing averages greater crowding than that of any other American racial category. In 1970, the Indian infant mortality rate was 49 per 1,000 live births in Canada (versus 21 per 1,000 for all Canadians), and 30 per 1,000 in the United States (versus 22 for all in the United States). Tuberculosis death rates were more than five times the national averages. Life expectancy was 63 for United States Indians, a shocking 36 for Canadian Indians. The suicide rate was about twice that of non-Indians. From half to two-thirds of United States Indian youth, depending on the region, dropped out before completing high school, and the median number of years of education for Indian adults in their early twenties was 9. In Canada, only 6 percent of Indians completed high school, versus 88 percent of all Canadians. There wasn't much incentive to complete high school, considering that the median annual earnings for Indians with a grade-12 education was only a few hundred dollars more than for those who dropped out earlier, in contrast with a considerably greater differential between Euro-American high-school graduates and dropouts. All these figures have shown fairly consistent improvement over the second half of the twentieth century, and a more marked rate of improvement since the 1970s; although the result is a lessening of the considerable gap between "white" and "Indian" figures, it is nothing like parity. One study pointed out that the greatest improvement in Indian health statistics occurred in the decade after responsibility for Indian health care was transferred from the Bureau of Indian Affairs to the U.S. Department of Health, Education, and Welfare.

Figures for Mexico show much greater poverty, which is shared by many who are not officially counted as Indians. For example, there are more than twice as many illiterates as persons listed as Indians—that is, persons who speak an Indian language. Perhaps a hint of the standard of living for the Mexican poor comes from 1960 census data that showed that one-third of all Mexicans were illiterate, one-third also did not wear shoes, and, again, one-third did not eat white bread. These illiterate, sandal-wearing or barefoot, tortilla-eating Mexicans may not all have regularly spoken Indian languages, but they were the "internal colony" descended from Mexico's native Indian peoples. Conditions for the Mexican poor improved in the last third of the twentieth century, although as in Anglo-America, never approaching the average of European-descended segments of the population. Hoping to raise their standard of living, many hundreds of thousands of Mexican workers, both Indian and mestizo, cross the border to find employment in the United States, legally or illegally. Some settle in the United States; large numbers of others voluntarily return periodically to families in Mexico. Among the settlers, intermarriage with United States Indian fellow laborers or neighbors is not uncommon.

The gross discrepancies in income, health, and education between the dominant Euro-Americans and American Indians clearly indict the policies of the three national governments: whether the intent was benevolent or exploitative, the effect has been pejorative. A radical shift in strategies is amply justified. Movements have taken two correlated lines of attack: one, to raise the image of the Indian so that self-determination appears appropriate; and two, to raise the basic standard of living and quality of life. Both these goals take money, and the money, Indians assert, is owed them by the Euro-American governments in compensation for their loss of nine-tenths of a continent.

The effort to raise the image of the Indian was directed more toward the Indians than toward the Euro-Americans who have been the source of denigration. There have been protests against caricatures of American Indians in cartoons, as mascots of athletic teams, in films, and in advertising, and against textbook promulgation of the view of the Indian as primitive and savage, but these protests are sporadic. What will really change Euro-

Americans' opinion of Indians, it is felt, will be public perception of Indians wielding political power. Hence, AIM's strategies emphasized dramatic confrontations in which Indians successfully resisted or manipulated Euro-American officials: the 1973 Wounded Knee siege, the 1972 trashing of the Bureau of Indian Affairs headquarters, the 1978 Longest Walk across the United States to stage a demonstration on the Mall in Washington. These "media events" projected a public image of strong young Indian men fighting for human rights, a scenario calculated to end television viewers' notions that the Indians disappeared with the settlement of the western frontier.

Exciting though it was to stage media events, AIM also worked with less public Indian organizations toward the more basic goal of uplifting Indians' self-image and thereby developing confidence and perseverance toward winning true self-determination. Foremost among these efforts has been the drive to control children's education. In place of schools controlled and staffed exclusively by Euro-Americans, often Euro-Americans who have been impelled by a missionary spirit, Indian leaders are insisting on schools with Indian teachers and administrators and school boards weighted with Indian parents. Public universities in western states and provinces, such as South Dakota and Saskatchewan, cooperate with Indian organizations in special teacher-training institutes to help Indian young people successfully complete teacher-certification courses, and in developing elementary- and secondary-school curricula in Indian languages and in English but with content and illustrations more familiar to most Indian youngsters than Dick and Jane in their suburban Euro-American home. Indian-led community colleges on reservations are another growing source of curricula and teachers that bridge over the differences between residents' heritages and the dominant society. Time is set aside in Indian-dominated schools for instruction in the local native language, folklore, dancing, and crafts by adults in the community respected for their skills in these areas, and in some northern Canadian Indian schools efforts are being made to schedule instruction in hunting and trapping in the bush during the school term. Where during the early 1960s, an Indian child was seen by teachers as "culturally deprived" because he or she had, for example, never used a flush toilet, today there is promotion of the Indian child's advantages in having the opportunity to become familiar with two cultural traditions. Indian children are being taught that there are abiding truths in their parental heritage as well as material benefits in mastering Euro-American literacy and political skills.

There is a tendency, especially among urban Indians, to teach children to find spiritual guidance and values in the Indian tradition and to contrast this with the gaining of pragmatic skills from the Euro-American content of their curriculum. This presentation of a carefully articulated cosmology and values set is said to be an answer to the more subtly indoctrinated Euro-American cosmology and values found in the Euro-American public schools, and to be necessary to the nurturing of dignified, responsible young Indian men and women. Not all Indian parents believe it desirable to shun the Euro-American schools: those who have stable skilled-trade or professional employment and homes in law-abiding neighborhoods frequently prefer their children to learn to live within the dominant society as their families do, maintaining native religious beliefs and values by activities in the homes and visits to the reservation where relatives live.

"Survival Schools" run by Indian activists in several large cities are aimed at youth from unstable homes in neighborhoods with high rates of delinquency, youth at great risk of arrest. Survival Schools draw upon the approaches developed during the 1960s and early 1970s "counterculture" movement for alternative schools opened by dissidents who believed the standard public schools stifled creativity and at the same time stimulated rebellion or apathy, but not a full and constructive

life. Like alternative schools for Euro-American and black youth, the Indian Survival Schools serve only a small proportion of the community's children, but are a source of ideas that are borrowed, modified, and incorporated in programs in those of the more standard schools that earnestly seek to respect and encourage students. Indian community schools and urban public "specialty" schools focusing on Indian culture serve children whose parents (some of them non-Indian) want a high awareness of Indian history and values in their children's daily lives. These schools may be, in effect, a reservation school for families living off the reservation in cities.

Priming the next generation for a life with less conflict and more material comfort than their parents obtained requires not only schools stressing the worth of an Indian heritage and the shrewdness of becoming capable of beating The Man at his own game, but also the building of real economic opportunities for Indians. All three national governments in North America have long histories of programs aimed toward the economic development of reservations or Indian communities, and poor records of success. One obvious cause of failure lies in the siphoning off of allotted funds to maintain the bureaucracies that administer the programs. Aside from this hidden bleeding of funds, a frequently cited cause of failure is the imposition of a program designed outside the community and decreed without opportunity for input by the supposed beneficiaries. Federal housing programs on many reservations have been resented because, in the first place, the houses are planned on the basis of Euro-American values—geometric lots, houses very close, no place for animals—while the people strongly prefer their traditional housing patterns: houses scattered over the land just within hailing distance (as on the Plains) or (in other regions) houses designed for small clusters of related families. A second source of resentment in many housing programs has been the letting out of construction to non-Indian contractors and labor, or relegation of

FIGURE 10.2 Homes in a reservation town, 1972. *(A. Kehoe)*

local Indian workers to unskilled jobs without opportunity for training in better-paying work. Complaints from Indians to the governments went unheeded, or were answered by citations of regulations that seemed to deny the possibility of modification to better serve the recipients' wishes.

Sovereignty for the First Nations

Affirmation of the worth of Indian values in recent years has led to insistence by many Indian leaders on community planning free of bureaucratic domination. These leaders want government money which they see as compensation for their

FIGURE 10.3 New homes built by the Blackfeet Tribe in the reservation town, 1972. Federal government monies were used for this project. *(A. Kehoe)*

forfeited lands, but not the government. They quite reasonably point to the egregious failure of nearly all government programs over the past two centuries and ask whether it is not time to try another tack. The demand for sovereignty voiced by the northern Canadian nations, the Iroquois activists, a number of Lakota Sioux, and the Assembly of First Nations of Canada—once the National Indian Brotherhood—rests in part on a conviction that only formal exclusion of the national governments' bureaucracies from the Indian homelands will allow real native control over funds and economic programs. Home Rule has been accepted as a viable structure for Kalaallit Nunaat (Greenland) by Denmark as well as by the Greenlandic Inuit, so it cannot be summarily rejected for other native nations. We can point out that Denmark itself is a small nation, that Norway and Sweden are independent nations that in the past were under Danish rule, and, in short, that there is ample precedent for sections of large nations to be constituted independent. Europe demonstrates that size, economic self-sufficiency, or military strength aren't necessary for nationhood (Luxembourg, Lichtenstein, San Marino, Iceland, Belgium, Ireland, Finland are examples).

The basis for a restoration of sovereignty to American Indian nations rests on British policy during the colonization era. In the sixteenth century, Elizabeth I's secretary of state, Sir Thomas Smith, first analyzed England's own political structure, then proposed the subjugation of "wicked, barbarous and uncivil people"—the Irish—and appropriation of "waste" land in their country. Smith assured his queen that taking over Ireland would render it both "pleasant and profitable" for the English, whom he noted were suffering from overpopulation. The model for Smith's ideas was the contemporary Spanish conquest of Latin America. A few years later, another member of Elizabeth's court recommended colonization of America in order to exploit its raw materials as well as to draw off surplus, unemployed English people. In 1608, Britain's manner of colonization was set

when an emissary of the king landed at Jamestown and, after negotiations, traveled up-river to Powhatan's capital to present the Indian ruler with symbols of lordship including a crown, scepter, and scarlet robe. The Englishman claimed that Powhatan's acceptance of these proffered symbols, though reluctant, signified his agreement to function as a subordinate to England's king, sharing his territory and its resources with the English. That Powhatan did not meekly accept the symbols of subordinate lordship, but actually *exchanged* symbols by insisting that the king's emissary take a robe and moccasins from Powhatan, was recorded without comment. As far as legal precedent goes, this first treaty between Britain and an American Indian nation acknowledged the sovereignty of the Indian ruler and the propriety of negotiating with him for territorial and exploitative rights. This was reinforced in 1620 when the governor of Jamestown stipulated that colonists settling beyond Jamestown's clearings must obtain consent from the Indian ruler, now Opechancanough. Jamestown's owners, the Virginia Company, were much agitated by the governor's concession of Opechancanough's sovereignty. They ordered the governor to henceforth respect the colony proprietors' power and in 1622 publicly reverted to the medieval concept that no "infidel" could lawfully rule: only Christians had God's mandate. Britain should overthrow the unlawful heathen sovereign as the European Crusaders had sought to overthrow the Muslims in the Holy Land. Thus, Anglo-American colonization policy, unlike that of Spain, interposed a stage of treaty-making between sovereigns before conquest.

From the British point of view, Indian sovereignty was conditional, existing only so long as no Christian nation overthrew it. (Strictly speaking, only *Protestant* Christian nations could exercise valid sovereignty, since the Catholic Irish were as ripe for conquest as any Indians.) Essentially, the early seventeenth century conception of native title was a feudal type, of a nation's land vested in its king who gave fiefs to loyal vassals. Vassals could exercise limited sovereignty on sufferance of their lord. If and when a British king's subjects overthrew the ruler of an opposing nation, that nation lost its sovereignty. By the 1770s, feudal political ideas had been eclipsed by the modern emphasis on rational universal principles, and in Britain's American colonies the prerogatives of the distant imperial government were criticized as obsolete and unjust. A 1757 ruling by Lord Camden and Solicitor General Yorke recognizing the legality of British purchases of land in India directly from "the Mogul or any of the Indian Princes" was interpreted, in America, to apply to purchases by British citizens directly from American "Indian Princes." The Crown, they held, had no superior right to such land after conquest. Revolutionary fervor backhandedly recognized Indians to possess true sovereignty. We can note that in 1776, events proved that thirteen colonies could form a confederacy preserving considerable autonomy for each of the thirteen while delegating foreign relations, currency issue, and certain other powers to the confederation as a whole, much as Home Rule in Kalaallit Nunaat today. Clear as "natural law" appeared to rebelling colonists in 1776, by the creation of the Constitution in 1787, the older notion of a conquering government's unilateral power was restored in respect to Indian rights—in plain language, Indians had no natural rights against a Christian conqueror. This was confirmed in 1823 by Chief Justice John Marshall in *Johnson v. M'Intosh*. Here, and reiterated in his 1831 *Cherokee Nation v. Georgia* and 1832 *Worcester v. Georgia*, Justice Marshall declared Indian nations to be no more than "dependent" nations, admittedly a relationship "perhaps unlike that of any other two people in existence." *Cherokee Nation v. Georgia* became pivotal: the United States was creating a new kind of relationship, neither feudal nor that upheld between modern European states.

Limited sovereignty seems, on the face of it, to be no sovereignty. The dictionary says sovereignty means to be supreme. United States Indians have generally compromised with the concept of sovereignty, accepting the pragmatic fact that the United States government is not about to relinquish its sovereignty to small economically dependent nations. Canada's Indians have been bolder. Seizing the moment when the patriation of the British North American Act (that is, Britain's formal recognition of Canada's sovereignty under its own constitution) necessitated explicit agreements between the federal and provincial governments about their relationship, the National Indian Brotherhood under Chief Noel Starblanket, a Saskatchewan Cree, demanded inclusion in the consultations between the first ministers of the provinces and the federal government. In preparation, the NIB had held a First Nations Constitutional Conference in April of 1980, drawing upon a platform and supporting arguments for Indian government originating since 1977 in the Federation of Saskatchewan Indians. That organization was the reincarnation of provincial Indian alliances paralleling, since the 1920s, Saskatchewan's unique agrarian socialist party, the CCF. Once the CCF came to power in 1944, it directly encouraged the province's Indians to form an association to identify problems and promulgate solutions. When the looser Union of Saskatchewan Indians reorganized in 1969 as the Federation to respond to the Trudeau government's notorious White Paper on Indians, it drew upon decades of political experience. Its sister group, the Indian Association of Alberta, was soon targeted for subversion after its leader, Harold Cardinal, articulated the NIB's adamant opposition to the proposed major shift in national policy. Saskatchewan's group of vigorous Indian politicians, a second generation in the province, then led the NIB to press on, publicizing through television appearances the government's perfidy on treaty rights. With AIM poised at the U.S. border, Trudeau quickly excused his White Paper as no more than a test of opinion, and the Department of Indian Affairs poured money into the reserves and Indian organizations as proof of good faith.

For Canada's Indians, the 1970s were an exhilarating decade of unprecedented funds and public support. On the crest of that support, the James Bay Agreement was forged, the Dene and Nishnawbe-Aski (Anishnabai) Declarations issued. Starblanket's insistence on Indian participation in the patriation of the constitution as "the 11th province" rode this tide. At first, the national government ignored the Chief's demand that the treaty Indian nations exercise sovereignty on a par with that exercised by the provinces. At the time in November 1981 that the government expected the provincial premiers to agree to the hammered-out constitution, a year of bitter Indian opposition to political exclusion had heightened these first ministers' distrust of Ottawa. Final institution of the Constitution Act in 1982 papered over the disagreements, only to have them surface in 1990 when a new version of federalism worked out in a conference at Meech Lake was to be approved. Mulroney, the Prime Minister, assiduously solicited Québec's agreement and sought to mollify the premiers of the Maritime and prairie provinces, only to have his house of cards collapse when one elected member of the Manitoba Legislature unexpectedly filibustered to prevent Manitoba ratification of the Meech Lake Accord before the announced deadline. He was a Cree Indian, Elijah Harper; single-handed, he reminded Canada that its First Nations, no less than Québec, had never been satisfied with the vague wording of the 1982 Constitution. Once Harper's strategy to prevent premature agreement was noticed, lawyers rallied to advise him on technical details. The former chief of the Red Sucker Lake band catalyzed the recalcitrant provinces to reject the Accord.

Up to the 1980s, Canada's colonization and subsequent Indian policies seemed to follow, and generally lag behind, precedents set in the United States. Canada continued to negotiate treaties, it extended the franchise to Indians a generation later than the United States did, it maintained Christian missionary operation of Indian schools, and its relocation and termination policy developed a decade after the United States' similar policy. When in the 1930s John Collier was reforming U.S. Indian Affairs, asserting the rights of Indians to preserve their religions and homelands, Canada's Department of Indian Affairs was threatening Indian leaders with jail if they left their reserves without their agents' permission. In the 1980s, the situation reversed. Canada's First Nations took the leadership in organizing the World Council of Indigenous Peoples, conceived in 1975 by George Manuel, a Shuswap who was then President of the National Indian Brotherhood. Realizing an internationally oriented strategy is the best means small numbers of people have to influence massive governments, Manuel developed the concept of "Fourth World" nations and worked to set these nations' issues on the agenda of the United Nations. By 1982, the U. N.'s Subcommission on the Prevention of Discrimination and the Protection of Minorities had a working group on indigenous peoples. The Assembly of First Nations of Canada carefully structures its membership and operations to meet ideals of representative democracy, with the 573 status-Indian band chiefs meeting annually to determine policy and direct the executive arm of the organization. In this way it constitutes a clear parallel to provincial governments and strengthens its demand that it and its member bands exercise similar jurisdiction. Canada in the 1990s must deal with two related models of Indian government, Home Rule in the Kalaallit Nunaat model for the broad territories of Denedeh and Nunavut, and a modified version for the scattered small reserves in which they would exercise all powers not expressly delegated to their representative Assembly or the federal government. The central tenet is that sovereignty resides in the bands, and it is they who may delegate it.

United States Indians have been less bold in insisting on sovereignty. Following United States practice, they look to the federal courts for relief, although logic would seem to indicate that to do so is surrendering sovereignty to the government behind the courts. While United States Indians have not neglected the international strategy utilized by

Canadian Indians, the principal users have been the Mohawk who straddle the St. Lawrence River boundary and thus are intimately familiar with their Canadian relatives' politics. United States Indians have obtained important success in recent years in the courts, notably in the Boldt decision of 1974 and the Voigt decision of 1983: Judge Boldt, in the state of Washington, affirmed the continuing validity of nineteenth-century treaty provisions for Indian fishing rights distinct from state regulation of its citizens, and Voigt issued a similar finding on the validity of 1836 and 1847 treaties accepting Chippewa rights to continue their hunting, fishing, and gathering activities in the territories they ceded to the United States for Euro-American settlement. Both decisions recognize the prior existence of Indian sovereignty and that treaties obtained specific cessions, not total oblivion of Indian rights. Unfortunately, both decisions occasioned immediate and continuing protests from Euro-Americans who cried "It isn't fair!" that Indians should have "privileges" denied other Americans. Unwilling to acknowledge the treaties as enduring agreements, the protesters mobbed boat landings, drinking Treaty Beer sold to raise money to finance an antitreaty campaign and taunting Indian fishermen.

Economic Strategies

An increasing number of Indian leaders and non-Indian critics familiar with Indian communities feel that a core plank in new programs for economic improvement must be enhancement of existing Indian patterns of work rather than dictatorial insistence on Euro-American structures. Indians had viable economies before Euro-American invasions, and their habits of more flexible work patterns may be just as productive as the tediously repetitive systems of Euro-American industrialism. (A number of Euro-Americans also question the sanctity of industrial work patterns, advocating more humane labor conditions.) A critical issue, though one not usually clearly articulated, is the

difference between economic betterment and economic development. Development connotes the infliction of alien patterns of exploitation upon the land or community, the extension or intensification of Euro-American practices to realize goals within the traditional Euro-American value system. Reinforcement of subsistence economies rather than routine application of "development" models is increasingly seen as a feasible option for many Indian communities. Offering that option along with access to critical medical care and educational opportunities gives families more choice in how they combine a valued heritage with a decently comfortable living.

An example of the difference between Euro-American and Indian planning can be seen in the case of the Lummi of coastal western Washington. In 1967, it appeared that the best chance for Lummi to improve their economic position would be to allow the construction of a magnesium oxide reduction plant on their reservation. The plant would have destroyed the tidal bay that was one of the beauties of the region and a traditional source of food, but it was promised that it would provide jobs. Fortunately, a biologist teaching at a nearby college did an ecological survey of the region and met Lummi who mentioned their dismay at the cost of the new jobs to their heritage. The biologist had been studying methods used by traditional Hawaiians to cultivate seafoods along their coasts, and suggested that the Lummi might use similar methods to cash-crop the tidal bay, preserving its beauty and traditional uses while adding jobs that would be much pleasanter and healthier than working in an industrial plant. Vine Deloria, Jr., the well-known Sioux writer and speaker on Indian concerns, suggested that other reservation communities should follow the Lummi example in developing local resources innovatively, aiming for employment rather than corporate profits. Aquaculture is an attractive answer because fish-farming is a relatively labor-intensive production requiring comparatively small enclosures, considerations that encouraged not only other Puget

Sound nations but also, for example, the Akwe-sasne Mohawks to explore such an enterprise. Co-lumbia River Indian nations are building a salmon-management program based on the re-gion's natural salmon life-cycle, planting juvenile hatchery-bred fish where spawning salmon popu-lations need to be reinforced and demanding fish ladders and flow control in the system's dams. The Columbia River Inter-Tribal Commission reminds us that the fishing station at Celilo Falls at The Dalles, traditionally seen as a gift from the Al-mighty to Indians who respect it, may be underwa-ter but is still there and still holy—affirmed by the Wanapam spiritual leader David Sohappy, descen-dant of the early nineteenth-century leader Souiepapie (So-Ha-Pe) and of later advocates of Smohalla's "Dreamer" religion. David Sohappy, jailed with his son in the early 1980s for selling fish out of season, fought for decades to remain at an off-reservation traditional fishing station on the river, living off its salmon as his forebears did.

The Lummis' future seemed to brighten further when Judge Boldt found the Puget Sound tribes entitled by their treaty to fishing rights independent of State of Washington regulations. A few years later, the Lummi were back in the news, now battling the IRS. In 1982, the Internal Revenue Service demanded Lummi fishermen pay federal income tax on what they earn from gillnetting salmon. The Lummi insisted their 1855 treaty means reservation Indians obtaining a living from local resources are exempt from federal taxes, while the IRS said this would be so only if the treaty specified income from selling fish would be ex-empt. That in 1855 there was no federal income tax should not affect the case, according to IRS. The Bureau of Indian Affairs disagreed, citing the gen-eral pattern of exemption of treaty lands, resources, and resident tribal members from taxes enacted by nonreservation governments. Other tribes guessed the IRS was using the thousand Lummi fishermen, most of whom, it admitted, probably would owe no tax once standard deductions were figured in their modest incomes, to test the likelihood it might

succeed in taxing the greater incomes foreseen by the Council of Energy Resource Tribes (CERT). If expected royalties and profits from CERT projects are taxed like ordinary corporation profits, the potential for significantly improving the general standard of living on western reservations would be substantially compromised. Eastern Indian na-tions were more directly affected by the IRS in a 1989 Tax Court decision claiming Senecas em-ployed off the reservation incurred federal income tax liability. The Grand Council of the Haudeno-saunee rejoined that its 1794 Treaty of Canan-daigua did not specify cession of any right to tax its citizens, therefore the United States does not have this right, regardless of where Six Nations citizens may be employed; the Haudenosaunee point out that it is because such a large extent of its nations' territories were taken over by the United States that too little is left to support all Six Nations citizens except as they find employment in the ceded portions of their country.

An increasing number of Indians, in company with many descendants of historic immigrants, have been questioning, since the mid-1950s, whether development is likely to equate with bet-terment. Some, such as the Cree Chief Robert Smallboy, who in 1968 led a number of families from the Hobbema reserve to camp and hunt year-round in the bush of north-central Alberta, have repudiated the Euro-American way of life as effete and contrary to humans' true nature, which they hold to properly be closely integrated with the rest of the natural world. From such a perspective, betterment lies in reviving Indian techniques of subsistence from hunting, fishing, and harvesting of plants, in teaching young people to find satisfac-tion in these activities, in the camaraderie of the extended family and small community and in a nonanalytical experiential kinship with an un-threatening wilderness. Other American Indians, such as the Mohawk and their friends who staff the newspaper *Akwesasne Notes*, choose a level of comfort closer to that considered minimal by most Euro-Americans, but eschew the accumulation of

FIGURE 10.4 Plains Cree rural reservation home, 1973. The "new" Government-built home is at left; in winter, the couple uses their old sod house, right background, because the frame house is difficult and expensive to heat. In this photo, the man is wringing out a deerskin that the woman is tanning. *(T. Kehoe)*

houses, cars, clothing, and appliances that appeals to the majority of their New York State neighbors. For these Indians, energies and income above what is needed to maintain a simple, though not aboriginal, life-style are channeled into political activities that may better all Indians. The Cree who live by subsistence hunting and fishing with the Income Security Programme incorporated in the James Bay and Northern Québec Agreement are not overtly political but quite aware that their success is a major test of the possibility that Fourth World nations may forge economies partially outside standard participation in the international capitalist system.

The basic theme of self-determination counters the common Euro-American subscription to the judgment of "experts" validated by academic credits, money, or governmental power. That many official experts are mentally locked into a particular tradition, a tradition that seems to despoil land and depress the creativity of persons in the lower social classes, has stimulated a number of American Indian leaders, along with their friends who campaign for ecological and human-rights causes, to reject what seem to be straightforward programs for development and instead insist on what may seem to be radical approaches. Pragmatic programs tuned to goals that from the Euro-American point of view are nontraditional are part of the larger picture of a vigorous assertion of the power of Indian belief systems. It was in 1973 that President Nixon signed the Indian Self-Determination Act allowing federally recognized tribes to contract to administer funds for programs up until then routinely administered by government agencies. Indians hailed the Act as a major turning point in United States policy, not only nullifying the termination and relocation goals adopted in 1953 but initiating an entirely new direction in United States Indian policy. Nixon's genuine concern for American Indians stemmed from his respect for his college football coach, Wallace "Chief" Newman, an

Indian. (Nixon believed that prejudice against Indians had robbed Newman of the big-league coaching position his abilities deserved.) With less ballyhoo, Canada's policy shifted to the same direction in the 1970s. "Self-determination" was held to be a basic human right by the United Nations' General Assembly in its 1960 Declaration on the Granting of Independence to Colonial Countries and Territories. The Declaration was not applied to Fourth World "internal colonies," although its wording would not preclude that. The term "self-determination" has been criticized as too much bound with European valuation of the individual "self," failing to reflect American Indian valuation of the community; in fact, the 1970s self-determination policies apply to communities and not to individuals, in spite of the somewhat misleading slogan.

Where the issue comes to a head is in the question of how independent Fourth World nations can be. Indigenous communities don't want to be "preserved" like wild orchids or blind cave fish. What land and resource bases would be sufficient to support growing populations even at a subsistence level? Medical services from the dominant society are necessary even if native medical knowledge is respected and used; how shall they be paid for? Some members of the Fourth World nation must obtain advanced professional education to deal with legal and business matters impinging on their nation. Economics can't be ignored—people gotta eat—and economics are part of politics.

To understand the present situation of American Indians, and to improve it, the isolation of American Indian history from world history must be overcome. American Indians have been systematically excluded from history texts and even from newsmagazines (*Time*'s founder and long-time publisher Henry Luce made it a policy not to print any articles about Indians). This exclusion prevented the majority of American citizens from learning their country's real history, allowed the imperialist myth of the "vanishing red man" to stand unchallenged, kept Indians out of economic policies, and let the Bureau of Indian Affairs become the least effective of all federal agencies. Looking at American Indians as an integral part of the international world for the last five hundred years, we see that they both produced and consumed goods and materials worth billions of dollars. The fur trade has been as major a factor in world history as the silk trade. Anthropologist John Moore has pointed out that Indians in the fur trade gave John Jacob Astor the fortune that made him the richest man in the United States when he died in 1848, the fortune that his great-grandson used to buy a British title and that man's daughter-in-law, Lady Nancy Astor, to become the first woman to sit in the British Parliament. (Yes, it also built New York's posh Waldorf-Astoria Hotel, named after the family.)

United States policies on Indians during the postfrontier century (1871–1970) have been analyzed by another anthropologist, Alice Littlefield, who found them correlated with the country's labor needs. After the Civil War, the government fostered Northern-style agriculture in which farm families worked their land and also participated in local manufacturing. To provide the base for this economy, the government forced Indians off the land at the frontier, by conquest and subsequently by the Dawes Allotment Act of 1887. Within a decade of that Act, the Indian land base was reduced by nearly two-thirds, compelling Indians into the rural labor market where they worked cheaply at peak labor demand times. The availability of such hired labor supported the "family" farm and allowed the Euro-American farmers' children to move into businesses. As European immigrants knew full well, in Europe they themselves were the reserve labor pool, the underemployed farm youth needed for seasonal labor demands. In America, immigrant homesteaders could hire Indians and blacks. The government built schools for Indians and blacks in which they were trained for manual labor and low-wage skills such as blacksmithing, carpentry, tailoring, and housekeeping; these schools did not teach a secondary-level curriculum that would qualify students for college. By the 1920s, farming had entered a recession that in the 1930s was exacerbated by the drought in the Plains states where significant numbers of Indians lived. The need for farm labor was further reduced by the steady increase in mechanization of farm work. John Collier's "Indian New Deal" of 1934 helped relieve the problem of excess rural labor by consolidating Indian land under tribal title, facilitating leasing by agribusinesses and mining and lumbering corporations. Indians' subsistence needs were met by federal programs, particularly the Indian Emergency Conservation Works (the equivalent of the Civilian Conservation Corps for non-Indians). Eighty-five thousand Indians, out of a total of some four hundred thousand federally recognized Indians, were employed in IECW pasture improvement, reforestation, and similar projects. Native crafts were encouraged at this time, to develop income outside the regional Euro-American economic structures. More community schools were opened, to keep Indians on the reservations rather than directly burdening the depressed national economy. World War II created a new demand for labor that continued over the generation it took for Europe and Japan to rebuild their economies. The Eisenhower administration's policy of termination and relocation of Indians to cities was designed to feed Indian labor to the industrial economy. The 1946 institution of the Indian Claims Commission to hear suits and award monetary compensation to quash Indian land claims was meant to be the final solution to "the Indian problem," settling once and for all how much Indians should have been paid for ceding the country and thereby getting on with assimilating this segment of the population into the labor force.

What the postwar policymakers did not anticipate was the level at which the Claims Commission drew Indians into national politics. With millions of dollars at stake, with fees that attracted big-time lawyers, Indians were no longer unseen parts of the dusty rural landscape. Tribal representatives went to Washington where, unlike their nineteenth-century forebears who had traveled there, they were treated not as a sideshow but instead rubbed shoulders with some of the country's most sophisticated movers and shakers. The administration in power intended to quit Indians' claims once and for all, pay money in just compensation and set Indians, and the United States, free of that anomalous wardship status. Indians back from serving in World War II in the armed forces or in factories had become accustomed to pursuing their needs like other Americans, looking out for a good deal. The United States said, "Let's deal." Indians allied with lawyers to figure out how to beat the old system. Many gross injustices of long standing would be addressed, but the Indians' goals were not so much to nullify old wrongs as to begin constructing economic foundations for their reservations.

Because the plaintiffs' aims were obtaining the wherewithal for economic bases, they usually insisted on money compensation without ceding land, for reservations need both land and capital. As the coalitions of lawyers, Indians, and "friends of the Indian" politically liberal organizations explored the historical data and precedent cases, they better understood the economic and political structures fettering the Indians. The National Congress of American Indians had been founded in 1944 to give stronger Indian direction to the changes initiated under Collier's Indian New Deal. In 1961, more radical younger Indians organized the National Indian Youth Council at a conference arranged through University of Chicago anthropologist Sol Tax. Ninety tribes were represented at the conference. Exactly one half-century earlier, in 1911, a small group of professionally educated Indians had formed the Society of American Indians. They included the medical doctors Charles Eastman (Dakota) and Carlos Montezuma (Yavapai), attorney Thomas Sloan (Omaha), Episcopalian minister Sherman Coolidge (Arapaho), anthropologist and museum director Arthur C. Parker (Seneca), and writer and musician Gertrude Bonnin, "Zitkala-sa" (Lakota). The Society had folded after a dozen years, unable to influence what Dr. Eastman bitterly termed the "Bureau Machine, which controls our property, our money, our children and our personal rights" (quoted in Iverson 1982:148). The Indian Claims Commission might be a means to circumvent the Bureau of Indian Affairs, to obtain capital under Indian control.

When the United States Indian Land Claims Commission completed its mission in 1974, the average length of time required for a case had been fifteen years. Two-thirds of the cases filed succeeded in obtaining settlements, but the long process drained much of the awards into legal expenses and fees. Meanwhile, President Lyndon Johnson's War on Poverty, in the late 1960s, was giving money to a number of programs on Indian reservations, from Head Start to prepare little children for school, to food and other welfare assistance. Though the War on Poverty was swallowed up in the outlay for the Vietnam War, it opened opportunities for working outside the Bureau Machine. Claims settlements could be invested in enterprises more or less independent of BIA controls. In Canada, although the 1970s outpour of funds to Indians came directly from the DIAND (Department of Indian Affairs and Northern Development), especially through the 1970 Indian Economic Development Fund, the Department was loosening its paternalistic hold as it sought to avoid radical confrontations.

The 1970s and 1980s saw hundreds of businesses created on Indian reservations. Many were tourist lodges, some quite luxurious. (If your land is remote from cities and about all it offers seems to be scenery, a tourist lodge is an obvious business.) Others were small industrial plants manufacturing items from fishing lures and pencils to prefabricated homes and electronic assemblies. Some tribal funds have been invested in shopping malls and the construction of houses and office buildings for the general market. On the opposite tack, "self-sufficiency" and craft cooperatives have been encouraged. The Mohawk in Cold Brook, New York, run the Native Self-Sufficiency

Center to produce and sell inexpensive complete log homes. In 1981, Wilma Mankiller (Principal Chief of the Cherokee Nation in 1990) and her husband Charlie Soap originated a community development department to balance the Cherokees' major enterprises such as the Nation's utilities company. Through small business loans and consultant advice, the Nation and the independent Gadugi Project assist local businesses valued by the Indian communities—for example, bakeries—and cooperatives capable of producing supplemental income where employment is scarce and wages low. Truly traditional crafts such as fine baskets, historically adapted crafts such as star quilts, and contemporary creations in native style can all be promoted by cooperatives and marketing undertaken by Indian nations. Farming can also be assisted, from developing drip irrigation on the Navajo reservation (for which an Israeli expert was brought in), through Cornell University agronomy consultants working with Haudenosaunee to select and distribute the best varieties of Iroquois crops, to the Five Sandoval Indian Pueblos' Blue Corn Project, which markets the pueblos' highly nutritious and suddenly ultra-fashionable blue maize. And, really cashing in on consumer demand (according to the *Wall Street Journal* in 1990), the largest supplier of potatoes for potato chips was the Navaho Agricultural Products Industry on the Navajo Reservation near Farmington, selling 30 million pounds to the Frito-Lay Company—not even their only customer!

Big money and Indians? After the extraordinary explosion of legal gambling on Indian lands in the 1980s, the average North American thinks of Indians as B-I-N-G-O. In the mid 1970s, Indian communities realized that because they are not under state jurisdictions, they should not be compelled to restrict gambling prizes to state restrictions. The Oneida Tribe of Wisconsin, with a small reservation on the edge of the city of Green Bay, changed a typical church-hall fundraising bingo game into a magnet for gambling addicts, offering games nearly every day, for hours each day, with more and larger prizes than the state of Wisconsin permitted in non-Indian jurisdictions. Busloads of players came from Milwaukee and Chicago. A new bingo hall was built, then enlarged to seat over a thousand players. A Radisson Hotel was constructed adjacent to the bingo hall. Several hundred Oneida found employment in the complex. The profits paid for day-care—the original goal of the developers—and a nursing home, then capital to develop convenience stores and an industrial park. The success story has been repeated in over a hundred Indian tribes. Tribes have pooled to offer mega-bucks pots via satellite hookup to patrons of Indian gaming. The publishers of the newspaper *News from Indian Country* spun off the monthly *Bingo and Casino Gaming Magazine*, promising on its cover "Fun & Entertainment ...Somewhere Near You." As feared, the Mafia moved in on some tribal gaming, according to testimony as early as 1989 by an FBI informant. Hoping to manage such threats, the United States Congress in 1988 had passed the Indian Gaming Regulatory Act, calling for agreements between tribes and the states in which their reservations lie; the Department of the Interior oversees the Act through its National Indian Gaming Commission, while forty-two tribes joined the National Indian Gaming Association, formed in 1983. Contracts between tribes and the non-Indian entrepreneurs who actually build the halls and operate the games should be approved by the Bureau of Indian Affairs. States cannot limit the amount of prizes offered, it seems, but can forbid certain types of gambling. One factor affecting the murky issues of what gambling is or should be legal is the competition that Indian bingo games and casinos offers to states' lotteries: both Indian gaming and state lotteries expanded tremendously during the 1980s. In the long run, the issue most likely to prove the strongest deterrent to unlimited gambling on Indian reservations is concern among residents that gambling adversely affects the communities' qualities as homes for their families. This erupted in 1990 among the Akwesasne Mohawks, many opposing the opening of a casino on the

reservation. Shootings and arrests proved the fears well grounded. It is ironic that Indian nations discovered the most practical way to reconstitute their long-depressed economies and strengthen the maintenance of their heritages seems to be pandering to non-Indians' craze for gambling.

By the closing decade of the twentieth century, it had become clear that Indians were not poor because they are an "ignorant and dependent race," as the nineteenth century wanted it, nor because their reservations lack resources, nor because they lack schooling or skills. Ethnohistorian Martha Knack, writing of Nevada's Pyramid Lake Paiutes, put it eloquently:

Pyramid Lake Paiutes became poor not because they were forgotten, but because they were integrated. They were integrated into a national economic system which transferred tribal lands of the West to Anglo ownership. Paiutes did not become poor because they were in an isolated backwater, but because they were drawn into the mainstream of historical events.....Against these exterior forces they were powerless to defend themselves because of their position under American law. Only when that position changed [under recent federal policies and increased outside advocacy] were the Pyramid Lake Paiutes able to fight again.

(Knack and Stewart 1984:349)

Indian nations needed capital, they needed banking services unimpeded by Bureau Machines in Washington or Ottawa, they needed acknowledgment of the validity of their values and goals. Economic viability and self-government—sovereignty—seem to be inextricably linked.

The Image of the Indian

The award of the Pulitzer Prize to the novel *House Made of Dawn*, published in 1968 by N. Scott Momaday, whose father is Kiowa and mother part Cherokee, recognized not only the talent of this well-educated man who remains sensitive to the beauty of the Kiowa land and philosophy, but also the fit between Momaday's work and a strong current in late-twentieth-century American literature and thought, a growing appreciation of diverse heritages. Quite different was the best-seller status of the several books by Carlos Casteneda, who began with *The Teachings of Don Juan* to build a cultic presentation of a philosophic system deliberately contrary to mainstream Americanism. Castaneda's purportedly Yaqui world (disowned by real Yaqui who read the books) opposed point by point the central tenets of the Euro-American tradition. With Casteneda and his imitator Lynn Andrews, the Indian becomes a mystic who knows and can teach the secrets of the universe to people who can shuck off their European heritage. Thousands of Euro-Americans dissatisfied with their lives buy these books to learn about an alternative to their disaffections.

Castaneda's supposed Yaqui seer and Andrews' "Cree medicine woman" (she seems more popular-stereotype "Sioux" than Cree) are exemplars of the modern myth projected by Euro-Americans upon the native nations of the continent. No more the brute driven back by the advancing frontier, the American Indian is now popularly endowed with wisdom and poetry, principles of conservation unremittingly pursued, and a noble kindness. No longer seen as a child of nature, the American Indian seems to have become an elder, a wrinkled brown grandparent of unfailing quiet dignity. On all the better-known reservations, there are a few Euro-Americans—most, but not all, young—seeking such a mythic guide to life. Occasionally, one of these seekers braids his hair—not a universal Indian hair style—passes himself off as Indian, and makes a living lecturing or writing "Indian" books emphasizing the mythic image. The immensely popular 1990 film *Dances with Wolves* won seven Academy Awards purveying the notion that Euro-Americans could find goodness only by rejecting their own society for that of the Lakota. Better sainted elders than brutish savages, perhaps, but neither mythic projection reflects the reality of the one and one-half million North Americans who grew up as Indians.

The five-hundredth anniversary of the first invasions of North America by conquest-minded Europeans transpired in 1992. The Indian nations have been devastated by war and disease and politically submerged, but the majority have persevered as conscious ethnic groups. In an international climate affirming the rights of the downtrodden, American Indians have begun a renaissance. Population increase combined with leaders sophisticated in legal maneuvers and media manipulation make American Indians a political force. Indian writers are being published, and artists exhibited, whose top-rank talent, drawing from non-Western traditions and from current techniques, expresses the visions of people very creatively alive in this modern world. Public opinion is being molded to recognize Indians as fellow humans: in films, the deservedly successful *Little Big Man* as well as the naively romantic *Dances with Wolves*; in novels such as James Welch's *Winter in the Blood*, sold on the popular-paperback-fiction racks (Welch is half Blackfoot, half Gros Ventre); and in shifts in law and policy. The Indian Child Welfare Act is the United States government's response to the growing anger over the frequency with which Indian children have been taken from parents or grandparents; in Wisconsin, for example, thirteen times as many Indian children as non-Indian were removed from their homes by welfare agencies, usually because poverty made the home appear "substandard" to the Euro-American social worker. The official reverse of these policies that for two centuries decried the raising of a child in its own heritage, perhaps more than any other change, signals the real renaissance of the Indian nations of North America.

This text has rejected any categorization of native peoples of North America as stages in cultural evolution or models of societal variants. North America has a human history that begins in the Pleistocene epoch over twelve thousand years ago and continues unbroken through the present.

Five hundred years ago, an expanding and industrializing Europe caused a long series of conflicts with the native nations of America. The North American nations that superseded the indigenous nations have at last reached geographic limits that have forced Mexico, the United States, and Canada to look to internal restructuring rather than to a frontier to accommodate population demands. The twentieth century has been a period of revolutions, open and covert. Late in this century, the persistent indigenous American peoples began to force a revolution of their unjust conditions. Wise to the ways of Euro-Americans, they refuse to suffer under the benign but destructive paternalism of official policies, or crass exploitation from the carriers of imperialist ideology. This book has drawn from primary histories and anthropological descriptions a factual account of the native nations of North America to serve as a framework for the new events through which these people will regain their just place in the world spectrum.

RECOMMENDED READING

Allen, Paula Gunn, ed. 1989 *Spider Woman's Granddaughters: Traditional Tales and Contemporary Writing by Native American Women.* New York: Fawcett Columbine. Allen, whose heritage combines Laguna Pueblo and Sioux, selects a broad cross-section of literature reflecting American Indian women's experiences.

Armstrong, William H. 1978 *Warrior in Two Camps.* Syracuse: Syracuse University Press. Life of Ely S. Parker, Seneca chief, brigadier general under U.S. Grant, Commissioner of Indian Affairs: the nineteenth century's ideal Indian.

Campbell, Maria. 1973 *Halfbreed.* New York: Saturday Review Press. Searing true story of a young Métis woman's battle for a decent life.

Crosby, Alfred W., Jr. 1972 *The Columbian Exchange.* Westport, Conn.: Greenwood Press. Balanced description of the major pragmatic consequences of the post-Columbian interaction between the "Old World" and the Americas.

Deloria, Vine, Jr. 1969 *Custer Died for Your Sins.* New York: Macmillan Co.

———1970 *We Talk, You Listen.* New York: Macmillan. Now-classic statements from a principal spokesman for American Indian activists.

Friedlander, Judith. 1975 *Being Indian in Hueyapan.* New York: St. Martin's Press. Friedlander describes the manipulation of Indian identity in a Nahuat village in central Mexico, including the "Aztec renaissance" movement.

Green, Rayna, ed. 1984 *That's What She Said: Contemporary Poetry and Fiction by Native American Women.* Bloomington: Indiana University Press. Green herself is Oklahoma Cherokee, and this anthology emphasizes the "contemporary."

Larson, Charles R. 1978 *American Indian Fiction.* Albuquerque: University of New Mexico Press. Detailed analysis of novels by American Indians, from the viewpoint of how they reflect Indian consciousness of status over a century.

Manuel, George and Michael Posluns. 1974 *The Fourth World.* New York: Free Press. Manuel, a Shuswap from British Columbia, was a founder and leader of the National Indian Brotherhood of Canada. His autobiography mixes memories of a Shuswap boyhood with a mature politician's analysis of Indian status.

Monthan, Guy and Doris Monthan. 1975 *Art and Indian Individualists.* Flagstaff, Ariz.: Northland Press. The authors emphasize the varied influences upon seventeen contemporary artists working in the Southwest who are Indian, effectively illustrating the creative tension between their heritages and the Indians as members of modern society.

Niatum, Duane, ed. 1988 *Harper's Anthology of Twentieth Century Native American Poetry.* San Francisco: Harper and Row. Niatum is Klallam. As the title indicates, his choices cover a broader spectrum of contemporary work than Allen's or Green's books.

O'Brien, Sharon. 1989 *American Indian Tribal Governments.* A good comparative survey of United States recognized tribes, looking in detail at history and a representative set of contemporary tribes.

Ruoff, A. LaVonne Brown. 1990 *American Indian Literatures: An Introduction, Bibliographic Review, and Selected Bibliography.* New York: Modern Language Association of America. From the perspective of college-level literature courses, an excellent guide to literature by American Indians.

Smith, Donald B. 1982 *Long Lance: The True Story of an Impostor.* Lincoln: University of Nebraska Press.

An extraordinary man born in North Carolina and classed as a black, who escaped Jim Crow in the South by claiming Indian ancestry. Athlete at Carlisle Indian School with the famous Jim Thorpe, successful journalist, actor, "Chief Buffalo Child Long Lance" ended up murdered in Hollywood. His dramatic, tragic life poignantly shows the rampant prejudice and consequent suffering of both Indians and blacks in early-twentieth-century America.

Turner, Frederick W., III. 1974 *The Portable North American Indian Reader*. New York: Viking Press. A well-balanced compendium of selections from Indian authors ranging from traditional myths and tales to poems and excerpts from recent work, plus material depicting Euro-American opinions of Indians, sympathetic and not.

Williams, Robert A., Jr. 1990 *The American Indian in Western Legal Thought*. New York: Oxford University Press. Not easy reading, but profoundly illuminating; by a legal scholar who is a Lumbee Indian.

SOURCES FOR THE FIRST EDITION

Bahr, Howard M., Bruce A. Chadwick, and Robert C. Day, eds. 1972 *Native Americans Today: Sociological Perspectives*. New York: Harper & Row, Publishers.

Bennett, Robert Lafollette. 1978 Tribal Government and Indian Self-determination. *América Indigena* 38:73-95.

Beuf, Ann H. 1977 *Red Children in White America*. Philadelphia: University of Pennsylvania Press.

Bowles, Richard P., James L. Hanley, Bruce W. Hodgins, and George A. Rawlyk, eds. 1972 *The Indian: Assimilation, Integration or Separation?* Scarborough, Ont.: Prentice-Hall of Canada, Ltd.

Brand, Johanna. 1978 *The Life and Death of Anna Mae Aquash*. Toronto: James Lorimer and Co.

Bureau of Indian Affairs, U.S. Department of the Interior. 1969 *Toward Economic Development for Native American Communities*. Washington, D.C.: Government Printing Office.

Byler, William. 1973 The Destruction of Indian Families. *Indian Affairs* 84:1-3.

Cahn, Edgar S., and David W. Hearne, eds. 1969 *Our Brother's Keeper: The Indian in White America*. New York: New American Library.

Capps, Walter Holden, ed. 1976 *Seeing with a Native Eye*. New York: Harper & Row, Publishers.

Conn, Stephen. 1977 The Extralegal Forum and Legal Power. In *Anthropology of Power*, ed. R. W. Adams and R. Fogelson. New York: Academic Press, pp. 217-224.

Fidler, Dick. 1970 *Red Power in Canada*. Toronto: Vanguard Publications.

Frideres, James S. 1974 *Canada's Indians: Contemporary Conflicts*. Scarborough, Ont.: Prentice Hall of Canada, Ltd.

Fuchs, Estelle, and Robert J. Havighurst. 1973 *To Live on This Earth: American Indian Education*. Garden City, N.Y.: Doubleday and Co.

Gendzier, Irene L. 1973 *Frantz Fanon: A Critical Study*. New York: Random House.

González Casanova, Pablo. 1965 *La Democracia en México*. Mexico City: Ediciones ERA, S.A.

González Navarro, Moises. 1970 *Sociología e Historia en Mexico*. Mexico City: El Colegio de Mexico.

Hoople, Joanne and J.W.E. Newbery. 1974 *And What About Canada's Native Peoples?* Ottawa: Canadian Council for International Co-operation.

Houghton, Ruth M. 1973 *Native American Politics: Power Relationships in the Western Great Basin Today*. Reno: Bureau of Governmental Research, University of Nevada.

Jacobs, Wilbur R. 1972 *Dispossessing the American Indian*. New York: Charles Scribner's Sons.

Josephy, Alvin M., Jr. 1971 *Red Power*. New York: American Heritage Press.

Kahl, Joseph A. 1976 *Modernization, Exploitation and Dependency in Latin America*. New Brunswick, N.J.: Transaction Books.

Leap, William L. 1974 Ethnics, Emics, and the New Ideology: The Identity Potential of Indian English. In *Social and Cultural Identity*, ed. T. K. Fitzgerald. Southern Anthropological Society Proceedings 8:51-62.

Levitan, Sar A. and Barbara Hetrick. 1971 *Big Brother's Indian Programs—With Reservations*. New York: McGraw-Hill Publishing Co.

Lukaczer, Moses. 1976 *The Federal Buy Indian Program*. Reseda, Calif.: Mojave Books.

Maestas, John R., ed. 1976 *Contemporary Native American Address*. Provo, Utah: Brigham Young University.

Milwaukee Journal. July 10, 1977; May 6, 1979; August 12, 1979.

Miner, H. Craig. 1976 *The Corporation and the Indian*. Columbia: University of Missouri Press.

Nammack, Georgiana C. 1969 *Fraud, Politics, and the Dispossession of the Indians*. Norman: University of Oklahoma Press.

Native American Rights Fund. 1978 Suppression of American Indian Culture and Religious Activities by Federal Policy. *Council for Museum Anthropology Newsletter* 3:7-10 (with Public Law 95-341, reprinted pp. 5-6).

Newsweek. 1978 Resources: The Rich Indians. March 20, 1978:61-64.

Pelletier, Wilfred, and Ted Poole. 1973 *No Foreign Land*. New York: Random House.

Prucha, Francis Paul. 1973 *Americanizing the American Indians*. Cambridge: Harvard University Press.

Saskatchewan Indian. 1973 Supplement: Indian Act. Prince Albert: Federation of Saskatchewan Indians.

Schultz, George A. 1973 *An Indian Canaan*. Norman: University of Oklahoma Press.

Sheehan, Bernard W. 1973 *Seeds of Extinction*. Chapel Hill: University of North Carolina Press.

Sorkin, Alan L. 1971 *American Indians and Federal Aid*. Washington: Brookings Institution.

Stanley, Sam, ed. 1978 *American Indian Economic Development*. The Hague: Mouton Publishers.

Svensson, Frances. 1973 *The Ethnics in American Politics: American Indians*. Minneapolis: Burgess Publishing Co.

Taylor, Theodore W. 1972 *The States and Their Indian Citizens*. Washington, D.C.: Government Printing Office.

Time. 1979 Fuel Powwow. August 20, 1979:17.

Waddell, Jack O., and O. Michael Watson, eds. 1973 *American Indian Urbanization*. West Lafayette, Ind.: Purdue University.

Zahar, Renate. 1974 *Frantz Fanon: Colonialism and Alienation*, trans. W. F. Feuser. New York: Monthly Review Press.

SOURCES FOR THE SECOND EDITION

Akwesasne Notes. 1986, 1989, 1990, January 1991 Nos. 18(3), 21(1), 22(1, 2, 3, 5). Rooseveltown, N.Y.: Akwesasne Notes.

Ambler, Marjane. 1990 *Breaking the Iron Bonds*. Lawrence: University Press of Kansas.

Anthropology and Education Quarterly. 1991 Issue on Indian children and classroom learning. *Anthropology and Education Quarterly* 22(1):21–94.

Association on American Indian Affairs. 1990 *Indian Affairs* 122:1–9, 123:4–7.

Barsh, Russel Lawrence, and James Youngblood Henderson. 1980 *The Road: Indian Tribes and Political Liberty*. Berkeley: University of California Press.

Bee, Robert L. 1982 *The Politics of American Indian Policy*. Cambridge, Mass.: Schenkman.

Berger, Thomas R. 1985 *Village Journey*. Toronto: Collins.

Boldt, Menno, and J. Anthony Long, eds. 1985 *The Quest for Justice*. Toronto: University of Totonto Press.

Bolt, Christine. 1987 *American Indian Policy and American Reform*. London: Allen & Unwin.

Brøsted, Jens et al. (Brøsted, Jens, Jens Dahl, Andrew Gray, Hans Christian Gulløv, Georg Henriksen, Jørgen Brøchner Jørgensen, Inge Kleivan) 1985 *Native Power*. Bergen: Universitetforlaget AS.

Burt, Larry W. 1982 *Tribalism in Crisis*. Albuquerque: University of New Mexico Press.

Cadwalader, Sandra L., and Vine Deloria, Jr. 1984 *The Aggressions of Civilization*. Philadelphia: Temple University Press.

Campisi, Jack, and Laurence M. Hauptman, eds. 1988 *The Oneida Indian Experience*. Syracuse: Syracuse University Press.

Carlson, Leonard A. 1981 *Indians, Bureaucrats, and Land*. Westport, Conn.: Greenwood Press.

Conference on Hunting and Gathering Societies. 1990 Precirculated Papers, Sixth International Conference on Hunting and Gathering Societies. Fairbanks: Department of Anthropology, University of Alaska.

Cornell, Stephen. 1988 *The Return of the Native*. New York: Oxford University Press.

Cox, Bruce Alden, ed. 1987 *Native People, Native Lands*. Ottawa: Carleton University Press.

D'Arcy McNickle Center for the History of the American Indian. 1985 *The Impact of Indian History on the Teaching of United States History*, nos. 2 and 3. Chicago Conference 1984, Sessions I–II, V–VI. Chicago: Newberry Library.

Deloria, Vine, Jr., and Clifford Lytle. 1984 *The Nations Within*. New York: Pantheon.

Deloria, Vine, Jr., ed. 1985 *American Indian Policy in the Twentieth Century*. Norman: University of Oklahoma Press.

Dippie, Brian W. 1982 *The Vanishing American: White Attitudes and U.S. Indian Policy*. Middletown, Conn.: Wesleyan University Press.

Doherty, Robert. 1990 *Disputed Waters: Native Americans and the Great Lakes Fishery.* Lexington: University Press of Kentucky.

Driben, Paul, and Robert S. Trudeau. 1983 *When Freedom Is Lost.* Toronto: University of Toronto Press.

Dyck, Noel, ed. 1985 *Indigenous Peoples and the Nation-State.* St. John's: Memorial University of Newfoundland, Institute of Social and Economic Research, Social and Economic Papers, No. 14.

Fixico, Donald L. 1986 *Termination and Relocation.* Albuquerque: University of New Mexico Press.

Fleckner, John A. 1984 *Native American Archives.* Chicago: Society of American Archivists.

Frideres, James S. 1983 *Native People of Canada* (2nd ed.). Scarborough: Prentice-Hall of Canada.

Geranious, Nicholas K. 1990 Sohappy Vows to Keep Fighting for Indian Treaty Fishing Rights. *News from Indian Country* 4(17):3.

Getty, Ian A. L., and Antoine S. Lussier, eds. 1983 *As Long As the Sun Shines and Water Flows.* Vancouver: University of British Columbia Press.

Getty, Ian A. L., and Donald B. Smith, eds. 1978 *One Century Later.* Vancouver: University of British Columbia Press.

Goodwill, Jean, and Norma Sluman. 1984 *John Tootoosis.* Winnipeg: Pemmican Publications.

Great Lakes Indian Fish and Wildlife Commission. 1990 *Masinaigan,* Spring 1990, Odanah, Wis.

Green, L. C., and Olive P. Dickason. 1989 *The Law of Nations and the New World.* Edmonton: University of Alberta Press.

Grobsmith, Elizabeth S. 1989 The Impact of Litigation on the Religious Revitalization of Native American Inmates in the Nebraska Department of Corrections. *Plains Anthropologist* 34(124):135–147.

Gross, Emma R. 1989 *Contemporary Federal Policy Toward American Indians.* New York: Greenwood Press.

Hauptman, Laurence M. 1981 *The Iroquois and the New Deal.* Syracuse: Syracuse University Press.

———1986 *The Iroquois Struggle for Survival, World War II to Red Power.* Syracuse: Syracuse University Press.

Höll, Otmar, ed. 1983 *Small States in Europe and Dependence.* Boulder: Westview Press.

Hoxie, Frederick E. 1984 *A Final Promise: The Campaign to Assimilate the Indians, 1880–1920.* Lincoln: University of Nebraska Press.

Indigenous Communications Resource Center. 1989 *The Web,* September 1989. Ithaca: Cornell University American Indian Program.

Iverson, Peter. 1982 *Carlos Montezuma.* Albuquerque: University of New Mexico Press.

Iverson, Peter, ed. 1985 *The Plains Indians of the Twentieth Century.* Norman: University of Oklahoma Press.

Jarvenpa, Robert. 1985 The Political Economy and Political Ethnicity of American Indian Adaptations and Identities. *Ethnic and Racial Studies* 8(1):29–48.

Joe, Jennie R., ed. 1986 *American Indian Policy and Cultural Values: Conflict and Accommodation.* Los Angeles: UCLA American Indian Studies Center.

Johnson, Dirk. 1991 Census Finds Many Claiming New Identity: Indian. *New York Times,* March 5, 1991.

Jorgensen, Joseph G., ed.. 1984 *Native Americans and Energy Development II.* Boston: Anthropology Resource Center.

Kehoe, Alice Beck. 1989 *The Ghost Dance: Ethnohistory and Revitalization.* New York: Holt Rinehart and Winston.

Keller, Robert H., Jr. 1983 *American Protestantism and United States Indian Policy, 1869–82.* Lincoln: University of Nebraska Press.

Kelly, Lawrence C. 1983 *The Assault on Assimilation.* Albuquerque: University of New Mexico Press.

Kerri, James Nwannukwu. 1978 *Unwilling Urbanites: The Life Experiences of Canadian Indians in a Prairie City.* Washington: University Press of America.

Kersey, Harry A., Jr. 1989 *The Florida Seminoles and the New Deal.* Boca Raton: Florida Atlantic University Press.

Knack, Martha C., and Omer C. Stewart. 1984 *As Long As the River Shall Run.* Berkeley: University of California Press.

LaDuke, Winona. 1989 Our Land is Our Life. *Radcliffe Quarterly* 75(4):13–16.

———1990 People Working Together. *Akwesasne Notes* 22(3):26.

Little Bear, Leroy, Menno Boldt, and J. Anthony Long, eds. 1984 *Pathways to Self-Determination.* Toronto: University of Toronto Press.

Littlefield, Alice. 1989 Native American Labor and Public Policy in the United States. Paper presented at Society for Economic Anthropology annual meeting, Mt. Pleasant, Mich., April.

Long, J. Anthony, and Menno Boldt, eds. 1988 *Governments in Conflict?* Toronto: University of Toronto Press.

Lopach, James J., Margery Hunter Brown, and Richmond L. Clow. 1990 *Tribal Government Today*. Boulder: Westview Press.

Los Angeles Times Service. 1990 You Can Thank Them for Potato Chips. Los Angeles Times Service, reprinted in *Milwaukee Journal*, October 24, 1990.

Marchione, Marilynn. 1991 Gambling on a School. *Wisconsin, the Milwaukee Journal Magazine*, April 14, 1991:7–16.

May, Elizabeth. 1990 Update from Cultural Survival (Canada). *Cultural Survival Quarterly* 14(4):69–70.

McDonnell, Janet A. 1991 *The Dispossession of the American Indian 1887–1934*. Bloomington: Indiana University Press.

Medicine, Bea. 1981 Native American Resistance to Integration: Contemporary Confrontations and Religious Revitalization. *Plains Anthropologist* 26(94):277–286.

Meeting Ground. 1989 Josephy Speaks. *Meeting Ground* 20:3–4. Chicago: D'Arcy McNickle Center for the History of the American Indian, Newberry Library.

Miller, J. R. 1990 Owen Glendower, Hotspur, and Canadian Indian Policy. *Ethnohistory* 37(4):386–415.

Milner, Clyde A., II. 1982 *With Good Intentions*. Lincoln: University of Nebraska Press.

Mohawk, John. 1989 International Principles of Indigenous Rights. *Daybreak* 3(1):14–17.

National Park Service. 1990 *Federal Archeological Contracting*. Washington, D.C.: U.S. Department of the Interior, National Park Service, Archeological Assistance Program, Technical Brief No. 7.

Native American Rights Fund. 1989, 1990 *NARF Legal Review* 14(2), 15(4), 16(1).

O'Brien, Sharon. 1989 *American Indian Tribal Governments*. Norman: University of Oklahoma Press.

Peterson, Nicolas, and Marcia Langton, eds. 1983 *Aborigines, Land and Land Rights*. Canberra: Australian Institute of Aboriginal Studies.

Philp, Kenneth R., ed. 1986 *Indian Self-Rule*. Salt Lake City: Howe Brothers.

Ponting, J. Rick, and Roger Gibbins. 1980 *Out of Irrelevance: A Socio-political Introduction to Indian Affairs in Canada*. Toronto: Butterworth.

Presidential Commission on Indian Reservation Economies. 1984 *Report and Recommendations*. Washington, D.C.: Presidential Commission on Indian Reservation Economies.

Price, John A., ed. 1978 *Native Studies*. Toronto: McGraw-Hill Ryerson.

Prpick, Sean. 1990 Just Say Chief. *The Third Degree: University of Regina Alumni Magazine*, Fall 1990:14–18.

Prucha, Francis Paul. 1984 *The Great Father*. Lincoln: University of Nebraska Press.

Rogel, Amy Lyn. 1990 *"Mastering the Secret of White Man's Power:" Indian Students at Beloit College, 1871 to 1884*. Archives Publication Number One, ed. Frederick A. Burwell. Beloit, Wis.: Beloit College.

Ross, Thomas E., and Tyrel G. Moore, eds. 1987 *A Cultural Geography of North American Indians*. Boulder: Westview Press.

Schrader, Robert Fay. 1983 *The Indian Arts & Crafts Board*. Albuquerque: University of New Mexico Press.

Schusky, Ernest L., ed. 1980 *Political Organization of Native North America*. Washington, D.C.: University Press of America.

Seventh Generation Fund. 1985 *Native Self-Sufficiency* 8(1).

Smith, Donald B. 1987 Aboriginal Rights a Century Ago. *The Beaver* 67(1):4–15.

Snipp, C. Matthew. 1989 *American Indians: The First of this Land*. New York: Russell Sage Foundation.

St. Clair, Robert, and William Leap, eds. 1982 *Language Renewal Among American Indian Tribes*. Rosslyn, Va: National Clearinghouse for Bilingual Education.

Stahl, Robert J. 1991 "Taking Medicine:" Demystifying the Peyote Experience in the Native American Church. Paper presented to the 67th annual meeting, Central States Anthropological Society, March 22, Ames, Iowa.

Sutton, Imre, ed. 1985 *Irredeemable America*. Albuquerque: University of New Mexico Press.

Swagerty, William R., ed. 1979 *Indian Sovereignty*, Proceedings of the Second Annual Conference on Problems and Issues Concerning American Indians Today. Chicago: Newberry Library.

Tanner, Adrian, ed. 1983 *The Politics of Indianness*. St. John's: Memorial University of Newfoundland, Institute of Social and Economic Research, Social and Economic Papers, no. 12.

Taylor, Graham D. 1980 *The New Deal and American Indian Tribalism*. Lincoln: University of Nebraska Press.

Taylor, Theodore W. 1984 *The Bureau of Indian Affairs*. Boulder: Westview Press.

Thornton, Russell. 1987 *American Indian Holocaust and Survival*. Norman: University of Oklahoma Press.

Trennert, Robert A., Jr. 1988 *The Phoenix Indian School*. Norman: University of Oklahoma Press.

United States Commission on Civil Rights. 1981 *Indian Tribes: A Continuing Quest for Survival*. Washington, D.C.: United States Commission on Civil Rights.

Unrau, William E. 1989 *Mixed-Bloods and Tribal Dissolution*. Lawrence: University Press of Kansas.

Vizenor, Gerald. 1990 *Crossbloods*. Minneapolis: University of Minnesota Press.

Waldram, James B. 1988 *As Long as the Rivers Run: Hydroelectric Development and Native Communities in Western Canada*. Winnipeg: University of Manitoba Press.

Walters, Robert. 1991 Sloppy Bureaucracy Hounds BIA. Cox New Service, reprinted in *Milwaukee Journal*, April 7, 1991.

Weaver, Sally M. 1981 *Making Canadian Indian Policy*. Toronto: University of Toronto Press.

Weiss, Lawrence David. 1984 *The Development of Capitalism in the Navajo Nation: A Political-Economic History*. Minneapolis: MEP Publications (University of Minnesota Anthropology Department).

White, Robert H. 1990 *Tribal Assets*. New York: Henry Holt.

Wilkinson, Charles R. 1987 *American Indians, Time, and the Law*. New Haven: Yale University Press.

Williams, Robert A., Jr. 1990 *The American Indian in Western Legal Thought*. New York: Oxford University Press.

———1990 Gendered Checks and Balances: Understanding the Legacy of White Patriarchy in an American Indian Cultural Context. *Georgia Law Review* 24:1019–1044.

Wolfe, Robert J., and Robert J. Walker. 1987 Subsistence Economies in Alaska: Productivity, Geography, and Development Impacts. *Arctic Anthropology* 24(2):56–81.

Appendix

ANTHROPOLOGY
AND AMERICAN INDIANS

Anthropology developed as a social science during the heyday of imperalism. Governmental support for anthropological research was frequently expected to yield information that could be used in the administration of colonies and subjugated people. Colonial powers that could insist on a native community receiving the researcher often facilitated anthropologists' access to peoples whose cultural patterns exemplified interesting alternative ways of life. Government agents, military officers, and missionaries sometimes provided accommodations, introductions, and background information for researchers in the field. Because of this apparent, and occasionally actual, alliance between anthropologists and colonial agents, some spokespeople for indigenous groups have accused anthropology of being an instrument of imperialism. It is true that anthropological data have been used by colonial agents, and even continue to be solicited by, for example, some Christian missionaries, but the relation between anthropology and the milieu that fostered it is complex.

It can be argued equally well that anthropology has contributed to the growing public sense of outrage at imperialism. To reduce the argument to very simple terms, there are a number of anthropologists who have studied or are studying native peoples of North America, who are themselves American Indians. Among the early employees of the Smithsonian Institution's Bureau of American Ethnology, in the late nineteenth century, were J.N.B. Hewitt, a Tuscarora, and Francis La Flesche, an Omaha. Others, with less formal education, were the fully acknowledged collaborators of professional anthropologists: George Hunt, life-long resident of a Kwakiutl village, who wrote thousands of pages with Franz Boas, or Robert Spott, a Yurok, coauthor with Alfred L. Kroeber. Arthur C. Parker, member of the well-known Seneca Iroquois family, was New York State Archaeologist, an ethnologist, and finally Director of the Rochester Museum in the early twentieth century. Somewhat later, Edward Dozier, whose mother was a Tewa, became a highly respected anthropologist, and a younger Tewa, Alfonso Ortiz, has gained a similar position today. The late D'Arcy McNickle, a Flathead, wrote powerful novels of his people as well as anthropological volumes. Ella Deloria, a Lakota, was trained by Boas as an anthropologist and prepared texts in her language, although her career was in applied rather than academic work. Her niece, Beatrice Medicine, is a professional anthropologist (and Vine Deloria, Jr., the writer and legal scholar, is a nephew). Robert K. Thomas, a Cherokee, has become known both for scholarly publications and as a leading applied anthropologist. Others, such as Joseph Medicine Crow, a Crow, have preferred work in programs with their own people after obtaining graduate degrees in anthropology. These examples, extending over four generations, show that anthropology is not incompatible with prideful active membership in an American Indian group.

More fundamentally, anthropology and American Indians have been in symbiosis even before the emergence of anthropology as a recognized scholarly discipline. Sahagún's sixteenth-century compendium of Aztec beliefs and practices was a stimulus to reflection upon the nature and possible worth of non-Western societies outside of the fringes of the classical world. By the eighteenth century, European philosophers such as Rousseau were discussing at length the significance of the reported differences between American and European peoples. The weighty questions formulated in those discussions called for directed research that developed through the nineteenth century as the traditionally broad field of philosophy became fragmented into independent disciplines. Observations of American Indians had honed many questions; now scholars would go to American Indian communities to obtain data in greater depth to perhaps answer the questions.

The first modern anthropological study is said to be Lewis Henry Morgan's *League of the Ho-de-no-sau-nee or Iroquois*, published in 1851. Morgan was an upstate New York lawyer fascinated since youth by the differences between his immi-grant people and the Seneca neighboring them. Noticing an Indian youth in a bookstore, Morgan struck up an acquaintance, and through this youth, Ely S. Parker, an introduction to other Seneca. From his visits to the Tonawanda and other Iroquois reservations, Morgan compiled his book. The matrilineal organization of the Iroquois intrigued him, and he decided to go West to interview other American Indians to discover how widespread this form of organization might be. He also sent questionnaires on kinship terms to missionaries and government agents in Asia and the Pacific islands. From his own and his correspondents' material, he prepared the landmark theoretical study, *Systems of Consanguinity and Affinity*, published by the Smithsonian Institution in 1871. As in any pioneering work on entirely new ground, Morgan's contains errors both of fact (especially where he had to use his correspondents' data) and of interpretation, but the volume inaugurated a whole new field of scholarly study, and much of its content remains usable. A more general work, *Ancient Society* (1877), attracted wide readership to its universal scheme of human societal and technical development, although the scheme was far too ambitious for the amount of data Morgan could obtain to support it. *Ancient Society* expounded stages of development tied to methods of subsistence, styles of crafts, and patterns of kinship and political organization. Insofar as it named non-European peoples as members of stages that Europeans had passed through and beyond, it seemed to justify imperialistic ethnocentric "development" forced upon these peoples. Morgan did not speak directly to this issue; he believed he was presenting a purely historical study, although one that required bold speculation to make history out of ahistorical descriptions. Karl Marx studied Morgan's popular book and Marx's disciple, Friedrich Engels, made it the basis of his revisions for publication of Marx's last notebooks. Engels' *The Origin of the Family, Private Property, and the State* (1884) in turn inspired Lenin and raised *Ancient Society* to reverence as a seminal influence upon Soviet social theory—ironic, for Morgan was a capitalist. *Ancient Society* was denounced as fantasy by Franz Boas, who privately inclined more toward socialism than Morgan ever did, and has had little direct influence upon anthropology outside the Slavic-speaking nations. Leslie White, a professor at the University of Michigan, attempted to revive Morgan for American anthropology beginning in the 1950s, but the schemes of White and his successor, Elman Service, resemble Morgan more in outline than in detail.

The Bureau of American Ethnology was organized in 1879 to compile records on the native peoples of the United States. Administered by the Smithsonian Institution, the Bureau's first director was Major John Wesley Powell, who as chief of the survey of the Rocky Mountain region had explored the Great Basin and Southwest and carefully described the peoples of these regions. Powell saw a critical need for data on the indigenous peoples if, as his successor put it, the government was to be capable of "intelligent administration." Such information had been specifically requested as early as 1795 from government agents to the Indians, and had been a major goal of the 1804–6 Lewis and Clark expedition instructed by President Jefferson. Henry Rowe Schoolcraft had a few years later kept, and soon published, journals of his surveys as a mineralogist in the upper Midwest, and his interest in the peoples of this frontier led to his appointment in 1822 as Indian agent based at Sault Ste. Marie. Schoolcraft married a woman who was part Ojibwa, and through her amassed volumes of notes on her mother's people and their neighbors, published in 1839 as *Algic Researches* (Algic = Algonkian). *Algic Researches* lacks the scientific acumen of Morgan's work, but perhaps on that very account was more popular with the general public. It was the source of Longfellow's notions of Indians embodied in his famous poem *The Song of Hiawatha*. Early in his own career, Morgan had consulted with Schoolcraft as with a mentor. Schoolcraft thus was influential in forming nineteenth-century images of northern American

Indians. His work culminated in a six-volume compendium that he prepared and published in the 1850s under the direction of the Bureau of Indian Affairs.

After the Civil War, Major Powell cited the Government's support of Schoolcraft's studies, his own series, Squier and Davis's *The Ancient Monuments of the Mississippi Valley* (1848), and other publications to argue that a systematic plan of research was not only feasible but likely to produce many volumes comparable in value to these. Successful, Powell hired several persons eager to work on the envisioned massive research project, and sent them to Indian communities not previously studied. The goal was an encyclopedic inventory of the native peoples—their languages, beliefs, customs, physical characteristics, populations, histories, and current situations. A century later, with the Bureau of American Ethnology title discarded and its staff merged into the Smithsonian's National Museum of Natural History's Department of Anthropology, the project continues toward its utopian goal. During this century, Powell's vision not only supported many hundreds of field research and archival studies through his Bureau, but also encouraged, guided, and occasionally helped support research by persons in museums and universities, the privately employed, or wealthy.

Powell's competitor was the German immigrant Franz Boas, who received some training in ethnography in Berlin in the early 1880s before going first to Baffin Land and then to the Northwest Coast on expeditions. Boas obtained a position as anthropologist at the American Museum of Natural History in New York, and soon after began teaching at Columbia University, where within a few years he established a department of anthropology that granted its first Ph.D. degree to Alfred L. Kroeber in 1901. Boas agreed with Powell that it was crucial to obtain first-hand information on prereservation Indian life before the last generation to live free should die out, and with his colleague Clark Wissler arranged for a series of field trips that would complement the work of the Bureau of

American Ethnology. Unlike Powell, Boas believed it important to train ethnologists formally, and for some years there was rivalry between "Washington" and "New York" on the merits of academic preparation. Boas's position prevailed. As Powell's first ethnographers retired, they were replaced, for the most part, by men with graduate degrees in anthropology. (Both Boas and Powell encouraged and employed women anthropologists, but once the two founders retired, administrators at their institutions and others were usually reluctant to hire women for professional positions.)

The Bureau of American Ethnology amassed priceless data, including detailed procedures of ceremonies that today are referred to by Indian priests whose own teachers may have been able, in the period of governmental suppression of Indian religions, to pass on only shortened versions. The Bureau's material was greatly augmented by the observations collected by the fieldworkers of the American Museum, the Field Museum in Chicago, the University of California, and other institutions. From these data, and from fieldwork designed to elucidate theoretical hypotheses but productive also of more data toward Powell's great goal, anthropologists selected whatever seemed to support one or another explanation of causes of human behavior. In other words, data from records of American Indian communities were drawn upon to test social-science hypotheses. Through this interaction—the designing of field work to produce relevant data, and the construction of hypotheses from American data—the recording of the cultural patterns of the native peoples of North America has been formative in the development of anthropology. Powell's plan was pragmatic and colonialist, though infused by his intellectual drive and curiosity; Boas, by concurring in the necessity of recording the memories of prereservation adult Indians, focused anthropological theory building upon American data. (Boas's contemporaries in Europe, such as the Polish-British anthropologist Bronislaw Malinowski, similarly combined the recording of cultures of colonial peoples in Africa and the Pacific with the building of theory. As in America, money to support student and professional researches was available from governments ostensibly seeking "intelligent administration.")

If their support money might seem, to some modern eyes, tainted, the majority of the anthropologists working in the late nineteenth and the twentieth centuries have sincerely believed that their work might improve the lot of the peoples they observed. The government was going to administer Indian communities, like it or no, so sympathetic descriptions of the dignity and complexity of the communities were a worthwhile attempt to sensitize bureaucrats. Bureaucrats don't always read all they should, or always follow recommendations in what they read, but better to try, if to no avail, than not to try at all. It is unfair to assume that anthropologists "mined" Indian communities for data primarily to advance their own careers. Instead, it should be recognized that many individuals who have been committed to cultural relativism as a foundation for human rights have chosen the unusual and not-very-well-paying career of anthropology in order to better live by humanitarian principles. When anthropologists' recommendations have proven ill advised, as when Alice Fletcher spoke in favor of the Dawes Act, it was not usually from dastardly motives, but from misplaced faith in government agents' capabilities to avert unscrupulous manipulation of their Indian charges. There are, of course, some anthropologists who were (or are) cads, or worse, but on the whole, anthropologists have been well-meaning friends whose principal sin has been the powerlessness of their small numbers and lack of wealth. Like everyone else, they have been molded by the beliefs and customary behavior of the societies in which they grew up. Even with anthropological training they cannot fully shake off these influences, and, like everyone else, they are frustrated by structures and processes they as individuals or as a tiny fraction of American society cannot control.

Often in reaction to these frustrations, anthropologists turned to theory building. Boas urged great caution in extrapolating from observations of a few American Indian communities to grand explanations of human behavior, and held up Morgan's *Ancient Society* as an example of the errors to which such schemes are prone. Taking their cue from Boas, the majority of American anthropologists have eschewed universal explanations; Leslie White was an exception. They have instead increasingly tended to examine the ecology in which a community lives, and emphasize the adaptation of the members of the community to that ecology through cultural patterns. One classic of this position is Julian Steward's *Theory of Culture Change* (1955). Steward drew heavily upon his ethnographic fieldwork in the Great Basin and the Southwest, published in part by the Bureau of American Ethnology as *Basin-Plateau Aboriginal Socio-Political Groups* (1938). He had been deeply impressed by the small size and highly flexible social structure of groups of Paiute and Shoshoni, and he attributed these features of their societies to the low density of food resources in the habitats in which he found them. His correlation of population size and structure with ecology was taken over by the archaeologist Jesse Jennings, who was excavating prehistoric sites in Utah, and Steward's ethnographic descriptions became the basis of Jenning's reconstruction of ancient Basin life. Steward failed to realize that the Numa he interviewed had been driven from their ancestral homelands along the lakes and streams by Euro-American colonists. Jennings eventually realized, as archaeological researches proved heavier prehistoric habitation in these localities, that his picture of the "Desert Culture" was skewed, but the more general application of Steward's emphasis on density of resources as a causal factor in societal structural complexity has remained a major explanatory principle. Part of its strength lies in its grounding in its intellectual forebears, Clark Wissler's 1914 "Material Culture of North American Indians" map of culture areas based upon principal subsistence resources, and Kroeber's 1939 *Cultural and Natural Areas of Native North America*, which refines the culture-area concepts of Boas, Otis Mason, and Wissler with the aid of better ecological studies. The conceptualization of culture areas was initially, in the late nineteenth century, a means of organizing American Indian data by criteria important to the peoples themselves; three generations later, Steward had been able to transcend the American data to produce a universal scheme, his "multilinear evolution."

The critical importance of American Indian data came to the fore again when several fieldworkers sharply took issue with the postulate of Steward and of Elman Service, another exponent of evolutionary schemes, that patrilocal bands were the norm for hunting peoples. June Helm and Richard Slobodin, working with Dene, David Damas with Central Inuit, Charles Bishop with Cree, and others were convinced that the northern hunting peoples did not blindly bind sons perpetually to their fathers, but rather weighed a number of factors to select the most pleasant and reliable family alliances. If anything, these northern peoples slightly favored matrilocality in that they expected a young couple to remain with the wife's parents for at least a couple of years. Debates over residence rules may look like quibbles, but there is a significant dimension in that these anthropologists, basing their arguments upon field observations, long discussions with members of the native communities, and historical archives, have exposed the limitations of evolutionary theories drawn from inadequately diversified field experience.

Much earlier, in 1917, a blow had been struck at the nineteenth-century notion that "primitive" peoples are simply organized in kinship structures when Kroeber published his *Zuñi Kin and Clan*. The matrilineal clans in Zuni are the basis for property rights, he admits, but non-kin-based religious fraternities and priesthoods and private friendships are also instruments through which Zuni people organize for tasks and personal goals. Kroeber's colleague, Robert Lowie, demonstrated the same situation for Plains Indian communities in his study of the sodalities so characteristic of these peoples in the nineteenth century. Post-World War II recognition by sociology and anthropology of the eminence of voluntary associations in many societies owes much to the data presented by Kroeber and Lowie decades earlier.

In the 1950s, some anthropologists concluded that at least under modern conditions on reservations, there are American Indian communities with very little societal structure. After conducting fieldwork with northern Wisconsin Chippewa (Ojibwa), Victor Barnouw and Bernard James could perceive so little organization other than federal bureaucracy among Chippewa that they termed them "atomistic." Much debate ensued, in part on the question of whether the prereservation hunting Chippewa were "atomistic" (game density being relatively low in the forest, each nuclear family had to look out for itself, the argument ran), or whether this was a breakdown caused by government paternalism. In time, the latter position seemed more defensible as new archival research on the Ojibwa indicated more formal and pervasive societal structures and alliances in the past, and the difficulties of combating the Bureau of Indian Affairs became better appreciated by outside observers. Contemporary with the debates on Chippewa "atomism," Oscar Lewis was using his work with Indian peasants in Mexico, especially those who had emigrated to urban slums, to develop his theory of the existence of a "culture of poverty" that he claimed characterizes all underclasses in modern societies and can be a major obstacle to betterment. Lewis's theory was rapidly extended from Mexican slums to American black ghettos. Most social scientists now seem to feel that Lewis overstated his case, that the bureaucratic and economic obstacles faced by the very poor are so overwhelming that their cynicism toward betterment programs is amply justified. One need not invoke any cultural tradition of cynicism to explain what are usually only too realistic perceptions.

Quite a different emphasis came, in the 1950s, from the research of Anthony F.C. Wallace on Iroquois. Wallace had become fascinated by the Seneca prophet Handsome Lake. Analyzing Ganioday'o's movement beginning in 1799, Wallace saw a pattern that he proposed was a general form of what he termed revitalization movements. From Wallace's perspective, there are striking parallels between Ganioday'o and his Longhouse religion, and Jesus and Christianity. In both cases, the prophet appears as a humble man revealing the will of God to a defeated people suffering demoralization and poverty. Disciples soon adapt the prophet's message into a code that appeals to a large segment of the populace as a new way of life. Wallace's well-presented study spurred many anthropologists and historians to be alert to revitalization movements as sound adaptations to new conditions. Formerly, because the prophet was not a formally educated theologian, such movements were often dismissed by scholars as merely "hysterical reactions" by "primitive" people to crises. The Ghost Dance religion preached by Wovoka (Jack Wilson) beginning in 1889 is a prime example of a true and intelligent religious movement maligned by popular commentators. The curious aspect of the disrespect paid to the Ghost Dance religion is that James Mooney's description of it, published in 1896 by the Bureau of American Ethnology, was entirely sympathetic and clearly stated that it was then, six years after the Wounded Knee Massacre, a strong and promising movement. The fiction that the Ghost Dance represented a year-long or two-year-long hysterical "dance" indulged in by "primitives" who could not understand modern civilization is a racist myth that has persisted among many Euro-American writers who seem loath to give up the nineteenth-century idea of a dichotomy between "civilized" and "primitive."

Whether there are differences between "primitive" and "civilized" minds has excited discussion for centuries in Europe. The majority of anthropologists have denied that there are real differences, and have cited many studies with American Indians to prove that the notion must be discarded. Mooney's great work is one example. Several of the studies have taken a psychoanalytical approach. Irving Hallowell, for one, used this general perspective in his descriptions of Berens River Ojibwa in northern Canada. Kroeber collaborated with Erik Erikson, the well-known psychologist, in an intriguing analysis in Freudian terms of Yurok beliefs and metaphors. Whatever one may think of the Freudian exercise, the underlying point is that neither Kroeber nor Erikson assumed there was any fundamental difference between Yurok and nineteenth-century Viennese minds. More recently, studies in cognition and learning processes have been made with American Indians to elucidate how different cognitive schemata, embodied in word structures and metaphors and transmitted as cultural patterns, produce the apparently different "ways of thinking" of the various peoples of the Americas, and the world. These studies include many that stem from pioneer work by the anthropologists Edward Sapir, an early student of Boas, and his student Benjamin Whorf. Sapir's researches on the Northwest Coast, and Whorf's in the Southwest, guided them to the fact that languages mold perception by the implicit classes or categorizations in grammatical structures and word meanings. For example, a Navajo sentence may not need a separate subject word because a particular verb-form choice implies a particular kind of subject, such as round or angular. Navajos, Whorf pointed out, are sensitive to noticing whether an object is round or angular because they must do so in order to select the correct grammatical form of the verb they wish to use. Blackfoot, to take another example, may be less sexist than English speakers because the pronouns in their Algonkian language refer to whether the referent is animate or inanimate, but not to its sex, so they may be less sensitized to always noticing a person's sex as a significant attribute of that individual in every situation.

Blackfoot speakers not infrequently have difficulty in using the correct pronoun in English because these grammatical differences mean they cannot translate directly from their thought in their own language, and this difficulty of course affects some children's schoolwork. Anthropological clarification of the causes of such difficulties can be useful in designing better curricula. Other anthropological studies of schoolchildren, such as Murray and Rosalie Wax's iconoclastic account of Oglala Sioux children in school, and Thomas Rhys Williams's thoughtful description of the largely nonverbal learning style of Papago ('O'odham), have been important contributions to the reassessment of traditional schooling. Anthropologists who have served as education consultants to reservation schools pointed out conflicts between traditional Euro-American classroom behavior, such as the expectation of eye contact between teacher and student, and etiquette in Indian communities where, for example, children are supposed to modestly lower their eyes when addressing an elder. More importantly, Indian children may learn it is bad manners to embarass others by "showing off" one's abilities, then be labeled passive or slow in a classroom where the Euro-American teacher assumes children will be competitive in gaining attention and higher grades. Adjusting teaching strategies to encourage cooperation not only revealed Indian children's capacities but merged with critiques of conventional classrooms to foster a general educational movement toward cooperative learning in all schools, even universities.

American Indian peoples have themselves hired anthropologists to research data on their heritages. A large number of anthropologists prepared testimony on land-claim cases. Some Indian communities, including the Makah in northwestern Washington and several British Columbia bands, Southern Utes, Zuni Pueblo, and the Navajo Nation, employ archaeologists to excavate their ancestors' villages in order to extend back the history of their people. The Makah and many others are building museums on their reservations to preserve and exhibit not only the results of excavations and historical archival work but also heirloom and contemporary crafts and art. Here, too, anthropologists have been invited in as consultants and plan-